HANDBOOK OF DATA MINING AND KNOWLEDGE DISCOVERY

HANDBOOK OF
DATA MINING
AND
KNOWLEDGE
DISCOVERY

EDITED BY

Willi Klösgen and Jan M. Żytkow

OXFORD
UNIVERSITY PRESS
2002

OXFORD
UNIVERSITY PRESS

Oxford   New York
Auckland   Bangkok   Buenos Aires   Cape Town
Chennai   Dar es Salaam   Delhi   Hong Kong   Istanbul
Karachi   Kolkata   Kuala Lumpur   Madrid   Melbourne   Mexico City   Mumbai
Nairobi   São Paulo   Shanghai   Singapore   Taipei   Tokyo   Toronto
and an associated company in
Berlin

Published by Oxford University Press, Inc.
198 Madison Avenue, New York, New York 10016
www.oup.com

Library of Congress Cataloging-in-Publication Data

Handbook of data mining and knowledge discovery/edited by Willi Klösgen and Jan M. Żytkow
p. cm.
Includes bibliographical references and index.
ISBN 0-19-511831-6 (alk. paper)
1. Data mining—Handbooks, manuals, etc. 2. Database management—Handbooks, manuals, etc.
I. Klösgen, Willi. II. Żytkow, Jan M.

QA76.9.D343 H39 2001

006.3–dc21   2001039746

EDITORIAL AND PRODUCTION STAFF

Acquiring Editor: Sean Pidgeon
Development Editor: Sean Pidgeon
Assistant Project Editor: Merilee Johnson
Manufacturing Controller: Donna Ng
Book Designer: Joan Greenfield
Managing Editor: Matthew Giarratano
Publisher: Karen Day

1 3 5 7 9 8 6 4 2

Printed in the United States of America
on acid-free paper

In Memorium

Jan M. Żytkow
September 9, 1944–January 16, 2001

Herbert A. Simon
June 15, 1916–February 9, 2001

CONTENTS

PART EIGHT: KDD IN PRACTICE: CASE STUDIES

Foreword

Enhancing the Intelligence of Discovery Systems

Discovery, finding things we did not know before, by observing and searching, is something we all have been doing since the day of our birth. Some of us even look for things that no one has known before, by doing scientific research, composing new music, painting pictures, or designing airplanes. In our formal education we have occasionally received a little instruction on how to discover. But most of us have acquired the bulk of such skills of discovery in casual ways and with little formal theory to guide us.

Now all of this is changing rapidly, in part because scientific discovery has become a legitimate domain of scientific inquiry. "Inspiration" and "intuition" are no longer eternal mysteries. They are now known to be produced by recognizing patterns in the things that strike our senses and by searching patiently through great labyrinths of possibilities. Recognition and selective search are the tools of discovery, acquired by long years of observing and learning about the world. Understanding this has already enabled us to build a sizable number of automated or human-machine discovery systems.

There is a second reason for our new interest in discovery. Our computer and communications technology has accumulated vast warehouses of information that are (in prospect, if not in present reality) vastly more accessible than in earlier times. We badly need a science of database design and of intelligent search that will permit us to use the new information resources efficiently.

We have shown that our computers and instruments can collaborate with us in data mining, in extracting new knowledge from old by original thought, and in obtaining new knowledge from nature by empirical observation. The pages of this handbook illustrate many of the ways in which computer intelligence is already complementing human intelligence in these tasks, and the many prospects for enlarging that collaboration.

Looking specifically at data mining, we see that the greatest need is not to enlarge our knowledge bases, however desirable that may be, but to be able to access in them the specific knowledge we need, whether or not we know it exists or even what it is. Because human capacity for attention is strictly limited (we cannot enlarge the number of hours in a day), our search engines must become more intelligent so that they can select and filter from the forests of information the particular items our eyes need to see. They must not only be able to respond to our specific requests, but also to use broader knowledge of our needs to retrieve important information we have not asked for and may be surprised by. We will design better data miners only if we remember that the scarce factor is not information but human attention, and that the task of the data miner is to conserve it for its most important uses.

In scientific discovery and design, we are already seeing the many ways in which computing devices that are intelligent can enhance the effectiveness of the scientist and the engineer. Automation of instrumentation and data analysis is proceeding apace. The challenge is to enhance our computing systems' intelligence both in the selectivity of their search and in their ability to communicate with their human collaborators and to understand their needs, whether expressed explicitly or not.

This handbook undertakes to summarize the stage we have reached in these endeavors as we enter a new millennium, and to set forth the basic ideas that can guide our efforts to use the powerful techniques of automatic knowledge acquisition now available to us. By introducing us to what we know today, it also highlights the many gaps in our knowledge that we will need to fill in order to grasp the great opportunities open to us.

—Herbert A. Simon

Foreword

Data Mining Coming of Age

The information revolution is generating mountains of data from sources as diverse as astronomy observations, credit card transactions, genetics research, telephone calls, and Web clickstreams. At the same time, faster and cheaper storage technology allows us to store ever greater amounts of data online, and better DBMS software provides an easy access to those databases. The Web revolution is also expanding the focus of data mining beyond structured databases to the analysis of text databases, hyperlinked Web pages, images, sounds, movies, and other multimedia data.

The progress in Data Mining and Knowledge Discovery since the first Knowledge Discovery in Databases workshop (KDD-1989) has been tremendous. While in 1989 a one-megabyte database was considered to be large, at KDD-1999 we saw examples of discovery in hundred-gigabyte databases. The number of researchers in the field has grown from a few dozen who attended KDD-1989 to many thousands, as measured by numerous publications and conferences all over the world. This handbook summarizes the best research in the field.

The first generation of what we would now call data mining systems appeared in the 1980s and consisted of research-driven tools focusing on single tasks such as building a classifier using a decision-tree tool, finding clusters in data, or visualizing data using only one approach. Such tools addressed a single generic data analysis problem and were intended for researchers only. While using these tools, the researchers realized that knowledge discovery is an iterative process encompassing many steps—from data warehousing and data cleaning to data analysis, model interpretation, and integration of the results.

The understanding of the process (see Part Three of the handbook) led to the second generation of data mining systems, called suites, which first appeared around 1995. The suites supported data preprocessing and cleaning and performed multiple discovery tasks.

In today's business world, good areas for applying data mining require knowledge-based decisions; have accessible, sufficient, and relevant data; have a changing environment; have suboptimal current methods; will not be obsoleted by imminent new technology; and provide high payoff for the right decisions. Such areas include marketing (especially database marketing), fraud detection, production control, and the Web (see Part Six). Development and deployment of data mining-powered applications in these areas led to third-generation data mining systems, which tightly integrate domain knowledge into the discovery process. These systems, also called solutions, are described in Parts Seven and Eight.

The Web creates unique challenges for miners. On one hand, almost all clickstreams are recorded and available for analysis. On the other hand, the drive to personalization needs to be balanced with respect for user privacy (see 22.1). Users need to be aware of how their information is being used, and marketing should eventually move to the opt-in model where users explicitly permit their information to be mined in exchange for some benefit to them.

Developing new algorithms for mining the rich multimedia data of the Web will be a major challenge for twenty-first-century miners. A second challenge is to integrate more complex forms of domain knowledge into mining algorithms—especially important in biotechnology. Finally, the miners will need to come up with standards for the knowledge discovery process and analytical models. This will allow software interoperability and facilitate seamless integration of knowledge discovery into business and scientific processes.

Looking at the future, I am optimistic that data mining and knowledge discovery systems will mature and become widely accepted. This handbook, which covers all aspects of building these systems, will serve as an excellent guide to both researchers and practitioners.

—Gregory Piatetsky-Shapiro

Preface

Explicit knowledge derived from data is gaining importance far beyond traditional domains of science and engineering. As companies merge, expand into new diverse markets, and strive to adapt to quick change, intuition and experience no longer suffice. Experience must be augmented by data that inform on remote markets and new trends. Such data can be abundant, for data gathering, storage, and retrieval follow the enormous growth of hardware and software technologies. Knowledge derived from data can provide a key competitive advantage and can be an instrument of company survival. In the current business world the margin between the two is thin.

Knowledge Discovery in Databases (KDD) has emerged as a new discipline that meets a need for knowledge derived from data by creating computer-conducted methods for knowledge discovery from large data sets.

KDD grows in synergy with computer technology, creating new analytical tools and using them for increasingly larger data volumes. It seeks useful and novel knowledge about real-world domains derived from empirical data and justified by well-understood and reliable evaluation methods. KDD has progressed remarkably in the past ten years and has reached maturity according to such standards as a large research and application community, conferences, journals, commercial software, many development projects, academic and industrial courses, substantial theory, and successful applications.

This handbook provides an extensive presentation of theory, methods, and applications of KDD. As a central resource of carefully designed chapters written by leading researchers and practitioners, the handbook summarizes the expertise of the whole community into a coherent structure that addresses many problems.

One problem addressed is the information overload caused by a rapid increase in the number of conferences and research and development projects, where the many papers published in the usual publication media of journals or conference proceedings and the new digital media created a first mature status of the field.

Another problem is the lack of a definitive textbook that not only provides a convenient entry to the field, but also elucidates KDD as a unique and fascinating combination of many founding fields, including artificial intelligence with its subfields of automated scientific discovery and machine learning, logical theory of knowledge, statistics, philosophy of science, databases, visualization, neural networks, fuzzy sets, and rough sets. Since KDD has emerged by the creative combination of so many fields, even an expert in one field lacks experience in many others, so that a broad summary of contributions from all the founding fields will facilitate interdisciplinary understanding and communication.

The handbook provides fast access to the basic concepts. Complementary views of statistics, logic, databases, rough sets, and fuzzy sets on data and knowledge are assembled in Part Two of the handbook along with the fundamental notions of search. Central to the field, the knowledge discovery process is described in Part Three. The main steps include data warehousing and other methods of data preparation, data visualization, a variety of fundamental data mining tasks and methods of discovery, and the use of available domain knowledge and of discovered knowledge.

The handbook presents contributions of many disciplines. It shows how artificial intelligence expertise helps in organizing large search processes and evaluating models and patterns in order to retain the really interesting knowledge. It shows how statistics derives nondeterministic knowledge patterns from data and how it handles hypothesis significance, how database scientists develop efficient query methods useful in data mining, and how visualization researchers combine the advantages of the human perception system and the analytic power of the computer in a synergistic way.

A representative sample of innovative discovery systems, each integrating many methods and designed for efficient and effective discovery processes, is presented in Part Four. Part Five addresses the opportunities for a mutual stimulation among KDD and its founding disciplines. The heterogeneous mix of backgrounds has resulted in a remarkably fast development of KDD, but the synergy will continue.

Domain experts and users of KDD technology want to see how effective the approach can be in their domains. Financial, marketing, production, and scientific professionals are interested in experiencing how the new methods can extend and complement their traditional analysis approaches. Problems and solutions useful in many fields are summarized in the chapters on these and other business and industry sectors in Parts Six and Seven. Inspiration for new applications can come from the analysis of case studies in Part Eight, which shows how knowledge discovery methods have been applied successfully in a broad range of environments.

The handbook summarizes the field for many categories of users: practitioners and data mining customers in many fields, researchers, system developers, teachers, and students in a variety of disciplines. A broad category of users are people in application domains such as medicine and finance, whom we call practitioners of data mining. They are interested in the assessment of their knowledge acquisition problems and in suitable KDD methods. Scientists, engineers, industry leaders, managers, and analysts alike will find Parts Six, Seven, and Eight particularly useful because they contain examples of problems and solutions from similar domains. They can trace the cases to methods and systems and educate themselves by working backward from case studies. Ultimately, KDD applications will be handled by motivated and well-educated domain experts who know what questions are important and what methods can provide answers.

Another category of users are research scientists. They have an in-depth knowledge of different parts of KDD. They need a well-organized reference that will help to develop new methods or improve existing ones, and that will develop new applications of KDD or contribute to the underlying theory and/or heuristic principles of KDD.

Systems developers use the existing and proven methods and put them into efficient systems for commercial or company use. The handbook provides them with examples of systems, techniques, and criteria by which discovery techniques are assessed.

Instructors who teach in academia and in the industry will find that the handbook can function in the role of a textbook. Different selections from the handbook can satisfy a variety of teaching needs and offer supplementary readings for motivated students, practical examples for projects, and so on.

Graduate students will find this handbook to be a convenient entrance point into the subject, while contributions in Part Five contain ideas for dissertation topics. The handbook is not designed to compete with journals or conference proceedings. The latter are well suited to the dissemination of leading-edge research. The handbook provides, instead, an overview of the field, collating and filtering the research findings into a sometimes less detailed but broader view of the domain, and satisfies the need for a broad-based reference book. In addition to allowing established practitioners to view the wider context of their work, it is designed to be used by newcomers to the field who need access to review-style articles.

The handbook was first conceived by Sean Pidgeon while at Oxford University Press. His idea for the project became our greatest challenge. Perfect organizational support provided by Oxford University Press made it possible to bring our project to completion. In particular, we would like to express our gratitude to Merilee Johnson, who worked on editorial and organizational issues. Our gratitude, last but not least, goes as well, of course, to the many editorial members and contributors, whom we identify as the best possible scientific and application experts.

—Willi Klösgen and Jan M. Żytkow

PART ONE

DATA MINING AND KNOWLEDGE DISCOVERY

1 KNOWLEDGE DISCOVERY IN DATABASES: THE PURPOSE, NECESSITY, AND CHALLENGES

Willi Klösgen and Jan M. Żytkow

ABSTRACT This section introduces knowledge discovery in databases (KDD) as a field that is driven by the need for knowledge derived from massive and varied data. We explain both the necessary role of KDD and the conditions under which KDD methods can be profitably applied. Together, application needs and successful methods stimulated the fast development of KDD into a field that is established both in academia and industry. To understand the results and challenges of knowledge discovery we categorize knowledge resulting from KDD along several dimensions. Then we outline many challenges crucial to the further growth of KDD.

1. What is Knowledge Discovery in Databases (KDD)?

Knowledge discovery in databases (KDD) has become a promising and widespread activity. It is an institution that is catching up with such established fields as artificial intelligence, databases, and statistics, and competes with them in many ways. Informal definitions contrast knowledge discovery in databases (KDD) with different fields.

In statistics, KDD was introduced as computer-automated exploratory data analysis of large complex data sets (Friedman, 1997a) or secondary analysis of large data sets (Hand, 1998). "Secondary" means that the primary business purpose for which a database was collected is not knowledge discovery. From a database perspective KDD was characterized as pattern querying (Imielinski and Virmani, 2000), that emphasizes a close coupling of search for patterns with queries executed by database management systems. In machine learning (ML), it was popular to treat KDD as a version of ML that applies to large data sets and a broader spectrum of unsupervised tasks and methods in addition to typical supervised concept learning from examples.

The definition frequently cited within the KDD community presents KDD as 'the non-trivial process of identifying valid, novel, useful and ultimately understandable patterns in data' (Fayyad et al., 1996). This definition is useful for selling KDD tools and services promising customers that they will get valid, novel, useful, and understandable results that they would not find on their own. But it does not describe a systematic intellectual domain of activities. If a discovery process does not obtain any results, because such is the content of the data, isn't it still a discovery process? If a discovery process is trivial and yet the results are important, are we going to say that this is not KDD? Isn't any knowledge ultimately useful? Are we looking for patterns in data or rather for knowledge about the domain represented by data?

While no definition is completely adequate for any extensive field of human activity, let us argue for a simple solution. Knowledge discovery in databases is exactly what it says under the normal meaning. No paraphrasing is required. Knowledge is any articulated and justified truth about a domain represented by a (formal) language.

Discovery of knowledge produces statements that describe real-world objects, concepts, and regularities. These statements are derived in a process of autonomous generation and verification of new hypotheses. Databases are well-structured and maintained repositories of data about real-world domains. KDD is more than data analysis (as explained in Section 3) and more than pattern detection in data. Many patterns in data do not represent knowledge on the domain represented by data.

The origin of the term KDD can be clearly traced to the first workshop on knowledge discovery in databases in 1989. Data mining is an older term, conceived in the statistically oriented data analysis community.

Actually, data mining is a misleading metaphor. We mine coal or gold rather than the dirt or rock from which they are extracted. Knowledge mining provides a better analogy, as knowledge is the intended outcome, similarly to coal and gold.

As proposed by Fayyad et al. (1996), KDD refers to the overall process of finding knowledge in data, while data mining is seen more narrowly as the central step in this process, that applies algorithms for extracting and verifying hypotheses. This restricted notion of data mining is not commonly accepted in the community. Many authors use data mining as a synonym for KDD, for instance the CRISP consortium when presenting a KDD process model (see Chapter 12). In this handbook we favor the CRISP terminology, and in general we see data mining as a synonymous, but miscoined term for KDD. Nevertheless some authors of this handbook support the restrictive meaning of data mining. This should not provide confusion, since each version can be clearly recognized.

The KDD process consists of many steps that are iteratively and interactively performed. These steps are often categorized into the phases of preprocessing, hypothesis generation and verification, and postprocessing. In Chapter 2 we argue that the practice of discovery goes beyond this sequence and the process should be viewed differently for the benefit of the continuing growth of KDD. As KDD provides solutions to business problems (Brachman et al., 1996), the full cycle of a practically useful discovery should be categorized into the phases of business problem analysis, data understanding and preparation, search for knowledge, solution to the business problem, and, finally, deployment and practical evaluation of the solution.

2. A Brief History

The KDD community originated in the early 1990s, stimulated by a sequence of KDD workshops. Gregory Piatetsky-Shapiro, supported by W. Frawley and C. Matheus, successfully welded together diverse approaches and results of KDD research at biennial and then annual workshops that started in July 1989. The rapidly increasing number of participants then met from 1995 at the International Conferences on Knowledge Discovery and Data Mining. Other conference series followed in short order, including PAKDD (Pacific-Asian conferences, which started in 1997), PKDD (European Conferences on Principles and Practice of KDD, organized from 1997), SPIE conferences from 1999, DAWAK (Data Warehousing and Knowledge Discovery, from 1999). New ICDM conferences (IEEE International Conferences on Data Mining) will start in 2001. Many other conference series include a substantial program on knowledge discovery, for instance ISMIS, and conferences in the areas of rough sets, neural networks, and evolutionary computation.

The rapid growth of KDD is partially owed to multidisciplinary contributions, initially from machine learning (Michalski, 1983) and automation of scientific discovery (Żytkow and Simon, 1986) and later from statistics and database communities. The roots of KDD are systematically discussed in Chapter 3 of this handbook.

Path breaking for the development of the field have been two books on KDD, edited by Piatetsky-Shapiro and Frawley (1991) and Fayyad et al. (1996). They brought together the most relevant recent research in KDD and consolidated the research paradigm.

A fast growing number of papers have been published on the topic, primarily in the many conference proceedings that appear each year. Among the many journals that publish KDD articles, the *Data Mining and Knowledge Discovery* journal has been dedicated to the field.

A Special Interest Group on KDD (SIGKDD) within the Association for Computing Machinery was recently organized (1998) reaching a substantial membership (about 1800 members in October 2000). It offers the KDD community many services and useful information on the field via the newsletter *Explorations* published twice a year since June 1999 and a dedicated web site (www.acm.org/sigkdd).

3. Why is KDD Needed?

Data analysis has a long and successful history that precedes KDD. Over many decades, many powerful methods were created to derive knowledge from data. Why do we need new methods for data analysis and what motivates the growth of KDD?

Traditional data analysis is time consuming for the analyst. Consider an analyst who determines the probability of a car accident by a policyholder, depending on variables like age, sex, marital status, region, type of car, and driving distance per day. The analyst would specify a generalized linear model, estimate its parameters using the client database, analyze the quality of the model, study the residuals, and reformulate the model several times by transforming, adding or removing variables. Problems would arise if the database is large and exceeds the limitations of the available statistical package.

As another example of manual data analysis consider a market researcher who studies changes of market shares in the last year and looks at a series of cross-tabulations of customer subgroups to identify interesting cells in these tables. The possibilities are combinatorially explosive, so when the problem includes many relevant variables, the available systems are often not applicable or need too much human time.

The number of data sets in business, official statistics, government, science, and elsewhere is estimated at tens of millions and is rapidly increasing. The volume of data is expected to double every twenty months. The computerization of business processes and automatization of administrative transactions make large supermarket chains, credit card companies, and other multinational companies produce daily volumes of hundreds of megabytes of data. The advances in scientific data collection make remote sensing instruments collect data at the rate of gigabytes per day.

Many data sets must be analyzed urgently, but manual data analysis is a bottleneck. Investigation in organizations collecting large data sets (NASA, etc.) shows that only a small portion of the collected data, estimated at 5/10 percent, is ever analyzed. According to Eurostat (1997) rapid advances in data capture, storage, and dissemination technologies have outrun the common techniques for analyzing data with the old methods.

New automated knowledge discovery methods try to overcome the bottleneck of traditional, time expensive, mainly manual techniques and increase the productivity of the analyst. This is achieved by automating generation, search, and evaluation of spaces of hypotheses and models, and assisting analysts in intelligently exploring large data sets. Compared to manual analysis, a computerized brute force search can be organized more systematically and more completely to cover larger parts of hypotheses spaces. Early implementations of this brute force paradigm have been tried in the statistics and data analysis community. Statistical packages like SPSS allow the generation of all cross-tabulations in a data set or offer heuristic approaches searching for good regression models by applying forward selection, backward elimination, and stepwise strategies. CART methods (Breiman et al., 1984) and their predecessors and successors generate classification and regression trees.

However, most early brute force techniques in data analysis had a bad reputation among statisticians. Data mining often had a negative connotation characterized as 'torture the data until they confess.' When many hypotheses are subjected to many tests, spurious results can occur by chance. This point has to be treated very seriously when developing and applying data mining methods. Bonferroni adjustment or similar techniques can adapt the test criteria to a huge number of automatic tests. Independent training and test data sets are useful to ensure statistically valid results and to exclude overfitting.

Statisticians postulate that 'every time the amount of data increases by a factor of ten we should totally rethink how we analyze it' (Friedman, 1997a). The large number of cases and high dimensionality (large number of variables) are the two most traditional aspects of data complexity. Other increasingly important complexities relate to multirelational data with several classes of linked objects (such as patients, hospitals, diagnoses, and therapies), incremental, spatial, distributed, and heterogeneous data consisting of transaction data, text, audio data, and images.

Advanced database management systems and data warehouse technology improve access to large amounts of collected data. However, the analytical tools of aggregation queries and OLAP still resemble the manual approach of statistics. In addition to aggregates produced by queries, pattern detection in aggregated data is needed. KDD provides automation of search, including automated detection of patterns. Such a search included in many KDD methods is much faster and yet flexible.

In addition to methods of machine learning that predominantly treat data as a source of concept learning from examples, KDD offers a broader scope of knowledge that it can detect. Methods of KDD are also needed because in contrast to machine learning, the majority of data are not prepared for the benefit of a learner.

4. When is KDD Useful?

Many knowledge discovery tools are available. They represent various views on data and knowledge developed in statistics, logics, artificial intelligence, databases, and visualization. A database user presented with those methods wants to know the conditions for their successful application. In particular, he would like to know when they provide better results than conventional data analysis methods.

An application must be data rich. The database must be conclusive, that is contain problem-relevant attributes and their values for many objects representative of the domain. KDD approaches prove particularly useful in comparison to standard statistical methods, when the problem includes a large number of potentially relevant variables, when it applies to multidimensional relations that vary in different subpopulations, when no proved (statistical) model has already been established for the problem, and when surprising results can be expected for subgroups.

For example, in one of our applications on a production control process (Klösgen, 1999), where production parameters that offer good production results were sought, it was necessary to study more than 100 variables that may influence the quality of a product. On the other hand, if a problem is well understood and a proven model exists to describe or analyze the domain, then there may be little need for new methods. Banks and insurance companies know client profiles, since they have regularly analyzed survey data with conventional data analysis tools for a long time. However, to detect sudden changes in the current year, KDD methods may prove useful in this well studied area, too. Unexpected changes in special subgroups that are not usually studied because they do not use the variables of the main model, can be detected by KDD methods while they would have been overlooked in traditional analyses.

It is sometimes not the question of choosing either standard modeling techniques established for a special application or new data mining approaches, but of deciding on how to combine them. There are several ways of combining standard statistical modeling approaches such as regression or advanced generalized linear models with knowledge mining methods. Data mining methods can be applied in the exploratory phase to get familiar with the data and find out about the relevant variables. Influenced by the data mining findings, models can be developed based on advanced statistical modeling techniques. But the reverse direction is often useful, too. Models are established that describe the main dependencies and trends, and data mining techniques are then applied to analyze the residual or incremental patterns of the models.

KDD applications are necessary when many dimensions can be relevant to the problem and many subgroups are to be studied. For example in a political planning application (Klösgen, 1994), the results of socioeconomic simulation models were analyzed to study the consequences of new tax and transfer laws. If an analyst or a politician is mainly interested in the overall cost of the new legislation and in a few fixed predefined groups of possible winners or losers of the legislation, he can study a small set of cross-tabulations. In contrast, when surprising results can be expected for an unknown subset of those subgroups, a KDD application can analyze a large open set of subgroups.

However, the role of surprising or unexpected results is often exaggerated in KDD. When the analyst has a strong background knowledge of the domain, she can typically explain most KDD results after some reflection, even though she did not think about all these factors before the analysis (see also Hand, 1998). For instance, changes in clients' behavior in the financial market can be explained by changes in marketing strategies, product policies, or legislation. Often the identification of a factor is not the most valuable discovery, but the weight of the factor and its detailed interaction with other factors.

5. Perspectives on Knowledge

In KDD applications, the problem specification may include necessary conditions on the type of knowledge to be discovered and dictate the purpose for which the knowledge shall be used. We will now discuss several dimensions for categorizing knowledge, important for selecting a potentially useful discovery method for a problem (Chapter 17).

We first distinguish five purposes for which knowledge can be used: prediction, description, explanation, optimization, and exploration.

Knowledge can be used to predict a property of a (future) case, for instance classify a client or transaction as fraudulent or predict the probability that a member of a category of car drivers will cause an accident. A predictor (or classifier) is some form of a function (e.g., decision tree, neural net, equation, etc.) from which the unknown value is inferred, given some known values. In addition, a prediction may include information on the confidence the user can have about it, for example, confidence intervals for the predicted values or accuracy of a classification.

Empirically verifiable predictions are among the main tools of knowledge verification. Any statement that cannot be verified can arguably not be considered knowledge.

Another frequent use of knowledge is description of a domain. It may take on the form of the dominant dependency among variables, for instance by a complete, but easily understandable overview of the winners and losers of a planned legislation, or products with decreasing market shares, or client groups that developed unprofitably. Here knowledge is not used for predictions (how future clients behave), but rather to present a dependency among variables that captures many customer behaviors. An empirical equation that captures the dependency between several economic variables or scientific measurements is another example of knowledge that can be used for descriptive purposes.

When identifying a specific combination of production control parameters that results in the highest quality or the most efficient production, we apply the discovered knowledge for optimization, seeking the best solution to a combinatorial problem. Knowledge that is useful in optimization can be derived from a database that includes many examples of production events, described in terms of different production parameters and qualities. The function that describes the dependence of the product quality from the production parameters is not known (in contrast to mathematical optimization problems).

Explanation is another application of knowledge. Here we use deep knowledge, at the level of principles, to derive a description that applies to a class of special situations. Such knowledge, however, is difficult to derive in KDD processes.

Knowledge can be also applied to support further discovery processes. The well articulated knowledge that can direct the discovery process is called background knowledge. Plenty of knowledge acquired during explorations is relatively weak, providing an analyst with the first insights into the data, for example, hints on dependencies between variables. They can be used for specifying KDD tasks such as selecting variables for a classification task. The analyst does not yet know which of the selected variables influence a target variable, how they are correlated among themselves, or which structural form governs the dependencies. The primary goal of an explorative analysis is to discover this kind of background knowledge.

Knowledge derived for one application purpose may be used for another purpose. An equation describing a domain can typically also be used for predictive purposes, and a derived classifier may also be useful as descriptive knowledge. This would, however, require that the classifier is understandable and compact which often is not ensured since maximizing classification accuracy is the main objective of a classification method.

The second perspective concerns the completeness of knowledge. Partial knowledge, illustrated by the metaphor of nuggets, can be contrasted with complete knowledge. For instance, a few subgroups of patients suffering from a special disease are identified without deriving a complete disease profile. Partial knowledge may be all we can get for several reasons, for example because of the limited quality of the available data, inconclusive data, missing relevant variables, or insufficient language used to express hypotheses. The nuggets results are not complete, because they do not allow the prediction of all new cases and do not represent a function for the whole input space.

Two types of knowledge, (local) patterns and (global) models, are closely related to the preceding dimension, because a local pattern is a nugget. However, a system of local patterns can be complete. Typical examples of local patterns are rules (Chapter 16.2) and subgroup findings (Chapter 16.3) or individual cells in a contingency table. In contrast to local patterns, global models describe the whole relation or cover the whole input space. Examples of global models are equations (Chapter 16.4), decision trees (Chapter 16.1.4), systems of clusters (Chapter 16.5), or Bayesian networks (Chapter 16.6). Local patterns can be derived from global models. For instance, an equation can be instantiated with a special value or a subgroup pattern derived from one leaf of a decision tree.

Mining methods that detect local patterns can be complemented with refinement techniques that convert a set of local patterns to their best system. The search for the best system of patterns, such as the best rule set, can be interpreted as model generation from a set of local patterns. When a rule set is complete, it can be seen as a model. A set of nonredundant local patterns that cover the input space is complete.

The next dimension is the understandability of knowledge. KDD responds to business concerns, thus understandability is a major concern. But black box approaches like neural networks or support vector machines (Burges, 1998) also play a role in KDD. Various recent approaches extract the easily understandable forms of knowledge from black boxes such as rules (see Chapter 31).

An important dimension that is extensively discussed in Chapter 5 is the structural form of knowledge such as rules, trees, nets, functions, and clusters. Table 1 summarizes the perspectives on knowledge.

6. Challenges for KDD

We do not lack new challenges in KDD. Many of them are simple requests for 'more of the same': handle more records, more variables, consider a broader range of hypotheses, reach better accuracy, or obtain the same results faster. Take any of the dimensions that characterize data, knowledge, and the process of discovery, and you may request improvements along one or more of these dimensions.

When we start working on an improvement, however, we realize that problems can be very subtle. Multi-relational, distributed, incremental, and heterogeneous data present much bigger challenges. In this chapter we enumerate many of the dimensions for improvements and we concentrate on some of the problems. Many challenges are also discussed in Chapters 3 and 25–33.

Several aspects of data can be complex. A single data table, the most popular source of data, may contain a large number of records, many dimensions, that is many attributes, may use attributes of many types and with large numbers of domain values per attribute. The preponderance of discovery methods were developed to operate on a single table of moderate size. Significant progress has been made, but we can seek further improvements in the analysis methods along all of those lines.

Table 1 Dimensions for Classifying Knowledge				
Application purpose	Classification/prediction	Optimization	Description/ summarization	Exploration
Completeness	Nugget	Complete		
Hypothesis type	Pattern	Model		
Understandability	High	Low: black box		
Structural form	Rule (-set)	Decision tree	Probabilistic net	Function
	Cluster (ing)	Concept hierarchy	Contingency table	Subgroup (-set)

For very large data sets including millions of tuples and several hundreds of variables, data reduction is important. Although high performance solutions can extend the applications of KDD methods from the usual boundaries of common KDD systems (10^6 tuples, a few hundreds of fields) by some orders, feature selection and sampling methods are often necessary to provide time efficient interactive discoveries. Interactivity of discovery systems is important because of the often explorative nature of the KDD process. Reduction of variables is also important for ensuring clear discovery results. Scaling techniques including parallelization options are discussed in Chapter 16.9.

Another source of big challenges comes from relationship between data and the real-world domains that they represent. In statistics, databases are often termed as a secondary source of data for the purpose of discovery, or the analysis is called secondary. Data are secondary because they are primarily collected for a purpose other than discovery of domain knowledge, for instance to support a business process. The statistical adequacy of objects represented in the data is often limited, and many conclusive variables can be missing. New statistical paradigms must be developed as statistical methods typically assume independently and identically distributed samples. For large secondary databases gathered over a period of time, these assumptions often do not hold.

Populations to which we can legitimately generalize regularities discovered in databases can be assessed with the help of external data, such as census data. That is an open research issue that requires systematic attention.

When we also consider that knowledge is generated by massive search, we realize that random results, that is regularities that correspond to random fluctuations, must be distinguished from statistically significant findings. Methods of statistics can help prevent data mining methods from treating random regularities as real.

Large scale search, central to many data mining methods, includes multiple comparisons. In each cycle of the search, a lot of alternative hypotheses are generated for which quality scores are estimated. The scores are used when selecting the best hypotheses to refine further. These procedures are responsible for three pathologies: attribute selection errors, overfitting, and oversearching (Jensen and Cohen, 2000). Statistical approaches like Bonferroni adjustment, randomization testing, and cross-validation can mitigate these problems.

When sampling is applied to reduce data and generate approximately correct results, we may have problems with not noticing weak yet real regularities (Danyluk and Provost, 1993). Given the broad range of statistical hypotheses considered by discovery systems, here is a big challenge that can lead to the growth of statistics and apply advanced sampling methods (Provost et al., 1999; Scheffer and Wrobel, 2000).

Recently statistics is developing more complex and flexible models. But especially for very high-dimensional data sets it has been observed that simple methods, such as Naive Bayes or nearest neighbors, yield higher performance than those complex models. Thus a new paradigm could be necessary to deal with the curse of dimensionality (Friedman, 1997b). Conditions must be derived on when simple search methods are more efficient than more powerful ones, when more powerful hypotheses lead to better results, or which simple models should be combined (Chan and Stolfo, 1995) instead of searching for a single best complex model.

Tukey (Friedman and Tukey, 1974) and other protagonists of exploratory data analysis often emphasize the principle of robustness. Applied in KDD this means that discovery results should not differ too sensitively respective to small alterations of the data, description language or selected values of the dependent variables. As an example, small modifications in the target group, which often is only vaguely defined, should not lead to a totally diverse set of derived rules. Robustness is also required with respect to invalid statistical assumptions, for example, on the distribution of variables. The main concern in KDD has been on accuracy. Strengthening the role of robustness in discovery research is a major challenge in KDD.

Hypotheses languages have roots in logic and statistics. The predominant attributive languages used to express rules, decision trees, and the like, have a limited expressive power. Sometimes first order language-based approaches can be helpful, including quantifiers and variables to distinguish different instances from one or several object classes (Quinlan, 1990). It is an open and substantial problem: which subsets of the first order language are sufficiently expressive and yet efficient for various KDD problems.

The subsets of the first order logic language are important for analyzing multirelational databases that include several object classes (Wrobel, 1997). Approaches for dealing with multirelational data, especially for multiple measurement data, also originate from the statistical field, for example, by developing multilevel modeling methods (Lindstrom and Bates, 1990).

Constructive induction is closely related to this problem. Here, additional variables are dynamically constructed during search that are better suited to describe regularities in the data. Especially for time and space related data, such derived variables can be useful when including descriptive terms based on means, slopes, or other (time-) series indicators. This problem area also includes methods of feature selection and aggregation (see Chapter 14).

Integrating several aspects of interestingness, for example, statistical significance, novelty, simplicity, and usefulness, is another problem. Discovered knowledge can be included in the domain knowledge base of a system and exploited in the continued discovery process. Discovery methods are used to learn from the users by monitoring and analyzing their reactions to the discovered and presented findings to assess the novelty of interestingness. See Chapter 18 for the role of domain knowledge in KDD. Substantive significance must be evaluated to deal with interestingness of hypotheses.

Ways for integrating KDD systems with other systems such as database systems, statistical packages, visualization systems, decision support systems, and knowledge management systems must be prepared. The need for integrating KDD systems with database systems is obvious, since most data are managed by database systems. Statistical query types must be determined that can be efficiently executed, so that KDD methods for very large databases can be designed that only use efficiently executable queries. When a search algorithm delegates the (next) generation of statistical queries to a database server that are jointly answered relying on very efficient processing of the database, for example, within a single pass over the data, employing specialized optimizers for bunches of queries (Graefe et al., 1998; Sarawagi et al., 2000), development and maintenance of mining methods will be easier and portable, robust, scalable, and parallel implementations will be supported.

Database integration can also support the development of spatial (Ester et al., 2000) and distributed data mining algorithms exploiting data that are distributed either because of business reasons or for scalability. In Chapter 2 we will present a number of challenges related to business processes that motivate the discovery process.

References

Brachman, R., T. Khabaza, W. Klösgen, G. Piatetsky-Shapiro, and E. Simoudis. 1996. "Mining Business Databases." *Commun. ACM* **39(11)**: 42–48.

Breiman, L., J. Friedman, R. Olshen, and C. Stone. 1984. In *Classification and Regression Trees*. Belmont, CA: Wadsworth.

Burges, C. 1998. "A tutorial on support vector machines for pattern recognition." *Data Mining and Knowledge Discovery* **2(2)**: 121–167.

Chan, P. and S. Stolfo. 1995. "Learning arbiter and combiner trees from partitioned data for scaling machine learning." In *Proceedings of the First International Conference on Knowledge Discovery and Data Mining*, pp. 39–44. Menlo Park, CA: AAAI Press.

Danyluk, A. and F. Provost. 1993. "Small disjuncts in action." In *Proceedings of the Tenth International Conference on Machine Learning (ICML-97)*, edited by P. Utgoff, pp. 81–88. San Mateo, CA: Morgan Kaufmann.

Ester, M., A. Frommelt, H. P. Kriegel, and J. Sander. 2000. "Spatial data mining: database primitives, algorithms and efficient DBMS support." *Data Mining and Knowledge Discovery* **4**: 193–216.

Eurostat. 1997. In *New Technologies and Techniques for Statistics*. Amsterdam, The Netherlands: IOS Press.

Fayyad, U., G. Piatetsky-Shapiro, P. Smyth, and R. Uthurusamy. 1996. In *Advances in Knowledge Discovery and Data Mining*. Cambridge, MA: MIT Press.

Friedman, J. H. and J. W. Tukey. 1974. "A projection pursuit algorithm for exploratory data analysis." *IEEE Trans. Comput.* **C-23**: 881–889.

Friedman, J. H. 1997a. "Data mining and statistics: what's the connection?" Available at: http://www-stat.stanford.edu/~jhf/.

Friedman, J. H. 1997b. "On bias, variance, 0/1-loss, and the curse-of-dimensionality." *Data Mining and Knowledge Discovery* **1(1)**: 55–77.

Graefe, G., U. Fayyad, and S. Chaudhuri. 1998. "On the efficient gathering of sufficient statistics for classification from large SQL databases." In *Proceedings of the Fourth International Conference on Knowledge Discovery and Data Mining*, pp. 204–208. Menlo Park, CA: AAAI Press.

Hand, D. 1998. "Data mining—reaching beyond statistics." *Research in Official Stat.* **1(2)**: 5–17.

Imielinski, T. and A. Virmani. 2000. "A query language for database mining." *Data Mining and Knowledge Discovery* **3(4)**: 373–408.

Jensen, D. and P. R. Cohen. 2000. "Multiple comparisons in inductive learning algorithms." *Machine Learning* **38(3)**: 309–338.

Klösgen, W. 1994. "Exploration of simulation experiments by discovery." In *Proceedings of AAAI-94 Workshop on Knowledge Discovery in Databases*, edited by V. Fayyad and R. Uthurusamy. Menlo Park, CA: AAAI Press.

Klösgen, W. 1999. "Applications and research problems of subgroup mining." In *Foundations of Intelligent Systems*, edited by Z. Ras and A. Skowron. Lecture Notes in Artificial Intelligence, pp. 1–15. Berlin: Springer.

Lindstrom, M. J. and D. M. Bates. 1990. "Nonlinear mixed-effects models for repeated measures data." *Biometrics* **46**: 673–687.

Michalski, R. S. 1983. "A Theory and methodology of inductive learning." In *Machine Learning: An Artificial Intelligence Approach*, edited by R. S. Michalski, J. Carbonell, and T. Mitchell, pp. 83–134. Palo Alto, CA: Tioga Publishing.

Piatetsky-Shapiro, G. and W. Frawley. 1991. In *Knowledge Discovery in Databases*. Menlo Park, CA: AAAI Press.

Provost, F., D. Jensen, and T. Oates. 1999. "Optimal progressive sampling." In *Proceedings of the Fifth International Conference on Knowledge Discovery and Data Mining*. San Diego, CA: ACM Press.

Quinlan, R. 1990. "Learning logical definitions from relations." *Machine Learning* **5(3)**: 239–266.

Sarawagi, S., S. Thomas, and R. Agrawal. 2000. "Integrating association rule mining with relational database systems: alternatives and implications." *Data Mining and Knowledge Discovery* **4**: 89–125.

Scheffer, T. and S. Wrobel. 2000. "A sequential sampling algorithm for a general class of utility criteria." In *Proceedings of the Fourth International Conference on Knowledge Discovery and Data Mining*, pp. 330–334. New York: ACM Press.

Wrobel, S. 1997. "An algorithm for multirelational discovery of subgroups." In *Proceedings of the First European Symposium on Principles of KDD*, edited by J. Komorowski and J. Żytkow, pp. 78–87. Berlin: Springer.

Żytkow, J. and H. Simon. 1986. "A theory of historical discovery: the construction of componential models." *Machine Learning* **1**: 107–136.

2 THE KNOWLEDGE DISCOVERY PROCESS

Willi Klösgen and Jan M. Żytkow

ABSTRACT   This chapter gives an overview of the knowledge discovery process. The full process starts from the definition and analysis of the business problem, followed by understanding and preparation of data, setup of the search for knowledge, the actual search, application of results in solving the business problem, and, finally, deployment and practical evaluation of the solutions. We outline the main tasks and methods that apply in each phase and we make references to the relevant chapters of this handbook. The discovery process is a combination of human involvement and autonomous methods of discovery. Autonomous methods may include automated task integration, for instance, integration of variable selection, knowledge mining, and result optimization. We also emphasize the iterative character of discovery including feedback loops and knowledge refinement.

1. Knowledge Discovery Process: The Main Phases

The search for knowledge in massive data, with the use of different hypothesis spaces, is the central and necessary phase within the discovery process. A large number of methods have been developed that handle many search tasks, but hypotheses inference and verification is only a part of the whole process of knowledge discovery, and often a short one at that. The entire process goes through many phases, which are listed in Table 1.

We will walk through each phase, providing examples and outlining the typical tasks and methods involved. Chapter 12 provides a systematic presentation of tasks and solutions.

Compared to the traditional manual analysis, KDD supplies a much higher degree of system autonomy, especially in processing large hypotheses spaces. However, at the current state of the art, a human analyst still makes many decisions in the course of a discovery process. Many situations cannot be specified in advance and they still require the analyst's intuitive understanding of the dynamic, intermediary results, and circumstances.

KDD and allied fields went through a long process of decomposing discovery tasks, and developed many alternative methods for these tasks. These resources can be best utilized when we systematically analyze which of the tasks should be accomplished and which methods are best for each task for each phase of the discovery process. Then we must decide on an appropriate way of applying a discovery method, which we call search setup and sometimes a strategy.

Search-based approaches are essential not only in hypothesis generation, evaluation, and refinement, but also in data preparation. The process iterates many times through the same application domain and feeds back on earlier findings. In particular, data preparation, search for knowledge, and knowledge refinement can be closely integrated by various feedback loops. For instance, numerical attributes are often discretized to enable a discovery method to be applied. In turn, discretization can be improved by feedback with knowledge revisions (Chapter 24.1.4).

Table 1 The Phases of a KDD Process	
1.	Definition and analysis of business problems
2.	Understanding and preparation of data
3.	Setup of the search for knowledge
4.	The actual search for knowledge
5.	Knowledge refinement
6.	Application of knowledge in solving the business problems
7.	Deployment and practical evaluation of the solutions

2. Business Problems

Large numbers of databases have been mined for knowledge. The main application fields and many case studies are described in Parts 6, 7, and 8 of this handbook. In this chapter we give examples of typical business problems and the knowledge applications they require, such as prediction and explanation.

Marketing belongs to the forefront of successful KDD applications with the overall aim of predicting and analyzing customer behavior. Typical business interests are customer and product profiles (which customer would want what product), predicting customer loyalty and retention, and evaluating the effectiveness of sales campaigns and of direct marketing or mailshot responses.

Strong competitive pressure, the often saturated market, and maturity of products cause a shift from product quality to a competition for information, where detailed and comprehensive knowledge on the behavior of customers and competitors is crucial. But simpler knowledge that leads to predictions and classifications is also useful.

Knowledge of exceptions and their explanation can be an important concern. A sales representative may want to know which products or regions are far above or below in levels of sales and which are the strongest contributors to an overall trend.

Market basket analysis is the study of data collected at the point of sale. The associated business problems are optimal shelf space allocation, store layout, product location, and promotion effectiveness.

In the financial area, knowledge is sought, for example, to predict a portfolio's return of investment, determine the credit worthiness of a customer, detect money laundering, or identify fraudulent use of credit cards.

Controlling and scheduling of production is another application field of KDD with a high potential profit. The target of discovery are conditions for optimal quality production. Initially, the engineers and operators can manually use such results for their process control decisions, while the long-range goal is automatic control of production. The broader task is understanding the relationship between the variables that describe the steering, the process, and product quality. A major challenge for KDD methods occurs when time and location play an important role, as they are only rudimentarily represented and analyzed by most of the mining methods.

Identification and understanding of dynamic behavior is another common business concern in many areas, such as identification of faults in telecommunications networks, analyzing customer interaction with a Web site, text and audio mining in e-mail collections and telephone calls.

Examples of scientific problems (see Chapter 48 of this handbook; and the special issue on data mining of CACM, November 1996) include explorations of complex data structures and often very large data sets of DNA sequences and other genetic data.

3. Understanding and Preparation of Data

KDD methods will supply knowledge useful in solving business problems only when such knowledge can be generated from the available data. Two questions must be answered positively:

1. Are relevant data available?
2. Can generalization from such data apply in target situations?

In answering the first question, for each data table and each attribute we should decide whether this attribute is even worth consideration. Then we must decide whether we have a minimum of such relevant attributes. If we seek predictors for the attribute C, we need C in the data as well as a number of potential predictor attributes whose values are known before the predictions of C must be made. We must also find out how can data from different tables be pulled together, because the preponderance of discovery tools apply to single tables.

We must also make sure that data cover a broad range of values of relevant variables. In particular data should be available for contrasting various generalizations with the appropriate control groups. If we consider the effectiveness of some treatment for a particular affliction then we need data on both treated and untreated individuals. The analysis will provide an even better understanding if we also have data on treated and untreated healthy individuals.

Suppose that we explored the existing data and found some generalizations. Can we use them to solve the business problems in target situations? It depends on the situations to which we want to generalize. They are typically different from those captured by the data.

When a set of data is collected to support the day-to-day business operation, we must be very careful about knowledge discovered from it, and the target groups to which we can generalize. The data are fine when a market research company performs a regular survey on a special market and therefore can usually collect the data that is relevant for the analysis. But if markets are different? Consider a marketing campaign in California. Can we apply the results to a future campaign in Kansas or British Columbia? Which of the results? Can we use them next month? Next year? Which attributes are more useful than others? By extending ANOVA analysis (Johnson and Bhattaharyya, 1992) we can select attributes that are distributed similarly in the data and in the target population. In general, we should demonstrate whether and in what ways the target population is similar to the source data.

But not always do we need to think in terms of populations. In science and engineering we rarely deal with populations, when target situations are under empirical control. We can repeatedly produce any situation as many times as we wish and the distribution of situations is not a reflection of any natural population. Consider knowledge used for optimization. The optimal control values can be used as many times as needed. In contrast, populations are useful when we apply knowledge to sets of objects that are produced by a natural process. Here statistical methods are particularly useful, as different attributes follow persistent distributions of values for objects in the same population.

If some data appear relevant, their preparation (Chapters 13 and 14) is commonly categorized into data cleaning, model selection, and data reduction. It is an iterative process including feedback loops, as the subsequent steps (see Sections 4–7) may generate insights in the domain that require additional data preparations.

As an important part of data preparation we should understand tables, attributes, and values in the domain of each attribute. Data cleaning tasks include investigation of odd and missing values and finding a legitimate replacement for each. Eventually the domain of each attribute should have a clear meaning. Various techniques to deal with missing data can be used. One possibility is to infer the missing values by exploiting relations with other variables. For example, the gender of a person in a questionnaire could be inferred from other information such as first name. However, it must be considered whether the fact that a data item is missing (some persons did not fill in their gender in the questionnaire) can provide useful information. In a customer retention analysis, the group of clients of a bank that did not fill in this field proved to be a client group with a critical tendency to desert to a business competitor.

Tables and attributes relevant to the mining task must be organized into a data model. Then, according to that model, data from various sources must be joined, transformed, and aggregated. Attribute domains may be binned into reduced sets of values. New attributes may be derived if they are more suitable to the analytical tasks. If the size of the data is too large for efficient analysis, data can be reduced in two ways: feature selection techniques (Chapter 14.2) select subsets of relevant attributes; and sampling methods (Chapter 14.1) select subsets of records.

As an example, consider a production control application with factory data on process conditions and laboratory data on the quality of products (Figure 1). Process conditions are continuously recorded and quality data are recorded several times a day. When fixing a data model, it must especially be decided how to represent time and space related data. The analysis unit must be determined (for which analysis objects or cases do we prepare variables?), such as a production day or production period of six hours. In a simple one-relational model, process variables can be discretized each hour and separate lag variables can be introduced at each hour and for different location measurements of pressures and

```
Problem:       Conditions for good productions
               target group: QKG1 < 0.16,  QKG3 < 0.41
Pattern:       Probabilistic rules
Strategy:      High accuracy, Low overlapping, Recursive exhaustive search
Productions:   Plant A, 1995
               20% of the productions are good

Subgroups describing the target group:

      66% of PG2L8 = 0, PG4 < 0.18
      94% of PG2L8 = 0, PG4 < 0.18, PG15 > 0.88,   PG15L8 > 0.88
     100% of PG2L8 = 0, PG4 < 0.18, PG1  = 0.25,   PG12 0.45-0.55
22% coverage of the target group, 9.8% overlapping

      55% of PG8 = 0.7, PG11L8 0.8-0.85
     100% of PG8 = 0.7, PG11L8 0.8-0.85, PG4 < 0.18, PG15L8 > 0.88
     100% of PG8 = 0.7, PG11L8 0.8-0.85, PG1L4 = 0.25
19% coverage of the target group, 5.4% overlapping

      63% of PG1 = 0.5, PG16 0.5-0.6
      90% of PG1 = 0.5, PG16 0.5-0.6, PG15 0.6-0.7, PG15L4 0.6-0.7
      86% of PG1 = 0.5, PG16 0.5-0.6, PG8L8 = 0.75, PG15L4 0.6-0.7
35% coverage of the target group, 9.4% overlapping

total coverage of target group: 66%
total overlapping: 19%
```

Figure 1 Conditions for good products

temperatures in the plant. Additionally, appropriately derived variables capturing maximum, minimum, average, and slope can be generated for the time or space indexed variables.

Data cleaning, selection, and reduction are some of the key steps in creating a data warehouse, which is a repository of data that summarizes the history of business operations and is created for the purpose of analysis. A large operational or transaction database may not be a practical source for knowledge mining. The analysis is hindered when data must be combined from several such databases, especially when held under multiple operational systems. A separate database, often a data warehouse, can be constructed to manage the data for mining purposes. It does not interfere with the ongoing transactions and has a well-defined state of the data. The size of data is reduced and data are augmented with structures suitable for efficient access and operation. The mining performance is improved as query performance can be tuned for aggregate queries typical to computationally intensive large-scale mining. Special purpose DBMS have been developed for storing multidimensional data and handling queries that aggregate over some dimensions. The main types and forms of data relevant within the KDD context are discussed in Chapter 4, and the role of database systems and data warehousing for KDD in Chapters 6 and 13.

4. Setup of the Search for Knowledge

Humanmade discoveries are considered very special intellectual achievements. Their cognitive and practical value is broadly recognized. Discoveries result from creative processes that notoriously escaped analytical reconstruction. Only recently have methods of artificial intelligence demonstrated that automated heuristic search is capable of humanlike discoveries (Langley et al., 1987). Automated discovery is based on a search that examines many possibilities before it eventually reaches accepted pieces of knowledge. Often, pieces of knowledge are rare in vast spaces of hypotheses, so that search is a necessary tool of discovery.

The practice of knowledge discovery in databases ranges from complex combinations of human-driven and automated search at the high end to the use of single and simple tools. Such tools conduct a limited search but can still produce results of practical value.

Huge numbers of discovery methods have been developed in the last decade. Each can be characterized by a hypotheses space it explores and the search control mechanism used in the exploration. To utilize these resources, the discovery process should include the following elements:

1. Select a search method appropriate to the discovery task.
2. Set up the search: the data, domain knowledge, and the search parameters.
3. Run the search.
4. Examine the results.

On one extreme, we can select a simple method, apply it, and exit. This is justified when a fast payoff is both needed and sufficient. At the other end of the spectrum, we may keep analyzing the data over and over, seeking deep understanding of a complex domain. In this section we consider simple tools and a single application cycle. In Section 6 we will consider knowledge refinement, which uses multiple tools and repeated human judgment.

Most of the development effort in KDD went into new method construction. Method selection is far more difficult. A few simple guidelines can be proposed if method selection is limited to simple and well-studied discovery tasks. As an example consider classification and prediction (Chapter 16.1), one of dominant knowledge applications (see Section 5). The vast majority of methods require a single data table $R(A_1, ..., A_n, C)$, where C is the class attribute, also called the decision attribute, while $A_1, ..., A_n$ are potential predictor attributes. The task is to derive knowledge (a classifier) that uses some attributes in $A_1, ..., A_n$ to predict values of the class attribute C for previously unseen objects. A typical example is fraud detection: use the training transactions already classified as fraudulent and nonfraudulent, to discover the conditions that determine whether a future transaction is fraudulent or not.

When the attributes $A_1, ..., A_n, C$ are symbolic, then target forms of knowledge are trees (Chapter 16.1.3) and rules (Chapters 16.1.4 and 16.3). In the case of numerical attributes, neural networks and equations are appropriate, but rules and trees can also be used, for instance trees produced by Quinlan's C4.5 and regression trees (Breiman et al., 1984). Sets of mean patterns (Chapter 16.3) can be derived in a similar way.

If we need complete predictors, then decision trees are preferred over rule sets. Decision trees can utilize information in highly dimensional data, but they have problems with spotting interactions among two or more variables and typically they have problems with highly uneven value distributions, such as a binary dependent variable with nearly all cases in one of the two classes. If strong and well-justified knowledge is needed, then selected rules may be preferred.

If we need understandable predictors, then rules and equations are generally preferred over neural networks and decision trees. Equation finders (Chapter 16.4.2), regression model constructors (Chapter 16.4.3) and advanced nonlinear modeling techniques (Friedman, 1991) are among the main choices. But black box methods such as neural networks (Chapter 16.1.8), support vector machines (Burges, 1998), and nearest neighbor methods (Chapter 16.1.6) can often be more effective, when a highly accurate classifier was derived and understandability of the classifier is not necessary.

Equations are very useful and compact summaries of domain knowledge, but results produced with rule searchers (Chapters 16.1.4 and 16.3) or decision tree methods (Chapter 16.1.3) can also be useful when the discovered rule sets or trees are compact and understandable.

The choice of appropriate methods presents big problems. Consider the vast numbers of methods available for rule and tree generation. First, many of the guidelines we already mentioned apply to knowledge discovered by a method, so that they can be used after a method was applied, not before. Second, many choices can be justified after the results of many methods are compared. This is because we seek knowledge about the domain, not just a pattern in a particular category. We will consider this in Section 6. Third, method selection is a multicriteria decision problem so that the choice must include external judgment on the importance of different criteria for the application. Among many trade-offs, consider the

Table 2 Usage of Several Types of Background Knowledge for Discovery Tasks

	Meta data	Taxonomies	Statistical measures	Constraints	User preferences	Previous discoveries
Selecting an analytic question	Types of variables	Taxonomies of problems	Distributions Sample properties	Expert rules	User profiled rules	Interestingness annotation
Selecting variables	Reliability annotations	Taxonomies of variables	Dependency nets Correlations	Clusters of variables	User profiled rules	Interestingness annotation
Specifying a mining strategy	Types and domains of variables	Taxonomies for value domains	Distributions Correlations	Background relations	User profiled rules	Performance measures
Guiding search in mining	Types and domains of variables	Nongreedy search: value domain tax	Distributions Correlations Significance	Cover constraints	User profiled rules	For initial nodes
Validating hypotheses	Reliability annotations	Reference groups	Confusion matrix sampl. prop.	Interestingness constraints	Usefulness & actionability preferences	For novelty evaluation
Refining the results	Reliability annotations, domains	Generalize: taxonomies on domains	Distributions Correlations Significance	Clusters of variables	Usefulness & actionability preferences	For novelty evaluation
Presenting the results	Lables and domain annotations	Ordering taxonomies variables & domains	Significance	Clusters of variables	User profiled rules	For ordering

derivation speed against adequacy, which is influenced by the scope of the search. Tree construction by hill climbing is fast because of the one step lookahead, nonbacktracking search through the space of decision trees, but that search tries only a limited set of all possible conjunctions of selectors that can be built with the (discretized) values of the variables. The more time-consuming rule-based methods often overcome that problem.

Each discovery method requires data, typically requires some search control decisions, and may use some domain knowledge for search guidance. Data relevant for the method must be a subset of the available data relevant to the problem (see Section 3). Search control is to a large degree fixed in simple search systems that generate trees and sets of rules. However, some decisions can still be introduced by the user. The depth of the tree can be often controlled, as well as the number of descriptors in the rule precondition. The minimum set of data that should not be sliced any further is another important parameter that received recognition as a safeguard of statistical significance.

The search space constraints (Chapter 18.2) can be motivated by interestingness. For example, the combinations of variables or their values that are potentially useful can be exploited as domain knowledge to exclude noninteresting hypotheses. A typical example is an association rule discovery task (Chapter 16.2.3), when sets of products are to be identified that are often bought jointly by clients in mail orders. The aim of this analysis may be to evaluate the efficiency of the catalogue issued by the mail-order company. Associations between products that appear on the same page of the catalogue may be declared as uninteresting by the same-page relation between products. By specifying appropriate constraints, uninteresting hypotheses can be excluded from search. Similar techniques are applied when a syntactical bias is defined for the hypotheses language, like a conjunctive description language for subgroups or an equation language. Similar variables, such as various income variables, can be grouped together, and constraints determine how many variables from a group and which combinations of variables are selected to build patterns or models. Evaluation by interestingness and the role of domain knowledge for supporting discovery tasks are discussed in Chapters 18 and 19.

Most KDD systems (Part 4 of this handbook) can only use some limited form of domain knowledge. Current systems typically exploit some meta data (Chapters 4 and 6.7) and taxonomical knowledge (Chapters 5.7 and 18.1) in the form of hierarchies on the domains of individual variables (e.g., a regional classification). They are useful in deriving interesting results on an appropriate aggregation level within the predefined hierarchy of subsets. For example, a finding that holds for nearly all subregions of a region should not be presented for each subregion, but be generalized to the regional level.

Search operators may be controlled by the user, too. For instance, a particular space of equations depends on the term-generating operators. Regression may or may not include second-degree terms, equation finders may or may not use functions such as logarithm or cosine.

The applications of domain knowledge at different stages of the discovery process are summarized in Table 2. The rows of this table include the main discovery tasks. The columns of the table distinguish between several types of background knowledge that can be exploited by KDD methods to support these tasks. For instance, statistical measures refer to background knowledge on the data in the form of descriptive summaries, and constraints restrict generally available options for an application. Hints for the exploitation of a subtype of knowledge or the objective of the exploitation are included in a cell of the matrix. Some of this domain or background knowledge such as meta data is often already available in a data dictionary, or has to be generated by preprocessing (statistical measures), specified by the user (constraints and preferences), or collected and learned by the KDD system (previous discoveries, analyzing actions of user).

In summary, methods are available for a broad range of mining tasks. The selection of a suitable task and method as well as method instantiation depends on the goals of the analysis: How shall the knowledge be used (classification, prediction, optimization, etc.)? Which properties of the results are most important (accuracy, compactness, homogeneity, understandability, etc.)? What data properties and background knowledge are to be used?

5. The Actual Search for Knowledge

Discovery methods perform a search for knowledge through their respective hypotheses spaces. We will illustrate such a search by a walk-through example that expands on the production control application already mentioned in Section 3.

A database of production cases includes some hundred variables relevant for steering a continuous production process and three variables measuring quality aspects of the product. The engineers define good quality products by specifying a condition for the quality variables, for example, a conjunction of their value intervals (Figure 1). The main business interest is to find production conditions that result in good quality products. These conditions shall be expressed as combinations of values of some production variables. The numerical data have been discretized: intervals are derived for each variable as values, and time references for the continuously measured process variables are considered by introducing lag variables for subperiods covering the time range of one production cycle. A single production cycle covers a time range of six hours. Within that period, measurements are aggregated into subperiods of half an hour. Since understandability of search results is a major concern and the target group of good products is only vaguely captured by the tentative and uncertain interval specification, rule-based methods have been selected to search in the space of all value combinations of production variables. Moreover, the results shall be robust against small modifications of the specification of the target group. The results for several such specifications are combined in a refinement step.

Figure 1 shows a rule set for this application that was generated using the system Explora (Klösgen, 1996). The results in Figure 1 were derived from an exhaustive search process of limited depth, which was run recursively. In each recursion, a space of at most $k = 2$ conjunctions was exhaustively searched considering, however, three pruning conditions: a rule describing a subgroup of productions is not expanded any more if (i) the statistical significance of the subgroup is already very high, or (ii) the generality of the subgroup is low (small size), or (iii) the number of target elements covered by the subgroup is low.

In preparation for the next recursion step, a small subset of all subgroups identified in the preceding step that exceed a minimum significance level (determined according to the number of statistical tests run in the hypotheses space) is selected that overlap below a specified threshold (10 percent in this case: low overlapping) and covers the target group maximally. Thus among the very many conditions built with two selectors found in the first recursion step, a small best subset of maximally different subgroups (small overlap) was selected. Each subgroup is further expanded in the next recursive step that, as in the first step, searches a complete space (in this example of up to $k = 2$) of additional conditions. To support the generation of relevant production conditions, the best subset selection after each recursion step can be reviewed and modified by the engineers. Figure 1 shows the rules discovered at the second level of recursion.

6. Knowledge Refinement

Substantial refinement may be required before elements of knowledge that result from an application of a discovery method are turned into reliable and well-organized knowledge.

Sometimes the results are validated against the data, but a closer scrutiny reveals their superficiality. For instance, in analyzing survey data, we were struck by unexpected and not substantively explainable results. Most of them led to the identification of some tricky behaviors of interviewers trying to speed up their interview efforts and other types of deficiencies or errors in data. It is always desirable to go beyond verification against the data and seek knowledge about the domain.

Granted that each method returns the best solution within its search space, knowing that each search space is limited, we must ask whether the best result is good enough. Can the best regression-based equation or the best C4.5 tree be treated as domain knowledge? Analysis by error propagation may sometimes give a positive answer, for instance when the values of a variable predicted by an equation are within the error of the values that occur in the data (Chapter 16.4.2).

But more typically we should continue the exploration as another method in the same category may produce a more accurate equation or a more accurate decision tree, or, what is also important, confirm the results of the first exploration. We should also try methods that result in different forms of knowledge and decide which form is more appropriate. Open-mindedness pays off as knowledge should be discovered in the form that reflects the real-world relationships, not one or another tool at hand (Chapters 24.1.4 and 29).

Another serious problem that requires knowledge refinement stems from the abundance of results. Such an abundance is one of the main challenges in many marketing applications. Often the analyst will need further support to master all the interesting groups of customers, products, and marketing actions derived for the various performance measures and to establish connections between them.

The flood of too many valid hypotheses is frequently the outcome of brute force approaches to mining. In the refinement phase we may seek a minimal subset of hypotheses that permits derivation of all hypotheses in the original set, which means that it is inferentially equivalent to the set originally discovered. Such minimal covers have been introduced for association rules (Kryszkiewicz, 1998), subset patterns, and the like.

For the selection of truly interesting and nonredundant hypotheses, methods from the following categories can be applied:

- Filtering (during and after search)
- Suppressing of hypotheses
- Ordering of hypotheses
- Statistical pruning
- Combination and generalization of hypotheses
- Grouping and clustering of hypotheses.

Good results in filtering and suppressing redundant hypotheses have been achieved in the Explora system with a suppression algorithm (Gebhardt, 1991; Klösgen, 1996), evaluating both the quality and the similarity of hypotheses. When the initial brute force search finds many similar hypotheses, the selection of the best system of nonredundant hypotheses is important (see Section 5). The degree of similarity between two hypotheses controls the suppression of a hypothesis with a weaker quality by a better-quality hypothesis. This algorithm can be applied, when a similarity and a quality measure are given for a class of hypotheses. Similarity of two subgroups can, for instance, be defined by the degree of overlap of the two subgroups, and quality can be measured by a statistical significance measure.

Methods of statistical pruning can prevent overfit. For instance, a hypothesis H that fits too closely a target set of data may be compared with simpler hypotheses resulting from dropping conjuncts in the "if" part of H. A simpler hypotheses will be chosen if it fits a separate test data set comparably.

To ensure robustness of results according to several small variations of, for example, target group specifications (see Figure 1), results from many instances of search processes can be generalized, for example, by identifying the main influence variables and their conditions.

In an attempt at the reduction of redundancy, hypotheses can be combined into groups by clustering approaches. Each cluster is presented by a typical hypothesis that is a member of the cluster.

Other general postprocessing tasks that operate on the derived knowledge are knowledge visualization, checking and resolution of conflicts with existing knowledge, and the incorporation of the derived knowledge into the application component of the overall application (see Section 7).

Knowledge visualization can be instrumental in knowledge refinement. Interactive visualization techniques, including dynamic statistical presentation techniques such as scatter diagrams linked with bar charts (see Wills, 1997), provide powerful examples of how to dynamically support an exploration process. Many knowledge visualization tools support interactive navigation through large knowledge constructs. The analyst can compare different branches of a tree, different elements of a rule set, or multicollinearity plots.

Pieces of knowledge are supported by visually represented information on sensitivity, confidence, and support. Visualization enhances understanding of data and knowledge, allowing the analyst to redirect and focus the search process. Visualization of mining results is discussed in Chapter 20.1.

7. Application of Knowledge to Business Problems

When knowledge relevant to the specified business objectives has been discovered, it is time to use that knowledge in deciding on actions that support those objectives. As before, our examples will focus on the predictive use of knowledge. Making reliable predictions is one of the main functions of knowledge. How can predictions be used in support of business decisions? It depends on the business problems and on what facts can be used in making predictions.

Knowledge may refer to objects, such as customers; events, such as transactions; or situations, such as production conditions. Let us call them, collectively, "entities." A prediction can be summarized by an if-then statement that links predictor variables $A_1, ..., A_n$ for an entity x with the predicted value of the target variable C:

For all x : if $A_1(x) = a_1$ and ... and $A_n(x) = a_n$ then $C(x) = c_1$.

If we are interested in entities that are c_1, that is, they satisfy $C(x) = c_1$, then we should seek entities that satisfy the *if* part. Predictions can be deterministic when the confidence of the rule is high or statistical when it is lower. In Section 3, when we discussed the choice of relevant data, we required that the values of predictors $A_1, ..., A_n$ are known before we can tell the value of C. Otherwise the predictions come too late. But some predictors may be excluded for additional reasons. Even though we may discover that race, age, or sex influence the desired outcome, for legal reasons a company may not be allowed to use any of these attributes in the selection process.

So why would we even consider such attributes? If a specific value of race, age, or sex is a proven predictor of inferior performance, we can use it to find disadvantaged students or workers and offer them additional help. Here we move to another category of actions: the use of knowledge in making the desired changes to entity x.

We can try to improve the success rate for at-risk students. We can try to move customers to a more profitable category, for instance, transform a single buyer into a multiple buyer. Here the relevant attributes are those whose values we can manipulate within the business process. We have a limited capability to manipulate some attributes. For instance, we cannot change a customer's age, although we can wait until he grows older, so it makes sense to keep a nonprofitable customer if our domain knowledge tells us that in a few years he will move to a profitable category. But we definitely cannot change sex or age of customers and we cannot change facts about their past. Many actions, however, are available. Students can be admitted into remedial education courses. Attractive loans can be offered to customers whom we want to retain. Of course, before they are applied, our knowledge should support credibility of such actions. If we changed the value of attribute B for a customer x from b_1 to b_2, and if one of the discovered rules says

For all x : if $A_1(x) = a_1$ and $B(x) = b_1$ then $C(x) = c_1$,

then there is a chance that the desired effect $C(x) = c_1$ will be reached. Whenever we want to make a change, for instance, make a customer accept an offer, we are trying to guess a causal relation. Some forms of knowledge, such as causal graphs offer more direct advice. But whenever we allege a causal relation, it is important to seek additional empirical verification, as soon as the data are available on the outcome of the implemented action.

We must be ready to withdraw from an action when the data show no relevance. When a regularity is missing while one was expected, we may withdraw from an action. Chapter 47.4 provides an example. The impact of remedial classes on the future performance of at-risk students was studied from many perspectives in many data subsets and it turned out that remedial classes do not help such students. Following that finding, the new action was to cancel the previously recommended remedial classes.

Causal graphs offer a more comprehensive domain model than sets of rules. The broader the understanding of the domain is, the better business decisions can be. Consider a marketing campaign. Using a couple of rules we can improve sales of a particular product. We may win a campaign, but lose the war. This can happen because of product cannibalization: purchase of the marketed product lowers the sales of another more profitable product. Such a situation can be noticed when we expand the scope of the domain model.

Data owners are the most qualified to apply knowledge creatively. Ideally, a KDD system should present as output a system of nonredundant and consolidated findings that answer the analysis questions. The findings are typically statements about the domain that are supported by the data. Various types and forms of statements that can represent knowledge derived from databases are summarized in Chapter 5.

Users can be in charge of knowledge applications if they understand the knowledge discovered. But users are often not familiar with tools and different data and knowledge formats that those tools use. The understandable presentation of knowledge is critical.

Rule-based presentation, with the rules expressed in English, is often considered particularly useful. But a large set of rules may not be understood, even if single rules are. Here, graphically oriented presentations of decision trees or probabilistic nets allow users to grasp the overall organization of domain knowledge.

The Spotlight (Anand and Kahn, 1992) and Coverstory marketing systems mimic the reports normally produced by human analysts. A basic search for exceptions and their explanations is scheduled by drilling down through a series of hierarchies. These drill-down systems are tailored toward solutions of a special class of marketing problems.

8. Deployment and Practical Evaluation

The KDD process starts from specification of business problems and data understanding, and ends with actionable conclusions from the discovered knowledge. After an action is deployed, we have an opportunity for practical evaluation of results.

We can, however, find little documented and detailed information about deployment of results in the corporate world. According to Adriaans and Zantinge (1996), KLM estimated that the implementation of a larger planning system, that included a substantial element of discovery from historical data, had a pay-back time of less than one year and led to a 2 percent reduction in total human resource costs.

There is yet another category of KDD results that are deployed in a different way. The KDD process has been captured to a varied degree by different KDD systems. Many have been commercially deployed and are available—for instance, SAS, SPSS-Clementine, as well as many systems described in Part 4 of this handbook. Both their sales and their use is substantial.

Many commercial systems specialize in narrow vertical applications, which provide the fastest return. Association rules (Chapter 16.2.3) are often sought in the retail area. IBM offers, for example, two products that discover association rules: Quest and Market Basket Analysis. These systems identify products that are sold together and exploit information on the demographics of the consumers.

Without doubt, current KDD systems provide a practical value. But they are still in the beginning stages of KDD process commercialization, and their consolidation into industrial standards is still a matter of the future.

References

Adriaans, P. and D. Zantinge. 1996. *Data Mining*. Reading, Mass: Addison-Wesley.

Anand, T. and G. Kahn. 1992. "SPOTLIGHT: a data explanation system." *Proceedings of the Eighth IEEE Conference on Applied AI*, pp. 2–8. Washington, D.C.: IEEE Computer Society.

Breiman, L., J. Friedman, R. Olshen, and C. Stone. 1984. *Classification and Regression Trees*. Belmont, CA: Wadsworth.

Burges, C. 1998. "A tutorial on support vector machines for pattern recognition." *Data Mining and Knowledge Discovery* **2(2)**: 121–167.

Friedman, J. H. 1991. "Multivariate adaptive regression splines." *Ann. Stat.* **19(1)**: 1–66.

Gebhardt, F. 1991. "Choosing among competing generalizations." *Knowledge Acquisition* **3**: 361–380.

Johnson, R. J. and G. K. Bhattaharyya. 1992. *Statistics Principles and Methods*. New York: John Wiley & Sons.

Klösgen, W. 1996. "Explora: a multipattern and multistrategy discovery assistant," edited by U. Fayyad, G. Piatetsky-Shapiro, P. Smyth, and R. Uthurusamy. *Advances in Knowledge Discovery and Data Mining*. Cambridge, MA: MIT Press.

Kryszkiewicz, M. 1998. "Representative association rules." *Proceedings of the Second Pacific–Asia Conference*, pp. 198–209. Berlin, Germany: Springer.

Langley, P., H. Simon, G. L. Bradshaw, and J. Żytkow. 1987. *Scientific Discovery: Computational Explorations of the Creative Processes*. Cambridge, MA: MIT Press.

Wills, G. 1997. "Visual exploration of large structured data sets," edited by Eurostat. In *New Technologies and Techniques for Statistics*. Amsterdam: IOS Press.

3 MULTIDISCIPLINARY CONTRIBUTIONS TO KNOWLEDGE DISCOVERY

Jan M. Żytkow and Willi Klösgen

ABSTRACT   We investigate interdisciplinary links that shaped and continue to influence KDD. Some of the key ideas can be traced far back into the history of science, logic, and philosophy, some originated with statistics in the nineteenth century, while some have been developed in the last few decades. We review the sources of concepts fundamental to KDD, such as data, knowledge, languages to express knowledge, inference, systems of knowledge, and their relations with real-world domains, including the imprecision inherent in data and knowledge.

1. Deep Roots of KDD

Frequently mentioned sources of knowledge discovery in databases (KDD) include artificial intelligence, databases, statistics, automated scientific discovery, machine learning, and visualization. Rarely mentioned but critical long-term contributors are sciences, philosophy (including philosophy of science), and logic. They shaped the basic concepts of data and knowledge, formal languages, and reasoning. We outline the influence of all these fields on KDD, and we emphasize several ways in which they can strengthen and expand the dominant KDD paradigm. We also discuss the influences of information theory and newer contributors, represented by large and active communities: neural networks, rough sets, and fuzzy sets.

The majority of direct contributors to KDD are a mere few decades old. These disciplines matured in a short time because they are built on many centuries of previous intellectual development. But at the same time they tend to be increasingly isolated and limited. This trend is common in the fast-growing field of information technology. Little time is left for understanding the foundations. Inside each of the growing number of subfields, the volume of research, publications, and conferences is large, so that the usually small fraction of time left to examine outside research cannot cover the increasing number of related disciplines. Different fields develop their own terminology to name the same things. Each develops its own simplifying assumptions needed in technical solutions but rarely made explicit. It becomes too costly for outsiders to penetrate the jargon and have any influence. This ignorance is often amplified by arrogance toward achievements made in competing domains. By examining the roots and by a better understanding of the history of ideas, we can enhance mutual respect, dialog, and unification.

2. Science

Demand for data collection and the emphasis on the quality of data is relatively new in human history. The role of data grew very slowly over centuries. Detailed quantitative theories such as Newtonian mechanics started to dominate science only some two centuries ago. When it turned out that theories, in conjunction with data, can yield precise, true, and useful empirical predictions, the respect for high-quality empirical data and theories grew enormously. One knowledge-based technological revolution followed another.

KDD is a big beneficiary of the recognition for empirical data and knowledge. When we analyze data and seek knowledge, we view ourselves as empirical scientists. But often we are poorly prepared for that role as modern education in computer science, mathematics, statistics, and logic, which raises the preponderance of data miners, teaches little about empirical inquiry. In this section we confront several such shortcomings.

2.1. Objective Knowledge

Typical to KDD is separation of data from their objective sources and the focus on patterns in data. In contrast, scientists seek objective knowledge, that is knowledge about the external world, not about patterns in data. Such knowledge allows us purposeful manipulation of material objects so that the rearranged objects behave as predicted. In KDD, when we mine a given data set we may see little room for the distinction between patterns in data and objective knowledge. But since we seek knowledge applicable in the external world, we must first ask to what degree is the external domain represented by the data. We should ask what objects and what relations are revealed by patterns in data. These concerns are critical as the majority of databases were not collected for the purpose of knowledge mining.

2.2. Public Verification of Data and Knowledge

Science requires repeatability of experiments and observations, and public verification of knowledge in independently researched situations. Weakening those requirements would compromise the value of empirical knowledge. We could confuse knowledge with coincidence or even with mistake and fraud. But the practice of repeatability and public verification in KDD is at best limited to repeated studies of an individual database, typically in the UCI repository. Even then, the comparisons concern the accuracy of predictions or the number of rules, not the regularities or objects revealed in the external domain. Data privacy and business competition are some of the obstacles to comparative investigation of related data sets, but how legitimate an advice can we derive from regularities detected by a limited tool in one data set?

2.3. From Empirical Regularities to Theories

Public verification is not only aimed at the objective elements of knowledge, but it also stimulates generalization. One of the first steps on the way to generalization is detecting a regularity between variables in a concrete empirical situation. For instance, empirical equations are commonly sought in data collected from a concrete experiment in physics or chemistry. At the next step, successful experiments are explored in different research centers and when regularities vary, new unification tasks follow. Eventually, basic laws may emerge that apply to a broad range of situations.

In KDD, the search for regularities in an individual relational table resembles the first steps of scientific inquiry. Further generalization steps should follow, transforming regularities into theories that fit many data sets. In the early stages of KDD we cherished any new regularities, but how long can we limit our attention to isolated sets of association rules or to decision trees derived from isolated data sets? It is common sense that customers differ from one shopping area to another and evolve over time. The discovery of generalizations that capture those changes is a task far more challenging and important than isolated studies of past behavior.

2.4. Let Data Speak

Diverse theories are needed to represent knowledge in physics, chemistry, biology, and social sciences. The history of science demonstrates the success of open-mindedness and the perils of preconceptions. Even within one domain the forms of knowledge can be very different, so that many must be tried in order to find the right ones.

In KDD this open and flexible quest is not sufficiently valued. Entire communities develop and apply tools of one kind and treat as knowledge the results generated by those tools. They resemble ancient astronomers who tried to fit planetary motions into systems of epicycles.

An axe treats everything like a tree. But most of the universe is not a forest. We can realize that when we apply other tools. Since discovery is a long process of gradual refinement, the selection of tools must be data driven.

3. Logic

Over centuries, logicians investigated the foundations of reasoning. In defining the validity of reasoning and the truth value of statements, they distinguished between a language and a domain described by that language (see Chapter 7). Languages talk about the external world or about limited domains, called models, viewed as sets of objects, properties, and relations on those objects.

Logicians introduced languages such as propositional logic and predicate logic, each described by a few simple rules of grammar. They introduced formal rules of logical inference, fully defined by the syntax of premises and conclusions. Computer applications are beneficiaries of syntactic representation. But the justification for syntactic operations comes from semantics. For instance, rules of deductive inference preserve truth: if premises are true, the conclusions are also true.

The framework of logic has been adopted by the theory of databases and is used in many textbooks (Elmasri and Navathe, 1999). Earlier it was used in the foundations of mathematics, in philosophy of science, and in artificial intelligence. Bits and pieces are used in KDD, especially by communities specializing in machine learning, inductive logic programming, and rough sets.

3.1. A Reference System for Knowledge

Logical knowledge representation is commonly known and widely applicable. This makes it a unified reference system for many forms of knowledge that are created in KDD. Translated to the logical form, they can be explained and compared in a unified framework. This approach was successful in philosophy of science (Hempel, 1966; Suppe, 1979) and in artificial intelligence (Rich and Knight, 1991; Russell and Norvig, 1995). It is an attractive feature of inductive logic programming (De Raedt, 1992). Complex forms of knowledge such as taxonomies can be expressed as conjunctions of simple statements (Chapter 5.7), so that a particular empirical contents of a taxonomy can be understood.

Theoretically, all nontautological and noncontradictory statements are candidates for empirical hypotheses, as their truth value is an empirical matter. But in KDD, only very simple statements have been used. Machine learning is likewise dominated by conjunctive classification rules. Although it is unrealistic to expect that any logic statement can be used to express practical empirical knowledge, in the future KDD will utilize many new categories of logic statements.

3.2. Deductive Systems

A deductive system includes all logical consequences of a set of axioms. An axiomatic approach is very successful in representing empirical theories, such as geometry and mechanics. AI uses logical knowledge representation and theorem provers based on the theory of deductive systems (Rich and Knight, 1991).

In KDD we also organize knowledge into deductive systems. Consider for instance a system that finds classification rules. In a large set of rules some can be treated as axioms while others can be derived from axioms. A minimal set of axioms can be the ultimate target of such pursuit.

Since deduction preserves truth, it is essential that axioms are true, as this guarantees the truth of all consequences. By accepting statements of limited accuracy, however, KDD is undermining the application of deductive systems. Association rules, for instance, can be approximately true with an accuracy as low as 70 percent, so that deductive reasoning may lead to false, paradoxical results (Suzuki, 1999). This suggests that the logical if-then form should be avoided when it becomes misleading. The *then* part can be replaced by the distribution of conditional probabilities.

3.3. Logic of Induction

A key element of logic is truth-preserving, deductive schemes of inference, developed over thousands of years. In analogy, other reasoning schemes were created, in the categories of induction, reduction, and abduction. An inductive conclusion is a generalization of premises that are often sets of data. The inductive schemes of Mill (1843) are some of the earliest and most celebrated attempts at a logic of induction. Other attempts followed in the nineteenth and twentieth century in logic and philosophy of science. Carnap and Reichenbach, followed by

Hintikka (Mortimer, 1989) proposed many solutions that approximate scientific inference of knowledge from data. Automation of scientific discovery also contributed to the logic of induction (Żytkow and Simon, 1988). Similarly, KDD develops many tools for inductive reasoning.

Inductive logic programming is a new attempt that expresses data as Prolog literals and knowledge as Prolog rules (DeRaedt, 1992; Dzeroski, 1996). Such knowledge, right after it is discovered by a Prolog-based discovery program, can be used by that program. Similarly, background knowledge can be used, often in the form of sophisticated Horn clauses. These are fine ideas and a large research community works on a variety of implementations. But current inductive logic programming is seriously limited. Neither probabilistic knowledge nor forms of knowledge such as systems of equations are supported by Prolog operation. In many respects the old logic of induction combined with deductive systems and probabilistic verification is more practical.

4. Philosophy of Science

Throughout the twentieth century, philosophy of science expanded our understanding of languages and theories used in empirical sciences. Since scientific knowledge is far more advanced than knowledge produced by KDD, the influence of philosophy of science on KDD is mainly indirect, through artificial intelligence and automated scientific discovery. We briefly signal some of the main directions in philosophy of science, as they will eventually be important in KDD.

A systematic analysis of the language of science is one of the main directions (Carnap, 1936). In particular, the meaning of complex linguistic constructs, terms, and statements is defined recursively, starting from the meaning of basic observational terms. All scientific terms acquire their meaning through a system of operational definitions, which are procedures that combine observations and computations (Bridgman, 1927). In KDD the data are given so there was no urge to examine the procedures for data acquisition. But when we want to share knowledge between database systems, we must compare the meanings of their attributes. We may also seek operational definitions of attributes that do not occur in a database in terms of the available attributes (Ras and Żytkow, 2000).

Logical structure and operational meaning capture the ways in which a given statement can be verified (Hempel, 1966). Widely accepted is Popper's (1961) doctrine of falsification, which requires of a scientific hypothesis that it would be false should certain data occur in the real world. Especially useful in KDD can be the theory of bootstrap confirmation (Glymour, 1980), which defines the conditions under which the same data can be derived from a theory and used for the theory's verification. Bootstrap confirmation does not require the naive approach in which data are divided into training and test data. It can also account for verification of theories, which use hidden objects and properties.

Philosophy of science has contributed in many ways to the logical view of scientific theories. In addition to treatment of individual theories as axiomatic deductive systems (Chapter 27), it has promoted the doctrine of reductionism in which all theories can be reduced to a few basic theories such as quantum mechanics and general relativity. Theory T1 can be reduced to T2 when T1 can be derived from a combination of T2 and conditions that describe the range of applications of T1 within T2. Reductionism becomes both natural and necessary when competing knowledge is acquired about the same domain. This is already happening in KDD.

5. Statistics

Statistics have been contributing to data analysis for more than a century. It provides tools that capture and utilize a nondeterministic component of empirical knowledge. Statistical distributions augment the language of logic, which is restricted to sharp statements and to two (or a few) truth values. The statistical counterpart of a deterministic equation $y = f(x)$, can be $y = S[f(x), e(x)]$, where $f(x)$ is now the expected value of y, given x, while e is one or more parameters that describe the statistical distribution S around the expected value. For instance, S can be a normal distribution of y with standard deviation $\sigma(x)$ and the mean value $\mu(x) = f(x)$. Both μ and σ can vary for different x. μ represents the deterministic component while σ characterizes statistical distribution of values, due to error or interpopulation differences.

5.1. Error and Population Distributions

Not long ago empirical error was not even sanctioned as an element of data. Even at the end of the eighteenth century, when the role of precise scientific measurements was widely accepted, error was not openly admitted. Only slowly, throughout the nineteenth century, was it accepted that valid observations of the same property can differ. Eventually, the information on empirical error was required for every piece of scientific data. But in KDD the error of data is still infrequently considered.

We must remember that empirical data without error are meaningless. Not knowing the error we cannot tell the accuracy required for fitting a hypothesis to the data. Error is not merely a number but a statistical distribution of values of the measured variable.

But a statistical distribution can also model the noise of transmission and statistical variation in a population. We must clearly know what the source of statistical distribution is in a given data set. The notion of a population makes sense when objects are sampled from a natural and steady group. But it makes no sense in scientific experiments, when the scientist can chose the pattern in which experiments are made.

5.2. Adapting the Methods of Statistics

At present, statistics is underutilized and sometimes ignored in KDD. We should not only apply but also expand the methods of statistics; sometimes knowingly leave them aside, but never ignore them. It is wise to start from implementing textbook solutions in KDD systems: formalisms of contingency tables, correspondence analysis, factor analysis, principal component analysis, and so forth. But then we must realize the limitations of traditional statistics. It was limited to small data sets where fifty cases were typical while one thousand was very big. It was applied to single data tables (matrices). The data were often obtained by carefully designed collection methods and experiment (Chapter 25). The analysis was manual, including human-intensive generation of hypotheses and assumptions about statistical distributions. A drive toward reasoning from assumptions made a significant portion of statistics deductive and detached from empirical inquiry.

KDD must overcome these limitations and it has means to do that. Databases include many tables, very many attributes, and huge numbers of tuples. The analysis of such data must be automated, including automated search in large hypothesis spaces. Data are often obtained for purposes other than knowledge mining, but the size of data sets permits verification of assumptions about statistical distributions or even inference of such distributions.

5.3. Hypotheses Testing

A deterministic empirical theory should be as general, complete, and adequate to the data as allowed by the domain under investigation. Logic and philosophy of science provide mechanisms that assess generality, completeness, and adequacy. But when statistical distributions become part of a theory, logical verification must be replaced by statistical tests. Measures such as the degree of determinism by Cramer's V (Press et al., 1992) or measures of association, as introduced by Goodman and Kruskal (1954), can be used to decide whether a deterministic approximation is justified.

In statistics, one of the standard concerns is whether a regularity induced from data is real. It can be a manifestation of another regularity or even a mere fluctuation in random data. The test of significance estimates the probability that the data could have been generated from the hypothesized distribution (Press et al., 1992). Historically, thresholds of acceptance were not usually demanding, to allow even a weak hypothesis to test positively against small amounts of data. In KDD, data are often plentiful, so the significance thresholds can be more demanding. They must be even more demanding when the numbers of hypotheses formed and tests applied are very large, as otherwise we would accept plenty of regularities in random data.

6. Information Theory

Information theory was initially developed as a theoretical foundation for data transmission. The main concern was adequate and efficient transmission. Adequacy required keeping the adverse influence of noise under control. Compression (encoding) of messages for transmission was used for efficiency. The main concepts of information, entropy and the minimum message length became the subject of both practical and theoretical interest. Brillouin (1956) created a systematic information theory perspective on scientific knowledge. Notions of expected information and information gain were adopted to tasks such as decision tree formation (Quinlan, 1986). The minimum message length was also used in support of tasks such as classification (Wallace and Boulton, 1968) and statistical inference (Wallace and Freeman, 1987). Eventually it was replaced by the minimum description length (Rissanen, 1983), which is frequently used to drive the search for regularities in data (Dowe et al., 1996) and considered the main target of discovery. It combines a simple way of comparing hypotheses by their length with a measure of adequacy by the complete fit to the given data.

The minimum message length can be viewed as optimal data compression, such that the original data can be fully restored. But in KDD we do not need to seek descriptions that capture the data in all details. Search for objective regularities in a domain represented by data is different from optimal data compression. Even though a regularity can be seen as a mechanism that produces data, we are not concerned with a faithful reproduction of an individual data set. Often a physically adequate description is longer than the minimal description under a given encoding schema.

The notion of minimal description makes sense with respect to a particular encoding schema. Different encoding schemas will result in different minimal descriptions. Encoding schemas work well for separate forms of knowledge such as decision trees. They are also very useful when it makes sense to pay attention to every bit of the data, for instance, in the study of DNA transformations (Milosavljevic and Jurka, 1993). There is no optimal encoding schema, however, that would cover all forms of knowledge.

7. Databases

KDD would not be possible if databases were not so common. In addition, relational database technology has been widely accepted. KDD benefits from a simple and uniform structure of relational data as well as from uniformity of database management systems (DBMS). Furthermore, databases embraced the logical world view. That view distinguishes (1) a real-world domain, represented conceptually by entity-relationship diagrams and database schemas, (2) data that represent specific objects within the domain, (3) operations on data, and (4) languages capable of describing data and operations on data. This is a popular view of data and a balanced foundation for KDD. Augmented by the logic-based theory of knowledge, this view allows for transfer of ideas and solutions among logic, philosophy of science, artificial intelligence, and KDD.

Data manipulation and access techniques provided by DMBS can furnish the KDD process with data. As business data are distributed in many tables optimized for business process support and data integrity control, the data relevant to the discovery tasks must be collected from the base tables. A well-designed query will create a view that combines information from several relational tables by the use of JOIN, SELECT, PROJECT, and aggregation operations. A view, as a relational table, can be mined for knowledge with the use of a broad range of KDD techniques that apply to single tables.

A tight coupling can be used to connect DBMS and knowledge discovery software: the DBMS performs all data manipulations, while KDD software proposes and evaluates hypotheses. But a discovery system can do its own data manipulations on a view prepared by a DBMS. This is called loose coupling, as DBMS is used occasionally to create a major view, that is explored as a discovery system. Loose coupling permits a discovery system to optimize generation of large numbers of short-lived views in the main memory and knowledge generation from those views, guided by the intermediate results, all within the boundaries of the discovery process.

In addition to view generation, the potential for increased interaction between DBMS and KDD is enormous. For instance, discovery systems should utilize data catalogs maintained by DBMS. A data catalog provides information important for discovery techniques. The type of an attribute tells what operations and relations on data are meaningful, while bounds on attribute domains can be used to guide the search.

Databases offer new challenges, not applicable to data resulting from scientific and statistical experiment design. In many databases, data are collected to support a business process. For example, business data acquisition can start by sending loan offers, receiving some responses, approving some of the responses, and accepting some loans by bank customers. Some loans turn bad; the status of many is unknown. What can be predicted from those data about future offers and loans? The set of records shrinks step by step. In statistical terms, data may be very skewed in several ways. When making a generalization, we should estimate the populations relevant to different steps in the business process. Recently, as data became an asset that has a market value, the process of data collection is often more carefully designed to assure that data represent valuable populations. Data warehousing is also helpful, as the main goal is transformation of business data to the knowledge acquisition perspective.

8. Artificial Intelligence

AI is one of the oldest fields in computer science. It started as a study of the principles of intelligence. The main engineering challenge was the construction of computer systems as intelligent as humans. Contrary to early estimates the task proved to be surprisingly hard, but many substantial accomplishments have been made. Some are a part of the modern teaching of AI (Jackson, 1999; Russell and Norvig, 1995).

AI is one of the founding domains for KDD, a provider of mechanisms for search and knowledge representation, ideas for knowledge acquisition, and elements of intelligent agent technology.

The discovery process always involves a search (Langley et al., 1987). Here the theory of search in AI provides many search mechanisms useful in KDD. They are well designed so it is easy to understand their properties and to modify them (Russell and Norvig, 1995).

Global and homogeneous knowledge representation is one of the objectives in AI. The attitude toward a global knowledge representation, however, is cautious. A universal representation is considered impractical. For instance, the predicate calculus is very useful in limited applications that use directed reasoning, but becomes hopeless in universal applications involving theorem provers. But there is a definite advantage in efficiently combining reasoning with knowledge in different forms. KDD adapted various AI techniques that support limited representations of knowledge. It is making slow progress toward knowledge unification.

Even if the influence of agent technology is still minor, it has already produced a big difference, by enabling large-scale multipurpose searches that have positioned KDD ahead of statistics and database methods.

9. Machine Learning

Machine learning took shape as a subfield of AI. In principle any form of knowledge can be learned from many sources, but the vast majority of research in machine learning was spent on concept learning from sets of attribute value tuples (Chapter 28). In this task, inherited from classification of feature vectors in pattern recognition, the data used for learning are well-prepared sets of examples and counterexamples (Shi, 1992), sometimes following the near-miss strategy (Winston, 1992).

KDD attracted substantial interest in the machine-learning community. Concept learning is often considered knowledge discovery, when concepts are learned from large data tables. Examples are no longer carefully prepared by a teacher so that statistical analysis infiltrates the earlier logical approach. We must remember, however, that concept learning is a very limited discovery task (Żytkow, 1997).

The use of symbolic forms of knowledge that are understandable and easy to explain is one of the main advantages of machine learning. Another advantage is a substantial number of mechanisms for evaluation of the induced knowledge and for evaluation of learning systems. Among the drawbacks is the limitation to single tables, and problems with missing data that are notorious in many databases.

10. Automation of Scientific Discovery

Research on automation of scientific discovery (ASD) has been active since the 1970s. It belongs to artificial intelligence and is motivated by intellectual curiosity about discovery and by the quest for automating intelligence.

A significant percentage of contributors to the first KDD meetings were researchers who established ASD. More than a decade of intensive research on automation of discovery prior to the origination of KDD legitimized the idea of automated discovery. Discovery, especially scientific discovery, employs the most sophisticated forms of human intelligence and was considered the most difficult, or even impossible, to automate. Popper (1961) argued that the logic of discovery is impossible. Research on automation of discovery initially progressed by demonstration that different isolated steps of scientific discovery can be done by computer systems. When a number of methods that provided such existential proofs became available, the next natural task was integration of many discovery capabilities into one system (Langley et al., 1987; Żytkow, 1996).

KDD can learn from the experience of ASD (Chapter 29), primarily from discovery systems that are more automated than KDD systems and can discover forms of knowledge yet to be considered in KDD. Discovery in scientific databases can especially be influenced, as the expected forms of knowledge are similar. ASD was occupied with discovery methods that can repeat some of the well-known scientific discoveries. It is clear that it will take a long time before a discovery system can make discoveries that are original and significant by scientific standards. In contrast, KDD aims at the present practical results. It is satisfied with discoveries in individual data sets.

11. Neural Networks

Neural networks compete with other discovery methods that approximate multidimensional numerical functions (Zurada, 1992). Such functions are a limited form of knowledge, but the field has been very creative in casting learning and discovery tasks for neural network application. Classical networks are limited to input from one data table and are slow learners. Arguably the main motivation for the broad use of networks is the metaphor of the human brain, and the broad success of simple neural network engines that support learning by backpropagation.

Knowledge in the form of a network was commonly criticized as nonintelligible, but recently a large effort has been dedicated to derivation of rules and other symbolic forms of knowledge from networks (Chapter 31).

12. Rough Sets

At the foundation of rough sets lies the idea that any empirical conceptual framework is granular. Each concept is measured with limited accuracy. That leads to indiscernibility of objects that are different but cannot be distinguished by attributes in the framework (Chapter 30).

The foundations of rough sets are close to those of machine learning. Data, called an information system, consist of a single table. The paradigmatic application is concept learning from examples, called concept approximation. Two tuples that are equal for all attributes but differ on their class assignment are called inconsistent in machine learning. Machine learning treats data inconsistency as an inconvenience that must be avoided, for instance, by expert advice. In contrast, rough sets developed a formalism that systematically uses data inconsistency (Chapter 9). All unproblematic examples of concept C determine its lower approximation C_*, while all inconsistent cases belong to the boundary. The lower approximation together with the boundary form the upper approximation C^*. So-called strong rules capture lower approximation while upper approximation is the target of possible rules.

Data inconsistency is a common result of data reduction, when only a subset of attributes is considered, and tuples become equal on the reduced set of attributes. Many rough sets techniques are used for data reduction, by determining special subsets of attributes called reducts, which are a popular contribution to KDD (Lin and Cercone, 1997). A classical reduct is a minimal set of attributes that retains indiscernibility in the original data.

In its early stages, similarly to early machine learning, the rough sets approach was used to learn from small well-prepared data sets, often called decision tables. Data reduction to decision tables is still one of the key methods. Recently concept approximation methods have been applied to large data sets.

13. Fuzzy Sets

Fuzzy sets are far less influential in KDD than neural networks and rough sets, but there are attempts to bring them into the KDD mainstream (Cios et al., 1998). The main ideas, which are (1) sets with a varied degree of membership, (2) combinations of such sets, and (3) application of fuzzy predicates, are motivated by modeling everyday knowledge and knowledge-based reasoning. For these reasons fuzzy sets may become useful in KDD as an appealing knowledge expression useful in business and other domains where other formalisms operate with unnecessary precision. Similar to rough sets, fuzzy sets simplify the formalism of statistics and bypass the unnecessary and unwarranted precision of many statistical inferences.

14. Visualization

Are our eyes smarter than our discovery systems? Even if many automated discoveries do not require inspection by the human eye, humans who operate discovery software want to understand the findings and verify the details of matching hypotheses against data. We should not neglect simple curiosity and aesthetic pleasure as other motivating factors.

Designing an appropriate visualization for a special type of knowledge is often very demanding. There are plenty of visualizations offered by discovery systems that do not satisfy even the most elementary rules of good visualizations. An effective visualization must immediately show why the presented hypothesis is interesting. Distraction and irrelevancy must be avoided. A number of textbooks introduce general visualization principles (e.g., Bertin, 1983; Tufte, 1997; Strothotte, 1998).

In this handbook we distinguish the visualization of discovery results from data visualization. Both have a long history. The latter is useful both in data preparation and as a discovery method selection. If our eyes notice a linear dependence, an equation finder can be invoked to determine the optimal parameter values and their error. But if our eyes notice a more complex functional dependence, discovery software must additionally determine the form of the dependence. Visualization of results follows and the best hypothesis is shown jointly with the data, so that the human eye can notice the areas of mismatch between the hypothesis and the data.

Interactive visualization is especially important for explorative discovery tasks (Chen, 1999; Card et al., 1999). It can guide a semiautomatic discovery process when many discovery subtasks are started by the user based on intermediate results. These intermediate results must be easy to capture. Good visualizations can support the user in selecting fruitful directions of further search tasks.

15. Computer Hardware

Exponential growth of computer hardware is perhaps the main underlying reason for the expansion of KDD and all computer-dependent fields that support KDD. Fast processors, large internal memories, and huge disk spaces are now available at low prices. Networks are fast and far reaching and their use is also inexpensive. Data acquisition hardware is widely available and can pump empirical data automatically into databases at the rate of terabytes per day. All that progress is matched by the growth in software, in system development expertise, and in numbers of specialists in all computer-related fields. Computational capabilities have created room for techniques that even ten to fifteen years ago would not be used. While old professions such as traditional statistics are now endangered (Friedman, 1997), new fields such as KDD must be cautious about new methods. When access to computers was expensive, users thought seriously about their methods and applied them prudently. Some techniques would not be proposed. N-fold cross-validation, bagging, and boosting are the products of fast and cheap computation.

References

Bertin, J. 1983. *Semiology of Graphics*. Madison, WI: The University of Wisconsin Press.

Bridgman, P. W. 1927. *The Logic of Modern Physics*. The Macmillan Company.

Brillouin, L. 1956. *Science and Information Theory*. Academic Press.

Card, S., J. Mackinlay, and B. Shneiderman. 1999. *Readings in Information Visualization*. San Francisco, CA: Morgan Kaufmann.

Carnap, R. 1936. "Testability and meaning." *Phil. Sci.* **3**.

Chen, C. 1999. *Information Visualisation and Virtual Environments*. London: Springer.

Cios, K., W. Pedrycz, and R. Swiniarski. 1998. *Data Mining Methods for Knowledge Discovery*. Kluwer.

De Raedt, L. 1992. *Interactive Theory Revision: An Inductive Logic Programming Approach*. Academic Press.

Dowe, D., K. B. Korb, and J. J. Oliver. (eds). 1996. *Information, Statistics and Induction in Science*. World Scientific.

Dzeroski, S. 1996. "Inductive logic programming." *Advances in Knowledge Discovery and Data Mining*, edited by U. Fayyad, G. Piatetsky-Shapiro, P. Smyth, and R. Uthurusamy, pp. 117–152. MIT Press.

Elmasri, R. and S. B. Navathe. 1999. *Fundamentals of Database Systems*. Addison-Wesley.

Friedman, J. H. 1997. *Data Mining and Statistics: What's the Connection?*

Glymour, C. 1980. *Theory and Evidence*. Princeton University Press.

Goodman, L. and W. Kruskal. 1954. *Measure of Association for Cross Classification*. Springer Series in Statistics, Springer-Verlag 1979. Reprinted from *J. Am. Stat. Assoc.* **49**, 732–764.

Hempel, C. 1966. *Philosophy of Natural Science*. Prentice-Hall.

Jackson, P. 1999. *Introduction to Expert Systems*. 3d ed. Addison-Wesley.

Johnson, R. J. and G. K. Bhattaharyya. 1992. *Statistics Principles and Methods*. John Wiley & Sons.

Langley, P. 1996. *Elements of Machine Learning*. Morgan Kaufmann.

Langley, P., H. A. Simon, G. L. Bradshaw, and J. M. Żytkow. 1987. *Scientific Discovery: Computational Explorations of the Creative Processes*. Cambridge, MA: MIT Press.

Lin, T. Y. and N. Cercone (eds). 1997. *Rough Sets and Data Mining: Analysis of Imprecise Data*. Kluwer Publishers.

Mill, J. S. 1843. *System of Logic*.

Milosavljevic, A. and J. Jurka. 1993. "Discovery by minimal length encoding: a case study in molecular evolution." *Machine Learning* **12**: 69–87.

Mitchell, T. 1997. *Machine Learning*. McGraw-Hill.

Mortimer, H. 1988. *The Logic of Induction*. Chichester, UK: Ellis Horwood Limited.

Popper, K. R. 1961. *The Logic of Scientific Discovery*. New York: Science Editions.

Press, W. H., B. P. Flannery, S. A. Teukolsky, and W. T. Vetterling. 1989. *Numerical Recipes in Pascal*. Cambridge, UK: Cambridge University Press.

Quinlan, J. R. 1986. "Induction of decision trees." *Machine Learning* **1**: 81–106.

Rich, E. and K. Knight. 1991. *Artificial Intelligence*. McGraw-Hill.

Rissanen. 1983. "A universal prior for integers and estimation by minimum description length." *Ann. Stat.* **11**: 416–431.

Russell, S. and P. Norvig. 1995. *Artificial Intelligence: A Modern Approach*. Prentice-Hall.

Shi, Z. 1992. *Principles of Machine Learning*. International Academic Publishers.

Shrager, J. and P. Langley. (eds). 1990. *Computational Models of Scientific Discovery and Theory Formation.* Morgan Kaufmann Publishers.

Strothotte, T. 1998. *Computational Visualization.* Berlin: Springer.

Suppe, F. (ed). 1979. *The Structure of Scientific Theories.* IL: University of Illinois Press.

Suzuki, E. 1999. "Scheduled discovery of exception rules." *Discovery Science, LNAI 1721,* pp. 184–195. Springer.

Tufte, E. 1997. *Visual Explanations.* Cheshire, CT: Graphics Press.

Valdés-Pérez, R. E., J. M. Żytkow, and H. A. Simon. 1993. "Scientific model-building as search in matrix spaces." *Proceedings of Eleventh National Conference on Artificial Intelligence,* pp. 472–478. The AAAI Press.

Wallace, C. S. and D. M. Boulton. 1968. "An information measure for classification." *Comput. J.* **11**: 185–194.

Wallace, C. S. and P. R. Freeman. 1987. "Estimation and inference by compact coding." *J. R. Stat. Soc. Series B* **49**: 240–265.

Winston, P. H. 1992. *Artificial Intelligence.* Addison-Wesley.

Ziarko, W. (ed). 1994. *Rough Sets, Fuzzy Sets and Knowledge Discovery.* Workshops in Computing. Springer-Verlag.

Zurada, J. M. 1992. *Introduction to Artificial Neural Systems.* West Publishing Company.

Żytkow, J. M. 1996. "Automated discovery of empirical laws." *Fund. Inform.* **27**: 299–318.

Żytkow, J. M. 1997. "Knowledge = concepts: a harmful equation." *Proceedings of KDD-97.* AAAI Press.

PART TWO

FUNDAMENTAL CONCEPTS

4 TYPES AND FORMS OF DATA

Willi Klösgen

ABSTRACT Knowledge discovery methods analyse data of quite diverse types such as cross sections, time series, texts, or multimedia data. We first summarize dimensions being important for identifying subtypes of these main general data types that require special analysis approaches. Thus, specifically for complex, that is, large, high-dimensional, multirelational, or dynamic, data sets problems occur with current views on data developed in statistics and other disciplines. Next, we deal with some organizational forms. Data are not collected as an unregulated set of numbers or strings, but appear in some organized form. Starting at the classical form used in data analysis for organizing cross-sectional data, the flat rectangular organization, we proceed to more complex forms and deal with time and space referenced data. Finally, we treat data aggregation levels and meta data. A classification of data types is useful to select appropriate mining tasks, analysis methods, and data management solutions for an application.

1. Overview

A few concepts from data analysis are important for organizing data. Typically, a population is studied which has a large number of analysis objects, but often with data available only for a sample. Each object is described by variables of different measurement scales. Populations have either a focussed time and space reference, or are temporally and spatially distributed. They are fixed, or evolving over time with additional data incrementally available.

Knowledge discovery in databases (KDD) usually deals with micro data (about individual objects), but macro data (on aggregated sets of objects; see Section 7) can also be analyzed. Different degrees of statistical quality of objects and variables, size, dimensionality, and dynamics of data, require specific analysis paradigms and an adaptation of current views on data predominant in statistics and other disciplines.

Table 1 contains some dimensions for classifying data. In the following sections, we summarize data types and organization forms along these dimensions. Whereas here we deal with the conceptual dimensions from a data analysis point of view, in Chapter 6 organization concepts are treated from the database implementation point of view.

2. Cross-sectional Data

Many statistical data analysis tools and most data mining systems assume that data are organized in a rectangular form compiled of rows and columns. The rows represent analysis objects, such as companies, clients, products, hospitals, patients, diagnoses, and therapies. The columns correspond to variables (statistical terminology) or attributes (database terminology). An attribute is a property of an object which in principle can be observed and described by a value (e.g., a number or label). That is, some measuring is applied to an object and a number or label results. Each variable can be seen as a dimension of a multidimensional space where each object is a point in that space. Conceptually this organization form is a two-dimensional matrix. Since typically very large sets of objects are analyzed in data mining, database systems are used to store these rectangular data (see Chapter 6). The corresponding matrix will usually not fit into main memory.

2.1. Object Populations and Samples

The individual objects that are analyzed in a data mining task are instances of an object class. The object class encompasses the generic properties of the object instances. In the simple rectangular data model, the object class is determined by the attributes, that is, a single object is defined by the values that describe the observations of the attributes for this object. Thus, two objects with the same values for all attributes captured in the data set cannot be

33

Table 1 Dimensions for Classifying Data

Main data type:	Observation/transaction	Textual	Multimedia	
Representativity:	Complete population	Sample of convenience	Random sample	Stratified sample
Variable type:	Binary	Categorical	Continuous	Mixed
Missing data:	No	Yes		
Conclusiveness:	Low	Medium	High	
Size:	Moderate	Large	Very large	Vast
Dimensionality:	Low	Medium	High	
Dynamics:	Static	Timely evolving		
Distribution:	Local	Fixed locations	Scattered on net	
Object heterogeneity:	One object class	Multivalued attributes	Multiple object classes	
Time reference:	One cross-section	2 Independent cross-sections	Series of independent cross-sections	Longitudinal data
	Continuous	Time series		
Space reference:	Point	Line	Area	Surface
Text structure:	Unstructured	Structured parts	Hypertext	
Text languages:	English	Other languages	Mixed collection	Multilingual text
Text quality:	High	Low (e.g., e-mail)		
Text size:	Full size	Abstract		
Hybrid forms:	No	Mixed observational data	Observational & text & multimedia	
Aggregation:	Micro data	Macro data		
Meta data:	No	Data dictionary	Domain knowledge	

distinguished. In data analysis terminology, objects are also called analysis units, entities, cases, individuals, and experimental units.

The set Ω of objects that is conceptually studied in a data mining task is called a population. It usually includes all potential objects that can be conceived in a given context and thus is the exhaustive or complete set of objects representing the target of the analysis about which findings shall be derived. Ω can be finite or infinite, concrete or hypothetical. Usually the objects of a population are appropriately focussed in space and time, for example, all cars running in the United States in 1998.

An example of an infinite, hypothetical population would be given by all the dollar exchange rates in the next 30 days, with the hypothetical currency rate of main currencies as attributes. In data mining, we mainly deal with finite and concrete, that is, physically existing, populations, assuming that populations are well defined collections of real objects.

A data mining task analyzes available data. A database may contain records for all the clients of a company, so that each client is represented. Often, however, data are only available for a subset of the population. Such a given subset of objects is called a sample. Typically in data mining, the given sample data set is not a random sample (in a strong statistical sense). It is an opportunistic sample or sample of convenience (Huber, 1997), where data have often been collected for an unrelated purpose. Their collection may be mandated by law (e.g., census data) or by the administration of transactions (e.g., financial transactions, sales in a supermarket).

The statistical view of a population assumes that some underlying random process generates the objects. A sample is then generated by a random experiment that is repeated n times (sample size n) to generate the n objects. Moreover, an independent and identically distributed sample is typically required, where the generation of an object occurs independently from another, that is, the generation of previous objects does not influence the subsequent objects, and the distribution from which the objects are sampled is the same. In this view, we regard a car in the United States in 1998 as the outcome of a random process that moves a car owner with special socioeconomic properties to run a car of a particular make. The underlying decision of the car owner is determined by very many properties. Usually only a small part of these properties is observable or available. The influence of the missing properties is then summarized in the random process. See statistical textbooks for a detailed discussion (e.g., Koopmans, 1981). The example shows that usually these assumptions are not exactly valid. The cars are not bought independently from one another and there may be a distribution shift during the year.

An ideal sample would have the property that any finding desired for the population could be inferred, without error, from the sample. Representative samples approximate this property. A random sample is often a useful solution to this problem. Random samples rely on a procedure for drawing a sample that is equivalent to lottery drawings and realized by the exploitation of random numbers. A random sampling procedure must generate, with an equal chance, every possible sample having the same number of objects. Although most data samples analyzed in typical data mining applications are only samples of convenience, there are some applications with data collected by a careful sampling design, for example, when opinion poll and market research institutes collect surveys. For these stratified samples, each object has a sample weight (possibly also an individual and a household weight) that must be exploited by analysis methods. Most data mining methods and systems (not originating from the statistical community), however, do not provide the option of analyzing weighted objects. A more detailed overview on sampling is given in Chapter 14.1 of this handbook.

Many data mining methods rely on statistical evaluations or models and more or less require a database representing an independent and identically distributed sample. Analyses of opportunistic data can then cause problems: assessing the accuracy and reliability of a fitted model by the usual statistical techniques can lack severity. This problem is not limited to the context of data mining, it has already often been neglected in many conventional applied data analysis projects. Huber (1997) describes this situation: 'If you have to tell your sponsor, that certain questions cannot be answered with the data at hand, he will easily find somebody else who will answer them anyway.' Therefore the degree of representativeness of available data for a given analysis purpose must be carefully assessed for a responsible data mining application.

Also in cases where the database includes the whole population, for example, all customers of a particular time period, methods of conventional statistical inference may not be appropriate for data mining applications, for example, for predictions on the next time period, which possibly has a different distribution. *P*-values and confidence intervals generally have no meaning when the sample is identical with the population, but that may depend on the statistical approach that is used for evaluating a special data mining pattern. For instance, when searching for deviating subgroups (see Chapter 16.3 of this handbook), the significance of a subgroup (e.g., young male clients) can be determined by the p-value, interpreting the subgroup as a sample from either the population of all clients (or of a sample of the population when the database does not include all clients) and rejecting that the subgroup distribution is identical with the overall distribution based on the p-value. Here the overall distribution is determined from the database, be it a sample or the whole population.

2.2. Variables and Their Types

The second organization dimension in the rectangular approach refers to the variables (or attributes) that describe an object and capture the properties and characteristics of objects that are of interest for the analytic investigation behind a data mining task. Thus we study a multivariate data set, because more than one variable is recorded for each object. In the simple rectangular organization usually applied, each variable has a simple value domain consisting of a set of numbers or labels. Each object can have only one number or label as the value of a variable. The values are typically captured by classification into categories represented by labels, or by a process of measurement producing numbers. The values thus result from a mapping from the population being studied to the value domain. In the theory of measurement (Narens, 1985) these mappings are studied.

Variables can be distinguished by their type: discussed as the concept of scale in measurement theory. Scale defines the extent of semantic content about the variable values provided by the measurement. Variable scale is essential in determining the kind of data mining tasks and methods that can be used for a given problem. The simplest type is a binary variable (dichotomous variable) allowing only two values. Sex is a typical two-valued variable that can be arbitrarily coded 0 for males and 1 for females. Numerical coding is not necessary here, since the only property of the numbers being used is their discernability, but it is useful, because of computing shares as averages.

A nominal variable (polytomous variable) has a finite (usually not too large) value domain, where no implication of a natural ordering between the values of this domain exists. For an ordinal variable, such a natural ordering exists. Binary, nominal, and ordinal variables are special subtypes of categorical variables, usually holding a value domain of labels, such as poor, fair, average, good, and excellent as an example of a domain belonging to an ordinal variable.

Measurement has been mentioned as another (often more precise) form of quantifying an attribute of an object. Measurement (or continuous) variables include interval scale and ratio scale variables. Measurement assumes the existence of an origin, the magnitude (of e.g., a physical property) of an object that receives the numerical value zero, and of a unit which is the increment in magnitude that will receive a numerical increment of one. Measurement then assigns to each object the numerical value of its magnitude in multiples and fractions of the unit of measure layered off from the chosen origin.

Interval scales require the same numerical increment to be assigned to equal differences of the magnitudes of objects. Ratio scales allow the possibility of ratio comparisons (a 200-pound man is twice as heavy as a 100-pound man) and need well defined points where the physical magnitudes begin and measurement origins that are located at these points.

Data mining methods typically do not differ between interval and ratio scaled continuous variables. Transforming continuous variables into categorical ones is sometimes necessary and achieved by discretization (see Chapters 14.4 and 18.1).

Missing data and not applicable are special values that can be used to indicate that a value could not be observed for an object (e.g., has been lost, has not been measured, has not been answered) or is not possible for logical reasons (e.g., the value pregnant for a male).

The statistical view of a random process generating the objects now means that a generated object is described by the values of the variables, that is, the values are generated by the random process, so that it makes sense to talk about the probabilities with which the various values of a variable occur. Thus, the variables are seen as random variables. They have a joint probability distribution which typically is unknown (see Chapter 8 for a more detailed discussion of the statistical view on data). Objects have, conceptually, an infinite number of attributes and one of the problems in assessing the appropriateness of available data is to be sure that the given variables are the relevant ones to address the application problem.

2.3. Conclusiveness, Size, and Dimensionality

Whereas representativity refers to the (statistical) quality of objects, conclusiveness is the next dimension for classifying data referring to the quality of variables. Perhaps three data types can be qualitatively distinguished that have a low, medium, or high conclusiveness and which require different analysis and inference approaches. In this context, Hand (1998) discusses the role of proxy variables in data mining. When a proxy variable is used in place of the variable one really wants to analyze (and which is not available in the data), a mismatch between the analysis results and the real situation of the application domain can arise. Hand argues that this may not matter, if only a few cases are involved, but for large data sets it can be very important.

Another problem about the quality of variables deals with the degree with which target variables are clearly defined. Consider a production control application and the target concept high production quality to be predicted. $QV1 > 0.8$ & $QV2 > 0.9$ and $QV1 > 0.9$ & $QV2 > 0.8$ may be equally legitimate definitions of high quality products used by engineers (referring to variables QV such as hydrousity). Sensitivity of data mining results to such definition differences then becomes an important topic and methods over-refining the results may not be appropriate.

Proxy variables and vague concepts are examples that the size of the data set influences the selection of data mining approaches because of a possible mismatch between accuracy of results and vagueness of concepts. Friedman (1998) argues that 'every time the amount of data increases by a factor of ten, we should totally rethink how and what we compute.' The size of the data set can be loosely defined by four categories, a moderate category defined by a size that still fits into main memory (e.g., <100,000 objects) and the other categories each involving an additional factor 10. These loose definitions are of course subject to rapid technological change. Run time efficiency is critical for data sizes which are not moderate. Usually an internal implementation is around ten to twenty times faster than an implementation based on external data access (for the same data size). Vast data sizes of over 100 millions of objects, for example, yearly transactions of credit card companies or phone calls of telecommunications companies, can only be exploited on the micro level by very special methods.

Size not only influences run time efficiency, but also the appropriateness of methods and underlying statistical or data analysis views. For instance, the role of significance must be carefully studied. In large data sets, slight deviations are highly statistically significant. Only some of the deviations might be important, and thus substantive significance has to be assessed.

Size of the data set with respect to the number of variables can be regarded as the dimensionality of the object space. It can be loosely defined by three categories with a low dimensionality referring to the usual upper limit (around ten) on the number of variables included into statistical models (e.g., linear regression, generalized linear models, projection pursuit, adaptive regression splines; Friedman, 1991). The following two categories each involve a factor 10. The number of possible models (or patterns) explodes with increasing dimensionality and also multicollinearity becomes a problem. Typically data preprocessing methods of variable selection (see Chapter 14) are then applied, but some data mining approaches do not preselect variables, instead they exploit all variables.

For big data sets (high dimensionality and large number of objects), analysis paradigms such as leisurely exploration to get familiar with the data might become problematic, especially when rapid results are necessary to influence immediate decisions. Then more autonomous methods are needed. Another direction is anytime algorithms that take into account not only the quality of models or patterns, but also the available resources, that is, time and memory. These algorithms can be interrupted at any time and still produce an output of a certain quality (Zilberstein and Russel, 1996).

2.4. Dynamic and Distributed Data

In Sections 3 and 4 below, we will discuss time and space related data and refer to domain objects that have a time or space reference. Here we deal with the time and space reference of the data, that is, collection time and physical location of data. A dynamic data set is temporarily evolving, with data on further objects incrementally arriving, for example, data on new clients or transactions. Often this is accompanied by real-time analysis constraints. The database owner wants to see the results early before a different population is set up by new objects and the previous results become obsolete. The time relation of objects can be explicitly represented and analyzed in both static and dynamic data sets (see Section 3), but dynamic data sets can also be analyzed without representing the time reference of objects. Thus, time reference of objects is independent from the dynamic aspect of evolving data sets.

The physical location of data sets can be centered in one computer, or distributed on a fixed number of sites, or even be scattered around the Web. Hand (1998) points to some difficulties that arise with scattered information, for example, the problem of obtaining random samples.

2.5. Extensions of the Rectangular Organization Form

A limitation of the simple rectangular form is the restriction on single values of attributes. Often several values from the value domain of an attribute can be observed for an object. A person can run several cars or a client can buy several items. If only the names of the makes or items are registered, multivalued (or set-valued) attributes are introduced (e.g., Cohen, 1996). Then subsets of values of an attribute are allowed when describing a single object. Some data mining systems offer this extension of the simple rectangular data organization. Often they use an inverted file organization, which is organized not by objects (records), but by some bit

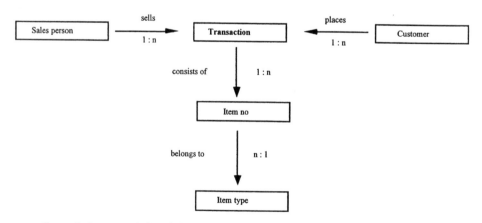

Figure 1 Conceptual view (schema) on data with multiple object classes

vector representation of attribute values. A bit vector represents all objects for an individual attribute value indicating whether this special value is set for an object. This solution with multivalued attributes is often more flexible than the explicit binarization, of attributes, where for each value of an attribute, for which multiple values are relevant, its own binary attribute is defined.

The multivalued attribute approach is a special case of multiple object classes. Then data do not belong to one object class only, but several classes are involved, such as persons and cars, or customers, transactions, and items. Each object class is then defined by several attributes, for example, not only the name (type) of an item is recorded for a transaction as can be implemented with multiple values, but also its price, purchase date, size. Thus the object class item-no holds instances representing a sale of an individual physical item identified by item or serial number. Typically the objects from different classes are linked by external link attributes, for example, transaction-id links and item-no objects with a transaction object.

Figure 1 shows the conceptual view of an example for multiple object classes. Five object classes (entity types) are involved: customers, sales persons, transactions, items, and item types. The schema presented in Figure 1 shows the relationships between object classes (entity relationship diagram). The type of database system used to store data consisting of multiple object classes influences appropriate data modeling on the next lower level, the database implementation level. The external link approach is used in, for example, relational systems, whereas object-oriented systems provide more powerful set-oriented data modeling capabilities. A more detailed discussion of these aspects is given in Chapter 6 from a database point of view. See Ullman (1988) for a detailed presentation of database modeling.

Thus, multiple object class data are not a problem for data management but for (statistical) analyses. Most data mining methods assume rectangular one-relational data. Then several relations must be joined during preprocessing and the analyses are run on the resulting one-relational data set. However, this approach sometimes lacks flexibility because of the non-dynamic join (independent from search in hypotheses spaces) and clumsy description languages (see Chapter 16.3 of this handbook).

Mixed-effects models (Lindstrom and Bates, 1990) are a recent statistical approach to deal with, for example, repeated measures data, longitudinal studies, and nested designs.

3. Time Related Data

Cross-sectional data have a focussed time and space reference. In this section, we discuss different subtypes of time related data, specifically series of cross-sections, panels, and time series. First, we assume that a time variable exists that associates a time reference to each object, typically expressing that the object has been observed during the recorded time point or time range. Second, we deal with time-series data.

3.1. Independent Cross-sections and Longitudinal Data

The simplest case is a binary time variable and a rectangular organization of objects and variables. Thus, we deal with two subpopulations observed for two different time points or ranges. Methods to analyze change (see Chapter 16.3.2) can be applied to these data. Two subtypes are important: independent cross-sections and longitudinal data (panels). Objects of independent populations must be generated independently from one another, necessarily this means that the two subpopulations do not contain the same objects. Panels include the same objects, so that each object is observed over time.

In cases with a categorical time variable, we have k subpopulations corresponding to k different time points, again with the independent cross-section and panel subtypes. The time points can be equidistantly or irregularly spaced. Methods to analyze trends (see Chapter 16.3.2) are important for these data.

Although the structure of longitudinal data is simple (rectangular form), many problems of heterogeneous data occur. The problems accompanying inhomogeneous data refer, for example, to different standards for measurement, different sets of observed variables, or different value domains changing over time.

Time can be also represented as a continuous variable. Then each object has a special individual time reference. Sometimes these time referenced objects represent actions or events extracted from a log-file. Methods for analyzing these data are presented in Chapter 16.2.4.

3.2. Time Series

A second popular data type of statistics and data analysis is the time series (Kendall, 1976). It is not easy to draw a boundary between longitudinal data and time-series data. A single time series consists of one variable (e.g., Gross National Product), measured for one object (for example, a country), on at least say ten and often many more occasions (e.g., consecutive years). Whereas longitudinal data rarely contain ten observations per object, but consist of many objects and many variables. But a time-series database, as for example, used in econometric modeling (West and Harrison, 1997), usually collects data for many objects and variables.

So the distinction between these data types relates more to the analysis methods, with forecasting and econometric methods for time series, and multivariate, categorical, and cross-sectional analyses for longitudinal data. To satisfy the data access needs of these methods, different database techniques are used to manage longitudinal and time-series databases (Chapter 6).

Time-series systems (e.g., for econometric modeling) offer data management facilities for storing, updating, and accessing a set of time series. A time series is a sequence of values where each single value corresponds to a time point. Time series have a periodicity, so that the time points are equidistant in time dimension (e.g., monthly, quarterly, yearly time series).

Since time series often refer to a longer time space, the heterogeneity problems mentioned above must be regarded. So time-series management systems include meta data on time series, such as definition breaks, reliability tags, and so on (see Section 8 below).

4. Space Related Data

Whereas time is a one-dimensional concept, space is at least two-dimensional. So, if the spatial context is reduced to one dimension, all the distinctions made in Section 3 also apply for spatial data, for example, simply comparing two populations located at two spatial objects. When referring to the two or three dimensions of space, some special spatial data subtypes can be distinguished. A more detailed discussion of these cases is presented together with the relevant analysis methods in Chapter 16.8 of this handbook. Here we only roughly classify spatial data into four subtypes.

First, we assume that a cross-section of spatial objects is given. We distinguish four types of spatial objects: points, lines, areas, and surfaces. Line data describe, for example, rivers, roads, and power lines. Area data represent a geographical region that is subdivided into smaller parts (states, counties, statistical districts, fields) called districts, which cover the whole region and do not overlap. In this case, the districts are the spatial objects.

Spatial (or location) variables measure properties of spatial objects. A variable can depend on a continuous spatial reference, that is, the variable is virtually known for all points. Elevation or air pressure are examples of spatially continuous variables (in two- or three-dimensional space on earth, measured for selected points and interpolated in between). A variable may alternatively depend on point, line, area, or surface spatial objects. Pollution concentration is actually a continuous variable, but measured only at a few points so that interpolation is infeasible and must be treated as point data.

Line, area, and surface objects are typically described by aggregated variables (see Section 7 below), for example, the unemployment rate in a district is aggregated from all persons living in the district. Spatial variables show a peculiarity: additionally the relative spatial position of two objects is an important feature. Thus, one may ask whether a variable shows a correlation between the values of neighboring objects (spatial autocorrelation). Another question is whether objects with some property are more or less evenly distributed in space or exhibit a spatial clustering.

Second, we refer to a multiple object class situation with several types of spatial objects. The objects have a spatial reference. For example, earthquake objects represent point data which exists only for some points in space. Then the epicenter of an earthquake would be the spatial object referenced by an earthquake object. The earthquake object is described by variables such as duration, magnitude, and time. Occurrences of cancer types or locations of plant species are other examples of two- or three-dimensional point referenced objects.

Data with multiple object classes can include all types of spatial objects, for example, to derive the relationship between the incidence of a disease (point data) and the distance from a power line (line data), the socioeconomic characteristics of a region (area data) and topography (surface data). Geographic information systems (GIS) specifically deal with the management and visualization of spatial data (Fotheringham and Charlton, 1994).

There are a few general data mining methods appropriate for exploiting spatial data. Most work is done with a technical emphasis supporting efficient spatial queries and operations for spatial database systems (Gueting, 1994). k-Medoid clustering algorithms partition a database into k clusters. A cluster is an enumeration of objects near a common center (medoid) and k is an input parameter (Ng and Han, 1994). These algorithms are fairly inefficient when applied to databases of more than a thousand objects and several techniques exploiting the capabilities of spatial index structures have been added.

Aside from clustering approaches, some attempts adapt other popular data mining methods in order to also include spatial attributes. Spatial decision tree classifiers have been developed by Koperski et al. (1998) and spatial association rules by Koperski and Han (1995).

A different branch of clustering approaches refers to a target variable and employs statistical tests to derive geographical regions with a significantly outstanding distribution of the target variable, for example, with an excess incidence of disease or crime. Two branches of spatial clustering have been proposed, related to discrete or continuous spatial references. In the discrete case, a set of (small) districts is given and a cluster consists of a set of neighboring, contiguous districts.

Gebhardt (1998) proposes an approach to identify clusters that are constructed independently from these regional hierarchies and which can consist of a set of districts across the hierarchy boundaries. These methods employ special statistical tests to avoid random clusterings. Various experiments with randomly generated data show that usually many contiguous groups of districts exist that show some outstanding behavior, for example, include an overproportionally large share of randomly distributed target objects. This can be explained by the relatively large number of neighbors each district has in a two-dimensional space. Thus, if a district is outstanding, often a not too small chance exists that some neighbor is also outstanding. The proposed method employs an iterative aggregation of partial clusters, initialized with a set of highly connected triplet districts, and some special statistical tests considering the degrees of freedom one has in joining partial clusters. Since the subsearch for spatial clusters can be very time consuming when scheduled very many times within an integrated search process, a global statistical test (Moran's I) is run first to check the appropriateness of such a dynamic subsearch.

Openshaw and Perree (1996) have developed various methods that deal with the continuous case. Typical events that are analyzed are diseases, crimes, and traffic accidents that occur in a population at risk at points in a $x-y$ space. A spatial cluster is a circle (of varying size) around some parent point that includes a significantly high number of events (compared to the risk rate in the population). Different variants of these methods employ diverse statistical tests depending on the rarity of the target events, based on the Poisson or binomial distribution, bootstrap or Monte Carlo methods, and search strategies such as exhaustive or genetic algorithms.

Recently, Openshaw et al. (1999) have developed methods that also identify spatial clusters in a combined attributive, temporal, and geographic space. However, tests with synthetically generated simulated data sets (Openshaw et al., 2000) show that all the compared methods do not (yet) succeed in finding the relevant clusters in the combined space.

5. Textual Data

Most information stored in digital form, however, appears in textual form. Textual databases contain collections of documents. The texts are preprocessed using linguistic methods (Allen, 1995), before being analyzed with mining methods. In the simplest form, a document is merely a string of text of variable length. Documents on the Web possess a complex hypertext form. So a first classification dimension distinguishes several degrees of structural information that is captured together with text components. This varies from missing structural information, over information on sentences, paragraphs, chapters, to relational structures for hypertexts.

The next dimension refers to the languages of texts. A text collection can only include English texts, or documents written in several languages (but each document in a single language), or multilingual documents that can individually use different languages. The extent of documents (e.g., full text or abstract) and the linguistic quality of texts (e.g., low quality e-mails) are further text dimensions important for the analysis of documents.

Multimedia documents represent complex data consisting of textual, image, and sound components. However, the general data mining approach to deal with these data relies on preprocessing methods to extract features from the multimedia documents and to represent the documents as feature vectors. Data mining is then operated on the feature vectors that typically have a simple rectangular organization form. An overview on data mining approaches for texts is given in Chapter 38, multimedia applications are described in Chapter 39.

6. Hybrid Data

The data types can also be combined, such as for a patient object described with cross-sectional variables (sex, age, . . .), time-series data (blood pressure measured over some time range), textual data (diagnosis report), image data (x-ray photograph), and sound data (heart sounds). Two problems have to be solved: modeling the complex data in a database system and analyzing the data.

Data mining methods can be type-specific and operate on their specific partial data, for example, rules on the cross-sectional data, time-series methods on the time series, text mining methods on the diagnosis reports. Another approach relies on transforming data from one type to another, for example, by feature extraction. In a preprocessing step, features are extracted from time series, texts, images, and sounds. On the resulting cross-sectional data, appropriate data mining tasks are run. Thus, both approaches reduce the hybrid case to one or more data mining tasks run on nonhybrid data.

7. Micro and Macro Data

Micro data can informally be introduced as observations on individual observational units, that is, data about single (micro) objects. These objects are individuals and thus are not aggregates of other objects. Individual persons, clients, patients, companies are usually micro objects.

Macro data describe macro objects that are constructed as aggregates of micro objects. The aggregates or macro objects describe a higher level of the unit of observation. Macro data are aggregated with respect to time, space, or subject-matter, usually cross-classified by a set of category attributes. The aggregated variables represent counts or frequencies, sums, averages or other statistics characterizing a set of individual objects. Macro data can occur both in cross-sectional and time-series form. Typically in data mining, we deal with micro cross-sections, but also macro cross-sections such as data about districts are possible. Time series often are macro data, for example, trade series on exports aggregated over product and country categories. Then macrodata are used as microdata for the higher level objects.

Macrodata are analyzed instead of the underlying microdata, when the microdata are no longer available, are not permissible because of confidentiality restrictions, or are simply too vast to be analyzed efficiently.

Variables for macro objects are typically aggregated from micro objects, for example unemployment in a district. But there are also inherent macro variables that describe a district (e.g., district is governed by a conservative party). Aggregated variables must be normalized, to make the districts comparable. Thus, the numbers of unemployed in districts should not be compared, but the proportion of unemployment should be taken. Finding the proper normalization can, however, sometimes be more difficult. The number of traffic accidents in a district certainly depends on the population, but also on other factors such as the number of licensed cars.

Even with normalization, the districts should for many analyses be comparable to achieve proper results. For example, when deriving rules for aggregates, the unequal size of the aggregates must be considered. Thus, it may be problematic to include districts with very different (population) sizes. Weighting of aggregates is sometimes a solution.

In the context of official statistics (Michalewicz, 1991) some other types of macro data are studied that cannot be seen as micro data for higher level objects and that are currently being treated in OLAP (see Chapter 6.3 and Chapter 13.2 of this handbook). This second type of macro data relates to tables with cells constructed by combining categorical attributes. A cell contains a single summary variable such as a count of the objects falling within the cell. Klensin (1991) discusses the special data analysis requirements of these data and concludes that the relational model and the SQL approach are not appropriate.

8. Meta Data

Meta data describe the data being investigated on the semantic, structural, statistical, and physical level to support tasks such as data validation and imputation, selection and application of (data mining) methods, and interpretation of the results. These tasks can be partially automated and thus both the analyst and KDD methods can exploit meta data. Much meta data is typically implicit in the head of the analyst, but it is aspired to make this more explicit to permit analysis tools to access and manipulate meta data and guide the discovery process. Meta data are informally defined as data about the data, descriptions of the data, or information about the meaning of the data and the context in which they arose. They include information about types of variables, value domains, data types, periodicities, units of measurement, reliability of measurements, changed definitions of categories, sampling techniques applied, and physical location. Meta data may also be connected to the analysis results and contain information on the execution and evaluation of data mining tasks. Thus, meta data cover the whole data life cycle from data collection to data dissemination. Meta data management (storage, transformation, retrieval) is addressed in Chapter 6.7 of this handbook.

Hand (1993) distinguishes context-free and context-specific meta data The measurement scale of a variable is given as an example of context-free meta data. Information that is usually included in data dictionaries (for example, codebooks of statistical systems) belong mostly to context-free meta data. Context-specific meta data are a partial and formalized representation of the context (domain knowledge). Theoretically-based laws on variables (electric potential difference is the product of current and resistance) and constraints (humans are less than nine feet tall) are examples given by Hand.

Apart from the statistical community, where meta data are studied because of the growth in official statistics, collected by people other than those who do the analyses, and the expansion in the availability of statistical software to protect, with statistical expert systems, the statistically naive user from misusing the tools, meta data have also recently been studied in the text domain. Specifically, meta data are used to describe the data contained on the Web. Although everything on the Web is machine-readable, these data are not machine-understandable. It is very hard to automate anything on the Web.

The Resource Description Framework (RDF), developed by the World Wide Web Consortium (W3C), enables the encoding, exchange, and reuse of structured meta data (Miller, 1998). RDF is a foundation for processing meta data; it provides interoperability between applications that exchange machine-understandable information on the Web. RDF thus supports automated processing of Web resources. The effective use of meta data among applications, however, requires common conventions about semantics and syntax. Individual resource description communities define the semantics, or meaning, of meta data that address their particular needs. Syntax, the systematic arrangement of data elements for machine-processing, facilitates the exchange and use of meta data among multiple applications.

RDF can be used in a variety of application areas; for example: in resource discovery to provide better search engine capabilities, in cataloging for describing the content and content relationships available at a particular Web site or digital library, in content rating, and in describing collections of pages that represent a single logical document.

References

Allen, J. 1995. *Natural Language Understanding*. Redwood City, CA: Benjamin Cummings.

Cohen, W. 1996. "Learning trees and rules with set-valued features." In *Proceedings of the Fourteenth National Conference on Artificial Intelligence*. Menlo Park, CA: AAAI Press.

Fotheringham, A. S. and M. E. Charlton. 1994. "GIS and exploratory spatial data analysis: an overview." *Geogr. Sys.* **1**: 315–327.

Friedman, J. 1991. "Multivariate additive regression splines." *Ann. Stat.* **19**: 1–66.

Friedman, J. 1998. Data mining and statistics: What's the connection? Available at http://stat.stanford.edu/~jhf/ftp/dm-stat.ps.

Gebhardt, F. 1998. Spatial cluster test based on triplets of districts. *GMD Report 20*, St Augustin, Germany.

Gueting, R. H. 1994. "An introduction into spatial database systems." *VLDB J.* **3(4)**: 357–399.

Hand, D. 1993. "Data, metadata and information." *Stat. J. United Nations* **10**: 143–151.

Hand, D. 1998. "Data mining—reaching beyond statistics." *Research in Official Stat.* **1(2)**: 5–17.

Huber, P. 1997. "From large to huge: a statistician's reactions to KDD & DM." In *Proceedings Third International Conference on Knowledge Discovery and Data Mining*, pp. 304–308. Menlo Park, CA: AAAI Press.

Kendall, M. 1976. *Time Series*. London: Charles Griffin.

Klensin, J. C. 1991. "Data analysis requirements and statistical database management systems." In *Statistical and Scientific Databases*, edited by Z. Michalewicz, pp. 35–49. New York: Ellis Horwood.

Koopmans, L. 1981. *An Introduction to Contemporary Statistics*. Boston, MA: Duxbury Press.

Koperski, K. and J. Han. 1995. "Discovery of spatial association rules in geographic information databases." In *Proceedings of the 4th International Symposium on Large Spatial Databases*, pp. 47–66. Berlin: Springer-Verlag.

Koperski, K., J. Han, and N. Stefanovic. 1998. "An efficient two-step method for classification of spatial data." In *Proceedings of the International Symposium on Spatial Data Handling*, pp. 45–54. Vancouver, Canada.

Lindstrom, M. J. and D. M. Bates. 1990. "Nonlinear mixed-effects models for repeated measures data." *Biometrics* **46**: 673–687.

Michalewicz, Z. 1991. *Statistical and Scientific Databases*. New York: Ellis Horwood.

Miller, E. 1998. An introduction to the resource description framework. *D-Lib Magazine*, May, 1998.

Narens, L. 1985. *Abstract Measurement Theory*. Cambridge, MA: MIT Press.

Ng, R. T. and J. Han. 1994. "Efficient and effective clustering methods for spatial data mining." In *Proceedings of the 20th International Conference on Very Large Data Bases*, pp. 144–155. Santiago, Chile.

Openshaw, S. and T. Perree. 1996. "User centred intelligent spatial analysis of point data." *Innovations in GIS* **3**: 119–134. London: Taylor & Francis.

Openshaw, S., I. Turton, J. Macgill, and J. Davy. 1999. "Putting the geographical analysis machine on the Internet." *Innovations in GIS* **6**: 121–131. London: Taylor & Francis.

Openshaw, S., A. Turner, I. Turton, J. Macgill, and C. Brunsdon. 2000. "Testing space-time and more complex hyperspace geographical analysis tools." *Innovations in GIS* **7**: 87–100. London: Taylor & Francis.

Ullman, J. 1988. *Principles of Database and Knowledge Base Systems*. Rockville, MD: Computer Science Press.

West, M. and J. Harrison. 1997. *Bayesian Forecasting and Dynamic Models*. New York: Springer.

Zilberstein, S. and S. J. Russel. 1996. "Optimal composition of real-time systems." *Artificial Intell.* **82**: 181–213.

5 TYPES AND FORMS OF KNOWLEDGE (PATTERNS)

5.1 Contingency Tables

Jan M. Żytkow

ABSTRACT Contingency tables are introduced as a form of knowledge. Their evaluation criteria are discussed, as well as applications, strengths, limitations, and relations to other forms of knowledge.

1. Introduction

Contingency tables are commonly used to express statistical relations between attributes (Gokhale and Kullback, 1978; Bhattacharyya and Johnson, 1986). They are particularly useful when knowledge is weak and undeterministic. Consider university records that include for each student information such as high school grade point average (HSGPA) and total credit hours taken at the university in the entire course of study (CRHRS). The contingency table given in Table 1 provides, for each pair of values of CRHRS and HSGPA indicated at the margins, the number of students in the university records who share these values. The numbers describe a cohort of students admitted in a particular year. For example, there are ninety-two records with CRHRS of 120+ and HSGPA = B.

Such a table is also known as an actual distribution, cross-tabulated data, cross-classified data, and a two-way frequency table.

We will concentrate on two-dimensional tables. A one-dimensional table is a histogram, which is a mapping from the set of attribute's values to the number of occurrences of each. In Table 1 the histogram of CRHRS includes the totals of all rows, while the histogram of HSGPA includes the totals of all columns. Many-dimensional tables can also be considered but are rarely used, as their size grows exponentially with the number of dimensions, as they are sparse when the number of records is small (this has been common in the past), and as their printing and viewing is awkward.

A typical size of two to ten values per attribute makes a two-dimensional table manageable and suitable for moderate-size data. Attribute values can be discretized (binned, grouped) when numbers of values are large. In our example, the number of original values of HSGPA and CRHRS is above 100 for each attribute. Those values have been grouped into the five and six categories shown in the table. The use of computers and large data sets will increase the admissible number of values. Grouping may utilize knowledge: the ordering scale of an attribute, a taxonomy of attribute values (see Chapter 18.1), or an equivalence relation between groups of values of two attributes.

2. Inductive Generalization from Data

A contingency table represents the data set D from which it was generated. But can it be used to infer knowledge about the domain represented by D? Let A_{ab} be the number of records that

Table 1 Example of a Histogram (One-Dimensional Table)

	Column totals:	4	242	583	240	184	1253
CRHRS	120+	0	11	102	92	73	278
	90–119	0	13	67	26	32	138
	60–89	0	6	54	25	25	110
	30–59	0	34	100	32	22	188
	1–29	4	164	243	60	29	500
	0	0	14	17	5	3	39
	HSGPA:	F	D	C	B	A	Row totals

include values a and b of two attributes. Let n be the total number of records in the data. We can make an instantaneous inductive generalization and claim that $p_{ab} = A_{ab}/n$ estimates the joint probability distribution of both attributes in the population represented by D.

Such a generalization can be very useful, but is not always valid. First, the number of data must be sufficient so that probability values are statistically significant. As a rule of thumb, the average number of data per category (cell) should be larger than a minimum of three or four. Second, not every data set represents a population. In engineering and sciences such as physics and chemistry, the notion of population is rarely useful. When data have been procured by experimentation or an observation strategy which selects the values of attribute A, the histogram of A represents the strategy, not a population. Instead of a joint probability distribution, conditional probabilities of other attributes, given the value of A, represent knowledge in the domain. Third, populations can change. As always, how far we can generalize is subject to future empirical verification.

Even if drawn from the same population, the actual frequency tables may be different in different samples. On the flip side, a given table can come from many distributions. The attributes used in the table can be independent, but an appearance of dependence may occur by a random fluctuation. Since attribute independence is common, it is customary to evaluate that possibility. A two-dimensional table shows the joint distribution of the values of both attributes, which is information additional to histograms of both attributes. When attributes A and B are independent, their joint distribution should be close to the product of histograms of both variables. The expected number of records with $A = a$ and $B = b$ is

$$E_{ab} = \frac{h(A, a) \cdot h(B, b)}{n},$$

where $h(A, a)$ is the number of records in data set D with the value a of attribute A, and similarly $h(B, b)$. E_{ab} is usually called the expected distribution.

How different can A_{ab} be from E_{ab} while we can still claim that E_{ab} is the true distribution? Here comes the theory of statistical significance. It can tell how probable it is that a sample generated from a specified probabilistic distribution has a parameter value that exceeds a specified threshold. An efficient but approximate way of making such an estimate starts from the value of chi-square:

$$\chi^2 = \sum_{a,b} \frac{(A_{ab} - E_{ab})^2}{E_{ab}}.$$

Given the χ^2 and the number ν of degrees of freedom in the table ($\nu = (M_{row} - 1)(M_{col} - 1)$; in our example $\nu = 20$), the probability Q can be computed (Jobson, 1991), estimating the likelihood that a table such as A_{ab} has been randomly drawn from distribution E_{ab}.

In our example, $\chi^2 = 229.0$, $Q = 1.66 \times 10^{-32}$. Such a low value of Q indicates that it is practically impossible that HSGPA and CRHRS can be independent. Thresholds of significance vary from the traditional $Q < 0.01$ or 0.05 to much smaller, more demanding Q values needed in massive searches for regularities in KDD (Zembowicz and Żytkow, 1996).

When a previously estimated joint distribution of A and B is available, we may use it instead of E_{ab} to estimate the probability that A_{ab} comes from that distribution. But lacking knowledge of the relationship between the attributes, the current A_{ab} table can be treated as an exact representation of the population.

3. Prediction and Explanation

A contingency table can be used to reason about objects in the domain (Gokhale and Kullback, 1978; Bhattacharyya and Johnson, 1986). Treated as a regularity, a contingency table can provide many predictions. In a two-dimensional table, p_{ab} are probabilities that randomly selected objects will have the pair of values a and b. If the value of one attribute is known, then the row or column corresponding to that value can be used to make predictions of values of the other attribute.

For instance, for an incoming student with the value A of HSGPA, we can predict probabilistically the value of CRHRS. The value 120+ will occur with probability 0.4 (73/184).

Predictive strength of a contingency table can be measured by various criteria, such as Cramer's V (Jobson, 1991) and lambda measures (Goodman and Kruskal, 1954). For a given $M_{row} \times M_{col}$ contingency table, Cramer's V, is defined as

$$V = \sqrt{\frac{\chi^2}{N \min(M_{row} - 1, M_{col} - 1)}}.$$

In our example, $V = 0.19$. When the values of one attribute can be uniquely predicted from values of the other, Cramer's $V = 1$. At the other extreme, when the actual distribution is equal to the expected, then $\chi^2 = 0$ and $V = 0$. V does not depend on the size of the contingency table nor on the number of records. Thus it can be used to compare regularities found in different subsets of records and for different combinations of attributes.

Missing values can be ignored. But contingency tables are convenient for determining why values are missing. When the missing value is one of the attribute values that occur at the margin, the counts of missing values may be related to the regular values of the other attribute. It may turn out, for instance, that test results are missing for students in a particular county.

4. Contingency Tables and Other Forms of Knowledge

Contingency tables can be seen as a very basic form of knowledge, especially useful for statistical, nondeterministic regularities, in which two variables are related but the relationship cannot be represented in a more concise form. A Bayesian network can combine many such tables.

Relations in the logical sense are special cases, when probabilities are zero in some cells. A special case of a relation is functional dependency. When a contingency table is diagram of a function, it is more convenient to represent it by a lookup table or an algebraic formula.

Rules can be derived from contingency tables when zero (or very small) probability values occur in the table. For instance, in our example, if HSGPA = F then CRHRS is 1–29. This and other logical formulas, such as equivalence among groups of values of two attributes can be inferred from special cases of contingency tables (Zembowicz and Żytkow, 1996).

References

Bhattacharyya, G. K. and R. A. Johnson. 1986. *Statistical Concepts and Methods*. New York: Wiley.

Gokhale, D. V. and S. Kullback. 1978. *The Information in Contingency Tables*. New York: Marcel Dekker.

Goodman, L. and W. Kruskal. 1954. *Measure of Association for Cross Classification*. Springer Series in Statistics. Berlin: Springer-Verlag. Reprinted from the *J. Am. Stat. Assoc.*, **49**, 732–764.

Jobson, J. D. 1991. *Applied Multivariate Data Analysis*. Berlin: Springer-Verlag.

Zembowicz, R. and J. Żytkow. 1996. "From contingency tables to various forms of knowledge in databases," edited by U. Fayyad, G. Piatetsky-Shapiro, P. Smyth and R. Uthurusamy. *Advances in Knowledge Discovery and Data Mining*. pp. 329–349. San Mateo, CA: AAAI Press.

5.2 Subgroup Patterns

Willi Klösgen

ABSTRACT Statistical findings on subgroups belong to the most popular and simple forms of knowledge we encounter in all domains of science, business, or even daily life. We are told such messages as: the unemployment rate is overproportionally high for young men with low educational level, young poor women are infected with AIDS at a much higher rate than their male counterparts, lung cancer mortality rate has considerably increased for women during the last ten years. In this article, we introduce description languages for subgroups, summarize general pattern classes for subgroup deviations and associations, and compare knowledge expressed by subgroup patterns with other popular knowledge types of KDD.

1. Introduction

Hand (1998) distinguishes between two types of data mining exercise: searching for models that typically display the complete relation between a dependent and a set of independent variables, or patterns describing some local finding for the variables referring, for example, to some subregion of the independent variable space. Subgroup patterns are such local findings identifying subgroups of a population with some unusual, unexpected, or deviating distribution of a target variable. Thus these patterns do not give a complete overview on the population, but refer only to subsets of cases. Nevertheless these local statements are often useful, either because the interest of the analyst is rather modest, or the available data do not allow the derivation an accurate model of the behavior for the whole population. In a production control application, the analyst may be satisfied if some conditions can be identified for the large number of process variables that lead to a very high quality of the product. Then these conditions can be used to improve the production process. In a medical application, the available variables often cannot sufficiently accurately model the dependencies between symptoms and diagnoses, because only a part of the relevant, and typically unknown, variables is available. But it is useful to know at least some subgroups of patients that can be diagnosed with a high accuracy.

To be useful, subgroup patterns must satisfy two conditions. Subgroup descriptions (which define a subgroup, e.g., young men with a low educational level) must be interpretable and application relevant, and the reported behavior for the subgroup must be interesting, which specifically means that it is statistically significant. If the pattern describes, for example, a deviation for the subgroup, significance requires a combined criterium for the subgroup size and deviation size. Two components of a subgroup hypothesis language are treated in this article as follows: description languages (Section 2) determine the space of subgroups, and pattern classes (Section 3) encompass the statistical conditions that define the interestingness of a subgroup and, thus, represent diverse analytic questions that can be answered with various specializations of subgroup patterns. These specializations and the inference aspect are treated in Chapter 16.3 of this handbook where search strategies and neighborhood operators in the subgroup space are also presented.

Subgroup patterns reveal subsets that can be important. Thus, a first modest objective of subgroup mining is a more or less brute force search for interesting local subgroups. However, many of the subgroups found overlap due to multicollinearities between independent variables, and they can only be seen as potential parts of a more complete model. Thus, more ambitiously, a best global system of subgroups is constructed. Such a refinement step has multiple objectives, trying to cover the target subset of the studied population by a small number of highly significant, little overlapping subgroups. For instance, Bayesian networks for the subgroups (as binary variables) can be constructed that show their interdependencies and influence on the target variable. This refinement step (see Chapter 16.3.1 of this handbook) can be seen as deriving a model for the target variable built with a subset of the subgroups as explanatory independent variables.

The search for subgroup patterns is a special subtype of a general inductive query task. Siebes (1995) formally introduced this task as a triple consisting of a description algebra, a quality function, and a search method. This approach encompasses many techniques from data mining and statistics. Projection pursuit introduced by Friedman and Tukey (1974), for example, is a statistical inductive query task searching for interesting projections of a n-dimensional space (given by n continuous variables) onto lower-dimensional spaces directed by a projection index. The descriptions are then projection planes and the quality function is given by a projection index, like a chi-square test, computing how far the projected density is away from a normal density. The low-dimensional projections can identify deviating subgroups. Thus, projection pursuit is a statistical method (mainly for continuous variables) with similar goals to subgroup mining.

2. Description Languages for Subgroups

A subgroup is informally defined as an interpretable and application-relevant subset of a studied population. A description of the subgroup is a statement in a subgroup description language that specifies the properties that characterize the subgroup objects. The subgroup consists of those objects for which these properties are true. We distinguish between the subgroup as a set of objects (extension) or defined by a subgroup description (intension). Ideally, a subgroup description language (Michalski, 1983) should be limited to subgroups that are interpretable and application relevant. This can of course often only be partially achieved, especially when the language is defined by syntactical constraints that cannot deal with the semantic aspects of application relevance.

Subgroup descriptions rely on variables (attributes) available in the database. A selector is a subset of the value domain of a variable. Conjunctive description languages consist of descriptions that are built as conjunctions of selectors. Description languages for subgroup mining are mostly conjunctive, propositional languages. We assume that the database consists of one or several relations, each with a schema $\{A_1, A_2, ..., A_n\}$ and associated domains D_i for the description variables A_i. A conjunctive, propositional description of a subgroup is then given by:

$$A_1 \in V_1 \wedge ... \wedge A_n \in V_n \quad \text{with} \quad V_i \subseteq D_i.$$

Conjunctive selectors with $V_i = D_i$ can, of course, be omitted in a description. Description languages allow in the simplest case only one-value selectors, or additionally also negations (one value excluded from the domain), or even any internal disjunction of values from the domain of a nominal or ordinal description variable.

One-relational languages handle a single relation table, possibly constructed in a preprocessing phase by joining several relations. Only the attributes belonging to the schema of this single relation can be used for subgroup descriptions.

Multirelational languages do not require a preprocessing join operation and allow descriptions with attributes from several relations. They are especially useful for applications that require different target object classes (e.g., patients or diagnoses or therapies) with flexible joins to be analyzed. In the Kepler system (see Chapter 24.2.3), the MIDOS subgroup miner (Wrobel, 1997) discovers subgroups of objects from a selected target relation. A subgroup description may include selectors from several relations, which are linked by foreign link attributes.

A database may, for instance, include relations on hospitals, patients, diagnoses of patients, and therapies for patient-diagnoses with obvious foreign links such as patient-id linking patient-diagnoses and patients. The analyst chooses a target object, for example, patients, and can decide on the other object classes, for example, hospitals and patient-diagnoses, and their attributes to be used for building subgroups of patients. Such a subgroup could, for example, be described by male patients with a cancer diagnosis treated in a small hospital.

By these foreign links and the implicit existential quantifier used for linking relations (e.g., patients with at least one diagnosis of a type), a very limited inductive logic programming (ILP) approach (see Chapter 16.2.4) is applied, extending the simple one-relational propositional approach. The full ILP approach has not (yet) been used for subgroup mining.

Description languages can be specialized by constraints on the types of domain subsets V_i and taxonomies (see Chapter 5.7) that can be used for subgroup descriptions. To restrict the number of descriptions and to ensure semantically relevant descriptions, usually not every subset V_i of the domain of an attribute A_i is allowed. A taxonomy H_i consisting of a set of subsets of D_i can define the allowed subsets. A taxonomy is a hierarchical partitioning of all values in subclasses. Usually the number of classes in H_i will be much smaller than that of the power set of D_i. A taxonomy can explicitly and statically be given for an attribute A_i included in the description language for a mining task, or dynamically and implicitly determined by a special subsearch process that generates and evaluates certain subsets of attribute values during a mining task.

3. Behavior Patterns for Subgroups

Patterns of many types can occur in a subgroup. We distinguish two general pattern classes: deviation and association patterns. A deviation pattern describes a subgroup with some type of deviation for one (or several) designated target variables (Klösgen, 1996) where typically the reference for the deviation relates to the whole population or the complementary set of the subgroup within the population. Various specializations of the general deviation pattern are treated in Chapter 16.3.1. An association pattern reports a type of association between two subgroups and thus identifies a pair of subgroups (see Chapter 16.2.3).

Unemployment is the designated target variable for the first example given in the abstract of this article. The subgroup description refers to gender = male & age = young & educational level = low, where young and low may designate entries from taxonomies on age and educational level. The deviation type is given by a target variable rate (unemployment rate) that deviates significantly from some reference value, for example, the rate in the whole population.

The second example (reported in the *New York Times* in August 1998) compares two subpopulations: males and females. Subgroups are searched, for which the designated target variable (AIDS infection rate) differs significantly in the two subpopulations. The interesting subgroup of poor, young persons is reported. The third example refers to a trend pattern identifying subgroups with a monotonic trend of a target variable, for example, the subgroup women and the target variable lung cancer mortality.

An example of an association pattern is given by: upload operations by experienced users are often followed by extensive comment operations. When analyzing logfiles of Web usage, a pair of subgroups of user actions (upload operations by experienced users and extensive comment operations) is identified as holding some association type. In this example, the association type is given by a mathematical relation between pairs of operations (executed in the same session, one after the other referring to time of execution) and some statistical association measure (often, i.e., with a high confidence rate). The statistical measure requires that the percentage of those operations in the first subgroup that have a related operation in the second subgroup is high.

A simpler association type (not including a time relation) is studied with association rules (see Chapter 16.2.3). The typical example is known as: most transactions that include beer, include sausages too. Besides pairs of subgroups sought with association patterns, partially ordered sets of subgroups can be studied. Special partial orderings such as parallel or serial sequences of subgroups are sought with sequences and episode rules (see Chapter 16.2.4). The next example relates to error logfiles: if an error of subgroup1 is followed by an error of subgroup2, then often an error of subgroup3 occurs immediately afterwards.

Statistical significance has already been mentioned as a necessary precondition for a subgroup being interesting. Subgroup patterns rely on statistical tests to decide on significance. The null hypothesis of such a test specifies the uninteresting case of a subgroup which does not deviate. The alternative hypothesis deals with the interesting deviation. Thus, a subgroup pattern, from a statistical point of view, captures knowledge in the form of a verified (alternative) hypothesis that rejects the null hypothesis of no difference between the subgroup and the reference group. Since these tests are run in large numbers in a subgroup mining task, very high significance thresholds can mitigate the problem of just discovering random fluctuations. Thus, subgroup patterns identified in an explorative way must be carefully interpreted by the analyst. See Chapter 16.3.1 for more details of this approach.

4. Subgroup Patterns and Other Types of KDD Knowledge

Whereas contingency tables (Chapter 5.1), decision trees (Chapter 5.4), and functional relations (Chapter 5.5) describe the complete relation between two or more variables, typically between one dependent and several independent variables, a subgroup pattern only represents some local knowledge which can specifically be seen as originating from a contingency table (Żytkow and Zembowicz, 1993), a leaf of a decision tree, or a special value instantiation of a functional equation. A cluster belonging to a collection of clusters (see Chapter 5.6) can also be seen as a subgroup, specifically when derived by conceptual clustering methods (see Chapter 16.5.2). Taxonomies and concept hierarchies (Chapter 5.7) are important for constructing subgroups, especially when they partition the value domain of a single variable (see Chapter 18.1). Rules (Chapter 5.3) are special subgroup patterns that typically deal with nominal target variables.

References

Friedman, J. H. and J. W. Tukey. 1974. "A projection pursuit algorithm for exploratory data analysis." *IEEE Trans. Comput.* **C-23**: 881–889.

Hand, D. 1998. "Data mining—reaching beyond statistics." *Research in Official Stat.* **1(2)**: 5–17.

Klösgen, W. 1996. "Explora: A multipattern and multistrategy discovery assistant." *Advances in Knowledge Discovery and Data Mining* edited by U. Fayyad, G. Piatetsky-Shapiro, P. Smyth, and R. Uthurusamy, pp. 249–271. Cambridge, MA: MIT Press.

Michalski, R. S. 1983. "A theory and methodology of inductive learning." *Machine Learning: an Artificial Intelligence Approach* edited by R. S. Michalski, J. Carbonell, and T. Mitchell, pp. 83–134. Palo Alto, CA: Tioga Publishing.

Siebes, A. 1995. "Data surveying: foundations of an inductive query language." *Proceedings of the First International Conference on KDD* edited by U. Fayyad and R. Uthurusamy, pp. 269–274. Menlo Park, CA: AAAI Press.

Wrobel, S. 1997. "An algorithm for multirelational discovery of subgroups." *Proceedings of the First European Symposium on Principles of KDD* edited by J. Komorowski and J. Zytkow, pp. 78–87. Berlin: Springer.

Żytkow, J. and R. Zembowicz. 1993. "Database exploration in search of regularities." *J. Intell. Inform. Sys.* **2**: 39–81.

5.3 Rules

Jan M. Żytkow

ABSTRACT Classification rules, characteristic rules, and association rules are presented. Their evaluation criteria are discussed, as well as rule applications, strengths, limitations, and relations to other forms of knowledge.

1. Introduction

Rules have the form "if P then Q," symbolically $P \rightarrow Q$ (or $P \Rightarrow Q$). Rules are commonly used for knowledge representation, owing their popularity to a simple shape, and to many ways in which they can be used.

One basic meaning is logical implication, also called "one-way conditional." P is called antecedent, Q is called "consequent." $P \rightarrow Q$ is true in all cases except when P is true while Q is false. $P \rightarrow Q$ is logically equivalent to $\sim P \vee Q$.

Rules are commonly used in logical reasoning. For instance, from $P \rightarrow Q$ and $Q \rightarrow R$ it logically follows that $P \rightarrow R$.

Logical implication is commonly called "descriptive," as distinct from procedural condition-action rules. "If condition then action" statements in programming languages consist of a test and an action performed when the test has succeeded. In languages such as Prolog and production systems (such as OPS5), rules form the core of any program. Inductive logic programming capitalizes on both descriptive and procedural roles of rules; rules are discovered as inductive generalizations from data and used as pieces of a program.

2. Classification Rules

The most common rules in KDD are classification rules, owing their popularity to their use in machine learning (Langley, 1996). They are inductively generated partial definitions of concepts. A rule of the form $\forall x(Dx \rightarrow Cx)$ is a partial definition of class C. The definition is limited to tuples (records, cases) that satisfy D and the rule cannot determine that a tuple is not C. Applied to new tuples, for which we cannot independently determine the truth value of C, rules work as normative definitions, true by convention.

A typical form for classification rules is $\forall x(P_1(A_1x)\&...\&P_k(A_kx) \rightarrow Cx = c_1)$, where $P_i(A_ix)$ is $A_ix = a$ (the value of SEX in record x is male), or $a \leqslant A_ix \leqslant b$ when the values of A_i are ordered. The antecedent of such a rule is typically a conjunction of conditions on single attributes. This allows problem decomposition and does not limit the rules for nominal variables. Discretization (grouping, binning) is useful when the number of values per attribute is large, as otherwise large numbers of classification rules may be needed.

Many rules may be needed to define a concept. Logically, any set of classification rules is still a partial definition. But a set of rules is often a tacit definition by equivalence, that is, a complete definition, when it is understood that "in all cases when rules do not apply to x, x is not in class C." However, if some values of the defining attributes were not present in the data, they will not occur in rules and thus objects that possess them may be included in the concept's complement.

3. Rule Evaluation

Two main criteria by which rules are evaluated against the available data are accuracy and coverage. Let Card(P) be the number of tuples in data which satisfy condition P. Accuracy of a rule $D \rightarrow C$ is defined as Card($C \wedge D$)/Card(D), which is the conditional probability of C, given $D : P(C|D)$. The maximum accuracy is 1.

For a set of rules r understood as a complete definition, let R be the disjunction of all rule antecedents. Classification accuracy is a ratio of cases classified correctly (number of cases in C and covered by R plus the number of negative cases not covered) to all cases Card($R \wedge C$) + Card($\sim R \wedge \sim C$)/n (Langley, 1996). n is the number of all tuples used in evaluation.

Coverage (recently also called support) of a rule is either Card(D) or Card($D \wedge C$) or Card($C \wedge D$)/n (Yao and Zhong, 1999). Coverage is not judged by the generality of the antecedent but by the number of the records. This resembles measures of statistical significance.

Rules are inductive generalizations, generated from the available data and evaluated against them, but intended as universal claims against all objects that satisfy their antecedents. One of the dangers is overfit, when rules are made accurate against the available data by being overly specific. The main technique for overfit prevention has been by decomposition of data into a training set and test set. Rules are induced from a training set and retained only when the accuracy against the test set is satisfactory. But that reduces the number of data from which the rules are induced, and may enter the test set into a loop that ultimately allows overfit. Statistical measures that would control rule overfitting are difficult to define.

4. Characteristic Rules

Characteristic rules answer the question: "Given that an object belongs to class C, what are the properties of that object?" (Cai et al., 1990). A rule of the form

$$\forall x(Cx \rightarrow D_1x)$$

claims that property D_i is shared by all objects in C. All such properties form the intension of a concept, as distinct from concept extension, which is the set of all objects in class C. Useful concepts possess a substantial intension.

Characteristic rules, equivalent to $\forall x(\sim D_1 x \rightarrow \sim Cx)$, can be treated as partial definitions that determine the complement of C. A pair consisting of a classification rule $\forall x(Dx \rightarrow Cx)$ and a characteristic rule $\forall x(Cx \rightarrow D_1 x)$ may lead to an empirical claim $\forall x(Dx \rightarrow D_1 x)$.

5. Association Rules and Itemsets

Consider a database of binary (boolean) attributes. Each attribute represents a particular item (object, event). The value of 1 means presence, while 0 means absence of that item in a tuple. All values of 1 in a tuple represent jointly an item set, that is a set of items that occurred jointly, for instance, have been purchased together. Frequent item sets can be viewed as clusters.

An association rule $X \rightarrow Y$, where $X = X_1 \wedge \ldots \wedge X_k$, and $Y = Y_1 \wedge \ldots \wedge Y_l$ means that when items $X_1, \ldots, X_k$ occur in a tuple, then with a specific confidence, items $Y_1, \ldots, Y_l$ occur in that tuple, too (Agrawal et al., 1993). Confidence (accuracy) of a rule is inductively determined as $P(Y|X)$.

Association rules are evaluated according to the same criteria as classification rules, but the acceptance thresholds are lower. For the rule $X \rightarrow Y$, a satisfactory support (coverage) can be in the order of 1 to 2 percent. Desired values of confidence are about 60 to 80 percent, as stronger rules can be obvious. Low accuracy makes the logical form of association rules misleading. For instance, it is possible that $X \rightarrow Y$ and $Y \rightarrow Z$, but not $X \rightarrow Z$.

6. Rule Application

A classification rule explains why a case has been included into category C: the reasons are stated in the antecedent. Rules help in domain understanding, by capturing dependencies between values of different variables.

Rules can be used to predict values of C for new data that satisfy the antecedent. Knowing the accuracy of a rule, we can also estimate the accuracy of prediction. A missing value for an attribute that occurs in the antecedent of a rule prevents the straightforward application of that rule.

Practical applications follow the mechanisms of understanding and prediction. If the consequence is desired, we select objects or modify them so they satisfy the antecedent. If the consequence is likely to occur, we may make it easier to accomplish. For instance, knowledge of frequent item sets and association rules may apply in planning the distribution of merchandise in a store. On the other hand, when the consequence is undesired, we may avoid objects or change them so that the antecedent is not satisfied. Directed by one rule, this remedy does not guarantee success when the same consequence occurs in many rules.

7. Rules and Other Forms of Knowledge

Classification rules and characteristic rules are a limited form of knowledge (Żytkow, 1997) and a limited form of concept definitions. When a definition by equation or equivalence applies, it is complete, that is, it works for all cases and explains the concept better than a set of rules.

Completeness and consistency of prediction by a rule set is difficult to achieve and verify in rule sets that include both classification and characteristic rules. In contrast, a decision tree is consistent and complete by virtue of its structure, when it partitions the population into exhaustive and nonoverlapping subsets. Predictions are more efficient with a decision tree or a taxonomy than with a rule set, because determining which rules are applicable to a given case is less efficient than tree traversal. Large decision trees may be more difficult to understand, however, while individual rules are often understandable and convincing. Missing values can be replaced by default values or probability distributions, but this can be done more systematically with decision trees (Quinlan, 1993) than with rule sets.

While statistical relations can generally be expressed by contingency tables, rules can be used to capture particularly interesting elements of such relations. For instance, a rule is very useful when there is only one nonzero cell in a column of a particular contingency table.

A rule does not say what happens when the antecedent is not satisfied. It misses explicit comparisons with various control groups that can be created by negating one or more conditions in the antecedent. Such comparative details can easily be seen in contingency tables. As it is difficult to use multidimensional contingency tables, rules gain competitive advantage when they involve more than two attributes.

References

Agrawal, R., T. Imielinski, and A. Swami. 1993. "Mining association rules between sets of items in large databases." *Proceedings of ACM SIGMOD Conference on Management of Data* edited by P. Buneman and S. Jajodia, pp. 207–216. Washington, DC.

Cai, Y., N. Cercone, and J. Han. 1991. "Learning in relational databases: an attribute oriented approach." *Computational Intelligence* **7(3)**: 119–132: NRCC.

Langley, P. 1996. *Elements of Machine Learning.* San Mateo, CA: Morgan Kaufmann.

Quinlan, R. 1993. *C5.4: Programs for Machine Learning.* San Mateo, CA: Morgan Kaufmann.

Yao, Y. Y. and N. Zhong. 1999. "An analysis of quantitative measures associated with rules." *Methodologies for Knowledge Discovery and Data Mining; Proceedings of PAKDD-99,* edited by N. Zhong and L. Zhou, pp. 479–488.

Żytkow, J. M. 1997. "Knowledge = concepts: a harmful equation." In *Proceedings of KDD-97,* pp. 104–109. Menlo Park, CA: AAAI Press.

5.4 Decision Trees

Jan M. Żytkow

ABSTRACT Decision trees are introduced in their role of concept definitions. Their acceptance criteria are discussed, as well as their applications, strengths, limitations, and relations to other forms of knowledge.

1. Introduction

Decision trees, also known as classification trees, have been increasingly popular as concept definitions induced from examples (Murthy, 1998). Their applications and properties are simpler than definitions by sets of rules. High accuracy decision trees can be built by simple recursive mechanisms.

2. Decision Tree Structure

Decision trees contain tests at internal nodes and decisions on leaves (Quinlan, 1986). Each branch corresponds to a specific result of a test at the parent node. When a tree is used as a definition of concept C, each leaf provides a value of C. Formally, a leaf carries a statement $Cx = c_i$, where c_i is a value in the domain of C. C is called a class attribute or a decision attribute. Classification of all values of C and definition of C are two equivalent ways of describing the use of a decision tree.

As a complement to a customary graphical representation of a tree, a simple and clear printed representation is often used. The following tree has 4 internal nodes and six leaves. Each line represents one branch. The branches are listed in the depth-first order of tree traversal.

```
A1 = yes :
| A2 = 1 : C = low
```

```
| A2 = 2 :
| | A3 = a : C = high
| | A3 = b : C = normal
| A2 = 3 : C = normal
A1 = no :
| A7 in [0...3] : C = low
| A7 in [4...9] : C = normal
```

Most frequently, as in our example, each test applies to values of a single attribute. Depending on the type of attribute and the number of values, the tests are of the form $Ax = a_i$ or $a_i \leqslant Ax \leqslant a_j$ (for example: A7 in $[0\ldots3]$).

However, multivariate tests can also be used (Murthy, 1998). Typically, parent nodes are split by inequalities on the linear combinations of values of many attributes. Such trees are called linear discriminant trees or regression trees (Breiman et al., 1984).

When the sets of tuples that branch out from any given node are disjoint and collectively exhaustive, a decision tree is a complete and consistent definition of concept C: it provides a unique value of C for each object (tuple).

3. Tree Evaluation

Decision trees are usually complete, so coverage (support) is not an issue. Predictive accuracy is the proportion of objects correctly classified to all objects available.

Trees share the tendency for overfit with rules. This can happen when tree nodes represent small numbers of records in a data set from which it has been generalized. Generalization from small numbers of cases, especially when the number of attributes to choose from is large, can lead to selection of accidental patterns. Discretization (grouping) of attribute values is needed when there is a large number of values per attribute, to reduce branching and prevent overfit.

4. Tree Application

Knowledge in the form of a decision tree can be used to predict (or define) values of a single attribute that is the target of classification and is represented at all leaves. This applies to all tuples that possess values required by tests. Starting from the root, apply the test to a given tuple, and follow the branch appropriate for the test result. Apply the test at the child node and continue until a leaf is reached. Retrieve a prediction $Cx = c_i$ at the leaf.

Missing values cause prediction problems. If a test requires a value of A that is missing, normal branch selection does not work. Several auxiliary mechanisms are described by Mitchell (1997) and Quinlan (1993). One selects the branch for the most common value of A. Another continues tree traversal on all branches following the missing value, each with the probability obtained from the histogram of A. Then it selects the value of C by the maximum total probability.

5. Trees and Other Forms of Knowledge

As concept definitions, decision trees are close relatives to sets of rules. A decision tree can be converted into a set of rules: one rule for each path from the root to a leaf. A decision tree is a more efficient prediction mechanism than a rule set produced that way. It is also easier to assess completeness and consistency of a definition by a decision tree than by a set of rules. However, there are situations in which other types of concept definitions work better than decision trees. When a definition by an equation applies, a decision tree is awkward. It can have many branches; it can be inaccurate; and it unnecessarily splits data that can be treated jointly.

Decision trees, as with all concept definitions, have a limited empirical content (Żytkow, 1997). Taxonomies use a similar tree structure, but provide empirical contents at each node (see Chapter 5.7).

References

Breiman, L., J. H. Friedman, R. A. Olshen, and C. J. Stone. 1984. *Classification and Regression Trees*. Belmont, CA: Wadsworth & Brooks.

Mitchell, T. 1997. *Machine Learning*. Boston, CA: McGraw-Hill.

Murthy, S. K. 1998. "Automatic construction of decision trees from data: a multi-disciplinary survey." *Data Mining and Knowledge Discovery* **2**: 345–389.

Quinlan, J. R. 1986. "Induction of decision trees." *Machine Learning* **1**: 81–106.

Quinlan, R. 1993. *C5.4: Programs for Machine Learning*. San Mateo, CA: Morgan Kaufmann.

Żytkow, J. M. 1997. "Knowledge = concepts: a harmful equation." In *Proceedings of KDD-97*, pp. 104–109. Menlo Park, CA: AAAI Press.

5.5 Functional Relations

Jan M. Żytkow

ABSTRACT Functional relations and their main varieties are presented. Their evaluation criteria are discussed, as well as applications, strengths, limitations, and relations to other forms of knowledge.

1. Introduction

Functional relations, especially in the form of equations, have become a common outcome of data mining, owing their popularity to the widespread use of regression methods and the abundant computational power needed for the search in large spaces of equations. In many domains of science and engineering, equations offer a fine approximation of data, in a concise and physically interpretable form, can be used in various forms of inference, and offer a superb generalization to unseen values. But equations have also been abused. Data conducive to generalization via functional relations are uncommon in many domains. Often the best equation provides a miserable match to data and an ostensible appearance of knowledge.

2. Varieties of Functional Relations

The basic mathematical definition of functional relation must be adapted to the realities of empirical knowledge, by relaxing the requirements, yet keeping them well defined. Various ways of expressing functional relations have been used, such as lookup tables, but equations are particularly useful and popular. Recently, neural networks have also been used to express numerical functional relations. Other useful representations include recursive definitions and various algorithmic mechanisms.

2.1. Mathematical and Empirical Functional Relations

According to mathematical definition, a two-dimensional relation R in a Cartesian product $\text{Dom}(B) \times \text{Dom}(A)$ is a function $B = f(A)$ if for every a in $\text{Dom}(A)$ there is exactly one b in $\text{Dom}(B)$ and in R such that $R(b, a)$. This can easily be generalized to a function of many variables $A_1, ..., A_n$.

The mathematical definition requires adjustments so that it can apply to empirical functions between variables. First, an empirical relation R captures all empirical data. Pairs that do not belong to R do not exist as results of physical experiments or observations. They are physically not possible.

Second, empirical data may not be available for some values in $\text{Dom}(A)$ or for many combinations of values (tuples) in $\text{Dom}(A_1) \times ... \times \text{Dom}(A_n)$. An empirical function is a generalization of the available data to all possible objects. The process of generalization must avoid many traps. For instance, when the number of data is small compared to the number of values, it may seem that a functional relationship holds, just because no two data have yet been collected with the same values of $A_1, ..., A_n$.

Third, the uniqueness requirement must be treated as approximation. Multiple measurements of B for the same object or for similar objects typically result in slightly different values. But if the values are close, we can treat them as approximations of one value. This is typical in empirical domains. A single value of B is commonly replaced by a statistical distribution.

2.2. Functional Dependencies

When our goal is discovery of knowledge that can be used to predict properties of new objects, we must disregard many of the so-called functional dependencies in databases. They tell us how we can retrieve information about known individuals, but they are not useful in making generalizations.

Consider for example a dependency Social Security Number (SSN)$\rightarrow$address or name $\rightarrow$ date of birth. A unique name and address accompanies each SSN and a unique date of birth is associated with each unique name. But given a new SSN, we cannot predict the address. A new name does not allow a prediction of the date of birth.

Such functional dependencies occur through a combination of two reasons. First, some attributes are unique identifiers (keys) for objects or events. Second, some attributes describe permanent properties of objects, so that their values do not change. Even if a value of such an attribute changes, the old value must be removed from data before the new value can be entered.

2.3. Lookup Tables

When a functional relation exists, it can be expressed as a lookup table, especially useful for nominal attributes with small numbers of values. Given the value of A, the value of B can be retrieved from the table. Interpolation and extrapolation extend the use of lookup tables. The use of the nearest neighbor in making predictions can be viewed as the use of a lookup table.

Lookup tables become awkward when the number of distinct values is too large. In the case of numerical attributes an analytical form of equations is preferred.

2.4. Equations

Equations are a very concise and useful expression of functional relationships. $B = f(A_1, ..., A_m)$ is an equation when $f(A_1, ..., A_m)$ is a term built from primitives that include numbers, $A_1, ..., A_m$, and algebraic or calculus operations.

Equations may hold in a subdomain, and then should be preceded by the range description:

if $P_1(B_1)\&...\&P_k(B_k)$ **then** $B = f(A_1, ..., A_m)$.

When the **if** part is satisfied and the values of $A_1, ..., A_m$ are given, the operations in f can be applied and $f(A_1, ..., A_m)$ predicts the value of B.

2.5. Deterministic and Statistical Components

In Section 2.1 we argued that it is impractical to require uniqueness from empirical functions. But if a range of values is allowed in place of a unique value, it is a good idea to use a formal range description that would be both empirically adequate and theoretically useful.

Statistical distribution can be added to an equation. The following form includes a deterministic part $f(A)$ and a statistical distribution $\epsilon(A)$:

$$B(x) = f(A(x)) + \epsilon(A(x)).$$

$\epsilon(A)$ represents the statistical component, for instance empirical error. It is important not to read $\epsilon(A)$ as error of A, because in fact it represents statistical distribution of values of B. A occurs in that term because the distributions of the corresponding values of B can be different for different values of A.

What error distribution applies in a given situation is a subject of empirical investigation. The most frequently used distribution is Gaussian (normal) with zero mean and standard deviation equal to $\sigma(A)$:

$$B = f(A) + N(0, \sigma(A)).$$

The mean value of zero indicates lack of systematic error. Each measured value of B is treated as drawn from the distribution $N(f(A), \sigma(A))$. When the distribution of values of B is the same for each value of A,

$$B = f(A) + N(0, \sigma).$$

In this model, error applies only to attribute B. This is justified when A is controlled by the experimenter and can be made very accurate, while the values of B are measured according to an empirically determined distribution. In such situations A is called an independent attribute, while B is called dependent. However, at the cost of more complex computations, error can be treated symmetrically. Two-dimensional normal distributions provide a useful model.

Statistical distributions may have meanings other than uncertainty of values that describe single data points. They may reflect a distribution of attribute values in a population. For instance, two attributes can be distributed normally in the entire population, while at the same time linearly correlated.

3. Evaluation Against Data

Lookup tables can be evaluated according to the mathematical definition of a functional relationship. $B = f(A_1, ..., A_n)$ holds in data table D when for each tuple in D which has the same values of $A_1, ..., A_n$, there is one value of B, possibly within a statistical distribution.

When differencies of values of B for the same values of $A_1, ..., A_n$, are unaccountable by error, by rounding, or another cause, the relationship between A and B is not functional. In that case, there is no need to seek analytical expressions such as equations. An equation becomes a crude approximation and may hold no knowledge.

Evaluation of equations and other analytical expressions is typically based on a global measure, such as χ^2. Given a set of numeric data points (A_i, B_i, σ_i), where σ_i approximates the error of measurement of B, and given an equation $B = f(A) + N(0, \sigma(B))$, the distance between the equation and the data can be computed as weighted χ^2 (Eadie et al., 1971; Press et al., 1989):

$$\chi^2 = \sum_{i=1}^{N} \left(\frac{B_i - f(A_i)}{\sigma_i} \right)^2. \tag{1}$$

The more precise data points are fitted more accurately.

Given the value of χ^2 and the number of degrees of freedom, which is the number of data minus the number of parameters in the equation, the probability can be computed that data with the same or higher value than χ^2 have been generated from the model. Such probability is then informally transformed into the evaluation of the model against empirical data. High probability means high likelihood that empirical data fit the model.

The procedure may seem circular, as parameters $a_1, ..., a_q$ in the equation are typically computed from data, by minimization of the weighted χ^2:

$$\chi^2 = \sum_{i=1}^{N} \left(\frac{B_i - f(A_i, a_1, ..., a_q)}{\sigma_i} \right)^2 \tag{2}$$

But the best fit may not be good enough, and that shows by the low value of probability.

The evaluation according to (1) is limited to the error of B. Similar, but more complex measures, using Mahalanobi distance, can be used to handle error of both independent and dependent variables.

Overfit is a common problem for any generalization. It occurs in particular in equations when the number of parameters is close to the number of data from which the equation has been generated. The fit is better than empirical error for the source data, but may be much worse for the new data.

4. Applications of Equations

Equations are commonly applied in engineering and sciences. Less frequently they can be used in other databases.

Equations can be used as predictors of attribute values: the values of B can be determined by values of $A_1, ..., A_n$; but many equations can be solved for some or all attributes. Then, an equation can be used as a many-ways predictor. Similarly to predictions, equations can be used as definitions of unknown values.

Equations are useful in logical reasoning. The strength of science and engineering is based on reasoning supported by precise or approximate transformations of equations.

Equations can support understanding of objects and phenomena. Terms that form an equation may have meaning such as energy, momentum, and the like, so that different parts of an equation represent components of a complex process. But if an equation is a poor match to data, the interpretation of terms in the equation can be misleading.

5. Functional Relations and Other Forms of Knowledge

Data conducive to generalization via functional relations may not be common. But if they occur, the use of functional relations and equations in particular is very worthwhile.

Equations are an alternative that satisfy the principle: "Do not divide what can be explained by a single regularity." Rather than dividing data into subsets and describing each subset by a rule or a node in a decision tree, an equation can match all data.

References

Eadie, W. T., D. Drijard, F. E. James, M. Roos, and B. Sadoulet. 1971. *Statistical Methods in Experimental Physics.* Amsterdam: North-Holland Publishers.

Press, W. H., B. P. Flannery, S. A. Teukolsky, and W. T. Vetterling. 1989. *Numerical Recipes in Pascal.* Cambridge, UK: Cambridge University Press.

5.6 Clusters

Padhraic Smyth

A fundamental cognitive activity is the treatment of entities as being equivalent or homogenous in some sense. For example, much scientific progress has relied heavily on the human ability to group entities into naturally-occurring categories of particles, stellar objects, flora and fauna, and so forth. A cluster can be thought of as an artificial construction that approximates a cognitively useful category. In data analysis, a cluster is typically defined by the similarity of its members, where similarity is often (but not always) captured by geometric notions of vector distances. For example, if our entities are described as d-dimensional tuples or points then it is natural to think of clusters in terms of the geometry of a d-dimensional space. In this context notions such as the centroid and shape of a cluster are natural. We will largely adopt this geometric notion in our discussion, while keeping in mind that while representing entities as tuples in a Euclidean space is convenient and widely used, it is not necessarily always appropriate.

There are numerous different definitions of a cluster available in the data analysis literature. One of the more confusing aspects is that cluster representation often arises as merely a byproduct of the particular clustering algorithm (i.e., the process of creating the cluster from the data). Thus, for example, an algorithm that builds clusters by adding points that are close to some member of the existing cluster will tend to produce long elongated clusters. An algorithm that incrementally adds points that are close to all members of an existing cluster will tend to produce more compact spherical clusters. One can nonetheless consider certain characteristics of a cluster representation to be somewhat generic: the location of the mean or centroid of the cluster, the overall shape and size of the cluster, the density of points within the cluster, the scale at which clusters are defined, and so forth. Indeed the notion of scale is inherent in any definition of a cluster. At the broadest scale the entire set of data points may be considered a single cluster (when viewed from a distance) while at the finest scale each data point is itself considered a cluster. Naturally, useful representations tend to lie somewhere between these two extremes, but the point remains valid that scale is inherent to any cluster description.

Central to all cluster representations is the notion of similarity or distance. Euclidean distance is often a convenient conceptual tool for entities that are represented as d-dimensional measurements. However, numerous alternative approaches are also possible, for example, for entities described by categorical measurements. There is no one universally superior method for defining distance in a clustering context. Ultimately the utility of a distance measure is application-dependent; the semantics of the distance measure should make sense for a given problem.

There are also some general frameworks in terms of how a set of clusters are defined in relation to each other. Clusters can be defined so that each entity is a member of one and only one cluster (a disjoint partition of the measurement space), or so that entities belong to different clusters with different probabilities or degrees of membership, or that entities can belong to multiple clusters without restriction (e.g., so-called overlapping clusters). Overlapping clusters can be completely unstructured, or (for example) can be structured in a multiscale hierarchical nested fashion where the root contains all of the data points, its two children contain a recursive partition into two clusters, and so on until the leaves contain only singleton data points. Alternatively, in the probabilistic approach, entities can belong to any of K clusters with a probability of membership, where these probabilities sum to 1 (Banfield and Raftery, 1993). Fuzzy clustering provides an alternative nonprobabilistic approach to clusters that allow for degree of membership (Bezdek, 1974). In contrast, additive clustering (Shepard and Arabie, 1979) allows entities to belong to multiple clusters in a general manner without the constraints of probabilistic or nested membership.

In conclusion, from a knowledge discovery viewpoint, clusters serve to summarize entities that are considered similar in some sense. Thus, clusters can serve as basic building blocks in a knowledge representation scheme, essentially defining equivalence classes for the entities they contain. For example, in a business application, modeling a heterogenous population of customers as a set of distinct clusters (each of which is relatively homogenous) may lead to more accurate models of predictive behavior. Clusters may also be of interest themselves, providing a summary description (e.g., location and variability) of a similar group of entities, for example, in scientific applications. The texts by Jain and Dubes (1988) and Everitt (1992) provide useful general introductions to different cluster representations and cluster analysis algorithms.

References

Banfield, J. D. and A. E. Raftery. 1993. "Model-based Gaussian and non-Gaussian clustering." *Biometrics* **49**: 803–821.

Bezdek, J. C. 1974. "Numerical taxonomy with fuzzy sets." *J. Math. Biol.* **1**: 57–71.

Everitt, B. S. 1992. *Cluster Analysis*. London: Edward Arnold.

Jain, A. K. and R. C. Dubes. 1988. *Algorithms for Clustering Data*. Englewood Cliffs, NJ: Prentice-Hall.

Shepard, R. N. and P. Arabie. 1979. "Additive clustering: representation of similarities as combinations of discrete overlapping properties." *Psychol. Rev.* **86**: 87–123.

5.7 Taxonomies and Concept Hierarchies

Jan M. Żytkow

ABSTRACT Taxonomies, also called concept hierarchies, are presented as a form of knowledge useful in knowledge discovery in databases (KDD). Their strength relies on compact description that can represent rich empirical contents. This results in predictive capabilities that can tolerate missing values. The applications and limitations of taxonomies are discussed and their relations to other forms of knowledge.

1. Introduction

Consider the way in which all animal species are organized into a taxonomy. Animal taxonomy is a hierarchical system in the form of a tree. The root represents all animals. All properties that are characteristic to all animals can be stored at the root. The category of all animals is divided into several major subcategories. All species within one category share many properties that, at the same time, differentiate them from species in other categories. Each subcategory can be divided into further subcategories. Each subcategory shares many further properties, and so on, until a single species is represented at a leaf. The partitioning of each category, at each level, is supposed to be exhaustive and disjoint, at least with respect to the known animal species.

Another example is an administrative taxonomy: a country is divided into provinces, each province into counties, and so on. The partitioning of the land is exhaustive and disjoint. Each unit has plenty of properties in common. Each province has one capital, governor, legislature, many special laws, and so forth.

Taxonomies are very common in biology, and they describe human-created artifacts and institutions because the species and products of human creativity grow by refinement and differentiation of the best existing products.

Discovery of taxonomies from data is an important task. In addition to a hierarchical partitioning of objects, knowledge specific to each partition guides the discovery process. Different approaches were used by Alberdi and Sleeman (1997), Fisher (1987), Fisher and Langley (1986), and Zembowicz and Żytkow (1997).

2. Taxonomy as a Form of Knowledge

Taxonomies can be represented by trees. Each node in a taxonomy represents a set (class, category) of objects. That set is partitioned into subsets, represented by children nodes. Similar partitioning applies in decision trees, but taxonomy contains additional knowledge at each

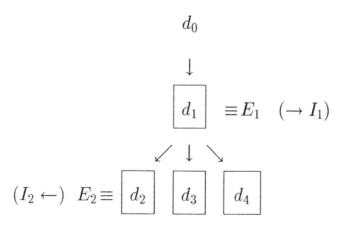

Figure 1 Fragment of taxonomy

node. Consider a generic building block of a taxonomy, including a parent node and its children nodes, as depicted in Figure 1. Category d_1 of the classified objects is partitioned into categories d_2, d_3, and d_4. d_0 represents the list of all supercategories of d_1 on the path to the root. Categories are described by descriptors, such as $A_i = a$ and $a < A_i < b$.

Let us now analyze knowledge contained in a taxonomy. It can be expressed as a conjunction of several types of statements. Our examples below refer to the situation depicted in Figure 1. All the occurrences of the free variable x in the formulas below are tacitly bound by the universal quantifier, which we skip for simplicity.

In Figure 1, d_0 represents the list of supercategories (superclasses) of class d_1, on the path from the root; d_1 represents a category that is further divided into subcategories; E_1 and I_1 are two sets of descriptors attached to d_1. E_1 is the set of alternative definitions of class d_1, while I_1 is the set of facts that can be inferred when it is known that an object belongs to category d_1. Similar sets of descriptors belong to all the children classes under d_1, that is to d_2, d_3, and d_4. For instance, E_2 and I_2 are sets of definitional and inferred descriptors at node d_2.

- Child class d_2 is a nonempty subset of parent class d_1:

  $$\exists x[d_0 x \,\&\, d_1 x \,\&\, d_2 x];$$

  and similarly for classes d_3 and d_4.

- The taxonomy is exhaustive and disjoint (xor is exclusive or):

  $$d_0 x \,\&\, d_1 x \rightarrow (d_2 x \text{ xor } d_3 x \text{ xor } d_4 x);$$

  when node d_1 has two children:

  $$d_0 x \,\&\, d_1 x \rightarrow (d_2 x \equiv \neg d_3 x).$$

- The empirical content of each class in a taxonomy is represented by statements such as:

  $$d_0 x \,\&\, d_1 x \equiv E_1 x, \quad d_0 x \,\&\, d_1 x \,\&\, d_2 x \equiv E_2 x,$$

  $$d_0 x \,\&\, d_1 x \rightarrow I_1 x, \quad d_0 x \,\&\, d_1 x \,\&\, d_2 x \rightarrow I_2 x,$$

  where $E_1 x = e_1 x \equiv ... \equiv e_k x$ and $e_i, i = 1, ..., k$ are the descriptors that are alternative equivalential definitions of class d_1.

  Similarly $I_1 x = i_1 x \,\&\, ... \,\&\, i_l x$, where $i_j x, j = 1, ..., l$, are the descriptors that can be inferred for d_1. Respectively, E_2 includes all equivalent descriptors of d_2, while I_2 all inferred descriptors for d_2.

  One definition is needed at each node, so that the node is defined, but if neither alternative definitions are available nor inferred descriptors, there is no empirical content on such a node. Such nodes occur in decision trees, and in taxonomies are limited to the values of a single attribute.

Statements that use class names are not observational, when by observation we mean noticing that a given object has a particular value of a particular observable property. In contrast, descriptors are observational statements. In database applications, attributes used in a relational table can be considered observational and concrete values are observations, from the perspective of knowledge miners. For each object, represented by a tuple of attribute values, all those values are observations. A typical task of taxonomy formation (discovery) requires categorization of tuples into classes. Class membership can be determined by attribute values available in the tuple.

From the perspective of the knowledge miner, class names are useful theoretical concepts, as they replace complex logical formulas formed from observational descriptors. For instance, to determine $d_1 a$ (a is in d_1) we may use any of the equivalent tests in E_1. If the test is positive, we can claim not only d_a but also all additional statements in E_1 and in I_1.

Consider an archeologist who examines a piece of bone b and wants to determine the species. He is successful when he can notice in b a definitional property of a particular species. Then he is allowed to infer membership in many superclasses, as well as many properties of b

captured in the taxonomy. Some of those properties may be observed in the piece of bone b and if they do, they constitute independent confirmations of the way b was classified.

A taxonomy must be exhaustive and disjoint only in relationship to the objects existing in the real world: no real object is excluded and each is included in one child category. While it is logically possible for there to be objects that may have some but not all of the properties in E_1 they should not occur physically. Of course, real world taxonomies are approximate, so limited exceptions are possible.

Normally, taxonomies do not include nodes for individuals. But COBWEB (Fisher, 1987) attaches individuals as leaves, which are used when the taxonomy is being revised.

Notice that a pair of concepts defined alternatively by $A_1 x \equiv A_2 x$, where A_1 and A_2 are two Boolean attributes, is a simple two-level taxonomy. One class under the root consists of all objects that are both A_1 and A_2, the other class consists of objects that are neither A_1 nor A_2. No other objects exist. Given an object a, if a is in A_1, then we can infer that a is in A_2.

3. Taxonomies and Knowledge in Databases

Consider a relational table $R = A_1, ..., A_n$. It represents a class of entities, such as an object or event, or a relation between them. Each record describes a vector of properties of an entity or a tuple of related entities. Depending on the specific situation captured in R, the table may justify the use of several taxonomies, each using a different subset of attributes in R. It is also possible that exactly one taxonomy is justified by R, but it may be the case that no taxonomy with empirical contents is justified by the data. This occurs when no inferences can be made from class membership, that is there are no equivalent or inferred descriptors.

It is always worthwhile considering taxonomies, but taxonomies may be rare, especially substantial taxonomies that include many attributes. A good indicator that a taxonomy may be appropriate is the occurrence of many relations that show equivalence among values of various attributes (Zembowicz and Żytkow, 1997).

4. Strengths and Applications

Taxonomies apply in domains where many equivalence and subset relations are present, such as medicine and biology, including molecular biology. They also apply in the analysis of humanmade artifacts and in analysis of questionnaires, which reflect group opinions.

Taxonomies may contain substantial empirical contents. Suppose that we determined that an object belongs to d_2 (Figure 1). We can infer each property in E_2 and I_2, each property in E_1 and I_1, as well as each definitional and inferred property for each node in d_0. Some of these properties were used in determining membership in d_2, but the majority are predictions.

Taxonomies are resilient to missing values. As each node in a taxonomy tree can be characterized by many equivalent descriptors, if a particular value is missing in a tuple, many other alternative values can classify the tuple.

Taxonomies on values of a single attribute are used in so-called attribute oriented induction (Chapters 18.1 and 24.1.1). In those cases, a taxonomy consists of classes defined by enumeration of members. Such a taxonomy can be used to guide inductive generalization, but its value is guaranteed by the provider of the taxonomy rather than by discovery from data. The provider guarantees that classes have empirical contents in the way outlined in this article.

5. Weaknesses and Limitations

Knowledge that is best represented in taxonomies is very specific. It belongs to the category of unary logic, that is, knowledge reduced to unary (one argument) predicates. This can be clearly seen in Section 2.

Elementary building blocks of a taxonomy are approximate equivalence relations (Zembowicz and Żytkow, 1997; Fisher, 1987). Subset relations are also useful. But since equivalence relations can seldom be found, taxonomies are rare. However, it is worthwhile to seek them, even if they are not common, because they are very useful.

If the values of a given attribute can be divided into a few subsets, each equivalent to a subset of values of another attribute, there is room for construction of a taxonomy. But such a mapping applies to numerical attributes, too. In that case it is a better idea to seek equations, as dividing numerical values into a large number of classes will produce unnecessarily large descriptions. We should keep in mind not to divide what can be explained jointly.

References

Alberdi, E. and D. Sleeman. 1997. "ReTAX: a step in the automation of taxonomic revision." *Artificial Intell.* **91**: 257–279.

Fisher, D. 1987. "Knowledge acquisition via incremental conceptual clustering." *Machine Learning* **2**: 139–172.

Fisher, D. and P. Langley. 1986. "Conceptual clustering and its relation to numerical taxonomy." *Artificial Intelligence and Statistics* edited by W. A. Gale, pp. 77–116. Reading, MA: Addison-Wesley.

Zembowicz, R. and J. Żytkow. 1997. "Contingency tables as the foundation for concepts, concept hierarchies and rules: the 49er system approach." *Fund. Inform.* **30**: 383–399.

5.8 Probabilistic and Causal Networks

Clark Glymour

ABSTRACT Bayes nets are directed acyclic graphs whose nodes or vertices are random variables with some definite joint probability distribution having conditional independence properties determined by the topology of the graph. If a directed edge $X \to Y$ is taken to represent the proposition that some variation in X produces a variation in Y, for some fixed values of other variables that are not descendants of Y, the Bayes net is a causal model. Bayes nets allow prediction of the probabilities of values of any represented variables conditional on values of any other disjoint set of represented variables. Causal Bayes nets also allow the prediction of the probabilities of variables, conditional on interventions that force values, or probabilities, on other variables. The two, predictions from conditioning and predictions from intervention, are not in general equal. Often the point of causal investigations is to enable prediction of the effects of interventions. Under appropriate assumptions, causal Bayes nets can be learned from experimental data, and features of them can be learned from observational data.

1. Bayes Nets and Causal Models

The Bayes net formalism, developed over the last twenty years, is used as a method for data analysis in the sciences and engineering. (For some recent applications, see Glymour and Cooper, 1999; and Shipley, 2000.) The formalism represents both causal claims and probabilistic dependencies. Using the representation, algorithms have been developed for inferring aspects of causal structure from appropriate observational data, for updating probabilities of variables given values of other variables in the network, and for predicting the indirect outcomes of interventions that directly alter some of the variables in the network. The representations are often called Bayes nets or directed graphical causal models. For causal features that are linearly related, the representations are isomorphic to structures variously called path models or structural equation models. Linear and nonlinear regression models are a special case of directed graphical models.

A possible causal structure is represented by a directed graph—an object with nodes (hereafter: vertices) and arrows between some of them. The vertices represent features or variables; a directed edge between two variables, $X \to Y$, means that for some values of all other variables represented, an action that varies X will cause variation in Y. For example,

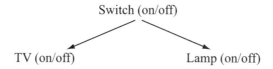

Figure 1

Figure 1 is the representation of a system consisting of a switch that turns on or off both a television and a lamp.

Factors that do not vary in the data under study are not represented. So, for example, if the electric power is always on, it has no corresponding vertex in the representation. If the power supply varies, the representation would be as shown in Figure 2.

Figure 1 explains the association of the state of the television and the state of the lamp by the state of the switch. If the power supply varies, the association between the state of the television and the state of the lamp is not entirely explained by the state of the switch, because there is another cause of both, the state of the power supply, which in Figure 2 is a common cause of the states of the television and the lamp—as is the switch. If no common causes are omitted from a set of variables, the set is said to be causally sufficient.

Bayes nets are especially appropriate for contexts in which the states of observed causes do not determine unique values for their effects, only probabilities. In the causal graph shown in Figure 3, not everyone who smokes has yellow fingers and lung cancer, and not all of those who do not smoke do not have yellow fingers and do not have lung cancer. Instead, there is a probability that those who smoke have yellow fingers and lung cancer, and it is different from the probabilities of those states for those who do not smoke. A Bayes net with yes/no variables includes a specification of the probability of each value of each variable for each vector of values of all of its direct causes. A specification of these probabilities is called a parameterization of the graph. For example, one complete parameterization of the graph in Figure 3 is:

pr(Smoking = yes) = 0.25

pr(Yellow fingers = yes | Smoking = yes) = 0.6

pr(Yellow fingers = yes | Smoking = no) = 0.1

pr(Lung cancer = yes | Smoking = yes) = 0.7

pr(Lung cancer = yes | Smoking = no) = 0.1

A parametrization determines values for all consistent sets of states of the variables of the system, and it determines the probability of any state of any variable given values for any other variables. For example, with the parametrization above, the probability of <yellow

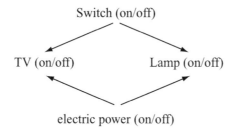

Figure 2

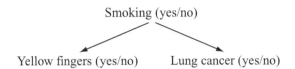

Figure 3

fingers = no, lung cancer = yes, smoking = no > equals pr(Yellow fingers = no | Smoking = no) × pr(Lung cancer = yes | Smoking = no) × pr(Smoking = no), or 0.9 × 0.1 × 0.75.
Again, the probability that Lung Cancer = yes is

(1) pr(Lung Cancer = yes | Smoking = yes) × pr(Smoking = yes) +

pr(Lung Cancer = yes | Smoking = no) × pr(Smoking = no) = 0.7 × 0.25

+ 0.1 × 0.75 = 0.425

The probability that Lung Cancer = yes given that Yellow fingers = no is 0.187

(2) pr(Smoking = no | Yellow fingers = no) × pr(Lung cancer = yes | smoking = no)

+ pr(Smoking = yes | Yellow fingers = no) × pr(Lung cancer

= yes | smoking = yes) = 0.187

which is different from the probability (0.425) that Lung cancer = yes. In other words, in the system described in Figure 3, the value of Yellow fingers provides information about the value of lung cancer. Since the probability of lung cancer changes if the absence of yellow fingers is conditioned on, lung cancer and yellow fingers are dependent in probability. A variety of exact and heuristic procedures is available for computing conditional probabilities in Bayes nets.
It is important that the conditional probability that Lung Cancer = yes given that Yellow fingers = no is not equal to the probability of lung cancer if Yellow fingers are prevented by some external means not represented in Figure 3—for example, by forcing everyone to wear gloves, or wash regularly with soap that prevents nicotine stains. Such a change is called an intervention and the variable directly altered is said to be manipulated. The result of an intervention that manipulates Yellow fingers, forcing the value no, is that Smoking no longer influences Yellow fingers, and the causal graph of the system with such an intervention is shown in Figure 4.
An intervention alters the parameterization of a causal Bayes net. The intervention fixes a value for the state of Yellow fingers, so that Yellow fingers and Smoking are probabilistically independent after the intervention. All other features of the original parameterization are unchanged. Thus the parameterization after an intervention that, for example, forces pr(Yellow fingers = no) = 1 is:

pr(Smoking = yes) = 0.25; pr(Yellow fingers = no) = 1

pr(Lung cancer = yes | Smoking = yes) = 0.7

pr(Lung cancer = yes | Smoking = no) = 0.1

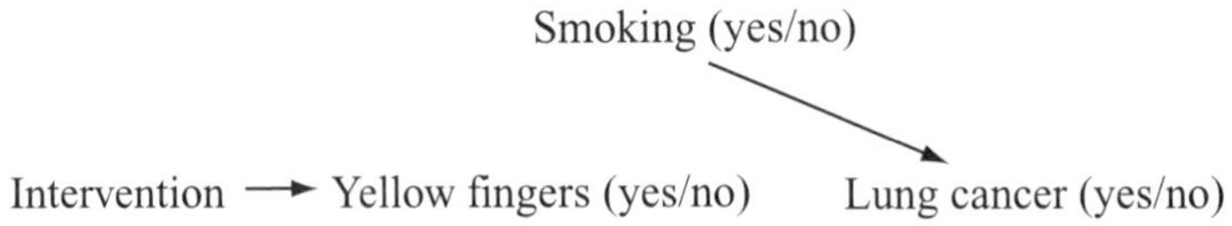

Smoking (yes/no)

Intervention ⟶ Yellow fingers (yes/no)   Lung cancer (yes/no)

Figure 4

The probability that Lung cancer = yes given an intervention that manipulates Yellow fingers to no is found by computing the probability of Lung cancer conditional on Yellow = no in Figure 4 rather than by conditioning on Yellow fingers = no in Figure 3. In Figure 4 the probability of Lung cancer is equal to its probability conditioning on any value of Yellow fingers, whereas in Figure 3 the probability of Lung cancer conditional on Yellow fingers = yes is different from its probability conditional on Yellow fingers = no. Or, put another way, the probability of lung cancer before an intervention that forces Yellow fingers = no is 0.425, and the probability of lung cancer after such an intervention is the same, 0.425. The causal Bayes net captures the fact that the state of Yellow fingers gives information about the state of Lung cancer but does not influence Lung cancer.

Bayes nets that are also linear models are parameterized by assigning a real number to each edge and a mean error (usually zero) and error variance to each variable, and specifying that the error terms are all uncorrelated with one another. So a Bayes net that is parameterized as a linear model asserting that the average SAT score of a college's entering class influences its dropout rate is

$$\text{SAT} \rightarrow \text{Dropout}$$

and would be parameterized so that:

$$\text{Dropout} = a\,\text{SAT} + e$$

where a is a real nonzero number, and e is a random variable distributed normally with zero mean. In addition to confusions between conditioning and intervening, the literature on linear path models contains a great many confusions about the causal significance of rewriting linear equations so that apparently dependent variables become independent. Pearl (2000) gives a systematic resolution in terms of causal Bayes nets.

Cyclic Bayes nets, in which there are closed directed paths, are also possible, and some of their (rather surprising) properties have been investigated (see Richardson, 1996). Many of their properties are, however, still little understood. For example, there is no generally accepted theory of prediction with conditionalization or with intervention for such networks, and their connections with time series are only partly explored.

To the extent that actual causal relations among features in a population of systems can be represented by some Bayes net, then features of the true representation can sometimes be discovered from observations alone, without experimental intervention and without prior knowledge of whether there are unobserved sources of covariation among observed variables. Thus if X, Y, Z, and W are four variables, only Bayes nets in which Z causes W can entail that X is independent of Y, and $\{X, Y\}$ is independent of W given any value of Z, and no other independencies. These sorts of constraints are exploited in two sorts of search algorithms. Scoring searches give an initial score to each possible Bayes net and update the scores based on the observed evidence. Search is generally heuristic hill-climbing through the space of graphs and their parameterizations. Conditional independence relations and other constraints implied by graphs implicitly influence their conditional scores, depending on how closely those constraints are satisfied in the sample data. Constraint searches use hypothesis tests to find independence or other relationships among the variables in the data, and they construct a class of alternative graphs as they do so. Both kinds of searches have proved fruitful in applications.

References

Glymour, C. and G. Cooper. 1999. *Computation, Causation and Discovery*. MIT/AAAI Press.

Shipley, B. 2000. *Cause and Correlation in Biology*. Oxford University Press.

Pearl, J. 2000. *Causality*. Oxford University Press.

Richardson, T. 1996. *Feedback and Cyclic Graphs*. Ph.D. Thesis, Department of Philosophy, Carnegie Mellon University.

5.9 Neural Networks

Witold Pedrycz

ABSTRACT   This article elaborates on the scope of knowledge representation in neural networks. In particular, we identify a list of properties of neural networks that are of interest in the context of data mining.

1. Introduction

As of today, the area of neurocomputing has its own highly visible identity of well-defined methodology and a profound range of areas of applications that spread from concept formation, control, pattern recognition, robotics, and so on, to specific target systems aimed at solving detailed tasks arising in these areas (Anderson and Rosenfeld, 1988; Fiesler and Beale, 1997; Golden, 1996; Grossberg, 1988; Hecht-Nielsen, 1991; Rocha, 1992; White, 1989). Neural networks are highly distributed and parallel processing architectures. One of their profound features lies in their learning capabilities. Our intent is to list and investigate the main aspects of neural networks that are of interest in the framework of data mining. The main advantages and shortcomings are also discussed.

2. Main Notions and Architectures of Neural Networks

The basic processing unit, the artificial neuron (or neuron, for short) is described as a static n-input single-output static nonlinear mapping of the form

$$y = f\left(\sum_{i=1}^{n} w_i x_i w_0\right) = f(\mathbf{w}^T \mathbf{x})$$

Here $\mathbf{x}$ forms a vector of inputs while $\mathbf{w}$ is a vector of adjustable connections. f is a nonlinear nondecreasing (say, sigmoid function) mapping from $\mathbf{R}^n$ to $[0, 1]$ (or $[-1, 1]$). Any neural network is composed of a significant number of neurons that are usually arranged in a number of layers. The layers that are not exposed to the original input or output signals are called hidden layers. If the neurons interact with most of the remaining elements in the successive layers, the network is fully connected. When the number of such connections is low, the network is sparsely connected. Depending on whether the processing is carried out starting from the input layer and proceeding towards the output layer or there is some feedback loop in the processing paths, we are concerned with a class of feedforward or feedback neural networks. Feedforward neural networks do not exhibit any elements of memory (do not have any ability to memorize) while feedback (or recurrence) provides the networks with the memorization mechanisms. The basic ideas are illustrated in Figure 1. Note that feedforward neural networks realize a direct flow of signals (processing) from the input to the output. The computed output fully depends on the input. Knowledge representation accomplished in this way embraces all forms of nonlinear mappings (functions) between highly-dimensional spaces. We can write it down concisely as $\mathbf{y} = f(\mathbf{x})$ with $\mathbf{x}$ and $\mathbf{y}$ being the inputs and outputs, respectively. The feedback mechanism, see Figure 1(b), leads to a representation of dynamical phenomena, namely all systems where the current state depends on the inputs as well as the previous states (history). The feedback loop leads to the expressions $\mathbf{q}$(current) = g ($\mathbf{q}$(previous), $\mathbf{x}$(current)) and $\mathbf{y} = h(\mathbf{q})$ with $\mathbf{q}$ denoting the state of the network. In this sense, we achieve the same knowledge representation capabilities as those encountered in state machines (and their continuous counterparts such as fuzzy or probabilistic state machines) augmented by learning schemes.

On the computational side, it is worth underlining that neural networks are universal approximators meaning that a multilayer network of a suitable size realizes an arbitrarily accurate approximation to any arbitrary continuous mapping (White, 1989). This is a fundamental underpinning that justifies the use (and successful performance) of neural networks.

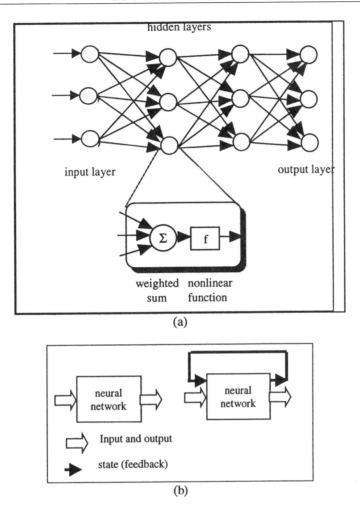

Figure 1 A basic topology of the neutral network (a) and feedforward and feedback neural networks (b)

3. Learning

A vast number of the learning procedures associated with neural networks are concerned primarily with their parametric learning. This means that the connections of the neurons are updated (modified) in such a way that an assumed performance index (objective function) becomes minimized. By the performance index we mean a way of expressing how well the outputs of the network follow the experimental data. Quite commonly, this performance index comes in the form of a sum of squared errors (differences between the data and the results of the network). Depending on the problem at hand, several main categories of learning are distinguished (Fiesler and Beale, 1997; Golden, 1996; Hecht-Nielsen, 1991).

- *Supervised learning.* This type of learning is the most evident and commonly exploited: the network is provided with inputs and expected outputs (targets). The outputs of the network should adhere to the target values; this is accomplished by changing (updating) the connections of the network. The dominant examples in this category are feedforward neural networks whose training is realized by using various versions of the backpropagation learning algorithm.

- *Reinforcement learning.* The network is provided with some general hints about its behavior (reinforcement signals). We generally deal with temporal or spatial reinforcement. The key difference between this form of learning and supervised learning lies in the way in which supervision is accomplished. Consider a network with many outputs. In supervised learning we are provided with the required values for each individual output. In reinforcement learning we are given only a global (scalar) reward signal. The reward signal is less detailed and the learning becomes more challenging.

- *Unsupervised learning.* In this case no labeling (desired output) is available and it is expected that the learning algorithm should provide a way of making sense of data and cluster the patterns by placing similar vectors in the same groups. Kohonen self-organizing maps (Golden, 1996; Hecht-Nielsen, 1991) are visible examples of neural networks falling in this category.

One may be faced with a mixture of these categories of learning, especially in more complex situations. For instance, most data may be fully labeled (which implies the mode of supervised learning) whereas another portion of data could be left unlabeled (and these patterns, that is data, call for an unsupervised style of learning).

To some extent there is a double-edged sword effect inherently associated with the distributed nature of representation and processing carried out in neural networks.

- A significant number of the connections support a high level of parametric flexibility so the network becomes capable of representing (approximating or interpolating) the experimental data. This flexibility may sometimes result in poor generalization abilities of the network meaning that its performance on a new set of data (testing data) may no longer be acceptable. An excessively high number of neurons usually results in a memorization effect (the training set is memorized and distributed across the connections of the neural network).

- The size of the search space (parameter space) contributes to an excessively long process of learning requiring a significant number of learning epochs. Depending on the algorithm itself, the learning procedure could get stuck at some local minima.

- The networks do no scale up very easily in terms of efficient learning procedures. As the number of inputs goes up, the number of the neurons increases. In fully connected neural networks this contributes to an even faster growth of the total number of the connections to be trained. Learning becomes less efficient and severely hampered by the existence of a number of local minima (because of high-dimensionality of the search space, a suitable visualization of such space is generally not feasible).

4. Knowledge Representation in Neural Networks and Interpretation Issues

Neural networks are highly distributed parallel structures. They support learning, make processing more robust but do not help in enhancing any interpretation capabilities. Available knowledge is accommodated by the network either through its architecture (topology) or during the process of training (that could be guided by some pieces of domain knowledge).

- Knowledge representation becomes crucial to the process of learning in the networks. The data, if represented properly, can contribute to faster and more efficient learning. The character of such representation is very much problem driven and requires some interaction with a system designer.

- Interpretation issues of neural networks are still open to a relatively high degree: the distributed nature of processing does not support the user in gaining a high level of interpretability of the network. Nevertheless, there is a significant advantage in using neural networks along the line of data analysis. Instead of searching for patterns in original data, we concentrate on the data generated by the neural network. This approach is fully legitimate as we concentrate on revealing meaningful and noise-free relationships in the data rather than coping with data sets including some erroneous records.

- Generation of an eventual representation of higher level (nonnumeric) constructs resulting from the network is essential to the use of neurocomputing in the realm of data mining.

- The critical point of learning and interpretation becomes even more apparent in cases of structured and heterogeneous data. In most current applications of neural networks, one is primarily concerned with the relatively homogeneous nature of their inputs. For instance, these could be vectors of real numbers. In this case a simple scaling (normalization) is usually sufficient to yield good learning results. In the case of a mixture of real and categorical inputs (which are common in databases), the choice of a proper representation space (from the perspective of which the network perceives the original data) is not that straightforward and calls for a well thought out and prudently arranged neural network interface that establishes an interaction between the network and its environment.

It becomes quite apparent that knowledge representation and its processing are crucial to the performance of neural networks. Table 1 provides a summary of several aspects of knowledge representation and their realizations completed in terms of the algorithms and architectures of neural networks.

It is instructive to elaborate in more detail on the architectures and algorithms associated with knowledge representation and processing. The role of interfaces is crucial as a conceptual vehicle to build an interaction between the world and the network so that these two can communicate effectively. The network perceives the world through its interface. The choice of the interface predetermines effectiveness of learning and quality of the network (say, its generalization abilities). Data normalization is one of these simple yet crucial aspects of any interface. To deal with uncertain (granular) data, one has to develop an interface in such a way so that the network becomes aware of the level of granularity of such data.

Radial basis functions could be also viewed as a sort of knowledge hints. By focusing and delineating highly homogeneous regions in the data space, they immensely accelerate learning, simplify a topology of the network and help avoiding eventual learning problems especially those concerning local minima in the highly-dimensional space of the connections of the network. In general, knowledge hints are crucial as they help reduce the size of the search space of the connections and avoid spurious and definitely ineffective search regions. For instance, one may know that symmetry of the problem may lead to symmetry in the connection space. This, in turn, may imply that we should maintain some symmetric

Table 1 Knowledge Representation in Neural Networks: Underlying Features and Examples

Main feature	Examples	Architectures and algorithms
Heterogeneous data	• Missing data • Granularity of data (numbers, numeric intervals, linguistic estimates, etc.) • Uncertain data	Development of neural network interfaces. The intent of the interfaces is to capture data, normalize them, and facilitate representation and quantification of granularity and uncertainty
Focus on selected regions of data space	• Data regions of high homogeneity	Radial basis function (RBF) neural networks; reliance on receptive fields that are crucial to ensuing learning processes
Available knowledge hints	• Type of data • Inclusion of general trends and relationships (e.g., symmetry)	Incorporation of hints through structural arrangements of the networks or some of its layers, use of various neurons of specific logic-inclined characteristics (such as weighted *and*, *or* etc.)

connections (weights). We make architectural provisions when dealing with positive numeric values or similar.

Overall, the realization of the associated neural network architectures addressing the above issues of knowledge representation calls for their integration with other technologies such as granular computing and fuzzy sets (in particular IEEE, 1992, cf. also Chapter 30).

5. Conclusions

We have elaborated on the main processing and knowledge representation issues in neural networks. It has been underlined that neural networks are equipped with high learning abilities and may deliver useful generalization. Neural networks are useful in data mining when careful attention is paid to the problems of knowledge representation and the aspects of scaling of the neural networks are completed in the presence of large volumes of highly-dimensional data.

References

Anderson, J. A. and E. Rosenfeld. (eds). 1988. *Neurocomputing: Foundations of Research*. Cambridge, MA: MIT Press.

Fiesler, E. and R. Beale. (eds). 1997. *Handbook of Neural Computation*. New York: IOP and Oxford University Press.

Golden, R. 1996. *Mathematical Methods for Neural Network Analysis and Design*. Cambridge, MA: MIT Press.

Grossberg, S. 1988. *Neural Networks and Natural Intelligence*. Cambridge, MA: The MIT Press.

Hecht-Nielsen, R. 1991. *Neurocomputing*. Reading, MA: Addison-Wesley.

IEEE, 1992. *IEEE Trans. Neural Networks*. Special issue on fuzzy logic and neural networks. **3**

Rocha, A. F. 1992. *Neural Nets: a Theory for Brain and Machine*. Lecture Notes in Artificial Intelligence. Volume 638. Berlin: Springer-Verlag.

White, H. 1989. "Learning in artificial neural networks: a statistical perspective." *Neural Comput.* **1**: 425–464.

6 DATA AND KNOWLEDGE IN DATABASE SYSTEMS

6.1 Relational Databases

Raghu Ramakrishnan

ABSTRACT Relational Database Management Systems (RDBMS) are widely used to store, manipulate, and query large data sets in a variety of applications. Complex application packages supporting human resource management, enterprise resource planning, and so on have been developed to run on top of RDBMS, and have helped to make RDBMS ubiquitous; virtually every major organization today relies upon an RDBMS to handle payroll, sales, inventory, and other mission-critical data. The underlying technology has been developed over the last three decades, and has proved itself in demanding situations involving vast data sets and requiring nonstop operations. We introduce the data model and query language used in relational systems. We also touch upon how an RDBMS stores data, optimizes and executes queries, handles concurrent requests, and recovers from system failures.

1. Introduction

A database management system, or DBMS, is software designed to assist in maintaining and utilizing large collections of data, and the need for such systems, as well as their use, is growing rapidly. The alternative to using a DBMS is to use *ad hoc* approaches that do not carry over from one application to another; for example, to store the data in files and write application-specific code to manage it.

Using a DBMS to manage data has many advantages:

- *Data independence.* Application programs should be as independent as possible from details of data representation and storage. The DBMS can provide an abstract view of the data to insulate application code from such details.

- *Efficient data access.* A DBMS utilizes a variety of sophisticated techniques to store and retrieve data efficiently. This feature is especially important if the data is stored on external storage devices.

- *Data integrity and security.* If data is always accessed through the DBMS, the DBMS can enforce integrity constraints on the data. For example, before inserting salary information for an employee, the DBMS can check that the department budget is not exceeded. Also, the DBMS can enforce access controls that govern what data is visible to different classes of users.

- *Data administration.* When several users share the data, centralizing the administration of data can offer significant improvements. Experienced professionals who understand the nature of the data being managed, and how different groups of users use it, can be responsible for organizing the data representation to minimize redundancy and for fine-tuning the storage of the data to make retrieval efficient.

- *Concurrent access and crash recovery.* As noted earlier, a DBMS schedules concurrent accesses to the data in such a manner that users can think of the data as being accessed by only one user at a time. Further, the DBMS protects users from the effects of system failures.

- *Reduced application development time.* Clearly, the DBMS supports many important functions that are common to many applications accessing data stored in the DBMS. This, in conjuction with the high-level interface to the data, facilitates quick development of applications. Such applications are also likely to be more robust than applications developed from scratch, because many important tasks are handled by the DBMS instead of being implemented by the application.

2. The Relational Model

In this section we provide a brief introduction to the relational model (Codd, 1970). The central data description construct in this model is a relation, which can be thought of as a set of records, each of which has the same number (and type) of fields.

A description of data in terms of a data model is called a *schema*. In the relational model, the schema for a relation specifies its name, the name of each field (or attribute or column), and the type of each field. As an example, student information in a university database may be stored in a relation with the following schema:

Students(*sid:* string, *name:* string, *login:* string, *age:* integer, *gpa:* real)

The preceding schema says that each row in the students relation has five fields, with field names and types as indicated. An example instance of the students relation appears in Table 1.

Each row in the students relation describes a student. The description is not complete—for example, the student's height is not included—but is presumably adequate for the intended applications in the university database. Every row follows the schema of the students relation, which can therefore be regarded as a template for describing a student.

We can make the description of a student more precise by specifying integrity constraints, which are conditions that the records in a relation must satisfy. For example, we could specify that every student has a unique *sid* value. Observe that we cannot capture this information by simply adding another field to the students schema; thus the expressiveness of the constructs available for specifying integrity constraints is an important aspect of a data model.

3. Query Languages

A relational database query is a question about the data, and the answer consists of a new relation containing the result. For example, we might want to find all students younger than eighteen or all students enrolled in Reggae203. A query language is a specialized language for writing queries.

Relational algebra is a formal query language that is the foundation for commercial query languages. It provides operators to select rows from a relation (σ), to project columns (π), and to join two relations ($\bowtie$). The first two operations allow us to manipulate data in a single relation, while the join operation allows us to combine information present in two relations. Every operator in the algebra accepts (one or more) relation instances as arguments and the result is always a relation instance. This makes it easy to compose operators to form a complex query.

The power of relational algebra derives from the ability to compose operators into expressions that can compute answers to a wide range of queries arising in practice. Further, many useful equivalence rules are known that allow us to replace one expression by another for the purposes of efficient query evaluation, as we will see in Section 4. Commercial query languages are based on extensions of relational algebra, and relational database systems typically convert a query into an internal form that is close to relational algebra; this representation of a query is used for query optimization and execution.

Table 1 An Instance of the Students Relation				
50 000	Dave	dave@cs	19	3.3
53 666	Jones	jones@cs	18	3.4
53 688	Smith	smith@ee	18	3.2
53 650	Smith	smith@math	19	3.8
53 831	Madayan	madayan@music	11	1.8
53 832	Guldu	guldu@music	12	2.0

SQL is the most popular commercial query language for a relational DBMS. We now present some SQL examples that illustrate how easily relations can be queried. We can compute the names and logins of students who are younger than eighteen with the following query:

```
SELECT S.name, S.login
FROM   Students S
WHERE  S. age<18
```

We can also combine information in the students and enrolled relations. If we want to obtain the names of all students who obtained an A and the id of the course in which they got an A, we could write the following query:

```
SELECT S.name, E.cid
FROM   Students S, Enrolled E
WHERE  S.sid = E.sid AND E.grade = 'A'
```

This query can be understood as follows: "If there is a students tuple S and an enrolled tuple E such that S.sid = E.sid (so that S describes the student who is enrolled in E) and E.grade = 'A,' then print the student's name and the course id." See Melton and Simon (1993) for a more detailed treatment of SQL.

4. Relational Storage System

A DBMS manages space on disk, where the data is to be stored, and effectively manages its own file system. Data pages are brought into main memory from disk as needed, through a DBMS component called the buffer manager, which partitions the available main memory into a collection of pages or frames. The buffer manager effectively supports virtual memory, but gives the DBMS complete over when pages are fetched from disk and written out. Such a high degree of control is required for implementing protocols used in recovering from system failures, and for exploiting knowledge of common DBMS page reference patterns.

The concept of a file in a DBMS is a collection of pages or a collection of records. The file layer typically supports a heap file, or file of unordered pages. In addition to keeping track of the pages in a file, this layer organizes the information within a page.

The file storage layer also supports the creation and maintenance of auxiliary data structures called indexes, which enable selection queries to be answered quickly. The most widely used index is called a B+ tree, and it provides efficient support for range searches, including sorted file scans as a special case.

An example B+ tree is shown in Figure 1. Data records (or pointers to them) are stored in the leaf level nodes of the tree, which are in the lowest layer shown in Figure 1. Nodes in higher levels serve to direct a search for a data record to the appropriate leaf. For example, a search for a data record containing the value eight in the search field begins at the root node, goes to the left child (because eight is less than the splitting value seventeen in the root node), then to the second leaf node (because eight is between the values five and thirteen, and the child pointer for this value range points to the second leaf node). To find all data records with values greater than eight in the search field, we would proceed as above until we get to the

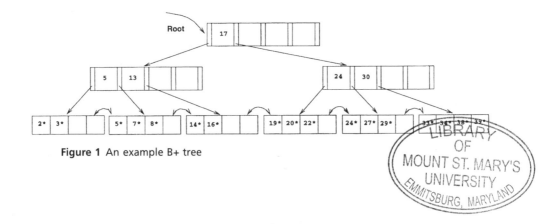

Figure 1 An example B+ tree

leaf node, then scan all leaf nodes from this point on toward the right, using the bidirectional links at the leaf level.

Unlike sorted files, B+ trees support efficient insertion and deletion. A new record is inserted into the tree by identifying the correct leaf (using the search algorithm). If the leaf has no space, a new leaf is created and added to the tree; this can be accomplished with minimal changes to the tree. B+ trees also provide support for equality selections, although they are not as efficient in this case as hash-based indexes, which are also supported in some systems.

For decision support and data mining, advanced index structures such as bitmap indexes are becoming popular. See Ramakrishnan and Gehrke (2000) for a more detailed coverage of storage and indexing techniques.

5. Relational Query Processing and Optimization

SQL queries are evaluated by considering their relational algebra form, to a first approximation. A query evaluation plan (or simply plan) consists of an extended relational algebra tree, with additional annotations at each node indicating the retrieval method for each relation and the implementation method to use for each relational operator. Several alternative implementation methods are typically supported for each of the basic relational operators, and the best method depends on the size of the input relations and the distribution of values in these relations.

Consider the following SQL query:

```
SELECT S.sname
FROM   Reserves R, Sailors S
WHERE  R.sid = S.sid
       AND R.bid = 100 AND S.rating > 5
```

This query can be expressed in relational algebra as follows:

$$\pi_{sname}(\sigma_{bid=100 \wedge rating > 5}(\text{Reserves} \bowtie_{sid=sid} \text{Sailors})).$$

The algebra expression partially specifies how to evaluate the query—we first compute the natural join of Reserves and Sailors, then perform the selections, and finally project the *sname* field. To obtain a fully specified evaluation plan, we must decide on an implementation for each of the algebra operations involved. For example, we can use a page-oriented simple nested loops join with Reserves as the outer relation and apply selections and projections to each tuple in the result of the join as it is produced; the result of the join prior to the selections and projections is never stored in its entirety.

An optimizer considers several alternative plans (which it generates by taking advantage of equivalences between relational algebra expressions), uses stored statistics about data distributions in the database to estimate the cost of each alternative plan, and chooses the plan with the least estimated cost.

The differences in cost between alternative plans for a query can be considerable. As an example, consider a query that retrieves all data records with a value greater than ten in the search field. One plan consists of a sequential scan of the file, which is indeed the only feasible plan if there is no index. If there is a B+ tree index, an alternative plan is to use the index to fetch only those records that satisfy the search condition. If the data records are stored in the leaf levels of the B+ tree, this is similar to a sequential scan over just the relevant portion of the file, and is superior to a sequential scan. If the leaf levels contain pointers to the data records, this plan requires us to follow one pointer per data record. Since these pointers are to locations on disk, rather than main memory, each such pointer traversal could result in fetching a separate disk page. The cost of this plan is lower than the cost of a sequential scan only if the search condition is highly selective (i.e., only a small fraction of the data records satisfy the condition). If we are able to estimate the selectivity of the search condition using statistics maintained by the system, such as a histogram of how values are distributed, we can estimate the cost of the two plans for a given query and choose the right one.

See Ramakrishnan and Gehrke (2000) for a more detailed coverage of query processing.

6. Concurrent Access and Crash Recovery

Consider a database that holds information about airline reservations. At any given instant, it is possible (and likely) that several travel agents are looking up information about available seats on various flights, and indeed, making new seat reservations. When several users access (and possibly modify) a database concurrently, the DBMS must order their requests carefully to avoid conflicts. For example, when one travel agent looks up Flight 100 on some given day and finds an empty seat, another travel agent may simultaneously be making a reservation for that seat, thereby making the information seen by the first agent obsolete.

An important task of a DBMS is to schedule concurrent accesses to data so that each user can safely ignore the fact that others are accessing the data concurrently. A DBMS allows users to think of their programs as if they were executing in isolation, and users need to think about other users' programs only to the extent that programs submitted concurrently could be executed in any order.

Further, the DBMS must protect users from the effects of system failures by ensuring that all data (and the status of active applications) is restored to a consistent state when the system is restarted after a crash. For example, if a travel agent asks for a reservation to be made, and the DBMS responds saying that the reservation has been made, the reservation should not be lost if the system crashes. On the other hand, if the DBMS has not yet responded to the request, but is in the process of making the necessary changes to the data while the crash occurs, the partial changes should be undone when the system comes back up. For example, if the DBMS is in the middle of transferring money from account A to account B, and has debited the first account but not yet credited the second when the crash occurs, the money debited from account A must be restored when the system comes back up after the crash.

A transaction is any one execution of a user program in a DBMS. (Executing the same program several times will generate several transactions.) A DBMS must ensure three important properties of transactions to correctly manage data, given concurrent access and the possibility of system failures:

1. *Isolation.* Users should be able to understand a transaction without considering the effect of other concurrently executing transactions, even if the DBMS interleaves the actions of several transactions for performance reasons.

2. *Atomicity.* Either all actions are carried out or none are. Users should not have to worry about the effect of incomplete transactions (say, when a system crash occurs).

3. *Durability.* Once the DBMS informs the user that a transaction has been successfully completed, its effects should persist even if the system crashes before all its changes are reflected on disk.

Transaction isolation is ensured by guaranteeing that even though actions of several transactions might be interleaved, the net effect is identical to executing all transactions in some serial order. For example, if two transactions T_1 and T_2 are executed concurrently, the net effect is guaranteed to be equivalent to executing T_1 followed by executing T_2 or executing T_2 followed by executing T_1. (The DBMS provides no guarantees about which order is effectively chosen.)

A DBMS typically uses a locking protocol to achieve isolation. For example, suppose that two kinds of locks are supported by the DBMS: shared locks on an object can be held by two different transactions at the same time, but an exclusive lock on an object ensures that no other transactions hold any lock on this object. Suppose that every transaction begins by obtaining a shared lock on each data object that it needs to read and an exclusive lock on each data object that it needs to modify, and then releases all its locks after completing all actions. Consider two transactions T1 and T2 such that T1 wants to modify a data object and T2 wants to read the same object. Intuitively, if T1's request for an exclusive lock on the object is granted first, T2 cannot proceed until T1 releases this lock, because T2's request for a shared lock will not be granted by the DBMS until then. Thus all of T1's actions will complete before any of T2's actions are initiated.

A DBMS ensures transaction atomicity by undoing the actions of incomplete transactions. In order to do so, the DBMS maintains a log of all writes to the database. A crucial property of the log is that each write action must be recorded in the log (on disk) before the corresponding change is reflected in the database itself—otherwise, if the system crashes just after making the change in the database but before the change is recorded in the log, the DBMS would be unable to detect and undo this change. This property is called Write-Ahead Log or WAL. To ensure this property, the DBMS must be able to selectively force a page in memory to disk. The log is also used to ensure durability. See Gray and Reuter (1992) for a more detailed coverage of transaction management issues.

Portions of this article were previously published in R. Ramakrishnan and J. Gehrke, *Database Management Systems*, 2d ed., 2000. Permission to reprint granted by McGraw-Hill.

References

Codd, E. 1970. "A relational model of data for large shared data banks." *Commun. ACM* **13(6)**: 377–387.
Gray, J. and A. Reuter. 1992. *Transaction Processing: Concepts and Techniques*. Morgan Kaufmann.
Melton, J. and A. Simon. 1993. *Understanding the New SQL: A Complete Guide*. Morgan Kaufmann.
Ramakrishnan, R. and J. Gehrke. 2000. *Database Management Systems*. 2d ed. McGraw-Hill.

6.2 Object-Oriented Databases

Klaus R. Dittrich and Anca Vaduva

ABSTRACT   An object-oriented database manages its data (i.e., the so-called objects) according to an object-oriented data model. An object encapsulates both state and behavior and has a unique object identity. Objects are instantiated from classes that may be organized in hierarchies with inheritance. Related to inheritance are the concepts of dynamic binding, polymorphism, overriding, and overloading.

1. Introduction

In analogy to relational database management systems (RDBMS), which are based on the relational data model (see Chapter 6.1 of this handbook), object-oriented database management systems (ODBMS) are defined as DBMS with an object-oriented data model. As such, they have to provide the usual database functionality: persistent data storage, management of large sets of data, secondary storage management, concurrency control, recovery, and a query facility. Their data model has to follow the typical object-oriented concepts. Recall that a data model is a set of conceptual tools for describing the representation of real-world structures in terms of data.

2. Features of Object-Oriented Data Models

The main concepts and notions of an object-oriented data model include the following (Atkinson et al., 1989; Cattell, 1994; Dittrich, 1994; Embley, 1998):

- An object-oriented database consists of a collection of objects. They are instantiated from classes, which constitute the database schema. An object is a representation of a real or conceptual entity. Each object has a state, specified by the value of its attributes, and a set of operations or methods (specifying the object behavior) that may be performed on that object. Methods are invoked by sending messages to an object.

  Object structures and relationships between objects can be built by means of references: attributes of an object may take on values that are references or collections of references to other objects. In particular, composite objects are built from simpler ones by applying constructors (e.g., tuples, sets, bags, lists) to them. Operations on composite objects can propagate transitively to all components. For example, when a composite object is deleted or copied, all the (possibly nested) components have to be deleted or copied automatically.

- In ODBMS, object identity plays a crucial role. Each object has an identity that distinguishes it from all other objects. This is achieved by, for example, assigning a unique internally generated identifier (like an ever-incrementing number) which is independent of the actual object state. Identifiers are the base for building object references. As an aside, they also bring a performance gain for retrieval since they support simple navigation through linked objects. In this way, the expensive table joins necessary in RDBMS can be avoided.

- A class is a description for objects having the same structure and behavior (intension). Similar to data types in programming languages, a class acts as a pattern for the creation of objects. Each object is created by instantiating a class and is thus called an instance. The set of instances of a class existing at a certain point in time represents the class extension.

- Encapsulation (sometimes called information hiding) is a descendant of the concepts of modularization and abstract data type. Both data (represented by the attribute values) and behavior are encapsulated in objects which are accessible from outside via their interface only. The interface consists of the specification of operations (i.e., methods signatures) that can be performed on that object. For the implementation of those methods, a computationally complete language has to be used that allows the expression of any desired algorithm. Encapsulation brings advantages especially for system maintenance: whenever the object interface is preserved, the hidden data structure and method implementation may be changed without any consequence for that object's access. In ODBMS, encapsulation is often weakened in order to improve performance, by allowing the declaration of public attributes. They can be directly used, for example, in queries to collections of objects.

- Inheritance allows classes to be organized in a subclass/superclass structure where subclasses inherit the structure and behavior defined in the superclasses. Instances of subclasses will have all the properties defined for their superclasses. However, subclasses may also extend the inherited class definition or override some of its behavior. As a consequence, subclasses will have the same operation names as their superclasses but with different implementations. The decision as to which method implementation should be executed when an operation has to be performed is postponed to runtime. This mechanism is called late or dynamic binding and is related to the notions of overriding, overloading (i.e., the redefinition of the method implementations), and to polymorphism (i.e., the property of messages to be dynamically bound to different classes).

3. Strengths and Weaknesses of ODBMS

Object-oriented databases evolved as the consequence of two facts: the breakthrough of object orientation and the shortcomings of the existing database technology, including their prominent representative, the relational approach.

The advent of object orientation imposed requirements for a seamless, transparent integration of database capabilities with object-oriented programming languages. The aim is the unification of the object-oriented data model used by applications with the data model of the DBMS used to store the application objects. In this way, the so-called impedance mismatch encountered with the use of RDBMS is significantly reduced. This provides benefits for modeling, system maintenance (including extensibility and reusing), and database administration.

The second reason for using ODBMS is the improved modeling power. Despite their popularity, relational database systems quickly reach their limitations when complex semantics, as required by advanced database applications, have to be modeled. For example, it is difficult to represent complex application objects that are naturally ordered in an array or list—such as chapters in a book or transistors on an integrated circuit—in relational tables. These impediments are partly related to the restricted, nonextensible choice of data type: no user-defined data types are supported and no composite objects can be represented (this applies, at least, to the traditional relational database systems).

Inherently, ODBMS go beyond the limitations of RDBMS and fulfill the requirements imposed by advanced object-oriented database applications like software engineering (CASE tools), mechanical and electrical engineering (CAD applications), scientific, and medical applications. As a rule, these applications have little data contention and consist of few long transactions. Besides the special modeling needs, they usually require additional features that could be effortlessly provided by ODBMS: support of versions, distribution of data, advanced transaction models, and schema evolution.

For these special kinds of applications, a substantial performance improvement may be achieved by using ODBMS instead of relational systems—according to Shasha (1992) 500-fold in certain situations. The reason is that these applications use graphs as the most natural data structure and thus traversal operations for them may be implemented more efficiently by ODBMS. In particular, when the same data items are accessed many times in a short time period, the inherent navigational facilities provided by memory-resident object structures may be exploited. However, relational queries are faster when applications need set-oriented instead of navigational query processing (Carey et al., 1997). Also for other features like database access or update requirements ODBMS do not have any performance advantage to offer. Carey et al. (1997) even noticed that the bulk load of databases from initial files becomes both more complex and more time-consuming than in the relational case.

4. State of the Art

There are a variety of practical approaches for the integration of the object-oriented paradigm with database technology. First of all, pure ODBMS blend an object-oriented language (like Smalltalk, C++, Java) with standard database functionality. The list of known products includes ObjectStore, Objectivity/DB, Gemstone, Versant, O2, and POET (Barry & Associates, 1998). Some of the vendors joined forces to specify ODMG (Catell and Barry, 1997), a standard for ODBMS. It includes an object model, an object specification language, and an object query language (OQL), which attempts to be the counterpart of SQL on the ODBMS side.

ODBMS have not reached the popularity of RDBMS because they still lack the same maturity with regard to their DBMS functionality. In addition, the instability of small companies like those marketing ODBMS at present, may be an impediment to the wider use of the technology.

A pragmatic alternative for combining existing DBMS with object-oriented concepts has been adopted by today's famous database software developers (Informix, Oracle, IBM) leading to object-relational databases (Stonebraker et al., 1999) as a hybrid approach. They extend the relational model with object-oriented features, providing support for tuple types, tuple identifiers, abstract data types, and inheritance. Due to their extensible nature, they can be customized to provide specialized solutions designed for specific data types or application domains, including data mining (e.g., the data mining cartridge provided for Oracle 8 (see Chapter 24.2.2 of this handbook)). However, object-relational databases still consider relational tables as the fundamental data modeling construct and thus a database is represented by a set of relations and the objects are second class entities. The query language is an extension of SQL.

Another possible form of integration between DBMS concepts and object orientation are middleware approaches including JavaBlend, PowerTier, and SQL Object Factory (Barry & Associates, 1998). They support object-oriented programming for applications while using nonobject-oriented databases to store the data for the objects created. At runtime, the middleware software automatically performs the mapping between the two different representations: objects on the one hand and the corresponding tuples stored in one or more relational tables on the other hand (assuming relational databases are used).

5. ODBMS and Data Mining

The advantages offered by object-oriented database applications can be exploited for data mining as well. Encapsulation provides for persistently managing both data and methods that apply for it. Thus, certain mining algorithm steps or even the hypothesis space to be validated may be represented as methods of the classes managing data (i.e., objects) to be mined. These objects may also encapsulate visualization methods that should make the identification of patterns and regularities in data sets easier.

Complex types of data such as those supported by ODBMS may require advanced data mining techniques. An example is the object cube based generalization technique presented in Han et al. (1998) that handles complex object structures, methods, class/subclass hierarchies, and object identifiers. Mining can then be performed on the multidimensional abstraction spaces provided by these object cubes.

References

Atkinson, M., F. Bancilhon, D. DeWitt, K. R. Dittrich, D. Maier, and S. Zdonik. 1989. "The object-oriented database system manifesto." In *1st International Conference on Deductive and Object-Oriented Databases (Kyoto, Japan)*, edited by W. Kim, J. M. Nicolas, and S. Nishio, pp. 223–240. Amsterdam: Elsevier Science Publishers 1990.

Barry & Associates. 1998. http://www.odbmsfacts.com/

Carey, M. J., D. J. DeWitt, J. F. Naughton, M. Asgarian, P. Brown, J. Gehrke, and D. N. Shah. 1997. "The BUCKY object-relational benchmark." In *Proceedings ACM SIGMOD International Conference on Management of Data (May 13–15, Tucson, Arizona)*, edited by Joan Peckham, pp. 135–146. New York, NY: ACM Press.

Catell, R. G. G. 1994. In *Object Data Management: Object Oriented and Extended Relational Database Systems*. Reading, MA: Addison Wesley.

Catell, R. G. G. and D. K. Barry. (eds). 1997. In *The Object Database Standard ODMG 2.0*. San Francisco, CA: Morgan Kaufmann.

Dittrich, K. R. 1994. "Object-oriented data model concepts." In *Advances in Object-oriented Database Systems*, edited by A. Dogac, M. T. Özsu, A. Biliris, and T. Sellis. Berlin: Springer-Verlag.

Embley, D. W. 1998. *Object Database Development: Concepts and Principles*. Reading, MA: Addison Wesley.

Han, J., S. Nishio, H. Kawano, and W. Wang. 1998. "Generalization-based data mining in object-oriented databases using an object cube model." *Data & Knowledge Engng* **25**: 55–97.

Shasha, D. E. 1992. *Database Tuning. A Principled Approach*. Englewood Cliffs, NJ: Prentice Hall.

Stonebraker, M., P. Brown, and S. Moore. 1999. *Object-relational DBMSs: Tracking the Next Great Wave*. San Francisco, CA: Morgan Kaufmann.

6.3 Multidimensional Databases and Online Analytical Processing

Surajit Chaudhuri and Umesh Dayal

ABSTRACT Multidimensional databases provide the conceptual framework and data model for enabling online analytical processing (OLAP). OLAP provides the technology to do *ad hoc* analysis of data stored in data warehouses. In this article, we introduce the multidimensional data model and its operators, and discuss implementation of OLAP over relational backend systems.

1. Introduction

With the proliferation and growth of database systems, their perceived role within organizations has started to evolve from being primarily data capture and reliable storage, to also enabling decision support, that is, enabling the richness of stored data to drive business decisions. In a nutshell, decision support requires database systems to get data out of storage and be made useful for analysis. Decision support includes data exploration, summarization, analysis, and advanced reporting. Thus, usage of databases is evolving from being purely transactional to being a repository of useful information (data warehouses), analyzed by decision support tools. The decision support tools are either natively supported in databases or are external client/middle-ware applications. Traditional data analysis over warehouses consists of predefined queries that are used to generate reports. More recently, a new class of analysis, called online analytical processing (OLAP) has been advocated as a natural way to view and operate business data stored in warehouses. E.F. Codd coined and used the term OLAP in Codd et al. (1993), where he set forth some of the requirements of *ad hoc* data analysis.

2. Multidimensional Data Model

OLAP has resulted in emphasizing a multidimensional view of data. A simple way of appreciating the multidimensional view of data is to think of databases as spreadsheets. In this view of data, a database consists of a set of facts. Each such fact represents one or more numerical measures in the context of one or more variables (referred to as dimensions).

The numeric measures are the objects of analysis. Examples of such measures are sales, budget, revenue, inventory, and ROI (return on investment). Each of the numeric measures depends on a set of dimensions, which provide the context for the measure. As shown in Figure 1, the dimensions associated with a sale amount can be the city, product name, and the date when the sale was made. The dimensions together are assumed to uniquely determine the measure. Thus, the multidimensional data views a measure as a value in the multidimensional space of dimensions. Each dimension is characterized by a set of attributes that represent properties associated with the dimension. For example, in the product dimension, every product entity may be characterized by the following three attributes: name, year (of its introduction), and the profit margin for the product. The dimensions may be related via a hierarchy. For example, as shown in Figure 1, each product is related through the dimension hierarchy to a product family and a company. The hierarchy captures the semantic relationship that products are organized in a set of product families and that product families belong to companies.

Another distinctive feature of the conceptual model for OLAP is its stress on aggregation of measures by one or more dimensions as one of the key operations; for example, computing and ranking the total sales by each country (or by each year). Other popular operations include comparing two measures (e.g., sales and budget) aggregated by the same dimensions. Time is a dimension that is of particular significance to decision support (e.g., trend analysis). Often, it is desirable to have built-in knowledge of calendars and other aspects of the time dimension.

We shall briefly discuss some of the popular operations that are supported by multidimensional spreadsheet applications. One such operation is pivoting. Consider the multidimensional schema of Figure 1 represented in a spreadsheet where each row

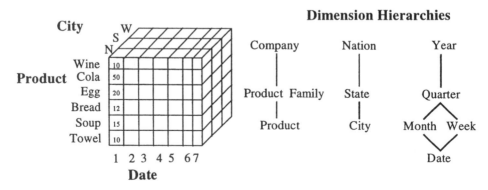

Figure 1 Multidimensional data

corresponds to a sale. Let there be one column for each dimension and an extra column that represents the amount of sale. The simplest view of pivoting is that it selects two dimensions that are used to aggregate a measure, for example, sales in the above example. The aggregated values are often displayed in a grid where each value in the (x, y) coordinate corresponds to the aggregated value of the measure when the first dimension has the value x and the second dimension has the value y. Thus, in our example, if the selected dimensions are city and year, then the x-axis may represent all values of city and the y-axis may represent the years. The point (x, y) will represent the aggregated sales for city x in the year y. Thus, what were values in the original spreadsheets have now become row and column headers in the pivoted spreadsheet.

Other operators related to pivoting are rollup or drill down. Rollup is the operation that enables a measure to be aggregated via one or more of the dimensions. The rollup operations can be cascaded. For example, it is possible to rollup the sales data, perhaps already aggregated on city, additionally by product. The drill-down operation is the converse of rollup. Thus, drill down makes it possible to identify the detailed data associated with an aggregated measure. Slice and dice corresponds to reducing the dimensionality of the data, that is, taking a projection of the data on a subset of dimensions for selected values of the other dimensions. For example, we can slice and dice sales data for a specific product to create a table that consists of the dimensions city and the day of sale. The other popular operators are ranking (sorting), selection, and defining computed attributes.

3. Implementation of OLAP

Implementing the multidimensional view of data so that the above data centric operations can be executed efficiently is a significantly challenging task. Several competing approaches to supporting such a view have emerged, often loosely referred to as relational OLAP (ROLAP), or multidimensional OLAP (MOLAP). The approach in MOLAP is to represent the data in the storage as an array. This approach has the advantage of directly supporting the multidimensional view at the storage layer. Unless the data is extremely sparse, such a storage representation can be efficient and enables easy implementations of cross-row calculations on multidimensional data. However, such an approach does not leverage the well-developed infrastructure of relational databases and must implement scalability, security, and other services that are expected of an enterprise database. Examples of products that represent a MOLAP implementation are Oracle Express (see the Oracle Corporation Home Page) and Essbase (see Hyperion Solutions Corporation Web Page). In ROLAP, a relational backend database is used to store the data. The ROLAP middleware translates a query over the multidimensional data as a sequence of one or more SQL queries against the relational databases. In order to be able to deliver fast response time to the user, such systems materialize results of selected queries, typically consisting of results of aggregation so that such pre-aggregated results can be leveraged for answering many queries. Therefore, identifying what information needs to be pre-aggregated is of vital importance for efficiency. Microstrategy (see the Microstrategy Inc. Home Page) and Microsoft OLAP Server (see the Microsoft SQL Server) represent examples of products that use a ROLAP implementation. In the rest of this section, we briefly discuss how the multidimensional model is implemented in ROLAP middleware. Such an implementation must take into account logical schema design, physical database design as well as considerations for processing OLAP queries against a relational backend. We briefly touch on each of these issues.

Star schema and its variations are used to represent the multidimensional data model. In a star schema, the database consists of a single fact table and a single table for each dimension. Each tuple in the fact table consists of a pointer (foreign key) to each of the dimensions that provide its multidimensional coordinates, and stores the numeric measures for those coordinates. Each dimension table consists of columns that correspond to attributes of the dimension. Figure 2 shows an example of a star schema. Star schemas do not explicitly provide support for attribute hierarchies. Snowflake schemas provide a refinement of star schemas where the dimensional hierarchy is explicitly represented by normalizing the dimension tables.

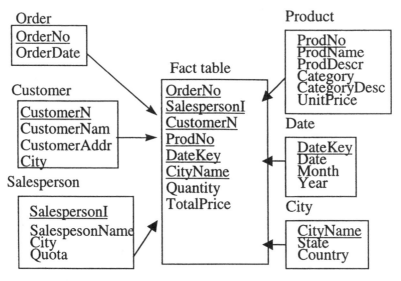

Figure 2 A star schema

Fact constellations are examples of more complex structures in which multiple fact tables share dimensional tables. For example, projected expense and the actual expense may form a fact constellation since they share many dimensions.

In order to ensure efficient processing of queries on the multidimensional view, OLAP middleware stores selected summary tables containing pre-aggregated data. In the simplest cases, the pre-aggregated data corresponds to aggregating the fact table on one or more selected dimensions. For example, in an investment environment, a large majority of the queries may be based on the performance of the most recent quarter and the current fiscal year. Having summary data on these parameters can significantly speed up query processing. Choosing which views (and which indexes) to materialize is an important physical design problem. The next challenge is to effectively use the existing indices and materialized views to answer queries. In order to ensure more predictable server behavior, OLAP middleware often transforms an OLAP program into a multistatement SQL query against the backend database. Finally, note that the efficiency of an OLAP implementation crucially depends on the server functionality available at the relational backend. For example, bitmap indexes can greatly aid processing of decision support queries generated by OLAP middleware against backend relational servers.

4. Relationship of OLAP to Other Decision Support Tools

Although OLAP has attracted a lot of interest since it empowers the end user to analyze business data, this has not replaced traditional analysis by means of a managed query environment. These environments use stored procedures and predefined complex queries to provide packaged analysis tools. Such tools often make it possible for the end-user to query business data using domain-specific terminology and concepts, for example, for a Web site data analysis, the concept of churn in the Web site visitors could be a useful predefined concept. Finally note that while OLAP systems provide a powerful infrastructure for manipulating and visualizing data, they are dependent on human-driven exploration and rely on the analyst to formulate and discover interesting patterns in data. In the future, data mining technology may be able to provide OLAP with a higher degree of analytical edge.

List of Web Sites

Below are details of the Web sites mentioned in this article.

(a) Microstrategy Incorporated Home Page: http://www.microstrategy.com

(b) Microsoft SQL Server OLAP Services, Microsoft Corporation: http://www.microsoft.com/sql/productinfo/olap.htm

(c) Oracle Corporation Home Page: http://www.oracle.com

(d) Hyperion Solutions Corporation, Essbase OLAP Server: http://www.hyperion.com/essbaseolap.cfm

(e) The Analytical Solutions Forum, Cambridge, MA: http://www.tasf.org. A consortium of OLAP and other database vendors; and intends to develop OLAP benchmarks and educate the market about OLAP.

References

Codd E. F., S. B. Codd, and C. T. Salley. 1993. Providing OLAP to user-analysts: An IT mandate. Technical report, E.F. Codd and Associates. Introduces OLAP to user analysts and discusses the services that are expected. Available for download from the Hyperion Solutions Corporation Web site http://www.hyperion.com.

Chaudhuri S. and U. Daya. 1997. An overview of data warehousing and OLAP technology. *ACM SIGMOD Record Newsletter*, March 1997. Also available for download from http://research.microsoft.com/~surajitc.

Kimball, R. 1996. *The Data Warehouse Toolkit*. Chichester, England: John Wiley. Discusses key aspects of implementing a multidimensional view and data warehousing strategy on a relational backend.

6.4 Deductive Databases

Carlo Zaniolo

ABSTRACT   The objective of deductive databases is to provide efficient support for sophisticated queries and reasoning on large databases; toward this goal, they combine the technology of logic programming with that of relational databases. Deductive database research has produced methods and techniques for implementing the declarative semantics of logical rules via efficient computation of fixpoints. Also, advances in language design and nonmonotonic semantics were made to allow the use of negation and set-aggregates in recursive programs; these yield greater expressive power while retaining polynomial data complexity and semantic well-formedness. Deductive database systems have been used in data mining and other advanced applications, and their techniques have been incorporated into a new generation of commercial databases.

1. Introduction

Relational databases, which support simple logic-based query languages, were proposed in the early 1970s (Codd, 1970). Initially considered too theoretical and not conducive to efficient implementation or commercial payoff, by the early 1980s they had become a stellar success, motivating research into more powerful languages and systems for querying and manipulating databases. After early work on logic and databases (Gallaire and Minker, 1978), most of the research work focused on a Prolog-like language called Datalog; this is due to the kinship of relational calculi and Prolog's Horn clauses (Abiteboul et al., 1995; Zaniolo et al., 1997), and the surge of interest in rule-based languages for expert systems of the mid-1980s. The main objectives of deductive databases are:

- logic-based extensions of database languages to support more powerful queries and reasoning, rule-based programming, and (ultimately) achieving Turing completeness, and

- the efficient and scalable implementation of these declarative languages on large databases.

2. Language Design and Semantics

Database query languages must be relationally complete, that is, they must be at least as powerful as safe relational calculus formulae and relational algebra expressions, which are known to be equivalent in terms of expressive power (Abiteboul et al., 1995). Relational database languages of the first generation, such as SQL, QUEL, and QBE, are relationally complete, but also include aggregates since these are not expressible in relational algebra (Abiteboul et al., 1995). Nonrecursive safe Datalog is also equivalent to relational algebra, and its expressive power can be extended by allowing recursion and complex objects (Abiteboul et al., 1995; Zaniolo et al., 1997).

Recursion is required to express many important queries, such as transitive closure queries (Chandra and Harel, 1980). The following Datalog rules compute the transitive closure of a directed graph stored as a binary relation $g(Outnode, Innode)$:

$$tc(X, Z) \leftarrow g(X, Z).$$

$$tc(X, Z) \leftarrow tc(X, Y), g(Y, Z).$$

These rules can also be viewed as defining a transformation T—in relational algebra, T is the union of (i) the relation g (first rule) with (ii) the natural join of relations tc and g with the Y-column projected out (second rule). Thus, T can first be applied to the empty set, and then, inductively, on the result from the last application, until no new tc-tuples are generated. The value of tc at this point is equal to the least fixpoint of T and to the transitive closure of g (Lloyd, 1987; Zaniolo et al., 1997).

The great increase in expressive power brought by recursion is not without a price, since the fixpoint semantics and other natural semantics no longer hold when negation or other nonmonotonic constructs are used in the program (Lloyd, 1987; Marek and Truszczynski, 1995). Negation is nonmonotonic because negative information is not stored explicitly, rather, it is derived by default (Marek and Truszczynski, 1995) under a closed-world assumption (Minker, 1996; Reiter, 1978). The notion of stable models (Gelfond and Lifschitz, 1988) that provides sound declarative semantics for programs with negated goals cannot be used as operational semantics because of its exponential complexity (Marek and Truszczynski, 1995). Thus, research focused on finding classes of Datalog programs whose stable models can be computed in polynomial time (Zaniolo et al., 1997). The notion of stratified programs, where negation can only be used on predicates defined in lower strata, represents an important concept in this area (Przymusinski, 1988). More powerful classes of programs include locally stratified programs (Przymusinski, 1988), whose well-founded models (Ross, 1994; Van Gelder et al., 1991) can be derived by an alternating fixpoint procedure (Van Gelder, 1989), and XY-stratified programs (Kemp et al., 1995; Zaniolo et al., 1993).

In general, aggregates are nonmonotonic and subject to the same restrictions as negation. However, some special classes of aggregates are monotonic (Ross and Sagiv, 1997; Zaniolo and Wang, 1999) and can be used in recursive rules; the choice construct that expresses nondeterminism in logic is also monotonic (Giannotti et al., 1991; Saccà and Zaniolo, 1990).

Most Datalog languages also support functors, which are used (i) to store complex objects in the database, and (ii) in recursive rules to process structures of unbound length, such as to achieve Turing completeness in the language. The aim of supporting more powerful objects and integrating two important programming paradigms has motivated research on deductive object-oriented databases (Kifer, 1995).

3. Compilation and Optimization

Unlike Prolog, deductive databases draw a sharp distinction between facts (extensional information) and rules (intensional information) (Minker, 1996). The rules are treated as program, and thus compiled and executed against the database, which contains a time-varying set of facts described by a time-invariant schema. The target for this compilation is code based on relational algebra operators (on sets of tuples) or on get-the-next-tuple kind of operators (Chimenti et al., 1990; Phipps et al., 1991; Zaniolo et al., 1997).

Sophisticated compilation techniques are used for recursion. The naive fixpoint computation consists of repeatedly firing the rules until saturation, using a table to memorize new results without duplicates. This forward-chaining, bottom-up computation is then optimized by minimizing repetitions between steps. For example, in the transitive closure computation of tc, only the Δtc produced in the last step need be considered in the following step. Symbolic differentiation techniques were developed by several authors to allow the compiler to implement this improvement, yielding the differential fixpoint (also known as the seminaive fixpoint) computation (Abiteboul et al., 1995; Zaniolo et al., 1997).

The differential fixpoint efficiently computes all pairs of nodes in the closure. But when only nodes reachable from a given node a are of interest (i.e., the query goal is $tc(a, W)$), then a top-down search, such as Prolog's backward chaining, can be much more efficient (Lloyd, 1987). Deductive databases address this problem by rule-rewriting methods that transform the original program into one that is specialized for this specific query. For the query goal $tc(a, W)$, our transitive-closure program is specialized by letting a become the first argument in every occurrence of tc (i.e., each X is replaced by a). However, if the query goal is $g(W, a)$, then this naive specialization approach does not work, and a left-to-right linear rule transformation is used instead (Abiteboul et al., 1995; Zaniolo et al., 1997), producing the following program:

$$tc(X, a) \leftarrow g(X, a).$$

$$tc(X, a) \leftarrow g(X, Y), tc(Y, a).$$

More sophisticated methods are needed for more general recursive rules, and many have been proposed for different situations; the most robust and widely used method is magic sets (Bancilhon et al., 1986; Beeri and Ramakrishnan, 1987; Saccà and Zaniolo, 1989). This method uses the rules of the program and the constraints in the query to generate a magic relation that is then applied to the original rules to act as a filter on the set of tuples produced by the differential fixpoint computation. The method was also shown to offer performance benefits when applied to nonrecursive SQL queries (Mumick et al., 1990).

As in the previous examples, a different execution plan is generated for each query— actually, for each template tc^{bf} describing goals, such as $tc(a, X)$, where the first argument of tc is bound and the second is free. Compilers use these bound/free adornments to select recursive methods and execution orders for rule goals so as to ensure a safe and optimized computation (Phipps et al., 1991; Zaniolo et al., 1997). These techniques have been incorporated into the new generation of database systems, which support recursive SQL queries (Seshadri et al., 1996).

4. Systems and Applications

Many interesting applications of deductive databases have been reported, ranging from the rapid prototyping of information systems and scientific databases, to data cleaning and stock market analysis (Ramakrishnan, 1995; Tsur, 1991). More recent applications include Web-searching (Lakshmanan et al., 1996), integration and mediation of heterogeneous information systems (Bayardo et al., 1997; Papakonstantinou et al., 1996), and GUI generation (Goyal et al., 1996).

Deductive database languages support rapid prototyping via rules that express both domain knowledge (either user-encoded or discovered) and database searches; these traits make them well-suited for data mining and knowledge discovery applications (Bonchi et al., 1999; Han et al., 1996; Shen et al., 1996; Tsur, 1991). The main obstacle to a wide deployment of deductive databases remains the lack of commercial systems. Indeed, while powerful prototypes are available (Chimenti et al., 1990; Ramakrishnan et al., 1993; Vaghani et al., 1994), they have not yet matured into commercial systems. These and other research prototypes are surveyed in Ramakrishnan and Ullman (1995).

References

Abiteboul, S., R. Hull, and V. Vianu. 1995. In *Foundations of Databases*. Reading, MA: Addison-Wesley.

Bayardo, Jr, R., W. Bohrer, R. Brice et al. 1997. "InfoSleuth: agent-based semantic integration of information in open and dynamic environment." In *Proceedings of the International ACM SIGMOD Conference on Management of Data*, pp. 195–206. New York: ACM.

Bancilhon, F., D. Maier, Y. Sagiv, and J. D. Ullman. 1986. "Magic sets and other strange ways to implement logic programs." In *Proceedings ACM SIGACT-SIGMOD-SIGART Symposium on Principles of Database Systems*, pp. 1–15. New York: ACM.

Beeri, C. and R. Ramakrishnan. 1987. "On the power of magic." In *Proceedings ACM SIGACT-SIGMOD Symposium on Principles of Database Systems*, pp. 269–283. New York: ACM.

Bonchi, F., F. Giannotti, G. Mainetto, and D. Pedreschi. 1999. "A classification-based methodology for planning audit strategies in fraud detection." In *Proceedings of the 5th ACM SIGKDD International Conference on Knowledge Discovery and Data, KDD'99*, pp. 175–184. New York: ACM.

Chandra, A. and D. Harel. 1980. "Computable queries for relational data bases." J. Comput. Sys. Sci. **21(2)**: 156–178.

Chimenti, D., R. Gamboa, R. Krishnamurthy, S. Naqvi, S. Tsur, and C. Zaniolo. 1990. "The LDL system prototype." *IEEE Trans. Knowledge and Data Engng* **2(1)**: 76–90. A Web demo of $\mathcal{LDL}$++ is available at http://www.cs.ucla.edu/ldl.

Codd, E. F. 1970. "A relational model of data for large shared data banks." *Commun. ACM* **13(6)**: 377–387.

Gallaire, H. and J. Minker (eds). 1978. *Logic and Databases*. New York: Plenum Press.

Gelfond, M. and V. Lifschitz. 1988. "The stable model semantics for logic programming." In *Proceedings of Joint International Conference and Symposium on Logic Programming*, pp. 1070–1080. Cambridge, MA: The MIT Press.

Giannotti, F., D. Pedreschi, D. Saccà, and C. Zaniolo. 1991. "Non-determinism in deductive databases." In *Proceedings of the 2nd International Conference on Deductive and Object-Oriented Databases, DOOD'91*, pp. 129–146. New York: Springer-Verlag.

Goyal, N., C. Hoch, R. Krishnamurthy, B. Meckler, and M. Suckow. 1996. "Is GUI programming a database research problem?" In *Proceedings of the International ACM SIGMOD Conference on Management of Data*, pp. 517–528. New York, NY: ACM.

Han, J., Y. Huang, N. Cercone, and Y. Fu. 1996. "Intelligent query answering by knowledge discovery techniques." *IEEE Trans. Knowledge and Data Engng* **8(3)**: 373–390.

Kemp, D., K. Ramamohanarao, and P. Stuckey. December 1995. "ELS programs and the efficient evaluation of non-stratified programs by transformation to ELS." In *Proceedings of the International Conference on Deductive and Object-Oriented Databases: DOOD95*, pp. 91–108. Berlin: Springer-Verlag.

Kifer, M. 1995. "Deductive and object-oriented data languages—a quest for integration." In *Proceedings of the International Conference on Deductive and Object-Oriented Databases, DOOD'95*, pp. 187–212. Berlin: Springer-Verlag.

Lakshmanan, L. V. S., F. Sadri, and I. Subramanian. February 1996. A declarative approach to querying and restructuring the World Wide Web. Post-ICDE Workshop on Research Issues in Data Engineering (RIDE'96), New Orleans.

Lloyd, J. W. 1987. *Foundations of Logic Programming*. New York: Springer-Verlag.

Marek, V. W. and M. Truszczynski. 1995. *Nonmonotonic Logic*. New York: Springer-Verlag.

Minker, J. 1996. "Logic and databases: a 20 year retrospective." In *Proceedings of the International Workshop on Logic in Databases (LID'96)*, edited by D. Pedreschi and C. Zaniolo, pp. 5–52. New York: Springer-Verlag.

Mumick, I. S., S. J. Finkelstein, H. Pirahesh, and R. Ramakrishnan. 1990. "Magic is relevant." In *ACM SIGMOD Conference*, pp. 247–258. New York, NY: ACM.

Papakonstantinou, Y., H. Garcia-Molina, and J. D. Ullman. 1996. "MedMaker: A mediation system based on declarative specifications." In *Proceedings of the IEEE International Conference on Data Engineering*, pp. 132–141. Los Alamitos, CA, NY: IEEE Computer Society.

Phipps, G., M. A. Derr, and K. A. Ross. 1991. "Glue-Nail!: a deductive database system." In *Proceedings International ACM SIGMOD Conference on Management of Data*, pp. 308–317. New York, NY: ACM.

Przymusinski, T. C. 1988. "On the declarative and procedural semantics of stratified deductive databases." In *Foundations of Deductive Databases and Logic Programming*, edited by J. W. Minker, pp. 193–216. San Francisco, CA: Morgan Kaufman.

Ramakrishnan, R. 1995. *Applications of Logic Databases*. Norwell, MA: Kluwer Academic.

Ramakrishnan, R. and J. D. Ullman. 1995. "A survey of research in deductive database systems." *J. Logic Programming* **23(2)**: 125–149.

Ramakrishnan, R., D. Srivastava, S. Sudanshan, and P. Seshadri. 1993. "Implementation of the CORAL deductive database system." In *Proceedings of the International ACM SIGMOD Conference on Management of Data*, pp. 167–176. New York, NY: ACM.

Reiter, R. 1978. "On closed world databases." In *Logic and Databases*, edited by J. W. Minker, and H. Gallaire, pp. 55–76. New York: Plenum Press.

Ross, K. A. 1994. "Modular stratification and magic sets for datalog programs with negation." *J. ACM* **41(6)**: 1216–1266.

Ross, K. A. and Y. Sagiv. 1997. "Monotonic aggregation in deductive database." *JCSS* **54(1)**: 79–97.

Saccà, D. and C. Zaniolo. 1989. "Implementation of recursive queries for a data language based on pure horn logic." In *Proceedings of the Fourth International Conference on Logic Programming*, pp. 104–135. Cambridge, MA: MIT Press.

Saccà, D. and C. Zaniolo. 1990. "Stable models and non-determinism in logic programs with negation." In *Proceedings ACM SIGACT-SIGMOD-SIGART Symposium on Principles of Database Systems*. New York, NY: ACM.

Seshadri, P., H. Pirahesh, and T. Y. Cliff Leung. 1996. In *Complex Query Decorrelation, ICDE* 450–458. Los Alamitos, CA: IEEE Computer Society.

Shen, W., K. Ong, B. Mitbander, and C. Zaniolo. 1996. "Metaqueries for data mining." Chapter 15 In *Advances in Knowledge Discovery and Data Mining*, edited by V. M. Fayyad et al. Cambridge, MA: MIT Press.

Tsur, S. 1991. "Deductive databases in action." In *Proceedings ACM SIGACT-SIGMOD-SIGART Symposium on Principles of Programming Languages*, pp. 142–154. New York, NY: ACM.

Vaghani, J., K. Ramamohanarao, D. B. Kemp et al. 1994. "The Aditi deductive database system." *VLDB J.* **3(2)**: 245–288.

Van Gelder, A. 1989. "The alternating fixpoint of logic programming with negation." In *Proceedings ACM SIGACT-SIGMOD-SIGART Symposium on Principles of Database Systems*, pp. 1–10. New York, NY: ACM.

Van Gelder, A., K. A. Ross, and J. S. Schlipf. 1991. "The well-founded semantics for general logic programs." *J. ACM* **38**: 620–650.

Zaniolo, C., N. Arni, and K. Ong. 1993. "Negation and aggregates in recursive rules: the $\mathscr{LDL}$++ approach." In *Proceedings International Conference on Deductive and Object-Oriented Databases, DOOD'93*. Berlin: Springer-Verlag.

Zaniolo, C., S. Ceri, C. Faloutsos, R. Snodgrass, V. S. Subrahmanian, and R. Zicari. 1997. *Advanced Database Systems*. San Francisco: Morgan Kaufmann.

Zaniolo, C. and H. Wang. 1999. "Logic-based user-defined aggregates for the next generation of database systems." In *The Logic Programming Paradigm: Current Trends and Future Directions*, edited by K. R. Apt, V. Marek, M. Truszczynski, and D. S. Warren. Berlin: Springer-Verlag.

6.5 Parallel Databases

Shahram Ghandeharizadeh and Frank Sommers

ABSTRACT Parallel databases based on the shared-nothing architecture are ideally suited for the increasingly demanding data management needs of enterprise decision support systems. In an ideal parallel system, twice as many nodes can perform twice as large a task in the same time, resulting in linear scale-up; or, twice as many nodes can perform the same task twice as quickly, resulting in linear speed-up. Round-robin, hash, range, hybrid, and other declustering techniques ensure that the needed data is available at each node for processing, and thus help approximate the ideal scalability characteristics. Parallelism can be applied to each of the relational operators. For the select operator, interquery parallelism executes several relational queries simultaneously; interoperator parallelism executes several operations within the same query simultaneously; and intraoperator parallelism is employed to each operator within a query.

1. Introduction

An increasing number of companies utilize decision support systems (DSS) for their day-to-day activities. These systems utilize data mining, data warehousing, data visualization, and other database management tools to empower their users to better understand the massive volume

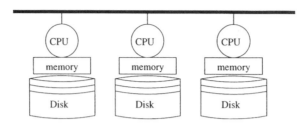

Figure 1 Shared-nothing parallel database architecture: A collection of nodes communicate via an interconnection network

of historical data gathered by an organization. These tools are data intensive and required to retrieve a large volume of information in order to provide summarized results that facilitate decisions. In addition, currently deployed DSS systems are growing at a rapid rate (Winter and Auerbach, 1997, 1998) for several reasons. First, within an organization, a larger number of individuals are trying to access historical data, increasing the daily load on the system. Second, organizations are increasingly storing a larger amount of information by: (a) expanding the length of history maintained online, and (b) increasing the details of each entry that is stored. A recent survey reports that while Wal-Mart's DSS nearly doubled in size from 2.4 terabytes (TB) to 4.4 TB in a span of twelve months in 1997, the Sears, Roebuck, and Co. DSS grew more than 350 percent in 1997 from 1.3 TB to 4.6 TB.

Parallel databases based on a shared-nothing architecture (Stonebraker, 1986) have established themselves as the architecture of choice for DSS primarily because of their scalability characteristics. As systems based on shared-nothing can grow in an incremental manner over time to satisfy both increasing storage and bandwidth requirements imposed by an application. A shared-nothing architecture consists of a collection of nodes that communicate with one another via an interconnection network (Figure 1). Each node consists of one or more CPUs, some memory, and one or more disk drives. In these systems, tuples of each relation in the database are horizontally declustered (Livny et al., 1987; Ries and Epstein, 1987) across multiple nodes (and, internally, across disk drives attached to each node) to enable multiple processors to scan large relations in parallel. Data redundancy techniques are employed to ensure availability of data in the presence of disk and node failures. This design is used by several commercial products, for example, Tandem (Tandem Performance Group, 1988), NCR's Teradata (Teradata Corp., 1985) and research prototypes, for example, Gamma (DeWitt et al., 1990), Bubba (Boral et al., 1990), Arbre (Lorie et al., 1989), Omega (Ghandeharizadeh et al., 1993), and Volcano (Graefe, 1993).

The ideal parallel system exhibits two performance characteristics: linear speed-up, which is when the execution of a task is reduced by a factor of two with twice as many nodes; and linear scale-up, which is when twice as many nodes can perform twice as large a task in the same elapsed time (DeWitt and Gray, 1992). Several factors might become barriers to these goals:

Coordination overhead. The time needed to initiate and terminate a parallel operation between nodes might dominate the execution time of the operation over only a few records using index structures (Ghandeharizadeh and DeWitt, 1990b). Parallel execution of operations brings greater benefits when the ratio of coordination to computation is low.

Load imbalance. Distributing the workload of an operation evenly across multiple nodes is not trivial (Scheuermann et al., 1993) because operations execute on those nodes that contain the data and the assignment of data to nodes is static.

Interference. In practice, when a new node is added to most parallel computer designs, it slows every other node down just a little bit (DeWitt and Gray, 1992).

A shared-nothing architecture may utilize several forms of parallelism to approximate the ideal performance characteristics. First, parallelism can be applied by executing several queries simultaneously. This form of parallelism is termed interquery parallelism. Second, interoperator parallelism can be employed to execute several operations within the same query concurrently. For example, multiple nodes could execute two or more relational join operators of a complex bushy join query in parallel. Finally, intraoperator parallelism can be applied to each operator within a query. For example, multiple nodes can be employed to execute a single relational selection operator.

2. Selection and Intraoperator Parallelism

It is beyond the focus of this short tutorial to describe the different forms of parallelism for each of the relational algebra operators, for example, join (Graefe, 1994; Schneider, 1990), aggregation operators (Graefe, 1994), et cetera. Instead, we focus on the select operator and the role of intraoperator parallelism in support of this operator. The selection operator is basic to any query plan. It consumes a relation—for example, products—as input and applies a predicate to each record of the relation—for example, price = $10—to produce those records that satisfy the predicate. This operator has a significant impact on the performance of a complex query because if it cannot be parallelized effectively, the performance and degree of parallelism of other operators in a complex query may be severely limited. This is especially true of those systems that utilize the concept of pipelining and data flow to execute complex queries.

In order to parallelize the selection operator, data must be horizontally declustered across multiple disks. Subsequently, a copy of the selection operator is initiated on each node or disk containing relevant records, and then their output is merged at the destination. There are several techniques to decluster a relation across multiple nodes: round-robin, hash, range, hybrid range (Ghandeharizadeh and DeWitt, 1990a), MAGIC (Ghandeharizadeh and DeWitt, 1994), CMD (Srivastava and Rotem, 1992), et cetera. These techniques differ on whether they decluster a relation based on one attribute or multiple attributes. With multiple attribute declustering techniques, while one class (Faloutsos and Bhagwat, 1993; Faloutsos and Metaxas, 1991; Faloutsos and Roseman, 1989; Moon and Saltz, 1998) of strategies strives to distribute the workload of a query across all disks, a second class (Ghandeharizadeh and DeWitt, 1994) tries to minimize the number of nodes that participate in the execution of a query. Choosing between these two conflicting objectives is dependent on the application and target hardware platform. If a query retrieves only a few tuples and the overhead of initiating and terminating it on all nodes is expensive then the second class is desirable. On the other hand, if the overhead of parallelism is negligible relative to the cost of executing the query then the first class is more appropriate.

3. Failure Management

While a single disk is fairly reliable with a mean time to failure of once every million hours (more than 100 years), the mean time to failure of a disk in a system consisting of 1,000 disks is once every 1,000 hours (42 days). A DSS system must continue operation in the presence of such failures. One can find a host of availability techniques in the database literature: disk mirroring (Borr, 1981), interleaved declustering (Copeland and Keller, 1989; Teradata Corp., 1985), chained declustering (Hsiao and DeWitt, 1990; Hsiao, 1990), et cetera. These techniques employ both a primary and backup copy of each relation to ensure availability of data in the presence of processor and/or disk failures. The trade-off between these techniques is one of (1) distributing the load of a failed disk evenly across the remaining disks in order to prevent a noticeable degradation in system performance, and (2) maximizing the level of data availability (Hsiao, 1990). For example, disk mirroring provides the highest level of availability when compared with both interleaved and chained declustering. However, it does a very poor job of distributing the load of a failed disk drive.

ACKNOWLEDGMENTS

This research was partially supported by the National Science Foundation under grants IRI-9258362 (NYI award) and ERC grant EEC-9529152.

References

Boral, H., W. Alexander, L. Clay, G. Copeland, S. Danforth, M. Franklin, B. Hart, M. Smith, and P. Valduriez. 1990. "Prototyping Bubba, a highly parallel database system." *IEEE Trans. Knowledge Data Engng* **2(1)**: 4–24.

Borr, A. 1981. "Transaction monitoring in Encompass[TM]: reliable distributed transaction processing." In *Proceedings of the 1981 VLDB Conference*, pp. 155–165. Cannes, France: IEEE Computer Society.

Copeland, G. and T. Keller. 1989. "A comparison of high-availability media recovery techniques." In *Proceedings of the 1989 SIGMOD Conference*, pp. 98–109. Portland, Oregon: ACM Press.

DeWitt, D. and J. Gray. 1992. "Parallel database systems." *Commun. ACM* **35(6)**: 85–89.

DeWitt, D., S. Ghandeharizadeh, D. Schneider, A. Bricker, H. Hsiao, and R. Rasmussen. 1990. "The Gamma database machine project." *IEEE Trans. Knowledge Data Engng* **2(1)**: 44–62.

Faloutsos, C. and P. Bhagwat. January 1993. "Declustering using fractals." In *Proceedings of the Second International Conference on Parallel and Distributed Information Systems*, pp. 18–25. San Diego, CA: IEEE Computer Society.

Faloutsos, C. and D. Metaxas. 1991. "Disk allocation methods using error correcting codes." *IEEE Trans. Comput* **40(8)**: 907–914.

Faloutsos, C. and S. Roseman. March 1989. "Fractals for secondary key retrieval." In *Proceedings of the Eighth ACM SIGACT-SIGMOD-SIGART Symposium on Principles of Database Systems*, pp. 247–250. Philedelphia, Pennsylvania: ACM Press.

Ghandeharizadeh, S. and D. DeWitt. 1990a. "Hybrid range partitioning strategy: a new declustering strategy for parallel database machines." In *Proceedings of the 1990 VLDB Conference*, pp. 481–492. Brisbane, Australia: Morgan Kaufmann.

Ghandeharizadeh, S. and D. DeWitt. February 1990b. "A multiuser performance analysis of alternative declustering strategies." In *Proceedings of the Sixth Data Engineering Conference*, pp. 466–475. Los Angeles, CA: IEEE Computer Society.

Ghandeharizadeh, S. and D. DeWitt. May 1994. "A multi-attribute declustering mechanism for multiprocessor database machines." In *IEEE Transactions on Parallel and Distributed Systems* **5(5)**: 509–524.

Ghandeharizadeh, S., V. Choi, S. Ker, and K. Lin. January 1993. "Omega: A parallel object-based system." In *Proceedings of the Second International Conference on Parallel and Distributed Information Systems*, pp. 182–186. San Diego, CA: IEEE Computer Society.

Graefe, G. 1993. "Query evaluation techniques for large databases." *Comput. Surveys* **25(2)**: 73–170.

Graefe, G. 1994. "Volcano: an extensible and parallel query evaluation system." *IEEE Trans. Knowledge and Data Engng* **6(1)**: 120–135.

Hsiao, H. I. 1990. *Availability in multiprocessor database machines.* Ph.D. diss. Wisconsin: University of Wisconsin—Madison.

Hsiao, H. I. and D. DeWitt. February 1990. "Chained declustering: a new availability strategy for multiprocessor database machines." In *Proceedings of the Sixth Data Engineering Conference*, pp. 456–465. Los angeles, CA: IEEE Computer Society.

Livny, M., S. Khoshafian, and H. Boral. May 1987. "Multi-disk management algorithms." In *Proceedings of the 1987 ACM SIGMETRICS International Conference on Measurement and Modeling of Computer Systems*, pp. 69–77. Alberta, Canada: ACM Press.

Lorie, R., J. Daudenarde, G. Hallmark, J. Stamos, and H. Young. 1989. "Adding intra-transaction parallelism to an existing DBMS." *IEEE Data Engng Newsletter* **12(1)**: 310–327.

Moon, B. and J. Saltz. 1998. "Scalability analysis of declustering methods for multidimensional range queries." *IEEE Trans. Knowledge Data Engng* **10(2)**.

Ries, D. and R. Epstein. 1987. "Evaluation of distribution criteria for distributed database systems." UCB/ERL Technical Report M78/22, UC Berkeley.

Schneider, D. 1990. "Complex query processing in multiprocessor database machines." Ph.D. diss. Wisconsin: University of Wisconsin–Madison.

Scheuermann, P., G. Weikum, and P. Zabback. 1993. "Adapative load balancing in disk arrays." In *Proceedings of the 1993 FODO Conference*, pp. 345–361. Chicago, Illinois: Kluwer.

Srivastava, J. and D. Rotem. 1992. "CMD: a multidimensional declustering method for parallel database systems." In *Proceedings of the 1992 VLDB Conference*, pp. 3–14. Vancouver, Canada: Morgan Kaufmann.

Stonebraker, M. 1986. "The case for shared-nothing." *Database Engng Bull.* **9(1)**: 4–9.

Tandem Performance Group. 1988. "A benchmark for non-stop SQL on the debit credit transaction." In *Proceedings of the 1988 ACM SIGMOD Conference.*

Teradata Corp., 1985. *DBC/1012 Data Base Computer System Manual.* Teradata Corp. Document No. C10-0001-02, Release 2.0.

Winter, R. and K. Auerbach. 1997. "Giants walk the earth: the 1997 VLDB survey." In *Database Programming and Design* **10(9)**: 19–23.

Winter, R. and K. Auerbach. 1998. "The big time: the 1998 VLDB survey." In *Database Programming and Design* **11(8)**: 118–125.

6.6 Distributed, Heterogeneous, and Federated Databases

Witold Litwin

ABSTRACT Distributed, heterogeneous, federated, and so on, multidatabases model complementary universes. Countless examples include banks, hospitals, car rentals, restaurants and so on. We overview the technical problems that the designer of a modern multidatabase system faces. We discuss solutions using object-relational databases, multidatabase access through the Internet, and current standards for database connectivity. We overview directions for efficient implementation: multidatabase queries with precomputing and aggregate data materialization, over-scalable and distributed data structures.

These popular terms refer to collections of autonomous interoperable databases that model similar or complementary universes (Bouguettaya et al., 1998; Gupta, 1989; Hurson et al., 1993). Examples include databases on banks, hospitals, car rentals, restaurants, jobs, and so on. The federated databases are typically subject to multidatabase queries, spanning several databases. A homebuyer may shop for the bank offering the cheapest mortgage. A doctor may need to pump comparative data about an illness from any hospital database accessible. A person may look in movie and restaurant database for a cinema and a reputable restaurant at the same street, and so on.

Systems for multidatabase operations are usually called multidatabase systems (Gupta, 1989; Hurson et al., 1993). These are invaluable tools for knowledge discovery, as they bring together information that does not exist in any of the databases separately. Modern relational database systems are multidatabase systems. The popular relational languages SQL and QBE have been enhanced with multidatabase capabilities over recent years. This was done generally for the SQL standard, and specifically for MS Access for QBE. Data warehouses are also multidatabase systems that manage their databases in a specific way that we show later on. Finally, there are data access systems, for example, MS Query, UNISQL/M, or Data Joiner, that do not have their own databases, but only provide a shell for multidatabase queries.

Heterogeneity of data from different sources has been a major technical challenge for multidatabase systems for more than a decade (Gupta, 1989). Databases are usually tuned for local use, making their multidatabase use hard. Terms for similar loans, as well loan schemes, often differ among banks. At the international level, monetary units (currencies) differ and the exchange rates vary all the time. The same patients in databases of different hospitals often have different attributes, or different values for the same attribute. Restaurant guides usually describe the same restaurant differently. The global decision as to whether a restaurant is good or disreputable, may be hard, as the ratings may differ largely.

The facets of multidatabase heterogeneity are often categorized into physical heterogeneity and semantic heterogeneity. Physical heterogeneity refers to the differences in data representation. It may concern the encoding of the same data values into integers or reals of different types. Next, it may concern different implementation of the data model, for example, of tables in different relational systems. The formats of manipulation procedures, for example, of SQL queries, also often differ. Finally, the data models themselves can differ. Data of interest may be in a relational database, and in an object-oriented database. Perhaps some data are in a spreadsheet or an e-mail file or in some legacy repository.

The physical heterogeneity is dealt with through interoperabiliy standards. The most common is the Open Database Connectivity (ODBC) standard for relational databases. Heterogeneous data and manipulations pass through the ODBC drivers that make them homogeneous. There are ODBC drivers for every major relational system. For data repositories, the OLE-DB standard allows data to be seen as if they were ODBC compatible relational tables. In this way, the user of an Ms Access database, for instance, can issue a query joining data in an MS Access database with those in Oracle, DB2, or Paradox databases, and perhaps in an Excel spreadsheet. Users of ODBC and of OLE-DB compliant systems usually do not need to worry about physical heterogeneity, although the current versions of these standards do not resolve all the discrepancies.

For Internet browser users, an emerging standard on the top of ODBC is the Java Database Connectivity (JDBC). This standard allows for queries from Java applets. At the browser, the data are typically formatted into HTML standard compliant pages. This standard, however, does not suffice. A new standard termed XML appears. For instance, the Junglee system uses XML for multidatabase retrievals delivered to the Internet portal Yahoo. By the same token, the Zenza system uses XML to generate forms and reports from multiple relational databases.

The discrepancies between relational and object data tend to disappear with the evolution of relational systems towards object-relational systems. The latter should be compatible with the object-oriented paradigm. A standard in the making for this paradigm is termed CORBA. A popular concept in the meantime, as long as we stay with heterogeneous data models and interoperability protocols, is also that of a wrapper. Wrappers are adapters, sometimes called mediators, that present relational and legacy data as if they were objects. A collection of wrappers allows for a homogenous object-oriented view of various databases and repositories, including heterogeneous object-oriented databases. Research is active in this domain. One example of an object-oriented data-access system is the AMOS object-relational system built at the University of Linkoping (Sweden) (see the AMOS Web site). The object-oriented interface is more flexible than the relational one. AMOS for instance may manipulate time series, popular with financial repositories. Another well-known research prototype is Tsimmis at Stanford University (see the Tsimmis Web site).

Semantic heterogeneity refers to the discrepancies between data names, vales, and the conceptual structures. These techniques are still largely at the research level, and there are no related standards. Prototype relational languages, for example, MSQL (Litwin et al., 1989) and IDEAL, (Hurson et al., 1993) were proposed specifically for semantic heterogeneity. It was shown that many of their specific functions need expressive power beyond that of relational systems at present, and of SQL specifically. They require multirelational operations and higher order predicate calculus, while SQL is based on relational algebra and first order predicate calculus. Knowledge processing techniques are also needed, for example, those of the MCC InfoSleuth project (see the InfoSleuth Web site), or in the IBM Garlic project (Fagin, 1998b). Semantic heterogeneity in object-oriented federated databases also requires specific capabilities (Ahmed et al., 1991; Chomicki and Litwin, 1994).

A practical solution for semantic heterogeneity at present is data cleansing. The process homogenizes the data using custom-made data extracting programs sometimes called data pumps. Some of the multidatabase queries that become possible can be processed online. Many others would have a prohibitively processing time. These are queries over large collections of databases calculating aggregate functions, such as the average or sum functions of SQL, or far more elaborated functions for data mining. Research on techniques for such queries now includes the distributed environment (e.g., Agrawal et al., The Quest Data Mining Project, see the Web site). That project gave rise recently to the line of commercial data mining products, able to pump data from multiple databases, and other repositories, especially text files. These products are tailored mainly for DB2 databases, but also support Oracle, Informix, and other popular DBMS through ODBC or JDBC interfaces.

One popular technique for complex queries is precomputing from the source databases. The aggregated values are materialized in dedicated databases. These are called warehouses, data marts or mining bases. They may materialize global or partial results, making the process hierarchical (Carino, 1997). The materialized data are refreshed incrementally when the source data change. The updates are forwarded instantly or, more often, grouped and sent with some user-defined delay.

For instance, the global values of daily sales of some products may be materialized in this way. The warehouse may store the sums for the whole company, while the data mart may materialize the departmental sales. Any time a sale enters the source database, its value is propagated to the data marts and the warehouse, where it is added to the results already accumulated. The warehouse may also store typically hard to compute data mining results, not available as SQL functions, like the correlation between different sales. Any query to a global value can be executed almost instantly, although it might miss the latest sale, not yet arrived at a data mart or warehouse. Chances are, however, that the user hardly notices the difference. Especially, since aggregate data are usually displayed in a graphical form.

A new related goal is scalable multidatabase queries (Quest Data Mining Project Web site; and Carino, 1997). Such queries transparently spread in parallel over as many sites as needed to keep the response time practical. Scalable systems may ease the need for precomputing. They are the only way to high-performance computations required by the multidatabase data mining. Recent years have seen intensive research in this direction. In particular, a new class of data structures has appeared, termed scalable distributed data structures (Litwin et al., 1996). Several SDDS were proposed, to allow large databases and hard queries to scale to very many sites under various application constraints, including data storage site failures (Litwin et al., 2000; SDDS Web site).

With the Internet gaining millions of users every year, efficient access to distributed, heterogeneous, and federated databases becomes a worldwide everyday need. New research problems appear for querying heterogeneous multimedia data, for example, those investigated by the Garlic project (Fagin, 1998a) and discussed in Carino (1997). Electronic commerce needs new techniques for the security and high-availability of multidatabase transactions. Although research in distributed, heterogeneous, and federated databases has greatly progressed for several years now, many exciting developments still lie ahead.

List of Web Sites

Below is a list of the Web sites mentioned in this article.

Agrawal et al. The Quest Data Mining Project: www.ibm.almaden.com

Risch, T. The Active Mediators Object System AMOS: www.ida.liu.se/labs/edslab/

Rusinkiewicz et al. The Infosleuth Project: www.mcc.com/projects/infosleuth/index.html

Scalable Distributed Data Structures. A New Class of Data Structures for Multicomputers: http://ceria.dauphine.fr/SDDS-bibliograhie.html

Tsimmis: The Stanford-IBM Manager of Multiple Information Sources: http://www-db.stanford.edu/tsimmis/tsimmis.html

References

Ahmed, R., Ph. De. Smedt, W. Du, W. Kent, M. Ketabchi, W. Litwin, A. Rafii, and M. Shan 1991. "The Pegasus heterogeneous multidatabase system." *IEEE Comput.* **24(12)**: 19–27.

Bouguettaya, A., B. Bentallah, and A. Elmagarmid. 1998. *Interconnecting Heterogeneous Information Systems.* Norwell, MA: Kluwer Academic Publishers.

Carino, F. 1997. Scalable multimedia data warehouse for the 21st century. Talk at Stanford DB Seminar. El Segundon, CA: NCR Parallel Systems Division.

Chomicki, J. and W. Litwin. 1994. "Declarative definition of object-oriented multidatabase mappings." In *Distributed Object Management*, edited by V. Dayal and T. Ozsu, pp. 375–392. San Francisco, CA: Morgan-Kaufman.

Fagin, R. 1998a. Fuzzy queries in multimedia database systems. Seventeenth ACM-SIGACT-SIGMOD-SIGART Symposium on Principles of Database Systems, June 1–3, Seattle, Washington: ACM Press.

Fagin, R. 1998b. "Combining fuzzy information from multiple systems." To appear in *J. Comput. Sys. Sci.*

Gupta, A. (ed.) 1989. *Integration of Information Systems: Bridging Heterogeneous Databases.* Piscataway, NJ: IEEE Press.

Hurson, A. R., M. W. Bright, and S. H. Pakzad. 1993. *Multidatabase Systems: an Advanced Solution for Global Information Sharing.* Piscataway, NJ: IEEE Press.

Litwin, W., A. Abdellatif, A. Zeroual, B. Nicolas, and Ph. Vigier 1989. "MSQL: A multidatabase Language." *Inform. Sci. J. Sys.* Special Issue on Database Systems, **48(2)**.

Litwin, W., M.-A. Neimat, and D. Schneider. 1996. "LH*—a scalable distributed data structure." *ACM Trans. Data Base Sys* **21(4)**: 480–525.

Litwin, W., J. Menon, T. Risch, and Th. Schwarz. 2000. "Design issues for scalable availability LH* schemes with record grouping." In *Distributed Data and Structures.* Waterloo, Canada: Carleton Scientific.

6.7 Meta-Data Management

Klaus R. Dittrich and Anca Vaduva

ABSTRACT Meta data facilitates managing, querying, and understanding of data. The generation, storage, and management of meta data promises to minimize the efforts required for administration and to better support the exploitation of information systems.

1. Introduction

Generally speaking, meta data is data about data. In particular, it may be defined as any information about data that both minimizes the efforts required for administration and improves the exploitation of an information system. For better understanding of the concept of meta data, we briefly present its evolution accompanied by multiple examples. Subsequently, we discuss the objectives and finally the management of meta data.

2. What is Meta Data?

The topic is as old as the existence of data: meta data has always been needed to describe the meaning or properties of data, with the aim being to better understand, sort out, manage, and control that data. Classical examples are libraries. The books (data) may be classified, managed, and retrieved only by means of appropriate meta-data (i.e., title, author, and content keywords).

In the context of database management systems (DBMS), meta data was first used in connection with the data dictionary, also called the system catalog (Elmasri and Navathe, 1994) (see Chapter 6.1 of this handbook). A data dictionary contains descriptions of the database structure, constraints, physical storage information (like storage details of each file, keys, and indexes), access rights, and so on. It may additionally include application documentation about users, the process of database design, and information about which applications use which parts of the database.

With the advent of general information systems consisting of distributed heterogeneous data sources (e.g., databases, flat files, Web sites), meta data expanded in scope. It covers the meta data of the original autonomous sources (e.g., the corresponding data dictionary entries) of the integrated system, as well as the meta data for the exploitation tools that perform tasks like query, analysis, and mining. That means meta data still contains descriptive information about data content and data structure, but also transformational information. Besides the information previously mentioned for data dictionaries, the former category contains meta data about the information types and sources in the integrated system, navigational meta data on how to access a source, and how the data is formatted. The specification of transformational meta data embodies procedural aspects that are needed to keep track of the processes that generate, aggregate, transform, and propagate data. For example, the administration of data warehouses (see Chapter 13) relies on meta data regarding data extraction, cleaning and loading, as well as transformation rules between data sources and the target warehouse database. Also, the transformation rules required for preprocessing data before applying data mining methods have to be represented as meta data as well.

With regard to their use, meta data may be classified as business (or application-driven) and technical meta data. The former category is used by end-users to better understand the application and thus use the information system better; it comprises application-specific documentation, business concepts and terminology, details about predefined queries, and reports. Also, context information like measurement units specification (currency, length), date format (American or European convention) or dictionaries, thesauri, and domain-specific ontological knowledge are considered as meta data.

In contrast, technical meta data are produced and used by database administrators or by other software tools. Considering again the example of a data dictionary, some of the meta data is produced by software modules of the DBMS (e.g., the data definition language compiler generates the database schema). Then, the data dictionary is used by other software modules like query optimizers and access control modules for carrying out their tasks.

The two classes, business and technical meta data, are not disjoint: often, the former is derived from the latter.

3. Purpose

Meta data generally serves two purposes: (1) to minimize the efforts for administration; and (2) to improve the exploitation of the information system.

The first objective concerns understanding and maintenance of the system, data source integration, analysis and design of applications, and business process modeling.

The second objective is concerned with:

- *Increasing query and retrieval quality.* Query quality may be enhanced through query optimization and database tuning that require knowledge about the database size and structure, and statistical meta data on how end-users access and use the information system. In the case of digital libraries, the effective and efficient retrieval of information relies on meta-data resulting from full-text indexing techniques (like those provided by Web search engines), resource descriptions, navigational meta data, and assumptions about user goals and preferences. Furthermore, query and information retrieval quality may be improved if the user is provided with assistance for precisely formulating a query or interpreting query results in a meaningful way. Inherently, business meta data plays a significant role in that case.

- *Improving data quality.* Data has to be up-to-date, reliable, and complete. Thus, information about the source credibility, when and who collected the data, whether some data are missing, and so on, has to be available.

- *Improving data analysis.* Known methods for data analysis include summarization, data mining, and OLAP (specific to data warehousing). In this context, meta data is necessary to understand the application domain and its representation in the data model (in the classical case the database schema) in order to adequately apply and interpret mined patterns. Meta data may also incorporate derived attributes or prior knowledge—which may be encoded as probabilities over data and distributions—that are then used to guide data mining.

4. Management

Meta data is stored and maintained in a repository, which is a structured storage and retrieval system, usually implemented on top of a database management system. According to Bernstein and Dayal (1994), the usual functionality of a repository include version and configuration management, checkout/checkin, notification, and interoperability.

The repository is a component in the architecture of an information system. It is accessed both by users and tools needing meta data. Thus, a user interface is required to offer suitable mechanisms for querying, navigating, browsing, and (possibly) manually updating the meta data of interest. For interacting with tools, a comprehensive set of operations, that is, the application programming interface, has to be available to read and write meta data into the repository.

The content and structure of the repository is directly related to the modeling of the information system. It is widely recognized that (at least) four levels are required for the modeling of complex information systems. Depending on the application, the levels may be refined. Each level contains the modeling constructs (or the modeling language) used to define the information on the level below. To start with, on the lowest level, level 0, there are the actual data items (e.g., the customer data). The levels above contain the meta information: level 1 contains meta data (e.g., the database schema); level 2 specifies the schema used to store the meta data, that means the meta model or the (conceptual) repository schema. The meta model should be easily extendable for additional information types when other meta-data sources have to be integrated. Level 2 also includes common modeling languages such as UML (Booch et al., 1999). Meta models are often defined as an extension (or specialization) of the UML core model. This is also the case for the meta data representation and interchange standards recently proposed by the Meta Data Coalition (1999) and OMG (1999). Finally, level 3 contains the meta meta model that unifies the different modeling languages specified on level 2.

Depending on their use, two kinds of systems managing meta data are commercially available today. General purpose repositories are typically used for providing information to the users. They provide a core meta model, which is easily extensible for any application requirements. Market leaders include Viasoft, Computer Associates, Unisys, and Microsoft (Data Warehousing Information Center, 1999). In contrast, tool-specific repositories are linked to certain tools that manage and use meta data in achieving different tasks. Inherently, the meta models of these repositories have to be compliant with their attached tools and thus they are less flexible as in the first case. Examples include extraction/transformation/loading tools known from data warehousing.

The ideal solution for meta-data management is to put all available meta data into a logically centralized repository (Bernstein and Dayal, 1994). In this way, since meta data is uniformly managed, consistency and maintainability are facilitated. However, centralization does not usually work well in practice. Often, meta data are spread across various repositories with different underlying data models and diverse representation standards, and are individually accessed by different tools or applications. The most widespread solution is decentralization, which imposes interoperability between these individual repositories. In this case, the shareability of meta data has to be ensured by a common interchange format. Extensive efforts are underway to produce meta-data standards, for example, OIM (Meta Data Coalition, 1999) and CWM (OMG, 1999).

Another solution is the integration of the repositories by means of federation (see Chapter 6.6), which strikes a trade-off between the advantages of centralization and those of local control.

References

Bernstein, P. A. and U. Dayal. 1994. "An overview of repository technology." In *Proceedings of the 20th International Conference on Very Large Data Bases* (September 12–15, Santiago de Chile, Chile), edited by J. B. Bocca, M. Jarke, and C. Zaniolo, pp. 705–713. San Francisco, CA: Morgan Kaufmann.

Booch, G., J. Rumbaugh, and I. Jacobson. 1999. *The Unified Modeling Language User Guide.* Reading, MA: Addison Wesley.

Data Warehousing Information Center. 1999: http://www.dwinfocenter.org/.

Elmasri, R. and S. B. Navathe. 1994. *Fundamentals of Database Systems*, pp. 479–489. Redwood City, CA: The Benjamin/Cummings Publishing Company.

Meta Data Coalition. 1999. *Open Information Model Version 1.0*: http://www.MDCinfo.com.

OMG (Object Management Group). 1999. *Common warehouse metamodel (CWM) specification.* OMG document ad/99-09-01, Initial Submission: http://www.omg.org.

7 LOGIC PERSPECTIVE ON DATA AND KNOWLEDGE

Lech Polkowski and Andrzej Skowron

ABSTRACT Logic understood as a study of mechanisms of inference, including inference of knowledge from data, has evolved into many reasoning schemes (languages) differing by understanding of semantics of inference. In this chapter, basic schemes are outlined along with their relation to KDD: classical calculi, many-valued logics, modal logics along with deductive mechanisms: axiomatized schemes, resolution in logic programming. An example of the system DATALOG is discussed. In complex tasks of AI and KDD like pattern recognition or machine learning, inductive reasoning is frequent in applications aimed at defining relevant concepts and dependencies among them. We discuss basic aspects of reasoning with knowledge, that is, making inferences in a chosen logical language from a given knowledge base, as well as basic aspects of reasoning about knowledge, that is, making inferences concerning properties of knowledge such as completeness, certainty.

1. Data, Knowledge, and their Representation

Perception, description, and analysis of real-life phenomena have dominated the intellectual activity of human beings; *a fortiori*, this activity has been assigned to machine systems exploiting various computing paradigms. Observation of a real-life phenomenon may be passive or active: by the former we mean perceiving the phenomenon and possibly rendering its impression, while by the latter we mean the process in which we create tools for a quantitative description of the phenomenon in terms of measurements, recordings, expert's knowledge, and so on. This latter process leads to the record of the phenomenon in the form of data. Data may therefore be of many various types: numerical data, symbolic data, pattern data including time series data, and so on. These types of data may be further elaborated to more complex types, for example, arrays of numerical data or audio or video series (e.g., documentary films). The choice of method of data collecting as well as the type of data depends on the particular problem to be solved about the given phenomenon; this data elicitation process may have a great complexity and it has been thoroughly studied by many authors (Gonzalez and Dankel, 1993). Data elicited from a phenomenon should undergo a representation process in which they are modeled by a certain structure. This structure allows for efficient knowledge representation and reasoning about it in order to solve some queries or problems. The relationship of data and knowledge, in particular how knowledge can be acquired from data, has attracted the attention of many philosophers and logicians (cf. Russell and Norvig, 1995).

From the logical point of view, data represent a model of a phenomenon, that is, a set of entities arranged in a certain space–time structure. Clearly, a real phenomenon may be associated with many distinct data structures.

Usually, the nature of the phenomenon suggests certain primitive concepts, that is, sets of entities in the data structure in terms of which we build more complex concepts and we carry reasoning about the phenomenon. Logic provides a widely accepted representation of properties of data structures, concepts, and their relationships or actions. A logic involves a set of formulas (well-formed expressions in a symbolic language) along with a family of relational structures (models) in which formulas are interpreted as concepts (i.e., sets of entities) of various relational complexities, as well as a mechanism allowing us to reason about properties of models. The choice of the language of formulas may be critical: on the one hand, this language should be expressive enough to render all essential concepts in data structures. On the other hand, a too expressive language may cause too complex an inference process (the phenomenon of language bias in machine learning, pattern recognition, knowledge discovery in databases (KDD); Fayyad and Piatetsky-Shapiro, 1996; Gonzalez and Dankel, 1993; Michalski and Tecuci, 1994; Mitchell, 1997; Nadler and Smith, 1993). The primitive data structures constructed according to selected way(s) of recording a phenomenon present possible models for various logics. Strategies for discovery of a particular logic, relevant for problems to be solved, present a challenge for KDD.

To illustrate the above ideas, we recall here a well-known logical language DATALOG used in relational databases (cf. Codd, 1970; Ullman and Widom, 1997).

1.1. Example: DATALOG

In relational databases, data are represented in two-dimensional tables called relations. Each row of the data table defines an instance of the relation among items occurring in this row. In DATALOG, relations are represented as predicates: for a relation R of arity n, we may introduce a predicate symbol P_R^n (often also written down simply as R) and we may define an atom (an elementary formula) $P_R^n(x_1, x_2, ..., x_n)$. From atoms, more complex formulas may be constructed by means of propositional connectives: $\wedge$ (AND), $\vee$ (OR), $\neg$ (NOT), for example, $P_R^n(x_1, x_2, ..., x_n) \wedge P_S^m(x_1, x_2, ..., x_m)$. In this way algebraic operations on relations are rendered in DATALOG in symbolic, logical form. We may have other atoms, for example, arithmetic ones, like $x + y > 1$. In DATALOG, we may also define rules as implications of the form $P_R^n(x_1, x_2, ..., x_n) \leftarrow \wedge_{i=1}^{k} P_{S_i}^{n_i}(x_{i_1}^i, ..., x_{i_{k_i}}^i)$; rules allow for symbolic rendering of a mechanism of new relation formation.

We have presented the syntax of DATALOG, that is, mechanisms of formula formation. The next aspect is its semantics, that is, meaning, interpretation of formulas. To interpret formulas, we must evaluate variables $x_1, x_2, ...$; to this end, we introduce a valuation v as a function that assigns to each variable x_i an element $a_i = v(x_i)$ in a specified set D called the domain of interpretation (for instance, D may be the set of objects occurring in data tables defining relations in our relational database). We have to select truth values, usually as T (true), F (false). Then we may define the meaning $[\alpha]_v$ of the atom $\alpha : P_R^n(x_1, x_2, ..., x_n)$ under the valuation v: $[\alpha]_v = T$ in case $R(a_1, ..., a_n)$ holds, that is, $a_1, ..., a_n$ is a row in the data table representing R, and $[\alpha]_v = F$, otherwise. Semantic rules assign meanings to complex formulas, for example, $[\alpha \wedge \beta]_v = T$ if and only if $[\alpha]_v = T = [\beta]_v$; $[\alpha \vee \beta]_v = T$ if and only if $[\alpha]_v = T$ or $[\beta]_v = T$; $[\neg \alpha]_v = T$ if and only if $[\alpha]_v = F$.

The logical structure of DATALOG allows for procedures not allowed by the original structure of data tables by, for example, a possibility to define new concepts.

In this example the two facets of a logical system: syntax and semantics are clearly visible and the logical language clearly matches the original data structure.

In fitting a logic to a data structure, some important intermediate steps are to be taken:

- in the data structure, certain sets of entities (concepts) and relationships among them are selected giving admissible relational structures in data (cf. relation representation in DATALOG);

- mechanisms of inference about properties of these admissible structures are selected (e.g., some deductive systems [see below] like propositional language in DATALOG).

Inference mechanisms of a logic may provide us with descriptors of complex concepts implicit in data structures; for various reasons, the formulas of logic may not describe concepts in data structures exactly but approximately only: one of the reasons is that we may not know exactly the concept in question (we usually know some positive or negative examples of this concept—this is typical for machine learning, data mining, and knowledge discovery). This makes it necessary to invoke inductive systems in addition to deductive ones allowing us to build models of inference from sets of examples. This leads to new logical systems for approximate reasoning allowing us to carry out reasoning about properties of data structures on the basis of uncertain, incomplete, or insufficient data (logics for reasoning under uncertainty). In these logics we encounter various phenomena not experienced by classical logics like nonmonotonicity, necessity of belief revision, and so on (see below). When a logic is selected that approximately specifies a data structure, this logic becomes an inference engine for using knowledge about a given phenomenon.

2. Concepts and Propositions

In general, the idea of a concept is associated with a set of entities; given a set U of entities, we call a concept any subset of the (universe set) U. For instance, in the DATALOG example in

Section 1.1, a concept may be any subset of the domain D of objects listed in the data table. This notion of a concept is what may be called a crisp (theoretical) concept: the subset is understood here in the classical sense, that is, for each element of U we can decide whether it is in X or not. However, concepts in data structures are often noncrisp (vague; see, e.g., Black (1937), Pawlak, 1991, Russell, 1923; and Zadeh, 1965): there are elements about which we cannot determine their membership in X with certainty due to, for example, imperfect knowledge about the concept or the object. A typical example is that provided by concepts expressed in natural language, for example, tall: it may be a matter of dispute whether a man of 175 cm is tall or not. Also concepts known by examples only (observational concepts) are such. To cope with such concepts various theories have been proposed, for example, probabilistic and statistical reasoning (Adams, 1975), fuzzy set theory (Zadeh, 1965), rough set theory (Pawlak, 1991), multivalued logics (Rescher, 1969), and so on.

Concept description may be either syntactic or semantic. In the classical case, syntactic description of a concept is provided by a formula of a logic (see Section 3.2, below). Semantic description relative to a model (the concept meaning) is provided by the meaning of this formula, that is, a set of entities in a model that satisfies this formula. This becomes more complex in cases of knowledge revision (Dubois and Prade, 1998), for example, for fuzzy or rough concepts where models learned from training data have to be revised after being tested against new cases.

A concept may also be characterized with respect to a set of formulas: given a crisp concept X and a set F of formulas, the intension of X with respect to F is the subset F' of F consisting of those formulas that are satisfied by each of the elements of X; assigning to a subset F' of F the family of all elements that satisfy each formula in F', we obtain a set (concept) called the extension of F' (in particular, we may start with X and find the extension X' of the intension F' of X; here, we work in the frame of Galois connections; Wille, 1996). This idea becomes more complicated in the case of noncrisp concepts where a formula is satisfied by an object in a degree usually less than 1.

In many applications there is need for analyzing dynamic structures involving changes of situations (concepts) by actions; from our point of view, actions are binary relations on concepts, that is, sets of pairs (precondition, postcondition; Sandewall and Shoham, 1995).

Reasoning with crisp concepts may be carried out by means of classical deductive systems. In nonclassical cases, where observational concepts are only approximated by theoretical concepts, an important additional ingredient in reasoning is provided by some measures of similarity (distance) among the concept and its approximation as well as by some mechanisms for propagation of these closeness measures or uncertainty coefficients (Zadeh, 1979).

3. Logic

3.1. General View on Logic

Logic gives us a mechanism for creating aggregates (collections) of propositions (see Section 3.2) in which one proposition (called the conclusion) is the consequence of the remaining propositions (called premises) in the sense that whenever we believe the premises we should also believe the conclusion. The conclusion and the premises are then in the consequence relation. The process of passing from believed premises to the believed conclusion (inference process) is at the heart of reasoning. Inference processes may be composed into chains of inferences and the overall inference mechanism may be very complex. Formal logic attempts to capture essential features and properties of inferential mechanisms applied in many contexts. Various logics differ with respect to the language in which they construct their propositions, the way in which they construct their consequence relations, and the way in which they understand the notion of belief. For instance, in classical logics (like in DATALOG), the belief is understood as the (absolute) truth, therefore consequence relations in these logics lead from true premises to the true conclusion. On the contrary, in nonclassical logics, belief may be understood as the probability of a statement to be true, the possibility of a statement to be true, the degree of belief in a statement to be true, and so on. Those consequence relations express the degree of belief in the conclusion as a function of degrees of belief in the premises.

Let us, however, observe that a logic *per se* may be inadequate for a complete description of a problem as it proposes a universal way of reasoning about the reality which is not feasible in sufficiently complex cases (e.g., distributed knowledge systems involving agents having different knowledge reasoning systems) because of imperfect knowledge about the environment. For this reason, some recent approaches advocate an implicit logic encoded directly in hardware translating sensor readings to actions (e.g., situated robots, Nehmzow, 2000; connectionistic approach, Rumelhart and McClelland, 1986). Clearly, this approach also involves a logic in which reasoning is realized by parameter adjustment. In complex cases the adjustment process requires decomposition and a search for proper decomposition schemes as well as a higher-level logic for controlling this process (Huhns and Singh, 1998; Polkowski and Skowron, 1996).

In order to illustrate these aspects, we begin with a description of basic classical logical systems. The reader may recall DATALOG as an example in the introductory part below.

3.2. Syntax and Semantics

Any logic needs a language in which its statements are constructed and its inference mechanisms are represented. Hence we should define an alphabet of symbols over which well-formed expressions of logic are to be constructed. Usually, the process of constructing formulas is of a generative character: one starts with simple (elementary, atomic) formulas and applies some generative rules for producing more complex formulas. This purely syntactic aspect of logic has its counterpart in the semantic aspect that deals with the meaning of formulas and the semantic aspect of consequence relations. Building semantics for a logic involves a certain world (or worlds) external to the set of formulas of this logic, in which we interpret propositions of the logic assigning to each of them its meaning, usually being relations in this world (worlds). A good example is a relational database providing a semantic frame for logic (e.g., DATALOG). With respect to given worlds, we can define truth values (in general, belief degrees) of formulas. When this is done, we can study semantically acceptable consequence relations as these inference mechanisms that lead from true premises to true conclusions (respectively, from premises in which we believe to a satisfactory degree to the conclusions in which we believe sufficiently; in both cases with respect to a chosen set of worlds).

Finding a model for a given formula (or set of formulas) in which these formula(s) are true (see Section on predicate logic below; called the satisfiability problem or model checking problem) is of high computational complexity (already NP-complete in the propositional case; Garey and Johnson, 1979). Although very important from a practical point of view, the satisfiability problem only has feasible approximate solutions for some simple logics (like the propositional logic).

With a logic we associate therefore two basic relations: the relation of syntactic consequence denoted $\vdash$, and the relation of semantic consequence (entailment) denoted $\vDash$; one of main problems of logic is to find relations between these two consequence notions (cf. the dicussion on completeness and soundness in Section 4.1).

3.3. Exemplary Classical Logical Systems (Calculi)

We review now some basic logical systems. We begin with propositional logic which deals with declarative statements. In this logic we may see in the simplest form all aspects discussed above.

PROPOSITIONAL LOGIC
Propositional reasoning turns out to be very effective for solving many KDD problems (see Boolean reasoning in Chapter 9 and Selman et al. (1997)). Despite high computational complexity of the satisfiability problem for propositional calculus, many efficient heuristics searching for, for example, relevant features, discretization of numeric features, grouping of symbolic values, association rules, have been developed at the cost of handling propositional formulas of very large size.

In this logic we consider propositions, that is, declarative statements like "London is the capital of Great Britain" or "$2 + 2 = 3$" about which we can establish with certainty whether they are true or false. The calculus of propositions is effected by means of propositional connectives that allow for constructions of complex propositions from simpler ones. Formally, we begin with the alphabet consisting of a countable number of propositional symbols $p_1, p_2, ..., p_k, ...$, functor symbols $\neg$, $\Rightarrow$, and auxiliary symbols: parentheses $)$, $($, $]$, $[$. An expression is any string of symbols over this alphabet. The set of formulas of propositional logic is defined as the smallest set X such that: (i) X contains all propositional symbols; and (ii) if expressions u, v are in X then expressions $\neg u$ and $u \Rightarrow v$ are also in X. To describe some useful subsets of the set X, a generative approach is also used: one singles out a set $A \subset X$ of formulas called axioms and one specifies derivation rules for generating some formulas (called theorems) from axioms. The idea is that theorems should coincide with tautologies, that is, true propositions. Axioms may be chosen in many distinct ways; a simple axiomatic (Mendelson, 1960) consists of the following axiom schemes (meaning that in each of these expressions we may substitute for $p, q, r, ...$ any formula and we obtain an axiom formula):

(Ax1) $(p \Rightarrow (q \Rightarrow p))$;

(Ax2) $(p \Rightarrow (q \Rightarrow r)) \Rightarrow ((p \Rightarrow q) \Rightarrow (p \Rightarrow r))$;

(Ax3) $((\neg p \Rightarrow \neg q) \Rightarrow ((\neg p \Rightarrow q) \Rightarrow r))$.

The set of derivation rules in this case consists of a single relation on expressions called *modus ponens* (MP) being the set of triples of the form $(p, p \Rightarrow q, q)$ meaning that: if $p, p \Rightarrow q$ are already derived from axioms, then q is also regarded as derived. The set of theorems is the set of formulas which can be obtained from instances of axioms by means of applying MP a finite number of times. The basic tool for efficient checking of syntactic properties of propositional logic is the Herbrand deduction theorem: For any set of formulas Γ

if $\Gamma, p \vdash q$ then $\Gamma \vdash p \Rightarrow q$.

This rule allows for incremental generation of formulas of increasing structural complexity. Now, we discuss semantics of propositional logic. We evaluate formulas with respect to their truth values: truth (denoted by T) and falsity (denoted by F) assuming that functors are truth-functional, that is, they are functions on truth values and they do not depend on the particular type of a formula. Under these assumptions one can characterize functors semantically by means of tables. We give the tables for $\neg$, $\Rightarrow$ (see Tables 1 and 2).

Semantics of propositional logic are defined with respect to a model that is the set of all boolean (i.e., 0, 1-valued) functions (called valuations) on the set of propositional symbols: given a formula $\alpha(p_{i_1}, p_{i_2}, ..., p_{i_k})$, which means that the propositional symbols $p_{i_1}, p_{i_2}, ..., p_{i_k}$ are the only variable symbols in α, and a valuation v we define the value $v(\alpha)$ with respect to α. An admissible state for α in the model is any valuation v such that $v(\alpha) = 1$. A formula α is true (is a tautology) when all states are admissible, that is, $v(\alpha) = 1$ for every valuation v.

Two important properties of this deductive system are: soundness (meaning that every theorem is true) and completeness (meaning that every true formula is a theorem). It is straightforward to check the soundness of propositional logic by induction on the formula length. Less obvious is the completeness of propositional logic established first by Gödel (Mendelson, 1960). Propositional logic is decidable: for each formula it is sufficient to check finitely many partial valuations restricted to the finite set of propositional symbols occurring in this formula to decide whether the formula is true. It is also effectively axiomatizable: for each formula one can decide in

Table 1 The Negation Functor $\neg$

p	$\neg p$
0	1
1	0

a finite number of steps whether the formula is an instance of an axiom scheme. Completeness implies consistency: for no formula α can both α and $\neg\alpha$ be theorems.

Let us add finally that in practical usage additional functors are introduced, familiar from DATALOG: the conjunction functor $\wedge$ defined by taking $\alpha \wedge \beta$ as a shortcut for $\neg(\alpha \Rightarrow \neg\beta)$, the disjunction functor $\vee$ defined by taking $\alpha \vee \beta$ as the shortcut for $\alpha \Rightarrow \beta$, and the logical equivalence functor $\neg$, $\leftrightarrow$ defined by taking $\alpha \leftrightarrow \beta$ as the shortcut for $(\alpha \Rightarrow \beta) \wedge (\beta \Leftarrow \alpha)$. Truth tables for these functors follow immediately from these definitions and Tables 1 and 2.

PREDICATE LOGIC

Propositional logic renders us good service by giving a formal treatment to propositions; however, in many practical situations, KDD applications included, we are concerned with properties of objects expressed as concepts, that is, sets of objects, and with relations among these properties.

In order to ensure the expressibility of relations, for example, inclusions (like every ripe tomato is red) we need to quantify statements involving object descriptors over concepts. The predicate logic is an extension of propositional logic enabling us to manipulate concept descriptors. Expressivenes of this logic is very powerful and it allows for encoding properties by short formulas, yet we pay the cost of high computational complexity or even algorithmic unsolvability of basic problems. Thus, in practice we use some simple fragments of this logic like relational calculus in DATALOG.

We will write $P(x)$ to denote that the object denoted x has the property denoted P; the symbol P is a (unary) predicate symbol (cf. DATALOG). With the expression $P(x)$ we associate two expressions: $\forall x P(x)$ and $\exists x P(x)$; the symbol $\forall x$ is called the universal quantifier and $\forall x P(x)$ denotes that for each object x the property P holds; the sympol $\exists x$ is called the existential quantifier and $\exists x P(x)$ denotes that there exists an object x such that P holds for x. Predicate calculus treats formally such utterances. For the sake of generality, we will give a formal analysis of deductive systems known as first-order theories of which predicate calculus is a specialization. To give a formal description of first order logical calculi, we begin with an alphabet that in general case consists of a few types of symbols:

1. individual variables $x_1, x_2, ..., x_k, ...$;

2. individual constants $c_1, c_2, ..., c_k, ...$;

3. predicate symbols $P_1^1, P_2^1, ..., P_{i_k}^k, ...$, where the upper index gives the arity of the predicate denoted thus;

4. functional symbols $f_1^1, f_2^1, ..., f_{i_k}^k, ...$;

5. symbols $\neg$, $\Rightarrow$, $\forall x$ (where x is a variable),), (.

First we define the set of terms by requiring it to be the set X with the properties that: (i) each individual variable or constant is in X; (ii) if $t_1, ..., t_k$ are elements of X and $f_{i_k}^k$ is a functional symbol of arity k then $f_{i_k}^k(t_1, t_2, ..., t_k)$ is in X; and (iii) if Y satisfies (i), (ii) then $X \subseteq Y$.

Next, the set of formulas is defined as the set Z with the properties: (i) for each predicate symbol $P_{i_k}^k$ and any set $\{t_1, t_2, ..., t_k\}$ of terms, the expression $P_{i_k}^k(t_1, t_2, ..., t_k)$ is in Z; (ii) for each pair α, β of elements of Z, the expressions $\neg\alpha, \alpha \Rightarrow \beta, \forall x\alpha$ are in Z for each variable x; and (iii) if Y satisfies (i), (ii) then $Z \subseteq Y$.

The existential quantifier is defined by duality: $\exists x P(x)$ is $\neg\forall x \neg P(x)$. We distinguish between free and bound occurrences of a variable x in a formula α: an occurrence is bound

Table 2 The Implication Functor $\Rightarrow$		
p	q	$p \Rightarrow q$
0	0	1
0	1	1
1	0	0
1	1	1

when this occurrence happens in a part of the formula (subformula) preceded by the quantifier sign; otherwise the occurrence is free. It is intuitively clear that a formula in which all occurrences are bound is a proposition, that is, either true or false in a given model.

To define the syntax, one should specify the axioms. Axioms of T can be divided into two groups: the first group consists of axioms of predicate logic, the second group consists of specific axioms (like commutativity in arithmetic); when the second group is present, we speak of a first order theory. The axiom schemes of the first group may be chosen as follows:

- (Ax1), (Ax2), (Ax3) are axiom schemes for propositional logic.
- (Ax4) $\forall x\alpha(x) \Rightarrow \alpha(t)$ where x is a variable, t is a term and t contains no variable such that x occurs in a subformula quantified with respect to that variable;
- (Ax5) $\forall x(\alpha \Rightarrow \beta) \Rightarrow (\alpha \Rightarrow \forall x\beta)$ where the variable x is not free in α.

Specific axioms depend on T; for instance the theory of equivalence relation may be expressed by means of a binary predicate symbol P_1^2 and axioms

$$\forall x P_1^2(x, x);$$

$$\forall x \forall y (P_1^2(x, y) \Rightarrow P_1^2(y, x));$$

$$\forall x \forall y \forall z (P_1^2(x, y) \Rightarrow (P_1^2(y, z) \Rightarrow P_1^2(x, z)))).$$

The set of derivation rules consists of two rules: *modus ponens* (MP), known from propositional logic; and quantification (generalization) rule (Q), which is the binary relation consisting of pairs of the form $(\alpha, \forall x\alpha)$, where x is any variable. A theorem of predicate logic is any formula which may be obtained from an instance of an axiom by applying a derivation rule a finite number of times.

Semantics of a first-order theory T is defined according to Tarski (1936) as follows.

A model (relational structure) M for the theory T is a pair (D, f), where D is a set and f is an interpretation of T in D, that is, f assigns to each individual constant c an element $f(c) \in D$, to each predicate symbol P_i^k a relation $f(P_i^k)$ on D of arity k, and to each functional symbol f_i^k a function $f(f_i^k)$ from D^k to D. Truth of a formula, relative to M, is defined inductively on structure of the formula. To this end, we consider the states of the model M as sequences $\sigma = (a_i)_i$ of elements of D. Given a formula α and a state σ, we need to declare when the formula α is satisfied by σ, in symbols, $\sigma \vDash \alpha$. We define a map F_σ that assigns an element of D to each term of T. Individual variables are interpreted via a given state σ: $F_\sigma(x_i) = a_i$. The mapping F_σ is equal to f on individual constants. The inductive condition is as follows: if F_σ is already defined on terms $t_1, t_2, ..., t_k$ and f_i^k is a functional symbol then

$$F_\sigma(f_i^k(t_1, t_2, ..., t_k)) = f(f_i^k)(F_\sigma(t_1), F_\sigma(t_2), ..., F_\sigma(t_k)).$$

The satisfiability $\vDash$ is defined inductively as follows:

1. $\sigma \vDash P_i^k(t_1, t_2, ..., t_k)$ if and only if $f(P_i^k)(F_\sigma(t_1), ..., F_\sigma(t_k))$ holds;
2. $\sigma \vDash \neg\alpha$ if and only if it is not true that $\sigma \vDash \alpha$;
3. $\sigma \vDash (\alpha \Rightarrow \beta)$ if and only if $\sigma \vDash \alpha$ implies that $\sigma \vDash \beta$;
4. $\sigma \vDash \forall x\alpha(x)$ if and only if $\sigma^x \vDash \alpha$ for each state σ^x, where (letting x be the variable x_i) σ^x is like σ except that the ith member of σ^x need not be equal to a_i.

These conditions allow each formula to be checked to see whether it is satisfied by a given state. A formula is true in the model M if and only if it is satisfied by every state σ. A formula is true (a tautology) if and only if it is true in every model M. Observe that a formula $\alpha(x_1, ..., x_n)$ is true if and only if its closure $\forall x_1 ... \forall x_n \alpha(x_1, ..., x_n)$ is true.

The first-order theory PC without specific axioms is called the predicate calculus. Properties of first-order theories depend on specific axioms so here we recapitulate the facts about the predicate calculus. The soundness of predicate calculus can be easily established by structural induction: each theorem of PC is true as all instances of axiom schemes (Ax1)–(Ax3) are true and truth is preserved by derivation rules *MP* and *Q*. The important Gödel completeness theorem (Gödel, 1930; Mendelson, 1960) states that predicate calculus is complete: each tautology is a theorem. Decidability problems for first-order theories involve questions about the formalizations of the intuitive notion of a finite procedure and can be best discussed in the frame of the fundamentally important first order-theory of arithmetic (cf. Mendelson, 1960): a predicate calculus without functional symbols and individual constants is called pure predicate calculus *PP* while predicate calculus with infinite sets of functional symbols and individual constants is called functional calculus *PF*. The classical theorem of Church (Davis, 1958; Mendelson, 1960) states that both *PP* and *PF* are recursively undecidable (algorithmically unsolvable). On the other hand, many problems are recursively decidable (algorithmically solvable), however, their time—or space—complexity makes them not feasible, for example, the satisfiability problem for propositional calculus is NP-complete (Garey and Johnson, 1979).

4. Deductive Systems (DS)

Here we sum up the features of deductive systems like propositional logic or predicate calculus. They are important for KDD because they provide tools for reasoning with knowledge. By a deductive system, we understand a tuple $(Ax, Gen, \vdash)$ where Ax is a set of axioms (meaning by an axiom a formula that is assumed to be well-formed and desirably true), Gen is a set of inference (derivation) rules, each rule R being a relation on the set of formulas and $\vdash$ is a relation on formulas such that whenever $\Gamma \vdash \alpha$ holds this means that there exists a formal proof of α from Γ (α is derivable from Γ), that is, there exists a finite sequence (the formal proof) $\alpha_1, ..., \alpha_k$ such that: (i) α_1 is either an axiom or an element of Γ; (ii) α_k is α; and (iii) each α_i ($i = 2, ..., k$) is either an axiom or is in Γ or satisfies $R(\alpha_{j_1}, ..., \alpha_{j_m}, \alpha_i)$ for some $R \in Gen$ and a subset $\{\alpha_{j_1}, ..., \alpha_{j_m}\}$ of $\{\alpha_1, ..., \alpha_{i-1}\}$. Any formula α such that $\vdash \alpha$ (meaning $\varnothing \vdash \alpha$) is said to be a theorem of the deductive system. From these definitions, the properties of $\vdash$ follow: (i) $\Gamma \subseteq Cn(\Gamma)$ where $Cn(\Gamma) = \{\alpha : \Gamma \vdash \alpha\}$; (ii) $Cn(\Gamma) = Cn(Cn(\Gamma))$; (iii) $Cn(\Gamma) \subseteq Cn(\Gamma')$ whenever $\Gamma \subseteq \Gamma'$ (the Tarski axioms for syntactic consequence; Tarski, 1956). Semantics of a deductive system are defined with respect to a class of specified structures called models: a mechanism exists that for each model and each formula assigns to this formula a subset of the model domain (called the interpretation of the formula in the model). A formula is true with respect to a given model when its interpretation in the model equals the model domain. A formula is true (is a tautology) when it is true with respect to all models (in the assumed class of models).

The semantic consequence $\vDash$ (entailment) is defined on sets of formulas as follows: $\Gamma \vDash \Gamma'$ if for any model M in which each formula in Γ is true, each formula in Γ' is true in M.

A closer look at KDD problems will assure that classical deductive systems are insufficient and they have to be augmented with inductive mechanisms (see Chapter 8) as well as with schemes for composition (fusion) of various deductive schemes in distributed knowledge bases.

4.1. Properties of DS: Soundness, Consistency, Completeness, Decidability, Expressiveness, Complexity

Among properties of deductive systems there are some whose importance deserves them to be mentioned separately. The first of them is soundness (of axiomatization), which means that all theorems of the system are true. The dual property of completeness means that each tautology has a formal proof in the system. As a rule, verification of soundness is straightforward while the completeness proofs are usually nontrivial. Another important property often intervening in completeness proofs is consistency: a set Γ of formulas is consistent if there is no formula α such that both α and its negation are derivable from Γ. Another important question is whether an algorithm exists which for each formula can decide if this formula is a theorem; if yes, we say that the deductive system is decidable. In this case, we may ask about the time—or space—complexity of the decidability problem. We may study complexity of other problems like satisfiability (whether the interpretation of the formula is nonempty). From the point of view of knowledge representation, it is important to decide what properties can be expressed by means of formulas of the deductive system. A useful meta rule is that the greater the expressibility the greater the complexity of problems about the deductive system. These properties are important for KDD; for example, if our reasoning system is complete, it is enough to remember only the axioms and inference rules to represent all theorems about our knowledge.

4.2. Resolution and Logic Programming

Logic programming in KDD allows encoding in a concise form of knowledge about more complex objects having a structure and dynamics (e.g., a model of cell behavior) and to extract more complex patterns. However, this approach is also limited by computational complexity bounds.

It is desirable from a computing point of view to have systems for automated deduction; the widely accepted technique for this is resolution due to J. A. Robinson (Eisinger and Ohlbach, 1993). It requires a clausal form of formulas, that is, a conjunction of disjunctions of literals (a literal is a variable or its negation). Symbols like $\{p, q\}$ mean a disjunction of literals p, q and symbols like $\{.\}; \{..\}; ...; \{...\}$ mean conjunctions of disjunctions, that is, a clause. Resolution uses the refutational proof technique: instead of checking validity of α it checks unsatisfiability of $\neg\alpha$; to this end $\neg\alpha$ is represented in a clausal form and the resolution rule: from clauses $a \cup p$ and $b \cup \neg p$ the clause $a \cup b$ is derived, is applied a finite number of times. The final appearance of the empty clause witnesses unsatisfiability of $\neg\alpha$ hence validity of α. The resolution calculus is sound and complete with respect to entailment $\vDash$. Resolution in predicate calculus involves unification, that is, the process of finding substitutions making two terms containing free variables identical. For extensions and refinements see Eisinger and Ohlbach (1993).

Particularly important from the computational point of view is the Horn clausal logic (Hodges, 1993) based on Horn clauses of which Horn facts are of the form

$$\forall x_1 ... \forall x_m P^k_{i_k}(\tau_1, ..., \tau_k),$$

and Horn rules are of the form

$$\forall x_1 ... \forall x_k \alpha_1(x) \wedge ... \wedge \alpha_n(x) \Rightarrow \beta(x).$$

A set of Horn clauses is a Horn clausal theory T. Inferences for T are based on inference rules of the form: $\alpha_1(c) \wedge ... \wedge \alpha_n(c)/\beta(c)$, where c is a ground term, that is, term without variables corresponding to Horn rules in T. A proof $T \vdash \gamma$ is a finite sequence of inferences starting from an inference based on a fact and ending with γ. This calculus is sound and complete. The Horn clausal logic can be considered as a generative device for incremental buildup of a set from Horn facts (alphabet) and Horn rules (generating rules). It has been applied in implementations of PROLOG and DATALOG in particular in logic programming (Lloyd, 1984).

The idea behind logic programming is that the logic program is a specification written as a formula in a logical language and the inference engine for the construction solution consists of a deduction system for this language. The system of deduction in logic programming is based on resolution. Logic programs can be of the form known as definite clause programs (a definite clause is a universally quantified disjunction of one or more literals, only one of which is negated). They are executed by adding a goal being a clause in a special form.

Semantics for logic programs can be defined by Herbrand interpretations. A Herbrand interpretation is based on the Herbrand universe, that is, the set of all ground atoms constructed from constants, function, and predicate symbols in the program. The least Herbrand model of a logic program can be defined as the least fixed point of a certain function from Herbrand universe into Herbrand universe. Any predicate calculus sentence can be transformed into a set of clauses and then resolution, can be used to test, by refutation, the validity of entailment in predicate calculus.

An example of a logic programming system is PROLOG (Colmerauer, 1972). More details can be found in Lloyd (1984). These systems may be regarded as engines for constructing knowledge bases from data.

One of the main tasks of inference is to obtain a description of a target object satisfying (exactly or to a satisfactory degree) a given specification (formulated in some logical language).

In constraint programming logic (Tsang, 1993) the construction schemes of such objects can be extracted from logical proofs.

4.3. Theorem Provers

Automated theorem proving was initiated in the 1950s and by 1960 various computer programs for theorem proving were implemented (Newell, Davis and Putnam, Gilmore, Prawitz, Hao Wang) and able to prove very simple theorems. Resolution technique (J. A. Robinson, 1965) proved to be much more powerful and by now most theorem provers use resolution. In spite of progress, much still remains to be done, in the first place in discovering proof strategies. This will need in particular to introduce some similarity measures on proofs. Moreover, KDD stimulates research towards revision of exact formal proofs by introducing schemes of approximate reasoning extracted from data instead (Polkowski and Skowron, 1999; see Chapter 9).

5. Other Logics

5.1. Modal Logic

In many applications in KDD, when our knowledge is incomplete or uncertain, for example, in mining association rules in databases with inconsistent decisions (Agrawal et al., 1993), we cannot have exact logical statements, but may only express certain modalities like property P is possible.

Modal propositional logics (cf. Hughes and Creswell (1968)) deal with formal rendering of phrases like "it is possible that...," "it is necessary that ...". These modalities are treated as generalized quantifiers: $[\alpha]$ is read as "it is necessary that α", $\langle\alpha\rangle$ is read as "it is possible that α". These operators are related by duality: $\langle\alpha\rangle$ is the shortcut for $\neg[\neg\alpha]$.

The rising importance of modal logic in KDD for knowledge representation and reasoning about knowledge (see Section 7) stems from its ability to express structural properties of objects and their dynamic changes.

The syntax of modal calculus is defined over an alphabet much like that of propositional logic: the only addition is the introduction of modal operator symbols [.] and $\langle.\rangle$. The set of formulas of modal logic is defined as the smallest set X such that (i) X contains all propositional variables, and (ii) with each pair α, β, X contains $\neg\alpha$, $\alpha\Rightarrow\beta$ and $[\alpha]$.

The axiomatics of modal logics depends essentially on properties of necessity that we intuitively deem as desirable; their rendering in axioms leads to various systems of modal calculi.

Semantics of modal logic are defined as the possible worlds (Kripke) semantics (Fitting, 1993). A model for a modal logic system is a triple $M = (W, R, v)$, where W is a collection of states (worlds) and R is a binary relation on W (called accessibility relation); the symbol v denotes a state of the model (a valuation), that is, the boolean function on the set of all pairs of the form (w, p), where $w \in W$ is a world and p is a propositional variable. The notion of satisfiability $M, v, w \vDash \alpha$ is defined by structural induction: (i) $M, v, w \vDash p$ if and only if $v(w, p) = 1$; (ii) $M, v, w \vDash \neg\alpha$ if and only if it is not true that $M, v, w \vDash \alpha$; (iii) $M, v, w \vDash \alpha \Rightarrow \beta$ if and only if either it is not true that $M, v, w \vDash \alpha$ or it is true that $M, v, w \vDash \beta$; and (iv) $M, v, w \vDash [\alpha]$ if and only if $M, v, w_1 \vDash \alpha$ for each world w_1 such that $R(w, w_1)$.

A formula α is true in the model M if and only if $M, v, w \vDash \alpha$ for each world $w \in W$ and every state v; a formula is true if and only if it is true in each model.

Recently modal logics have played an important role in many theoretical branches of computer science and artificial intelligence, for example, in formalization of reasoning by groups of intelligent agents (Fagin et al., 1995); in applicational domains, we may mention hand-written digit recognition (Bazan et al., 1998) where modal formulas are used to express properties discerning between structural objects.

5.2. Temporal and Dynamic Logics

There are some particular contexts in which formulas of modal logic may be specialized and tailored to specific usage. Let us mention two such cases, that is, temporal as well as dynamic logics. These logics are useful to express changes of knowledge in a changing environment, for example, in geographic information systems (GIS; Egenhofer and Golledge, 1997).

In temporal logics (Van Bentham, 1995), the set W of possible worlds is interpreted as the set of time instances, and the accessibility relation R is the precedence in time relation, that is, wRw_1 means that w precedes w_1 in time (in particular, it may happen that $w = w_1$).

Dynamic logic is applied in the context of properties of programs (Harel, 1994). In this case the set W is the set of states of an abstract computing machine. Given a program P, the modality $[.]_P$ acts on formulas describing states of the machine and its semantics are defined by the accessibility relation R_P, which holds on a pair (w, w_1) if and only if an execution of P starting at w terminates at w_1; specifically, a state w satisfies the formula $[\alpha]_P$ if and only if each state w_1 such that $R_P(w, w_1)$ satisfies α. This means that the state in which P terminates necessarily satisfies α.

5.3. Epistemic Logics

These are logics of knowledge and belief. Logics for reasoning about knowledge, belief, obligations, norms, and so on, have to deal with statements that are not merely true or false but which are known or believed, and so on, to be true at a moment; an additional complication is of pragmatic character: knowledge, belief, and so on, may be considered with respect to particular intelligent reasoners (agents) hence we may also need to express statements about group or common knowledge, belief, and so on. Modal logics have proved suitable as a general vehicle for carrying out the task of constructing such logics. These logics are useful in KDD in, for example, tasks of describing problems of distributed/many–agent nature, in building networks of reasoning agents (e.g., belief networks), and so on. Epistemic logics for reasoning about knowledge (Halpern, 1995; Hintikka, 1962; Von Wright, 1951) are built as modal logics with a family $K_i : i = 1, 2, ..., n$ of necessity operators, K_i interpreted as the modal operator the agent i knows that.... Syntax of such logic is like that of modal propositional logic except for the above family K_i instead of a single $[.]$ modal operator symbol. Formulas are defined as usual, in particular given a formula α, the expression $K_i\alpha$ is a formula, each i. We therefore have formulas like $K_iK_j\alpha$, which are read as the agent i knows that the agent j knows that α, and so on. Semantics are the usual Kripke semantics of possible worlds except that to accommodate all K_is, a model is now a tuple $M = (W, v, R_1, ..., R_n)$, where R_i is an accessibility relation of K_i, that is, $v, w \vDash K_i\alpha$ if and only if $v, w' \vDash \alpha$ for every w' with $R_i(w, w')$. One may also want to express in this logic statements like every agent in a group G knows that... or it is common knowledge among agents in G that.... This may be done by introducing additional symbols E_G, C_G for each subset $G \subseteq \{1, 2, ..., n\}$, requiring that for each formula α and each G, expressions $E_G\alpha, C_G\alpha$ are formulas, and defining semantics of these formulas as follows: $v, w \vDash E_G\alpha$ if and only if $v, w \vDash K_i\alpha$ for each $i \in G$ and $v, w \vDash C_G\alpha$ if and only if $v, w \vDash K_{i_1}K_{i_2}, ..., K_{i_j}\alpha$ for each sequence $i_1i_2 ... i_j$ over G. In other words, the accessibility relation for E_G is $\cap\{R_i : i \in G\}$ and the accessibility relation for C_G is the transitive closure of $\{R_i : i \in G\}$. These logics are axiomatized soundly and completely in analogy to modal logics of respective types; additional axiom schemes for logics endowed with operators E_G, C_G may be chosen as follows (Halpern, 1995): $E_Gp \leftrightarrow \wedge K_ip$; $C_Gp \leftrightarrow E_G(p \wedge C_Gp)$ along with the additional derivation rule $(p \Rightarrow E_G(\alpha \wedge \beta)) \Rightarrow (\alpha \Rightarrow C_G\beta)$. These logics are decidable (to check truth of a formula it is sufficient to examine at most 2^n worlds where n is the formula length).

5.4. Nonmonotonic Logics

In the presence of inconsistencies nonmonotonicity may arise: a greater set of premises may lead to a smaller set of consequents because of the need for revision of our knowledge. Attempts at formal rendering of this phenomenon has led to nonmonotonic logics (Makinson, 1993). Nonmonotonic reasoning is central to intelligent systems dealing with common-sense reasoning being nonmonotonic. These logics answer the call for such tools in KDD, to be applied in incremental extraction of patterns and knowledge, for example, in synthesis of adaptive systems.

The nonmonotonic logics deal with nonmonotonic consequence $\vdash_{nm}$; a general idea for rendering $\vdash_{nm}$ may be as follows: try to define $\alpha \vdash_{nm}\beta$ as holding when there exists a belief set Γ of formulas, $\alpha \vdash \beta$ and $\alpha \vdash \gamma$ for sufficiently many $\gamma \in \Gamma$.

This idea is realized in various ways: in default logic (Poole, 1993), probabilistic logic (Adams, 1975), circumscription (MacCarthy cf., Konolige, 1993), auto-epistemic logic (Lifschitz, 1993). Reiter's default logic is built over predicate calculus L by enriching it with inference rules (called defaults) of the form $\alpha(x); \beta(x)/\gamma(x)$, where $\alpha(x), \beta(x), \gamma(x)$ are formulas called, respectively the precondition, the test condition, and the consequent of the default. For a constant a, the default permits $\alpha(a)$ to be derived from $\gamma(a)$ under the condition that not $\vdash \neg\beta(a)$; we denote this consequence by $\vdash_d$. Formally, a default theory T may be represented as a pair (K, E) where K, a background context, contains rules and E, the evidence set, contains facts. Rules in K are of two kinds: rules of L and defaults D.

Let us consider one example of characterization of nonmonotonic inference $\vdash_{K,E}$ from given (K, E). It may be done by a set of postulates of which we mention: (Defaults) $p \vdash_d q \in D$ implies $p \vdash_{K,E} q$; (Deduction) $\vdash p$ implies $\vdash_{K,E} p$; (Augmentation) $\vdash_{K,E} p$ and $\vdash_{K,E} q$ imply $\vdash_{K,E \cup \{p\}} q$; (Reduction) $\vdash_{K,E} p$ and $\vdash_{K,E \cup \{p\}} q$ imply $\vdash_{K,E} q$; (Disjunction) $\vdash_{K,E \cup \{p\}} r$ and $\vdash_{K,E \cup \{q\}} r$ imply $\vdash_{K,E \cup \{p \vee q\}} r$. As shown in Geffner (1992), these rules are sound and complete under a probabilistic interpretation of ϵ-entailment (Adams, 1975). In this interpretation, probability distributions P_K ϵ-consistent with K in the sense of ϵ-entailment, that is, such that $P_K(\alpha) = 1$ for each $\alpha \in L$, $P_K(\beta \mid \alpha) \geq 1 - \epsilon$ and $P_K(\alpha) \geq 0$ for each rule $\alpha \vdash_d \beta$ in D (where ϵ is a fixed parameter), are considered. A proposition p is ϵ-entailed by T when for each ϵ there exists a δ such that $P_K(p \mid E) \geq 1 - \epsilon$ for each δ-consistent probability distribution P_K.

One of the main problems for nonmonotonic logics is to define for a given set A of sentences a family $E(A)$ of all its extensions, that is, sets of sentences acceptable by an intelligent agent as a description of the world. Different formal attempts to solve this problem are known. Some of them are trying to implement the principle called closed world assumption (facts which are not known are false). Having the set of extensions $E(A)$ one can define the skeptical consequence relation by taking the intersection of all possible extensions of A.

Let us finally observe that, for example, classification problems can be treated as problems of constraints satisfaction, with constraints specified by discernibility conditions, and some optimality measures (see Chapter 9). Two consistent sets describing situations (objects) are satisfying the discernibility relation if their union creates an inconsistent (or inconsistent in some degree) set.

5.5. Many-Valued Logics

The need for many-valued logics in KDD follows from using imprecise concepts, propositions true in degree, the need for knowledge reduction, and lossless compression, for example, granulation, and from using beliefs characterized by their degrees of truth (certainty).

Yet another treatment of inference, comparing the above discussed, was proposed by Jan Łukasiewicz (1930) by assigning to propositions other logical values than truth and falsity. In the first 3-valued logic L_3 propositions were additionally assigned the value $1/2$ (possible); the meaning of implication $p \Rightarrow q$ was determined as $\min(1, 1 - v(p) + v(q))$, where $v(p)$ is the logical value of the proposition p; similarly negation was determined by the condition $v(\neg p) = 1 - v(p)$.

The same formulas were used to define semantics of n-valued Łukasiewicz logic L_n and infinite-valued logic L_ω (where logical values are rational numbers from the interval $[0, 1]$). A complete axiomatization for these logics was proposed by Wajsberg (Rosser and Turquette, 1952). Other systems for many-valued logic were proposed by Post, Kleene and others (Rosser and Turquette, 1952; Urquhart, 1993).

In general, one may consider, for example, Łukasiewicz implication, negation, and so on, as interpreted as functions of suitable arity on the interval $[0, 1]$ *a fortiori* truth values may be regarded as real numbers from the interval $[0, 1]$. In real-valued logics, truth-functional definitions of propositional functors rely on real functions on $[0, 1]$ in particular on so-called t-norms and t-co-norms that, respectively, define semantics of conjunction and disjunction. Implications are usually defined by Łukasiewicz or Kleene implications or so-called residuated implications and negations are interpreted as decreasing idempotent functions on $[0, 1]$ (Kruse et al., 1994). The interest in many-valued logics grew rapidly after introduction of fuzzy logic by Lotfi A. Zadeh (see below).

6. Inductive Reasoning

Particular areas of importance for inductive reasoning are machine learning, pattern recognition, and knowledge discovery in data. Various specific approaches have been proposed for inductive (approximate) inference in these areas. In addition some universal paradigms for inductive reasoning have been developed like inductive logic programming (Muggleton, 1995), for example, fuzzy inference, rough inference, probabilistic and statistical reasoning. In what follows we will outline the basic ideas of these approaches.

Inductive reasoning (inference) can be described as an art of hypothesizing a set of premises P for a given set C of consequences in order to satisfy $P \vDash C$ (Michalski, 1993).

In the above scheme, the unknown element is a set P of premises but the semantic inference $\vDash$ also has to be specified. Contrary to logical deductive semantic consequence, the inductive inference $\vDash$ is not concerned with absolute truth-preserving but deals with approximations of concepts and, along with mechanisms for concept approximations, it should also possess mechanisms for generating degrees of closeness between any concept approximated and its approximation. These degrees may be expressed as numerical values or logical expressions. It is hardly expected that the inductive inference $\vDash$ may be defined abstracting from the specific background knowledge BK, that is, from the application context; one should rather expect a variety of inference mechanisms dependent on the context and extracted from data by using appropriate algorithmic tools. This seems to be a challenge for further development of logic.

A general scheme for inductive reasoning may thus consist of a mechanism for primitive concept formation and a mechanism for construction of complex concepts from primitives. All concepts are of approximate character and mechanisms for their construction must rely on some measures of closeness among concepts. It is important to realize that concepts may be defined in various languages and their comparison is effected by imposing measures of closeness on their extensions.

6.1. General View: Experimental Concepts and Approximate Definability

Background knowledge is often expressed by means of data tables (e.g., training and test examples in machine learning, pattern recognition, inductive logic programming). These data tables contain positive as well as negative examples for concepts to be learned or recognized; most often, the given examples form a relatively small part of the concept extension so we may not learn these concepts exactly but approximately only. In constructing approximations to concepts, the choice of a language for concept description (e.g., a language of logical [boolean] formulas) involving the choice of primitive formulas as well as inference mechanisms is very important. Finding a suitable language is itself a challenging problem in scientific discovery. Approximate definability is effected by means of some measure μ of closeness (similarity) on concept extensions; one of the more often applied measures is the Łukasiewicz measure μ_L (Łukasiewicz, 1913) based on frequency count, $\mu_L(A, B) = \mathrm{card}(A \cap B)/\mathrm{card}(A)$, where A, B are concept extensions, which was recently rediscovered by machine learning and KDD communities.

Some natural constraints can be put on concept approximations: (i) the extension of concept approximation should be consistent with the concept extension or, at least almost consistent, that is, consistent on training examples and having small error on test examples; (ii) some minimality (economy) conditions, for example, minimal length of concept description, universality of description or best adaptability. These conditions are applied in machine learning, pattern recognition, and KDD. Satisfying (i) as well as (ii) may be computationally hard (finding a minimal consistent description is NP-hard for propositional logic (Anthony and Biggs, 1992; Mitchell, 1997). Hence there are strategies for suboptimal approximations and as a solution to the concept approximation problem we usually obtain a family of concept descriptions parameterized by languages chosen or strategies applied for particular solutions.

The choice of a particular solution may be motivated by ease of adaptivity, computational complexity of procedures of parameter tuning, and so on. Let us observe that the choice of primitive concepts is actually a choice of an initial model (relational structure), which itself is to be discovered; an essential criterion is its expressiveness for concept approximations (see Chapter 9).

6.2. Relationships to Machine Learning, Pattern Recognition, and Inductive Logic Programming

To illustrate the relationship of logic to machine learning, pattern recognition, and inductive logic programming, we borrow an example from KDD. A decision rule may be expressed in the form:

$$a_1 = v_1 \land a_2 = v_2 \land ... \land a_k = v_k \Rightarrow d = v,$$

where $a_1, a_2, ..., a_k$ are relevant features (predicates) used to build formulas expressing approximating concepts and d is a (vector of) feature(s) used in formulas discerning concepts (decisions) approximated. An association rule (Agrawal et al., 1993; Fayyad and Piatetsky-Shapiro, 1996) is a decision rule in which the concept defined by the premise of the rule approximates the concept defined by the consequent of the rule in high degree (high confidence), that is, sufficient fraction of examples satisfying the premise satisfy the consequent as well and there is a sufficient (defined by a set threshold) number of examples supporting both the premise and the consequent. Similar ideas are exploited in machine learning and pattern recognition for estimating the strength of a rule.

The problem of selecting relevant features (Michell, 1997; Nadler and Smith, 1993) involves some searching procedures like discretization, grouping of symbolic values, clusterization, and morphological filtering. These procedures may be conveniently written down in propositional logic (see Chapter 9). These preliminary procedures define primitive concepts (features) for a given problem of concept approximation. This process leads from primitive features (variables; e.g., real-valued features, pixel-valued features to new intrinsic features (variables) at the gain being a more compact and a more general description of concepts. Another alternative in the search for features is to search for hidden features (variables)—possibly better suited for concept approximation—in terms of which one may define (possibly near-to-functionally) the existing features (variables).

Along with decision rules some strategies for classifying new objects (involving matching and conflict resolution strategies) are selected. The received classifier provides a concept approximation.

Inductive logic programming (ILP; Muggleton, 1995) bridges machine learning to logic programming (cf. Section 4). It gives approximate descriptions of relational concepts from given background knowledge and examples in the language of logical programs. Schematically, ILP may be expressed as inductive hypothesis H formation by means of Logic Programming tools such as relative least general generalizations and inverse entailment (Muggleton, 1997; Muggleton and Feng, 1992) in order to satisfy the implication $B \land H \vDash E$, where B, E are, respectively, background knowledge and examples. ILP systems have been applied to various problem domains (Muggleton, 1997; Muggleton and Feng, 1992).

7. Reasoning about Knowledge

In addition to reasoning with knowledge, that is, making inferences from a given knowledge base by means of a chosen inference mechanism, reasoning about knowledge involves inferences concerning properties of knowledge (e.g., complete/incomplete), fusion of knowledge from different sources (e.g., in distributed or many-agent systems), and communication and interface among various sources and bases of knowledge (e.g., fuzzy/ rough controller). These aspects are very important for KDD (e.g., data mining in the Internet).

As examples of logics reasoning about knowledge we mention fuzzy logic (Kruse et al., 1994; Zadeh, 1979; see Chapter 10), rough logic (Pawlak, 1991; see also Chapter 9), probabilistic logic (Adams, 1975; Pearl, 1988). The latter is based on evaluating evidence based on probabilities of inferences $p \Rightarrow q$. In these evaluations often one applies Bayesian reasoning based on the Bayes formula. Complex inferences may be carried out in semantic networks known as Bayesian belief networks, that is, graphical representations of causal relations in a domain.

An example of a logical system dealing with fusion of knowledge is mereological (cf. Leśniewski (1992)) logic based on rough inclusion (Polkowski and Skowron, 1996), that is, a predicate $\mu(X, Y)$, which for concepts X, Y returns the value of degree in which X is a part of Y. This idea involves necessity of a calculus for fusion of local rough inclusions at any agent as well as for propagation of rough inclusion degrees among agents.

8. KDD as a Logical Process

Data mining can be described as searching data for relevant structures (semantic models) and their primitive properties, that is, patterns. These relevant constructs are then used to discover knowledge. The process of knowledge discovery can be treated as a kind of inference process (classical, commonsense, and so on) based on the constructs found in the data mining stage, leading to efficient solutions of tasks like classification, prediction, and so on. The solutions provide us with descriptions of concepts of interest having satisfactory quality. The inference process has its own logic: in some cases it may be based on classical logic but in many cases, due to uncertainty, the logic of inference should be extracted from data as schemes for approximate reasoning (Polkowski and Skowron, 1996; Zadeh, 1979). In this latter case a very important issue is knowledge granulation and reasoning with information granules (Polkowski and Skowron, 1999; Zadeh, 1996, 1997), making feasible the reasoning process in case of complex problems like spatial reasoning (http://agora.leeds.ac.uk/spacenet/spacenet.html) where the perception mechanisms play an important role. Finally, let us mention that the inference process should be dynamically adapted to changing data. This causes the necessity to develop adaptive reasoning strategies that tune parameters of logical models (structures) and formulas to induce the optimal (suboptimal) concept approximations.

KDD currently faces problems related to cognitive and information aspects of perception and reasoning (Roddick and Spiliopoulou, 1999). This certainly stimulates investigations on foundations of logic toward the revision and redefining of its traditional notions (van Bentham, 1999). For example, the notion of a proof seems to evolve toward the notion of an approximate scheme of reasoning (extracted from data) due to uncertainty or complexity of search in possible proof space. Such a notion of a proof involves aspects of cooperation, negotiation, and conflict resolution among various agents attached to distinct (local) knowledge bases as well as admits a reduction of the proof size under acceptable loss of its exactness.

ACKNOWLEDGMENT

This work has been supported by grant No. 8T11C02417 from the State Committee for Scientific Research (KBN) of the Republic of Poland and by the ESPRIT-CRIT 2 project No. 20288. Andrzej Skowron has also been partially supported by a grant from the Wallenberg Foundation and by a grant from the State Committee for Scientific Research (KBN) of the Republic of Poland, No. 8T11C02519.

References

Adams, E. W. 1975. *The Logic of Conditionals, An Application of Probability to Deductive Logic*. Dordrecht, Netherlands: D. Reidel Publishing Company.

Agrawal, R., T. Imieliński, and A. Swami. 1993. "Mining association rules between sets of items in large databases." *Proceedings ACM SIGMOD Conference on Management of Data*, pp. 207–216. Washington, DC: Assoc. Comp. Mach.

Anthony, M. and N. Biggs. 1992. *Computational Learning Theory*. Cambridge, UK: Cambridge University Press.

Bazan, J. G., S. H. Nguyen, T. T. Nguyen, A. Skowron, and J. Stepaniuk. 1998. "Decision rules synthesis for object classification." *Incomplete Information: Rough Set Analysis*, edited by E. Orlowska, pp. 23–57. Heidelberg: Physica-Verlag.

Bentham, J. van 1995. "Temporal logic." In *Handbook of Logic in Artificial Intelligence and Logic Programming*, edited by D. M. Gabbay, C. J. Hogger, and J. A. Robinson 4: 241–350. New York: Oxford University Press.

Bentham, J. van 1999. "Logic after the Golden Age." *IILC Magazine*, December 1999. Institute for Logic, Language and Computation, Amsterdam: Amsterdam University.

Black, M. 1937. "Vagueness—an exercise in logical analysis." *Philosophy Sci.* **4**: 427–455.

Codd, E. F. 1970. "A relational model for large shared data banks." *Commun. ACM.* **13**: 377–387.

Davis, M. 1958. *Computability and Unsolvability.* New York: McGraw-Hill.

Dubois, D. and H. Prade. 1998. "Belief Change." In *Handbook of Defeasible Reasoning and Uncertainty Management Systems*, edited by D. M. Gabbay and Ph. Smets, Volume 3. Dordrecht, Netherlands: Kluwer Academic Publishers.

Egenhofer, M. J. and R. G. Golledge. (eds). 1997. *Spatial and Temporal Reasoning in Geographic Information Systems.* Oxford: Oxford University Press.

Eisinger, M. and H. J. Ohlbach. 1993. "Deduction systems based on resolution." In *Handbook of Logic in Artificial Intelligence and Logic Programming*, edited by D. M. Gabbay, C. J. Hogger, and J. A. Robinson, **3**: 183–271. New York: Oxford University Press.

Fagin, R., J. Y. Halpern, Y. Moses, and M. Y. Vardi. 1995. *Reasoning about Knowledge.* Cambridge, MA: MIT Press.

Fayyad, U. and G. Piatetsky-Shapiro. (eds). 1996. *Advances in Knowledge Discovery and Data Mining.* Cambridge, MA: MIT and AAAI Press.

Fitting, M. 1993. "Basic modal logic." In *Handbook of Logic in Artificial Intelligence and Logic Programming*, edited by D. M. Gabbay, C. J. Hogger, and J. A. Robinson, **3**: 368–438. New York: Oxford University Press.

Garey, M. R. and D. S. Johnson. 1979. *Computers and Intractability. A Guide to the Theory of NP-completeness.* New York: W. H. Freeman and Company.

Geffner, H. 1992. *Default Reasoning: Causal and Conditional Theories.* Cambridge, MA: MIT Press.

Gonzalez, A. J. and D. D. Dankel. 1993. *The Engineering of Knowledge Based Systems: Theory and Practice.* Englewood Cliffs, NJ: Prentice-Hall.

Gödel, K. 1930. "die Vollständigkeit der Axiome des Logischen Funktionenkalküls." *Monatshefte für Mathematik und Physik* **37**: 349–360.

Halpern, J. Y. 1995. "Reasoning about knowledge: a survey." In *Handbook of Logic in Artificial Intelligence and Logic Programming*, edited by D. M. Gabbay, C. J. Hogger, and J. A. Robinson, **4**: 1–34. New York: Oxford University Press.

Harel, D. 1994. "Dynamic logic." *Handbook of Philosophical Logic*, edited by D. M. Gabbay, and F. Guenthner **2**: 497–604. Dordrecht, Netherlands: Kluwer Academic Publishers.

Hintikka, J. 1962. *Knowledge and Belief.* Ithaca, NY: Cornell University Press.

Hodges, W. 1993. "Logical features of Horn clauses." In *Handbook of Logic in Artificial Intelligence and Logic Programming*, edited by D. M. Gabbay, C. J. Hogger, and J. A. Robinson, **3**: 449–503. New York: Oxford University Press.

Hughes, G. E. and M. J. Creswell. 1968. *An Introduction to Modal Logic.* London: Methuen.

Huhns, M. N. and M. P. Singh. (eds). 1998. *Readings in Agents.* San Mateo, CA: Morgan Kaufmann.

Konolige, K. 1993. "Autoepistemic logic." In *Handbook of Logic in Artificial Intelligence and Logic Programming*, edited by D. M. Gabbay, C. J. Hogger, and J. A. Robinson, **3**: 217–295. New York: Oxford University Press.

Kruse, R., J. Gebhardt, and F. Klawonn. 1994. *Foundations of Fuzzy Systems.* New York: J. Wiley.

Lifschitz, V. 1993. "Circumscription." *Handbook of Logic in Artificial Intelligence and Logic Programming*, edited by D. M. Gabbay, C. J. Hogger, and J. A. Robinson, **3**: 297–352. New York: Oxford University Press.

Leśniewski, S. 1992. "On the foundations of mathematics." In *Stanisław Leśniewski. Collected Works*, edited by S. Surma, J. T. Srzednicki, D. I. Barnett, and F. V. Rickey, pp. 174–382. Dordrecht, Netherlands: Kluwer Academic Publishers.

Lloyd, J. W. 1984. *Foundations of Logic Programming.* Berlin: Springer-Verlag.

Lukasiewicz J. 1913. *Die logischen Grundlagen der Wahrscheinchkeitsrechnung*, Krakow. Also in: L. Borkouski (ed.), Jan Lukasiewicz—Selected Works, North-Holland Publ. Co., Amsterdam, 1970

Lukasiewicz, J. 1930. "Philosophische Bemerkungen zu mehrwertigen Systemen des Aussagenkalküls." *Comptes rendus de la Société des Sciences et des Lettres de Varsovie* **23**: 57–77.

Makinson, D. 1993. "General patterns in non-monotonic reasoning." In *Handbook of Logic in Artificial Intelligence and Logic Programming*, edited by D. M. Gabbay, C. J. Hogger, and J. A. Robinson, **3**: 35–110. New York: Oxford University Press.

Mendelson, E. 1960. *Introduction to Mathematical Logic.* New York: Van Nostrand.

Michalski, R. 1993. "Inferential theory of learning as a conceptual basis for multistrategy." *Machine Learning* **11**: 111–151.

Michalski, R. and G. Tecuci. 1994. *Machine Learning. A Multistrategy Approach*, Volume 4. San Francisco, CA: Morgan Kaufmann.

Mitchell, T. M. 1997. *Machine Learning.* Boston, MA: McGraw-Hill.

Muggleton, S. 1995. *Foundations of Inductive Logic Programming.* Englewood Cliffs, NJ: Prentice Hall.

Muggleton, S. 1997. "Learning from positive data." *Proceedings of the Sixth International Workshop on Inductive Logic Programming.* Lecture Notes in Artificial Intelligence, Volume 1314. Berlin: Springer-Verlag.

Muggleton, S. and C. Feng. 1992. "Efficient induction of logical programs." In *Inductive Logic Programming*, edited by S. Muggleton. New York: Academic Press.

Nadler, M. and E. P. Smith. 1993. *Pattern Recognition Engineering.* New York: Wiley.

Nehmzow, U. 2000. *Mobile Robots: An Introduction.* Berlin: Springer-Verlag.

Pawlak, Z. 1991. *Rough Sets—Theoretical Aspects of Reasoning about Data.* Dordrecht, Netherlands: Kluwer Academic Publishers.

Pearl, J. 1988. *Probabilistic Reasoning in Intelligent Systems: Networks of Plausible Inference.* San Francisco, CA: Morgan Kaufmann.

Polkowski, L. and A. Skowron. 1996. "Rough mereology: a new paradigm for approximate reasoning." *Int. J. Approximate Reasoning* **15(4)**: 333–365.

Polkowski, L. and A. Skowron. 1999. "Towards adaptive calculus of granules." *Computing with Words in Information/Intelligent Systems*, edited by L. A. Zadeh and J. Kacprzyk. **1**: 201–227. Heidelberg: Physica-Verlag.

Poole, D. 1993. "Default logic." In *Handbook of Logic in Artificial Intelligence and Logic Programming*, edited by D. M. Gabbay, C. J. Hogger, and J. A. Robinson, **3**: 189–216. New York: Oxford University Press.

Rescher, N. 1969. *Many-valued Logics.* New York: McGraw Hill.

Roddick, J. F. and M. Spiliopoulou. 1999. "A bibliography of temporal, spatial, and temporal data mining research." *Newsletter of the Special Interest Group (SIG) on Knowledge Discovery and Data Mining* **1(1)**: 34–38.

Rosser, J. B. and A. R. Turquette. 1952. *Many-valued Logics.* Amsterdam: North-Holland.

Rumelhart, D. E. and J. L. McClelland. 1986. *Parallel Distributed Processing: Explorations in the Microstructure of Cognition 1–2: Foundations/Psychological and Biological Models.* Cambridge, MA: The MIT Press.

Russell, B. 1923. "Vagueness." *Aust. J. Philosophy* **1**: 84–92.

Russel, S. J. and P. Norvig. 1995. *Artificial Intelligence. A Modern Approach.* Englewood Cliffs, NJ: Prentice-Hall.

Sandewall, E. and Y. Shoham. 1995. "Non-monotonic temporal reasoning." In *Handbook of Logic in Artificial Intelligence and Logic Programming*, edited by D. M. Gabbay, C. J. Hogger, and J. A. Robinson. **4**: 439–498. New York: Oxford University Press.

Selman, B., H. Kautz, and D. McAllester. August, 1997. "Ten challenges in propositional reasoning and search." *Proceedings of the Fifteenth International Joint Conference on Artificial Intelligence (IJCAI'97).* San Fransisco: Morgan Kaufmann Publ., pp. 50–54. Nagoya, Aichi, Japan.

Tarski, A. 1956. "On the concept of logical consequence." In *Logic, Semantics, Metamathematics.* Oxford: Oxford University Press.

Tarski, A. 1936. "Der Wahrheitsbegriff in den Formalisierten Sprachen." *Studia Philosophica* **1**: 261–405.

Tsang, E. 1993. *Foundations of Constraint Satisfaction.* London: Academic Press.

Ullman, J. D. and J. Widom. 1997. *A First Course in Database Systems.* Englewood Cliffs, NJ: Prentice-Hall.

Urquhart, A. 1993. "Many-valued logic." In *Handbook of Logic in Artificial Intelligence and Logic Programming*, edited by D. M. Gabbay, C. J. Hogger, and J. A. Robinson, **3**: 71–116. New York: Oxford University Press.

Wille, R. 1996. *Formale Begriffsanalyse: Mathematische Grundlagen.* Berlin: Springer-Verlag.

Von Wright, G. H. 1951. *An Essay in Modal Logic.* Amsterdam: North-Holland.

Zadeh, L. A. 1965. "Fuzzy sets." *Inform. Control* **8**: 333–353.

Zadeh, L. A. 1979. "A theory of approximate reasoning." In *Machine Intelligence*, edited by J. E. Hayes, D. Michie, and L. C. Mikulich, **9**: 149–194. New York: John Wiley.

Zadeh, L. A. 1996. "Fuzzy logic = computing with words." *IEEE Trans. Fuzzy Sys.* **4**: 103–111.

Zadeh, L. A. 1997. "Toward a theory of fuzzy information granulation and its certainty in human reasoning and fuzzy logic." *Fuzzy Sets Sys.* **90**: 111–127.

8   STATISTICS PERSPECTIVE ON DATA AND KNOWLEDGE

David Madigan and Martha Nason

ABSTRACT   We describe some classical statistical ideas concerning samples and populations, testing, estimation, and prediction. We briefly discuss the Bayesian approach to statistical inference and also provide some cautionary notes.

1. Introduction

The field of Statistics develops methodology for data analysis. Key statistical activities include experimental design, exploratory data analysis, prediction, sampling, stochastic modeling, and testing. Traditionally statistics has closely aligned itself with mathematics, and much statistical research has focused on often arcane mathematical properties of statistical artifacts. Increasingly, however, major developments in statistics draw as much from computer science as from mathematics. The emergence of massive data sets and ever more sophisticated modeling requirements are having a profound effect on the cutting edge of statistical research and practice.

In what follows we will attempt to touch on some of the big ideas in statistics such as:

- *Sampling.* A random sample of 1500 from a population of millions or even billions can estimate the percentage of the entire population who have a certain trait or opinion to within 3 percent. That is, the difference between the sample-based estimate and the correct answer is no more than 3 percent for 95 percent of such random samples.

- *Experimentation.* Advances in experimental design have revolutionized fields as diverse as medicine and manufacturing. Standard methods allow us to routinely and reliably infer causation from practically-sized experiments.

- *Prediction.* A staggering array of statistical techniques is now available to facilitate well-calibrated predictions about future observables. No forecaster has a crystal ball, but intelligently chosen statistical approaches can properly account for uncertainty and improve the quality of decision making under uncertainty.

- *Visualization.* Developments in statistical graphics now enable viewing of up to 100,000 data points in 20 or more dimensions—see, for example, http://www.research.att.com/andreas/xgobi/ or http://www.visualinsights.com.

- *Bayesian inference.* Until quite recently, Bayesian inference occupied a quirky statistical backwater. Bayesians were long on talk but short on action. Developments in Monte Carlo methods combined with raw computing power have changed all that, and the frontline statistical journals are packed with elaborate Bayesian applications.

The diversity of activity within statistics is striking and no two statisticians would agree on what constitutes the core of the field (not even the two authors of this chapter). In what follows we will endeavor to cover a broad spectrum of ideas and topics but we will fail in our effort to be comprehensive. We should also note at the outset that the statistical process spans a range of activities from gathering data to looking at data to making inferences about unobserved quantities. In what follows we will focus almost entirely on this last activity. For an overview of state-of-the-art statistical practice see, for example, Venables and Ripley (1999).

Section 2 introduces some of the basic ideas that, for better or for worse, define elementary statistics as taught the world over. Section 3 briefly introduces the idea of statistical hypothesis testing. Section 4 introduces the Bayesian perspective. Finally, Section 5 provides cautionary advice on nonexperimental data.

2. A Nonrandom Sample of Mathematical Statistics

The canonical mathematical statistical task is to use a sample to estimate some characteristic of a (possibly apocryphal) population. Examples of populations include all Amazon.com shoppers in 1999, telephone calls on the AT&T network during 2000, or freeway interchanges in the United States. The goal is to estimate (guess) some characteristic of the population, such as the population mean μ. For example, Amazon.com might be interested in estimating the average customer household income in 1999. Imagine that Amazon is somehow able to obtain a simple random sample of n customers and record their household incomes as $x_1, ..., x_n$. We can then compute the sample mean household income $\bar{x}_n$. The value of the sample mean is an obviously reasonable guess for the value of the population mean (although not the only possible guess). For more discussion of simple random sampling and other sampling schemes, see Chapter 14.1 of this handbook.

This model of sampling from a fixed and countable population has the advantage that its theoretical properties are well understood. It is important to be aware, however, that it abstracts away many practically important issues such as the fact that samples are rarely random and populations are often ill-defined and dynamic in nature. With that caveat, we now explore some of the basic theory.

The general idea is that while we can't say much about the discrepancy between μ and the particular $\bar{x}_n$ that our random sample has provided, we can make precise statements about the family of $\bar{x}_n$'s, ($\mathscr{F}$) that our sampling procedure might have provided:

1. The sample mean is an unbiased estimate of the population mean. That is, the average value of the $\bar{x}_n$'s in $\mathscr{F}$ is μ.

2. The standard deviation of the $\bar{x}_n$'s in $\mathscr{F}$ is equal to the standard deviation of the population (σ), divided by the square root of n.

3. For n bigger than 30 or so, the probability distribution of the $\bar{x}_n$'s in $\mathscr{F}$ is Gaussian with mean μ and standard deviation $\frac{\sigma}{\sqrt{n}}$. This result is known as the central limit theorem.

4. The sample mean is a consistent estimate of the population mean. That is, as the sample size n gets larger, $\bar{x}_n$ converges to μ.

2.1. Random Variables

Our goal in this section is to introduce abstractions that allow us to prove statements like "the average of sample means is the population mean" or "the standard deviation of sample means decreases like $1/\sqrt{n}$, where n is the sample size." (This section draws in part from lecture notes prepared by Werner Stuetzle.)

We refer to the process of randomly sampling an individual from the population, and recording the number associated with that individual (for example his or her age), as observing a random variable. We denote random variables by capital letters $X, Y, ...$ Note that a random variable is not a number; you obtain a number by observing a random variable.

Random variables can be continuous or discrete. A random variable is discrete if observing it can only give a countable set of values. Common examples of discrete variables include sex or ethnic group. If it can take any value within a range of values, such as income, it is called continuous.

A random variable is characterized by its distribution. Suppose X is a discrete random variable with k possible values. Then its distribution is specified by the corresponding probabilities $p_1, ..., p_k$. If X is a continuous random variable, its distribution is specified by a density function $p(x)$. In either case we refer to p as the probability density of the random variable.

The average or expected value of the random variable X is defined as

$$\mathbf{E}(X) = \sum_i x_i p_i$$

if X is discrete, or

$$\mathbf{E}(X) = \int x \ p(x) \ dx$$

if X is continuous.

The variance of the random variable X is defined as

$$\mathbf{var}(X) = \mathbf{E}(X - \mathbf{E}(X))^2.$$

Suppose we have two random variables X and Y with probability densities p_X and p_Y. For example, let X be the dollar value of the 1999 book purchases of a randomly chosen amazon. com shopper, and let Y be the dollar value of the shopper's 1999 music purchases. Clearly, the densities p_X and p_Y do not completely describe the situation, because we lose the information that, in general, customers who spend a lot on books at amazon.com are probably more likely to also spend a lot on music products. To completely describe the situation we need to know the joint density $p(x, y)$. Specifically, the probability of picking a shopper with book purchases between x_{low} and x_{high}, and music purchases between y_{low} and y_{high} is

$$\text{Prob}([x_{low}, x_{high}] \times [y_{low}, y_{high}]) = \int_{x=x_{low}}^{x_{high}} \int_{y=y_{low}}^{y_{high}} p(x, y) \, dx \, dy.$$

An analogous equation holds if both random variables are discrete, with the integrals replaced by sums.

In contrast to the joint density $p(x, y)$ of the two random variables X and Y, the densities p_X and p_Y are called the marginal densities. Joint and marginal densities are directly related:

$$p_X(x) = \int_{y=-\infty}^{\infty} p(x, y) \, dy,$$

with an analogous formula holding for p_Y.

Suppose we restricted our attention to shoppers with a specific level of book purchases x_0. Within this group of customers there would be a distribution of music purchases, called the conditional density of music purchases, given book purchases $= x_0$, abbreviated $p(y \mid X = x_0)$. This conditional density $p(y \mid X = x_0)$ is proportional to $p(y, x_0)$, because all densities must integrate to 1; the following formula expresses this, and can be used as a definition for $p(y \mid X = x_0)$:

$$p(y \mid X = x_0) = \frac{p(y, x_0)}{\int p(y, x_0) \, dy} = \frac{p(y, x_0)}{p_X(x_0)}.$$

Two random variables X, Y are defined to be independent if the conditional density $p(y \mid X = x_0)$ does not depend on x_0 and thus is equal to p_Y. Intuitively, any two variables are independent if knowing something about the value of one gives you no information as to the value of the other. Straightforward calculations show that

$$\frac{p(y, x)}{p_X(x)} = p_Y(y),$$

and

$$p(y, x) = p_Y(y)p_X(x).$$

In other words, Y, X are independent if, and only if, the joint density is the product of the marginal densities.

The book purchases and music purchases of a randomly picked shopper presumably are not independent. On the other hand, suppose we randomly sample two shoppers, with replacement, and let X_1 be the book purchases of the first shopper, and X_2 be the book purchases of the second. It is reasonable that the distribution of the book purchases of the second shopper does not depend on the book purchases of the first shopper, so X_1 and X_2 are independent.

Now suppose we are not so much interested in the random variables themselves, but in some combination of them. For instance, $S = X + Y$ is also a random variable: we observe S by observing X and Y, resulting in two numbers x and y, and then adding the numbers, obtaining $s = x + y$.

We might now ask what the population average $E(S)$ of S is. As before, let $p(x,y)$ be the joint distribution of X and Y. The population average is the sum of the possible values, weighted with their probabilities:

$$E(S) = \int_x \int_m (x+y)p(x,y)\, dx\, dy = E(X) + E(Y).$$

So we have shown that the expected value of the sum of two random variables is the sum of the expected values.

This result applies to the context of estimating a population mean from a sample of size n. Let X_1 be a random variable that we observe by randomly choosing a member of the population, recording the property of interest, and putting it back. As discussed above, the expected value $E(X_1)$ is simply the population average μ. Define $X_2, ..., X_n$ accordingly. Obviously, $X_1, ..., X_n$ all have the same distribution and the same expected value μ. Now consider the sum $S_n = X_1 + X_2 + \cdots + X_n$, and the mean $\bar{X}_n = S_n/n$. Keep in mind that we observe S_n by observing $X_1, ..., X_n$, obtaining n numbers $x_1, ..., x_n$, and then computing their sum $s_n = \sum x_i$. Analogously, $\bar{x}_n = s_n/n$ is an observation of $\bar{X}_n$.

By the above fact,

$$E(S_n) = E(\sum X_i) = \sum E(X_i) = n\mu$$

and

$$E(\bar{X}_n) = E(S_n/n) = \frac{1}{n} E(S_n) = \mu.$$

In words: 'The average of sample means is the population mean'. We have proven mathematically that the sample mean is unbiased.

Now consider products of random variables. Let X and Y be random variables with joint density $p(x,y)$ and define $T = X\ Y$. The expected value of T is

$$E(T) = \int_x \int_y x\ yp(x,y)\, dy\, dx.$$

In general there is no simple formula for that. However, if X and Y are independent and thus $p(x,y) = p_X(x)p_Y(y)$, then

$$E(T) = \int_x \int_y x\ yp_X(x)\ p_Y(y)\, dy\, dx = E(X)E(Y).$$

So we have shown the analogous fact to the one about sums: if random variables X and Y are independent, then the expected value of the product $X\ Y$ is the product of the expected values.

In summary, the expected value of a sum of random variables is always the sum of the expected values. The expected value of a product is the product of the expected values if X and Y are independent.

Consider next the variance of a sum of random variables. Let X and Y be random variables with joint density $p(x,y)$ and define $S = X + Y$. To simplify notation, define $\mu_X = E(X)$ and $\mu_Y = E(Y)$. By definition,

$$\begin{aligned}\mathbf{var}(S) &= E(S - E(S))^2 = E(X + Y - E(X+Y))^2 = E((X - \mu_X) + (Y - \mu_Y))^2 \\ &= \mathbf{var}(Y) + \mathbf{var}(Y) + 2E((X - \mu_X)(Y - \mu_Y)).\end{aligned}$$

The last term is called the covariance of X and Y, abbreviated $\mathbf{cov}(X,Y)$:

$$\mathbf{cov}(X, Y) = E((X - \mu_X)(Y - \mu_Y)).$$

The covariance measures the degree of (linear) association between the two variables. In our example of books and music, the covariance will be positive. If X and Y are independent, then

$$\mathbf{cov}(X, Y) = E((X - \mu_X)(Y - \mu_Y)) = E(X - \mu_X)\ E(Y - \mu_Y) = 0$$

and thus $\mathbf{var}(X + Y) = \mathbf{var}(X) + \mathbf{var}(Y)$.

These calculations have established that if random variables X and Y are independent, then the variance of the sum $X + Y$ is the sum of the variances.

We will now apply this result to the context of estimating a population mean from a sample of size n. As before, let X_1 be a random variable that we observe by randomly choosing a member of the population, recording the property of interest, and putting it back. Define $X_2, \dots, X_n$ accordingly. As before, $X_1, \dots, X_n$ all have the same distribution and the same expected value, namely the population average μ. They also have all the same variance, namely the population variance σ^2, and they can reasonably be assumed to be independent. Now consider the sum $S_n = X_1 + X_2 + \cdots + X_n$, and the mean $\bar{X}_n = S_n/n$. We have already shown that $\mathbf{E}(\bar{X}_n) = \mu$, that is, the expected value of the sample mean is the population mean.

Let's now look at the variance of $\bar{X}_n$. We would expect $\mathbf{var}(\bar{X}_n)$ to decrease as n increases.

$$\mathbf{var}(\bar{X}_n) = \mathbf{var}\left(\frac{1}{n}\sum X_i\right) = \frac{1}{n^2}\mathbf{var}\left(\sum X_i\right) = \frac{1}{n^2}\sum \mathbf{var}(X_i) = \frac{1}{n}\sigma^2.$$

We have shown that the variance of means of samples of size n is $1/n$ times the population variance.

2.2. Confidence Intervals for a Population Mean

In the previous section we established that:

- The average of sample means is the population mean: $\mathbf{E}(\bar{X}_n) = \mu$.

- The variance of means of samples of size n is $1/n$ times the population variance: $\mathbf{var}(\bar{X}_n) = \sigma^2/n$.

Moreover, the larger the sample size n, the closer the distribution of sample means will be to a Gaussian distribution—this is the central limit theorem. Therefore, $\bar{X}_n$ has a distribution which is approximately Gaussian with mean μ and variance σ^2/n. Using known facts about the Gaussian distribution, we can say that on average, 95 percent of sample means fall in the interval $[\mu - 2\sigma/\sqrt{(n)}, \mu + 2\sigma/(\sqrt{n})]$. More practically, we can turn this statement around: for 95 percent of the sample means, the population mean falls in the (confidence) interval $[\bar{x}_n - 2\sigma/\sqrt{(n)}, \bar{x}_n + 2\sigma/\sqrt{(n)}]$.

This result does, however, depend on the usually unknown population variance, $\sigma^2 = \mathbf{E}(X - \mu)^2$. To proceed, one can use an estimate in its place. A natural choice for this estimate is $s^2 = 1/n\sum(x_i - \bar{x}_n)^2$. Simply replacing the unknown σ^2 by its estimate s^2 shows that $[\bar{x}_n - 2s/\sqrt{(n)}, \bar{x}_n + 2s/\sqrt{(n)}]$ is an (approximate) 95 percent confidence interval for the population mean μ. To compensate for the fact that we are estimating the standard deviation, it is common practice to make the interval a little wider, that is, going out a bit more than $2s/\sqrt{(n)}$ from the sample mean. Such intervals are called t-intervals and are based on the t-distribution. With a reasonably sized sample (say bigger than 30), however, this adjustment becomes irrelevant.

2.3. Some of the Notions Underlying Estimation

So far we have examined the properties of the arithmetic average of random sample as an estimate of a particular parameter, namely, the population mean.

In general there are three established ways of finding a point estimate for a parameter. The method of moments (MoM) is the simplest, and was the first historically, dating back at least to the 1800s. Method of moments estimates are found by setting the sample average (called the first moment) equal to the population average, the sample variance (the second moment) equal to the population variance, and so on as needed. We are using the method of moments whenever we estimate the population average by the sample average.

Another method which has significantly gained in popularity as computing power has increased is maximum likelihood; this is now the most common technique for finding estimators. Intuitively, the maximum likelihood estimate (MLE) for a parameter is the value of the parameter that makes the observed data the most likely. Likelihood plays a large role in

Bayesian analysis, and this technique which has become such a staple of frequentist statisticians has much in common with the Bayesian approach. In many straightforward situations, the MLE and the MoM estimates will agree.

The Bayesian approach (see Section 4 below) provides a variety of estimators, the most common being the posterior Bayes estimators. A posterior Bayes estimator for a parameter is the mean of the posterior probability distribution for the parameter.

Estimation almost always requires some set of enabling assumptions. One of the aims of statistical research is to find ways of obtaining good estimates while weakening the necessary assumptions. The subfield of robust statistics (Huber, 1981) looks for estimators which work satisfactorily with large families of distributions and have small errors when their assumptions are violated.

When comparing different estimators for the same parameter, all else being equal, an estimator with smaller variability will be preferred. Estimator variability is often measured by mean sqaure error (MSE). When closed-form expressions for the MSE do not exist, a variety of resampling and simulation techniques can assist with assessing estimator uncertainty. Several concepts have been developed to describe the important features of a good estimator. Paramount among these are the ideas of unbiasedness, sufficiency, efficiency, and consistency; we will touch on each of these briefly.

A statistic is said to be unbiased for a parameter if the expected value of the statistic is the parameter. That is, if you were to take an infinite number of independent samples from the same population and compute the value of the statistic in question for each of them, the average of these statistics would be exactly the parameter of interest. The discussion on random variables in Section 2 above proved that the sample mean is an unbiased estimate of the population mean. There may be an infinite number of unbiased estimators for a parameter, including some that make little sense: for instance, simply using the first value drawn for the sample as the estimate would be unbiased for the mean. Of these unbiased estimators, the one with the smallest variance is called the uniform minimum variance unbiased estimator (UMVUE), and is often a reasonable choice.

While unbiasedness is obviously a very important quality for an estimator, there are situations in which it may be willingly compromised. For instance, for some important parameters the only unbiased estimators have fairly large variance. That is, while they will average out in the long run to the true value of the parameter, they can be very far away from it in any specific instance. Other potential estimators for this statistic might have much smaller variance. While these candidates might be somewhat biased and not be expected to average out to exactly the true parameter value, with the smaller variance these estimators might be likely to fall closer to the desired value than their unbiased counterparts. We note in passing that maximum likelihood estimators are not necessarily unbiased.

For most meaningful estimators, the variance will decrease as the sample size increases. In fact, for many estimators the variance is inversely proportional to the sample size. When two estimators with this quality are compared, the ratio of the sample sizes necessary to have equal variances for the two is defined to be the efficiency of one relative to the other. Using a theoretical notion, the Cramer–Rao lower bound, it is possible to quantify the smallest possible variance for an estimator in any given situation. If an estimator achieves this lowest possible variance, the estimator is said to be efficient.

Sufficiency refers to an estimate's ability to capture all the information that is in the data about that parameter. For instance, if we were interested in estimating the average income of the customers for a particular business, and had collected information on 100 incomes, we could choose our estimate to be simply the income of the customer whose name came first in the alphabet. While this could serve as an estimator, it is clear that we would lose all the information provided by the other 99 customers in our sample. This would not be a sufficient statistic for the true population mean.

In order for an estimate to be considered consistent for a parameter, it must, with probability 1, approach the true value of whatever it is supposed to estimate as the sample size grows to infinity. It is worth noting that, while the example in the previous paragraph is indeed unbiased because we expect the average incomes of people whose names come early in the alphabet to be the same as the overall average, this estimate is not consistent. There is no reason to believe, no matter how large our sample got, that we would be closer to the truth by using the income of people whose names were alphabetically earlier and earlier. All of these criteria are important to consider when deciding on an appropriate estimator, and there is extensive information available as to the merits and usefulness of each in the statistical literature. Standard references include: Mood et al. (1974), Cox and Hinkley (1974), and Rice (1994).

3. Statistical Hypothesis Testing

The preceding section explored some of the basic ideas in statistical estimation. Now we turn to a more specialized form of statistical inference, namely testing. The basic idea is to test the plausibility of certain hypotheses in the light of the available data. Rather than repeating some of the mathematics of the previous section, we present an approach that is more computationally based. We begin with a simple example.

3.1. Pepsi and Coca-Cola

Several years ago, *Consumer Reports* set out to establish whether or not cola drinkers can tell the difference between Pepsi and Coca-Cola. They conducted the following experiment. They located 19 regular cola drinkers and 27 diet cola drinkers. They then gave each subject four unidentified samples of cola one at a time, regular colas for the one group and diet versions for the other. The subjects were charged with identifying each sample as Pepsi or Coke. According to *Consumer Reports*, "only" 7 of the 19 regular cola drinkers correctly identified all four samples. The diet cola drinkers did a little worse: "Only" 7 of the 27 diet cola drinkers identified all four samples correctly.

Consumer Reports' experiment raises several troublesome questions, but for now, we take the results on face value, and focus on the regular cola part of the experiment. Implicitly, *Consumer Reports* is considering two possible hypotheses. Either the subjects are just guessing the correct identity of each of the samples, or, alternatively, they are doing better than guessing. We refer to the former hypothesis as the *null hypothesis* (denoted by H_0) and the latter as the *alternative hypothesis* (denoted by H_A). By interjecting "only" in their text, it seems *Consumer Reports* is leaning towards the null hypothesis. It is clear that we cannot definitively rule out either hypothesis on the basis of this little experiment—even if H_0 is true and people are just guessing, they might be lucky and correctly identify many of the samples. None the less, we should be able to shed some light on the issue.

We proceed as follows. Suppose the null hypothesis is true (that is, the subjects were just guessing). How likely is it that as many as 7 of the 19 subjects would have gotten all four correct? We can calculate this exactly using the binomial formula:

$$\sum_{i=7}^{19} \frac{19!}{i!(19-i)!} \frac{1^i}{16} \frac{15^{19-i}}{16} \approx 0.0001$$

So, if the subjects were just guessing, the probability that as many as 7 of the 19 would have gotten all 4 samples correct is about 0.0001. So, it is possible that that they would have done that well even if they were just guessing, but it is unlikely. This certainly sheds doubt on H_0 (although we can't entirely rule out the possibility that H_0 is true).

To summarize, we started with two hypotheses: the null hypothesis and the alternative hypothesis. Next, we designed an experiment and gathered the data. Then we constructed a reference distribution of what results we would be likely to see if the null hypothesis was true (a binomial distribution in this case), and used this to calculate the probability that the data would have given as much support as it did for the alternative hypothesis (i.e., as many as 7 out of 19 correctly identifying all 4 samples), if the null hypothesis was actually true. That probability is called a significance level or *P*-value. In this example, it turned out to be fairly small, shedding doubt on the null hypothesis. Incidentally, the $\frac{7}{19}$ upon which we based the test is called a test statistic—a single number that measures the evidence against H_0.

Note that the kind of reasoning we just performed is sort of backward. What you'd perhaps like to do is reason forward from the data to make inference about the two competing hypotheses. Instead we assumed that one of the hypotheses was true (the null hypothesis) and computed how probable our data would have been in that case.

3.2. Two-Sample Tests

Consider an experiment to compare two classification algorithms, say naive Bayes (naive) and a multilayer perceptron (net). The experiment comprised five exchangeable replications for each algorithm and Table 1 shows the resultant test data misclassifications.

The mean number of test data misclassifications for the net algorithm is 100.0 as against 105.2 for the naive algorithm, so there is some evidence that the more expensive net procedure might be better. Do you find the evidence convincing?

On the basis of just ten replications, we could hardly expect to make a definitive statement one way or the other. However, we should be able to proceed as we did in the cola example and find some way to quantify the evidence.

Now we want to test:

H_0 : Naive TrueMean = Net TrueMean

versus

H_A : Naive TrueMean $\neq$ Net TrueMean.

As before, we will proceed backward. We will calculate the probability that we would have seen a difference as extreme as what we found in our pair of samples, if H_0 is actually true. The natural test statistic here is the difference between the two sample means, that is, $105.2 - 100.0$ or 5.2, and the question of interest then reduces to this: what is the probability that we would have gotten a difference between averages-of-five as far away from 0 as 5.2, if the true average difference really is 0?

To answer this we need to have some idea of the kinds of difference-between-averages-of-five that one would ordinarily expect to find when in fact H_0 is true. For instance, if differences-between-averages-of-five are always between -1 and 1, then we might consider that the evidence in favor of the net algorithm is very strong. On the other hand, if differences-between-averages-of-five are usually between -10 and 10, then the evidence in favor of the net algorithm would be very weak.

We need a reference distribution in order to figure out if 5.2 represents convincing evidence against H_0 or not. To find the reference distribution, we proceed as follows. If H_0 is actually true then any one misclassification tally in the set of ten could just as well be due to the naive algorithm as to the net algorithm. For instance, the data set of Table 2 (which we generated by randomly permuting the net and naive labels) would have been just as likely as the data set we actually got. This would have given a test statistic of $\frac{95+104+105+109+108}{5} - \frac{103+101+97+100+104}{5}$ or 3.2.

Table 1 Numbers of Misclassified Test Cases in Five Replications with Each Algorithm

Net	103	
Net	95	
Net	101	
Net	97	
Net	104	Sample Mean = 100.0
Naive	100	
Naive	105	
Naive	109	
Naive	104	
Naive	108	Sample Mean = 105.2

Table 2 A Random Permutation of the Labels in Table 1	
Net	103
Naive	95
Net	101
Net	97
Naive	104
Net	100
Naive	105
Naive	109
Net	104
Naive	108

We can continue in this manner and generate all permutations of the labels, or a random sample of say 100 of them, if exhaustive enumeration takes too long. In this case, there are actually only 252 permutations, so we can fairly easily compute all possible values of the test statistic. We end up with Table 3.

This provides the requisite reference distribution. Figure 1 shows a histogram of the values of the test statistic in Table 3. If the null hypothesis is true, the probability of getting a test statistic as far away from zero as 5.2 is about 8 percent. So, there is some evidence against H_0 but perhaps not very convincing evidence. Even if the algorithms are equivalent, you could get an average difference between two samples of five replications as large as 5.2 just by chance 8 percent of the time.

Historically, the computing power required to carry out an exercise like this was not widely available, so various short cuts were developed. Most of these depend on the central limit theorem: they rely on the fact the reference distributions which we have been calculating are well approximated by Gaussian distributions (or t-distributions). For the previous example, the standard approximation is the two sample t-test. You can find the formula for the two-sample t-test in any statistics textbook (e.g., Utts, 1996) and almost all statistical software and even spreadsheets like Microsoft Excel will perform t-test calculations.

3.3. Discussion

The hypothesis test comparing naive with net was a two-sided test. That is, the tests were of the form: $H_0 : x = y$ versus $H_A : x \neq y$. With this sort of test, we don't distinguish between positive evidence and negative evidence. For instance, in the classifier example of Section 3.2, if the test statistic had been −5.2 (indicating that the naive algorithm was better than the net algorithm) we would have gotten exactly the same significance level. In certain situations, you might be interested in conducting a one-sided test, where you look for evidence in one direction only.

Traditionally when researchers get a significance level of 5 percent or less, they declare their results to be statistically significant and reject the null hypothesis. This unfortunate practice has established itself despite long-standing warnings to the contrary. Neyman and Pearson (1933) and countless others have argued that the decision to reject or not reject a null

Table 3 Reference Sample of Differences of Averages-of-Five			
	Naive	Net	Test Statistic
1	100 105 109 104 101	103 95 108 97 104	2.4
2	95 108 104 105 109	103 97 100 104 101	3.2
3	103 95 104 109 101	97 104 108 100 105	−0.4
⋮	⋮	⋮	⋮
252	108 109 105 104 104	97 95 103 101 100	6.8

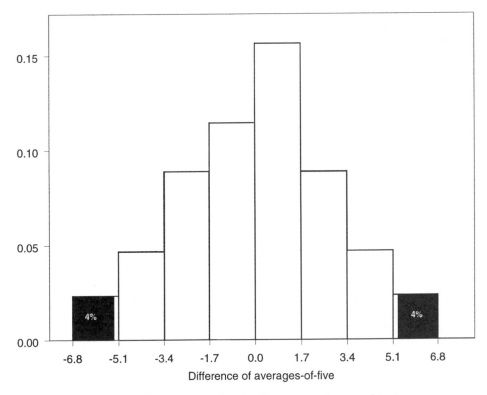

Figure 1 Reference distribution for the classifier comparative experiment

hypothesis must depend on the costs associated with the two types of error that we might make: we might reject the null hypothesis when it is, in fact, true (Type I error), or, we might accept the null hypothesis when it is, in fact, false (Type II error). (We note in passing that the statistical literature refers to the probability of not making a Type II error as the power.)

For instance, suppose an AIDS researcher develops a treatment that is cheap, has no side effects, and appears to be effective. Here we would not worry too much about a Type I error (i.e., concluding that the treatment really is effective when in fact it is not), since the cost of that kind of mistake is small. On the other hand, a Type II error in this situation (i.e., concluding that the treatment really is useless when in fact it is effective) has an enormous cost associated with it. In this case we would presumably want to adopt the treatment and make it widely available, even if the significance level was relatively large.

If instead the new treatment had significant morbidity and mortality associated with it, we would try to protect ourselves against the possibility of a Type I error by insisting on a smaller significance level before rejecting the null hypothesis. As a direct consequence, we would have a greater risk of making a Type II error with this same sample size, but this may well be justifiable here.

Traditionally, hypothesis tests center around P-values. There are, however, many specific difficulties concerning P-values, including:

- Raftery (1995) points out that the whole hypothesis testing framework rests on the basic assumption that only two hypotheses are ever entertained. In practice, data analysts will often consider very large numbers of possible hypotheses. As a consequence, indiscriminate use of P-values with standard fixed α-levels can lead to undesirable outcomes such as selecting models with parameters that are highly significantly different from zero, even when the training data are pure noise (Freedman, 1983).

- The *P*-value is the probability associated with the event that the test statistic was as extreme as the value observed, or more so. However, the event that actually happened was that a specific value of the test statistic was observed. Consequently, the relationship between the *P*-value and the veracity of the null hypothesis is subtle at best. Jeffreys (1980) puts it this way:

  I have always considered the arguments for the use of *P* absurd. They amount to saying that a hypothesis that may or may not be true is rejected because a greater departure from the trial value was improbable; that is, that it has not predicted something that has not happened.

- Schervish (1995) suggests a simple logical condition that any measure of evidential support should satisfy, namely that if hypothesis H implies hypothesis H′, then there should be at least as much support for H′ as for H. Schervish points out that *P*-values fail to satisfy this condition.

- Grimmett and Ridenhour (1996) demonstrate that while in general one might expect an outlying data point to lend support to the alternative hypothesis in, for instance, a one-way analysis of variance, it may in fact detract from the significance. Indeed, the value of the outlying data point that minimizes the significance level may even lie within the range of the remaining points.

In short, important, real-world decisions are complex. It is unrealistic to expect that a significance level on its own can provide a basis for a sensible and informed decision. To quote Deming (1940):

> So-called modern "theories of estimation" are not theories of estimation at all, but are rather theories of distribution and are a disappointment to one who is faced with the necessity of making a prediction from his data, that is, of basing some critical course of action on them. The conviction that such devices as confidence limits and Student's *t* provide a basis for action regardless of the size of the sample whence they were computed, even under conditions of statistical control, is too common a fallacy.

4. The Bayesian Viewpoint

The standard classical or frequentist approach to statistics revolves around the idea that we are trying to estimate fixed unknowns (or parameters) and it regards the data values before us as but one possible outcome of the supposedly random process of data generation. Thus with this approach the data are viewed as random and the unknowns as fixed.

With the Bayesian approach, we hold constant things we know, including the data values, and use the machinery of probability to quantify uncertainty about the unknowns. With this approach the data are fixed and the unknowns are random. This makes it easy to explicitly acknowledge the sequential nature of most learning: before the current data arrive, you know something about the unknowns (the prior information); then the data arrive, and your job is to quantify what you now know about the unknowns in the light of the data (the posterior information).

As a result of this distinction, Bayesian inferential statements tend to be easier to interpret, and it is often easier with the Bayesian approach to build highly complex models when such complexity is realistic.

As an example of the former assertion, consider the interpretation of interval estimates. A Bayesian 90 percent probability interval for a mean, for instance, has a 90 percent probability of containing the unknown mean. A classical 90 percent confidence interval, on the other hand, can only be interpreted in relation to a sequence of similar inferences that might be made with other data sets.

For a simple example of the second assertion, in medicine when researchers conduct, for example, blood enzyme studies on a representative cross-section of a population of interest, they often observe unexplained heterogeneity (which will appear in histograms or density traces as two or more distinct modes), and scientific interest then focuses on how many subpopulations have in effect been mixed together. Such *mixture* analyses with an unknown number of components are vexedly difficult to undertake using frequentist inferential methods, but are straightforward with a Bayesian formulation (e.g., Richardson and Green, 1997).

These advantages, however, come at an apparent price: the Bayesian approach requires the quantitative specification of prior information, which may be regarded either as a bug (it can be hard to do) or a feature (if you can do it well, you will get better answers) or a nonissue (default priors usually work just fine). Computational requirements also continue to be a big issue—notwithstanding the rapid progress of recent years, the application of Bayesian methods to massive data sets remains challenging. (This section draws in part from Draper and Madigan 1997.)

4.1. A Simple Example

Here we consider an example (adapted from Berry, 1997) that exemplifies differences between the Bayesian and frequentist perspectives. Consider an experiment in which a medical device is used to treat 100 patients and a particular outcome measurement is made on each. The design value for the device is a measurement of 0, but as is usual, there is variability from the design value even under ideal conditions. The goal of the experiment is to assess whether the mean μ of the measurements in some population of devices is in fact 0. That is, the null hypothesis is that $\mu = 0$. Suppose that the average $\bar{x}$ of the 100 measurements is 1.96 and the standard deviation is 10.

In a frequentist analysis one calculates a z-score:

$$z = \frac{\bar{x}}{\frac{10}{\sqrt{100}}} = 1.96.$$

Since 1.96 is the 97.5 percentile of the standard Gaussian distribution, the null hypothesis is rejected at the (two-sided) 5 percent level of significance. Put another way, the results are statistically significant with a P-value of 0.05. More precisely, if the population mean μ is indeed 0, observing a value of $\bar{x}$ as more extreme than that observed (that is, either larger than 1.96 or smaller than −1.96) has probability 0.05.

The 95 percent confidence interval for μ is given by (0, 3.92). If we imagine future repetitions of this experiment, then in 95 percent of them the interval thus constructed will contain μ.

In the Bayesian approach one computes probabilities for the parameters given all the available information. (There is a single parameter in the above example, the population mean μ.) The following questions are typical of those addressed when taking a Bayesian approach: What is the probability that $\mu = 0$ given the currently available data? What is the probability that μ is between −1 and +1 given the data? What is the probability that the next observation will be between −1 and +1 given current information? Such questions require Bayes' theorem and cannot be answered from a frequentist perspective. Addressing the first question, Bayes' theorem says:

$$p(\mu = 0 \mid \bar{x}) = \frac{p(\bar{x} \mid \mu = 0)p(\mu = 0)}{p(\bar{x})},$$

where

$$p(\bar{x}) = p(\bar{x} \mid \mu = 0)p(\mu = 0) + p(\bar{x} \mid \mu \neq 0)p(\mu \neq 0).$$

Bayes theorem is sometimes called the theorem of inverse probabilities because it relates $p(\mu = 0 \mid \bar{x})$ with $p(\bar{x} \mid \mu = 0)$. The former is called a posterior probability—posterior to the current data—and the latter is called a likelihood, the likelihood of $\mu = 0$. The probabilities for μ without conditioning on the data $\bar{x}$, such as $p(\mu = 0)$, are called prior probabilities because they apply separate from or before observing the data in the experiment at hand.

To proceed we need to specify prior probabilities for the various possible values of μ, including values different from 0. For expository purposes, let us make the (unrealistic) assumption that 0, 1, 2, and 3 are the only possible values of μ. Then the denominator of Bayes' theorem is

$$p(\bar{x}) = p(\bar{x} \mid \mu = 0)p(\mu = 0) + p(\bar{x} \mid \mu = 1)p(\mu = 1) + p(\bar{x} \mid \mu = 2)p(\mu = 2)$$
$$+ p(\bar{x} \mid \mu = 3)p(\mu = 3).$$

The likelihoods $l(\mu) = p(\bar{x} \mid \mu)$ can be probabilities or, as in the current case, densities. Under normal sampling where the standard deviation of $\bar{x}$ is 1,

$$l(\mu) \propto \exp - \left(\frac{\bar{x} - \mu}{2}\right)^2.$$

In addition to the likelihoods, evaluation of the posterior probabilities for μ requires prior probabilities $p(\mu)$. For now assume that the four possible models are equally likely: $p(\mu = 0) = p(\mu = 1) = p(\mu = 2) = p(\mu = 3) = \frac{1}{4}$. We now have the pieces in place to use Bayes' theorem and Table 4 shows the consequent results. The interpretation is now direct—the a posteriori probability that $\mu = 0$ is 6.2 percent.

A more realistic prior distribution for μ might be something like a Gaussian distribution with mean zero and variance 2. This leads to a posterior distribution for μ which is Gaussian with mean 1.31 and standard deviation 0.82. In turn, this drives conclusions such as $p(\mu > 0) = 0.945$ and $p(-1 \leqslant \mu \leqslant 1) = 0.35$. As for a 95 percent interval, the common choice is mean plus or minus 1.96 standard deviations which is $(-0.29, 2.91)$. There is a 95 percent probability that this interval contains μ.

4.2. Bayesian Modeling

For the pragmatic data analyst concerned more with functionality and flexibility than with interpretative niceties and philosophical drumbeating, the Bayesian approach to modeling also has much to offer. To begin with, however, we briefly describe the idea of the statistical model from a general perspective.

The construction and analysis of statistical models plays a key role in statistical practice. While modeling can be used as a descriptive tool, modelers are usually more concerned with prediction of future observables and making inference about relationships between variables. On some level, all statistical modeling draws on the idea that observed data comprise signal and noise. The two-fold hope is that the model can capture the signal and that the model can suitably hedge its estimates and predictions to reflect the noisiness of the data-generating mechanism.

Regression models are perhaps the most widely used statistical model class. In general, regression assumes that the outcome variable of interest is made up of a combination of functions of the other variables (signal), plus random variation (noise). For instance, suppose we have collected data on age and height from a group of children of both genders, and we wish to model height as a function of age and gender. A simple linear regression model would look like this:

$$\text{Height} = B0 + (B1 * Age) + (B2 * Male) + (B3 * Age * Male) + error,$$

where height is measured in inches, male is set to 0 for girls and 1 for boys, and we use a technique such as maximum likelihood to estimate the intercept B0 and the coefficients B1, B2, and B3. Suppose, for instance, after plugging in our estimates we arrived at a model such as

Table 4 Demonstration of Bayes' Theorem in Discrete Case

μ	Prior	Likelihood	Prior × Likelihood	Posterior
0	$\frac{1}{4}$	147	$\frac{147}{4}$	0.062
1	$\frac{1}{4}$	631	$\frac{631}{4}$	0.267
2	$\frac{1}{4}$	999	$\frac{999}{4}$	0.423
3	$\frac{1}{4}$	582	$\frac{582}{4}$	0.247

the following:

$$\text{Height} = 20 + (2 * \text{Age}) + (0.25 * \text{Male}) + (1 * \text{Age} * \text{Male}) + \text{error}.$$

From this, we would predict that a one-year-old girl would be 22 inches tall, and a one-year-old boy would be 23.25 inches tall. The difference between two girls one year apart in age would be predicted to be 2 inches, no matter what the ages of the girls are; for two boys a year apart we would predict a difference of 3 inches.

There are a few common-sense warnings about a model such as this. The first is that the model is no better than data upon which it relies. For instance, if the maximum age in the data set is 12, don't expect the model to make a good prediction for a 35-year-old male. Equally, if the modeler gathered the data at an NBA players union meeting, inferences about the general population will probably not be very useful.

The second warning is that any predictions or inferences we draw from it are only as good as our original assumptions were. If age is not in truth an approximately linear predictor of height then this model may not be appropriate and may moreover be misleading. Instead, we could explore using a different function of age in our model, such as an unknown coefficient times the logarithm of age. Since the logarithm changes faster for small numbers than for larger numbers, this model would postulate that the effect of age on height decreased as the child got older. Clearly a myriad choices exist here and a methodology for model selection is a must-have. The idea of model scoring is important here. A model score is any rule that maps models and data to numbers that specify a preference ordering over the space of models, given the data. Typical rules assign models a value determined by the likelihood function associated with the model, the number of parameters, and the data. Popular rules include the Akaike information criterion (AIC), Bayesian information criterion (BIC), and the minimum description length. In large samples, the Bayesian information criterion approximates the Bayesian posterior model probability, which is itself a scoring function. There is a notion of consistency appropriate to scoring rules; in the large sample limit, the true model should almost surely be among those receiving maximal scores. AIC models are not, in general, consistent. In some contexts, inference made using Bayesian scores can differ a great deal from inferences made with traditional hypothesis tests. Raftery (1995) gives examples of models that account for almost all the variance of an outcome of interest, and have very high Bayesian scores, but are overwhelmingly rejected by classical statistical tests.

The Bayesian approach to models such as the regression model just described is conceptually straightforward. The analyst first associates prior distributions with each of the parameters B0, B1, B2, and B3. Bayes theorem combines these priors with the likelihood to derive posterior distributions for the parameters. From these we can compute probabilities of arbitrary assertions about the parameters, as well as derive uncertainty bands for predictions. The form of the likelihood will depend on our model for the error term. If we assume independent and identically distributed Gaussian errors, then expressions for the various posterior and predictive distributions are available in closed form.

Whilst this is all well and good, perhaps a more compelling reason for adopting a Bayesian approach to modeling is the notion of a Bayesian hierarchical model. There are classical analogues but the Bayesian approach to hierarchical modeling is exquisitely straightforward. Consider the following fictitious example. Columbo Inc., a large healthcare corporation, owns 50 major hospitals. Total hip replacements (THR) are performed at each of these hospitals although the frequency with which the hospitals performed the procedure in 1997 varies from a minimum of 18 at one hospital to a maximum of 650 at another hospital. Columbo wishes to compare THR outcomes across the hospitals. One common outcome measure for THR is length of stay. A naive comparison of length-of-stay measures across the hospitals clearly could be quite misleading since it could well be the case that some hospitals handle more risky patients than others. A standard approach in these situations (Iezzoni, 1994) is to adjust for risk using a regression model like the one discussed above. So, here we have:

$$\text{Length-of-stay} = \text{B0} + (\text{B1} * \text{Risk}) + \text{error}.$$

(Customized risk scores exist for a large number of procedures and disease—see Iezzoni, 1994.) How should we estimate the parameters of this model? One possibility would be to lump all the patients together and ignore the fact that they attended different hospitals. This will almost certainly lead to tricky heterogeneity issues in modeling the error however, and affords no way to incorporate known hospital covariates such as hospital size or location. Another possibility would be fit a single model for each hospital, and then compare the risk-adjusted lengths of stay across the hospitals. However, it is clear that the model for the hospital with 18 procedures will be considerably less reliable than the model for the hospital with 650 procedures. Furthermore, the B1's for the different hospitals will presumably be somewhat similar, as will the B0's and the error distributions—fitting separate models ignores this fact. The Bayesian hierarchical approach allows us to bridge the gap between these two extremes. On the one hand it does use all the data. On the other hand, it allows for heterogeneity among the hospitals. How does it do this? The basic idea is to fit a separate model for each hospital, but to assume that the parameters of the 50 models represent a sample from a population of parameters. For instance, we might assume that the B1's for the 50 hospitals arise from a Gaussian distribution with some mean and variance *a priori*. In this way the different hospitals can borrow strength from each other—what we learn from the hospital with 650 procedures will sharpen our inferences about the hospital with 18 procedures, and to a lesser extent, vice versa. Incorporation of hospital-level data is also straightforward.

Draper and Madigan (1997) sketch a more detailed hierarchical modeling example. Freely available software called BUGS can fit quite elaborate hierarchical and nonhierarchical Bayesian models (Spiegelhalter et al., 1995; Gilks et al., 1996). See http://www.mrc-bsu.cam. ac.uk/bugs/ for further details.

5. The Pitfalls of Nonexperimental Data

Data mining applications typically rely on observational (as opposed to experimental) data. Interpreting observed associations in such data is challenging; sensible inferences require careful analysis, and detailed consideration of the underlying factors. Here we offer a detailed example to support this position.

Wen et al., (1995; WHN hereafter) analyzed administrative records of all Ontario general hospital separations (discharges, transfers, or in-hospital deaths) from 1981 to 1990, focusing specifically on patients who had received a primary open cholecystectomy. Some of these patients had in addition received an incidental (i.e., discretionary) appendectomy during the cholecystectomy procedure. Table 5 displays the data on one outcome, namely in-hospital deaths. A chi-square test comparing this outcome for the two groups of patients shows a statistically significant difference. This finding is surprising since long-term prevention of appendicitis is the sole rationale for the incidental appendectomy procedure—no short-term improvement in outcomes is expected. This finding might lead a naive hospital policy maker to conclude that all cholecystectomy patients should have an incidental appendectomy to improve their chances of a good outcome! Clearly something is amiss—how could incidental appendectomy improve outcomes?

WHN did separately consider a subgroup of low-risk patients. For these patients (using ten different definitions of low risk), incidental appendectomy indeed resulted in poorer outcomes. Paradoxically, it could even be the case that appendectomy adversely affects

Table 5 In-hospital Survival of Patients Undergoing Primary Open Cholecystectomy With and Without Incidental Appendectomy

	With Appendectomy	*Without Appendectomy*
In-hospital deaths, No. (%)	21 (0.27%)	1394 (0.73%)
In-hospital survivors, No. (%)	7825 (99.73%)	190 205 (99.27%)

Table 6 Fictitious Data Consistent with the Wen et al. (1995) Data

| | With Appendectomy | | Without Appendectomy | |
	Low Risk	High Risk	Low Risk	High Risk
Death	7 (0.09%)	14 (10.07%)	100 (0.06%)	1294 (4.71%)
Survival	7700 (99.91%)	125 (89.93%)	164 009 (99.94%)	26 196 (95.29%)

outcomes for both high-risk patients and low-risk patients, but appears to positively affect outcomes when the low-risk and high-risk patients are combined. WHN do not provide enough data to check whether this so-called Simpson's Paradox (Simpson, 1951) occurred in this example. However, Table 6 presents data that are plausible and consistent with WHN's data.

Table 7 displays the corresponding proportions of in-hospital death for these fictitious data. Clearly the risk and death categories are directly correlated. In addition, appendectomies are more likely to be carried out on low-risk patients than on high-risk ones. Thus, if we did not know the risk category (age) of a patient, knowing that they had an appendectomy allows us to infer that they are more likely to be lower risk (younger). However, this does not in any way imply that having an appendectomy will lower one's risk. None the less, when risk is omitted from the table, exactly such a fallacious conclusion appears justified from the data.

Returning to the original data, WHN provide a more sophisticated regression analysis, adjusting for many possible confounding variables (e.g., age, sex, admission status). They conclude that 'there is absolutely no basis for any short-term improvement in outcomes' due to incidental appendectomy. This careful analysis agrees with common sense in this case.

In general, analyses of observational data demand such care, and come with no guarantees. Glymour et al. (1997) list some of the potential pitfalls.

- Associations in the database may be due in whole or part to unrecorded common causes (latent variables).

- The population under study may be a mixture of distinct causal systems, resulting in statistical associations that are due to the mixing rather than to any direct influence of variables on one another or any substantive common cause.

- Missing values of variables for some units may result in misleading associations among the recorded values.

- Membership in the database may be influenced by two or more factors under study, which will create a spurious statistical association between those variables.

- Many models with quite distinct causal implications may fit the data equally or almost equally well.

- The frequency distributions in samples may not be well approximated by the most familiar families of probability distributions.

- The recorded values of variables may be the result of feedback mechanisms which are not well represented by simple nonrecursive statistical models.

Table 7 Proportion of In-hospital Deaths Cross-Classified by Incidental Appendectomy and Patient Risk Grouping for the Fictitious Data of Table 6

	With Appendectomy	Without Appendectomy
Low Risk	0.0009	0.0006
High Risk	0.10	0.05
Combined	0.003	0.007

There is research that addresses aspects of these problems, but there are few statistical procedures yet available that can be used off the shelf—the way randomization is used in experimental design—to reduce, but not necessarily eliminate, these risks. Standard techniques such as multiple regression, and logistic regression may work in many cases, such as in the appendectomy example, but they are not always adequate guards against these hazards. Indeed, controlling for possibly confounding variables with multiple regression can in some cases produce inferior estimates of effect sizes. Procedures recently developed in the artificial intelligence and statistics literature (Pearl, 2000; Spirtes et al., 1993) address some of the problems associated with latent variables and mixing.

It is important to keep in mind that there are almost always many different ways of looking at the same question. For example, suppose we were interested in investigating the existence of gender discrimination within a university. Perhaps the most obvious approach would be to compare the average salaries of men and women in, say, 1998; a *t*-test might then suffice to test the statistical significance of any observed difference. Since we would expect there to be other factors that influence an individual's salary, however, we might well want to take this analysis a step farther, using say linear models to compare these two groups of salaries while adjusting for other variables, such as degree or year hired. Once we have made this decision, a myriad choices face us regarding which variables we are going to include in our model. Not only are there likely to be a large number of combinations of variables for us to choose from, there are many ways of evaluating the importance of any given variable or set of variables. We could start with only our predictor of interest and add other covariates one at a time, or we could start with everything that might be relevant in the model and try to pare it down, or we could base our choice for a model solely on what we felt was appropriate for the scientific question, or we could try to choose the model that predicted a subset of the data with the smallest error, or we could aim for a simple model that allowed easy interpretations of its coefficients, or . . . Even once we have decided on our modeling strategy and our priority, there are still a multitude of choices to be made. Supposing we have set our mind towards regression, we must decide whether we will use linear regression or one of the many available nonlinear or even nonparametric techniques. Different analysts may make different choices about which variable to consider the response variable: for instance, instead of average salary in any given year, we could compare the magnitude of salary increases, or the probability of getting hired in the first place, or the length of time to promotion.

There is comfort to be had in the fact that different statistical techniques applied sensibly to the same problem will often lead to similar conclusions. However, this is not always the case. While Bayesian analysis is often attacked for its subjective nature, it should be kept in mind that the conclusions of most statistical analyses, classical and Bayesian alike, can often be drastically affected by the analyst's choices in selecting, displaying, and modeling the data.

References

Berry, D. A. 1997. Using a Bayesian approach in medical device development. http://www.stat.duke.edu/people/personal/db/CDRH.doc.

Cox, D. R. and D. V. Hinkley. 1974. *Theoretical Statistics*. London, UK: Chapman and Hall.

Deming, W. E. 1960. "Discussion of Professor Hotellings paper." *Ann. Math. Stat.* **11(4)**: 470–471.

Draper, D. and D. Madigan. 1997. "The scientific value of Bayesian statistical methods." *IEEE Intell. Sys. Appl.* **12**: 18–21.

Freedman, D. A. 1983. "A note on screening regression equations." *Am. Stat.* **37**: 152–155.

Gilks, W. R., S. Richardson, and D. J. Spiegelhalter. 1996. *Markov Chain Monte Carlo in Practice*. London: Chapman and Hall.

Glymour, C., D. Madigan, D. Pregibon, and P. Smyth. 1997. "Statistical themes and lessons for data mining." *J. Data Mining and Knowledge Discovery* **1**: 11–28.

Grimmett, D. R. and J. R. Ridenhour. 1996. "The effect of a variable data point on hypothesis tests for means." *Am. Stat.* **50**: 145.

Huber, P. J. 1981. *Robust Statistics*. New York: Wiley.

Iezzoni, L. I. 1994. *Risk Adjustment for Measuring Health Care Outcomes*. Chicago, IL: Health Administration Press.

Jeffreys, H. 1980. *Theory of probability*. Oxford: Clarendon Press.

Mood, A. M., F. A. Graybill, and D. C. Boes. 1974. *Introduction to the Theory of Statistics*. Chicago, IL: McGraw Hill.

Neyman, J. and E. S. Pearson. 1933. "On the problem of the most efficient tests of statistical hypotheses." *Philos. Trans. R. Soc. (Series A)* **231**: 289–337.

Pearl, J. 2000. *Causality: Models, Reasoning and Inference*. New York: Cambridge University Press.

Raftery, A. E. 1995. "Bayesian model selection in social research (with discussion)." In *Sociological Methodology*, edited by P. V. Marsden, pp. 111–196. Oxford: Blackwells.

Rice, J. A. 1994. *Mathematical Statistics and Data Analysis*. Stanford, CT: Wadsworth.

Richardson, S. and P. J. Green. 1997. "On Bayesian analysis of mixtures with an unknown number of components (with discussion)." *J. R. Stat. Soc. (Series B)* **59**: 731–792.

Schervish, M. J. 1995. *Theory of Statistics*. New York: Springer-Verlag.

Simpson, C. H. 1951. "The interpretation of interaction in contingency tables." *J. R. Stat. Soc. B* **13**: 238–241.

Spiegelhalter, D. J., A. Thomas, N. G. Best, and W. R. Gilks. 1995. BUGS: Bayesian inference using Gibbs sampling, Version 0.50. Cambridge, England: MRC Biostatistics Unit.

Spirtes, P., C. Glymour, and R. Scheines. 1993. *Causation, Prediction and Search*. Springer Lecture Notes in Statistics. New York: Springer-Verlag.

Utts, J. M. 1996. *Seeing Through Statistics*. Belmont, CA: Wadsworth.

Venables, W. N. and B. D. Ripley. 1999. *Modern Applied Statistics with S-PLUS*. Third Edition. New York: Springer-Verlag.

Wen, S. W., R. Hernandez, and C. D. Naylor. 1995. "Pitfalls in nonrandomized studies: the case of incidental appendectomy with open cholecystectomy." *J. Am. Med. Assoc.* **274**: 1687–1691.

9 ROUGH SETS PERSPECTIVE ON DATA AND KNOWLEDGE

Andrzej Skowron, Jan Komorowski, Zdzisław Pawlak, and Lech Polkowski

ABSTRACT   Rough set theory was proposed by Zdzisław Pawlak (1982, 1991) in the early 1980s. Since then we have witnessed a systematic, worldwide growth of interest in rough set theory and its applications. The rough set approach has been introduced to deal with vague or imprecise concepts, to derive knowledge from data, and to reason about knowledge derived from data. In the first part of this chapter we outline the basic notions of rough sets, especially those that are related to knowledge extraction from data. Searching for knowledge is usually guided by some constraints (Langley et al., 1987). A wide class of such constraints can be expressed by discernibility of objects. Knowledge derived from data by the rough set approach consists of different constructs. Among them there are reducts, which are the central construct in the rough set approach, different kinds of rules (such as decision rules or association rules), dependencies, and patterns (templates), or classifiers. The reducts are of special importance since all other constructs can be derived from different kinds of reducts using the rough set approach. Strategies for searching reducts apply Boolean (propositional) reasoning (Brown, 1990), since the constraints (e.g., constraints related to the discernibility of objects) are expressible by propositional formulas. Moreover, using Boolean reasoning, minimal description-length data models (Mitchell, 1997; Rissanen, 1978) can be induced since they correspond to constructs of Boolean functions called prime implicants (or their approximations). The second part of this chapter includes illustrative examples of applications of this general scheme to inducing from data various forms of knowledge.

1. Basic Rough Set Approach

We start by presenting the basic notions of the rough set approach (Pawlak, 1991), which was introduced to deal with imprecise or vague concepts.

1.1. Information Systems

A data set can be represented by a table where each row represents, for instance, an object, a case, or an event. Every column represents an attribute, or an observation, or a property that can be measured for each object; it also can be supplied by a human expert or user. This table is called an information system. More formally, it is a pair $\mathscr{A} = (U, A)$, where U is a nonempty finite set of objects called the universe and A is a nonempty finite set of attributes such that $a : U \to V_a$ for every $a \in A$. Set V_a is called the value set of a. By $Inf_B(x) = \{(a, a(x)) : a \in B\}$, we denote the information signature of x with respect to B, where $B \subseteq A$ and $x \in U$.

1.2. Decision Systems

In many cases the target of the classification, that is, the family of concepts to be approximated, is represented by an additional attribute called a decision. Information systems of this kind are called decision systems. A decision system is any system of the form $\mathscr{A} = (U, A, d)$, where $d \notin A$ is the decision attribute and A is a set of conditional attributes or simply conditions.

Let $\mathscr{A} = (U, A, d)$ be given and let $V_d = \{v_1, ..., v_{r(d)}\}$. Decision d determines a partition $\{X_1, ..., X_{r(d)}\}$ of the universe U, where $X_k = \{x \in U : d(x) = v_k\}$ for $1 \leqslant k \leqslant r(d)$. The set X_i is called the ith decision class of $\mathscr{A}$. By $X_d(u)$ we denote the decision class $\{x \in U : d(x) = d(u)\}$, for any $u \in U$.

One can generalize the above definition to a case of decision systems of the form $\mathscr{A} = (U, A, D)$, where the set of decision attributes $D = \{d_1, ... d_k\}$ and A are assumed to be disjoint. Formally, this system can be treated as a decision system $\mathscr{A} = (U, A, d_D)$, where $d_D(x) = [d_1(x), ..., d_k(x)]$ for $x \in U$.

Decision tables may be identified with training samples known in machine learning and used to induce concept approximations in the process known as supervised learning (Mitchell, 1997).

The rough set approach allows precise definition of the notion of concept approximation. It is based (Pawlak, 1991) on the indiscernibility relation between objects defining a partition (or covering) of the universe U of objects. Since objects are perceived by means of the values of the available attributes, objects having the same (or similar) values of attributes are indiscernible.

1.3. Indiscernibility Relation

Let $\mathscr{A} = (U, A)$ be an information system. Then with any $B \subseteq A$ there is associated an equivalence relation $IND_{\mathscr{A}}(B)$:

$$IND_{\mathscr{A}}(B) = \{(x, x') \in U^2 : \forall a \in B \, a(x) = a(x')\}.$$

$IND_{\mathscr{A}}(B)$ [or, $IND(B)$, for short] is called the B-indiscernibility relation and its equivalence classes are denoted by $[x]_B$. X/B denotes the partition of U, which is defined by the indiscernibility relation $IND(B)$.

We will now discuss what sets of objects may be expressed (defined) by formulas constructed by means of attributes and their values. The simplest formulas, called descriptors, are of the form $a = v$, where $a \in A$ and $v \in V_a$. (It is also possible to consider generalized descriptors of the form $a \in S$ where $S \subseteq V_a$.) The descriptors can be combined into more complex formulas using propositional connectives. The meaning $|\varphi|_{\mathscr{A}}$ of formula φ in $\mathscr{A}$ is defined inductively as follows:

1. If φ is of the form $a = v$, then $| \varphi |_{\mathscr{A}} = \{x \in U : a(x) = v\}$;
2. $| \varphi \wedge \varphi' |_{\mathscr{A}} = | \varphi |_{\mathscr{A}} \cap | \varphi' |_{\mathscr{A}}$; $| \varphi \vee \varphi' |_{\mathscr{A}} = | \varphi |_{\mathscr{A}} \cup | \varphi' |_{\mathscr{A}}$; $| \neg \varphi |_{\mathscr{A}} = U - | \varphi |_{\mathscr{A}}$.

The above definition may easily be extended to generalized descriptors.

Any set of objects $X \subseteq U$ definable in $\mathscr{A}$ by some formula φ (i.e., $X = | \varphi |_{\mathscr{A}}$) is referred to as a *crisp* (exact) set; otherwise, the set is rough (inexact, vague). Vague concepts may only be approximated by crisp concepts; these approximations are defined in the next section (Pawlak, 1991).

1.4. Lower and Upper Approximation of Sets, Boundary Regions

Let $\mathscr{A} = (U, A)$ be an information system and let $B \subseteq A$ and $X \subseteq U$. We can approximate X using only the information contained in B by constructing the so-called B-lower and B-upper approximations of X, denoted $\underline{B}X$ and $\overline{B}X$, respectively, where $\underline{B}X = \{x : [x]_B \subseteq X\}$ and $\overline{B}X = \{x : [x]_B \cap X \neq \varnothing\}$.

The lower approximation corresponds to certain rules while the upper approximation to possible rules (rules with confidence greater than 0). The B-lower approximation of X is the set of all objects which can be certainly classified to X using attributes from B. The set $U - \overline{B}X$ is called the B-outside region of X and consists of those objects that can be classified with certainty as not belonging to X using attributes from B. The set $BN_B(X) = \overline{B}X - \underline{B}X$ is called the B-boundary region of X, thus consisting of those objects that on the basis of the attributes from B cannot be unambiguously classified into X. A set is said to be rough (respectively, crisp) if the boundary region is nonempty (respectively, empty). Consequently, each rough set has boundary-line cases, that is, objects that can neither be certainly classified as members of the set nor of its complement. Obviously, crisp sets have no boundary-line elements at all. It follows that boundary-line cases cannot be properly classified by employing the available knowledge. The size of the boundary region can be used as a measure of the quality of set approximation (in U).

It can be seen easily that the lower and upper approximations of a set are, respectively, the interior and the closure of this set in the topology generated by the indiscernibility relation.

It is possible to consider weaker indiscernibility relations defined by so-called tolerance relations defining coverings of the universe of objects by tolerance (similarity) classes. An extension of the rough set approach based on tolerance relations has been used for pattern extraction and concept approximation (see, e.g., Nguyen, 2000; Nguyen et al., 1998; Skowron and Stepaniuk, 1996; Słowiński and Vanderpooten, 1999).

1.5. Quality Measures of Concept Approximation and Measures of Inclusion and Closeness of Concepts

We now present some examples of measures of quality approximation as well as of inclusion and closeness (approximate equivalence). These notions are instrumental in evaluating the strength of rules and closeness of concepts. They are also applicable in determining plausible reasoning schemes (Polkowski and Skowron, 1996, 1999). An important role is also played by entropy measures (see, e.g., Duentsch and Gediga, 2000).

Let us consider first an example of a quality measure of approximations.

ACCURACY OF APPROXIMATION

A rough set X can be characterized numerically by the following coefficient

$$\alpha_B(X) = \frac{| \underline{B}(X) |}{| \overline{B}(X) |},$$

called the accuracy of approximation, where $|X|$ denotes the cardinality of $X \neq \emptyset$ and B is a set of attributes. Obviously, $0 \leqslant \alpha_B(X) \leqslant 1$. If $\alpha_B(X) = 1$, X is crisp with respect to B (X is exact with respect to B); otherwise, for example, if $\alpha_B(X) < 1$, X is rough with respect to B (X is vague with respect to B).

ROUGH MEMBERSHIP FUNCTION

In classical set theory an element either belongs to a set or it does not. The corresponding membership function is the characteristic function of the set, that is, the function takes values 1 and 0, respectively. In the case of rough sets, the notion of membership is different. The rough membership function quantifies the degree of relative overlap between the set X and the equivalence class to which x belongs. It is defined by

$$\mu_X^B(x) : U \rightarrow [0,1] \quad \text{and} \quad \mu_X^B(x) = \frac{| [x]_B \cap X |}{| [x]_B |}.$$

The rough membership function can be interpreted as a frequency-based estimate of $\Pr(y \in X \mid u)$, the conditional probability that object y belongs to set X, given the information signature $u = Inf_B(x)$ of object y with respect to attribute set B. The value $\mu_X^B(x)$ measures the degree of inclusion of $\{y \in U : Inf_B(x) = Inf_B(y)\}$ in X.

POSITIVE REGION AND ITS MEASURE

If $X_1, ..., X_{r(d)}$ are the decision classes of $\mathscr{A}$, then the set $\underline{B}X_1 \cup ... \cup \underline{B}X_{r(d)}$ is called the B-positive region of $\mathscr{A}$ and is denoted by $POS_B(d)$. The number $|POS_B(d)|/|U|$ measures the degree of inclusion of the partition defined by attributes from B in the partition defined by the decision.

DEPENDENCIES TO A DEGREE

Another important issue in data analysis is discovering dependencies among attributes. Intuitively, a set of attributes D depends totally on a set of attributes C, denoted $C \Rightarrow D$, if all values of the attributes from D are uniquely determined by the values of the attributes from C. In other words, D depends totally on C, if a functional dependency exists between values of D and C. Dependency can be formally defined as follows.

Let D and C be subsets of A. We will say that D depends on C to a degree k ($0 \leqslant k \leqslant 1$), denoted $C \Rightarrow_k D$, if

$$k = \gamma(C, D) = \frac{| POS_C(D) |}{| U |},$$

where $POS_C(D) = POS_C(d_D)$.

Obviously,

$$\gamma(C, D) = \sum_{X \in U/D} \frac{|\underline{C}(X)|}{|U|}.$$

If $k = 1$, then D depends totally on C, and if $k < 1$, then D depends partially (to a degree k) on C. $\gamma(C, D)$ describes the closeness of the partition U/D and its approximation with respect to the conditions from C.

The coefficient k expresses the ratio of all elements of the universe that can be properly classified to blocks of the partition U/D by employing attributes C. It will be called the degree of the dependency.

INCLUSION AND CLOSENESS TO A DEGREE

Instead of classical exact set inclusion, inclusion to a degree is often used in the process of deriving knowledge from data. A well-known measure of inclusion of two nonempty sets $X, Y \subseteq U$ is described by $|X \cap Y| / |X|$ (see Agrawal et al., 1996; Polkowski and Skowron, 1996); their closeness may be defined by

$$\min(|X \cap Y| / |X|, |X \cap Y| / |Y|).$$

2. Searching for Knowledge

We have pointed out that the rough set approach was introduced by Z. Pawlak (1991) in order to deal with vague or imprecise concepts. More generally, it is an approach for deriving knowledge from data and for reasoning about knowledge derived from data. Searching for knowledge is usually guided by some constraints (Langley et al., 1987). A wide class of such constraints can be expressed using the rough set framework or its generalizations (e.g., rough mereology [Polkowski and Skowron, 1996] or granular computing [Polkowski and Skowron, 1999]). Knowledge derived from data by the rough set approach may consist of different constructs. Among these constructs are reducts, which are fundamental to the rough set approach; different kinds of rules (e.g., decision rules or association rules); dependencies; and patterns (also called templates); or classifiers. The reducts are of special importance since all other constructs may be derived from different kinds of reducts.

Searching strategies for reducts are based on Boolean (propositional) reasoning (Boole (1854), Brown, 1990) since constraints (e.g., related to discernibility of objects) are expressible by propositional formulas. Moreover, using Boolean reasoning, it is possible to induce data models with a minimum description length (Mitchell, 1997; Rissanen, 1978), since they correspond to the constructs of Boolean functions called prime implicants (or their approximations).

Searching for knowledge can be performed in a language close to data or in a language with more abstract concepts; this is closely related to the issues of feature selection and feature extraction in machine learning or pattern recognition (Mitchell, 1997). Let us also mention that data models derived from data by using the rough set approach are controlled using statistical test procedures (for more details see, e.g., Duentsch and Gediga, 2000). A thorough analysis of the quality of rough set classifiers, including discrimination and callibration, as well as the so-called ROC analysis (Swets and Picket, 1982), was originally introduced to rough sets in Øhrn (1999) and is available in the ROSETTA system (see Chapter 24.1.3).

In this section we present illustrative examples showing how the general scheme outlined above is used for deriving knowledge.

Finally, we would like to mention that extensions of rough sets (e.g., rough mereology [Polkowski and Skowron, 1996] or granular computing [Polkowski and Skowron, 1999]), have been developed for extracting knowledge and reasoning about knowledge related to more complex data models such as, for instance, those in distributed environments or related to qualitative reasoning (e.g., spatial reasoning [Roddick and Spiliopoulou, 1999]).

It is also worth making some remarks on Boolean reasoning here, since most of the methods discussed later in this chapter are based on generation of reducts using Boolean reasoning.

2.1. Boolean Reasoning

The combination of the rough set approach with Boolean reasoning (Brown, 1990) has created a powerful methodology that allows formulation and efficient solution of searching problems for different kinds of reducts and their approximations.

The idea of Boolean reasoning is as follows. Given problem P, construct a corresponding Boolean function f_P. This function has the property that solutions of problem P may be recovered from prime implicants of f_P. We recall that an implicant of a Boolean function f is any conjunction of literals (variables or their negations) such that if the values of these literals are true under an arbitrary valuation v of variables, then the value of the function f under v is also true. A prime implicant is a minimal implicant.

Using the rough set approach, searching strategies for data models under a given partition of objects are based on discernibility and Boolean reasoning (see, e.g., Komorowski et al., 1999; Nguyen, 2000; Nguyen et al., 1998; Polkowski and Skowron, 1998b,c; Skowron and Nguyen, 1999; Słowiński and Vanderpooten, 1995, 1999). This process also covers tuning parameters, such as threshold, used to extract relevant partitions (or coverings), to measure the degree of inclusion (or closeness) of sets, or to extract parameters measuring the quality of approximation.

It is necessary to deal with Boolean functions of a large size in order to solve real-life problems. Consequently, a successful methodology has been developed for computing many of the constructs important for applications such as reducts and their approximations, decision rules, association rules, discretization of real value attributes, symbolic value grouping, searching for new features defined by oblique hyperplanes or higher order surfaces, and pattern extraction from data as well as conflict resolution or negotiation. The methodology is based on discernibility of objects and Boolean reasoning.

Reducts are also basic tools for extracting from data functional dependencies or, to a degree, functional dependencies (for references see the papers and bibliography in Pal and Skowron, 1999; Polkowski and Skowron, 1998b,c; Skowron and Nguyen, 1999).

Most of the problems related to generation of the above mentioned constructs are of high computational complexity (i.e., they are NP-complete or NP-hard). This also shows that most of the problems related to, for example, which feature selection or pattern extraction from data, have a high intrinsic computational complexity. However, using the reasoning in the above methodology, it was possible to discover efficient heuristics returning suboptimal solutions to the problems.

The reported results of experiments on many data sets are very promising. In comparison with other methods reported in literature (see, e.g., Michie et al. (1994)), they show (see, e.g., Bazan, 1998) very good quality of solutions (expressed by the classification quality of unseen objects and time necessary for the construction of solutions) as generated by the heuristics. Moreover, a method to deal with large relational databases (see, e.g., Nguyen, 1999) and a decomposition method based on patterns called templates have been developed for processing large data sets (see, e.g., Nguyen, 2000; Nguyen et al., 1998). The former method (see, e.g., Nguyen, 1999) has shown that Boolean reasoning methodology can be extended to large relational databases. Its main idea is based on the observation that Boolean variables relevant to a very large formula (corresponding to an analyzed relational database) may be discovered by analyzing some statistical information. This statistical information can be efficiently extracted from large databases. The latter method is based on a decomposition of large data into regular subdomains that are of a size feasible for processing with previously developed methods. We will discuss this approach later.

Another interesting statistical approach is based on different sampling strategies. Samples are analyzed using the developed strategies, and stable constructs for a sufficiently large number of samples are considered as relevant for the whole table. This approach has been successfully used for generating different kinds of so-called dynamic reducts (see, e.g., Bazan, 1998). It has been used for example for generation of so-called dynamic decision rules. Experiments on different data sets have proven that these methods are applicable to large data sets.

Our approach is strongly related to propositional reasoning (Selman et al., 1997) and progress in propositional reasoning will bring further progress in the development of our methods. It is important to note that our methodology allows the construction of heuristics that have a very important approximation property. It may be formulated as follows: expressions (i.e., implicants) generated by heuristics close to prime implicants define approximate solutions for the problem (Selman et al., 1997). This property is important since the time complexity of heuristics generating implicants close to prime implicants may be much lower than for generating prime implicants.

In the following sections, we will discuss different kinds of reducts and their applications in deriving different forms of knowledge from data.

2.2. Reducts in Information Systems and Decision Systems

We begin with reducts of information systems. Given an $\mathscr{A} = (U, A)$, a reduct is a minimal set of attributes $B \subseteq A$ such that $IND_{\mathscr{A}}(B) = IND_{\mathscr{A}}(A)$. In other words, a reduct is a minimal set of attributes from A that preserves the original classification defined by the set A of attributes. Finding a minimal reduct is NP-hard (Skowron and Rauszer, 1992); one can also show that for any m there exists an information system with m attributes that has an exponential number of reducts. Fortunately, good heuristics exist that can compute sufficiently many reducts in an acceptable time.

Let $\mathscr{A}$ be an information system with n objects. The discernibility matrix of $\mathscr{A}$ is a symmetric $n \times n$ matrix with entries c_{ij} as given below. Each entry consists of the set of attributes upon which objects x_i and x_j differ.

$$c_{ij} = \{a \in A \mid a(x_i) \neq a(x_j)\} \text{ for } i, j = 1, ..., n.$$

A discernibility function $f_{\mathscr{A}}$ for an information system $\mathscr{A}$ is a Boolean function of m Boolean variables $a_1^*, ..., a_m^*$ (corresponding to the attributes $a_1, ..., a_m$) defined by

$$f_{\mathscr{A}}(a_1^*, ..., a_m^*) = \bigwedge \left\{ \bigvee c_{ij}^* \mid 1 \leqslant j \leqslant i \leqslant n, c_{ij} \neq \varnothing \right\},$$

where $c_{ij}^* = \{a^* \mid a \in c_{ij}\}$. In the following we will write a_i instead of a_i^*.

The discernibility function $f_{\mathscr{A}}$ describes constraints that should be preserved in order to maintain discernibility between all pairs of discernible objects from $\mathscr{A}$. It is necessary to keep at least one attribute from each nonempty entry of the discernibility matrix, which corresponds to any pair of discernible objects. One can observe (Skowron and Rauszer, 1992) that the sets of all minimal sets of attributes preserving discernibility between objects, that is, reducts, correspond to prime implicants of the discernibility function $f_{\mathscr{A}}$.

The intersection of all reducts is called core.

In general, the decision is not constant on the indiscernibility classes. Let $\mathscr{A} = (U, A, d)$ be a decision system. The generalized decision in $\mathscr{A}$ is the function $\partial_A : U \to \mathscr{P}(V_d)$ defined by $\partial_A(x) = \{i \mid \exists x' \in U \; x' IND(A)x \text{ and } d(x') = i\}$. A decision system $\mathscr{A}$ is called consistent (deterministic), if $\mid \partial_A(x) \mid = 1$ for any $x \in U$; otherwise $\mathscr{A}$ is inconsistent (non-deterministic). Any set consisting of all objects with the same generalized decision value is called a generalized decision class.

It is easy to see that a decision system $\mathscr{A}$ is consistent if and only if $POS_A(d) = U$. Moreover, if $\partial_B = \partial_{B'}$, then $POS_B(d) = POS_{B'}(d)$ for any pair of nonempty sets $B, B' \subseteq A$. Hence the definition of a decision-relative reduct: a subset $B \subseteq A$ is a relative reduct if it is a minimal set such that $POS_A(d) = POS_B(d)$. Decision-relative reducts may be found from a discernibility matrix: $M^d(\mathscr{A}) = (c_{ij}^d)$ assuming $c_{ij}^d = c_{ij} - \{d\}$ if $(\mid \partial_A(x_i) \mid = 1 \text{ or } \mid \partial_A(x_j) \mid = 1)$ and $\partial_A(x_i) \neq \partial_A(x_j)$, $c_{ij}^d = \varnothing$, otherwise. Matrix $M^d(\mathscr{A})$ is called the decision-relative discernibility matrix of $\mathscr{A}$. Construction of the decision-relative discernibility function from this matrix follows the construction of the discernibility function from the discernibility matrix. It has been shown (Skowron and Rauszer, 1992) that the set of prime implicants of $f_M^d(\mathscr{A})$ defines the set of all decision-relative reducts of $\mathscr{A}$.

In some applications, instead of reducts, we prefer to use their approximations called α-reducts, where $\alpha \in [0, 1]$ is a real parameter. For a given information system $\mathscr{A} = (U, A)$, the set of attributes $B \subseteq A$ is called α-reduct if B has a nonempty intersection with at least $\alpha \cdot 100\%$ of the nonempty sets $c_{i,j}$ of the discernibility matrix of $\mathscr{A}$.

2.3. Reducts and Boolean Reasoning: Examples of Applications

We will present examples showing how a combination of rough set methods with Boolean reasoning may be successfully used to solve several KDD problems. Reducts are the crucial constructs. They are (prime) implicants of suitably chosen Boolean functions expressing discernibility conditions, which should be preserved during reduction.

FEATURE SELECTION

Selection of relevant features is an important problem and has been extensively studied in machine learning and pattern recognition (see, e.g., Mitchell, 1997). It is also a very active research area in the rough set community.

One of the first ideas (Pawlak, 1991) was to consider the core of the reduct set of the information system $\mathscr{A}$ as the source of relevant features. One can observe that relevant feature sets, in a sense used by the machine learning community, can be interpreted in most cases as the decision-relative reducts of decision systems obtained by adding appropriately constructed decisions to a given information system.

Another approach is related to dynamic reducts (for references see, e.g., Polkowski and Skowron, 1998b). The attributes are considered relevant if they belong to dynamic reducts with a sufficiently high stability coefficient that is, they appear with sufficiently high frequency in random samples of a given information system. Several experiments (see Polkowski and Skowron, 1998b) show that the set of decision rules based on such attributes is much smaller than the set of all decision rules. At the same time the quality of classification of new objects increases or does not change if one only considers rules constructed over such relevant features.

The idea of attribute reduction can be generalized through the introduction of the concept of significance of attributes, which enables one to evaluate attributes not only in the two-valued scale dispensable–indispensable, but also in the multivalue case by assigning to an attribute a real number from the interval [0, 1], which expresses the importance of an attribute in the information table.

Significance of an attribute can be evaluated by measuring the effect of removing the attribute from an information table.

Let C and D be sets of condition and decision attributes, respectively, and let $a \in C$ be a condition attribute. It was shown previously that the number $\gamma(C, D)$ expresses the degree of dependency between attributes C and D, or the accuracy of the approximation of U/D by C. It may now be checked how the coefficient $\gamma(C, D)$ changes when attribute a is removed. In other words, what the difference is between $\gamma(C, D)$ and $\gamma(C - \{a\}, D)$. The difference is normalized and the significance of attribute a is defined by

$$\sigma_{(C,D)}(a) = \frac{[\gamma(C, D) - \gamma(C - \{a\}, D)]}{\gamma(C, D)} = 1 - \frac{\gamma(C - \{a\}, D)}{\gamma(C, D)}.$$

Coefficient $\sigma_{C,D}(a)$ can be understood as a classification error that occurs when attribute a is dropped. The significance coefficient can be extended to sets of attributes as follows:

$$\sigma_{(C,D)}(B) = \frac{[\gamma(C, D) - \gamma(C - B, D)]}{\gamma(C, D)} = 1 - \frac{\gamma(C - B, D)}{\gamma(C, D)}.$$

Another possibility is to consider as relevant the features that come from approximate reducts of sufficiently high quality.

Any subset B of C is called an approximate reduct of C, and the number

$$\varepsilon_{(C,D)}(B) = \frac{[\gamma(C,D) - \gamma(B,D)]}{\gamma(C,D)} = 1 - \frac{\gamma(B,D)}{\gamma(C,D)}$$

is called an error of reduct approximation. It expresses how exactly the set of attributes B approximates the set of condition attributes C with respect to determining D. Using a similar approach, Komorowski and Øhrn (1999) showed how feature selection can be applied to identify population subgroups.

Several other methods of reduct approximation based on measures different from positive region have been developed. All experiments confirm the hypothesis that by tuning the level of approximation, the quality of the classification of new objects may be increased in most cases. It is important to note that it is once again possible to use Boolean reasoning to compute the different types of reducts and to extract from them relevant approximations.

FEATURE EXTRACTION

The rough set community has been committed to constructing efficient algorithms for (new) feature extraction (Polkowski and Skowron, 1998c). Rough set methods combined with Boolean reasoning (Brown, 1990) have lead to several successful approaches to feature extraction. The most successful methods are: (i) discretization techniques (see, e.g., Nguyen, 1997; Skowron and Nguyen, 1999); (ii) methods of partitioning of nominal attribute value sets (see, e.g., Nguyen, 2000; Skowron and Nguyen, 1999); and (iii) combinations of the above methods (see, e.g., Nguyen and Skowron, 1999). The discretization problems and symbolic value partition problems are NP-complete or NP-hard which clearly justifies the importance of designing efficient heuristics.

Our illustrative example concerns symbolic (nominal, qualitative) attribute value grouping. We also present some experimental results of heuristics based on our methods that are applied to the case of mixed nominal and numeric attributes.

In the case of symbolic value attributes (i.e., without pre-assumed order on values of given attributes), the problem of searching for new features of the form $a \in V$ is, in a sense, from practical point of view more complicated than for the real value attributes. However, it is possible to develop efficient heuristics for this case using Boolean reasoning.

Let $\mathscr{A} = (U, A, d)$ be a decision table. Any function $P_a : V_a \rightarrow \{1, ..., m_a\}$ (where $m_a \leqslant |V_a|$ $a \in A$) is called a partition of V_a. The rank of P_a is the value $rank\ (P_a) = |P_a(V_a)|$. The family of

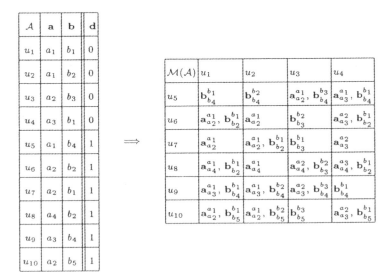

Figure 1 A decision table and its discernibility matrix

partitions $\{P_a\}_{a\in B}$ is consistent with B (B-*consistent*) iff any two objects u, u' discerned by B and d must be discerned by partition attributes defined by $\{P_a\}_{a\in B}$. We consider the following optimization problem:

Problem 1 (Partition Problem: Symbolic Value Partition Problem):
Given a decision table $\mathscr{A} = (U, A \cup \{d\})$ and a set of attributes $B \subseteq A$, search for the minimal B-consistent family of partitions (i.e., such that B-consistent family $\{P_a\}_{a\in B}$ that $\sum_{a\in B} rank\,(P_a)$ is minimal).

In order to discern between pairs of objects, will use new binary features $a_v^{v'}$ (for $v \neq v'$) defined by $a_v^{v'}(x,y) = 1$ iff $a(x) = v \neq v' = a(y)$. One can apply Johnson's heuristics (Johnson, 1974) for the new matrix with these attributes to search for the minimal set of new attributes that discerns all pairs of objects from different decision classes. After extracting these sets, for each attribute a_i we construct graph $\Gamma_a = \langle V_a, E_a \rangle$, where E_a is defined as the set of all new attributes (propositional variables) found for the attribute a. Any vertex coloring of Γ_a defines a partition of V_a. The colorability problem is solvable in polynomial time for $k = 2$, but it remains NP-complete for all $k \geqslant 3$. However, similarly to discretization, it is possible to apply some efficient heuristics searching for optimal partition.

Let us consider the example in Figure 1 of a decision table (presented on the left-hand side) and (a reduced form) of its discernibility matrix (presented on the right-hand side).

From the Boolean function $f_{\mathscr{A}}$ with Boolean variables of the form $\mathbf{a}_{v_1}^{v_2}$, one can find the shortest prime implicant: $\mathbf{a}_{a_2}^{a_1} \wedge \mathbf{a}_{a_3}^{a_2} \wedge \mathbf{a}_{a_4}^{a_1} \wedge \mathbf{a}_{a_4}^{a_3} \wedge \mathbf{b}_{b_1}^{b_1} \wedge \mathbf{b}_{b_4}^{b_2} \wedge \mathbf{b}_{b_3}^{b_2} \wedge \mathbf{b}_{b_3}^{b_1} \wedge \mathbf{b}_{b_5}^{b_3}$, which can be represented by graphs (see Figure 2).

We can color vertices of those graphs as shown in Figure 2. The colors correspond to the partitions:

$$P_{\mathbf{a}}(a_1) = P_{\mathbf{a}}(a_3) = 1; \quad P_{\mathbf{a}}(a_2) = P_{\mathbf{a}}(a_4) = 2$$

$$P_{\mathbf{b}}(b_1) = P_{\mathbf{b}}(b_2) = P_{\mathbf{b}}(b_5) = 1; \quad P_{\mathbf{b}}(b_3) = P_{\mathbf{b}}(b_4) = 2.$$

At the same time one can construct a new decision table (Figure 2).

One can extend this approach to the case when a given decision system contains nominal and numeric attributes (see, e.g., Nguyen and Nguyen, 1998). The heuristics obtained are of a very good quality. Experiments with classification methods (see Nguyen and Nguyen, 1998) have been carried over decision systems using two techniques called train-and-test and n-fold-cross-validation. Table 1 shows some experimental results obtained by applying the proposed methods MD (using only discretization based on MD-heuristics using Johnson's approximation strategy; see Nguyen, 1997; Skowron and Nguyen, 1999); and MD-G (using discretization and symbolic value grouping; see Nguyen, 2000; Skowron and Nguyen, 1999) to the classification tasks for some data tables from the UC Irvine repository. The results reported in Friedman et al. (1996) are summarized in the columns labeled S-ID3 and C4.5 (see Quinlan (1993)) in Table 1. Note that the heuristics MD and MD-G are also very efficient with respect to time complexity.

In the case of real value attributes, one can search for features in the feature set that contains the characteristic functions of half-spaces determined by hyperplanes, or parts of

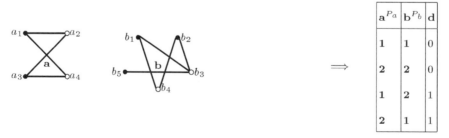

Figure 2 Coloring of the attribute value graphs and the reduced table

Table 1 A Quality Comparison of Various Decision Tree Methods and Our Heuristics

Names of Tables	Classification accuracy			
	S-ID3	C4.5	MD	MD-G
Australian	78.26	85.36	83.69	84.49
Breast (L)	62.07	71.00	69.95	69.95
Diabetes	66.23	70.84	71.09	76.17
Glass	62.79	65.89	66.41	69.79
Heart	77.78	77.04	77.04	81.11
Iris	96.67	94.67	95.33	96.67
Lympho	73.33	77.01	71.93	82.02
Monk-1	81.25	75.70	100	93.05
Monk-2	69.91	65.00	99.07	99.07
Monk-3	90.28	97.20	93.51	94.00
Soybean	100	95.56	100	100
TicTacToe	84.38	84.02	97.7	97.70
Average	78.58	79.94	85.48	87.00

Abbreviations: MD: MD-heuristic; MD-G: MD-heuristic with symbolic value partition.

spaces defined by more complex surfaces in multidimensional spaces. Genetic algorithms have been applied in searching for semioptimal hyperplanes (Nguyen, 1997). The reported results show a substantial increase in the quality of classification of unseen objects but at the price of increased time for searching for a semioptimal hyperplane.

DECISION RULES

Reducts serve the purpose of inducing minimal decision rules. Any such rule contains a minimal number of descriptors in the conditional part so that their conjunction defines the largest subset of a generalized decision class (decision class, if the decision table is deterministic). Hence, information included in the conditional part of any minimal rule is sufficient for predicting the generalized decision value for all objects satisfying this part. The conditional parts of minimal rules define the largest object sets relevant for generalized decision classes approximation. It turns out that the conditional parts of minimal rules can be computed (by using Boolean reasoning) as the so-called reducts relative to objects or local reducts (see, e.g., Bazan, 1998; Skowron, 1995). Once the reducts have been computed, the conditional parts of rules are easily constructed by laying the reducts over the original decision system and reading off the values. In the case discussed, the generalized decision value is preserved during the reduction. One can consider stronger constraints that should be preserved. For example, in Ślęzak (1998) the constraints are described by probability distributions corresponding to information signatures of objects. Once more, the same methodology can be used to compute the reducts corresponding to these constraints.

The main challenge in inducing rules from decision systems lies in determining which attributes should be included in the conditional part of the rule. Using the strategy outlined above, minimal rules are first computed. Their conditional parts describe the largest object sets (definable by conjunctions of descriptors) with the same generalized decision value in a given decision system. Hence, they create the largest sets still relevant for defining the decision classes (or sets of decision classes when the decision system is inconsistent). Although such minimal decision rules can be computed, this approach can result in a set of rules with an unsatisfactory quality of classification. These rules will be too detailed and will over-fit so that unseen cases will be poorly classified. Shorter rules should be synthesized instead. Although they will not be perfect on the known cases, there is a good chance that they will be of high quality when classifying new cases. They can be constructed by computing approximations of the above mentioned reducts. Approximations of reducts received by dropping some descriptors from the conditional parts of minimal rules define larger sets, not entirely included in the decision classes but included to a satisfactory degree. It means that these shorter descriptions may be more relevant for decision class (concept) approximation than the exact reducts. This leads to the following observation: if dropping a descriptor from the conditional part provides a description of the object set that is almost included in the approximated decision class, then this descriptor is a good candidate for removal. For example Bazan (1998), Ågotnes et al. (1999) use systematic approaches to pruning sets of classification rules.

For estimation of the quality of decision classes approximation, global measures based on the positive region (Skowron, 1995) or entropy (Duentsch and Gediga, 2000) are used. Methods of boundary region thinning (Ziarko, 1993) can be based, for example, on the idea that neighborhoods included in decision classes to a satisfactory degree can be treated as parts of the lower approximations of decision classes. Hence the lower approximations of decision classes are enlarged and decision rules generated for them are usually stronger (e.g., they are supported by more examples). The degree of inclusion is tuned experimentally to achieve, for example, high classification quality of new cases.

When a set of rules has been induced from a decision system containing a set of training examples, they can be used to classify new objects. However, to resolve conflict between different decision rules recognizing new objects, one should develop strategies for resolving conflicts between them when they are voting for different decisions (see the bibliography in Polkowski and Skowron, 1998b,c). Recently (see, e.g., Szczuka, 1999), it has been shown that rough set methods can be used to learn from data the strategy for resolving conflict between decision rules when they are classifying new objects contrary to existing methods using some fixed strategies.

α-Reducts and Association Rules

In this section we discuss the relationship between association rules (Agrawal et al., 1996) and approximations of reducts

We consider formulas called templates that are conjunctions of descriptors. Templates will be denoted by $\mathbf{T}$, $\mathbf{P}$, $\mathbf{Q}$ and descriptors by D with or without subscripts. $support_{\mathscr{A}}(\mathbf{T})$ denotes the cardinality of $|\mathbf{T}|_{\mathscr{A}}$ and $confidence_{\mathscr{A}}(\mathbf{P} \rightarrow \mathbf{Q})$ denotes the ratio $support_{\mathscr{A}}(\mathbf{P} \wedge \mathbf{Q})/support_{\mathscr{A}}(\mathbf{P})$ assuming $support_{\mathscr{A}}(\mathbf{P}) \neq \phi$.

The reduct approximations mentioned above are descriptions of the object sets matched by templates. They describe these sets in an approximate sense expressed by coefficients called support and confidence.

There are two main steps in rule generation methods for a given information system $\mathscr{A}$ and two parameters (support s and confidence c):

1. Extract from the data as many as possible frequent templates $\mathbf{T} = D_1 \wedge D_2 \ldots \wedge D_k$ such that $support_{\mathscr{A}}(\mathbf{T}) \geqslant s$ and $support_{\mathscr{A}}(\mathbf{T} \wedge D) < s$ for any descriptor D different from descriptors of $\mathbf{T}$ (i.e., generation of maximal templates among those supported by more than s objects);

2. Search for a partition $\mathbf{T} = \mathbf{P} \wedge \mathbf{Q}$ for any generated template $\mathbf{T}$ satisfying the following conditions:

    (a) $support_{\mathscr{A}}(\mathbf{P}) < \frac{support_{\mathscr{A}}(\mathbf{T})}{c}$

    (b) $\mathbf{P}$ has the shortest length among templates satisfying the previous condition.

We show that the second step can be solved using rough set methods and a Boolean reasoning approach.

Let $\mathbf{T} = D_1 \wedge D_2 \wedge \ldots \wedge D_m$ be a template with $support_{\mathscr{A}}(\mathbf{T}) \geqslant s$. For a given confidence threshold $c \in (0; 1)$, the decomposition $\mathbf{T} = \mathbf{P} \wedge \mathbf{Q}$ is called c-irreducible if $confidence_{\mathscr{A}}(\mathbf{P} \rightarrow \mathbf{Q}) \geqslant c$ and for any decomposition $\mathbf{T} = \mathbf{P}' \wedge \mathbf{Q}'$ such that $\mathbf{P}'$ is a subtemplate of $\mathbf{P}$, we have $confidence_{\mathscr{A}}(\mathbf{P}' \rightarrow \mathbf{Q}') < c$.

We now explain that the problem of searching for c-irreducible association rules from the given template is equivalent to the problem of searching for local α-reducts (for some α) from a decision table. The last problem is a well-known problem in rough set theory.

Let us define a new decision table $\mathscr{A}\mid_{\mathbf{T}} = (U, A\mid_{\mathbf{T}}, d)$ from the original information system $\mathscr{A}$ and the template $\mathbf{T}$ by

1. $A\mid_{\mathbf{T}} = \{a_{D_1}, a_{D_2}, ..., a_{D_m}\}$ is a set of attributes corresponding to the descriptors of $\mathbf{T}$ such that

$$a_{D_i}(u) = \begin{cases} 1 & \text{if the object } u \text{ satisfies } D_i, \\ 0 & \text{otherwise.} \end{cases}$$

2. The decision attribute d determines if the object satisfies template $\mathbf{T}$; that is,

$$d(u) = \begin{cases} 1 & \text{if the object } u \text{ satisfies } \mathbf{T}, \\ 0 & \text{otherwise.} \end{cases}$$

The following facts (Nguyen and Nguyen, 1999; Skowron and Nguyen, 1999) describe the relationship between association rules and approximations of reducts.

For the given information table, $\mathscr{A} = (U, A)$, the template $\mathbf{T}$, and the set of descriptors $\mathbf{P}$. The implication $\left(\bigwedge_{D_i \in \mathbf{P}} D_i \rightarrow \bigwedge_{D_j \notin \mathbf{P}} D_j\right)$ is:

1. 100%-Irreducible association rule obtained from $\mathbf{T}$ if and only if $\mathbf{P}$ is a reduct in $\mathscr{A}\mid_{\mathbf{T}}$.

2. c-Irreducible association rule obtained from $\mathbf{T}$ if and only if $\mathbf{P}$ is an α-reduct of $\mathscr{A}\mid_{\mathbf{T}}$, where $\alpha = 1 - \left(\frac{1}{c} - 1\right)/\left(\frac{n}{s} - 1\right)$, n is the total number of objects from U, and $s = support_{\mathscr{A}}(\mathbf{T})$.

It can be shown that the problem of searching for the shortest α-reducts is NP-hard (Nguyen and Nguyen, 1999). From the above facts it follows that extracting association rules from data is strongly related to extraction of reduct approximations (Nguyen and Nguyen, 1999).

2.4. Decomposition of Large Data Tables

Several methods based on rough sets have been developed in order to deal with large data tables, in other words, in order to generate strong decision rules for such tables. We will discuss one of the methods based on a decomposition of tables using patterns, called templates, which describe regular subdomains of the universe (e.g., they describe a large number of customers having a large number of common features).

Long templates with large support are preferred in many data mining tasks. Several quality functions can be used to compare templates. For example, they can be defined by $quality^1_{\mathscr{A}}(\mathbf{T}) = support_{\mathscr{A}}(\mathbf{T}) + length(\mathbf{T})$ and $quality^2_{\mathscr{A}}(\mathbf{T}) = support_{\mathscr{A}}(\mathbf{T}) \times length(\mathbf{T})$. Problems of high-quality template generation (using different optimization criteria) are of high computational complexity. However, efficient heuristics have been developed for solving them (see, e.g., Agrawal et al., 1996; Nguyen, 2000; Zaki et al., 1997). Templates extracted from data are used to decompose large data tables. Consequently, a decision tree is built. Its internal nodes are labeled by the templates extracted from the data, and the edges outgoing from them are labeled by 0 (false) and 1 (true). Any leaf is labeled by a subtable (subdomain) consisting of all objects from the original table matching all templates or their complements appearing on the path from the root of the tree to the leaf. The process of decomposition is continued until the size of subtables attached to leaves is feasible for the rough set algorithms at hand (e.g., decision rules for them can be generated efficiently). The reported experiments show that such decomposition returns interesting patterns of regular subdomains of large data tables (for references, see Nguyen, 2000; Nguyen et al., 1998; Polkowski and Skowron, 1998b,c).

It is also possible to search for patterns that are almost included in the decision classes, that is, default rules (Mollestad and Komorowski, 1998). For a presentation of generating default rules, see the bibliography in Polkowski and Skowron (1998b,c).

3. Conclusions

We have shown that rough set theory constitutes a sound basis for KDD: minimal concept descriptions, classifiers, dependencies, et cetera are systematically synthesized and their quality can be evaluated using statistical methods. Features can be extracted and selected. The strict concepts are extended by the approximate ones that usually improve the quality of classification. Methods for processing very large data sets are developed. Successful software tools have been implemented and used by thousands of researchers worldwide (e.g., ROSETTA).

There has been substantial progress in developing rough set methods for KDD, such as methods for extracting rules from data, partial or total dependencies, methods for elimination of redundant data, methods dealing with missing data, dynamic data, and others (reported, for example, in Cios et al., 1998; Czyżewski, 1998; Deogun et al., 1997; Gryzmała-Busse, 1998; Komorowski and Żytkow, 1997; Lin and Cercone, 1997; Mollestad and Komorowski, 1998; Nguyen, 1997; Pal and Skowron, 1999; Polkowski and Skowron, 1998b,c,d; Ziarko, 1998). New methods for extracting patterns from data (see e.g., Kowalczyk, 1998; Krawiec et al., 1998; Mollestad and Komorowski, 1998; Nguyen et al., 1998; Piasta and Lenarcik, 1998), decomposition of decision systems (see e.g., Nguyen et al., 1998), as well as a new methodology for data mining in distributed and multi-agent systems (see, e.g., Polkowski and Skowron, 1998), have been reported. Recently, rough set based methods have been proposed for data mining in very large relational databases.

There are numerous areas of successful applications of rough set software systems (see Polkowski and Skowron (1998c) and http://www.idi.ntnu.no/~aleks/rosetta/ for the ROSETTA system). Many interesting case studies are reported (see, e.g., Pal and Skowron, 1999; Polkowski and Skowron, 1998b,c; and the references therein, in particular Czyżewski, 1998; Grzymała-Busse, 1998; Kowalczyk, 1998; Tsumoto, 1998; Ziarko, 1998).

We would like to mention some generalizations of the rough set approach such as the rough mereological approach (see Polkowski and Skowron, 1996, 1999). The inclusion relation $x\mu_r y$ with the intended meaning x is a part of y to a degree r has been taken as the basic notion of rough mereology, being a generalization of the Leśniewski mereology. Rough mereology offers a methodology for synthesis and analysis of objects in a distributed environment of intelligent agents, in particular, for synthesis of objects satisfying a given specification to a satisfactory degree, that is, objects sufficiently close to standard objects (prototypes) satisfying the specification. Moreover, rough mereology has recently been used (Polkowski and Skowron, 1998) for developing foundations of the information granule calculus, an attempt toward a formalization of the Computing-with-Words paradigm, recently formulated by Lotfi Zadeh (1996, 1997). Let us also note that one of the prospects for rough mereological applications is to look for algorithmic methods of extracting logical structures from data such as, for instance, finding relational structures corresponding to relevant feature extraction, synthesizing default rules (approximate decision rules), constructing connectives for uncertainty coefficients propagation, and synthesizing schemes of approximate reasoning creating a higher-level knowledge extracted from data (e.g., qualitative schemes of reasoning). The development of such methods is crucial to further progress in many applications. It is also one of the central issues of KDD as pointed out in Fayyad and Piatetsky-Shapiro (1996).

Several other generalizations of rough sets have been investigated and some of them have been used for real life data analysis (see e.g., Cattaneo, 1998; Greco et al., 1998; Kryszkiewicz, 1997; Lin, 1989; Paun et al., 1996; Pawlak, 1981; Polkowski and Skowron, 1998; Ras, 1996; Ziarko, 1993).

Finally, we would like to point out that the algebraic and logical aspects of rough sets have been intensively studied since the beginning of rough set theory. The reader interested in that topic is referred to the bibliography in Polkowski and Skowron (1998b) and, for example, Orłowska (1998), Marek et al. (1999).

ACKNOWLEDGMENTS

The number of people who are involved in this research is very large and we can only express our general thanks to all colleagues, collaborators, reviewers, students, wives, and funding agencies who have contributed to this chapter in very many direct and indirect ways, and who supported us over the years. The authors would like to thank Willi Klösgen, Jan Żytkow, and the anonymous reviewer for their criticism and comments on the previous version of the paper. Jan Komorowski has been supported in part by the European Union 4th Framework Telematics Project CARDIASSIST, and by the Norwegian Research Council (NFR) grants No. 74467/410, and No. 110177/730. Lech Polkowski has been supported by grant No. 8T11C02417 from the State Committee for Scientific Research (KBN) of the Republic of Poland. Andrzej Skowron has been supported by a grant from the Wallenberg Foundation, by the ESPRIT-CRIT 2 Project No. 20288, and by the grant 8T11C02519 from the State Committee for Scientific Research (KBN) of the Republic of Poland.

References

Ågotnes, T., J. Komorowski, and T. Løken. 1999. "Taming large rule models in rough set approaches." In *Proceedings of the Third European Conference of Principles and Practice of Knowledge Discovery in Databases, September 15–18, 1999, Prague, Czech Republic.* Lecture Notes in Artificial Intelligence **1704**: 193–203. Berlin: Springer-Verlag.

Agrawal, R., H. Mannila, R. Srikant, H. Toivonen, and A. Verkano. 1996. "Fast discovery of association rules." In *Advances in Knowledge Discovery and Data Mining*, edited by U. M. Fayyad, G. Piatetsky-Shapiro, P. Smyth, and R. Uthurusamy, pp. 307–328. Menlo Park, CA: The AAAI Press/The MIT Press.

Bazan, J. G. 1998. "A comparison of dynamic and non-dynamic rough set methods for extracting laws from decision system." In *Rough Sets in Knowledge Discovery 1: Methodology and Applications*, edited by L. Polkowski and A. Skowron, pp. 321–365. Heidelberg: Physica-Verlag.

Boole, G. 1854. *An Investigation of the Laws of Thought on which are Founded the Mathematical Theories of Logic and Probabilites.* London: Walton and Maberly.

Brown, F. M. 1990. *Boolean Reasoning.* Dordrecht, The Netherlands: Kluwer Academic Publishers.

Cattaneo, G. 1998. "Abstract approximation spaces for rough theories." In *Rough Sets in Knowledge Discovery 1: Methodology and Applications*, edited by L. Polkowski and A. Skowron, pp. 59–98. Heidelberg: Physica-Verlag.

Cios, J., W. Pedrycz, and R. W. Swiniarski. 1998. *Data Mining in Knowledge Discovery.* Boston: Academic Publishers.

Czyżewski, A. 1998. "Soft processing of audio signals." In *Rough Sets in Knowledge Discovery 2: Applications, Case Studies and Software Systems*, edited by L. Polkowski and A. Skowron, pp. 147–165. Heidelberg: Physica-Verlag.

Deogun, J., V. Raghavan, A. Sarkar, and H. Sever. 1997. "Data mining: trends in research and development." In *Rough Sets and Data Mining. Analysis of Imprecise Data*, edited by T. Y. Lin and N. Cercone, pp. 9–45. Boston: Kluwer Academic Publishers.

Duentsch, I. and G. Gediga. 2000. "Rough set data analysis." *Encyclopedia of Computer Science and Technology*, vol 43 281–301. New York: Marcel Dekker.

Fayyad, U. M., G. Piatetsky-Shapiro, P. Smith and G. Uthurusamy. (eds). 1996. *Advances in Knowledge Discovery and Data Mining.* Menlo Park, CA: MIT/AAAI Press.

Friedman, J., R. Kohavi, and Y. Yun. 1996. "Lazy decision trees." *Proceedings of AAAI-96.* Menlo Park, CA: AAAI Press/The MIT Press, pp. 717–724.

Greco, S., B. Matarazzo, and R. Słowiński. 1998. "Rough approximation of a preference relation in a pairwise comparison table." In *Rough Sets in Knowledge Discovery 2: Applications, Case Studies and Software Systems*, edited by L. Polkowski and A. Skowron, pp. 13–36. Heidelberg: Physica-Verlag.

Grzymała–Busse, J. W. 1998. "Applications of the rule induction system LERS." In *Rough Sets in Knowledge Discovery 1: Methodology and Applications*, edited by L. Polkowski and A. Skowron, pp. 366–375. Heidelberg: Physica-Verlag.

Huber, P. J. 1981. *Robust Statistics.* New York: Wiley.

Johnson, D. S. 1974. "Approximation algorithms for combinatorial problems." *J. Comp. Sys. Sci.* **9**: 256–278.

Komorowski, J. and A. Øhrn. 1999. "Modelling prognostic power of cardiac tests using rough sets." *Artificial Intell. Med.* **15(2)**: 167–191.

Komorowski, J., Z. Pawlak, L. Polkowski, and A. Skowron. 1999. "Rough sets: a tutorial." In *Rough Fuzzy Hybridization: A New Trend in Decision-making*, edited by S. K. Pal and A. Skowron, pp. 3–98. Singapore: Springer-Verlag.

Kowalczyk, W. 1998. "Rough data modelling, A new technique for analyzing data." In *Rough Sets in Knowledge Discovery 1: Methodology and Applications*, edited by L. Polkowski and A. Skowron, pp. 400–421. Heidelberg: Physica-Verlag.

Krawiec, K., R. Słowiński, and D. Vanderpooten. 1998. "Learning decision rules from similarity based rough approximations." In *Rough Sets in Knowledge Discovery 2: Applications, Case Studies and Software Systems*, edited by L. Polkowski and A. Skowron, pp. 37–54. Heidelberg: Physica-Verlag.

Kryszkiewicz, M. 1997. "Generation of rules from incomplete information systems." In *The First European Symposium on Principles of Data Mining and Knowledge Discovery (PKDD'97). June 25–27, Trondheim, Norway*, edited by J. Komorowski and J. Żytkow. Lecture Notes in Artificial Intelligence **1263**: 156–166, pp. 1–396. Berlin: Springer-Verlag.

Langley, P., H. A. Simon, G. L. Bradshaw, and J. M. Żytkow. 1987. *Scientific Discovery, Computational Explorations of the Creative Processes*. Cambridge, MA: The MIT Press.

Lin, T. Y. 1989. "Granular computing on binary relations I, II." In *Rough Sets in Knowledge Discovery 1: Methodology and Applications*, edited by L. Polkowski and A. Skowron, pp. 107–140. Heidelberg: Physica-Verlag.

Marek, V. M. and M. Truszczyński. 1999. "Contributions to the theory of rough sets." *Fund. Inform.* **39(4)**: 389–409.

Michie, D., D. J. Spiegelhalter, and C. C. Taylor. (eds). 1994. *Machine Learning, Neural and Statistical Classification*. New York: Ellis Horwood.

Mitchell, T. M. 1997. *Machine Learning*. Portland, ME: McGraw-Hill.

Mollestad, T. and J. Komorowski. 1998. "A Rough Set Framework for Propositional Default Rules Data Mining." In *Rough–Fuzzy Hybridization: New Trend in Decision Making*, edited by S. K. Pal and A. Skowron. Singapore: Springer-Verlag, pp. 233–262.

Nguyen, H. S. 1997. "Discretization of real value attributes, Boolean reasoning approach." Ph.D. diss. Poland: Warsaw University.

Nguyen, H. S. 1999. "Efficient SQL-learning method for data mining in large data bases." In *Proceedings of the Sixteenth International Joint Conference on Artificial Intelligence (IJCAI'99)*. San Fransisco: Morgan Kaufmann, pp. 806–811.

Nguyen, H. S. 2000. "Data regularity analysis and applications in data mining." Ph.D. diss. Poland: Warsaw University.

Nguyen, H. S. and S. H. Nguyen. 1998. "Pattern extraction from data." *Fund. Inform.* **34**: 129–144.

Nguyen, H. S. and S. H. Nguyen. 1999. "Rough sets and association rule generation." *Fund. Inform.* **40/4**: 383–405.

Nguyen, S. H., A. Skowron, and P. Synak. 1998. "Discovery of data patterns with applications to decomposition and classification problems." In *Rough Sets in Knowledge Discovery 2: Applications, Case Studies and Software Systems*, edited by L. Polkowski and A. Skowron, pp. 55–97. Heidelberg: Physica-Verlag.

Øhrn, A. 1999. "Discernibility and rough sets in medicine: tools and applications." PhD diss. Trondheim, Norway: Norwegian University of Science and Technology. IDI-rapport 1999:14.

Orłowska, E. (ed). 1998. *Incomplete Information, Rough Set Analysis* 1–613: Physica-Verlag.

Pal, S. K. and A. Skowron. 1999. *Rough-Fuzzy Hybridization: New Trend in Decision Making*. Singapore: Springer-Verlag.

Paun, G., L. Polkowski, and A. Skowron. 1996. "Parallel communicating grammar systems with negotiations." *Fund. Inform.* **28/3-4**: 315–330.

Pawlak, Z. 1981. "Information systems—theoretical foundations." *Inform. Sys.* **6**: 205–218.

Pawlak, Z. 1982. "Rough sets." *Int. J. Comput. Inform. Sci.* **11**: 341–356.

Pawlak, Z. 1991. *Rough Sets—Theoretical Aspects of Reasoning About Data*. Dordrecht, The Netherlands: Kluwer Academic Publishers.

Piasta, Z. and A. Lenarcik. 1998. "Rough Clarifiers Sensitive to Costs Varying from Object to Object." *Proc. of RSCTC'98, Warsaw, Poland, Lecture Notes in Artificial Intelligence 1424*. Berlin: Springer-Verlag, 222–230.

Polkowski, L. and A. Skowron. 1996. "Rough mereology: a new paradigm for approximate reasoning." *Int. J. Approx. Reasoning* **15/4**: 333–365.

Polkowski, L. and A. Skowron. 1998. "Rough sets: a perspective." In *Rough Sets in Knowledge Discovery 1: Methodology and Applications*, edited by L. Polkowski and A. Skowron, pp. 31–58. Heidelberg: Physica-Verlag.

Polkowski, L. and A. Skowron. 1999. "Towards adaptive calculus of granules." In *Computing with Words in Information/Intelligent Systems*, edited by L. A. Zadeh and J. Kacprzyk **1–2**: 201–227. Heidelberg: Physica-Verlag.

Quinlan, J. R. 1993. *C4.5. Programs for Machine Learning*. San Mateo, CA: Morgan Kaufmann.

Rissanen, J. J. 1978. "Modeling by shortest data description." *Automatica* **14**: 465–471.

Roddick, J. F. and M. Spiliopoulou. 1999. "A bibliography of temporal, spatial, and temporal data mining research." *Newsletter of the Special Interest Group (SIG) on Knowledge Discovery & Data Mining* **1/1**: 34–38.

Selman, B., H. Kautz, and D. McAllester. 1997. "Ten challenges in propositional reasoning and search." *Proceedings of IJCAI'97*. Nagoya, Japan. San Francisco: Morgan Kaufmann, pp. 50–54.

Ras, Z. W. 1996. "Cooperative knowledge-based systems." *J. Intell. Automation Soft Comput.* **2/2**: 193–202.

Skowron, A. 1995. "Synthesis of adaptive decision systems from experimental data." In *Proceedings of the Fifth Scandinavian Conference on Artificial Intelligence (SCAI'95), May 1995, Trondheim, Norway*, edited by A. Aamodt and J. Komorowski, pp. 220–238. Amsterdam: IOS Press.

Skowron, A. and H. S. Nguyen. 1999. "Boolean reasoning scheme with some applications in data mining." In *Proceedings of the Third European Conference on Principles and Practice of Knowledge Discovery in Databases, September 1999, Prague Czech Republic*. Lecture Notes in Computer Science **1704**: 107–115. Berlin: Springer-Verlag.

Skowron, A. and C. Rauszer. 1992. "The Discernibility Matrices and Functions in Information Systems." In *Intelligent Decision Support—Handbook of Applications and Advances of the Rough Sets Theory*, edited by R. Słowiński, pp. 331–362. Dordrecht, The Netherlands: Kluwer Academic Publishers.

Skowron, A. and J. Stepaniuk. 1996. "Tolerance approximation spaces." *Fund. Inform.* **27**: 245–253.

Ślęzak, D. 1998. "Approximate reducts in decision tables." In *Proceedings of the Sixth International Conference, Information Processing and Management of Uncertainty in Knowledge-Based Systems (IPMU'96)* **3**: 1159–1164, July 1–5, Granada, Spain: Universidad de Granada.

Słowiński, R. and D. Vanderpooten. 1995. "Similarity relation as a basis for rough approximations." In *Advances in Machine Intelligence & Soft Computing*, edited by P. Wang, pp. 17–33. Raleigh, NC: Bookwrights.

Słowiński, R. and D. Vanderpooten. 2000. "A generalized definition of rough approximations based on similarity." *IEEE Trans. Data Knowledge Engng* **12**, 331–336.

Swets, J. A. and R. M. Picket. 1982. *Evaluation of Diagnostic Systems: Methods from Signal Detection Theory*. New York, NY: Academic Press.

Szczuka, M. 1999. "Symbolic and neural network methods for classifiers construction." Ph.D. diss. Poland: Warsaw University.

Tsumoto, S. 1998. "Modelling diagnostic rules based on rough sets." In *Proceedings of the First International Conference on Rough Sets and Soft Computing (RSCTC'98), Warszawa, Poland, June 22–27*, edited by L. Polkowski and A. Skowron. Lecture Notes in Artificial Intelligence **1424**: 475–482. Berlin: Springer-Verlag.

Zadeh, L. A. 1996. "Fuzzy logic = computing with words." *IEEE Trans. Fuzzy Sys.* **4**: 103–111.

Zadeh, L. A. 1997. "Toward a theory of fuzzy information granulation and its certainty in human reasoning and fuzzy logic." *Fuzzy Sets Sys.* **90**: 111–127.

Zaki, M. J., S. Parthasarathy, M. Ogihara, and W. Li. 1997. "New parallel algorithms for fast discovery of association rules." *Data Mining Knowledge Discovery: Int. J.* **1/4**: 343–373.

Ziarko, W. 1993. "Variable precision rough set model." *J. Comput. and Sys. Sci.* **46**: 39–59.

Ziarko W. (ed.) 1994. *Rough Sets, Fuzzy Sets and Knowledge Discovery (RSKD'93)*. Workshops in Computing. London, Berlin: Springer–Verlag & British Computer Society.

Ziarko, W. 1998. "Rough sets as a methodology for data mining." In *Rough Sets in Knowledge Discovery 1: Methods & Applications*, edited by L. Polkowski and A. Skowron, pp. 554–576. Heidelberg: Physica-Verlag.

10 FUZZY SETS PERSPECTIVE ON DATA AND KNOWLEDGE

Witold Pedrycz

ABSTRACT This study delivers a comprehensive overview of the fundamentals of the technology of fuzzy sets, regarded as one of the essential conceptual and algorithmic settings of data mining. We review the underlying concepts of fuzzy sets and discuss their role in information granulation. The basic computing aspects of fuzzy sets are studied; these include operations on fuzzy sets, transformations of fuzzy sets, and quantification of information granularity. Our conjecture is that granularity of information plays a pivotal role in knowledge-based computing that dominates data mining pursuits. We contrast probability with fuzzy sets and underline their orthogonal character manifested in data mining.

1. Introduction: Fuzzy Sets as a Conceptual and Algorithmic Framework of Information Granulation

The inherent feature of data mining pursuits (Fayyad et al., 1996a,b; Frawley et al., 1991) lies in a multitude of activities depending upon the category of potential users. Data mining tasks are carried out at various levels of detail. For instance, a corporate report usually requires pieces of knowledge about associations (relations) between various factors (variables) collected at a highly general level. The report produced at this level helps users gain a global look at the problem, identify the most crucial relationships, and undertake strategic decisions. To carry out such activities, the decisionmaker has to concentrate on the most essential aspects of the problem and identify the most profound trends. Any detailed underpinnings should be hidden on purpose to avoid eventual blurring of the overall picture by overloading it with massive records of numeric data. At the other end of the spectrum arise far more specific situations in which we require detailed, very local information. What is common to these two decision scenarios (and many others) is the concept of information granularity. In a nutshell, information granularity concerns information summarization (compression). Fuzzy sets, as well as sets (at least to some extent), support this essential feature. They can be regarded as conceptual filters (focal elements) that help us concentrate on some specific level of detail to be searched for and eventually discovered throughout databases. Consider a few examples of information granules shown in Figure 1 as they point at the underlying nature of the data mining processes. They reflect an intuitive capture of the notion of information granularity. For instance, the fuzzy set in the upper part of Figure 1 is far more specific (detailed) than the one displayed at the bottom in which we are not concerned about details (and, in fact, they become hidden in the linguistic descriptor of interest).

The process of information granulation changes the way in which we carry out data mining (or any exploratory data analysis). As illustrated in Figure 2, the mechanisms of information granulation allow us to move away from clouds of data and concentrate on revealing associations at a more transparent and easy to interpret level of nonnumeric granular entities. Thus information granules become the essential building blocks supporting the resulting data mining activities and leading to more computationally-driven procedures.

The objectives of this chapter are three-fold:

1. To provide a comprehensive yet highly concise introduction to fuzzy sets.

2. To cast the discussion in the broader context of information granularity and granular computing, in general. This helps underline the main features of fuzzy sets in comparison to other environments such as set theory.

3. To reveal key links between fuzzy sets and data mining, both in terms of underlying concepts as well as pertinent algorithms.

The chapter is arranged into eleven sections. First, we provide the reader with the basic notions and computing mechanisms of fuzzy sets, including a discussion on logic operations (Sections 2–5). Special attention is then paid to the issues of information granularity captured

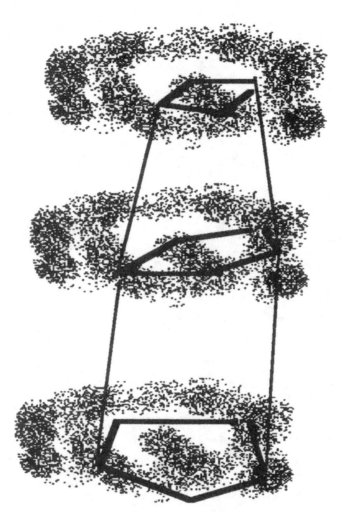

Figure 1 Information granules and resulting processes of data mining; note that larger chunks (information granules) spread over larger regions of the data set

by fuzzy sets; here we concentrate on expressing granularity and showing some direct applications to rule-based architectures (Sections 6 and 7). A comparative analysis of set theory and fuzzy sets carried out with respect to the resulting granulation properties, such as robustness and reconstruction issues, is covered in Section 8. The concept of linguistic approximation is studied in Section 9. Finally, Section 10 is devoted to the issues of probability and fuzziness, regarded as two highly complementary technologies. Conclusions (Section 11) finish the study.

The leitmotiv of this study is to present fuzzy sets as one, among several, of the useful technologies of data mining. We underline those key points of fuzzy sets that are important in data processing and data mining: information granularity, uncertainty representation, and its management; and interpretation aspects of fuzzy sets carried out with the aid of linguistic approximation. The chapter does not cover all fundamental ideas of fuzzy sets. Those aspects of fuzzy sets that are marginal to the agenda of data mining are intentionally left out. For more details on fuzzy sets, the reader may refer to a number of monographs and handbooks solely devoted to the fundamentals of fuzzy sets; in particular one may consider Klir and

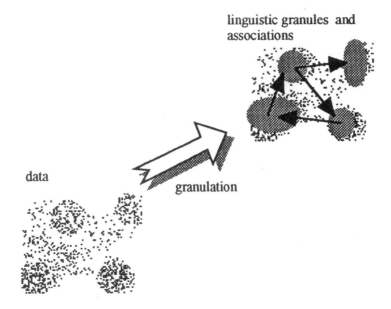

Figure 2 Granulation of data and its role in revealing associations between information granules

Folger (1988), Pedrycz (1995), Pedrycz and Gomide (1998), Dubois et al. (1993), and the *Handbook of Fuzzy Computation* (Ruspini et al., 1998).

2. Fuzzy Sets: Basic Definitions and Examples

A characteristic function of a set (A), $A : \mathbf{X} \to \{0, 1\}$ induces a constraint, with a well-defined boundary, on the objects (elements) of a domain $\mathbf{X}$, which may be assigned to a set A. Sets are two-valued quantified constructs (producing common quantification as yes–no, true–false). We either fully admit an element to be in a certain set (yes–true) or fully exclude it from this set (no–false). The cornerstone idea of fuzzy sets is to relax this requirement of dichotomy and admit intermediate values of class membership. This allows for an enriched and more realistic interpretation framework accommodating statements with a partial quantification of membership. Interestingly enough, most of the categories being used in description of real world objects do not possess well-defined boundaries. In these circumstances, the property of belongingness of an object to a category is a matter of degree, expressed, for example, by a real number defined in the unit interval [0, 1]. The closer the value of this degree to one, the higher the level of binding of the object to a category. In data mining, such notions with continuous membership become an integral part of the various development environments. It does not necessarily mean that we always represent them in the setting of fuzzy sets. It could well be that the specific formal framework within which these concepts are realized is implemented via sets or probabilistic structures.

A fuzzy set (Zadeh, 1965) is characterized by a membership function mapping the elements of a domain, space or an universe of discourse $\mathbf{X}$ to the unit interval [0 1], that is

$$A : \mathbf{X} \to [0, 1].$$

Thus, a fuzzy set A defined in $\mathbf{X}$ may be represented as a set of ordered pairs of a generic element $x \in \mathbf{X}$ and its grade of membership, namely $A = \{A(x) | x \in \mathbf{X}\}$. Clearly, a fuzzy set is a generalization of the concept of a set whose membership function takes only a yes–no form of quantification. The value of $A(x)$ describes a degree of membership of an element x in A. For instance, consider the concept of high temperature discussed in the setting of control indoor temperature with temperatures distributed in the interval $X = [0, 50]$. Clearly $0°C$ is not understood to be a high temperature value and we may assign to it a zero membership degree to express its grade of compatibility with the high temperature concept. Likewise, $30°C$ (that is $A(30°C)$) and over are certainly high temperatures and we may assign a full degree of compatibility with the concept.

Fuzzy sets can be defined in either finite or infinite universes. Based on that, the reader should be aware of different notations being used throughout the literature. Especially, if the universe X is discrete and finite, of cardinality n, then a fuzzy set is given in a form of a n-dimensional vector whose entries denote grades of membership of the corresponding elements of X.

Fuzzy relations (Klir and Folger, 1988; Pedrycz and Gomide, 1998) are multidimensional extensions of fuzzy sets. These are constructs defined in a Cartesian product of several universes of discourse. The key concept conveyed by fuzzy relations is the one dealing with partial association between some variables. For instance, a fuzzy relation named "approximately equal" links any two elements and quantifies a degree of their association. This type of relationship can be modeled through the following expression:

$$R(x, y) = \exp(-\alpha(x-y)^2),$$

where α is a positive scaling factor controlling the spread of the membership function.

If $R(x, y)$ attains values close to 1, we say that x and y are strongly linked. The lower the grade of membership, the weaker the association between the elements of interest. The notion of relation (and fuzzy relation, in particular) is fundamental in revealing dependencies between elements (objects). As we are not constrained in any sense to a specific direction (as envisioned in the case of functions), the formalism of fuzzy relations and relations is of genuine interest in the area of data mining. As a matter of fact, fuzzy relations are models of associations. Relations are more generic than functions (any function is a relation but not vice versa). This eliminates some restrictions that come into play when we start working with functions.

3. Selected Classes of Fuzzy Sets

A panoply of problems in which we are concerned with partial membership implies a diversity of ways in which this notion needs to be captured through the respective membership functions. In this section we elaborate on some main classes of membership functions. The list is not exhaustive; our intention is to focus on the most commonly used classes of fuzzy sets. In most cases such membership functions are also computationally attractive.

Triangular fuzzy sets are defined by the following piecewise membership functions:

$$A(x) = \begin{cases} 0 & \text{if } x \leq a \\ \dfrac{x-a}{m-a} & \text{if } x \in [a, m] \\ \dfrac{b-x}{b-m} & \text{if } x \in [m, b] \\ 0 & \text{if } x \geq b. \end{cases}$$

Here m is a modal value of A while the lower and upper bounds of a range of nonzero values of $A(x)$ are denoted by a and b, respectively. The equivalent, and more concise, notation of the triangular membership function assumes the form:

$$A(x; a, m, b) = \max\{\min[(x-a)/(m-a), (b-x)/(b-m)], 0\}.$$

The three parameters of the triangular membership functions carry a straightforward interpretation. The lower and upper bound identify the region where there are nonzero grades of membership. The modal value identifies the most likely element of the fuzzy set. As no additional hints are available, it is legitimate to anticipate a linear form of changes in the membership values when moving across the universe of discourse. It is worth underlining that the triangular membership functions are the simplest model of uncertain quantities.

The S-membership functions of this class are governed by a three-parameter function of the form:

$$A(x) \begin{cases} 0 & x \leqslant a \\ 2\left(\dfrac{x-a}{b-a}\right)^2 & x \in [a, m] \\ 1-2\left(\dfrac{x-b}{b-a}\right)^2 & x \in [m, b] \\ 1 & x > b. \end{cases}$$

The point $m = \frac{a+b}{2}$ is known as a crossover of the S-function.

Trapezoidal membership functions are described in the following fashion:

$$A(x) = \begin{cases} 0 & \text{if } x < a \\ \dfrac{x-a}{m-a} & \text{if } x \in [a, m] \\ 1 & \text{if } x \in [m, n] \\ \dfrac{b-x}{b-n} & \text{if } x \in [n, b] \\ 0 & \text{if } x > b. \end{cases}$$

The equivalent notation reads as

$$A(x; a, m, n, b) = \max\{\min[(x-a)/(m-a), 1, (b-x)/(b-n)], 0\}.$$

Gaussian membership functions are two-parameter functions of the form

$$A(x) = \exp\left(\frac{(x-m)^2}{\sigma^2}\right).$$

Here m is a modal value of the membership function (*viz.* $A(m) = 1$), while σ denotes a spread of this fuzzy set.

4. Logic Operations on Fuzzy Sets

Before getting into the operations on fuzzy sets, it is highly instructive to start with the basic operations encountered in set theory and highlight relationships between them and fuzzy set counterparts. The main properties of these operations form a suitable reference one can apply when analyzing various models of fuzzy set operations. These, in particular, concern the properties of commutativity, idempotency, associativity, distributivity, and transitivity. As characteristic functions are equivalent representations of sets, the basic intersection, union, and complement operations are conveniently represented by taking the minimum, maximum, and complement of the corresponding characteristic functions for all $x \in \mathbf{X}$, that is:

$$(A \cap B)(x) = \min(A(x), B(x)) = A(x) \wedge B(x)$$

$$(A \cup B)(x) = \max(A(x), B(x)) = A(x) \vee B(x)$$

$$\bar{A}(x) = 1 - A(x),$$

where A and B are sets defined in a universe (universe of discourse) $\mathbf{X}$, and $(A \cap B)(x)$, $(A \cup B)(x)$ denote the values of the membership functions of the set resulting from the intersection and union of A and B, respectively.

While the main features to be expressed below use standard set notation, the same formulas can be immediately re-expressed in the language of characteristic functions:

Commutativity

$$A \cup B = B \cup A$$

$$A \cap B = B \cap A$$

Associativity

$$A \cup (B \cup C) = (A \cup B) \cup C = A \cup B \cup C$$

$$A \cap (B \cap C) = (A \cap B) \cap C = A \cap B \cap C$$

Idempotency

$$A \cup A = A$$

$$A \cap A = A$$

Distributivity

$$A \cap (B \cup C) = (A \cap B) \cup (A \cap C)$$

$$A \cup (B \cap C) = (A \cup B) \cap (A \cup C)$$

Boundary conditions

$$A \cup \varnothing = A \quad A \cup \mathbf{X} = \mathbf{X}$$

$$A \cap \varnothing = \varnothing \quad A \cap \mathbf{X} = A$$

Involution

$$\overline{\overline{A}} = A$$

Transitivity

$$A \subset B \text{ and } B \subset C \text{ implies } A \subset C.$$

The inclusion operation is meant in the usual sense, that if $A \subset B$ means that $A(x) \leqslant B(x)$ for all values of the argument. The original proposal of fuzzy sets (Zadeh, 1965) included the maximum and minimum functions as the two basic fuzzy set operators. Due to the existence of intermediate membership values, it has been realized that there are far more realizations of logic operations on fuzzy sets. The commonly accepted models rely on triangular norms (see Menger, 1942; Schweizer and Sklar, 1983; Weber, 1983; Butnariu and Klement, 1993). Triangular norms form general classes of intersection and union operators. Formally they are introduced as follows:

4.1. t-norm

A t-norm is a binary operation $t : [0, 1]^2 \rightarrow [0, 1]$ satisfying the requirements of

commutativity	$xty = ytx$
associativity	$xt(ytz) = (xty)tz$
monotonicity	if $x \leqslant y$ and $w \leqslant z$ then $xtw \leqslant ytz$
boundary conditions	$0tx = 0; \ 1tx = x.$

s-norms are regarded as constructs dual to the t-norms.

4.2. s-norm

An s-norm (known also as a triangular co-norm) is a binary operation $s : [0, 1]^2 \rightarrow [0, 1]$ satisfying the requirements of

commutativity	$xsy = ysx$
associativity	$xs(ysz) = (xsy)sz$
monotonicity	if $x \leqslant y$ and $w \leqslant z$ then $xsw \leqslant ysz$
boundary conditions	$xs0 = x;\ \ xs1 = 1.$

Clearly, the min operator ($\wedge$) is a t-norm whereas the max operator ($\vee$) is an s-norm. They correspond to set intersection and union operators, respectively, when membership degrees are constrained to the two-element set of grades of belongingness, that is $\{0, 1\}$. Thus, they may be regarded as natural extensions of set intersection and union operations to fuzzy sets. Some of the most frequently encountered triangular norms include product and Lukasiewicz AND connective, $\max(0, x + y - 1)$. In the case of s-norms, we can point out at the probabilistic sum $(x + y - xy)$ and Lukasiewicz OR connective, $\min(1, x + y)$. A selection of a certain t-norm and s-norm is guided by two criteria: interactivity of the information granules and computational complexity. By interactivity of A and B we mean a way in which the two information granules interact. If there is no interaction, the min (and max, respectively) could serve as good models of the logic operators. If there is an interaction, one should favor some other t- and s-norms that are interactive. For instance, the semantics of the two information granules "expensive car" and "fast car" suggests that these granules (fuzzy sets) interact. Thus the result of such AND combinations should incorporate the fact that these granules interact (one may expect that if the car is expensive it is also fast). On the other hand, the combination of the granules "new car" and "red car" involves two pieces that are highly noninteractive (a new car is not necessarily red).

On the computational side, the lack of interaction is well represented by the min and max operations: note that $\min(x, a)$ returns x once x is less than a and this result does not reflect the value of a. Obviously, this does not happen in the case of the product operation whose result depends on the values of the two arguments.

For each t-norm there exists a dual s-norm; this means that the equality holds

$$xsy = 1 - (1 - x)t(1 - y)$$

or, alternatively,

$$xty = 1 - (1 - x)s(1 - y).$$

Once rewritten in the form:

$$1 - xsy = (1 - x) + (1 - y), \quad 1 - xty = (1 - x)s(1 - y).$$

It is seen immediately that these two relationships are De Morgan laws, as commonly encountered in set theory:

$$\overline{A \cup B} = \bar{A} \cap \bar{B}$$

$$\overline{A \cap B} = \bar{A} \cup \bar{B}.$$

In general, fuzzy sets do not support two fundamental relationships encountered in set theory, namely,

$$A \cap \bar{A} \neq \varnothing$$

$$A \cup \bar{A} \neq \mathbf{X}.$$

More specifically the following inclusions hold:

overlap

$$A \cap \bar{A} \supset \varnothing$$

underlap

$$A \cup \bar{A} \subset \mathbf{X}.$$

This departure from the essential dependencies encountered in set theory is inherently associated with the continuous membership functions. The existence of membership values different than 0 or 1 contributes to the effect of fuzzy set overlap and underlap.

5. Transformations of Fuzzy Sets

The extension principle plays a fundamental role in translating set-based concepts into their fuzzy-set oriented counterparts. Typical examples include arithmetic operations with fuzzy numbers. Essentially, the extension principle is used to transform fuzzy sets via functions (Kandel, 1986; Klir and Folger, 1988).

Let X and Y be two universes of discourse (spaces) and f be a mapping from X to Y,

$$f : X \rightarrow Y.$$

Let A be a fuzzy set in X. The extension principle states that the image of A under this mapping is a fuzzy set $B = f(A)$ in Y such that, for each $y \in Y$,

$$B(y) = \sup_x A(x)$$

subject to $x \in X$ and $y = f(x)$

as illustrated in Figure 3 below.

6. Specificity of Fuzzy Sets

Fuzzy sets are information granules that encapsulate a number of elements and provide their unique name (label). We have already discussed the role of information granularity although not getting into detail as far as the quantification of the concept itself is concerned. While highly intuitive, the notion still calls for a more detailed description. Let us concentrate on normal fuzzy sets (that is fuzzy sets whose membership functions assume values equal to 1). The simplest way of handling this concept is to use an idea of σ-count (cardinality, Zadeh, 1975a,b,c). Recall that the σ-count is expressed in the form:

$$\sigma(A) = \int_x A(x)\, dx$$

(we assume that the above integral makes sense). Subsequently, we define specificity using any decreasing transformation of the σ-count, say

$$Sp(A) = \exp(-\sigma(A) - 1)$$

that brings the values of the s-count to the unit interval. Following this definition we count the number of elements in the fuzzy set. As these elements belong to the fuzzy set to a different degree of membership, the overall integral (or sum in the case of finite spaces) meets our intuitive sense of distinction between fuzzy sets containing a large number of elements versus the constructs embracing a small number of elements. If $\sigma(A) = 1$ then the specificity of this fuzzy set assumes one, $Sp(A) = 1$. In light of the normality, this implies that the information granule consists only of a single element. If the A is spread over the entire universe of discourse then its specificity is low, $Sp(A) = \exp(-(card(X) - 1))$.

As an example, let us compute the σ-count of the following fuzzy sets: $A = (1.0\ 0.6\ 0.5\ 0.2\ 0.0)$ and $B = (0.2\ 0.6\ 1.0\ 1.0\ 1.0)$. The specificity of A is equal $Sp(A) = \exp(-(2.3 - 1)) = \exp(-1.3)$ whereas $Sp(B) = \exp(-(3.8 - 1)) = \exp(-2.8)$. This is highly intuitive: we regard A to be more specific than B as it embraces (even partially) less elements than the concept described by the another fuzzy set.

It is interesting to note that specificity can be modified by operations on fuzzy sets as well as applying hedges (linguistic modifiers). The linguistic modifiers such as more or less (more or less $A(x) = A^{0.5}(x)$) decrease specificity. The linguistic modifiers such as very (very $A(x) = A^2(x)$) concentrate the concept and increase their specificity. As far as logic operations on fuzzy sets go, the union operation results in the decreasing specificity, namely:

$$Sp(A \cup B) \geqslant \max(Sp(A), Sp(B)).$$

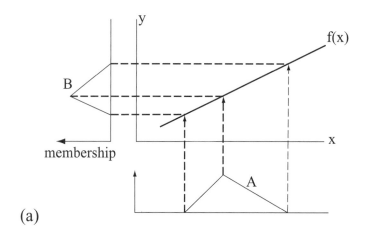

(a)

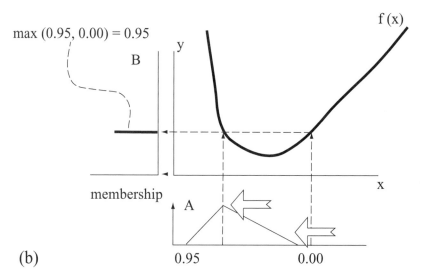

(b)

Figure 3 Computing induced fuzzy set B through a function (f): (a) invertible functions (f^{-1} exists); (b) noninvertible functions (f^{-1} does not exist)

We cannot draw general conclusions regarding an intersection of fuzzy sets. The main reason is that the resulting fuzzy set is subnormal while the definition has been introduced to handle normal fuzzy sets. In such situations we may consider the definition of specificity introduced by Yager (1982, 1983) which holds for subnormal fuzzy sets. The specificity of A defined in $\mathbf{X}$, $Sp'(A)$, assigns to a fuzzy set A a nonnegative number such that it satisfies the following conditions:

- $Sp'(A) = 1$ if and only if there exists only one element of $\mathbf{X}$ for which A assumes 1 while the remaining membership values are equal zero.
- If $A(x) = 0$ for all elements of $\mathbf{X}$ then $Sp'(A) = 0$.

- If $A_1 \supset A_2$ then

$$Sp'(A_1) \leqslant Sp'(A_2).$$

Then the specificity measure is defined as the integral

$$Sp'(A) = \int_0^{\alpha_{\max}} \frac{d\alpha}{card(A_\alpha)},$$

where $\alpha_{\max}$ is the maximal membership value of A (height of A) and A_α is an α-cut of A, $A_\alpha = \{x | A(x) \geqslant \alpha\}$.

For the finite universe of discourse (that implies a finite number of membership values), the integration is replaced by a summation:

$$Sp(A) = \sum_{i=1}^{n} \frac{1}{card(A_{\alpha_i})} \Delta\alpha_i,$$

where

$$\Delta\alpha_i = \alpha_i - \alpha_{i-1}$$

and $\alpha_{i-1} = 0$ whereas n denotes a number of the membership values of A.

In general, if we are concerned with normal fuzzy sets, the use of the previous definition is computationally less demanding and equally appealing.

7. Granularity of Fuzzy Sets in Rule-based Systems

It is beneficial to relate the effect of modifiable granularity with the behavior of the commonly used structures of data mining such as rules and rule-based systems. The main advantage of rule-based systems lies in their high readability and modularity. The rules can be added and deleted quite easily. The knowledge represented in this way is thus highly modifiable. An important and relevant aspect of rules comes from their ability to cope with various levels of information granularity (see Figure 1). By changing the granularity of conditions and conclusions, the rule can be made more specific or more general. For example, if the granularity of the conclusion increases then the rule becomes more general. Evidently, the rule:

If speed is 60 mph then fuel consumption is 30 mpg

is far more specific than the rule whose conclusion arises as an interval of possible values:

If speed is 60 mph then fuel consumption is [25, 35] mpg.

On the other hand, if we make the condition less specific, then the rule gets more general. Analogically, by dropping a subcondition in the rule, the rules gains in generality. As an example, consider the rule:

If speed is [45, 65] mph then fuel consumption is 30 mpg

where the condition is replaced by an interval containing speed values. One can make this condition more realistic and less brittle (which is associated with set-based representation) by using a fuzzy set named moderate speed:

If speed is moderate then fuel consumption is 30 mpg.

It is also quite evident that by increasing the granularity of the condition we make the rule more general up to the point where the rule becomes an unconditional (condition-free) statement. For instance, we have

If speed is ANY SPEED then fuel consumption is 30 mpg

where ANY SPEED is a fuzzy set with the membership function equal identically to 1 over the space of feasible speed values. The granulation of information effect is schematically visualized in Figure 4.

The rules can be induced from data in two main modes:

1. The information granules are provided by the designer or the user of the data mining tool; then all required associations are learned automatically and captured in the form of

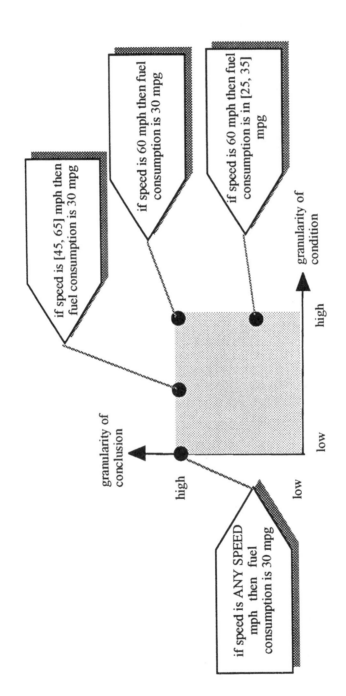

Figure 4 Granulation effect in rules realized by modifiable fuzzy sets

detailed rules (usually equipped with some confidence factors) or multidimensional contingency tables. In this sense, this approach is user-driven: it is the user who furnishes the basic information granules to be used in the ensuing activities of data mining and building pertinent associations.

2. In this option, both information granules as well as associations between them are optimized simultaneously (e.g., using neural networks).

8. Fuzzy Set and Set-Based Information Granulation

Sets and fuzzy sets are the two conceptual and algorithmic frameworks in which an information granulation takes place. The aim of this section is to contrast these two frameworks and underline the advantages of fuzzy sets over the set-theoretic environment. More specifically, we set up two criteria using which this comparison can be completed. We discuss a problem of robustness as emerging in granular computing and afterward pose a question of reconstruction of granular information. In these two tasks we will deal with a family of information granules $A_1, A_2, ..., A_c$ that are used to granulate the variable. Refer, for example, to the speed variable and its granulation through three terms of low, medium, and high speed.

8.1. Robustness Properties

The noise component associated with the original datum produces a certain effect within the family of information granules. Any modification of the datum is clearly reflected in the values of the membership functions. A sound index quantifying this effect can be given in the form:

$$Q_x = \int_x \sum_{i=1}^{c} | A_i(x) - A_i(x') | \, dx,$$

where x' denotes a datum affected by a noise component. Furthermore we consider a local index $q(x)$, whose values depend on the current element of the universe of discourse, that is

$$q(x) = \sum_{i=1}^{c} | A_i(x) - A_i(x') | \, \Delta x,$$

where Δx is a slice of the arguments of $\mathbf{X}$ situated around x. We may anticipate, which will be illustrated by a number of examples, that the distribution of q over x becomes very different in these two cases. In the case of set-based information granules, one ends up with an error that forms spikes situated right around the boundaries of the individual sets whereas in the fuzzy set case we have a far more uniform distribution of the values of the performance index.

As an illustrative example, we consider a collection of overlapping Gaussian fuzzy sets illustrated in Figure 5.

These fuzzy sets are described by their mean values and spreads

$$m_1 = -2.0, \quad \sigma_1 = 2.5$$
$$m_2 = 0.0, \quad \sigma_2 = 2.5$$
$$m_3 = 1.5, \quad \sigma_3 = 2.0$$
$$m_4 = 3.0, \quad \sigma_4 = 3.5$$
$$m_5 = 5.0, \quad \sigma_5 = 2.5$$
$$m_6 = 7.0, \quad \sigma_6 = 2.0.$$

In the experiment, we construct a noise-affected version of the original input (x) by additively combining this particular datum with a uniform random variable centered around zero with amplitude σ, that is

$$x' = x + U(0,0)\sigma,$$

where $U(0, 0)$ denotes a uniform distribution located around zero. For comparative reasons we

membership

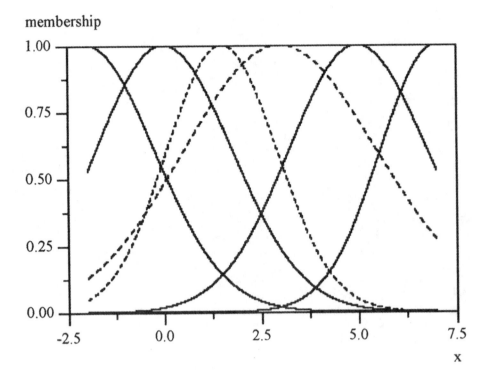

Figure 5 A collection of fuzzy sets

discuss a collection of sets induced by the original fuzzy sets (these sets are generated by taking 1/2 cuts of the respective fuzzy sets). As we are dealing with a family of these fuzzy sets, we span sets between intersection points of the consecutive fuzzy sets.

The plot of $q(x)$ is shown in Figure 6. It contains the values of this local measure obtained for the fuzzy sets as well as the resulting sets. The distribution of $q(x)$ is very different for sets and fuzzy sets. Fuzzy sets promote continuity of membership values. This is very much reflected in the way in which the local performance index looks. The values of q are nonzero over the entire universe of discourse but they are distributed relatively evenly. Furthermore $q(x)$ assumes low values. In contrast, sets absorb noise (in some regions the local values of q assume zero) yet there are significant bursts of this index in the regions located at the boundaries of the corresponding sets. The magnitude of $q(x)$ is also significantly higher than in the previous situation. To make this more visible, the reader may superimpose Figure 6 on top of the second figure summarizing the values of q.

Finally, Figure 7 shows the values of Q plotted versus a variable magnitude of noise. The effect of noise absorption is better in case of fuzzy sets than sets. The differences in the values of Q become more profound for higher values of σ. An importance of this finding lies in avoidance of the brittleness of rules containing fuzzy sets over those realized in the setting of set theory (numeric intervals). The brittleness pertains to the effect of complete firing or disabling of the rule depending on a location of the given fact versus the condition part of the rule. Avoidance of the brittleness effect is essential to the development (training) of the rules as well as their further usage.

8.2. Reconstruction Problem in Granular Computing

As we are concerned with operations on information granules, there could emerge situations when one becomes interested in producing a numeric representative of the granules. Here the difference between sets and fuzzy sets regarded as information granules becomes

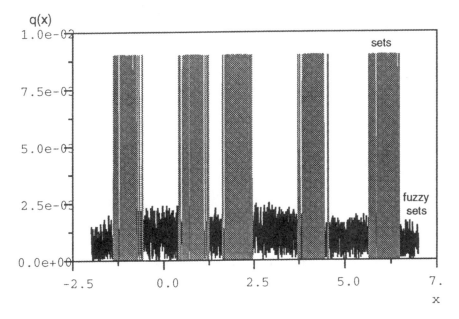

Figure 6 A distribution of local performance index $q(x)$ in the universe of discourse

profound. When it comes to sets, it becomes apparent that once we state that "x is included in A" (here A is viewed as a set) there is no way to reconstruct x. Simply, one can only state that x is located somewhere in set A (see Figure 8). In contrast, for the information

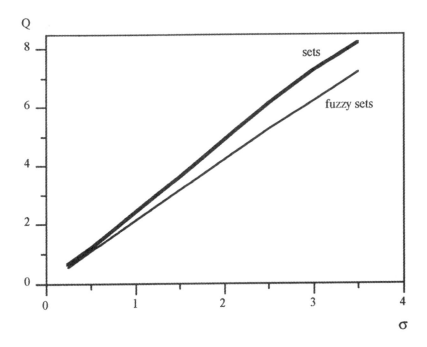

Figure 7 Q versus magnitude of noise (σ) for a collection of fuzzy sets and their set-based counterpart

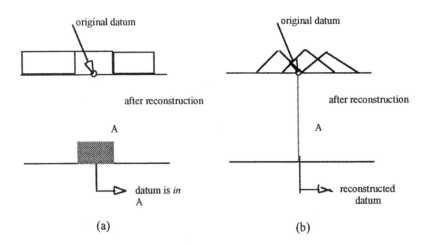

Figure 8 Encoding and decoding with sets (a) and fuzzy sets (b)—note an evident decrease in the granularity of the reconstructed results in case of sets and lossless reconstruction in the case of fuzzy sets

granules represented in the form of fuzzy sets there exists an efficient way of reconstructing original numeric information. Especially if the contributing fuzzy sets are defined by triangular fuzzy sets with 1/2 overlap between two successive linguistic terms, then the reconstruction becomes lossless, that is, one reconstructs an original entity. The reconstruction formula takes into consideration the modal values of the A_is (that is m_i) and the corresponding degrees of membership:

$$\tilde{x} = \frac{\sum_{i=1}^{c} A_i(x_0)m_i}{\sum_{i=1}^{c} A_i(x_0),}$$

where x_0 is an original numeric datum.

9. Linguistic Approximation

The key objective of linguistic approximation (Zadeh, 1975a,b,c) is to produce results of fuzzy computing that, by being approximated using a collection of the generic linguistic terms, deliver highly interpretable results. This activity becomes crucial to the high level of user-friendliness of the overall data mining environment. The term linguistic approximation underlines the character of the approximation process occurring there: any information granule arising at any phase of granular computing is expressed in terms of the finite collection of linguistic terms. These terms consist of two main categories of entities:

1. n generic fuzzy sets with clearly defined semantics that are regarded as fundamental building blocks conveying clearly defined semantics (for example, seven fuzzy sets labelled as negative large, negative medium, negative small, zero, positive small, positive medium, positive large constitute a meaningful basis for describing any variable in the process of being captured). Denote these fuzzy sets by $T_1, T_2, ..., T_n$. Additionally, this collection of fuzzy sets is denoted by $\mathcal{T}$.

2. Linguistic hedges (modifiers) such as more or less, very, more or less, unknown are used to modify any generic fuzzy set. They contribute to the enhancement of the descriptive capabilities of these fuzzy sets and produce compound expressions of the form more or less positive small, very positive large, et cetera. Denote the modifiers by $M_1, M_2, ..., M_p$

$(= \mathscr{M})$. A common way of defining membership functions of these compound expressions is by affecting the original membership functions in the following ways

$$M_j[A_i(x)] = A_i^{r_j}(x),$$

where r_j is an exponent of the respective linguistic modifiers. For instance, the linguistic modifier more or less comes with the exponent equal to $1/2$. The hedge very exhibits a concentration effect and is associated with $r = 2$.

Formally, the problem of linguistic approximation can be regarded as a straightforward enumeration task:

Given an information granule X, find a generic linguistic term $T^* \in \mathscr{T}$ along with a linguistic modifier $M^* \in \mathscr{M}$ that represents (approximates) X to the highest extent meaning that

$$\min_{M \in \mathscr{M}, T \in \mathscr{T}} \|X - MT\| = \|X - M^*T^*\|.$$

The result of the linguistic approximation is M^*T^*. To express the quality of approximation we may use any distance $\| \cdot \|$ (e.g., the Hamming one) that is calculated between X and its approximation $\|X - M^*T^*\|$. The optimization mechanism comprises of two phases (refer to Figure 9):

1. Finding an optimal linguistic term T^*.
2. Refining (improving) the result by applying one among the linguistic modifiers M^* being at our disposal.

This optimization scheme is the simplest one may envision. Longer approximation chains such as $M^* M^{**} T^*$ could be possible (even though they could be difficult to interpret). One may also think of compound logical expressions that are developed over the generic terms, say T^* and T^{**}, T^* or T^{**}, T^* and (not T^{**}), et cetera.

10. Fuzzy Sets and Probability Theory

There is an interesting, contentious, and important issue regarding an identification of symbiotic links arising between the calculus of probability and fuzzy sets. These relationships

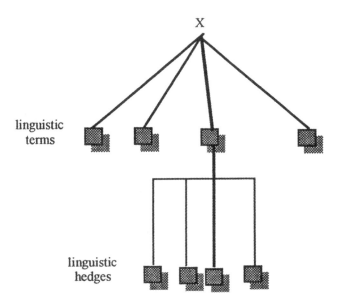

Figure 9 A two-stage process of linguistic approximation

are crucial in the setting of any application pursuit of data mining where each of them starts playing a visible role. There is currently a widely recognized consensus that fuzzy sets and probability calculus are highly orthogonal concepts. Fuzziness deals with granular concepts and fuzzy sets attempt to capture an aspect of gradual membership. Fuzzy sets deal with an array of problems of graduality of concepts. Probability is concerned with quantifying phenomena of sharp boundaries whose occurrence may not be certain, namely the events under consideration may occur with some probability. Hence the occurrence of an event becomes a central notion of probability: the calculus of probability deals with occurrences of events. As the leading research agendas of fuzzy sets and probability theory are different and complementary, we may anticipate several possible avenues of synergy. In particular, we may talk about probabilities of fuzzy events, *viz.*, events characterized by fuzzy sets. The notion itself goes back to the very inception of fuzzy sets as first introduced by Zadeh (1968) under the name of expected value of a fuzzy set. Formally, this probability is computed in the form

$$P(A) = \int_X A(x)p(x)\,dx,$$

where A is a fuzzy set defined in $\mathbf{X}$ while $p(.)$ is a probability density function (or probability function) expressed over the same space. The obvious, yet highly relevant, relationships are satisfied:

- if $A < A'$ then $Sp(A) \geqslant Sp(A')$ and $E(A) \leqslant E(A')$
- if $A = \mathbf{X}$ then its relevance attains its maximum equal to 1;
- if $p(x)$ is located in a single point $x0$ then the fuzzy set is relevant if $x0$ is included in its support.

In light of these findings, there is a certain compromise (trade-off) between a specificity of the fuzzy set and its probabilistic relevance. On the one hand, we are usually after quite detailed (specific) information granules. On the other, we expect these granules to be highly relevant and supported in the sense of available data. Too specific fuzzy sets will loose relevance. Highly relevant (from the probabilistic standpoint) information granules become less specific up to the point of becoming useless. Treating relevance and specificity as two important characteristics of any information granule, we can use them in completing data mining activities. Assuming some values of the threshold levels γ_1 and γ_2 such that

$$Sp(A) > \gamma_1$$

$$E(A) > \gamma_2.$$

Each information granule, no matter if introduced externally at the beginning of data mining activity or derived as an effect of some data mining algorithm, can be readily evaluated. The satisfaction of the above given requirements helps us control a scope of data mining. For example, if we are interested in data nuggets (which by definition are rare yet very essential findings), the threshold value for the expected value of the fuzzy set can be made low. On the other extreme, if we are interested in revealing facts that commonly hold, then the specificity criterion may assume lower values with the expected value of this fuzzy set taking on high values. We can capture the specificity–relevance requirements by locating fuzzy sets in a so-called specificity-relevance plane (see Figure 10).

11. Conclusions

This study serves as a brief introduction to fuzzy sets regarded as an important conceptual and algorithmic framework for granular computing. We have enumerated a number of key features of fuzzy sets that make them a useful vehicle in the area of data mining:

- An ability to represent a broad spectrum of granular information in a flexible manner.
- Useful robustness properties that help eliminate a cumbersome brittleness effect.
- A broad class of operations on fuzzy sets is useful in developing models being capable of working with a broad range of practical problems.

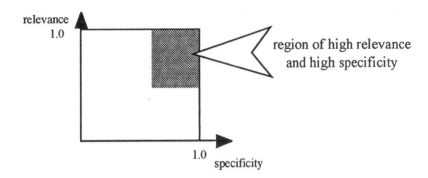

Figure 10 A specificity–relevance plane used to quantifity orthogonal aspects of fuzziness and randomness (probability)

In summary, Figure 11 paints a concise picture as to the role of fuzzy sets (and granular computing, in general) in the framework of data mining. Information granules cast all data mining activities in a certain framework. The user approaches a database through the focal entities—information granules. These granules address the issues of semantics of all ensuing granular computing. As a result of data mining, as shown on the right-hand side of this figure, we obtain new information granules (these may be a result of a certain revision of those previously used based on some experimental evidence) and derive relationships between them (either in the form of a web of associations or rule-based architectures). Figure 11 also identifies the position of the individual concepts discussed in this study (relevance, specificity, linguistic approximation, etc.).

The study has not tackled any detailed fuzzy-set augmented data mining algorithms. These were left out on purpose as they are beyond the scope of this chapter. In general, two avenues of development can be sought:

1. A granulation of the existing methods where we do not change the backbone of the method that already exists but modify it to perform at the level of information granules. Some representative examples may concern computing correlation coefficients (matrices) for multivariable data. Instead of determining strengths of correlation among individual variables (as done so far), we compute values of the correlation coefficients between particular information granules. There is a striking difference: the correlation coefficients used in a standard way describe relationships between variables taken over their

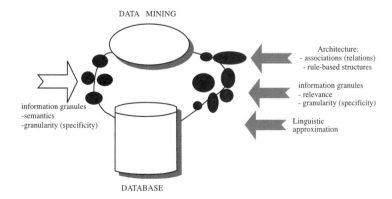

Figure 11 Granular computing and its role in data mining

complete ranges of values (where a linear relationship may not be globally present). The correlation coefficient determined over some information granules forms a far more precise and adjustable instrument that helps reveal dependencies in databases. Another example deals with fuzzy contingency tables where such tables are constructed over a series of linguistic granules forming their entries. Finally, one can think of granular regression models equipped with fuzzy sets (fuzzy numbers) serving as parameters of such models.

2. A development of new methods that are even more profoundly geared toward granular computing. One may allude here to a broad class of relational calculus including relational equations.

Acknowledgment

Support from the Natural Sciences and Engineering Research Council (NSERC) is gratefully appreciated.

References

Butnariu, D. and P. Klement. 1993. *Triangular Norm Based Measures and Games with Fuzzy Coalitions.* Dordrecht: Kluwer Academic Publishers.

Dubois et al. (eds). 1993. *Readings in Fuzzy Sets for Intelligent Systems.* San Mateo, CA: Morgan Kaufmann.

Fayyad, U. M., G. Piatetsky-Shapiro, and P. Smyth. 1996a. "From data mining to knowledge discovery in databases." *AI Magazine* **17**: 37–54.

Fayyad, U. M., G. Piatetsky-Shapiro, G. Smyth, and R. Uthurusamy. 1996b. *Advances in Knowledge Discovery and Data Mining.* Menlo Park, CA: AAAI Press.

Frawley, W., G. Piatetsky-Shapiro, and C. Matheus. 1991. "Knowledge discovery in databases: an overview." In *Knowledge Discovery in Databases,* edited by G. Piatetsky-Shapiro and W. Frawley, pp. 1–27. Menlo Park, CA: AAAI Press.

Kandel, A. 1986. *Fuzzy Mathematical Techniques with Applications.* Redwood, CA: Addison-Wesley.

Klir, G. J. and T. A. Folger. 1988. *Fuzzy Sets, Uncertainty and Information.* Saddle Back, NJ: Prentice-Hall.

Menger, K. 1942. "Statistical metric spaces." *Proc. Nat. Acad. Sci. (USA)* **28**: 235–237.

Pedrycz, W. 1995. *Fuzzy Sets Engineering.* Boca Raton, FL: CRC Press.

Pedrycz, W. and F. Gomide. 1998. *An Introduction to Fuzzy Sets. Analysis and Design.* Cambridge, Mass: MIT Press.

Ruspini, E., P. Bonnisone, and W. Pedrycz. 1998. *Handbook of Fuzzy Computation.* Bristol and Philadelphia: Institute of Physics Publishers.

Schweizer, B. and A. Sklar. 1983. *Probabilistic Metric Spaces.* Amsterdam: North-Holland.

Weber, S. 1983. "A general concept of fuzzy connectives, negations and implications based on *t*-norms." *Fuzzy Sets Sys.* **11**: 115–134.

Yager, R. R. 1982. "Measuring tranquility and anxiety in decision making: an application of fuzzy sets." *Int. J. Gen. Syst.* **8**: 139–146.

Yager, R. R. 1983. "Entropy and specificity in a mathematical theory of evidence." *Int. J. Gen. Sys.* **9**: 249–260.

Zadeh, L. A. 1965. "Fuzzy sets." *Inform. Control* **8**: 338–353.

Zadeh, L. A. 1968. "Probability of fuzzy events." *J. Math. Anal. Appl.* **22**: 421–427.

Zadeh, L. A. 1975a. "The concept of a linguistic variable and its application to approximate reasoning." *Inform. Sci.* **8**: 199–249.

Zadeh, L. A. 1975b. "The concept of a linguistic variable and its application to approximate reasoning." *Inform. Sci.* **8**: 301–357.

Zadeh, L. A. 1975c. "The concept of a linguistic variable and its application to approximate reasoning." *Inform. Sci.* **9**: 43–80.

11 SEARCH TECHNIQUES

Weixiong Zhang

ABSTRACT   Search plays an important role in knowledge discovery in databases (KDD) and data mining. Given hypothesis representation schemas and hypothesis evaluation criteria, a search process explores a hypothesis space to find useful knowledge from given data. The effectiveness and efficiency of the underlying search methods determine the success and performance of the overall KDD process. In this chapter, we briefly describe the basic concepts of hypothesis space and hypothesis evaluation, discuss in detail the basic search techniques, and highlight their performance and complexity. Particularly, we consider systematic enumerative search methods, including best-first search, depth-first branch-and-bound and iterative deepening, and neighborhood search methods, including gradient descent, artificial neural networks, tabu search, and simulated annealing. We also describe beam search, complete beam search, and genetic algorithms.

1. Introduction and Overview

Knowledge discovery in databases (KDD) and data mining refers to the process of finding useful knowledge from a set of data for a particular application. The targeted knowledge for discovery includes patterns and regularities that are embedded in the data, decision rules that can be induced from the data, and models such as functions and probability and causal networks (see Chapter 5). The goal of a KDD process is to find useful knowledge about the given data with a high confidence.

A KDD process is a feedback loop of two steps, hypothesis formation and hypothesis evaluation and verification. At an early stage of a discovery process, hypotheses are merely speculations or conjectures about possible knowledge that the given data may provide. The hypotheses need to be verified, and further refined and enhanced. This hypothesis formation and verification process can be repeated many times until high quality hypotheses have been found.

According to Fayyad et al. (1996), a data mining method may consist of three components: knowledge (hypothesis) representation (see Chapter 5), knowledge evaluation (see Chapter 19), and search. The representation component is concerned with the selection of a language for the hypotheses to be developed. The evaluation component focuses on using the right quantitative function to measure the quality or fitness of the hypotheses in the overall KDD process, as well as in the process of searching for a set of hypotheses that satisfy a criterion. The search component is the subject of this chapter.

Given a representation schema and hypothesis evaluation criterion, a KDD process concentrates on finding a set of qualified hypotheses. This is a combinatorial optimization problem that requires extensive search in the space of hypotheses. Although developing the right hypothesis formats in the first place is important to the overall KDD process, finding qualified hypotheses is equally critical. The effectiveness and efficiency of the search methods used can largely determine the success and performance of the KDD process.

In this chapter, we give an overview of the basic search techniques. These search techniques can be classified into two major categories, although the boundary between the two groups is not a straight, clear line.

The first group consists of exhaustive search methods. The basic idea of this class of search methods is to enumerate intelligently the combinations of possible hypotheses and their parameters. The main search algorithms of this group include best-first search, depth-first branch-and-bound, iterative deepening, recursive best-first search, and fixed-memory best-first search. These search algorithms employ evaluation functions or cost functions to prune the hypotheses that are inferior to the best one found so far, as well as to guide the search process itself. The most important feature of this class of algorithms is that they are guaranteed to provide an optimal hypothesis under the current representation schema.

The second group consists of neighborhood search or local search methods. These search methods in principle conduct (random) walks in the space of a neighborhood of hypotheses. The important search algorithms in this class include gradient descent or hill climbing, artificial neural networks, tabu search, and simulated annealing. These search algorithms first define the structure of the search neighborhood by developing operators that make local perturbations to transform one hypothesis to its neighboring hypotheses. They then define a policy on how the neighborhood should be explored. With a defined neighborhood structure and search strategy, neighborhood search algorithms then search for a hypothesis that is better than its neighbors.

This chapter is organized as follows. In Section 2, we describe the basic concepts of hypothesis space. We consider hypothesis evaluation for the purpose of guiding a search algorithm in Section 3. In Section 4, we describe the basic search techniques in detail. Our discussion is organized around the two groups of search algorithms, enumerative search and neighborhood search. We first discuss the basic concepts and features of these two types of search algorithms, and we then present individual search algorithms. We then briefly discuss the performance and complexity of enumerative search and neighborhood search algorithms in Section 5. We highlight the most important results regarding the worst-case and average-case performance of these algorithms. Finally, our conclusions are given in Section 6.

2. Hypothesis Space

To reiterate, the knowledge that a KDD process tries to discover can be represented in various forms, including patterns, regularities, decision rules (decision trees and decision lists), and models (functions and probability and causal networks; see Chapter 5). These different forms of knowledge are categorically referred to as hypotheses in the process of knowledge discovery, as their validity and usefulness need to be examined in practice. After settling on a particular hypothesis format, which largely depends on the application at hand, the KDD process turns to a combinatorial optimization problem of finding the hypothesis to best fit the given data or a set of hypotheses that satisfy a quality criterion.

The process of finding a set of hypotheses that meet a criterion is a search in the space of possible hypotheses. Depending on how the search is carried out, a hypothesis space may contain partially specified hypotheses, which may satisfy a quality criterion, or fully specified hypotheses, which may not necessarily be invalid. A hypothesis space contains partially specified hypotheses if fully specified hypotheses are to be constructed in steps during an enumerative search, as described in Section 4.1. Consider the problem of finding the best decision tree based on a set of features as an example. The search process starts with an empty tree with all features unbound. It then selects one feature and binds it to all its possible values, resulting in a new set of more constrained, partially specified hypotheses. This process continues until all the features are specified, with more and more specific hypotheses being generated.

A hypothesis space contains fully specified but invalid hypotheses organized in a neighborhood of hypotheses, which is used in a neighborhood search, as described in Section 4.2. Consider a neighborhood of decision rules as an example. A decision rule, such as an IF–THEN rule, can be encoded as a string of 0 and 1 bits. A local operator can simply flip a single bit from 0 to 1 or vice versa, swap the positions of two substrings, or perform other similar local perturbations. The hypothesis space thus consists of all possible 0–1 strings representing valid and invalid decision rules. Two decision rules (strings) are connected to each other in the hypothesis space if an operator can change one to the other.

In short, the search space of a KDD problem is typically a graph, in which a node represents a hypothesis to be evaluated and an edge represents a relationship between the two hypotheses to which the edge is connected.

3. Hypothesis Evaluation

Hypothesis evaluation plays a critical role in the whole KDD process, which is the main topic of Chapter 19. The reader is referred to Chapter 19 on issues regarding how to develop evaluation functions for the purpose of KDD.

Hypothesis evaluation plays equally important roles in the process of searching for the best hypothesis within a huge space of possible hypotheses. An evaluation function provides guidance to a search algorithm, determining if a hypothesis can be eliminated from further consideration as well as deciding the order in which hypotheses are explored. Furthermore, the accuracy of an evaluation function determines the efficiency of the search.

An evaluation function can measure the quality of a hypothesis or the quality of the best hypothesis it can lead to. An evaluation function typically appears in the form of a cost function used by a search algorithm. A quality measure of a hypothesis can be represented as the estimated cost of an optimal hypothesis that can be found by exploring the space underneath the node representing the hypothesis. Specifically, the estimated cost of a node, $f(n)$, is an estimate of the actual cost of the node n, $f^*(n)$, which is the cost of the best hypothesis underneath the node.

The evaluation functions used in enumerative search and neighborhood search may have completely different features. One important feature of the evaluation functions employed in enumerative search is lower boundedness. A lower-bound evaluation function can guarantee the optimality of the final solution found by an enumerative search algorithm. A cost function is a lower bound if it never overestimates the actual cost of a node, that is, $f(n) \leqslant f^*(n)$, for all nodes n in the state space. A cost function is monotonic if the cost of a child node n', $f(n')$, is always greater than or equal to the cost of its parent node n, that is, $f(n') \geqslant f(n)$. The monotonic property comes from the fact that a child node typically represents a more constrained problem than its parent, and hence costs at least as much. The monotonic property is slightly stronger than the lower bound property, and the former implies the latter, but not vice versa. Given a lower bound function, a monotonic function can be constructed by taking the cost of a node as the maximum cost of all nodes on the path from the root to the node, guaranteeing that $f(n') \geqslant f(n)$, where n is the parent of n'.

Lower-bound cost functions are available for almost all practical problems. They can be developed by removing constraints on the problem to be solved (Pearl, 1984). This is a general method called constraint relaxation schema. One simple example of constraint relaxation is the Manhattan distance that is the direct distance between two points on a map. This gives a lower bound on the actual distance between the two points by ignoring the constraint of physical obstacles on the straight line connecting these two points.

Evaluation functions used in neighborhood search do not necessarily require lower boundedness. As the hypothesis space contains fully specified hypotheses, the evaluation function used is only required to correctly compute the actual value of a hypothesis.

4. Basic Search Techniques

A hypothesis space is a search space as far as the search process is concerned, and hypotheses correspond to states or nodes in a search graph. A search method is a strategy that defines the order in which nodes in a search space are explored or the order in which hypotheses are evaluated. The overall goal of a search process is to find an optimal or high quality hypothesis for the KDD problem at hand, or a set of hypotheses that satisfy a quality criterion. Such targeting hypotheses are goal nodes for a search algorithm.

According to the order of node exploration, search methods fall into enumerative search and neighborhood search paradigms. An enumerative search method is an intelligent enumeration of the states of a search space. An enumerative search algorithm is also called constructive enumeration, as it systematically constructs possible solutions by enumeration. A neighborhood search method, on the other hand, can be viewed as a walk in a space or neighborhood of solutions, which repeatedly and iteratively improves the best solution found so far.

In this section, we describe the basic concepts of these two different search paradigms and their most important search algorithms.

4.1. Enumerative Search

A search using systematic enumeration is usually used to find optimal solutions. The basic idea of systematic enumeration is to decompose a difficult problem into problems of a smaller scale so that solving some of the subproblems gives rise to the solution to the original problem. In order to guarantee that a solution to a problem is found, a decomposition must generate all subproblems that can cover the original problem in terms of providing solutions. In other words, all possible subproblems must be constructed using the decomposition and all possible solutions will potentially be generated.

The main focus of systematic enumeration is to arrange a search space in such a way that many nodes in the space do not have to be generated or visited during the search. This is done by pruning some nodes based on their merit of leading to (optimal) goal nodes. If the current node is believed to have no chance of leading to a solution better than the best solution found so far, this node can be discarded from further consideration.

In short, an enumerative search can be represented by a state space. A state space consists of a set of states and a collection of operators. The states are configurations of the problem to be solved. The operators are actions that map one state to another. The number of children of a node is referred to as the branching factor of the node.

In general, a state space is a graph, in which nodes represent states, and edges represent decompositions or operators. A state space tree is a special state space graph without cycles. In the rest of this section, we focus on the state space tree. Note that a tree is a realistic model for problem solving in practice. Almost all combinatorial optimization problems can be decomposed by the principle of inclusion and exclusion (Liu, 1968). If the problem is decomposed such that one entity included in one subproblem is excluded from its siblings, then we have a partition of the state space, which is a tree without any duplicate nodes. Many search algorithms, especially those that use memory linear in search depth (Korf, 1995; Zhang and Korf, 1995), explore a state space graph as a tree, since these algorithms are generally unable to verify if a node has been visited before.

In order to decide the order of node exploration and to carry out pruning to avoid enumerating all possible states, a node's merit of leading to an optimal goal needs to be measured. This merit measure comes from evaluation or cost functions, which are discussed in Chapter 19 and Section 3. In the following discussion, we assume the cost functions used are lower bound functions.

BEST-FIRST SEARCH

The first algorithm we consider is best-first search (BFS). BFS maintains a partially expanded state space, and at each cycle expands a node of minimum cost, among all nodes that have been generated but not yet expanded, until an optimal goal node is chosen for expansion. To maintain the partially expanded space, BFS typically requires space that is exponential with regard to search depth, making it impractical for most applications. Pseudocode for the algorithm for searching in a state space tree is given in Figure 1, where the list open is used to maintain current frontier nodes. The algorithm starts with BFS (root).

A special case of BFS is the A^* algorithm (Hart et al., 1968), which uses the cost function $f(n) = g(n) + h(n)$, where $g(n)$ is the sum of the cost of the path from the initial state to the current node n, and $h(n)$ is an estimated cost from node n to a goal node. An important feature

```
     BFS(root)
1)   open ← ∅;
2)   n ← root;
3)   WHILE (n is not a goal node)
4)       Delete n from open;
5)       Expand n, generating and evaluating all its children;
6)       Insert all its children into open;
7)       n ← a minimum-cost node in open
```

Figure 1 Best-first search algorithm

of A^* is that for a given consistent heuristic estimate h, it expands the minimum number of nodes among all algorithms guaranteed to find an optimal goal, up to tie-breaking among nodes whose cost is equal to the optimal goal cost (Dechter and Pearl, 1985).

Depth-First Branch-and-Bound

Depth-first branch-and-bound (DFBnB) uses space that is only linear in the search depth. Starting at an initial node, and with a global upper bound u on the cost of an optimal goal, DFBnB always selects the most recently generated node, or the deepest node to expand next. Whenever a new leaf node is reached whose cost is less than u, u is revised to the cost of this new leaf. Whenever a node is selected for expansion whose cost is greater than or equal to u, it is pruned, because node costs are nondecreasing along a path from the root, and all descendents of a node must have costs at least as great as that of their ancestors.

In order to find an optimal goal node quickly, the newly generated child nodes should be searched in increasing order of their costs. This is called node ordering. Throughout this paper, when we refer to DFBnB, we mean DFBnB with node ordering. A recursive version of the algorithm with node ordering is given in Figure 2. The top-level call is made on the root node, DFBnB (*root*), with initial upper bound $u = \infty$.

The penalty for running DFBnB in linear space is that it expands some nodes that are not explored by BFS, or some nodes whose costs are greater than the optimal goal cost. In addition, DFBnB does not work very well on a graph with cycles, since it may keep expanding the nodes on a cycle. In this case, DFBnB requires either a finite tree, or a cutoff depth in order to guarantee termination.

Iterative Deepening

One remedy to the problem caused by unknown cutoff depth in depth-first branch-and-bound is to use iterative deepening (Korf, 1985). Iterative deepening also uses space with a linear search depth, and it never expands a node whose cost is greater than the optimal goal cost.

Using a global variable called the cutoff threshold, initially set to the cost of the root, iterative deepening performs a series of depth-first search iterations. In each iteration, it expands all nodes with costs less than or equal to the threshold. If a goal node is chosen for expansion, then it terminates successfully. Otherwise, the threshold is increased to the minimum cost of all nodes that were generated but not expanded on the last iteration, and a new iteration is begun. The algorithm is shown in Figure 3.

Iterative deepening is a general search algorithm, and includes a number of special cases, depending on the cost function. For example, depth-first iterative deepening (DFID) uses depth as cost and expands all nodes at a given depth before expanding any nodes at a greater depth. Uniform cost iterative deepening, an iterative version of Dijkstra's single-source shortest-path algorithm (Dijkstra, 1971), uses the sum of the costs on the path from the root to a node as the node cost. Iterative deepening A* (IDA*) employs the A^* cost function $f(n) = g(n) + h(n)$.

```
    DFBnB(n)
1)  Generate all k children of n: n_1, n_2, ···, n_k;
2)  Evaluate and Sort the children in increasing order of cost;
3)  FOR (i from 1 to k)
4)      IF ( cost(n_i) < u)
5)          IF (n_i is a leaf node and a solution)
7)              u ← cost(n_i);
8)          ELSE DFBnB(n_i);
9)      ELSE RETURN;
10) RETURN
```

Figure 2 Depth-first branch-and-bound algorithm

```
        ID(root)
1)      threshold  ←  cost(root);
2)      next_threshold  ←  ∞;
3)      REPEAT
4)          DFS(root)
5)          threshold  ←  next_threshold
6)          next_threshold  ←  ∞

        DFS(n)
7)      FOR (each child n_i of n)
8)          IF (n_i is a goal node and cost(n_i) ≤ threshold
9)              EXIT with optimal goal node n_i
10)         IF (cost(n_i) ≤ threshold)
11)             DFS(n_i)
12)         ELSE IF (cost(n_i) < next_threshold)
13)             next_threshold  ←  cost(n_i)
14)     RETURN
```

Figure 3 Iterative deepening algorithm

Although iterative deepening will not expand a node whose cost is greater than the cost of the optimal goal node, it may expand some nodes more than once. For instance, the number of times that the root is expanded is equal to the number of total iterations.

4.2. Neighborhood Search

In contrast with enumerative search methods, neighborhood search methods do not enumerate the states of a search space, and are usually used to find high quality approximate solutions quickly. Typically an optimal solution is not guaranteed.

The search space explored by a neighborhood search is defined by a neighborhood of feasible solutions, which are considered as states of the search space. Two states are connected if there is an operator that changes one state to the other by a local perturbation. Therefore, a neighborhood search is also called a local search. Neighborhood search has been studied extensively under the name of local search for solving combinatorial optimization problems (Aarts and Lenstra, 1997). In practice, local search emphasizes the operators making local perturbations that transform one state to another. All the carefully crafted operators for a particular problem define a neighborhood structure. How to develop effective operators and therefore smooth neighborhood structures are the main challenges for neighborhood search or local search methods.

A neighborhood search can be viewed as a (random) walk in a search space. When exploring a neighborhood of solutions, a neighborhood search method focuses on the current state and the states that can be directly reached from the current state. It repeatedly moves from the current state to one of its neighboring states to find solutions better than the best one encountered so far. The simplest strategy is to move to the best neighbor of the current state. However, this simple strategy, as well as all the other sophisticated ones, cannot guarantee the optimality of the final solution with limited computation. The problem is caused by the local minima in a search space, which are solutions better than their neighbors defined by the neighborhood structure. The biggest challenges to a neighborhood search include how to define a neighborhood that leads to high quality local minima, and how to escape from a local minimum when the search process reaches it. The answer to the first challenge depends, in principle, on the particular problem to be solved. The answer to the second challenge leads to different neighborhood search algorithms, which include gradient descent or hill climbing, tabu search (Glover, 1986; Glover et al., 1993), and simulated annealing (Kirkpatrick et al., 1983).

GRADIENT DESCENT OR HILL CLIMBING

Gradient descent or hill climbing are the simplest strategies of neighborhood search, and all other strategies can be considered as variants or improvements on this basic method. This method is called gradient descent, if solutions are measured by a minimizing function, or hill climbing, if solutions are quantified by a maximizing function. Without loss of generality, we will use gradient descent in our discussion.

Given a neighborhood structure, gradient descent simply moves from the current state to the best neighboring state, that is, the one with the least cost among all the neighboring states. It repeats this process until it reaches a local minimum, a state that is better than all of its neighbors. It may then restart the process of searching for another local minimum from a new starting point. This is called a multiple restart schema. This whole process of iterative search of local minima can terminate when the best solution encountered so far is satisfactory, or the total computation is exhausted. A prototypical gradient descent algorithm is shown in Figure 4, where $f(n)$ is the cost of state n.

A minor variant of the basic gradient descent is to move from the current state to a neighbor that has better quality than the current state, rather than moving to the one with the best quality among all neighboring states. However, whether this variant can improve performance in terms of final solution quality with the same computation time depends on particular problem domains.

TABU SEARCH

Repeated starts from a new initial state followed by subsequent search for a new local minimum is just one method to escape from a local minimum. There may exist neighborhood structures in which local minima are clustered, that is, local minima may not be far away from each other. In such neighborhood structures, it makes much more sense to restart the search for new local minima from the most recently found local minimum rather than a randomly generated starting point. This is the essence of tabu search (Glover, 1986; Glover et al., 1993).

Starting from an initial state, a neighborhood search can keep moving to the best neighbor, regardless of if the best neighbor is or is not better than the current state. In other words, the search process makes the deepest downhill move possible, which leads to the best neighbor with better quality than the current state, until it reaches a local minimum. It then

```
 1)  Set the best solution n* ← ∅;
 2)  DO
 3)     Choose an initial solution n′;
 4)     DO
 5)        n ← n′;
 5)        Generate the neighboring solutions of n, N(n);
 6)        Select the best neighbor n′ in N(n);
 7)     WHILE (f(n′) < f(n));
 8)     IF (f(n) < f(n*))
 9)        n* ← n;
10)  WHILE (no stopping criterion is met)
```

Figure 4 Basic gradient descent algorithm

makes the best uphill move to escape from the local minimum, and subsequently makes downhill moves again, if possible, to another local minimum.

However, when local minima are located in a vicinity, this modified gradient descent, which includes uphill moves, is very likely to visit the same local minima over and over again. In other words, the new gradient descent allows escape from individual local minima, but it cannot overcome the problem of being trapped by a set of clustered local minima. To solve this problem comes the tabu list or lists of tabu search, which is introduced to prevent previously encountered solutions or tabu solutions being revisited. A tabu list is used to keep track of some of the previous moves. The basic rule of tabu search is to avoid the neighbors if they happen to be on the tabu list. There are many exceptions to the basic tabu rule (Glover et al., 1993). One important exception is the use of aspiration level conditions. The aspiration level of a state on the tabu list measures the state's possibility of leading to a new local minimum from the perspective of the current state. The rule of aspiration level conditions allows a move to a state on the tabu list if the state's aspiration level is above a predefined value. Figure 5 gives a prototypical tabu search algorithm. Note that the tabu list may contain only uphill moves, so that an uphill move will take place.

A tabu list plays a central role in tabu search. It helps to intensify the search in areas of the neighborhood that are more likely to have high quality local minima, as well as to diversify the search to unexplored regions. However, effective use of the limited memory for the tabu list is problem dependent and requires experimental tests in practice. In addition, how to compute aspiration level and choose a corresponding effective threshold also remains an art. Nevertheless, it is worth mentioning that the very well-known Lin–Kernighan local search algorithm (Lin and Kernighan, 1973) is a special case of tabu search (Johnson and McGeoch, 1997).

SIMULATED ANNEALING

Simulated annealing (Kirkpatrick et al., 1983) is another search strategy for escaping local minima in neighborhood search. As the name indicates, simulated annealing simulates a physical annealing process (Metropolis et al., 1953; Kirkpatrick et al., 1983). In condensed matter physics, annealing is a thermal process for obtaining a solid of low-energy states. The process first heats the material until it melts, and then decreases the temperature slowly and carefully so that the particles of the material can reach the ground state in which the particles form a highly structured lattice and the energy of the material is minimal. Compared to other neighborhood search algorithms, simulated annealing has a solid theoretical background and enjoys a favorable, although less practical, feature of convergence to a global optimum if sufficient running time is given.

Similar to tabu search, simulated annealing allows uphill moves. Different from tabu search, however, simulated annealing does not always make the best downhill move, and

1)   Choose an initial solution n, and
     set the best state $n^* \leftarrow n$;
2)   DO
3)   Generate the neighboring solutions of n, $N(n)$;
4)   Choose the best neighbor n' from $N(n)$ that does not
         violate the tabu and aspiration conditions;
5)   IF $(f(n') < f(n^*))$
6) $n^* \leftarrow n'$;
7)   Update the tabu list and aspiration conditions;
8)   WHILE (no stopping criterion is met)

Figure 5 Tabu search algorithm

furthermore can make an uphill move at any point, depending on a random test to be explained below. Instead of always moving to the best neighbor of the current state, simulated annealing makes random moves. It moves to a randomly chosen neighbor if its quality is better than the quality of the current state. It may also move to the chosen neighbor with a probability less than one, even if the quality of the chosen neighbor is worse than that of the current state.

The random test is the most important ingredient of simulated annealing. This test determines which states will be visited and in what order, and most importantly what final state can be reached. The probability of accepting a randomly chosen uphill move is determined by two factors. The first is the measure of the badness of the uphill move, which is the difference Δ between the quality of the chosen state and the quality of the current one. The second factor is a parameter T, which corresponds to the temperature in a physical annealing process. At a high temperature, an uphill move is more likely to be taken; while at a very low temperature, almost all moves are downhill moves, and at temperature zero, only a downhill move is allowed in order to reach a local minimum. The final local minimum reached by this simulated annealing process is also the global minimum, if the temperature is lowered slowly and carefully. How the temperature is reduced over time is controlled by a schedule. A prototypical simulated annealing algorithm is given in Figure 6.

4.3. Other Search Methods

In this section, we consider three important search methods, artificial neural networks, genetic algorithms, and beam search, which do not exactly fall into the two classes of algorithms discussed above.

ARTIFICIAL NEURAL NETWORKS

Artificial neural networks (ANN) have their origin in biological neural networks' encoding and solving problems (Hertz et al., 1991). Solving a problem using ANN requires two steps. The first is to formulate the problem as the minimization of an objective function of an ANN. The second step is to find an approximate solution to the objective function that correctly classifies the training examples. The basic assumption of this approach is that the objective function that correctly classifies the training examples can also do so on future problem instances.

One type of ANN system is built upon basic units called perceptrons, as shown in Figure 7. A perceptron functions as a step function on a linear combination of a set of inputs. If the linear combination is greater than a threshold, then the output is 1, otherwise it is −1.

```
           SimulatedAnnealing(problem, schedule)
    1)   Choose an initial state n;
    2)   FOR (t from 1 to ∞) DO
    3)       T ← schedule(t);
    4)       IF (T = 0)
    5)           RETURN n;
    6)       n' ← a randomly selected neighbor of n;
    7)       Δ ← value(n') − value(n);
    8)       IF (Δ > 0)
    9)           n ← n'
    10)      ELSE
    11)          n ← n' with probability e^(Δ/T)
```

Figure 6 Simulated annealing algorithm

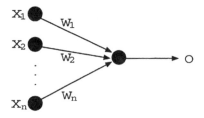

Figure 7 A perceptron

Specifically, the output of a perceptron can be written as

$$o(x_1, \cdots, x_n) = \begin{cases} 1, & \text{if } \sum_{i=1}^{n} w_i x_i > 0; \\ \\ -1, & \text{otherwise.} \end{cases} \tag{1}$$

which can be written as

$$o(\vec{x}) = \vec{w} \cdot \vec{x}, \tag{2}$$

where $\vec{x}$, $\vec{w}$, and $o(\vec{x})$ are the vector representations of the input, weights, and output, respectively.

ANN can be organized hierarchically using multilayer interconnected perceptrons. The goal is to minimize an objective function of an ANN using a backpropagation algorithm (Rumelhart and McClelland, 1986), whose basis is a gradient descent search in the space of possible weights of individual perceptrons to find the weights that best fit the given training examples. Due to space limitations and for illustrative purposes, we describe below the gradient descent search of a single perceptron.

The goal of the search is to find the weights of the perceptron that give the best classification results for the given examples V. From an optimization point of view, this can be formulated as a problem of minimizing an error function of the differences between the outputs from perceptron and the targeted values of the given examples. One such common error function is

$$E = \frac{1}{2} \sum_{v \in V} (t_v - o_v)^2, \tag{3}$$

where t_v is the target output for training example v, o_v is the output of the perceptron for the example v, and E is the error function. E is a function of the weights of the perceptron $\vec{w}$, as the output of the perceptron depends on $\vec{w}$. E represents a high-dimensional surface defined in terms of weights $\vec{w}$. The search is to find the point on this error surface that yields the minimum error. The idea of gradient descent is to move along the direction of steepest descent toward this minimum error point. This direction of steepest descent is the negation of the gradient of E with respect to $\vec{w}$, which can be computed as the derivative of E with respect to each component of $\vec{w}$. Specifically, the gradient, denoted as $\nabla E(\vec{w})$, can be calculated as,

$$\nabla E(\vec{w}) = \left[\frac{\partial E}{\partial w_0}, \frac{\partial E}{\partial w_1}, \cdots, \frac{\partial E}{\partial w_n} \right], \tag{4}$$

where $\frac{\partial E}{\partial w_i}$ is the partial derivative on w_i.

The gradient descent algorithm works as follows to find the set of weights that gives the minimum error. It starts with an arbitrary set of weights $\vec{w}$, and repeatedly updates $\vec{w}$ or its component w_i as follows,

$$w_i \leftarrow w_i + \Delta w_i, \quad \Delta w_i = -\sigma \frac{\partial E}{\partial w_i}, \tag{5}$$

where σ is a positive constant called the convergence rate, which determines the step size of the gradient descent. Using (3), it can be easily shown that

$$\Delta w_i = \sigma \sum_{v \in V} (t_v - o_v) x_{iv}, \tag{6}$$

where x_{iv} is the single input component x_i for training example v. Figure 8 lists the gradient descent algorithm for finding the best weights of a perceptron for a given set of training examples.

GENETIC ALGORITHM

Genetic algorithm (GA; Goldberg, 1989; Holland, 1975) was inspired by natural evolution processes. It falls into a general class of evolutionary algorithms (Bremermann et al., 1966). The overall process of a GA comprises two steps. The first is to design a coding schema for the problem to be solved. A common coding schema uses bit strings that can be conveniently manipulated by genetic operations. The second step is to manipulate and evolve a population of objects, such as a collection of encoded hypotheses, and to search for a generation containing an object that best fits an objective function.

From a search point of view, GA can be viewed as a combination of a neighborhood search and a beam search. The overall search space is a neighborhood of object populations. States are directly connected to each other if one can be changed to the other by a generic operator. General generic operators include mutation and crossover. A mutation operator can mutate an object in the current population to generate a new object in the next generation. For instance, a point mutation operator simply flips a bit within a 0–1 string-encoded decision rule to change the rule to a new one. A crossover operator switches the positions of substrings from two strings of objects to produce two new objects.

The idea of beam search comes into play in two places. It is used to select which and how many objects can participate in the genetic operations, and to prune some less favorable objects in the next generation to keep the population within a fixed size. A prototypical genetic algorithm is given in Figure 9.

Two general stopping criteria can be applied. The first is to stop the algorithm when the fitness of an object of the current population P reaches a predefined threshold. The second is to stop the algorithm when the population reaches an equilibrium state in which no new object can be generated. This second stopping criterion comes from the observation that objects tend to inherit the genetic features of their parents, and some features are more likely to pass along from one generation to the next. After a certain number of generations, some strong features may spread over the whole generation so that no new object can be produced.

BEAM SEARCH

Beam search (Bisiani, 1992; Winston, 1992) is a heuristic technique for reducing complexity of an enumerative search. It has existed for more than two decades and has been successfully

```
GradientDescent(V, σ)
1)   For each w_i in w⃗, set w_i to an initial, small value;
2)   WHILE (no stopping criterion met)
3)      Δ w_i ← 0;
4)      FOR (all v ∈ V)
5)         compute perceptron's output o;
6)         Δ w_i ← Δ w_i + σ (t - o) x_i;
7)      FOR (all v ∈ V)
8)         w_i ← w_i + Δ w_i.
```

Figure 8 Gradient descent algorithm for finding weights of a perceptron

```
1)   Generate a population of k hypotheses P = {s_1, ..., s_k};
2)   WHILE (no stopping criterion met)
3)       Compute Fitness(s_i) for each member in the population P;
4)       Apply mutation operator to k_1 uniformly selected
         members of P, and add the result to P'.
5)       Randomly select k_2 pairs of members from P,
         with a member s_i being selected with probability
         proportional to its relative fitness
         Pr(s_i) = Fitness(s_i)/∑ Fitness(s_j),
         produce two offspring for each pair using
         Crossover operator, and add all offsprings to P';
6)       Choose k survivors from P and P' based on a selection
         strategy, and replace the members of P with the
         survivors.
```

Figure 9 Genetic algorithm

applied to many real-world applications, such as machine learning (Dietterich and Michalski, 1981), jobshop scheduling (Fox, 1983), speech recognition (Lee, 1988), planning (Muscettola et al., 1989), and vision (Rubin, 1978).

Beam search executes a best-first search or breadth-first search, but may restrict the search to a set of selected alternatives using a fixed amount of memory. It also applies problem-specific heuristics to prune nonpromising search alternatives. The set of active search alternatives at any moment is collectively referred to as the beam of the search, hence the name "beam search."

Figure 10 gives the beam search algorithm using best-first search as its underlying search method, where hypothesis represents the hypothesis to be evaluated, and R the set of heuristic pruning rules. It is invoked with BeamSearch (initial hypothesis, R).

The only difference between beam search and its underlying best-first search method is line 5 of Figure 10, where heuristic pruning rules are used to prune nodes. The algorithm terminates in two cases. It may stop when a required goal node is reached at line 3. It may also terminate when no nodes are left for further exploration, which is a failure if a goal exists. This failure makes beam search incomplete, an unfavorable feature for practical use.

Beam search's pruning power and its possibility of finding a solution depend on the accuracy of the heuristic pruning rules used. Effective heuristic rules are generally problem

```
     BeamSearch(hypothesis, R)
1)   open ← ∅;
2)   n ← hypothesis;
3)   WHILE (n is not a goal)
4)       Delete n from open;
5)       Expand n, generating and evaluating all its children;
6)       Discard a child node if it is pruned by a rule in R;
7)       Insert all remaining children into open;
8)       If the size of open, p, is greater than m,
             remove m − p worst nodes from open.
9)       n ← a minimum-cost node in open
```

Figure 10 Beam search algorithm

dependent, and their effectiveness comes from deep understanding of problem domains. In practice, it is difficult to find effective heuristic rules that can strike the right balance of finding the desired goal and using the minimum amount of computation.

To make beam search complete, this simple search technique has been extended to depth-first branch-and-bound, and used to develop a complete beam search algorithm for finding optimal solutions (Zhang, 1998). Figure 11 gives the generalized, complete beam search algorithm using depth-first branch-and-bound as its underlying search method, where problem represents the problem to be solved, R the set of heuristic pruning rules, and α the current upper bound on the cost of an optimal goal. It is invoked with CompleteBeamSearch(initial_hypothesis, R, ∞).

5. Performance of Search Algorithms

A search algorithm needs to be measured by the quality of the solution that it provides and the execution time that it requires. As an enumerative search can find an optimal solution, its performance can be measured by the total execution time. The performance of a neighborhood search, on the other hand, must be measured by the solution quality and the execution time. In principle, solution quality and execution time go hand in hand, that is, more execution time leads to better solutions.

5.1. Enumerative Search

One of the major results regarding the performance of enumerative search is the optimality of best-first search, the A^* algorithm in particular. This hard and long-standing problem was finally settled by Detcher and Pearl (1985). They showed that the A^* algorithm is optimal, in terms of the number of nodes expanded, among all search algorithms that use the same heuristic information and are guaranteed to find an optimal solution. However, the optimality of a best-first search comes with the penalty of large memory requirements. In order to expand nodes in a best-first order, best-first search has to store all the open nodes, the ones that have

```
        CompleteBeamSearch(problem, R, α)
    1)  Do
    2)      Call BeamSearch_DFBnB(problem, R, α);
    3)      Weaken heuristic pruning rules in R;
    4)  WHILE (no desired goal has been found and
                    a rule in R was applied in the last iteration)

        BeamSearch_DFBnB(n, R, α)
    5)  Generate all children of n;
    6)  Discard a child node if it is pruned by a rule in R;
    7)  Sort the remaining k children in increasing order of cost:
        n_1, n_2, ···, n_k
    8)  FOR (i from 1 to k)
    9)      IF (cost(n_i) < α)
   10)          IF (n_i is a goal node)
   11)              α ← cost(n_i);
   12)          ELSE
   13)              BeamSearch_DFBnB(n_i, R, α);
   14)      ELSE RETURN
   15)  RETURN
```

Figure 11 Complete beam search algorithm

been generated but not yet expanded, in the memory. For a typical application, the number of open nodes grows exponentially with the size of the problem. Thus, best-first search is usually not the choice in practice.

Depth-first branch-and-bound and iterative deepening are search algorithms using space that is linear in search depth. The linear-space requirement often makes them the choice of search algorithms in practice. On the other hand, these algorithms usually expand more nodes than a best-first search. Depth-first branch-and-bound may explore nodes that are not visited by best-first search. Iterative deepening may expand a node more than once. Although these algorithms typically expand more nodes than best-first search, they generally run faster than best-first search on large state spaces, as experimentally shown in Zhang and Korf (1995). The reason is the time needed to expand a node is a constant in a linear-space search algorithm, as the algorithm uses a stack to maintain the search path, while the time required to expand a node increases logarithmically with the number of current open nodes in a best-first search.

The running time of a search algorithm in the KDD process depends on two factors. The first is the total number of nodes the algorithm needs to generate; and the second is the time to evaluate a node. Generating and evaluating a node in a KDD process typically involves accessing a database and performing some database queries. As the complexity and the size of underlying databases vary, a canonical form of time measure for a search algorithm is the number of nodes generated.

In the worst case, an enumerative algorithm has to expand every node in a state space in order to find and verify an optimal solution. As the worst case rarely occurs, a more meaningful performance measure is an average-case complexity. There are two important sets of analytical results regarding average-case complexity of enumerative search algorithms, based on two types of random tree models.

The first analytical model is a random tree of fixed depth d and fixed branching factor b (Pearl, 1984). With this model, the expected complexity of the A^* algorithm was analyzed. It was shown that the necessary and sufficient condition for A^* to run with a polynomial expected complexity, in terms of the tree depth, is that the error of the heuristic evaluation has logarithmic precision, which is typically difficult to obtain (Pearl, 1984). As these results can be readily applied to best-first search, they lead to the conclusion that highly precise heuristic information must be devised if the complexity of best-first search is to be contained within a reasonable growth rate.

The second analytical model is a random tree with depth d, and independent and identically distributed random branching factors with mean value b (McDiarmid, 1990; McDiarmid and Provan, 1991; Zhang and Korf, 1995). In this tree, edges are assigned with nonnegative costs, which are independently drawn from a common probability distribution. The cost of a node is the sum of the edge costs along the path from the root to that node. An optimal goal node is a node of minimum cost at depth d. On this incremental random tree, best-first search can run in linear expected time if the expected number of children of a typical node that have the same cost as their parent is greater than or equal to one. Only when the cost function is very accurate does best-first search run polynomially with the search depth. Despite these negative results regarding the expected complexity of best-first search, it was shown that on this analytical model, depth-first branch-and-bound and iterative deepening are asymptotically optimal when the complexity of best-first search is exponential in search depth (Zhang and Korf, 1995). This result further supports the result that linear-space search algorithms are the choice in practice.

5.2. Neighborhood Search

Neighborhood search algorithms are designed to find approximate solutions quickly, and their performance is measured by the quality of the solution found and the time needed to find such a solution.

As mentioned above, one of the main tasks of neighborhood search is to develop a set of local operators that defines the underlying neighborhood structure. The ultimate goal may be to develop a complete neighborhood structure that contains only one local minimum, which is also the global minimum. However, for all NP-complete problems (Garey and Johnson, 1979), no complete neighborhood structure has been found in which the number of steps that is required to reach the only local minimum is polynomial in the worst case.

The most important theoretical result regarding the worst-case complexity of neighborhood search is the complexity class PLS of polynomial time neighborhood (local) search problems. PLS is introduced to define those neighborhood search problems for which local optimality can be verified in polynomial time. As NP-complete problems are the hardest decision problems in NP, PLS-complete problems are the hardest search problems in PLS. Many important neighborhood search problems have been identified as PLS-complete, including uniform graph partitioning with the Kernighan-Lin variable-depth neighborhood (Johnson, et al., 1988), satisfiability with the analog of a flip neighborhood (Schäffer and Yannakakis, 1991), and a variant of the well-known Lin-Kernighan neighborhood for the traveling salesman problem (Papadimitriou, 1992). No PLS-complete problem is known to be solvable in polynomial time, and if one PLS-complete problem can be solved in polynomial time, so are all problems in the class PLS. The interested reader is referred to Johnson et al. (1988) for detailed information on the PLS class and PLS-complete problems.

Given a neighborhood structure, one important issue regarding the behavior of a neighborhood search algorithm is its convergence, which concerns whether the algorithm can eventually find a global minimum. A neighborhood search algorithm is not usually guaranteed to reach a global minimum, although it finds high quality local minima fast. One exception is simulated annealing, thanks to its statistical nature of selecting the next state. It has been shown that under certain conditions, simulated annealing asymptotically converges to a global minimum (Aarts and Korst, 1989). However, convergence to a global minimum generally takes an exponential number of steps, making the algorithm impractical for finding optimal solutions. Nevertheless, neighborhood search algorithms have the favorable features of being generally applicable, flexible, and fast for finding good approximate solutions.

6. Conclusions

Search plays a very important role in knowledge discovery and data mining. Given hypothesis representation schemas and hypothesis evaluation criteria, it relies on search to find the best hypotheses for the overall KDD process and the application problem at hand. The effectiveness and efficiency of the search methods employed can determine the success and performance of the KDD process.

ACKNOWLEDGMENT
The author was funded in part by the NSF under grant No. IRI-9619554.

References

Aarts, E. and J. Korst. 1989. *Simulated Annealing and Boltzmann Machines*. Chichester, England: Wiley.

Aarts, E. and J. K. Lenstra. 1997. *Local Search in Combinatorial Optimization*. Chichester, England: John Wiley & Sons.

Bisiani, R. 1992. "Search, Beam." In *Encyclopedia of Artificial Intelligence*, edited by S. C. Shapiro. 2d ed., pp. 1467–1468. New York: Wiley-Interscience.

Bremermann, H. J., J. Roghson, and S. Salaff. 1966. "Global properties of evolution processes." In *Natural Automata and Useful Simulations*, edited by H. H. Pattee, E. A. Edelsack, L. Fein, and A. B. Callahan, pp. 3–42. London: Macmillan.

Dechter, R. and J. Pearl. 1985. "Generalized best-first search strategies and the optimality of A*." *J. ACM* **32**: 505–536.

Dietterich, G. and R. S. Michalski. 1981. "Inductive learning of structural descriptions: evaluation criteria and comparative review of selected methods." *Artificial Intell.* **16**: 257–294.

Dijkstra, E. W. 1971. "A note on two problems in connexion with graphs." *Numerische Math.* **1**: 269–271.

Fayyad, U., G. Piatetsky-Shapiro, and P. Smyth. 1996. "From data mining to knowledge discovery in databases." *AI Magazine* **17(3)**: 37–54.

Fox, M. S. 1983. "Constraint directed search: a case study of job-shop scheduling." Ph.D diss. Pittsburgh: Carnegie Mellon University.

Garey, M. R. and D. S. Johnson. 1979. *Computers and Intractability: A Guide to the Theory of NP-Completeness.* New York: Freeman.

Glover, F. 1986. "Future paths for integer programming and links to artificial intelligence." *Comput. Oper. Res.* **13**: 533–549.

Glover, F., E. Taillard, M. Laguna, and D. de Werra. 1993. *Tabu Search. Annals of Operations Research 41.* Basel: Baltzer.

Goldberg, D. E. 1989. *Genetic Algorithms in Search, Optimization, and Machine Learning.* Reading, MA: Addison-Wesley.

Hart, T. P., N. J. Nilsson, and B. Raphael. 1968. "A formal basis for the heuristic determination of minimum cost paths." *IEEE Trans. Sys., Sci. Cybernet.* **4**: 100–107.

Hertz, J., A. Krogh, and R. G. Palmer. 1991. *Introduction to the Theory of Neural Computation.* Reading, MA: Addison-Wesley.

Holland, J. H. 1975. *Adaptation in Natural and Artificial Systems.* Ann Arbor: University of Michigan Press.

Johnson, D. S. and L. A. McGeoch. 1997. "The traveling salesman problem: a case study." In *Local Search in Combinatorial Optimization,* edited by E. Aarts and J. K. Lenstra, pp. 215–310. Chichester, England: John Wiley & Sons.

Johnson, D. S., C. H. Papadimitriou, and M. Yannakakis. 1988. "How easy is local search." *J. Comput. Sys. Sci.* **37**: 79–100.

Kirkpatrick, S., Jr., C. D. Gelatt, and M. Vecchi. 1983. "Optimization by simulated annealing." *Science* **220**: 671–680.

Korf, R. E. 1985. "Depth-first iterative-deepening: an optimal, admissible tree search." *Artificial Intell.* **27**: 97–109.

Korf, R. E. 1995. "Space-efficient search algorithms." *ACM Comput. Survey* **27**: 337–339.

Lee, K. F. 1988. "Large-vocabulary speaker-dependent continuous recognition: the sphinx system." Ph.D. diss. Pittsburgh: Carnegie Mellon University.

Lin, S. and B. W. Kernighan. 1973. "An effective heuristic algorithm for the traveling salesman problem." *Oper. Res.* **21**: 498–516.

Liu, C. L. 1968. *Introduction to Combinatorial Mathematics.* McGraw-Hill.

McDiarmid, C. J. H. 1990. "Probabilistic analysis of tree search." In *Disorder in Physical Systems,* edited by G. R. Gummett and D. J. A. Welsh, pp. 249–260. Oxford Science.

McDiarmid, C. J. H. and G. M. A. Provan. August 1991. "An expected-cost analysis of backtracking and non-backtracking algorithms." In *Proceedings of the Twelfth International Joint Conference on Artificial Intelligence, (IJCAI-91),* pp. 172–177. Sydney, Australia.

Metropolis, N., A. Rosenbluth, M. Rosenbluth, A. Teller, and E. Teller. 1953. "Equation of state calculations by fast computing machines." *J. Chem. Phys.* **21**: 1087–1092.

Muscettola, N., S. F. Smith, G. Amiri, and D. Patak. 1989. "Generating space telescope observation schedules." Technical Report CMU-RI-TR-89-28. Pittsburgh: The Robotics Institute, Carnegie Mellon University.

Papadimitriou, C. H. 1992. "The complexity of the Lin-Kernighan heuristic for the traveling salesman problem." *SIAM J. Comput.* **21**: 450–465.

Pearl, J. 1984. *Heuristics: Intelligent Search Strategies for Computer, Problem Solving.* Reading, MA: Addison-Wesley.

Rubin, S. 1978. "The ARGOS image understanding system." Ph.D. diss. Pittsburgh: Carnegie Mellon University.

Rumelhart, D. E. and J. L. McClelland. 1986. *Parallel Distributed Processing: Exploration in the Microstructure of Cognition,* Volumes 1 & 2. Cambridge, MA: MIT Press.

Schäffer, A. A. and M. Yannakakis. 1991. "Simple local search problems that are hard to solve." *SIAM J. Comput.* **20**: 56–87.

Winston, P. H. 1992. *Artificial Intelligence.* 2d ed. Addison-Wesley.

Zhang, W. July 1998. "Complete anytime beam search." *Proceedings of the Fifteenth National Conference on Artificial Intelligence (AAAI-98).* Reading, MA: Madison, WI.

Zhang, W. and R. E. Korf. 1995. "Performance of linear-space search algorithms." *Artificial Intell.* **79**: 241–292.

PART THREE

THE PROCESS OF KNOWLEDGE DISCOVERY
IN DATABASES

12 STAGES OF THE DISCOVERY PROCESS

Thomas Reinartz

ABSTRACT   This chapter describes the stages of the knowledge discovery process and presents a joint perspective on Part 3 of this handbook. We first motivate the need for a standardization of the knowledge discovery process and we then adopt the CRISP-DM view on the knowledge discovery and data mining process. We describe the CRISP-DM process model for knowledge discovery and data mining in detail, which consists of six phases: business understanding, data understanding, data preparation, modeling, evaluation, and deployment. For each phase, we outline its tasks and the resulting outputs of each task. Concluding remarks recapitulate directions for future research toward a unified standard for knowledge discovery and data mining.

1. Toward the Standardization of the Discovery Process

While early research in knowledge discovery and data mining mainly focused on algorithms and techniques, the current view in the field clearly considers knowledge discovery and data mining as a complex, iterative, and interactive process. The first, and probably most prominent, comprehensive attempt to define knowledge discovery as a process states:

> "Knowledge Discovery in Databases is the non-trivial process of identifying valid, novel, potentially useful, and ultimately understandable patterns in data." (Fayyad et al., 1996)

This definition is sufficiently general to cover most of the activities related to knowledge discovery. However, this definition and its description of single steps in the process does not provide any guidance in performing data mining projects. Furthermore, Fayyad et al. (1996) refer to data mining as a single step in the knowledge discovery process. Since data mining is often used as a synonym for knowledge discovery, this distinction frequently leads to confusion.

Hence, we propose to define a process model for knowledge discovery and data mining that provides initial guidance in performing knowledge discovery and data mining projects, and use data mining in the same way as knowledge discovery to avoid unnecessary misinterpretations.

Since the communication of this definition many attempts to describe the knowledge discovery process have been published. Among others, textbooks describe the process and give initial guidance in performing data mining projects as well as report on numerous case studies in data mining (e.g., Adriaans and Zantinge, 1996; Berry and Linoff, 1997; Dhar and Stein, 1997; Cabena et al., 1997; Groth, 1998; Weiss and Indurkhya, 1998).

All these definitions of knowledge discovery processes share high-level aspects but differ to some extent at more detailed levels. One of the dangers in defining divergent process descriptions is that each organization follows its own process model, and comparing and evaluating knowledge discovery and data mining efforts and tools is hardly possible in systematic ways.

Consequently, we conclude the need for a standardization of the knowledge discovery process to propose a unified view on knowledge discovery and data mining based on existing process descriptions and to allow an appropriate usage of this emerging technology to solve business problems in practice.

Recently, the CRISP-DM (CRoss-Industry Standard Process for Data Mining) initiative started to push forward the standardization of the knowledge discovery and data mining process. In this chapter, we adopt the CRISP-DM approach to identify a process model for data mining that is both a promising step to defining a standard methodology as well as initial guidance in performing data mining projects (Reinartz et al., 1998). For more detailed information on CRISP-DM, we refer the reader to http://www.crisp-dm.org.

2. The CRISP-DM Process Model for Data Mining

The CRISP-DM view on knowledge discovery and data mining consists of six phases. Figure 1 outlines these phases and their most important relations to each other. In general, relations between all phases possibly exist, and moving back and forth between phases is always required.

- The business understanding phase focuses on understanding the business objectives and requirements, and converting them into a data mining problem definition and a preliminary plan designed to achieve the objectives.

- The data understanding phase starts with an initial data collection and proceeds with activities to become familiar with the data, to identify data quality problems, to discover first insights into the data, or to detect interesting subsets for further examination.

- The data preparation phase covers all activities to construct the data set for modeling. Data preparation tasks are likely to occur multiple times and not in any prescribed order. They include table, record, and attribute selection as well as transformation and cleaning.

- In the modeling phase, we select and apply modeling techniques, and calibrate their parameters to optimal values. Since most techniques have specific requirements on the form of data, close interaction with data preparation is generally expected.

- At this stage, we hold models that have high quality from a data mining perspective. In the evaluation phase, we validate the models according to business perspectives, and review the steps executed to construct the models.

- Creation of models is generally not the end of knowledge discovery and data mining. Depending on the objectives, the deployment phase is as simple as generating a report or as complex as implementing a repeatable data mining process.

Each phase contains a number of tasks which produce specific outputs (see Table 1 for an overview). In the following sections, we briefly characterize these tasks and outputs and relate them to more detailed descriptions of related issues in the following chapters of Part 3.

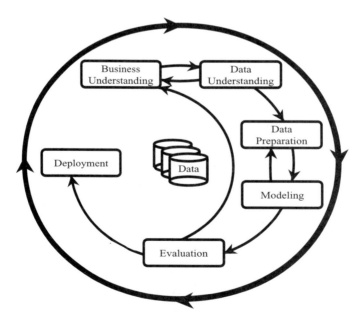

Figure 1 The CRISP-DM process model for data mining

Table 1 Phases (Bold), Tasks (Plain), and Outputs (Italic) of the Knowledge Discovery Process

Business Understanding	*Data Understanding*	*Data Preparation*	*Modeling*	*Evaluation*	*Deployment*
Determine Business Objectives	**Collect Initial Data**	*Data set*	**Select Modeling Technique**	**Evaluate Results**	**Plan Deployment**
Background	*Initial data collection report*	*Data set description*	*Modeling technique*	*Approved Models*	*Deployment plan*
Business objectives	**Describe Data**	**Select Data**	Modeling assumptions	*Assessment of Data Mining Results w.r.t. Business Success Criteria*	**Plan Monitoring and Maintenance**
Business success criteria	*Data description report*	*Rationale for inclusion/ exclusion*			*Maintenance plan*
Assess Situation	**Verify Data Quality**	**Clean Data**	**Generate Test Design**	**Review Process**	**Produce Final Report**
Inventory of resources	*Data quality report*	*Data cleaning report*	*Test design*	Review of Process	*Final report*
Requirements, assumptions, and constraints	**Explore Data**	**Construct Data**	**Build Model**	**Determine Next Steps**	*Final presentation*
Risks and contingencies	*Data exploration report*	*Derived variables*	*Parameter settings*	*List of Possible Actions*	**Review Project**
Terminology		*Generated records*	*Models*	Decision	*Experience documentation*
Costs and benefits		*Transformed data*	*Model description*		
Determine Data Mining Goals		**Integrate Data**	**Assess Model**		
Data mining goals		*Merged data*	*Model assessment*		
Data mining success criteria		*Aggregated data*	*Revised parameter settings*		
Produce Project Plan		**Format Data**			
Project plan		*Reordered records*			
		Rearranged attributes			
		Reformatted within-values			

2.1. Business Understanding

DETERMINE BUSINESS OBJECTIVES

The first objective is to understand, from business perspectives, what we want to accomplish. Neglecting this step means potentially expending a great deal of effort producing the right answers to the wrong questions.

The first output of this task is the background, which details information known about the business situation at the beginning of the process. This information includes any available background knowledge that is eventually of use for the knowledge discovery process (Chapter 18). The business objectives describe primary goals from business perspectives. Finally, business success criteria define measures for sufficiently high-quality results of the project from business points of view.

ASSESS SITUATION

This task details background information on all resources, constraints, assumptions, and other factors considered in determining the data mining goals and the project plan.

An important output of this task is the inventory of resources, which lists all available resources, including personnel, data, computing, and software resources. The requirements, assumptions, and constraints list all restrictions on the project including schedule of completion, comprehensibility and quality of results, security, as well as legal issues (Chapter 22), assumptions about the data, conditions on the validity of results, and constraints on availability of resources. An additional output, risks and contingencies, describes jeopardies and corresponding actions. A glossary of terminology covers business as well as data mining terminology, relevant to the business problem in question. Finally, a cost-benefit analysis unveils costs and benefits to compare expenditures of the project with potential gains to the business.

DETERMINE DATA MINING GOALS

The main concern of this task is to transform business objectives into data mining goals. Business objectives state general aims in business terminology, whereas data mining goals describe project objectives in technical terms. Typical data mining goals include classification (Chapter 16.1), rule discovery (Chapter 16.2), subgroup discovery (Chapter 16.3), equation fitting (Chapter 16.4), clustering (Chapter 16.5), probabilistic and causal networks (Chapter 16.6), time-series analyses, and spatial analyses (Chapter 16.7). The appropriate selection of data mining goals is an important and often neglected issue in knowledge discovery (Chapter 17.1).

Along with data mining goals, this task also specifies data mining success criteria to define measures for successful results in technical terms. For example, a typical data mining success criterion is a certain level of predictive accuracy.

PRODUCE PROJECT PLAN

At the end of the business understanding phase, we describe the intended plan for achieving the data mining goals, and thereby achieving the business objectives.

The project plan specifies the anticipated set of steps for the rest of the project, along with duration, required resources, inputs and outputs, and dependencies.

2.2. Data Understanding

COLLECT INITIAL DATA

The first task within data understanding acquires or accesses relevant data listed in the inventory of resources. For example, large organizations build and maintain data warehouses (Chapter 13), which then contain the data for knowledge discovery. This initial collection includes data loading if necessary (Chapter 13.1).

The output of this task is an initial data collection report, which lists the data with locations, methods used to acquire them, and any problems encountered.

DESCRIBE DATA

In this task, the project first examines properties of the data and then reports on the results.

As a consequence, this task provides a data description report. It describes the data in terms of format, quantity, identities of fields, and any other surface features which are discovered.

VERIFY DATA QUALITY

After an initial understanding of the data, we inspect the quality of the data, addressing questions such as completeness, correctness, and missing information.

As a result, the data quality report lists findings of the data quality verification. If quality problems exist, it also discusses possible solutions.

EXPLORE DATA

Finally, data exploration starts to deal with the data mining goals by using querying, visualizing, and reporting techniques and tools (Chapter 15). For example, this task considers distributions of key attributes, relations between pairs of attributes, results of simple aggregations, properties of significant subpopulations, and simple statistical analyses.

In the end, a data exploration report describes all results of this task, including first findings or hypotheses and their impact on the remainder of the project.

2.3. Data Preparation

In general, data preparation generates two outputs, the data set for subsequent phases and a data set description that lists all characteristics of performed data preparation.

SELECT DATA

An important task in data preparation is data selection. It covers manual and automatic selection of tuples (Chapter 14.1), selection of attributes or features (Chapter 14.2), as well as reducing the number of values, for example, by applying discretization techniques (Chapter 14.4). Selection criteria include relevance to the data mining goals as well as quality and technical constraints, such as limits on data volume or data types. If the main concern of data selection is data reduction due to large volumes of data, parallel approaches (Chapter 16.9) and other efforts on scalability (Chapter 16.8) provide alternative methods.

The output rationale for inclusion/exclusion states which data is retained and why selections are made.

CLEAN DATA

According to the output of data quality verification, data cleaning raises data quality to the required level. This involves selection of clean data subsets, insertion of suitable defaults or more ambitious techniques such as estimation of missing data by modeling.

A data cleaning report describes decisions and actions to address data quality problems and lists data transformations for cleaning and possible impacts on analysis results.

CONSTRUCT DATA

The next task includes constructive data preparation operations such as generation of derived variables, entire new records, or transformed values for existing variables.

Consequently, the outputs of this task include derived variables, generated records, and single-variable transformed data.

INTEGRATE DATA

The integration task aims at combining information from multiple tables or records to create new records or values.

The outputs are merged data, which refers to joining two or more tables that contain different information about the same objects, or aggregated data, which involves operations to compute new values by summarizing information from multiple tables or records (Chapter 14.3).

FORMAT DATA

One of the most important tasks in data preparation is formatting the data. Formatting mainly covers syntactic modifications that do not change meanings, but are required by the modeling tool.

Typical outputs of this task are reordered records, rearranged attributes, and reformatted within-values.

2.4. Modeling

SELECT MODELING TECHNIQUE

As the first step in modeling, we select the actual modeling technique among pre-selected techniques and tools. If multiple techniques are applied, we perform this task for each technique separately.

The outputs are the modeling technique and any modeling assumptions by this technique. Many modeling techniques make specific assumptions on the data; for example, all attributes have uniform distributions, no missing values are allowed, or the class attribute must be symbolic. It is important to select the potentially best-suited technique to solve the present data mining goal given the existing data (Chapter 17.2).

GENERATE TEST DESIGN

Before we build models, we usually generate a procedure to test the quality of models. For example, in supervised data mining tasks such as classification, it is common to use error rates as quality measures for data mining models. Therefore, we typically separate the data into a training and a test set, build models on the training set, and estimate their quality on the separated test set.

The test design as the output of this task describes the intended plan for training, testing, and evaluating models.

BUILD MODEL

Within this task, we run the modeling technique on the prepared data to create one or more models.

Since most modeling techniques allow calibration of various parameters, we consider parameter settings, along with rationales for their choice, and the models as outputs of this task. Separate model descriptions, including its expected accuracy, robustness, and possible shortcomings, also result from this task.

ASSESS MODEL

In this task, we interpret modeling results according to data mining success criteria and the desired test design. Typically, we apply statistical evaluations (Chapter 19.1) and other available mechanisms (Chapter 19.2) during this task.

The output model assessment summarizes results of this task, lists qualities of generated models, and ranks their quality in relation to each other. In addition, this assessment possibly leads to revised parameter settings, which then in turn lead to more fine-tuned modeling results in iterated modeling steps.

2.5. Evaluation

EVALUATE RESULTS

Whereas model assessment deals with factors such as accuracy and generality of models, this task evaluates models according to the original business objectives and success criteria.

The result of this task is an overall assessment of data mining results with respect to business success criteria, including a final statement as to whether the project already meets the initial business objectives.

REVIEW PROCESS

In addition to model evaluation, the entire process is considered in order to determine if there is any important factor or task that is neglected or to identify a generic procedure to generate similar models in the future.

The output review of process consolidates this review and provides recommendations for further activities. If there is a generic procedure to create relevant models, this procedure is documented for planning deployment.

DETERMINE NEXT STEPS

Finally, the last task in evaluation determines the next steps in the project. According to assessment of results and process review, we decide how to proceed. Here, we conclude whether to finish this project and move on to deployment if appropriate; whether to initiate further iterations; or whether to set up new data mining projects.

A list of possible actions along with reasons for and against each option leads to the final decision as outputs of this task.

2.6. Deployment

PLAN DEPLOYMENT

In order to deploy the data mining results into the business, this task develops a strategy for deployment (Chapter 21).

The output is a deployment plan and summarizes the deployment strategy.

PLAN MONITORING AND MAINTENANCE

Monitoring and maintenance are important issues if data mining results are to become part of day-to-day business and its environment. Careful preparation of a maintenance strategy helps to avoid unnecessarily long periods of incorrect usage of data mining results.

In order to monitor deployment of data mining results, we generate a maintenance plan on the monitoring process as an output of this task.

PRODUCE FINAL REPORT

At the end of the project, we write up a final report. It depends on the deployment plan, if the report is to be a summary of the project and its experiences or a final presentation of data mining results (Chapter 20). Online analytical processing techniques and tools often provide assistance in creating reports of results (Chapter 13).

As the outputs of this task, we find a final report or a final presentation or both.

REVIEW PROJECT

Finally, we review the entire project and assess what went right and what went wrong, what was done well and what needs to be improved.

The output experience documentation consolidates important experiences made for future engagements. For example, pitfalls, misleading approaches, or hints for selecting the best-suited data mining techniques in similar situations are part of this documentation.

3. Concluding Remarks

In this chapter, we presented the stages of the knowledge discovery process based on the CRISP-DM methodology and gave a joint perspective on Part 3 of this handbook. The CRISP-DM effort is one of the first steps toward a common standard in knowledge discovery and data mining. Future activities will attempt to enhance the CRISP-DM methodology to become a well-established and commonly accepted standard in the area of knowledge discovery and data mining.

Enhancements will possibly include universal definitions of all stages of the process, including some interchange standard for mutual exchange between different tools that supply techniques for different stages in the process.

The standard will help researchers and business users of knowledge discovery and data mining to discuss issues in the same framework, to aid data mining applications, and to detect further research challenges.

ACKNOWLEDGMENTS

The partners of the CRISP-DM consortium are NCR Systems Engineering Copenhagen (USA and Denmark), DaimlerChrysler AG (Germany), SPSS Inc. (USA), and OHRA Verzekeringen en Bank Groep B.V. (The Netherlands). The CRISP-DM Project was particulary funded by the European Commission as part of the ESPRIT program. I particularly thank Pete Chapman, Julian Clinton, Jens Hejlesen, Tom Khabaza, Randy Kerber, and Rüdiger Wirth for the collaborative work in developing the CRISP-DM process model for data mining.

References

Adriaans, P. and D. Zantinge. 1996. *Data Mining*. Harlow, England: Addison-Wesley.

Berry, M. J. A. and G. Linoff. 1997. *Data Mining Techniques for Marketing, Sales, and Customer Support*. New York: John Wiley & Sons.

Cabena, P., P. Hadjinian, R. Stadler, J. Verhees, and A. Zanasi. 1997. *Discovering Data Mining*. Upper Saddle River, NJ: Prentice-Hall.

Dhar, V. and R. Stein. 1997. *Seven Methods for Transforming Corporate Data into Business Intelligence*. Upper Saddle River, NJ: Prentice-Hall.

Fayyad, U., G. Piatetsky-Shapiro, and P. Smyth. 1996. "Knowledge discovery and data mining: towards a unifying framework." In *Proceedings of the Second International Conference on Knowledge Discovery and Data Mining. August 2–4, Portland, Oregon*, edited by E. Simoudis, J. Han, and U. Fayyad, pp. 82–88. Menlo Park, CA: AAAI Press.

Groth, R. 1998. *Data Mining: A Hands-On Approach for Business Professionals*. Upper Saddle River, NJ: Prentice-Hall.

Reinartz, T., R. Wirth, J. Clinton, T. Khabaza, J. Hejlesen, P. Chapman, and R. Kerber. 1998. "The current CRISP-DM process model for data mining." In *Proceedings of the Annual Meeting of the German Machine Learning Group FGML-98, August 17–19, Berlin*, edited by F. Wysotzki, P. Geibel, and K. Schädler, pp. 14–22. Germany Technical Report 98/11. Berlin: Technical University.

Weiss, S. and N. Indurkhya. 1998. *Predictive Data Mining*. San Francisco, CA: Morgan Kaufmann.

13 DATA WAREHOUSING

13.1 Data Cleaning and Loading

Toby Bloom

ABSTRACT   The process of preparing data for mining includes extracting the data from multiple sources, cleaning it, transforming it to a common format, and finally, writing the data to the target warehouse(s) or file(s). Because data mining applications look for patterns and correlations that were not previously predicted, these applications are particularly susceptible to spurious results if the input data are bad. Important patterns may be missed, and nonexistent correlations detected. The data must be cleaned and transformed into a structure usable by the data mining application. The process involves moving and processing very large amounts of data on a regular basis, and significant challenges exist in performing these steps efficiently. This article describes the kinds of corrections that must be made and techniques for managing and optimizing the transformation process.

1. Identifying and Cleaning Dirty Data

It is often a surprise that data coming from operational databases are quite dirty. Dirty data may result from typographical errors, inconsistencies among the various input data sources, or intentional encodings of data in ways that cannot be interpreted by a data mining application. We discuss the kinds of problems encountered, and techniques for correcting them, below.

1.1. Invalid and Missing Fields

Data entry is always very error-prone. If a field has a known domain, for example, a two-letter state abbreviation or a product code, then invalid entries are easily detected by table lookups. Detecting misspelled names or addresses is more difficult and is discussed later.

If a value is determined to be invalid, there are several actions available. One is to eliminate the records with invalid values and run the data mining application against the known good records. However, if data entry errors are more likely to occur on some values than others, then elimination of bad records may skew the resulting data set and lead to invalid data mining results.

In some cases, it is possible to correct the value. In the case of product codes, there may be a product name field that can be used to look up the correct code. It may also be possible to use a default value.

Sometimes the data just aren't there. An empty field may mean something specific: an empty field for children's names may mean no children. Or it may mean the information is unknown. The data mining application cannot differentiate between those cases: the data must be transformed into a consistent format. Missing fields are handled in the same way as invalid values: the record can be dropped; the value can be derived from other data; or a default value can be used.

Missing or partial values may sometimes be found via external sources. Missing gender fields can be determined to some degree of accuracy using standard name lists. Nine-digit ZIP codes can be derived from street addresses using postal service data. There are name and address cleansing products on the market that include these standard sources and perform the brute-forcing cleaning and enrichment.

1.2. Duplicate Data and Fuzzy Matches

If a data mining application is trying to predict buying patterns based on past purchase histories, then it is critical that all purchases for a given customer are properly associated with that customer. However, data entry errors, nicknames, and so on, may result in the same person appearing in the data as multiple customers. Steve Jones, Steven Jones, and Stephen

Jones might well be the same person, but if his purchases are spread across three different records, then the data mining application might miss patterns.

INDIVIDUALIZATION TECHNIQUES

The process of identifying and merging all the data associated with one entity is called individualization or householding. There is no universally applicable approach for identifying individuals. Sound-alike matching is a common method for names. Lists of nicknames and alternative spellings for common names are often used. It is common to use business rules such as: If two people with different last names live at the same address, then if they share any joint account, all of their accounts are in one household. If they share no accounts, then they are in separate households. Obviously, none of these approaches is entirely accurate.

Even within a single company, different matching criteria might be used in different circumstances. A financial services firm sending out advertising brochures might use fairly loose matching rules to avoid sending duplicate brochures to a single household. However, when they send out annual reports mandated by law, they may use much stricter matching rules to ensure no one is missed. The same kinds of decisions must be made with respect to the data needed for a given data mining application.

There are different ways in which matching rules can be applied. The rule is a distance function between two values. But such rules are not necessarily transitive. If the rule for address matching is that the street number must be off by no more than one on any digit, then 512 matches 522, and 522 matches 532, but 512 does not match 532. Starting with 512 and matching all records against it yields different individuals than starting with 522. Comparing all pairs yields yet other results, but in practice, this is too inefficient. Most frequently, a randomly selected record becomes the reference record for that individual: anything matching it is considered to be the same individual, even if records in that set may not match each other at all.

RECONCILING CONFLICTING DATA FOR AN INDIVIDUAL

Once it is determined that two records represent the same individual or household, another problem arises. The data in those records might conflict. For example, they might have different phone numbers or addresses. Resolving the conflict is often done by prioritizing the sources for different fields. In the phone number case, the value from the Recent_Phone_Inquiries source might be considered more reliable than the value in the existing customer table. If both records come from the same source, a rule like most recent value is often used.

1.3. Hidden Data

Some legacy databases have schemas that have not been allowed to change in years. Because the needs of the organization have certainly changed during that time, processes develop to overcome this mismatch. Often comment fields serve multiple purposes. If the organization wants to track who served which customers, the service rep's initials are placed, by convention, at the beginning of the comment field. Other data are added to the same field, with other tags. If these hidden data are to be available to the data mining application, the fields must be parsed and the various pieces of tagged data separated.

1.4. Pivot Tables

Pivot tables are another kind of encoding common when source data comes from a relational database. If the data in some columns is sparse, DBA's will define schemas that try to save space by sharing columns. For example, Column A might identify whether the person owns a home or rents a home. Column B contains the home value for owners, but the monthly rent for renters. These values must be split before any standard analysis tools can be used on that data.

1.5. Integrating Disparate Sources

When multiple independent data sources are integrated, it is often the case that each source uses different codes for the same data. One source, for example, might use a numeric key to represent age ranges: 1 for under 20, 2 for 21–40, 3 for 41–65, 4 for over-65. A second uses the actual age. A third uses date-of-birth. And finally, there is a source that uses different ranges: 1 for under 15, 2 for 16–25, 3 for 26–50, and so on. Not only does the meaning of the value 5 vary with the source, merging the sources involves defining an encoding that meets the needs of the data mining application, and for which sufficient information exists in all the sources.

The data from the various sources must also be combined into a common record format and massaged into the structure needed by the data mining application. That often includes complex joins of the various tables to merge the data.

1.6. Aggregations and Derived Data

While there may be no errors in the data, the level of detail may be inappropriate for the data mining application in use. For example, if the desired result is information about sales by quarter, point-of-sale data that has time by hour and minute is not ready for mining. The data must be aggregated to provide groupings at a level of granularity useful for the data mining application. Knowledge of the application, and of the data, is needed to select usable groupings.

2. Techniques for Data Loading

The process of loading a data warehouse includes extracting the data from sources, cleaning it, transforming it to a common format, and finally, writing the data to the target warehouse(s). The previous section described the issues and techniques in cleaning the data. This section describes the issues and techniques involved in integrating those cleaning steps into a full extract–transform–load process.

The major issue driving techniques for data loading is performance. With terabyte-class warehouses becoming more commonplace, and with complex transformation techniques needed to load data into those warehouses, it becomes essential to make maximal use of parallelism, to optimize the transformation process, and to perform incremental updates rather than bulk loads.

2.1. Incremental Loading

When data warehouses were smaller, it was common practice to reload a warehouse in its entirety on a regular basis, rather than updating the existing warehouse. With warehouse sizes growing, it becomes important to update the warehouse with new data, rather than entirely reload it.

There are two phases to performing an incremental load: capturing the changes in the data sources, and updating the warehouse records.

There are many ways to capture changes, depending on the type of data source, and the application making changes to the source. One method available for relational databases is reading logs to find recent updates. Another is to timestamp all records in the source database and run queries to find all changes since the last warehouse update. (Deletes get a bit tricky with this one.) Tools are also available that provide a middleware layer that logs all updates before sending them to the source databases. A good overview of change capture can be found in Bokun and Taglienti (1998).

The second step—incrementally updating the warehouse—can still present significant problems. Any cleaning step that requires the aggregation or comparison of multiple records is problematic for incremental load. The problem arises because some of the records involved will have been processed previously, and some will be new updates. All records associated with the update record must be found and accessed from either the warehouse or the original sources.

For example, suppose the warehouse is maintaining only a maximum value for some field in a table. Adding a new record can be easily accomplished, since it involves comparing the new record to the max value already in the warehouse. But updating or deleting a record makes it difficult to determine how the aggregate value should change. If the deleted record matched the max value, how does the load process know whether another record also provided that value, and if not, what the new maximum is? Research on incremental update in the presence of aggregation has been done by Quass (1996).

If the step involves a join, it may be difficult to determine whether updates to the warehouse tables are needed, and or even whether sufficient information exists in the warehouse to perform the update. For example, suppose a warehouse table C is the result of a join of source tables A and B. If a new record is added to B, there may not be sufficient information in the warehouse to determine how C changes without entirely rerunning the join between A and B (Huyn, 1997).

These problems are related to the problem of maintaining materialized views. Further discussion of these issues can be found in Quass et al. (1996), Gupta and Blakeley (1995), Huyn (1997), and Mumick and Gupta (1999).

Individualization, or fuzzy matching, presents other problems for incremental update. Since finding fuzzy matches often depends on the weight of various values in a set of records, comparing a new record to the current values in the warehouse may not yield the same result as rerunning the matching on the full set of original records. But the larger problem is that, since the match rules often cannot be expressed in SQL, the tables in the warehouse to which a new record must be compared must be unloaded from the warehouse, updated, and reloaded. Thus, while incremental updates are feasible, they can be very expensive. The cost of incremental update will often be relative to the size of the warehouse rather than the size of the update set.

2.2. Parallelism and Optimization of Warehouse Loading

There are two major factors that affect data throughput for a given set of cleaning steps. One is the amount of parallelism that can be introduced within or between steps. The other is how many passes must be made over the data to perform all the steps.

Since data cleaning involves performing the same actions on every record in a potentially very large set, the cleaning process is very conducive to both pipeline parallelism and data parallelism. In data parallelism, each process handles one partition of the data, and all the processes perform the same sequence of steps on different partitions at the same time. In pipeline parallelism, a different thread or process executes each step. When the current step completes processing on a record, it passes the resulting record to the next step and picks up the next record to process in this step. In fact, the result of any one step can be sent to several processes next, rather than to just one, so that multiple steps can be executed in parallel. This is useful when many warehouse tables are being generated from one or more sources.

Both forms of parallelism can be used effectively in reducing load time for large data sets. How the two can be used together, and which is more effective in which circumstances, are questions still to be answered. While a great deal is understood about parallel query optimization (Graefe, 1993, 1994), much less is understood about how to optimize parallel bulk loading of warehouses (Garcia-Molina et al., 1998)

Minimizing the number of passes through the source data is another technique for reducing processing time in data transformation. As an example, suppose there is a customer table and a new orders list, and that it is necessary to generate a list of existing customers who have recent orders, a list of existing customers with no recent orders, and a list of new customers. If three joins must be performed on those two tables to get the three results, it could be very expensive. It would be much cheaper to cull all three pieces of information from the two source tables in one pass, rather than three. While performing the transformations in SQL requires multiple passes through the data to produce multiple tables, some transformation and loading tools do provide the ability to extract multiple outputs in a single step. This ability is critical to efficiently cleaning and loading very large data sets for data mining.

3. Current Products

There are numerous products currently on the market for cleaning and loading data. The product offerings in this area change relatively frequently and so the listing provided here may be out of date by the time of publication of this book. We mention below a small sampling of the products currently available. Those mentioned are not necessarily considered superior to others in the market, but merely representative of the various categories. One excellent resource for finding extensive listings of available products is the Data Warehousing Information Center web site (Greenfield, 2000).

The products fall into several categories: name and address-cleaning; general data accuracy; deduplication; and ETL tools (extract, transform, and load).

Group 1 Software and FirstLogic, as well as many other companies, provide name- and address-checking tools. These tools include extensive postal service address listings and standard name lists that are used to identify and correct errors in addresses, add gender-based titles, add postal codes, and so on. When evaluating these tools, it is essential to check whether they provide support for all of the countries needed. Because the tools are dependent on actual postal service data, they are not inherently internationalized.

Tools such as those from Vality Technology can be used for more general data quality and business rule checking.

Data extraction, transformation, and loading (ETL) tools can pull data from multiple disparate sources, merge it, and transform it into the format needed for warehousing or mining. The actual functionality provided varies greatly among these tools. Ardent's DataStage is currently a leading ETL vendor. It provides an easy-to-use graphical interface for defining transformations. Evolutionary Technologies' Extract product is known particularly for its ability to interface with mainframe databases and migrate data to other systems, as well as other databases. It also provides a full complement of transformation capability. Informix's Formation product focuses on complex transformations, providing capabilities for fuzzy matching and deduplication, as well as support for highly parallel execution and optimization techniques discussed in the previous section. Ab Initio and Torrent also provide tools that emphasize concurrent execution for very large datasets. Sagent also offers an ETL product. Overall, the Data Warehousing Information Center site lists over two hundred products in this category.

4. Summary

Data requires significant preparation before they can be used effectively by a data mining application. By validating data values, finding equivalences that tend to weed out data entry errors, and properly aggregating the data, we can reduce the likelihood that the data mining applications will find spurious correlations, or miss real ones, due to data anomalies. The size of the data to be processed, as well as the complexity of the processing, present challenges to performing the entire cleaning and loading process in reasonable timeframes. Parallel processing techniques and multistep single-pass processing are essential tools in increasing throughput for loading of very large warehouses.

References

Barclay, T., R. Barnes, J. Gray, and P. Sundaresan. 1994. "Loading databases using dataflow parallelism." DEC Technical Report 94.2. July 1994.

Bokun, M. and C. Taglienti. 1998. "Incremental data warehouse updates: approaches and strategies for capturing changed data." *Data Mgmnt Rev.* **8(5)**.

Garcia-Molina, H., W. J. Labio, J. L. Wiener, and Y. Zhuge. 1998. "Distributed and parallel computing issues in data warehousing." In *ACM Principles of Distributed Computing Conference* (Invited Paper).

Graefe, G. 1993. "Query evaluation techniques for large databases." *ACM Comput. Surv.* **25(2)**.

Graefe, G. 1994. "Volcano, an extensible and parallel query evaluation system." *IEEE Trans. on Knowledge and Data Engng* **6(1)**: 120–135.

Greenfield, L. 2000. "The Data Warehouse Information Center." www.dwinfocenter.org.

Gupta, A. and J. A. Blakely. 1995. "Using partial information to update materialized views." *Inform. Sys.* **20(8)**: 641–662.

Huyn, N. 1997. "Multiple-view self-maintenance in data warehousing environments." In *Proceedings of the Twenty-Third VLDB Conference*, Athens.

Mumick, I. and A. Gupta. 1999. *Materialized Views: Techniques, Implementations and Applications*: MIT Press.

Quass, D. June 1996. "Maintenance expressions for views with aggregations." In *Proceedings of the ACM Workshop on Materialized Views: Techniques and Applications*. Montreal, Canada.

Quass, D., A. Gupta, I. Mumick, and J. Widom. 1996. "Making views self-maintainable for data warehousing." In *PDIS*, pp. 158–169. Miami, Florida.

Further Reading

Bacon, J. 1992. *An Integrated Approach to Operating Systems, Databases and Distributed Systems*. Addison-Wesley. This book provides a good overview of the terminology and types of concurrency that can be applied to warehousing, as well as more general applications.

Berry, M. J. A. and G. Linoff. 1997. *Data Mining Techniques For Marketing, Sales, and Customer Support*. Wiley Computer Publishing. This overview of data mining techniques includes a good section on cleaning data for data mining.

Bischoff, J. and T. Alexander. 1997. *Data Warehouse: Practical Advice from the Experts*. Prentice Hall. This book on building data warehouses has an excellent section on cleaning and loading.

Meyer, D. and C. Cannon. 1998. *Building a Better Data Warehouse*. Prentice Hall.

Morse, S. and D. Isaac. 1998. *Parallel Systems in the Data Warehouse*. Prentice Hall.

Moss, L. 1998. "Data cleansing: a dichotomy of data warehousing?" *Data Mgmnt Rev.* **9(2)**. An excellent article that describes the various cases in which the need for data cleaning arises, and presents some arguments for why it may not always be best to perform all the cleaning possible.

13.2 Warehouse Administration

Wolfgang Lehner

ABSTRACT Running an organizational-wide reliable data warehouse requires a huge administration effort. This article outlines data warehouse-specific administrational issues from the two perspectives of administration roles and administration tasks. The roles of a data administrator, application administrator, and systems administrator are identified and outlined in the first part. Subsequently, different administrational tasks, such as activities from data acquisition to publication, are described and assigned to one or more administrational roles. This article stresses the fact that the task of data administration in the context of a data warehouse is of high complexity and embraces a mixture of technical system administration tasks and of administrational tasks in new areas, such as quality assurance and security.

1. Introduction

A data warehouse reflects, without doubt, a strategic asset for an organization. Since a data warehouse must be considered an ongoing process (Bontempo and Zagelow, 1998) the task of data warehouse administration is of paramount importance for a successful data warehouse project. This is even more important as data warehouse installations are classified a mission-critical application in many organizations. Setting up a data warehouse initially requires a tremendous effort (Srivastava and Chen, 1999), but running a long-term and reliable data warehouse smoothly requires even more effort.

This article discusses the topic of data warehouse administration in two major parts. The first part identifies three major administrational roles and explains their main responsibilities. The second part focuses on different administrative tasks in the context of a data warehouse. Issues like data acquisition and publication, database tuning, data warehouse backup and recovery, quality assurance, and data warehouse security are explained and warehouse-specific perspectives are detailed.

2. Different Roles in Data Warehouse Administration

Since self-administrating systems are unrealistic, the persons involved in data warehouse administration are crucial for the success of a data warehouse project and thus are becoming strategic players within organizations. The complex architecture of a data warehouse system requires multifaceted administrative tasks that may be assigned to multiple administrative roles, each of which is played by one or more persons. Therefore, the role of the classical database administrator and its administrative tasks are changing tremendously according to the new working areas in the context of a specific warehouse environment. More significant, however, is the fact that the general focus of a data warehouse administrator is responsibility and strategic thinking instead of executing predefined procedures and reacting to special events (Cox, 1999; Dyck, 1998).

The complexity of a data warehouse system implies the need for a classification of administrative tasks and different roles that are responsible for these administrative tasks (Mullins, 1998). Each role must be defined and exactly specified by means of relevant tasks and responsibilities through the data warehouse project organization, that is, data warehouse project manager. The following three major roles are identified:

- *Data Administrator.* Responsible for the strategic management of the organization's data and meta data.

- *System Administrator.* Responsible for maintenance of the production database and system-related infrastructure.

- *Application Administrator.* Responsible for the design and development of new data warehouse applications, help desk, and education.

All persons working in the data warehouse administration group should be involved in the design and building process of the data warehouse and participate in all technical and strategic decisions, so that expert knowledge may be disseminated from the early beginnings of the data warehouse project. Moreover, all data, information, and knowledge regarding the techniques, processes, and overall experiences should be recorded in a data warehouse specific database often called a meta-data repository (Bernstein, 1998).

2.1. Data Administrator

A data administrator, often called a business systems analyst, is responsible for the correct flow of data and meta data through the entire warehouse process. The responsibility starts with identifying potential source systems and conducting negotiations between single departments owning the data sources about how these sources may be used, integrated, and published for data warehouse users. The most critical task connected with the role of a data administrator is meta-data management, which is commonly known as the key prerequisite for a successful data warehouse project. The data administrator alone is in charge of meta data, that is, defining and enforcing a corporate-wide terminology. Therefore, the data administrator has knowledge about where and which meta data officially exists, is supported, and is useful for the warehouse project, who or which department owns which part of the meta data, and who is allowed to update the meta data. Budgeting-related data and customer-related data, for example, may be maintained by different departments using different applications. Strongly related to this point is the task of defining the semantics of the data and possible queries. Warehouse users from different departments may have a different understanding of terms like running costs or weighted distribution analysis. Furthermore, the data administrator is responsible for getting the data out of the warehouse. This implies defining strategies on how and when to populate dependent data marts or synchronize data marts in the case of a virtual warehouse architecture.

This characterization of the role of a data administrator implies that the person(s) fulfilling this role work(s) closely together with the warehouse management and must exhibit a strong technical background as well as excellent communications skills and a certain political sense.

2.2. Application Administrator

The main responsibility of an application administrator is to design, develop, and maintain the applications of a data warehouse system. Thus, the application administrator has to demonstrate in-depth knowledge of user requirements and possess a strong database background to understand fully the impacts of the applications on the underlying database system. The application administrator is usually also involved in the process of designing and refining the conceptual data schema of the warehouse database. A further task, which is part of the application administrator role, is to provide a help desk facility to resolve existing problems or route problems to the appropriate person. Within this context, the application administrator is responsible for data warehouse education by explaining data content and data access through prebuilt applications to the end users.

Since the users of a data warehouse decide upon the success of a data warehouse project, the importance of an application administrator is often underestimated. Depending on the specific installation, an application administrator is supported by the business system analyst and by one or more end user application developers.

2.3. System Administrator

The role of a (database) system administrator in a data warehouse environment resembles the classical operations DBA. A system administrator is responsible for performing periodic maintenance and preventive tasks following a predefined checklist and promptly reacting to specific events, such as a data segment overflow. The system administrator uses commercial database analysis tools like Control Center (IBM Corp, 1999; see Figure 1) or Enterprise Manager (Oracle Corp, 1999a), as well as sophisticated and self-developed tools like scripts and stored procedures.

Although many database system-oriented tasks, such as performing "reorgs," extension of table spaces, adapting load balancing, and partitioning schemas, are performed automatically by state-of-the-art database engines, there are still traditional as well as newly emerging tasks for a system administrator. Examples encompass the definition of the degree of

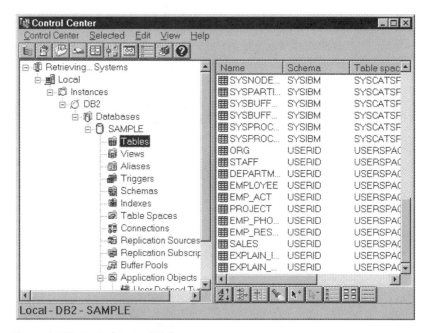

Figure 1 DB2 ControlCenter (IBM)

redundancy within the database introduced through the use of indexes and summary tables, control of the loading process, and carrying out backups of the data warehouse database.

The role of a system administrator is of such importance that it should always be fulfilled by at least two persons sharing the same knowledge and being able to act for each other. System administrators are sometimes supported by specific computer systems and network administrators who are generally responsible for the computer machinery, network devices, peripherals, and client machines.

3. Tasks of Data Warehouse Administration

The following section details data warehouse specific administrational tasks, including data acquisition and publication, database tuning, data warehouse backup and recovery, quality assurance, and data warehouse security. Each task will be assigned to one or more roles introduced in the preceding section (O'Neil et al., 1997).

3.1. Data Acquisition and Publication

Since the content of data sources is permanently changing, these changes must be reflected in the data warehouse database by importing data on a regular basis. The process of data acquisition, which may be very error-prone, is outlined from a theoretical point of view in Chapter 13.1. In general, the process of data acquisition is a sequence of extracting data from multiple source systems, transporting and transforming the data, and integrating it into the production database of the data warehouse. Most important from the administrative point of view is that each step be controlled and checked for success and that the complete process must be finished and must have passed quality assurance under a certain time constraint (load window).

Extracting data from a source system requires the existence of well-specified interfaces that must be defined during the data warehouse installation process. A general rule for the extraction process itself is to carry out as little processing as possible inside the source system, in order to prevent any interference with the operational environment. For the ability to perform incremental database loads, it is important to know whether delta information, that is, the set of changed data according to the last extraction process, can be retrieved from a source system.

Transporting data to another platform requires the appropriate bandwidth of the underlying network. This often-neglected aspect must be part of the capacity planning during the initial data warehouse architecture design. Moreover, the transportation of multiple gigabytes of data requires special network transportation protocols (ATM, IP-switching), providing the ability for error detection and check pointing.

Transforming data may be seen from two different perspectives. From the technical perspective, data must be converted to a common data format, such as, for example, from EBCDIC to ASCII. At the conceptual layer, the data must be aligned according to its semantics by detecting homonyms, synonyms, missing values, and so on. An optional step in the transformation procedure happening outside of the database system is to presort and preaggregate the data to speed up the subsequent loading process.

Loading data into the production database may again be seen from two perspectives. From a physical perspective, external data is loaded into an interim database (staging area), taking strong advantage of database mechanisms like specialized loading tools or tables in append-only mode. After a successful import, the data must be checked from a conceptual perspective, that is, enforcing data integrity rules like not-nullable columns and checking the consistency of relationships (e.g., Are there new sales figures for products without a product description?). Finally, the data is integrated into the production database.

Publishing data implies that the design and population strategy of data marts provide a specific view of a data warehouse. From an administration point of view, this task consists of preparing customized (preaggregated) portions of the data warehouse database in a format that is easily loadable or directly usable by OLAP-servers.

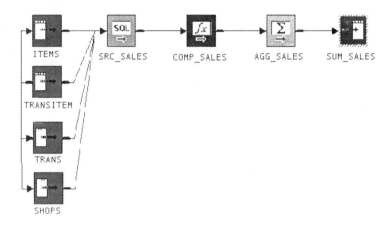

Figure 2 PowerMart Designer (Informatica)

The complete data acquisition and publication process may be supported by powerful cleansing and transformation tools. Commercial representatives are PowerMart (Informatica Corp, 1999), Warehouse Workbench (Systemfabrik Inc., 1999), and many more. Using these tools, the data acquisition process may be graphically configured, automatically executed, and monitored. Figure 2 shows the graphical specification of translations using Informatica's PowerMart. Accrued meta data are stored in specialized repositories that can be tapped by OLAP tools (e.g., Microstrategy DSS Suite; MicroStrategy Inc., 1999) to trace single warehouse figures back to the source systems.

Usually data and system administrators are involved in the task of data acquisition and publication. In data warehouse systems with a high number of heterogeneous source systems, there might be the explicit role of a data staging system designer, who is responsible for the complete data acquisition process.

3.2. Database Tuning

The most common task of a database administrator is database tuning. As in traditional database scenarios, well-known recommendations for tuning are still valid and should be applied to warehouse databases. Additional challenges for the system administrator are aggregate queries, which are typical for decision support environments. To speed up aggregation queries, most relational database engines provide special index structures (bitwise-index, star-join index, and so on) and/or the concept of summary tables. Summary tables hold preaggregated data and are used to answer aggregation queries referring to precomputed summary values of equal or coarser granularity (Roussopoulos, 1997). On the one hand, the right combination of specialized indexes and summary tables usually results in a boost in query performance. On the other hand, these techniques increase the size and complexity of a data warehouse installation enormously. Although there is already some support in automatically finding the best set of indexes (IBM Corp., 1999) and/or summary tables (Microsoft Corp., 1998; Oracle Corp., 1999b), the management, that is, the control of creation, deletion, and usage, is mostly left to the system administrator (Gupta, 1997). In the case of deferred refresh summary tables, the system administrator must manually initiate the recomputation of summary tables in case of an update of the base data.

3.3. Data Warehouse Backup and Recovery

As in the case of database tuning, the task of database backup and recovery in a data warehouse environment shows similarities as well as differences from the traditional way of operating a database system. For example, carrying out a cold backup of a data warehouse database is usually not feasible. The fundamental goal of database backup is to enable the recovery of essential data in an emergency. A backup strategy, which is as important as any other module in a data warehouse project, has to consider the following factors:

- Is it acceptable to lose data that can be reconstructed by either initiating the data acquisition process for the base data (or only the data loading step in case of temporary stored staging data) or recomputing derived data, such as, for example, indexes and summary tables?

- What are the external requirements for mean time between failure (MTBF) and mean time to repair (MTTR)?

- Which types of error should be covered (user error, system failure, media error, ...)?

When developing the backup strategy for a data warehouse, these factors should be kept in mind in order to come up with a sound recovery plan, especially if the data warehouse is classified as a mission-critical application.

3.4. Quality Assurance

The task of quality assurance in the context of data warehousing is of vital importance (Jarke et al., 1998) and has to be considered under two orthogonal perspectives. Quality, from the system-oriented perspective, addresses reliability, availability, load efficiency, and query performance of a warehouse system. Quality assurance must monitor these factors, compare them with the expectations of the end users and dependent data marts, and potentially demand changes to the current capacity plan.

The second perspective of quality assurance is dataoriented. The quality assurance has to ensure that the right data is loaded, the data is loaded in the correct order, and the loaded data and meta data are consistent and plausible. Consistency checks are necessary even if all underlying source systems enforce their local data consistency. Plausibility checks are useful to detect source systems that do not act as expected by the warehouse system as well as to enable prediction about the quality of the data.

For large warehouse systems, it is advisable to set up a mini-warehouse system for all quality related data, such as load and query statistics. This system may be used to perform analyses to detect specific events as well as long-term trends.

The system administrator role is responsible for the system oriented perspective of quality assurance, whereas the data oriented perspective is part of the role of a data administrator.

3.5. Data Warehouse Security

As more and more warehouse systems are connected to thousands of users via intranets or the Internet, security requires more and more attention. Security becomes even more crucial when all of the strategic and decisionmaking-related information of an organization is stored within a single warehouse system.

Therefore, classical techniques for authentication and authorization have to be applied to a warehouse system as to any other system storing sensitive information. From a system-oriented view, password aging, expiration, complexity verification, and session-level auditing are mandatory.

Data warehouse–related security concerns address the question of whether everyone needs access to everything and up to which level of detail. Technically, this implies that distinct roles are defined for each group of users and for each warehouse subject area, and that each user needs privileges from both directions to access the required data. A more sophisticated strategy is required to detect and reject tracker queries (Michalewicz, 1991), by which detailed information may be derived by issuing a set of intelligently specified aggregate queries. Current strategies include monitoring the users' access behavior and limiting the number of queries referring to similar database objects.

Security assurance has an impact on all data warehouse administration roles. Some organizations assign security responsibility to an explicit security administrator to control access to all data warehouse–related resources.

Table 1 Major Administrational Tasks as Assigned by Administrational Roles

	Data Acquisition	Data Publication	Database Tuning	Backup and Recovery	Data Quality	Data and System Security	Help Desk
Data Administrator	X				X	X	
Application Administrator		X			X		X
System Administrator	X	X	X	X	X	X	

4. Summary and Conclusion

This article addresses data warehouse–specific administrational issues. The three major roles of a data administrator, application administrator, and systems administrator have been identified and explained in the first part of this article. In the second part, the major administrational tasks are described and assigned to one or more administrational roles (see Table 1). These tasks include descriptions of activities during the data acquisition and publication phase, specific requirements according to database tuning and backup in a warehouse environment, and issues in the context of quality and security assurance.

This survey shows that the administration of a data warehouse is of high complexity and consists of a mixture of well-known and traditional techniques in database system administration, and of administrational tasks in new areas, such as quality assurance and security, which are vital for a successful data warehouse project.

References

Bernstein, P. A. 1998. "Repositories and object oriented databases." *ACM SIGMOD Record* **27(1).**
Bontempo, C. and G. Zagelow. 1998. "The IBM data warehouse architecture." *CACM* **41(9).**
Cox, T. 1999. "The strategic DBA." *Oracle Magazine.* March 1999.
Dyck, T. 1998. "10 design tips." *PC Week Magazine*, June 1998.
Gupta, G. 1997. *Selection of Views to Materialize in a Data Warehouse. ICDT.*
IBM Corp. 1999. *DB2 IBM DB2 Universal Database Administration Guide.* IBM Corp.
Informatica Corp. 1999. "PowerMart." Available at http://www.informatica.com.
Jarke, M., M. Jeusfeld, C. Quix, and P. Vassiliadis. 1998. *Architecture and Quality in Data Warehouses.* CAiSE.
Michalewicz, Z. (ed). 1991. *Statistical and Scientific Databases.* Chichester, England: Ellis Horwood Limited.
Micorsoft Corp. 1998. "Microsoft Decision Support Services—Administrator's Guide." Available at http://www.microsoft.com.
MicroStrategy Inc. 1999. "DSS-Suite." Available at http://www.microstrategy.com.
Mullins, C. S. 1998. "Data warehouse administration." *The IDUG Solutions Journal* **5(2).**
O'Neil, B., M. Schrader, J. Dakin, K. Hardy, M. Townsend and M. Withney. 1997. *Oracle Data Warehousing.* Indianapolis: Sams Publishing. Northern Lights Software Ltd.
Oracle Corp. 1999a. *Oracle DBA Management Pack.* Oracle Corp.
Oracle Corp. 1999b. *Oracle 8i Tuning.* Oracle Corp.
Roussopoulos, N. 1997. *Materialized Views and Data Warehouses*: KRDB.
Srivastava, J. and P.Y. Chen 1999. "Warehouse creation–a potential roadblock to data warehousing." *TKDE* **11(1).**
Systemfabrik Inc. 1999. "Warehouse Workbench." Available at http://www.systemfabrik.com.

Further Reading

Bischoff, J., T. Alexander, and J. Biscoff. *Data Warehouse: Practical Advice from the Experts.* Englewood Cliffs, NJ: Prentice Hall, 1997.
Chamberlin, D. *A Complete Guide to DB2 Universal Database.* San Francisco, CA: Morgan Kaufmann Publishers, Inc., 1998.
Devlin, B. *Data Warehouse from Architecture to Implementation.* Reading, MA: Addison-Wesley, 1997.
Dodge, G. and T. Gorman. *Oracle 8 Data Warehousing.* New York: John Wiley & Sons, Inc., 1998.
Inmon, W. H., J. D. Welch, and K. L. Glassey. *Managing the Data Warehouse.* New York: John Wiley & Sons, Inc., 1998.
Kimball, R., Reeves, L., Ross, M. and Thornthwaite, W. *The Data Warehouse Lifecycle Tool-kit.* New York: John Wiley & Sons, Inc., 1998.

14 DATA REDUCTION

14.1 Sampling

David Madigan and Martha Nason

ABSTRACT Beginning with the fundamental concept of simple random sampling, we describe the main uses and types of classical sampling techniques. Issues that arise include stratification, clustering, and sample size. We briefly mention how these issues are relevant and are being addressed in the context of data mining.

1. Introduction

Sampling theory is one of the great success stories of modern statistics. Using routine sampling methods, characteristics of populations can be estimated in a reliable, unbiased, and efficient manner. For example, a simple random sample of size 1500 from a population of millions of people can almost certainly estimate the percentage of the entire population who have a certain trait or opinion to within 3 percent. It is hardly surprising that opinion polls and sample surveys have become so widespread and influential.

Samples are taken all the time: at factories, in political races, from databases. Whenever it is impossible, impractical, or unnecessary to examine all the objects in a population, a sample can potentially provide valuable insights. The goal of a sample is usually to distill from it an estimate of some quantity of interest in the population: an average, a difference between two groups, relationships between sets of variables. In order for these estimates to be useful, they should be fairly precise (if we can say with 95 percent confidence that our customers' average income lies somewhere between $10,000 and $100,000, we have not gained much).

The precision of an estimator depends in part on the natural variability inherent in the population. However, the sampling method can increase the precision of an estimator in two ways. First, in the most common situations, the variability of the estimate is inversely proportional to the square root of the size of the sample. Therefore, the precision of an estimator will increase as the sample gets larger. Second, careful choice of the sampling method can result in more precise estimators—we will briefly discuss some examples below.

2. Types of Sampling

2.1. Simple Random Sampling

This is the most straightforward type of sampling; in it, every conceivable group of objects of the required size has the same chance of being the selected sample. While it is possible to get a very atypical sample in this manner, the laws of probability dictate that the larger a sample is, the more likely it will be representative of the population whence it came. In general, the method leads to samples in which the characteristics of individuals are distributed similarly to the population.

The traditional method of choosing a random sample begins with a numbering of the members of the target population. The order in which they are numbered is irrelevant. Once each member in the population has a number, the sampler consults a random number table to select the indices of the members to be included in the sample. In practice, a computer carries out this task, but the concept is identical.

There are two types of simple random samples: with and without replacement. If a sample is taken without replacement it means that after each member is chosen for the sample, it is removed from consideration and the rest of the sample is selected from the remaining members. In random sampling with replacement, after each member is selected for the sample, that member is returned to the pool of eligible members. In this type of sample, any one member may appear more than once. If the population is large compared to the sample, there is a very small probability that any member will be chosen more than once and the two techniques are essentially the same.

2.2. Stratified Random Sampling

A stratified random sample first divides the population into strata, or groups, and then uses simple random sampling within each group. These strata are based on a variable or variables that might be related to the variable(s) of interest but are not of primary concern. Dividing the population into groups that are similar before sampling yields two advantages: first, the analyst can control the number of observations within each stratum. This is particularly useful if one stratum has a much smaller membership than the others, but the analyst wishes to look at effects within that stratum. For instance, suppose that a large majority of a particular population of interest falls into one racial group, such as Caucasian, with relatively few individuals falling into another category, such as Native American. In this situation, a simple random sample will likely reflect the racial distribution in the population. This could result in no or few members of the smaller ethnic group, resulting in low quality estimates of characteristics of this subpopulation. On the other hand, a sample that stratifies on race and includes an appropriate number of members from each subpopulation can yield high quality estimates of target characteristics in each of the subpopulations. This is clearly an important consideration in many data mining applications.

The second advantage of stratifying has to do with the amount of error or variance of the data. If the members within strata are more similar to each other than members from different strata, stratum-specific estimates will be more precise than ones from the entire sample. This technique does come with the warning that it is important to adjust for the overrepresentation when generalizing to the original sample.

2.3. Cluster Sampling

Cluster sampling is a related idea, useful when the members in the population naturally form clusters, such as patients within hospitals or employees within a company. One approach samples within each cluster; this is essentially stratified sampling. The other approach, which is often easier to implement, is to randomly sample clusters and then to include every member of each sampled cluster. Two-stage (or more generally, multistage) sampling combines the two ideas by randomly choosing clusters, and then sampling members within each cluster.

Because it is likely that members of a cluster are more alike than members of different clusters (if not, there would be no gain to either type of cluster sampling), statistical approaches which assume that the data are independent will lead to biased inferences. Approaches such as hierarchical or random effects modeling can explicitly model the sampling-induced structure in the data.

In the context of large databases, a common application of cluster sampling is to randomly select blocks of data, and then use all data on these blocks. The motivation behind this approach is that to retrieve one database record from a particular block, the entire block must be read into memory. This type of sampling, known as block sampling, has been the subject of much recent attention by researchers (see for example Chaudhuri et al., 1998).

2.4. Systematic Sampling

When individuals in a population are numbered in some way, systematic sampling is an option. Also known as every kth sampling, systematic sampling involves choosing one member at random from those numbered between 1 and k, then including every kth member after this in the sample. Because the selection is not random, systematic samples may not be representative of the population and must be used carefully.

2.5. Two-phase Sampling

Two-phase sampling may be useful when we wish to organize our sampling based on the values of one or more variables, but we do not know the range or distribution of these variables in our population. An initial sample may facilitate more educated decisions about sampling strategies. For instance, suppose we believe that a relationship we are examining might vary by age. We might wish to know whether there are certain age groups that are more or less represented in our database than others; this would help us decide whether we should take a stratified sample, or whether random sampling would be likely to give us a sample in which a variety of ages are represented. If we decide to stratify, we might find it useful to have information on the age range of the people from whom we are choosing.

An initial sample might also help in determining sample size. Sample size calculations frequently need estimates of certain population parameters, such as the strength of the relationship between two variables. In the absence of prior knowledge and/or data, an initial sample would provide estimates for these quantities, and these estimates would determine the sample size for the second phase sample. Toivonen (1996) explores a related idea in the context of association rule mining. See also Haas and Swami (1992) and Lipton and Naughton (1990).

2.6. Uncertainty Sampling

In the context of predictive modeling, uncertainty sampling can provide dramatic improvements over random sampling. Uncertainty sampling methods iteratively request class labels for training instances whose classes are uncertain despite the previous labeled instances. See Lewis and Catlett (1994) for more details.

3. Other Considerations

3.1. How Large Should a Sample Be?

There are straightforward mechanisms in statistics for estimating the sample size necessary to have a certain probability of detecting an effect of a pre-specified size or greater. These tools, grouped under the heading of power analysis, are based on estimates of the relevant means and variances of the variables in the population to be sampled. If good estimates are not available a priori, a two-phase sampling design can be used to generate them, or a set of power analyses can be used. These calculations can give a high probability of detecting the smallest effect that would be meaningful.

In clustered or stratified sampling, sample sizes can be estimated for each group separately. In this case, an estimate of desired precision should be formed for each stratum—this can be the same for each group, but does not need to be. Once a size has been determined for the subsample within each group, the total sample size is easily calculated by adding these numbers together.

An alternative to setting a predetermined sample size is to let the data choose the size of the sample. The basic idea is to continue to increase the sample size until the results or summaries no longer change very much (where very much is set in advance). Variations on this idea are known as progressive sampling, adaptive sampling or sequential sampling, and have been getting substantial attention lately—see, for example, Provost et al. (1999).

3.2. Finite Population Correction

When a random sample is taken from a very large population, the variance of the estimates (such as the sample average) is easily calculated and used throughout statistical analyses, as well as in power calculations. However, when the population is small, the formulas that give the variance of these estimates must strictly speaking be multiplied by a finite population correction factor. Practically, this correction factor will not have an effect if the size of the sample is small when compared to the size of the population. A common rule of thumb is that the correction factor can be ignored as long as not more than 5 percent of the population is sampled.

3.3. Design Effect

In circumstances where a specialized technique such as stratified sampling is used, the gain in precision over simple random sampling can be estimated. The design effect, as this gain is known, comes when an existing structure in the population, such as the similarity of customers within the same region, is successfully incorporated into the sampling design.

3.4. Warnings and Caveats

Many of the common tools for statistical inference, including t-tests and logistic regression, assume that the data comprise a simple random sample from some population, and that the individual data points are therefore statistically independent. Many of the sampling techniques will violate this assumption unless the structure of the data is incorporated into the analysis. Specialized statistical techniques exist for dealing with data generated by any number of complex sampling schemes—see for example Thompson et al. (1996) or Diggle et al. (1994). Obviously the extent of the bias introduced by ignoring the sampling scheme depends on the specifics of the application.

For data miners, it is certainly comforting that random sampling from a database provides unbiased estimates of characteristics of the database. However, if the database itself represents a haphazardly or systematically biased sample from the real population of interest, no statistical technique can rescue the resulting inferences.

References

Cochran (1977) is the classic text in the area of sampling. Thompson (1992) provides a review of the current state of the art including such topics as spatial sampling, double sampling, and capture–recapture methods. See also Thompson et al. (1996) and Deming (1984). For an excellent basic introduction see Utts (1996).

Chaudhuri, S., R. Motwani, and V. Narasayya. 1998. "Random sampling for histogram construction: how much is enough." In *Proceedings of the ACM SIGMOD Conference*, pp. 436–447. New York: ACM.
Cochran, W. G. 1977. *Sampling Techniques*. 3d ed. New York: Wiley.
Deming, W. E. 1984. *Some Theory of Sampling*. New York: Dover Publications.
Diggle, P. J., K-Y. Liang, and S. L. Zeger. 1994. *The Analysis of Longitudinal Data*. London: Clarendon.
Haas, P. J. and A. N. Swami. 1992. "Sequential sampling procedures for query size estimation." In *Proceedings of the ACM SIGMOD Conference*, pp. 341–350.
Lewis, D. and J. Catelett. 1994. "Heterogeneous uncertainty sampling for supervised learning." In *Machine Learning: Proceedings of the 11th International Conference*. San Francisco: Morgan Kaufmann.
Lipton, R. J. and J. F. Naughton. 1990. "Query size estimation by adaptive sampling." In *Proceedings of the ACM PODS*, pp. 40–46. New York: ACM.
Provost, F., D. Jensen, and F. T. Oates. 1999. "Efficient progressive sampling." In *Proceedings of the Fifth ACM International Conference on Knowledge Discovery and Data Mining*, pp. 23–32. New York: ACM.
Thompson, S. K. 1992. *Sampling*. New York: Wiley.
Thompson, S. K., G. A. F. Seber, and G. F. Seber. 1996. *Adaptive Sampling*. New York: Wiley.
Toivonen, H. 1996. "Sampling large databases for association rules." In *Proceedings of the 22nd VLDB Conference*, pp. 134–145.
Utts, J. 1996. In *Seeing Through Statistics*. Belmont, CA: Duxbury.

14.2 Feature Selection

Hiroshi Motoda and Huan Liu

ABSTRACT Feature selection is introduced as a search problem that consists of feature subset generation, evaluation, and selection. The purpose of feature selection is three-fold: reducing the number of features, improving classification accuracy, and simplifying the learned representation. We review major evaluation measures and various feature selection approaches, list some existing methods, and show by example the role of feature selection in data mining.

1. Introduction

The study of feature selection can be explained via inductive learning in which a learning algorithm constructs a description of a function from a set of input/output instances. The learning model adopted here is inductive learning from observation. We use a learning task for classification to elaborate on the idea of induction from observation—there are many other types of learning tasks. Some examples are conceptual clustering, reinforcement learning, macro operator learning (speedup learning), and so on. The observation is summarized in a data set, which consists of input/output instances in terms of feature-values plus one feature of class labels. The learning task is to find a function (or classifier here) that generalizes from the data so that the classifier is able to predict the classes for new instances.

Features are primitive units in defining a problem and convenient to use and manipulate. The use of features decouples data acquisition from data mining and machine learning. Features are also called attributes, properties, or characteristics. A collection of features with their values forms a flat data file that describes an application in which each line describes an instance (or pattern, case, example, record, tuple). Each feature can have discrete, continuous, or mixed values. The continuous features may have values from the domain of real numbers, which implies that the number of possible values is infinite. Discrete features are variables with only a limited number of values. Discrete features can further be divided into ordinal (such as the winning places in a tournament) and nominal (such as names of colors; see Chapter 4).

Many real-life databases contain very many attributes. The problem of feature selection arises because search complexity in the hypothesis space must be reduced for practical reasons and redundant or irrelevant features can have significant effects on the quality of results of analysis methods. Feature selection is a process that chooses an optimal subset of features according to a certain criterion. The criterion specifies the details of measuring feature subsets. The choice of a criterion can be influenced by the purpose of feature selection. An optimal subset can be a minimal subset; other things being equal, it can be a subset that gives the best estimation of predictive accuracy. In some cases, if the number of features is given (as in data visualization and projection, this number can be 2 or 3), we need to find a subset with the specified number that best satisfies the criterion. Intuitively, choosing a subset of M features from a full set of N features is equivalent to a reduction in the hypothesis space. This would make it easier for a data-mining algorithm to mine the available data. For example, if we want to learn a binary function from a binary domain, reducing the number of features from N to M means reducing the data by a factor of $O(2^{N-M})$. The reduction of data leads to the reduction of hypotheses.

As data are usually not designed and collected for the sole purpose of data mining, feature selection can facilitate data mining in many ways: data/dimensionality reduction, (partial) noise removal, model selection, comprehensibility enhancement, and evaluation improvement. All these are made possible because feature selection can choose features relevant to a particular application and relevant features make many tasks much easier. In the following, we introduce the basic ideas of various feature selection methods with pointers to many existing algorithms, and provide some guidelines on applying feature selection.

2. Various Methods of Feature Selection

The problem of feature selection can be viewed as a problem of search with various criteria for good or relevant features. According to whether feature selection is involved with a classification algorithm or not, two types of feature selection are commonly defined: a filter model vs. a wrapper model (John et al., 1994; Blum and Langley, 1997). The filter model does not rely on a classifier to determine whether a subset of features is good, but the wrapper does. If a classifier is not used during feature selection, we need some measures to discern good features from bad ones. In other words, the filter model requires such measures. The commonly used measures are information measures, distance measures, dependence measures, and inconsistency measures (Liu and Motoda, 1998). As a matter of fact, if we consider accuracy estimated by a classifier as another measure, we can unify the filter and wrapper

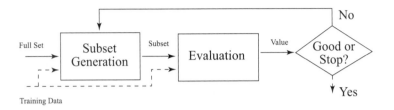

Figure 1 A unified model of feature selection

models into a general model as shown in Figure 1. Given a training data set with features, there are three main components for feature selection: (1) generating subsets of features, (2) evaluating subsets of features to find the best subset, and (3) deciding when the loop of generation and evaluation should stop. Each component could have several choices. The various combinations of these choices are the basis of many existing feature selection algorithms.

Feature subset generation. One intuitive way is to generate subsets of features sequentially. If we start with an empty subset and gradually add one feature at a time, we adopt a scheme called sequential forward selection; if we start with a full set and remove one feature at a time, we have a scheme called sequential backward selection. We can also randomly generate a subset so that each possible subset (in total, 2^N, where N is the number of features) has an approximately equal chance of being generated. One extreme way is to exhaustively enumerate 2^N possible subsets.

Feature evaluation. No matter which method of feature subset generation is adopted, we need some measure to decide which feature should be added or removed, or which subset should be kept. One of the five above-mentioned measures is typically used for this evaluation purpose.

Given an uncertainty function U and the prior class probabilities $P(c_i)$ where $i = 1, 2, ..., d$, the information gain from a feature X, $IG(X)$, is defined as the difference between the prior uncertainty $\sum_i U(P(c_i))$ and the expected posterior uncertainty using X, that is

$$IG(X) = \sum_i U(P(c_i)) - \mathbf{E}\left[\sum_i U(P(c_i \mid X))\right].$$

A feature evaluation rule derived from the concept of information gain states that feature X is preferred to feature Y if $IG(X) > IG(Y)$. That is, a feature should be selected if it can reduce more uncertainty. Another typical type is derived from distances between the class-conditional density functions. For the two-class case, if $D(X)$ is the distance between $P(X|c_1)$ and $P(X|c_2)$, a feature evaluation rule based on distance $D(X)$ states that X is preferred over Y if $D(X) > D(Y)$. This is because we try to find the feature that can separate the two classes as far as possible. The larger the distance, the easier to separate the two classes. Instead of checking how a feature changes information gain or a posterior class probability, we look at how strongly a feature is associated with the class. Denoting by $R(X)$ a dependence measure between feature X and class C, we prefer feature X to feature Y if $R(X) > R(Y)$. Put it another way, we select a feature that associates more closely with class C.

One common problem with the above three measures is that they cannot break ties between two equally good features. Therefore these measures cannot detect whether one of them is redundant. Inconsistency measures, however, attempt to find a minimum number of features that separate classes as consistently as the full set of features can. In other words, inconsistency measures aim to achieve $P(C \mid \text{FullSet}) = P(C \mid \text{SubSet})$. Feature evaluation rules derived from inconsistency measures state that we should select the minimum subset of features that can keep the consistency of the data maintained by the full set of features

(Almuallim and Dietterich, 1994; Liu and Setiono, 1996b).

Obviously, accuracy measures stand out from the above four categories. The rationale is that since we want to have a good set of features to improve the accuracy of a classifier, why don't we use the classifier's accuracy as a measure? With this type of measure come some considerations. One is how to truly estimate predictive accuracy and avoid overfitting. Another is that a classifier takes time to be learned from the data by a learning algorithm (by the way, the first consideration often further slows down a classifier). Yet another consideration is that sometimes data are too huge to run a learning algorithm so we need to reduce its dimensionality.

Stopping criteria. In any case, we should ensure that the loop of generation and evaluation in Figure 1 terminates. For exhaustive or sequential feature subset generation, the loop will naturally stop when a full set becomes empty, or an empty subset becomes full. In other cases, we need to force the loop to terminate, such as when a subset is good enough (e.g., using accuracy as the evaluation measure) or when a certain percentage of the total search space has been searched (a variation of this criterion is the number of subsets that have been generated).

With the above three components, we can build a customized feature selection method for an application at hand.

2.1. Representative Feature Selection Methods

Many feature selection algorithms exist. Using the general model described earlier, we can regenerate these existing algorithms by having proper combinations for each component.

Exhaustive/complete approaches. Focus (Almuallim and Dietterich, 1991; Almuallim and Dietterich, 1994) applies an inconsistency measure and exhaustively evaluates subsets starting from subsets with one feature (i.e., sequential forward search); branch-and-bound (Narendra and Fukunaga, 1977; Siedlecki and Sklansky, 1988) evaluates estimated accuracy; and ABB (Liu et al., 1998) checks an inconsistency measure that is monotonic. The latter two start with a full feature set until the preset bound cannot be maintained.

Heuristic approaches. SFS (sequential forward search) and SBS (sequential backward search; Siedlecki and Sklansky, 1988; Dash and Liu, 1997; Blum and Langley, 1997) can apply any of five measures. DTM (Cardie, 1993) is the simplest version of a wrapper model—just learn a classifier once and use whatever features found in the classifier.

Nondeterministic approaches. LVF (Liu and Setiono, 1996b) and LVW (Liu and Setiono, 1996a) randomly generate feature subsets but test them differently: LVF applies an inconsistency measure, LVW uses accuracy estimated by a classifier. Genetic algorithms and simulated annealing are also used in feature selection (Siedlecki and Sklansky, 1988; Jain and Zongker, 1997). The former may produce multiple subsets, the latter produces a single subset.

Instance-based approaches. Relief (Kira and Rendell, 1992; Kononenko, 1994) is a typical example for this category. There is no explicit procedure for feature subset generation. Many small data samples are sampled from the data. Features are weighted according to their roles in differentiating instances of different classes for a data sample. Features with higher weights can be selected.

2.2. Other Related Issues

For data mining tasks, data can be huge so that we often need to consider the scalability of a feature selection algorithm. For nonclassification data mining tasks (no class labels available), the algorithms introduced above will not work and alternative algorithms for feature selection should be considered.

Scalable feature selection. LVS (Liu and Setiono, 1998) is one such algorithm. The basic idea is to identify the most time-consuming part in a feature selection process and delay it until really necessary. LVS is an extension of LVF. As mentioned before, LVF uses an inconsistency measure (IC) with a run-time complexity of checking IC being $O(P)$, where P is the number of instances. If P is huge, it is still costly to compute IC many times. It is also noticed that the feature subset generation component will generate more and more invalid subsets that do not satisfy IC as the cardinality of a valid subset decreases. Therefore, it makes sense to separate the computation of IC for the whole data from feature subset generation. But we need data to generate subsets of features. The compromise is that instead of using the whole data set, we just use a portion of it for feature subset generation. When a subset is tested valid on the portion of the data, the IC for the whole data is calculated. Two cases ensue: (1) IC is still satisfied, then feature selection is completed; and (2) IC is not satisfied, then those inconsistent instances are added into the portion of the data and another round of feature subset generation is carried out on the enlarged portion of data. Empirical study shows that this method is effective only when P is sufficiently large, due to the overhead involved in LVS.

Supervised vs. unsupervised approaches. Unsupervised data do not have class labels. Feature selection algorithms using any of the five abovementioned evaluation measures cannot work. If there is a need for dimensionality reduction, another approach should be considered. In Dash et al. (1997), an entropy measure is introduced to sequentially rank features. The basic idea is that features are relevant if they can describe instances in terms of relatively clearly defined clusters. Consider a case of sequential forward selection. The essence of the algorithm is this: first, we find the feature with the minimum entropy when we just describe the data with one feature; second, we find another feature with the minimum entropy when pairing with the selected feature; we continue in this fashion and introduce one feature at a time into the selected feature subset until all features are selected. A ranked list of features is obtained. We can choose the first m features if we wish.

3. Application of Feature Selection Methods

Given many feature selection algorithms, we often encounter a problem of which one is more suitable for a particular task. In order to solve this problem, we need some extra information. One example is to study statistical characteristics or information theoretic measures of the data (Michie et al., 1994). We can also make use of simple measures such as number of instances (P), number of features (N), number of classes (C), and number of relevant features (M). For example, if we know the value of M but do not know which M features, then based on the difference d of N and M, we can decide whether to choose Focus, ABB, or LVF: the rule of thumb is if d is small, use ABB; if d is large, use Focus; otherwise, consider LVF. The purpose of performing feature selection can also play an important role. If accuracy is the major concern, we should adopt a wrapper model. More detailed discussion can be found in Liu and Motoda (1998). All in all, extra information can help us choose the proper method or build a customized algorithm for feature selection.

4. Summary

We have briefly introduced the components of a feature selection process (feature subset generation, feature evaluation, and stopping criteria) and representative algorithms, mentioned issues such as scalability and unsupervised feature selection, and also provided some guidelines on how to apply a feature selection algorithm. Many issues still remain untouched, such as how to handle noise and missing values and how to treat mixed data types. Some work has been done on hybrid feature selection methods (Dash and Liu, 1998). This chapter only serves an introductory purpose, and interested readers can find many more details through the references cited here. Feature selection has been studied in many fields like statistics, pattern recognition, machine learning, and now data mining. Feature selection has found applications in all these fields. One recent example (Ng et al., 1998) is to use feature selection to identify objective relevant indicators and capture concept drifts in order to assist human experts in customer retention—a typical data mining application.

Part of this section is reproduced, with permission, from Liu, H. and Motoda, H., *Feature Selection for Knowledge Discovery and Data Mining*, Boston: Kluwer Academic Publishers (1998).

References

Almuallim, H. and T. Dietterich. 1991. "Learning with many irrelevant features." In *Proceedings of the Ninth National Conference on Artificial Intelligence*, pp. 547–552. Menlo Park, CA: AAAI Press/The MIT Press.

Almuallim, H. and T. Dietterich. 1994. "Learning Boolean concepts in the presence of many irrelevant features." *Artificial Intell.* **69(1–2)**: 279–305.

Blum, A. and P. Langley. 1997. "Selection of relevant features and examples in machine learning." *Artificial Intell.* **97**: 245–271.

Cardie, C. 1993. "Using decision trees to improve case-based learning." In *Proceedings of the Tenth International Conference on Machine Learning*, edited by P. Utgoff, pp. 25–32. Amherst, MA: University of Massachusetts.

Dash, M. and H. Liu. 1997. "Feature selection methods for classifications." *Intelligent Data Analysis: An International Journal IOS Press* **1**.

Dash, M. and H. Liu. 1998. "Hybrid search of feature subsets." In *Proceedings of the Fifth Pacific Rim International Conference on AI (PRICAI'98), November 22–27, 1998*, edited by P. Lee and H. Motoda. Singapore: Springer-Verlag.

Dash, M., H. Liu, and J. Yao. 1997. "Dimensionality reduction of unsupervised data." In *Proceedings of the Ninth IEEE International Conference on Tools with AI (ICTAI'97), November 1998*, pp. 532–539. Newport Beach, CA: IEEE Computer Society.

Jain, A. and D. Zongker. 1997. "Feature selection: evaluation, application, and small sample performance." *IEEE Trans. Pattern Anal. Machine Intell.* **19(2)**: 153–158.

John, G., R. Kohavi, and K. Pfleger. 1994. "Irrelevant feature and the subset selection problem." In *Machine Learning: Proceedings of the Eleventh International Conference*, edited by W. A. H. H. Cohen, pp. 121–129. New Brunswick, NJ: Rutgers University.

Kira, K. and L. Rendell. 1992. "The feature selection problem: traditional methods and a new algorithm." In *Proceedings of the Tenth National Conference on Artificial Intelligence*, pp. 129–134. Menlo Park, CA: AAAI Press/The MIT Press.

Kononenko, I. 1994. "Estimating attributes: analysis and extension of RELIEF." In *Proceedings of the European Conference on Machine Learning, April 6–8*, edited by F. Bergadano and L. De Raedt, pp. 171–182. Berlin: Springer-Verlag.

Liu, H. and H. Motoda. 1998. *Feature Selection for Knowledge Discovery Data Mining*. Boston: Kluwer Academic Publishers.

Liu, H. and R. Setiono. 1996a. "Feature selection and classification—a probabilistic wrapper approach." In *Proceedings of the Ninth International Conference on Industrial and Engineering Applications of AI and ES*, edited by T. Tanaka, S. Ohsuga, and M. Ali, pp. 419–424. Fukuoka, Japan. The Netherlands: Gordon and Breach Publishers.

Liu, H. and R. Setiono. 1996b. "A probabilistic approach to feature selection—a filter solution." In *Proceedings of International Conference on Machine Learning (ICML-96), July 3–6, 1996*, edited by L. Saitta, pp. 319–327. San Francisco, CA: Morgan Kaufmann Publishers.

Liu, H. and R. Setiono. 1998. "Scalable feature selection for large-sized databases." In *Proceedings of the Fourth World Congress on Expert Systems (WCES'98)*, edited by F. Cantu, R. Soto, J. Liebowitz, and E. Sucar. New York: Morgan Kaufmann Publishers.

Liu, H., H. Motoda, and M. Dash. 1998. "A monotonic measure for optimal feature selection." In *Machine Learning: ECML-98, April 21–23, 1998*, edited by C. Nedellec and C. Rouveirol, pp. 101–106. Berlin: Springer-Verlag.

Michie, D., D. Spiegelhalter, and C. Taylor. (eds). 1994. *Machine Learning, Neural and Statistical Classification*. England: Ellis-Horwood.

Narendra, P. and K. Fukunaga. 1977. "A branch and bound algorithm for feature subset selection." *IEEE Trans. Comput.* **C-26(9)**: 917–922.

Ng, K., H. Liu, and H. Kwah. 1998. "A data mining application: customer retention at the Port of Singapore Authority (PSA)." In *Proceedings of ACM SIGMOD International Conference on Management of Data*, edited by L. Haas and A. Tiwary, pp. 522–525. New York: ACM Press.

Siedlecki, W. and J. Sklansky. 1988. "On automatic feature selection." *Int. J. Pattern Recognition Artificial Intell.* **2**: 197–220.

14.3 Feature Aggregation

Hiroshi Motoda and Huan Liu

ABSTRACT Feature aggregation is a process through which a set of new features is created. Its purpose is improving performance such as estimated accuracy, visualization, and comprehensibility of learned knowledge. Feature aggregation is briefly reviewed in the framework of constructive induction and functional mapping. In the former we introduce basic operators for constructing new features and a typical algorithm; in the latter, we introduce some statistical methods and a neural network method.

1. Introduction

Feature aggregation is a process through which a set of new features is created. Two major groups under feature aggregation are feature construction and feature extraction. Both are sometimes called feature discovery.

Feature construction is a process that discovers missing information about the relationships between features and augments the space of features by inferring or creating additional features (Matheus, 1991; Wnek and Michalski, 1994; Matheus and Rendell, 1989). Assuming the original set consists of n features, after feature construction, we may have an additional m features. For example, a new feature could be constructed by performing a logical operation on the original features. An example would be that a new feature $C_k(= A_i \wedge A_j)$ is formed from original features A_i and A_j. Let S_n be the original feature set and S_m be the new feature set. Usually, the dimensionality of the new feature set is expanded and is bigger than that of S_n because the constructed features are used with the original features. All new features are defined in terms of existing features, as such no inherently new information is added through feature construction. Feature construction can be applied repeatedly to generate more compound features.

Feature extraction is a process that extracts a set of new features from the original features through some functional mapping (Wyse et al., 1980). After feature extraction, we have m new features. For example, a new feature may be a linear combination of some of the original features. A common characteristic of feature extraction methods is that they all produce a new feature set S_m based on the original feature set S_n. Usually, the dimensionality of S_m is reduced and is smaller than that of S_n because the original features are replaced by the new features.

Methods of feature aggregation are not solely designed for reducing dimensionality of S_n, as does feature selection (Chapter 14.2), but also for enabling purposes. After feature aggregation, the representation of data is changed so that many techniques such as visualization, decision-tree building, and rule extraction can be used more efficiently. Feature aggregation and feature selection are not two totally independent issues. They can be viewed as two sides of the representation problem. We can consider features as the core of a representation language. In some cases, where this language contains more features than necessary, feature selection helps simplify the language; in other cases, where this language is not proper to directly describe the problem, feature aggregation helps enrich the language by constructing compound features or transforming the features. It is common that some constructed features are not useful at all. Feature selection can then be used to remove these useless features. The use of feature aggregation and feature selection depends on the purpose—for simpler concept description or for better classification. The former aims at preserving the topological structure of the data whereas the latter targets on enhancing the predictive (discriminative) power.

2. Various Methods of Feature Aggregation

2.1. Constructive Induction

Feature aggregation can best be viewed in the framework of constructive induction. New compound features are constructed out of the original features. The primary goals of constructing new features include improving the overall predictive accuracy of a classifier, decreasing the overall complexity of learned concepts, or both.

Wnek and Michalski (1994) offer a classification of constructive induction systems: data-driven (DCI), hypothesis-driven (HCI), knowledge-driven (KCI), and multistrategy constructive induction (MCI) based on what is used to construct compound features. DCI is the most common approach. It builds new attributes based on an analysis of the training data. New features are constructed based on a generate-and-test method using generic domain-independent arithmetic and Boolean operators (see Section 2.2). HCI approaches construct new features based on the hypotheses generated previously. Useful concepts in the induced rules (hypotheses) can be extracted and used to define new features. These new features are useful because they explicitly express hidden relationships in the data. Instances are redescribed by the derived features and the original ones, and the same process is repeated until no good new features could be found. HCI approaches have the advantage of relying on previous knowledge/hypotheses but at the same time have the disadvantage of being strongly dependent on the quality of previous knowledge. On the other hand, DCI approaches cannot benefit from previous hypotheses, but can avoid the strong quality dependency. KCI approaches make use of background knowledge (such as unit dimensions of variables) as an external bias to direct constructive induction. This is needed because the search space of new features is sometimes huge and beyond the reach of the constructive operators. The types of new features derived depend on the learning strategy applied. The process bias of a learning strategy affects the formation of new features. There is no universal learning process bias that could cover the whole feature spectrum. As the target concept becomes more complicated, any single constructive induction system is no longer adequate. MCI approaches combine multiple learning strategies to cover a wider portion of the feature spectrum than a single strategy. In Bloedorn et al. (1993), results are summarized when DCI, HCI, and MCI are applied to a modified second Monk problem. All of these constructive induction methods give a more compact description of the target concept than a selective induction method. Further, MCI gives improved performance in terms of predictive accuracy and hypothesis complexity over either one of the single strategy methods.

Constructive induction systems contribute to overcoming the limitation of representation in original features and attack the problems of replication, repetition, and fragmentation. Many selective inductive learning systems employ the divide-and-conquer strategy (see Chapter 16.1). Examples are CART (Breiman et al., 1984), ID3 and C4.5 (Quinlan, 1986, 1993), and CN2 (Clark and Niblett, 1989), among many. This strategy brings with it the above problems. For example, in decision-tree induction, the replication problem can be observed if some subtrees are replicated in a decision-tree; the repetition (or repeated testing) problem is present if features are repeatedly tested (more than once) along a path in a decision tree; and the fragmentation problem exists if data is gradually partitioned into small fragments (Pagallo and Haussler, 1990; Brodley and Utgoff, 1995). Replication and repetition always imply fragmentation, but fragmentation may occur without any replication or repetition if many features need to be tested (Friedman et al., 1996).

2.2. Feature Construction

Through years of research, many constructive operators have been designed and implemented. Conjunction, disjunction, and negation are commonly used constructive operators for nominal feature values. Another two constructive operators are M-of-N (M-of-N is true iff at least M out of N conditions are true; conjunction and disjunction can be thought of as N-of-N and 1-of-N, respectively) and X-of-N (X-of-N takes a number between 0 and N; its value is x iff x of N conditions are true; Zheng, 1998). Yet another operator is the Cartesian product (Pazzani, 1998). It is the direct product of two or more attributes (e.g., if height with values tall and short were joined to weight with values heavy and light, a new attribute formed is height_weight with values tall_heavy, tall_light, short_heavy and short_light). All these operators work on and produce binary features. For numerical features, simple algebraic operators such as equivalence (i.e., a new feature's value is 1 if two features $x = y$, otherwise 0), inequality, addition, subtraction, multiplication, division, maximum (i.e., a new feature's value is the maximum value of all features in feature set), minimum, and average are often used to construct compound features. How to apply these constructive operators efficiently is a difficult task. In many cases, greedy local search or genetic algorithms are used.

One extremely useful constructive operator is Count(S, C) shown in Bloedorn and Michalski (1998). It denotes how many features there exist in set S satisfying condition C. The new feature found for the second Monk's problem (Monk2) is, after feature construction, Count($\{A_1, \ldots A_6\}$, FirstValue) $= 2$, which actually states the concept to be learned: an instance belongs to the concept, if exactly two of six features take their first value. After this new feature is defined, Monk2 is simplified to a linearly separable problem from a problem with high interdependence between features. This example clearly shows the power of feature construction.

A straightforward algorithm incorporating a data-driven constructive induction approach is summarized below for a decision-tree induction. At each decision node the algorithm generates one new feature based on original features using the local training set. If the new feature constructed at a node is better than all original features and all previously created new features, the algorithm uses it as the test for the node; otherwise it discards it and uses the best of the original features and previously constructed new features. To construct a new feature, the algorithm performs a greedy search in the instance space defined by original features. The search starts from an empty set. At each search step, it either adds one possible feature-value pair or deletes one possible feature-value pair. For comparing and selecting new features, an evaluation function that takes both class entropy (information gain ratio) and model complexity (coding cost) into account (e.g., AIC criterion [Akaike, 1974]) can be used. The search stops when the maximum possible size of representations is reached or no better new feature has been found in a certain number of consecutive search steps.

2.3. Feature Extraction

Finding a good functional mapping from the original features is the heart of feature extraction. There are well-established statistical methods that can be directly applied to numeric features for this purpose. Linear discriminant analysis and principal component analysis (also called the Karhunen–Loeve (K-L) method) are two such methods. Most statistical software packages (e.g., SAS [http://www.sas.com/SASHome.html]) include these standard methods.

One application of linear discriminant analysis often attempted is inducing an oblique decision tree, where the decision surface of each test node is oblique to the axes defined by the original features. Each test node is a linear discriminant, which is a linear combination of the original features. The new feature extracted this way, can be propagated downwards through the tree, thus allowing nonlinear fittings (Gama and Brazdil, 1998).

Principal component analysis is often used to reduce dimensionality of the data for visualization purposes because data of high dimensions cannot be analyzed visually. It is based on the eigenvalues of a covariance matrix ($\mathbf{R}$) computed from the data. The M eigenvectors corresponding to the M largest eigenvalues of $\mathbf{R}$ define a linear transformation from the N-dimensional space to an M-dimensional space in which the features are uncorrelated. This property comes from the fact that if the eigenvalues of a matrix are distinct, the associated eigenvectors are linearly independent (Pettofrezzo, 1966). The ratio of the sum of the M largest eigenvalues of $\mathbf{R}$ to the trace of $\mathbf{R}$ is the fraction of the variance retained in the M-dimensional space. When the ratio is sufficiently large (0.9 or more), M is taken as an estimate of the intrinsic dimensionality. This method is computationally inexpensive, but it requires characterizing data with covariance matrix $\mathbf{R}$ and some shortcomings may ensue. One of them is that correlations among multiple features cannot be characterized because it is possible that there is interdependency among the features and these features are co-correlated with the class attribute. Another disadvantage is that class information is left out, even if it is available.

The last problem of using class information in feature extraction can be overcome by employing a feedforward neural network. Basically, the hidden unit activations of a network are interpreted as new features extracted from the original dataset (Hu, 1998; Setiono and Liu, 1998; Utgoff and Precup, 1998). The usual procedure is to train the network until a prespecified predictive accuracy (or a threshold) is achieved, prune it while maintaining the accuracy (or simplifying the network without sacrificing the accuracy), and then take hidden units in the pruned network as the new features. Pruning is based on the magnitudes of the connections between units and is terminated when the removal of a connection would cause a decrease in the accuracy below the threshold. Irrelevant and/or redundant connections are removed in the pruning process. More often than not, the number of hidden units in the pruned network is much smaller than the number of input units. Thus, it is possible to extract a smaller number of features out of the original features. This feature extraction algorithm can handle both discrete and continuous data in addition to taking into account class information. In Liu and Motoda (1998) the Iris data are used to view the different results of several feature extraction methods. The interested reader is advised to read further.

3. Summary

Feature construction has long been considered a powerful tool for increasing both the accuracy and understanding of structure, particularly in high-dimensional problems (Breiman et al., 1984). Constructed features help alleviate replication and fragmentation problems and build compact and accurate classifiers. How to find good compound features is still an art. Constructive operators must be carefully designed. Once a good set of operators is prepared, the constructed features are very powerful for characterizing the structure of the data. Feature construction is also an effective tool to handle concept drifting (Widmer, 1996). This is because we can perform features construction, from time to time, on original features and form compound features to capture drifted concepts. Main types of feature construction include hypothesis-driven, data-driven, knowledge-driven, and multistrategy induction.

Most work in knowledge-guided constructive induction has assumed approximately complete background knowledge; however, in practice, domain knowledge can be partial. For domains that are barely understood, even fragmentary knowledge could be used to narrow the search space of constructed features (Donoho and Rendell, 1996).

Little work has been devoted to studying how human experts come up with good representations. We know little about how human experts relate original features to higher-level abstract intermediate concepts in real-world domains. It would be very useful if we could know more about involving human efforts in the process of developing good representations.

Part of this section is reproduced, with permission, from Liu, H. and Motoda, H. (eds), *Feature Extraction, Construction and Selection: A Data Mining Perspective*. Boston: Kluwer Academic Publishers (1998), and Liu, H. and Motoda, H. *Feature Selection for Knowledge Discovery and Data Mining*. Boston: Kluwer Academic Publishers (1998).

References

Akaike, H. 1974. "A new look at the statistical model identification." *IEEE Trans. Automatic Control* **AC-19**: 716–723.

Bloedorn, E. and R. Michalski. 1998. "Data-driven constructive induction: a methodology and its applications." In *Feature Extraction, Construction and Selection: A Data Mining Perspective*, edited by H. Liu and H. Motoda, pp. 51–68. Boston: Kluwer Academic Publishers.

Bloedorn, E., R. Michalski, and J. Wnek. 1993. "Multistrategy constructive induction: AQ17-MCI." In *Proceedings of the Second International Workshop on Multistrategy Learning*, pp. 188–203. Harpers Ferry, VM. Machine Learning and Inference Laboratory M.S. 5C3, George Mason University, Fairfax, VA.

Breiman, L., J. Friedman, R. Olshen, and C. Stone. 1984. *Classification and Regression Trees*. Belmont, CA: Wadsworth & Brooks/Cole Advanced Books & Software.

Brodley, C. and P. Utgoff. 1995. "Multivariate decision trees." *Machine Learning* **19**: 45–77.

Clark, P. and T. Niblett. 1989. "The CN2 induction algorithm." *Machine Learning* **3**: 261–283.

Donoho, S. and L. Rendell. 1996. "Constructive induction using fragmentary knowledge." In *Proceedings of the International Conference on Machine Learning (ICML-96)*, edited by L. Saitta, pp. 113–121. San Francisco, CA: Morgan Kaufmann Publishers.

Friedman, J., R. Kohavi, and Y. Yun. 1996. "Lazy decision trees." In *Proceedings of the Thirteenth National Conference on Artificial Intelligence*, pp. 717–724.

Gama, J. and P. Brazdil. 1998. "Constructive induction on continuous spaces." In *Feature Extraction, Construction and Selection: A Data Mining Perspective*, edited by H. Liu and H. Motoda, pp. 289–303. Boston: Kluwer Academic Publishers.

Hu, Y. 1998. "Constructive induction: covering attribute spectrum." In *Feature Extraction, Construction and Selection: a Data Mining Perspective*, edited by H. Liu and H. Motoda, pp. 257–272. Boston: Kluwer Academic Publishers.

Liu, H. and H. Motoda. 1998. *Feature Selection for Knowledge Discovery and Data Mining*. Boston: Kluwer Academic Publishers.

Matheus, C. 1991. "The need for constructive induction." In *Machine Learning—Proceedings of the Eighth International Workshop*, edited by L. Birnbaum and C. G. Collins, pp. 173–177. San Mateo, CA: Morgan Kaufmann Publishers.

Matheus, C. and L. Rendell. 1989. "Constructive induction on decision trees." In *Proceedings of the International Joint Conference on AI*, pp. 645–650. San Mateo, CA: Morgan Kaufmann Publishers.

Pagallo, G. and D. Haussler. 1990. "Boolean feature discovery in empirical learning." *Machine Learning* 5: 71–99.

Pazzani, M. J. 1998. "Constructive induction of cartesian product attributes." In *Feature Extraction, Construction and Selection: A Data Mining Perspective*, edited by H. Liu and H. Motoda, pp. 341–354. Boston: Kluwer Academic Publishers.

Pettofrezzo, A. 1966. *Matrices and Transformations*. New York: Dover Publications, Inc.

Quinlan, J. 1986. "Induction of decision trees." *Machine Learning* 1(1): 81–106.

Quinlan, J. 1993. *C4.5: Programs for Machine Learning*. San Francisco, CA: Morgan Kaufmann.

Setiono, R. and H. Liu. 1998. "Feature extraction via neural networks." In *Feature Extraction, Construction and Selection: A Data Mining Perspective*, edited by H. Liu and H. Motoda, pp. 191–204. Boston: Kluwer Academic Publishers.

Utgoff, P. E. and D. Precup. 1998. "Constructive function approximation." In *Feature Extraction, Construction and Selection: a Data Mining Perspective*, edited by H. Liu and H. Motoda, pp. 219–235. Boston: Kluwer Academic Publishers.

Widmer, G. 1996. "Recognition and exploitation of contextual clues via incremental meta-learning." In *Machine Learning: Proceedings of the Thirteenth International Conference*, edited by L. Saitta, pp. 525–533. San Fransisco, CA: Morgan Kaufmann Publishers.

Wnek, J. and R. Michalski. 1994. "Hypothesis-driven constructive induction in AQ17-HCI: a method and experiments." *Machine Learning* 14: 139–168.

Wyse, N., R. Dubes, and A. Jain. 1980. "A critical evaluation of intrinsic dimensionality algorithms." In *Pattern Recognition in Practice*, edited by E. Gelsema and L. Kanal, pp. 415–425. Amsterdam: North Holland Publishing Company.

Zheng, Z. 1998. "A comparison of constructing different types of new feature for decision tree learning." In *Feature Extraction, Construction and Selection: A Data Mining Perspective*, edited by H. Liu and H. Motoda, pp. 239–255. Boston: Kluwer Academic Publishers.

14.4 Discretization of Numerical Attributes

Jerzy W. Grzymala-Busse

ABSTRACT Discretization is the process of converting a numerical attribute into a symbolic attribute by partitioning the attribute domain. This chapter presents the taxonomy of currently developed discretization systems. Discretization techniques based on equal interval frequency, equal interval width, minimum class entropy, minimum description length, and clustering are briefly described. In addition, other methods of discretization are also outlined.

1. Introduction

Many knowledge discovery in databases (KDD) algorithms require symbolic (categorical) attributes. On the other hand, many real-world databases contain numerical attributes (also called continuous attributes), with integers or real numbers as values. Thus it is necessary to preprocess input data for knowledge discovery: numerical attributes should be converted into

Table 1 Data with Numerical Attributes

IQ	Weight	Height	Class
109	63	175	no
105	90	170	yes
115	61	178	yes
107	85	182	no
107	62	179	no
115	92	172	yes

symbolic attributes. This conversion is accomplished by partitioning of a numerical attribute domain into intervals. The conversion process of numerical attributes into symbolic attributes is called discretization (or quantization). Usually, the process of discretization contributes to more efficient use of knowledge discovery, even for systems that may discretize data during the main process of knowledge discovery. However, the most important issue is maximizing the resulting accuracy of the rule set induced from discretized data.

An example of a decision table with numerical attributes is presented in Table 1. The decision table from Table 1 has six examples. Attributes are the variables *IQ*, *Weight*, and *Height*.

The variables from Table 1 are too specific for any immediate generalization. For example, attribute *IQ* is as good in determining the class membership for any example as the set of all attributes. Hence a machine learning system could induce the following rules using *IQ* as the only attribute:

(IQ, 105) → (Class, yes)

(IQ, 107) → (Class, no)

(IQ, 109) → (Class, no)

(IQ, 113) → (Class, yes)

(IQ, 115) → (Class, yes)

Rules induced in this way are not useful, because they are over-specialized. With any new example characterized by different value of *IQ* than listed in the original decision table, it will be impossible to determine *Class*. Thus, the accuracy of the above rule set will be close to 0 percent.

In KDD, in general, this problem is solved by a technique called discretization. According to this technique, if a variable has numerical values from an interval $[a, b]$, then this interval is divided into subintervals $[a_1, b_1), [a_2, b_2), ..., [a_{m-1}, b_{m-1}), [a_m, b_m]$, where $a_1 = a, b_1 = a_2, ..., a_{m-1} = b_{m-2}, b_{m-1} = a_m, b_m = b$ and $a_1 > b_1, a_2 > b_2, ..., a_m > b_m$ In the following these subintervals will be denoted $a_1 ... b_1, a_2 ... b_2, ..., a_m ... b_m$, respectively. Numbers $a_2, a_3, ..., a_m$ are called cut points. In some discretization algorithms, cut points are actual attribute values; in others, cut points are averages of consecutive actual attribute values. We will follow the first approach.

Obviously, the first step in discretization of any numerical attribute is sorting values of the attribute.

2. Taxonomy of Discretization Methods

Discretization methods in which information about class membership is not taken into account are called unsupervised (Dougherty et al., 1995) or class-blind (Pfahringer, 1995). When information about classes is utilized, the methods are called supervised. Usually unsupervised discretization methods lead to low accuracy of knowledge induced from discretized data (Kerber, 1992).

Some discretization methods process all attributes, selecting not only cut points but also attributes during computation. Such methods are called global in Chmielewski and Grzymala-Busse (1994, 1995, 1996) or dynamic in Dougherty et al. (1995). On the other hand, methods working separately on attributes, one attribute at a time, are called local in Chmielewski and

Grzymala-Busse (1994, 1995, 1996) or static in Dougherty et al. (1995). Most of the discretization algorithms currently in existence belong to this last class.

Methods that discretize all the required numerical attributes before rule induction, as a kind of preprocessing, are called global in Kohavi and Sahami (1996). When discretization is done during rule induction, corresponding methods are called local. Examples of systems using this last type of discretization are CART (Breiman et al., 1984) and C4.5 (Quinlan, 1993). Simultaneous discretization and rule induction restricts the choice of search strategy for discretization.

If small intervals are merged into larger and larger intervals, discretization is called bottom-up. When intervals are recursively split into smaller and smaller intervals, the methods are top-down.

3. Equal Interval Frequency and Equal Interval Width

In some cases discretization is done by experts, for example in our example, an expert may decide that the variables *IQ*, *Weight*, and *Height* should have cut points of 109, 85, and 178, respectively. Thus, each interval represents the same number of examples (three examples). The table obtained this way from Table 1 is presented as Table 2. This method of discretization is called the equal interval frequency method.

An example of the rule set induced from Table 2 is:

(Weight, 61 ... 85) & (Height, 170 ... 178) → (Class, no)

(IQ, 105 ... 109) & (Height, 178 ... 182) → (Class, no)

(Weight, 85 ... 92) & (Height, 170 ... 178) → (Class, yes)

(IQ, 109 ... 115) & (Height, 178 ... 182) → (Class, yes)

The above rule set was induced by the system LERS (Grzymala-Busse, 1992).

A similar discretization method, called equal interval width, is based on dividing the domain of the attribute into equal subintervals. For example, attribute *IQ* may be divided into two subintervals: 105 ... 110 and 110 ... 115.

In both methods, equal interval frequency and equal interval width, discretization does not need to produce binary attributes. In general, for any attribute, the user may want a number k of subintervals. Both of these methods are unsupervised, that is, discretization is independent of class membership.

4. Minimal Class Entropy

Supervised discretization methods take into account class membership of attribute values. An example of such a method is the minimal class entropy method. For an attribute A over the set S of all examples, entropy $H(S)$ is defined by

$$-\sum_{i=1}^{n} P_i \cdot \lg P_i,$$

where P_i is the probability of occurrence of the class C_i in attribute A and n is the total number of classes. Logarithms in the formulas are of the base two. Probability P_i is computed as the

Table 2 Data Discretized by Equal Frequency Method

IQ	Weight	Height	Class
109 ... 115	61 ... 85	170 ... 178	no
105 ... 109	85 ... 92	170 ... 178	yes
109 ... 115	61 ... 85	178 ... 182	yes
105 ... 109	85 ... 92	178 ... 182	no
105 ... 109	61 ... 85	178 ... 182	no
109 ... 115	85 ... 92	170 ... 178	yes

ratio of all values of A for which class is C_i to the cardinality $|S|$ of the set S of all examples. In our example,

$$H(S) = -\frac{3}{6} \cdot \lg\frac{3}{6} - \frac{3}{6} \cdot \lg\frac{3}{6} = 1.$$

For a cut point T dividing the set S into two subsets S_1 and S_2 a conditional entropy $H(A, S \mid T)$ is defined as

$$\frac{|S_1|}{|S|} \cdot H(S_1) + \frac{|S_2|}{|S|} \cdot H(S_2).$$

For example, for attribute IQ and cut point $T = 107$, S_1 contains one example (the second one), S_2 contains the five remaining examples, and

$$H(IQ, S \mid 107) = \frac{1}{6}(-1 \cdot \lg 1) + \frac{5}{6}\left(-\frac{3}{5} \cdot \lg\frac{3}{5} - \frac{2}{5} \cdot \lg\frac{2}{5}\right) = 0.809.$$

The best cut point, selected by the method, is the one with the smallest conditional entropy. An important observation by Fayyad and Irani (1992) simplifies computation. They showed that the best cut point will never cut examples within the same class. For example, for attribute IA, the sorted list of values is 105, 107, 109, 113, 115 with class labels yes, no, no, yes, yes, respectively. Potential best cut points are 107 and 113. There is no need to compute conditional entropy for $T = 109$ and $T = 115$. Thus, we need to compute only one extra entropy: $H(A, S \mid T)$ for $A = IQ$ and $T = 113$.

$$H(IQ, S \mid 113) = \frac{4}{6}\left(-\frac{1}{4} \cdot \lg\frac{1}{4} - \frac{3}{4} \cdot \lg\frac{3}{4}\right) + \frac{2}{6}(-1 \cdot \lg 1) = 0.541.$$

The cut point $T = 113$ is the best cut point for attribute IQ over the entire set S. If we would like to find the second cut point for IQ, it should be done recursively, for both S_1 and S_2 separately. Let us say that instead of further discretizing attribute IQ we want to discretize the remaining attributes, *Weight* and *Height*. Using similar computations as for IQ we conclude that for *Weight* the best cut point is $T = 90$ and that for *Height* the best cut point is $T = 175$. It is not difficult to observe that the two discretized attributes, IQ and *Weight*, are sufficient to classify all examples. The new discretized data are presented in Table 3.

An example of the rule set induced from Table 3 is:

(IQ, 105 ... 113) & (Weight, 61 ... 90) → (Class, no)

(Weight, 90 ... 92) → (Class, yes)

(IQ, 113 ... 115) → (Class, no)

The rule set induced from Table 3 is not only much simpler but also easier to interpret than the rule set induced from Table 2. A few discretization systems utilizing minimal conditional entropy were developed, for example, D2 (Catlett, 1991) and systems described in Dougherty et al. (1995) and Kohavi and Sahami (1996).

Table 3 Data Discretized by Minimal Entropy Method

IQ	Weight	Height	Class
105 ... 113	61 ... 90	175 ... 182	no
105 ... 113	90 ... 92	170 ... 175	yes
113 ... 115	61 ... 90	175 ... 182	yes
105 ... 113	61 ... 90	175 ... 182	no
105 ... 113	61 ... 90	175 ... 182	no
113 ... 115	90 ... 92	170 ... 175	yes

5. Minimum Description Length Principle

A modification of the minimal entropy algorithm is an algorithm based on the minimum description length principle. The principle is justified by a tendency to favor the simplest description that explains the same facts. The minimum description length principle, introduced by Rissanen (1978) and then further developed by Quinlan and Rivest (1989), is cited here as presented by Fayyad and Irani (1993). According to the minimum description length principle, the cut point should be accepted if

$$\text{Gain}(A, S \mid T) = H(S) - H(A, S \mid T)$$

$$> \frac{\lg(\mid S \mid -1) + \lg(3^n - 2) - n \cdot H(S) + n_1 \cdot H(S_1) + n_2 \cdot H(S_2)}{\mid S \mid},$$

where n, n_1, n_2 are the number of classes in S, S_1, and S_2, respectively. The above formula was derived from the idea that the cut point should be accepted if the cost of transmitting the shortest description through the channel, assuming that the cut point was accepted, is smaller than the same cost associated with rejection of the cut point. In our example, for $T = 107$, $\mid S \mid = 6$, $n = 2, n_1 = 1, n_2 = 2$, the condition

$$\text{Gain}(IQ, S \mid 107) = H(S) - H(A, S \mid 107) = 1 - 0.809 = 0.191$$

$$> \frac{\lg(6 - 1) + \lg(3^2 - 2) - 2 \cdot H(S) + 1 \cdot H(S_1) + 2 \cdot H(S_2)}{6}$$

$$= \frac{\lg 5 + \lg 7 - 2 \cdot 1 + 1(-1 \cdot \lg 1) + 2\left(-\frac{3}{5} \cdot \lg \frac{3}{5} - \frac{2}{5} \cdot \lg \frac{2}{5}\right)}{6} = 0.845$$

is not satisfied.

Systems using the minimum description length principle were described, for example, in Fayyad and Irani (1993), Pfahringer (1995), and Quinlan (1996). Results are favorable. This principle was used by Friedman and Goldszmidt (1996) for Bayesian networks.

6. Discretization Based on Clustering

The KDD system LERS (Learning from Examples based on Rough Sets) is equipped with a global method based on an agglomerative method of cluster analysis (Chmielewski and Grzymala-Busse, 1994, 1995, 1996). During agglomerative cluster formation, objects that exhibit the most similarity are fused into clusters. Once this process is completed, clusters are projected on all attributes to determine initial intervals on the domains of the numerical attributes. During the second step (merging) adjacent intervals are merged together. Using discretization implemented in LERS, the original data from Table 1 are transformed into a new data set, presented in Table 4.

Rules induced by LERS from Table 4 are:

(IQ, 105 ... 110) & (Weight, 61 ... 90) → (Class, no)

(Weight, 90 ... 92) → (Class, yes)

Table 4 Data Discretized by Discretization Based on Clustering

IQ	Weight	Height	Class
105 ... 110	61 ... 90	175 ... 182	no
105 ... 110	90 ... 92	170 ... 175	yes
110 ... 115	61 ... 90	175 ... 182	yes
105 ... 110	61 ... 90	175 ... 182	no
105 ... 110	61 ... 90	175 ... 182	no
110 ... 115	90 ... 92	170 ... 175	yes

(IQ, 110 ... 115) → (Class, yes)

The above rules are similar to rules induced from Table 3. The above method performed well, as reported in Chmielewski and Grzymala-Busse (1994, 1995, 1996). Another system based on clustering was developed by Van de Merck (1993), also with promising results.

7. Other Discretization Methods

Chan et al. (1991) developed a method of discretization based on adaptive discretization. First the attribute domain is divided into two equal width intervals. Then a rule set is induced. If an error rate falls below some limit, one of intervals is divided further and the process is repeated.

A system merging intervals was presented in Grzymala-Busse and Lakshmanan (1996) and Grzymala-Busse and Stefanowski (1997). An algorithm performing discretization during rule induction was developed by Stefanowski (1998). The idea was further developed by introducing the algorithm MODLEM (Grzymala-Busse and Stefanowski, 1999), a modification of the rule induction algorithm LEM2 (Grzymala-Busse, 1992).

Different systems for finding discretization by testing all possible partitions were presented by Chlebus and Nguyen (1998), Nguyen and Skowron (1995), and Zighed et al. (1997). Some approaches to discretization use rough set theory (Chlebus and Nguyen, 1998; Nguyen, 1998; Nguyen and Nguyen, 1998; Nguyen and Skowron, 1995, 1997) and some a combination of rough set theory and genetic algorithms (Sun and Gao, 1999).

A kind of unsupervised discretization, based on maximum entropy, was suggested in Chiu et al. (1991). A discretization system using the χ^2 statistic was developed by Kerber (1992). A visual tool for discretization was described in Subramonian et al. (1997). In Ho and Scott (1997) a discretization method based on a new measure of strength of variable association was presented.

8. Conclusions

It is a well-accepted opinion that discretization is an art rather than a science. There is no one superior discretization method. However, there is a kind of agreement that discretization methods based on conditional entropy perform very well; see, for example, Dougherty et al. (1995) and Kohavi and Sahami (1996).

For an overview and comparison of discretization methods see Chmielewski and Grzymala-Busse (1996), Dougherty et al. (1995), and Fayyad and Irani (1993).

References

Breiman, L., J. H. Friedman, R. A. Olshen, and C. J. Stone. 1984. *Classification and Regression Trees.* Monterey, CA: Wadsworth & Brooks.

Catlett, J. March 1991. "On changing continuous attributes into ordered discrete attributes." In *Machine Learning EWSL-91, Proceedings of the European Working Session on Learning, Porto, Portugal.* Lecture Notes in Artificial Intelligence, pp. 164–178. Berlin: Springer-Verlag.

Chan, C.-C., C. Batur, and A. Srinivasan. 1991. "Determination of quantization intervals in rule based model for dynamic systems." In *Proceedings of the IEEE Conference on Systems, Man, and Cybernetics, Charlottesville, VA, October 13–16*, pp. 1719–1723. Los Alamitos, CA: IEEE Press.

Chiu, D. K. Y., A. K. C. Wong, and B. Cheung. 1991. "Information discovery through hierarchical maximum entropy discretization and synthesis." In *Knowledge Discovery in Databases*, edited by G. Piatetsky-Shapiro and W. J. Frawley, pp. 125–140. Cambridge, MA: MIT Press.

Chlebus, B. S. and S. H. Nguyen. 1998. "On finding optimal discretizations for two attributes." In *Proceedings of the First International Conference on Rough Sets and Current Trends in Computing, Warsaw, Poland, June 22–26.* Lecture Notes in Artificial Intelligence, pp. 537–542. Berlin: Springer-Verlag.

Chmielewski, M. R. and J. W. Grzymala-Busse. 1994. "Global discretization of continuous attributes as preprocessing for machine learning." In *Proceedings of the Third International Workshop on Rough Sets and Soft Computing, San Jose, CA, November 10–12*, pp. 474–480. San Jose, CA: San Jose State University.

Chmielewski, M. R. and J. W. Grzymala-Busse. 1995. "Global discretization of continuous attributes as preprocessing for machine learning." In *Soft Computing: Rough Sets, Fuzzy Logic, Neural Networks,*

Uncertainty Management, Knowledge Discovery, edited by T. Y. Lin and A. M. Wilderberger, pp. 294–297. San Jose, CA: Simulation Councils, Inc.

Chmielewski, M. R. and J. W. Grzymala-Busse. 1996. "Global discretization of continuous attributes as preprocessing for machine learning." *Int. J. Approximate Reasoning* **15**: 319–331.

Dougherty, J., R. Kohavi, and M. Sahami. 1995. "Supervised and unsupervised discretization of continuous features." In *Proceedings of the Twelfth International Conference on Machine Learning, Tahoe City, CA, July 9–12*, pp. 194–202. San Fransisco, CA: Morgan Kaufmann Publ.

Fayyad, U. M. and K. B. Irani. 1992. "On the handling of continuous-valued attributes in decision tree generation." *Machine Learning* **8**: 87–102.

Fayyad, U. M. and K. B. Irani. 1993. "Multi-interval discretization of continuous-valued attributes for classification learning." In *Proceedings of the Thirteenth International Joint Conference on AI, Chambery, France, 28 August–3 September*, pp. 1022–1027. San Francisco, CA: Morgan Kaufmann Publ.

Friedman, N. and M. Goldszmidt. 1996. "Discretizing continuous attributes while learning Bayesian networks." In *Proceedings of the Thirteenth International Conference on Machine Learning, Bari, Italy, July 3–6*, pp. 157–165. San Francisco, CA: Morgan Kaufmann Publ.

Grzymala-Busse, J. W. 1992. "LERS—a system for learning from examples based on rough sets." In *Intelligent Decision Support Handbook of Applications and Advances of the Rough Sets Theory*, edited by R. Slowinski, pp. 3–18. Norwell, MA: Kluwer Academic Publishers.

Grzymala-Busse, J. W. and A. Lakshmanan. 1996. "LEM2 with interval extension: an induction algorithm for numerical attributes." In *Proceedings of the Fourth International Workshop on Rough Sets, Fuzzy Sets and Machine Discovery (RSFD'96), Tokyo, Japan, November 6–8*, pp. 67–73. Japan: The University of Tokyo.

Grzymala-Busse, J. W. and J. Stefanowski. 1997. "Discretization of numerical attributes by direct use of the rule induction algorithm LEM2 with interval extension." In *Proceedings of the Sixth Symposium on Intelligent Information Systems (IIS'97), Zakopane, Poland, June 9–13*, pp. 149–158. Warsaw, Poland: IPIPAN.

Grzymala-Busse, J. W. and J. Stefanowski. 1999. "Two approaches to numerical attribute discretization for rule induction." In *Proceedings of the Fifth International Conference of the Decision Sciences Institute (D.S.I.'99), Athens, Greece, July 4–7*, pp. 1377–1379. Athens, Greece: New Technologies Publ.

Ho, K. M. and P. D. Scott. 1997. "Zeta: a global method for discretization of continuous variables." In *Proceedings of the Thirteenth International Conference on Machine Learning, Bari, Italy, July 3–6*, pp. 191–194. San Fransisco, CA: Morgan Kaufmann Publ.

Kerber, R. 1992. "ChiMerge: discretization of numeric attributes." In *Proceedings of the Tenth National Conference on AI, San Jose, CA, July 12–16*, pp. 123–128. Menlo Park, CA: AAAI Press.

Kohavi, R. and M. Sahami. 1996. "Error-based and entropy-based discretization of continuous features." In *Proceedings of the Second International Conference on Knowledge Discovery and Data Mining, Portland, OR, August 2–4*, pp. 114–119. Menlo Park, CA: AAAI Press.

Nguyen, S. H. 1998. "Discretization problem for rough sets methods." In *Proceedings of the First International Conference on Rough Sets and Current Trends in Computing, Warsaw, Poland, June 22–26*. Lecture Notes in Artificial Intelligence, pp. 545–552. Berlin: Springer-Verlag.

Nguyen, S. H. and H. S. Nguyen. 1998. "Discretization methods in data mining." In *Rough Sets in Knowledge Discovery*, edited by L. Polkowski and A. Skowron, pp. 451–482. Heidelberg: Physica-Verlag.

Nguyen, S. H. and A. Skowron. 1995. "A quantization of real value attributes: rough set and Boolean reasoning approach." In *Proceedings of the Second Joint Annual Conference on Information Science, Wrightsville Beach, NC, 28 September–1 October*, pp. 34–37. Durham, NC: P. P. Wang.

Nguyen, S. H. and A. Skowron. 1997. "Boolean reasoning for feature extraction problems." In *Proceedings of the Tenth International Symposium on Methodologies for Intelligent Systems (ISMIS'97), October 15–18, Charlotte, NC*, pp. 117–126. Heidelberg: Springer Verlag.

Pfahringer, B. 1995. "Compression-based discretization of continuous attributes." In *Proceedings of the Twelfth International Conference on Machine Learning, Tahoe City, CA, July 9–12*, pp. 456–463. San Francisco, CA: Morgan Kaufmann Publ.

Quinlan, J. R. 1993. In *C4.5: Programs for Machine Learning*. San Mateo, CA: Morgan Kaufmann Publishers.

Quinlan, J. R. 1996. "Improved use of continuous attributes in C4.5." *J. AI Res.* **4**: 77–90.

Quinlan, J. R. and R. L. Rivest. 1989. "Inferring decision trees using the minimum description length principle." *Inform. Comput.* **80**: 227–248.

Rissanen, J. R. 1978. "Modeling by shortest data description." *Automatica* **14**: 465–471.

Stefanowski, J. 1998. "Handling continuous attributes in discovery of strong decision rules." In *Proceedings of the First International Conference on Rough Sets and Current Trends in Computing, Warsaw, Poland, June 22–26*. Lecture Notes in Artificial Intelligence, pp. 394–401. Berliny: Springer-Verlag.

Subramonian, R., R. Venkata, and J. Chen. 1997. "A visual interactive framework for attribute discretization." In *Proceedings of the Third International Conference on Knowledge Discovery and Data Mining, Newport Beach, CA, August 14–17*, pp. 82–88. Menlo Park, CA: AAAI Press.

Sun, L. and W. Gao. 1999. "The discretization of continuous attributes based on compatibility rough set and genetic algorithm." In *Proceedings of the Seventh International Workshop: New Directions in Rough Sets, Data Mining, and Granular-Soft Computing (RSFDGrC'99), Yamaguchi, Japan, November 9–11*. Lecture Notes in Artificial Intelligence, pp. 188–192. Berlin: Springer-Verlag.

Van de Merck, T. 1993. "Decision trees in numerical attribute spaces." In *Proceedings of the Thirteenth International Joint Conference on AI, Chambery, France, 28 August–3 September*, pp. 1016–1021. San Francisco, CA: Morgan Kaufmann Publ.

Zighed, D. A., R. Rakotomala, and F. Feschet. 1997. "Optimal multiple intervals discretization of continuous attributes for supervised learning." In *Proceedings of the Thirteenth International Conference on Machine Learning, Bari, Italy, July 3–6*, pp. 295–298. San Francisco, CA: Morgan Kaufmann Publ.

15 DATA VISUALIZATION FOR DOMAIN EXPLORATION

15.1 Interactive Statistical Graphics

Graham J. Wills and Daniel Keim

ABSTRACT   This chapter describes the use of interactive statistical graphics such as bar charts, histograms, scatterplots, etc. It briefly outlines their history, and enumerates the important features of an interactive graphic: simplicity, focusing on data, robustness and integration. The linked views paradigm is expounded on and a demonstration of a set of interactive views is given using a well-known set of baseball data.

1. History

Examining data using graphical tools, such as histograms, bar charts, quantile plots, scatterplots and other statistical graphics, is a necessary part of any serious analysis effort. Statistical graphics are typically most useful at two stages of an analysis. Initially, plots are useful for data cleaning (see Chapter 13.1), where unusual sets of values can be investigated, attribute distributions can be evaluated, and transformations can be suggested using graphical techniques. After a data mining model has been built, similar techniques can be used to validate the results of the model, highlight unusual or atypical results, and present the model in a way that facilitates understanding (Chapters 19.1 and 20).

With the advent of cheap graphics-capable desktop computing, these tools have become widely available. But the use of computers enables more than simply reproducing static plots on a display; it allows users to interact with plots; changing parameters, querying, zooming, and linking plots together, so that interesting features of one plot can be seen in the light of the others. Interactive statistical graphics explore data by manipulating a graphical representation of the data. Becker et al. (1987) define the process thus: "The data analyst takes an action through manual manipulation of an input device and something happens on the screen. These computing capabilities provide a new medium for the invention of graphical methods for data analysis."

The roots of interactive statistical graphics lie in exploratory data analysis (EDA) as described by Tukey (1977): a set of techniques for investigating data in order to spot trends, patterns, errors, and features. A key feature of EDA is the use of simple, robust plots to show characteristics of the data. According to Tukey, EDA is about "looking at data to see what it seems to say" (Tukey, 1977, p. v); "It is detective work—numerical detective work—or counting detective work—or graphical detective work." (Tukey, 1977, p. 1); and "Unless exploratory data analysis uncovers indications, usually quantitative ones, there is likely to be nothing for confirmatory data analysis to consider" (Tukey, 1977, p. 3).

Interactive graphics (also known as direct manipulation graphics or dynamic graphics) provide a satisfying extension of the principles of EDA to the computing environment. Many of the graphic facilities developed for exploratory data analysis are present in interactive graphic analysis, but in an enhanced form. Compared to the centuries-old history of static graphics for data display, dynamic display and high interaction techniques for the analysis of statistical data are relatively recent phenomena. One of the earliest pieces of work in this area was PRIM-9, a system that enabled the user to view a multidimensional cloud of data and rotate it on the computer screen in realtime (Fisherkeller et al., 1974; reprinted in Cleveland and McGill, 1988). The system projected a multivariate data set into a three-dimensional point cloud and allowed the user to spin the cloud, manipulate the data visibility, and alter the projection. PRIM stands for picturing, rotation, isolation, and masking, the four major components of its operation In this early work, interaction was necessarily somewhat crude—using only an alphanumeric keyboard, light-pen, and a function keyboard with thirty-two buttons—but the principle was of lasting importance.

In more recent years other interactive techniques, such as dynamic scatterplot brushing, have been introduced into statistical thought. Dynamic scatterplot brushing is a technique for visualizing several numerical variables by the creation of a matrix of scatterplots, one for each pair of variables in a data set. Then, using a pointing device, a small region (denoted a brush) is moved over one of the scatterplots, with the result that points that lie within this region are highlighted both in that scatterplot and in the other scatterplots that comprise the matrix. This early work in the field of interactive graphics focused on individual plots. The idea was to create unique views with which the user would interact to gain a more thorough understanding of the data. More recently, the emphasis has been on making interaction pervasive throughout the analysis process. Environments such as LISP-Stat (Tierney, 1990), Data Desk (Velleman, 1988), and XGOBI (Swayne et al., 1991) have provided statistical environments where interaction is an integral part of the analysis. Furthermore, there has been much research into designing specific interactive systems to solve more narrowly defined problems. Examples of these systems include REGARD (Haslett et al., 1991), which applies these techniques to geographic information systems, and SeeSoft (Eick et al., 1992), which applies them to the analysis of software change management data.

2. General Features of Statistical Graphical Views

Since interactive graphics methods are mainly exploratory and diagnostic in intent, the graphical displays must be easy to interpret. Preferably, the results of an analysis should jump out, as in the case of a bivariate outlier in a scatterplot. A good display will

- have an obvious encoding method,
- focus attention on the data, and
- integrate into the environment.

Note that the goals of interactive statistical graphics and presentation graphics are not the same; the former seeks to help the analyst discover, hypothesize, and explore. The latter seeks to present a known result in the clearest possible manner. The characteristics listed above play mainly to the former goals. An analyst may look at many views without knowing whether there are any interesting features in them and so it is critical that views can be evaluated rapidly without requiring laborious deciphering. This motivates the desire for an intuitive encoding mechanism.

Achieving an intuitive encoding can be quite difficult. Suppose that we wish to encode a third variable on a scatterplot. Should we use a glyph whose size encodes the variable? Or should we use color? Or type of glyph (circle, square)? And if we decide on size, should the area encode the value or should the radius? Psychophysical experiments have provided much guidance in this area (see, e.g., Stevens, 1975), and Cleveland (1985) has translated some important principles into the statistical graphics arena, but much care is still needed to ensure a clear, intuitive display.

Focusing attention on the data means that labels, grid lines, and other additional view elements should be minimized. In an interactive setting, the user should be able to query the view for labels and values, often rendering the default display of labels and grid lines unnecessary.

Because interactive statistical graphics is an enabling technology, it is necessary that views be integrated into an environment in which they can add value to each other and to the overall analysis. The analyst should be able to interrogate views and see the results of either formal or informal queries (e.g., pointing at view elements or brushing data items) in all available views. In the next section we introduce a method of integrating views that has been used in a wide variety of contexts and is becoming a standard feature of modern interactive statistical graphic environments.

3. The Linked Views Paradigm

Linking is not a new concept, as can be seen from examination of the relevant literature (Becker et al., 1987; Tierney, 1990; Velleman, 1988). For static graphics, a number of methods have been employed, possibly the most widespread of which is to split points into a number of classes and to assign a unique symbol or color to each class and use that symbol or color to draw points within that class within each plot that is displayed. An excellent example of this is shown in Chambers et al. (1983, p. 172) where a data set of measurements on a set of flowers has been displayed via a scatterplot matrix of petal width, petal length, sepal width, and sepal length.

The symbol used to plot each point in each scatterplot is a dot, circle, or cross (".," "○," or "×") depending on the variety of iris on which the measurements were made. This coding links the scatterplots together in a way that augments the natural linking caused by the juxtaposition of the scatterplots within the matrix structure. As an aside, note that Cleveland and McGill (1984) point out that plotting symbols of different colors provide the most acceptable coding mechanism, but that limitations on reproduction of color images can require the use of non-optimal encodings in black and white media. Linking is an intuitively attractive idea for increasing the information content of a set of data plots. Linking shows visually which parts of one data plot correspond to those of another. This allows the interesting or anomalous areas of one view of the data to be seen in the context of other views of the data in a rapid and intuitive fashion.

For data analysis one common method used to implement view linking is to associate a binary state with each data item, either highlighted or unhighlighted. The subset of data that is marked highlighted is assumed to be the focus of interest to the user. The user should be able to highlight a subset of data dynamically in one plot and see the results of that selection in another plot. The scatterplot brushing technique mentioned in Section 1 is a limited example of this method.

4. Interactive Statistical Graphics Scenario

In this section we will look at a small data set that describes the career performances and salaries of baseball players in 1987. Our purpose is to use this data set to illustrate the utility of interactive statistical graphics at several stages of analysis.

If the analyst wanted to examine players' fielding performances, they might create a scatterplot such as Figure 1. This figure shows the joint distribution of PutOuts (an opposition hitter is retired by the player) and Assists (where the player throws the ball to another player who performs a PutOut). The analyst has examined the distribution of both these variables in histograms or normal score plots and has determined that a square root transform should be applied to each variable (this makes sense statistically as both variables are counts). The resulting figure shows two distinct clusters, each with a strong linear pattern. The user then uses the mouse to select the lower right cluster which highlights those items in it, and the resulting highlighting (Figure 2) is examined in a bar chart of fielding position (Figure 3). It is immediately apparent, without requiring any knowledge of baseball, that the relationship between PutOuts and Assists is conditional on the fielding position, with the positions 2B, 3B, SS having more assists than PutOuts. Note that UT denotes a utility fielder, one who might play anywhere, which explains why that bar is partially selected.

Following this analysis further, selecting one of the fielding positions from the bar chart, the analyst can see that the clusters themselves are composed of unions of even more linear features associated with each position. In Figure 4 the analyst has selected two positions—one in each cluster—using the bar chart and has coded the number of AtBats (a measure of how much playing time each player had in the year) as color for the highlighted points. The color scale runs through shades of gray from black (few AtBats) to white (many AtBats). The unhighlighted points have been displayed as points to make them less noticeable in the scatterplot view. The analyst is now in a good position to propose a model; PutOuts and

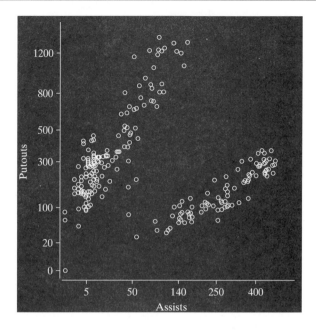

Figure 1 Scatterplot of player's main fielding statistics

Assists have a linear relationship whose slope is determined by the fielding position, and players who have more playing time have increased counts of both PutOuts and Assists.

One of the original goals of the analysis of this data set was to explore the relationship between players' salaries and players' performances. Are players paid based on their ability?

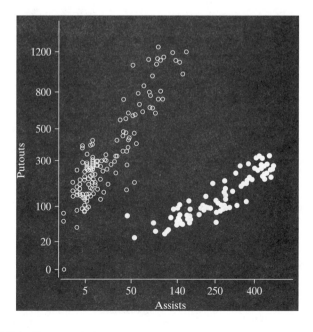

Figure 2 Selecting one cluster

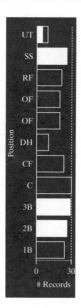

Figure 3 Linked fielding positions

There are many measures of hitting performance that could be used in a model. For this data set, career averages of seven such measures (Runs, Hits, Runs Batted In, Walks, Home Runs, AtBats, Years) were used. These were used as inputs into a feedforward neural net (see Chapters 5.9 and 16.1.8) with one hidden layer containing four nodes and trained by back-propagation to predict a single output, a logarithmic transform of the salary. The resulting predictions for the training data were very good; probably due to over-training on this small data set of only 262 players. A scatterplot of prediction error against predicted value (Figure 5) shows generally good shape with a few poorly predicted points and one extremely poorly predicted point toward the bottom of the plot. The highlighted values are indicated by the error term Log(Salary)-Predicted. In Figure 6 we show a diagnostic plot to help us explore these outliers.

Figure 6 shows a vertical strip for each variable used in the analysis. The Year variable, shown on the far right, has been shown as a form of bar chart where circles are used instead of rectangles. The other variables are continuous and have been shown via a modified form of boxplot (as defined in Tukey, 1977). The dark rectangles show where 95 percent of the data values are expected to lie and the inner gray boxes contain exactly the middle 50 percent of the data, with the central line being the median. Note that these statistics are relatively robust. Superimposed on these plots we draw a line for each of our unusual players, which links the

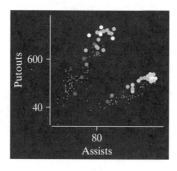

Figure 4 AtBats related to fielding statistics for two positions

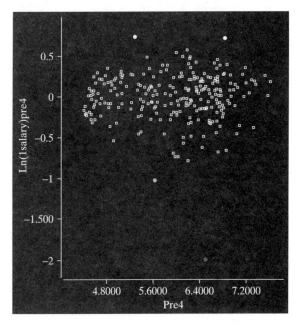

Figure 5 Prediction errors

player's statistics on each variable. By comparing the trajectories these take, we can immediately compare individuals' performances. When we select the outliers in Figure 5, the corresponding players trajectories are shown on this linked display.

In this example, if we examine the outlier with the highest salary among the outliers, shown in white, with the outlier with the least, shown in black, we see that they follow each other very closely except for Years (in which they differ by three) and in Log(Salary) (in which they are very different). These are players who have very similar hitting ability, have both been playing for a while and therefore our model predicts they have very similar salaries, whereas in fact one of them is paid $90,000 and the other $1,940,000. Clearly the model is not at fault; there must be other factors at work that may or may not be present in the rest of the

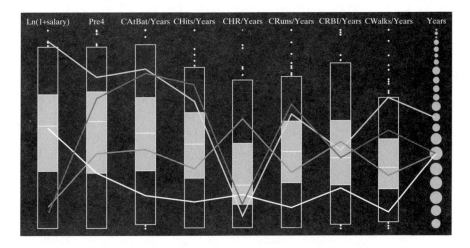

Figure 6 Parallel axes superimposed on Boxplots and a bubble plot showing outliers in relation to the overall data trends

data. The analyst can either accept the current model, noting that there is at least one exception to the model, or they can examine the data and maybe collect more data in an effort to expand the model and improve it for all cases.

5. Challenges

Interactive statistical graphics are sets of general purpose views that allow users to look at data in different ways to explore features and focus attention on unusual items, both pre- and post-modeling. The roots in exploratory data analysis have given the analyst a set of standard plots such as histograms, boxplots, scatterplots, and bar charts. These have been augmented and adapted for interactive environments so as to add to their utility, and a number of new views are making their way into more common usage. Current research challenges lie in two main directions. The first of these is in dealing with large data sets, both in terms of numbers of data items and numbers of variables. In gigabyte- and terrabyte-sized data sets, statistical significance becomes less and less useful a concept and robust summaries are important. Moreover, small percentages of a data set represent sizable amounts of data and cannot be ignored by a technique or graphic display. When there are numerous variables, standard views can become overly complex, and views that summarize multiple relationships become necessary.

The second challenge is to build interactive graphical views for specific types of analysis; for geographic and spatial analysis, for time series, for neural net and decision-tree analyses, for clustering, for document and text analysis, for real-time analysis, network analysis, and many other emerging areas. The use of interactive statistical graphics techniques for database discovery will continue to grow in importance over time as these challenges are addressed.

References

Becker, R. A., W. S. Cleveland, and A. R. Wilks. 1987. "Dynamic graphics for data analysis." *Stat. Sci.* **2**: 355–395.

Chambers, J., W. S. Cleveland, B. Kleiner, and P. Tukey. 1983. *Graphical Methods for Data Analysis.* CA: Wadsworth.

Cleveland, W. S. 1985. *The Elements of Graphing Data.* CA: Wadsworth.

Cleveland, W. S. and R. McGill. 1984. "Graphical perception: theory, experimentation and application to the development of graphical methods." *J. Am. Stat. Assoc.* **79**: 531–554.

Cleveland, W. S. and R. McGill. (eds). 1988. *Dynamic Graphics for Statistics.* CA: Wadsworth and Brooks.

Eick, S., J. Steffan, and E. Sumner. 1992. "Seesoft—a tool for visualizing line oriented software statistics." *IEEE Trans. Softw. Engng* **18(11)**: 957–968.

Fisherkeller, M. A., J. H. Friedman, and J. W. Tukey. 1974. *Prim-9: An Interactive Multi-dimensional Data Display and Analysis System, SLAC-Pub-1408.* Stanford, CA: SLAC Publications Office.

Haslett, J., R. Bradley, P. S. Craig, G. Wills, and A. R. Unwin. 1991. "Dynamic graphics for exploring spatial data, with application to locating global and local anomalies." *Am. Stat.* **45**: 234–242.

Stevens, S. 1975. *Psychophysics.* New York: Wiley.

Swayne, D. F., D. Cook, and A. Buja. 1991. "Xgobi: interactive dynamic data visualization in the X window system." *J. Comput. Graph. Stat.* **7**: 113–130.

Tierney, L. 1990. *LISP-STAT: An Object-oriented Environment for Statistical Computing and Dynamic Graphics.* New York, NY: Wiley.

Tukey, J. W. 1977. *Exploratory Data Analysis.* Reading, MA: Addison-Wesley.

Velleman, P. F. 1988. *The Datadesk Handbook.* Cornell, NY: Odesta Corporation.

15.2 Highly Multivariate Interaction Techniques

Martin Theus

ABSTRACT Linking and highlighting interactive statistical graphics increases the dimensionality of data that can be explored. For highly multivariate data (i.e., more than ten to twenty variables) insight into the data by linking low-dimensional plots can be limited. Thus the need for high-dimensional plots arises. These plots—for example, rotating plots (grand tour, projection pursuit), parallel coordinate plots, or mosaic plots—can incorporate up to ten or more variables in a single plot. Linked highlighting and alterations inside these plots (e.g., zooming, reordering, or sorting) offer high-dimensional insights into data sets. Multiple selections via selection sequences offer a convenient way of interacting with high-dimensional subsets of the data using low-dimensional plots.

1. High-Dimensional Plots and Interaction Techniques

A common characteristic of high-dimensional plots is that these plots can only be used in an interactive environment on computers. Static versions of the plots introduced in this section are weak and are not even as insightful as their low-dimensional counterparts.

The basic selection and highlighting techniques already described in Chapter 15.1 apply to all plots mentioned in this article.

1.1. Rotation Plot

THREE DIMENSIONS

A rotation plot in three dimensions is a simple generalization of the two-dimensional scatterplot. Since any projection of a three-dimensional point cloud onto a two-dimensional plane—typically the computer screen—is nothing but an ordinary scatterplot, usually with nonorthogonal axes, the basic interaction technique for a three-dimensional rotation plot is the rotation. Only smooth rotation suggests the presence of a three-dimensional object. Rotation can thus reveal three-dimensional structures that are not visible in any of the two-dimensional projections. Basically two methods exist for rotating a point cloud:

1. Controls are provided for each axis to rotate back and forth around this axis. This implementation allows—often in addition to a direct manipulation of the rotations parameter—rotation exactly around certain axes (Figure 1).

2. Given an imaginary ball which surrounds the point cloud, the user can grab the surface of this ball at any position with the mouse and rotate the enclosed point cloud to any new projection (Figure 1). Although this method is very flexible, it sometimes lacks the exact control given in (1).

In order to support the three-dimensional effect of the point cloud two methods can be applied:

1. A tripod (that is, a symbolic representation of the three coordinate axes) can be added to the plot to show the actual orientation of the natural axes of the data set. These three axes can be extended to a whole cube along the three axes that enclose the data set.

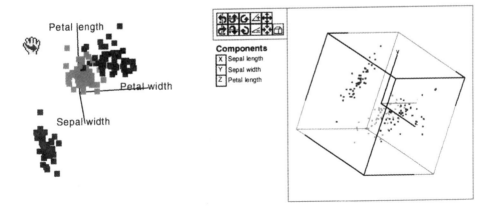

Figure 1 Rotation control using a virtual ball (left) and axis rotation (right). Depth cueing has been applied to the enclosing cube for better three-dimensional support (right)

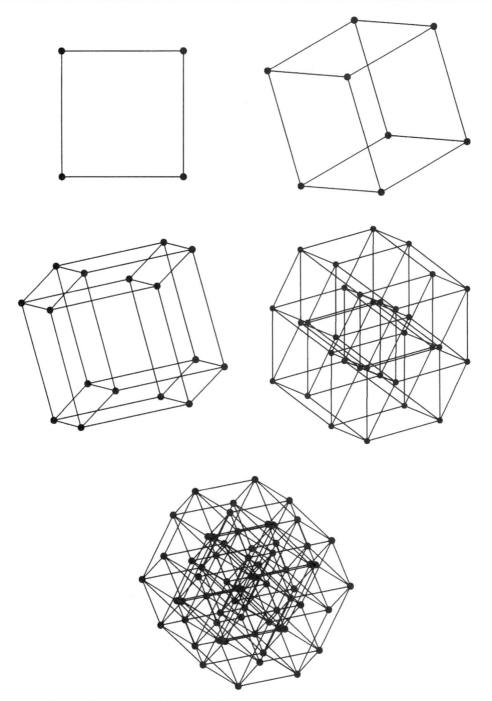

Figure 2 Hypercubes of dimension three to six

2. Depth cueing is a method where points that are virtually further away from the observer are plotted smaller or lighter in order to mimic the effect of depth that would arise with a real three-dimensional object.

INTERACTION TECHNIQUES FOR MORE THAN THREE DIMENSIONS

Since the human perception of objects of dimensionality four and higher is very limited, we need assistance and guidance from the computer for rotating plots of point clouds of more than three dimensions. Figure 2 gives an example of a hypercube in three dimensions, which is an ordinary cube, to six dimensions, which already has $2^6 = 64$ edges. Although this hypercube of order six is a very regular object it is far beyond human imagination. The same effect holds true for statistical variables. If the number of variables is not too large, it is still feasible to display a generalization of the tripod in three dimensions in order to give the observer a chance to keep track of the projection.

The grand tour introduced by Asimov (1985) and described by Cook et al. (1995) is a method for viewing multivariate data via orthogonal projections onto a sequence of two-dimensional subspaces. The sequence of the subspaces is chosen so that it is dense in the set of all two-dimensional subspaces. Whenever the grand tour passes projections which reveal patterns like clusters, gaps, regular lower-dimensional shapes, and so on, the user may halt the grand tour in order to investigate these features more closely. This can be done by marking the patterns with specific colors to see their representation in linked lower-dimensional plots.

Whereas the grand tour searches the space randomly, the projection pursuit guided grand tour optimizes certain features of the projection and thus hopefully visits more interesting projections. This feature—found by the so-called projection pursuit index—depends on the pattern (e.g., deviation from normality, clusters, holes, etc.) that is targeted in the data. Typically the user spots an interesting pattern during the grand tour and then invokes the optimization, in order to get an even more revealing projection of the feature. Usually the optimization process leads to a local optimum of the index until the optimization is canceled and the grand tour proceeds.

The most powerful support for analyzing interesting projections is to mark the groups or features with specific colors to investigate the representation of this feature in lower-dimensional plots and other projections. The XGobi (Buja et al., 1996) software implements high-dimensional rotating scatterplots along with the grand tour and projection pursuit. Figure 3 shows a typical XGobi session.

The left part of the upper window shows various controls, the middle part the actual projection, and the right part the different variables, along with a symbolic representation of the projection of its axis to the screen. The lower window shows a trace of the projection index along with three snapshots of interesting projections. Note the increasing index, until a local maximum is reached. These projections can be revisited with a single mouse-click.

1.2. Parallel Coordinates

Unlike a usual scatterplot or a three-dimensional rotating plot, the axes in a parallel coordinate plot are not plotted perpendicular but parallel. Since this arrangement does not allow the observations to be naturally placed into a two-dimensional or three-dimensional space, the points are placed along the particular axis, that is, a one-dimensional projection of the data onto its axis. All points of adjacent axes are then connected via straight lines. This parallel layout allows as many as ten to thirty variables to be plotted simultaneously on a computer screen.

Figure 4 shows how points on a straight line with positive or negative slope in cartesian coordinates translate into parallel coordinates. Although a lot can be said about the geometrical properties of parallel coordinates (see Inselberg, 1998) we will focus on the main use in data analysis, which is cluster analysis and outlier detection.

Like all plots discussed in this article, parallel coordinate plots are mainly useful in an interactive environment. Whereas the interaction with rotating plots is basically the rotation, that is a systematic change of the projection parameters, the most effective interactions with parallel coordinate plots are selection and highlighting. In focusing on particular subsets it is often necessary to select stepwise over several axes. This stepwise selection is an example for selection sequences, described in Section 2.

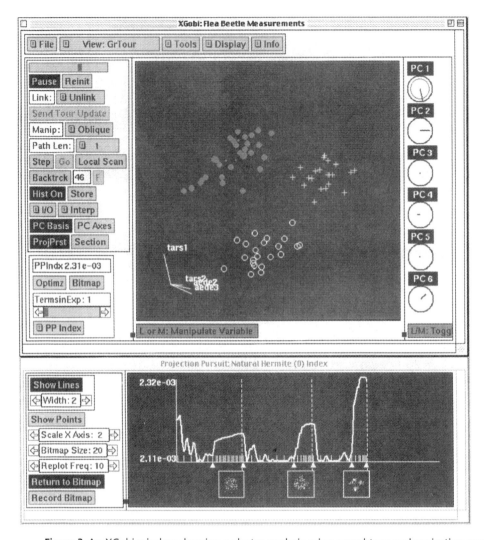

Figure 3 An XGobi window showing a cluster analysis using grand tour and projection persuit

Given a few hundred observations, the plot gets cluttered due to heavy overplotting, which makes highlighting indispensable. One way to avoid this loss of information is to use different intensities to indicate the amount of overplotting. By using a nonwhite background and adding the brightness of overplotting lines, the density of lines can still be observed, even if a large number of observations is plotted. The way the brightness actually is increased in the case of overplotting offers various degrees of freedom in estimating the density. For related work see Wegmann and Lou (1997), who developed the ExplorN package, an advanced implementation of parallel coordinate plots. Figure 5 compares the same data set using parallel coordinates with and without density estimation.

Another way to avoid overplotting is by simply de-selecting observations, which prevents them from being plotted. This is useful in scenarios where an analysis focuses on a specific subgroup. In this case only the data for this particular subgroup is plotted. Although specialized selection tools have been developed, the methods described in Chapter 15.1 are all that are necessary for this task.

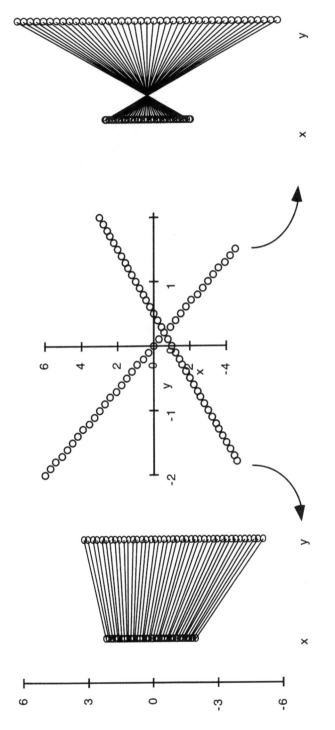

Figure 4 An example of how straight lines translate into parallel coordinates

Another important interaction with parallel coordinate plots is the possibility of permuting the axes interactively. Interesting features are more likely to be detected for adjacent axes. Although we could think of $n*(n-1)/2$ possible plots to display all $n*(n-1)/2$ adjacencies, Wegman (1990) showed that floor $(n+1)/2$ permuted plots are sufficient to show all adjacencies.

If variables in the parallel coordinate plot have been measured on the same scale, it should be possible to scale these axes equally. An initial display of a parallel coordinate plot should have each axis scaled individually.

Figure 5 Density estimation in parallel coordinates to solve overplotting

Some additional interactive features that are desirable include individual transformation (Box-Cox, translation, etc.) and zooming.

Clusters and outliers in a data set are usually detected by gaps between data points on any axis. Because of the connectedness of the multidimensional parallel coordinate plot it is then easy to see whether the clustering propagates through other dimensions. Another simple way to distinguish between clusters is by identifying groups that all have the same slope. That is, if a group of line segments slopes at twenty degrees to the horizontal and another group slopes at −50 degrees, then even though the lines fully overlap on the adjacent axes—that is, no gap is found on one of these axes—these sets represent distinct clusters in the data. This leads to selection techniques that allow the user to select all lines that have a certain slope, or a slope that is in a certain interval.

The methods for finding clusters presented so far all assume clusters that show up orthogonally to the natural axis. Since this a very restrictive assumption that will probably leave many clusters unrevealed, the parallel coordinate display can be extended by the grand tour already mentioned in Section 1.1.

1.3. Mosaic Plot

Mosaic plots (Hartigan, 1981; Friendly, 1994; Theus, 1997) are defined as a recursive generalization of bar charts. In a simple bar chart, bars represent categories. The heights of the bars are proportional to the number of observations falling into this particular category. Since the width of each bar is identical, the area is proportional to the number of observations.

Starting with a bar chart, Figure 6 shows the systematic construction of a mosaic plot for the Titanic data, given in Table 1 below. These data consist of survival and descriptive information for passengers on the Titanic steamship.

The bar chart of the variable *Class* of the Titanic data set is shown in the upper left plot in Figure 6. In every bar of the bar chart the proportion of survivors is highlighted. It is not easy to compare the proportions in each class, since the bars have different heights.

To solve this problem we modify the bar chart to have identical height instead of width, and proportional width instead of height. In this plot, called a spineplot (cf. Theus, 1997), the proportions of survivors, still drawn from bottom to top, can be compared easily. A spineplot for the variable *Class* is shown in Figure 6 (top right).

A spineplot can be regarded as a one-dimensional mosaic plot. In the lower right plot in Figure 6 an example of a two-dimensional mosaic plot is shown. Whereas we divided the first variable along the x-axis, we divide the second variable along the y-axis. This division is done conditional upon the different levels of variable one.

In the Titanic example the different classes have been divided according to the conditional proportions of adults and children inside the classes. The areas are thus proportional to the absolute numbers inside the particular class. Since there were no children in the crew, this category is empty, indicated by an area of size zero—that is, a line. To distinguish between very small nonempty groups, which may be rendered by just a single line, and really empty groups, an additional zero ("0") is drawn centered in this line. This feature extends the definition of mosaic plots, and can be found implemented in the MANET software (Hofmann and Theus, 1998).

The highlighting of the proportion of survivors, formerly drawn from bottom to top, is now drawn from left to right. This is sensible, since further divisions in a mosaic plot will alternate between the x and y directions. If the last division in a mosaic plot was made along x, a potential highlighting is drawn along y, and vice versa.

Incorporating the variable *Gender* we get a three-dimensional mosaic plot, which is shown in the lower left plot of Figure 6. Following the above algorithm this subdivision is done along x, conditional upon each combination of the variables *Class* and *Age*.

INTERACTION TECHNIQUES

The selection and highlighting techniques inside mosaic plots generalize those found in bar charts. Interaction techniques specific to mosaic plots deal with the reordering of the variables

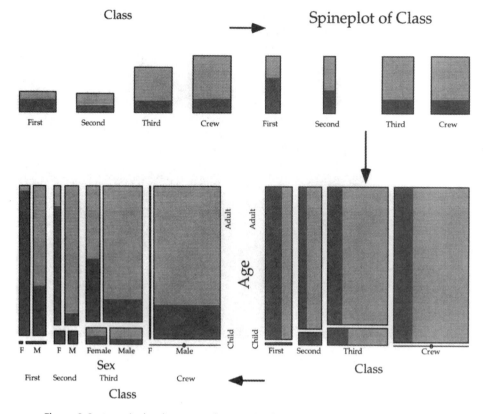

Figure 6 Systematic development of a mosaic plot using the Titanic example

displayed in the plot. For a better understanding of the mosaic plot, it can be essential to develop the mosaic step by step starting with the first variable (as shown in Figure 6). The order in which the variables are included into the plot depends on the questions that are to be solved. In many cases the order cannot be determined prior to an analysis. Two rules of thumb can be given to choose the most insightful order of the variables. The variables that are at position one and two obviously show their interaction most clearly. Given n variables, the variables at position $n-1$ and n can be investigated, conditioned upon the different subgroups of variables 1 to $n-2$.

Table 1 Data on the 2201 Titanic Passengers

| Survived | Age | Gender | Class | | | |
			First	Second	Third	Crew
No	Child	Male	0	0	35	0
No	Child	Female	0	0	17	0
No	Adult	Male	118	154	387	670
No	Adult	Female	4	13	8	3
Yes	Child	Male	5	11	13	0
Yes	Child	Female	1	13	14	0
Yes	Adult	Male	57	14	75	192
Yes	Adult	Female	140	80	76	20

In the typical response situation—as already seen in Figure 6—the proportions of the selected response can be compared between the categories of variable n, for all subgroups of the variables 1 to $n-1$. In the Titanic example we can compare the proportions of survivors (response) between the different groups of *Gender* (male and female) given the eight subgroups of the variables *Class* and *Age*, that is (first, second, third, crew), × (child, adult).

2. Selection Sequences

One of the main tasks in analyzing massive data sets is to condition views, that is, graphs and/or statistics, of the data on subsets. One approach to do so is trellis displays, introduced by Cleveland (1993). But whereas trellis displays are static and show all views of all subgroups at a time, the exploration of data sets is iterative and often focuses on particular subgroups.

Selection sequences (Theus et al., 1998) are an intuitive extension to the established linked-highlighting paradigm and allow highly multivariate selections of subsets using low-dimensional plots. Selection sequences store the whole hierarchical path of a selection and allow an easy editing, redefinition, and interrogation of each selection in this path. This enables the user to analyze even massive data sets without losing the aim he or she was heading for. Implementations of parallel coordinates usually make use of multiple selections. Starting with an initial selection that replaces all previous selections we can narrow down a subset by adding further selections with different selection modes, for example, OR, XOR, AND, and so on.

Since all selection parameters (selection step, mode, variable(s), and range) are stored in a sequence, a generalization to graphical database queries is easy to achieve.

Implementations of selection sequences can be found in the research software tools MANET (cf. Hofmann and Theus, 1998) and Mondrian (cf. Theus, 1999).

References

Asimov, D. 1985. "The grand tour: a tool for viewing multidimensional data." *SIAM J. Sci. Stat. Comput.* **6**: 128–143.

Buja, A., D. Cook, and D. F. Swayne. 1996. "Interactive high-dimensional data visualization." *J. Comput. Graphical Stat* **5(1)**: 78–99.

Cleveland, W. S. 1993. *Visualizing Data*. Summit, NJ: Hobart Press.

Cook, D., A. Buja, and J. Cabrera. 1995. "Grand tour and projection pursuit." *J. Comput. Graphical Stat.* **4(3)**: 155–172.

Friendly, M. 1994. "Mosaic displays for multi-way contingency tables." *J. Am. Stat. Assoc.* **89**: 190–200.

Hartigan, J. A. and B. Kleiner. 1981. "Mosaics for contingency tables." *Computer Science and Statistics: Proceedings of the Thirteenth Symposium on the Interface*, pp. 268–273.

Hofmann, H. and M. Theus. 1998. "Selection sequences in MANET." *Comput. Stat.* **13(2)**.

Inselberg, A. 1989. "Visualizing multi-dimensional structure using parallel coordinates." *Computer Science and Statistics: Proceedings of the Twenty-First Symposum on the Interface*, pp. 175–190.

Inselberg, A. 1998. "Visual data mining with parallel coordinates." *Comput. Stat.* **13(2)**.

Theus, M. 1997. "Visualisation of categorical data." *Advances in Statistical Software 6, Softstat '97*, edited by F. Faulbaum and W. Bandilla, pp. 47–55. Stuttgart: Lucius and Lucius.

Theus, M. 1999. "MONDRIAN—interactive statistical graphics in JAVA." To appear in *Stat. Comput. Graphics Newsletter* **10**.

Theus, M., H. Hofmann, and A. Wilhelm. 1998. "Selection sequences—interactive analysis of massive data sets." *Computing Science and Statistics, Proceedings of the Twenty-Ninth Symposium on the Interface*.

Wegman, E. J. 1990. "Hyperdimensional data analysis using parallel coordinates." *J. Am. Stat. Assoc.* **85**: 664–675.

Wegman, E. and Q. Luo. 1997. "High dimensional clustering using parallel coordinates and the grand tour." *Computing Science and Statistics, Proceedings of the Twenty-Eighth Symposium on the Interface*, pp. 361–368.

15.3 Geographical Information Systems

Martin Theus

ABSTRACT A geographic information system (GIS) is a collection of computer hardware, software, and geographic data designed to support the capture, management, manipulation, analysis, modeling, and display of spatially referenced information for solving a variety of spatial problems. In contrast to pure statistical or cartographic approaches, which will always leave an important part of the information in the data unrevealed, GISs have the capability to combine attribute and spatial information and are thus powerful analytical tools. Strong links between the cartographic and analytical components of the GIS result in more sophisticated analytical possibilities. The complex nature of spatial relationships means that GISs require sophisticated data structures to encapsulate the geographical aspects of the information. These usually make the use of database management systems (DBMS) indispensable. Thus database considerations are an important aspect of a GIS. The effort to acquire and collate suitable geographical data for analysis is often underestimated.

1. Geographic Questions

GIS analysis can be illustrated by a series of typical queries:

1. *Identification: What is there?* By pointing at a symbol on the map, stored information that is related to the feature represented by the symbol can be retrieved. Although an interrogation in the attribute space would be possible as well, the geographical context and additional local knowledge provided by a map view can aid inquiry.

2. *Location: Where is?* The reverse process of querying the map is to select objects in the attribute space that satisfy certain criteria. The locations of selected objects can then be identified in the map representation using visual cues. A typical example is the visualization of the locations of good customers in a customer database in order to study their distribution.

3. *Trends: What has changed since?* If the spatial data has a temporal component, the development over time is often of great interest. The temporal component can consist of a single variable that holds the times that objects exist or events occur, or a complete dimension representing the attributes over a specified time period.

4. *Optimal path: What is the best route between?* When dealing with network or flow data the calculation of optimal paths can be a useful technique. Network data sets containing vertices with associated attributes can be sought for optimal paths in a variety of different aspects, for example, distance, costs, time, et cetera.

5. *Patterns: What relation exists between?* Whereas the investigation of relations of spatial data measured on the same support (base units) is relatively easy—that is, the data is associated with the same objects (point locations, regions, lines)—the investigation of relations of data measured in different spatial units is much harder. For example, an investigation of air quality might include data on the number of registered cars (region layer: counties), amount of pollutant in the air (point layer: weather stations), and number of cars on major roads (lines layer: traffic flow along highways). Obviously the combination of these numbers is not trivial. A GIS provides some standard solutions.

6. *Models: What if?* Once a GIS is established certain models can be developed. Based on these models planning and forecasting can be carried out. For example, if a model can be built for the traffic flow in a city, it is easy to study the influence of the opening or closing of roads, a change in public transportation or a general increase of the traffic. The accuracy of these investigations obviously depends strongly on the accuracy of the model and as with all other GIS analysis, the quality of the data.

2. Spatial Data

2.1. Sources of Spatial Data

The preparation of a digital representation of the geographical information often accounts for the majority of the cost and effort that goes into performing GIS analysis. A diversity of problems explains this situation. In most studies the geographic data that are used have already been gathered for previous studies. Only very large-scale projects can afford to survey new geographical data for the study. Many forms of map can be bought on CD-ROMs today, but the accuracy and utility of these data is often restricted. Another limitation is the various formats in which geographical data is stored. But even if an accurate database containing the spatial information can be set up, the underlying geography often changes over time, which makes regular updates of the data necessary. For example an accurate map of the outlines of all countries of the world produced in 1992 will not reflect the splitting of the former USSR and former Yugoslavia, and thus miss more than fifteen states only a few years later.

Basic geographic information is often available from governmental census organizations. For example, the U.S. Census Bureau distributes the TIGER lines database, which covers all information on streets, railroads, rivers, and so on, along with the common administrative borders. This database is updated at regular intervals.

2.2. Types of Spatial Data

Geographic information systems have traditionally dealt with two fundamentally different data models, those of vector data and raster data. The vector model includes information about points, lines, and areas/regions. Each of these representations is based on points stored as x,y-coordinates. Lines and regions are assembled out of these coordinates and additional structural information to build more complex shapes. Whereas the vector model is ideal to describe discrete features, the raster model (which represents data on a regular grid) is used to represent continuous features like temperature or rainfall, which could have been measured, at least in principle, at any location. Raster data is often gathered by remote sensing methods, or generated by interpolation between features sampled on an irregular grid. The vector model is ideal for storing information about point samples, land units, and route-ways. It is also appropriate for the enumerated unit model through which population data are often released and ties in neatly with the traditional map production process and automated cartography. The raster model represents continuous environmental information well.

To map the real world in a GIS it is often necessary to combine various layers of vector and/or raster data. Such mapping operations require that data be projected onto a plane using a suitable algorithm and geo reference. In the simple case of data measured at different locations (points) it might be helpful to add a static backdrop layer that holds a simple street map of the area under investigation. In many applications, thematic data sets (where each set represents the distribution of one particular phenomenon) are systematically assigned to different layers.

A unique feature of geographical information systems in contrast to other information systems is the possibility of logically combining information on different layers, as is done in Figure 1, which shows an example of six different layers for the city of Exeter in the United Kingdom.

Tomlin (1990) has produced a formal map algebra for raster data sets. The most common operations on vector data are as follows:

1. *Point Data.* A scatter-plot(-map) showing the x- and y-coordinates of a series of points is an appropriate view if no further geographical data or other layers are involved. Standard statistics packages can analyze point data very easily, using the whole range of statistical procedures. However, the importance of the geographical context must not be underrated.

   Properties like interpoint distances, point densities, and spatial statistics can be calculated and visualized with GIS. Symbol point locations showing multivariate spatial

Layer Model of Exeter, UK

Elevation

Topography

Satellite Imagery

Population Density Surface

Enumerated Census Data

Aspect

Figure 1 A layer model of Exeter, UK including six different layers

distributions are a typical cartographic display mechanism. For instance weather maps combine wind speed and wind direction in a single symbol.

2. *Lines/flows.* Lines are used in geographical information systems to model information on flows or binary relationships between pairs of objects. The attribute data, such as imports and exports between two countries can be attached to the line that connects two points. For two points that are not connected directly the optimal path that connects them may be of interest, as may the nature of the network. The optimality criteria can use any of the attributes; in the simplest case it might just be the distance between two points.

In some applications, objects correspond to a whole sequence of lines. Looking at the path of a hurricane, notice that we have several anchor points that make up the path. Although we might have data measured at each of these anchor points we also refer to a hurricane as a whole, made up by several points.

Figure 2 visualizes the above scenario for hurricane data in the northern Atlantic over a period of more than thirty years. Storms that hit the land are plotted in red (not shown here).

3. *Regions.* Most census data are collected and distributed according to areas for reasons of administration and privacy. Once defined, these areas (counties, states, area codes, ZIP Codes, etc.) are often adapted by nongovernmental organizations to organize their geographical data.

In contrast to points and lines, regions have the property of adjacency. The effort of calculating adjacencies on the fly is usually large. Thus geographic information systems often store adjacency information in a separate matrix. Many geographical statistical methods use the property of adjacency. Since the length of the common border between two regions might determine the quality of their adjacency, it is useful to allow not only binary entries in the adjacency matrix, but weights. In a typical implementation, all neighbor weights for a region will sum up to one.

The handling of regional data must enable more than one region to be attached to any attribute record as enumeration areas are often noncontinuous and may be completely enclosed by other areas (islands, see Figure 3). Such complex topology requires a sophisticated data storage and retrieval mechanism.

While these models have given GIS an enormous initial thrust, recent developments have tried to model geographic phenomena more suitably either by mixing models or creating more

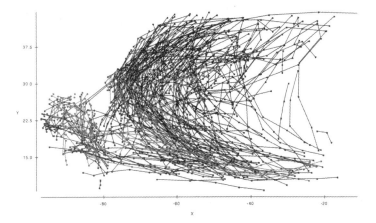

Figure 2 Connected lines are used to visualize the paths of hurricanes in the Northern Atlantic

suitable ones. Producing continuous population density information from enumerated data is an example of the former (Martin, 1989) and an object-based approach to geographic phenomena is another (Raper and Livingston, 1995). Both require specialist GIS software, and developments continue.

3. Scope of GIS

3.1. *From Analysis to Presentation to Analysis*

When working with a geographic information system, essentially five tasks are performed. Table 1 classifies these five tasks according to the use of methods from statistics, cartography

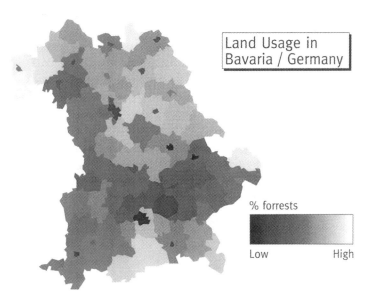

Figure 3 A choropleth map of the land usage in Bavaria. Several polygons are totally enclosed by other areas (islands)

Table 1 Five Stages of Implementing a GIS

	Statistics	*Cartography*	*Data(base) Management*
1. Data Input			•
2. Data Manipulation		•	–
3. Data Management			•
4. Query and Analysis	•		–
5. Visualization	•	•	

and data(base) management. Solid dots "•" indicate a strong impact, dashes "-" a weaker impact of each field at the five stages.

The smooth integration of these methods is required to create an efficient and useful implementation of a GIS. Tasks 1–3 are concerned with data handling. Based on this preparation, Tasks 4 and 5 then can analyze the data and finally present results.

The visual inspection of geographic patterns, clusters, and outliers takes advantage of the human visual system in ways utilized by cartographers over the centuries. New dynamic mapping techniques mean that a series of successive inquiries can be made rapidly in an iterative process of exploration and confirmation termed "visualization" (MacEachren and Taylor, 1994). This new form of map use that incorporates query and analysis and traditional visualization was depicted by MacEachren and Taylor (1994) in the (Cartography)[3] diagram shown in Figure 4.

This form of map use, and the types of map that are appropriate, have more in common with exploratory statistical graphics and less with production cartography, the map use to which many geographical information systems are geared. The exploratory techniques that MacEachren and Taylor (1994) termed visual thinking can be considered a spatial and cartographic equivalent of data mining.

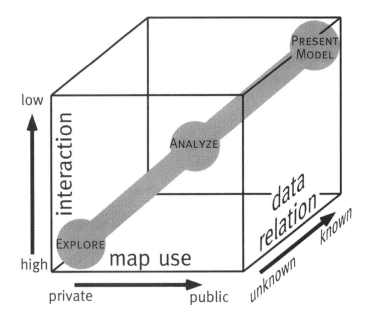

Figure 4 The (Cartography)3 diagram displays the relationship between exploration, analysis and presentation in a map-based information system

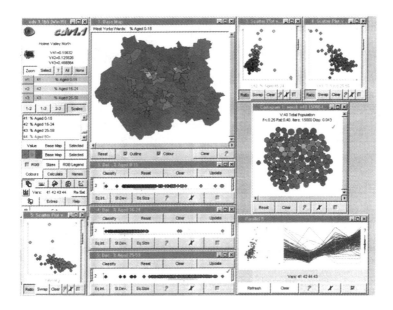

Figure 5 A sample screen of a CDV session

Since the main goal of a data exploration in a GIS is not only the visualization of the data, the last stage along the diagonal is not restricted to the visual presentation of the data, but might also be a model, used for prediction, and so on.

Starting with little knowledge of the data relation, the analyst uses a series of unique transient maps with which they interact quickly and often. As the knowledge of the data relations increases, the amount of interaction with the maps tend to decrease and the maps will get more presentable.

Final results are often presented as static maps, a ubiquitous medium with which large audiences are familiar and confident. Obviously the path from one edge of the cube to the opposite is not necessarily a linear one, but can move back and forth as analysis progresses. Newer developments (cf. Section 3.3) with more user-friendly graphical user interfaces allow the combination of the "analysis" and "present/model" steps, which make GIS more and more conducive to nonspecialists.

3.2. GIS Systems

GIS systems can be distinguished into three broad categories: (1) systems with a focus on the geographic aspects of the data, (2) systems that are statistical data analysis/visualization systems with extra capabilities for geographical data handling; and (3) hybrid systems that are a combination of systems (1) and (2).

1. The most common systems are those that offer strong functionality in drawing maps of the attribute data. Most off-the-shelf packages—for example, ArcInfo, MapInfo, Grass, and so on—fall into this category. They offer the best support in Steps 1–3 as defined in Section 3.1.

    The traditional cartographic approach is to code a large variety of attributes into a single, static, production map. This is an appropriate method for a single presentation map with multiple uses and users, but does not support the flexibility required for visual data analysis.

    The Descartes system (Andrienko and Andrienko, 1999) (Chapter 24.2.3) offers these traditional map-drawing functions along with basic statistical graphs of the attribute data.

2. Most interesting for data mining applications are packages that originate in the statistics domain. SAS offers the SAS/GIS module, which adds GIS functionality to the basic SAS statistics system.

Both the REGARD (Unwin, 1994) and MANET (Unwin, 1996) software are statistical data visualization tools, which allow work with geographical data in conjunction with highly interactive multivariate graphics of the attribute data.

The cartographic data visualizer (CDV, cf. Figure 5; Dykes, 1996) is a unique implementation of various cartographic views of the data along with statistical graphs, implemented in a highly interactive environment.

3. To offer the best of both worlds (geography and statistics) some solutions combine a geographical information system with a statistical analysis/visualization tool to form a hybrid system. Symanzik et al. (1997) describe a series of links between the XGobi data visualization tool, and ArcInfo GIS. Another, commercial package is the ArcInfo connection to S-Plus.

These loose links require the user to deal with two packages. Tighter coupling would be a more preferable solution as the interaction between these hybrid systems is not as smooth as desired.

Whereas packages in category (1) are relatively weak in the exploration and analysis steps, the packages in category (2) often lack functionality in geographical data manipulation.

3.3. Current Developments

The integration of techniques and development of new appropriate methods are proceeding rapidly. Notable research areas are in multimedia mapping that allows for interactive integration of sound, animation, text, and digital video images. In a GIS environment, which usually only works on relatively primitive graphical elements, their attributes, and spatial relation, this new technology offers a link, often through the map, to various kinds of exogenous information of a geographic nature. This ranges from simple text documents and photographs to video animations that describe objects in the GIS database.

The World Wide Web (WWW) and JAVA applets have had a great impact on the accessibility of geographical data. Numerous data sources exist on the WWW, for example, the TIGER database provided from the U.S. Bureau of Census is fully accessible at http://tiger.census.gov, and sensors such as satellites, weather stations, and Web Cams stream data online. A growing collection of satellite images is provided at http://www.terraserver.com.

The integration of the full range of stages from 1–5 as outlined in Table 1 may be possible with Internet technology and would be of great benefit to geographic data miners.

References

Andrienko, G. L. and N. V. Andrienko. 1999. "Interactive maps for visual data exploration." *Int. J. Geograph. Inform. Sci.* **13(4)**: 355–374.

Dykes, J. A. 1996. "Dynamic maps for spatial science: a unified approach to cartographic visualization." *Innovations in Geographical Information Systems*, edited by D. Parker, pp. 171–181: Taylor & Francis.

Hearnshaw, H. M. and D. Unwin. (eds). 1994. *Visualization in Geographical Information Systems*. Chichester, England: Wiley.

Kraak, M. J. and F. J. Ormeling. 1996. *Cartography—Visualization of Spatial Data*. Edinburgh: Addison Wesley Longman.

MacEachren, A. M. and Taylor. (eds). 1994. *Visualization in Modern Cartography*. Oxford: Pergamon.

Martin, D. 1989. "Mapping population data from zone centroid locations." *Trans., Inst. British Geographers* **14(1)**: 90–97.

Raper, J. and D. Livingston. 1995. "Development of a geomorphological spatial model using object-oriented design." *Int. J. Geograph. Inform. Sys.* **9(4)**: 359–384.

Symanzik, J., J. J. Majure, and D. Cook. 1997. "The linked ArcView 2.1 and XGobi environment—GIS, dynamic statistical graphics, and spatial data." *Proceedings of the Fourth ACM Workshop on Advances in Geographic Information Systems, Rockville, MD, November 15–16*, edited by S. Shekhar and P. Bergougnoux, pp. 147–154. New York: ACM Press.

Tomlin, C. D. 1990. *Geographic Information Systems and Cartographic Modelling*. Englewood Cliffs, NJ: Prentice Hall.

Unwin, A. 1994. "REGARDing geographic data." *Computational Statistics*, edited by Dirschedl and Ostermann. Heidelberg: Physica.

Unwin, A. 1996. "Interactive graphics for data sets with missing values—MANET." *J. Comput. Graphical Stat.* **5(2)**: 113.

15.4 Animation Techniques

Stephen G. Eick

ABSTRACT In visualization, animation is a technique for displaying a sequence of images in rapid succession that shows changes in a display. The most common data to animate involve time-varying information. In this case each frame shows the value statistic at one point in time. For animations to be perceptually effective, the information must vary smoothly from frame to frame.

1. Introduction

Animating a data visualization involves rapidly displaying a sequence of images showing change. This technique extends a static visualization to show one additional dimension of information. Each image in the animation sequence is called a frame, and for the animation to be effective, the frames must change smoothly. The sorts of visual properties suitable for animation include:

- position of an object
- shape, color, transparency, texture, or other retinal property
- lighting changes
- viewing angle

One of the most common applications of animation for information discovery involves animating time-varying data. In this case the additional data dimension is the time at which the data were recorded. Each frame then corresponds to one point in time. The animation is like a movie showing the evolution of the data set through time.

Illustrating the technique, Figure 1 contains six frames from an animation showing the spread of an infectious disease (mumps) over a two-year period. (These images are reproduced from Eddy and Mockus, 1994). The surface elevation and shading show the disease incidence rate, by region, smoothed both spatially and through time and rendered over a U.S. map. The highest surface elevations (brightest tones) correspond to the highest incidence rates. Initially in spring, the epidemic starts in the midwestern and mountain states (upper-left frame), subsides over the summer (middle and top-right frames), and resumes in the fall and spreads eastward (lower frames), touching more states, including Texas, California, Nebraska, and the Dakotas in the winter. Some states (e.g., Nebraska) remain unaffected and form a barrier to the spread of the epidemic.

Although it is quite common to animate over the time dimension, it is also possible to animate over an arbitrary dimension. In medical visualization, for example, it is common to show two-dimensional sequences of MRI images. In general, each frame in the animation corresponds to one slice along the dimension being animated across. Unfortunately, not all dimensions and animations lead to useful and interpretable displays. Certain perceptual constraints apply.

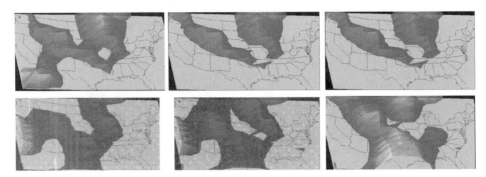

Figure 1 Six frames from an animation showing the spread of an infectious disease (mumps) over a two-year period. Although the outbreak pattern is obvious from the two-minute animation, it is quite difficult to see even from the carefully selected six frames. In particular, it is virtually impossible to notice that the outbreak spread in a counter-clockwise fashion

2. Perceptual Issues

Three perceptual issues constrain the sorts of data and animations that are useful for information discovery. First, for humans to perceive smooth motion, the frames must be displayed at a sufficiently fast rate. Films use a frame rate of 24 frames per second and NTSC TV (U.S. standard) uses a frame rate of 30 per second. Perceptual studies show that the minimum frame rate to perceive smooth motion is about 10 per second or 100 milliseconds per image. For interactive renderings, this constraint limits scene complexity to what can be rendered within one short time step.

Second, human ability to detect motion is preattentive and dates to our evolutionary history. We effortlessly and instantly perceive motion changes. In our evolutionary history, detecting motion helped ensure that we found predators before they found us. Applying this ability to animation, users perceive smooth motions and instantly detect jerky events. Perceptually these events jump out. Thus, for animations to be effective, the information between frames must change slowly. Furthermore, the sorts of analysis tasks that are supported frequently involve detecting unusual and sudden events. Often, as in Figure 1, it is necessary to smooth both in time and space to avoid visually jarring effects due to rapid changes.

Third, since each frame in an animation is displayed for only a fraction of a second, it is not possible to display as rich an image in an animation as in a static display. This limits the complexity of the data that is suited for animation.

3. Uses of Animation for Information Discovery

Animation is useful for:

Scanning huge data archives. Even at the lowest frame rate it is possible to scan a huge data set. As a rough calculation, if each frame in a four-minute animation displays 1,000 data items, the total volume of raw information scanned is nearly 10 gigabytes (at four bytes per item).

Detecting outliers or unusual events. Leveraging our perceptual abilities, animations are well suited for detecting unusual events and sudden changes.

Discovering local patterns. Patterns that are masked and obscured by overall trends. In Figure 1, the counter-clockwise spread of mumps is readily apparent in the animation, but masked in the static images.

Adding excitement to a visualization. Bringing data to life by adding motion and interactivity make static presentations more interesting and engaging.

As a presentation mechanism for sharing analysis results. Entertainment companies such as Disney have discovered that carefully crafted animations are well suited for story telling. The same story-telling techniques apply well for sharing analysis results.

Understanding in three-dimensional space. Motion is often crucial for understanding complex three-dimensional scenes. It is often necessary to move objects using animations in relation to each other or in relation to the background to perceive three-dimensional relationships correctly.

4. Implementation Issues

There are two basic methods for constructing animations. The first involves precomputing a sequence of images that are saved and played back. A small number of images may be stored on disk, while a larger number may be written to video tape for subsequent viewing. The second, and arguably more interesting technique, involves dynamically rendering each image during playback. The disadvantage of the first is that it supports only limited interaction with a carefully crafted visual display, for example, pause, forward, and backward. Its advantage, however, is that arbitrarily complex images can be rendered offline. The second method reverses these, permitting arbitrary interaction by requiring simpler images.

Beyond obvious implementation issues such as providing good graphic design, three more subtle issues arise when building interactive animation systems:

1. Maintaining constant frame rates throughout the animation as the level of detail varies from frame to frame. For accurate perception of the information in an animation, it is important that the frames be displayed at a constant rate. This means, for example, that the effective frame rate is limited by the time required to redraw the most complex frame. In practice many animation systems use a governor to monitor the frame rate and drop out rendering detail when the rate becomes too slow.

2. Providing effective navigation controls helps the user maintain a sense of context. When viewing animations, it is easy to become lost and lose track of the interesting frames. Providing useful navigation controls avoids user frustration. Important operations include, for example, stopping, restarting, marking significant frames, and choosing the current frame to view. It is useful, for example, to have sliders and controls to manipulate the frame rates and to exclude uninteresting frames.

3. Supporting common analysis tasks such as calculating differences between frames, transforming the data, displaying residuals from a statistical model, and manipulating visual characteristics of the image.

Sound is particularly effective in helping users navigate through animations. Triggering an audible click with each frame change, perhaps with increasing pitch, helps users maintain a sense of time change. Sound is often more effective than a visual indicator showing the current frame, since checking the indicator distracts the visual focus. Sound utilizes a channel independent of the human visual system and therefore does not interfere with the main focus of the user's attention.

5. Applications

This section includes two examples of network animations. Animation is a particularly useful technique for studying networks for three reasons. First, huge volumes of time-stamped network data are collected. This data is difficult to analyze and overwhelms traditional statistical methods. Second, network traffic often varies smoothly, as it results from many independent operations. Third, the interesting cases often involve network events, where something unusual happens.

The first example, Figure 2, includes four frames from an animation showing worldwide Internet traffic (Cox et al., 1996). In this animation three visual properties vary: lighting showing the time of day, arc height and shading coding the intercounty traffic volumes, and node height representing the total traffic volumes into and out of each country.

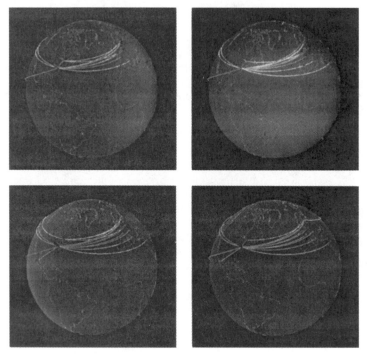

Figure 2 Four frames from an animation showing how worldwide Internet traffic patterns vary by time of day. Lighting and visual clues show the time of day and shaded arcs between the countries show the volume of traffic

Using lighting to convey time of day is particularly effective on a globe. The first frame (upper left) shows predawn (North America) traffic, the second (upper right) morning, the third (lower left) daytime, and the fourth (lower right) shows nighttime traffic. As might be expected, traffic between the United States and Europe is highest in the morning (upper right) and lowest in the evening (lower right). The barely visible arc between Finland and Australia (lower right) indicates a high level of traffic between these two countries during their daytimes.

The second example involves the CICNet network, one of the regional data networks of the U.S. portion of the Internet. CICNet connects thirteen universities and research facilities in the Great Lakes region. Figure 3 shows large circles at each of the facilities. These large circles represent the packet routers. Lines are drawn between the routers to show which pairs of them are physically connected. The smaller circles represent local area networks attached to the routers. Each router counts the number of bytes it sends to and receives from each of the local area networks and the other routers to which it is connected. The nodes of Figure 3 occur where line segments terminate at routers, and at each node a rectangle is represented. The size of the rectangle is determined by the number of incoming and outgoing bytes during a ten-minute period corresponding to each frame. The color of the rectangle shows the predominant direction of the traffic with red indicating source and green sink.

Figure 3 is one frame from a series of frames representing all ten-minute periods for one month. Animating over the frames provides an excellent dynamic view of the network. In this particular frame the two sequences of red-green rectangles show two ftp conversations, one between ARGON and MINN and another between UIUC and the rest of the Internet through the UMN gateway. Without animation it would be nearly impossible to discover fine details, such as ftp conversations, in such a large data set. For more detail and other interesting insights see, Becker and Wilks (1993) and Becker et al. (1995).

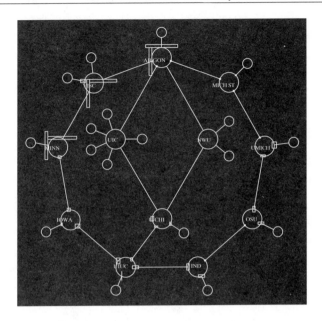

Figure 3 A schematic representation of the CICNet regional network, showing routers (larger circles), local area networks (smaller circles), connections between them (line segments), and byte flows along the connections (rectangles where the line segments terminate on the router circles). A flow from the ARGON (Argonne National Labs) to the MINN (University of Minnesota) local area networks can be discerned clearly, in spite of the lack of explicit information about this pair

6. Other Applications for Animation

Animation has been applied in the financial markets, for example, by showing stock market ticker-tape activity, share prices through time, and fund flows between market sectors.

7. Comparing Animation and Small Multiples

Small multiples, the graphical technique used in Figures 1, 2, and 3, tile several related images on a single display (Tufte, 1983). Animations extend small multiples from a few images, say ten, to large sequences of images. Small multiples are better suited for sharp, careful comparisons between a few images. Animations, however, are more effective when the number of images is large, for example, one hundred, and it becomes tedious to compare them pairwise.

References

Becker, R. A. and A. R. Wilks. February 1993. "Final report: network traffic analysis project." *BBN Subcontract agreement #20510.*

Becker, R. A., S. G. Eick, and A. R. Wilks. 1995. "Visualizing network data." *IEEE Trans. Visualization Comput. Graphics* **1(1)**: 16–28.

Cox, K. C., S. G. Eick, and T. He. 1996. "3D Geographic network displays." *ACM Sigmod Record* **25(4)**: 50–54.

Eddy, W. F. and A. Mockus. 1994. "An example of the estimation and display of a smoothly varying function of time and space—the incidence of mumps disease." *J. Am. Soc. Inform. Sci.* **45(9)**: 686–693.

Tufte, E. R. 1983. *The Visual Display of Quantitative Information.* Cheshire, CT: Graphics Press.

16 DATA MINING TASKS AND METHODS

16.1 Classification

16.1.1 The Goal of Classification

Hans-Hermann Bock

ABSTRACT This article informally introduces the basic problems and approaches related to classification. It distinguishes three basic interpretations: classification systems, discrimination, and clustering. The essential steps of discrimination and clustering methods are outlined, including the preprocessing of data. The text establishes links to statistical approaches (such as prediction) and conceptual learning methods (such as decision trees), and illustrates the problems by practical examples.

1. What is Classification?

Classification is a basic intellectual ability that proceeds by ordering or dissecting complex phenomena (e.g., a set of objects described by high-dimensional data) into small and comprehensive units, classes, substructures, or parts that serve for better understanding or control, and to assign new situations to one of these classes on the basis of suitable information. Classification may also be the *result* of a classificatory activity. We distinguish (at least) three interpretations:

1. *Classification as an ordering or classification system for objects.* Ordering of objects and empirical knowledge results in classification systems for further use. Well-known examples include: the classification of books in a library (e.g., by Dewey's decimal classification), patent classification systems in the European patent agency, the ordering of chemical elements (e.g., in the periodic system), classifying products and merchandises (e.g., for international standardisation). Classification systems are typically constructed by a detailed intellectual and structural analysis of the underlying situation supported by tools from concept theory, linguistics, and terminology, with the idea to facilitate the processing, the retrieval, or the understanding of the underlying facts, objects, or entities. This topic is beyond the scope of this handbook.

2. *Classification as discrimination or class assignment, also termed supervised learning, learning with a teacher, identification or pattern recognition.* This interpretation is typical for the engineering, statistics, and data mining communities and relates to examples such as: recognizing a disease from the symptoms of a patient (in medicine), distinguishing normal blood cells or chromosomes from abnormal ones on the basis of blood smears or differential counts (in cytology, pathology and prenatalogy), classifying consumers as reliable or risky from sociological or income data (in credit scoring), automatic recognition of letters or digits from handwritten addresses (in pattern recognition), identification of speakers, images or scenarios on the basis of acoustical or visual data (sonograms, photos, satellite signals) in speech recognition and image restoration, recognition of real and falsified banknotes from physical measurements, reading bar codes at the cashier of a supermarket, and so on.

   In these situations it is known that each object (e.g., a consumer, a digit) originates from one of m classes (types, subpopulations) $\Pi_1, ..., \Pi_m$ and is described by a data vector $x = (x^{(1)}, ..., x^{(k)})'$ (column vector). But it is unknown to which class the object belongs to, and this class must be reconstructed from x. In principle, this is possible if the classes are clearly distinguished by different data distributions such that the objects show a strictly class-specific behavior. In practice, however, there is typically some overlap between classes and often also some random variation inside the classes such that a perfect separation cannot be attained and misclassifications may occur with positive (but hopefully small) probabilities. Formally, the class properties are described either by m probability distributions for the underlying observable random feature vector $X = (X^{(1)}, ..., X^{(k)})'$, or by a learning (training) sample $\{x_{i1}, ..., x_{in_i}\}$ for each class $i = 1, ..., m$, such that for each sampled object $j = 1, ..., n_i$ its class index $I = i$ and its feature vector x_{ij} are both known (supervised learning). The basic problem is to assign a new object to one of the m classes on the basis of its observed measurement vector x. A classifier (in data mining) or discrimination rule (in statistics) is a decision rule ϕ that specifies, for each data point x, the index $\phi(x) \in \{1, ..., m\}$ of the class to which a data point x will be assigned. As an alternative, a randomized rule $\phi = (\phi_1, ..., \phi_m)$ provides m probabilities or plausabilities $\phi_1(x), ..., \phi_m(x)$ for assigning the data point x to the classes $1, ..., m$, respectively (see the posterior probabilities in Chapter 16.1.2). An appropriate or an optimum classifier is typically obtained by tools from statistics and informatics and may use, for example, discriminant functions, dissimilarity measures or a decision tree. In the engineering, neural network, and data mining communities, classification is often identified with discrimination.

3. *Classification as class construction or clustering, also termed grouping, numerical taxonomy, unsupervised classification or learning without a teacher.* Here we start from a set of objects (subjects, entities) $\mathcal{M} = \{1, ..., n\}$, say, where the relevant properties of the objects are described by suitable data (e.g., by n feature vectors $x_1, ..., x_n$) that specify, in particular, the mutual similarities or dissimilarities existing among the objects. The basic problem is to find those subsets $C_1, C_2, ...$ of objects in $\mathcal{M}$ (termed classes or clusters) which are homogeneous in some sense, that is, such that objects (data points) from the same cluster tend to be more similar than those belonging to different clusters, and clusters are sufficiently separated. Thus, in contrast to discrimination, the classes are unknown in the clustering framework and must be detected or (re-)constructed from the data.

Practically relevant clustering problems include: grouping consumers into life-style or consumption types for promotion purposes, building market segments for product scheduling, subdividing the clients of an insurance into risk groups, typifying enterprises according to their organizational structure, finding disease types with class-specific symptom constellations and therapies (in medicine), quantizing electronic signals into a discretized form, and so on. In many applications the clusters found by clustering methods will correspond to natural types or subpopulations $\Pi_1, \Pi_2, ...$ in $\mathcal{M}$. Clustering methods will be described in Chapter 16.5. Typically the resulting classes must be checked for their validity and significance.

2. Classification (Discrimination) as a Prediction Problem

From a general point of view, classification (discrimination) can be seen as a special type of prediction or multiple regression problem. The unknown target variable is the index $I \in \{1, ..., m\}$ of the class to which an object belongs, and the k components of the object's data vector $x = (x^{(1)}, ..., x^{(k)})'$ are interpreted as k explanatory variables (predictors, regressors). Then the decision function $\phi(x)$ has the role of a regression function and is a prediction or estimate of the true, but unknown class index I of the object with data x. This regression analogy underlies, for example, Fisher's linear discriminant function for a two-class problem (see Chapter 16.1.4), or a multilayer neural network for estimating the posterior probabilities of the classes (see Chapter 16.1.8).

The general *discrimination* approach includes the following steps:

1. The selection of variables and measurements which can discriminate between the considered classes, including preprocessing steps, data compression and data sampling.

2. The collection of information on the statistical properties of the classes, either by designing a class-specific probability model for the random observation vector X (as is typical, e.g., for Bayesian classifiers) or by providing, for each class Π_i, a learning or training sample $\{x_{i1}, ..., x_{in_i}\}$ of representative data vectors.

3. The construction of a practicable, good, or even optimum classifier ϕ from the available information on the existing classes (see Step 2).

4. The evaluation of the performance of the classifier ϕ, for example, by determining error rates (see Chapter 16.1.2), robustness studies, and so on.

5. The application of the resulting classifier ϕ to a new object with measurement vector x, typically implemented by some electronic device (e.g., a scanning machine in a supermarket or the TV equipment in a personal identification system).

The general *clustering* approach includes the following steps:

1. The selection of variables and measurements that characterize the properties of the given objects and can separate the hidden classes (clusters) of the set of objects $\mathcal{O}$.

2. The specification of quantitative measures for the similarity (or dissimilarity) between pairs of objects, objects and classes, or pairs of classes, often based on appropriate distances $d(x, y)$ for data vectors x, y.

3. A decision on the type of clustering to be constructed: partitional, hierarchical, overlapping, pyramidal, and so on.

4. A decision on the type of clusters to be found, either in geometrical terms (e.g., spherical or ellipsoidal shape in R^k, hyperplane-type), in graph theoretical concepts (e.g., cliques, connected components = single-linkage clusters), or by probabilistic models (e.g., normal distributions).

5. Specification of a clustering criterion that assesses the performance of a classification with respect to the data and must be optimized with respect to all classifications.

6. A clustering algorithm that finds or approximates the best classification defined in Step 5.

7. Validation steps that control the significance or realness of the obtained clustering(s), determine a suitable class number, check for stability and robustness, and so on.

8. Descriptive characterization and practical interpretation of the constructed clusters.

3. Classification as a Learning Process

Any method that estimates parameters or (re-)constructs a classification rule from data, may be termed *learning* from data. Learning may proceed batchwise or sequentially: In batch learning the method uses a fixed number n of data points $x_1, ..., x_n$ in a simultaneous way. In sequential or incremental learning data points $x_1, x_2, ...$ are sequentially observed and provide a continuous stream of information on the underlying classes, for example, when sampling more and more patients in a clinic, or when tuning a speaker recognition device by replicated presentation of this speaker's voice. Then learning proceeds by a successive updating of the classifier $\phi^{(n)}(\cdot)$ or the clustering $\mathscr{C}^{(n)} = (C_1^{(n)}, ..., C_m^{(n)})$ obtained for $x_1, ..., x_n$ after observing a new data point x_{n+1} in order to obtain $\phi^{(n+1)}(\cdot)$ or $\mathscr{C}^{(n+1)} = (C_1^{(n+1)}, ..., C_m^{(n+1)})$, respectively (which are expected to converge to optimum constellations in well-behaving situations). The learning terminology is typically used in the context of empirical Bayes methods, computational learning theory, pattern recognition, and neural networks.

4. Conceptual Learning and Decision Trees

Classical discriminant rules such as Fisher's linear discriminant rule, Bayesian methods, minimum-distance approaches or logistic discrimination (see Chapters 16.1.4 to 16.1.8) are primarily designed, and often optimal, for classical data with, for example, quantitative, categorical, ordinal, or binary predictors. Basically, they assign a data vector $X = x = (x^{(1)}, ..., x^{(k)})'$ to the class Π_i, which maximizes (or minimizes) a discriminant function $d_i(x)$ among m functions $d_1(x), ..., d_m(x)$ that are calculated simultaneously from all k predictors $x^{(1)}, ..., x^{(k)}$ in x, for example, as a distance between x and the class centroid μ_i or as a linear combination $d_i(x) = \sum_{t=1}^{k} a_{it} x^{(t)}$ ($i = 1, ..., m$; polythetic approach). Even if optimal in theory, these (linear, quadratic) discriminant functions will often be difficult to interpret in practice. Therefore, practitioners will often prefer classification or clustering rules which combine simple assertions on single variables by logical conjunctions and thereby yield, for example, decision rules of the type 'If $[x^{(1)} \leqslant 3.5]$ and $[x^{(3)} \in \{red, green\}]$ and $[x^{(6)} = yes]$, then assign x to the class Π_2'. Such approaches are termed conceptual and corresponding classifiers are typically developed in the form of a decision tree where appropriate monothetic queries such as $[x^{(1)} \leqslant 3.5]$, $[x^{(3)} \in \{red, green\}]$ and so on, are successively combined and yield a characterization of classes by (disjunctions of) conjunctions of logical assertions. This approach is realized, for example, in the CART algorithm (Breiman et al., 1984) or by the conceptual learning algorithms of Quinlan (1992) and Michalski et al. (1983, 1986). These methods construct partially optimum rules in the sense that at each step ($\hat{=}$ node of the tree) the query is built from one variable and a threshold, which are chosen in a (locally) optimum way.

5. Preprocessing of Data

In most practical classification problems, it is not at all obvious which data or variables to use for assigning objects to given classes since different choices of variables may result in a quite different class separation performance (e.g., in speech recognition). Moreover, the data gathering process can provide, for each single object, such a multitude of data that it is impossible to process them directly in a reasonable time or even on-line. For example, satellite photos may contain several thousands of pixels each with 256 grey values or spectral measurements, changing every 1/10 second, and warehouse enterprises have to face thousands of sale, price, and customer data every day. Therefore, common classification strategies comprise various tricky preprocessing steps which transform, reduce, and compress the original, high-dimensional data in order to attain an acceptably low dimension, but nevertheless to maintain the essential information (factors) that distinguish the underlying classes. Whereas practical experience and substantial knowledge of the application field will provide general guidelines for data selection, there are many statistical or mathematical techniques for selecting important variables (feature selection; see Chapter 14.2) and for reducing data, such as principal component analysis, Karhunen–Loève expansion, fast Fourier transformation, and so on.

References

General sources of information on discrimination are Young and Calvert (1974), Lachenbruch (1975), Krishnaiah and Kanal (1982), Fukunaga (1990), Goldstein and Dillon (1978), Hand (1986, 1997), McLachlan (1992), Niemann (1990) and Devroye, Györfi and Lugosi (1997). A survey of clustering methods is given by Bock (1974), Duran and Odell (1974), Späth (1983), Jain and Dubes (1988), Kaufman and Rousseeuw (1990), and Arabie et al. (1996).

Arabie, Ph., L. Hubert, and G. De Soete (eds). 1996. *Clustering and Classification*. River Edge, NJ: World Science Publishers. Survey articles on recent developments in cluster analysis.
Bock, H. H. 1974. *Automatische Klassifikation*. Göttingen: Vandenhoeck and Ruprecht. An introduction and survey for clustering methods and their mathematical and statistical bases.
Breiman, L., J. H. Friedman, R. A. Olshen, and Ch. J. Stone. 1984. *Classification and Regression Trees*. Belmont: Wadsworth. Introduces the classical CART methods.
Devroye, L., L. Györfi, and G. Lugosi. 1997. *A Probabilistic Theory of Pattern Recognition*. New York: Springer. A theoretical presentation of and survey on classical and recent results in pattern recognition, classification, and neural networks.
Duran, R. O. and P. L. Odell. 1974. *Cluster Analysis—A Survey*. Berlin: Springer-Verlag.
Fukunaga, K. 1990. *Introduction to Statistical Pattern Recognition*. New York: Academic Press. An engineering-oriented presentation.
Goldstein, M. and W. R. Dillon. 1978. *Discrete Discriminant Analysis*. New York: Wiley. Concentrates on categorical data.
Hand, D. J. 1986. *Discrimination and Classification*. New York: Wiley.
Hand, D. J. 1997. *Construction and Assessment of Classification Rules*. New York: Wiley. A survey on discrimination methods with practical comments and evaluation strategies.

Jain, A. K. and R. C. Dubes. 1988. *Algorithms for Clustering Data*. Englewood Cliffs, NJ: Prentice Hall.

Kaufman, L. and P. J. Rousseeuw. 1990. *Finding Groups in Data*. New York: Wiley. A computational approach with a software program.

Krishnaiah, P. R. and L. N. Kanal. (eds). 1982. *Classification, Pattern Recognition and Reduction of Dimensionality*, Volume 2. Handbook of Statistics. The Netherlands: North Holland/Elsevier, Amsterdam. With survey articles on many special topics in classification.

Lachenbruch, P. A. 1975. *Discriminant Analysis*. London, England: Hafner/Macmillan. A classical reference with emphasis on normal theory discrimination.

McLachlan, G. J. 1992. *Discriminant Analysis and Statistical Pattern Recognition*. New York: Wiley. An invaluable source for all topics of discriminant analysis and its applications, with emphasis on the statistical background.

Michalski, R. S., J. Carbonnel, and T. Mitchell (eds). 1983. *Machine Learning: an Artificial intelligence approach*, Volume 1. Berlin: Springer-Verlag.

Michalski, R. S., J. Carbonnel, and T. Mitchell. 1986. *Machine Learning: an Artificial intelligence approach*, Volume 2. Palo Alto, CA: Kaufmann. Decision trees and conceptual methods for classification.

Niemann, H. 1990. *Pattern Analysis and Understanding*. Berlin: Springer-Verlag. A survey on classical pattern recognition and its applications in technology and knowledge processing.

Quinlan, J. R. 1992. *Programs for Machine Learning*. Palo Alto, CA: Kaufmann. Describes decision trees and conceptual classification.

Späth, H. 1985. *Cluster Dissection and Analysis. Theory, FORTRAN Programs, Examples*. Chichester, England: Horwood. Presents mathematical bases and computational tools.

Young, T. Y. and T. W. Calvert. 1974. *Classification, Estimation and Pattern Recognition*. New York: Elsevier. A classical standard reference.

16.1.2 Classification Methodology

Hans-Hermann Bock

ABSTRACT This article surveys a range of classification (discrimination) methods, which are based on probabilistic or statistical models such as Bayes methods, maximum likelihood, nearest neighbor classifiers, nonparametric kernel density methods, plug-in rules, and so on. Additionally, we point to various algorithmic approaches for classification such as neural networks, support-vector machines, and decision trees which are, however, fully discussed in subsequent sections of this handbook. A major part of this article is devoted to the specification and estimation of various types of recovery rates and misclassification probabilities of a (fixed or data dependent) classifier. Finally, we describe some preprocessing methods for the selection of most informative variables.

1. Introduction

This article is devoted to the discrimination or classification problem, that is, the problem of assigning an object O to one of m given classes (populations) $\Pi_1, ..., \Pi_m$, on the basis of a data vector $x = (x^{(1)}, ..., x^{(k)})'$ from a sample space $\mathcal{X}$ (e.g., $\mathbb{R}^k$) that collects the values of k explanatory or predictive variables $X^{(1)}, ..., X^{(k)}$, which were observed for this object O (see Chapter 16.1.1). Depending on the information available on the classes and the type of classification rule, we may distinguish the following cases:

1. Probabilistic approach with known parameters.

2. Probabilistic approach with estimated parameters.

3. k-nearest-neighbor rules, Fisher's geometrical approach.

4. Neural network classification.

5. AI algorithms such as: decision trees, rule-based approaches, and so on.

The performance of classifiers is often measured in terms of (various types of) recovery rates and misclassification probabilities. Their specification and estimation is addressed in Section 4 below.

2. Probabilistic Approach with Known Parameters

The decision-oriented approach for classification starts from a probabilistic model and minimizes either an expected loss or a total misclassification probability. The basic model assumes:

1. An object $\mathcal{O}$ is randomly sampled from a heterogeneous population Π with m subpopulations (classes) $\Pi_1, ..., \Pi_m$ and corresponding prior probabilities (class frequencies) $\pi_1, ..., \pi_m > 0$ with $\sum_{i=1}^{m}\pi_i = 1$. Thus, π_i is the probability that the object $\mathcal{O}$ is actually sampled from the class Π_i. The random index I of the class to which $\mathcal{O}$ belongs cannot be observed.

2. The observable feature vector $X = (X^{(1)}, ..., X^{(k)})'$ for $\mathcal{O}$ is a random vector with values in a space $\mathcal{X}$ (e.g., $\mathcal{X} = \mathbb{R}^k$) and with a class-specific distribution density $f_i(x)$, where $i \in \{1, ..., m\}$ denotes the index of the population Π_i to which $\mathcal{O}$ belongs. In many cases $f_i(x)$ is taken from a parametric density family $f(x; \vartheta)$ such that $f_i(x) = f(x; \vartheta_i)$ with a class-specific parameter $\vartheta = \vartheta_i$, for example, from a normal distribution $\mathcal{N}_k(\mu_i, \Sigma_i)$ where the unknown parameter vector $\vartheta_i = (\mu_i, \Sigma_i)$ comprises the class mean $\mu_i \in \mathbb{R}^k$ and the covariance matrix Σ_i of X (for $i = 1, ..., m$). For discrete data $f_i(x)$ is the probability that X takes the value x (in the ith class).

A nonrandomized decision rule (classifier) is a function $\delta : \mathcal{X} \rightarrow \{1, ..., m\}$ that specifies, for each $x \in \mathcal{X}$, the index $\delta(x) = i$ of the class Π_i to which an object $\mathcal{O}$ with data x (but with unknown class membership) is assigned. In contrast, a randomized decision rule ϕ or $\phi(x) = (\phi_1(x), ..., \phi_m(x))$ specifies, for each $x \in \mathcal{X}$ and each class Π_i, a probability or plausability $\phi_i(x) \geq 0$ for assigning the observation x to the ith class Π_i (with $\phi_1(x) + \cdots + \phi_m(x) = 1$).

In the (unrealistic) case where all π_i, $f_i(\cdot)$ or ϑ_i are known, there are some well-established methods for defining optimum classifiers ϕ, which are then typically used in practice and implicitly underly many algorithms of pattern recognition, artificial intelligence, and supervised learning.

2.1. The Bayesian Classification Rule for a General Loss Function

The Bayesian approach assumes that each decision is related to a specified loss (or gain): Let $L_{ti}\text{tf} = \}Pi2\}50$ be the loss incurred when assigning an object from Π_t to the class Π_i, which means a misclassification if $t \neq i$ and a correct classification if $t = i$. Then, each classification rule $\phi = (\phi_1, ..., \phi_m)$ has an expected (average) loss, also termed the Bayesian loss of ϕ, which is given by:

$$r(\phi, \pi) := \int_{\mathbb{R}^k} \sum_{i=1}^{m}\phi_i(x)\left[\sum_{t=1}^{m}L_{ti}\pi_t f_t(x)\right]dx = \sum_{i=1}^{m}\sum_{t=1}^{m}L_{ti}\pi_t \cdot \alpha_{ti}(\phi). \tag{1}$$

Here $\alpha_{ti}(\phi) = \int \phi_i(x)f_t(x)dx$ denotes the probability of assigning an object from Π_t to Π_i when using ϕ. For $t \neq i$ this is the error probability of type (t, i), whereas for $t = i$ $\alpha_{ii}(\phi)$ is termed the recovery probability of type i.

A decision rule ϕ^* that minimizes the loss (1) is called a Bayesian classifier. It appears that ϕ^* is essentially given by the rule:

$$h_i(x) := \sum_{t=1}^{m}L_{ti}\pi_t f_t(x) \rightarrow \min_{i \in \{1, ..., m\}}. \tag{2}$$

Thus, an object $\mathcal{O}$ with observation vector x is assigned to the class Π_i with minimum value $h_i(x)$ among $h_1(x), ..., h_m(x)$. This is equivalent to saying that the class index i minimizes the a posteriori loss given by $L_i(x) := h_i(x)/[\sum_{t=1}^{m}\pi_t f_t(x)]$. Here the denominator $f(x) := \sum_{t=1}^{m}\pi_t f_t(x)$ is the marginal density of the random data vector X, it is a mixture of the m class densities

$f_1, ..., f_m$. Formally, we may put $\phi_i^*(x) = 1$ for this minimizing index i (whereas $\phi_j^*(x) = 0$ for all classes $j \neq i$) and see that ϕ^* is a nonrandomized classifier.

In particular, the set $A_i := \{x \in \mathbb{R}^k \mid h_i(x) = \min\{h_1(x), ..., h_m(x)\}\} = \{x \in \mathbb{R}^k \mid \phi_i^*(x) = 1\}$ of all data vectors x that are assigned to the same class Π_i is called the acceptance region for Π_i. The form of these regions A_i and of their boundaries ∂A_i depends primarily on the densities $f_1, ..., f_m$. If these boundaries ∂A_i are linear, quadratic, ... we speak of a linear, quadratic, ... classifier; the practical usefulness of a classifier is largely dependent on the substantial interpretability of these boundaries.

2.2. The Bayesian Rule for a 0–1 Loss Function

In the case of the two-valued 0–1 loss function $L_{ti} = 1$ or 0 for $t \neq i$ and $t = i$, respectively, the expected loss (1) reduces to the total error probability

$$r(\phi, \pi) = \sum_{i=1}^{m} \sum_{t \neq i} \pi_t \alpha_{ti}(\phi) = 1 - \sum_{i=1}^{m} \pi_i \alpha_{ii}(\phi) =: 1 - \alpha(\phi), \tag{3}$$

where $\alpha(\phi) := \sum_{i=1}^{m} \pi_i \alpha_{ii}(\phi) = 1 - r(\phi, \pi)$ is the total probability for a correct decision (overall recovery rate, hitting probability). Since the corresponding Bayesian classifier ϕ^* minimizes (3), it maximizes the recovery rate $\alpha(\phi)$. Substitution of L_{ti} into (2) yields $h_i(x) = f(x) - \pi_i f_i(x) \rightarrow \min_i$, therefore ϕ^* assigns an observed data vector $x \in \mathcal{X}$ to the class Π_i with maximum value of $\pi_i f_i(x)$ or, equivalently, with maximum a posteriori probability $p_i(x)$ for the class Π_i:

$$p_i(x) := \frac{\pi_i f_i(x)}{f(x)} \rightarrow \max_{i \in \{1, ..., m\}}. \tag{4}$$

The minimum attainable total error probability is then given by $r(\phi^*, \pi) = 1 - \alpha(\phi^*) = 1 - \int m(x) dx$ with the maximum $m(x) := \max_i \{\pi_i f_i(x)\}$.

Note that the m posterior probabilities $(p_1(x), ..., p_m(x))$ define a fuzzy classification for each data point x: In this interpretation $p_i(x)$ is the degree of membership of x in the ith class, and the 'fuzzy class i' is characterized by the function $p_i(x)$ from $\mathcal{X}$ to the unit interval $[0, 1]$ (see, e.g., Bandemer and Gottwald, 1995).

2.3. The Bayesian Rule for Uniform Priors: the Maximum-Likelihood Classifier

If all classes are equally likely, that is, $\pi_i = 1/m$ for all i, then (4) reduces to the maximum likelihood discrimination rule:

$$f_i(x) \rightarrow \max_{i \in \{1, ..., m\}}. \tag{5}$$

Thus each data vector x is assigned to the class i with maximum density (probability) $f_i(x)$.

2.4. Detection of Unclassifiable Objects

Various modifications are possible in the formulation of the classification or discrimination problem, in particular the consideration of an $(m + 1)$th decision category $i = 0$, which corresponds to postponing the decision and in so far collects unclassifiable objects. If in the case of uniform priors all losses L_{t0} for postponing are assumed to have the same value d with $0 = L_{tt} \equiv d < L_{ti} = 1$ (for all t, $i \geqslant 1$, and $t \neq i$), then the corresponding Bayes rule ϕ^* is formulated in terms of the maximum function $m(x)$:

Decide for 'x is unclassifiable'   if $m(x) < (1 - d)f(x)$.

Assign x to the class Π_i if $f_i(x) = m(x) \geqslant (1 - d)f(x)$.

2.5. Normal Distribution Models

A commonly used (but often inappropriate) distribution model is provided by the normal distribution: Each Π_i is characterized by a k-dimensional normal distribution that is, $f_i(x; \vartheta_i) \triangleq \mathcal{N}_k(\mu_i, \Sigma)$ with the class-specific mean $\vartheta_i \equiv \mu_i \in \mathbb{R}^k$ and a positive definite covariance matrix Σ.

The corresponding Bayesian classifier (4) reduces (after some elementary calculations) to the rule:

$$d_i(x) := \|x - \mu_i\|^2_{\Sigma^{-1}} - 2 \log \pi_i \to \min_{i \in \{1,\dots,m\}}, \tag{6}$$

that is, it involves the squared Mahalanobis distance $\|x - \mu_i\|^2_{\Sigma^{-1}} := (x - \mu_i)'\Sigma^{-1}(x - \mu_i)$ and can be equivalently written with Fisher's linear discrimination function $L_{ti}(x)$: Decide for class Π_i if

$$L_{ti}(x) := \tfrac{1}{2}[\|x - \mu_t\|^2_{\Sigma^{-1}} - \|x - \mu_i\|^2_{\Sigma^{-1}}] = \left(x - \frac{\mu_i + \mu_t}{2}\right)' \Sigma^{-1} (\mu_i - \mu_t) \geqslant \log \frac{\pi_t}{\pi_i} \tag{7}$$

for $t = 1, \dots, m$. For a uniform prior with $\pi_i \equiv 1/m$ the rules (6) and (7) reduce both to the minimum distance rule:

$$d_i(x) := \|x - \mu_i\|^2_{\Sigma^{-1}} \to \min_{i \in \{1,\dots,m\}}, \quad \text{in other words } L_{ti}(x) \geqslant 0 \text{ for all } t. \tag{8}$$

If, more generally, each class has its specific covariance matrix such that Π_i is described by a normal density $f_i(x) \triangleq \mathcal{N}_k(\mu_i, \Sigma_i)$ with the parameter $\vartheta_i = (\mu_i, \Sigma_i)$, the Bayes rule (4) is given by:

$$d_i(x) := \|x - \mu_i\|^2_{\Sigma_i^{-1}} + \log |\Sigma_i| - 2 \log \pi_i \to \min_{i \in \{1,\dots,m\}} \tag{9}$$

and may be formulated with quadratic discriminant functions $L_{ti}(x)$: Decide for the class Π_i if

$$L_{ti}(x) := \|x - \mu_t\|^2_{\Sigma_t^{-1}} - \|x - \mu_i\|^2_{\Sigma_i^{-1}} \geqslant \log \frac{\pi_t}{\pi_i} \quad t = 1, \dots, m. \tag{10}$$

3. Probabilistic Approach with Estimated Parameters

In practical applications, the priors π_i, class-specific densities $f_i(x)$, and/or the class parameters ϑ_i are unknown or only partially known. Then the typical approach consists of (a) estimating the unknown densities or parameters from appropriate training data (learning samples) and (b) using the previously described optimum classification rules (see Section 2) with the proviso that unknown densities or parameters are substituted by their estimates (plug-in rules). In the most simple case, the data consist of n pairs $(x_1, z_1), \dots, (x_n, z_n)$, where $x_j \in \mathcal{X}$ are the data points and $z_j \in \{1, \dots, m\}$ is the known class membership of data point x_j (which is, e.g., provided by a teacher: learning with a teacher, supervised classification). Collecting all data from the same class Π_i (i.e., with $z_j = i$) in a set C_i, this yields m samples or training sets $C_i = \{x_{i1}, \dots, x_{in_i}\}$, where n_i is the number of data points originating from the ith class Π_i, with $n = n_1 + \cdots + n_m$. Basically, we have to distinguish between parametric and nonparametric models.

3.1. Parametric Models

In the case of a parametric density model $f_i(x) = f(x; \vartheta_i)$, the unknown parameters ϑ_i can be replaced, for example, by their maximum likelihood estimates $\hat{\theta}_i$ obtained from the training data in $C_1, \dots, C_m$. This yields the plug-in version $\phi^{(n)}$ of the maximum likelihood classifier (5):

$$\hat{f}_i(x) := f(x; \hat{\vartheta}_i) \to \max_{i \in \{1,\dots,m\}}. \tag{11}$$

For a normal distribution model with $f_i \triangleq \mathcal{N}_k(\mu_i, \Sigma_i)$ or $f_i \triangleq \mathcal{N}_k(\mu_i, \Sigma)$ with unknown μ_i, Σ_i, and Σ, the estimates are given by the class centroids $\hat{\mu}_i = \bar{x}_i. := (1/n_i)\sum_{i=1}^{n_i} x_{ij}$ and the empirical covariance matrices $\hat{\Sigma}_i = (1/n_i)\sum_{j=1}^{n_i}(x_{ij} - \bar{x}_i.)(x_{ij} - \bar{x}_i.)'$ or $\hat{\Sigma} = (1/n)\sum_{i=1}^{n} n_i \hat{\Sigma}_i$, respectively, and lead to minimum distance rules of the type:

$$\hat{d}_i(x) := \|x - \bar{x}_i.\|^2_{\hat{\Sigma}_i^{-1}} \to \min_i \quad \text{or} \quad \hat{d}_i(x) := \|x - \bar{x}_i.\|^2_{\hat{\Sigma}^{-1}} \to \min_i \tag{12}$$

with quadratic and linear discrimination functions, respectively.

Plug-in versions for Bayesian rules with unknown priors π_i require a sampling scheme that allows for the estimation of the parameters π_i as well (which is not possible when fixing the sizes $n_1, ..., n_m$ of the training samples C_i beforehand). This can be attained by sampling the n training objects randomly from the entire population $\Pi = \Pi_1 + \cdots + \Pi_m$ such that π_i is the probability of membership to Π_i (this is the probability model in Section 2; mixture sampling). Then, if N_i is the random number of objects sampled from Π_i (with $\sum_{i=1}^{m} N_i = n$ and a joint polynomial distribution for $N_1, ..., N_m$), the relative frequency $\hat{\pi}_i := N_i/n$ provides an unbiased and consistent estimate for π_i, which can be used for a Bayesian plug-in rule corresponding, for example, to (4): $\hat{\pi}_i f(x; \hat{\vartheta}_i) \to \max_i$.

3.2. Nonparametric Models

In cases where a parametric distribution model is inappropriate (e.g., since the boundaries between the acceptance regions $A_1, ..., A_m$ for the classes are expected to be nonlinear or irregular), a nonparametric density estimate will be used, for example, the Parzen or kernel density estimator given by:

$$\hat{f}_i(x) := \frac{1}{nh^k} \cdot \sum_{j=1}^{n_i} K\left(\frac{x - x_{ij}}{h}\right) \quad x \in \mathbb{R}^k. \tag{13}$$

Here the kernel function $K(\cdot)$ is typically a distribution density such as $K(x) = (2\pi)^{-k/2} \exp\{-\|x\|^2/2\}$ (other options: uniform density in the unit cube or in the unit ball, Epanechnikov kernel, etc.). It is common experience that the performance of a density-based classifier depends not so much on the choice of the kernel function, but mainly on the choice of the bandwidth $h > 0$ which specifies the neighborhood of data points and can also be chosen in dependence on the data. For a large dimension k, a primary requirement is a sufficiently large number n_i of samples for each class (curse of dimensionality). In order to attain consistent rules when $n_i \to \infty$, the bandwidth $h \to 0$ must approach 0, but sufficiently slowly such that $hn_i^k \to \infty$.

3.3. Nearest-Neighbor Discrimination, k-Nearest-Neighbor Classifier

The minimum distance classifiers (12) can be generalized in many ways in order to comply with geometrical intuition or nonquantitative data (qualitative or mixed data, symbolic data, etc.). Common methods are provided by the nearest-neighbor classification rule (NN classifier) and the k-nearest-neighbor (k-NN) classifier.

Both methods start from a measure $d(x, y)$ for the dissimilarity or distance between two elements x, y of the sample space $\mathcal{X}$ (e.g., the Euclidean or Mahalanobis distance). Let $d(x, C_i) := \min_{y \in C_i} d(x, y)$ denote the minimum distance between a data point x and the ith training sample C_i ($i = 1, ..., m$). Then the inverse $1/d(x, C_i)$ is a measure for the density of points from C_i in the neighborhood of x and in so far an estimate for $f_i(x)$. With this interpretation, the NN classification rule: $d(x, C_i) \to \min_i$, is a plug-in version of the maximum likelihood classifier (5): the NN rule assigns a data point x to the class Π_i with minimum distance $d(x, C_i)$ that is, to the class of the nearest neighbor of x among all training data.

A generalized version considers, for a fixed integer k (typically $1 \leqslant k \leqslant 10$), the set $S^{(k)}(x)$, which contains the k-nearest-neighbors of x within the total set $\mathcal{X}^{(n)} = C_1 + \cdots + C_m$ of all n data. Denote by $k_i(x) = \|C_i \cap S^{(k)}(x)\|$ the number of data points from the learning sample C_i, which are among those k-nearest-neighbors of x such that $k_i(x)/n$ might be considered as an estimate for $f_i(x)$. Then the k-NN classifier assigns a new data point x to the class Π_i, which contains the maximum number of k-nearest-neighbors in the training samples, that is, with $i := \text{argmax}_{j=1,...,m} \{k_{j(x)}\}$. The theory of minimum distance and k-NN classifiers is surveyed, for example, in Devroye et al. (1997) where consistency and error bounds are derived (e.g., for $n \to \infty$ with $k = k_n \to \infty$).

3.4. Mixture Models

A special plug-in rule derives from the probabilistic model described in Section 2 if we consider the marginal density $f(x; \pi, \theta) = \sum_{i=1}^{m} \pi_i f_i(x) = \sum_{i=1}^{m} \pi_i f(x; \vartheta_i)$ (mixture density) of an observation $X = (X^{(1)}, ..., X^{(k)})'$ (i.e., without considering its class membership). The unknown parameter vector $\theta := (\vartheta_1, ..., \vartheta_m)$ and the prior $\pi = (\pi_1, ..., \pi_m)$ are estimated from a training sample $\{x_1, ..., x_n\}$ (without class memberships) by the maximum likelihood method, that is, by minimizing the negative loglikelihood:

$$-\text{loglik}(\pi, \theta) := \sum_{j=1}^{n} -\log\left(\sum_{i=1}^{m} \pi_i f(x_j; \vartheta_i)\right) \to \min_{\pi, \theta}. \tag{14}$$

Optimum parameter values are found by iterative numerical methods such as the EM or SEM algorithm (SEM is stochastic expectation maximization; see McLachlan and Krishnan, 1997). The resulting estimates $\hat{\pi}, \hat{\vartheta}_i$ are used for obtaining plug-in rules as previously described.

3.5. Neural Networks

Neural networks are often used for classification purposes, for example, in pattern recognition, credit scoring, robot control, and so on. Relevant types of neural networks can be seen as devices or algorithms for approximating an unknown function $y = g(x)$ by a semi-parametric ansatz function $y = g(x; w)$ with an unknown (and typically high-dimensional) parameter vector w (typically termed a weight vector), for example, in the form of a radial basis function or a multilayer network. The optimum approximation to $g(\cdot)$ is found by observing data points of the form $y_j = g(x_j)$ or $y_j = g(x_j) + U_j$ (with a random error U_j) and minimizing the deviation between the data $y_1, ..., y_n$ and their predictions $\hat{g}(x_1; w), ..., \hat{g}(x_n; w)$ with respect to w (various deviation measures can be used). This process is often performed in a recursive way such that $x_1, x_2, ...$ are observed sequentially and, after observing x_{n+1}, the previous estimate $w^{(n)}$ for w is suitably updated (sequential learning).

Neural network classifiers result if such a procedure is applied to a classification problem where y denotes, for example, the observed class membership, and $g(x; w)$ is a discrimination rule. Corresponding methods use a neural network in order to estimate the unknown class densities $g(x) = f_i(x)$ or the posterior probabilities $g(x) = p_i(x)$ of the classes, and then use the estimates $f_i(x)$ or $p_i(x)$ in the formulas for the classical (Bayes, maximum likelihood, minimum distance) classifiers such as (4) or (5). For details see Chapter 16.1.8 of this handbook.

4. Estimating the Error Probabilities of a Classification Rule

The performance of a (fixed, nonrandomized) classification rule ϕ with acceptance regions $A_1, ..., A_m \in \mathbb{R}^k$ is characterized by:

- the m true recovery rates $\alpha_{ii}(\phi) := \int \phi_i(x) f_i(x) dx = \int_{A_i} f_i(x) dx$; and
- the $m(m-1)$ true error probabilities $\alpha_{ti}(\phi) := \int \phi_i(x) f_t(x) dx = \int_{A_i} f_t(x) dx$ (for $t \neq i$).

If the densities $f_i(x)$ or the parameters ϑ_i in $f(x; \vartheta_i)$ are estimated from a training sample $\mathcal{X}^{(n)} = \{x_{ij} \mid i = 1, ..., m, j = 1, ..., n_i\}$ of size n, these formulas will depend on n and on the data set $\mathcal{X}^{(n)}$. A similar remark holds in the case of a data-dependent classifier $\phi(\cdot) = \phi^{(n)}(\cdot) = \phi^{(n)}(\cdot; \mathcal{X}^{(n)})$ with data-dependent acceptance regions $A_i^{(n)}$ (e.g., a plug-in rule). As a consequence, we must distinguish among various conceptually different specifications of an error or recovery probability and also among various different error estimates:

1. The plug-in estimate $\hat{\alpha}_{ti}(\phi)$ for the probability $\alpha_{ti}(\phi)$, for a fixed known classifier ϕ:

$$\hat{\alpha}_{ti}(\phi) = \int \phi_i(x) \hat{f}_t(x) dx = \int_{A_i} \hat{f}_t(x) dx. \tag{15}$$

2. The actual (true) error/recovery rate of a data-dependent classifier $\phi^{(n)}$:

$$\alpha_{ti}(\phi^{(n)}) = \int \phi_i^{(n)}(x) f_t(x) dx = \int_{A_i^{(n)}} f_t(x) dx. \tag{16}$$

3. The estimated error/recovery rate of $\phi^{(n)}$ obtained by substituting an estimated density (e.g., with estimated parameters):

$$\hat{\alpha}_{ti}(\phi^{(n)}) = \int \phi_i^{(n)}(x)\hat{f}_t(x)dx = \int_{A_i^{(n)}} \hat{f}_t(x)dx. \tag{17}$$

4. The apparent error/recovery rate of $\phi^{(n)}$ (also termed resubstitution estimate):

$$\alpha_{ti,\text{app}}(\phi^{(n)}) = U_{ti}/n_t, \tag{18}$$

where $U_{ti} = \sum_{j=1}^{n_i} \phi_i^{(n)}(x_{tj}) = \sum_{j=1}^{n_i} I_{A_i^{(n)}}(x_{tj})$ is the number of data from the tth training sample C_t which are assigned to the class Π_i by the classifier $\phi^{(n)}$ (confusion matrix). Unfortunately, this estimator is much too optimistic: For example, the estimated recovery rate $\alpha_{ii,\text{app}}(\phi^{(n)})$ is typically quite a lot larger than the true value $\alpha_{ii}(\phi^{(n)})$ to be estimated since the latter one is estimated from the same data $\mathscr{X}^{(n)}$ that have tuned the classifier $\phi^{(n)}$.

5. The expected error/recovery probability $E_T[\hat{\alpha}_{ti}]$:

   For any of the data-dependent estimates $\hat{\alpha}_{ti}$ given before, $E_T[\hat{\alpha}_{ti}]$ is defined as the expected value of $\hat{\alpha}_{ti}$ with respect to all training samples $\mathscr{X}^{(n)}$ (e.g., under the mixture model). This is a fixed (i.e., non data-dependent) probability, which characterizes the overall quality of the entire classification process, including the learning of the (plug-in) classifier $\phi^{(n)}$ from the fluctuating data.

In practice, these definitions are often confounded or uncritically used.

Considering a Bayesian classifier ϕ^* and a corresponding plug-in rule $\phi^{(n)}$, it is expected that for an increasing sample size $n \to \infty$ and, when using consistent parameter estimates, $\vartheta_i^{(n)}$ or $\hat{f}_i(x)$, the true and estimated error/recovery rates $\alpha_{ti}(\phi^*)$, $\alpha_{ti}(\phi^{(n)})$, $\hat{\alpha}_{ti}(\phi^{(n)})$, and so on, should all be close to each other. In this context, there are a range of convergence theorems, for example, for $\hat{\alpha}_{ti}(\phi^{(n)}) \to \alpha_{ti}(\phi^*)$, and finite sample inequalities for the (maximum) deviation between true and estimated error/recovery probabilities. Similar results hold for the empirical Bayesian risk $r(\phi^{(n)}, \pi)$, which converges to the minimum risk $r^* = r(\phi^*, \pi)$ of the Bayesian rule ϕ^*. These topics are investigated in the context of computational learning theory, which also yields bounds for the risk difference $r(\phi^{(n)}, \pi) - r^*$, which are formulated in terms of the so-called Vapnik–Chervonenkis dimension (Devroye et al., 1997).

The quality of a classification rule should not be evaluated by considering error rates exclusively (which can be large even for an optimum classifier if the underlying populations Π_i are not well separable). Other properties of a classifier such as its generalization ability, the ease of application, its stability, or its robustness (against departures from the underlying model; Kharin, 1996) will sometimes be equally or even more important when selecting an appropriate decision rule (see Hand, 1997).

4.1. Test Samples and Cross-Validation Methods

A commonly used method for obtaining an unbiased, consistent estimate for the actual error/recovery probabilities $\alpha_{ti}(\phi^{(n)})$ of a classifier $\phi^{(n)}$ (obtained from the training data in $\mathscr{X}^{(n)}$) proceeds as follows: We observe, in addition to the training data, from each population Π_i a new test sample $T_i = \{y_{i1}, ..., y_{im_i}\}$, which is independent from $\mathscr{X}^{(n)}$, and calculate the relative error/recovery frequencies inside T_t:

$$\hat{\alpha}_{ti}(\phi^{(n)}) = (1/m_t)\sum_{j=1}^{m_t} \phi_i^{(n)}(y_{tj}) = (1/m_t)\sum_{j=1}^{m_t} I_{A_i^{(n)}}(y_{tj}) \tag{19}$$

for $t = 1, ..., m$. This approach is typically realized in the way that the original n data points are randomly split into a training set (of size $2n/3$, say, with m training classes C_i), which yields the classifier, and a test set (the remaining $n/3$ data points with test samples T_i), which is used for evaluation afterwards. Since this splitting process needs (spoils) a lot of data, some more refined and economical tools have been designed under the heading cross-validation methods where one single or some few elements are singled out in turn.

A common approach is the jackknife or leave-one-out method for evaluating a data-dependent (plug-in) classifier $\phi^{(n)}$ (e.g., a plug-in version of the Bayesian rule ϕ^*): Given n training data x_j with known class memberships $z_j \in \{1, ..., m\}$ (for $j = 1, ..., n$), we eliminate in turn each data point x_j, build the decision rule $\phi^{(n-1,j)}$ from the remaining $n-1$ data points (in the same way as $\phi^{(n)}$ has been constructed from the entire data set) and classify the jth point using $\phi^{(n-1,j)}$. Denote by d_j the index of the class obtained for x_j. Then we estimate the true probabilities $\alpha_{ti}(\phi^*)$, $\alpha_{ti}(\phi^{(n)})$, or $E_T[\alpha_{ti}(\phi^{(n)})]$ by the relative frequency $\tilde{U}_{ti}/n$, where $\tilde{U}_{ti} :=$ $\#\{j \in \{1, ..., n\} \mid c_j = t, d_j = i\}$ is the number of data x_j from Π_t, which were classified by the rule $\phi^{(n-1,j)}$ into the class Π_i. Similarly, $\hat{\alpha} := \sum_{i=1}^{m} \tilde{U}_{ii}/n$ provides an estimate for the overall recovery rate $\alpha(\phi^{(n)})$. Theoretical results as well as simulations show that this method yields quite precise estimates, even for moderate sample sizes.

4.2. The Bootstrapping Method

This method is commonly used for estimating the error rates $\alpha_{ti}(\phi^{(n)})$, (16), of a (plug-in) rule $\phi^{(n)}$. Basically, it works by replacing in (16) the unknown distribution density $f_i(\cdot)$ of X by the empirical distribution of data points from Π_i, for example, taken from the training set C_i. Thus, for given sample sizes $m_1, ..., m_m$ (often: $m_i \equiv n_i$), the method repeatedly takes (N times, say) a random subsample of size m_i from each training set C_i and iterates the following Steps (1) to (3) for $v = 1, ..., N$:

1. Sample m_i data points (with replacement) from C_i, obtaining a bootstrap data set $C_i^{[v]}$ (typically with repetitions) for each $i = 1, ..., m$.

2. Using the data in $C_1^{[v]}, ..., C_m^{[v]}$, construct the corresponding plug-in rule $\phi^{[v]}$ (in the same way as $\phi^{(n)}$ is constructed from $C_1, ..., C_m$).

3. Let $U_{ti}^{[v]}$ and $\tilde{U}_{ti}^{[v]}$ denote the number of data points from C_t and $C_t^{[v]}$, respectively, which were assigned to the class Π_i by $\phi^{[v]}$. Calculate $D_{ti}^{[v]} := U_{ti}^{[v]}/n_t - \tilde{U}_{ti}^{[v]}/m_t$, that is, the difference of the corresponding resubstitution estimates.

Finally, the bootstrap estimator for $\alpha_{ti}(\phi^{(n)})$ is given by:

$$\hat{\alpha}_{ti,\text{boot}} := \alpha_{ti,\text{app}}(\phi^{(n)}) + (1/N)\sum_{v=1}^{N} D_{ti}^{[v]}, \tag{20}$$

where $\alpha_{ti,\text{app}}(\phi^{(n)}) = U_{ti}/n_t$ is the resubstitution estimator for $\phi^{(n)}$. This estimator yields quite accurate estimates for the actual error probability $\alpha_{ti}(\phi^{(n)})$ even for close classes and small class sizes n_i.

5. Fisher's Classical Linear Discriminant Analysis

A geometrical point of view underlies the classical linear discriminant theory developed by R.A. Fisher. This approach can be interpreted as the search for an s-dimensional hyperplane H in $\mathbb{R}^k$, such that the known classification $C_1, ..., C_m$ of the training data x_{ij} is best reproduced by the n projection points $y_{ij} = \pi_H(x_{ij})$ of x_{ij} onto H in the sense that the variance between the classes $\sum_{i=1}^{m} n_i \|\bar{y}_i - \bar{y}\|^2$ is minimized by H. It appears that the optimum hyperplane is spanned by the s first eigenvectors $v_1, ..., v_s \in \mathbb{R}^k$ of the between-class covariance matrix $B :=$ $\sum_{i=1}^{m} n_i(\bar{x}_i - \bar{x})(\bar{x}_i - \bar{x})'$ and that, in so far, the discrimination process may be based on the n reduced, s-dimensional feature vectors $z_{ij} := (v'_1 x_{ij}, ..., v'_s x_{ij})'$ (with $j = 1, ..., n_i$; $i = 1, ..., m$). For $s = 2$ dimensions these vectors can easily be shown on the screen and the separating boundaries $L_{ti}(z) = 0$ for the projected classes (for the minimum-distance classifier [12]) can be simultaneously displayed in $\mathbb{R}^2$.

6. Selection and Preprocessing of Variables

A major step in classification and pattern recognition concerns the specification of variables that are able to distinguish the underlying or conjectured classes $\Pi_1, ..., \Pi_m$. In data mining, this problem is superposed by the fact that most databases in enterprises or marketing institutions typically store so much information and details about the underlying subjects (customers, products, bank transfers) that it makes no sense to use all these variables for the classification process (for technical as well as for economic reasons). Therefore, any classification process is usually preceded by a selection of a sufficiently small number of (hopefully) informative, discriminating, or predictive variables.

There are various statistical methods for selecting or transforming variables: principal components (identical or related to the Karhunen–Loève expansion), Fisher's projection method described in Section 5, projection pursuit methods, and so on. These methods typically yield a small set of s, say, linear combinations of the k original variables $X^{(1)}, ..., X^{(k)}$. In contrast, the decision tree approach constructs a higly nonlinear classification rule and acceptance regions A_i in a recursive, monothetic way: First by dissecting the entire set of training samples optimally on the basis of a single variable that is optimally selected (i.e., such that the m classes are best separated in the training set), and then by iterating this dissection process iteratively for each of the attained subsamples (until a stopping criterion precludes further splitting). As a result we obtain a decision tree where the acceptance regions A_i result from a recursive combination of rules relating to single variables only. Further details are described in Chapters 16.1.3 and 16.1.4.

Another type of method concentrates on the selection of a suitable subset of variables $S \subset \{1, ..., k\}$ of a given size $s = |S|$ from the original k variables (with $2 \leqslant s < k$), and then using this reduced number of variables instead of the original ones in the formerly described Bayesian, maximum likelihood and NN classifiers. This classical model selection approach typically works with information measures (Akaike, Schwarz, ICOMP), which are to be optimized. A more recent approach looks for a selection S, which minimizes (an estimate of) the total error probability of the corresponding (optimum or plug-in) classifier built from the s selected variables. Both approaches proceed by successively eliminating a single variable from the entire set of all k variables (backward method), or by successively adding one more variable to an initial choice of one variable (forward method). The method is locally optimum in so far as, in each step, it eliminates (includes) the variable that leads to the smallest (estimated) total error probability of the corresponding (optimum, Bayes, plug-in, or empirical) decision rule until the given dimension s is attained or the error will be too large.

Finally, we point to the approaches developed under the heading of support-vector machines and potential function method. In this approach, the acceptance regions A_i for the underlying classes Π_i are computationally optimized in order to attain small error rates for the training samples. For linear boundaries between the regions A_i, the classical Fisher approach might suffice. Since, however, many practical applications require the consideration of nonlinear class boundaries, the linear approach is combined with a suitable nonlinear transformation $\psi(x)$ of the original data vector x. Then the support vector classifier is formulated in terms of the transformed data $y = \psi(x)$ with linear boundaries (instead of using nonlinear boundaries for the original data x). This approach is also investigated in the framework of computational learning theory, a good reference is provided by Cristianini and Shawe-Taylor (2000).

References

Classical sources on classification, discrimination, and pattern recognition are Young and Calvert (1974), Lachenbruch (1975), Krishnaiah & Kanal (1982), Fukunaga (1990), Goldstein & Dillon (1978), Niemann (1990), Läuter (1992) and Hand (1986). Modern viewpoints are considered, for example, in Breiman et al. (1984), McLachlan (1992), Ripley (1996), Kharin (1996), Devroye et al. (1997) and Bock and Diday (2000). Nonparametric density estimation is presented in Tapia and Thompson (1978), Devroye (1987) and Silverman (1986).

Bandemer, H. and S. Gottwald. 1995. *Fuzzy Sets, Fuzzy Logic, Fuzzy Methods with Application*. Chichester, England: Wiley.

Bock, H. H. and E. Diday. 2000. *Analysis of Symbolic Data. Exploratory Methods for Extracting Information from Complex Data*. Berlin: Springer-Verlag. Presents classification and data analysis methods for set-valued and probabilistic data.

Breiman, L., J. H. Friedman, R. A. Olshen, and Ch. J. Stone. 1984. *Classification and Regression Trees*. Belmont: Wadsworth. Describes rule-based classification methods (decision trees).

Cristianini, N. and J. Shawe-Taylor. 2000. *An Introduction to Support Vector Machines.* Cambridge, England: Cambridge University Press.

Devroye, L. 1987. *A Course on Density Estimation.* Basel: Birkhäuser.

Devroye, L., L. Györfi, and G. Lugosi. 1997. *A Probabilistic Theory of Pattern Recognition.* New York: Springer. An excellent and comprehensive survey on classical and recent results in pattern recognition, classification, computational learning theory, and neural networks.

Fukunaga, K. 1990. *Introduction to Statistical Pattern Recognition.* New York: Academic Press. An engineering-oriented presentation.

Goldstein, M. and W. R. Dillon. 1978. *Discrete Discriminant Analysis.* New York: Wiley. Concentrates on categorical data.

Hand, D. J. 1986. *Discrimination and Classification.* New York: Wiley.

Hand, D. J. 1997. *Construction and Assessment of Classification Rules.* New York: Wiley. A survey on discrimination methods and the evaluation of their performance, with applications and practical comments.

Kharin, Y. 1996. *Robustness in Statistical Pattern Recognition.* Dordrecht, The Netherlands: Kluwer Academic Publishers. Concentrates on robustness studies for discrimination and clustering methods.

Krishnaiah, P. R. and L. N. Kanal. (eds). 1982. *Classification, Pattern Recognition and Reduction of Dimensionality. Handbook of Statistics,* Volume 2. Amsterdam: North Holland/Elsevier. With survey articles on many special topics in classification.

Lachenbruch, P. A. 1975. *Discriminant Analysis.* London, England: Hafner/Macmillan. A classical reference with an emphasis on normal theory discrimination.

Läuter, J. 1992. *Stabile multivariate Verfahren. Diskriminanzanalyse, Regressionsanalyse, Faktoranalyse.* Berlin, Germany: Akademie Verlag. Discusses error probabilities as a function of n and p, contains discrimination methods for badly behaving data, e.g., by using penalty functions and ridge methods.

McLachlan, G. J. 1992. *Discriminant Analysis and Statistical Pattern Recognition.* New York: Wiley. An invaluable source for all topics of discriminant analysis and its applications, with an emphasis on the statistical background.

McLachlan, G. J. and Th. Krishnan. 1997. *The EM Algorithm and Extensions.* New York: Wiley.

Niemann, H. 1990. *Pattern Analysis and Understanding.* Berlin: Springer-Verlag. The new version of a classical survey on pattern recognition and its applications in technology and knowledge processing.

Ripley, B. D. 1996. *Pattern Recognition and Neural Networks.* Cambridge, England: Cambridge University Press. A very appealing survey on the statistical bases of neural network classification methods.

Silverman, B. W. 1986. *Density Estimation for Statistics and Data Analysis.* London: Chapman and Hall.

Tapia, R. A. and J. R. Thompson. 1978. *Nonparametric Probability Density Estimation.* Baltimore: John Hopkins University Press.

Young, T. Y. and T. W. Calvert. 1974. *Classificaton, Estimation and Pattern Recognition.* New York: American Elsevier. A classical standard reference.

16.1.3 Decision-Tree Discovery

Ronny Kohavi and J. Ross Quinlan

ABSTRACT We describe the two most commonly used systems for induction of decision trees for classification: C4.5 and CART. We highlight the methods and different decisions made in each system with respect to splitting criteria, pruning, noise handling, and other differentiating features. We describe how rules can be derived from decision trees and point to some differences in the induction of regression trees. We conclude with some pointers to advanced techniques, including ensemble methods, oblique splits, grafting, and coping with large data sets.

1. C4.5

C4.5 belongs to a succession of decision-tree learners that trace their origins back to the work of Hunt and others in the late 1950s and early 1960s (Hunt, 1962). Its immediate predecessors were ID3 (Quinlan, 1979), a simple system consisting initially of about 600 lines of Pascal, and C4 (Quinlan, 1987). C4.5 has grown to about 9,000 lines of C that is available on diskette with Quinlan (1993). Although C4.5 has been superseded by C5.0, a commercial system from RuleQuest Research, this discussion will focus on C4.5 since its source code is readily available.

1.1. Input and Output

Input to C4.5 consists of a collection of training cases, each having a tuple of values for a fixed set of attributes (or independent variables) $A = \{A_1, A_2, ..., A_k\}$ and a class attribute (or dependent variable). An attribute A_a is described as continuous or discrete depending on whether its values are numeric or nominal. The class attribute C is discrete and has values $C_1, C_2, ..., C_x$.

The goal is to learn from the training cases a function

$$DOM(A_1) \times DOM(A_2) \times ... \times DOM(A_k) \rightarrow DOM(C)$$

that maps from the attribute values to a predicted class.

The distinguishing characteristic of learning systems is the form in which this function is expressed. We focus here on decision trees (Chapter 5.4), a recursive structure that is

- a leaf node labeled with a class value, or

- a test node that has two or more outcomes, each linked to a subtree.

Figure 1 shows a simple example in which the tests appear in ovals, the leaves in boxes, and the test outcomes are labels on the links.

To classify a case using a decision tree, imagine a marker that is initially at the top (root) of the tree.

- If the marker is at a leaf, the label associated with that leaf becomes the predicted class.

- If the marker is at a test node, the outcome of that test is determined and the marker moved to the top of the subtree for that outcome.

1.2. Divide-and-Conquer

Decision-tree learners use a method known as divide-and-conquer to construct a suitable tree from a training set S of cases:

- If all the cases in S belong to the same class (C_j, say), the decision tree is a leaf labelled with C_j, assuming equal costs.

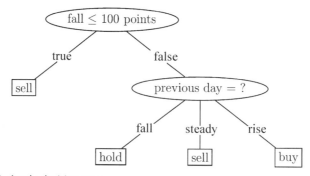

Figure 1 A simple decision tree

- Otherwise, let B be some test with outcomes $b_1, b_2, ..., b_t$ that produces a nontrivial partition of S, and denote by S_i the set of cases in S that has outcome b_i of B. The decision tree is

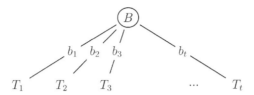

where T_i is the result of growing a decision tree for the cases in S_i.

1.3. Candidate Tests

C4.5 uses tests of three types, each involving only a single attribute A_a. Decision regions in the instance space are thus bounded by hyperplanes, each orthogonal to one of the attribute axes.

- If A_a is a discrete attribute with z values, possible tests are:

  "$A_a = ?$" with z outcomes, one for each value of A_a. (This is the default.)

  "$A_a \in G?$" with $2 \leqslant g \leqslant z$ outcomes, where $G = \{G_1, G_2, ..., G_g\}$ is a partition of the values of attribute A_a. Tests of this kind are found by a greedy search for a partition G that maximizes the value of the splitting criterion (discussed below).

- If A_a has numeric values, the form of the test is "$A_a \leqslant \theta$" with outcomes *true* and *false*, where θ is a constant threshold. Possible values of θ are found by sorting the distinct values of A_a that appear in S, then identifying one threshold between each pair of adjacent values. (So, if the cases in S have d distinct values for A_a, $d-1$ thresholds are considered.)

1.4. Selecting Tests

In the divide-and-conquer algorithm, any test B that partitions S nontrivially will lead to a decision tree, but different Bs give different trees. Most learning systems attempt to keep the tree as small as possible because smaller trees are more easily understood and, by Occam's Razor arguments, are likely to have higher predictive accuracy (see, for instance, Quinlan and Rivest, 1989). Since it is infeasible to guarantee the minimality of the tree (Hyafil and Rivest, 1976), C4.5 relies on greedy search, selecting the candidate test that maximizes a heuristic splitting criterion.

Two such criteria are used in C4.5, information gain and gain ratio. Let $RF(C_j, S)$ denote the relative frequency of cases in S that belong to class C_j. The information content of a message that identifies the class of a case in S is then

$$I(S) = -\sum_{j=1}^{x} RF(C_j, S) \log(RF(C_j, S)).$$

After S is partitioned into subsets $S_1, S_2, ..., S_t$ by a test B, the information gained is then

$$G(S, B) = I(S) - \sum_{i=1}^{t} \frac{|S_i|}{|S|} I(S_i). \tag{1}$$

The gain criterion chooses the test B that maximizes $G(S, B)$.

A problem with this criterion is that it favors tests with numerous outcomes—for example, $G(S, B)$ is maximized by a test in which each S_i contains a single case. The gain ratio criterion sidesteps this problem by also taking into account the potential information from the partition itself:

$$P(S, B) = -\sum_{i=1}^{t} \frac{|S_i|}{|S|} \log\left(\frac{|S_i|}{|S|}\right). \tag{2}$$

Gain ratio then chooses, from among the tests with at least average gain, the test B that maximizes $G(S, B)/P(S, B)$.

1.5. Missing Values

Missing attribute values are a common occurrence in data, either through errors made when the values were recorded or because they were judged irrelevant to the particular case. Such lacunae affect both the way that a decision tree is constructed and its use to classify a new case.

When a decision tree is constructed from a set S of training cases, the divide and conquer algorithm selects a test on which to partition S. Let B be a potential test based on attribute A_a with outcomes $b_1, b_2, ..., b_t$. Denote by S_0 the subset of cases in S whose values of A_a are unknown, and hence whose outcome of B cannot be determined. As before, let S_i denote those cases with (known) outcome b_i of B. The information gained by B is reduced because we learn nothing about the cases in S_0; Equation 1 now becomes

$$G(S, B) = \frac{|S - S_0|}{|S|} G(S - S_0, B).$$

The split information is increased to reflect the additional outcome of the test (namely, the fact that it cannot be determined for the cases in S_0). Equation (2) is modified to

$$P(S, B) = -\frac{|S_0|}{|S|} \log\left(\frac{|S_0|}{|S|}\right) - \sum_{i=1}^{t} \frac{|S_i|}{|S|} \log\left(\frac{|S_i|}{|S|}\right).$$

Both changes have the effect of reducing the desirability of tests involving attributes with a high proportion of missing values.

When a test B has been chosen, C4.5 does not build a separate decision tree for the cases in S_0. Instead, they are notionally fragmented into fractional cases and added to the subsets corresponding to known outcomes. The cases in S_0 are added to each S_i with weight $|S_i| / |S - S_0|$.

Missing attribute values also complicate the use of the decision tree to classify a case. Instead of a single class, the initial result of the classification is a class probability distribution determined as follows: Let $CP(D, Y)$ denote the result of classifying case Y with decision tree T.

- If T is a leaf, $CP(D, Y)$ is the class probability distribution of training cases that reach T as estimated by the relative frequencies of the class.
- If D is a tree whose root is test B, and the outcome of B on case Y is known (b_i, say), then

$$CP(D, Y) = CP(T_i, Y),$$

where, as before, T_i is the decision tree for outcome b_i.

- Otherwise, all outcomes of B are explored and combined probabilistically, giving

$$CP(D, Y) = \sum_{i=1}^{t} \frac{|S_i|}{|S - S_0|} CP(T_i, Y).$$

Note that the weight of the subtree T_i depends on the proportion of training cases that have outcome b_i, interpreted as the prior probability of that outcome.

When the class probability distribution resulting from classifying case Y with the decision tree has been determined, the class with the highest probability is chosen as the predicted class.

1.6. Avoiding Overfitting

The divide-and-conquer algorithm partitions the data until every leaf contains cases of a single class, failing only if two cases have the same values for each attribute but belong to different classes. Consequently, the decision tree will correctly classify all training cases. This so-called overfitting is generally thought to lead to a loss of predictive accuracy in most applications (Quinlan, 1986) The loss of predictive accuracy due to overfitting is explained well by the bias-variance tradeoff (Geman and Bienenstock, 1992, Kohavi and Wolpert, 1996).

Overfitting can be avoided by a stopping criterion that prevents some sets of training cases from being subdivided (usually on the basis of a statistical test of the significance of the best test), or by removing some of the structure of the decision tree after it has been produced. Most authors agree that the latter is preferable since it allows potential interactions among attributes to be explored before deciding whether the result is worth keeping.

C4.5 employs two mechanisms of the latter kind. Before discussing this, we introduce the heuristic on which it is based.

1.7. Estimating True Error Rates

Consider some classifier Z formed from a (sub)set S or training cases, and suppose that Z misclassifies M of the cases in S. The true error rate of Z is its accuracy over the entire universe from which the training set was sampled. The true error rate is usually markedly higher than the classifier's resubstitution error rate on the training cases (here $M/|S|$), which might be near zero for an unpruned decision tree.

The true error rate is often estimated by measuring Z's error rate on a collection of unseen cases that were not used in its construction; this is the best strategy when a substantial set of unseen cases is available. In many applications, though, data is scarce and all of it is needed to construct the classifier. C4.5 estimates the true error rate of Z using only the values M and $|S|$ from the training set as follows.

If an event occurs M times in N trials, the ratio M/N is an estimate of the probability p of the event. We can go further and derive confidence limits for p; for a given confidence CF, an upper limit p_r can be found such that $p \leqslant p_r$ with probability $1 - CF$. Following (Ed, 1962, p. 185), p_r satisfies the following equations:

$$CF = \begin{cases} (1 - p_r)^N & \text{for } M = 0 \\ \sum_{i=0}^{M} \binom{N}{i} p_r^i (1 - p_r)^{N-i} & \text{for } M > 0 \end{cases}$$

(The same source gives a quickly computable approximation for p_r in the latter case.)

Now, the classifier Z can be viewed as causing M error events in $n = |S|$ trials. Since Z was constructed to fit the cases in S, and so tends to minimize the apparent error rate, the upper bound p_r is used as a more conservative estimate of the error rate of Z on unseen cases. In the following, we will use $U_{CF}(M, N)$ to denote the error bound p_r above. C4.5 uses a default CF value of 0.25, but this can be altered to cause higher or lower levels of pruning.

1.8. Pruning Decision Trees

After a decision tree is produced by the divide-and-conquer algorithm, C4.5 prunes it in a single bottom-up pass. Let T be a nonleaf decision tree, produced from a training set S, of the form

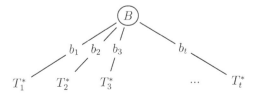

where each T_i^* has already been pruned. Further, let T_f^* be the subtree corresponding to the most frequent outcome of B, and let L be a leaf labeled with the most frequent class in S. Let the number of cases in S misclassified by T, T_f^*, and L be E_D, $E_{T_f^*}$, and E_L, respectively. C4.5's tree pruning algorithm considers the three corresponding estimated error rates

- $U_{CF}(E_D, |S|)$,
- $U_{CF}(E_L, |S|)$, and
- $U_{CF}(E_{T_f^*}, |S|)$.

Depending on whichever is lower, C4.5

- leaves T unchanged;
- replaces T by the leaf L; or
- replaces T by its subtree T_f^*.

This form of pruning is computationally efficient and gives quite reasonable results in most applications.

2. CART

CART, an acronym for Classification And Regression Trees, is described in the book by Breiman et al. (1984). The use of trees in the statistical community dates back to AID (Automatic Interaction Detection) by Morgan and Sonquist (1963), and to later work on THAID by Morgan and Messenger in the early 1970s.

CART® is also the name of the system currently implementing the methodology described in the above book. It is sold by Salford Systems.

The basic methodology of divide-and-conquer described in C4.5 is also used in CART. The differences are in the tree structure, the splitting criteria, the pruning method, and the way missing values are handled.

2.1. Tree Structure

CART constructs trees that have only binary splits. This restriction simplifies the splitting criterion because there need not be a penalty for multiway splits (Kononenko, 1995b). It also allows optimal partitioning of categorical attributes in linear time (in the number of attribute values) if the label is binary (Breiman et al., 1984, theorem 4.5). The restriction has its disadvantages, however. The tree may be less interpretable with multiple splits occurring on the same attribute at adjacent levels. There may be no good binary split on an attribute that has a good multiway split (Kononenko, 1995a), which may lead to inferior trees.

2.2. Splitting Criteria

CART uses the Gini diversity index as a splitting criterion. Let $RF(C_j, S)$ denote the relative frequency of cases in S that belong to class C_j. The Gini index is defined as:

$$G(S) = 1 - \sum_{j=1}^{x} RF(C_j, S)^2.$$

A class probability tree predicts a class distribution for an example instead of a single class. The common measure of performance for a class probability tree is the mean squared error. For each class j, let C_j be the indicator variable, which is one if the class for the example is j and zero otherwise. The mean squared error, or MSE, is defined as:

$$MSE = E_e \left[\sum_{j=1}^{x} (C_j - P_j(e))^2 \right],$$

where the expectation is over all examples, and $P_j(e)$ represents the probability assigned to class j for example e by the probabilistic classifier.

The interesting observation about the Gini diversity index is that it minimizes the resubstitution estimate for the mean squared error.

CART also supports the twoing splitting criterion, which can be used for multiclass problems. At each node, the classes are separated into two superclasses containing disjoint and mutually exhaustive classes. A splitting criterion for a two-class problem is used to find the attribute and the two superclasses that optimize the two-class criterion. The approach gives strategic splits in the sense that several classes that are similar are grouped together.

2.3. Pruning

CART uses a pruning technique called minimal cost complexity pruning, which assumes that the bias in the resubstitution error of a tree increases linearly with the number of leaf nodes. The cost assigned to a subtree is the sum of two terms: the resubstitution error and the number of leaves times a complexity parameter α. Formally,

$$R_\alpha = R(T) + \alpha \cdot \text{number-of-leaves}.$$

It can be shown that, for every value of α, there exists a unique smallest tree minimizing R_α (Breiman et al., 1984, proposition 3.7). Note that, although α runs through a continuum of values, there are at most a finite number of possible subtrees. There is thus a sequence of trees minimizing $R_\alpha, T_1 \succ T_2 \succ \cdots \succ \{T_t\}$, created by varying α from zero to infinity. The trees are nested: each tree is contained in the previous one. An efficient weakest-link pruning algorithm can be constructed to compute T_{k+1} from T_k.

When a large data set is available, selecting the best α to minimize the true error can be done by setting aside a holdout set (e.g., a third of the data) and constructing $T_1 \succ T_2 \succ \cdots \succ \{T_t\}$ from the data, excluding the holdout set. The examples in the holdout set can then be classified using each tree, giving an estimate of the true error of each tree. The α matching the tree that minimizes the error can then be used as the pruning parameter to prune the tree built from the whole data set.

The pruning step described above is relatively fast, but building a second tree using the whole data set effectively doubles the induction time. Moreover, if the data set is small, the error estimates have high variance and precious data (held out) are not used in building the initial tree.

CART therefore uses ten-fold cross-validation (Stone, 1974; Kohavi, 1995) to improve the error estimates and utilize more data. The procedure for pruning using ten-fold cross-validation is more complex since multiple trees must be built and pruned. We refer the reader to Breiman et al. (1984) for details. The time complexity of the pruning step when ten-fold cross-validation is used is a factor of 10 more expensive than C4.5's pruning, but it does tend to produce smaller trees (Oates and Jensen, 1997).

Even when cross-validation is used, the pruning parameter is sometimes unstable. Also, to improve comprehensibility, it is sometimes preferable to choose a smaller tree that has comparable accuracy to the best tree. CART employs the "1 SE rule," which chooses the smallest tree whose estimated error is within one standard deviation of the estimated error of the best tree.

2.4. Missing Values

Unlike C4.5, CART does not penalize the splitting criterion during the tree construction if examples have unknown values for the attribute used in the split. The criterion uses only those instances for which the value is known. Unlike C4.5, CART finds several surrogate splits that can be used instead of the original split. During classification, the first surrogate split based on a known attribute value is used.

The surrogates cannot be chosen based on the original splitting criterion because the subtree at each node is constructed based on the original split selected. The surrogate splits are therefore chosen to maximize a measure of predictive association with the original split. This procedure works well if there are attributes that are highly correlated with the chosen attribute.

2.5. Regression Trees

As its name implies, CART also supports building regression trees. Regression trees are somewhat simpler than classification trees because the growing and pruning criteria used in CART are the same. The regression tree structure is similar to a classification tree, except that each leaf predicts a real number.

The resubstitution estimate is the mean squared error:

$$R(S) = \frac{1}{n}\sum_i (y_i - h(t_i))^2,$$

where y_i is the real-valued label, for example, t_i and $h(t_i)$ is the (real-valued) prediction. The splitting criteria is chosen to minimize the resubstitution estimate. Pruning is done in a manner similar to the cost complexity pruning described above.

In CART, each leaf predicts a constant value; model trees generalize to building a model at each leaf (Quinlan, 1995; Frank et al., 1998).

3. Advanced Methods

Decision trees have been extended in many ways. We provide a short list of pointers to important topics.

1. The induction of oblique decision trees allow tests at the nodes to be linear combinations of attributes. Murthy et al. (1994) describe an induction system that allows such tests. Breiman et al. (1984) also describe some mechanisms for supporting such splits in CART. The main advantage of oblique splits is their ability to create splits that are not axis-orthogonal. The disadvantage is loss of comprehension.

2. Many different pruning methods have been proposed in the literature. Esposito et al. (1995) provide a comparison of pruning and grafting methods. Kearns and Mansour (1998) provide a theoretically-justified pruning algorithm. Quinlan and Rivest (1989), Mehta et al. (1995), and Wallace and Patrick (1993) describe MDL- (minimum description length) and MML- (minimum message length) based pruning methods.

3. C4.5 also contains a mechanism to re-express decision trees as ordered lists of if–then rules. Each path from the root of the tree to a leaf gives the conditions that must be satisfied if a case is to be classified by that leaf. C4.5 generalizes this prototype rule by dropping any conditions that are irrelevant to the class, guided again by the heuristic for estimating true error rates. The set of rules is reduced further based on the MDL principle described above. There are usually substantially fewer final rules than there are leaves on the tree, and yet the accuracy of the tree and the derived rules is similar. Rules have the added advantage of being more easily understood by people.

4. Ensemble methods that build multiple trees can dramatically reduce the error, but usually result in huge structures that are incomprehensible. Breiman (1996) describes a bagging (bootstrap aggregating) procedure. Schapire (1990) introduced boosting, which was later enhanced in Freund and Schapire (1995). Kohavi and Kunz (1997) describe option trees, which provide the advantages of voting methods, yet keep a tree-like structure that can be shown to users. Empirical comparisons were done in Quinlan (1996) and Bauer and Kohavi (2000).

5. Most implementation of decision trees requires loading the data into memory. Shafer et al. (1996) describe the SPRINT algorithm, which can scale out of core. Variants and other methods for scaling to larger data sets are described in Freitas and Lavington (1998). Several commercial systems implementing decision trees also provide parallel implementations.

6. Decision trees choose a split and do not revisit choices. Lookahead methods are described in Murthy and Salzberg (1995).

7. Utgoff (1997) describes how to update decision trees incrementally as more data is made available.

8. Most algorithms assume 0–1 costs for mistakes. Descriptions on how to generalize to loss matrices are given in Breiman et al. (1984) and a comparison is given in Pazzani et al. (1994). More information can be found in Turney (1997). A recent method for dealing with costs is described in Domingos (1999).

9. Lazy decision trees (Friedman et al., 1996) conceptually choose the best tree for a given test instance. In practice, only a path needs to be constructed.

10. Oblivious decision trees conduct the same split across a whole level (Kohavi and Li, 1995) and can be converted into a graph or a decision table (Kohavi and Sommerfield, 1998).

References

Bauer, E. and R. Kohavi. 2000. "An empirical comparison of voting classification algorithms: bagging, boosting, and variants." *Machine Learning* **36**: 105–139.

Breiman, L. 1996. "Bagging predictors." *Machine Learning* **24**: 123–140.

Breiman, L., J. H. Friedman, R. A. Olshen, and C. J. Stone. 1984. *Classification and Regression Trees*. Belmont, CA: Wadsworth International Group.

Domingos, P. 1999. "Metacost: A general method for making classifiers cost-effective." *Proceedings of the 5th International Conference on Knowledge Discovery and Data Mining*, edited by S. Chaudhuri and D. Madigan, pp. 155–164. New York: ACM Press.

Eposito, F., D. Malerba, and G. Semeraro. 1995. "Simplifying decision trees by pruning and grafting: new results." *Machine Learning: ECMIL-95 (Proceedings of the European Conference on Machine Learning, 1995)*, edited by N. Lavrac and S. Wrobel. Lecture Notes in Artificial Intelligence 914, pp. 287–290. Berlin, Germany: Springer-Verlag.

Frank, E., Y. Wang, S. Inglis, G. Holmes, and I. H. Written. 1998. "Using model trees for classification." *Machine Learning* **32(1)**: 63–76.

Freitas, A. A. and S. H. Lavington. 1998. *Mining Very Large Databases With Parallel Processing*. Dordrecht, the Netherlands: Kluwer Academic Publishers.

Freund, Y. and R. E. Schapire. 1995. "A decision-theoretic generalization of on-line learning and an application to boosting." *Proceedings of the Second European Conference on Computational Learning Theory*, pp. 23–27. Berlin: Springer-Verlag.

Friedman, J., R. Kohavi, and Y. Yun. 1992. "Lazy decision trees." *Proceedings of the Thirteenth National Conference on Artificial Intelligence*, pp. 717–724. Menlo Park, CA: AAAI Press and the MIT Press.

Geman, S., E. Bienenstock, and R. Doursat. 1996. "Neural networks and the blas/variance dilemma." *Neural Computation* **4**: 1–58. Cambridge, MA: The MIT Press.

Hunt, E. B. 1962. *Concept Learning: An Information Processing Problem*. New York, NY: Wiley.

Hyafil, L. and R. L. Rivest. 1976. "Constructing optimal binary decision trees in NP-complete." *Inform. Process. Lett.* **5(1)**: 15–17.

Kearns, M. and Y. Mansour. 1998. "A fast, bottom-up decision tree pruning algorithm with near-optimal generalization." *Machine Learning: Proceedings of the Fifteenth International Conference*, edited by J. Shavlik, pp. 269–277. San Francisco, CA: Morgan Kaufmann Publishers, Inc.

Kohavi, R. 1995. "A study of cross-validation and bootstrap for accuracy estimation and model selection." *Proceedings of the Fourteenth International Joint Conference on Artificial Intelligence*, edited by C.S. Mellish, pp. 1137–1143. San Francisco, CA: Morgan Kaufmann. Available at http://robotics.stanford.edu/~ronnyk.

Kohavi, R. and C. Kunz. 1997. "Option decision trees with majority votes." *Machine Learning: Proceedings of the Fourteenth International Conference*, edited by D. Fisher, pp. 161–169. San Francisco, CA: Morgan Kaufmann Publishers, Inc. Available at http://robotics.standard.edu/users/ronnyk.

Kohavi, R. and C.-H. Li. 1995. "Oblivious decision trees, graphs, and top-down pruning." *Proceedings of the Fourteenth International Joint Conference On Artificial Intelligence*, edited by C. S. Mellish, pp. 1071–1077. San Francisco, CA: Morgan Kaufmann.

Kohavi, R. and D. Sommerfield. 1998. "Targeting business users with decision table classifiers." *Proceedings of the Fourth International Conference on Knowledge Discovery and Data Mining*, edited by R. Agrawal, P. Stoloroz, and G. Piatetsky-Shapiro, pp. 249–253. Menlo Park, CA: AAAI Press.

Kohavi, R. and D. H. Wolpert 1996. "Bias plus variance decomposition for zero-one loss functions." *Machine Learning: Proceedings of the 13th International Conference*, edited by L. Saitta, pp. 275–283. San Fransisco, CA: Morgan Kaufmann Publishers July 1996. Available at http://robotics.stanford.edu/users/ronnyk.

Kononenko, I. 1995a. "A counter example to the stronger version of the binary tree hypothesis." *ECML-95 workshop on Statistics, Machine Learning, and Knowledge Discovery in Databases*, pp. 31–36. San Fransisco, CA.

Kononenko, I. 1995b. "On biases in estimating the multivalued attributes." *Proceedings of the Fourteenth International Joint Conference on Artificial Intelligence*, edited by C. S. Mellish. San Fransisco, CA: Morgan Kaufmann Publishers, pp. 1034–1040. Available at http://ai.fri.uni-lj.si/papers/index.html.

Konrad, D. (ed.) 1962. *Documenta Geigy Scientific Tables*. Basle, Switzerland: Geigy Pharmaceuticals.

Mehta, M., J. Rissanen, and R. Agrawal. 1995. "MDL-based decision tree pruning." *Proceedings of the First International Conference on Knowledge Discovery and Data Mining*, edited by U. M. Fayyad and R. Uthurusamy, pp. 216–221. Menlo Park, CA: AAAI press.

Morgan, J. N. and J. A. Sonquist. 1963. "Problems in the analysis of survey data, and a proposal." *J. AM. Stat. Assoc.* **58**: 415–434.

Murthy, S. K., S. Kasif, and S. Salzberg. 1994. "A system for the induction of oblique decision trees." *J. Artificial Intell. Res.* **2**: 1–33.

Murthy, S. and S. Salzberg. 1995. "Lookahead and pathology in decision tree induction." *Proceedings of the Fourteenth International Joint Conference on Artificial Intelligence*, edited by C. S. Mellish, pp. 1025–1031. San Francisco, CA: Morgan Kaufmann.

Oates, T. and D. Jensen. 1997. "The effects of training set size on decision tree complexity." *Machine Learning: Proceedings of the Fourteenth International Conference*, edited by D. Fisher, pp. 254–262. San Francisco, CA: Morgan Kaufmann.

Pazzani, M., C. Merz, P. Murphy, K. Ali, T. Hume, and C. Brunk. 1994. "Reducing misclassification costs." *Machine Learning: Proceedings of the Eleventh International Conference*. San Francisco, CA: Morgan Kaufmann, pp. 217–226.

Quinlan, J. R. 1979. "Discovering rules from large collections of examples: a case study." *Expert Systems in the Micro Electronic Age*, edited by D. Michie. Scotland: Edinburgh University Press.

Quinlan, J. R. 1986. "Induction of decision trees." *Machine Learning* **1**: 81–106.

Quinlan, J. R. 1987. "Inductive knowledge acquisition: a case study." *Applications of Expert Systems*, edited by Quinlan, pp. 157–173. Wokingham, England: Addison-Wesley.

Quinlan, J. R. 1993. *C4.5: Programs for Machine Learning*. San Mateo, CA: Morgan Kaufmann.

Quinlan, J. R. 1995. "Learning with continuous classes." *Proceedings of the 5th Australian Joint Conference on Artificial Intelligence*, edited by A. Adams and L. Sterling, pp. 343–348. Singapore: World Scientific.

Quinlan, J. R. 1996. "Bagging, boosting, and C4.5." *Proceedings of the Thirteenth National Conference on Artificial Intelligence*, pp. 725–730. Menlo Park, CA: AAAI Press and the MIT Press.

Quinlan, J. R. and R. L. Rivest. 1989. "Inferring decision trees using the minimum description length principle." *Inform. Comput.* **80**: 227–248.

Schapire, R. E. 1990. "The strength of weak learnability." *Machine Learning* **5(2)**: 197–227.

Shafer, J., R. Agrawal, and M. Mehta. 1996. "Sprint: Scalable parallel classifier for data mining." *Proceedings of the Twenty-Second International Conference on Very Large Databases (VLDB)*. San Fransisco, CA: Morgan Kaufmann Publishers, pp. 544–555.

Stone, M. 1974. "Cross-validatory choice and assessment of statistical predictions." *J. R. Stat. Soc. B* **36**: 111–147.

Turney, P. 1997. "Cost-sensitive learning." Available at http://extractor.iit.nrc.ca/bibliographies/cost-sensitive.html.

Utgoff, P. E. 1997. "Decision tree induction based on efficient tree restructuring." *Machine Learning* **29**: 5.

Wallace, C. and J. Patrick. 1993. "Coding decision trees." *Machine Learning* **11**: 7–22.

16.1.4 Decision Rules

Willi Klösgen

ABSTRACT Decision rules are the most prominent subtype of subgroup patterns (see Chapter 16.3). They are expressed as if–then rules with preconditional left-hand-side subgroups and conclusive right-hand-side target groups. The subgroups and target groups are constructed as conjunctions of propositional selectors. More expressive rules based on first-order Horn clauses are treated in Chapter 16.2.4. In this article, we discuss algorithms that derive rule sets that are going to be used for classification purposes. Specifically, we focus on description languages for constructing left-hand-side preconditional subgroups, evaluation functions measuring the quality of rules, and search strategies deriving rule sets.

1. Introduction

Decision rules are a special subtype of subgroup patterns (see Chapters 5.2 and 16.3). A disjoint and exhaustive set of target groups (classes) is given, and a set of rules is searched that can be used to classify a new object, that is, to predict the target group (class) to which the object belongs. A decision rule thus identifies a subgroup of objects in the studied population that has a dominant probability of belonging to one of the classes. Typically it is assumed that the set of target groups is given by a nominal target variable so that each target group corresponds to a selector built with a single value of this target variable. The left-hand-side preconditional part of a rule describes a subgroup of objects (cases of the database) and is constructed as a conjunction of propositional selectors. Thus decision rules represent the upper left cell in Table 1 in Chapter 16.3.1, which summarizes various subtypes of subgroup patterns, that is, decision rules deal with only one population of objects and a nominal target variable.

In this article we assume a one-relational, propositional description language for constructing left-hand-side conditional subgroups; more advanced description languages are discussed in Chapter 5.2. Thus we regard a database consisting of one relation with a schema $\{A_1, ..., A_{n+1}\}$ and associated domains D_i for the attributes A_i. A rule is then given by:

$$\text{if } A_1 \in V_1 \wedge ... \wedge A_n \in V_n \text{ then } A_{n+1} = a \text{ with } V_i \subseteq D_i \text{ and } a \in D_{n+1}.$$

Conjunctive selectors with $V_i = D_i$ can of course be omitted in a left-hand-side condition. Without loss of generality we assume the target attribute to be A_{n+1}.

A rule description language is defined in more detail by the type of subsets V_i that can be constructed for a left-hand side of a rule. With respect to nominal variables A_i, a basic description language is given by including one-value selectors ($A_i = a$, e.g., *marital status = single*). The first extension also includes negations built with one value, that is, $A \neq a$. The next extension includes any internal disjunction of values ($A_i = a \vee ... \vee b$, e.g., *marital status = single ∨ widowed ∨ divorced*). Dependent on these extensions of the basic description language, the number of potential left-hand-side conditions gets larger, specifically much larger for internal disjunctions.

For an ordinal variable A_i, intervals of values are dynamically constructed by most rule-search algorithms and used as selectors. Several discretization methods are available (see Chapters 14.4 and 18.1).

Decision rules can be applied to different data mining tasks. Besides for classification, which is the main focus of this article, they can also be used for understanding domains and nugget detection. The main reason for this wide application of decision rules is their expressive and easily human-readable representation, as well as the broad range of evaluation and search strategies that can be applied to find rule sets. When using decision rules for classification or prediction purposes, prediction accuracy plays a major role in evaluating rules and rule sets. The prediction accuracy of a rule set can be estimated by applying the rule set for a test set of objects and calculating the relative frequency of correct classifications. Rule searchers mainly differ in the evaluation functions used to rank rules and in search strategies applied to heuristically traverse the space of potential left-hand sides.

A set of rules is first derived in a data mining task and then applied in a subsequent performance task to predict the class to which a new object belongs. Three forms of rule sets can be distinguished: only one rule set that specifically refers to a single distinguished class, a system of k-rule sets where each rule set is related to one of the k-classes, and a single rule set jointly treating all classes. In the first case, the user is only interested in one distinguished class and wants to know whether an object belongs to the class. If no rule of the single rule set can be applied to a new object, the object is predicted not to belong to the class. In the second case, the k-rule sets are typically derived separately one after the other.

Usually a vector of probabilities is connected with a rule where, for each class, the probability is included that an object satisfying the precondition of the rule belongs to the class. The probabilities are estimated with the database calculating the relative frequencies of objects that belong to the class within the preconditional subgroup. The class corresponding to the largest probability in the vector is usually predicted by a rule. When a rule set refers to a distinguished class, the probability is calculated that an object in the subgroup belongs to the class. This probability must be larger than 0.5 for a rule to be applied for classification. For overlapping rules (from k-rule sets or jointly dealing with k-classes), that is, when several rules cover an object, some conflict resolving procedure has to be applied. This can be solved by rules ordered in the form of decision lists, so that the first rule in the given order that is applicable for an object predicts its class, or by a combination of techniques when, for example, the sum of the probability vectors of the competing applicable rules is calculated and the class with the highest resulting probability is predicted.

2. Sequential Covering Approaches

Because of their expressive and easily understandable representation, decision rules are often also applied for classification purposes, making the prediction transparent to the user. In contrast to applications that focus on domain understanding, classification accuracy plays the major role in classification applications and simplicity of the rule set is only a secondary goal. Thus the sequential covering search heuristic of exploring the space of potential rule sets by iteratively searching for a best rule for data still to be uncovered is very attractive for classification applications. The interpretation problems that exist with this approach specifically occur for domain understanding applications. Therefore we concentrate on the sequential covering algorithm in this classification section and only briefly summarize other approaches.

The general control of the sequential covering algorithm is simple: it iteratively searches for the best rule (with some basic best rule search heuristic) and explicitly or implicitly eliminates all objects in the database that are covered by this rule before applying the next iteration step for the remaining data. This is only a greedy hill climbing approach in the space of rule sets without backtracking, which does not guarantee to find the best set of rules. In classification applications, (best) rule sets are assessed primarily by their classification accuracy, but simplicity (e.g., number of rules) also plays a role in avoiding overfitting. Other criteria for assessing rule sets are discussed in Chapter 16.3.1.

Let us use a simple example to demonstrate the interpretation drawbacks of this sequential covering approach. If the first best rule identifies *males*, all males are eliminated from the database, the next rule is searched among the remaining females and, for example, *married* is found as the second best condition for a given target group (for simplicity reasons we assume the same right-hand-side target group in both rules). Because the second rule is found only in the subpopulation of females, it must correctly be presented as a rule for *married females*. However, the rule "if married and female then target group" does not necessarily get the same evaluation in the whole population as the rule "if married then target group" in the subpopulation of females. Both rules have the same probability or certainty (the percentage of married females with the target property within married females), but different reference probabilities (the percentage of persons with the target property within the whole population, respectively the subpopulation of females). Thus the evaluation will be different, if the reference probability is used for the evaluation of a rule.

Also the rule "if married then target group" does not necessarily hold in the whole population. Thus presenting both rules on males and married persons is misleading for the purpose of understanding the domain. Comprehension of the ordered rule set generated can be difficult, because the interpretation of a single rule depends on the other rules that precede it. Nevertheless, for classification, this works when the rules are executed in their generation order for classifying new objects in a classification task. If a new object is a male, the target group is predicted. The second rule is applied only when the first rule is not applicable, that is, it is applied correctly for a married female.

Within this sequential covering approach and the large and noisy data context of data mining, some variations of a heuristic, general-to-specific, and generate-and-test search strategy are applied in the partially ordered space of conditional left-hand-side subgroups to find the best rule (see Chapter 11). We summarize now some of these variants, especially the CN2 (Clark and Niblett, 1989), GoldDigger (Riddle et al., 1994), RIPPER (Cohen, 1995), and PRIM (Friedman and Fisher, 1999) approaches.

The description languages for rules include the much larger search space of internal disjunctions both for CN2 and PRIM; RIPPER allows single-valued selectors that can also be negated. Additionally, RIPPER is applicable for multiple value attributes (see Chapter 4), called set-valued features, constructing selectors such as $red \in color$ or $blue \notin color$. In this case, a single object can have several colors and the first selector defines the set of objects for which at least one color is red.

Whereas the description language defines the set of all potential left-hand-side preconditions, the expansion operator (neighborhood operator) that is used by a general to specific search strategy to construct the specializations of a description, fixes the space of really processed descriptions. Usually one must differentiate between nominal and ordinal variables. Using a nominal expansion variable V that does not yet occur in the current description, specializations are generated by adding for all values v of V a further conjunctive selector $V = v$, or also $V \neq v$ when negations are allowed. If the description language includes internal disjunctions, the description is specialized by eliminating one internal disjunctive term from a selector of the description, including the case that internal disjunctions of all values of the variable V are implicitly given in a selector, which means that V does not really occur in the description. For ordinal expansion variables V, usually the selectors $V < v$, $V > v$ are added for all values v. PRIM uses a more patient discretization, cutting only small upper and lower boundary quantiles (e.g., deciles corresponding to 10 percent) from a current ordinal selector, which, however, is problematic for U-form dependencies.

The expansion operators are applied in steps by a search heuristic, where the first step starts with the most general subgroup of all objects. Usually a hill-climbing or beam-search strategy is used, selecting the best expansion or the best w expansions in case of a beam search with width w at each expansion step. To identify the best expansions and the currently best overall description in an expansion step, a quality function is used for ranking the expanded descriptions. A broad spectrum of quality functions is used by diverse rule generating systems, mainly on a statistical or information theoretic (entropy measure) background.

The next distinction refers to the option of only searching rules for some fixed value of the target variable or treating all values of the target variable in parallel. This option influences the quality function that specifically refers to the distinguished target value when only rules for that value shall be derived. When a symmetric quality function such as entropy is used (not directed to a special selected target value), that target value is associated with the left-hand side of the rule hand, which meets the majority of objects of the left-hand side.

In addition to a quality function, a filter is sometimes used to select only those expanded descriptions (and corresponding rules) that are statistically significant. This implicitly includes a cutoff criterion stopping further specialization when no expanded description generated is statistically significant. Again various significance tests are applied by diverse rule algorithms. Besides statistical significance, some other constraints may be applied by rule finders, for example, that the precondition covers at least a specified minimal number of objects or consists of at most d conjunctions.

The next component of a rule-search procedure is the inclusion of backtracking for modifying the heuristically-found best rule(s) by trying more general preconditions (e.g., eliminating conjunctive terms) to check if they have a still better quality. Due to the heuristic nature of rule searching, not all of these generalizations may have been processed during the previous search.

When the best rules are generated with a separate training data set, statistical pruning approaches check on a test data set if more general rules have a better quality. Thus overfitting is addressed to avoid rules that are too special adapting to the pecularities of the given training data set.

Another distinction refers to the elimination of objects in the sequential covering strategy. Especially when only positive rules (for one value of a target variable) are searched, one can eliminate only the positive examples, which favors selectors that are less correlated to the subgroups already found.

RIPPER developed an optimization method for a rule set. Each rule of the derived rule set is considered in turn and an alternative new rule is constructed from scratch with pruning guided so as to minimize the error rate of the modified rule set. A decision based on the minimum description length heuristic (see Chapter 19.2.1) is then made as to whether the new rule or the original rule is included. This optimization algorithm can be iterated. An overview on these features of rule-finding algorithms as they are applied in some systems is given in Table 1.

3. Other Approaches

We focused in Section 1 on general-to-specific, generate-and-test search heuristics that are dominantly applied in the data mining context of large and noisy data. Especially in the early machine-learning environment concentrating on exact rules classifying training data perfectly, bottom-up search strategies have also been applied. These are mainly directed by a single

Table 1 Comparison of Four Sequential Covering Strategies

Search aspect	(1) CN2	(2) GoldDigger	(3) RIPPER	(4) PRIM
Description language	Internal disjunctions	Positive or negated one-value conjunctions	Positive one-value conjunctions, also set-valued	Internal disjunctions
Expansion (specialization) with nominal variable V	Remove a disjunctive element in a selector	For all values v of V: add conjunctive selector $V = v, V \neq v$	For all values v of nominal (set valued) V $V = v, (V \in v)$	Remove a disjunctive element in a selector
Discretization: specialization with ordinal variable V	User provided subrange values v: $V < v, V > v$	For all occurring values v of V: $V < v, V > v$	For all occurring values v of V: $V < v, V > v$	Remove upper, lower quantile of current interval
Search strategy	Beam search	Hill climber	Hill climber	Hill climber
Backtrack strategy	No	Yes, separate data	Yes, separate data	Yes, separate data
Quality for ranking	Entropy = $-\sum p_i \log p_i$, p_i = targetshare class$_i$	Percentage of positive examples for distinct target value	Information gain	Average of continuous or binary target
Significance test	Likelihood ratio for expected, observed frequency distribution	No	No	No
Other constraints	No	Precondition: at least p positive exps	No	Precondition: at least p examples
Refinement of rule set	No	No	Optimizing, pruning rule set	No

positive example, that is, apply example-driven search strategies (as opposed to generate-and-test strategies). The main problem with these example-driven strategies is that the examples can mislead the search when they are noisy. AQ (Michalski, 1969) is a very prominant representative of example-driven (but general-to-specific) approaches. Within the family of AQ algorithms, some extensions also deal with noisy data (Michalski et al., 1986), but are not so appropriate for large data sets.

Another approach not using the sequential covering technique is based on association rules (Liu et al., 1998). In the first step all association rules (see Chapter 16.2.3) are found that have as a right-hand-side conclusion a simple selector built with the given target attribute (for a selected confidence and low support parameter). In the second step, these rules are hierarchically ordered by first using confidence and then support values. In the next iteration, which similar to the sequential covering approach eliminates all covered objects, a subset of the association rules is identified that is used as final rule set for classification. Results are reported that show some better classification accuracy than those induced by the sequential covering approach.

CWS (Domingos, 1996) dynamically interleaves rule induction and performance evaluation of a current rule set. Thus, a new rule (which can also be a refinement of an existing rule) is not evaluated independently from the rules already found, but the accuracy of the rule set consisting of the current rules and the new rule is assessed, and that new rule is added to the current rule set that achieves the highest increase in evaluation.

4. Time Complexity and Performance

To assess the applicability of rule searching in very large databases, analyzing time complexity of rule searchers is important. Most comparisons use decision-tree methods or CN2 as a reference. The C4.5 system (Quinlan, 1993) generates rules from decision trees (see Chapter 16.1.3) by statistical postpruning of decision trees. C4.5 has been empirically observed to require $O(N^3)$ computation time, dependent on the number of objects N of the database (Cohen, 1995). For CWS, a time complexity of $O(N)$ is claimed (Domingos, 1996) and a better accuracy on large data sets than C4.5RULES and CN2 has been empirically shown. RIPPER is competitive with C4.5 in accuracy, but has time complexity of $O(N \log N)$.

But the number A of attributes is also important for analyzing time complexity. A worst case bound for CN2 is given by $O(N^2 A^2 W)$ with beam width W. $O(NA^2)$ is also reported for C4.5 when there are no numeric attributes (no discretization). Some pruned, near-exhaustive search methods (Segal and Etzioni, 1994) cause running time to become exponential in A. Thus often an efficient preselection of attributes would be necessary to ensure time-efficient rule discoveries.

These figures are only approximate values to assess the appropriateness of a rule searching method for a given very large data set. A comprehensive, detailed, and authoritative comparative study of time complexity and other performance figures—for example—accuracy, is still missing.

References

Clark, P. and T. Niblett. 1989. "The CN2 induction algorithm." *Machine Learning* **3**: 261–284.

Cohen, W. 1995. "Fast effective rule induction." *Proceedings of the Twelfth International Conference on Machine Learning*, pp. 115–123. Tahoe City, CA: Morgan-Kaufmann.

Domingos, P. 1996. "Linear time rule induction." *Proceedings of the Second International Conference on Knowledge Discovery and Data Mining*, pp. 96–101. Menlo Park, CA: AAAI Press.

Friedman, J. and N. Fisher. 1999. "Bump hunting in high-dimensional data." *Stat. Comput.* **9(2)**: 1–20.

Liu, B., W. Hsu, and Y. Ma. 1998. "Integrating classification and association rule mining." *Proceedings of the Fourth International Conference on Knowledge Discovery and Data Mining*, pp. 80–86. Menlo Park, CA: AAAI Press.

Michalski, R. S. 1969. "On the quasi-minimal solution of the general covering problem." *Proceedings of the First International Symposium on Information Processing*, pp. 125–128. Bled, Yugoslavia.

Michalski, R. S., I. Mozetic, J. Hong, and H. Lavrac. 1986. "The multi-purpose incremental learning system AQ15 and its testing application in three medical domains." *Proceedings of the Fifth National Conference on AI*, pp. 619–625. Seattle, WA: AAAI Press.

Quinlan, J. R. 1993. *C4.5: Programs for Machine Learning*. San Mateo, CA: Morgan-Kaufmann.

Riddle, P., R. Segal, and O. Etzioni. 1994. "Representation design and brute-force induction in a Boeing manufacturing domain." *Appl. Artificial Intell.* **8**: 125–147.

Segal, R. and O. Etzioni. 1994. "Learning decision lists using homogeneous rules." *Proceedings of the Twelfth National Conference on AI*, pp. 1041–1045. Philadelphia: Morgan-Kaufmann.

16.1.5 Bayesian Classification

Nir Friedman and Ronny Kohavi

ABSTRACT Bayesian classification addresses the classification problem by learning the distribution of instances given different class values. We review the basic notion of Bayesian classification, describe in some detail the naive Bayesian classifier, and briefly discuss some extensions.

1. Introduction

The goal of classification (see Chapter 16.1.1) is to classify an instance to a class based on the value of several attributes. Many approaches to classification attempt to explicitly construct a function from the joint set of values of the attributes to class labels. Example of such classifiers include decision trees (see Chapter 16.1.3), decision rules (see Chapter 16.1.4), and neural networks (see Chapter 16.1.8).

Bayesian classification takes a somewhat different approach to this problem. In this approach, we approximate the joint probability distribution of the class and the attributes: $\Pr(C, A_1, ..., A_k)$, where C is a random variable describing the class, and $A_1, ..., A_k$ are random variables describing the attributes. Thus, learning in Bayesian classification amounts to estimation of this joint probability distribution. After we construct such an estimate, we classify a new instance by examining the conditional probability of C given the particular attribute values, and returning the class that is most probable.

The standard approach to Bayesian classification uses the chain rule to decompose the joint distribution:

$$\Pr(C, A_1, ..., A_k) = \Pr(C) \Pr(A_1, ..., A_k \mid C). \tag{1}$$

The first term on the right-hand side of (1) is the prior probability of the class labels which can be directly estimated from the training data, or from a larger sample of the population. For example, we can often get statistics on the number of breast cancer occurrences in the general population. The second term on the right-hand side of (1) is the distribution of attribute values given the class label. The estimation of this term is usually more complex, and we elaborate on it below.

Once we have an estimate of $\Pr(C)$ and $\Pr(A_1, ..., A_k \mid C)$ we can use Bayes rule to get the conditional probability of the class given the attributes:

$$\Pr(C \mid A_1, ..., A_k) = \alpha \Pr(C) \Pr(A_1, ..., A_k \mid C), \tag{2}$$

where α is a normalization factor that ensures that the conditional probability of all possible class labels sums up to 1. (In practice, we do not need to explicitly evaluate this factor because it is constant for a given instance.) Using (2) we can classify new instances by combining the prior probability of each class with the probability of the given attribute values given that class.

2. Properties of Bayesian Classifiers

Bayesian classification does not attempt to learn an explicit decision rule. Instead, learning reduces to estimating probabilities. As a consequence there are some differences compared to other approaches to classification. In this section, we briefly touch on the main ones.

A basic property that we often require is asymptotic correctness; the classification system should learn the best possible classifier if we provide it with a sufficient number of training instances, ignoring computational limitation.

It can be shown that induction of a Bayesian classifier is asymptotically optimal (i.e., reaches the smallest possible classification error given a sufficiently large training set) if the method of estimating $Pr(A_1, ..., A_k \mid C)$ is consistent, that is, will converge to the true underlying conditional distribution given a sufficiently large sample. Thus, the asymptotic properties depend on our choice of methods for estimating $Pr(A_1, ..., A_k \mid C)$. Note that in contrast to some learning methods, in Bayesian classification it is possible that the class of hypotheses we consider contains an optimal classifier, and yet we would not learn it even with an infinite amount of data. This can happen if the probabilistic model that corresponds to this optimal classification rule does not provide the best approximation to the observed probability distribution.

This asymptotic guarantee suggests that if our knowledge about the domain leads us to believe that a particular model (i.e., class of hypotheses) for $Pr(A_1, ..., A_k \mid C)$ allows for a good approximation of the true distribution, then we would expect the Bayesian classifier to perform well. On the other hand, this does not imply that an unrealistic model that does not give good approximation to the distribution is necessarily a bad classifier. For example, the model used in the naive Bayesian classifier of the next section makes unrealistic assumptions, yet often leads to competitive classification performance (Domingos and Pazzani, 1997).

Probabilistic semantics of Bayesian classification yield several advantages over other methods.

First, Bayesian classification can be combined with methods for dealing with asymmetric loss functions. For example, in cancer screening, a misdiagnosis of a malignant tumor is more costly than a misdiagnosis of a benign tumor, since the detection of cancer at an early stage can dramatically improve the chances of curing the cancer. To deal with such situations, we can rely on decision theory to provide methods for combining probability estimates with the utility (or cost) of different decisions. See, for example, Duda and Hart (1973) and Bishop (1995).

Second, probabilistic methods provide methods for dealing with missing values. Probability theory allows us to deal with missing values in classification by averaging over the possible values that the attribute might have taken. For example, if the value of A_1 is not provided, then the probability of $Pr(A_2, ..., A_k \mid C)$ is $\sum_{x \in DOM(A_1)} Pr(A_1 = x, A_2, ..., A_k \mid C)$. Using Bayes rule we can then compute the conditional probability $Pr(C \mid A_2, ..., A_k)$ for classification. Similar considerations apply training with missing values as well, although these come at some computational cost; see Dempster et al. (1977) and Gelman et al. (1995). We note that this approach assumes that the values are missing at random, that is, that the process by which these values were removed does not depend on the actual missing values, given the values we do observe (Rubin, 1976). When this assumption is not reasonable, then we have to either include a model of this hiding process (i.e., the probability that the values are missing) or use other approaches (see below).

Finally, probabilistic methods allow for use of prior knowledge and for combining knowledge from other sources. Probabilistic semantics provide a clear way of using prior knowledge about the domain, and knowledge gathered from other sources (e.g., different training data) in the classification process. This knowledge can be used in various ways. For instance, prior knowledge may determine the type of model we use for estimating $Pr(A_1, ..., A_k \mid C)$. In speech recognition, for example, the attributes are measurements of the speech signal, and the probabilistic model is a *hidden Markov model* (Rabiner, 1990) that is usually composed from phoneme models. This highly structured model is motivated by our prior knowledge on speech. Note that the choice of model usually reflects our knowledge about the process that generated the observations. In contrast, choice of model class (e.g., decision trees vs. neural networks) in other classification methods usually depends on the type of decision surface we expect to learn and the amount of data we can learn with. Depending on the domain, either way of thinking of the choice of models can be more natural.

Prior knowledge can be also used in other ways. For example, it can be used to determine our prior estimate of probabilities. This leads to shifting our estimate toward specific values. If training data for a particular parameter of the model are sparse, then the final estimate is heavily dependent on the prior, and if there is sufficient training data, then the final estimate is usually not sensitive to the prior. Additionally, the probabilistic semantic, and the representation tools (such as probabilistic networks; see Chapter 16.6, and Pearl, 1988) allow the combination of learning with modeling assumptions and knowledge about the domain. That is, we might fix part of the model in advance and learn the other parts.

3. The Naive Bayesian Classifier

We now turn to the question of estimating $\Pr(A_1, ..., A_k \mid C)$. This is a density estimation problem, since we are attempting to learn the probability distribution of the attributes among all the instances with the same label. We first note that we cannot use counting to estimate this probability because most of the counts will be zero.

To see this, suppose that all the attributes are binary. Then there are 2^k possible assignments to the attributes, and even for a moderate number of attributes, we do not expect to see most of these assignments in the training data.

One way of addressing this problem, is to use the so-called *naive Bayesian classifier* (Duda and Hart, 1973; Langley et al., 1992), sometimes called the *simple Bayesian classifier* (Domingos and Pazzani, 1997). We assume that each attribute is independent of the rest, given the value of the class. We easily establish that, given this assumption, we can write

$$\Pr(A_1, ..., A_k \mid C) = \Pr(A_1 \mid C) \cdot \Pr(A_2 \mid C) \cdots \Pr(A_k \mid C). \tag{3}$$

Now the estimation problem is easier, since we need to estimate the probability of each attribute, given the class, independently of the rest. Combining (2) and (3), we get the naive Bayesian classier classification rule:

$$\Pr(C \mid A_1, ..., A_k) = \alpha \Pr(C) \, \Pr(A_1 \mid C) \cdots \Pr(A_k \mid C), \tag{4}$$

where, again, α is a normalization constant.

The probabilities above are estimated from the training set and the posterior probability for each class is computed. The prediction is made for the class with the largest posterior probability. The model works well in areas where the conditional independence assumption is likely to hold, such as medical domains (Kononenko, 1993). In recent years, the model has been found to be very robust and continues to perform well even in the face of obvious violations of this conditional independence assumption (Domingos and Pazzani, 1997; Kohavi and Sommerfield, 1995; Friedman, 1997).

Estimating the probabilities can be done using simple frequency counts, but this creates problems if the counts of an attribute and a class are zero because assigning a probability of zero to one of the terms, $\Pr(A_i \mid C)$ causes the whole expression to evaluate to zero and rule out a class. This is especially problematic when attributes have many values and the distribution is sparse: several (or even all) classes get a probability of zero. Several methods have been proposed to overcome this issue. The zero probability can be replaced by a small constant, such as $0.5/n$ or $\Pr(C)/n$, where n is the number of instances in the training set (Clark and Niblett, 1989; Kohavi et al., 1997b). Another, more theoretically justified, approach is to apply a generalized Laplace correction (Cestnik, 1990; Kohavi et al., 1997a).

Unknown (missing, null) values are commonly handled in one of two ways. In evaluating the probabilities $\Pr(A_i \mid C)$, when A_i is unknown, one can simply ignore the term,

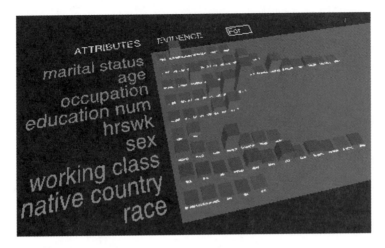

Figure 1 Visualization of naive Bayes in MineSet™ (see Chapter 24.2.4), showing U.S. census data for working adults. The attributes are sorted by their discrimination power. For each continuous attribute the range is discretized. For each value (or range), the bar height shows the evidence (log of the conditional probability). In this case, the label chosen in the GUI was gross income over $50,000. The high bars indicate that there is most evidence for people to earn over $50,000 when they satisfy one or more of the following criteria: they are married; their age is between 36 and 61; their occupation is executive managerial or professional specialist; they are highly educated; they work over 40 hours a week, etc.

which is equivalent to marginalizing over the attribute, something done in MLC++ (see Chapter 24.1.2; Kohavi et al., 1997b). Another alternative is to estimate the probabilities from unknown values in the data. The second alternative works better if there is a special meaning to a missing value (e.g., a blank entry for the army rank of a person usually indicates the person did not serve in the army).

An important advantage of naive Bayes is that the simple structure lends itself to comprehensible visualizations (Becker et al., 1997; Kononenko, 1993). Figure 1 shows an example of visualization used in MineSet (Silicon Graphics, 1998; Brunk et al., 1997).

As can be expected from the form of (4), the decision surfaces learned by the naive Bayesian classifier are of limited form. In particular, if the attributes are binary, then it is easy to show that the decision between any two classes is made by a hyperplane. (A linear decision surface also occurs when the attributes are nominal and the conditional distributions are Gaussians.) This fact has been known since the 1960s, for example, Duda and Hart (1973), and has been frequently rediscovered. Notice, however, that the decision rule learned by the naive Bayesian classifier would not, in general, coincide with the ones learned by other linear methods, such as perceptrons.

4. Alternative Approaches

There are several possible extensions of Bayesian classification beyond the naive Bayesian classifier. These works fall into several categories.

Work in the first category, such as that of Langley and Sage (1994) and of Kohavi and John (1997), attempted to improve classification accuracy by restricting attention to only a subset of the attributes. This approach can reduce errors due to a strong correlation among attributes by removing one or more of the correlated attributes.

Work in the second category (Ezawa and Schuermann, 1995; Friedman et al., 1997; Kononenko, 1991; Pazzani, 1995; Sahami, 1996) attempts to improve classification accuracy by removing some of the independence assumptions made in the naive Bayesian classifier. It turns

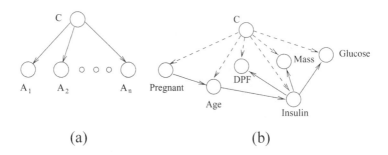

(a)   (b)

Figure 2 Description of two Bayesian classifiers for diabetes type classification using the probabilistic network representation: (a) the naive Bayesian classifier, (b) a TAN model learned from data. The dashed lines are those edges required by the naive Bayesian classifier. The solid lines are the dependency edges between attributes that were learned by Friedman et al.'s algorithm

out that probabilistic networks (also known as Bayesian networks) provide a useful language to describe such independencies. Friedman et al. (1997) discuss several ways of using these networks for Bayesian classification. Figure 2(a) shows how the naive Bayesian classifier is represented as a probabilistic network.

For brevity, we will briefly describe one of these approaches that Friedman et al. (1997) call the tree-augmented naive Bayesian classifier, or TAN, which is based on ideas that go back to Chow and Liu (1968). In this approach, instead of assuming that each attribute is independent of the rest, we allow each one to depend on, at most, one other attribute. An example of such a dependency structure, in a probabilistic network notation, is shown in Figure 2(b). The choice of these dependencies implies a different decomposition of the attributes' joint distribution. For example, the decomposition corresponding to the network shown in Figure 2(b) is

$$\Pr(P, A, I, D, M, G \mid C) = \Pr(P \mid C)\Pr(A \mid P, C)\Pr(I \mid A, C)\Pr(D \mid I, C)\Pr(M \mid I, C)\Pr(G \mid I, C),$$

where we use the obvious abbreviation for each attribute name. In this augmented dependency structure, an edge from A_i to A_j implies that the influence of A_i on the assessment of the class variable also depends on the value of A_j. For example, in Figure 2(b), the influence of the attribute "Glucose" on the class C depends on the value of "Insulin", while in the naive Bayesian classifier the influence of each attribute on the class variable is independent of other attributes. These edges affect the classification process in that a value of "Glucose" that is typically surprising (i.e., $\Pr(g \mid c)$ is low) may be unsurprising if the value of its correlated attribute, Insulin, is also unlikely (i.e., $\Pr(g \mid c, i)$ is high). In this situation, the naive Bayesian classifier will overpenalize the probability of the class variable by considering two unlikely observations, while the augmented network of Figure 2(b) will not.

We are now faced with the question of how to choose the dependency arcs. Friedman et al. (1997) describe a procedure that finds the decomposition function that maximizes the likelihood (see Chapter 8) of the data. In addition, this procedure has attractive computational properties, its running time is linear in the number of training instances and quadratic in the number of attributes, k. The TAN method is a compromise between the complexity of the learned model and the generalization ability and computational cost of learning the model. Because only pairwise interactions are modeled directly, the learned model only requires estimates of pairs of attributes, which are relatively robust and efficient to compute. It is clear that in some domains other points on this trade-off might be explored. In general, for more complex models, it is NP-hard to find the maximal likelihood structure, and thus we need to resort to some heuristic search.

Finally, in the last category there are approaches that use domain-specific models. For example, speech recognition (Rabiner, 1990) and protein classification (Durbin et al., 1998) use specialized hidden Markov models to learn the distribution of the observed attributes (sound-wave frequencies and amino acids). Approaches in these categories rely on knowledge of special structure in the domain to construct the density estimates.

References

Becker, B., R. Kohavi, and D. Sommerfield. 1997. "Visualizing the simple bayesian classifier." *KDD Workshop on Issues in the Integration of Data Mining and Data Visualization*. Menlo Park, CA: AAAI Press.

Bishop, C. M. 1995. *Neural Networks for Pattern Recognition*. Oxford: Oxford University Press.

Brunk, C., J. Kelly, and R. Kohavi. 1997. "MineSet: an integrated system for data mining." *Proceedings of the Third International Conference on Knowledge Discovery and Data Mining*, edited by D. Heckerman, H. Mannila, D. Pregibon, and R. Uthurusamy, pp. 135–138. Menlo Park, CA: AAAI Press. Also available at: http://mineset.sgi.com.

Cestnik, B. 1990. "Estimating probabilities: a crucial task in machine learning." *Proceedings of the Ninth European Conference on Artificial Intelligence*, edited by C. Aiello, pp. 147–149. San Francisco, CA: Morgan Kaufmann.

Chow, C. K. and C. N. Liu. 1968. "Approximating discrete probability distributions with dependence trees." *IEEE Trans. on Inform. Theory* **14**: 462–467.

Clark, P. and T. Niblett. 1989. "The CN2 induction algorithm." *Machine Learning* **3(4)**: 261–283.

Dempster, A. P., N. M. Laird, and D. B. Rubin. 1977. "Maximum likelihood from incomplete data via the EM algorithm." *J. R. Stat. Soc.* **B39**: 1–39.

Domingos, P. and M. Pazzani. 1997. "Beyond independence: conditions for the optimality of the simple Bayesian classifier." *Machine Learning* **29(2/3)**: 103–130.

Duda, R. and P. Hart. 1973. *Pattern Classification and Scene Analysis*. New York, NY: Wiley.

Durbin, R., S. Eddy, A. Krogh, and G. Mitchison. 1998. *Biological Sequence Analysis: Probabilistic Models of Proteins and Nucleic Acids*. Cambridge: Cambridge University Press.

Ezawa, K. J. and T. Schuermann. 1995. "Fraud/uncollectable debt detection using a Bayesian network based learning system: a rare binary outcome with mixed data structures." *Proceedings of the Eleventh Conference on Uncertainty in Artificial Intelligence (UAI '95)*, edited by P. Besnard and S. Hanks, pp. 157–166. San Francisco, CA: Morgan Kaufmann.

Friedman, J. H. 1997. "On bias, variance, 0/1-loss, and the curse of dimensionality." *Data Mining and Knowledge Discovery* **1(1)**: 55–77.

Friedman, N., D. Geiger, and M. Goldszmidt. 1997. "Bayesian network classifiers." *Machine Learning* **29**: 131–163.

Gelman, A., J. B. Carlin, H. S. Stern, and D. B. Rubin. 1995. *Bayesian Data Analysis*. London: Chapman & Hall.

Kohavi, R. and G. H. John. 1997. "Wrappers for feature subset selection." *Artificial Intell.* **97(1–2)**: 273–324.

Kohavi, R. and D. Sommerfield. 1995. "Feature subset selection using the wrapper model: overfitting and dynamic search space topology." *The First International Conference on Knowledge Discovery and Data Mining*, pp. 192–197.

Kohavi, R., B. Becker, and D. Sommerfield. 1997a. "Improving simple bayes." *The Ninth European Conference on Machine Learning, Poster Papers*. New York: Springer-Verlag.

Kohavi, R., D. Sommerfield, and J. Dougherty. 1997b. "Data mining using MLC++: a machine learning library in C++." *Int. J. Artificial Intell. Tools* **6(4)**: 537–566.

Kononenko, I. 1991. "Semi-naive Bayesian classifier." *Proceedings of the Sixth European Working Session on Learning*, edited by Kodratoff, pp. 206–219. Berlin: Springer-Verlag.

Kononenko, I. 1993. "Inductive and Bayesian learning in medical diagnosis." *Appl. Artificial Intell.* **7**: 317–337.

Langley, P. and S. Sage. 1994. "Induction of selective Bayesian classifiers." *Proceedings of the Tenth Conference on Uncertainty in Artificial Intelligence*, pp. 399–406. Seattle: Morgan Kaufmann.

Langley, P., W. Iba, and K. Thompson. 1992. "An analysis of Bayesian classifiers." *Proceedings of the Tenth National Conference on Artificial Intelligence*, pp. 223–228. Menlo Park, CA: AAAI Press and MIT Press.

Pazzani, M. J. 1995. "Searching for dependencies in Bayesian classifiers." *Proceedings of the Fifth International Workshop on Artificial Intelligence and Statistics*, edited by D. Fisher and H. Lenz. New York: Springer-Verlag.

Pearl, J. 1988. *Probabilistic Reasoning in Intelligent Systems*. San Mateo, CA: Morgan Kaufmann.

Rabiner, L. R. 1990. "A tutorial on hidden Markov models and selected applications in speech recognition." *Proc. IEEE* **77(2)**: 257–286.

Rubin, D. R. 1976. "Inference and missing data." *Biometrica* **63**: 581–592.

Sahami, M. 1996. "Learning limited dependence Bayesian classifiers." *KDD-96: Proceedings of the Second International Conference on Knowledge Discovery and Data Mining*, pp. 335–338. Menlo Park, CA: AAAI Press.

Silicon Graphics. 1998. *MineSet User's Guide*: Silicon Graphics Inc. Available at: http://mineset.sgi.com.

16.1.6 Nearest-Neighbor Approaches

Belur V. Dasarathy

ABSTRACT   This article discusses the role and significance of nearest-neighbor (NNR)[1] approaches (and its conceptual equivalents in the field of artificial intelligence, such as instance-based learning, lazy learning, memory-based reasoning, case-based reasoning, and the like) in the data mining and knowledge discovery process. The presentation first traces the development of NNR approaches from its origins in the early fifties to the present day with appropriate historical references. In the context of data mining applications, which necessarily involve large databases, computational concerns become a major issue and NNR techniques are particularly vulnerable in this sphere. Accordingly, this aspect of NNR techniques is discussed next in great detail to provide a panoramic view of the latest developments in this area. The associated issues of attribute selection and weighting are also addressed. This is followed by an overview of the different metrics that have been proposed in the literature to meet the special needs of the data mining community in contrast to the traditional Euclidean metric and its variants such as the Manhattan (city-block) distance generally employed in the pattern recognition field. A brief but direct discussion on the well-recognized problem of the curse of dimensionality is offered next, although this subject matter is indirectly covered in prior subsections. The article concludes with a brief closing summation of the objective and scope of the presentation highlighting some of the outstanding issues in this arena.

1. Introduction

Data mining, the precursor to the knowledge discovery process, is accomplished by a variety of means, many of which had their origins in statistics and subsequently in the field of pattern recognition. Within this statistical pattern recognition domain, nearest neighbor (NNR) approaches (Dasarathy, 1991) hold a unique status. They represent a bridge between the parametric techniques that require *a priori* knowledge of the distributions underlying the various categories of data (pattern classes) and nonparametric techniques, which presuppose the functional form of the discriminant surfaces separating the different pattern classes. The importance of NNR techniques to the field of data mining and knowledge discovery has been brought out in many of the survey articles in the area by Fayyad and associates (Fayyad, 1996; Fayyad et al., 1996a,b). Books on data mining (Berson and Smith, 1997) almost invariably include NNR techniques as an essential part of their repertoire. Indeed, commercial packages for data mining applications such as Darwin[R] (a product of Thinking Machines Corporation) have incorporated NNR techniques as part of their suite under the name memory-based reasoning (MBR) (Waltz and Kasif, 1995). MBR is one terminology among the many used in the artificial intelligence community to represent a conceptual generalization of the NNR concept that had its roots in the pattern recognition world. This generalization offered by MBR

---

[1] Nearest neighbor is generally abbreviated as NN. However, to avoid the confusion between this and neural network discussed elsewhere in the handbook, we have chosen the modified acronym NNR.

Figure 1 A two-class, two-attribute scenario with an as yet unidentified data record

is in terms of flexibility of adaptive distance metric and local interpolating functions (which are not common under traditional NNR techniques). In the image data mining context, NNR techniques have been rejuvenated as techniques for similarity retrieval. A review of these, by White and Jain, is available as a university technical report (White and Jain, 1996).

In layman's terms, NNR techniques can be aptly described by the adage: Judge a person by the company (s)he keeps. This translates into a practical tool by which an incoming data record gets categorized on the basis of its nearness or similarity to the data records previously collected and identified in the knowledge base. This is illustrated in Figure 1, which shows multiple data records each with two attributes that are representations of two classes of data. The unknown incoming data record, shown as a question mark lies closest to a data record from Class 1 (star symbol) and the NNR rule accordingly assigns it to Class 1.

NNR techniques originated conceptually from the parametric domain in the works of Fix and Hodges (1951, 1952) in the early fifties. However, in practice, these NNR techniques require no *a priori* knowledge of the probabilistic models of the pattern classes. While in that sense they are akin to the nonparametric tools, unlike them, they need no assumptions on the shape of the discriminant functions. Additionally they have asymptotic error bounds expressible in terms of the theoretically minimum Bayes error (Cover and Hart, 1967). There are indeed extensive studies on the topic of error estimation in the context of NNR techniques (see for example, chapters 1 and 4 in Dasarathy, 1991) but these are not discussed here as they are outside the immediate scope of this article.

Nearest-neighbor techniques, since their first birth in the early 1950s, have been reincarnated in the artificial intelligence (AI) community under a variety of names including instance-based learning algorithms (Aha et al., 1991), lazy learning (Aha, 1997), memory-based learning (Dietterich et al., 1994), case-based reasoning (CBR) (Kolodner, 1993), the latter term often being encountered in the context of industrial applications (Miyashita, 1994; Miyashita and Sycara, 1995). As is to be expected, each of these reincarnations has developed its own mutations, resulting in numerous studies under each nomenclature. MBR is viewed as a means of combining the merits of CBR with those of more traditional probabilistic reasoning (Pearl, 1993).

The basic principle of the NNR approach is that an unknown entity or data case is best assigned to the category that is closest to it in a suitably defined information (data/attribute) space under an appropriate metric. We shall address the question of appropriate metric a little later on in this article. A variety of modifications to this basic principle or rule have been proposed in the literature (see chapters 1, 2, and 3 in Dasarathy, 1991), the simplest of which, analyzed by Patrick and Fischer (1970) is the use of k-nearest-neighbors (instead of just a single) in making the decision. This involves maintaining a roster of k-nearest-neighbors during the search process instead of a single one and at the end of the search process identify the majority class within the final list of k-nearest-neighbors. Referring back to Figure 1, if we choose k to be 3, it is easy to see that the unidentified data record has among its three nearest neighbors two from Class 2 and one from Class 1. Accordingly the 3-NNR rule would assign the data record to Class 2, while the 1-NNR rule had assigned it to Class 1. Such a contrasting behavior does not occur in general when the value of k is changed from 1 to 3 and the example is contrived only to illustrate the possibility of such a change. Obviously the use of multiple neighbors has its advantages and disadvantages. The advantage is that it places less reliance on a single data record that could be corrupted in some fashion and hence is likely to be more robust than the single NNR rule. This is clearly the case in the example shown in Figure 1. The flip side of it is that it is computationally more expensive. Also, one cannot increase k indefinitely without considering the number of data records available in the database. Obviously k has to be small relative to the total number of records. For example, consider the limiting case of k being increased to the maximum, that is, to the total number of data records in the knowledge base. Then the NNR based class assignment would be decided purely on the basis of which class has the maximum representation in the knowledge base and the actual location of the data record in the attribute space becomes irrelevant, which of course makes the decision process meaningless. Studies dealing with this issue in more detail (choice of k relative to the size of the knowledge base) are available in the literature and are beyond the scope of this survey, which at the editor's directive, is being kept at an elementary level. An early interesting variation of the k-NNR rule was the weighted k-NNR rule by Dudani (1976) wherein the votes of the neighbors are weighted inversely according to their distances from the data point under consideration. That is, the closer the neighbor, the greater its influence on the decision, an intuitively acceptable variation. Applying this to the example shown in Figure 1, the decision becomes a close call and depends on the actual distances of the neighbors, the metric used, and the specifics of the weighting scheme. There are very many studies in the literature aimed at improving the performance of NNR techniques. A recent example is that of Djouadi (1998), that studies the NNR performance in terms of its finite sample size risk (the risk associated with the finiteness of the training sample set) relative to the asymptotic risk (the best possible performance given an infinite training set). This is based on a 2-NN rule previously proposed by Fukunaga and Flick (1985) to eliminate the first order effects of samples in the NNR risk estimation. NNR techniques have also been employed in conjunction with other classifiers under an innovative composite classifier construct (Dasarathy and Sheela, 1979), which permits a dynamic selection of the NNR classifier only when required through an optimal partitioning of the attribute space learned in a prior training phase. This can be best appreciated looking at Figure 2, wherein, as before, multiple data records each with two attributes which belong to two different classes are shown plotted using two different symbols. If the two classes were well separated with no overlap, then one could conceive of a single line or simple curve separating the two groups. However, in a real-world situation, this is rarely the case. In such cases, one can conceive of a pair of lines as shown therein, that partitions the attribute space such that the overlapping areas are bounded by a pair of straight lines (or hyper planes). One needs to employ the computationally more expensive NNR tool only when the incoming to-be-identified data record falls within this overlapping area and the rest of the time, when the incoming data record falls outside this domain, it gets automatically tagged by the label corresponding to that subspace. The determination of the position of these lines in the attribute space is structured as an optimization problem that aims to minimize the number of data records within the bounded

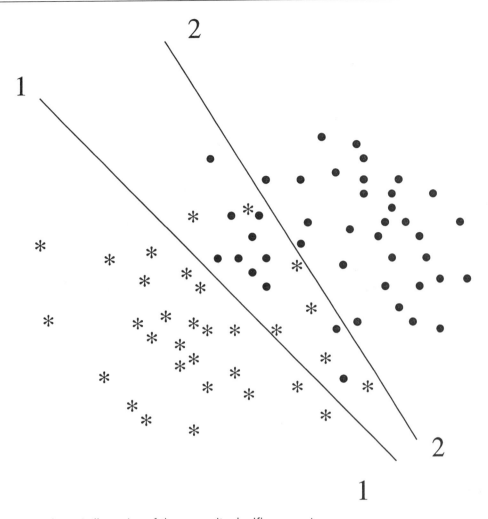

Figure 2 Illustration of the composite classifier concept

domain. This minimizes the need for the NNR tool as well as the burden thereof when its use becomes unavoidable. The computational burden associated with NNR techniques is discussed in more detail in the next section.

It is clear that the accuracy of the decision provided by NNR in terms of identification of the category of the incoming data record is dependent upon the correctness of the identity of the individual data records in the knowledge base. If the identity of the data records in the knowledge base were of questionable accuracy, then this would have a direct impact on the quality of the decisions made by NNR. NNR techniques have been developed to address this problem of imperfectly or incorrectly designated data records in the knowledge base. This is particularly critical in the context of data mining applications (more so than in classical pattern recognition applications), since manual data entry (a prime source for errors) is likely at various points in the network linked to the database. The first such study was by Whitney and Dwyer (1966) who assessed the performance of NNR classifiers under such imperfect learning, assuming that the probability of correctness was at least greater than half in a two-class environment. Later studies include that of Joussellin and Dubuisson (1987) who reported on a method to tackle the problem of learning in imperfectly known environments in the context of knowledge-based system design and hence could be of particular interest to the data mining community. The NNR method has also been extended to cover more complex problem environments involving data categories for which no representatives are available within the database. This is a realistic problem in the data mining arena since new categories not foreseen by the designer may show up in the operational phase after the system has been designed and put into operation. This is known in pattern recognition literature as learning and classification in partially exposed environments. That is one is operating in an environment which initially is only partially known (in terms of the categories of records) to the user and new categories may surface during the operational phase. This problem has been studied in the context of NNR techniques, among others, by Dasarathy in a series of papers, exemplified by the neighborhood census rule (NCR) (Dasarathy, 1980a) and the alien rule (Dasarathy, 1980b). NCR admits into the k-NNR voting procedure only those data records adjudged acceptable on the basis of a qualifying test designed *a priori* using the training database. The alien rule is more adaptive in that it employs a complementary concept to those used in all the prior studies and explores the neighborhood of the data point to identify the subset in whose neighborhood the data under consideration appears. This permits the user to adaptively define different thresholds in different regions of the attribute space rather than being forced to employ a single global threshold in the entire decision space, as was the case under most other previous studies of this nature. For additional information on the tools employed for learning in imperfectly and/ or imprecisely defined environments, the reader can look up chapters 1 and 5 in the NNR book (Dasarathy, 1991). Nearest-neighbor based techniques (Dasarathy, 1996) have also been employed for fusion of information from multiple data sources (multiple databases). Nearest-neighbor techniques have also been conceptually linked (Denoeux, 1995) to evidential reasoning concepts such as Dempster–Shafer theory, which helps in handling uncertainty and imperfect knowledge within the training database. NNR techniques have also been implemented as forms of neural networks, for example multilayer perceptrons (Smyth, 1992).

2. Computational Concerns

One of the major issues associated with the use of NNR techniques, especially in the context of large databases that is common in the domain of data mining and knowledge discovery, is their computational demands. Each time, an incoming data record has to be labeled, the system has to compute its distance (or inversely its similarity) to all the data records in the knowledge base. This is essential to be able to identify the one (or more) nearest (or most similar) data record(s), depending on the specific type of k-NNR technique employed. This represents an enormous computational burden, especially in data mining applications wherein the knowledge base accumulated over periods of time can be very large indeed. This problem has been addressed at length in NNR literature, (see chapters 1, 6, and 7 in Dasarathy, 1991) over the years through two fundamentally different approaches.

One approach has been development of algorithmic innovations that reduce the computational effort needed to identify the nearest-neighbor(s). There is vast literature in this field as surveyed in the compendium on NNR techniques (Dasarathy, 1991). Most involve · some innovative algorithmic constructs of ordering the search database and organizing a dynamic search that can take advantage of this pre-ordering and thereby avoid having to compute distances to each and every data record in the knowledge base. These approaches do incur the overhead of pre-ordering the database as well as of the cost of organizing the dynamic search process. The trade-off of the savings achieved versus these overhead costs vary from application to application depending on the number of categories, number of attributes, number of data records in each category, and so on. Each of the approaches proposed in the literature has a different trade-off in terms of these parameters and a discussion thereof is beyond the scope of this brief survey. Suffice to say that such a trade-off has to be evaluated in the context of one's application environment. Some recent examples of these innovations include a branch-and-bound approach by Mico et al. (1996), a relative-distances-based tree construct by Portegys (1995), a set of four alternative schemes by Grother et al. (1997) and a feature-space partitioning scheme by Djouadi and Bouktache (1997). A complexity analysis of partitioning NNR search algorithms has been reported by Zakarauskas and Ozard (1996). This issue has also been addressed in the context of memory-based reasoning by Greene (1994), who proposed a scheme for efficient retrieval from sparse associative memory, that is, the data is spread sparsely in the attribute space. It should be noted that many of these techniques are closely linked to the specific type of metric employed for the closeness measure and hence not effective under a change in the metric employed.

The other major avenue for addressing the computational issue is that of reducing the number of prototypes for representation of the different classes within the database. Within this domain, there are two subclasses of approaches. The first one essentially picks a direct subset of the original training data set as the prototype set. An example of such a study is the so-called minimal consistent set (MCS) approach by Dasarathy (1994a). MCS does not analytically guarantee minimality, but in practice yields unique and close to minimal subsets. Skalak (1994) offers two algorithms, a Monte Carlo sampling and random mutation hill climbing (RMHC), which drastically reduce, at least in the examples shown, the training set sizes without loss of predictive accuracy. It is, however, not clear as to what the limitations of these processes are in terms of their applicability to other data sets, although the author does provide some discussion in this regard. Another interesting aspect of this study is that it also simultaneously explores the complementary problem of attribute selection by letting the RMHC jointly select various subsets of both prototypes and attributes during the random mutation process.

The second class of approaches artificially generates a small number of representative prototypes through some process such as averaging. Recent examples include a comparative study by Bezdek et al. (1998) that covers six different methods of generating representative prototypes and a companion study by Kuncheva and Bezdek (1998) using genetic algorithms (GAs). GAs, which are orders of magnitude slower than MCS, also do not always produce a unique result being sensitive to initial conditions. However, if the user has sufficient resources to make repeated runs, GAs can occasionally lead to a smaller consistent prototype set than MCS, as the latter is not analytically guaranteed to lead to minimality. On the other hand, the major claim of the GA approach is that it can be used to derive truly small prototype sets which may not necessarily be consistent with the original set but have some tolerable error levels.

These prototype reduction techniques can alternatively be further categorized as either an editing tool, or as a data condensing tool. As an editing tool, the primary aim is to edit or cleanse the data set to eliminate prototypes that are erroneous and likely to cause classification errors in the test phase with data set size reduction being an incidental objective. As a data-condensing tool the main objective is indeed data set size reduction while minimizing the effect of such a reduction on the expected classification accuracy. The proximity graph based study by Sanchez et al. (1997), is primarily an example of the former, although it also applies a tool of the latter type as a postedit processor. MCS, on the other hand, is essentially a representation of the latter type. The proximity graph approach is computationally very much more expensive than direct approaches such as MCS. The scope for exploiting the synergy between these two types of tools through a tandem fusion of the proximity graph and MCS approaches was illustrated in a recent study by Dasarathy et al. (2000).

An example, which combines elements of both of the major approaches to this problem of high computational demands, is that of Lee and Chae (1998). Their approach is to define and select a subset of training data vectors as anchor vectors. These anchor vectors control the logic for determining whether or not distances to the rest of the data set need to be computed. The determination is based on the concept of triangular inequality elimination (TIE). Equivalent computational demand minimization approaches have been proposed in the context of instance-based learning under the nomenclature of instance-pruning techniques (Wilson and Martinez, 1997a). Thus, while there indeed exist a host of schemes for reducing the computational burden of nearest-neighbor like techniques, there is unfortunately no single authoritative quantitative (as opposed to qualitative) comparison of all the proposed alternatives.

As mentioned previously, the dimensionality of the attribute space also dictates (albeit linearly) the computational demands of the NNR search process. A reduction in the dimensionality of the search space would therefore seem advisable. However, the relevancy of the different components (attributes) of the data vectors in the database to the specific data mining query may differ and hence the decision process has to take this into account in some fashion. For example, the color of the eyes may have little to do with the type of purchases expected of a potential customer defined in the database of a catalog merchandiser. The alternatives are attribute selection and/or attribute weighting. In the former, some of the features or attributes are pre-selected based on an understanding of the specific classification problem and evaluation of the significance of the attribute relative to this problem through statistical analysis of the available training data possibly combined with human perception of the relevancy as well. While many attribute evaluation/selection tools have been proposed in the literature and have been addressed elsewhere in this handbook in detail, a brief discussion is deemed appropriate in this article as well. In the context of data mining applications, it is necessary to look for one that can handle a truly large number of attributes in as rapid a manner as possible. An example of such a tool is CORPS: Class Overlap Region Partitioning Scheme (Dasarathy, 1993) which is eminently suited for fast independent evaluation of a large number of attributes. CORPS provides a measure of effectiveness of each attribute normalized to be in the range 0–1 and thus can be employed as not only an attribute-ranking tool but also an attribute-weighting determination process. The method has also been extended to environments with either imperfect (Dasarathy, 1994b) or imprecise (Dasarathy, 1995) supervision.

In traditional NNR techniques, all the attributes are by default weighted equally, that is, the separation (or inversely similarity) along each attribute is deemed to be equally significant. One could, however, visualize a more flexible approach wherein there is a provision for weighting the separation along each attribute differently. This calls for a rational method for determining such weights. Feature weighting, in the context of nearest-neighbor and lazy learning algorithms, has been the topic of several studies by Aha and associates (Aha, 1998; Wettschereck et al., 1997), as well as others such as Kohavi et al. (1997). In a similar vein, a methodology for deriving attribute weights through genetic algorithms in the context of instance-based learning has been proposed by Wilson and Martinez (1996). The weighting of attributes under case-based reasoning nomenclature is addressed in the study by Wettschereck and Aha (1995).

3. Modified Metrics

The Euclidean metric has been the standard bearer for measuring the separation between data points in the field of NNR techniques. Frequently encountered modifications to this classical metric include the city-block or Manhattan distance metric and their combinations (Chaudhuri et al., 1992). But these are mostly suited only for cases where the attribute values are continuous variables. However, in real-world data mining applications, one can expect to encounter a spectrum of different types of attributes such as integers and symbolic valued attributes. Various metrics have therefore been defined in the literature for tackling such a mix of the different types of variables. Examples of such modified metrics (Wilson and Martinez, 1997b) proposed in the context of instance-based learning (NNR methods in AI parlance), are:

- value difference metric (VDM)
- modified value difference metric (MVDM)
- heterogeneous euclidean-overlap metric (HEOM)
- heterogeneous value difference metric (HVDM)
- interpolated value difference metric (IVDM)
- discretized value difference metric (DVDM)
- windowed value difference metric (WVDM).

The VDM (Stanfill and Waltz, 1986) is intended as a metric for defining a distance function for nominal attributes. Various attribute-weighting schemes have been introduced in the literature in the context of the VDM. One of the drawbacks of this metric is that the initial set of nominal values should be exhaustive to span all the expected cases, as introduction of new values requires a complete restructuring of the metric. That is, application to another case study, with possibly different nominal values than are currently present within the training database, would not be a very simple task. MVDM (Cost and Salzberg, 1993) is a modification of the VDM with weighting that is instance-based rather than attribute-based. It handles continuous-valued attributes by a process of discretization. HEOM, which is similar to the distance functions used by Aha for certain types of instance-based learning algorithms (Aha, 1992), is designed to handle both continuous and nominal valued attributes. This is essentially a fused metric combining normalized Euclidean distance for linear continuous valued variables and an overlap metric for the nominal valued variables. HVDM (Wilson and Martinez, 1997b) essentially combines the Euclidean distance measure for continuous-valued attributes with the VDM designed for nominal-valued attributes. It differs from HEOM in that it substitutes VDM for the overlap metric for the nominal-valued attributes and also uses a different normalization. IVDM (Wilson and Martinez, 1997b) modifies VDM to permit VDM to become directly applicable to continuous-valued attributes also. This overcomes the need for separate normalization of the attributes. DVDM (Wilson and Martinez, 1997b), the discretized version of the VDM, has also been defined in the literature, which although conceptually similar has certain computational differences in its implementation. WVDM (Wilson and Martinez, 1997b) is a further variation in terms of using a sampling method for the implementation of the basic VDM concepts. The cited reference (Wilson and Martinez, 1997b) provides a detailed comparative analysis and discusses the pros and cons of the different metrics, which have to be interpreted in the context of the specific application of interest. Modifications to the classical metrics have also been offered by, among others, Fukunaga and his associates (Short and Fukunaga, 1981, Fukunaga and Flick, 1984) to improve performance in the context of finite sample sizes by minimizing the mean square error between the finite sample risk and the asymptotic risk. Similarity metric learning is another interesting approach, proposed by Lowe (1995) to improve upon the generalization capability of traditional NNR methods. An incidental computational benefit claimed therein is that the similarity metric optimization (through conjugate gradient methods) results in a *de facto* dimensionality reduction because of the variable weighting of the different dimensions (attributes).

4. Dimensionality Demons

One of the major motivations for the development of new customized techniques for data mining applications (instead of just using well-known techniques from the field of pattern recognition and classical NNR techniques) is the huge volumes of data and associated high data dimensionality in data mining applications. This, more commonly referred to as the curse of dimensionality, has been addressed by several researchers, a recent example of which is the study by Friedman (1997). The problem can be either one of a large number of data records (which increases the number of distance computations) or one of a large number of attributes descriptive of the data records (which increases the cost of each distance computation) or both. One of the approaches to tackling this dimensionality curse problem is to be selective of the attributes describing the database. The attribute selection techniques discussed earlier in this article can be useful in addressing this issue. Deleting from consideration irrelevant attributes can alleviate this problem of high-dimensionality. An interesting discussion of irrelevant attributes including a definition of strong and weak relevance is provided in the study by John et al. (1994). Strong relevance in this context implies that the attribute concerned is critical to the data mining process and whose removal can be expected to cause a loss in the accuracy of the results of the data mining and knowledge discovery process. A study dealing with the concept of relevant attributes in machine learning is given by Langley (1994). Another recent study, by Hastie and Tibshirani (1996), offers a modification to the NNR approach in the context of high-dimensionality data. Since NNR classification assumes the class conditional probabilities to be locally constant, certain bias is likely in high dimensions. The study proposes a locally adaptive form of NNR classification to minimize this curse of dimensionality. It also offers a method for global dimensionality reduction that combines local dimension information and illustrates it with examples. This issue of the dimensionality curse is also addressed by Motwani and Indyk (1998), who exploit the concept of approximate NNR under the Euclidean norm towards this end. Here, instead of looking for the true nearest-neighbor in an absolute sense, one seeks to identify an ϵ-approximate nearest-neighbor, which is not farther from the test sample by more than certain ϵ fraction of the distance to the true nearest-neighbor. Two algorithms are offered that lead to significant reductions in computational demands of the query (operational) phases without incurring prohibitively large preprocessing costs, a common problem under many of the schemes proposed for reduction of query phase costs.

5. Concluding Comments

NNR techniques, being a field unto themselves, have been covered extensively elsewhere (Dasarathy, 1991). As such, this treatment has to be viewed only as an invitation to pique the interest of the reader and briefly illustrate how NNR techniques are related to the field of data mining and knowledge discovery, the main topic of this handbook. NNR techniques represent but one tool, albeit an important and powerful one, in the toolbox of the knowledge engineer. The extensive bibliographic references cited here can aid in the selection of the most appropriate techniques within this domain to address any specific problem one might have on hand. Computational concerns still remain the single most significant issue but with the continued leap-frogging advancements in computational power, this is becoming a less and less serious factor in the selection of the most appropriate processing technology.

References

Aha, D. W. 1992. "Tolerating noisy, irrelevant, and novel attributes in instance-based learning algorithms." *Int. J. Man–Machine Studies* **36**: 267–287.

Aha, D. W. 1997. "Editorial, special AI review issue on lazy learning." *Artificial Intell. Rev.* **11(1–5)**: 7–10.

Aha, W. 1998. "Feature weighting for lazy learning algorithms." *Feature Extraction, Construction and Selection: a Data Mining Perspective*, edited by H. Liu and H. Motoda. Norwell, MA: Kluwer.

Aha, D. W., D. Kibler, and M. K. Albert. 1991. "Instance based learning algorithms." *Machine Learning* **6**: 37–66.

Berson, A. and S. J. Smith. 1997. *Data Warehousing, Data Mining, and Olap*: McGraw-Hill, Inc.

Bezdek, J. C., T. R. Reichherzer, G. S. Lim, and Y. Attikiouzel. 1998. "Multiple-prototype classifier design." *IEEE Trans. Sys., Man, Cybernet. C* **28(1)**: 67–79.

Chaudhuri, D., C. A. Murthy, and B. B. Chaudhuri. 1992. "A modified metric to compute distance." *Pattern Recognition* **25(7)**: 667–677.

Cost, S. and S. Salzberg. 1993. "A weighted nearest neighbor algorithm for learning with symbolic features." *Machine Learning* **10**: 57–78.

Cover, T. M. and P. E. Hart. 1967. "Nearest neighbor pattern classification." *IEEE Trans. Inform. Theory* **IT-13(1)**: 21–27.

Dasarathy, B. V. 1980a. "Nosing around the neighborhood—a new system structure and classification rule for recognition in partially exposed environments." *IEEE Trans. Pattern Anal. Machine Intell.* **PAMI-2(1)**: 67–71.

Dasarathy, B. V. 1980b. "There goes the neighborhood—an alien identification approach to recognition in partially exposed environments." *Proceedings of the 5th International Conference on Pattern Recognition*, pp. 91–93.

Dasarathy, B. V. 1991. *Nearest Neighbor (NN) Norms—NN Pattern Classification Techniques*. Los Alamitos, CA: IEEE Computer Society Press.

Dasarathy, B. V. April 1993. "CORPS: class overlap region partitioning scheme—a tool for feature assessment." *Proceedings of the SPIE—Architecture, Hardware, and Forward-Looking Infrared Issues in Automatic Target Recognition*, **1957**: 215–226.

Dasarathy, B. V. 1994a. "Minimal consistent subset (MCS) identification for optimal nearest neighbor decision systems design." *IEEE Trans. on Sys., Man, Cybernet* **24(3)**: 511–517.

Dasarathy, B. V. April 1994b. "Feature assessment in imperfectly supervised environment." *Proceedings of the SPIE—Automatic Object Recognition IV*, **2234**: 360–371.

Dasarathy, B. V. 1995. "CORPS_F: a new tool for feature assessment in imperfectly supervised or fuzzy environments." *Int. J. Uncertainty, Fuzziness and Knowledge-based Sys.* **3(4)**: 451–464.

Dasarathy, B. V. 1996. "Adaptive fusion processor paradigms for fusion of information acquired at different levels of detail." *Optical Engng* **35(3)**: 634–649.

Dasarathy, B. V. and B. V. Sheela. 1979. "A composite classifier system design: concepts and methodology." *Proc. IEEE* **67(5)**: 708–713.

Dasarathy, B. V., J. S. Sanchez, and S. Townsend. 2000. "Nearest neighbor editing and condensing tools—synergy exploitation." *Pattern Anal. Appl.* **3(1)**: 19–30.

Denoeux, T. 1995. "A *k*-nearest neighbor classification rule based on Dempster–Shafer theory." *IEEE Trans. on Sys., Man, Cybernet* **SMC-25(5)**: 804–813.

Dietterich, T. G., D. Wettschereck, C. G. Atkeson, and A. W. Moore. 1994. "Memory-based methods for regression and classification." *Neural Information Processing Systems*, Volume 6, edited by I. Cowan, G. Tesauro, and J. Alspector. Denver: Morgan Kaufmann.

Djouadi, A. 1998. "On the reduction of the nearest neighbor variation for more accurate classification and error estimates." *IEEE Trans. on Pattern Anal. and Machine Intell.* **PAMI-20(5)**: 567–571.

Djouadi, A. and E. Bouktache. 1997. "A fast algorithm for the nearest neighbor classifier." *IEEE Trans. Pattern Anal. Machine Intell.* **PAMI-19(3)**: 277–282.

Dudani, S. A. 1976. "The distance-weighted *k*-nearest-neighbor rule." *IEEE Trans. on Sys., Man, Cybernet* **SMC-6(4)**: 325–327.

Fayyad, U. M. 1996. "Data mining and knowledge discovery—making sense out of data." *IEEE Expert—Intell. Sys. Appl.* **11(5)**: 20–25.

Fayyad, U. M., G. Piatetsky-Shapiro, and P. Smyth. 1996a. "From data mining to knowledge discovery in databases." *AI Magazine* **17(3)**: 37–54.

Fayyad, U. M., S. G. Djorgovski, and N. Weir. 1996b. "From digitized images to online catalogs—data mining a sky survey." *AI Magazine* **17(2)**: 51–66.

Fix, E. and J. L. Hodges, Jr. 1951. Discriminatory analysis—nonparametric discrimination: consistency properties. Project 21-49-004, Report No. 4, pp. 261–279. Randolph Field, TX: USAF School of Aviation Medicine.

Fix, E. and J. L. Hodges, Jr. 1952. Discriminatory analysis—nonparametric discrimination: small sample performance. Project 21-49-004, Report No. 11, pp. 280–322. Randolph Field, TX: USAF School of Aviation Medicine.

Friedman, J. H. 1997. "On bias, variance, 0/1—loss, and the curse of dimensionality." *Data Mining and Knowledge Discovery* **1**: 55–77.

Fukunaga, K. and T. Flick. 1984. "An optimal global nearest neighbor metric." *IEEE Trans. Pattern Anal. Machine Intell.* **PAMI-6(3)**: 314–318.

Fukunaga, K. and T. Flick. 1985. "The 2-NNRule for More Accurate Risk Estimation." *IEEE Trans. Pattern Anal. Machine Intell.* **PAMI-7(1)**: 107–111.

Greene, R. L. 1994. "Efficient retrieval from sparse associative memory." *Artificial Intell.* **66(2)**: 395–410.

Grother, P. J., G. T. Candela, and J. L. Blue. 1997. "Fast implementations of nearest neighbor classifiers." *Pattern Recognition* **30(3)**: 459–465.

Hastie, T. and R. Tibshirani. 1996. "Discriminant Adaptive nearest neighbor classification." *IEEE Trans. Pattern Anal. Machine Intell.* **18(6)**: 607–616.

John, G. H., R. Kohavi, and K. Pfleger. 1994. "Irrelevant features and the subset selection problem." *Machine Learning: Proceedings of the Eleventh International Conference*, pp. 121–129. San Francisco, CA: Morgan Kaufmann Publishers.

Joussellin, A. and B. Dubuisson. 1987. "A link between *k*-nearest neighbor rules and knowledge based systems by sequence analysis." *Pattern Recognition Lett.* **6(5)**: 287–295.

Kohavi, R., P. Langley, and Y. Yun. April 23–25, 1997. "The utility of feature weighting in nearest-neighbor algorithms." *9th European Conference on Machine Learning*. Prague, Czech Republic.

Kolodner, J. 1993. *Case-based Reasoning*. San Mateo, CA: Morgan Kaufmann.

Kuncheva, L. I. and J. C. Bezdek. 1998. "Nearest prototype classification: clustering, genetic algorithms, or random search?" *IEEE Trans. Sys., Man, Cybernet. C* **28(1)**: 160–164.

Langley, P. 1994. "Selection of relevant features in machine learning." *Proceedings of the AAAI Fall Symposium on Relevance*. New Orleans: AAAI Press.

Lee, E.-W. and S.-I. Chae. 1998. "Fast design of reduced-complexity nearest-neighbor classifiers using triangular inequality." *IEEE Trans. Pattern Anal. Machine Intell.* **PAMI-20(5)**: 562–566.

Lowe, D. G. 1995. "Similarity metric learning for a variable-kernel classifier." *Neural Comput.* **7(1)**: 72–85.

Mico, L., J. Oncina, and R. C. Carrasco. 1996. "A fast branch & bound nearest neighbour classifier in metric spaces." *Pattern Recognition Lett.* **17(7)**: 731–740.

Miyashita, K. 1994. "A case-based approach to improve quality and efficiency in ill-structured optimization: an application to job shop scheduling". Ph.D Thesis. Japan: Osaka University.

Miyashita, K., and K. Sycara. 1995. "CABINS—A framework of knowledge acquisition and iterative revision for schedule improvement and reactive repair." *Artificial Intell.* **76(2)**: 377–426.

Motwani, R. and P. Indyk. May 1998. "Approximate nearest neighbor: towards removing the curse of dimensionality." *Proceedings of the 30th Annual ACM Symposium on Theory of Computing*, pp. 604–613.

Patrick, E. A. and Fischer, F. P. III 1970. "A generalized *k*-nearest neighbor rule." *Inform. Contr.* **16**: 128–152.

Pearl, J. 1993. *Probabilistic Reasoning in Intelligent Systems*. San Mateo, CA: Morgan Kaufmann.

Portegys, T. E. 1995. "A search technique for pattern recognition using relative distances." *IEEE Trans. Pattern Anal. Machine Intell.* **PAMI-17(9)**: 910–914.

Sanchez, J. S., F. Pla, and F. J. Ferri. 1997. "Prototype selection for the nearest neighbor rule through proximity graphs." *Pattern Recognition Lett.* **18**: 507–513.

Short, R. D. and K. Fukunaga. 1981. "The optimal distance measure for nearest neighbor classification." *IEEE Trans. on Inform. Theory* **IT-27**: 622–627.

Skalak, D. B. 1994. "Prototype and feature selection by sampling and random mutation hill-climbing algorithms." *Proceedings of the Eleventh International Conference on Machine Learning*, pp. 293–301. New Jersey: New Brunswick.

Smyth, S. G. 1992. "Designing multilayer perceptrons from nearest-neighbor systems." *IEEE Trans. Neural Networks* **3(2)**: 329–333.

Stanfill, C. and D. Waltz. 1986. "Towards memory-based reasoning." *Commun. ACM* **29**: 1213–1228.

Waltz, D. and S. Kasif. 1995. "On reasoning from data." *ACM Comput. Surv.* **27(3)**: 356–359.

Wettschereck, D. and D. W. Aha. 1995. "Weighting features." *First International Conference on Case-Based Reasoning*, Sesimbra, Portugal, pp. 347–358. Berlin: Springer-Verlag.

Wettschereck, D., D. W. Aha, and T. Mohri. 1997. "A review and empirical evaluation of feature-weighting methods for a class of lazy learning algorithms." *Artificial Intell. Rev.* **11(1–5)**: 273–314.

White, D. A. and R. C. Jain. 1996. Algorithms and strategies for similarity retrieval. *Technical Report VCL-96-101*. Visual Computing Laboratory, University of California, San Diego, La Jolla, CA 92093-0407. USA.

Whitney, A. W. and S. J. Dwyer, III. 1966. "Performance and implementation of the *k*-nearest neighbor decision rule with incorrectly identified training samples." *Proceedings of the 4th Annual Allerton Conference on Circuits and System Theory*, pp. 96–106.

Wilson, R. and T. R. Martinez. August 1996. "Instance-based learning with genetically derived attribute weights." *Proceedings of the International Conference on Artificial Intelligence, Expert Systems, and Neural Networks (AIE'96)*, pp. 11–14.

Wilson, R. and T. R. Martinez. July 1997a. "Instance pruning techniques." *Proceedings of the International Conference on Machine Learning (ICML'97)*.

Wilson, D. R. and T. R. Martinez. 1997b. "Improved heterogeneous distance functions." *J. Artificial Intell. Res.* **6(1)**: 1–34.

Zakarauskas, P. and J. M. Ozard. 1996. "Complexity analysis for partitioning nearest neighbor searching algorithms." *IEEE Trans. Pattern Anal. Machine Intell.* **PAMI-18(6)**: 663–668.

16.1.7 Regression

Robert Henery

ABSTRACT Regression methods for classification are based on population means, and usually, though by no means always, a linear combination of attributes is the starting point for predicting the population means, even if subsequently the linear combination is subjected to a nonlinear transformation as in logistic regression. In this sense, neural networks are extensions to logistic regression, but they are treated in Chapter 16.1.8 of this handbook. We begin by describing the classical approach to statistical discrimination, which is based on multivariate normal distributions. In logistic regression, although the underlying method is identical, an alternative justification is given for choosing the coefficients, and this leads to more efficient solutions in some circumstances. When the basic assumptions of linear or logistic regression are not satisfied, for example when there are many outliers, more robust and flexible approaches are required, and some modern statistical approaches have been developed to deal with this problem. Finally, Fisher's canonical discriminants may be used to display multivariate data to good effect, either to investigate relationships between the population means or to investigate the assumptions of multivariate normality.

1. Theory

Classification has several meanings, but in this article we deal only with supervised learning, which is generally known as discrimination in the statistical community. We begin by giving an outline of the main ideas behind the classic linear discriminant approach given by Fisher (1936, 1938) for the simple two-class problem.

Given a vector $X = (X_1, X_2, ..., X_p)$ of p attributes, we predict the class via a linear predictor or linear discriminant

$$L = \beta_0 + \beta_1 X_1 + \beta_2 X_2 + ... \beta_p X_p.$$

This linear predictor should be chosen to minimize the Bayes risk, that is, to minimize the probability of misclassifying observations. When the random vector X has a multivariate normal distribution and the covariance matrix Σ is the same in the two classes, it is not too difficult to show that the optimal discriminant is indeed linear in the observations. We will discuss the formula for the optimal linear discriminant in a moment, but three important points should be made at the outset. Firstly, the linear discriminant is optimal from another standpoint, which we arrive at by treating the classes as numeric-valued and predicting the class value by least squares. Secondly, empirical methods can be used to give some kind of check on the validity of various assumptions, or even to improve performance when the assumptions fail, for example, in the presence of outliers. Thirdly, the basic linear discriminant model has been elaborated and extended to deal with much more general situations, with more general error distributions. These lead to discriminants that are nonlinear functions of the linear predictor, as in logistic regression and loglinear models.

We treat the two-class problem because it is conceptually simple and also because it is often used as a first step in the k-class problem by considering all $k(k-1)/2$ pairs of classes as in pairwise coupling (Friedman, 1996; Hastie and Tibshirani, 1998) and DIPOL92 (Taylor et al., 1994). Generalizations to the k-class problem are straightforward, but the reader is referred to McLachlan (1992) for details. We use the notation $E_I(X)$ to denote the expectation of X over population I.

Since the discriminant L is a linear combination of variates, it is simple to work out the mean value of L for both populations (the variance of L is the same in the two populations by virtue of our assumption of a common covariance matrix for X).

$$\lambda_1 = E_I(L) = \beta_0 + \beta_1 \mu_{11} + \beta_2 \mu_{12} + ... \beta_p \mu_{1p}$$

$$\lambda_2 = E_{II}(L) = \beta_0 + \beta_1 \mu_{21} + \beta_2 \mu_{22} + ... \beta_p \mu_{2p}.$$

We assume, with no loss of generality, that $\lambda_1 < \lambda_2$. Then it is clear that we should allocate a new observation to class I if the linear discriminant L is small and to class II if L is large. The precise boundary between the two decision regions depends on the prior probabilities of the two populations. If the two populations are equally likely to occur, the optimal boundary is midway between the two class mean discriminants, so the decision rule is to allocate to class I if $L < \frac{1}{2}(\lambda_1 + \lambda_2)$, and to class II if $L > \frac{1}{2}(\lambda_1 + \lambda_2)$. Let us denote the (conditional) variance of the discriminant scores by V, that is, the variance of L given the observation is from I, or the variance of L given the observation is from II (by assumption these variances are the same).

To achieve good discrimination, we would like the variance V of the discriminant L to be small, so that class I values are clustered near their mean value λ_1, and class II values are clustered near λ_2, with very little overlap. This is the same as saying that we wish the difference in the mean discriminants $\lambda_2 - \lambda_1$ to be large in relation to the standard deviation of the discriminant. Fisher (1936) expressed this last condition as maximizing the between group variation $(\lambda_2 - \lambda_1)^2$ relative to the within group variation V.

When the multivariate assumptions hold, L has a normal distribution as it is a linear combination of normal variates. Even if the multivariate normal assumptions do not hold, when the number p of variates is moderately large, the distribution of L will be approximately normal as predicted by the central limit theorem, so that some parts of the following discussion will still hold in more general circumstances. Then the theoretical probability α of misclassifying an observation from class I is the probability that the linear discriminant exceeds $\frac{1}{2}(\lambda_1 + \lambda_2)$, giving

$$\alpha = P(L > \tfrac{1}{2}(\lambda_1 + \lambda_2) \mid \text{class} I) = \Phi\!\left(\tfrac{1}{2}(\lambda_1 - \lambda_2)/\sqrt{V}\right).$$

This error will be minimized if we choose the coefficients β to maximize $\{(\lambda_1 - \lambda_2)/\sqrt{V}\}^2 = (\lambda_1 - \lambda_2)^2/V$, and thus the Bayes optimal rule reduces to a least squares criterion when the parent populations are multivariate normal.

The optimal coefficients are given by

$$\beta = \Sigma^{-1}(\mu_2 - \mu_1)$$

and with this choice of coefficients, the error rate α can be written as

$$\alpha = \Phi(-\tfrac{1}{2}(\mu_2 - \mu_1)'\Sigma^{-1}(\mu_2 - \mu_1)).$$

For the theoretical error rate in the case of unequal population sizes see Ripley (1994).

When the parent distributions are not normal, as for example when there are outliers, or when the attributes are binary, other criteria are often used, rather than least squares. A common alternative is to use logistic regression, as this has some theoretical advantages with binary attributes. Although these alternative procedures may lead to substantially different values of the parameters, it is more often the case that the parameters β are only slightly different from the linear discriminant values.

1.1. More Than Two Classes

When there are more than two classes, the simplest procedure is to calculate a separate linear discriminant for every class (although one class may be taken as a reference class with discriminant zero). Each of the k classes has its own vector of coefficients $\beta_j, j = 1, \ldots k$, giving k linear discriminants $L_1, \ldots L_k$, one for each class. A new observation is allocated to the class that has the largest discriminant. See McLachlan (1992) for details.

2. Empirical

The above discussion assumes that the true population means and variances are known. In the more likely case that we only have samples from the populations, the parameters β_i are usually estimated, perhaps naively, by replacing theoretical quantities by their sample estimates, for example replacing population means by sample means, and population variances by the pooled sample variances. When there are outliers in the data, however, it is usual to use robust methods to estimate means and variances, as in McLachlan (1992).

Kendall et al. (1983) give an expression for standard errors derived for the most common situation where the data have arisen by random sampling within each population. Although most statistical computing packages contain a discriminant procedure that will provide estimates of the parameters, they usually give standard errors of the parameters based on a model in which the attributes are nonrandom (i.e., inference is conditional on the observed data matrix). A variable X_k may be dropped from the discriminant rule, with no appreciable loss in accuracy, if the coefficient β_k is small compared to its standard error. The two most common ways of selecting attributes for the final model are forward and backward selection. In backward selection, all attributes are fitted and the least significant attribute (among the nonsignificant attributes) is then dropped. Once an attribute has been dropped, it is necessary to recompute the estimates and standard errors for the remaining coefficients before judging if any other attribute may be dropped.

If no explicit discriminant procedure is available, a standard multiple regression package can be persuaded to give the parameters β_i (with standard errors) by predicting the classes as numerical values using the attributes X as predictors in a multiple regression. With unequal data in the two classes, say with sample sizes of n_1 and n_2 in the two classes, the cut-off point is chosen to be $L > \{(n_1\lambda_2 + n_2\lambda_1)/(n_1 + n_2)$.

3. Quadratic Discrimination

Even if observations satisfy the multivariate normal assumption reasonably well, the assumption of equal covariance matrices is seldom true. When the covariances in the two populations are different, as is often the case when the means differ for example, the optimal decision surfaces are quadratic, and the number of parameters increases to $(k-1) * p(p+1)/2$ compared to only $(k-1)(p+1)$ for the linear case. This generally requires substantially larger samples to justify the use of the quadratic rule.

For larger data sets, Box's M-test may be used to decide if the covariance matrices differ: this is described in Taylor et al. (1994) for example. However, it is not always sensible to rely entirely on a single test statistic for the complex question of whether the data are multivariate normal with common covariance, and it is better to plot the scatter diagram, and make a subjective judgment on this (see Section 6).

Regularized discriminant analysis (Friedman, 1989; Randles et al., 1978) seeks to improve the performance of quadratic discriminants when the training data set is small, as then the quadratic procedure tends to be strongly biased. The bias may also be reduced by cross-validation methods (See Chapter 19.1), or by rescaling the computed probabilities as in Henery (1997).

4. Logistic Regression

The basic linear regression approach can be generalized in two ways: (i) to deal with nonGaussian distributions, and (ii) to deal with nonlinear transformations of the predicted mean. Among these generalized linear models, the most relevant generalization is logistic regression for predicting class membership via the binomial error distribution. In principle, this is fully Bayesian and the parameters are estimated by maximum likelihood. The method also has the advantage of directly estimating posterior probabilities for class membership. This is done by expressing the conditional probability P of belonging to class I via the nonlinear function

$$\log\frac{P}{(1-P)} = \beta_0 + \beta_1 X_1 + \beta_2 X_2 + ... \beta_p X_p.$$

Note that the discriminant function is still linear in the attributes, but that the predicted value of the probability is constrained to lie in the interval $(0, 1)$.

Logistic regression is usually fitted by regarding each observation in the training set as a single Bernoulli trial, with an occurrence of class I as a success. Most techniques from linear regression carry over to logistic regression, such as goodness-of-fit measures, and standard errors of coefficients. Some care is needed with degrees of freedom, however, particularly if the attributes are all binary, and the number of data n is larger than the number 2^k of possible attribute vectors. In the latter case, it is best to count the number of successes in each of the 2^k cells in attribute space, and model this number as a binomial variable with probability p depending on the attribute values as above.

5. Flexible and Robust Approaches

More recently, since around 1980, several more flexible approaches to classification have emerged: these seek to deal with more awkward data sets, where, for example, there may be many outliers, or there may be doubt about the correct identification of some classes in the training data. Smart is an improved version of projection pursuit (Friedman et al., 1984). Multivariate adaptive regression splines (MARS) (Friedman, 1991) use splines as a basis for the regression. Hastie and Tibshirani (1998) combine pairwise discriminants using a loglinear model analogous to using logistic regression on the pairwise class probability estimates. In the ACE procedure of Breiman and Ihaka (1984), the aim is to find arbitrary nonlinear transformations of the attributes so that the discriminant takes the form:

$$L = t_1(X_1) + t_2(X_2) + ... + t_k(X_k),$$

where $t_i()$ is the required nonlinear transformation for attribute X_i. ACE, Smart, and MARS are available as standard procedures, or as add-on libraries, in the commonly used programming environments such as Splus or the freeware R.

Relying as they do on the Gaussian distribution for residuals, least squares methods are very susceptible to outliers. There are many ways of reducing the influence of outliers. Robust methods usually function by defining a set of weights for every observation, giving reduced weight to observations with large residuals. The weights are often calculated iteratively, with weights for the next iteration being calculated from the current residuals. Then population means and variances are estimated by calculating weighted averages over the observations. McLachlan (1992) gives more details.

5.1. Categorical Attributes

Occasionally, when a categorical attribute is ordered, it might be sensible to interpret the category itself as a rank, and use the rank as a numerical valued attribute. Even when ordered, it can be illuminating to treat the categorical variable as unordered and then plot the coefficients against attribute rank, to see if some transformation might suggest itself (or to confirm a working hypothesis of linearity in the ranks). Usually, however, it is better to make a transformation of the ranks, perhaps as suggested by a preliminary analysis using ACE.

For a particular categorical attribute, in the two-class problem, a separate marginal contingency table of class versus attribute value might be drawn up (i.e., ignoring all other attributes). Then the log-odds of the classes in a contingency table of class by attribute value may be used as scores to be given to the categories. Correspondence analysis is another procedure that aims to give scores to categorical variables: these scores can be used to order the categories or as numerical values to be used in prediction.

6. Canonical Discriminants

A plot of the data often leads to a better understanding of the relative positions of the class centroids (do the class centroids lie along a line in attribute space as in Fisher (1938) in his original derivation?). The best way to plot the data, in 2-D at any rate, is to use the first two canonical discriminants. Canonical discriminants give a low-dimensional representation of high-dimensional data that maximizes the separation of the classes. This differs from principal components, a closely related concept, in that the class information in the data is used to emphasize differences in the centroids of the various classes. A plot also gives a qualitative test of the assumptions of multivariate normality, and of common covariance. A more formal test of multivariate normality is based on a QQ plot of the Mahalanobis distances (see Taylor et al., 1994, for a description), but there is no single test of normality, and for this reason the graphical method is all the more practical.

Figure 1 shows the plot of the Iris data using the first two canonical discriminants. Note how the three class centroids lie approximately along the horizontal axis. This means that the three classes may be approximately separated using only a single discriminant, that is, using only the first canonical discriminant. If the distributions were truly multivariate normal, the clusters would all have circular shapes with the same radius. This is approximately true, except that the class **S** is perhaps too elliptical. As a footnote, it should be observed that decision trees function best when the decision surfaces are orthogonal to the attributes. The first canonical discriminant may be thought of as that projection of the attributes for which the decision surfaces are most nearly in planes normal to it. Canonical discriminants are therefore to be

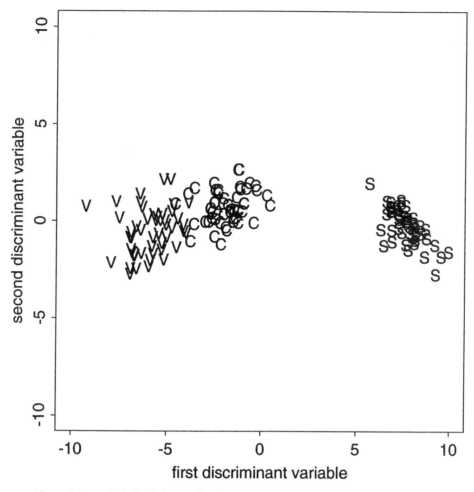

Figure 1 Canonical discriminants for the Iris data

preferred over principal components if the aim is to build a decision tree with minimal number of nodes.

References

Standard references to statistical approaches to discrimination include: Hand (1981), Kendall et al. (1983), and Lachenbruch and Mickey (1975). Breiman et al. (1984) describe CART, which is a partitioning algorithm that deals with classification (categorical classes) and regression (where the classes are numerical-valued or ordered). More modern approaches to statistical discrimination are given in McLachlan (1992) and Ripley (1994).

Breiman, L. and R. Ihaka. 1984. Nonlinear discriminant analysis via scaling and ace. Technical Report No. 40. Department of Statistics, University of California: Berkeley.

Breiman, L., J. H. Friedman, R. A. Olshen, and C. J. Stone. 1984. *Classification and Regression Trees*. Monterey, CA: Wadsworth and Brooks.

Fisher, R. 1936. "The use of multiple measurements in taxonomic problems." *Ann. Eugenics* **7**: 179–188.

Fisher, R. 1938. "The statistical utilization of multiple measurements." *Ann. Eugenics* **8**: 376–386.

Friedman, J. H., W. Stuetzle, and A. Schroeder 1984. "Projection pursuit density estimation." *J. Amer. Statist. Assoc.* **79**: 599–608.

Friedman, J. 1989. "Regularized discriminant analysis." *J. Am. Stat. Assoc.* **84**: 165–175.

Friedman, J. 1991. "Multivariate adaptive Regression Splines (with discussion)." *Ann. Stat.* **19**: 1–141.

Friedman, J. 1996. Another approach to polychotomous classification. Technical Report. Stanford University.

Hand, D. J. 1981. *Discrimination and Classification*. Chichester, England: John Wiley.

Hastie, T. and R. Tibshirani. 1998. "Classification by pairwise coupling." *Ann. Stat.* **26**: 451–471.

Henery, R. 1997. "Combining classification procedures." *Machine Learning and Statistics: the Interface*, edited by G. Nakhaeizadeh and C. Taylor, pp. 153–178. New York: Wiley.

Kendall, M. G., A. Stuart, and J. K. Ord. 1983. *The Advanced Theory of Statistics*, fourth edition. Design and Analysis and Time Series. Chapter 44, Volume 3. London: Griffin.

Lachenbruch, P. A. and M. R. Mickey. 1975. *Discriminant Analysis*. New York: Hafner Press.

McLachlan, G. J. 1992. *Discriminant Analysis and Statistical Pattern Recognition*. New York: John Wiley.

Randles, R., J. Broffitt, J. Ramberg, and R. Hogg. 1978. "Generalized linear and quadratic discriminant functions using robust estimates." *J. Am. Stat. Assoc.* **73**: 564–568.

Ripley, B. 1994. "Neural networks and related methods for classification (with discussion)." *J. R. Stat. Soc. B* **56**: 410–456.

Taylor, C., D. Michie, and D. Spiegelhalter. 1994. *Machine Learning, Neural and Statistical Classification*. Englewood Cliffs, NJ: Prentice Hall.

16.1.8 Neural Network Approaches

Andreas Nürnberger, Witold Pedrycz and Rudolf Kruse

ABSTRACT This article elaborates on the role of neural networks in data mining, especially classification, and presents various ways of using them in this area. In order to do this the main architectures of neural networks (including multilayer perceptrons and radial basis function networks) are reviewed, and an overview of the classification process and the training of neural networks is given. Furthermore, the interpretation of neural networks and the generation of rules based on already trained networks are discussed and exemplified on a number of rule extraction algorithms. Finally, the role of neuro-fuzzy systems in the process of designing interpretable neural networks is described.

1. Introduction

Neural networks offer a powerful and distributed computing architecture equipped with significant learning capabilities (see Chapters 5.9 and 31). They are able to represent highly nonlinear and multivariable relationships.

Besides their biological heritage, neural networks have a strong relation to statistics (Sarle, 1994). For example, many neural network models are similar or identical to statistical methods. Linear neural networks and perceptrons are linear regression or discriminant models (see Chapters 16.1.7). Multilayer perceptrons are nonlinear regression models, possibly multiple and multivariable, if there are multiple input and output neurons.

Compared to statistical methods, a neural network is useful if there is no knowledge about the relationship between input (independent) and output (dependent) variables. Furthermore, neural networks are easy to extend to multiple inputs and multiple outputs without an exponential increase in their parameters, as would be the case for splines or polynomials, which can also be used for regression problems. Therefore, the role of neural networks in the context of data mining nicely corresponds with the class of problems addressed therein. Quite often, the phenomena we would like to comprehend, describe, and quantify have no physical underpinnings. For instance, economical time series (stock market, trends in real-estate business, etc.) are not governed by any specific physics-oriented phenomenon. This stipulates that the black-box nature of a neural network does not imply any detrimental effect, as there is no danger of ignoring any piece of otherwise available domain knowledge.

Neural networks that use competitive learning and adaptive vector quantization are similar to c-means clustering (Duda and Hart, 1973; see Chapter 16.5). Kohonen's self-organizing feature maps (Kohonen, 1982, 1984) also use a form of competitive learning, but do not have a statistical equivalent. The same is true for models based on reinforcement learning. In general, learning in neural networks is the same as parameter estimation in statistical methods. In statistical terms neural networks are nonparametric models (Neal, 1996). This term is used to contrast them with simpler parametric models that use few parameters, which often have meaningful interpretations, to represent input-output relations. Neural networks have parameters, of course, but they are more numerous and less interpretable than those of parametric models.

In the following we present different neural network architectures, give an overview of a classification process, and finally present techniques to interpret neural networks. In addition, we discuss the pros and cons concerning the use of neural networks for classification.

2. Neural Network Architectures

Neural networks (see Chapter 5.9), also known as connectionist models, consist of a number of independent, simple processors: the neurons. Every neuron is able to store an activation value. The neurons communicate with each other via weighted connections: links and synaptic weights. Neural networks differ in the way in which the neurons are connected, in the way the neurons process their input, and in the propagation and learning methods used. Learning in this context is usually restricted to modifying the weights; the structure of the initial network is usually left unchanged during a learning process. Therefore, an appropriate network structure must be selected for a specific problem. Furthermore, a general learning problem has to be transferred into a problem, which can be solved by a neural network. That is, all nonnumeric data attributes have to be converted into numeric values. Furthermore, in the case of a classification problem, the classes must be coded into a binary vector, so that each output neuron represents a single class. A class i is encoded by setting all elements of a binary vector y to 0, except the element y_i of the corresponding class i, which is set to 1. In the same way categorical attributes must be coded. Then a network with one input neuron for each attribute and one output neuron for each class can be constructed.

In the following, we present selected neural network architectures that are usually used for classification tasks. All of these are feed forward structures, since these types of networks are more appropriate for the representation of static input-output mappings, while its (mathematically more complex) recurrent variants, that is, networks that have feedback connections between neurons, are more appropriate for dynamic problems, such as, analysis of time-series data, optimization problems, or control applications (Medsker and Jain, 1999). Nevertheless, recurrent networks are also used for classification purposes, for example, Hopfield networks (Hopfield, 1982) for pattern classification (Lippmann, 1987; Palcic et al., 1992). Here, a representative vector of each class is coded as the attractor of the network. When the network is applied to unseen data, the network is propagated until it finally rests in one of the predefined attractors. Therefore, this recurrent network can be used as an associative memory.

For a more general description and introduction to neural networks see, for example, Haykin (1994) or Rojas (1996).

2.1. Multilayer Perceptron (MLP)

A multilayer perceptron is a neural network that consists of one input layer, one or multiple hidden layers, and one output layer of neurons (Figure 1). The units of the input layer do not perform any computation; they just pass on their input values. The other neurons of the network are simple processing units combining (multiple) input(s) to a single output. The MLP is an extension of the simple perceptron introduced by Rosenblatt (1958), which consists of

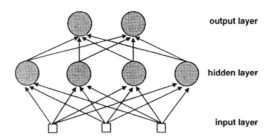

output layer

hidden layer

input layer

Figure 1 Structure of a multilayer perceptron with one hidden layer

only one input and one output layer of neurons without any hidden layer. The introduction of hidden units (Minsky and Papert, 1969) solved the restriction of the simple perceptron, which cannot solve a certain class of problems, the so-called linearly nonseparable problems.

More formally, the multilayer perceptron computes a function f: $\mathbb{R}^n \to \mathbb{R}^m$, where n is the number of input units and m is the number of output units. The output of an MLP is calculated by propagating the input from layer to layer through the network (feedforward architecture). During this process each neuron calculates its new activation and output until the output layer of the network is reached. For this, each neuron j of the hidden and output layers calculates an output o_j and its current activation a_j based on the input from the preceding layer by use of an input function net_j, an activation function $A_j(x)$: $a_j = A_j(net_j)$ and an output function $O_j(x)$: $o_j = O_j(net_j)$. The input function net_j simply sums up the products of the output o_i from each unit of the preceding layer and the weight w_{ij} by which it is connected to the neuron j:

$$net_j = \sum_i w_{ij} o_i.$$

The activation function must be differentiable, since this property is required for the learning process. Frequently, the so-called logistic function,

$$f(x) = \frac{1}{1 + e^{-\beta x}}, \quad \beta > 0,$$

is used. The logistic function approximates a threshold function and asymptotically approaches the value 0 for $x \to -\infty$ and 1 for $x \to +\infty$. The parameter β determines the steepness of this sigmoid function. A linear transformation is usually used as the output function, generally the identity function. In this case the output of the network is restricted to the interval [0, 1].

The learning methods used for multilayer perceptrons are based on the backpropagation learning algorithm (Rumelhart et al., 1986a,b). After propagating a pattern through the network, the output pattern is compared with a given target pattern and the error of each output unit is calculated. This error is propagated backward—that is, toward the input layer—through the network. Based on this error signal, the hidden units can determine their own error. Finally, the errors of the units are used to modify the weights. Since a correct weight cannot be derived exactly, the weights are varied slightly during each learning step. Therefore, the whole learning process must be repeated until a desired output is obtained. This method extends the idea of the delta rule learning algorithm for the perceptron introduced by Widrow and Hoff (1960) to multilayer neural networks, hence it is also called the generalized delta rule. Improved backpropagation learning methods are, for example, Quickprop (Fahlmann, 1989) and resilient propagation (RPROP), developed by Riedmiller and Braun (1993).

A multilayer perceptron with one hidden layer can be used to approximate arbitrary continuous functions (see, for example, Funahashi, 1989, or Hornik et al., 1989). Nevertheless, it may be useful to introduce more than one hidden layer if rules are to be extracted from the trained network. To use a multilayer perceptron for classification, the learning problem has to be modified and the network has to be defined as described at the beginning of this section. Furthermore, the number of hidden units must be estimated. The index $(m + n)/2$ hidden units can be used, where m and n are the number of input and output neurons. After training, the

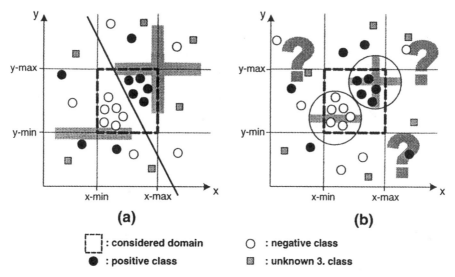

Figure 2 Classification by a multilayer perceptron (a) and a radial basis function network (b)

network associates an output vector $y = [y_1, y_2, ..., y_n]$ to (prior unknown) input data. Each y_i can be considered as a confidence value that the input data belong to class i. The class with the largest activation is usually chosen as the final classification output.

A multilayer perceptron used in this way classifies data by dividing the input space by hyperplanes. The class of a data point depends on its position relative to the hyperplanes. This kind of procedure corresponds to a global view, since all points on the same side of a hyperplane belong to the same class with regard to this special hyperplane. However, such a global classification can cause problems. For example, it is possible that points are counted as members of a class even if they are, for example, outside the domain being considered. Figure 2(a) illustrates this situation.

2.2. Radial Basis Function Networks (RBF Networks)

Another way to classify data is to encircle points of a class, that is, to specify a closed region or a cluster. All points within the same cluster belong to the same class. If for a certain class it is not possible to indicate a single region that would not include members of other classes, multiple clusters can be defined. This situation is shown in Figure 2(b). Due to this local view of the classification problem, points in far distant areas cannot also be interpreted as members of the class being considered. It is usually preferable to obtain the output "unknown" instead of a wrong classification, even if a unique assignment were possible. In general, the regions used for classification are not of arbitrary shape but are radial symmetric. In two-dimensional space the result is a circle, as shown in the example. In the n-dimensional case we are dealing with hyperspheres. To represent the clusters, radial (symmetric) functions can be used.

A radial function has a center where it assumes its highest absolute value. With increasing distance from this center the absolute value of the function decreases continuously in all directions and approaches zero. That is why these functions are also called center functions. For example, the following functions in $\mathbb{R}$ are radial symmetric around c $(d, \sigma > 0)$:

(i) $\quad h_c(x) = \exp\left(-\frac{1}{2\sigma^2}(x-c)^2\right)$

(ii) $\quad h_c(x) = \dfrac{1}{\sqrt{\left(\dfrac{x-c}{\sigma}\right)^2 + d^2}}.$

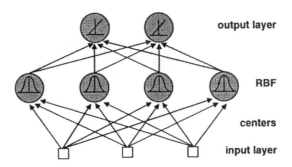

Figure 3 Structure of a Radial Basis Function network

If patterns can have arbitrary degrees of class membership, the (binary-encoded) classification is generalized to function approximation. For a multilayer perceptron this means that not just a two-valued decision concerning the location of a point relative to a hyperplane is made. The same generalization can be performed with local classification by considering the distance of a point to the center of a cluster. In fact, the idea of considering radial functions comes from mathematical interpolation theory (Powell, 1985). The goal is to interpolate a function of multiple variables by specifying several basis functions that are superimposed:

$$f(x) = \sum_i w_i \cdot h_c(x).$$

Radial basis functions turn out to be especially suitable for this approach. The first neural networks that were developed to compute and learn such models were presented by Broomhead and Lowe (1988) and Moody and Darken (1989). Radial basis function networks (RBF networks) are constructed by use of three different layers. The first layer simply passes the input values on to the hidden layer, while the output layer is used to superimpose the radial basis functions, which are implemented as activation functions of the neurons in the hidden layer. The connection weights from the input to the hidden layer are used to encode the centers of the respective clusters defined by the hidden neurons. Therefore, a neural network constructed by use of n radial basis functions in the hidden layer can distinguish between n hyperspheres or clusters. An example of an RBF network is presented in Figure 3.

One of the main advantages of RBF neural networks in the realm of data mining is that detailed numeric connections in the network can be designed in a more transparent way:

- RBF helps capture domain knowledge about the problem itself (e.g., a certain classification task) by defining (even in an approximate fashion) a series of receptive fields capturing regions of the data space that consists of data with a high level of heterogeneity.

- Introduction of the RBF is useful in reducing the inherent complexity of the data. A simple example is the well-known exclusive-OR problem: introducing a suitably located RBF changes the linearly nonseparable problem into one that is linearly separable.

The parameters of radial basis function networks can be derived by a supervised learning procedure. For this, the classification problem and the RBF network must be defined as described before. The number of hidden neurons, which implement the radial basis functions, now represents the number of clusters searched for. The network is trained analogously to a multilayer perceptron.

In contrast to the multilayer perceptron, the parameters of the hidden layer (centers and radii) can be set directly using known clusters. Then, the weights of the output layer can be computed by solving an (overdetermined) system of linear equations. A fixed number of centers can be defined, for example, by randomly chosen input patterns. A more suitable

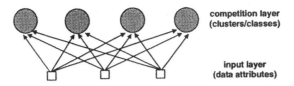

Figure 4 Network architecture for competitive learning

selection of centers can be obtained by vector quantization approaches, by clustering methods (see Chapter 16.5), or by self-organizing systems.

2.3. Self-Organizing Systems (Competitive Learning)

Self-organizing systems are neural networks that can be used to solve free learning problems, that is, the neural network determines an output pattern for each input pattern, such that similar input patterns result in similar output patterns on the basis of a suitable distance measure. A learning algorithm that uses a free learning problem is called an unsupervised learning algorithm, in contrast to supervised learning algorithms, which use a given set of pairs of input and output patterns (fixed learning problem). Classification problems of this type are also discussed in clustering analysis. Thus, self-organizing systems can solve a clustering problem during learning and a trained system can be used for classification.

Typically, self-organizing systems use neural networks with two layers to which an unsupervised learning procedure is applied (see Figure 4). The number of neurons in the input layer corresponds, as usual, to the number of features of the examined data. The only task of the input layer is to forward the values of an input pattern to the second layer of neurons (competition layer). The number of classes (clusters) into which the data is divided is determined by the output layer. The class that is assigned to a certain neuron is determined by the weights of the connections from the input neurons to this particular neuron. If a pattern is presented to the input layer, then each output neuron compares the input pattern with the information encoded in the weights of its incoming connections. The neuron that detects the strongest similarity between its weight vector and the input pattern obtains activation 1. Activation 0 is assigned to all other output neurons. The neuron with activation 1 is called the winner neuron (winner-takes-all principle). The network can be trained by modifying the weight vector of the winner neuron after propagation, such that for the next presentation of the same input vector a higher similarity is obtained.

A refined model of these networks is the self-organizing feature map developed by Kohonen (1982). This model enables the definition of a topological structure on the competition layer (e.g., straight line, rectangle, or cuboid), so that adjacent clusters are represented by adjacent neurons and thus a similarity measure on the data can be represented more appropriately.

3. Configuring and Training a Neural Net (for Classification)

Before a neural network can be configured, that is, before a specific architecture can be selected and its structure defined (number of neurons in each layer), and the network can be trained, the data should be reduced and preprocessed as described in Chapters 13 and 14. Furthermore, missing values have to be removed. This must be done using conventional techniques (e.g., deletion of all data sets with missing values, random replacement of missing values or replacement by mean value over the attribute, estimation of the missing parameter(s) by statistical approaches). After this data-preprocessing phase, an appropriate network architecture has to be selected. In general, a multilayer perceptron can be used for any classification purpose. Nevertheless, if it is expected that the data can be classified more appropriately by use of hyperspheres, an RBF network should be used instead.

Define number of input units i according to input data dimensionality

Define number of output units o according to output data dimensionality (number of classes)

Estimate number of hidden units:

    For RBF networks estimate number of clusters, for a MLP (with one hidden layer) estimate the number of hyperplanes or use the estimated value: (number of input units + number of output units)/2

Split your data set in p subsets S_i

repeat

    reset error and training estimator

    for all subsets S_i

        merge all subsets but S_i to a training set T

        train the network with T until the error no longer decreases

        add the (local) training error to the training estimator

        test the network with S_i

        add the (local) test error to the error estimator

    end for

    if the error estimator is not sufficiently low

        if the error on the training set is sufficiently low

            decrease the number of hidden units (probably overfitting occurred)

            if no hidden unit is left

                exit (training data is insufficient to train network)

            end if

        else

            increase the number of hidden units (problem can not be approximated well enough by the current network structure)

            if too many hidden units are created

                exit (network can not approximate the problem well enough)

            end if

        end if

    end if

Figure 5 Design and training process for a neural network (sample)

A possible training process for a neural network is described in Figure 5. The process presented is based on cross-validation (see, for example, Stone, 1974; see Chapter 19.1) to ensure the quality and robustness of the trained network. A further advantage of cross-validation in contrast to the simple splitting of the available data into a training and a test set is that all data patterns can be used for training. Nevertheless, the quality/performance of the neural network can be estimated. This is very important if only a few patterns of training data are available.

The presented process uses leave-k-out cross-validation: The whole data set is divided in p subsets of k elements (obviously, one set may consist of less than k elements, but it should be ensured that the size of the subsets differs by only about one element). Before each training cycle of the network, one set is selected as the test set; the remaining $p-1$ sets are merged to form a training set. The network is trained and tested by the respective sets until every subset has been used as a test set. Then, the error of each training cycle is combined into a single estimation value to describe the quality of the classification obtained. Usually $k = 10$ is used (10-fold cross-validation). If the number of available training patterns is very small, then $k = 1$ (leave-one-out cross-validation) should be used as much as possible as the pattern for training. A refined method, which reduces the computational costs for leave-one-out cross-validation drastically, was presented by Leisch and Hornik (1997). This method only cross-validates patterns with a high aggregated output error.

The process presented also includes a simple structure adaptation mechanism, which supports the user in finding an appropriate number of hidden neurons. The number of hidden units is enlarged if the network is not able to approximate the problem sufficiently. Thus, the learning capability of the neural network is enhanced. The number of hidden neurons is reduced (node pruning) if the network tends to interpolate some specific patterns in the learning set. In this case, even outliers will be learned and thus the generalization capability is reduced. This situation is also called overfitting and can (generally) be detected by a small error on the training set combined with a large error on the test set. Unfortunately, this situation can also occur if the available data is insufficient (number or type of sample patterns) to train the network. In this case, the presented process will terminate with an error.

The process can be refined by weight pruning techniques to improve the generalization capabilities of the network. For example, weights (connections) could be removed that are below a defined threshold (magnitude-based pruning). More refined pruning techniques respect the error change during the learning process to remove specific weights, for example, the optimal brain surgeon (OBS) technique developed by Hassibi and Storck (1993).

An overview of the interactive development and training of multilayer perceptrons is also presented in Swingler (1996) and Berry et al. (1997).

4. Interpretation of Neural Networks: Extracting Rules

The induction of rules using an already trained neural network is one of the important issues of data mining, and it determines to a high degree the usability of the networks in this environment. In general, one should stress that the networks can approximate data and eliminate eventual outliers. Thus, the determination of rules based on the network's outcomes rather than raw data is legitimate, and we may also hope for more stable and meaningful rules.

4.1. Current Techniques

Currently, most rule-extracting techniques are restricted to represent the network description as a set of if-then-else rules by use of conventional (two-valued Boolean) logic. This group of algorithms can be separated into decompositional, pedagogical, and eclectic approaches (Andrews et al., 1995).

Decompositional approaches extract rules at the level of individual (hidden and output) units of the trained network. For this, the output from each hidden and output unit is mapped into a binary outcome that corresponds to a rules consequent. Since each hidden or output unit can be interpreted as a step function (Boolean rule), only situations in which the summed input of a set of incoming links guarantees the activation of the unit, regardless of the activation on the other incoming links, have to be determined to construct (local) rules for the respective unit. Then, a rule base for the neural network can be constructed by aggregation of the local

for each hidden and output unit

    extract up to β_p subsets P_i of the positively weighted incoming links for which the summed weight

    is greater than the bias of the unit.

    for each subset P_i

        extract up to β_n minimal subsets N_i of negatively weighted links such that the summed

        weights are greater than the sum of P_i less the bias of the unit.

        let Z be a new predicate used nowhere else.

        for each subset N_i

            create the rule 'if N_i then Z'.

        end for

        create the rule "if P_i and not Z then the concept designated by the unit."

    end for

end for

Figure 6 The subset algorithm of Towell and Shavlik (1993)

rules. Examples of these methods are the KT algorithm developed by Fu (1991) and the subset algorithm developed by Towell and Shavlik (1993). Subset algorithms search for subsets of incoming weights that exceed the bias on a unit. They usually search at first for single links (i.e., the smallest subsets) that guarantee that the bias is exceeded. Then the size of the subsets is increased until all possible subsets have been analyzed and finally subsumed, and the overly general rules are removed. The subset algorithm proposed by Towell and Shavlik (1993) is presented in Figure 6. The decompositional approaches are usually combined with a special network structure and/or learning technique, which ensures in some manner the quality of the extracted rules, for example, the RuleNet technique of McMillan et al. (1991).

Pedagogical approaches treat the networks as a black box. The rule extraction process is constructed as a learning task, which uses the trained network just to generate examples. Such techniques are typically used in conjunction with a symbolic learning algorithm. Examples of such methods are the VI-analysis (VIA) technique developed by Thrun (1994), which uses validity intervals to derive the rules, and the RULENEG algorithm of Pop et al. (1994). This algorithm (see Figure 7) is designed to extract conjunctive rules using the training pattern of the network.

The third group, eclectic approaches, combines decompositional and pedagogical methods. An example of this is the DEDEC technique developed by Tickle et al. (1994), which focuses on extracting rules that include the most important input units (based on a ranking).

A different method, which can also be seen as a pedagogical approach, since it treats the network as a black box, is presented in the following. The main idea of this approach is to construct fuzzy relations based on a trained neural network (Pedrycz, 1998).

4.2. Interpretation Based on Fuzzy Relations

As mentioned before, neural networks realize a nonlinear static mapping $y = f(x)$, where x and y are vectors of reals. This, unfortunately, does not directly support any interpretation activities. Conditional statements of the form (see Chapter 5.3):

    if input is x_0 then output is y_0

```
let the rule base R be empty

for every pattern s from the training set

        find the class C for s using the network ( C = f(s) )

        if s is not classified by any rule r ∈ R

                initialize a new rule r for class C

                for every input unit i

                        s' = s

                        negate the i-th entry in s'

                        find the class C' for s' using the network ( C' = f(s') )

                        if C is not equal to C'

                                add i-th input and its truth value to r

                        end if

                end for

                add r to R

        end if

end for
```

Figure 7 The RULENEG algorithm

are too detailed to be easily interpretable. One possible way to alleviate this problem is to introduce an auxiliary interface to the neural network (see Figure 8).

It is composed of a number of linguistic granules (fuzzy relations) defined in the input space, for example, $A_1, A_2, \ldots A_c$ and a series of the corresponding granules showing in the output space $B_1, B_2, \ldots, B_p$. The interface works as follows: each numeric input activates the network as well as activates the linguistic terms in the input space. The level of activation of A_i is the membership value of A for this particular value of the argument. The result of the computation by the network is projected to the collection of linguistic terms in the output space. Thus, we may interpret the result obtained at the linguistic level in the form of the conditional statement "if a then b," where a and b are vectors of the activation levels of the fuzzy relations. The use of fuzzy relations, therefore, can greatly improve the interpretability.

As already mentioned, the linguistic granules must be chosen according to the particular data mining task. For this, two main aspects have to be emphasized:

- The size of the information granules depends heavily on the way we want to produce rules; the more detailed the description, the more fuzzy sets (relations) should be defined.

- One may relate the size as well as the location of the linguistic term with the experimental data. Basically, we make sure that the probability of the corresponding fuzzy relation does not fall below a certain threshold. In other words, we require that the following inequality holds

$$\int_X A(x)p(x)\,dx \geqslant \gamma,$$

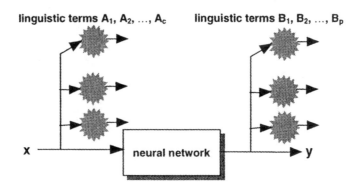

Figure 8 An interpretation environment of neural networks

where p is the probability density function of the experimental data, A is a membership function of the linguistic term, while γ denotes an assumed threshold level.

There is an important issue of characterization of the conditional statements appearing in the form "if a then b." Assume the following rule:

if $a = [0\ 0\ 0\ 1\ 0\ 0\ 0]$ then $b = [0.1\ 0.5\ 0.9\ 0\ 0]$.

This could be interpreted as three conditional statements (arranged according to their level of confidence):

1. If input is A_4 then output is B_3 with confidence level 0.9.
2. If input is A_4 then output is B_2 with confidence level 0.5.
3. If input is A_4 then output is B_1 with confidence level 0.1.

Therefore, such rules can be derived by defining an input vector that includes only one input equal to one and the rest of the entries equal to zero. The associated output vector results from the computing completed by the neural network. Unfortunately, two extreme types of output behavior can occur:

- The entries of the vector assume low values, for example, $[0.2\ 0.4\ 0.1\ 0.2]$. In other words, the conditional statement does not carry enough confidence associated with the conclusion. This signals a lack of evidence.

- The entries of the vector assume high values but this happens for several entries, for example, $[0.9\ 0.8\ 0.2\ 0.9]$. In this pattern the conclusion lacks specificity; the statement can arise in the form

  if input then output is B_i or B_k or B_j.

A rule should show neither of these; that is, a rule is a conditional statement "if a then b," whose conclusion is strong and specific.

One may easily quantify the notions of strength and specificity. In the first case we allude to the height of b, hgt(b). The notion of specificity (Yager, 1992), Sp(b), can serve as a useful indicator of specificity of the conclusion. If b is normal, then one may also consider a σ-count of b.

> **Remark.** *In case of RBF networks it is also possible, as mentioned before, to extract and insert knowledge in the form of cluster centers and radii directly using the network parameters. In the case of self-organizing systems, the cluster centers can usually be obtained using the weights.*

A different approach to simplifying the interpretability of neural networks by the use of fuzzy techniques is the use of fuzzy rules. This method is realized in so-called neuro-fuzzy systems.

4.3. Neuro-Fuzzy Systems

The main idea of neuro-fuzzy systems is to combine the advantages of fuzzy systems (see Chapters 10 and 30; e.g., interpretability, use of prior knowledge for initialization) with the learnability of neural networks. Thus, using fuzzy rules, it is possible to interpret the network structure and to introduce prior knowledge to the learning process in a convenient way.

Modern neuro-fuzzy systems are usually represented as special multilayer feedforward neural networks (see, for example, models like ANFIS, Jang, 1993; FuNe, Halgamuge and Glesner, 1994; Fuzzy RuleNet, Tschichold-Gürman, 1995; GARIC, Berenji and Khedkar, 1992; or NEFCLASS and NEFCON, Nauck et al., 1997). However, fuzzifications of other neural network architectures are also considered, as with, for example, self-organizing feature maps (Bezdek et al., 1992). In those neuro-fuzzy networks, connection weights and propagation and activation functions differ from common neural networks. Although there are many different approaches (see, for example, Buckley and Hayashi, 1994, 1995), the term neuro-fuzzy system is usually used for approaches that display the following properties (Nauck et al., 1997):

- A neuro-fuzzy system is based on a fuzzy system, which is trained by a learning algorithm derived from neural network theory. The (heuristical) learning procedure operates on local information, and causes only local modifications in the underlying fuzzy system.

- A neuro-fuzzy system can be viewed as a three-layer feedforward neural network. The first layer represents input variables, the middle (hidden) layer represents fuzzy rules, and the third layer represents output variables. Fuzzy sets are encoded as (fuzzy) connection weights. (Sometimes a five-layer architecture is used, where the fuzzy sets are represented in the units of the second and fourth layer.)

- A neuro-fuzzy system can always (i.e., before, during, and after learning) be interpreted as a system of fuzzy rules. It is also possible to create the system out of training data from scratch, as it is possible to initialize it by prior knowledge in the form of fuzzy rules. (Not all neuro-fuzzy models specify learning procedures for fuzzy rule creation, structure learning.)

- The learning procedure of a neuro-fuzzy system takes the semantical properties of the underlying fuzzy system into account. This results in constraints on the possible modifications applicable to the system parameters. (Not all neuro-fuzzy approaches have this property.)

- A neuro-fuzzy system approximates an n-dimensional (unknown) function that is partially defined by the training data. The fuzzy rules encoded within the system represent vague samples, and can be viewed as prototypes of the training data. A neuro-fuzzy system should not be seen as a kind of (fuzzy) expert system, and it has nothing to do with fuzzy logic in the narrow sense.

A neuro-fuzzy system is a good choice if interpretability is required or prior knowledge must (should) be used to initialize the learning process. A disadvantage of this approach is that in most cases the quality of the classification result is reduced due to the constraints that ensure interpretability. For a detailed overview of neuro-fuzzy (classification) systems see, for example, Lin and Lee (1996), Nauck et al. (1997), or Pedrycz (1998). Discussions concerning classification behavior can be found in Nürnberger et al. (1999b, 2000), a comparison to naive Bayes classifiers in Nürnberger et al. (1999a).

5. Conclusion

Compared to statistical methods, neural networks are useful if there is no knowledge about the relationship between input (data attributes) and output (classifier) variables. They offer a powerful and distributed computing architecture equipped with significant learning abilities and they are able to represent highly nonlinear and multivariable relationships.

However, it must be noted that neural networks cannot be seen as a general and easy solution for all types of classification problems. As described before, the selection of a network architecture and the design of an appropriate structure for a specific problem has to be done carefully. Furthermore, the data must be preprocessed as usual for all classification methods, and the learning process has to be done thoroughly. Nevertheless, if these points are considered, neural networks offer an efficient and robust method for classification.

References

Andrews, R., J. Diederich, and A. B. Tickle. 1995. "A survey and critique of techniques for extracting rules from trained artificial neural networks." *Konnektionismus und Neuronale Netze: Beiträge zur Herbstschule HeKoNN 95 (GMD Studien Nr. 272).* Sankt Augustin, Germany: GMD Forschungszentrum Informationstechnik.

Berenji, H. R. and P. Khedkar. 1992. "Learning and tuning fuzzy logic controllers through reinforcements." *IEEE Trans. Neural Networks* 3: 724–740.

Berry, M. J. A. and G. Linoff. 1997. *Data Mining Techniques: For Marketing, Sales and Customer Support.* New York: John Wiley and Sons.

Bezdek, J. C., E. C. K. Tsao and N. R. Pal. 1992. "Fuzzy Kohonen clustering networks." *Proceedings of the IEEE International Conference on Fuzzy Systems.* San Diego, NJ: IEEE, pp. 1035–1043.

Broomhead, D. S. and D. Lowe. 1988. "Multivariable functional interpolation and adaptive networks." *Complex Sys.* 2: 321–355.

Buckley, J. J. and Y. Hayashi. 1994. "Fuzzy neural networks: a survey." *Fuzzy Sets Sys.* 66: 1–13.

Buckley, J. J. and Y. Hayashi. 1995. "Neural networks for fuzzy systems." *Fuzzy Sets Sys.* 71: 265–276.

Duda, R. and P. Hart. 1973. *Pattern Classification and Scene Analysis.* New York: John Wiley and Sons.

Fahlmann, S. E. 1989. "An empirical study of learning speed in back-propagation networks." *Proceedings of the 1988 Connectionist Models Summer School,* edited by D. Touretzky, G. Hinton, and T. Sejnowski. San Mateo, CA: Morgan Kaufmann, and Carnegie Mellon University.

Fu, L. M. 1991. "Rule learning by searching on adapted nets." *Proceedings of the Ninth National Conference on Artificial Intelligence.* Anaheim, CA: AAAI/MIT Press, pp. 590–595.

Funahashi, K. 1989. "On the approximate realization of continuous mappings by neural networks." *Neural Networks* 2: 183.

Halgamuge, S. K. and M. Glesner. 1994. "Neural networks in designing fuzzy systems for real world applications." *Fuzzy Sets Sys.* 65: 1–12.

Hassibi, B. and D. G. Storck. 1993. "Second order derivatives for network pruning: optimal brain surgeon." *Advances in Neural Information Processing 5 (NIPS-5),* edited by S. J. Hansen, J. D. Cowan, and C. L. Giles. San Mateo, CA: Morgan Kauffmann.

Haykin, S. 1994. *Neural Networks.* Englewood Cliffs, NJ: Prentice-Hall.

Hopfield, J. J. 1982. "Neural networks and physical systems with emergent collective computational abilities." *Proc. Nat. Acad. Sci.* 79: 2554–2558.

Hornik, M., M. Stinchcombe, and H. White. 1989. "Multilayer feedforward networks are universal approximators." *Neural Networks* 2: 359–366.

Jang, J. S. R. 1993. "ANFIS: adaptive-network-based fuzzy inference systems." *IEEE Trans. Sys., Man Cybernet.* 23: 665–685.

Kohonen, T. 1982. "Self-organized formation of topologically correct feature maps." *Biol. Cybernet.* 43: 59–69.

Kohonen, T. 1984. "Self-organization and associative memory." Berlin: Springer-Verlag.

Leisch, F. and K. Hornik. 1997. "Error-dependent resampling for artificial neural network classifiers." *Proceedings of Neuronale Netze in Ingenieuranwendungen (NNIIA'97),* edited by B. Kröplin, pp. 1–14. Stuttgart: Universität Stuttgart.

Lin, C. T. and C. S. G. Lee. 1996. *Neural Fuzzy Systems: A Neuro-fuzzy Synergism to Intelligent Systems.* Englewood Cliffs, NJ: Prentice-Hall Inc.

Lippmann, R. P. 1987. "An introduction to computing with neural nets." *IEEE Mag. Acoust. Signal Speech Process* 4: 4–22.

McMillan, C., M. C. Mozer, and P. Smolensky. 1991. "The connectionist scientist game: rule extraction and refinement in a neural network." *Proceedings of the Thirteenth Annual Conference of the Cognitive Science Society.* Hillsdale, NJ, pp. 424–430. Chicago: Erlbaum.

Medsker, L. and L. C. Jain. 1999. *Recurrent Neural Networks: Design and Applications.* Boca Raton, FL: CRC Press.

Minsky, M. L. and S. Papert. 1969. *Perceptrons.* Cambridge, MA: MIT Press.

Moody, J. E. and C. Darken. 1989. "Fast learning in networks of locally-tuned processing units." *Neural Comput.* 1: 281–294.

Nauck, D., F. Klawonn, and R. Kruse. 1997. *Foundations of Neuro-Fuzzy Systems*. Chichester: John Wiley and Sons, Inc.

Neal, R. M. 1996. *Bayesian Learning for Neural Networks. Lecture Notes in Statistics 118*. New York: Springer-Verlag.

Nürnberger, A., C. Borgelt, and A. Klose. 1999a. "Improving naive Bayes classifiers using neuro-fuzzy learning." *Proceedings of the Sixth International Conference on Neural Information Processing '99 (ICONIP'99), Perth, Australia*, pp. 154–159. Piscataway, NJ: IEEE.

Nürnberger, A., A. Klose, and R. Kruse. 1999b. "Discussing cluster shapes of fuzzy classifiers." *Proceedings of the Eighteenth International Conference of the North American Fuzzy Information Processing Society (NAFIPS 99)*. Piscataway: IEEE 546–550.

Nürnberger, A., A. Klose, and R. Kruse. 2000. "Analyzing borders between partially contradicting fuzzy classification rules." *Proceedings of the Nineteenth International Conference of the North American Fuzzy Information Processing Society (NAFIPS 2000)*. Piscataway: IEEE, pp. 59–63.

Palcic, B. C., C. MacAulay, S. Shlien, W. Treurniet, H. Texcan, and G. Anderson. 1992. "Comparison of three different methods for automated classification of cervical cells." *Anal. Cellular Pathol* 4: 429–461.

Pedrycz, W. 1998. *Computational Intelligence: An Introduction*. Boca Raton, FL: CRC Press.

Pop, E., R. Hayward, and J. Diederich. 1994. *RULENEG: Extracting Rules from a Trained ANN by Stepwise Negation*. Queensland, Australia: Queensland University of Technology, Neurocomputing Research Center.

Powell, M. J. D. 1985. "Radial basis functions for multivariable interpolation: a review." *IMA Conference on Algorithms for the Approximation of Functions and Data*, pp. 143–167. Shrivenham, UK: RMCS.

Riedmiller, M. and H. Braun. 1993. "A direct adaptive method for faster backpropagation learning: the RPROP algorithm." *Proceedings of IEEE International Conference on Neural Networks (ICNN-93)*. Piscataway, NJ: IEEE, pp. 586–591.

Rojas, R. 1996. *Neural Networks—A Systematic Introduction*. Berlin: Springer-Verlag.

Rosenblatt, F. 1958. "The perceptron: a probabilistic model for information storage and organization in the brain." *Psychol. Rev.* 65: 386–408.

Rumelhart, D. E., G. E. Hinton, and R. J. Williams. 1986a. "Learning internal representations by error propagation." *Feature Discovery by Competitive Learning*, edited by D. E. Rumelhart and D. Zipser, pp. 318–362. Cambridge, MA: MIT Press.

Rumelhart, D. E., G. E. Hinton, and R. J. Williams. 1986b. "Learning representations by back-propagating errors." *Nature* 323: 533–536.

Sarle, W. S. 1994. "Neural networks and statistical models." *Proceedings of the Nineteenth Annual SAS User Group International Conference*, pp. 1538–1550. Cary, NC: SAS Institute.

Stone, M. 1974. "Cross-validation choice and assessment of statistical predictions." *J. R. Stat. Soc. B* 36(2): 111–147.

Swingler, K. 1996. *Applying Neural Networks: A Practical Guide*. London: Academic Press.

Tickle, A. B., M. Orlowski, and J. Diederich. 1994. *DEDEC: Decision Detection by Rule Extraction from Neural Networks*. Queensland, Australia: Queensland University of Technology, Neurocomputing Research Center.

Towell, G. and J. Shavlik. 1993. "The extraction of refined rules from knowledge based neural networks." *Machine Learning* 13: 71–101.

Thrun, S. B. 1994. "Extracting provably correct rules from artificial neural networks." Technical Report IAI-TR-93-5. Bonn, Germany: Institut für Informatik III, Universität Bonn.

Tschichold-Gürman, N. 1995. "RuleNet—a new knowledge-based artificial neural network model with application examples in robotics." Ph.D. diss. Zürich, Switzerland: ETH Zürich.

Yager, R. R. 1992. "On the specificity of a possibilistic distribution." *Fuzzy Sets Sys.* 50: 279–292.

Widrow, B. and M. E. Hoff. 1960. "Adaptive switching circuits." *IRE WESCON Convention Record*, pp. 96–104. New York: IRE.

16.1.9 Multicriteria Classification

Salvatore Greco, Benedetto Matarazzo, and Roman Slowinski

ABSTRACT In this article we consider multicriteria classification, which differs from usual classification problems since it takes into account preference orders in the description of objects by condition and decision attributes. The well-known methods of knowledge discovery do not use information about preference orders in multicriteria classification. It is worthwhile, however, to take this information into account as many practical problems involve evaluation of objects on preference-ordered domains. To deal with multicriteria classification we propose to use a dominance-based rough set approach (DRSA). This approach is different from the classical rough set approach (CRSA) because it takes into account preference orders in the domains of attributes and in the set of decision classes. Given a set of objects partitioned into predefined and preference-ordered classes, the new rough set approach is able to approximate this partition by means of dominance relations (instead of indiscernibility relations used in the CRSA). The rough approximation of this partition is a starting point for induction of "if..., then..." decision rules. The syntax of these rules is adapted to represent preference orders. The DRSA keeps the best properties of the CRSA: it only analyzes facts present in data and possible inconsistencies are not corrected. Moreover, the new approach does not need any prior discretization of continuous-valued attributes. The usefulness of the DRSA and its advantages over the CRSA are presented in a real study of evaluation of the risk of business failure.

1. Multicriteria Classification

The traditional meaning of classification concerns an assignment of a set of objects to a set of predefined classes. The objects are characterized by a set of attributes and the classes are not necessarily ordered according to a preference. In practice, however, very often the attribute domains and classes are preference ordered. Attributes with preference-ordered domains are called criteria. For example, classification of bank clients from the viewpoint of bankruptcy risk may involve such characteristics as return on equity (ROE), return on investment (ROI), and return on sales (ROS). The domains of these attributes are not simply ordered but involve a preference order since, from the viewpoint of bank managers, greater values of ROE, ROI, or ROS are better for clients being analyzed for bankruptcy risk. Neglecting this information in knowledge discovery may lead to the wrong conclusions being drawn. Consider, for example, two firms, A and B, evaluated by a set of attributes including ROE. If firm A has a high value of ROE while firm B has a low value of ROE, and evaluations of these firms on other attributes are equal, then, from a bankruptcy-risk point of view, firm A is better than (dominates) firm B. If, however, in the data sample set firm A has been assigned to a class of higher risk than firm B, then this is obviously inconsistent. This inconsistency will not be detected by usual knowledge discovery methods and possible conclusions derived by them from these data could be: if ROE of a firm is low, then the firm is safe, and if ROE of a firm is high, then the firm is risky, which is paradoxical. In order to discover this inconsistency one should analyze the data sample set from the viewpoint of the dominance principle, which requires that an object having a better (in general, not worse) evaluation on considered attributes cannot be assigned to a worse class.

The above deficiency of knowledge discovery methods in the context of multicriteria classification can be repaired by proposing concepts and algorithms respecting the dominance principle.

A knowledge discovery method that deals with multicriteria classification is the dominance-based rough set approach (DRSA) proposed in Greco et al. (1998, 1999). It generalizes the classical rough set approach (CRSA; Pawlak, 1982, 1991; Slowinski, 1992) by substituting the indiscernibility relation, used in CRSA, by a dominance relation, enabling discovery of inconsistencies with respect to the dominance principle. DRSA prepares, moreover, a conceptual ground for discovering rules that have syntax concordant with the dominance principle.

2. Dominance-Based Rough Set Approach (DRSA)

As is usual in knowledge discovery methods, in DRSA, information about objects is represented in a data matrix, in which rows are labeled by objects and represent the values of attributes for each corresponding object, whereas columns are labeled by attributes and represent the values of each corresponding attribute for the objects.

Let U denote a finite set of objects (universe), Q a finite set of attributes, V_q a domain of the attribute q, and $f(x, q)$ a function assigning to each object-attribute pair (x, q) a value from V_q. The set Q is, in general, divided into a set C of condition attributes and a decision attribute d.

In multicriteria classification, condition attributes are criteria. The notion of criterion involves a preference order in its domain while the domains of attributes, usually considered in machine discovery, are not preference ordered.

Furthermore, decision attribute d makes a partition of U into a finite number of classes $Cl = \{Cl_t, t \in T\}$, $T = \{1, ..., n\}$. Each $x \in U$ belongs to one and only one class $Cl_t \in Cl$. The classes from Cl are preference-ordered according to increasing order of class indices, that is, for all $r, s \in T$, such that $r > s$, the objects from Cl_r are preferred to the objects from Cl_s.

In multicriteria classification, due to the preference order in the set of classes Cl, the sets to be approximated are not the particular classes but upward unions and downward unions of classes, respectively:

$$Cl_t^{\geq} = \bigcup_{s \geq t} Cl_s, \quad Cl_t^{\leq} = \bigcup_{s \leq t} Cl_s, \quad t = 1, ..., n.$$

Union $Cl_t^{\geq}$ is the set of objects belonging to class Cl_t or to a more preferred class, while $Cl_t^{\leq}$ is the set of objects belonging to class Cl_t or to a less preferred class.

Notice that for $t = 2, ..., n$ we have $Cl_t^{\geq} = U - Cl_{t-1}^{\leq}$, that is, all the objects not belonging to class Cl_t or better belong to class Cl_{t-1} or worse.

Let us remark that in usual classification problems, knowledge discovery methods extract knowledge with respect to a given class Cl_t dividing the universe U into class Cl_t (set of positive examples) and its complement $U - Cl_t$ (set of negative examples), $t = 1, ..., n$. However, such bipartitions do not take into account the preference order among classes. Thus, in multicriteria classification we need another type of bipartitions that divide the universe into upward and downward unions of classes $Cl_t^{\geq}$ and $Cl_{t-1}^{\leq}$, $t = 2, ..., n$. As a result of this division, each object from the upward union $Cl_t^{\geq}$ is preferred to each object from the downward union $Cl_{t-1}^{\leq}$. When extracting knowledge with respect to an upward union $Cl_t^{\geq}$, we consider as positive all objects belonging to $Cl_t^{\geq}$ and as negative all objects belonging to $Cl_{t-1}^{\leq}$. Analogously, when extracting knowledge with respect to a downward union $Cl_{t-1}^{\leq}$, we consider as positive all objects belonging to $Cl_{t-1}^{\leq}$ and as negative all objects belonging to $Cl_t^{\geq}$. In this approach to knowledge discovery the dominance principle is applied as follows.

Let $\succeq_q$ be a weak preference relation on U (often called outranking; see Roy, 1985) representing a preference on the set of objects with respect to criterion q; $x \succeq_q y$ means that x is at least as good as y with respect to criterion q. We say that x dominates y with respect to $P \subseteq C$ (or, shortly, x P-dominates y), denoted by $x D_P y$, if $x \succeq_q y$ for all $q \in P$. Assuming, without loss of generality, that domains of all criteria are ordered such that preference increases with the value, $x D_P y$ is equivalent to: $f(x, q) \geq f(y, q)$ for all $q \in P$. Observe that for each $x \in U$, $x D_P x$, that is, P-dominance is reflexive.

Given $P \subseteq C$ and $x \in U$, the granules of knowledge used in DRSA for approximation of the unions $Cl_t^{\geq}$ and $Cl_t^{\leq}$ are:

- A set of objects dominating x, called P-dominating set, $D_P^+(x) = \{y \in U : y D_P x\}$.
- A set of objects dominated by x, called P-dominated set, $D_P^-(x) = \{y \in U : x D_P y\}$.

Given a set of criteria $P \subseteq C$, the inclusion of an object $x \in U$ to the upward union of classes $Cl_t^{\geq}$, $t = 2, ..., n$, creates an inconsistency in the sense of dominance principle if one of the following conditions holds:

- x belongs to class Cl_t or better but it is P-dominated by an object y belonging to a class worse than Cl_t, that is, $x \in Cl_t^{\geq}$ but $D_P^+(x) \cap Cl_{t-1}^{\leq} \neq \varnothing$.

- x belongs to a worse class than Cl_t but P-dominates an object y belonging to class Cl_t or better, that is, $x \notin Cl_t^{\geq}$ but $D_P^-(x) \cap Cl_t^{\geq} \neq \varnothing$.

If, given a set of criteria $P \subseteq C$, the inclusion of $x \in U$ to $Cl_t^{\geq}$, $t = 2, ..., n$, creates an inconsistency in the sense of dominance principle, we say that x belongs to $Cl_t^{\geq}$ with some ambiguity. Thus, x belongs to $Cl_t^{\geq}$ without any ambiguity with respect to $P \subseteq C$, if $x \in Cl_t^{\geq}$ and there is no inconsistency in the sense of dominance principle. This means that all objects P-dominating x belong to $Cl_t^{\geq}$, that is, $D_P^+(x) \subseteq Cl_t^{\geq}$.

Furthermore, x could belong to $Cl_t^{\geq}$ with respect to $P \subseteq C$ if one of the following conditions holds:

- According to decision attribute d, x belongs to $Cl_t^{\geq}$.

- According to decision attribute d, x does not belong to $Cl_t^{\geq}$ but is inconsistent in the sense of dominance principle with an object y belonging to $Cl_t^{\geq}$.

In terms of ambiguity, x could belong to $Cl_t^{\geq}$ with respect to $P \subseteq C$, if x belongs to $Cl_t^{\geq}$ with or without any ambiguity. Due to reflexivity of the dominance relation D_P, the conditions above can be summarized as follows: x could belong to class Cl_t or better, with respect to $P \subseteq C$, if among the objects P-dominated by x there is an object y belonging to class Cl_t or better, that is, $D_P^-(x) \cap Cl_t^{\geq} \neq \varnothing$.

For $P \subseteq C$, the set of all objects belonging to $Cl_t^{\geq}$ without any ambiguity constitutes the P-lower approximation of $Cl_t^{\geq}$, denoted by $\underline{P}(Cl_t^{\geq})$, and the set of all objects that could belong to $Cl_t^{\geq}$, constitutes the P-upper approximation of $Cl_t^{\geq}$, denoted by $\bar{P}(Cl_t^{\geq})$:

$$\underline{P}(Cl_t^{\geq}) = \{x \in U : D_P^+(x) \subseteq Cl_t^{\geq}\}, \quad \bar{P}(Cl_t^{\geq}) = \{x \in U : D_P^-(x) \cap Cl_t^{\geq} \neq \varnothing\}, \quad \text{for } t = 1, ..., n.$$

Analogously, one can define P-lower approximation and P-upper approximation of $Cl_t^{\leq}$ as follows:

$$\underline{P}(Cl_t^{\leq}) = \{x \in U : D_P^-(x) \subseteq Cl_t^{\leq}\}, \quad \bar{P}(Cl_t^{\leq}) = \{x \in U : D_P^+(x) \cap Cl_t^{\leq} \neq \varnothing\}, \quad \text{for } t = 1, ..., n.$$

All the objects belonging to $Cl_t^{\geq}$ and $Cl_t^{\leq}$ with some ambiguity constitute the P-boundary of $Cl_t^{\geq}$ and $Cl_t^{\leq}$, denoted by $Bn_P(Cl_t^{\geq})$ and $Bn_P(Cl_t^{\leq})$, respectively. They can be represented in terms of upper and lower approximations as follows:

$$Bn_P(Cl_t^{\geq}) = \bar{P}(Cl_t^{\geq}) - \underline{P}(Cl_t^{\geq}), \quad Bn_P(Cl_t^{\leq}) = \bar{P}(Cl_t^{\leq}) - \underline{P}(Cl_t^{\leq}), \quad \text{for } t = 1, ..., n.$$

P-lower and P-upper approximations of unions of classes $Cl_t^{\geq}$ and $Cl_t^{\leq}$ have the important property of complementarity. It says that if object x belongs without any ambiguity to class Cl_t or better, it is impossible that it could belong to class Cl_{t-1} or worse, that is, $\underline{P}(Cl_t^{\geq}) = U - \bar{P}(Cl_{t-1}^{\leq})$. Due to complementarity property, $Bn_P(Cl_t^{\geq}) = Bn_P(Cl_{t-1}^{\leq})$, for $t = 2, ..., n$, which means that if x belongs with ambiguity to class Cl_t or better, it also belongs with ambiguity to class Cl_{t-1} or worse.

From the knowledge discovery point of view, P-lower approximations of unions of classes represent certain knowledge provided by criteria from $P \subseteq C$, while P-upper approximations represent possible knowledge and the P-boundaries contain doubtful knowledge.

The above definition of rough approximations is based on a strict application of the dominance principle. However, when defining nonambiguous objects, it is reasonable to accept a limited proportion of negative examples, particularly for large data matrices. Such an extended version of DRSA is called the variable-consistency DRSA model (VC-DRSA; Greco et al., 2000).

For every $P \subseteq C$, the objects being consistent in the sense of dominance principle with all upward and downward unions of classes are P-correctly classified. For every $P \subseteq C$, the quality of approximation of multicriteria classification Cl by set of criteria P is defined as the ratio between the number of P-correctly classified objects and the number of all the objects in the data sample set. Since the objects P-correctly classified are those that do not belong to any P-boundary of unions $Cl_t^{\geq}$ and $Cl_t^{\leq}$, $t = 1, ..., n$, the quality of approximation of multicriteria classification Cl by set of criteria P, can be written as

$$\gamma_P(Cl) = \frac{\text{card}\left(U - \left(\bigcup_{t \in T} Bn_P(Cl_t^{\leq})\right)\right)}{\text{card}(U)} = \frac{\text{card}\left(U - \left(\bigcup_{t \in T} Bn_P(Cl_t^{\geq})\right)\right)}{\text{card}(U)}.$$

$\gamma_P(Cl)$ can be seen as a measure of the quality of knowledge that can be extracted from the data matrix, where P is the set of criteria and Cl is the considered classification.

Each minimal subset $P \subseteq C$ such that $\gamma_P(Cl) = \gamma_C(Cl)$ is called a reduct of Cl and is denoted by RED_{Cl}. Let us remark that a data sample set can have more than one reduct. The intersection of all reducts is called the core and is denoted by $CORE_{Cl}$. Criteria from $CORE_{Cl}$ cannot be removed from the data sample set without deteriorating the knowledge to be discovered. This means that in set C there are three categories of criteria:

1. Indispensable criteria included in the core.
2. Exchangeable criteria included in some reducts but not in the core.
3. Redundant criteria being neither indispensable nor exchangeable, thus not included in any reduct.

3. Extraction of Decision Rules

Dominance-based rough approximations of upward and downward unions of classes can serve to induce a generalized description of objects contained in the data matrix in terms of "if..., then..." decision rules. For a given upward or downward union of classes, $Cl_t^{\geq}$ or $Cl_s^{\leq}$, decision rules induced under a hypothesis that objects belonging to $\underline{P}(Cl_t^{\geq})$ or $\underline{P}(Cl_s^{\leq})$ are positive and all the others negative suggest an assignment to class Cl_t or better, or to class Cl_s or worse, respectively. On the other hand, decision rules induced under a hypothesis that objects belonging to the intersection $\bar{P}(Cl_s^{\leq}) \cap \bar{P}(Cl_t^{\geq})$ are positive and all the others negative are suggesting an assignment to some classes between Cl_s and Cl_t ($s < t$).

In multicriteria classification it is meaningful to consider the following five types of decision rules:

1. Certain $D_{\geq}$-decision rules, providing lower profile descriptions for objects belonging to $Cl_t^{\geq}$ without ambiguity: if $f(x, q_1) \geq r_{q1}$ and $f(x, q_2) \geq r_{q2}$ and $...f(x, q_p) \geq r_{qp}$, then $x \in Cl_t^{\geq}$
2. Possible $D_{\geq}$-decision rules, providing lower profile descriptions for objects belonging to $Cl_t^{\geq}$ with or without any ambiguity: if $f(x, q_1) \geq r_{q1}$ and $f(x, q_2) \geq r_{q2}$ and $...f(x, q_p) \geq r_{qp}$, then x could belong to $Cl_t^{\geq}$
3. Certain $D_{\leq}$-decision rules, providing upper profile descriptions for objects belonging to $Cl_t^{\leq}$ without ambiguity: if $f(x, q_1) \leq r_{q1}$ and $f(x, q_2) \leq r_{q2}$ and $...f(x, q_p) \leq r_{qp}$, then $x \in Cl_t^{\leq}$
4. Possible $D_{\leq}$-decision rules, providing upper profile descriptions for objects belonging to $Cl_t^{\leq}$ with or without any ambiguity: if $f(x, q_1) \leq r_{q1}$ and $f(x, q_2) \leq r_{q2}$ and $...f(x, q_p) \leq r_{qp}$, then x could belong to $Cl_t^{\leq}$
5. Approximate $D_{\geq \leq}$-decision rules, providing lower and upper profile descriptions simultaneously for objects belonging to $Cl_s \cup Cl_{s+1} \cup ... \cup Cl_t$ without possibility of discerning to which class: if $f(x, q_1) \geq r_{q1}$ and $f(x, q_2) \geq r_{q2}$ and $...f(x, q_k) \geq r_{qk}$ and $f(x, q_{k+1}) \leq r_{qk+1}$ and $...f(x, q_p) \leq r_{qp}$, then $x \in Cl_s \cup Cl_{s+1} \cup ... \cup Cl_t$.

In the left-hand side of a $D_{\geq \leq}$-decision rule we can have $f(x, q) \geq r_q$ and $f(x, q) \leq r_q'$, where $r_q \leq r_q'$, for the same $q \in C$. Moreover, if $r_q = r_q'$, the two conditions boil down to $f(x, q) = r_q$.

Since a decision rule is an implication, by a minimal rule we mean an implication for which there is no other implication with a left-hand side of at least the same weakness (in other words, a rule using a subset of elementary conditions and/or weaker elementary conditions) and a right-hand side of at least the same strength (in other words, a $D_{\geq}$- or a $D_{\leq}$-decision rule assigning objects to the same union or sub-union of classes, or a $D_{\geq,\leq}$-decision rule assigning objects to the same or larger set of classes).

Rules of type (1) and (3) represent certain knowledge extracted from the data matrix, while rules of type (2) and (4) represent possible knowledge, and rules of type (5) represent doubtful knowledge.

The rules of type (1) and (3) are exact, if they do not cover negative examples, and they are probabilistic, otherwise. In the latter case, each rule is characterized by a confidence ratio, representing the probability that an object matching the left-hand side of the rule also matches its right-hand side. Probabilistic rules are concordant with the VC-DRSA model mentioned above.

Let us comment on application of decision rules to the objects described by criteria from C. When applying $D_{\geq}$-decision rules to object x, it is possible that x either matches the left-hand side of at least one decision rule or does not match the left-hand side of any decision rule. In the case of at least one matching, it is reasonable to conclude that x belongs to class Cl_t, being the lowest class of the upward union $Cl_t^{\geq}$ resulting from the intersection of all the right-hand sides of rules covering x. Precisely, if x matches the left-hand side of rules $\rho_1, \rho_2, ..., \rho_m$, having a right-hand side $x \in Cl_{t1}^{\geq}, x \in Cl_{t2}^{\geq}, ..., x \in Cl_{tm}^{\geq}$, then x is assigned to class Cl_t, where $t = \max\{t1, t2, ..., tm\}$. In the case of no matching, it is concluded that x belongs to Cl_1, that is, to the worst class, since no rule with a right-hand side suggesting a better classification of x is covering this object.

Analogously, when applying $D_{\leq}$-decision rules to object x, it is concluded that x belongs either to class Cl_z, being the highest class of the downward union $Cl_t^{\leq}$ resulting from intersection of all the right-hand sides of rules covering x, or to class Cl_n, that is, to the best class, when x is not covered by any rule. Precisely, if x matches the left-hand side of rules $\rho_1, \rho_2, ..., \rho_m$, having a right-hand side $x \in Cl_{t1}^{\leq}, x \in Cl_{t2}^{\leq}, ..., x \in Cl_{tm}^{\leq}$, then x is assigned to class Cl_t, where $t = \min\{t1, t2, ..., tm\}$. In the case of no matching, it is concluded that x belongs to the best class Cl_n because no rule with a right-hand side suggesting a worse classification of x is covering this object.

Finally, when applying $D_{\geq,\leq}$-decision rules to object x, it is concluded that x belongs to the union of all classes suggested in the right-hand side of rules covering x.

A set of decision rules is complete if it is able to cover all objects from the data matrix in such a way that consistent objects are reclassified to their original classes and inconsistent objects are classified to clusters of classes referring to this inconsistency. We call each set of decision rules that is complete and nonredundant minimal, that is, exclusion of any rule from this set makes it noncomplete.

One of three induction strategies can be adopted to obtain a set of decision rules (Stefanowski and Vanderpooten, 1994; Stefanowski, 1998):

- generation of a minimal description, that is, a minimal set of rules,

- generation of an exhaustive description, that is, all rules for a given data matrix,

- generation of a characteristic description, that is, a set of rules covering relatively many objects each, however, all together not necessarily all objects from U.

In the following we present a rule induction algorithm, called DOMLEM (Greco et al., 2000), built on the idea of LEM2 (Grzymala-Busse, 1992) and generating a minimal description.

In the algorithm, E denotes a complex (conjunction of elementary conditions e) being a candidate for the left-hand side of the rule. Moreover, $[E]$ denotes a set of objects matching complex E. Complex E is accepted as the left-hand side of the rule iff $\varnothing \neq [E] = \bigcap_{e \in E}[e] \subseteq B$, where B is the considered approximation corresponding to the right-hand side of the rule. For

the sake of simplicity, in the following we present the general scheme of the DOMLEM
algorithm for type (1) decision rules.

Procedure DOMLEM
(**input:** L- a family of P-lower approximations of upward unions of classes:
$\{\underline{P}(Cl_t^{\geqslant}), \underline{P}(Cl_{t-1}^{\geqslant}), \ldots, \underline{P}(Cl_2^{\geqslant})\}$, where $P \subseteq C$,
output: $R_{\geqslant}$ set of $D_{\geqslant}$-decision rules);
begin
　　　　$R_{\geqslant} := \varnothing;$
　　　for each $B \in L$ **do**
　　　begin
　　　　　　$E := \mathbf{find\_rules}\,(B);$
　　　　　　$R_{\geqslant} := R_{\geqslant} \cup E;$
　　　end
end.
Function find_rules
(**input:** a set B;
output: a set of rules $\mathbf{E}$ covering set B);
begin
　　　　$G := B;$ {a set of objects from the given approximation}
　　　　$E := \varnothing;$
　　　while $G \neq \varnothing$ **do**
　　　begin
　　　　　　$E := \varnothing;$ {starting complex}
　　　　　　$S := G;$ {set of objects currently covered by E}
　　　　while $(E = \varnothing)$ **or not** $([E] \subseteq B)$ **do**
　　　　begin
　　　　　　　　$best := \varnothing;$ {best candidate for elementary condition}
　　　　　　　for each criterion $q_i \in P$ **do**
　　　　　　　begin
　　　　　　　　　　$Cond := \{(f(x, q_i)\mathrm{tf} = \}\mathrm{Pi2}\}5 r_{qi}) : \exists x \in S\,(f(x, q_i) = r_{qi})\};$
　　　　　　　　　　{for each positive object from S create an elementary
　　　　　　　　　　condition}
　　　　　　　　　for each $elem \in Cond$ **do**
　　　　　　　　　if $evaluate(\{elem\} \cup E)$ is_better_than $evaluate(\{best\} \cup E)$
　　　　　　　　　then $best := elem;$
　　　　　　　　　　　　{evaluate if new condition is better than previous
　　　　　　　　　　　　best};
　　　　　　　end;
　　　　　　　$E := E \cup \{best\};$
　　　　　　　$S := S \cap [best];$
　　　　end; {while not $([E] \subseteq B)$}
　　　　for each elementary condition $e \in E$ **do**
　　　　　　　　if $[E - \{e\}] \subseteq B$ **then** $E := E - \{e\};$
　　　　$\mathbf{E} := \mathbf{E} \cup \{E\};$
　　　　$G := G - [E];$
　　　end; {while $G \neq \varnothing$}
　　　create rules on the basis of $\mathbf{E}$
end {function}

Let us comment on the choice of the best condition using the function *evaluate*(E). Complex E,
being a candidate left-hand side for a rule, can be evaluated by various measures. In the
current version of DOMLEM the complex E with the highest ratio $|[E] \cap G| / |[E]|$ is
considered the best. In case of a tie, the complex E with the highest value of $|[E] \cap G|$ is
chosen.

The procedure of rule extraction makes clear the utility of the concept of inconsistency in the sense of the dominance principle in the knowledge discovery process. Decision rules are created by appending descriptors to a complex until a consistency is reached. For instance, in the case of type (1) decision rules, the descriptors are appended until there is no object dominating the complex while not belonging to the upward union of classes indicated in the right-hand side of the rule being created. The concept of inconsistency is similarly applied in calculation of reducts. These remarks justify the use of DRSA in the discovery of rules and reducts even if there is no inconsistency in the sample data set for the complete set of criteria C.

4. Example

To illustrate the application of DRSA to multicriteria classification we will use part of some data provided by a Greek industrial bank, ETEVA, which finances industrial and commercial firms in Greece (Slowinski and Zopounidis, 1995). A sample composed of thirty-nine firms was chosen for the study in cooperation with ETEVA's financial manager. The manager has classified the selected firms into three classes of the bankruptcy risk. The sorting decision is represented by decision attribute d making a trichotomic partition of the thirty-nine firms:

- $d = A$ means acceptable,
- $d = U$ means uncertain,
- $d = NA$ means unacceptable.

The partition is denoted by $Cl = \{Cl_A, Cl_U, Cl_{NA}\}$ and, obviously, class Cl_A is better than Cl_U, which is better than Cl_{NA}.

The firms were evaluated using the following twelve criteria (↑ means preference increasing with value and ↓ means preference decreasing with value):

- A_1 = earnings before interests and taxes/total assets(↑)
- A_2 = net income/net worth(↑)
- A_3 = total liabilities/total assets(↓)
- A_4 = total liabilities/cash flow(↓)
- A_5 = interest expenses/sales(↓)
- A_6 = general and administrative expense/sales(↓)
- A_7 = managers' work experience(↑), (very low = 1, low = 2, medium = 3, high = 4, very high = 5),
- A_8 = firm's market niche/position(↑), (bad = 1, rather bad = 2, medium = 3, good = 4, very good = 5),
- A_9 = technical structure-facilities(↑), (bad = 1, rather bad = 2, medium = 3, good = 4, very good = 5),
- A_{10} = organization-personnel(↑), (bad = 1, rather bad = 2, medium = 3, good = 4, very good = 5),
- A_{11} = special competitive advantage of firms(↑), (low = 1, medium = 2, high = 3, very high = 4),
- A_{12} = market flexibility(↑), (very low = 1, low = 2, medium = 3, high = 4, very high = 5).

The first six criteria are continuous (financial ratios) and the last six are ordinal. The data matrix is presented in Table 1.

The main questions to be answered by the knowledge discovery process were the following:

- Is the information contained in Table 1 consistent?
- What are the reducts of criteria ensuring the same quality of approximation of the multicriteria classification as the whole set of criteria?

Table 1 Financial Data Matrix

Firm	A_1	A_2	A_3	A_4	A_5	A_6	A_7	A_8	A_9	A_{10}	A_{11}	A_{12}	d
F1	16.4	14.5	59.82	2.5	7.5	5.2	5	3	5	4	2	4	A
F2	35.8	67.0	64.92	1.7	2.1	4.5	5	4	5	5	4	5	A
F3	20.6	61.75	75.71	3.6	3.6	8.0	5	3	5	5	3	5	A
F4	11.5	17.1	57.1	3.8	4.2	3.7	5	2	5	4	3	4	A
F5	22.4	25.1	49.8	2.1	5.0	7.9	5	3	5	5	3	5	A
F6	23.9	34.5	48.9	1.7	2.5	8.0	5	3	4	4	3	4	A
F7	29.9	44.0	57.8	1.8	1.7	2.5	5	4	4	5	3	5	A
F8	8.7	5.4	27.4	3.3	4.5	4.5	5	2	4	4	1	4	A
F9	25.7	29.7	46.8	1.7	4.6	3.7	4	2	4	3	1	3	A
F10	21.2	24.6	64.8	3.7	3.6	8.0	4	2	4	4	1	4	A
F11	18.32	31.6	69.3	4.4	2.8	3.0	4	3	4	4	3	4	A
F12	20.7	19.3	19.7	0.7	2.2	4.0	4	2	4	4	1	3	A
F13	9.9	3.5	53.1	4.5	8.5	5.3	4	2	4	4	1	4	A
F14	10.4	9.3	80.9	9.4	1.4	4.1	4	2	4	4	3	3	A
F15	17.7	19.8	52.8	3.2	7.9	6.1	4	4	4	4	2	5	A
F16	14.8	15.9	27.94	1.3	5.4	1.8	4	2	4	3	2	3	A
F17	16.0	14.7	53.5	3.9	6.8	3.8	4	4	4	4	2	4	A
F18	11.7	10.01	42.1	3.9	12.2	4.3	5	2	4	2	1	3	A
F19	11.0	4.2	60.8	5.8	6.2	4.8	4	2	4	4	2	4	A
F20	15.5	8.5	56.2	6.5	5.5	1.8	4	2	4	4	2	4	A
F21	13.2	9.1	74.1	11.21	6.4	5.0	2	2	4	4	2	3	U
F22	9.1	4.1	44.8	4.2	3.3	10.4	3	4	4	4	3	4	U
F23	12.9	1.9	65.02	6.9	14.01	7.5	4	3	3	2	1	2	U
F24	5.9	−27.7	77.4	−32.2	16.6	12.7	3	2	4	4	2	3	U
F25	16.9	12.4	60.1	5.2	5.6	5.6	3	2	4	4	2	3	U
F26	16.7	13.1	73.5	7.1	11.9	4.1	2	2	4	4	2	3	U
F27	14.6	9.7	59.5	5.8	6.7	5.6	2	2	4	4	2	4	U
F28	5.1	4.9	28.9	4.3	2.5	46.0	2	2	3	3	1	2	U
F29	24.4	22.3	32.8	1.4	3.3	5.0	2	3	4	4	2	3	U
F30	29.7	8.6	41.8	1.6	5.2	6.4	2	3	4	4	2	3	U
F31	7.3	−64.5	67.5	−2.2	30.1	8.7	3	3	4	4	2	3	NA
F32	23.7	31.9	63.6	3.5	12.1	10.2	3	2	3	4	1	3	NA
F33	18.9	13.5	74.5	10.0	12.0	8.4	3	3	3	4	3	4	NA
F34	13.9	3.3	78.7	25.5	14.7	10.1	2	2	3	4	3	4	NA
F35	−13.3	−31.1	63.0	−10.0	21.2	23.1	2	1	4	3	1	2	NA
F36	6.2	−3.2	46.1	5.1	4.8	10.5	2	1	3	3	2	3	NA
F37	4.8	−3.3	71.9	34.6	8.6	11.6	2	2	4	4	2	3	NA
F38	0.1	−9.6	42.5	−20.0	12.9	12.4	1	1	4	3	1	3	NA
F39	13.6	9.1	76.0	11.4	17.1	10.3	1	1	2	1	1	2	NA

- What decision rules can be extracted from Table 1?
- What are the minimal sets of decision rules?

We have answered these questions using the dominance-based rough set approach.

The first result of the DRSA is the discovery that the financial data matrix is consistent for the complete set of criteria C. Therefore, the C-lower approximation and C-upper approximation of $Cl_{NA}^{\leqq}$, $Cl_U^{\leqq}$ and $Cl_U^{\geqq}$, $Cl_A^{\geqq}$ are the same. In other words, the quality of approximation of all upward and downward unions of classes is equal to 1.

The second discovery is a set of eighteen reducts of criteria ensuring the same quality of classification as the whole set of 12 criteria:

$$RED_{Cl}^1 = \{A_1, A_4, A_5, A_7\},$$
$$RED_{Cl}^2 = \{A_2, A_4, A_5, A_7\},$$
$$RED_{Cl}^3 = \{A_3, A_4, A_6, A_7\},$$

$$RED_{Cl}^{4} = \{A_4, A_5, A_6, A_7\},$$

$$RED_{Cl}^{5} = \{A_4, A_5, A_7, A_8\},$$

$$RED_{Cl}^{6} = \{A_2, A_3, A_7, A_9\},$$

$$RED_{Cl}^{7} = \{A_1, A_3, A_4, A_7, A_9\},$$

$$RED_{Cl}^{8} = \{A_1, A_5, A_7, A_9\},$$

$$RED_{Cl}^{9} = \{A_2, A_5, A_7, A_9\},$$

$$RED_{Cl}^{10} = \{A_4, A_5, A_7, A_9\},$$

$$RED_{Cl}^{11} = \{A_5, A_6, A_7, A_9\},$$

$$RED_{Cl}^{12} = \{A_4, A_5, A_7, A_{10}\},$$

$$RED_{Cl}^{13} = \{A_1, A_3, A_4, A_7, A_{11}\},$$

$$RED_{Cl}^{14} = \{A_2, A_3, A_4, A_7, A_{11}\},$$

$$RED_{Cl}^{15} = \{A_4, A_5, A_6, A_{12}\},$$

$$RED_{Cl}^{16} = \{A_1, A_3, A_5, A_6, A_9, A_{12}\},$$

$$RED_{Cl}^{17} = \{A_3, A_4, A_6, A_{11}, A_{12}\},$$

$$RED_{Cl}^{18} = \{A_1, A_2, A_3, A_6, A_9, A_{11}, A_{12}\}.$$

All the above subsets of criteria are equally good and sufficient for perfect approximation of the classification performed by ETEVA's financial manager on the thirty-nine firms. The core of Cl is empty ($CORE_{Cl} = \varnothing$), which means that no criterion is indispensable for the approximation. Moreover, all the criteria are exchangeable and no criterion is redundant.

The third discovery is the set of all decision rules. We obtained seventy-four rules describing $Cl_{NA}^{\leqslant}$, fifty-one rules describing $Cl_{U}^{\leqslant}$, seventy-five rules describing $Cl_{U}^{\geqslant}$, and seventy-nine rules describing $Cl_{A}^{\geqslant}$.

The fourth discovery is the finding of minimal sets of decision rules. Several minimal sets were found; one of them is shown below (in parenthesis there is the number of objects supporting the rule):

1. if $f(x, A_3) \geqslant 67.5$ and $f(x, A_4) \geqslant -2.2$ and $f(x, A_6) \geqslant 8.7$, then $x \in Cl_{NA}^{\leqslant}$, (4),

2. if $f(x, A_2) \leqslant 3.3$ and $f(x, A_7) \leqslant 2$, then $x \in Cl_{NA}^{\leqslant}$, (5),

3. if $f(x, A_3) \geqslant 63.6$ and $f(x, A_7) \leqslant 3$ and $f(x, A_9) \leqslant 3$, then $x \in Cl_{NA}^{\leqslant}$, (4),

4. if $f(x, A_2) \leqslant 12.4$ and $f(x, A_6) \geqslant 5.6$, then $x \in Cl_{U}^{\leqslant}$, (14),

5. if $f(x, A_7) \leqslant 3$, then $x \in Cl_{U}^{\leqslant}$, (18),

6. if $f(x, A_2) \geqslant 3.5$ and $f(x, A_5) \leqslant 8.5$, then $x \in Cl_{U}^{\geqslant}$, (26),

7. if $f(x, A_7) \geqslant 4$, then $x \in Cl_{U}^{\geqslant}$, (21),

8. if $f(x, A_1) \geqslant 8.7$ and $f(x, A_9) \geqslant 4$, then $x \in Cl_{U}^{\geqslant}$, (27),

9. if $f(x, A_2) \geqslant 3.5$ and $f(x, A_7) \geqslant 4$, then $x \in Cl_{A}^{\geqslant}$. (20).

As the minimal set of rules is complete and composed of $D_{\geqslant}$-decision rules and $D_{\leqslant}$-decision rules only, application of these rules to the thirty-nine firms will result in their exact reclassification to classes of risk.

Minimal sets of decision rules represent the most concise and nonredundant knowledge representations. The above minimal set of nine decision rules uses eight criteria and eighteen elementary conditions, that is, 3.85 percent of descriptors from the data matrix.

5. Comparison with Other Classification Methods

The well known machine discovery methods cannot deal with multicriteria classification because they do not consider preference orders in the domains of attributes and among the classes. Within multicriteria decision analysis there are methods for multicriteria classification, however, they are not discovering classification patterns from data; they simply apply a preference model, like the utility function in scoring methods (see e.g., Thomas et al., 1992), to a set of objects to be classified. In this sense, they are not knowledge discovery methods.

Comparing DRSA to CRSA, one can see the following differences between the two approaches. CRSA extracts knowledge about a partition of U into classes that are not preference ordered; the granules used for knowledge representation are sets of objects indiscernible by a set of condition attributes. In the case of DRSA and multicriteria classification, the condition attributes are criteria and classes are preference ordered. The extracted knowledge concerns a collection of upward and downward unions of classes and the granules used for knowledge representation are sets of objects defined using dominance relation. This is the main difference between CRSA and DRSA.

There are three remarkable advantages of DRSA over CRSA. The first one is the ability to handle criteria, preference-ordered classes, and inconsistencies in the set of decision examples that CRSA is not able to discover—inconsistencies in the sense of violation of the dominance principle. In consequence, rough approximations separate the certain part of the information from the doubtful part, which is taken into account in rule induction. The second advantage is the analysis of a data matrix without any preprocessing of data, in particular, any discretization of continuous attributes. The third advantage of DRSA lies in the richer syntax of decision rules induced from rough approximations. The elementary conditions (criterion *rel.* value) of decision rules resulting from DRSA use $rel. \in \{ \leqslant, =, \text{tf} = \}Pi2\}5\}$, while those resulting from CRSA use $rel. \in \{=\}$. The DRSA syntax is more understandable to practitioners and makes the representation of knowledge more synthetic, since minimal sets of decision rules are smaller than minimal sets of decision rules resulting from CRSA. Other extensions and characteristics of DRSA can be found in Greco et al. (2001).

6. Conclusion

Multicriteria classification differs from the usual classification problems since it involves preference orders in domains of attributes and in the set of classes. This requires that a knowledge discovery method applied to multicriteria classification respects the dominance principle. As this is not the case for well known methods of data mining and knowledge discovery they are not able to discover all relevant knowledge contained in the analyzed data sample set and, even worse, they may yield unreasonable discoveries, because they are inconsistent with the dominance principle. These deficiencies are repaired in DRSA based on the concept of rough approximations consistent with the dominance principle.

ACKNOWLEDGMENT

The research of the first two authors was supported by the Italian Ministry of University and Scientific Research (MURST). The third author wishes to acknowledge financial support from the State Committee for Scientific Research, KBN research grant no. 8T11F 006 19, and from the Foundation for Polish Science, subsidy no. 11/2001.

References

Greco, S., B. Matarazzo, and R. Slowinski. 1998. "A new rough set approach to evaluation of bankruptcy risk." In *Operational Tools in the Management of Financial Risk*, edited by C. Zopounidis, pp. 121–136. Boston: Kluwer Academic Publishers.

Greco, S., B. Matarazzo, and R. Slowinski. 1999. "The use of rough sets and fuzzy sets in MCDM." In *Advances in Multiple Criteria Decision Making*, edited by T. Gal, T. Hanne, and T. Stewart, Chapter 14, pp. 14.1–14.59. Boston: Kluwer Academic Publishers Detailed description of the dominance-based rough set approach to multicriteria classification and other multicriteria decision problems, i.e., choice and ranking problems. Heterogeneous information (qualitative and quantitative, ordered and nonordered, crisp and fuzzy evaluations, as well as ordinal, quantitative, and numerical nonquantitative scales of preference) can be processed within the new rough set approach.

Greco, S., B. Matarazzo, R. Slowinski, and J. Stefanowski. 2000. "Variable consistency model of dominance-based rough set approach." In *Proceedings of the RSCTC'2000 Conference*, Banff.

Greco, S., B. Matarazzo, and R. Slowinski 2001. "Rough sets theory for multicriteria decision analysis." *Eur. J. Oper. Res.* **129**: 1–47.

Grzymala-Busse, J. W. 1992. "LERS—a system for learning from examples based on rough sets." In *Intelligent Decision Support. Handbook of Applications and Advances of the Rough Sets Theory*, edited by R. Slowinski, pp. 3–18. Dordrecht, Netherlands: Kluwer Academic Publishers.

Pawlak, Z. 1982. "Rough sets." *Int. J. Inform. Comput. Sci.* **11**: 341–356.

Pawlak, Z. 1991. *Rough Sets. Theoretical Aspects of Reasoning about Data*. Dordrecht, Netherlands: Kluwer Academic Publishers.

Roy, B. 1985. *Méthodologie Multicritère d'Aide à la Décision*. Paris: Economica.

Slowinski, R. (ed). 1992. *Intelligent Decision Support. Handbook of Applications and Advances of the Rough Sets Theory*. Boston: Kluwer Academic Publishers.

Slowinski, R., J. Stefanowski, S. Greco, and B. Matarazzo. 2000. "Rough sets based processing of inconsistent information in decision analysis." *Control and Cybernetics* **29**: 379–404.

Slowinski, R. and C. Zopounidis. 1995. "Application of the rough set approach to evaluation of bankruptcy risk." *Intell. Sys. Accounting, Finance Mgmnt* **4**: 27–41.

Stefanowski, J. 1998. "On rough set based approaches to induction of decision rules." In *Rough Sets in Data Mining and Knowledge Discovery*, edited by L. Polkowski and A. Skowron, **1**: 500–529. Heidelberg, Germany: Physica-Verlag.

Stefanowski, J. and D. Vanderpooten. 1994. "A general two-stage approach to inducing rules from examples." In *Rough Sets, Fuzzy Sets and Knowledge Discovery (Banff, Canada)*, edited by W. P. Ziarko, pp. 317–325. Berlin: Springer-Verlag.

Thomas, L. C., J. N. Crook, and D. B. Edelman. (eds). 1992. *Credit Scoring and Credit Control*. Oxford: Clarendon Press.

16.2 Rule Discovery

16.2.1 Rough Set Approaches for Discovering Rules and Attribute Dependencies

Wojciech Ziarko

ABSTRACT This article presents an elementary overview of techniques for data analysis and predictive modeling from data using the rough set approach. The specific knowledge discovery-related data analysis problems discussed are the discovery of functional and partial functional dependencies and the discovery of rules in data. The presentation is focused on the application of the basic rough set model to knowledge discovery and does not include discussion of the application of the extended probabilistic model of rough set for that purpose.

1. Introduction

The theory of rough sets was introduced by Pawlak in early eighties (Pawlak, 1984, 1991, 1982; Pawlak and Orlowska, 1984; Pawlak et al., 1988; Wasilewska, 1989; Pawlak et al., 1995). The intuition behind this idea is derived from the simple fact that in real life, when dealing with sets we often have no means of distinguishing individual set elements. The elements may possess some measurable characteristics but in principle, due to limited resolution of our perception mechanism, we can distinguish only classes of elements rather than individuals. Elements within classes are indistinguishable.

For example, assume that we have a large database of hospital patient records and that all what we know about each patient is whether the patient's body temperature (BT) is low, normal or high, whether patients blood pressure (BP) is low, normal or high, and whether the heart rate (HR) is normal or abnormal. If that's all we know, then regardless of how many records we have in our database, we will have a maximum of eighteen classes of patients corresponding to different combinations of the values BP, BT, and HR, such as the combination (BT = NORMAL, BP = High, HR = ABNORMAL). Each combination potentially corresponds to thousands of patient records, each of which is not different, as far as blood pressure and body temperature are concerned, from any other record from this group. We say that the patients have been classified into a certain number of categories, or elementary sets in rough set terminology. Such a classification has several advantages:

1. Reduction in the complexity of information representation (rather than analyzing huge information files about individual patients we deal with relatively small tables corresponding to observed combinations of generalized features).

2. The ability to discover repetitive patterns in data since each combination potentially corresponds to a large number of patients.

3. The ability to reason about relations among features (attributes) of objects occurring in a large data collection based on results of analysis of relatively small and size-constrained tables, referred to as decision tables, representing classifications of the domain of interest.

The theory of rough sets provides a collection of methods that can be applied to the analysis and reduction of such tables. The methods are in particular applicable to data-mining or knowledge discovery problems but also have other applications such as trainable control and pattern recognition (Slowinski and Stefanowski, 1992; Plonka and Mrozek, 1995; Lin, 1996; Ziarko, 1996, 1998, 1999; Tsumoto et al., 1995; Munakata, 1998; Polkowski and Skowron, 1998; Son, 1997; Zhong et al., 1998; Tsumoto, 1998).

For the purpose of illustration, we will use the decision table given in Table 2, which was derived from data collection partially shown in Table 1 by replacing the original attribute values with some discrete ranges. In this table, the column headings S, H, E, C, T are abbreviations for attribute names size, height, energy, current, and temperature, respectively. The attributes are generalized properties of objects, identified by sequence numbers in the column OBJ of Table 1. The classes of objects with the same combinations of attribute values are identified in Table 2 in the column CLASS.

2. Discovering Attribute Dependencies

An important aspect of KDD is the discovery, analysis, and characterization of dependencies among attributes. The problem of discovery of attribute dependencies was studied independently by many researchers (Piatetsky-Shapiro, 1993; Piatetsky-Shapiro and Frawley, 1991; Schlimmer, 1993). In this article, we specifically focus on discovering functional and partial functional dependencies using rough set theory. The probabilistic extension of this theory, called the variable precision rough set model, allows for discovery of probabilistic dependencies among attributes (Ziarko, 1999; Polkowski and Skowron, 1998) using essentially the same techniques as presented in the rest of this section.

Table 1 Example Raw Data Representing 9558 Objects

OBJ	S	H	E	C	T
1	12.0	132.2	1715	7.0	75
2	18.2	148.0	3015	32.3	130
3	19.0	175.8	1826	11.2	60
.	...	...	...	...	...
9555	17.5	199.1	1917	4.0	143
9556	18.0	111.0	2001	17.1	95
9557	19.6	186.6	4222	29.9	152
9558	15.7	103.2	3832	41.1	161

Table 2 The Decision Table Derived from Table 1

CLASS	S	H	E	C	T
E_1	0	0	1	0	0
E_2	1	0	2	1	1
E_3	1	1	1	0	0
E_4	0	2	1	1	1
E_5	1	2	1	0	1
E_6	1	0	1	0	0
E_7	1	2	2	1	1
E_8	0	0	2	1	1

In the rough set approach to discovery of dependencies, the subject of the analysis are decision tables derived from the original data rather than the data itself. As demonstrated in the example shown in the Section 1, the decision table is obtained by performing a suitably selected multidimensional mapping converting the original data into finite-valued secondary attribute-value vectors. The definition of the mapping is domain-dependent and often requires significant domain expertise for proper definition. Typically, the values of the secondary attributes correspond to some generalized qualitative categories, such as low, medium, high, et cetera. The key issue is to have a sufficient amount of representative data points so that classification of the universe of discourse *OBJ* (i.e., domain of interest containing objects represented by data points accumulated in the database) is complete. The complete classification covers all feasible combinations of values of the generalized secondary attributes. For example, we will assume that the decision table in Table 2 exhausts all feasible combinations of discretized attributes S, H, E, C, T. In the absence of the complete classification of the domain, any conclusions derived from the decision table should be constrained to the accumulated data only. They can be false in the whole domain from which the data were collected. In particular, the dependencies discovered in the decision table will hold in the data on hand, but may not hold in the whole domain, if the decision table is incomplete.

In the search for dependencies, we are interested not only in functional dependencies but also in a spectra of partial functional dependencies. In more detail, in the context of the data-derived decision table, we ask the question as to whether there is any functional or partial functional dependency between groups of attributes $P \subseteq A$ and $Q \subseteq A$, where A is a set of all attributes of the decision table.

To precisely define the notions of partial functional dependency, deterministic and nondeterministic decision rules, we need to use some elementary ideas of rough sets theory, as presented below (Pawlak, 1991).

Let $R(P)$ be the equivalence relation among objects in the universe *OBJ*. The pair [*OBJ*, $R(P)$] will be called an approximation space (Pawlak, 1991). Also, let $R^*(P)$ be the collection of equivalence classes (also called elementary sets) of $R(P)$. That is, elements of $R^*(P)$ are groups of objects having the same values of attributes belonging to P. The elementary sets reflect our basic knowledge about the domain, the knowledge in the sense of knowing which categories of objects occur in the domain, and being able to classify each object into one of the categories. With this kind of knowledge it is not possible, in general, to construct a discriminating description of any arbitrary subset of the domain. What it means in practice is that some concepts can never be learned precisely with the available information. Instead, rough approximations of these concepts can be learned. These approximations are defined below. They are fundamental notions of rough set theory, which are necessary to evaluate the quality of information describing objects of the domain of interest, relative to the target set of objects Y. The quality of the information is expressed in these definitions in terms of the ability to form tight lower and upper approximations of the target set Y.

The lower approximation in the approximation space $(OBJ, R(P))$, or alternatively the interior $INT(Y)$ of an arbitrary subset $Y \subseteq OBJ$, is defined as the union of those equivalence classes of $R^*(P)$, which are completely contained by Y, that is

$$INT(Y) = \bigcup \{E \in R^*(P) : E \subseteq Y\}.$$

The lower approximation characterizes objects that can be classified into Y without any uncertainty, based on the available information. In other words, the lower approximation is the largest set of objects that has discriminating description and is contained in the target set Y.

The upper approximation defines objects that possibly belong to the target set. It is the smallest set of objects having discriminating description and containing the target set. The upper approximation of Y, denoted here as as $UPP(Y)$, is a union of these elementary classes, which have some overlap with Y, that is

$$UPP(Y) = \bigcup \{E \in R^*(P) : E \cap Y \neq \varnothing\}.$$

Because the set of the attributes Q corresponds to the partitioning $R^*(Q)$ of the universe OBJ, the degree $K(P, Q)$ of the deterministic, or functional dependency in the relationship between attribute collections P and Q can be defined as the total relative size of lower approximations of classes of the partition $R^*(Q)$ in the approximation space $(OBJ, R(P))$. That is, if $R^*(Q) = \{Y_1, Y_2, ..., Y_m\}$ then

$$K(P, Q) = \frac{\sum_{i=1}^{m} card(INT(Y_i))}{card(OBJ),}$$

where $card$ is a set cardinality. $K(P, Q)$ assumes values in the range $[0, 1]$ with $K(P, Q) = 1$ for functional dependency and $K(P, Q) = 0$ when no value of Q attributes can be uniquely determined by values of P attributes. $K(P, Q)$ can be interpreted as a proportion of such objects in the domain for which it suffices to know the values of attributes in P to determine the values of attributes in Q. In practice, we are most often interested in analyzing dependencies where Q contains only a single attribute.

For example, it is easy to verify, based on the Table 2, that for $P = \{SIZE, HEIGHT, ENERGY, CURRENT\}$ and $Q = \{TEMPERATURE\}$ the degree of dependency of $K(P, Q)$ is 1. This means that this dependency is functional whereas the dependency between $P = \{ENERGY, CURRENT\}$ and $Q = \{TEMPERATURE\}$ is only partially functional with $K(P, Q) = 0.5$. The methodology for the dependency computation can be summarized in the following algorithm. In the algorithm, it is assumed that there is only one finite-valued target attribute. In the case of several target attributes, any subset of them can be treated as a compound single attribute and processed in the same way.

Algorithm DEP: Attribute Dependency Computation:

1. *Construct decision table from the original data according to predefined mapping of data records into secondary attribute vectors.*

2. *For each value V_i of the target attribute identify the set of objects (represented by data records) Y_i containing that value.*

3. *Compute the cardinality of the lower approximation of each set Y_i.*

4. *Output the degree of dependency as the ratio of the total size of all lower approximations of the sets Y_i to the total number of objects (data records here).*

In the rough set approach, any full or partial function reflecting dependency occurring in data is represented by the decision table. The decision table plays the same role as the analytical formula for numeric dependencies (functions). The tabular representation can be simplified to eliminate any redundant attributes and analyzed to determine the relative significance of the attributes involved in such a dependency. This step would be equivalent to finding a simpler formula representing a numeric function. The simplification of table dependencies is based on the concept of relative reduct of rough sets theory (Pawlak, 1991), as presented below. The relative reduct of the attribute collection P, with respect to the dependency $K(P, Q)$, is defined as a subset $RED(P, Q) \subseteq P$ such that:

1. $K(RED(P, Q), Q) = K(P, Q)$, that is, relative reduct preserves the degree of interattribute dependency, and

2. For any attribute $a \in RED(P, Q)$, $K(RED(P, Q) - \{a\}, Q) \neq K(P, Q)$, that is, the relative reduct is a minimal subset with respect to Property 1.

A single relative reduct can be computed in linear time with the following attribute elimination procedure. The outcome of the process depends on the predetermined priority ordering of attributes.

Algorithm RRED: Computation of Relative Reduct:

1. *Consider all attributes of the initial collection of attributes P, one by one, in the reverse order of priority. For each attribute a do the following:*

    1. *Remove the attribute a from P temporarily.*

    2. *Check if the dependency K(P, Q) changed. If yes, return a back to P, else remove the attribute a from P permanently.*

2. *Output the set of attributes remaining in P at the end of the process. It is a relative reduct of the initial set of attributes P.*

For example, one possible relative reduct with respect to the dependency between $P = \{SIZE, HEIGHT, ENERGY, CURRENT\}$ and $Q = \{TEMPERATURE\}$ is $RED(P, Q) = \{HEIGHT, ENERGY\}$. This means that the discovered dependency can be characterized by fewer attributes, leading to possible savings in information representation, better understanding of the nature of the dependency and stronger patterns. In general, a number of alternative reducts can be computed for each analyzed dependency and the one of the lowest total cost can be selected to represent the discovered dependency. The dependency represented in reduced form is usually more regular as it reflects stronger data patterns. This is illustrated in Table 3. For computing all attribute reducts, the decision matrix methodology, described in the next section, can be used. The details are provided in Shan and Ziarko (1995). More research results and algorithms related to finding reducts can be also found in Kryszkiewicz and Rybinski (1994).

To find fundamental factors contributing to the discovered dependency the idea of relative core can be used. The relative core set of attributes with respect to the dependency $K(P, Q)$ is a subset $CORE \subseteq P$ such that for all $a \in CORE$, $K(P - \{a\}, Q) \neq K(P, Q)$. In other words, $CORE$ is a set of the essential attributes that cannot be eliminated from P without affecting the dependency between P and Q.

For example, the core of the dependency between $P = \{SIZE, HEIGHT, ENERGY, CURRENT\}$ and $Q = \{TEMPERATURE\}$ is $\{HEIGHT\}$. That is, $HEIGHT$ is the fundamental dependency factor, and it is included in every relative reduct representing this dependency (Pawlak, 1991). The relative core is a context-sensitive notion (depends on other attributes in the decision table) and can be empty. This can be interpreted as a case of a highly over-specified system with superfluous attributes. In a reduct, all attributes are core attributes (relative to the reduct attributes only) since the elimination of any attribute from the reduct results in a drop of the dependency. The percentage drop of the dependency can be used as a

Table 3 Reduced Representation of the Dependency Between *P* and *Q*

HEIGHT	ENERGY	TEMPERATURE
0	1	0
0	2	1
1	1	0
2	1	1
2	2	1

measure of relative significance of an attribute in the reduct: the higher the drop the more significant the attribute is with respect to the dependency $K(RED(P, Q), Q)$. For instance, in the dependency between reduct attributes $RED(P, Q) = \{HEIGHT, ENERGY\}$ and the attribute $\{TEMPERATURE\}$, as represented in the Table 3, the relative significance of HEIGHT is 60 percent whereas the significance of ENERGY is 40 percent.

3. Rule Discovery

Discovering rules from data is one of the most important tasks of knowledge discovery in databases. Many systems and approaches for rule computation have been used for rule or decision-tree discovery (Ziarko, 1994; Piatetsky-Shapiro, 1994; Ziarko and Shan, 1996; Piatetsky-Shapiro, 1991; Major and Mangano, 1993; Gawrys and Sienkiewicz, 1994; Grzymala-Busse and Grzymala-Busse, 1994; Lenarcik and Piasta, 1993; Slowinski and Stefanowski, 1992; Fayyad and Uthurusamy, 1995; Pawlak et al., 1995; Polkowski and Skowron, 1998; Son, 1997; Zhong et al., 1998; Tsumoto, 1998). Rules can be perceived as data patterns that represent relationships between attribute values. In the rough sets approach, we distinguish certain or deterministic rules, and possible or nondeterministic rules. In addition to the above, in the variable precision rough set model, the probabilistic rules can be computed (Katzberg and Ziarko, 1994; Ziarko and Shan, 1994; Ziarko, 1993; Katzberg and Ziarko, 1994). Since the rule computation methodology developed within the original rough set framework is directly applicable to computation of probabilistic rules by using probabilistic definitions of set approximations, in this section we will focus on rule discovery with the original rough set model only. In the data mining context, maximally general rules are the most useful, the ones that minimize the number of rule conditions. We will refer to such rules as minimal rules. They correspond to value reducts known in rough set theory, or to prime implicants of digital circuit–design theory. The rough set-based algorithms for rule discovery can either compute rules forming minimal cover or approximation of minimal cover of the target class, or they can be used to find all minimal rules for the target class. Representative algorithms of both kinds are presented in the rest of this section.

To define the concept of rules in the rough set approach precisely some additional notational conventions are needed. Let V denote a selected value of the decision (target) attribute $d \in A$ and let $supp(d = V)$ denote the set of objects matching this value, referred to as the target set of objects. The rules can be computed either with respect to a lower approximation $INT[supp(d = V)]$ or an upper approximation $UPP[supp(d = V)]$ of the target set. When the lower approximation is selected then deterministic rules are obtained. Nondeterministic rules are obtained from the upper approximation of the target set. In either case, the computational procedure is the same. Therefore, to describe the methods we can assume, without loss of generality, that $supp(d = V)$ is an exact set, or not rough, that is, $supp(d = V) = INT[supp(d = V)] = UPP[supp(d = V)]$, as otherwise $supp(d = V)$ would be substituted by either $INT[supp(d = V)]$ or $UPP[suppd = V)]$.

In our notation, the rule derived from data is a logical implication formula corresponding to the combination of values of some attributes such that the set of all objects matching this combination is contained in the target set of objects. The rule r can be expressed as

$$r : (a_{i1} = V_{i1}) \wedge (a_{i2} = V_{i2}), \wedge ... \wedge (a_{in} = V_{in}) \rightarrow (d = V),$$

where a_{ij}, V_{ij} denote condition attributes and attribute values, respectively. The set of attribute-value pairs occurring on the left-hand side of the rule r is referred to as the rule condition part, denoted $cond(r)$, and the right-hand side is the decision part, $dec(r)$, so the rule can be expressed as $cond(r) \rightarrow dec(r)$. The set of all objects $supp(cond(r))$ in the universe OBJ whose attribute values match the rule conditions is called the rule support. To define minimal rules, the notion of value reduct is introduced first. The value reduct of the set of attribute-value pairs $cond(r)$ is a subset $red(r) \subseteq cond(r)$ such that

1. $supp(red(r)) \subseteq supp(d = V)$, that is, value reduct preserves the relation of inclusion of the rule support set in the target set.

2. For any attribute-value pair $(a_{ij} = V_{ij}) \in red(r)$, $supp(red(r) - \{(a_{ij} = V_{ij})\}) \not\subseteq supp(d = V)$, that is, the value reduct is a minimal subset with respect to Property 1.

Similar to a relative reduct, a single value reduct can be computed in linear time with the following value elimination procedure. The outcome of the process depends on the predetermined priority ordering of attributes.

Algorithm VRED: Computation of Value Reduct:

1. *Consider all attribute-value pairs of the set cond(r), one by one, in the reverse order of priority. For each pair x do the following:*

   1. *Remove the pair x from cond(r) temporarily.*

   2. *Check if the support set of cond(r), supp(cond(r)) is included in supp(d = V). If not, return x back to cond(r), else remove the pair x from cond(r) permanently.*

3. *Output the set of attribute-value pairs remaining in cond(r) at the end of the process. It is a value reduct of the original contents of cond(r).*

Every value reduct corresponds to a minimal rule $red(r) \rightarrow dec(r)$ derived from the initial rule $cond(r) \rightarrow dec(r)$. For example, some of the value reducts of the set of attribute–value pairs of the rule corresponding to the first row of the Table 2, with respect to target value $T = 0$, are $\{(H = 0), (E = 1)\}$, and $\{(S = 0), (C = 0)\}$. These value reducts translate into rules such as, for example the following:

$$(HEIGHT = 0) \wedge (ENERGY = 1) \rightarrow (TEMPERATURE = 0)$$

$$(SIZE = 0) \wedge (CURRENT = 0) \rightarrow (TEMPERATURE = 0).$$

As follows from the above, a single minimal rule can be computed in linear time in the number of attributes. Some minimal rules, selected according to a predefined heuristic and covering the target set, or rough approximation of it, can be computed relatively easily in time proportional to the number of attributes and number of elementary sets in lower (or upper) approximation of the target class. Algorithms for computing such rules have been implemented in several systems for machine learning and data mining (Ziarko and Shan, 1994; Grzymala-Busse, 1992; Shan and Ziarko, 1995; Slowinski and Stefanowski, 1992; Lin, 1996; Son, 1997; Zhong et al., 1998; Munakata, 1998; Tsumoto, 1998). A representative simplified algorithm is presented below. It is aimed at generating close to minimum covering of the lower (or upper) approximation of the target class with the support sets of selected value reducts.

Algorithm MinRul: Computation of Minimal Rules:

1. *Compute lower (or upper) approximation of the target class. Initialize the list L of value reducts to empty.*

2. *In the decision table, consider one by one every row corresponding to the selected lower (or upper) approximation of the target set. Compute a single value reduct from the current row. If the support set of the computed value reduct is contained in the union of support sets of the value reducts in the list L, go to the next row; otherwise add the computed value reduct to the list L.*

3. *Output the list L. At the end of the process, the list L will contain a nonredundant set of value reducts whose support sets will cover the selected approximation of the target set. These reducts will directly correspond to the set of rules discriminating either the lower, or the upper approximation of the target class.*

For illustration, let's compute minimal rules for $T = 1$ from the decision table shown in Table 2. The lower approximation of $supp(T = 1)$ is the union of elementary classes E_2, E_4, E_5, E_7, E_8. Consequently, we will compute value reducts for rows 2, 4, 5, 7, 8 of the decision table using the VRED algorithm (the assumed order of value elimination is from left to right). It can easily be verified that the value reduct of rows 2, 4, 7, and 8 is $\{(C = 1)\}$. The value reduct of row 5 is $\{(H = 2)\}$. Since the support set of $\{(H = 2)\}$ is not covered by the support set of

Table 4 The Decision Table with Additional Class Indexes

i	j	CLASS	S	H	E	C	T
–	1	E_1	0	0	1	0	0
1	–	E_2	1	0	2	1	1
–	2	E_3	1	1	1	0	0
2	–	E_4	0	2	1	1	1
3	–	E_5	1	2	1	0	1
–	3	E_6	1	0	1	0	0
4	–	E_7	1	2	2	1	1
5	–	E_8	0	0	2	1	1

$\{(C=1)\}$, the result consists of the value reducts $\{(C=1)\}$ and $\{(H=2)\}$, and rules corresponding to them:

$$(CURRENT = 1) \rightarrow (TEMPERATURE = 1)$$

$$(HEIGHT = 2) \rightarrow (TEMPERATURE = 1).$$

For knowledge discovery applications, finding all possible minimal rules rather than minimal covering rules is more desirable. However, the problem of computing all minimal rules is NP-hard. All minimal rules can be computed, if the problem size permits, using the techniques of discernibility matrix (Skowron and Rauszer, 1992), or decision matrix (Ziarko and Shan, 1996), which is described below.

Before we define the concept of a decision matrix, we will assume some notational conventions. That is, we will assume that all classes containing objects belonging to $supp(d = V)$ and all classes with objects belonging to the complement of $supp(d = V)$ are separately numbered with subscripts i ($i = 1, 2, \dots \gamma$) and j ($j = 1, 2, \dots \rho$), respectively. The modified example decision table with additional indexes is shown in Table 4.

A decision matrix $M(S) = (M_{ij})$ of a decision table with respect to value V of the decision attribute d is defined as a matrix whose entries are sets of attribute-value pairs

$$M_{ij} = \{(a, a(E_i)) : a(E_i) \neq a(E_j)\},$$

where $a(E_i)$ denotes the common value of the attribute a on all objects belonging to the class E_i. The set M_{ij} contains all attribute-value pairs (*attribute, value*) whose values are not identical between E_i and E_j. In other words, M_{ij} represents the complete information distinguishing E_i from E_j. For example, the entry M_{11} of the decision matrix given in Table 5 reflects the fact that class E_1 differs from the class E_2 in values of attributes *SIZE, ENERGY,* and *CURRENT*. These values are $SIZE = 1$, $ENERGY = 2$, and $CURRENT = 1$ for the class E_2.

Table 5 Decision Matrix for *TEMPERATURE* = 1 of Table 3.

i	CLASS	j 1 E_1	2 E_3	3 E_6
1	E_2	(S, 1)(E, 2) (C, 1)	(H, 0)(E, 2) (C, 1)	(E, 2)(C, 1)
2	E_4	(H, 2)(C, 1)	(S, 0)(H, 2) (C, 1)	(S, 0)(H, 2) (C, 1)
3	E_5	(S, 1)(H, 2)	(H, 2)	(H, 2)
4	E_7	(S, 1)(H, 2) (E, 2)(C, 1)	(H, 2)(E, 2) (C, 1)	(H, 2)(E, 2) (C, 1)
5	E_8	(E, 2)(C, 1)	(S, 0)(H, 0) (E, 2)(C, 1)	(S, 0)(E, 2) (C, 1)

The set of all minimal value reducts of the collection of attribute–value pairs corresponding to row i of the decision table and consequently the set of all minimal decision rules for that row can be obtained by forming the Boolean expression

$$B_i = \bigwedge_j \bigvee M_{ij},$$

where $\bigwedge$ and $\bigvee$ are, respectively, generalized conjunction and disjunction operators (Ziarko and Shan, 1996; Skowron and Rauszer, 1992).

The Boolean expression, called a decision function B_i, is constructed out of row i of the decision matrix, that is, $(M_{i1}, M_{i2}, \ldots M_{ip})$, by formally treating each attribute–value pair occurring in the matrix entry M_{ij} as a Boolean variable and then forming a Boolean conjunction of disjunctions of attribute-value pairs belonging to each set M_{ij}.

The decision rules are obtained by turning each decision function into disjunctive normal form and using the absorption law of Boolean algebra to simplify it. The conjuncts or prime implicants of the simplified decision function correspond to the minimal decision rules (Ziarko and Shan, 1996; Skowron and Rauszer, 1992).

The major steps in computing all minimal rules for the selected approximation (lower or upper) of the target class are summarized in the following algorithm.

Algorithm AllRul: Computation of All Minimal Rules:

1. *Split the rows of the input decision table into two categories: lower (or upper) approximation rows of the target set versus all other rows.*

2. *Construct the decision matrix by comparing decision table rows belonging to the categories obtained in Step 1.*

3. *Form decision functions out of rows of the decision matrix and turn them into disjunctive normal form.*

4. *Identify prime implicants of the simplified decision functions obtained in Step 3.*

5. *Perform the set union operation on the sets of prime implicants associated with the rows of the decision matrix.*

6. *Output minimal rules for lower (or upper) approximation of the target class by translating all prime implicants obtained in Step 5 into rule format. Each prime implicant is translated into rule conditions with the rule conclusion corresponding to the selected value V of the decision attribute.*

For example, for the target class corresponding to *TEMPERATURE* $= 1$ of the decision table shown in Table 4, we can compute and simplify the following decision functions, as derived from the decision matrix presented in Table 5.

$$B_1 = ((S,1) \vee (E,2) \vee (C,1)) \wedge ((H,0) \vee (E,2) \vee (C,1))$$

$$\wedge ((E,2) \vee (C,1)) = (E,2) \vee (C,1)$$

$$B_2 = ((H,2) \vee (C,1)) \wedge ((S,0) \vee (H,2) \vee (C,1))$$

$$\wedge ((S,0) \vee (H,2) \vee (C,1)) = (H,2) \vee (C,1)$$

$$B_3 = ((S,1) \vee (H,2)) \wedge ((H,2)) \wedge ((H,2)) = (H,2)$$

$$B_4 = ((S,1) \vee (H,2) \vee (E,2) \vee (C,1))$$

$$\wedge ((H,2) \vee (E,2) \vee (C,1))$$

$$\wedge ((H,2) \vee (E,2) \vee (C,1)) = (H,2) \vee (E,2) \vee (C,1)$$

$$B_5 = ((E,2) \vee (C,1)) \wedge ((S,0) \vee (H,0) \vee (E,2) \vee (C,1))$$

$\wedge\,((S,0)\vee(E,2)\vee(C,1))=(E,2)\vee(C,1).$

The prime implicants are $(E, 2)$, $(C, 1)$ and $(H, 2)$. After translation, the following rules are obtained:

$(ENERGY=2)\rightarrow(TEMPERATURE=1)$

$(CURRENT=1)\rightarrow(TEMPERATURE=1)$

$(HEIGHT=2)\rightarrow(TEMPERATURE=1).$

All the minimal rules for the decision class "0" can be computed in a similar way.

The level of difficulty with applying the decision matrix method in practical situations depends on the complexity of the decision table obtained through classification of the original data based on values of generalized secondary attributes. Typically, the attributes used to construct a decision table are the functions of the original data values, their number is small and each attribute has a small number of domain values. This leads to a relatively small and constrained number of classes of the decision table. The size of the decision table is constrained by the product of cardinalities of attribute domains and is independent of the size of the original data set. Consequently, careful definition of the decision table attributes is an essential prerequisite before applying the decision matrix method and, in fact, any other rough set-based rule discovery method. On the other hand, the computation of prime implicants associated with decision functions, the most time-consuming aspect of the algorithm AllRul, can be done independently, for each row of the decision matrix. This means that the decision matrix method can take full advantage of a parallel implementation in a multiprocessor system to speed up the rule computation process.

4. Final Remarks

The theory of rough sets is a fundamental mathematical model that has been extensively studied by mathematicians, logicians, and computer scientists. The simplicity and mathematical clarity of the model makes it attractive for both theoreticians and application-oriented researchers. Although its introduction was not motivated by any particular application, it touched the essence of many old problems in AI, pattern recognition, and control. More recently, it became clear that rough set theory provides a framework for studying data mining and for developing data analysis algorithms for this research area. However, it should be emphasized that, while providing a sound theoretical basis for designing new algorithms, rough set theory is not associated with any particular method or algorithm for data mining or other applications. The choice of rough set-based techniques for data mining presented in this article reflects only the author's preferences and experiences and by no means pretends to cover the whole subject area.

ACKNOWLEDGMENTS

The research reported in this article was partially supported by a research grant awarded to the author by the Natural Sciences and Engineering Research Council of Canada. Many thanks to Jan Z´ytkow and the anonymous referees for precise and inspiring comments.

References

Fayyad, U. and R. Uthurusamy. (eds). 1995. *Proceedings of the First International Conference on Knowledge Discovery and Data Mining*. Montreal, Canada.

Gawrys, M. and J. Sienkiewicz. 1994. "RSL—the rough set library version 2.0." ICS Research Report 27/94. Warsaw, Poland: Institute of Computer Science, W. U. of T.

Grzymala-Busse, J. W. 1992. "LERS—a system learning from examples based on rough sets." In *Intelligent Decision Support: Handbook of Applications and Advances of Rough Sets Theory*, edited by R. Slowinski. Kluwer.

Grzymala-Busse, D. and J. Grzymala-Busse. 1994. "Comparison of machine learning and knowledge acquisition methods of rule induction based on rough sets." In *Rough Sets, Fuzzy Sets and Knowledge Discovery*, edited by W. Ziarko, pp. 282–289. Springer-Verlag.

Hu, X., N. Cercone, and J. Han. 1994. "An attribute-oriented rough set approach for knowledge discovery in databases." In *Rough Sets, Fuzzy Sets and Knowledge Discovery*, edited by W. Ziarko, pp. 90–99. Springer-Verlag.

Katzberg, J. and W. Ziarko. 1994. "Variable precision rough sets with asymmetric bounds." In *Rough Sets, Fuzzy Sets and Knowledge Discovery,* edited by W. Ziarko, pp. 167–177. Springer-Verlag.

Kryszkiewicz, M. and H. Rybinski. 1994. "Finding reducts in composed information systems." In *Rough Sets, Fuzzy Sets and Knowledge Discovery,* edited by W. Ziarko, pp. 261–274. Springer-Verlag.

Lenarcik, A. and Z. Piasta. 1993. "Probabilistic approach to decision algorithm generation in the case of continuous condition attributes." *Found. Comput. Decision Sci.* **18(3–4)**: 213–224.

Lin, T. Y. (ed). 1996. "Special issue on rough sets and soft computing." *Intell. Automation and Soft Comput. Int. J.* **2(2)**.

Major, J. and J. Mangano. 1993. "Selecting among rules induced from a hurricane database." In *Proceedings of AAAI Workshop on Knowledge Discovery in Databases*, pp. 28–41. Washington D.C.

Marek, W. and Z. Pawlak. 1984. "Rough sets and information systems." *Fund. Inform.* **17(1)**: 105–115.

Munakata, T. 1998. *Fundamentals of the New Artificial Intelligence: Beyond Traditional Paradigms.* Springer Verlag.

Pawlak, Z. 1982. "Rough sets." *Int. J. Inform. Comput. Sci.* **11(5)**: 341–356.

Pawlak, Z. 1984. "Rough classification." *Int. J. Man–Machine Studies* **20**: 469–483.

Pawlak, Z. 1991. *Rough Sets: Theoretical Aspects of Reasoning About Data.* Kluwer Academic Publishers.

Pawlak, Z. 1994. "Rough sets present state and further prospects." In *Proceedings of the Third International Workshop on Rough Sets and Soft Computing*, edited by T. Y. Lin and A. M. Wildberger, pp. 3–5. San Jose, CA.

Pawlak, Z. and E. Orlowska. 1984. "Expressive power of knowledge representation." *Int. J. Man–Machine Studies* **20**: 485–500.

Pawlak, Z., S. K. M. Wong, and W. Ziarko. 1988. "Rough sets: probabilistic versus deterministic approach." *Int. J. Man–Machine Studies* **29**: 81–95.

Pawlak, Z., J. Grzymala-Busse, R. Slowinski, and W. Ziarko. 1995. "Rough sets." *Commun. ACM* **38(11)**: 89–95.

Piatetsky-Shapiro, G. 1991. "Discovery, analysis, and presentation of strong rules." In *Knowledge Discovery in Databases*, edited by G. Piatetsky-Shapiro and W. Frawley, pp. 229–248. AAAI/MIT Press.

Piatetsky-Shapiro, G. (ed). 1993. *Proceedings of AAAI-93 Workshop on Knowledge Discovery in Databases.* Washington, D.C.

Piatetsky-Shapiro, G. 1994. "Knowledge discovery in databases: progress and challenges." In *Rough Sets, Fuzzy Sets and Knowledge Discovery*, edited by W. Ziarko, pp. 1–10. Springer-Verlag.

Piatetsky-Shapiro, G. and W. J. Frawley. (eds). 1991. *Knowledge Discovery in Databases*: AAAI/MIT Press.

Plonka, L. and A. Mrozek. 1995. "Rule-based stabilization of the inverted pendulum." *Comput. Intell. Int. J.* **11(2)**: 348–356.

Polkowski, L. and A. Skowron. (eds). 1998. *Rough Sets in Knowledge Discovery*, Volume 1–2. Physica Verlag.

Schlimmer, J. V. 1993. "Using learned dependencies to automatically construct sufficient and feasible editing views." In *Proceedings of AAAI Workshop on Knowledge Discovery in Databases*, pp. 186–196. Washington, D.C.

Shan, N. and W. Ziarko. 1995. "Data-based acquisition and incremental modification of classification rules." *Comput. Intell. Int. J.* **11(2)**: 357–370.

Skowron, A. and C. Rauszer. 1992. "The discernibility matrices and functions in information systems." In *Intelligent Decision Support: Handbook of Applications and Advances of Rough Sets Theory*, edited by R. Slowinski: Kluwer.

Slowinski, R. and J. Stefanowski. 1992. "'ROUGHDAS' and 'ROUGHCLASS' software implementation of the rough sets approach." In *Intelligent Decision Support: Handbook of Applications and Advances of Rough Sets Theory*, edited by R. Slowinski: Kluwer.

Son, N. 1997. "Rule induction from continuous data." In *Proceedings of the Joint Conference of Information Sciences*, edited by P. Wang, **3**: 81–84. Duke University.

Tsumoto, S. 1998. "Formalization and induction of medical expert system rules based on rough set theory." In *Rough Sets in Knowledge Discovery,* edited by L. Polkowski and A. Skowron, **2**: 307–323. Physica Verlag.

Tsumoto, S., N. Shan, W. Ziarko, and H. Tanaka. 1995. "Knowledge discovery in clinical databases based on variable precision rough sets." *J. Am. Med. Inform. Assoc.* pp. 270–274.

Wasilewska, A. 1989. "Syntactic decision procedures in information systems." *Int. J. Man–Machine Studies* **30**: 273–285.

Wong, S. K. M. and W. Ziarko. 1986. "Comparison of the probabilistic approximate classification and the fuzzy set model." *Int. J. Fuzzy Sets Sys.* **21**: 357–362.

Ziarko, W. 1993. "Variable precision rough sets model." *J. Comput. Sys. Sci.* **46(1)**: 39–59.

Ziarko, W. (ed). 1994. *Rough Sets, Fuzzy Sets and Knowledge Discovery*: Springer-Verlag.

Ziarko, W. (ed). 1996. "Special issue on rough sets." *Fund. Inform.* **27(2–3)**.

Ziarko, W. 1998. "Approximation region-based decision tables." In *Rough Sets and Current Trends in Computing*, edited by L. Polkowski and A. Skowron, Lecture Notes in AI, **1424**: 178–185. Berlin: Springer Verlag.

Ziarko, W. 1999. "Predictive modelling with probabilistic decision tables." In *Proceedings of the Eighteenth IASTED Conference on Modelling, Identification and Control*, pp. 59–62. Innsbruck.

Ziarko, W. and N. Shan. 1994. "KDD-R: a comprehensive system for knowledge discovery in databases using rough sets." In *Proceedings of the International Workshop on Rough Sets and Soft Computing*. RSSC'94, San Jose, CA.

Ziarko, W. and N. Shan. 1996. "A method for computing all maximally general rules in attribute-value systems." *Comput. Intell. Int. J.* **12(2)**: 223–234.

Zhong, N., J. Dang, and S. Ohsuga. 1998. "Soft techniques to data mining." In *Rough Sets and Current Trends in Computing*, edited by L. Polkowski and A. Skowron, Lecture Notes in AI, **1424**: 231–238. Berlin: Springer Verlag.

16.2.2 Characteristic Rules

Jiawei Han

ABSTRACT Descriptive data mining is the description of a set of data in a concise and summary manner and the presentation of the general properties of the data. Mining characteristic rules and discriminant rules from the data are two essential components in descriptive data mining. In contrast to online analytical processing, data description puts more emphasis on (1) automated processing, helping users determine which dimensions (or attributes) should be included in the analysis and to what abstraction level the data set should be generalized in order to obtain interesting summarization; and (2) handling complex data types. Mining data characteristics and discriminant descriptions can be implemented based on a data cube method or an attribute-oriented induction method. Moreover, data description can be enhanced by data dispersion analysis, multifeature data cubes, and discovery-driven data cubes.

1. Concept Description: Mining Characteristic Rules and Discriminant Rules

From the data analysis point of view, data mining can be classified into descriptive data mining and predictive data mining. The former describes a set of data in a concise and summary manner and presents general properties of the data; whereas the latter constructs one or a set of models from the data and attempts to predict the behavior of new data sets.

The simplest kind of descriptive data mining is concept description (or class description when the concept to be described refers to a class of objects). A concept usually refers to a collection of data, such as winners, frequent buyers, best sellers, and so on. As a data mining task, concept description is not simple enumeration of the set of objects. Instead, it generates characteristic and/or comparative descriptions of the objects: concept characterization provides a concise and succinct summary of a concept, whereas concept comparison (also known as discrimination) provides a comparative summary of the concept being examined (often called the target class) in contrast to one or a set of comparative concepts (often called the contrasting classes). Besides description of data based on their general properties, such as average cost or count, one may also describe data based on their clustering or dispersion properties, such as variance or deviation.

Concept description can be presented in many forms, including generalized relation, cross-tabulation, chart, graph, and so on. It can also be presented in the form of a logical rule.

A rule as a conjunction of properties shared by all the entities in the class is called a characteristic rule of the class; whereas a rule as a conjunction of properties shared by all the entities in the target class and that distinguishes its entities from that of contrasting classes is called a discriminant rule of the target class (in comparison with the contrasting classes).

2. Concept Description versus Online Analytical Processing

Concept description has close ties with data generalization. Given the large amount of data in a database, it is useful to describe concepts in concise terms by generalization. Allowing data sets to be generalized at multiple levels of abstraction facilitates the examination of the general behavior of the data. For example, given a sales database, instead of examining individual customer transactions, one may prefer to view the data generalized to higher levels, such as summarized by geographic region, purchase frequency, and customer group. Such multidimensional, multilevel data generalization is similar to multidimensional data analysis in data warehouses.

However, there are some notable differences between concept description and online analytical processing (OLAP) in data warehouses. First, OLAP in data warehouses relies heavily on the user's control. The selection of dimensions and the application of OLAP operations, such as drill-down, roll-up, dicing, and slicing, are directed and controlled by users. This requires users to have a good understanding of the role of each dimension and to spend time in the search for interesting patterns. In contrast, concept description in data mining strives for more automated processing to help users determine which dimensions (or attributes) should be included in the analysis and at which level the data set should be generalized in order to generate interesting summarization. Second, many current OLAP systems confine dimensions to categorical data and measures to numerical data only. For concept description, the attributes can be of various data types, including numerical, categorical, spatial, text, or image data. The aggregation of attributes in a database may include sophisticated data types, such as the collection of categorical data, the merging of spatial regions, the composition of images, the integration of texts, and the grouping of object pointers. Therefore, OLAP, with its restrictions on the possible dimension and measure types, represents a simplified model for data analysis. Concept description in databases should be able to handle complex attribute data types and their aggregations.

3. Mining Characteristic Rules

Data generalization, which generalizes a large set of task-relevant data from a low level of abstraction to high levels, is an essential operation in mining data characterization. For example, items sold in the Christmas season can be generalized according to region, customer group, and so on, for further analysis. Methods for efficient and flexible generalization of large data sets can be categorized into two approaches: (1) the data cube approach (Chaudhuri and Dayal, 1997; Gray et al., 1997) and (2) the attribute-oriented induction approach (Han and Fu, 1996; Han et al., 1993).

In the data cube approach, a multidimensional database is constructed that consists of a set of dimensions and measures. A dimension is usually defined by a set of attributes that form a hierarchy or a lattice structure. For example, the date may consist of the attributes day, week, month, quarter, year, which form a lattice structure and define a data cube dimension, time. A data cube can store precomputed aggregates for all or some of its dimensions. Generalization and specialization can be performed on a multidimensional data cube by roll-up or drill-down operations. A roll-up operation reduces the number of dimensions in a data cube or generalizes attribute values to higher level concepts. A drill-down operation does the reverse. Since many aggregate values may need to be used repeatedly in data analysis, the storage of precomputed aggregates in a multidimensional data cube will ensure fast response time and offer flexible views of data from different angles and at different levels of abstraction. Data cubes, their architectures, implementations, and OLAP applications are discussed in Chapter 13.2. However, generalization by the data cube approach is controlled by users, and some important analyses, such as attribute relevance analysis, are not performed in this approach.

The attribute-oriented induction approach (Han et al., 1993) may handle complex types of data and perform attribute relevance analysis in characterization. In general, the approach consists of the following steps:

1. *Data collection.* Based on the user's mining query, where the concept is provided either explicitly (such as a winning team) or implicitly (such as where the score is no less than ninety), a set of task-relevant data in the database is collected by query processing.

2. *Attribute relevance analysis.* Based on feature reduction techniques studied in decision-tree induction or other classification analysis methods (see Chapters 5.4 and 14.2), attribute relevance analysis can be performed on the dimensions relevant to the mining task. The analysis ranks the dimensions and their corresponding abstraction levels and excludes weakly relevant attributes from further analysis.

3. *Data generalization.* Data generalization is performed based on two techniques: (1) attribute removal and (2) attribute generalization.

   The first technique is based on the rule: If there is a large set of distinct values for an attribute in a relation, but either (1) there is no generalization operator on the attribute (e.g., there is no concept hierarchy or taxonomy [see Chapter 5.7] defined for the attribute) or (2) there are other attributes representing the higher-level concepts, then the attribute should be removed from the relation. This is because the removal of a conjunct implies eliminating a constraint and thus generalizes the data.

   The second technique is based on a rule similar to concept hierarchy ascension in machine learning (Michalski, 1983; also see Chapter 28): If there is a large set of distinct values for an attribute in a relation, and there exist a set of generalization operators on the attribute, then a generalization operator should be selected and applied to the attribute in the relation. This is because the use of a generalization operator to generalize an attribute value within a tuple or an object, or rule, will make the rule cover more of the original data and thus generalizes the concept it represents.

   After such generalization, aggregation is performed by merging identical, generalized objects, and accumulating their corresponding counts and other aggregate values. This reduces the size of the generalized data set.

4. *Drilling, dicing, and other adjustments.* The degree of generalization can be controlled by the attribute generalization threshold, which indicates how many distinct values one may have in each dimension in the generalized relation. One may either adopt a default threshold value (typically ranging from two to eight), or allow experts or users to specify the desired values. Furthermore, the generalized results should be interactively adjustable by users with drilling, dicing, and other OLAP-like operations to ensure that the desirable characterization result is obtained.

5. *Presentation of characterization results.* The characterization results can be mapped to different forms for presentation, including cross-tabulation, charts, graphs, or characteristic rules.

4. Mining Discriminant Rules

The method for mining discriminant rules (Han et al., 1993) is similar to that of mining characteristic rules except that mining should be performed in both target class and contrasting classes synchronously to ensure that the comparison is performed at comparative levels of abstraction.

In particular, concept discrimination is performed in the following steps:

1. *Data collection.* Similar to mining characteristic rules, the set of task-relevant data is collected by query processing. However, the set of task-relevant data is partitioned into a target class and one or a set of contrasting class(es).

2. *Attribute relevance analysis.* A feature reduction method is used to rank the attributes. Only highly relevant attributes are included in the further analysis.

3. *Synchronous generalization.* Generalization is performed on the target class to a desired level, such as by year and country, based on a user- or expert-specified generalization threshold, which results in a prime target class. Since comparison can only be performed at the same level of abstraction, the concepts in the contrasting class(es) should be generalized to the corresponding level, such as also by year and country, forming the prime contrasting class(es).

4. *Drilling, dicing, and other adjustments.* The generalized results should be interactively adjustable by users with drilling, dicing, and other OLAP-like operations, and such operations should be performed synchronously on the target and contrasting classes.

5. *Presentation of the discrimination results.* The discrimination results can be mapped to different forms for presentation, including cross-tabulation, charts, graphs, or discriminant rules.

5. Example

We examine an example to see how to perform concept description in large databases. Suppose one would like to comparatively describe the sales of laptop computers versus cellular phones in all the branches of a store E-City in North America in 1999. There are many features (attributes) to be considered, such as transaction time (year, month, day), store (continent, country, city, branch, manager, telephone), merchandise (category, model, maker, production date), customer (name, age, payment method), and so on, and these features are all stored in a relational database.

The descriptive mining is performed as follows. First, the task-relevant set of data is collected by selecting only two categories of items sold, laptop computer and cellular phone, in 1999, joining related relations and partitioning the data into two classes: laptop computer sales and cellular-phone sales. Second, attribute relevance analysis is performed. Only highly relevant attributes are retained in the subsequent analysis, such as transaction time (year, month), and store (country, city). Third, synchronous generalization is performed on the target class laptop computers and the contrasting class cellular phones, which leads to two dimensions, each containing only one level: transaction time (month), store (country). Fourth, drilling, dicing, and other adjustments can be performed synchronously on the target and contrasting classes, based on the user's instructions to derive the desired description. Suppose the user drops the attribute transaction time (month) and leaves only store (country) in the table. Finally, the result comparison can be presented in the form of a cross-tabulation, a graph, and/or a rule.

To present descriptive mining results in the form of rules, two weighted measures, t-weight and d-weight, are introduced. The former indicates how typical a term is in the concept/class; whereas the latter indicates how discriminative the term is in the target class in comparison with the other classes.

More formally, the t-weight of a generalized term t_a is the ratio that the objects covered by t_a in the target class versus all the objects in the initial target class; whereas the d-weight of a generalized term t_a in the target class is the ratio of the number of objects in the initial target class that are covered by t_a versus the total number of objects in both the initial target and contrasting classes that are covered by t_a.

Table 1 shows the number (in thousands) of laptop computers and cellular phones sold by region in 1999, with t-weight and d-weight information associated. The t-weight for (laptop computer, Canada) is 25 percent because the number of laptop computers sold in Canada (two hundred thousand) represents only 25 percent of the laptop computer sales in both regions (eight hundred thousand); whereas the d-weight for (laptop computer, Canada) is 66.67 percent because the number of laptop computers sold in Canada (two hundred thousand) represents 66.67 percent of the total units sold in Canada (which is three hundred thousand).

Table 1 The Cross-tabulation with *t*-Weight and *d*-Weight Associated with Each Class

	Canada			U.S.			Both regions		
Class/region	Count	t-weight	d-weight	Count	t-weight	d-weight	Count	t-weight	d-weight
laptop computer	200	25%	66.7%	600	75%	25%	800	100%	29.63%
cellular phone	100	5.26%	33.3%	1,800	94.74%	75%	1,900	100%	70.37%
both classes	300	11.11%	100%	2,400	88.89%	100%	2,700	100%	100%

Table 1 can be transformed into bidirectional, quantitative description rules. For example, for the target class, laptop computers, we have the following rule,

$$\forall X, \quad \text{class}(X) = \text{"laptop computer"} \iff (\text{region}(X) = \text{"Canada"})(t:25\%, \quad d:66.7\%)$$

$$\vee (\text{region}(X) = \text{"U.S."})(t:75\%, \quad d:25\%)$$

It states that for all the sales of laptop computers and cellular phones in 1999, if the sale item is a laptop computer (i.e., in the forward direction), the probability of being sold in Canada is 25 percent, whereas that of being sold in the United States is 75 percent. On the other hand (i.e., in the reverse direction), if we compare the sales in the two classes in Canada, 66.7 percent sold were laptop computers (and 33.3 percent were cellular phones).

Notice that many different interestingness thresholds can be set up to filter out some terms that are minor either in its own class or in comparison with the contrasting classes to simplify the resulting rules or other forms of presentation.

6. Variations and Extensions of Descriptive Data Mining

Besides mining characteristic and discriminant rules, another interesting task is to mine descriptive statistics (Elder and Pregibon, 1996), especially data dispersion properties. One can demonstrate such properties using boxplot (which is a graph showing median, first and third quarters, whiskers, and outliers), quantile plot, scatter plot, histogram, outlier analysis tools, and so on.

Although most data warehouse systems require users to define concept hierarchies for multidimensional data analysis, concept hierarchies can be constructed automatically by discretization, clustering and outlier analysis, and the analysis of the number of distinct values in database attributes. Automatic construction of concept hierarchies help explore data from different angles and find unexpected patterns.

Mining characteristic rules, discriminant rules, and descriptive statistics are implemented in the DBMiner system (see Chapter 24.1.1) as modules for online analytical mining (Han, 1998).

Recently, proposals have been made about the construction of variants of data cubes to facilitate data mining. For example, one may construct a multiple-feature cube (Ross et al., 1998), a special kind of data cube based on sophisticated queries. For example, consider a special data cube that may help analyze high-performance companies by region, by year, and so on, where a high-performance company is a company whose annual revenue increase in percentage is over 150 percent of the average annual revenue increase in percentage in its region. Moreover, one may annotate cells/regions in a cube to form a discovery-driven cube (Sarawagi et al., 1998) which may highlight the exceptions or other distinct features on a cube plane, along its drilling paths, and/or on its lower-level planes. These techniques and their further development may substantially enhance the power and flexibility of descriptive data mining.

References

Chaudhuri, S. and U. Dayal. 1997. "An overview of data warehousing and OLAP technology." *ACM SIGMOD Record* **26**: 65–74.

Elder, J. IV and D. Pregibon. 1996. "A statistical perspective on knowledge discovery in databases." In *Advances in Knowledge Discovery and Data Mining*, edited by U. M. Fayyad, G. Piatetsky-Shapiro, P. Smyth, and R. Uthurusamy, pp. 83–115. Menlo Park, CA: AAAI/MIT Press.

Gray, J., S. Chaudhuri, A. Bosworth, A. Layman, D. Reichart, M. Venkatrao, F. Pellow, and H. Pirahesh.
1997. "Data cube: a relational aggregation operator generalizing group-by, cross-tab and sub-totals."
Data Mining and Knowledge Discovery **1**: 29–54.

Han, J. 1998. "Towards on-line analytical mining in large databases." *ACM SIGMOD Record* **27**: 97–107.

Han, J., Y. Cai, and N. Cercone. 1993. "Data-driven discovery of quantitative rules in relational databases."
IEEE Trans. Knowledge Data Engng. **5**: 29–40.

Han, J. and Y. Fu. 1996. "Exploration of the power of attribute-oriented induction in data mining." In
Advances in Knowledge Discovery and Data Mining, edited by U. M. Fayyad, G. Piatetsky-Shapiro,
P. Smyth, and R. Uthurusamy, pp. 399–421. Menlo Park, CA: AAAI/MIT Press.

Michalski, R. S. 1983. "A theory and methodology of inductive learning." In *Machine Learning: An Artificial
Intelligence Approach,* edited by Michalski et al. **1**: 83–134. Los Altos, CA: Morgan Kaufmann.

Ross, K. A., D. Srivastava, and D. Chatziantoniou. 1998. "Complex aggregation at multiple granularities."
In *Proceedings of the International Conference of Extending Database Technology (EDBT'98),* pp. 263–277.
Berlin: Springer-Verlag.

Sarawagi, S., R. Agrawal, and N. Megiddo. 1998. "Discovery-driven exploration of OLAP data cubes." In
Proceedings of the International Conference of Extending Database Technology (EDBT'98), pp. 168–182.
Berlin: Springer-Verlag.

16.2.3 Association Rules

Heikki Mannila

1. Introduction

Association rules are a simple class of sentences that can be efficiently discovered from large
sets of 0/1 valued data. These rules are not particularly powerful, but their usefulness stems
from the ability of the algorithms to find all association rules satisfying certain conditions that
hold in the data.

Given a schema $R = \{A_1, ..., A_p\}$ of attributes with domain $\{0, 1\}$, and a relation r over R,
an association rule (Agrawal et al., 1993) about r is an expression of the form $X \Rightarrow B$, where
$X \subseteq R$ and $B \in R \backslash X$. If $X = \{A_{i_1}, ..., A_{i_k}\}$, we can also write

$$A_{i_1}, ..., A_{i_k} \Rightarrow B.$$

The intuitive meaning of the rule is that if a row of the matrix r has a 1 in each column of X,
then the row also tends to have a 1 in column B. That is, the rule expresses the implication

$$A_{i_1} = 1 \wedge \cdots \wedge A_{i_k} = 1 \Rightarrow B = 1.$$

As a trivial example, consider Table 1. In this table the rule $A \Rightarrow B$ is true with accuracy
2/6. Examples of data where association rules might be applicable include the following:

- A student database at a university: rows correspond to students, columns to courses, and
  a 1 in entry (s, c) indicates that the student s has taken course c.

- Data collected from bar-code readers in supermarkets: columns correspond to products,
  and each row corresponds to the set of items purchased at one time.

- A database of publications: the rows and columns both correspond to publications, and
  $(p, p') = 1$ means that publication p refers to publication p'.

- A set of measurements about the behavior of a system, say exchanges in a telephone
  network. The columns correspond to the presence or absence of certain conditions, and
  each row corresponds to a measurement: if entry (m, c) is 1, then at measurement m
  condition c was present.

Given $W \subseteq R$, we denote by $s(W, r)$ the frequency of W in r: the fraction of rows of r that
have a 1 in each column of W. The frequency of the rule $X \Rightarrow B$ in r is defined to be

Table 1 An Artificial Example of 0/1 Data

Basket-id	A	B	C	D	E
t_1	1	0	0	0	0
t_2	1	1	1	1	0
t_3	1	0	1	0	1
t_4	0	0	1	0	0
t_5	0	1	1	1	0
t_6	1	1	1	0	0
t_7	1	0	1	1	0
t_8	0	1	1	0	1
t_9	1	0	0	1	0
t_{10}	0	1	1	0	1

$s(X \cup \{B\}, r)$, and the confidence or accuracy of the rule is $s(X \cup \{B\}, r)/s(X, r)$. The frequency of the rule is often called the support of the rule; support is also used to denote the fraction of rows that have a 1 in each column of $W \cup \{B\}$.

2. Discovery Task

In the discovery of association rules, the task is to find all rules $X \Rightarrow B$ such that the frequency of the rule is at least a given threshold σ and the confidence of the rule is at least another threshold θ. Note that the task really is to find all rules satisfying the criteria, not just selected ones or the ones with the highest confidence.

What properties should an algorithm for this task have? In large retailing applications the number of rows might be 10^6 or even 10^8, and the number of columns around 5,000. The frequency threshold σ is typically around 10^{-2}–10^{-4}. The confidence threshold θ can be anything from 0 to 1. From such a database one might obtain thousands or hundreds of thousands of association rules. (Of course, one has to be careful in assigning any statistical significance to findings obtained from such methods.)

Note that there is no predefined limit to the number of attributes on the left-hand-side X of an association rule $X \Rightarrow B$, and B is not fixed either; this is important so that unexpected associations are not ruled out before the processing starts. It also means that the search space of the rules has exponential size in the number of attributes of the input relation. Handling this requires some care with the algorithms, but there is a simple way of pruning the search space.

We call a subset $X \subseteq R$ frequent in r, if $s(X, r)\text{tf} = \}Pi2\}5\sigma$. Once all frequent sets of r are known, finding the association rules is easy. Namely, for each frequent set X and each $B \in X$, verify whether the rule $X \setminus \{B\} \Rightarrow B$ has sufficiently high confidence.

How can one find all frequent sets X? This can be done in a multitude of ways (Agrawal et al., 1993, 1996; Han and Fu, 1995; Holsheimer et al., 1995; Savasere et al., 1995; Toivonen, 1996). A typical approach (Agrawal et al., 1996) is to use the fact that all subsets of a frequent set are also frequent.

3. The A Priori Algorithm

A simple but efficient algorithm for the association rule discovery task operates as follows. First find all frequent sets of size 1 by reading the data once and recording the number of times each attribute A occurs. Then form candidate sets of size 2 by taking all pairs $\{B, C\}$ of attributes such that $\{B\}$ and $\{C\}$ are both frequent. The frequency of the candidate sets is again evaluated against the database. Once frequent sets of size 2 are known, candidate sets of size 3 can be formed; these are sets $\{B, C, D\}$ such that $\{B, C\}$, $\{B, D\}$, and $\{C, D\}$ are all frequent. This process is continued until no more candidate sets can be formed.

As an algorithm, the process for finding the set F of all frequent sets is as follows.

```
1. C := {{A}|A ∈ R};
```

```
2. ℱ := ∅
3. i := 1;
4. while 𝒞 ≠ ∅ do
5.    ℱ' := the sets X ∈ 𝒞 that are frequent;
6.    add ℱ' to ℱ;
7.    𝒞 := sets Y of size i + 1 such that
8.       each subset W of Y of size i is frequent;
9.    i := i + 1;
10. Od;
```

The algorithm has to read the database at most $K + 1$ times, where K is the size of the largest frequent set. In the applications, K is small, typically at most 10, so the number of passes through the data is reasonable.

A modification of the above method is obtained by computing for each frequent set X the subrelation $r_X \subseteq r$ consisting of those rows $t \in r$ such that $t[A] = 1$ for all $A \in X$. Then it is easy to see that for example $r_{\{A,B,C\}} = r_{\{A,B\}} \cap r_{\{B,C\}}$. Thus, the relation r_X for a set X of size k can be obtained from the relations $r_{X'}$ and $r_{X''}$, where $X' = X \setminus \{A\}$ and $X'' = X \setminus \{B\}$ for some $A, B \in X$ with $A \neq B$. This method has the advantage that rows that do not contribute to any frequent set will not be inspected more than once. For comparisons of the two approaches see Agrawal et al. (1996), Holsheimer et al. (1995), and Savasere et al. (1995).

The algorithms described above work quite nicely on large input relations. Their running time is approximately $O(NF)$, where $N = np$ is the size of the input and F is the sum of the sizes of the sets in the candidate collection $\mathscr{C}$ during the operation of the algorithm (Mannila and Toivonen, 1996b). This is nearly linear, and the algorithms seem to scale nicely to tens of millions of examples. Typically, the only case when they fail is when the output is too large, that is, there are too many frequent sets.

The methods for finding frequent sets are simple: they are based on one nice but simple observation (subsets of frequent sets must be frequent) and use straightforward implementation techniques.

4. Database Implementation Issues

A naive implementation of the algorithms on top of a relational database system would be easy: we need to pose to the database management system (DBMS) queries of the form What is $s(\{A_1, ..., A_k\}, r)$? or in SQL

select count (*) from r t
where t[A₁] = I and · · · and t[Aₖ] = I

The number of such queries can be large: if there are thousands of frequent sets, there will be thousands of queries. The overhead in performing the queries on an ordinary DBMS would probably be prohibitive.

The customized algorithms described above are able to evaluate masses of such queries reasonably efficiently, for several reasons. First, all the queries are very simple and have the same general form; thus, there is no need to compile each query individually. Second, the algorithms that make repeated passes through the data evaluate a large collection of queries during a single pass. Third, the algorithms that build the relations r_X for frequent sets X use the results of previous queries to avoid looking at the whole data for each query.

5. Extensions

Many variants of the basic association rule algorithm exist. The methods typically strive toward one or more of the following three goals: minimizing the number of passes through the data, minimizing the number of candidates that have to be inspected, and minimizing the time needed for computing the frequency of individual candidates.

One important way of improving the speed of computation of the frequencies of candidates is to use data structures that make it easy to find out which candidate sets in C_i occur for each row in the data set. A possible way of organizing the candidates is to use a treelike structure with branching factor p (the number of attributes). For each attribute A occurring in a candidate set, the root of the tree has a child labeled with A. This subtree contains those candidate sets whose first attribute (according to some ordering of the attributes) is A. The subtree is constructed in a recursive manner, that is, it has a subtree for each attribute B such that there is a candidate set with A as the first attribute and B as the second.

Another important way of speeding up the computation of frequent sets is to use sampling. Since we are interested in finding patterns describing large subgroups, that is, patterns having support higher than a given threshold, it is clear that just using a sample instead of the whole data set will give a fairly good approximation for the collection of frequent sets and their frequencies. A sample can also be used to obtain a method that, with high probability, only needs two passes through the data. First, compute from the sample the collection of frequent sets $\mathcal{F}$ using a threshold that is slightly lower than the one given by the user. Then, compute the frequencies in the whole data set of each set in $\mathcal{F}$. In most cases this produces the exact answer to the problem of finding the frequent sets in the whole data set. The only situation that can cause problems is the existence of a set Y of attributes all of whose subsets turned out to be frequent in the whole data set but which was not frequent in the sample. In this case, we know from the whole data set that Y could be frequent in the whole data set, but we did not compute its frequency in the whole data set. One has to make an extra pass through the database to guarantee an exact result.

Association rules are a simple formalism and they produce nice results for binary data. The basic restriction is that the relation should be sparse in the sense that there are no frequent sets that contain more than about fifteen attributes. Namely, the framework of finding all association rules typically generates at least as many rules as there are frequent sets, and if there is a frequent set of size K, there will be at least 2^K frequent sets.

The information about the frequent sets can actually be used to approximate fairly accurately the confidences and supports of a far wider set of rules, including negation and disjunction (Mannila and Toivonen, 1996a).

One of the big problems in the whole framework of association rules is that the approach is inherently tied to finding rules that have a high frequency. This can be motivated in terms of typical applications of data mining. In market basket analysis, for example, the retailer is probably not interested in finding rules that show connections between very rarely bought items. However, if those items are quite expensive, it might still be interesting to know what the most significant associations between the attributes are. Another problem (or strength) of the association rule idea is the asymmetry between 0s and 1s in the definition.

Recently, approaches have been presented for finding the most significant correlations between variables. Given p binary variables $A_1, ..., A_p$ and a set $r = \{t_1, ..., t_n\}$ of n observations with p values, define the correlation of the pair A_i and A_j to be $c(A_i, A_j) = Pr(A_i = A_j)$, that is, the probability that a randomly chosen row $t \in r$ has the same value for attributes A_i and A_j. The task is to find the pair (A_i, A_j) that has the highest correlation. This problem has been called the lightbulb problem (Paturi et al., 1995).

A straightforward method would be to investigate each pair (A_i, A_j) and to compute the actual probability $Pr(A_i = A_j)$. The complexity of such a method would be $O(p^2 n)$, which is prohibitively large for large values of p. If we have tens of thousands of attributes, we simply cannot investigate each pair of attributes separately.

A beautiful solution to this problem has been suggested in Paturi et al. (1995). The algorithm finds, with high probability, a pair of attributes whose correlation is not too far from the largest one. The basic idea is to repeatedly sample m rows $\{u_1, ..., u_m\}$ from the relation r. Given a variable A_i, denote by $s(A_i)$ the values of A_i for the rows in the sample, that is, the string $u_1[A_i], u_2[A_i], ..., u_m[A_i]$.

If m is not too large, then for a highly correlated pair (A_i, A_j) of attributes we have with high probability that $s(A_i) = s(A_j)$. On the other hand, if m is large enough, then the number of pairs of attributes (A_i, A_j) such that $s(A_i) = s(A_j)$ is at most linear in the total number of attributes.

Repeating the sampling sufficiently many times, it is relatively easy to show that the pair with the highest correlation satisfies the condition $s(A_i) = s(A_j)$ more frequently than all the other pairs.

References

Agrawal, R., T. Imielinski, and A. Swami. May 1993. "Mining association rules between sets of items in large databases." In *Proceedings of ACM SIGMOD Conference on Management of Data (SIGMOD'93)*, edited by P. Buneman, and S. Jajodia, pp. 207–216. Washington DC.

Agrawal, R., H. Mannila, R. Srikant, H. Toivonen, and A. I. Verkamo. 1996. "Fast discovery of association rules." In *Advances in Knowledge Discovery and Data Mining*, edited by U. M. Fayyad, G. Piatetsky-Shapiro, P. Smyth, and R. Uthurusamy, pp. 307–328. Menlo Park, CA: AAAI Press.

Han, J. and Y. Fu. September 1995. "Discovery of multiple-level association rules from large databases." In *Proceedings of the 21st International Conference on Very Large Data Bases (VLDB'95)*, edited by U. Dayal, P. M. D. Gray, and S. Nishio, pp. 420–431. Zurich: Morgan Kaufmann.

Holsheimer, M., M. Kersten, H. Mannila, and H. Toivonen. August 1995. "A perspective on databases and data mining." In *Proceedings of the First International Conference on Knowledge Discovery and Data Mining (KDD-'95)*, edited by U. M. Fayyad, and R. Uthurusamy, pp. 150–155. Montreal: AAAI Press.

Mannila, H. and H. Toivonen. August 1996a. "Multiple uses of frequent sets and condensed representations." In *Proceedings of the Second International Conference on Knowledge Discovery and Data Mining (KDD-'96)*. Portland, OR: AAAI Press, pp. 189–194.

Mannila, H. and H. Toivonen. April 1996b. "On an algorithm for finding all interesting sentences." In *Cybernetics and Systems, Volume II, The Thirteenth European Meeting on Cybernetics and Systems Research*. Vienna: Austrian Society for Cybernetic Studies, pp. 973–978.

Paturi, R., S. Rajasekaran, and J. H. Reif. 1995. "The light bulb problem." *Inform. Comput.* **117(2)**: 187–192.

Savasere, A., E. Omiecinski, and S. Navathe. September 1995. "An efficient algorithm for mining association rules in large databases." In *Proceedings of the Twenty-First International Conference on Very Large Data Bases (VLDB'95)*. Zurich: Morgan Kaufmann, pp. 432–444.

Toivonen, H. September 1996. "Sampling large databases for association rules." In *Proceedings of the Twenty-Second International Conference on Very Large Data Bases (VLDB'96)*, edited by T. M. Vijayaraman, A. P. Buchmann, C. Mohan, and N. L. Sarda, pp. 134–145. Mumbay, India: Morgan Kaufmann.

16.2.4 Inductive Logic Programming Approaches

Sašo Džeroski

ABSTRACT Inductive logic programming (ILP) is concerned with the development of tools for multirelational data mining. Besides the ability to deal directly with data stored in multiple tables, ILP systems are usually able to take into account generally valid background (domain) knowledge in the form of a logic program. They also use the powerful language of logic programs for describing discovered patterns. This article gives a brief introduction to the basic notions of ILP, presents some of the main ILP approaches, and points out some successful applications of ILP methods.

1. Introduction

From a KDD perspective, we can say that inductive logic programming (ILP) is concerned with the development of tools for multirelational data mining. In a typical relational database, data reside in multiple tables. ILP tools can be applied directly to such multirelational data to find patterns that involve multiple relations. This is a distinguishing feature of ILP approaches: most other data mining approaches can only deal with data that reside in a single table and require preprocessing that integrates data from multiple tables (e.g., through joins or aggregation) into a single table before they can be applied.

Integrating data from multiple tables through joins or aggregation can cause loss of meaning or information. Suppose we have relations *customer(CustID, Name, Age, SpendsALot)* and *purchase(CustID, ProductID, Date, Value, PaymentMode)*, where each customer can make multiple purchases, and we are interested in characterizing customers that spend a lot. Integrating the two relations via a natural join will give rise to a relation *purchase1*, where each row corresponds to a purchase and not to a customer. One possible aggregation would give rise to the relation *customer1(CustID, Age, NumOfPurchases, TotalValue, SpendsALot)*. Some information, however, has been clearly lost during the aggregation process.

A pattern discovered by an ILP system in the above case might look as follows: *customer(CID, Name, Age, yes)* ← *Age* > 30 ∧ *purchase(CID, PID, D, Value, PM)* ∧ *PM* = *creditcard* ∧ *Value* > 100. It says: a customer spends a lot if she is older than 30, has purchased a product of value more than 100 and paid for it by credit card. It would not be possible to induce such a pattern form the relations *purchase1* and *customer1*.

Besides the ability to deal with data stored in multiple tables directly, ILP systems are usually able to take into account generally valid background (domain) knowledge in the form of a logic program. The ability to take into account background knowledge and the expressive power of the language of discovered patterns are also distinctive for ILP.

2. Logic Programming, Relational Databases and Deductive Databases

The patterns discovered by ILP systems are typically expressed as clauses in first-order (predicate) logic. We can think of clauses as first-order rules, where the conclusion part is termed the head and the condition part the body of the clause. The head and body of a clause consist of atoms, where an atom is a predicate applied to some arguments (e.g., variables). A set of clauses is called a clausal theory.

As an example, consider the clause *father(X, Y)* ∨ *mother(X, Y)* ← *parent(X, Y)*. This clause is read as follows: "if X is parent of Y, then X is the father of Y or X is the mother of Y." *Parent(X, Y)* is the body of the clause, and *father(X, Y)* ∨ *mother(X, Y)* is the head. *Parent, father,* and *mother* are predicates, X and Y are variables, and *parent(X, Y), father(X, Y)*, and *mother(X, Y)* are atoms. Variables in clauses are implicitly universally quantified.

As opposed to full clauses, definite clauses contain exactly one atom in the head. As compared to definite clauses, program clauses can also contain negated atoms in the body. Logic programs are sets of program clauses. While the clause in the paragraph above is a full clause, the clause *ancestor(X, Y)* ← *parent(Z, Y)* ∧ *ancestor(X, Z)* is a definite clause. It is also a recursive clause since it defines the relation *ancestor* in terms of itself and the relation *parent*. The clause *mother(X, Y)* ← *parent(X, Y)* ∧ *not male(X)* is a program clause. A set of program clauses with the same predicate in the head is called a predicate definition.

A relational database (RDB) is a set of relations. A predicate in logic programming corresponds to a relation in an RDB, and the arguments of a predicate correspond to the attributes of a relation. The major difference is that the attributes of a relation are typed (i.e., a domain is associated with each attribute). Database clauses are thus typed program clauses. A deductive database is a set of database clauses.

The language of deductive databases is more expressive than the language of relational databases. In deductive databases, relations can be defined extensionally as sets of tuples (as in RDBs) or intensionally as sets of database clauses (views). Note that full clauses, such as *father(X, Y)* ∨ *mother(X, Y)* ← *parent(X, Y)*, can be used to express integrity constraints on databases. ILP approaches can be used to learn views (logical definitions) from extensional relations (Quinlan, 1990), as well as integrity constraints (De Raedt and Dehaspe, 1997).

For a full treatment of logic programming, relational databases and deductive databases, we refer the reader to Lloyd (1987) and Ullman (1988).

3. Learning Logical Definitions of Relations

The most commonly addressed task in ILP is the task of learning a logic program that defines a target relation p in terms of other relations.

A set of examples is given, that is, tuples that belong to p (positive examples) and tuples that do not belong to p (negative examples). Also given are background relations (or background predicates) q_i that constitute the background knowledge and can be used in the learned definition of p. Finally, a hypothesis language, specifying syntactic restrictions on the definition of p, is also given (either explicitly or implicitly).

The task is to find a definition of the target relation p that is consistent and complete, that is, explains (derives) all the positive and none of the negative tuples. When dealing with incomplete or noisy data, which is most often the case, the criteria of consistency and completeness are relaxed. Statistical criteria are typically used instead, based on the number of positive and negative examples explained by the definition and the individual constituent clauses.

We can say we are dealing with a binary classification problem, where one of two classes is assigned to the examples (tuples): $\oplus$ (positive) or $\ominus$ (negative). If our task is to learn to distinguish customers that spend a lot from those that don't, the target relation could be *SpendsALot(CustID, Name, Age)* and the two tuples *customer(1, jane_doe, 35, yes)* and *customer(2, john_smith, 28, no)* would yield the examples *(spendsalot(1, jane_doe, 35), $\oplus$)* and *(spendsalot(2, john_smith, 28), $\ominus$)*. Given the background relation *purchase*, the clause *spendsalot(CID, Name, Age) ← Age > 30 ∧ purchase(CID, PID, D, Value, PM) ∧ PM = creditcard ∧ Value > 100* could be induced.

The hypothesis language is typically a subset of the language of program clauses. As the complexity of learning grows with the expressiveness of the hypothesis language, restrictions have to be imposed on hypothesized clauses. Typical restrictions are the exclusion of recursion and restrictions on variables that appear in the body of the clause but not in its head (so-called new variables).

The top-level induction algorithm does not vary much among different ILP systems that learn logical definitions of relations: most systems use the covering approach. While there are unexplained positive examples, a clause is constructed explaining some of them, the explained positive examples are removed and the loop is repeated. Individual clauses are constructed by searching through a lattice of clauses ordered by a generalization or a specialization operator.

A part of the lattice of clauses for the *spendsalot* ILP problem is given in Figure 1. A specialization operator is first applied to the clause *spendsalot(CID, Name, Age) ←*, then to its specializations, and so on. The operator adds conditions to the body of a clause: these introduce new relations/predicates or place constraints on the existing variables (attributes).

A typical ILP algorithm starts with the clause *spendsalot(CID, Name, Age) ←*, which covers all positive and negative examples of the target relation *spendsalot*. It then greedily

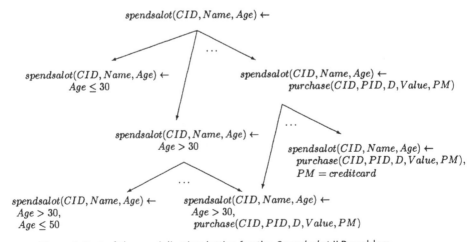

Figure 1 Part of the specialization lattice for the *Spendsalot* ILP problem

searches the specialization lattice and keeps adding conditions to the clause currently estimated as best until it covers no negative examples. This is roughly what the system FOIL (Quinlan, 1990) does.

The search for individual clauses to be included in the definition of the target relation can proceed top-down (using a specialization operator) or bottom-up (using a generalization operator). Generalization operators typically remove conditions from the body of a clause. Generalization and specialization operators are known as refinement operators and the corresponding graphs/lattices are known as refinement graphs/lattices (Shapiro, 1983).

A problem with searching refinement graphs for program clauses is that they can be very large and even infinite. Searching refinement graphs is thus computationally expensive. Their size can be reduced by introducing language restrictions (i.e., imposing a limit on the number of conditions in the body or the number of new variables).

The search through the refinement graph can be focused by first calculating the most specific clause that covers one or several given positive examples. Such a clause is called a bottom clause and bounds the refinement lattice from below. Roughly speaking, only conditions that appear in this clause need to be considered for addition to a partially built clause in the search process, thus making search more efficient.

The bottom clause can be calculated from several examples by least general generalization, that is, by calculating the most specific clause that explains/derives the selected examples. Relative least general generalization, on the other hand, also takes into account the background knowledge (relations). This approach is taken in the ILP system GOLEM (Muggleton and Feng, 1990). The bottom clause can also be calculated from a single example using mode-directed inverse resolution, as done in the ILP system PROGOL (Muggleton, 1995).

For an impression of how (relative) least general generalization and inverse resolution work, consider a simplified example. Consider two positive examples of the relation *mother*: *mother(ann, mary)* and *mother(eve, tom)*. Suppose the background knowledge contains (implicitly or explicitly) the following facts about *ann*, *mary*, *eve*, and *tom*: *parent(ann, mary)*, *parent(eve, tom)*, *female(ann)*, *female(eve)*, *blond(ann)*, *tall(eve)*. The least general generalization of *mother(ann, mary)* ← *female(ann)*, *parent(ann, mary)*, *blond(ann)* and *mother(eve, tom)* ← *female(eve)*, *parent(eve, tom)*, *tall(eve)* is the clause *mother(X, Y)* ← *female(X)*, *parent(X, Y)*. This is also (a reduced variant of) the relative least general generalization of the two examples with respect to the given background knowledge. For details, we refer the reader to Muggleton and Feng (1990).

Inverse resolution (Muggleton and Buntine, 1988) reverses the direction of inference for the deductive operator of resolution. We can derive *mother(ann, mary)* from the clause $c = mother(X, Y)$ ← *female(X)*, *parent(X, Y)* and the facts *female(ann)* and *parent(ann, mary)* in two resolution steps. The first step, applying the substitution X/ann, $Y/mary$ derives the clause *mother(ann, mary)* ← *female(ann)* from clause c above and *parent(ann, mary)*. In contrast, inverse resolution would derive *mother(X, mary)* ← *female(X)* from the example *mother(ann, mary)* and the fact *female(ann)*, applying the inverse substitution ann/X.

State-of-the-art ILP algorithms include mechanisms for handling imperfect, for example, noisy, data, as well as numerical data including numerical classes. Suitable techniques from single-table learning approaches have been adapted to that end.

4. Clausal Discovery

In the ILP setting described above, classification rules are induced. If the induced rules are sufficiently accurate, they may replace the examples; namely, the examples can be derived from the rules. A radically different approach is taken in the setting of clausal discovery: given a database, a set of constraints from a given language is to be found that hold for the database (De Raedt and Dehaspe, 1997). The constraints can have the form of full first-order clauses. A clause of the form *Head* ← *Body* holds for a database if the query *Body* ∧ *not Head* fails, that is, has an empty answer set.

To illustrate clausal discovery, consider a database containing facts about the family relations *mother*, *father*, and *parent*. The following integrity constraints, among

others, can be discovered: $mother(X, Y) \vee father(X, Y) \leftarrow parent(X, Y), parent(X, Y) \leftarrow father(X,$
$Y), \leftarrow mother(X, Y) \wedge father(X, Y),$ and $\leftarrow parent(X, X).$ The third and fourth constraints state
that it is impossible that X is at the same time both the mother and the father of Y, and that it
is impossible for a person to be their own parent. The constraints learned are not necessarily
sufficient for classification or to define some relations in terms of other: if we discard the
database, the learned theory may be unable to reconstruct it.

An ILP system for clausal discovery is CLAUDIEN (De Raedt and Dehaspe, 1997). It
searches a refinement (specialization) graph for full clauses. Since the clauses discovered are
not intended for classification, the covering approach cannot be used. Instead, CLAUDIEN
searches the complete lattice of clauses within a given hypothesis language, returning the most
general valid clauses found. The structure of the lattice is exploited to prune the search.

Since essentially a complete search of the hypothesis language has to be performed, it is
crucial that the hypothesis language is of manageable size. The facility of declarative bias is a
powerful tool in this respect: CLAUDIEN comes equipped with DLAB, a language for
describing clauses that belong to the hypothesis language in a generative way. In DLAB, clause
templates may also contain second-order variables, that is, variables that stand for predicates.
For example, the clauses $female(X) \leftarrow mother(X, Y)$ and $human(Y) \leftarrow parent(X, Y)$ can be
generated from the DLAB template $P(\{X, Y\}) \leftarrow Q(X, Y),$ where P and Q are second-order
variables. Finally, let us mention that CLAUDIEN is an anytime algorithm that reports valid
regularities ordered by their generality/complexity: more general/simpler constraints are
found first and we can look for as complex constraints as time allows.

5. Other ILP Approaches

While initial efforts in ILP focused on classification rule induction (more precisely on concept
learning in first-order logic and synthesis of logic programs, cf. Muggleton [1991]), state-of-the-
art ILP approaches now span most of the spectrum of KDD tasks and techniques. The
distinguishing features of using multiple relations directly and discovering patterns expressed
in first-order logic are present throughout: ILP approaches can thus be viewed as upgrades of
traditional approaches. For example, the systems for induction of first-order classification and
regression trees SRT (Kramer, 1996) and TILDE (Blockeel and De Raedt, 1998) upgrade
techniques found in CART (Breiman et al., 1984) and C4.5 (Quinlan, 1993).

The relational instance-based learning approach of Emde and Wettschereck (1996)
upgrades the nearest-neighbor approach to classification. ILP approaches to clustering, such as
relational distance-based clustering (Kirsten and Wrobel, 1998) and logical clustering trees
(Blockeel et al., 1998) have also been developed. Finally, the very popular approach of frequent
pattern discovery, used for the discovery of association rules, has been upgraded to the
discovery of frequent queries (Dehaspe and Toivonen, 1999), thus enabling the discovery of
association rules in first-order logic.

6. Successful ILP Applications

ILP approaches have been successfully applied to a number of knowledge discovery problems
in different areas, ranging from environmental sciences through mechanical engineering to
molecular biology. ILP has been successfully used by Srinivasan et al. (1996) to discover
structural alerts for mutagenesis. It has also been successfully used for predicting the activity
of drugs in drug design (King et al., 1992) and for predicting carcinogenicity (Srinivasan et al.,
1997). A recent application where ILP approaches clearly outperformed traditional approaches
involved the classification of NMR spectra of a range of natural products (diterpenes)
important for the pharmaceutical industry (Džeroski et al., 1998). A common property of the
above-mentioned applications is that they involve chemical compounds: they thus require
effective ways for dealing with structures and substructures, as well as the use of existing
domain knowledge and an expressive language of discovered patterns. These requirements are
most easily met by ILP approaches, as confirmed by the success of ILP techniques.

References

Blockeel, H. and L. De Raedt. 1998. "Top-down induction of first order logical decision trees." *Artificial Intell.* **101**: 285–297.

Blockeel, H., L. De Raedt, and J. Ramon. 1998. "Top-down induction of clustering trees." In *Proceedings of the Fifteenth International Conference on Machine Learning*, pp. 55–63. San Francisco, CA: Morgan Kaufmann.

Breiman, L., J. H. Friedman, R. A. Olshen, and C. J. Stone. 1984. *Classification and Regression Trees.* Belmont, NY: Wadsworth.

De Raedt, L. and L. Dehaspe. 1997. "Clausal discovery." *Machine Learning* **26**: 99–146.

Dehaspe, L. and H. Toivonen. 1999. "Discovery of frequent DATALOG patterns." *Data Mining and Knowledge Discovery* **3**: 7–36.

Džeroski, S., S. Schulze-Kremer, K. Heidtke, K. Siems, D. Wettschereck, and H. Blockeel. 1998. "Diterpene structure elucidation from ^{13}C NMR spectra with inductive logic programming." *Appl. Artificial Intell.* **12**: 363–383.

Emde, W. and D. Wettschereck. 1996. "Relational instance-based learning." In *Proceedings of the Thirteenth International Conference on Machine Learning*, pp. 122–130. San Mateo, CA: Morgan Kaufmann.

King, R. D., S. H. Muggleton, and M. J. E. Sternberg. 1992. "Drug design by machine learning: the use of inductive logic programming to model the structure-activity relationships of trimethoprim analogues binding to dihydrofolate reductase." In *Proceedings of the National Academy of Sciences* **89**: 11322–11326.

Kirsten, M. and S. Wrobel. 1998. "Relational distance based clustering." In *Proceedings of the Eighth International Conference on Inductive Logic Programming*, pp. 261–270. Berlin: Springer.

Kramer, S. 1996. "Structural regression trees." In *Proceedings of the Thirteenth National Conference on Artificial Intelligence*, pp. 812–819. Cambridge, MA: MIT Press.

Lloyd, J. 1987. *Foundations of Logic Programming.* 2nd edition. Berlin, Germany: Springer.

Muggleton, S. H. 1991. "Inductive logic programming." *New Generation Comput.* **8**: 295–318.

Muggleton, S. H. 1995. "Inverse entailment and PROGOL." *New Generation Comput.* **13**: 245–286.

Muggleton, S. H. and W. Buntine. 1988. "Machine invention of first-order predicates by inverting resolution." In *Proceedings of the Fifth International Conference on Machine Learning*, pp. 339–352. San Mateo, CA: Morgan Kaufmann.

Muggleton, S. H. and C. Feng. 1990. "Efficient induction of logic programs." In *Proceedings of the First Conference on Algorithmic Learning Theory*, pp. 368–381. Tokyo: Ohmsha.

Quinlan, J. R. 1990. "Learning logical definitions from relations." *Machine Learning* **5**: 239–266.

Quinlan, J. R. 1993. *C4.5: Programs for Machine Learning.* San Mateo, CA: Morgan Kaufmann.

Shapiro, E. 1983. *Algorithmic Program Debugging.* Cambridge, MA: MIT Press.

Srinivasan, A., R. D. King, S. H. Muggleton, and M. J. E. Sternberg. 1997. "Carcinogenesis prediction using inductive logic programming." In *Intelligent Data Analysis in Medicine and Pharmacology*, edited by N. Lavrač, E. Keravnou, and B. Zupan, pp. 243–260. Dordrecht, Netherlands: Kluwer.

Srinivasan, A., S. H. Muggleton, R. D. King, and M. J. E. Sternberg. 1996. "Theories for mutagenicity: a study of first-order and feature based induction." *Artificial Intell.* **85**: 277–299.

Ullman, J. 1988. *Principles of Database and Knowledge Base Systems*, vol. I. Rockville, MA: Computer Science Press.

Further Reading

Džeroski, S. 1996. "Inductive logic programming and knowledge discovery in databases." In *Advances in Knowledge Discovery and Data Mining*, U. Fayyad, G. Piatetsky-Shapiro, P. Smyth, and R. Uthurusamy, eds, pp. 118–152. Cambridge, MA: MIT Press. A brief account on ILP from the KDD perspective.

Džeroski, S. and N. Lavrač, eds. 1999. *Data Mining and Knowledge Discovery* **3**(1). Special issue on inductive logic programming. Most recent advances in ILP relevant to KDD. Attention paid to scaling-up ILP methods to deal with large databases.

Džeroski, S. and N. Lavrač, eds. 2001. *Relational Data Mining.* Berlin: Springer. An overview of state-of-the-art ILP approaches and their applications from the KDD perspective.

Fuernkranz, J. and B. Pfahringer, eds. 1998. *Appl. Artificial Intell.* **12**(5). Special issue on first-order knowledge discovery in databases. Includes accounts of several applications of ILP.

Lavrač, N. and S. Džeroski. 1994. *Inductive Logic Programming: Techniques and Applications.* Chichester, England: Ellis Horwood. Practically oriented introductory textbook. Freely available at http://www-ai.ijs.si/SasoDzeroski/ILPBook.

16.3 Subgroup Discovery

16.3.1 Deviation Analysis

Willi Klösgen

ABSTRACT The two general data analytic questions of subgroup mining (see Chapter 5.2 of this handbook) deal with deviations and associations (see Chapters 16.2.3 and 16.2.4). A deviation pattern describes a deviating behavior (distribution) of a target variable in a subgroup. Target variable and behavior type are selected by the analyst for an individual mining task, the deviating subgroups are determined by the mining method. Deviation patterns rely on statistical tests and thus capture knowledge about a subgroup in the form of a verified alternative hypothesis on the distribution of a target variable. Typically the rejected null hypothesis assumes an uninteresting, not deviating subgroup. Search for deviating subgroups is organized in two phases. In a first brute force search, different search heuristics can be applied to find a set of deviating subgroups. In a second refinement phase, redundancy elimination operators construct the best system of subgroups from the brute force search results. We discuss the role of tests for subgroup mining, introduce specializations of the general deviation pattern, summarize search and automatic refinement algorithms, and deal with navigation and visualization operations that support an analyst when interactively constructing the best system of deviating subgroups.

1. Motivation for Subgroup Mining and Role of Hypothesis Testing

The motivation for this large scale and direct search approach is caused by a frequent analysis situation where a user is interested in a special property or behavior of one or several selected target variables. Those regions of the input variable space are searched where the target variables show this behavior. The analyst could be interested in regions, for example, with a high average value of a continuous target, with a high share of one value of a nominal target (see Chapter 20.1 for results of such a subgroup mining task), or for which this share has increased significantly more during two years than in the complementary region, or that show a special time trend of a target variable. Thus many different data analysis questions can be represented as special behavior types of target variables.

One approach for many of these data analyses relies on an approximation of the unknown function that describes the dependency between target and input variables. The approximating function is then studied to identify the interesting regions. However, it is difficult to find a good approximation when there are many input variables, the approximation must be global (covering the whole input space), and be derived with a sample of noisy data. So, often the direct approach of searching for the interesting subgroups without relying on an intermediary functional approximation is more efficient (Friedman and Fisher, 1999).

To formalize the subgroup mining approach, a specification of the description language to build subgroups and a formalization of behavior patterns are needed. The behavior of target variables $y = (y_1, ..., y_k)$ is captured by assuming a probabilistic approach and referring to their joint distribution with the input variables $x = (x_1, ..., x_m)$. We are interested in some designated property of the unknown joint distribution with density $p(y, x)$, for example, a large average of $E[y \mid x]$ in a subgroup. The interesting behavior is now defined by a statistical test. In the null hypothesis of the test, an assumption on the distribution of the target variable(s) in the subgroup is specified that is regarded as expected or uninteresting. The alternative hypothesis defines the deviating or interesting subgroup. When a given data set spots the null hypothesis for a subgroup as very unlikely (under a given confidence threshold), the subgroup (i.e., the behavior of the target variable(s) in the subgroup defined by the distribution property) is identified as interesting. In this way, a broad spectrum of statistical tests and of associated data analysis questions is applicable for subgroup mining.

Thus, subgroup mining does not rely on an estimation of the density function (kernel density estimation), or more simply on an estimation of the first moment $E[y \mid x]$ of the density function (function approximation), but a direct search for significant subgroups is scheduled.

Now the problem remains to formulate appropriate null hypotheses to represent analytic questions. In principal, one can rely on a priori assumptions on the behavior regarded as uninteresting, or on measurements within the population which with a given sample database estimate the real population behavior. For instance, the probability of a binary event for members of a subgroup could be regarded as uninteresting, if it does not deviate from the overall probability for the total population. The probability for the population can be estimated with the given sample database and used for the null hypothesis of a parametric statistical test.

A subgroup is interesting depending on a selected confidence threshold. Since very many tests are performed in a mining task, based on Bonferroni adjustment for multiple tests, a very high confidence threshold must be specified. Even if, due to clever heuristic search strategies (see Section 3 below), only a small part of the whole subgroup space is processed, conceptually very many tests are considered. This must be regarded when setting the confidence level, either automatically or by the user. The problem is further aggravated by secondary search processes, for example, for discretization of continuous variables or geographical clustering of values of spatial independent variables.

The test approach has three advantages for subgroup mining. It allows a broad spectrum of data analytic questions to be treated, offers intelligent solutions to balance the trade-off between diverse criteria for assessing the statistical interestingness of a deviation, for example, size of subgroup versus amount of deviation, and finally mitigates the problem of discovering random fluctuations of the target variables in the given noisy sample as interesting.

2. Specializations of the General Deviation Pattern

Special analytic questions can be classified with two main dimensions. Firstly, the type of the target variable is important. For a binary target, a single share is analyzed, for example, the percentage of good productions. In the case of a nominal target, a vector is studied, for example, the joint percentages of bad, medium, and good productions. When the target is ordinal, the median, or alternatively, the probability of a better value in the subgroup than in a reference group can be analyzed. For example, the probability that a production from a subgroup is better than a production from the complementary subgroup. Finally, the target can be continuous. Then statements on the mean or the variance of the variable can be inferred. If several target variables are selected, their joint distribution must be analyzed. The second dimension for classifying analytic questions is given by the number of populations studied. Populations may, for example relate to several time points (see Chapter 16.3.2), or countries, or rely on other segmentation variables like gender for comparing males and females.

A verification and a quality function evaluate the deviation of a subgroup. Together they deal with three goals: reducing random results, including application-dependent preferences for interestingness criteria, and efficiently directing search. The verification test operationalizes a special analytic question. Table 1 lists some tests according to the classification of analytic questions. When relying on parametric tests, a property of one of the distribution parameters of the target determines the meaning of the analytical question. Nonparametric tests are also appropriate in the data mining context, because the smaller test power (adhering longer to the null hypothesis) is generally not a problem, and the modest distribution assumptions and calculation efforts of these tests are preferable. Furthermore, the large sample and explorative situation in data mining favours nonparametric tests. The verification function is used as a filter constraint for subgroups. Only those deviations are selected that have a very low probability of being generated just by random fluctuations of the targets.

The quality function is used by the search algorithm to rank the subgroups when processing the search space. For instance, in a beam search strategy (see Section 3 below), only the best n subgroups according to their quality are further expanded to construct the next nodes to be evaluated in the search space. In this step, application-dependent interestingness criteria and search efficiency are important. While the verification test deals with the problems

Table 1 Some Statistical Verification Tests for Subtypes of the Subgroup Deviation Pattern

Type of dependent variable(s)	One cross-section	Two independent cross-sections	k independent cross-sections and time series
Binary	Binomial test Chi square test Confidence intervals Information gain	Bin.test:pooled variance Chi square test Log odds ratio: z-scores (each with absolute/ relative version)	Chi square tests Trend test
Nominal	Chi square: goodness-of-fit Independence test Gini diversity index Information gain Twoing criterium	Chi square tests Gini diversity index	Chi square test Trend analysis
Ordinal	Ridit analysis	Ridit analysis	Ridits & trend analysis
Continuous	Median test Median-quantile test U-test H-test 1 or 2 sample t-test	Median test Median-quantile test U-test H-test Two-sample t-test	Analysis of variance

of executing very many tests and is applied as a statistical significance filter, the quality function includes application-dependent criteria capturing the interestingness of subgroups (e.g., preferring either large subgroups or large deviations). Quality computation can rely on statistical and other interestingness aspects such as simplicity, usefulness, and novelty (see Chapter 18). The quality can be given by the P-value or test statistic calculated in the verification method, or by a function exploiting this significance value only as one component for the final quality. A typical statistical quality function (e.g., defined by z-scores) combines several aspects of interestingness such as strength (deviation of parameter from *a priori* value) and generality (subgroup size).

Alternative tests for an analytical question, for example, the tests listed in each cell of Table 1, can be assessed by their statistical properties (e.g., power or type II error). It is also important for deciding between several test options, how the single interestingness aspects are combined. We will discuss this representatively for the tests listed in Table 1 for the simplest case, the binary event.

$$Q_1 = \frac{p - p_0}{\sqrt{p_0(1 - p_0)}} \sqrt{n} \tag{1}$$

$$Q_2 = \frac{p - p_0}{\sqrt{p_0(1 - p_0)}} \sqrt{n} \sqrt{\frac{N}{N - n}}. \tag{2}$$

Tests for a binary event in a subgroup include several criteria. The z-score quality function based on comparing the subgroup with the total population (1) balances three criteria to measure the interestingness of a subgroup: the size of the subgroup (n), the difference of the target shares ($p - p_0$), and the level of the target share in the total population (p_0).

If the target share in the subgroup is compared with the share in its complementary subset (2), a fourth criterion is added, the relative size of the subgroup with respect to total population size (N). Then large subgroups are favored, which is also useful for patient search strategies (see Section 3 below). Thus option (2) is generally more appropriate. Test options (1) and (2) combine the diverse evaluation criteria in an evident way.

Option (2) has a factor $g/(1 - g)$ instead of relative subgroup size g for option (1). These two factors also appear in other quality functions, for example, in the two χ^2 tests of Table 1, or the two-sample t-test. Option (2) is symmetric with the same value for a subgroup and its complementary group, which is often more appropriate (e.g., for discretization subsearch).

But the appropriate balance of criteria may depend on application requirements. Thus, typically the analyst decides, based on background knowledge, which criteria are more important for a specific application. Specifically, the role of subgroup size usually is application-dependent. For some applications (e.g., production control), very small subgroups with large deviations are relevant, for other applications (e.g., marketing), subgroup size is important. Thus, an appropriate selection of a quality function must include application requirements. Another aspect of the quality function relates to its appropriateness for efficient search, for example, its behavior for hill climbing approaches.

Monotony axioms (Klösgen, 1996), that refer to monotonic behavior of the four basic criteria subgroup size, population size, subgroup target share, and population target share, set constraints on reasonable quality functions. Furthermore, symmetry properties, invariances, and equivalences (Klösgen, 1996) are important for quality functions. Sometimes families of quality functions (Klösgen, 1996; Kaufman and Michalski, 1999) are introduced involving a parameter to adjust the generality versus deviation trade-off.

3. Search

Search for deviations is determined by such aspects as search space dimensionality, strategies, pruning, and constraints. The main search dimension is the space of subgroup descriptions, partially ordered by the generality of the intensional descriptions or by the subset relation of their extensions. In Explora (Klösgen, 1996), a search algorithm for multidimensional spaces with an induced product ordering additionally exploits a space of target subgroups, which are built as conjunctions of taxonomical values for target variables, and a space of range subgroups. Searching in this three-dimensional space is scheduled from general to specific groups regarding the product ordering and is constrained by redundancy filters pruning successor subgroups. So interesting subgroups are at first identified for the most general target groups (e.g., clients) and the whole population. These patterns are then refined for more specialized target groups (e.g., product specific clients) and range restrictions. Typically the complete search space of all subgroups is exponentially large (relating to the number of conjunctions, values of attributes, and internal disjunctions, etc.) and cannot be processed exhaustively such that heuristic search strategies are necessary.

3.1. Search Strategies

Generate and test search strategies (see Chapter 11) usually iterate over two main steps: validating hypotheses (subgroups) and generating new hypotheses. Operating on a current population of hypotheses, neighborhood operators generate the neighbors, for example, by expanding subgroup descriptions with additional selectors, or genetic operators create the next generation by mutation and cross-over. Both the validation and generation steps consist of four substeps as summarized in Table 2. Simple neighborhood operators expand a current subgroup description by adding a further conjunctive selector (or removing an internal disjunction). These operators cannot guarantee that from a current description any other description can be reached by a sequence of neighborhood operators. Exchange operators modifying a part of a description (e.g., a selector) do not involve this limitation.

Search strategies fix the details within this general search frame, for example, the order in which the hypotheses are evaluated, expanded and validated, the selection and pruning criteria, and the iteration, recursion or backtracking. In Table 2, these steps are summarized for some simple search strategies implemented in Data Surveyor (see Chapter 24.2.2). All these strategies perform a brute force search to identify a set of hypotheses (subgroups) with high quality. Whereas beam search only expands the best hypotheses at each step to find more specialized, better subgroups, the broad view strategy is complementary. If a high quality subgroup is found, it is not further expanded. So subgroups can be identified that consist of a conjunction of selectors, where each selector alone is not interesting. The best n strategy is exhaustive, so that an efficient pruning is necessary for large hypothesis spaces. This can be achieved by a restrictive cover constraint (requiring a large size of subgroup). The optimistic

Table 2 Four Simple Brute Force Search Strategies for Subgroup Mining

Search Step	1. Beam Search	2. Broad View	3. Best n	4. Sequential
Select hypotheses to validate from list of generated, not validated hypotheses	All	All	All	All
Validate	Apply verification test and quality computation			
Evaluation of validated hypotheses	Sort successfully verified, not prunable hypotheses (cover constraint) by quality and put best n on list of hypotheses to be expanded	Put not successfully verified, not prunable hypotheses (cover constraint) on list of hypotheses to be expanded. Put successfully verified hypotheses on result list	Update list of best n hypotheses with successfully verified hypotheses. Put not prunable hypotheses (cover constraint, optimistic estimate) on list of hypotheses to be expanded	Sort successfully verified, not prunable hypotheses by quality and put best one on list of hypotheses expanded. If no better hypotheses, repeat process, but eliminate or disregard all cases covered by found subgroups
Update list of not yet validated hypotheses		Not applicable: all have been validated		
Select hypotheses for expansion	All	All	All	All
Expand hypotheses	Depending on type of expansion attribute: discretization, regional clustering nominal attributes: add selector, if internal disjunctions: eliminate one term			
Evaluation of expanded hypotheses	Eliminate successors of results			
Update list of hypotheses to be expanded		Not applicable: all have been expanded		

estimate evaluation of a subgroup checks if any specialization can have a better quality than the worst of the currently best n hypotheses.

Another aspect of search strategies relates to greediness. The usual general to specific search realized by successively adding further conjuncts is very greedy, that is, the size of the next subgroup is much reduced by a further conjunct. Especially for hill climbing strategies, this is often a problem. Friedman and Fisher (1999) therefore propose a patient strategy based on a description language offering all internal disjunctions for categorical and quantiles for continuous variables. At each specialization step, one internal disjunction is eliminated or one small upper or lower quantil is taken away from the current interval. So only a small part of the objects of a current subgroup is reduced in a specialization step. A more patient search is further supported by a nongreedy quality function (e.g. (2) in Section 2 above).

3.2. Search Constraints

Pruning criteria are special constraints (see Chapter 18.2) limiting the search space and, thus, are important for an efficient algorithm. The main pruning criterion for subgroup mining is the cover constraint. Other criteria are given by syntactical details of the description language, for example, maximal number of conjunctions. Depending on the search strategy, quality estimates can be exploited. When for example, searching for the best n subgroups, all those subgroups can be pruned for which all successors that fulfill the cover constraint cannot have a higher quality than the current nth best subgroup (Smyth and Goodman, 1992). These optimistic estimates depend on the quality function, so that for each function an estimate must be derived. In Klösgen (1996), some general classes of quality functions are analyzed, for which an easy calculation of such an estimate is possible. However, these estimates show some different power, that is, the pruning potential for the diverse quality functions is very different.

3.3. Search Refinement

In the brute force phase, subgroups are determined satisfying constraints and goals of the specified search task. In a refinement phase, subgroups are elaborated, redundancies eliminated, and general patterns specialized. Elaborations analyze a single hypothesis (typically using an independent test data set) by filtering, bottom up refinement (backward elimination of selectors), sensitivity analysis of description boundaries, statistical pruning and cross-validation, or analyzing the homogeneity of the subgroup to avoid only a subset being relevant but not the subgroup as a whole. Redundancies relate to the correlation between subgroups which may include spurious effects. Redundancies are eliminated by suppressing and ordering, combining, generalizing, or clustering of hypotheses (Klösgen, 1996; Gebhardt, 1991). Examples of specializations of general patterns are treated in Chapter 16.3.2. Brute force and refinement subtasks can be scheduled iteratively. This can be done automatically or in a user controlled exploratory mode.

The overall goal is to find a consolidated set of subgroups. Thus, criteria are needed to evaluate a set of subgroups. A selection process selects or produces (by constructing additional subgroups) a best set of subgroups. Specifically, four criteria are important:

1. The overlapping degree of the selected subgroups should be low.
2. The covering degree of subgroups should be high. If, for example the target objects are determined on an individual level, the covering degree is given by the percentage of target objects that are included in the union of the selected subgroups.
3. The quality of the union of the selected subgroups (regarded as a single subset) should be high.
4. Finally, the number of selected subgroups should be low.

Trade-offs between these criteria can be automatically scheduled by thresholding parameters.

Suppression algorithms employ diverse criteria to suppress a subgroup S2 by a subgroup S1 with a higher quality. Elementary criteria suppress S2 if there are not enough additional objects in S2 or underproportionally many targets in S2 − S1. Criteria based on conditional independence (Mitchell, 1997, Chapter 6.11.1) of the target subgroup of S2 given S1 (and other subgroups) are constitutive for the construction of Bayesian networks describing the interdependencies of subgroups and their influence on the target subgroup. Usually Bayesian suppression based on conditional independence is weaker than the mentioned elementary criteria, so that less subgroups are suppressed and a larger set of best subgroups is constructed with the Bayesian net.

In contrast to an automatic refinement, user involvement in this process supported by navigation and visualization tools is sometimes more appropriate.

4. Navigation and Visualization

The kind and extent of user involvement into a data mining step considerably varies dependent on applications and user preferences. Subgroup mining systems differ in the degree of autonomy that is incorporated in the system by the parameterization of decision processes and treatment of trade-offs between evaluation aspects. Because the autonomy requirements of an analyst are so different, a system should provide both a nearly fully automatic search and refinement system, identifying a consolidated best set of pattern instances for a mining task, and a user controlled iterative and explorative search for such a set of patterns. A user centered search is incrementally scheduled and supported by navigation operators to specify and redefine search tasks to be run in subspaces of a hypothesis space.

Including the user in an interactive and explorative search is also preferable because of brute force and large scale search and hypothesis testing to exclude random results and select the valid patterns based on background knowledge of the user. Examples generated using an explorative visualization system for subgroup mining are discussed in Chapter 20.1.

For the visualization of subgroup results, appropriate graphical presentations of subgroups and their deviation figures must be determined. For example, a simple share pattern (binary dependent variable, one population) can be graphically represented as a four-fold display including the confidence intervals of the share (Friendly, 1993). In case of a nominal dependent variable, the set of percentages could be represented as a pie chart. However, the application of pie charts to illustrate a single frequency distribution has already been heavily discussed, because of the limited capacities of humans to compare a set of angles. Using many pie charts to compare several subgroups and their frequency distributions for the values of a nominal variable is even more doubtful.

Additional visualizations to explain mining results can, for example, support the analyst in selecting between subgroups by assessing the trade-off between generality and strength. Friedman and Fisher (1999) propose a trajectory visualization of subgroups in a two-dimensional generality vs. strength space. Another example relates to the multi-collinearity problem. A frequency distribution of the values of an input variable for a subgroup and the population can help to identify those correlations. Other visualizations can uncover the degree of overlapping between subgroups and explain a suppression refinement. Friedman and Fisher (1999) also propose sensitivity plots that can be used to judge the sensitivity of the subgroup quality to the subgroup description boundaries. These plots address the overfitting problem.

5. Conclusion

The generic components of deviation patterns include a description language to construct subgroups, a verification method to test the significance of a subgroup, quality functions to measure the interestingness of subgroups and direct the search, constraints limiting the space of admissible subgroups, and search goals and controls defining additional properties of the subgroups to be found. Interactive visualization of individual subgroups and sets of interdependent subgroups is fixed in the presentation component of a pattern class. Subgroup mining is a pragmatic exploration approach that can be applied for various analytic questions.

Although subgroup mining has reached a quite impressive development status, it is an evolving area for which a lot of problems must still be solved.

Assessing the validity of discovery results must be elaborated for subgroup patterns, for example, to avoid a situation where they overfit the given data. A second problem relates to providing adequate description languages, such as multirelational languages and dynamic, constructive induction of additional variables that are better suited to describe the given data. Especially for time and space related data, such derived variables can be useful when including descriptive terms, for example, based on means, slopes or other time series indicators. Finding a best set of hypotheses among a large set of significant hypotheses and integrating several aspects of interestingness, for example, significance, novelty, simplicity, usefulness, are the next problems. Robustness means that discovery results (e.g., definitional boundaries of subgroup descriptions) should not differ too sensitively with respect to small alterations of the data, description language or selected values of the dependent variables. The main concern in KDD has been on accuracy, whereas robustness up to now has only played a minor role in discovery research. Second order discovery to compare and combine the results for different pattern types could be necessary, especially if many analysis questions are issued to the data. Another point relates to changing data and domain knowledge. This problem area includes incremental mining methods adapting existing results according to the addition or modification of a small number of objects and comparing new discovery results with the preceding results. Besides sequential subgroup mining approaches to deal with incremental batches of new objects, parallel methods are important for distributed data sets. These sequential and parallel subgroup miners are not only useful for corresponding to institutionally determined data organizations, but also in providing scalable and anytime solutions. Finally, there are a lot of technical challenges to ensure efficient and interactive KDD processes. High performance solutions are necessary for VLDB applications. Other problems relate to the integration of KDD systems with other systems such as database systems or statistical packages.

References

Friedman, J. and N. Fisher. 1999. "Bump hunting in high-dimensional data." *Stat. Comput.* **9(2)**: 1–20.

Friendly, M. 1993. "Conceptual and visual models for categorical data." *The American Statistician* **49**: 153–160.

Gebhardt, F. 1991. "Choosing among competing generalizations." *Knowledge Acquisition* **3**: 361–380.

Kaufman, K. and R. Michalski. 1999. "Learning from inconsistent and noisy data: The AQ18 approach." In *Foundations of Intelligent Systems*, edited by Z. Ras and A. Skowron, pp. 411–418. Lecture Notes in Artificial Intelligence 1609. Berlin: Springer-Verlag.

Klösgen, W. 1996. "Explora: a multipattern and multistrategy discovery assistant." In *Advances in Knowledge Discovery and Data Mining*, edited by V. Fayyad, G. Piatetsky-Shapiro, P. Smyth, and R. Uthurusamy, pp. 249–271. Cambridge, MA: MIT Press.

Mitchell, T. 1997. *Machine Learning*. Boston, MA: McGraw-Hill.

Smyth, P. and R. Goodman. 1992. "An information theoretic approach to rule induction." *IEEE Trans. Knowledge and Data Engng* **4**: 301–316.

16.3.2 Change Analysis

Willi Klösgen

ABSTRACT   Micro data are often available for several time points, especially when new data are incrementally collected, for instance by regularly adding new batches of objects (e.g., daily or monthly). In this article, we summarize subgroup mining approaches to analyze several cross-sections of data, each representing a special time point. We assume the more general case of independent cross-sections not necessarily containing the same objects. Change patterns are then typically more useful for an analyst, since in this regularly proceeding or incremental situation, the main static patterns related to a special time point (see Chapter 16.3.1 of this handbook) are often quite stable over time and mostly well known. Specifically we deal with analyzing change (two time points) or trend (sequence of equidistant time points), and we discuss pattern elaboration to refine or combine diverse types of patterns and to deal with some pecularities (Simpson's paradox).

1. Introduction

Many interesting questions in analyzing data deal with change. It is useful for market analysts to know the distribution of market shares for competing products, but it may be also important to know in which subgroups of clients the market shares have developed in an extraordinary way. These dynamic questions can be answered when data have been collected over some time rather than studying a particular point in time represented by a single cross-section.

Analyzing global change usually is based on complex models, such as regression, logistic or loglinear models (Plewis, 1985). For causal models of global change, see also Chapter 16.6. Methods for analyzing time series data bases are described in Chapter 16.7. Concentrating in this article on the data mining approach of identifying deviating local subgroups, we are interested in change and trend behavior of target variables in subgroups. Specifically, we discuss several specializations of the general deviation pattern (Table 1 of Chapter 16.3.1) to analyze change when two independent cross-sections are available for two time points. We also deal with some trend analyses for the investigation of a sequence of independent cross-sections (k time points).

Three measurements of change can be distinguished: individual, absolute, and relative change. When the database includes data on the same objects for different time points (panel data), so that for each object the values of all variables are known for all time points, individual change can be studied for each object. This can partially be reduced to the one cross-section case by simply deriving variables with the individual difference between the two time points as values. However, when these individual differences are not available for analyzing subgroups, a three-dimensional cross table is studied (time × target variable × subgroup & complementary group). Thus, more analysis perspectives are available compared to the two-dimensional tabulations used for the single cross-section case. We regard the more general case of independent cross-sections, that is, we do not require that the cross-sections include the same objects. A typical example is a market survey when in each month persons of a new (different) sample are asked about their market preferences. Thus, individual changes are not available. Within the (large scale) search based data mining context, which is characterized by large samples, exploratory processes, modest distribution assumptions, and limited calculation possibilities for each single subgroup, one typically relies on simple test statistics for analyzing change.

2. Two Time Points: Change Analysis

We first treat two independent cross-sections, for example, samples for two time points. Again we refer to one target variable, for which changes of distributions shall be found. The first approach finds subgroups, for which the distributions belonging to the two time points are different (absolute change). A relative approach compares the differences of the distributions for the subgroup with the difference for a reference group (e.g., the whole population or the complementary subgroup). Different specializations depend again on the type of the target variable.

For a binary target variable, the first data analytic goal is to find subgroups, for which the shares, that is, Bernoulli parameter $P(Y = 1)$, are different for the two cross-sections. An example of such an absolute change pattern could describe the subgroup of young male persons whose accident rate has increased within one year from 15 to 20 percent. Under the null hypothesis of equal shares for the two years, the test statistic, which is defined analogously to (2) in Chapter 16.3.1, is asymptotically Gaussian distributed. Subgroups for which the value of this test statistic rejects the null hypothesis are selected as statistically interesting. With this approach, absolute change is analyzed, that is, we look for subgroups that have changed.

The next goal is to analyze relative change. Then the change of a subgroup is compared with the change of a reference group, for example, the whole population. The increase of the accident rate from 15 to 20 percent for young males is compared with the difference of the rates for the whole population. This increase might be not significant, when the rates for the whole population also increase, say from 10 to 13 percent. For a relative comparison, the statistical quality of a subgroup measures the significance of the difference between change in the subgroup and change in the whole population (or complementary subgroup), where change is given by the difference of the binary target shares for the two time points. The z-scores for the difference of changes that are asymptotically Gaussian distributed under the null hypothesis of equal change in the subgroup and the whole population (or its complementary subgroup) are used as the quality function.

Other options rely on the log odds ratio for analyzing absolute change, respectively on the difference of log odds ratios for relative change. The odd value is, for example, 2, if the probability of having an accident is twice as high as not having an accident. The odd ratio is the ratio of the odd values for the two time points. The simple difference of shares does not consider the level (e.g., the difference between 50 percent and 30 percent is the same as beween 100 percent and 80 percent), which is different for odds and the underlying logistic model. Another option for measuring changes of shares is the quotient $(p_2 - p_1)/(1 - p_1)$. z-Scores are calculated for all these options as quality functions.

The analyst has to decide which option is more appropriate for a special mining task. By comparing the different test statistics (see example in Chapter 16.3.1), some rules can be given that support this decision.

For ordinal target variables and analyzing change, a first option is to use ridits to make a statement on the probability of a larger value of the ordinal target variable in a subgroup for the second time point (compared to a reference group, for example, subgroup for the first time point). Consider for example the ordinal target variable production quality with five qualitative values from very low to very high. Then subgroups of production could be identified (defined by a combination of special steering parameters of the production process) having a, say, 80 percent probability of higher quality in the second time period than in the first period. Especially when assuming ordinal variables are being derived by discretization of continuous variables, ridits are defined by:

$$r_i = \sum_{j=1}^{i-1} p_j + \frac{p_i}{2} \quad i = 1 \dots k \quad \text{(reference ridits; } p_i \text{ : percentages for the } k \text{ variable values)}$$

$$r_g^{(2)} = \sum_{i=1}^{k} r_i p_{i2} \quad \text{mean ridit for subgroup } g \text{, second time point.} \tag{1}$$

For continuous target variables, methods based on median tests, order statistics, t-tests, and analysis of variance can be used. For very skewed distributions, mean-based approaches may cause problems. However, large samples (subgroups) allow an approximation with a normal distribution.

Some pecularities may arise with change patterns relying on the analysis of three-dimensional contingency tables. A well known example is Simpsons's paradox (Simpson, 1951). For example, the proportion of accidents for some population of insured drivers has decreased between two time points from 30 to 27 percent, but the subgroup proportions for both complementary subgroups male and female drivers have increased (from 50 to 55, respectively, from 10 to 15 percent). To explain this counter-intuitive result, one has to regard the proportions of male drivers at the total population for the two time points that has decreased, say from 50 to 30 percent (the complementary proportion of female drivers has increased). Since the overall decreasing proportions of accidents are weighted averages of the increasing accident proportions for the subgroups with weights changing over time, the incorrect intuitive assumption of equal weights for the two time points explains the paradox.

Due to the three-dimensional structure of the underlying contingency table, there are several types of deviation patterns which can be combined. Thus, when identifying subgroups for which the target share has changed (e.g., increasing accident rate for males and females), one can elaborate this pattern by studying the corresponding change pattern for the subgroup share (e.g., proportion of male drivers has decreased) to explain the overall decrease of accidents. Additionally one can study the proportion of the subgroup of the target group and its change, for example, the proportion of males out of the drivers having an accident.

4. *k* Time Points: Trend Analysis

To analyze trends, we deal with more than two independent cross-sections, for example, samples for several time points. Some basic analytic questions are: Is there a variability in time? Is there a positive trend in time? A possible approach is first to find subgroups with variability in time, and then to elaborate this pattern by subsequent more specialized analyses, for example, for trends. These trends are again studied for the different types of target variable, for example, for shares (binary target), ridits or medians (ordinary target), medians or means (continuous target).

Variability of discrete target variables for the *m* time points are identified with a chi-square test. Special tests can be used to derive quality functions that measure the continuous increase (e.g., gradient test), or a positive trend for shares or ridits. Instead of using special trend tests for elaborating the variability pattern, one can also rely on heuristic methods to detect patterns such as monotony or *U*-form in the time dependency of shares, ridits, medians, or means of target variables in a subgroup.

Elaboration of patterns can be seen as another refinement approach (Chapter 16.3.1). In a first search phase, only general patterns are searched such as a heterogeneous set of association measures for a subgroup and a dependent variable in a sequence of populations (analysis of *k* populations). A simple chi-square test can identify subgroups with these heterogeneous association measures. For selected subgroups, a more elaborated statistical test can now determine if the *k* association values for a subgroup can be grouped together in homogeneous sets, or if there is a time trend. Similar approaches have been realized in the context of automatic scientific discovery (see Chapter 29) to first identify simple types of patterns as a precondition for more elaborate patterns in data.

References

Plewis, I. 1985. *Analysing Change*. New York: John Wiley.
Simpson, E. H. 1951. "The interpretation of interaction in contingency tables." *J. R. Stat. Soc. B* **13**: 238–241.

16.3.3 Drill-Down Methods

Tejwansh S. Anand

ABSTRACT   Drill down is the process of discovering one or more subgroups of individuals within a population whose behavior partially or completely explains or accounts for the aggregate behavior of the entire population. Drill down is an analytic technique that is usually employed when all individuals in a population can be described by the same set of attributes. The term drill down has gained popularity since the advent of OLAP tools. OLAP tools allow business users to understand business behavior by drilling down from the aggregate to the detail along hierarchies that the business user considers significant. Knowledge representation systems provide a robust way of maintaining hierarchies that are used during drill down. Heuristics used by business users determine interesting or significant business behaviors. Clustering algorithms can be used to generate hierarchies that can be examined for interesting or significant business behaviors. Attribute focusing is an example of an algorithm that generates a hierarchy that is likely to be significant.

1. Introduction

Drill down is the process of discovering one or more subgroups of individuals within a population whose behavior partially or completely explains or accounts for the aggregate behavior of the entire population. Drill down further involves the characterization of the subgroup of individuals using their common attributes for the purpose of human decisionmaking. Drill down is an analytic technique that is usually employed when all individuals in a population can be described by the same set of attributes.

Consider that we are interested in understanding the declining sales of shirts. Furthermore, all shirts can be described by the attributes fabric, collar size, and collar style. For human decisionmaking purposes, it is a valuable discovery that the subgroup cotton shirts with a button-down collar account for most of the decline in sales of shirts. Drill down is the analytic process that enables such a discovery.

Formally, let us consider a population P where $P_i \in$ P. Each individual P_i in P can be described by the relational schema R[U]. U is the set of attributes A_i that describe P_i. DOM (A_i) is the finite set of values that A_i can take. Restricting the values in DOM (A_i) that A_i can take results in subgroups within P. Creation of subgroups in P is sometimes referred to as partitioning. In business terminology, subgroups are sometimes referred to as segments. The process of drill down assumes that partitioning leads to segments that are exhaustive and mutually exclusive. In other words, within a partition an individual can belong to only one segment and the segments within a partition should account for all individuals in the population. The number of attributes that are used to describe an individual is referred to as dimensionality and the number of values of an attribute that different individuals in a population may have is referred to as variability. Most real-life analysis situations involve populations that have high dimensionality as well as high variability. Most real-life situations also involve successive partitioning of segments to create a hierarchy (see also Chapter 5.7 of this handbook). Figure 1 shows a hierarchy for a population of retail products. Knowledge representation systems integrated with a relational database are ideal tools for manipulating hierarchies of segments. IMACS (Brachman et al., 1993) is an excellent example of such a tool.

The analytic process of drill down can now be restated as the creation of one or more partitions over a population followed by the discovery of those partitions that contain subgroups of interest. We will now examine three approaches for implementing the drill-down process.

2. OLAP

Online analytic processing (OLAP) involves the analysis of data along multiple dimensions (multidimensional analysis—in the terminology used in this article an attribute is a dimension, but the term *dimension* has been used differently within different OLAP implementations; also see Chapter 13.2). The term *drill down* has gained popularity since the advent of OLAP tools. Within OLAP, analysts who are knowledgeable about the business analysis that needs to be conducted manually create hierarchies of partitions and segments. These hierarchies are then represented in OLAP data structures known as cubes or hypercubes. These data structures allow multiple points of entry along the various attributes into the data for analysis. Depending on performance requirements and memory constraints, aggregate behaviors (or rollups) for each segment may be precomputed and stored or may be computed at the time they are required for analysis. In OLAP tools hierarchies of partitions and segments are usually known prior to application development. A business analyst does not usually define new segments during analysis. The drill-down process is performed manually by analysts. They

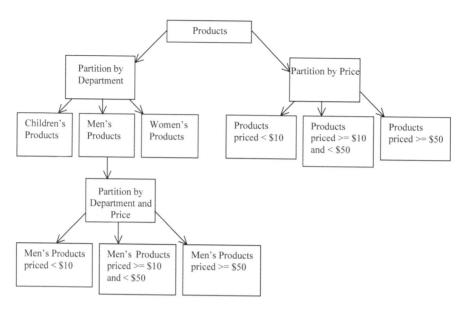

Figure 1 Hierarchy of retail products

evaluate the behaviors of segments in a partition and if they want to further understand the behavior of a segment, they analyze subsegments within the segment of interest. The hierarchy being traversed during drill down can be prespecified. OLAP works very effectively for populations with low dimensionality and low variability. OLAP tools usually come in two broad flavors:

1. Relational OLAP (ROLAP) tools store the data in a relational database management system; and

2. Multidimensional OLAP (MOLAP) tools store the data in a proprietary data structure that is optimized for drill down.

3. Knowledge-Based Drill Down

Rather than representing hierarchies of partitions and segments implicitly in data structures during design, a knowledge representation system coupled with a relational database management system allows for explicit representation of hierarchies. Analysts can easily adapt these hierarchies by creating new segments of likely interest to the business. When an analyst creates a new segment, the knowledge representation system automatically classifies this segment into the existing hierarchy. Knowledge representation systems make it possible for managing multiple partitions at each drill-down level. The drill-down process in such implementations can be a manual process as in OLAP tools or it can be automated by using heuristics. During drill down, partitions at each drill-down level are examined by a set of heuristics that determine if a partition is likely to contain interesting information. Heuristics depend on the behavior that is being analyzed: specifically, the mathematical operator used to compute the aggregate behavior for a segment. For example, to compute the aggregate behavior sales for the segment Children's products in Figure 1, the system adds the sales of all individual products whose department attribute has the value Children. Similarly, to compute the aggregate behavior retail price for the segment Children's products in Figure 1, the system takes the mean of the retail price of all individual products whose department attribute has the value Children. Knowledge-based drill down with heuristics has been implemented in a system called the management discovery tool (MDT). The user interface of MDT is described by Knutson et al.

(1997). The architecture and heuristics used in MDT are described by Anand et al. (1997). The following are some of the heuristics implemented in MDT for discovering interesting partitions:

If 20 percent of the segments in a partition account for 80 percent of the behavior of the entire population.

If more than 10 percent of the segments in a partition are two standard deviations away in either direction from the behavior of the entire population.

If more than 20 percent of the segments have changed in a direction opposite to the change in behavior of the entire population.

Once a heuristic is triggered, MDT produces an explanation of the behaviors of the segments in the interesting partition.

For the most part, MDT relies on partitions that are manually created by business analysts. In the event that none of the partitions created by a business analyst are deemed interesting for drill down by the MDT heuristics, then MDT automatically creates partitions by restricting the values of enumerated attributes of individuals in the population. MDT heuristics have been tested in a wide range of industries: health insurance, telecommunications, retail, and finance. MDT has proven to be more effective in populations with higher dimensionality and variability than OLAP tools.

Recently, research based on MDT has focused on using clustering algorithms to automatically create partitions for evaluation by MDT heuristics (Li and Biswas, 1998; also see Chapter 16.5).

Rather than employing heuristics to identify interestingness, projection pursuit, a standard statistical tool, can be used. However, in populations with high dimensionality and variability this can be computationally very expensive.

4. Attribute Focusing

Attribute focusing (AF) is an algorithm (Bhandari et al., 1996) that helps an analyst find a segment that is most interesting for a particular behavior. Drill down from this segment does not lead to any further insight. AF looks at the overall distribution of the behavior being analyzed and tries to find segments that have a characteristically different distribution for this behavior than the overall population. AF has been successfully used in a system called Advanced Scout that helps teams in the National Basketball Association discover interesting matchups during a game.

5. Conclusions

Drill down is a widely used technique during the knowledge discovery process. In this article the process of drill down was explained with a discussion of three methods for implementing drill down.

References

Anand, T., M. Georgantos, Y. Hu, J. Knutson, D. Lettington, M. Lindsay, A. Meyer, K. O'Flaherty, R. Schubert, and P. Selfridge. 1997. "System and method for generating reports from a computer database." United States Patent Numbers 5,692,181, 5,710,900, and 5,721,903.

Bhandari, I., E. Colet, J. Parker, Z. Pines, R. Pratap, and K. Ramanujam. 1996. "Advanced Scout: data mining and knowledge discovery in NBA data." Research Report RC 20443. IBM T. J. Watson Research Center.

Brachman, R., P. Selfridge, L. Terveen, B. Altman, F. Halper, T. Kirk, A. Lazar, D. McGuiness, L. Resnick, and A. Borgida. 1993. "Integrated support for data archaeology." *Int. J. Intell. Cooperative Inform. Sys* **2(2)**: 159–185.

Knutson, J. F., T. Anand, and R. L. Henneman. 1997. "Evolution of a user interface design: NCR's management discovery tool." In *Proceedings of CHI 97*, pp. 526–533, ISBN 0-201-32229-3. Atlanta: ACM/Addison-Wesley March 22-27, 1997.

Li, C. and G. Biswas. 1998. "Drill down the database with feature segmentation." Technical Report VU-CS-TR-98-06. Department of Computer Science, Vanderbilt University.

16.4 Equation Fitting

16.4.1 Methodology for Equation Fitting

Takashi Washio and Hiroshi Motoda

ABSTRACT   This article describes basic methods for equation fitting to a set of data acquired under static and dynamic environments. First, the dependency checking technique to identify a set of variables appearing in each equation is explained. Second, the principles and algorithms to discover a single equation and multiple equations are described. Finally, representative approaches to use a priori and generic knowledge to enhance the plausibility of the discovered equation formulas are mentioned.

1. Introduction

The numerical data acquired in various domains, for example, science, frequently indicate regularities that can be represented in the form of equations that are a standard expression of deterministic relations among continuous variables. The scope of this article is to discover one or multiple deterministic equations embedded in a given set of continuous numerical data. In the framework of deterministic equation discovery, the artificial disturbance and/or natural noise components contained in the data are represented by some residual terms. The key technique to discover equations from the data is an equation formulas and parameters search through numerical data fitting to minimize the residual terms while avoiding overfitting in some measures. This article describes basic methods for equation fitting to a given set of data. The problems of equation fitting are grouped into two categories depending on how the data are acquired. One is a static environment where the data are obtained through observations of an object without disturbing the state of the object by the observer. Another is a dynamic environment where the data are acquired through experiments on an object in which the state of the object is artificially controlled over a wide range by experimenters. Some assumptions are usually introduced in the static case on the form of the equation to search because the information acquired in the observation is limited to a set of some specific states of the object due to various reasons. For example, the observed combination of rotation speed and electric current for a motor in a subway train are bounded by the practical condition of the electric voltage of the power supply and the torque loaded to the motor in the subway operation. Under such limited observations, a certain feasible formula for the equation governing these variables needs to be presumed based on related background knowledge to make up for the lack of sufficient data. In contrast, the assumptions about the equation formulation are very weak in the latter where the data can be acquired for various conditions allowing the identification of the possible classes of the equation. Accordingly, different basic approaches are used for equations search and parameters fitting for the two categories.

2. Dependency Checking among Variables

Given a set of variables $S = \{x_i \mid i = 1, 2, ..., n\}$, these variables may be mutually dependent when some deterministic relations are represented by equations. Dependency checking techniques among variables provide the preliminary knowledge to infer the appropriate combination of variables appearing in each equation.

In a static environment, the basic principle of dependency checking is cross-correlation analysis. The cross-correlation of x_i and x_j is defined as

$$C(x_i, x_j) = \frac{c_{ij}}{\sqrt{c_{ii}}\sqrt{c_{jj}}},$$
(1)

$$\text{where} \quad c_{ij} = \frac{1}{n-1} \sum_{k=1}^{n} (x_{ik} - \bar{x}_i)(x_{jk} - \bar{x}_j).$$

k is the numbering of data in a given data set, and $\bar{x}$ represents the average of variable x over the data set. If $|C(x_i, x_j)|$ is very close to 0, then x_i and x_j are not correlated, and both are independent of each other. In contrast, if $|C(x_i, x_j)|$ is very close to 1, x_i and x_j are correlated.

Although this criterion indicates candidate combinations of relevant variables, it does not provide a more detailed dependency structure representing a set of variables appearing in each equation. For example, if three variables x_1, x_2, and x_3 have the dependency structure $x_1 \rightarrow x_3 \leftarrow x_2$, where x_1 and x_2 are mutually independent, then they must appear in an equation $f(x_1, x_2, x_3) = 0$ because the value of x_3 should not be independently determined via more than one equation under the assumption of deterministic relations among the variables. On the other hand, if x_2 is fully dependent on x_1, and x_3 is fully dependent on x_2, that is, $x_1 \rightarrow x_2 \rightarrow x_3$, x_1 and x_2 must be related by the equation $g_1(x_1, x_2) = 0$, and x_2 and x_3 must follow another equation $g_2(x_2, x_3) = 0$. The criterion of the cross-correlation analysis that indicates the dependency of x_3 on x_1 and x_2 in both cases is insufficient to differentiate these dependency structures. Blalock (1961) proposed an approach named causal inference to overcome this limitation where multiple cross-correlation coefficients are used to determine the dependency structure. For instance, $C(x_1, x_2)$ may be close to 0 in the former case, because x_1 and x_2 are independent. In contrast, $C(x_1, x_2)$ may be close to 1 in the latter case. Blalock proposed a set of rules to identify every type of dependency structure among up to four variables by introducing partial correlation analysis. A study by Glymour et al. (1987) systematically extended this principle to identify the dependency structure among more than four variables. Their approach allows the introduction of latent variables that are not directly observed in the analysis. They implemented the extended approach into a tool named TETRAD (Chapter 24.4.1). These correlation-based approaches, that is, nonparametric approaches, have a strong advantage in that their consequences are quite robust against the nonlinearity in relations among variables. Unless the nonlinearity is so strong that the explicit correlations among variables are not preserved, these approaches indicate appropriate candidate dependency structures among variables. Another advantage of these approaches is that they can suggest the part of the structure that may possibly contain some feedback and/or cyclic dependency. This property of the approaches is highly beneficial for inferring the appropriate configuration of variables in multiple equations, especially simultaneous equations.

Another line of studies to find dependency structure among variables from a given data set is ongoing in the research field of Bayesian networks (Heckerman, 1999). The recent extended version of TETRAD has also introduced such techniques (Glymour, 1995). The framework of Bayesian networks techniques has a significant advantage in that it can analyze the stochastic dependency structure among a large number of variables in a highly efficient manner. They have been successfully applied to various practical problems. However, state-of-the-art Bayesian networks do not meet the requirements of dependency structure discovery sufficiently for equation fitting in the following sense. First, Bayesian networks are essentially stochastic models. Its consequences on the dependency among variables are not deterministic dependency that can be embedded into equations. In addition, the probability distribution functions on the states of the variables, which must be estimated in the techniques, are not well defined in problems for equation fitting, since exogenous disturbances to an object under observation are often artificial and do not follow any presumed probability distribution. Second, due to the tractable computation of the structure and the probability, most of the techniques presume acyclic dependency structures and linear or independent combinations of influences among variables. These modeling assumptions do not fit the dependency structure analysis for fitting deterministic equations including nonlinear and simultaneous relations.

When the given data set consists of time series, the information on the temporal order of the observations is applicable to dependency analysis. Akleman et al. (1999) reported the applications of TETRAD and an autoregressive analysis technique to model time-series data on corn exports and currency exchange rates. They succeeded in clarifying the dependency structure among observed and latent variables by explicitly introducing the temporal order information in concert with the loss function criteria (Akaike, 1974). Their basic interest is to derive the dependency structure in time and variable amplitude domains. The autoregressive model presented in the latter half of their paper is an example of a deterministic model where the probability distribution of the variables is not explicitly introduced. Although the autoregressive model can only represent linear dependency, it has a powerful ability for analyzing detailed dependency structures in the frequency domain by applying Fourier transformation to the model, whenever linear model approximation is feasible. Akaike (1968) proposed the technique of signal transmission path (STP) analysis, which enables detailed analysis of the signal transmission dependency among variables at every frequency point based on this idea. Because an object containing some temporal dynamics for observation frequently shows various dependency structures among variables at each frequency, this type of analysis for both deterministic and stochastic systems is expected to become important in the future.

In the dynamic environment, directly controllable variables are experimentally changed to investigate the dependency structure among variables. The bivariate test is the most popular strategy of manipulation (Langley et al., 1985). A pair of variables in S, say x_i and x_j, is chosen to check their dependency, where one of the two must be directly controllable. When a variable, say x_i, is directly controllable, the influence of manipulation on the other variable, x_j, is evaluated under the experimental setting in which all other variables are maintained to their steady values. If the manipulation of x_i is observed to have an influence on the value of x_j, x_j is known to be directly dependent on x_i, and both variables must appear in the same complete equation. This test is applied to every pair of variables in which one is directly controllable. After bivariate tests on all possible pairs of variables, the subset of S in which the variables belong to a complete equation is obtained. Although this approach works well in most deterministic and continuous systems, the dependency between two variables can be hidden under certain value combinations of the other variables when the objective system has strong nonlinearity. Accordingly, this test must be carefully repeated under various value combinations of the other variables when the existence of strong nonlinearity in the object is supposed.

3. Finding a Single Equation

Suppose that the dependency checking technique derives a set of variables E composing a complete equation. In a static environment, a complete equation can be identified through equation fitting to the given data based on the set of variables for the equation and assumptions made for the equation formulas. The equation to be fitted is represented as $0 = f(x_1, x_2, ..., x_m)$, where $E = \{x_1, x_2, ..., x_m\}$ is the set of variable appearing in an equation. Many methods have been developed to utilize various types of the formula f. The most common approach is linear regression analysis in which a linear combination of variables is used as f when the relationship among variables is supposed to be linear or very weakly nonlinear (Chatterjee and Hadi, 1986). For cases where the relation is quite strongly nonlinear, many approximation methods have been proposed by using some presumed function formulas f, including the piecewise linear and/or local polynomial regression method and spline smoothing (Simonoff, 1996). The former approach basically partitions the variable space formed by E into multiple subspaces having appropriate granularity, where the nonlinearity of the relationship among the variables is not very significant, and applies linear or low-order polynomial equation fitting within each subspace. The curves represented by the equations in the subspaces are simply joined at the borders of the subspaces. The latter also partitions the variable space and applies low-order polynomial equation fitting in each subspace in the same manner, but what makes it different from the former approach is that it smoothly connects the curve edges at the borders of the subspaces by applying weighted mixing of the curves across both sides. A well-known approach for representing a nonlinear relation by a global function f

is the neural network, where some variables in E are linearly combined and related to some intermediate variables (units) through a nonlinear logistic function, and those units are multilayered to relate with another variable in E (Wasserman, 1989). Another nonlinear approach similar to the neural network technique is the group method of data handling (GMDH), which also uses a multilayered function. Its unit function is a nonlinear polynomial of the Kolmogorov–Gabor type as follows (Ivakhnenko, 1970),

$$y = a_0 + \sum_{i=1}^{m} a_{1i} x_i + \sum_{i=1}^{m}\sum_{j=1}^{m} a_{2ij} x_i x_j + ...,\tag{2}$$

where y is an intermediate variable in the multilayers. An advantage of a linear regression formula is its simplicity and independent contribution of each variable to the entire relation. However, any nonlinear phenomena that are widely observed cannot be captured. In contrast, local approximation methods and the neural network model are well known for their ability of capturing the various nonlinear features of the objects. A disadvantage of these approaches is the lack of comprehensibility of the resultant equation. The GMDH can also handle nonlinear modeling, and the equation formula used for data fitting has moderate comprehensibility for assessing the influence of each variable on the others. The basic principle of equation fitting to the data in every method is based on the least-square error criterion. The neural network technique uses an iterative least-square fitting called backpropagation. The GMDH also uses a different iterative and bottom-up algorithm of least-square fitting. The computational complexity of equation fitting is of a low polynomial order such as $O(n)$ or $O(n^2)$ in these approaches, where n is the number of terms in the equation formula.

   Another major drawback of these methods is that the class of the equation formula f is presumed and not inductively changed during the course of the computation. For instance, the linearity, a specific class of nonlinearity, and/or certain independence of the influence among the variables, are assumed in most of the methods. To overcome this difficulty, an approach to construct an equation based on a given set of logical rules has been studied (Dzeroski, 1994). It basically takes a generate-and-test approach, while an efficient formulas generation including differential equations is performed by using techniques that borrows the idea from inductive logic programming. Starting from the order zero to its upper limit order, the time derivatives of variables in E are introduced first. Then new terms are introduced by repeatedly applying multiplication to variables from E and their time derivatives. The values of the new terms at all time points are calculated as the terms are introduced. Finally, various types of equation formulas consisting of those terms are generated and tested by using linear regression analysis. The disadvantages of this approach are the high computational complexity and the derivation of redundant equations representing an identical relation in different shapes.

   In the dynamic environment, partial formulas to relate variables in each subset of E reflecting the relation observed in the experimental data are searched, and partial formulas discovered for some subsets are successively composed into a complete equation formula for the variables in E. It is possible to check the validity of each partial formula in the experiment because the data representing the relationship among the variables in the partial formula can be acquired while maintaining constant values of the other variables. This framework has a significant advantage in that the type of equation formula f is not presumed and is inductively constructed through the experiments. The most representative approach to deriving each partial formula of the equation is bivariate checking, which is utilized in many scientific equation discovery systems (Langley, 1985; Falkenhainer and Michalski 1986; Koehn and Z'ytkow, 1986). Given a set of variables E to appear in a complete equation, a pair of variables in E is chosen to evaluate their relationship where one of the two must be directly controllable. When a variable x_i is directly controllable, the data to represent its relationship to the other x_j is acquired under an experimental setting in which other variables are maintained to steady values. To this extent, bivariate checking is identical to the bivariate test. However, after this data acquisition, quantitative least-square data fitting of a candidate bivariate formula is applied to the data, and the appropriateness of the candidate is evaluated by statistically checking if the coefficients in the formula remain constant over the data. When necessary, intermediate variables are artificially introduced to represent some partial formulas. The bivariate formulas discovered are successively composed into a complete equation representing the entire relation. The search ability of the type of the objective equation is limited by the variety of candidate bivariate formulas used in the search. If various candidate bivariate formulas are provided for the search, the resultant complete equation captures a relationship among the wide varieties. Since the complete equation reflects no presumed relations among variables, it brings many insights to help in understanding the mechanisms involved in the object system. A drawback of this framework is its nonpolynomial computational complexity to generate and search the partial formulas. The variables that may appear in the formulas during the search are not only the original ones in E but intermediately generated variables. This increase in variables causes a combinatorial explosion to choose variable pairs in the search.

4. Finding Multiple Equations

In a static environment, the dependency structure of simultaneous equations among variables can be guessed in many cases by applying the aforementioned dependency checking techniques. The basic frameworks for finding a single equation are also applicable to finding multiple equations. Given a set of variables E_p appearing in the pth equation ($p = 1, 2, ..., k$), the least-square fitting of some equation formulas $0 = f_p(x_{p1}, x_{p2}, ... x_{pm})$, where $x_{pi} \in E_p$, is adopted. Any of the aforementioned methods to find a single equation, for example, neural networks, and/or a set of local equations, for example, piecewise linear regression, can be used for f_p. Similarly, the heuristic approach of generate-and-test is applicable to searching for multiple equations (Dzeroski, 1994).

In a dynamic environment, two cases for finding multiple equations have been studied. One is to find an equation for each mode of the object for the observation (Falkenhainer and Michalski, 1986; Koehn and Z'ytkow, 1986). For example, this approach automatically identifies the phase transient points, such as boiling point and melting point of water, and discovers the state equation of the water for each phase. First, discontinuous changes in the relationship among variables in E are searched. This is done by a certain qualitative relation analysis. For example, if x_i and x_j show a positive proportional relation in a region in the variable space of E, but a negative proportional relation in the other region, then the former region is separated from the other. After partitioning the value space of the variables into some regions, a single complete equation to represent the relation among variables is sought in each region.

Another case is to find simultaneous equations to represent an objective system under observation. In this case, prior to equation finding, the simultaneous dependency structure among variables must be experimentally determined. The bivariate test mentioned in the previous section cannot determine the exact dependency among variables in simultaneous equations. Instead, a test to find complete subsets is used to check the dependency (Washio and Motoda, 1998). For example, consider the following four simultaneous equations,

$$x_1 = x_2 x_3, \quad x_4 = x_5 x_6, \quad x_7 = x_1, \quad \text{and} \quad x_7 = x_4. \tag{3}$$

If we directly control one variable in the subset $\{x_1, x_4, x_7\}$, then the values of the rest of the subset are determined by the relations $x_7 = x_1$ and $x_7 = x_4$, while the values of $x_2, x_3, x_5,$ and x_6 remain undetermined. Through this experiment, the variables in $\{x_1, x_4, x_7\}$ are known to be constrained by two simultaneous equations. The subset $\{x_1, x_4, x_7\}$ is said to be a complete subset of the second order because two variables are simultaneously determined in the subset. After the values of $x_1, x_4,$ and x_7 have been determined, if we directly control a variable in $\{x_2, x_3\}$, then the other variable in this subset is determined. Based on this experiment, a subset of $\{x_1, x_2, x_3, x_4, x_7\}$ is known to be constrained by an extra equation. A subset of $\{x_1, x_4, x_5, x_6, x_7\}$ also is known to be constrained by another equation in the same manner. Consequently, the simultaneous dependency structure of the objective system under experiment is identified by tests on the complete subsets without knowing the original simultaneous equations. Once this structure is obtained, each equation can be found by a single equation fitting. The computational complexity of the search algorithm currently available is nonpolynomial in the number of variables included in the simultaneous equations.

5. Use of A Priori Knowledge

All the methods explained in the preceding sections can possibly derive equations whose generality over the unseen data is not highly guaranteed. In some cases, equations that are different from the actual constraints show a high degree of good fit in the least-square sense on the values of variables given in the experiments. To alleviate this difficulty, some approaches use *a priori* but generic knowledge to limit the types of equations within mathematically admissible formulas. The bounding of the mathematical equation type greatly reduces the possibility of discovering pretend equations over given data.

The most representative approach uses knowledge of unit dimensions of the variables (Falkenhainer and Michalski, 1986; Dzeroski, 1994). The principle is to check the dimensional homogeneity of every term in the equation. For example, given an equation $0 = f(x_1, x_2, ...) + g(x_1, x_2, ...)$, if the unit dimension of the first term f is $[m/s^2]$ and that of the second $g[kgm/s]$, then these two terms are not additive. Thus, this formula is not admissible. The search space of the equation is reduced, and the degree of plausibility of the discovered equation in terms of physical semantics is increased by the introduction of this knowledge.

Another approach to applying knowledge of unit dimension in a more strict manner is to use the following two theorems on the admissible type of formula among variables (Buckingham, 1914; Bridgman, 1922).

Theorem 1 (Buckingham Π-theorem). *If $\phi(x_1, x_2, x_3, ...) = 0$ is a complete equation, and if all of its arguments are of the ratio-scale type, then the solution can be written in the form*

$$F(\Pi_1, \Pi_2, ..., \Pi_{n-r}) = 0,$$

where n is the number of arguments of ϕ, and r is the number of basic units in $x_1, x_2, x_3, ...$. For all i, Π_i is a dimensionless quantity.

The variables of ratio-scale type are the variables having absolute origin and their admissible unit conversion $x' = kx$. Examples of ratio scale–type variables are mass, length, and currency value. The basic units are such primary scaling units independent of the other scaling units such as length (L), mass (M), and time (T) of physical unit dimension. The relation of each dimensionless Π_i, that is, an intermediate variable having no unit, to the arguments of ϕ is given by the following theorem.

Theorem 2 (Product Theorem). *Assuming primary quantities, $x_1, x_2, x_3, ...$ are ratio-scale type, the function ρ relating an intermediate dimensionless quantity Π to $x_1, x_2, x_3, ...$ has the form*

$$\Pi = \rho(x_1, x_2, x_3, ...) = \Gamma x^\alpha y^\beta z^\gamma ...,$$

where $\Gamma, \alpha, \beta, \gamma, ...$ are constants.

Any complete equation whose arguments are physical and ratio-scale type follows these theorems. In other words, the relationship between physical and ratio scale–type variables is highly likely to have this type of formula, and if it has, the power coefficients $\alpha, \beta, \gamma, ...$ can be calculated based on the knowledge of unit dimension and the principle of dimensional homogeneity. In the procedure for searching bivariate partial formulas, the formula indicated in the product theorem is applied with high priority to efficiently find a physically plausible equation (Kokar, 1986).

A drawback of these approaches is their limited applicability to objective systems under experiment where knowledge of the unit dimension of each variable is available. This knowledge is rarely available except in physical domains. As an efficient remedy to this problem, a new method using only the knowledge of scale types of variables has been proposed (Washio and Motoda, 1997). Most of the numerical variables measured in the experiment or observation are categorized into two scale types. One is the aforementioned ratio-scale type and the other the interval-scale type. Examples of interval scale–type variables are temperature in Celsius/Fahrenheit and sound pitch, where the origin of the measurement is arbitrarily set, and only the ratio of the interval on the scale is meaningful. Thus, its admissible unit conversion follows $x' = kx + c$. The following two theorems provide the generic plausible equation formulas is terms of scale-type constraints.

Theorem 3 (Extended Buckingham Π-theorem). *If $\phi(x_1, x_2, x_3, ...) = 0$ is a complete equation, and if each argument is either an interval or ratio-scale type, then the solution can be written in the form*

$$F(\Pi_1, \Pi_2, ..., \Pi_{n-r-s}) = 0, \tag{4}$$

where n is the number of arguments of ϕ, r the number of basic units in the arguments and s the number of their basic origins, respectively. For all i, Π_i is an intermediate dimensionless quantity.

Theorem 4 (Extended Product Theorem). *Assuming primary quantities in a set R are ratio-scale type, and those in another set I are interval-scale type, the function ρ relating an intermediate dimensionless quantity Π to $x_i \in R \cup I$ has the forms*

$$\Pi = \left(\prod_{x_i \in R} |x_i|^{a_i} \right) \left(\prod_{I_k \subseteq I} \left(\sum_{x_j \in I_k} b_{kj} |x_j| + c_k \right)^{a_k} \right) \tag{5}$$

$$\Pi = \sum_{x_i \in R} a_i \log |x_i| + \sum_{I_k \subseteq I} a_k \log \left(\sum_{x_j \in I_k} b_{kj} |x_j| + c_k \right) + \sum_{x_\ell \in I_g \subseteq I} b_{g\ell} |x_\ell| + c_g, \tag{6}$$

where all coefficients except Π are constants and $I_k \cap I_g = \phi$.

The relationship among variables of the two scale types is highly likely to have these types of formulas. In the procedure to search for bivariate formulas, high priority is placed on these formulas. This *a priori* knowledge is widely applicable because the scale types of variables are easily found by analyzing their measurement processes in most domains.

The other type of *a priori* knowledge applicable to limiting equation formula candidates is the identity constraint (Washio and Motoda, 1997). The basic principle of identity constraints comes from answering the question: What is the relationship among Θ_h, Θ_i and Θ_j, if $\Theta_i = f_{\Theta_j}(\Theta_h)$ and $\Theta_j = f_{\Theta_i}(\Theta_h)$ are known? For example, if $a(\Theta_j)\Theta_h + \Theta_i = b(\Theta_j)$ and $a(\Theta_i)\Theta_h + \Theta_j = b(\Theta_i)$ are given, the following identity equation is obtained by solving each for Θ_h:

$$\Theta_h \equiv -\frac{\Theta_i}{a(\Theta_j)} + \frac{b(\Theta_j)}{a(\Theta_j)} \equiv -\frac{\Theta_j}{a(\Theta_i)} + \frac{b(\Theta_i)}{a(\Theta_i)} \tag{7}$$

Because the third expression is linear with Θ_j for any Θ_i, the second must be so. Accordingly, the following must hold.

$$1/a(\Theta_j) = \alpha_1 \Theta_j + \beta_1,$$

$$b(\Theta_j)/a(\Theta_j) = -\alpha_2 \Theta_j - \beta_2.$$

By substituting these to the expression (7),

$$\Theta_h + \alpha_1 \Theta_i \Theta_j + \beta_1 \Theta_i + \alpha_2 \Theta_j + \beta_2 = 0 \tag{8}$$

is obtained. This principle is generalized to various relations among multiple terms. Accordingly, the entire formula of an admissible equation can be deduced by knowing the fragments of the equation.

References

Akaike, H. 1968. "On the use of a linear model for the identification of feedback systems." *Ann. Inst. Stat. Math.* **20**: 425–439.

Akaike, H. 1974. "A new look at the statistical model identification." *IEEE Trans. Automatic Control* **19(6)**: 234–241.

Akleman, D. G., D. A. Bessler, and D. M. Burton. 1999. "Modeling corn exports and exchange rates with directed graphs and statistical loss functions." In *Computation, Causation, Discovery*, pp. 497–520. Menlo Park, CA: AAAI Press.

Blalock, H. M. 1961. *Causal Inferences in Nonexperimental Research.* Chapel Hill, NC: The University of North Carolina Press.

Bridgman, P. W. 1922. *Dimensional Analysis.* New Haven: Yale University Press.

Buckingham, E. 1914. "On physically similar systems; illustrations of the use of dimensional equations." *Phys. Rev.* **IV(4)**: 345–376.

Chatterjee, S. and A. S. Hadi. 1986. "Influential observations, high leverge points, and outliers in linear regression." *Stat. Sci.* **1**: 379–416.

Dzeroski, A. 1994. "Discovering dynamics: from inductive logic programing to machine discovery." *J. Intell. Inform. Sys.* **3**: 1–20.

Falkenhainer, B. C. and R. S. Michalski. 1986. "Integrating qualitative and quantitative discovery: the ABACUS system." *Machine Learning* **1**: 367–401.

Glymour, C. 1995. "Available technology for discovering causal models, building Bayes nets, and selecting predictors: the TETRAD II program." In *Proceedings of the First International Conference on Knowledge Discovery and Data Mining (KDD '95)*, pp. 130–135. Menlo Park, CA: AAAI Press.

Glymour, C., R. Scheines, R. Spirtes, and K. Kelly. 1987. *Discovering Causal Structure.* London, England: Academic Press Inc.

Heckerman, D. 1999. "A tutorial on learning with Bayesian networks." In *Learning in Graphical Models*, edited by M. I. Jordan, pp. 301–354. Cambridge, MA: MIT Press.

Ivakhnenko, A. G. 1970. "Heuristic self-organization problems of engineering cybernetics." *Automatica* **6**: 207–219.

Koehn, B. and J. M. Żytkow. 1986. "Experimenting and theorizing in theory formation." In *Proceedings of the International Symposium on Methodologies for Intelligent Systems*, pp. 296–307. New York: ACM Press.

Kokar, M. M. 1986. "Determining arguments of invariant functional descriptions." *Machine Learning* **1**: 403–422.

Langley, P. W., H. A. Simon, G. Bradshaw, and J. M. Żytkow. 1985. *Scientific Discovery; Computational Explorations of the Creative Process.* Cambridge, MA: MIT Press.

Simonoff, J. S. 1996. *Smoothing Methods in Statistics.* New York: Springer-Verlag.

Washio, T. and H. Motoda. 1997. "Discovering admissible models of complex systems based on scale-types and identity constraints." In *Proceedings of IJCAI-97: the Fifteenth International Joint Conference on Artificial Intelligence*, pp. 810–817. San Francisco, CA: Morgan Kaufmann Publishers, Inc.

Washio, T. and H. Motoda. 1998. "Discovering admissible simultaneous equations of large scale systems." In *Proceedings of AAAI-98: Fifteenth National Conference on Artificial Intelligence*, pp. 189–196. Menlo Park, CA: AAAI Press/MIT PRESS.

Wasserman, P. D. 1989. *Neural Computing: Theory and Practice.* New York: Van Nostrand Reinhold.

16.4.2 Equation Finders

Jan M. Żytkow

ABSTRACT Equation finders discover equations that fit numerical data. We present them in a common framework that captures commonalities of many systems: model forming, fitting and testing, term generation, term coupling, and search control. We then describe testing of equation finders.

1. Equation Finders Seek Equations That Fit Numerical Data

The search for equations has been the most common feature of discovery systems since the 1970s (see Chapter 29), and in the 1990s it became an important task in KDD.

With a few simplifications, the task addressed by equation finding systems can be defined as:

- given an input of N numeric data points $(x_i, y_i, \varepsilon_i), i = 1, ..., N$, where x_i are values of the independent variable x, y_i are values of the dependent variable y, ε_i represents the uncertainty of y_i, called error, deviation, or noise,

- find a list of acceptable equations, in the form $y = f(x)$, that fit the data within the limits of error, including numerical parameter values and their error.

In this article we focus on one independent variable. For methods that apply to many independent variables, see Chapters 16.4.1 and 16.4.3.

In distinction from statistical regression methods (see Chapter 16.4.3), equation finders run a large automated search for equations, including automated generation of terms and a variety of search heuristics. Various systems have been reported by Cheng and Simon (1992), Dzeroski and Todorovski (1993), Gerwin (1974), Langley et al. (1987), Falkenhainer and Michalski (1986), Kokar (1986), Koza (1992), Moulet (1992), Nordhausen and Langley (1993), Zhong and Ohsuga (1995), Schaffer (1993), Washio and Motoda (1997), Wu and Wang (1989), Wong (1991), Zembowicz and Zˇytkow (1992), and others.

2. Equation Finders Are an Important Part of Discovery Systems

In distinction from statistical regression mechanisms, equation finders are often designed as a part of larger discovery systems, for which equations are one of several types of knowledge. BACON (Langley et al., 1987), ABACUS (Falkenhainer and Michalski, 1986), FAHRENHEIT (Zˇytkow, 1987, 1996), IDS (Nordhausen and Langley, 1993), and KOSI (Zhong and Ohsuga, 1995) repeatedly use modules that find equations in two variables from a sequence of data and build them into a broader framework of knowledge.

In order to handle discovery tasks in sciences, engineering, and other applications, a useful equation finder must combine a broad range of attainable equations with a modular design, flexible control, and a systematic use of error. We will now examine the basic building blocks used in equation finders.

3. Equation Finders Use the Same Building Blocks

Consider an equation $e^y = 1.1 + 0.5/x + 0.07/x^2$. e^y is expressed as a quadratic function of $1/x$. Different steps are needed to find the relation between x and y described by this equation. Terms e^y and $1/x$ must be constructed, the quadratic model must be proposed, parameter values must be computed, and the equation must be tested. Finally, the equation may be solved for y to reach the form $y = \log(a + b/x + c/x^2)$. We will now consider the modules needed to perform these tasks.

3.1. Model Fitting

Model fitting has evolved since its nineteenth century origins. Simple and efficient, modern statistical model fitters use chi-square fitting, often modified to weighted least-squares (Eadie et al., 1971; Press et al., 1992), to fit a set of numerical data points (x_i, y_i, σ_i) to a finite number of polynomial models. The model is a function template $y = f(x, a_1, ..., a_q)$ (for example, $y = a_1 + a_2 x + a_3 x^2$). A model fitter seeks values of $a_1, ..., a_q$ that minimize the value of χ^2,

$$\chi^2 = \sum_{i=1}^{N} \left(\frac{y_i - f(x_i, a_1, ..., a_q)}{\sigma_i} \right)^2. \tag{1}$$

The value of χ^2 is the sum of squares of deviations (residua) of data points (x_i, y_i) from the values predicted by the model, weighted by errors σ_i, so that measurements that are more precise acquire a closer fit. The minimum of χ^2 can be found as a point where the derivatives with respect to a_j, $j = 1, ..., q$, all vanish,

$$\sum_{i=1}^{N} \frac{y_i - f(x_i, a_1, ..., a_q)}{\sigma_i^2} \cdot \frac{\partial f(x_i, a_1, ..., a_j, ..., a_q)}{\partial a_j} = 0. \tag{2}$$

In general, the set (2) of equations is nonlinear and not easy to solve. For a polynomial model, however, it can efficiently produce a unique solution by algebraic or matrix operations.

The error of parameter values can and should be estimated. Standard deviations of parameters $a_1, ..., a_q$, at the values that minimize χ^2, can be calculated from the error of data, according to the formula for error propagation (Eadie et al., 1971):

$$\sigma_{a_j}^2 = \sum_{i=1}^{N} \left(\frac{\partial a_j}{\partial y_i} \right)^2 \cdot \sigma_i^2, \quad j = 1, ..., q, \quad \sigma_i = 0.5\varepsilon_i. \tag{3}$$

The canon of empirical science, followed by statistics, calls for the estimation of parameter errors. A measured value has no meaning if the error is not known. Discovery systems can use that error both to generalize and to simplify the discovered equations. First, BACON-like generalization of equations to additional variables builds equations on parameter values and thus requires knowledge of parameter error. Second, if the absolute value of a_j is smaller than the corresponding error σ_{a_j}, then zero is an acceptable value for a_j. EF (Zembowicz and Z'ytkow, 1992) uses this technique to eliminate spurious higher-degree polynomials, which can be always created. But it can also eliminate lower polynomial terms, so that equations such as $e^y = a + b\sqrt{x}$ can be simplified to $e^y = b\sqrt{x}$.

Even the best fit may not be satisfactory. Equation finders evaluate equations against data. BACON, IDS, and ABACUS use simple criteria of acceptance within error, requiring that at most a small fixed percentage of residua exceed empirical error. However, a more adequate statistical criterion totals the contributions of all residua. The value of χ^2 defined in (1) and applied to the best-fit equation, and the number of degrees of freedom $N - q$ in the data left after the fit, can be used to assign the probability $Q = Q(\chi^2, N - q)$ with which the data $(x_i, y_i, \varepsilon_i)$ could have been generated from the model $y = f(x, a_1, ..., a_q) + N(0, \sigma(x))$. The probability must exceed a threshold of acceptance. Press et al. (1992) argue for a threshold of 0.001.

3.2. Generation of New Terms

The class of polynomial models is too narrow for many applications, but polynomial fitting is very efficient. Thus to extend the scope of functions detectable by polynomial fitting, equation finders construct new terms from variables x and y, transform data to new terms, assemble terms into new models, all in preparation for polynomial model fitting.

The majority of equation finders include a module that explores the space of new terms. It creates new variables by applying a number of transformation rules, initially to the original variables x and y, and then to the transformed variables. EF (Zembowicz and Z'ytkow, 1992) includes error propagation into transformation schemas

$$x \rightarrow x' = t_1(x), \tag{4}$$

$$(x, y, \varepsilon) \rightarrow (y', \varepsilon') = \left(y'(x, y), \left| \frac{\partial y'}{\partial y} \right| \cdot \varepsilon \right). \tag{5}$$

Each time y is used in a transformation, the associated ε should be also transformed according to (5). Examples of transformations include the product of two terms, logarithm, exponent, and the inverse of a term. Dzeroski and Todorovski (1993) use numerical differentiation. Application of one transformation generates terms such as

$$\log x, \frac{1}{x}, xy, \quad \log y, \frac{1}{y}. \tag{6}$$

At the next level, the same transformations generate terms such as:

$$\log(\log x), \quad y \log x, \quad x^2 y, \quad \log(xy), \quad \frac{\log x}{y}.$$

The number of variables grows rapidly.

3.3. Combining Terms and Other Tasks

Terms are combined into tuples (most often pairs x', y') in such a way that each tuple contains exactly one (or at least one) term with variable y in it. Then polynomial models $y' = \text{poly}(x')$ are proposed for those tuples.

Several additional tasks can be useful. In systems such as BACON.1 and EF, each new term is simplified and then compared against all the previous terms to ensure its uniqueness. Similarly, a system can detect and remove equivalent equations before fitting the parameters. A mechanism that solves equations for the original dependent variable y simplifies predictions and understanding of the results.

Some of the first-degree polynomials produced from terms in (6) and solved for y are:

$$y = a + b/x, \quad y = ax^b, \quad y = \frac{1}{a + b \log x}, \quad y = \frac{a}{x} + \frac{b}{x^2}, \quad y = \frac{x}{a + bx}, \quad y = ae^{b/x}.$$

4. The Search Combines Steps in Several Spaces

Equation finders perform search in a combined space of terms, tuples (pairs) of terms, and equations for tuples of terms. We can outline the multisearch in the following way:

```
TERMS := (x y); the initial list of terms for term space search
OLD-TERMS := NIL; the list of terms already used
E := a set of polynomial equation models ; list of models for model fitting
LOOP UNTIL TERMS exceed threshold of complexity
   TUPLES := list of new tuples (pairs) of terms made of TERMS and OLD-TERMS
   FOR each tuple in TUPLES and FOR each model in E
     fit and evaluate the best equation
   IF at least one equation accepted,
     THEN RETURN all accepted equations and HALT the search
   OLD-TERMS := OLD-TERMS union with TERMS
   TERMS := list of new terms created from OLD-TERMS
END LOOP
```

The search terminates when an acceptable model is found or else it will continue until it reaches a user-specified limit. The user can decide on the maximum depth of each search, that is, the maximum polynomial degree, the maximum transformation search depth, and the maximum size of a tuple.

5. Empirical Evaluation of Equation Finders

Equation finders can be tested in many ways. They can be used in a scientific laboratory, on a robot, and in KDD. In each application the user can compare the equation(s) generated by the system against data or against his own findings. Such applications, however, do not provide easy and systematic testing on a broad range of equations. In addition, they do not provide us with undisputed right answers, against which we can compare the outcome. Schaffer (1993) used the actual equations proposed by scientists for their data as the standard of validity. Although the result proposed by a scientist should be among those proposed by an equation finder within the measurement error, this approach is not appropriate for stand-alone testing of an equation finder. Scientific standards of acceptance combine several criteria not available to equation finders, such as plausible interpretation of parameters, derivation from a theoretical model, and susceptibility to generalization to additional dimensions.

Equation finders can use convergence tests on data generated from known equations (Zembowicz and Zytkow, 1992). For each test equation $y = f(x)$ in the scope of equation finder, f is used to generate data, with the addition of a controlled Gaussian error of y. The source equation $y = f(x)$ should be among the solutions returned by the equation finder. One cannot require, however, that the source equation is the unique solution. First, the larger the experimental errors, the more models fit the data with a similar probability measure. Second, the number of acceptable models increases with the decreasing range of values of the independent variable x represented in data. A convergence test verifies whether a gradual reduction of error and the expanded range of x eventually leave the source function as the only acceptable model.

References

Cheng, P. C. and H. A. Simon. 1992. "The right representation for discovery: finding the conservation of momentum." In *Proceedings of the Ninth International Conference on Machine Learning*, edited by D. Sleeman and P. Edwards. San Mateo, CA: Morgan Kaufmann 62–71.

Dzeroski, S. and L. Todorovski. 1993. "Discovering dynamics." In *Proceedings of the Tenth International Conference on Machine Learning*. San Mateo, CA: Morgan Kaufmann, pp. 97–103.

Eadie, W. T., D. Drijard, F. E. James, M. Roos, and B. Sadoulet. 1971. *Statistical Methods in Experimental Physics*. Amsteeerdam, Netherlands: North-Holland Publishers.

Falkenhainer, B. C. and R. S. Michalski. 1986. "Integrating quantitative and qualitative discovery: the ABACUS system." *Machine Learning* 1: 367–401.

Gerwin, D. G. 1974. "Information processing, data inferences, and scientific generalization." *Behav. Sci.* 19: 314–325.

Kokar, M. M. 1986. "Determining arguments of invariant functional descriptions." *Machine Learning* 1: 403–422.

Koza, J. R. 1992. *Genetic Programming: On the Programming of Computers by Means of Natural Selection.* Cambridge, MA: MIT Press.

Langley, P., H. A. Simon, G. Bradshaw, and J. M. Zytkow. 1987. *Scientific Discovery: Computational Exploration of the Creative Processes.* Boston, MA: MIT Press.

Moulet, M. 1992. "A symbolic algorithm for computing coefficients' accuracy in regression." In *Proceedings of the Ninth International Conference on Machine Learning*, edited by D. Sleeman and P. Edwards. San Mateo, CA: Morgan Kaufmann, pp. 339–352.

Nordhausen, B. and P. Langley. 1993. "An integrated framework for empirical discovery." *Machine Learning* 12: 17–47.

Press, W. H., S. A. Teukolsky, W. T. Vetterling, and B. P. Flannery. 1992. *Numerical Recipes in C.* Cambridge, UK: Cambridge University Press.

Schaffer, C. 1993. "Bivariate scientific function finding in a sampled, real-data testbed." *Machine Learning* 12: 167–183.

Washio, T. and H. Motoda. 1997. "Discovering admissible models of complex systems based on scale-types and identity constraints." *Proceedings of IJCAI-97*: Morgan Kaufmann. San Mateo, CA, pp. 810–817.

Wong, P. 1991. Machine discovery of function forms. Ph.D. diss. Waterloo, Canada, University of Waterloo.

Wu, Y. and S. Wang. 1989. "Discovering knowledge from observational data." *Proceedings of IJCAI-89 Workshop on Knowledge Discovery in Databases*, edited by G. Piatetsky-Shapiro. Detroit, MI, pp. 369–377.

Zembowicz, R. and J. M. Zytkow. 1992. "Discovery of equations: experimental evaluation of convergence." In *Proceedings of the Tenth National Conference on Artificial Intelligence*, pp. 70–75. Menlo Park, CA: AAAI Press.

Zhong, N. and S. Ohsuga. 1995. "KOSI—an integrated discovery system for discovering functional relations from databases." *J. Intell. Inform. Sys.* 5: 25–50.

Zytkow, J. M. 1987. "Combining many searches in the FAHRENHEIT discovery system." In *Proceedings of the Fourth International Workshop on Machine Learning*, pp. 281–287. Los Altos, CA: Morgan Kaufmann.

Zytkow, J. M. 1996. "Automated Discovery of Empirical Laws." *Fundamenta Informatica*, 27, pp. 299–318. Los Altos, CA: Morgan Kaufmann.

16.4.3 Multidimensional Regression Analysis

J. Sunil Rao and William J. E. Potts

ABSTRACT Multidimensional regression analysis relates a target outcome Y to a vector of predictors **X** through a variety of possible link functions depending on the distribution of Y. The predictors may be used in a linear fashion or given a more data-driven nonparametric functional form. These variations on the modeling paradigm cover the standard linear model, generalized linear model, and generalized additive model. This article details these connections and provides algorithms for model fitting. A database-marketing example illustrates the use of multidimensional regression models.

1. Introduction

A fundamental data-mining task is modeling the relationship between a vector of predictor variables, $\mathbf{X} = \{X_1, ..., X_p\}$, (also known as inputs), and the expected value of an outcome variable, Y (also known as response, target). Data on the outcome and predictors is collected on a number (n) of cases (also known as observations). The functional form of the relationship is specified up to a vector of unknown parameters, **b**.

$$E(Y) = g(\mathbf{X}, \mathbf{b}), \tag{1}$$

where $E(Y)$ is the expected value of Y, sometimes denoted μ, and the function g can have many forms, which will be discussed later. Fitting consists of determining values of the parameters that satisfactorily explain the observed data. This analytical process is known as (multiple) regression analysis.

   The purpose of regression analysis can be to gain an understanding of the effects of the predictors on the outcome. In data mining, the principal purpose is applying the model to new cases where only the predictors are known in order to predict the outcome. This process is known as scoring.

2. Model Specification

Regression analysis can be viewed as fitting a multivariate surface on the input space. Various assumptions can be made about the shape of the surface.

2.1. Linear Models

The simplest way of relating the response to the predictors is through the model:

$$E(Y) = \mathbf{X}\mathbf{b} = b_0 + b_1 X_1 + ... + b_p X_p. \tag{2}$$

This is known as the multiple linear regression (MLR) model. Here the function g from (1) gives a linear combination of the predictors. Model (2) is used for continuous valued outcomes that are generally assumed to follow normal distributions (Weisberg, 1981).

2.2. Generalized Linear Models

The class of generalized linear models (GLMs) relates the outcome to a linear combination of the predictors through a link function $G(\mu) = \mathbf{X}\mathbf{b}$. The link function constrains the predicted target to a sensible range. For example, the logit link constrains the expected value of binary outcomes to lie between zero and one.

$$G(\mu) = \text{Logit}(E(Y)) = \ln\frac{E(Y)}{1 - E(Y)} = \mathbf{X}\mathbf{b}.$$

Binary outcomes are, perhaps, the most common type of targets used in data mining. For example, in database marketing, the outcome is an indicator of response to an offer. In credit scoring, the outcome is an indicator of default. The expected value of a binary target is the posterior probability that the event occurred (given the predictors). Hence, it must lie between zero and one.

The log link constrains the expected value of a nonnegative, continuous outcome to be positive.

$$\ln(E(Y)) = h \iff E(Y) = \exp(h).$$

A wide class of GLMs can be derived using different link functions and the reader is directed to McCullagh and Nelder (1989) for more details.

2.3. Generalized Additive Models

The nonlinearity in generalized linear models is due to the measurement scale of the outcome. Generalized additive models (GAMs) can accommodate nonlinear effects of the original predictors.

$$G(E(Y)) = G(\mu) = b_0 + f_1(X_1) + \ldots + f_p(X_p), \tag{3}$$

where the $f's$ are arbitrarily defined functions usually estimated from the data through some sort of smoother like a cubic smoothing spline or regression spline or the like (see Hastie and Tibshirani, 1990, for a full discussion of smoothing). Note that the multiple linear regression model is a special form of equation (3). Once the model is fit, we can examine predictor effects in the absence of interactions. Model (3) is composed of univariate functions, one for each predictor, that are nonparametric estimates of trends holding the other predictors in the model constant.

3. Model Fitting

Maximum likelihood estimation (MLE) is the classic approach to model fitting. The likelihood function, denoted by $L(y, \theta)$, is the joint probability density of the data. For a given data set, the likelihood is a function of the unknown parameters. The MLEs are the estimates that maximize $L(y, \theta)$. Consequently, the MLEs are the parameter values that most likely generated the observed data. It is usually more convenient to work with the natural logarithm of L, denoted $l(y, \theta)$, as this often simplifies the functional form.

For the multiple linear regression model, the usual likelihood function is based on the assumption of normality of the outcome. Maximizing the normal likelihood is equivalent to minimizing a loss function based on the sum of squared deviations between the observed and fitted values. These estimates are called the ordinary least squares (OLS) estimates.

For a generalized linear model, the likelihood function is based on the assumption that the distribution of the outcome is from the exponential family (McCullagh and Nelder, 1989). The exponential family contains many continuous and discrete distributions in addition to the normal distribution. For example, the Bernoulli likelihood is typically used for binary outcomes. Coupled with the logit link function, this method is known as logistic regression. An example of this is shown in Figure 1 where a two-parameter linear predictor is fit in a logistic regression model with a binary outcome. The likelihood function is the mesh over the axes with the MLE for the parameters clearly marked. This plot was generated using simulated data.

In linear regression, the OLS (ML) estimates can be determined analytically. This is not the case with nonlinear models. Iterative numerical optimization algorithms are usually needed. For generalized linear models, a similar ML estimation process can be used, typically employing some sort of numerical optimization technique like Newton–Raphson. This process is also known as Fisher scoring. An equivalent approach is known as iteratively reweighted least squares (IRLS). This turns the MLE problem into a sequence of updated weighted regressions (McCullagh and Nelder, 1989).

A further generalization of Fisher scoring is known as backfitting for handling GAMs. This uses the updated weighted regression scheme of IRLS but substitutes weighted regressions with iteratively weighted smooths. This process has been called local Fisher scoring (Hastie and

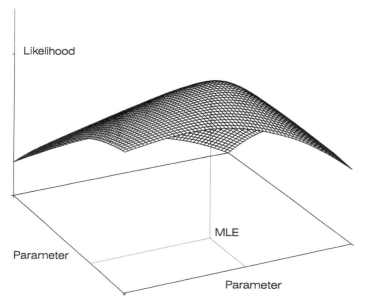

Figure 1 Maximum likelihood estimate from logistic regression model

Tibshirani, 1990). A simplified version of the backfitting is presented below where all of the weights are identity weights and an additive model (AM) is fit to a continuous-valued outcome:

The Backfitting Algorithm

i) Initialize: $f_j(X_j)$, $j = 1, ..., p$ and $f_0 = \text{ave}(y_i)$

ii) Cycle: $j = 1, ..., p, 1, ..., p, ...$

$$f_j = S_j\left(\left(Y - f_0 - \sum_{k \neq j} f_k(X_k)\right) \mid X_j\right)$$

iii) Continue (ii) until individual functions do not change. Step (ii) is simply doing individual scatterplot smooths of a partial residual on the individual predictors in a sequential fashion. This is indicated by the notation S_j for the jth predictor.

4. Example

In database marketing, customer history data is used to support decisions about future marketing campaigns. This example concerns 1,299 responders to a direct-mail offer. All cases represent existing customers. The outcome was the dollar amount purchased (REVENUE) in a recent test campaign. Revenues ranged from 50 to 250 dollars. Five predictors were considered in the analysis:

VALUE—the lifetime total amount purchased (prior to the current campaign)

LASTAMT—the most recent amount purchased (prior to the current campaign)

ORDERS—the number of previous purchases (prior to the current campaign)

RECENCY—the length of time (in years) since their last purchase (prior to the current campaign)

AGE—the customer's age (in years) at the time of the current campaign.

One use of such data is in the second part of a two-stage method for estimating expected revenue. In the first stage, the unconditional probability of response versus nonresponse is

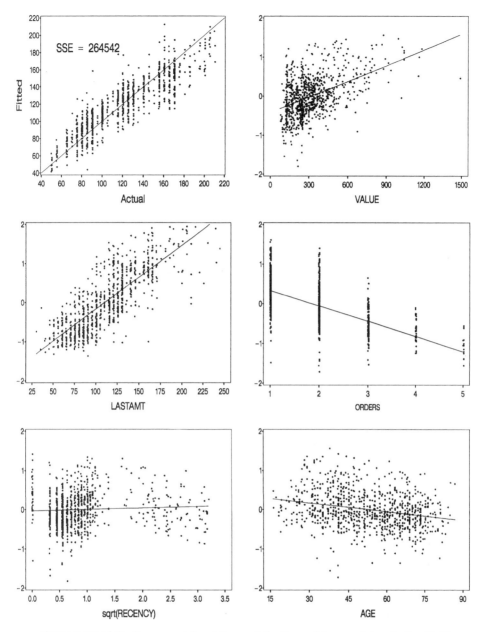

Figure 2 Fit of the linear model and the contributions of the predictors to the fit. The upper left panel is a plot of the predicted versus actual values of REVENUE. The other panels show the linear effect of each predictor overlaid with the standardized partial residuals

estimated from a sample of responders and nonresponders. The second stage consists of estimating the revenue, conditional on response. The two models are then combined to give the unconditional expected revenue (Heckman, 1979; Levin and Zahavi, 1998).

The 1,299 cases were split into a training set of 866 cases and a test set of 433 cases. The test set was reserved for model assessment. A linear regression model (identity link function)

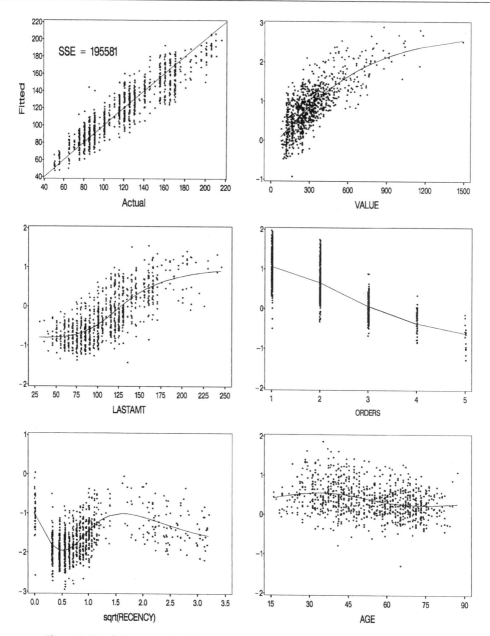

Figure 3 Fit of the generalized additive model and the contributions of the predictors to the fit. The upper left panel is a plot of the predicted versus actual values of REVENUE. The other panels show the additive functions for each predictor overlaid with the partial residuals; both have been standardized

was fitted to the training data using ordinary least squares (normal maximum likelihood)

$$REVENUE = 76.9 + 0.0506(VALUE) + 0.618(LASTAMT) - 14.6(ORDERS)$$

$$+ 1.39(\sqrt{RECENCY}) - 0.283(AGE).$$

The square root transformation was applied to RECENCY to reduce skewness and better differentiate among the early times. The error sum of squares (SSE) of the fitted model was

264,542. The regression coefficients are estimates of the slopes in each dimension of the approximating plane. For example, a 0.618 increase in revenue is achieved with a 1-dollar increase in LASTAMT, while all other predictors are held constant at any value. These linear effects are displayed graphically in Figure 2. The fitted effects are overlaid on the partial residuals (Larsen and McCleary, 1972).

The comparison of the raw slopes can be misleading because they may be measured on different scales and estimated with different precision. More formal inferential methods, such as hypothesis tests and confidence intervals, can be used to evaluate the effect of the input variables (Draper and Smith, 1981). In this example, all slopes are significantly different from zero ($P < 0.0001$) except for the slope of RECENCY ($P = 0.17$). However, statistical significance does not entail practical or predictive importance (e.g., AGE). The validity of standard statistical inference can be compromised by the elaborate *ad hoc* data preparation and variable selection methods used in predictive data mining (Hurvich and Tsai, 1990; Chatfield, 1995; Ye, 1998).

A GAM that allowed for nonlinear predictor effects gave a better fit to the training data. The SSE was reduced to 195,581. A graphical comparison of the effects of each predictor reveals some conspicuous differences (Figure 3). The effect of VALUE increases at a decreasing rate. The effect of LASTAMT shows a sigmoidal trend. The effect of RECENCY shows a sinusoidal trend. The most striking difference in the fitted values of the linear and nonlinear models was the effect of RECENCY. The fit of the GAM shows that customers with current, outstanding orders (RECENCY = 0) appear to generate more revenue. However, the revenue diminishes as RECENCY approaches three months and then rises until approximately three years, at which time it gradually declines.

Evaluating a model on the training data usually gives an optimistically biased assessment (Efron, 1986). A flexible (complex) model has the ability to accommodate the true systematic signal as well as random noise in the sample data. Many methods have been devised to give an honest assessment of the ability of the model to generalize to cases outside the training sample (Efron, 1983). A simple, though somewhat inefficient, method is data splitting. For this example, the SSE on the test set was 145,329 for the linear model and 112,637 for the GAM.

5. Summary

We have presented an overview of multidimensional regression models showing how the simplest linear regression model can be expanded to handle noncontinuous outputs through the generalized linear model, and how this can further be expanded to relax the parametric form imposed on the inputs via the generalized additive model. The revenue example clearly shows the richness of these models and their particular appeal for prediction purposes. This review, however, is by no means exhaustive. These models simply present some approaches to estimating the multidimensional surface over the input space. They all assume the absence of interactions between the inputs. There is a wealth of techniques available for expanding these classes of regression models to deal with interactions. A good review of this work can be found in Hastie and Tibshirani (1990) or Ripley (1996).

References

Chatfield, C. 1995. "Model uncertainty, data mining and statistical inference (with discussion)." *J. R. Stat. Soc., Series B* **158**: 419–466.

Draper, N. R. and H. Smith. 1981. *Applied Regression Analysis*. 2d ed. Wiley.

Efron, B. 1983. "Estimating the error rate of a prediction rule: improvement on cross-validation." *J. Am. Stat. Assoc.* **78**: 316–331.

Efron, B. 1986. "How biased is the apparent error rate of a prediction rule?" *J. Am. Stat. Assoc.* **81**: 461–470.

Hastie, T. J. and R. J. Tibshirani. 1990. *Generalized Additive Models*. New York: Chapman and Hall.

Heckman, J. 1979. "Sample selection bias as a specification error." *Econometrika* **47**: 153–161.

Hurvich, C. M. and C. L. Tsai. 1990. "The impact of model selection on inference in linear regression." *Am. Stat.* **44**: 214–217.

Larsen, W. A. and S. J. McCleary. 1972. "The use of partial residual plots in regression analysis." *Technometrics* **14**: 781–790.

Levin, N. and J. Zahavi. 1998. "Continuous predictive modeling, a comparative analysis." *J. Interactive Marketing* **12**: 5–22.

McCullagh, P. and J. A. Nelder. 1989. *Generalized Linear Models*. 2d ed. New York: Chapman and Hall.

Ripley, B. 1996. *Pattern Recognition and Neural Networks*. Cambridge, England: Cambridge University Press.

Weisberg, S. 1981. *Applied Linear Regression*. New York: Wiley Publishers.

Ye, J. 1998. "On measuring and correcting the effects of data mining and model selection." *J. Am. Stat. Assoc.* **93**: 120–131.

16.5 Clustering

16.5.1 Numerical Clustering

Padhraic Smyth

Numerical clustering algorithms are typically cast in a number of different basic forms. We can distinguish three general approaches to the problem:

1. Partition-based algorithms (sometimes called optimization-based), which seek to partition the d-dimensional measurement space into K disjoint clusters.

2. Density-based algorithms, which use a probabilistic model to determine the location and variability of potentially overlapping density components, again in a d-dimensional measurement space.

3. Hierarchical clustering algorithms, which recursively construct a multiscale hierarchical cluster structure in either a top-down or bottom-up fashion.

The first two techniques are most suitable for multidimensional tuples of measurements, while the third is naturally (though not necessarily) suited to data in the form of proximity matrices. Each is briefly described below.

Partition-based clustering algorithms have a common two-part generic structure: a score function that determines how well any given set of clusters describes the data, and a search method that seeks a particular set of cluster centers that optimizes the score function for a given data set (e.g., Jain and Dubes, 1988). A well-known example of this type of clustering algorithm is the K-means algorithm, which uses a prototype mean as the representation for each of the K clusters, a square error score function that measures the distance of each data point to the mean of the nearest cluster, and a greedy search technique to iteratively move the centers such that the square error is gradually decreased to a minimum (MacQueen, 1967). In the standard instantiation of the algorithm, at each iteration data points are assigned in a greedy fashion to the closest mean (usually in a Euclidean distance sense) and the resulting new means then computed. This continues until no points change assignment, or equivalently, the means do not move. The search problem of optimizing the score function is inherently hard due to the combinatorics of the number of ways to assign N points to K clusters. Thus, typically, only a local optimum of the score function can be guaranteed by the greedy search heuristic. Nonetheless, the greedy method is often quite useful in practice, although the use of the square-error clustering criterion (or equivalently, the use of Euclidean distance as a metric between data points and their means) leads to a favoring of compact spherical clusters, which may not necessarily be appropriate for a given problem.

Density-based techniques go one step further than partition-based clustering, and assume a functional form of a specific type for the probability distribution of the data points that belong to each cluster (Banfield and Raftery, 1993; Cheeseman and Stutz, 1996; Fraley and Raftery, 1998). The overall distribution of the data is then assumed to be a weighted linear sum (mixture) of K component distributions (Titterington et al., 1985; McLachlan and Basford, 1988). Examples of component distributions are a multinomial for categorical data or a multivariate Gaussian for real-valued data. If the assumption on the functional form of the component distributions is reasonable, this can be a powerful technique. For example, in the Gaussian case, each cluster is described by both its location (mean) and variability (covariance matrix), allowing for a relatively flexible fitting of general elliptically shaped clusters. The score function in this context is quite naturally the widely used statistical concept of likelihood, namely the probability of the observed data as a function of a particular setting of the parameters. Here the parameters consist of the individual parameters of each component model as well as their relative weights. The likelihood is then maximized as a function of the unknown parameters, usually a difficult nonlinear optimization problem, often solved by gradient techniques or the expectation-maximization (EM) algorithm. Density-based clustering is particularly useful when there is sufficient prior knowledge to support the necessary assumptions on the functional forms. For example, one can use relatively objective techniques (such as cross-validation; Smyth, 2000) to determine the most appropriate value for K given the data. Note that finding the best K in this manner means that one has found the best number of components K from a density estimation viewpoint, given the observed data. In general, across all clustering methods, there is no universally objective answer to the question "How many clusters are best?"—It largely depends on one's viewpoint and goals.

Hierarchical clustering algorithms take a proximity (distance) matrix on $N \times N$ data points and produce a multiscale set of nested partitions of the data. The primary differences between this technique and the aforementioned partitional and density-based clustering are the overlapping hierarchical nature of the clusters and the use of pairwise distance matrices rather than attribute-value representations. Agglomerative algorithms operate in a bottom-up fashion, beginning with each data point being assigned to its own cluster and gradually merging clusters until all points belong to a single cluster at the root node. The merging criterion largely determines the shape of the resulting clusters. For example, if clusters are merged based on the pairwise distance of their closest two points, one can expect relatively elongated clusters (compared to merging based on the pairwise distance of the centroids, for example). Divisive methods operate in a complementary top-down fashion and are less widely used since the search for partitions is more difficult in this direction. A useful feature of hierarchical clustering is the resulting visualization of the hierarchical structure (known as a dendrogram). If multi-scale structure does in fact exist in the data, the dendrogram will often clearly indicate this structure compared, say, to a dendrogram built on purely random data. A known disadvantage of the hierarchical approach is the fact that the algorithms scale as $O(N^2)$, limiting their applicability to relatively small data sets, for example, $N < 10^4$, compared to the other two techniques that have a performance closer to linear in N.

Scaling in terms of computational efficiency becomes important when applying clustering algorithms to very large data sets, where much of the data may reside in secondary disk memory. Various heuristics, such as sampling the data in a clever fashion, have been developed to deal with this problem (e.g., Bradley et al., 1998). Systematic search techniques, such as branch and bound, have also been found useful in speeding up standard clustering algorithms (Koontz et al., 1975).

There are numerous variations on the basic themes outlined above as well a number of less widely used clustering techniques that do not naturally fall under any of these headings. General discussions of clustering algorithms can be found in a number of books on the topic, for example, Jain and Dubes (1988), Kaufman and Rousseeuw (1990), and Everitt (1992). There is no universal criterion for judging the quality of one clustering algorithm over another. Each has its own advantages and disadvantages, and the true judge of a clustering algorithm is the knowledge imparted to the user by the discovered clusters (e.g., to the scientist, medical researcher, or business person).

References

Banfield, J. D. and A. E. Raftery. 1993. "Model-based Gaussian and non-Gaussian clustering." *Biometrics* **49**: 803–821.

Bradley, P. S., U. Fayyad, and C. Reina. 1998. "Scaling clustering algorithms to large databases." In *Proceedings of the Fourth International Conference on Knowledge Discovery and Data Mining*, edited by R. Agrawal, P. Stolorz, and G. Piatetsky-Shapiro, pp. 9–15. Menlo Park, CA: AAAI Press.

Cheeseman, P. and J. Stutz. 1996. "Bayesian classification (AutoClass): theory and results." In *Advances in Knowledge Discovery and Data Mining*, edited by U. M. Fayyad, G. Piatetsky-Shapiro, P. Smyth, and R. Uthurusamy, pp. 153–180. Cambridge, MA: AAAI/MIT Press.

Everitt, B. S. 1992. *Cluster Analysis*. London: Edward Arnold.

Fraley, C. and A. E. Raftery. 1998. "How many clusters? Which clustering method? Answers via model-based cluster analysis." *Comput. J.* **41**: 578–588.

Jain, A. K. and R. C. Dubes. 1988. *Algorithms for Clustering Data*. Englewood Clifs, NJ: Prentice-Hall.

Kaufman, L. and P. J. Rousseeuw. 1990. *Finding Groups in Data: An Introduction to Cluster Analysis*. New York: Wiley.

Koontz, W. L. G., P. M. Narendra, and K. Fukunaga. 1975. "A branch and bound clustering algorithm." *IEEE Trans. Comput.* **24**: 908–915.

MacQueen, J. 1967. "Some methods for classification and analysis of multivariate observations." In *Proceedings of the Fifth Berkeley Symposium on Mathematical Statistics and Probability*, edited by L. M. Le Cam and J. Neyman, pp. 281–297. Berkeley: University of California Press.

McLachlan, G. J. and K. E. Basford. 1988. *Mixture Models: Inference and Applications to Clustering*. New York: Marcel Dekker.

Titterington, D. M., A. F. M. Smith, and U. E. Makov. 1985. *Statistical Analysis of Finite Mixture Distributions*. New York: Wiley.

Smyth, P. 2000. "Model selection for probabilistic clustering using cross-validated likelihood." *Stat. Comput.* **9**: 63–72.

16.5.2 Conceptual Clustering

Douglas Fisher

ABSTRACT   Clustering methods of machine learning place great importance on the utility of conceptual descriptions, which logically or probabilistically express patterns found in clusters. Conceptual descriptions are important for cluster interpretation, inference tasks such as pattern completion and problem solving, and for data compression, memory management, and runtime-efficiency enhancements. This article surveys a wide variety of themes and algorithms found in the clustering literature of machine learning, including the various forms of conceptual representation, inference tasks that exploit the conceptual summaries of clusters, cluster validation strategies, clustering relational data, the use of background knowledge to guide clustering, and promising scale-up strategies.

1. Introduction

Michalski (1980) defined conceptual clustering as measuring the quality of a clustering by the quality of intensional (summary, conceptual) descriptions (see Chapters 5.6 and 7) used to represent clusters. Conceptual clustering was inspired by earlier work in numerical taxonomy (see Chapter 16.5.1) and supervised learning of disjunctive concepts from positive-only examples (see Chapter 16.1). The motivation for conceptual clustering was to automate what is typically a manual and iterative process of applying a clustering technique, followed by a supervised technique to characterize clusters, in search of interpretable clusters.

Conceptual clustering systems have since proliferated and differ along many dimensions, including the form of their summary representations, the measures used to judge the quality of summary descriptions, and the strategies used to search the space of clusterings.

2. Summary Descriptions of Clusters

Most conceptual clustering systems assume that clustering occurs over tuples. A conjunctive summary description lists all attribute values that are common to all cluster members, sometimes with limited forms of disjunction allowed (Michalski and Stepp, 1983a,b). Probabilistic cluster summaries used by Autoclass (Cheeseman et al., 1988; Cheeseman and Stutz, 1996), Cobweb (Fisher, 1987), Snob (Wallace and Boulton, 1968; Wallace, 1990; Wallace and Dowe, 1999), Dido (Scott and Markovitch, 1991), and other systems (Hanson and Bauer, 1989; Anderson and Matessa, 1991; Biswas et al., 1991; Kilander and Jansson, 1993; De Alte Da Veiga, 1994; Fisher, 1996; Sahami et al., 1998) specify probability distribution (or density) functions over the domains of attributes.

It has been pointed out (Stepp, 1987; Shavlik and Dietterich, 1990) that the term "conceptual clustering" has often been misused relative to the initial motivation for the paradigm. Nonetheless, this survey will continue with a liberal treatment (e.g., we include probabilistic, model-based approaches), with citations that cross the line to traditional (i.e., numerical taxonomy) methods where a common theme is shared across clustering paradigms. We concentrate on the ways that summary descriptions are exploited during clustering, be they logical, probabilistic, or even prototypes/centroids. In fact, the variety of representations correspond nicely to various psychological theories of human concept representation (Smith and Medin, 1981).

3. The Structure of Clusterings

Partitional clustering algorithms such as Cluster/2 (Michalski and Stepp, 1983a,b) partition the tuples into mutually-exclusive clusters. In some probabilistic (model-based) approaches, however, a tuple is fractionally assigned to each cluster based on the estimated probability (computed from summary descriptions) that the tuple belongs to that cluster (Kearns et al., 1997; Meilă and Heckerman, 1998), as opposed to a hard assignment to only one cluster (e.g., the most probable host cluster for the tuple). Fractional assignment in probabilistic approaches is typically motivated by uncertainty about a tuple's true host cluster, as opposed to the motivations for fractional assignment in fuzzy clustering systems (Bezdek, 1987).

Hierarchical methods, such as extensions of Cluster/2 and Autoclass, as well as Cobweb, form tree-structured clusterings, in which sibling clusters partition the objects covered by their common parent. A hierarchical clustering may take the form of a decision tree (see Chapters 5.4 and 16.1.3) over the tuples, where a path from root to node/cluster is a conjunctive representation of the cluster (Fisher and Langley, 1986; Fisher and Hapanyengwi, 1993; Blockeel et al., 1998).

Overlapping clusters, which may place each tuple in multiple clusters (via a hard assignment), are also possible (Martin and Billman, 1994), including cluster-mining approaches (Perkowitz and Etzioni, 1999), which seek good clusters without requiring complete coverage of the tuples, and without regard to a larger (partitional, hierarchical) organizational scheme. Early artificial intelligence (AI) memory management systems such as Unimem (Lebowitz, 1982, 1987), Cyrus (Kolodner, 1983), and others (Scott and Markovitch, 1991; Martin and Billman, 1994) form hierarchies of overlapping clusters. A number of systems form a lattice of clusters (Levinson, 1984; Wilcox and Levinson, 1986; Carpineto and Romano, 1996), one for each unique, conjunctive, maximally specific generalization (see Chapters 7 and 16.1) that can be formed for any member of the power set of the tuples.

4. Categorization and Inference

One benefit of summary descriptions is that they support efficient inference. For example, using probabilistic concepts, one can predict a cluster member's attribute values with varying degrees of certainty (Fisher, 1987; Cheeseman et al., 1988; Anderson and Matessa, 1991; Martin and Billman, 1994; Fisher, 1996).

Of course, determining the cluster membership of a tuple is a prerequisite to making attribute inferences. Ideally, summary descriptions make it easy to categorize tuples that were not originally used for clustering, as well as making inferences upon categorization if the tuple is incomplete. In many cases, clustering methods can be viewed as optimizing a trade-off between the predictability of attributes (given cluster membership) and the predictiveness of attributes (for determining cluster membership). This trade-off can also be expressed as a trade-off between the coverage (size, generality) of a cluster and attribute predictability (specificity). Importantly, automatically managing this trade-off, which is analogous to concerns with intracluster and intercluster similarity in traditional techniques (see Chapter 16.5.1) eliminates or mitigates the need to specify the number of clusters *a priori*.

Within a hierarchical setting, summary descriptions at one level of description offer default predictions that can be controverted or otherwise qualified if a tuple is categorized to a deeper level (Lebowitz, 1982; Fisher, 1987, 1996; Hanson et al., 1991; Scott and Markovitch, 1991; Martin and Billman, 1994; Hoffman and Puzicha, 1998). In general, hierarchical schemes allow for richer categorization and inference possibilities (see Chapters 5.7, 7, and 18.1).

An objective way to assess the merits of one clustering over another is the extent that the clustering facilitates accurate and low-cost inferences about all or selected attributes (Fisher, 1987, 1996; Anderson and Matessa, 1991; Reich and Fenves, 1991; Matthews and Hearne, 1991; Cheeseman and Stutz, 1996; Blockeel et al., 1998; Meilă and Heckerman, 1998). There are other objective ways of evaluating clusterings such as their promotion of fast query (e.g., nearest-neighbor) searches (Talbert and Fisher, 1999; see Chapter 16.1.6). Together with run-time and memory costs, these cluster validation measures and others suggest objective ways to assess clustering systems.

Unfortunately, a common practice to assess clusterings is to compare them against *a priori* established (typically human) classifications to see whether the gold-standard classification is rediscovered. Unless the comparison delves into which bias, of the many possibilities, went into forming the gold standard, and the (mis)match with the clustering system's bias, such a rediscovery evaluation is of very limited utility.

A second admonition is that in many real-world applications, clustering is but a tool in a larger, iterative search for scientific (e.g., causal) explanations for structure/patterns in data (Cheeseman and Stutz, 1996), which involves data engineering and expert interpretation. In fact, in some cases the rediscovery-evaluation strategy may only be successful because the data to which clustering is applied have evolved, during an earlier exploration by experts and analysts, to a state where rediscovery is easy. However, a clustering tool should be an effective participant in such an exploration, not simply a beneficiary of it. Unfortunately, evaluating the extent that a clustering tool advances analyst/expert exploration in a new domain of study is not amenable to formalization, though case studies like those of Cheeseman and Stutz (1996) enumerate many important issues. Thus, the objective assessment strategies above only provide part of the picture when determining the expected utility of a clustering system within a real application.

5. Searching for Clusterings

In a strict interpretation of conceptual clustering, the search for clusterings is guided by the quality of cluster summary descriptions. Thus, the search for cluster descriptions is a subroutine (and not an afterthought) of the search for clusterings (Fisher and Langley, 1985, 1986; Stepp, 1987).

Given extensional representations of one or more clusters, the search for probabilistic, centroid, or maximally specific conjunctive representations is trivial. Cluster/2 goes through a more extensive search because it is not limited to maximally specific conjunctions for each cluster. Further, we could allow disjunctive representations for each cluster by using a supervised system like C4.5 (Quinlan, 1993) to summarize and discriminate clusters. In principle, the strategies that can be used to search the space of summary descriptions is coextensive with the plethora of supervised learning methods (see Chapter 16.1) though the strategies that are actually exploited across existing conceptual clustering methods is very much smaller and often trivial.

There have been many strategies used to search the space of clusterings, including the EM algorithm (Cheeseman et al., 1988; Meilă and Heckerman, 1998), branch-and-bound (Nevins, 1995), greedy divide-and-conquer (Fisher and Langley, 1986; Blockeel et al., 1998; see Chapter 16.1.3), agglomeration (Fisher et al., 1992; Meilă and Heckerman, 1998; Talavera and Béjar, 1999), separate-and-conquer (Mirkin, 1998; see Chapter 16.1.4), and other methods of set covering (Michalski and Stepp, 1983a,b).

A strategy that appears particularly useful for scale-up to massive data sets, however, is sorting, in which tuples are incrementally categorized relative to a number of contrast clusters. If a tuple is sufficiently novel, then a new cluster may be created. Sorting is used by a variety of systems (Lebowitz, 1982; Kolodner, 1983; Fisher, 1987, 1996; Gennari et al., 1989; Hadzikadic and Yun, 1989; Anderson and Matessa, 1991; McKusick and Langley, 1991; Zhang et al., 1997; Biswas et al., 1998). Sorting can be viewed as a component of the K-means algorithm (Duda and Hart, 1973) and EM. Not coincidentally, sorting's early appearance in machine learning stemmed from cognitive concerns with modeling the computational limitations of human learning, in which memory constraints were also an issue.

Sorting is greedy and scans the data only once. It yields a view of the data quickly, but a view that may be far from optimal because the final clustering depends on the order that data are processed. There are several ways to iteratively optimize/refine this initial clustering, but a strategy that seems especially promising for scale-up is to cluster clusters, which in effect reclusters large numbers of tuples simultaneously by exploiting summary descriptions to guide the reclustering process. Fisher (1996) exploits probabilistic representations, Bradley and Fayyad (1998) and Cutting et al. (1993) exploit centroid summaries, and Zhang et al. (1997) and Fayyad et al. (1998) exploit extended-centroid representations. The summary description can also replace a large number of instances, thus freeing up critical main memory in the face of massive data sets.

6. Variations of Conceptual Clustering

There have been notable variations on the conceptual clustering theme, many in directions that extend the form of input data.

Cluster/S (Stepp and Michalski, 1986) uses background knowledge (see Chapter 18) to augment the data definition in a manner that is guided by user goals. Occam (Pazzani, 1987) and other systems (Carpineto and Romano, 1996; Talavera and Béjar, 1999) also exploit background knowledge.

Clustering over relational or structural data (e.g., where each datum is represented in terms of relations over attributes, as well as the attributes themselves; see Chapter 4) includes Stepp and Michalski (1986), Lebowitz (1987), Levinson (1984), Segen (1990), Thompson and Langley (1991), Iba and Gennari (1991), Bisson (1992), Kietz and Morik (1994), Wrobel (1994), Ketterlin et al. (1995), Blockeel et al. (1998), and Kirsten and Wrobel (1998). Again, methods used for relational supervised learning can be adapted to find summary descriptions for relational clustering systems.

Conceptual clustering of sequential or time series data, in which the value of one or more attributes of a tuple varies with time, has also been explored (Fisher et al., 1993; Li and Biswas, 1999; Smyth, 1999).

Some clustering systems treat attributes differently. Consistent with human categorization studies, for example, (extensionally defined) clusters of tuples can be established based on common functional attributes, and summary descriptions of these clusters can then be obtained from form (perceptual, observable, operational) properties (Fisher and Pazzani, 1991). Several systems can be regarded as clustering using function and form distinctions for purposes of theory revision and shift of bias (Utgoff, 1986; Mooney, 1991; Thompson and Langley, 1991; Wrobel, 1994) and scientific discovery (Langley et al., 1986, pp. 438–446) (see Chapter 29). In a similar vein, utility-based clustering (Rendell et al., 1987; Horvitz and Klein, 1993; Chajewska et al., 1998) groups tuples based on similarities along utility dimensions (e.g., of outcomes), and these clusters can then be summarized in terms of other properties (e.g., actions). Of course, if there is only one functional (i.e., dependent) attribute to guide the formation of extensionally defined clusters, then this (degenerate-clustering) task is simply supervised learning (classification or regression; see Chapter 16.1).

More generally, various methods have been used in support of problem solving, including the discovery of Strips-style operators from execution traces (Vere, 1978), and to cluster explanations or Strips-style (macro-)operators in support of more efficient problem solving (Yoo and Fisher, 1991a,b), game-playing (Levinson and Snyder, 1991), diagnosis (Fisher et al., 1993), expert system inference (Biswas et al., 1998), and planning (Scott and Markovitch, 1991; Langley and Allen, 1993; Yang and Fisher, 1992; Alterman and Garland, 1998).

Clustering in the context of problem solving, together with a lineage of systems that began with Lebowitz (1982) and Kolodner (1983), suggests the efficacy of using clustering to organize (human or artificial) agent memories. Various Web applications (e.g., Zamir et al., 1997; Sahami et al., 1998; Perkowitz and Etzioni, 1999) are an obvious point of intersection between data mining and agent technology.

7. Directions for Research and Application

An important direction in furtherance of scale-up is anytime clustering algorithms, which can be queried at any time for the best solutions uncovered to point of query (Smyth and Wolpert, 1997). These methods should exploit structure in the data so that a large percentage of the best clusters tend to be discovered relatively quickly. A user may continue optimizing and searching in the background for an indefinite time, albeit with (ideally) rapidly diminishing returns. Systems that partition the search for clustering into a greedy (but informed) phase, followed by (or interweaved with) an iterative optimization phase (Cutting et al., 1993; Fisher, 1996; Zhang et al., 1997; Biswas et al., 1998; Bradley et al., 1998; Goldszmidt and Sahami, 1998) have this flavor. Conceptual cluster-mining approaches (Perkowitz and Etzioni, 1999) are also amenable to an anytime variation. However, none of these approaches has been well evaluated as anytime algorithms.

Different organizations for clusterings should also be explored. In particular, directed acyclic graphs (DAGs) that are far more sparse than full lattices have been little studied (cf. Scott and Markovitch, 1991; Martin and Billman, 1994), but would be advantageous in many contexts, as would strategies that do not insist on full coverage of the data (Perkowitz and Etzioni, 1999).

Different unsupervised paradigms provide unique views of data that probably can be combined to good effect. Some work already has combined clustering with construction of probabilistic networks (Connolly, 1993; see Chapters 5.8 and 16.6) and association rule learning (Lent et al., 1997; see Chapter 16.2.3). In fact, frequent set discovery (in support of association rule learning) can be also viewed as conceptual cluster mining, albeit with attention limited to only the coverage aspect of the coverage/specificity trade-off that we noted earlier.

Finally, we have suggested the utility of clustering for organizing agent memories in support of problem solving. Work on problem solving and clustering may also inform attempts to (semi-)automate many of the vital problem-solving activities that surround the clustering process in a data mining application (Cheeseman and Stutz, 1996; see Chapter 16.5.1), thus building upon the modest but important initial motivations for conceptual clustering to semi-automate cluster interpretation (Michalski, 1980).

ACKNOWLEDGMENTS
We thank Paul Bradley, Luc De Raedt, Eric Horvitz, Ray Liere, Mehren Sahami, Willi Klösgen, Jan Z'ytkow, and Clark Glymour for helpful comments on an earlier draft of this article.

References

Alterman, R. and A. Garland. 1998. "Conventions in joint activity." Technical Report CS-98-199. Waltham, MA: Department of Computer Science, Brandeis University.

Anderson, J. and M. Matessa. 1991. "An incremental Bayesian algorithm for categorization." In *Concept Formation: Knowledge and Experience in Unsupervised Learning*, edited by D. Fisher, M. Pazzani, and P. Langley, pp. 165–178. San Francisco, CA: Morgan Kaufmann.

Bezdek, J. 1987. "Some non-standard clustering algorithms." In *Developments in Numerical Ecology*, edited by P. Legendre and L. Legendre, pp. 225–287. New York: Springer.

Bisson, G. 1992. "Learning in FOL with a similarity measure." In *Proceedings of the Tenth National Conference on Artificial Intelligence (San Jose, CA)*, pp. 82–87. Menlo Park, CA: AAAI/MIT Press.

Biswas, G., J. Weinberg, and D. Fisher. 1998. "Iterate: a conceptual clustering algorithm for data mining." *IEEE Trans. Sys., Man, Cybernet.* **28**: 219–230.

Biswas, G., J. Weinberg, Q. Yang, and G. Koller. 1991. "Conceptual clustering and exploratory data analysis." In *Proceedings of the Eighth International Workshop on Machine Learning (Evanston, IL)*, pp. 591–595. San Francisco, CA: Morgan Kaufmann.

Blockeel, H., L. De Raedt, and J. Ramon. 1998. "Top-down induction of clustering trees." In *Proceedings of the Fifteenth International Conference on Machine Learning (Madison, WI)*, pp. 55–63. San Francisco, CA: Morgan Kaufmann.

Bradley, P. and U. Fayyad. 1998. "Refining initial points for K-means clustering." In *Proceedings of the Fifteenth International Conference on Machine Learning (Madison, WI)*, pp. 91–99. San Francisco, CA: Morgan Kaufmann.

Bradley, P., U. Fayyad, and C. Reina. 1998. "Scaling clustering algorithms to large data sets." In *Proceedings of the Fourth International Conference on Knowledge Discovery and Data Mining (New York, NY)*, pp. 9–15. Menlo Park, CA: AAAI/MIT Press.

Carpineto, C. and G. Romano. 1996. "A lattice conceptual clustering system and its application to browsing retrieval." *Machine Learning* **24**: 95–122.

Chajewska, U., L. Getoor, J. Norman, and Y. Shahar. 1998. "Utility elicitation as a classification problem." In *Uncertainty and Artificial Intelligence*, pp. 79–88. San Francisco, CA: Morgan Kaufmann.

Cheeseman, P., J. Kelly, M. Self, J. Stutz, W. Taylor, and D. Freeman. 1988. "Autoclass: a Bayesian classification system." In *Proceedings of the Fifth International Conference on Machine Learning (Ann Arbor, MI)*, pp. 54–64. San Francisco, CA: Morgan Kaufmann.

Cheeseman, P. and J. Stutz. 1996. "Bayesian classification (AutoClass): theory and results." In *Advances in Knowledge Discovery and Data Mining*, edited by U. Fayyad, G. Piatetsky-Shapiro, P. Smyth, and R. Uthurusamy, pp. 153–180. Cambridge, MA: AAAI/MIT Press.

Connolly, D. 1993. "Constructing hidden variables in Bayesian networks via conceptual clustering." In *Proceedings of the Tenth International Conference on Machine Learning (Amherst, MA)*, pp. 65–72. San Francisco, CA: Morgan Kaufmann.

Cutting, D., D. Karger, and J. Pederson. 1993. "Constant interaction-time scatter/gather browsing of very large document collections." In *Proceedings of the Sixteenth International ACM SIGIR Conference on Research and Development in Information Retrieval (Pittsburgh, PA)*, pp. 126–134. New York: ACM Press.

De Alte Da Veiga, F. 1994. "Data analysis in biomedical research: a novel methodological approach and its implementation as a conceptual clustering algorithm." Ph.D. diss. Columbia, Portugal: Universidade de Coimbra, Unidade de Biomatemática e Informática Médica da Faculdade de Medicina.

Duda, R. and P. Hart. 1973. *Pattern Classification and Scene Analysis*. New York: Wiley and Sons.

Fayyad, U., C. Reina, and P. Bradley. 1998. "Initialization of iterative refinement clustering algorithms." In *Proceedings of the Fourth International Conference on Knowledge Discovery and Data Mining (New York, NY)*, pp. 194–198. Menlo Park, CA: AAAI/MIT Press.

Fisher, D. 1987. "Knowledge acquisition via incremental conceptual clustering." In *Machine Learning* **2**: 139–172.

Fisher, D. 1996. "Iterative optimization and simplification of hierarchical clusterings." *J. Artificial Intell. Res.* **4**: 147–179.

Fisher, D. and G. Hapanyengwi. 1993. "Database management and analysis tools of machine induction." *J. Intell. Inform. Sys.* **2**: 5–38.

Fisher, D. and P. Langley. 1985. "Approaches to conceptual clustering." In *Proceedings of the International Joint Conference on Artificial Intelligence (Los Angeles, CA)*, pp. 691–697. San Francisco, CA: Morgan Kaufmann.

Fisher, D. and P. Langley. 1986. "Methods of conceptual clustering and their relation to numerical taxonomy." In *Artificial Intelligence and Statistics*, edited by W. Gale, pp. 77–113. Reading, MA: Addison-Wesley.

Fisher, D. and M. Pazzani. 1991. "Theory-guided concept formation." In *Concept Formation: Knowledge and Experience in Unsupervised Learning*, edited by D. Fisher, M. Pazzani, and P. Langley, pp. 165–178. San Francisco, CA: Morgan Kaufmann.

Fisher, D., L. Xu, J. Carnes, Y. Reich, S. Fenves, J. Chen, R. Shiavi, G. Biswas, and J. Weinberg. 1993. "Applying AI clustering to engineering tasks." *IEEE Expert* **8**: 51–60.

Fisher, D., L. Xu, and N. Zard. 1992. "Ordering effects in clustering." In *Proceedings of the Ninth International Conference on Machine Learning (Aberdeen, Scotland)*, pp. 163–168. San Francisco, CA: Morgan Kaufmann.

Gennari, J., P. Langley, and D. Fisher. 1989. "Models of incremental concept formation." *Artificial Intell.* **40**: 11–62.

Goldszmidt, M. and M. Sahami. 1998. "A probabilistic approach to full-text document clustering." Technical Report ITAD-433-MS-98-044. Palo Alto, CA: SRI International.

Hadzikadic, M. and D. Yun. 1989. In *Proceedings of the International Joint Conference on Artificial Intelligence (Detroit, MI)*, pp. 831–836. San Francisco, CA: Morgan Kaufmann.

Hanson, R., J. Stutz, and P. Cheeseman. 1991. In *Proceedings of the International Joint Conference on Artificial Intelligence (Sydney, Australia)*, pp. 692–698. San Francisco, CA: Morgan Kaufmann.

Hanson, S. and M. Bauer. 1989. "Conceptual clustering, categorization, and polymorphy." *Machine Learning* **3**: 343–372.

Hoffman, T. and J. Puzicha. 1998. "Statistical models for co-occurrence data." Technical Report A.I. Memo 1625. Cambridge, MA: Massachusetts Institute of Technology.

Horvitz, E. and A. Klein. 1993. "Utility-based abstraction and categorization." In *Proceedings of Uncertainty in Artificial Intelligence (Washington, D.C.)*, pp. 128–135. San Francisco, CA: Morgan Kaufmann.

Iba, W. and J. Gennari. 1991. "Learning to recognize movements." In *Concept Formation: Knowledge and Experience in Unsupervised Learning*, edited by D. Fisher, M. Pazzani, and P. Langley, pp. 355–386. San Francisco, CA: Morgan Kaufmann.

Kearns, M., Y. Mansour, and A. Ng. 1997. "An information-theoretic analysis of hard and soft assignment methods for clustering." In *Proceedings of the Thirteenth Annual Conference on Uncertainty in Artificial Intelligence (Providence, RI)*, pp. 282–293. San Francisco, CA: Morgan Kaufmann.

Ketterlin, A., P. Gançarski, and J. Korczak. 1995. "Conceptual clustering in structured databases: a practical approach." In *Proceedings of the First International Conference on Knowledge Discovery and Data Mining (Montreal, Canada)*, pp. 180–185. Menlo Park, CA: AAAI/MIT Press.

Kietz, J. and K. Morik. 1994. "A polynomial approach to the constructive induction of structural knowledge." In *Machine Learning* **14**: 193–218.

Kilander, F. and C. Jansson. 1993. "Cobbit: a control procedure for Cobweb in the presence of concept drift." In *Machine Learning: ECML-93*, edited by P. Brazdil. Lecture Notes in Computer Science, **667**: 244–261. New York: Springer.

Kirsten, M. and S. Wrobel. 1998. "Relational distance-based clustering." In *Inductive Logic Programming*, edited by D. Page. Lecture Notes in Computer Science, vol. 1446. New York: Springer.

Kolodner, J. 1983. "Maintaining organization in a dynamic long-term memory." *Cognitive Sci.* **7**: 243–280.

Langley, P. and J. Allen. 1993. "A unified framework for planning and learning." In *Machine Learning Methods for Planning and Scheduling*. San Francisco, CA: Morgan Kaufmann.

Langley, P., J. Żytkow, H. Simon, and G. Bradshaw. 1986. "The search for regularity: four aspects of scientific discovery." In *Machine Learning: An Artificial Intelligence Approach*, edited by R. Michalski, J. Carbonell, and T. Mitchell **2**: 425–470. San Francisco, CA: Morgan Kaufmann.

Lebowitz, M. 1982. "Correcting erroneous generalizations." *Cognition and Brain Theory* **5**: 367–381.

Lebowitz, M. 1987. "Experiments with incremental concept formation: UNIMEM." *Machine Learning* **2**: 103–138.

Lent, B., A. Swami, and J. Widom. 1997. "Clustering association rules." In *Proceedings of the Thirteenth International Conference on Data Engineering (Birmingham, UK)*, pp. 220–231. Piscataway, NJ: IEEE Press.

Levinson, R. 1984. "A self-organizing retrieval system for graphs." In *Proceedings of the National Conference on Artificial Intelligence (Austin, TX)*, pp. 203–206. Menlo Park, CA: AAAI/MIT Press.

Levinson, R. and R. Snyder. 1991. "Adaptive pattern-oriented chess." In *Proceedings of the Ninth National Conference on Artificial Intelligence (Anaheim, CA)*, pp. 601–606. Menlo Park, CA: AAAI/MIT Press.

Li, C. and G. Biswas. 1999. "Temporal pattern generation using hidden Markov model-based unsupervised classification." In *Advances in Intelligent Data Analysis*, edited by D. Hand, J. Kok, and M. Berthold. Lecture Notes in Computer Science, vol. 1642. New York: Springer.

Martin, J. and D. Billman. 1994. "Acquiring and combining overlapping concepts." *Machine Learning* **16**: 121–155.

Matthews, G. and J. Hearne. 1991. "Clustering without a metric." *IEEE Trans. Pattern Anal. Machine Intell.* **13**: 175–184.

McKusick, K. and P. Langley. 1991. "Constraints on tree structure in concept formation." In *Proceedings of the Twelfth International Joint Conference on Artificial Intelligence (Sydney, Australia)*, pp. 810–816. San Francisco, CA: Morgan Kaufmann.

Meilă, M. and D. Heckerman. 1998. An experimental comparison of several clustering and initialization methods. Technical Report MSR-TR-98-06. Redmond, WA: Microsoft Research.

Michalski, R. 1980. "Knowledge acquisition through conceptual clustering: a theoretical framework and algorithm for partitioning data into conjunctive concepts." *Int. J. Policy Anal. Inform. Sys.* **4**: 219–243.

Michalski, R. and R. Stepp. 1983a. "Automated construction of classifications: conceptual clustering versus numerical taxonomy." *IEEE Trans. Pattern Anal. Machine Intell.* **5**: 396–409.

Michalski, R. and R. Stepp. 1983b. "Learning from observation: conceptual clustering." In *Machine Learning*, edited by R. Michalski, J. Carbonell, and T. Mitchell, pp. 331–363. San Francisco, CA: Morgan Kaufmann.

Mirkin, B. 1998. "Concept learning and feature selection based on square-error clustering." *Machine Learning* **35**: 25–40.

Mooney, R. 1991. "Explanation-based learning as concept formation." In *Concept Formation: Knowledge and Experience in Unsupervised Learning*, edited by D. Fisher, M. Pazzani, and P. Langley, pp. 179–206. San Francisco, CA: Morgan Kaufmann.

Nevins, A. 1995. "A branch and bound incremental conceptual clusterer." *Machine Learning* **18**: 5–22.

Pazzani, M. 1987. "Inducing causal and social theories: a prerequisite for explanation-based learning." In *Proceedings of the Fourth International Workshop on Machine Learning (Irvine, CA)*, pp. 230–241. San Francisco, CA: Morgan Kaufmann.

Perkowitz, M. and O. Etzioni. 1999. "Adaptive Web sites: conceptual cluster mining." In *Proceedings of the International Joint Conference on Artificial Intelligence (Stockholm, Sweden)*, pp. 264–269. San Francisco, CA: Morgan Kaufmann.

Quinlan, J. R. 1993. *C4.5: Programs for Machine Learning.* San Francisco, CA: Morgan Kaufmann.

Reich, Y. and S. Fenves. 1991. "The formation and use of abstract concepts in design." In *Concept Formation: Knowledge and Experience in Unsupervised Learning*, edited by D. Fisher, M. Pazzani, and P. Langley, pp. 323–354. San Francisco, CA: Morgan Kaufmann.

Rendell, L., R. Seshu, and D. Tcheng. 1987. "More robust concept learning using dynamically-variable bias." In *Proceedings of the Fourth International Workshop on Machine Learning (Irvine, CA)*, pp. 66–78. San Francisco, CA: Morgan Kaufmann.

Sahami, M., S. Yusufali, and M. Baldonado. 1998. "Sonia: A service for organizing networked information autonomously." In *Proceedings of the Third ACM Conference on Digital Libraries*, pp. 200–209. New York: ACM.

Scott, P. and S. Markovitch. 1991. "Representation generation in an exploratory learning system." In *Concept Formation: Knowledge and Experience in Unsupervised Learning*, edited by D. Fisher, M. Pazzani, and P. Langley, pp. 387–422. San Francisco, CA: Morgan Kaufmann.

Segen, J. 1990. "Graph clustering and model learning by data comparison." In *Proceedings of the Seventh International Conference on Machine Learning (Austin, TX)*, pp. 93–100. San Francisco, CA: Morgan Kaufmann.

Shavlik, J. and T. Dietterich. 1990. "Unsupervised concept learning and discovery." In *Readings in Machine Learning*, edited by J. Shavlik and T. Dietterich, pp. 263–266. San Francisco, CA: Morgan Kaufmann.

Smith, E. and D. Medin. 1981. *Categories and Concepts.* Cambridge, MA: Harvard University Press.

Smyth, P. 1999. "Probabilistic model-based clustering of multivariate and sequential data." In *Proceedings of Artificial Intelligence and Statistics '99 (Fort Lauderdale, FL)*, pp. 299–304. San Francisco, CA: Morgan Kaufmann.

Smyth, P. and D. Wolpert. 1997. "Anytime exploratory data analysis for massive data sets." In *Proceedings of the Third International Conference on Knowledge Discovery and Data Mining (Newport Beach, CA)*, pp. 54–60. Menlo Park, CA: AAAI/MIT Press.

Stepp, R. and R. Michalski. 1986. "Conceptual Clustering: Inventing Goal-oriented Classifications of Stuctured Objects." In *Machine Learning II*, edited by R. Michalski, J. Carbonell, and T. Mitchell, pp. 471–498. San Francisco, CA: Morgan Kaufmann.

Stepp, R. 1987. "Concepts in Conceptual Clustering." In *Proceedings of the Tenth International Joint Conference on Artificial Intelligence (Milan, Italy)*, pp. 211–215. San Francisco: Morgan Kaufmann.

Talavera, L. and J. Béjar. 1999. "Integrating declarative knowledge in hierarchical clustering tasks." In *Advances in Intelligent Data Analysis*, edited by D. Hand, J. Kok, and M. Berthold. Lecture Notes in Computer Science, vol. 1642. New York: Springer.

Talbert, D. and D. Fisher. 1999. "Exploiting sample-data distributions to reduce the cost of nearest-neighbor searches with KD-trees." In *Advances in Intelligent Data Analysis*, edited by D. Hand, J. Kok, and M. Berthold. Lecture Notes in Computer Science, Volume 1642. New York: Springer.

Thompson, K. and P. Langley. 1991. "Concept formation in structured domains." In *Concept Formation: Knowledge and Experience in Unsupervised Learning*, edited by D. Fisher, M. Pazzani, and P. Langley, pp. 127–161. San Francisco, CA: Morgan Kaufmann.

Utgoff, P. 1986. "Shift of bias for inductive concept learning." In *Machine Learning II*, edited by R. Michalski, J. Carbonell, and T. Mitchell, pp. 107–148. San Francisco, CA: Morgan Kaufmann.

Vere, S. 1978. "Inductive learning of relational productions." In *Pattern Directed Inference Systems*, edited by D. Waterman and F. Hayes-Roth, pp. 281–295. New York: Academic Press.

Wallace, C. 1990. "Classification by minimum-message-length principal." In *Advances in Computing and Information*, edited by S. Akl, F. Fiala, and W. Koczkodaj. Lecture Notes in Computer Science, **468**: 72–81. New York: Springer.

Wallace, C. and D. Boulton. 1968. "An information measure for classification." *Comput. J.* **11**: 185–194.

Wallace, C. and D. Dowe. 1999. "Minimum message length and Kolmogorov complexity." *Comput. J.* **42(4)**: 270–283.

Wilcox, C. and R. Levinson. 1986. "A self-organized knowledge base for recall, design, and discovery in organic chemistry." In *Artificial Intelligence in Chemistry*, edited by T. Haas and B. Hohne, pp. 209–230. Washington, DC: American Chemical Society.

Wrobel, S. 1994. "Concept formation during interactive theory revision." *Machine Learning* **14**: 169–192.

Yang, H. and D. Fisher. 1992. Similarity-retrieval and partial reuse of macro-operators. Technical Report CS-92-13. Nashville, TN: Department of Computer Science, Vanderbilt University.

Yoo, J. and D. Fisher. 1991a. "Concept formation over explanations and problem-solving experiences." In *Proceedings of the Twelfth International Joint Conference on Artificial Intelligence (Sydney, Australia)*, pp. 630–636. San Francisco, CA: Morgan Kaufmann.

Yoo, J. and D. Fisher. 1991b. "Concept formation over problem solving experiences." In *Concept Formation: Knowledge and Experience in Unsupervised Learning*, edited by D. Fisher, M. Pazzani, and P. Langley, pp. 279–303. San Francisco, CA: Morgan Kaufmann.

Zamir, O., O. Etzioni, O. Madani, and R. Karp. 1997. "Fast and intuitive clustering of Web documents." In *Proceedings of the Third International Conference on Knowledge Discovery and Data Mining (Newport Beach, CA)*, pp. 287–290. Menlo Park, CA: AAAI/MIT Press.

Zhang, T., R. Ramakrishnan, and M. Livny. 1997. "Birch: a new data clustering algorithm and its applications." *Data Mining and Knowledge Discovery* **1**: 141–182.

16.6 Probabilistic and Causal Networks

16.6.1 Methodology for Probabilistic Networks

Peter L. Spirtes

ABSTRACT This article provides an overview of the uses, methods of construction, and interpretations of Bayesian networks. Bayesian networks have two distinct interpretations. Under the probabilistic interpretation, a Bayesian network consists of a directed acyclic graph over a set of random variables, and represents a set of probability distributions, all of which share certain conditional independence relations described by a Markov property. Interpreted in this way, a Bayesian network is a device that provides a means of eliciting probabilities from an expert, a compact representation of a probability distribution, and a means for quickly calculating arbitrary conditional probabilities. Under the causal interpretation, a Bayesian network is a directed acyclic graph where an edge represents direct causal relations between random variables. Under the causal intepretation, the Bayesian network can be used to calculate the effects of intervening on an existing causal system by manipulating the values of variables. Methods of construction are briefly described, and several examples are given.

1. Introduction

There is a long history of using directed acyclic graphs (DAGs) to describe both probability distributions over a set of random variables V and causal relations among members of V (Wright, 1921, 1934). When used to describe probability distributions, DAGs are useful for calculating conditional probabilities, which can in turn be used for purposes of classification (Chapter 16.1). When used to describe causal relations, DAGs can be used to predict the effects of manipulating an existing causal structure (Chapter 5.8), which can in turn be used to select the best action.

2. Classification Problems

Bayesian networks aid the use of the theory of probability to solve classification problems. A Bayesian network is interpreted as a representation of a particular probability distribution over the observed and target features. (This representation is explained in more detail in Section 4.) The advantages of using Bayesian networks to classify or diagnose include the ability to solve a wide variety of different classification problems with a single model, to perform classifications with respect to multiple features, and to calculate arbitrary conditional probabilities (relatively) quickly. The Bayesian network representation also aids users in combining background knowledge as well as data in the construction of a probability distribution, and allows users to construct probability distributions from data that is incomplete. The automatic construction of probabilistic Bayesian networks from background knowledge and data is discussed in more detail in Chapter 16.6.2.

3. Predicting the Effects of an Action

Bayesian networks can be used to represent causal relations among features, as well as probability distributions over features (Chapter 5.8). Under the causal interpretation, a Bayesian network (henceforth called a causal Bayesian network) can be used to calculate the effects of carrying out an action when the values of all of the relevant variables have been measured. There are also algorithms for using a causal Bayesian network to calculate (in some instances) the effects of carrying out a proposed policy when the causal structure is only partially known, or contains unobserved features that influence the outcome. The causal Bayesian network representation also aids users in combining background knowledge as well as data in the construction of a causal theory. The automatic construction of causal Bayesian networks from background knowledge and data is discussed in more detail in Chapter 16.6.2.

4. Probabilistic Bayesian Networks

A directed graph G is a pair $\langle V, E \rangle$ in which V is a set of vertices and E is a set of directed edges between distinct members of V. G is a directed acyclic graph (DAG) if G contains no cyclic directed paths. In the DAG G in Figure 1, the members of V are the random variables *Sex*, *PE* (Parental Encouragement), and *CP* (College Plans), where *PE* has two values ($0 =$ low, $1 =$ high), *CP* has two values ($0 =$ yes, $1 =$ no), and *Sex* has two values ($0 =$ male, $1 =$ female). (*CP* is a measure of whether high school students plan to go to college, and *PE* is a measure of whether their parents encourage them to go to college. The variables in V relate to data collected in an actual data set by Sewell and Shah, 1968, also discussed in Chapter 16.6.2.)

In the probabilistic interpretation of a DAG G, V is a set of random variables, and associated with each G is a set of probability distributions over V, all of which satisfy certain conditional independence constraints among the members of V, determined by G. There are several essentially equivalent ways of specifying the set of probability distribution associated with G.

Say that $P(V)$ satisfies the local directed Markov condition for G if for each $V \in V$, V is independent of its nondescendants in G who are not parents, given its parents. The local directed Markov condition for G implies that *CP* is independent of *Sex* given *PE*, *PE* is independent of the empty set given *Sex* (we interpret independence of the empty set as being trivially true), and *Sex* is independent of the empty set given the empty set. A (probabilistic) Bayesian network is a pair $\langle G, P \rangle$, where P is a probability distribution (or density function) that satisfies the local directed Markov condition for DAG G. Any conditional independence relation shared by every distribution that satisfies the local directed Markov condition for G is said to be entailed by G.

Table 1 Example of a Parameterization

$P(Sex = 0) = 0.4837$	$P(PE = 0|Sex = 0) = 0.4178$	$P(CP = 0|PE = 0) = 0.0630$
	$P(PE = 0|Sex = 1) = 0.5406$	$P(CP = 0|PE = 1) = 0.5724$

Say that a probability distribution $P(V)$ factors according to DAG G if

$$P(V) = \prod_{V \in V} P(V|\textbf{\textit{Parents}}(V)),$$

where $\textbf{\textit{Parents}}(V)$ is the set of parents of V in G. In the example, if $P(Sex, PE, CP)$ factors according to G, the

$$P(Sex, PE, CP) = P(Sex) \times P(PE|Sex) \times P(CP|PE).$$

Under weak assumptions (Lauritzen et al., 1990) about the distribution P, the set of distributions that factor according to G equals the set of distributions that satisfy the local directed Markov condition for G. (The definition of factoring according to a graph carries over to continuous variables by substituting a density function for the probability distribution in the definition.)

Many sorts of familiar statistical models, including various kinds of regression models (Chapter 16.1.7), item response models, recursive structural equation models (Bollen, 1989), factor analytic models, and Hidden Markov models (Smyth et al., 1997) are special cases of Bayesian networks.

The parameters associated with a given Bayesian network depend upon the distribution of the random variables in G. Common assumptions are that the variables are multivariate Gaussians, multinomial, conditional Gaussian, or sigmoid. The set of distributions associated with a DAG can be parameterized by specifying $P[V|\textbf{\textit{Parents}}(V)]$ for each variable V, for each value of V, and for each set of values of $\textbf{\textit{Parents}}(V)$. Using the example of Figure 1, an example of a parameterization is shown in Table 1.

(Note that when the variables are discrete, the sum over all the values of a vertex V, of the probability of V conditional on a fixed value for $\textbf{\textit{Parents}}(V)$, is equal to one, e.g., $P(CP = 1|PE = 0) + P(CP = 0|PE = 0) = 1$. A redundant parameter such as $P(CP = 1|PE = 0)$ has not been listed explicitly, because its value is determined by $P(CP = 0|PE = 0)$.)

4.1. Calculating Conditional Probabilities with Bayesian Networks

The problem of calculating a conditional probability from a Bayesian network is NP-hard (Cooper, 1990). However, there are a number of algorithms that have been developed to calculate conditional probabilities quickly for Bayesian networks with discrete variables and some commonly occurring kinds of DAGs (Howard and Matheson, 1981; Pearl, 1986; Lauritzen and Spiegelhalter, 1988; Jensen et al., 1990; Dawid, 1992). A number of approximation techniques have also been developed (Saul et al., 1996; Jaakkola and Jordan, 1996). In addition Gibbs sampling techniques have been developed (Pearl, 1986). See Heckerman (1996) for further references.

4.2. Construction of Bayesian Networks

Constructing a probabilistic Bayesian network naturally falls into two parts: construction of the DAG G, and estimating either the values or the distributions over the values of the associated

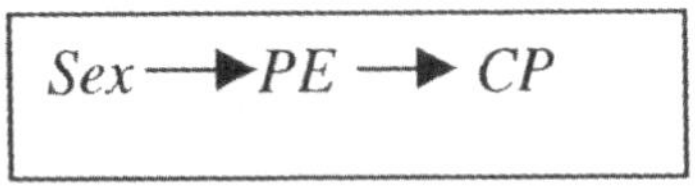

$$Sex \longrightarrow PE \longrightarrow CP$$

Figure 1 Example of a DAG G

parameters. However, the process may be an iterative one, in which the graph is constructed, the parameters estimated, and then both are repeatedly modified.

One common method of constructing the graph G among a set of random variables is by eliciting from an expert whether a variable A directly causes a variable B, and then adding a directed edge from A to B if it is a direct cause. The justification of this procedure for constructing G is discussed in Section 5. There are also automated methods for constructing DAGs from background knowledge and data, which are discussed in detail in Chapter 16.6.2.

There are methods for calculating maximum likelihood estimates of the parameters, maximum posterior probability estimates of the parameters, or a posterior distribution over the parameters. Since the parameters of a Bayesian network are of the form $P(V|\textbf{Parents}(V))$, any method that outputs a probabilistic classification model can be used to estimate the parameters. Such methods include various kinds of regression, kernel density estimation methods, and probabilistic neural networks.

In the case of complete discrete data, the maximum likelihood estimate of $P(V = 0|\textbf{Parents}(V) = v)$ for a given sample is equal to the sample relative frequency of $V = 0$ among units with $\textbf{Parents}(V) = v$. An expression for the posterior distribution of the parameters of a Bayesian network is given in Spiegelhalter and Lauritzen (1990).

When there is missing data, it is known in principle how to calculate the posterior distribution of the parameters, but it is often computationally infeasible to do so. Gibbs's sampling techniques and a variety of approximations have been developed (see Heckerman, 1996, for references).

5. The Causal Interpretation of DAGs

There are two basic rules for causally interpreting a DAG G with vertices V.

1. There is a directed edge in the DAG from A to B if and only if A is a direct cause of B, relative to V. (We will take direct cause relative to a set of variables as a primitive term here. The inferences that are made under the causal interpretation do not depend upon the definition of cause, but rather depend upon some axiomatic connections between cause and probability stated in the next subsection. See Sosa and Tooley, 1993, for discussions of the definition of cause.)

2. Every random variable that is a direct cause (relative to V) of a pair of variables in V is itself in V.

Under the causal interpretation, G of Figure 1 implies that the set of direct causes of CP in V is $\{PE\}$, the set of direct causes of PE in V is $\{Sex\}$, and there are no direct causes of Sex in V.

DAGs do not represent feedback, reversibility, logical relationships, interunit causation, or certain kinds of mixtures. See Spirtes (1995) and Koster (1996) for a discussion of feedback.

5.1. Causal Markov Assumption

The two different interpretations of DAGs can be connected by the following causal Markov assumption: If $G = \langle V, E \rangle$ is a DAG that describes the causal structure in a population X, then the joint distribution $P(V)$ in X satisfies the local directed Markov condition for G. In the example of Figure 1, the causal Markov assumption implies that Sex is independent of CP given PE.

Probability distributions for the vertices of causal DAGs in which each vertex is a function of its parents in the DAG plus an independent error term satisfy the causal Markov assumption. The warrant for the conditions lies in this fact, and in the history of human experience with systems that we can largely control or manipulate. Electrical devices, mechanical devices, and chemical devices all satisfy the condition. Large areas of science and engineering—from auto mechanics to chemical kinetics to digital circuit design—would be impossible without using the principles to diagnose failures and infer mechanisms. An instance of the causal Markov assumption is used in randomized experiments. A more complete discussion of the justification of the causal Markov assumption and putative counterexamples is given in Spirtes et al. (1993).

5.2. Predicting the Effects of an Action

It is possible to use a DAG given only a probabilistic interpretation to calculate a conditional probability, for example, $P(CP = 0|PE = 1)$ or $P(Sex = 0|PE = 1)$. The calculation of these quantities depends only upon the joint probability distribution, and is not dependent upon the causal relations between the variables. In the Sewell and Shah (1968) data, $P(CP = 0|PE = 1) = 0.5724$ and $P(Sex = 0|PE = 1) = 0.5428$.

In contrast, it is not possible to calculate the effects of adopting a new policy using only the probabilistic interpretation of a DAG; it is necessary to use the causal interpretation. Suppose, for example, one contemplated adopting a policy of increasing $P(PE = 1)$ via some method whose only direct effect is on PE (in which case the manipulation is called an ideal manipulation). What are the values of $P(CP = 0)$ and $P(Sex = 0)$ in this hypothetical population?

In this hypothetical population, the joint probability $P(Sex, PE, CP)$ is different than the joint probability in the actual population. Let us distinguish these two joint probability distributions by using $P_{Unman(PE)}(Sex, PE, CP)$ to refer to the joint probability in the real world, and $P_{Man(PE)}(Sex, PE, CP)$ to refer to the joint probability in the hypothetical world where the intervention to increase parental encouragement has taken place. It is clear that if the manipulation is successful then $P_{Unman(PE)}(Sex, PE, CP) \neq P_{Man(PE)}(Sex, PE, CP)$.

If more parents encourage their children to go to college, using common-sense intuitions we expect that $P_{Man(PE)}(CP = 0) \neq P_{Unman(PE)}(CP = 0)$, but that $P_{Man(PE)}(Sex = 0) = P_{Unman(PE)}(Sex = 0)$. There is nothing about the probability distribution by itself to indicate why some of the manipulated probabilities are different than their unmanipulated counterparts, and others are not. The intuition that $P_{Man(PE)}(CP = 0) \neq P_{Unman(PE)}(CP = 0)$ is based upon the intuition that PE causes CP; the intuition that $P_{Man(PE)}(Sex = 0) = P_{Unman(PE)}(Sex = 0)$ is based upon the intuition that CP does not cause Sex. Calculating the effects of manipulating a variable requires knowing the causal relations among the variables.

One way to formalize these intuitions is to represent the effect of an ideal manipulation by introducing a new policy variable representing the effect of the ideal manipulation, with a directed edge from the policy variable to the variable being manipulated, as in Figure 2.

In this case, $P_{Unman(PE)}(Sex, PE, CP) = P(Sex, PE, CP|Policy = Off)$ and $P_{Man(PE)}(Sex, PE, CP) = P(Sex, PE, CP|Policy = On)$.

It follows from this representation and the causal Markov assumption that whenever a policy variable for manipulating X is entailed by the graph to be independent of Y given Z, then $P_{Unman(X)}(Y|Z) = P_{Man(X)}(Y|Z)$. Hence

$$P_{Man(PE)}(Sex, PE, CP) =$$

$$P_{Man(PE)}(Sex) \times P_{Man(PE)}(PE|Sex) \times P_{Man(PE)}(CP|PE) =$$

$$P_{Unman(PE)}(Sex) \times P_{Man(PE)}(PE|Sex) \times P_{Unman(PE)}(CP|PE).$$

It follows from this factorization of $P_{Man(PE)}(Sex, PE, CP)$ that $P_{Man(PE)}(CP = 0) \neq P_{Unman(PE)}(CP = 0)$, but that $P_{Man(PE)}(Sex = 0) = P_{Unman(PE)}(Sex = 0)$.

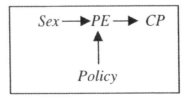

Figure 2 Representation of manipulation of *PE*

In general, if G is a causal graph $\langle V, E \rangle$ that describes the causal structures of a population, and there is an ideal manipulation of $V \in V$ to $P_{Unman(PE)}[V|Parents(V)]$ then

$$P_{Man(V)}(V) = P_{Man(V)}[V|Parents(V)] \times \prod_{X \in V \setminus V} P_{Unman(V)}[X|Parents(X)].$$

The quantities in this formula can be estimated from the data if the causal DAG is completely known and all of the variables in it are measured; this is generally not a realistic assumption. Spirtes et al. (1993) considers the case where the causal graph is only partially known, Pearl (1995) considers the case where some of the variables are unmeasured, and Pearl and Robins (1995) consider the case of sequential ideal manipulations. Robins (1986) considers some of the same issues in a nongraphical framework.

6. Examples

Bayesian networks used as classification tools have been successfully used for medical diagnosis in the Pathfinder system (Heckerman et al., 1992), for providing intelligent help in Lumière (Horvitz et al., 1998), in computer vision (Levitt et al., 1993), and for information retrieval (Fung and Favaro, 1995). For a list of other applications see Jensen (1996).

A number of Bayesian networks under their causal interpretation are described in Spirtes et al. (1993), including an analysis of causes of Spartina grass biomass, the causes of mathematical marks, and causes of whether or not students plan to go to college.

7. Further Reading

A variety of different kinds of graphs have been used to describe probability distributions: these include directed graphs, undirected graphs, chain graphs, influence diagrams, summary graphs, and partial ancestral graphs. Each of them associates a graph with a set of probability distributions that share certain conditional independence relations specified by the graph. General introductions to graphical models can be found in Lauritzen (1996). Pearl (1986) and Jensen (1996) give introductions to the use of graphical models in expert systems. Spirtes et al. (1993) is a comprehensive description of the use of directed graphs for performing causal inferences. Heckerman (1996) and Buntine (1996) are articles that provide general overviews of construction of graphical models. Influence diagrams, which are a modification of directed acyclic graphs that include representations of utilities and possible decisions, as well as representations of probability distributions, can be used to help solve the computational problem of finding the best action (see Schacter, 1986).

The use of directed graphs to represent both causal theories and probability distributions dates back to Wright's path analysis (Wright, 1934) and was subsequently applied via the structural equation modeling literature to economics and social science (Wold, 1954; Blalock, 1971). More general theories of directed graphical models were subsequently developed in Wermuth and Lauritzen (1983) and Pearl (1988). The use of directed graphs in expert systems was pioneered in Pearl (1988) and Lauritzen and Spiegelhalter (1988). The use of directed graphs to calculate the effects of adopting a particular policy is due to Spirtes et al. (1993), although similar rules are given in a nongraphical context in Strotz and Wold (1960) and Robins (1986).

Useful programs for building and using graphical models include HUGIN (Andersen et al., 1989), Bugs (Gilks et al., 1994), BIFROST (Højsgaard and Thiesson, 1995), and TETRAD II (Scheines et al., 1994; Chapter 24.4.1).

The proceedings of the Uncertainty in Artificial Intelligence, and Artificial Intelligence and Statistics meetings contain many articles describing methods for using and constructing Bayesian networks.

References

Andersen, S., K. Olesen, F. Jensen, and F. Jensen. 1989. "HUGIN—a shell for building Bayesian belief universes for expert systems." In *Proceedings of the Eleventh Conference on Uncertainty in Artificial*

Intelligence, edited by P. Besnard and S. Hanks, pp. 1080–1085. San Mateo: CA: Morgan Kaufmann Publishers, Inc.

Balke, A. and J. Pearl 1994. "Universal formulas for treatment effects from noncompliance data." In *Lifetime Data: Models in Reliability and Survival Analysis*, edited by N. Jewell, A. Kimber, M. Lee, and G. Whitmore, pp. 39–43. Dordrecht, Netherlands: Kluwer Academic Publishers.

Blalock, H. (ed). 1971. *Causal Models in the Social Sciences*. Chicago, IL: Aldine-Atheston.

Bollen, K. 1989. *Structural Equations with Latent Variables*. New York: Wiley.

Buntine, W. 1996. "A guide to the literature on learning graphical models." *IEEE Trans. Knowledge Data Engng* **8**: 195–210.

Darroch, J., S. Lauritzen, and T. Speed. 1980. "Markov fields and log-linear models for contingency tables." *Ann. Stat.* **8**: 522–539.

Dawid, P. 1992. "Applications of a general propagation algorithm for probabilistic expert systems." *Stat. Comput.* **2**: 25–36.

Cooper, G. 1990. "Computational complexity of probabilistic inference using Bayesian belief networks." *Artificial Intell.* **42**: 393–405.

Fung, R. and B. Favero. 1995. "Applying Bayesian networks to information retrieval." *Commun. ACM* **38**: 42–48.

Gilks, W., A. Thomas, and D. Spiegelhalter. 1994. "A language and a program for complex Bayesian modeling." *The Statistician* **43**: 169–178.

Heckerman, D. 1996. "A tutorial on learning with Bayesian networks." Microsoft Research Technical Report MSR-95-06. This is also available on the Web at http://www.research.microsoft.com/research/dtg/heckerma/heckerma.html.

Heckerman, D., E. Horvitz, and B. Nathwani. 1992. "Towards normative expert systems: Part I. The Pathfinder project." *Meth. Inform. Med.* **31**: 90–105.

Højsgaard, S. and B. Thiesson. 1995. "BIFROST—Block recursive model induced from relevant knowledge, observations and statistical techniques." *Comput. Stat. Data Anal.* **19**: 155–175.

Horvitz, E., J. Breese, D. Heckerman, D. Hovel, and K. Rommelse. 1998. "The Lumière project: Bayesian user modeling for inferring the goals and needs of software users." In *Proceedings of the Fourteenth Conference on Uncertainty in Artificial Intelligence*, edited by G. Cooper and S. Moral, pp. 256–265. San Francisco, CA: Morgan Kaufmann.

Howard, R. and J. Matheson. 1981. "Influence diagrams." In *Readings on the Principles and Applications of Decision Analysis*, edited by R. Howard and J. Matheson, **II**: 721–762. Menlo Park, CA: Strategic Decisions Group.

Jaakkola, T. and M. Jordan. 1996. "Computing upper and lower bounds on likelihoods in intractable networks." In *Proceedings of the Twelfth Conference on Uncertainty in Artificial Intelligence*, edited by F. Jensen and E. Horvitz, pp. 330–348. Portland, OR: Morgan Kauffman.

Jensen, F. 1996. *An Introduction to Bayesian Networks*. London: University College London Press.

Jensen, F., S. Lauritzen and K. Olesen. 1990. "Approximations in Bayesian belief universes for knowledge based systems." Technical Report. Aalborg, Denmark: Institute of Electronic Systems.

Koster, J. 1996. "Markov properties of non-recursive causal models." *Ann. Stat.* **24**: 2148–2177.

Lauritzen, S. 1996. *Graphical Models*. Oxford, England: Clarendon Press.

Lauritzen, S., A. Dawid, B. Larsen, and H. Leimer. 1990. "Independence properties of directed Markov fields." *Networks* **20**: 491–505.

Lauritzen, S. and D. Spiegelhalter. 1988. "Local computations with probabilities on graphical structures and their applications to expert systems." *J. R. Stat. Soc. B* **50**: 157–224.

Levitt, T., M. Hedgcock, J. Dye, S. Hohnston, V. Shadle, and D. Vosky. 1993. "Bayesian inference for model-based segmentation of computed radiographs of the hand." *Artificial Intell. Med.* **5**: 365–387.

Pearl, J. 1986. "Fusion, propagation, and structuring in belief networks." *Artificial Intell.* **29**: 241–288.

Pearl, J. 1988. *Probabilistic Reasoning in Intelligent Systems*. San Mateo, CA: Morgan Kaufman.

Pearl, J. 1995. "Causal diagrams for empirical research." *Biometrika* **82**: 669–710.

Pearl, J. and J. Robins. 1995. "Probabilistic evaluation of sequential plans from causal models with hidden variables." In *Eleventh Conference on Uncertainty in Artificial Intelligence*, edited by P. Besnard and S. Hanks, pp. 444–453. San Francisco, CA: Morgan Kaufmann.

Robins, J. 1986. "A new approach to causal inference in mortality studies with sustained exposure results." *Math. Modelling* **7**: 1393–1512.

Saul, L., T. Jaakkola, and M. Jordan. 1996. "Mean field theory for sigmoid belief networks." *J. Artificial Intell. Res.* **4**: 61–76.

Sewell, W. and V. Shah. 1968. "Social class, parental encouragement, and educational aspirations." *Am. J. Sociol.* **73**: 559–572.

Schacter, R. 1986. "Evaluating influence diagrams." *Oper. Res.* **34**: 871–882.

Scheines, R., P. Spirtes, C. Glymour, and C. Meek. 1994. *TETRAD II: Tools for Causal Modeling*. Hillsdale, NJ: Lawrence Erlbaum.

Smyth, P., D. Heckerman, and M. Jordan. 1997. "Probabilistic independence networks for hidden Markov probability models." *Neural Comput.* **9**: 221–270.

Sosa, E. and M. Tooley. (eds). 1993. *Causation*. Oxford: Oxford University Press.

Spiegelhalter, D. and S. Lauritzen. 1990. "Sequential updating of conditional probabilities on directed graphical structures." *Networks* **20**: 579–605.

Spirtes, P., C. Glymour, and R. Scheines. 1993. *Causation, Prediction, and Search*. New York: Springer-Verlag.

Spirtes, P. 1995. "Directed cyclic graphical representation of feedback models." In *Proceedings of the Eleventh Conference on Uncertainty in Artificial Intelligence*, edited by P. Besnard and S. Hanks, pp. 491–498. San Mateo, CA: Morgan Kaufmann Publishers, Inc.

Strotz, R. and H. Wold. 1960. "Recursive versus nonrecursive systems: an attempt at synthesis." *Econometrica* **28**: 417–427.

Wermuth, N. and S. Lauritzen. 1983. "Graphical and recursive models for contingency tables." *Biometrika* **72**: 537–552.

Wold, H. 1954. "Causality and econometrics." *Econometrica* **22**: 162–177.

Wright, S. 1921. "Correlation and causation." *J. Agric. Res.* **20**: 557–585.

Wright, S. 1934. "The method of path coefficients." *Ann. Math. Stat.* **5**: 161–215.

16.6.2 Mining for Probabilistic Networks

Peter L. Spirtes

ABSTRACT This article provides an overview of how to handle uncertainty about which Bayesian network to use for calculating the effect of an ideal manipulation or a classification. The Bayesian approach to handling uncertainty is to put a prior distribution over all of the Bayesian networks and their parameters, and then use this to calculate a posterior distribution over the quantity of interest. This is in general computationally infeasible, due to the huge number of different Bayesian networks over a given set of variables. Other approaches approximate the Bayesian answer using Monte Carlo Markov chain algorithms, or Bayesian model averaging, where all Bayesian networks except for a few good Bayesian networks are ignored in order to simplify the calculations. The latter approach requires searching among the vast space of Bayesian networks for the good Bayesian networks. Several methods for scoring Bayesian networks, and several search algorithms are described. It is shown how the problems of equivalent models and latent variables complicate both searching and scoring. Finally, it is shown how searching over equivalence classes of Bayesian networks, instead of searching over Bayesian networks can simplify both scoring and search.

1. Introduction

Chapter 16.6.1 discussed how to use a given Bayesian network either to calculate the effect of an ideal manipulation or as a classifier. This section discusses how to handle uncertainty about which Bayesian network to use for calculating the effect of an ideal manipulation or a classification.

Consider again the Sewell and Shah (1968) data set described in Chapter 16.6.1. Suppose that G_1 of Figure 1 below is the true causal graph, and the problem is to calculate the effect of an ideal manipulation of *PE* on *CP*. For the sake of simplicity, the possibility of unmeasured common causes of measured variables will be postponed until Section 8. Figure 1 contains 5 directed acyclic graphs (DAGs), all of which can be parameterized to produce P(*Sex, PE, CP*) as given in Table 1. G_1 and G_2 make the same prediction about the effect on *CP* of an ideal manipulation of *PE* that sets $P(PE = 1) = 1$ (i.e., $P(CP = 0)$ becomes 0.5724), and G_3, G_4, and G_5, make the same prediction about the effect of an ideal manipulation of *PE* on *CP* (i.e., no effect).

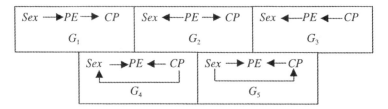

Figure 1 Five DAG models of Sewell and Shah (1968) data

Since the different DAGs predict different effects of an ideal manipulation of PE on CP, if there is uncertainty about which DAG is correct, how should the effect of an ideal manipulation of PE on CP be calculated? An analogous question arises for calculating conditional probabilities.

2. Bayesian Approach to Model Uncertainty

Let G be the space of DAGs over a set of given variables, I be an ideal manipulation of some variable in the DAGs, and D be the observed data. The Bayesian approach to calculating the effect of an intervention is via the formula

$$P(I|D) = \sum_{k=1}^{K} P(I|G_k, D)P(G_k|D),\tag{1}$$

where

$$P(G_k|D) = \frac{P(D|G_k)P(G_k)}{\sum_{k=1}^{K} P(D|G_k)P(G_k)}\tag{2}$$

and

$$P(D|G_k) = \int P(D|\theta, G_k)P(\theta|G_k)\,d\theta.\tag{3}$$

θ is the vector of parameters for DAG G_k, $P(\theta|G_k)$ is the prior probability of the parameters given G_k, and $P(D|\theta, G_k)$ is the likelihood of the data for DAG G_k with parameters θ.

This approach explicitly takes into account the uncertainty over which DAG G_k is correct. Unfortunately, the number of DAGs grows superexponentially with the number of variables in the DAG so in many cases the number of terms in (1) is astronomically large. If DAGs with unobserved variables are allowed the number of terms in (1) is even larger, and there are often no closed-form formulas for (3). See Heckerman et al. (1994) for details.

2.1. Monte Carlo Markov Chain

The posterior distribution over the effect of an ideal intervention I can be approximated by Monte Carlo Markov chain model composition methods. Let G be a set of DAGs. An aperiodic irreducible Markov chain $\{G(t), t = 1 \ldots N\}$ whose state space is G and which has an equilibrium distribution $P(G_k|D)$ is constructed. It follows under weak assumptions that for any function $g(G_k)$ defined on each $G \in G$

$$\frac{1}{N}\sum_{t=1}^{N} g(G(t))$$

converges to the expected value of $g(G)$ with probability 1. To compute $P(I|D)$, $g(G_k)$ can be set to $P(I|G_k, D)$. See Madigan and York (1995) for details.

One problem with this approach is that the sequence may take a long time to approach the expected value, and it is not possible to tell when the sample average is near the population expected value.

2.2. Bayesian Model Averaging

Another approach to solving the computational problem associated with (1) is to reduce the number of terms in (1) by including only good models in the sum. The question that will be considered next is how it is possible to judge from the data whether a model is good or not. See also Madigan and Raftery (1994).

3. Scoring DAGs

The relative posterior $P(G_1|D)/P(G_2|D)$ can be used to compare two models. Cooper and Herskovits (1992) gave a closed form formula for comparing two DAGs with discrete variables.

It is possible to score a DAG G_1 by comparing the extent to which the set of conditional independence relations entailed by G_1 matches the set of conditional independence relations judged to hold in the population (as judged by, e.g., a hypothesis test; see Spirtes et al., 1993, for details).

There are a variety of scores for DAGs that trade off how simple the DAG is with how likely the DAG makes the data. These include the Bayes Information Criterion (BIC), which is equal to $\log L_G(\theta) - 1/2 \dim(G) \log(n)$, where G is a DAG, $L_G(\theta)$ is the likelihood of the data evaluated at the maximum likelihood estimate θ of the parameters θ, and n is the sample size (Schwartz, 1978). Under suitable assumptions, BIC is asymptotically an $O(1)$ approximation of the posterior of G (see Lauritzen, 1996, for a list of other related scores, and references).

There are parameterizations of DAG G_5 of Figure 1 that lead to joint probability distributions that satisfy the local directed Markov condition for G_1. In those cases in which a distribution P satisfies the local directed Markov condition for G, and some conditional independence relation is true of P that is not entailed by G, say that P is unfaithful to G; otherwise P is faithful to G. Any distribution P that satisfies the local directed Markov condition for both G_1 and G_5 is unfaithful to G_5.

If G_1 is selected on the basis of its greater simplicity, but G_5 were the correct causal DAG, then the inference of the effect of the ideal manipulation is incorrect even in the large sample limit. In order for the true causal DAG to receive a score no lower than any other DAG, it has to be assumed that if the population distribution satisfies the local directed Markov condition for G_1, then it was not generated by G_5. A general simplicity assumption that entails this is:

Causal Faithfulness Assumption: *If a distribution P is generated by DAG G, then P is faithful to G.*

For discrete variables, or multivariate Gaussian variables, any prior over the parameters that is absolutely continuous with the Lebesgue measure entails that violations of the Faithfulness Assumption are measure 0. Assuming the causal Markov and causal Faithfulness Assumptions, if G is the true causal DAG, then in the large sample limit with probability 1 no other DAG receives a higher BIC score than G. However, there might be false causal DAGs that receive BIC scores equal to the true causal DAG.

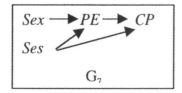

Figure 2

4. The Problem of Equivalent DAGs

For a variety of interesting kinds of scores, including BIC, G_1, G_2, and G_3 receive the same score for every data set. Hence they are BIC-score equivalent. Moreover, G_1, G_2, and G_3 entail the same set of conditional independence constraints—hence they are conditional independence equivalent. BIC and related scores will not help select which of these three DAGs is the true causal DAG. If the goal is to classify, then the fact that their BIC scores are equal does not matter, because each of the DAGs classifies in the same way; so an arbitrary choice from among the three DAGs can be made. However, if the goal is to predict the effects of an ideal intervention, then the equal BIC scores of the three DAGs does matter because the different DAGs make different predictions about the effects of an ideal manipulation. This leaves several possibilities for making causal inferences.

One approach would be to average the predictions about the effects of an ideal manipulation made by each of the DAGs in the conditional independence equivalence class (as in Bayesian model averaging). Unfortunately, in many cases, this posterior would have a very large variance.

A second approach would be to use domain knowledge to eliminate some of the alternatives. Sometimes a partial time order allows a reliable conclusion about the effects of an ideal manipulation of PE on CP to be drawn. For example, given that Sex occurs before PE, and that the only conditional independence in the joint distribution is that CP is independent of Sex given PE, and the causal Markov and causal Faithfulness Assumption, in the large sample limit with probability 1, any DAG with the highest score has no edge between Sex and PE, and does have an edge $PE \rightarrow CP$ (see Cooper, 1997). This information allows the effect of an ideal manipulation of PE on CP to be calculated.

A third approach is possible in some cases. Although in the example of Figure 1 the members of the conditional independence equivalence class with the highest score disagree about the effects of an ideal manipulation of PE on CP, there are other cases where all the members of the conditional independence class with the highest score do agree.

For example, the conditional independence equivalence class of G_7 contains only G_7, and hence in this case, the problem of BIC score equivalent DAGs making different predictions does not exist. Even when the conditional independence equivalence class contains more than one DAG, there are cases in which all of the DAGs still make the same prediction about the effect of a particular ideal intervention.

A pattern is a graphical object containing a mixture of directed and undirected edges that compactly represents an entire conditional independence equivalence class of DAGs, as well as representing the edges that all of the members of the equivalence class have in common (Pearl and Verma, 1991; Spirtes et al., 1993). This allows the calculation of the effect of an ideal manipulation from a pattern, rather than a DAG, in some cases.

5. Search

Since the number of DAGs grows exponentially to the number of vertices, it is completely impractical to do an exhaustive search of the space of DAGs.

5.1. Searching the Space of DAGs

A number of different kinds of searches take a current best DAG G, examine all of the one-edge changes that can be made to G (either deletions, additions, or reversals that do not introduce cycles), and assign scores to each of the changes.

A greedy search always chooses the change that most increases the score, and terminates when no change increases the score. This produces incorrect results in some cases, where a local maximum is found instead of a global maximum.

Solutions to the problem of local maxima include greedy search with restarts, and simulated annealing. In best-first search, the space of DAGs is searched using a heuristic that determines which is the next most promising DAG to examine. See Heckerman (1996) for brief descriptions of these searches. Other searches are described in Dai et al. (1997), Wedelin (1993), and Sebastiani and Ramoni (1998).

5.2. Searching the Space of Patterns

Without domain background assumptions, it is generally not possible to tell from the data which of the different DAGs represented by a pattern is the true causal DAG. If the goal is to calculate the effect of an ideal manipulation the proper output of a search algorithm is a pattern (assuming there are no latent common causes).

Moreover, searching the space of patterns, rather than the space of DAGs, has several advantages. The space of patterns is smaller than the space of DAGs and certain kinds of local maxima that occur in DAGs (due to the BIC score-equivalence of some DAGs) do not occur with patterns.

Spirtes and Meek (1995) and Chickering (1995) describe greedy search of the space of patterns.

The PC algorithm (Spirtes and Glymour, 1991; Spirtes et al., 1993) uses a sequence of conditional independence tests together with optional background knowledge to construct a pattern. It attempts to construct a pattern that entails all and only the conditional independence relations judged to hold in the population. If the true causal DAG is sparse (no variable has a large number of parents) it is able to construct a pattern using only a small number of conditional independence tests. Assuming causal Markov and faithfulness, in the large sample limit, with probability 1, the output is a pattern that represents the conditional independence equivalence class of the true causal DAG. If it is assumed the true causal DAG is sparse then the number of tests performed grows polynomially with the number of variables. If the true causal DAG is sparse, the output patterns are both more reliable and more informative (there are fewer possible alternative DAGs represented by the output pattern.)

6. Latent Variable DAGs

Adding latent variable DAGs to a search increases the difficulty of search in a number of ways. It is currently not clear what concept of simplicity should be used for latent variable DAGs, nor how they should be scored (Geiger and Meek, 1998). Calculating the maximum likelihood estimates of the parameters is much more difficult than in the nonlatent case, and generally there is no closed form expression for doing so. The posterior distribution of DAGs is much more computationally expensive to calculate. The search space is infinite if one allows no limit to the number of latents, and structuring the search is more difficult.

However, time order and the causal Markov and Faithfulness Assumptions do make consistent estimation of some ideal interventions possible. For example, even when there may be latent variables, given that *Sex* occurs before *PE*, the only conditional independence in the marginal distribution over *CP*, *PE*, and *Sex* is that *CP* is independent of *Sex* given *PE*, and the causal Markov and causal Faithfulness Assumptions, in the large sample limit with probability 1, the DAG with the highest score has no edge between *Sex* and *PE*, and does have a directed path from *PE* to *CP* (see Cooper, 1997; and Spirtes et al., 1993).

In addition, the PC algorithm can be generalized to the FCI algorithm (Spirtes et al., 1993), which in the large sample limit with probability 1 constructs the conditional independence equivalence class over the margin of the observed variables of the true causal DAG, assuming causal Markov and causal Faithfulness, even when latent variables (or sample selection bias) may be present. In the worst case, the algorithm is exponential in the number of variables. (The FCI algorithm is implemented in TETRAD II; see http://hss.cmu.edu/html/departments/philosophy/TETRAD/tetrad.html; see Chapter 24.4.1.)

Other searches over latent variable DAGs are described in Friedman (1998), Thiesson et al. (1998), and Geiger and Meek (1998). Spirtes et al. (1996) describe a greedy search over conditional independence equivalence classes of latent variable DAGs.

7. Examples

More extensive discussions of the results of searching for causal DAGs to fit the Sewell and Shah college plans data are given in Spirtes et al. (1993) and Heckerman (1996). In general, it is difficult to evaluate the results of a search for a set of DAGs that contains the true causal DAG, because the true causal DAG is not known. There are a few cases where some features of the output of such searches have received some independent confirmation. These include causal models of the biomass of Spartina grass (Spirtes et al., 1993), satellite calibration (Waldemark and Norqvist, 1995), and prediction of college retention (Druzdzel and Glymour, 1994). Other applications include studying mechanisms in plant biology (Shipley, 1995, 1997). Finding better tests of the overall reliability of causal search methods remains an important problem.

References

Buntine, W. 1996. "A guide to the literature on learning graphical models." *IEEE Trans. Knowledge Data Engng* **8**: 195–210.

Chickering, D., D. Geiger, and D. Heckerman. 1995. "Learning Bayesian networks: search methods and experimental results." In *Proceedings of the Fifth Conference on Artificial Intelligence and Statistics*, pp. 112–128. Fort Lauderdale, FL: Society for Artificial Intelligence in Statistics.

Chickering, D. 1995. "Learning equivalence classes of Bayesian-network structures." In *Proceedings of the Twelfth Conference on Uncertainty in Artificial Intelligence*, edited by F. Jensen and E. Horvitz, pp. 150–157. Portland, OR: Morgan Kauffman.

Cooper, G. 1995. "Causal discovery from data in the presence of selection bias." In *Preliminary Papers of the Fifth International Workshop on Artificial Intelligence and Statistics*, pp. 140–150. Fort Launderdale, FL. January 5–7.

Cooper, G. 1997. "A simple constraint-based algorithm for efficiently mining observational databases for causal relationships." *J. Data Mining Knowledge Discovery* **1**: 203–224.

Cooper, G. and E Herskovits. 1992. "A Bayesian method for the induction of probabilistic networks from data." *Machine Learning* **9**: 309–347.

Dai, H., K. Korb, C. Wallace, and X. Wu. 1997. "A study of causal discovery with weak links and small samples." *Fifteenth International Joint Conference on Artificial Intelligence*, Nagoya, Japan, 23–29 August, 1997.

Druzdzel, M. and C. Glymour. 1994. "Application of the TETRAD II program to the study of student retention in U.S. colleges." In *Proceedings of the AAAI-94 Workshop on Knowledge Discovery in Databases (KDD-94)*, pp. 419–430. Seattle.

Friedman, N. 1998. "The Bayesian structural EM algorithm." In *Proceedings of the Fourteenth Conference on Uncertainty in Artificial Intelligence*, edited by G. Cooper and S. Moral, pp. 129–138. San Francisco, CA: Morgan Kaufmann.

Geiger, D. and C. Meek. 1998. "Graphical models and exponential families." In *Proceedings of the Fourteenth Conference on Uncertainty in Artificial Intelligence*, edited by G. Cooper and S. Moral, pp. 156–165. San Francisco, CA: Morgan Kaufmann.

Heckerman, D., D. Geiger, and D. Chickering. 1994. "Learning Bayesian networks: the combination of knowledge and statistical data." In *Proceedings of the Tenth Conference on Uncertainty in Artificial Intelligence*, edited by R. de Mantaras and D. Poole, pp. 293–301. San Mateo, CA: Morgan Kaufmann.

Korf, R. 1993. "Linear-space best-first search." *Artificial Intell.* **62**: 41–78.

Madigan, D. and A. Raftery. 1994. "Model selection and accounting for model uncertainty using Occam's window." *J. Am. Stat. Assoc.* **89**: 1535–1546.

Madigan, D. and J. York. 1995. "Bayesian graphical models for discrete data." *Int. Stat. Rev.* **63**: 215–232.

Pearl, J. and T. Verma. 1991. "A theory of inferred causation." In *Principles of Knowledge Representation and Reasoning: Proceedings of the Second International Conference*. San Mateo, CA: Morgan Kaufmann.

Schwartz, G. 1978. "Estimating the dimension of a model." *Ann. Stat.* **6**: 461–464.

Sebastiani, P. and M. Ramoni. 1998. "Induction of graphical models from incomplete samples." In *Proceedings of the Thirteenth Conference of the International Association for Statistical Computing (COMPSTAT-98), Bristol, UK.*

Sewell, W. and V. Shah. 1968. "Social class, parental encouragement, and educational aspirations." *Am. J. Sociol.* **73**: 559–572.

Shipley, B. 1995. "Structured interspecific determinants of specific leaf are in 34 species of hebaceous angiosperms." *Functional Ecol.* **9**: 312−319.

Shipley, B. 1997. "A quantitative interspecific model of functional coordination involving foliar nitrogen, stomatal regulation and photosynthetic capacity in a wetland flora." *Am. Naturalist* **149**: 1113−1138.

Spirtes, P. and C. Glymour. 1991. "An algorithm for fast recovery of sparse causal graphs." *Soc. Sci. Comput. Rev.* **9**: 62−72.

Spirtes, P. and C. Meek. 1995. "Learning Bayesian networks with discrete variables from data." In *Proceedings of The First International Conference on Knowledge Discovery and Data Mining*, edited by U. Fayyad and R. Uthurusamy, pp. 294−299. AAAI Press.

Spirtes, P., T. Richardson, and C. Meek. 1996. "Heuristic greedy search algorithms for latent variable models." In *Proceedings of the Sixth International Workshop on Artificial Intelligence and Statistics*. Fort Lauderdale, FL, January 4−7, 1997, pp. 481−488.

Thiesson, B., C. Meek, D. Chickering, and D. Heckerman. 1998. "Learning mixtures of DAG models." In *Proceedings of the Fourteenth Conference on Uncertainty in Artificial Intelligence*, edited by G. Cooper and S. Moral, pp. 504−513. San Francisco, CA: Morgan Kaufmann.

Waldemark J. and P. Norqvist. 1995. "In-flight calibration of satellite ion composition data using artificial intelligence methods." Manuscript. Department of Applied Physics and Electronics. Sweden: Umea University, S-90187 Umea.

Wedelin, D. 1993. "Efficient algorithms for probabilistic inference, combinatorial optimization, and the discovery of causal structure from data." Unpublished Ph.D. diss. University of Gothenburg.

Further Reading

Spirtes et al. (1993), Heckerman (1996), and Buntine (1996) provide general overviews of search methods and the underlying assumptions and problems. The proceedings of the Uncertainty in Artificial Intelligence, and Artificial Intelligence and Statistics meetings contain many articles describing different search methods.

Information about a number of programs implementing either automatic discovery procedures, or environments that aid uses in constructing Bayesian networks, including BAYDA 1.0, Bayesian Knowledge Discoverer 1.0, Belief Network Constructor, Microsoft MSBN, AT-Sigma Data Chopper, BMR, Hugin, Strategist, and TETRAD II can be found at http://www.kdnuggets.com/.

16.7 Spatial Analysis

Martin Ester

ABSTRACT The number and the size of spatial databases are rapidly growing in applications such as geomarketing, astrophysics, and molecular biology. This is mainly due to the amazing progress in scientific instruments such as satellites with remote sensors or X-ray crystallography. While a lot of algorithms have been developed for knowledge discovery in relational databases, the field of knowledge discovery in spatial databases has only recently emerged (see Koperski et al., 1996, for an overview). The assumption of independently and identically distributed attributes, which is implicit in classical data mining, may not be applicable for spatial data. Attributes of the neighbors of some object of interest may have an influence on the object itself. For instance, a new industrial plant may pollute its neighborhood depending on the distance and on the major direction of the wind. In Section 1, we introduce spatial database systems and some basic operations for mining in such databases. Then, we discuss the major data mining tasks of spatial clustering (Section 2), spatial classification (Section 3), and spatial characterization (Section 4).

1. Basic Operations for Spatial Data Mining

A spatial database system (SDBS) is a database system (see Chapter 6) offering spatial data types in its data model and query language and supporting efficient implementation of these data types with their operations and queries (Gueting, 1994).

1.1. Spatial Data Types

Spatial objects may be either point objects or spatially extended objects such as lines, polygons, or polyhedrons. Spatial data types (Gueting, 1994) define classes of spatial objects with common attributes and operations. Spatial objects typically also have nonspatial attributes, that is, attributes such as name or population with a domain of strings or numbers. Sets of points can be used as a generic representation of spatial objects. The points are elements of a d-dimensional Euclidean vector space called *Points*, and spatial objects are elements of $P(Points)$. For instance, $d = 2$ for geographic objects such as cities or rivers and $d = 3$ for objects in biological applications such as proteins.

Typical operations on spatial data types include the calculation of the distance and the intersection for pairs of objects. Important query types are, for example, region queries, obtaining all objects intersecting a specified query region, and spatial joins yielding all pairs of objects satisfying some spatial predicate.

1.2. Neighborhood Relations

We distinguish three types of spatial neighborhood relations, which are introduced below: topological, distance, and direction relations.

Topological relations are those relations that are invariant under topological transformations, that is, they are preserved if both objects are, for example, rotated, translated, or scaled simultaneously. The topological relations between two objects A and B are derived from the nine intersections of the interiors, the boundaries, and the complements of both A and B with each other (Egenhofer, 1991). In the case of two-dimensional objects without holes, there are eight different topological relations.

Distance relations are those relations comparing the distance of two objects with a given constant using one of the arithmetic predicates $<$, $>$, or $=$.

Unlike distance relations and some of the topological relations, direction relations are not symmetric. Therefore, we distinguish between the source object and the destination object of a direction relation. The direction relation of two spatially extended objects may be define (Papadias and Sellis, 1993) based on one representative point of the source object (e.g., its center) and on all points of the destination object.

Let A and B be two-dimensional spatial objects and let rep(A) denote the representative point of A. The following are examples of direction relations that can be defined for A and B:

$$B \text{ northeast } A \text{ iff } \forall b \in B : b_x \text{tf} = \}Pi2\}5rep(A)_x \wedge b_y \text{tf} = \}Pi2\}5rep(A)_y$$

$$B \text{ northwest } A \text{ iff } \forall b \in B : b_x \leqslant rep(A)_x \wedge b_y \text{tf} = \}Pi2\}5rep(A)_y$$

Figure 1 illustrates some topological as well as distance and direction relations for two-dimensional spatial objects.

1.3. Neighborhood Graphs and Their Operations

Based on spatial neighborhood relations, Ester et al. (2000) define the concepts of neighborhood graphs and neighborhood paths for knowledge discovery in spatial databases.

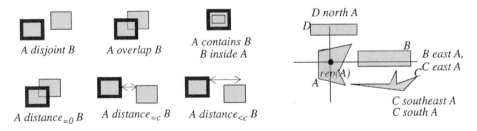

Figure 1 Sample neighborhood relations

Graphs are used as an abstract representation allowing a uniform treatment of the different types of neighborhood relations.

Let *neighbor* be a neighborhood relation and $DB \subseteq P(\text{Points})$ be a database of objects. A neighborhood graph with aspect to *neighbor* and *DB*, denoted by

$$G^{DB}_{neighbor},$$

is a directed graph (N, E) with a set of nodes N and a set of edges $E \subseteq N \times N$, where node presents one object in *DB* and two nodes n_1 and $n_2 \in N$ are connected via some edge of E iff n_1 *neighbor* n_2 holds. A sequence of nodes $[n_1, n_2, ..., n_k]$, $n_i \in N, 1 \leqslant i \leqslant k$, is called a neighborhood path iff $(n_i, n_{i+1}) \in E$ holds for all $1 \leqslant i < k$. n_1 is called the source and n_k is called the destination of the neighborhood path. The number k of nodes is called the length of the neighborhood path.

Several basic operations are defined on neighborhood graphs and paths (Ester et al., 2000). We only sketch the two major operations. The operation neighbors (graph, object, pred) returns the set of all object o connected to object by a single edge of graph and satisfying the conditions expressed by the predicate pred.

The operation extensions (graph, paths, max, filter) returns the set of all neighborhood paths in graph extending one of the elements of paths to a length of max edges. All objects on these extended paths must satisfy the predicate filter, which expresses further constraints on the paths to be created. Filtering is very important for the computational complexity of data mining algorithms operating on sets of paths because the number of all paths in a neighborhood graph tends to become very large. For instance, the filter starlike requires that the direction of a path p may not be generalized by an extending edge (n_k, n_{k+1}), that is, the direction of the edge (n_k, n_{k+1}) has to specialize the direction of p. For instance, a path with direction northeast may only be extended by a node of an edge with direction northeast but not by an edge with direction north or east.

1.4. Efficient DBMS Support

In order to speed up query processing, many spatial index structures have been developed to restrict the search to the relevant part of the space (see Gueting, 1994, for a survey). For instance, an *R*-tree (Guttmann, 1984; see Figure 2) manages spatial objects such as polygons or polyhedrons by using minimum bounding boxes (BB) as approximations. An entry of an R-tree node consists of one BB and a pointer to the exact geometry (for leaf nodes, so-called data nodes) or of one BB and a pointer to a child node (for interior nodes, so-called directory nodes). Each BB covers all spatial objects in the subtree referenced by the corresponding pointer. To answer a region query, starting from the root, the set of all BBs intersecting the

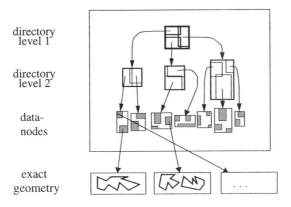

directory
level 1

directory
level 2

data-
nodes

exact
geometry

Figure 2 Sample R-tree for two-dimensional data

query region is determined and then their referenced child nodes are searched until the data nodes are reached.

Spatial operations such as the intersection test on two polygons tend to be very expensive. Therefore, the idea of a join index is to maintain a precomputed structure containing all pairs of objects satisfying the join predicate. A distance associated join index (Lu and Han, 1992), consists of tuples of the form (object$_1$, object$_2$, distance) for each pair of database objects.

Ester et al. (2000) introduces the more general technique of neighborhood indices. Let DB be a set of spatial objects and let D be a direction relation and T be a topological relation. Then the neighborhood index for DB with maximum distance max, denoted by I_{max}^{DB}, is defined as follows:

$$I_{max}^{DB} = \{(O_1, O_2, \text{dist}, D, T) \mid O_1, O_2 \in DB,$$

$$O_1 \ \text{distance}_{=\text{dist}} \ O_2 \wedge \text{dist} \leqslant \max \wedge O_2 \, D \, O_1 \wedge O_2 \, T \, O_1\}.$$

The critical distance of a neighborhood relation r is the maximum possible distance for a pair of objects O_1 and O_2 satisfying $O_1 r O_2$. A neighborhood index with a maximum distance of max is applicable for a neighborhood graph with relation r if the critical distance of r does not exceed max.

2. Spatial Clustering

Clustering (see Chapter 16.5) is the task of grouping the objects of a database into meaningful subclasses (that is, clusters) so that the members of a cluster are as similar as possible whereas the members of different clusters differ as much as possible from each other. Applications of clustering in spatial databases are, for example, the detection of seismic faults by grouping the entries of an earthquake catalog or the creation of thematic maps in geographic information systems by clustering feature spaces.

2.1. k-Medoid Algorithms

k-Medoid clustering algorithms (Kaufmann and Rousseeuw, 1990) construct a partition of a database DB into a set of k clusters, where k is an input parameter. Each cluster is represented by a medoid, that is, one of its objects located near its center, and each database object is assigned to the cluster of the closest medoid. The basic *k*-medoid algorithm PAM (partitioning around medoids; Kaufmann and Rousseeuw, 1990) starts from an initial set of medoids and iteratively replaces one of the medoids by one of the nonmedoids as long as the total distance of the resulting clustering, that is, the sum of the distances of all objects from their respective medoid, is reduced.

Ng and Han (1994) propose the *k*-medoid clustering algorithm, CLARANS (Clustering Large Applications based on RANdomized Search), with a new heuristic search strategy. The key idea is not to consider all possible replacements of one medoid by one nonmedoid and then select the optimal one, but to perform the first replacement that improves the quality of the clustering (i.e., reduces its total distance). The clustering obtained after performing a single replacement is called a neighbor of the current clustering. The number of neighbors tried is restricted by a parameter provided by the user (maxneigbor) and the selection of these neighbors is random. Each iteration of CLARANS yields a local optimum, that is, a clustering for which no neighbor with a better quality was found. The parameter numlocal allows the user to define the number of these local optima to be maintained by the search.

A performance evaluation (Ng and Han, 1994) demonstrates that CLARANS is significantly more efficient than the well-known *k*-medoid algorithms (Kaufmann and Rousseeuw, 1990), but it is still too inefficient to be applied to large databases of more than several thousand objects. Therefore, several techniques exploiting the capabilities of index structures have been developed to speed up CLARANS and similar algorithms, which are discussed in the next section.

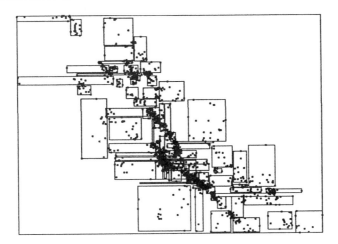

Figure 3 Data node structure of a sample R-tree

2.2. Exploiting Index Structures

Ester et al. (1995) propose to select a relatively small number of representatives from the database and to apply the clustering algorithm only to these representatives. Their method called focusing on representatives exploits the clustering capabilities of a spatial index structure, for example, an R-tree. The clustering strategy of the R-tree, which minimizes the overlap between directory BBs, yields a set of BBs for the data nodes truly reflecting the distribution of the database objects (see Figure 3). From each leaf node of an R-tree, one or several representatives are selected as input for a clustering algorithm such as CLARANS. Experimental results (Ester et al., 1995) show that the efficiency is improved by a very large factor whereas the clustering quality decreases only slightly when comparing CLARANS with and without focusing on representatives.

Zhang et al. (1996) present the clustering method BIRCH (Balanced Iterative Reducing and Clustering using Hierarchies), which is based on a highly specialized tree structure for the purpose of clustering BIRCH incrementally computes so-called clustering features:

$$CF = \left(n, \sum_{l=1}^{n} \vec{x}_i, \sum_{i=1}^{n} \vec{x}_i^2 \right)$$

consisting of the number of points, the vector representing the linear sum, and the scalar product of all points in the cluster. The CF-values are sufficient for computing information about subclusters like centroid, radius, and diameter and constitute an efficient storage method since they summarize information about subclusters instead of storing all points.

The clustering features are organized in a balanced tree with branching factor B and a threshold T (see Figure 4). A nonleaf node represents a cluster consisting of all the CF-values contained in its subtree. A leaf node has to contain at most L entries and the diameter of each entry in a leaf node has to be less than T.

In the first phase, BIRCH performs a linear scan of all data points and builds a CF-tree. A point is inserted by inserting the corresponding CF-value into the closest leaf of the tree. If an entry in the leaf can absorb the new point without violating the threshold condition, then the CF-values for this entry are updated, otherwise a new entry in the leaf node is created. In an optional phase 2, the CF-tree can be further reduced until a desired number of leaf nodes is reached. In phase 3 an arbitrary clustering algorithm (e.g., CLARANS) is used to cluster the CF-values stored in the leaf nodes of the CF-tree.

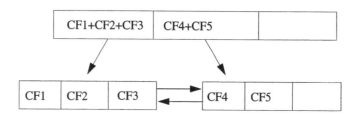

Figure 4 Sample CF-tree

2.3. Single-Scan Algorithms

The basic idea of single-scan algorithm is to group neighboring objects of the database into clusters based on a local cluster condition thus performing only one scan through the database. Single-scan clustering algorithms are very efficient if the neighbors operation is efficiently supported by the spatial DBS, that is, by a spatial index structure or by a neighborhood index.

The cluster condition of GDBSCAN (generalized density-based spatial clustering of applications with noise; Sander et al., 1998) is density-based: for example, for each point of a cluster the neighborhood of a given radius (*Eps*) has to contain at least a minimum number of points (*MinPts*), that is, the density in the neighborhood has to exceed some threshold. GDBSCAN starts with an arbitrary object *p* and retrieves all objects density-reachable from *p* with respect to *Eps* and *MinPts*. This procedure is iteratively applied to each object *p* that has not yet been classified.

This cluster condition can be generalized in the following ways (Sander et al., 1998): First, any neighborhood relation can be used if it is symmetric and reflexive. A distance-based neighborhood is a natural notion for point objects, but it is not clear how to apply it for the clustering of spatially extended objects such as a set of polygons of considerably differing sizes. Neighborhood relations such as intersects or meets are more appropriate in such cases. Second, instead of simply counting the objects in a neighborhood of an object, other measures to define the cardinality of that neighborhood can be used as well. For instance, one may sum up the values of some nonspatial attribute for all elements of the neighborhood.

3. Spatial Classification

The task of classification (see Chapter 16.1) is to assign an object to one class from a given set of classes based on the attribute values of this object. Classification rules are learned from a preclassified training set. The goal of spatial classification is to discover classification rules considering the spatial attributes and spatial relations as well as the nonspatial attributes of the database objects.

3.1. Basic Spatial Decision Tree Classifier

Ester et al. (2000) extends the ID3 algorithm (see Chapter 16.1.3) for spatial databases. It does not only consider the attributes of the object to be classified but also considers the attributes of neighboring objects, that is, objects connected by a neighborhood path starting from *o* with length limited by an input parameter max_length.

The algorithm presented in Ester et al. (2000) starts creating the set of all neighborhood paths having a length of max_length starting from one of the objects satisfying the nonspatial predicate sel. Then, the recursive procedure classify is called for this set of paths and the specified attribute determining the class membership of the database objects. The information gain of attribute attr is calculated with respect to the classification defined by attribute class _attr and the specified set of neighborhood paths. Figure 5 depicts a spatial decision tree discovered by algorithm discover-spatial-classification (Ester et al., 2000).

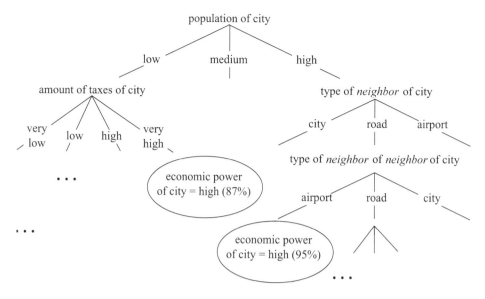

Figure 5 Sample spatial decision tree

3.2. *Improved Spatial Decision-Tree Classifier*

Koperski et al. (1998) follows the approach of Ester et al. (1997) and modifies it in several important ways. First, not all nonspatial attributes are used for learning classification rules. The relevant attributes are extracted by comparing the attribute values of the target objects with the attribute values of the nearest neighbors. Second, it does not consider the neighbors of target objects individually. Instead, so-called buffers are created around the target objects and non-spatial attribute values are aggregated over all objects contained in the buffer.

The determination of relevant attributes is based on the concepts of the nearest hit (the nearest neighbor belonging to the same class) and the nearest miss (the nearest neighbor belonging to a different class). If the nearest hit (miss) has the same (a different) attribute value than the target object, then the weight for the respective attribute is increased. Otherwise, the weight of this attribute is decreased. Finally, only attributes with weights larger than some predefined threshold are used for the classification.

Buffers represent areas around an object that have an impact on the class membership of this object. For instance, in the case of shopping malls a buffer may represent the area where its customers live or work. The relevant attribute values are aggregated over all objects of the buffer. The size of the buffer yielding the maximum information gain is chosen and this size is applied to compute the aggregates for all relevant attributes.

Koperski et al. (1998) present an experimental evaluation demonstrating that the proposed algorithm is both more efficient and yields decision trees with higher classification accuracy than the method of Ester et al. (1997).

4. Spatial Characterization

The task of characterization (see Chapter 16.2.2) is to find a compact description for a set of objects. For example, a bounding box may summarize the points of some cluster with respect to their location. In this section, we discuss the task of characterization in the context of spatial databases and introduce several methods.

4.1. Attribute Oriented Induction with Spatial Hierarchies

In Lu et al. (1993), algorithms for mining spatial characteristic rules are presented that use the method of attribute-oriented generalization. Attribute-oriented generalization of a relation is the process of replacing the attribute values of all objects by more general values, for one attribute at a time, until the number of objects becomes less than a specified threshold. The generalized values are taken from a predefined concept hierarchy that is assumed to be available for each of the attribute. A spatial concept hierarchy represents the successive merging of neighboring regions into larger regions.

Two alternative algorithms are proposed in Lu et al. (1993). The spatial-dominant-generalization algorithm merges spatial objects according to the spatial hierarchy obtaining a small number of regions. Then, a nonspatial description of each region is produced generalizing the relevant nonspatial attribute values of all objects of a region. The nonspatial-dominant-generalization algorithm starts with attribute-oriented generalization on the selected nonspatial attributes. Then, the neighboring objects with the same generalized attribute values are merged into a region.

4.2. Spatial Association Rules

Extending the concept of association rules (see Chapter 16.2.3), Koperski and Han (1995) introduce spatial association rules that describe associations between objects based on spatial neighborhood relations. For instance, a user may want to discover the spatial associations of towns in British Columbia with roads, waters, or boundaries having some specified support and confidence. Then, the following spatial association rule may be discovered:

$$\forall X \in DB \, \exists Y \in DB : is - a(X, town) \rightarrow close - to(X, Y) \land is - a(Y, water) \ (80\%).$$

This rule states that 80 percent of the selected towns are close to water, that is, the rule characterizes towns in British Columbia as generally being close to some lake, river, and so on.

Koperski and Han (1995) present an algorithm consisting of five steps. Step 2 and Step 4 involve spatial aspects of the objects and thus are examined in the following. Step 2 computes spatial joins of the object type to be characterized (such as town) with each of the other specified object types (such as water, road, boundary, or mine) using the neighborhood relation. For each of the candidates, in Step 4 the exact spatial relation, for example, overlap, is determined. The resulting set of candidates provides the input for the final step of rule generation, which uses a standard algorithm for mining association rules.

4.3. Proximity Relationship Analysis

Knorr and Ng (1996) study the task of discovering characteristic properties of clusters of points in terms of the features of the neighbors that are close to them. The goal is to explain a cluster by the existence of certain neighboring objects that may cause the existence of that cluster.

First an algorithm is presented that can efficiently find the top-k objects that are closest to a given cluster. The distance between a cluster C and some spatial object O is measured by the so-called aggregate proximity, denoted by ap(C, O), which is defined as:

$$ap(C, O) = \sum_{p \in C} dist(p, O).$$

Methods of computational geometry are applied to efficiently retrieve the k objects O that have the smallest ap(C, O) values without using a spatial index structure. In a multistep approach, the number of candidate objects is progressively reduced by using more and more exact approximations of the spatial objects: first the encompassing circle, then the bounding rectangle, and finally the convex hull is used as an approximation.

For each of the clusters of interest, the k closest objects are determined, and a second algorithm finds the commonalities of most of the clusters. For example, it is unlikely that a specific school will be close to all the clusters. However, each cluster may have some school that is near by. Therefore, concept generalization is used to find more common characteristic

Global trend 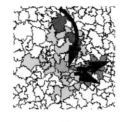 Local trends

➤ direction of decreasing attribute values

Figure 6 Sample spatial trends

features. Characteristic properties such as "most of the clusters of expensive houses are close to private schools and parks" may be discovered.

4.4. Spatial Trend Detection

Ester et al. (1998) define a spatial trend as a regular change of one or more nonspatial attributes when moving away from a given start object o. Neighborhood paths starting from o model the movement and a regression analysis is performed on the respective attribute values for the objects of a neighborhood path to describe the regularity of change. The distance from o is used as the independent variable and the difference of the attribute values is the dependent variable(s). The correlation of the observed attribute values with the values predicted by the regression function yields a measure of confidence for the discovered trend.

Ester et al. (1998) present two algorithms for discovering spatial trends. Algorithm globaltrend creates all neighborhood paths with source o of the same length simultaneously—starting with min-length and continuing until max-length. The regression is performed once for each of these sets of all paths of the same length. The existence of a global trend for a start object o indicates that if considering all objects on all paths starting from o the values for the specified attribute(s) in general tend to increase (decrease) with increasing distance. Algorithm local-trends performs a regression once for each of the neighborhood paths with length ⩾min-length and a path is only extended further if it has a significant trend. Figure 6 illustrates the global trend and some local trends for attribute average rent starting from the city of Regensburg discovered in a geographic information system on Bavaria.

References

Egenhofer, M. J. 1991. "Reasoning about binary topological relations." In *Proceedings of the Second International Symposium on Large Spatial Databases*. Berlin: Springer, pp. 143–160.

Ester, M., H.-P. Kriegel, and X. Xu. 1995. "Knowledge discovery in large spatial databases: focusing techniques for efficient class identification." In *Proceedings of the Fourth International Symposium on Large Spatial Databases Portland, ME*, Lecture Notes in Computer Science, **951**: 67–82. Berlin: Springer-Verlag.

Ester, M., H.-P. Kriegel, and J. Sander. 1997. "Spatial data mining: a database approach." In *Proceedings of the Fifth International Symposium on Large Spatial Databases*, pp. 47–66. Berlin: Springer.

Ester, M., A. Frommelt, H.-P. Kriegel, and J. Sander. 1998. "Algorithms for characterization and trend detection in spatial databases." In *Proceedings of the Fourth International Conference on Knowledge Discovery and Data Mining*. Menlo Park, CA: AAAI Press.

Ester, M., A. Frommelt, H.-P. Kriegel, and J. Sander. 2000. "Spatial data mining: database primitives, algorithms and efficient DBMS support." Special Issue on Integration of Data Mining with Database Technology. *Int. J. Data Mining and Knowledge Discovery*, **4** (2/3).

Gueting, R. H. 1994. "An introduction to spatial database systems." *The VLDB J.* **3(4)**: 357–399.

Guttmann, R. 1984. "R-trees: a dynamic index structure for spatial searching." In *Proceedings of the ACM SIGMOD Conference*. New York: ACM Press.

Kaufman, L. and P. J. Rousseeuw. 1990. *Finding Groups in Data: An Introduction to Cluster Analysis*. New York: John Wiley & Sons.

Koperski, K. and J. Han. 1995. "Discovery of spatial association rules in geographic information databases." In *Proceedings of the Fourth International Symposium on Large Spatial Databases (SSD'95)*, pp. 47–66. Berlin: Springer.

Koperski, K., J. Adhikary, and J. Han. 1996. "Spatial data mining: progress and challenges." In *SIGMOD'96 Workshop on Research Issues on Data Mining and Knowledge Discovery (DMKD'96)*. New York: ACM Press.

Koperski, K., J. Han, and N. Stefanovic. 1998. "An efficient two-step method for classification of spatial data." In *Proceedings of the International Symposium on Spatial Data Handling (SDH'98)*. Vancouver, Canada.

Knorr, E. M. and R. T. Ng. 1996. "Finding aggregate proximity relationships and commonalities in spatial data mining." *IEEE Trans. Knowledge and Data Engng* **8(6)**: 884–897.

Lu, W. and J. Han. 1992. "Distance-associated join indices for spatial range search." In *Proceedings of the Eighth International Conference on Data Engineering*, pp. 284–292. Los Alamitos, CA: IEEE Computer Society.

Lu, W., J. Han, and B. C. Ooi. 1993. "Discovery of general knowledge in large spatial databases." In *Proceedings of the Far East Workshop on Geographic Information Systems*, pp. 275–289. Singapore.

Ng, R. T. and J. Han. 1994. "Efficient and effective clustering methods for spatial data mining." In *Proceedings of the Twentieth International Conference on Very Large Databases*, pp. 144–155. San Mateo, CA: Morgan Kaufmann.

Papadias, D. and T. Sellis "The semantics of relations in 2D space using representative points: spatial indices." In *Spatial Information Theory: A Theoretical Basis for GIS, Lecture Notes in Computer Science*, edited by A. V. Frank and I. Csampari, **716**: 234–247. Berlin: Springer-Verlag.

Sander, J., M. Ester, H.-P. Kriegel, and X. Xu. 1998. "Density-based clustering in spatial databases: a new algorithm and its applications." *Int. J. Data Mining and Knowledge Discovery* **2(2)**: 169–194.

Zhang, T., R. Ramakrishnan, and M. Linvy. 1996. "BIRCH: an efficient data clustering method for very large databases." In *Proceedings of ACM SIGMOD International Conference on Management of Data*, pp. 103–114. New York: ACM Press.

16.8 Scalability

Foster Provost and Venkateswarlu Kolluri

ABSTRACT   One of the defining challenges for the KDD research community is scaling up data mining algorithms to mine very large collections of data. This article summarizes, categorizes, and compares existing work on scaling up data mining algorithms. In order to provide focus and specific details, we concentrate on algorithms that build decision trees and rule sets; the issues and techniques generalize to other types of data mining. We discuss the important issues related to scaling up and highlight similarities among scaling techniques by categorizing them into three main approaches. We describe in detail the characteristic features of each category, using specific examples as needed, and we compare and contrast different constituent techniques.

1. Introduction

With the proliferation of large-scale data repositories, the data mining community is faced with the challenge of developing scalable techniques that can be used to extract useful information. This article summarizes, categorizes, and compares various existing methods for scaling up inductive learning methods to large data. It focuses on issues related to scalable algorithms, and it does not consider issues of efficient file system design, storage design, network interface design, or problem formulation, except as they relate to the design of inductive algorithms. Although we focus primarily on algorithms that build feature vector–based classifiers (rather than those that include structural or relational terms) in the form of decision trees or rule sets, the categorization and lessons apply more generally.

The most commonly cited reason for scaling up is that increasing the size of the training set often increases the accuracy of learned classification models (Catlett, 1991b). In many cases, the degradation in accuracy when learning from smaller samples stems from overfitting due to the need to allow the program to learn small disjuncts (Holte et al., 1989), elements of a class description that cover few data items, which in some domains together account for a large portion of the class description (Danyluk and Provost, 1993). In such domains, high accuracy depends on the ability to learn small disjuncts to account for these special cases.

Overfitting from small data sets also may be due to the existence of a large number of features describing the data. Having many features increases the size of the space of models. Searching through and evaluating more candidate models increases the likelihood that, by chance, the program will find a model that fits the data well (Jensen and Cohen, 1999), and thereby increases the need for larger example sets (Haussler, 1988).

Some data mining applications are concerned not with predictive modeling, but with the discovery of interesting knowledge from large databases. In such cases, increasing accuracy may not be a primary concern. However, scaling up may still be an issue. For example, the ability to learn small disjuncts well is of interest to scientists and business analysts, because small disjuncts often capture special cases that were previously unknown (the analysts often know the common cases).

2. What is Scaling Up?

For all its theoretical considerations, the issue of scaling up is inherently pragmatic. For scaling up learning algorithms, the issue is not as much one of speeding up a slow algorithm as one of turning an impracticable data mining task into a practicable one. The crucial issue is seldom how fast can one run on a certain problem, but instead how large a problem can one deal with. From the point of view of complexity analyses, for most scaling problems the limiting factor has been the number of data items (training examples). A large number of examples introduces potential problems with both time and space complexity. For time complexity, the appropriate algorithmic question is: what is the growth rate of the algorithm's run time as the number of examples increases? Also important is the number of attributes describing each example and the number of values for each attribute. As may be expected, time-complexity analyses do not tell the whole story. As the number of instances grows, certain space constraints become critical—most importantly, the absolute size of the main memory with which the computing platform is equipped.

It is important to consider that evaluating the effectiveness of a scaling technique becomes complicated if a degradation in the quality of the learning is permitted. For example, the vast majority of work on learning algorithms uses classification accuracy as the metric by which different algorithms are compared. In such cases, it is particularly useful to identify methods that can process a certain number of examples more efficiently without a substantial decrease in accuracy. More generally, one can think of scaling techniques as lossless or lossy. As we describe below, some scaling techniques make induction algorithms more efficient without changing the induced knowledge: efficiency is gained but no loss of information is incurred. In contrast, other techniques scale up by introducing approximations and heuristics: efficiency is gained, but there may be a loss in information. However, as with data compression, in certain cases the loss of information has little effect on the target application. Indeed, given the empirical nature of data mining research, it may be the case that more efficient heuristics actually induce better knowledge (Domingos, 1999).

3. Methods for Scaling Up

Many diverse techniques have been proposed and implemented for scaling up inductive algorithms. Figure 1 summarizes the general methods that make up each of three general approaches.

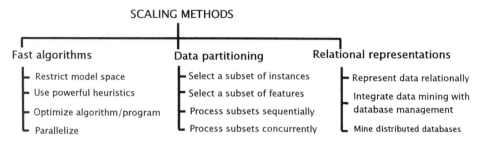

Figure 1 Techniques for scaling up learning

3.1. *Fast Algorithms*

The most straightforward approach to scaling up inductive learning is to produce more efficient algorithms or to increase the efficiency of existing algorithms. Fast algorithm approaches include a wide variety of algorithm design techniques for reducing asymptotic complexity, for optimizing the search and representation, for finding approximate solutions instead of exact solutions, or for taking advantage of a task's inherent parallelism. As shown in Figure 1, the set of techniques that falls under the category of fast algorithms can be broadly divided into four subcategories.

RESTRICTED MODEL SPACE

One approach to designing a fast learning algorithm is to restrict it to searching an easy model space. The clearest example of effective restricted model space algorithms are the long-lived and still viable linear-discriminant methods for learning classifiers (Duda and Hart, 1973). One-level decision trees, also known as decision stumps, and simple perceptrons have been shown to achieve high accuracy on many common benchmark databases (Shavlik et al., 1991; Iba and Langley, 1992). Also, because of their restricted model spaces, these simple learning algorithms can be trained very quickly (Haussler, 1988).

POWERFUL SEARCH HEURISTICS

Certainly, in some domains there is advantage to be gained with more complex models. The size and structure of the space of models, the size of the sample necessary to learn well, and the computational complexity of algorithms that search the space are intimately related. Generally, searching is harder for more complex models. (This is somewhat of an oversimplification. The interested reader should consult literature on computational learning theory; Haussler, 1988). However, several heuristics have proven effective for fast search of even very large spaces. For example, for a vast model space, it is unusual for learning algorithms to search the space directly (i.e., by generating many alternative models and choosing one). In most cases, a single model is built up by evaluating and composing components. Divide-and-conquer learners recursively partition the instance space until regions of roughly uniform class membership are obtained, whereas separate-and-conquer learners induce one rule at a time, removing the newly covered examples from the training set after each step. Designers of inductive algorithms have had much success with greedy, divide-and-conquer approaches to building class descriptions. In fact, the decision tree generator C4.5 (Quinlan, 1993), a successor to ID3 (Quinlan, 1986), has become a *de facto* standard for comparison in machine learning research, because it produces good classifiers very quickly (Lim et al., 2000).

In many situations, rule sets are preferred because of their modularity and increased comprehensibility (Catlett, 1991a). The most common technique for producing high accuracy rule sets, known as reduced-error pruning, is to grow rules via one algorithm or another, and then prune the rules in order to increase accuracy (Quinlan, 1987). First the training set is split into two subsets: a growing set and a pruning set. A concept description explaining all of the examples in the growing set is generated with a rule learning algorithm. The resulting concept is then generalized by deleting literals and clauses from the theory until any further deletion would result in a decrease of predictive accuracy measured on the pruning set. Reduced-error pruning generally does not scale well (Cohen, 1995; Domingos, 1996b), but significant speedups can be obtained by pruning each rule as it is learned and then applying a separate-and-conquer strategy based on the pruned rule (Fürnkranz and Widmer, 1994).

A different style of rule learning can be traced back to the search-based data mining program MetaDENDRAL (Buchanan et al., 1976; Buchanan and Feigenbaum, 1978). Examples of MetaDENDRAL-style rule learning include the Brute programs (Riddle et al., 1994; Segal and Etzioni, 1994a), PVM (Weiss et al., 1990), ITRULE (Smyth and Goodman, 1992), the RL programs (Clearwater and Provost, 1990; Provost and Buchanan, 1995; Fawcett and Provost, 1997), SE-trees (Rymon, 1993), and even Schlimmer's determination-learning algorithm (Schlimmer, 1993). These programs view rule learning as an explicit search of a straightforward rule space. The space of possible conjunctive rules is structured as a tree at the most general rule, that with no conditions, which covers all data trivially. The search operators specialize rules. In its most basic form, each successive level of the search specializes the rules with a single additional condition. To allow for massive searches of very large rule spaces, the search space is reduced with various forms of pruning (Provost et al., 1999b), both admissable (guaranteed not to discard a good rule) and heuristic. For example, consider a problem where rules are considered not to be interesting if they cover fewer than a predetermined number of examples (Buchanan and Feigenbaum, 1978). If a given rule does not exceed the threshold, neither will any of its specializations, and these can be eliminated from further consideration. Such admissable rule space pruning is guaranteed never to eliminate interesting rules from consideration, and can yield tremendous search efficiencies (Clearwater and Provost, 1990; Segal and Etzioni, 1994a; Webb, 1995). Alternatively, search-based data mining programs can use *heuristic* pruning. As a simple example, consider a beam search of the rule space. At each level of a breadth first search, each node is given a score based on a numeric interestingness criterion—which is to indicate the interestingness of this path in the search space, presumably because it will eventually lead to an interesting rule. Instead of expanding all nodes, the beam search expands the best w nodes, where w is predetermined. Such heuristic pruning methods can result in even greater efficiency gains, but may discard potentially interesting rules.

ALGORITHM/PROGRAMMING OPTIMIZATIONS
Optimization with efficient data structures (e.g., bit vectors, hash tables, binary search trees) and clever programming techniques complements the other methods of scaling up, and in practice often can give very large speedups. These optimizations differ from powerful search heuristics in that they concentrate on eliminating redundant or unnecessary computations; the models induced will not be affected. For example, when learning decision trees, repetitive sorting reduces the efficiency when dealing with numeric attributes. SLIQ (Mehta et al., 1996a) overcomes this problem by sorting the training data just once for each numeric attribute at the beginning of tree growth.

Domingos (1996b) explored ways to improve rule learning efficiency by not growing each rule to its full length in the first place. To avoid superfluous growth, each rule is evaluated in the context of the rule set currently held; doing so efficiently requires careful bookkeeping. As mentioned above, some of the rule space pruning techniques used in MetaDENDRAL-style rule learners can be guaranteed not to discard good rules (Clearwater and Provost, 1990; Segal and Etzioni, 1994b; Webb, 1995). Webb (1995) takes this idea even further, introducing techniques for dynamic search space restructuring to maximize the amount of search space removed with each pruning.

Most inductive algorithms load all data into main memory, and hence in practice are limited by the main memory size (otherwise virtual memory thrashing will render the inductive algorithms useless). An alternative is never to load all the data into the memory, instead accessing them on secondary storage as needed. Since secondary storage devices do not typically provide random access to data, algorithms must be designed to process data via sequential scans—as few as possible (Mehta et al., 1996b; Shafer et al., 1996).

A simple bookkeeping technique has been pointed out recently by several independent research groups. The main insight is that matching hypotheses against the data is not necessary at all: for most of the processing, statistics from which the results of matching can be inferred are sufficient. For example, the fundamental operation of rule-space search is the specialization of a hypothesis by adding conjuncts, namely, attribute-value pairs, and counting the matches of the resulting specializations against the training database. These counts are used to define statistics-based interestingness measures. Matching is also the central operation of other rule learning programs and of decision tree learning programs. Decision tree learning programs use the counts to compute interestingness values, using information-theoretic principles, to select among the candidate attributes at each step while growing the tree. Separating the generation of sufficient statistics from their use in the evaluation of hypotheses allows each to be treated separately—first using the data to populate the statistics data structure and then operating only on the data structure—which affords both optimized use of memory and improved run-time complexity (Aronis and Provost, 1997; John and Lent, 1997; Gehrke et al., 1998; Moore and Lee, 1998). A straightforward data structure to store such statistics is a contingency table of example counts for each attribute, indexed by attribute-value and class. Gehrke et al. (1998) provide a thorough treatment of the use of sufficient statistics to build decision trees when the size of the data set exceeds main memory.

PARALLELIZATION

Finally, algorithms can be fast because of parallelization. The process of inductive learning is decomposable at two levels, illustrated by two methods for parallel learning: search-space parallelization and parallel matching.

Search-space parallelization decomposes the search space such that different processors search different portions of the space in parallel (Cook and Holder, 1990), similar to the parallelization of other forms of heuristic search (Kumar and Rao, 1987; Rao and Kumar, 1987). For loosely coupled processors, this type of parallelization does not address the problem of very large data sets, because each processor will have to deal with all the data (or subsample, which we discuss below). However, search-space parallelization may take advantage of shared memory multiprocessors (Zaki et al., 1999).

Parallel learning has been more successful when the problem is decomposed at a lower level. Parallel matching relies on the fact that search for inductive learning is different from most other parallel searches. In inductive learning the cost of evaluating a node is very high, but is also highly decomposable. Nodes in the search space (e.g., partial rules or decision tree branches) are hypothesized and each is matched against many data to gather statistics. In the parallel matching approach, this computationally intensive matching process is farmed out, migrating the data set and matching routines to a parallel machine, while the main learning algorithm (the master) runs on a sequential front end (Lathrop et al., 1990; Provost and Aronis, 1996). Access to parallel hardware may not be a concern if the data are already resident in a data warehouse with a parallel infrastructure (Freitas and Lavington, 1996; Zaki, 1998).

3.2. Data Partitioning

The second general category of scaling techniques, data partitioning, can be subdivided based on whether data are partitioned into subsets of examples or subsets of features. In either case, a single sample may be taken, or multiple samples may be processed sequentially or concurrently.

Figure 2 depicts a general model showing the similarities among partitioned-data approaches. Systems using data partitioning approaches select one or more subsets $S_1, ..., S_n$ of the data based on a selection procedure. Learning algorithms $L_1, ..., L_n$ are run on the corresponding subsets, producing concept descriptions $C_1, ..., C_n$. Then the concept descriptions are processed by a combining procedure, which either selects from among the different concept descriptions $C_1, ..., C_n$ or combines them to produce a final concept description. The systems differ in the particular procedures used for selection and combining. They also differ in the

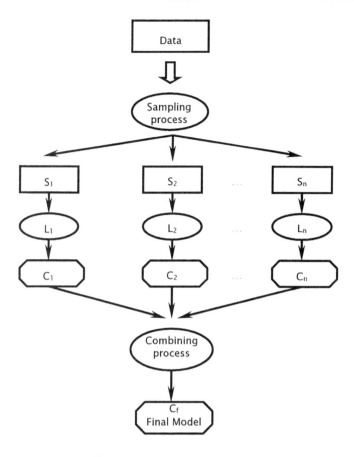

Figure 2 Learning using data partitioning

amount and style of interaction among the learning algorithms and learned concept descriptions.

SELECT A SUBSET OF THE INSTANCES

Sampling is a degenerate form of data partitioning: only a single subset is chosen. If sampling produces models with lower accuracy than otherwise, its usefulness for scaling up is questionable. On the other hand, if using sampling produces equivalent (or better) models, then sampling is an effective scaling mechanism.

For anyone wanting to mine a large data set, an important question is: must I process the whole thing? Or will sampling be effective? The answer is: it depends on the data set and the inductive algorithm. Just because one has a massive data set does not necessarily imply that one must mine it all. In practice, as the amount of data grows, the rate of increase in accuracy slows, forming the familiar learning curve. Whether sampling will be effective depends on how dramatically the rate of increase slows. Oates and Jensen (1997) studied decision tree induction for nineteen data sets, and looked specifically at the number of examples necessary before the learning curves reached a plateau, that is, when the accuracy estimate is within a certain tolerance of the maximum. They found that plateaus were reached quite soon. Provost et al. (1999a), explored efficient progressive sampling techniques, that is, using progressively larger samples as long as model accuracy improves. Such procedures reduce the need for users to know beforehand how many examples are necessary. Inductive algorithms can also sample actively based on intermediate results, as induction progresses. Catlett (1991a,b) and Musick et al. (1993) studied the active, tactical use of sampling to process large data sets efficiently.

SELECT A SUBSET OF THE FEATURES
In instance sampling, the rows of a data table are selected; in feature sampling, the columns are selected. The space trade-off is symmetric because the amount of space needed to store the table is the product of the number of rows and the number of columns.

The majority of the existing work on feature selection has not focused directly on scaling. Instead it has focused on the phenomenon that reducing the size of the feature set, when done well, can often increase the accuracy of the resultant class description. However, selecting a subset of features is such a common method for reducing problem size that it is often neglected in discussions of scaling. When setting up a learning problem, only a small set of the possibly relevant variables are chosen for representation. Sometimes this restriction is based on the data collection apparatus, but often it is based on knowledge of relevance.

An alternative approach is first to describe the problem with as many features as possible, and then to do inexpensive empirical studies to select a subset using, for example, statistical (Kaufmann and Michalski, 1996) or information-theoretic approaches (Wettschereck and Dietterich, 1995).

PROCESSING SUBSETS SEQUENTIALLY
Several efforts have addressed processing multiple samples sequentially and combining the results. For example, Fayyad et al. (1993) use a sequential independent multi-subset approach in which decision-tree learners are used to extract rule sets from multiple samples; the trees are converted to rules and a greedy covering algorithm is used to combine the rule sets, as shown in Figure 2.

When multiple subsets are being processed sequentially, it is possible to take advantage of knowledge learned in one iteration to guide learning in the next iteration. Model-guided instance selection, as shown in Figure 3(a), is an iterative, active sampling technique, with which C_i, the knowledge mined from sample S_i, helps to determine the next sample, S_{i+1}. Quinlan (1983) used a model-guided instance selection approach, called windowing; data that are misclassified by C_i are used to populate the next window, S_{i+1}.

Incremental batch learners (Clearwater et al., 1989; Provost and Buchanan, 1995; Domingos, 1996a) are hybrids of sampling and incremental learning. Class description C_i induced using a sample of instances S_i is given as prior knowledge to learning algorithm L_{i+1}, along with the next subset of samples S_{i+1}, as shown in Figure 3(b). The learning algorithm uses this sample S_{i+1} to evaluate the previous C_i, and uses C_i as a basis for building C_{i+1}. As with windowing, the combining procedure chooses C_n as the final concept description, where C_n is constructed across the n learning runs.

Sequential multisample techniques can process example sets that are too large for pure batch processing because of limits on main memory, as discussed above, leading to increased accuracy over simple sampling (Provost and Buchanan, 1995). They may also transform an algorithm whose run-time is superlinear in the size of the example set to a linear algorithm (Domingos, 1996a). Not unexpectedly, as with single subsets, sequential multisubset techniques may degrade classification accuracy as compared to learning from the entire data set at once, if that is possible.

All of these approaches incrementally process instance subsets. Similarly, feature subsets can be processed incrementally using a wrapper approach (Kohavi, 1995). Wrapper approaches run an underlying inductive algorithm within different contexts, in an attempt to maximize some criteria. By considering the problem of feature selection as a state space search, each state representing a subset of features whose goal is to find the state with the best performance measure, wrapper approaches can be used to repeatedly run an inductive algorithm using different sets of features to select the best set of features. Two classic methods are sequential forward selection and sequential

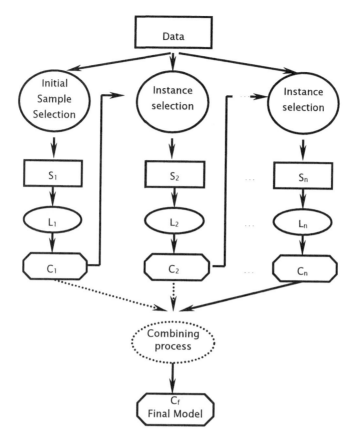

Figure 3(a) Sequential multisubset learning: model-guided instance selection

backward elimination (Devijver and Kittler, 1982). However, these wrapper approaches to feature selection (Kohavi, 1995) typically address increasing accuracy, rather than scaling up.

Provost and Buchanan (1992, 1995) discuss how a wrapper approach unifies the different multisubset scaling approaches (examples, features) with other policy choices that must be made (and remade) to focus a learning algorithm on a particular problem.

PROCESS SUBSETS CONCURRENTLY

To further increase efficiency, partitioned-data approaches can be parallelized by distributing the subsets to multiple processors, mining models in parallel, and then combining them. This approach differs from parallel matching (described above) in the degree of autonomy afforded the individual learners. Rather than simply parallelizing a subprocedure of an existing algorithm, and returning results to the master, these techniques are loosely coupled collections of otherwise independent algorithms. Recently this type of algorithm has been called *distributed data mining*, and was the subject of a KDD-98 workshop (Kargupta and Chan, 1998).

Referring back to Figure 3, concurrency precludes partitioned-data approaches where a prior concept description is needed as input to a subsequent learning stage, such as incremental batch learning. However, for independent multisubset approaches, as shown in Figure 2, the classification models, C_i, can be learned concurrently—even with different learning algorithms (Chan and Stolfo, 1996; Ali and Pazzani, 1996). Combining the different models C_i can take place as a sequential post-process, or can be parallelized (as by Kufrin,

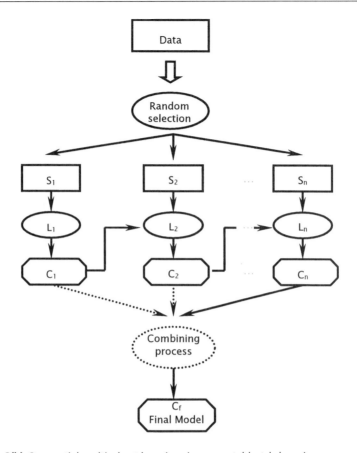

Figure 3(b) Sequential multisubset learning: incremental batch learning

1997). The final model can be generated as a hybrid of all models C_i. Alternatively, instead of combining all models into a hybrid model by composing pieces of the C_i, the individual C_i can be saved and the predictions made using these individual models can be combined (using a simple voting scheme, for example) to obtain the final prediction (Domingos, 1996a).

As above, with concurrent partitioned-data techniques, accuracy may be degraded as compared to running a single inductive algorithm with all the data. If the group of distributed learners cooperates to obtain a global view of the problem as depicted in Figure 4, it may be possible to guarantee that as a group they discover the same knowledge (Provost and Hennessy, 1996).

3.3. Relational Representations

Most existing inductive learning programs were not designed to handle very large data sets. In particular, the majority were designed under the assumption that the data set would be represented as a single, memory-resident table. Unfortunately, producing flat files from real-world, multitable, relational databases is fraught with problems. The flattening-out process can be quite time consuming, substantial storage space is needed, and keeping the flat files around leads to the problems that relational databases are designed to avoid (e.g., update and delete anomalies). Indeed, flattening may create, from otherwise manageable databases, data sets that can no longer fit in main memory. Also, flattening often demands choosing a subset of all the attributes that could be used to describe the data, which places an inflexible restriction on the unexpected discoveries that a KDD system may make.

Recently several techniques to mine relationally represented data have been proposed, which scale up either because the representation is more efficient, or because the data are stored on a fast database machine (although the latter has been questioned by Musick et al. (1993)).

MINING RELATIONAL DATA

A simple form of relational data—data with hierarchical, or tree-structured, attributes (Almuallim et al., 1995)—has received relatively much attention in the literature on inductive learning. The data compression afforded by tree-structured attributes can be substantial, especially with tall trees. Efficient mining with tree-structured attributes is treated in depth by Almuallim et al. (1995), and improvements are described by Aronis and Provost (1997). Tree-structured attributes allow the representation of a simple relation, the isa relation, between attribute-value pairs. Each such relation can be seen as a separate table in a relational database, as in, for example, a state/county table or a county/ZIP code table.

Mining general multitable, relational data is an obvious next step. The ability to handle multitable data not only allows practitioners to compress otherwise unwieldy flat files, it also creates possibilities for augmenting learning systems with more and more related knowledge. For each field of an example record, practitioners can consider whether additional tables of knowledge describing that field exist. This view unifies learning from relational databases with learning with large amounts of background knowledge. Parallel marker-passing techniques can be used to aid in augmenting inductive learners with large networks of relational background knowledge (Aronis and Provost, 1994).

The field of inductive logic programming (ILP; Muggleton, 1992) concentrates on mining data and knowledge expressed in a relational format. However, ILP addresses a harder problem than the type of mining we are considering. Specifically, not only are the data represented relationally, the results of the mining may also be represented relationally. Because learning relational descriptions is harder than learning propositional ones, relational algorithms are considerably slower than propositional ones, and the scaling problem is correspondingly harder. However, Blockeel et al. (1999) observe that "the full power of standard ILP is not used for most practical applications." Therefore, a general approach to speeding up learning with relational data is to avoid expensive but seldom used constructs. Aronis et al. (1996) investigate induction from feature vector-based data items linked to relational background knowledge. For the sake of efficiency, they purposely avoid n-ary and recursive relational terms, and limit the induced models to propositional concept descriptions. Blockeel et al. (1999) study an efficient subset of ILP known as learning from interpretations, and in particular, first- order-logic decision trees.

DATA MINING/DBMS INTEGRATION

For many applications, data are already stored in an efficient relational representation—a multitable relational database, most easily accessible via a commercial database management system (DBMS). Although many data mining systems access data stored in a commercial DBMS, most of these do not actually mine the relational data directly. Rather, they extract the data from the DBMS into a memory-resident flat file. Such approaches only take advantage of the DBMS's efficient data retrieval, not its efficient representation.

Relational data, stored in a commercial DBMS, can be mined directly by implementing the core data manipulation operations within the DBMS. As discussed in Section 3.1, the speed of inductive programs is often determined primarily by the speed of the matching or the gathering of sufficient statistics. If these operations can be cast as SQL requests for statistics (Agrawal and Shim, 1995, 1996; John and Lent, 1997; Sarawagi et al., 1998), a data mining program can avoid massive data uploads and problems due to main memory restrictions, and can take advantage of fast database machines optimized for query processing. In their proposal for a SQL interface protocol, John and Lent (1997) discuss how the basic operations for various types of data mining programs can be cast as SQL queries. However, Graefe et al. (1998) show that a straightforward implementation for deriving sufficient statistics from a SQL database (using select and union operators) results in unacceptably poor performance. This poor performance stems from the

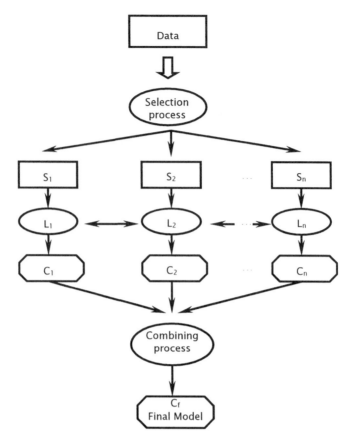

Figure 4 Cooperation among concurrent learners

manner in which the database system will implement the query; specifically, most database systems will implement a union query by performing a separate scan for each clause in the union. However, for deriving sufficient statistics the unions will be very similar. The authors propose to take advantage of this similarity by extending SQL to include a new operator (unpivot), which minimizes the number of scans required to produce sufficient statistics.

Sarawagi et al. (1998) discuss several alternatives for data mining/DBMS integration. Their focus is on mining association rules, but they illustrate principles that apply more generally. In particular, they point to several efforts to extend SQL to support mining operations, and they discuss expressing mining algorithms in SQL. Also, scaling can be extended further by making use of parallel database server technology to speed up data-intensive SQL operations (Freitas and Lavington, 1996).

DISTRIBUTED DATABASES

Enabling inductive programs to learn from multitable relational data makes the vast amount of data and background knowledge distributed across a local network, or scattered about the Internet available to data mining. For example, companies are interested in mining federations of similar data (Stolfo et al., 1997a), and digital library research is working to facilitate access to networked data and information (Fox et al., 1995). Along with the desire to take advantage of these collections comes the need to scale up to massive amounts of distributed data and background information. This scaling problem manifests all the issues discussed so far in this survey, plus some additional constraints and opportunities.

Not only do distributed data provide the opportunity for concurrent mining of different subsets, similar to the more straightforward uses of parallelism and data partitioning, distributed data may *require* distributed mining. Combining already-distributed databases may be out of the question for a variety of reasons. They may simply be too big to combine on a local system. The bandwidth of the communications channel may make combining databases infeasible, because it would take too long to download the data. Finally, privacy issues may prevent unrestricted access to the data. For any of these reasons, a database of interest may be accessible over the network, but transferring it may not be feasible. Stolfo et al. (1997a,b) present their approach and an implemented system, and discuss how privacy concerns restrict the federation of banking data.

Ribeiro et al. (1995) propose a method for performing knowledge discovery across multiple databases by using foreign key values to augment tables. Specifically, they propose tracing through multiple databases following the foreign keys, and learning individual knowledge segments for each database. The WoRLD system (Aronis et al., 1997) learns across multiple distributed databases spread across the network, using spreading activation techniques. These require only limited communication in order to pass sets of markers (implemented with SQL queries).

4. Conclusion

In summary, the many techniques for mining large data sets can be grouped into three main approaches: (i) choose or design a fast algorithm, (ii) mine a subset or multiple subsets of the data, and (iii) use a compact, relational representation. At a high level, these three approaches are independent and can be applied in combination. In fact, doing so may be necessary, as the size of available data sets continues to grow.

New ideas are constantly emerging that may cause us to adjust our classification of approaches. As just one example, recently DuMouchel and his coauthors introduced the notion of squashing large data sets (DuMouchel et al., 1999). Instead of selecting a subset of the existing data, the data are summarized statistically and a much smaller set of pseudodata points is generated based on the statistics. The synthetic data are a dense representation of the statistical regularities in the original data, and can be fed into traditional data mining programs. Besides illustrating that the characterization of approaches above may not be perfect, this example can also highlight its utility. If we expand our notion of sampling to include squashing, then we can infer that the techniques for processing multiple samples (sequentially or in parallel) may be beneficial when squashing alone is insufficient. Questions from other multi-sample techniques are relevant, for example, should the results of mining the first squashed sample influence subsequent squashing?

As KDD has gelled as a field of study, concentrating in part on mining very large data sets, the production of research results has accelerated. More comprehensive descriptions, analysis, and references can be found in the survey paper that this article summarizes (Provost and Kolluri, 1999). At the time of writing, the first approach (fast algorithm) has received considerably more attention than the latter two. However, this is changing. For example, distributed data mining was the topic of a recent workshop (Kargupta and Chan, 1998) and subsequent book (Kargupta and Chan, 2000). The growth of the volume of data available for mining shows no signs of slowing (and in fact is accelerating). Therefore, the scaling problem for KDD will only get more intense. It is likely that future systems for successful mining of large data will have to combine methods from all three high level categories.

ACKNOWLEDGMENTS

We are indebted to many, including John Aronis, Lars Asker, Bruce Buchanan, Jason Catlett, Pedro Domingos, Phil Chan, Doug Fisher, Dan Hennessy, David Jensen, Ronny Kohavi, Rich Segal, Sal Stolfo, and anonymous referees of previous papers, who have influenced our views of scaling up through many discussions.

This article is adapted from F. Provost and V. Kolluri, "A survey of methods for scaling up inductive learning algorithms," in *Data Mining and Knowledge Discovery*, 1999, **3(2)**: 131–169. Reprinted by permission of Kluwer Publishers.

References

Agrawal, R. and K. Shim. 1995. "Developing tightly-coupled applications on IBM DB2/CS relational database system: methodology and experience". Research Report RJ 10005(89094). IBM Corporation.

Agrawal, R. and K. Shim. 1996. "Developing tightly-coupled data mining applications on a relational database system." In *Proceedings of Second International Conference on Knowledge Discovery and Data Mining (KDD'96)*, pp. 287–290. Menlo Park, CA: AAAI Press.

Ali, K. M. and M. J. Pazzani. 1996. "Error reduction through learning multiple descriptions." *Machine Learning* **24(3)**: 173–202.

Almuallim, H., Y. Akiba, and S. Kaneda. 1995. "On handling tree-structure attributes in decision tree learning." In *Proceedings of the Twelfth International Conference on Machine Learning*. San Francisco, CA: Morgan Kaufmann.

Aronis, J. and F. Provost. 1994. "Efficiently constructing relational features from background knowledge for inductive machine learning." In *Working Notes of the AAAI-94 Workshop on Knowledge Discovery in Databases (KDD-94)*. Seattle.

Aronis, J. M. and F. J. Provost. 1997. "Increasing the efficiency of data mining algorithms with breadth-first marker propagation." In *Proceedings of the Third International Conference on Knowledge Discovery and Data Mining*, edited by D. Heckerman, H. Mannila, D. Pregibon, and R. Uthurusamy, pp. 119–122. Menlo Park, CA: AAAI Press.

Aronis, J., F. Provost, and B. Buchanan. 1996. "Exploiting background knowledge in automated discovery." In *Proceedings of the Second International Conference on Knowledge Discovery and Data Mining (KDD '96)*, pp. 355–358. Menlo Park, CA: AAAI Press.

Aronis, J. M., V. Kolluri, F. J. Provost, and B. G. Buchanan. 1997. "The WoRLD: knowledge discovery from multiple distributed databases." In *Proceedings of the Tenth International Florida Artificial Intelligence Research Symposium*, edited by D. D. Dankel, pp. 337–341. Menlo Park, CA: AAAI Press.

Blockeel, H., L. D. Raedt, N. Jacobs, and B. Demoen. 1999. "Scaling up inductive logic programming by learning from interpretations." *Data Mining and Knowledge Discovery* **3(1)**: 59–93.

Buchanan, B. and E. Feigenbaum. 1978. "DENDRAL and METADENDRAL: their applications dimensions." *Artificial Intell.* **11**: 5–24.

Buchanan, B. G., D. H. Smith, W. C. White, R. Gritter, E. A. Feigenbaum, J. Lederberg, and C. Djerassi. 1976. "Applications of artificial intelligence for chemical inference, XXII. Automatic rule formation in mass spectrometry by means of the meta-DENDRAL program." *J. Am. Chem. Soc.* **96**: 6168.

Catlett, J. 1991a. "Megainduction: a test flight." In *Proceedings of the Eighth International Workshop on Machine Learning*, pp. 596–599. San Francisco, CA: Morgan Kaufmann.

Catlett, J. 1991b. "Megainduction: machine learning on very large databases". Ph.D. diss. Sydney: University of Technology, School of Computer Science.

Chan, P. and S. Stolfo. 1996. "On the accuracy of meta-learning for scalable data mining." *J. Intell. Inform. Sys.* **8**: 5–28.

Clearwater, S., T. Cheng, H. Hirsh, and B. Buchanan. 1989. "Incremental batch learning." In *Proceedings of the Sixth International Workshop on Machine Learning*, pp. 366–370. San Francisco CA: Morgan Kaufmann.

Clearwater, S. H. and F. J. Provost. 1990. "RL4: a tool for knowledge-based induction." In *Proceedings of the Second International IEEE Conference on Tools for Artificial Intelligence*, edited by A. Dollas, W. T. Tasi, and N. G. Bourbakis, pp. 24–30. Los Alamitos, CA: IEEE Computer Society Press.

Cohen, W. W. 1995. "Fast effective rule induction." In *Proceedings of the Twelfth International Conference on Machine Learning*, pp. 115–123. San Francisco, CA: Morgan Kaufmann.

Cook, D. and L. Holder. 1990. "Accelerated learning on the connection machine." In *Proceedings of the Second International IEEE Conference on Tools for Artificial Intelligence*, pp. 366–370. San Francisco, CA: Morgan Kaufmann.

Danyluk, A. and F. Provost. 1993. "Small disjuncts in action: learning to diagnose errors in the telephone network local loop." In *Machine Learning: Proceedings of the Tenth International Conference*, edited by P. Utgoff, pp. 81–88. San Francisco, CA: Morgan Kaufmann.

Devijver, P. A. and J. Kittler. 1982. *Pattern Recognition: A Statistical Approach*. Upper Saddle River, NJ: Prentice Hall.

Domingos, P. 1996a. "Efficient specific-to-general rule induction." In *Proceedings of the Second International Conference on Knowledge Discovery and Data Mining (KDD'96)*, pp. 319–322. Menlo Park, CA: AAAI Press.

Domingos, P. 1996b. "Linear time rule induction." In *Proceedings of the Second International Conference on Knowledge Discovery and Data Mining (KDD'96)*, pp. 96–101. Menlo Park, CA: AAAI Press.

Domingos, P. 1999. "The role of Occam's razor in knowledge discovery." *Data Mining and Knowledge Discovery* **3(4)**: 409–425.

Duda, R. O. and P. E. Hart. 1973. *Pattern Classification and Scene Analysis*. New York: John Wiley.

DuMouchel, W., C. Volinsky, T. Johnson, C. Cortes, and D. Pregibon. 1999. "Squashing flat files flatter." In *Proceedings of The Fourth International Conference on Knowledge Discovery and Data Mining (KDD-97)*. Menlo Park, CA: AAAI Press.

Fawcett, T. and F. Provost. 1997. "Adaptive fraud detection." *Data Mining and Knowledge Discovery* **1(3)**: 291–316.

Fayyad, U., N. Weir, and S. Djorgovski. 1993. "SKICAT: a machine learning system for automated cataloging of large scale sky surveys." In *Proceedings of the Tenth International Conference on Machine Learning*. San Francisco, CA: Morgan Kaufmann.

Fox, E. A., R. M. Akscyn, R. Furuta, and J. Leggett. 1995. "Digital Libraries: Introduction." *Commun. ACM* **38(4)**: 22–28.

Freitas, A. and S. Lavington. 1996. "Using SQL primitives and parallel DB servers to speed up knowledge discovery in large relational databases." In *Cybernetics and Systems '96: Proceedings of the Thirteenth European Meeting on Cybernetics and Systems Research*, pp. 955–960. Vienna, Austria: Grobrialand Helscher.

Fürnkranz, J. and G. Widmer. 1994. "Incremental reduced error pruning." In *Proceedings of the Eleventh Annual Machine Learning Conference*. San Francisco, CA: Morgan Kaufmann.

Gehrke, J., R. Ramakrishnan, and V. Ganti. 1998. "RAINFOREST—a framework for fast decision tree construction of large data sets." In *Proceedings of the Twenty-Fourth International Conference on Very Large Data Bases*. New York: Morgan Kaufman.

Graefe, G., U. Fayyad, and S. Chaudhuri. 1998. "On the efficient gathering of sufficient statistics for classification of large SQL databases." In *Proceedings of the Second International Conference on Knowledge Discovery and Data-Mining*. Menlo Park, CA: AAAI Press.

Haussler, D. 1988. "Quantifying inductive bias: AI learning algorithms and Valiant's learning framework." *Artificial Intell.* **36**: 177–221.

Holte, R., L. Acker, and B. Porter. 1989. "Concept learning and the problem of small disjuncts." In *Proceedings of the Eleventh International Joint Conference on Artificial Intelligence*, pp. 813–818. San Francisco, CA: Morgan Kaufmann.

Iba, W. and P. Langley. 1992. "Induction of one-level decision trees." In *Proceedings of Ninth International Conference on Machine Learning*, pp. 233–240. San Francisco, CA: Morgan Kaufmann.

Jensen, D. and P. R. Cohen. 2000. "Multiple comparisons in induction algorithms." *Machine Learning*.

John, G. and B. Lent. 1997. "SIPping from the data firehose." In *Proceedings of the Third International Conference on Knowledge Discovery and Data Mining*, pp. 199–202. Menlo Park, CA: AAAI Press.

Kargupta, H. and P. Chan, P. 1998. KDD-98 workshop on distributed data mining. Available at http://www.eecs.wsu.edu/~hillol/kdd98ws.html.

Kargupta, H. and P. Chan. 2000. "Distributed and parallel knowledge discovery: a brief introduction." In *Advances in Distributed and Parallel Knowledge Discovery*, edited by H. Kargupta and P. Chan. Cambridge, MA: The MIT Press.

Kaufmann, K. and R. Michalski. 1996. "A method for reasoning with structured and continuous attributes in the INLEN-2 knowledge discovery system." In *Proceedings of the Second International Conference on Knowledge Discovery and Data Mining*, pp. 232–237. Menlo Park, CA: AAAI Press.

Kohavi, R. 1995. "Wrappers for performance enhancement and oblivious decision graphs." Ph.D. diss. Computer Science Department, Stanford University. STAN-CS-TR-95-1560. Available at ftp://starry.stanford.edu/pub/ronnyk/teza.ps.

Kufrin, R. 1997. "Generating C4.5 production rules in parallel." In *Proceedings of the Fourteenth National Conference on Artificial Intelligence (AAAI-97)*, pp. 565–670. Menlo Park, CA: AAAI Press.

Kumar, V. and V. Rao. 1987. "Parallel depth-first search. Part 2: analysis." *Int. J. Parallel Programming* **16**: 501–519.

Lathrop, R., T. Webster, T. Smith and P. Winston. 1990. "ARIEL: a massively parallel symbolic learning assistant for protein structure/function." In *AI at MIT: Expanding Frontiers*, edited by P. Winston and S. Shellard. Cambridge, MA: MIT Press.

Lim, T. J., W. Y. Loh, and Y. S. Shih. 2000. "A comparison of prediction accuracy, complexity, and training time of thirty-three old and new classification algorithms." *Machine Learning* **40**: 203–209. New York: Kluwer.

Mehta M., R. Agrawal and J. Rissanen. 1996a. "SLIQ: a fast scalable classifier for data mining." In *Proceedings of the Fifth International Conference on Extending Database Technology (EDBT)*, Heidelberg, Germany: Spinger Verlag.

Mehta, M., R. Agrawal, and J. Rissanen. 1996b. "Sliq: a fast scalable classifier for data mining." In *Proceedings of the Fifth International Conference on Extending Database Technology (EDBT)*. Avignon, France.

Moore, A. and M. Lee. 1998. "Cached sufficient statistics for efficient machine learning with large data sets." *J. Artificial Intell. Res.* **8**: 67–91.

Muggleton, S. 1992. *Inductive Logic Programming*, Volume 8. London: Academic Press, Ltd.

Musick, R., J. Catlett, and S. Russell. 1993. "Decision theoretic subsampling for induction on large databases." In *Proceedings of the Tenth International Conference on Machine Learning*, pp. 212–219. San Francisco, CA: Morgan Kaufmann.

Oates, T. and D. Jensen. 1997. "The effects of training set size on decision tree complexity." In *Proceedings of the Fourteenth International Conference on Machine Learning*, pp. 254–262. San Francisco, CA: Morgan Kaufmann.

Provost, F. J. and J. M. Aronis. 1996. "Scaling up inductive learning with massive parallelism." *Machine Learning* 23: 33–46.

Provost, F. and B. Buchanan. 1992. "Inductive policy." In *Proceedings of AAAI-92*, pp. 255–261. Menlo Park, CA: AAAI Press.

Provost, F. and B. Buchanan. 1995. "Inductive policy: the pragmatics of bias selection." *Machine Learning* 20: 35–61.

Provost, F. and D. Hennessy. 1996. "Scaling up: distributed machine learning with cooperation." In *Proceedings of the National Conference on Artificial Intelligence*. Menlo Park, CA: AAAI Press.

Provost, F. and V. Kolluri. 1999. "A survey of methods for scaling up inductive learning algorithms." *Data Mining and Knowledge Discovery* 3(2): 131–169.

Provost, F., T. Oates, and D. Jensen. 1999a. "Efficient progressive sampling." In *Proceedings of the Fifth International Conference on Knowledge Discovery and Data Mining*. San Diego, CA: ACM Press.

Provost, F. J., J. Aronis, and B. Buchanan. 1999b. "Rule-space search for knowledge-based discovery." Research Report IS 99-012. New York: New York University, Stern School of Business.

Quinlan, J. 1983. "Learning efficient classification procedures and their application to chess endgames." In *Machine Learning: an AI approach*, edited by R. C. J. Michalski and T. Mitchell. Los Altos, CA: Morgan Kaufmann.

Quinlan, J. R. 1986. "Induction of decision trees." *Machine Learning* 1: 81–106.

Quinlan, J. 1987. "Simplifying decision trees." *Int. J. Man-Machine Studies* 27: 221–234.

Quinlan, J. R. 1993. *C4.5 Programs for Machine Learning*. San Mateo, CA: Morgan Kaufmann.

Rao, V. and V. Kumar. 1987. "Parallel depth-first search. Part 1: Implementation." *Int. J. Parallel Programming* 16: 479–499.

Ribeiro, J., K. Kaufmann, and L. Kerschberg. 1995. "Knowledge discovery from multiple databases." In *Proceedings of The First International Conference on Knowledge Discovery and Data Mining (KDD-96)*, pp. 240–245. Menlo Park, CA: AAAI Press.

Riddle, P., R. Segal, and O. Etzioni. 1994. "Representation design and brute-force induction in a boeing manufacturing domain." *Appl. Artificial Intell.* 8: 125–147.

Rymon, R. 1993. "An SE-tree based characterization of the induction problem." In *Proceedings of the Tenth International Conference on Machine Learning*. San Francisco, CA: Morgan Kaufmann.

Sarawagi, A., S. Thomas, and R. Agrawal. 1998. "Integrating association rule mining with databases: alternatives and implications." In *Proceedings of the ACM SIGMOD International Conference on Management of Data*. pp. 343–354. New York: ACM Press.

Schlimmer, J. C. 1993. "Efficiently inducing determinations: a complete and systematic search algorithm that uses optimal pruning." In *Proceedings of the Tenth International Conference on Machine Learning*, edited by P. Utgoff, pp. 284–290. San Mateo, CA: Morgan Kaufmann.

Segal, R. and O. Etzioni. 1994a. "Learning decision lists using homogeneous rules." In *Proceedings of the Twelfth National Conference on Artificial Intelligence*, pp. 619–625. Menlo Park, CA: AAAI Press.

Segal, R. and O. Etzioni. 1994b. "Learning decision lists using homogenous rules." In *Proceedings of the Twelfth National Conference on Artificial Intelligence*, pp. 619–625. Seattle, WA: AAAI Press.

Shafer, J., R. Agrawal, and M. Mehta. 1996. "SPRINT: a scalable parallel classifier for data mining." In *Proceedings of the Twentysecond VLDB Conference*. Mumbai, India: Morgan Kaufmann.

Shavlik, J. W., R. J. Mooney, and G. G. Towell. 1991. "An experimental comparison of symbolic and connectionist learning algorithms." *Machine Learning* 6(2): 111–143.

Smyth, P. and R. Goodman. 1992. "An information theoretic approach to rule induction from databases." *IEEE Trans. Knowledge and Data Engng* 4(4): 301–316.

Stolfo, S., D. Fan, W. Lee, A. Prodromidis, and P. Chan. 1997a. "Credit card fraud detection using meta-learning: issues and initial results." In *Proceedings of the AAAI-97 Workshop on AI Approaches to Fraud Detection and Risk Management*, pp. 83–90. Menlo Park, CA: AAAI Press.

Stolfo, S., A. Prodromidis, S. Tselepis, D. Fan, W. Lee, and P. Chan. 1997b. "JAM: Java agents for meta-learning over distributed databases." In *Proceedings of the AAAI-97 Workshop on AI Approaches to Fraud Detection and Risk Management*, pp. 91–98. Menlo Park, CA: AAAI Press.

Webb, G. 1995. "OPUS: an efficient admissible algorithm for unordered search." *J. Artificial Intell. Res.* 3: 383–417.

Weiss, S. M., R. S. Galen, and P. V. Tadepalli. 1990. "Maximizing the predictive value of production rules." *Artificial Intell.* **45**: 47–71.

Wettschereck, D. and T. G. Dietterich. 1995. "An experimental comparison of the nearest-neighbor and nearest-hyperrectangle algorithms." *Machine Learning* **19(1)**: 5–28.

Zaki, M. 1998. "Scalable data mining for rules." Ph.D. diss, University of Rochester.

Zaki, M. J., C. Ho, and R. Agrawal. 1999. "Scalable parallel classification for data mining on shared memory multiprocessors." In *Proceedings of IEEE International Conference on Data Engineering*. Los Alamitos, CA: IEEE Computer Society Press.

16.9 Parallel Methods for Scaling Data Mining Algorithms to Large Data Sets

Robert Grossman and Yike Guo

ABSTRACT   In this article, we describe some approaches and specific techniques for scaling data mining algorithms to large data sets through parallel processing. We then analyze in more detail three core algorithms that can be scaled to large data sets: building decision trees, discovering association rules, and creating clusters.

1. Introduction

A fundamental challenge is to extend data mining to large data sets. In this article, we introduce some of the basic approaches and techniques that have proved successful and describe in some detail work on scaling three fundamental data mining algorithms: trees, clustering algorithms, and association rules.

Section 2 introduces computational models for working with large data sets. By "large" we mean data that does not fit into the memory of a single processor. Parallel RAM computational models describe algorithms that are distributed between several processors. Hierarchical memory computational models describe algorithms that require working with data both in memory and on disk. Parallel disk computational models describe algorithms in which data is distributed over several processors and disks.

Section 3 surveys some of the basic approaches to scaling data mining algorithms. The most basic approach is to manipulate the data until it fits into memory. Another fundamental technique is to use specialized data structures to work with data that is disk resident. We also describe techniques for distributing algorithms between several processors, precomputing various quantities, and intelligently reducing the amount of data.

Sections 4, 5, and 6 describe work on scaling tree-based algorithms, association rules, and clustering algorithms to large data sets.

2. Computational and Programming Models

In this section, we briefly describe some of the different computational and programming models that are used in high-performance and parallel computing. We begin by discussing the cost of computation. We describe four models: a RAM model, a parallel RAM model, a disk model, and a parallel disk model. Next, we describe two basic distinctions between the various programming models used in high-performance computing. The first distinction is whether the data itself is used to determine the parallelism (data parallelism) or whether the parallelism is determined explicitly by the programmer (task parallelism). The second distinction is how different processors communicate: this can be done with shared memory, with message passing, or with remote memory operations.

2.1. Computational Models

The standard model for measuring the complexity of an algorithm is the random access machine model (RAM Aho et al., 1974). A RAM model has a single processor with unlimited memory, which can store and access data with unit cost. With the RAM model, sorting N records has cost $O(N \log N)$.

Parallel computers exploit multiple processors. Shared-memory parallel computers allow more than one processor to share the same memory space. With the P-RAM model, different processors may simultaneously read the same memory location, but may not simultaneously write to the same memory. In distributed-memory parallel computers, each processor has its own memory and processors communicate by explicitly sending messages to each other over an interconnection network. See Kumar et al. (1994) for more details about shared-memory and distributed-memory parallel computers.

In practice, accessing data from disk can affect the running time of an algorithm by one or two orders of magnitude so that an order $O(N^3)$ algorithm effectively becomes an order $O(N^5)$ algorithm. To model this, the most basic i/o model assumes that data is either in memory or on disk, and that data in memory can be accessed uniformly with unit cost, while data on disk can be accessed uniformly, but at a higher cost. On a parallel computer, there will usually be several disks that can read and write blocks in parallel. With the parallel disk model (Vitter and Shriver, 1994), B data records (a block of data) can be read from disk into memory at unit cost and D blocks of data can be read or written at once. A typical algorithm will read $M = DB$ records into memory, compute with them, and write out necessary information to disk. An external memory algorithm is designed to work with $N > M$ records so that several memory loads of M records must be used to examine all of the data. With the parallel disk model (see Table 1), sorting has cost (Vitter and Shriver, 1994)

$$O((N/DB) \log(N/B)/\log(M/B)).$$

2.2. Communication Primitives

Certain communication patterns in parallel algorithms are very common and typically special hardware and software is provided to support them. We describe three of these here. Scatter takes a value at one processor and sends it to all the other processors. Gather takes values at all the processors and brings them to a common processor. Reduction takes values at all of the processors, computes the sum, and places the sum in each of the processors. Reduction can also be used for computing the max, min, and similar operations.

2.3. Data Parallelism

With data parallelism, data is divided into different partitions, the same program is run on each partition, and the results combined. Finding the maximum value in a list of N elements has an easy data-parallel solution. If the list is divided into P sublists and one is stored in the local memory of each processor, then each processor can determine its local maximum and send the maximum to a central processor or place it in common shared memory. The global maximum is then the largest of the P values. As another example, a data-parallel approach to growing a tree, splits the data into P partitions, grows a single tree on each partition, and then produces an ensemble of P trees (Grossman et al., 1996).

Table 1 Parallel Disk Model

N	Number of input records
P	Number of processors
M	Number of records that fit into the aggregate internal memories of the P processors
B	Number of records that can be transferred in a single block
D	Number of disks, and more generally the number of disk blocks that can be transferred with one parallel read or parallel write operation

2.4. Task Parallelism

Task parallelism is specified explicitly by the programmer. For example, a task-parallel approach to growing a tree uses P processors to speed up the computation of locating the best split for a single node in the tree. In the simplest task-parallel approach, the data is distributed evenly between the P processors and, for each attribute, each processor computes the class distribution information for that attribute using its local data. See Section 3 for an example of class distribution information. Reduction is used to exchange local class distribution information with each of the other $P-1$ processors to compute global class distribution information. A single split value is computed and scattered to each of the other $P-1$ processors. Using this split value, the data is distributed between the two nodes produced by the split and the process repeats. Notice that, unlike the ensemble-based approach described above, the different processors need to communicate class distribution information before a split can be determined. On the other hand, a single tree is computed, whereas the ensemble-based approach yields a collection of trees.

2.5. Shared Memory

The simplest way for different processors to communicate is for each to share some global memory. Locking is used to control conflicts when different processors write to the same memory location. As the number of processors grows, it becomes more difficult to design machines in which all the global memory can be accessed uniformly. Some architectures allow each processor access to global memory, but different processors may require different amounts of time to read and write the common shared memory. A variant is for each processor to have some local memory and some global memory.

2.6. Message Passing

With message passing, each processor has its own memory, and different processors communicate by explicitly sending and receiving messages between them with a send and receive command. Messages are simply buffers of data of specified length.

2.7. Remote Memory Operations

With remote memory operations, a processor can explicitly access memory of other processors, but different operations are used for accessing local and remote memory. For example, local memory access is implicit, while remote memory access requires explicit get or put commands. Unlike message passing, in which the remote processor must explicitly receive the message, with remote memory operations, all the work is done by the local processor.

3. Five Basic Approaches for Scaling Data-Intensive Computing

3.1. Approach 1. Manipulate the Data so that it Fits into Memory

We begin with the most common approach. There are four basic variants. The first is to sample the data until the number of records N is smaller than the memory of a single processor. The second is to select features until the amount of data is smaller than the memory of a single processor. The third is to partition the data so that although it doesn't fit into the memory of a single processor, it does fit into the aggregate memory M of the processors. The fourth technique is to summarize the data in some fashion so that the summarized or partly summarized data can fit into memory. These four techniques can be used in any combination with each other. Broadly speaking, these techniques arose from the statistical community.

3.2. Approach 2. Reduce the Time to Access Out of Memory Data

Special care is required when accessing data from disk. No more time is required to access all B records in a block on disk than is required to access any single one of them. Three basic techniques are common. The first uses specialized data structures to access data on disk. The most familiar is the B+-tree, which uses a tree structure to determine which block contains a desired record and which has efficient operations for adding new blocks and merging existing blocks (Ramakrishnan, 1997). The second technique is to lay out the data on disk to benefit from block reads. For example, some algorithms proceed faster if data is organized by record and others if data is organized by attribute. The third technique organizes data on disk to benefit from parallel block reads. A basic example is provided by matrix transpose. Instead of organizing the disk by row or column, a slightly more complicated organization can cut the number of reads by a factor of two (Shafer et al., 1996). Broadly speaking, these techniques arose from the database community.

3.3. Approach 3. Use Several Processors

One of the easiest ways to speed up algorithms on large data sets is to use more than one processor. The success depends upon how easy it is to break up the problem into subproblems that can be assigned to the different processors. As described above, there are two basic techniques. The first technique is data parallelism. With this technique, essentially the same program is applied to different partitions of the data. The second technique is task parallelism. With this technique, the program itself is broken into subtasks, which are distributed among the available processors. We will examine several examples of both techniques later in this article. Broadly speaking these techniques come from the high-performance computing community.

3.4. Approach 4. Precompute

The most expensive part of building tree-based classifiers on continuous attributes is sorting. For example, Table 2 contains the class distribution information for the continuous attribute 8. Computing the best split value for the tree requires sorting the data by the attribute's values as indicated. Precomputing these sorts reduces the cost of the algorithm (Mehta et al., 1996). For efficiency, specialized data structures are usually employed (Shafer et al., 1996).

Intermediate computations can sometimes be shared across algorithms. For example, cross-tab tables, such as Table 3 for ordinal attribute 5, are of intrinsic interest and are also used by different algorithms, including trees. Precomputing such tables can often save significant amounts of time.

A closely related approach is to provide very efficient implementations for certain basic operations, such as computing statistics on columns, which can be shared across algorithms. Sometimes these are known as data mining primitives. Broadly speaking, these techniques were developed by the data mining system implementation community.

3.5. Approach 5. Reduce the Amount of Data

This approach is very similar to Approach 1, except that there is no expectation that the data will be able to fit into memory. Three of the techniques mentioned in Approach 1 apply here without change: sampling, selecting features, and summarizing data. We also mention three more specialized techniques, which can also sometimes be used in Approach 1. Discrete data points can be smoothed and replaced by a continuous approximation specified by one or more parameters. For example, a set of points can be replaced by its center, a measure of dispersion, the number of points, the sum of the errors, and the sum of the squared errors. Data can also

Table 2 Class Distribution Information for Attribute 8

Attribute value	Fraud	
	Fraud	No Fraud
0	2	284
0.04	3	296
0.15	1	672
0.18	1	485
0.26	1	794
etc.	etc.	etc.

Table 3 Class Distribution Information for Attribute 5

	Fraud	
Attribute value	Fraud	No Fraud
0 (codes 0–1)	129	48,484
1 (codes 2–5)	494	58,492
2 (codes 5–9)	696	54,040
3 (codes >9)	789	40,949

be compressed and computations done directly on the compressed data. Finally, data can be transformed with more complicated transformations that reduce the size of the data and variants of algorithms can be applied directly to the transformed data. For example, data can be reduced with a principal components analysis.

4. Parallel Tree Induction

In this section we describe some of the ways that have been used to scale tree algorithms. For simplicity we describe these approaches in the context of the C4.5 system (Quinlan, 1993). C4.5 attempts to find the simplest classification tree that describes the structure of the data by applying search heuristics based on information theory. At any given node in the tree, the algorithm chooses the most suitable attribute to further expand it based on the concept of information gain, a measure of the ability of an attribute to minimize the information needed to classify the cases in the resulting subtrees. The algorithm constructs a tree recursively using a depth first divide-and-conquer approach. Other tree induction algorithms share a similar computation structure. See Chapter 16.1.3.

There are three main approaches for building trees in parallel.

4.1. Move Class Distribution Information

This approach is based on dividing the initial data set evenly among the P processors. The processors leave the data in place but move the class distribution information (see Section 3) using reduction in order to compute the splitting values, as described in Section 2.4 on task parallelism. In more detail, consider the expansion of a single node into its children using splitting values. Each processor computes the class distribution information for each attribute using its local data. Each processor then uses reduction with the other $P-1$ processors to compute the global class distribution information. The processors then simultaneously compute the splitting criteria and scatter the value of the attribute with the best split value. Using these splitting values, the data is then assigned to the children and the process continues.

The main advantage of this approach is that no data needs to be moved. On the other hand, moving the class distribution information can have a high communication cost and can result in a load imbalance. In particular, the deeper the tree, the less the data, and the greater the overhead of the communication.

4.2. Move Data

The advantage of this approach is that, when possible, different processors can work on different nodes at the same time. The basic idea is simple. Assume a group of processors are assigned to a node. The processors work together to compute the split value as described for the move class distribution information approach above. Assume that the number of children computed by the split is less than the number of processors available. Split the processors between the children and then distribute the data to the processors that are assigned to it. This partitions the underlying data between several processors so that they can work simultaneously. The processors are then used to compute the split value. Processors assigned to different nodes can proceed independently. Cases in which the number of children is greater than the number of processors are handled similarly. Joshi et al. (1998) gives a performance formula for this approach.

This method is also referred to as search parallelization (Provost and Kolluri, 1999) since the search space is divided among the processors so that different processors search different portions of the space in parallel.

A disadvantage of this approach is that moving data can result in a high communication overhead. Another disadvantage is that the workload can become unbalanced. On the other hand, an advantage of this approach is that once a single processor is assigned to a node it can compute the subtree without any communication overhead. Zaki et al. (1999) applies this approach to parallel tree induction by taking advantage of shared-memory multiprocessor architecture.

4.3. Ensemble-Based Methods

With this approach, the data is divided into partitions, perhaps overlapping, and one or more processors are used to build a separate tree for each partition (Grossman et al., 1996; Grossman and Poor, 1996). This produces an ensemble of trees, which can be combined using a variety of methods. An ensemble is a collection of statistical models, together with a rule for combining the models into a single model. For example, the models may be combined with a voting function or a function that averages the various values produced by the separate models. See Dietterich (1997) for additional information about ensembles in data mining.

Two or more of these approaches may be combined to produce hybrid algorithms. For example, Joshi et al. (1998) describe an algorithm that starts by exploiting the approach of moving class distribution information. When the interprocessor communication and synchronization requirements increase past a certain threshold, the implementation switches to exploiting a mixture of approaches, involving moving both data and class distribution information. This method is also referred to as parallel matching (Provost and Kolluri, 1999). This approach has been adopted in the work of Provost and Aronis (1996) and in the parallelization of the SPRINT algorithm (Shafer et al., 1996) as well as in the recently proposed ScalParC parallel tree induction system (Joshi et al., 1998). Other examples are given by Pearson (1994), who uses a vertical partitioning strategy, and Han et al. (1999), who use a horizontal partitioning strategy.

Ensemble-based methods have also been combined with approaches that move both data and class distribution information (Grossman et al., 1996).

It should be noted that after generating a classification tree by an algorithm such as C4.5, several postprocessing steps might still be required. These are applied in order to simplify the tree and to translate it into a set of production rules (Quinlan, 1993). Kufrin (1997) has noted that these postprocessing steps may require more computation time than the actual tree generation phases and has described how such steps can be parallelized.

5. Parallel Association Rule Discovery

Algorithms for uncovering associations were introduced in Agrawal et al. (1993). The well-known A priori algorithm (Agrawal et al., 1993) generates association rules by computing frequent item sets (Chapter 16.2.3). Frequent item sets of length one are simply singleton sets. Given a frequent item set of length n, there are efficient algorithms for computing frequent item sets of length $n + 1$ (Agrawal and Srikant, 1994). The A priori algorithm uses a hash tree to maintain items of length n while it computes frequent item sets of length $n + 1$. The hash tree is required to remain in main memory, although the transaction data set is not. Association rules can be read easily from frequent item sets.

There are two steps to construct frequent item sets of length $n + 1$. In the first step, a set of candidate frequent item sets is created. In the second step, the entire database is scanned to count the number of transactions that the candidate sets contain. Concurrency can be used in both steps—parallel processing can be used to speed the creation of candidate frequent item sets and to speed up the counting of transactions.

Data parallel approaches that distribute the transaction data among several processors and count the transactions in parallel have been proposed by Park et al. (1995) and Agrawal and Shafer (1996). The count distribution (CD) algorithm of Agrawal et al. is an adaptation of the A priori algorithm. At each iteration, the algorithm generates the candidate sets at each local processor by applying the same generation function as that used in the A priori algorithm. Each processor then computes the local support counts of all the candidate sets and uses a reduction for computing the global frequent item sets for that iteration. In this way, the CD algorithm scales linearly with the number of transactions. On the other hand, since the CD algorithm, like A priori, requires the hash tree to fit into the memory of a single processor, it does not scale as the number of candidates in the frequent item sets increases.

To scale as the number of candidates in the frequent item sets increases, the frequent item sets themselves can be distributed among the processors. In this case, a simple hash tree fitting into the memory of a single processor can no longer be used. Simple implementations of this idea require moving all the data to each of the processors in order to compute the counts. Sometimes this is called the data distribution (DD) method. Simple DD algorithms do not perform well due to the communications overhead, but more complex implementations have been developed with better performance.

CD-style algorithms scale to large transaction data sets since the transactions are partitioned. DD-style algorithms scale to problems with large candidate sets since the candidates are partitioned. Some algorithms combine these two approaches to achieve scalability along both dimensions (Han et al., 1997).

Cheung et al. (1996) observed that a global frequent item set must be a local frequent item for some processor. With this property, much smaller candidate sets can be generated in parallel at each processor. Moreover, local pruning can be applied by removing those sets that are not locally large. The communication required for exchanging support counts is therefore reduced from the $O(P^2)$ of directly parallelizing A priori, to $O(P)$, where P is the number of distributed processors or computers. This type of algorithm can be extended easily to parallelize any pattern discovery algorithm that employs a level by level monotonic search component like that of A priori.

Speeding up association rules through sampling is discussed in Lee et al. (1998).

In their recent paper, Pei et al. (2000) proposed the CLOSET algorithm for computing association rules. Instead of generating frequent item sets, the algorithm computes a much smaller set of candidates. Their algorithm also employs a compact representation of association rules. This algorithm is based on a memorization mechanism that avoids redundant computations. A partition-based approach can be used to scale this algorithm to large data sets. At this time, parallel versions of this algorithm have not been studied in detail.

6. Parallel Clustering Algorithms

Clustering algorithms can be broadly divided into three types: distance-based clustering, hierarchical clustering, and density-based clustering (Chapter 16.5). In general, clustering algorithms employ a two-stage search: an outer loop over possible cluster members and an inner loop to fit the best possible clustering for a given number of clusters.

With distance-based clustering, n clusters are constructed by computing a locally optimal solution to minimize the sum of the distances within the data clusters. This is either done by starting from scratch and constructing a new solution or by using a valid cluster solution as a starting point for improvements. A common distance-based algorithm is the k-means algorithm, which minimizes the sum of the distance between each data point and its nearest cluster center (Selim and Ismail, 1984). Parallelism in distance-based clustering methods can be exploited at both the outer level, by trying different cluster numbers concurrently, and at the inner level by computing the distance metrics in parallel.

Hierarchical clustering groups data with a given similarity measurement into a sequence of nested partitions. Two different approaches can be employed. One is to start with each data point as a single cluster and then at each step, merge pairs of points together. This is known as the agglomerative approach. The alternative is to start with all data points in one cluster and then divide one cluster into clusters in each step. This is the divisive approach. For both methods, $O(N^2)$ algorithms are known. Recent attempts have been made to develop parallel algorithms for hierarchical clustering using several distance metrics in parallel (Olson, 1995).

With the density-based clustering approach, clustering is done by postulating a hidden density model indicating the cluster membership. The data is assumed to be generated from a mixture model with hidden cluster identifiers. The clustering problem is then one of finding parameters for each individual cluster that maximize the likelihood of the data set given the mixture model. A typical density-based clustering method is the EM algorithm, which employs an iterative search procedure to find the best parameters of a mixture model to fit the data. The iteration procedure comprises the following steps:

1. Initialize the model parameters, thereby producing a current model.

2. Decide memberships of the data items to clusters, assuming that the current model is correct.

3. Re-estimate the parameters of the current model assuming that the data memberships obtained in (2) are correct, producing a new model.

4. If the current model and new model are sufficiently close to each other then terminate, else go to (2).

This procedure has the same structure as the k-means method where the only model parameter is the distance between assumed cluster centers and data points. The search hierarchy in EM algorithms includes an outermost-level search on cluster numbers, a middle-level search for functional forms, and an inner-level search for parameter values. The rich inherent parallelism of the algorithm may be exploited by combining the decomposition of loops (task parallelism) and partitioning of data (data parallelism). Subramonian and Parthasarathy (1998) present a parallelization of the EM algorithm. The model employs three different methods for parallelizing each of the three levels of search loops:

• Vectorize the computation of parameters (inner-level search).

• Exploit data parallelism in computing the cluster model given the cluster number (middle-level search).

• Concurrently search cluster numbers using parallel machine clusters.

This method provides a general framework for parallelizing iterative clustering procedures.

7. Discussion and Summary

Broadly speaking, techniques for scaling data mining algorithms can be divided into five basic categories: (1) manipulating the data so that it fits into memory, (2) using specialized data structures to manage out of memory data, (3) distributing the computation so that it exploits several processors, (4) precomputing intermediate quantities of interest, and (5) reducing the amount of data mined.

During the past few years there have been successes scaling tree-based predictors and association rules to large data sets that do not fit into memory but rather fill the memories of several processors, spill onto disks, or both. More recently, techniques have been introduced that scale clustering algorithms. These successes have typically involved combining two or more of the approaches described above.

References

Agrawal, R. and J. Shafer. 1996. "Parallel mining of association rules." *IEEE Trans. Knowledge Data Engng* **8(6)**: 962–969.

Agrawal, R. and R. Srikant. 1994. "Fast algorithms for mining association rules in large databases." In *Proceedings of the Twentieth International Conference on Very Large Databases*. CA: Morgan Kaufmann, pp. 487–499.

Agrawal, R., T. Imielinski, and A. Swami. 1993b. "Mining association rules between sets of items in large databases." In *Proceedings of the ACM SIGMOD International Conference on Management of Data*, p. 207. NY: ACM Press.

Aho, A., J. Hopcroft, and J. Ullman. 1974. *The Design and Analysis of Computer Algorithms*. Reading, MA: Addison-Wesley.

Breiman, L., J. H. Friedman, R. A. Olshen, and C. J. Stone. 1984. *Classification and Regression Trees*. Belmont, CA: Wadsworth.

Cheung, D. W., J. Han, V. T. Ng, and C. Y. Wong. 1996. "Maintenance of discovered association rules in large databases: an incremental updating techniques." In *Proceedings of International Conference on Data Engineering*. CA: IEEE Computer Society, pp. 106–114.

Dietterich, T. G. 1997. "Machine learning research." *AI Magazine* 18: 97–136.

Grossman, R. L. and H. V. Poor. 1996. "Optimization driven data mining and credit scoring." In *Proceedings of the IEEE/IAFE 1996 Conference on Computational Intelligence for Financial Engineering (CIFEr)*, pp. 104–110. Piscataway, NY: IEEE.

Grossman, R. L., H. Bodek, D. Northcutt, and H. V. Poor. 1996. "Data mining and tree-based optimization." In *Proceedings of the Second International Conference on Knowledge Discovery and Data Mining*, edited by E. Simoudis, J. Han, and U. Fayyad, pp. 323–326. Menlo Park, CA: AAAI Press.

Guo, Y. and J. Sutiwaraphun. 1998. "Knowledge probing in distributed data mining." In *Working Notes of the KDD-97 Workshop on Distributed Data Mining*, pp. 61–69.

Han, E., G. Karypis, and V. Kuma. 1997. "Scalable parallel data mining for association rules." In *Proceedings of the 1997 ACM-SIGMOD International Conference on the Management of Data*. NY: ACM Press, pp. 277–288.

Han, E. H., A. Srivastava, V. Kumar, and V. Singh. 1999. "Parallel formulations of decision-tree classification algorithms." In *Data Mining and Knowledge Discovery: An International Journal*, 3(3): 237–261. Boston: Kluwer Academic Publishers.

Joshi, M. V., G. Karypis, and V. Kumar. 1998. "ScalParc: a new scalable and efficient parallel classification algorithm for mining large data sets." In *Proceedings of the International Parallel Processing Symposium*. CA: IEEE Computer Society, pp. 573–597.

Kufrin, R. 1997. "Generating C4.5 production rules in parallel." In *Proceedings of the Fourteenth National Conference on Artificial Intelligence (AAAI-97)*. Menlo Park, CA: AAAI Press, pp. 565–570.

Kumar, V., A. Grama, and G. Karypis. 1994. *Introduction to Parallel Computing: Design and Analysis of Algorithms*. Redwood City, CA: Benjamin Cummings Publishing Company.

Lee, S. D., D. W. Cheung, and B. Kao. 1998. "Is sampling useful in data mining? A case study in the maintenance of discovered association rules." *Data Mining and Knowledge Discovery* 2: 233–262.

Mehta, M., R. Agrawal, and J. Rissanen. 1996. "SLIQ: a fast scalable classifier for data mining." In *Proceedings of the Fifth International Conference on Extending Database Technology*. NY: Springer-Verlag, pp. 18–32.

Olson, C. F. 1995. "Parallel algorithms for hierarchical clustering." *Parallel Comput.* 21(8): 1313–1325.

Park, J. S., M. Chen, and P. S. Yu. 1995. "An effective hash-based algorithm for mining association rules." In *Proceedings of the ACM SIGMOD International Conference on Management of Data*. pp. 175–186. New York, NY: Association for Computing Machinery.

Pearson, R. A. 1994. "A coarse grained parallel induction heuristic." In *Parallel Processing for Artificial Intelligence 2*, edited by H. Kitano, V. Kumar, and C. B. Sutter, pp. 207–226. New York, NY: Elsevier Science.

Pei, J., J. Han, and R. Mao. 2000. "CLOSET: an efficient algorithm for mining frequent closed itemsets (PDF)." In *Tenth International Workshop on Research Issues in Data Engineering: RIDE 2000*. Los Alamitos: IEEE Computer Society Press, pp. 11–20.

Provost, F. and J. Aronis. 1996. "Scaling up inductive learning with massive parallelism." *Machine Learning* 23: 33–46.

Provost, F. and V. Kolluri. 1999. "A survey of methods for scaling up inductive algorithms." To appear in *Data Mining and Knowledge Discovery 2 (1999)*. pp. 131–169. Boston: Kluwer Academic Publishers.

Quinlan, J. 1993. *C4.5 Programs for Machine Learning*. San Mateo, CA: Morgan Kaufmann.

Ramakrishnan, R. 1997. *Database Management Systems*. New York: McGraw-Hill.

Shriver, E. and M. Nodine 1996. "An introduction to parallel I/O models and algorithms." In *Input/output in parallel and distributed computer systems*. Chapter 2. pp. 31–68. NY: Kluwer Academic Publishers.

Selim, S. Z. and M. A. Ismail. 1984. "K-means-type algorithms: a generalized convergence theorem and characterization of local optimality." *IEEE Trans. Pattern Anal. Machine Intell.* 6: 81–87.

Shafer, J., R. Agrawal, and M. Mehta. 1996. "SPRINT: a scalable parallel classifier for data mining." In *Proceedings of the Twenty-Second International Conference on Very Large Databases (VLDB 1996)*. San Francisco, CA: Morgan Kaufmann, pp. 544–44.

Subramonian, R. and S. Parthasarathy. 1998. "A framework for distributed data mining." In *Proceedings of the KDD-98 Workshop on Distributed Data Mining*. New York, NY: Association for Computing Machinery, pp. 444–59.

Vitter, J. S. and E. A. M. Shriver. 1994. "Algorithms for parallel memory I: two level memories." *Algorithmica* **12**: 110–147.

Zaki, M. J., C. Ho, and R. Agrawal. 1999. "Scalable parallel classification for data mining on shared memory multiprocessors." In *Proceedings of IEEE International Conference on Data Engineering*. Los Alamitos: IEEE Computer Society Press, pp. 198–205.

17 TASK AND METHOD SELECTION

17.1 Selection of Tasks

Padhraic Smyth

One of the more subtle aspects of the practical art of knowledge discovery and data mining is the matching of data mining tasks (see Chapter 16) to real-world applications. This matching process can often be highly nontrivial since real-world applications tend to be relatively complex and involve many details that are not necessarily of direct relevance to the discovery problem, while definitions of data mining tasks tend to be quite abstract and high level.

To make this a little more concrete, consider the example of using data mining methods to build a system for detecting fraudulent behavior in a transaction data setting (see Chapter 35) (e.g., detecting fraudulent use of a credit card). Classification (see Chapter 16.1) is a task that potentially may match this application quite well. We can consider the problem to consist of two classes, namely normal and fraudulent transactions, and build a classifier for this two-class problem. (Note that the selection of a particular classification method is at the next level of the matching problem and will be dealt with in Chapter 17.2.) However, classification may not be entirely appropriate for this application since in monitoring potential fraud activity one may also wish to have an estimate of the probability of fraud given the observed activity (allowing one to rank and select the most likely cases). This task of probability estimation could in turn be solved as a regression task (see Chapter 16.4.3), such as logistic regression.

Furthermore, framing our fraud detection problem as a supervised learning task requires that we have labeled data with which to train our classifier or regression model (an alternative of course would be to build a hand-crafted fraud detection system, but here we are interested in a data mining approach—see Fawcett and Provost (1997) for a comparison of the two approaches on a large-scale real-world fraud detection problem). In many practical fraud detection settings there may be very little or no labeled data available. Thus, unsupervised tasks may be more appropriate than supervised tasks such as classification, using methods such as rule discovery with characteristic rules (see Chapter 16.2.2), subgroup discovery (see Chapter 16.3), or clustering (see Chapter 16.5). To further complicate the picture, the task of time-series analysis may be relevant to handle the problem of handling observations that occur over time as well for dealing with the inherent nonstationarity and drift that is likely to be present in real-world fraud applications. At another level, the task of spatial analysis (see Chapter 16.7) may provide benefit in that it could model useful geographical patterns of fraudulent activity.

The point of this particular example is to illustrate that the problem of matching a real-world application to a data mining task rarely has a simple single solution. Many different tasks may match a particular application, depending on how one approaches the problem. Unfortunately, there are relatively few standard rules to guide the novice data miner in this matching process. Most papers and textbooks do not discuss this practical engineering issue, nor do most software packages provide much guidance on how to map a practical application problem to a specific data mining task. Nonetheless a few general points are worth making in this context:

- While there may be many different tasks that are potentially relevant to one's application (as in the example above), it is possible that it is sufficient to use only one of these tasks to achieve good performance. For example, while time-series and spatial modeling may in principle be useful for the fraud detection problem, they may not be worth trying if a simple rule-induction method can provide almost 100 percent accuracy without temporal or spatial information. Thus, the familiar advice of starting with the simpler tasks, and working up to the more complex ones only if necessary, is quite relevant here.

- Selecting tasks is in essence a matching process, matching somewhat abstract descriptions of tasks to much more complex real-world situations. To perform this matching, it is often necessary to transform or abstract the original formulation of the real-world problem into a framework that more closely resembles a standard textbook task description (Langley and Simon, 1995 provide an excellent discussion of real-world examples of this transformation process). The art here is not to transform or simplify the problem so much that it is no longer close to the original problem, but instead to remove only the irrelevant details or those that can be deemed inconsequential. This transformation process is typically learned from experience rather than learned in the classroom.

- To properly select a knowledge discovery task for a given problem it is essential that the data miner has a fairly complete understanding of both the problem and the task to which it is matched. This will typically require a time investment on the part of the data miner to understand the domain in some depth and/or on the part of the domain expert to understand the general principles of the selected data mining task. This type of careful understanding of both halves of the application seems somewhat obvious but, nonetheless, is often skipped in practice in practitioners's haste to generate results. However, if one looks at large-scale successful KDD applications it is usually very clear that both the data miners and the domain experts invested considerable time in learning the basics of each other's area.

- A final comment, well known in applied statistical practice, is that it is better to approximate the solution to the right problem than it is to solve the wrong problem exactly. This is a cautionary note to academic researchers who sometimes have a tendency to become somewhat enamoured with rather exotic algorithms and techniques while forgetting to try much less complex methods that might in fact provide a simple, robust, and interpretable solution (albeit one that is more difficult to publish a paper on!).

General discussions on the issue of matching tasks to applications can be found in Langley and Simon (1995) and Brodley and Smyth (1997; with particular focus on classification), as well as the editorial by Provost and Kohavi (1998) for the special issue of the *Machine Learning Journal* (1998) on the "Applications of Machine Learning and the Knowledge Discovery Process" and the paper by Saitta and Neri (1998) in the same issue.

References

Brodley, C. and P. Smyth. 1997. "Applying classification algorithms in practice." *Stat. Comput.* **7(1)**: 45–56.

Fawcett, T. and F. Provost. 1997. "Adaptive fraud detection." *Data Mining and Knowledge Discovery* **1(3)**: 291–316.

Langley, P. and H. A. Simon. 1995. "Applications of machine learning and rule induction." *Commun. ACM* **38**: 55–64.

Provost, F. and R. Kohavi. 1998. "Guest editor's introduction: on applied research in machine learning." *Machine Learning* **30(2/3)**: 127–132.

Saitta, L. and F. Neri. 1998. "Learning in the 'real-world'." *Machine Learning* **30(2/3)**: 133–163.

17.2 Selection of Data Mining Methods for Tasks C5.1–C5.8

Guido Lindner, Robert Engels, and Rudi Studer

ABSTRACT Once a data mining task is determined, as described in Chapter 17.1, appropriate methods have to be selected for execution of this task. In this article, issues are discussed that play a part in choosing among alternative models for performing such data mining tasks. We argue that method selection depends highly on the application context as given by initial task analysis, on the properties of the data the analysis is performed on, on previous experiences with similar domains, and on user-specified requirements on the results.

1. Introduction

Several factors influence the success of knowledge discovery in databases (KDD) projects. An important success factor is the choice of an appropriate data mining method for the selected data mining task, for example, the choice of a technique that generates appropriate results with respect to the task definition. Up to now, method selection has been performed by experts. These experts, ideally, possess knowledge about method selection that is based on their experience with the application of data mining techniques. Since a continuously increasing number of such techniques is available today, ever more specialized knowledge about the techniques is necessary for the selection process. It is easy to see that keeping this knowledge up to date forms a major problem even for experts in this field.

It is theoretically proved (cf. Schaffer, 1994; and Wolpert, 1994) that no algorithm is the overall best, with a generally superior performance in all possible contexts. This theory is commonly known as the "no free lunch" theorem (NFL theorem). However, the relevance of the NFL theorem is limited with respect to practical applications, since the NFL theorem is only valid as long as no properties of the domain are known.

Method selection also plays a part in data analysis paradigms in statistics (cf. Hand, 1994a,b), as well as in machine learning (cf. the MLT project with its Consultant System [Consortium, 1993] as well as the Statlog project [Michie et al., 1994]). These projects compared the performance of a fixed set of algorithms on several data sets.

A similar perspective on method selection can be found in Kohavi et al. (1997), where these ideas form the background motivation for the MLC++ library. In accordance with the Statlog approach, the MLC++ approach also advises the application of all available algorithms in order to select the best method for the current application. Obviously, such an approach is ineffient. However, what exactly is defined as best strongly depends on application-specific goals and the data. Where application-specific goals are requested from the user, meta data on the data can be calculated automatically. An approach integrating this user interaction and domain characteristics as a top-down and bottom-up strategy is described in the user guidance modeling (UGM) approach by Engels et al. (1997). It is our firm opinion that retracting users restrictions on the functionality of an application has to form an integral part of every approach to method selection. Such an approach is also pursued in the METAL project (a meta-learning assistant for providing user support in machine learning and data mining; ESPRIT project 26357).

At the same time there is a growing interest in these problems, as shown by workshops that elaborate on these ideas; two recent examples are the workshop on Upgrading Learning to the Meta-level: Model Selection and Data Transformation (Giraud-Carrier and Hilario, 1998) and the AAAI/ICML Workshop on The Methodology of Applying Machine Learning (Engels et al., 1998).

The relationship between the application goal, data properties, and method selection will be discussed in more detail in Section 2. Section 3 discusses techniques for collecting data properties, while Section 4 discusses different approaches to support method selection.

2. Application Restrictions on Method Selection

Selecting an appropriate method is a bidirectional process of mapping application restrictions and data on methods. The advantage of a bidirectional approach is that the integration of additional algorithms does not require a complete overhaul of the knowledge about algorithms that have already been modeled. The understandability of the representation format of the final model, model restrictions that follow from the type of processes, model complexity, model accuracy, and requirements on execution speed are examples of such restricting properties. For example, in critical application areas like medicine, it is often important to thoroughly understand generated knowledge before it can be deployed, whereby the time needed for generating output is often less important than its quality.

Generally, a preselection of algorithms that will probably be applicable is based on application requirements. This preselected set of methods forms the basis for a further selection of a (possibly) single method that can fulfil all requirements and constraints of the application at hand. There are a variety of properties that make up the application restrictions:

- *Run-time restrictions.* Is time a critical factor for model applications? For classification tasks, for instance, time could be critical at the training and at the classification phase. On the one hand, some classifiers (such as neural networks) are fast in classifying but slow in training, and, depending on the data that is used, can be extremely slow when certain unfortunate properties are found in the input data. On the other hand, there is a group of algorithms that does not focus on learning models beforehand but concentrates on deploying the information in the data at hand at the time of execution. These algorithms, sometimes called lazy algorithms (Aha, 1997), are represented by nearest-neighbour algorithms, among others.

- *Kind of model.* Different model types might be able to fulfill similar tasks. Which one is selected highly depends on the exact requirements posed by the user. The main properties of models are

    their ability to generalize,

    their interpretability,

    their compactness, and

    their transportability, which describes to what extent a model can be used on new data independently from the historical data.

    For instance in applications, where the knowledge acquisition aspect is important, the ability to generalize and interpretability are more relevant than compactness or transportability. In other applications (for instance, medical diagnosis), the combination of interpretability and transportability is more important.

- *Model fitness.* Can one say that a model is fit when it has a high accuracy?

    Examples of measurements that can contribute to model fitness are accuracy on unseen data, confidence (the error rate of a specific decision on the unseen data), and support (percentage of training data supporting a decision). But the complexity of the model also has to be considered when defining the fitness of a model for solving a particular problem.

- *System restrictions.* In applications the choice of algorithms is highly correlated with the available hardware platform, and therefore system restrictions have to be taken as an input for the selection process. (Also known as nonfunctional requirements in software engineering.)

    Access to specific software (KDD tools) generally restricts the variety of algorithms that can be used.

3. How Can We Characterize Data?

Data characteristics play an important part in the second stage of method selection, where the preselected set of algorithms is drilled down to leave just a few.

The Statlog project (cf. Michie et al., 1994) analyzed the relationship between characteristics of the data and result quality, aiming at finding ways for the determination of applicable algorithms for a given data set.

It became clear that the data characteristics used in the Statlog project are not powerful enough to determine an optimal choice of algorithms. In several experiments it was possible to create data sets that, although not different in their data characteristics, delivered significantly different results.

Engels and Theusinger (1998) and Lindner and Studer (1999) extended this set of characteristics with several statistical measurements that facilitate method selection and data preprocessing.

The characteristics can be divided into simple characteristics, statistical characteristics, and information theoretical characteristics. While simple characteristics refer to measurements that can be objectively calculated on all data sets, the other two groups refer to more sophisticated measurements for specific groups of tasks.

3.1. Simple Characteristics

Relatively simple measurements give a general insight into the data. Next to the number of vectors, their size (typically the number of attributes) and the data types of the single elements in the vectors play a part. For each attribute the number of unique values is useful. In case of a continuous attribute, it makes more sense to represent its range. In cases where an attribute is defined as the goal attribute for learning, the number of such unique values defines the number of classes that are present in the data.

Often, the ratio of basic measurements can be useful, for instance,

$$\frac{\|\text{number of discrete attributes}\|}{\|\text{number of continuous attributes}\|}.$$

This measurement describes the relation between discrete and continuous attributes in the data set. For instance, a data set that contains mostly discrete attributes with a high range of instances indicates that neural nets could not be the first choice because each symbolic value will typically be represented by a separate neuron of the input layer.

3.2. Statistical Characteristics

In addition to simple statistical measurements, information on the location and dispersion of attributes can be useful to estimate the complexity of the mining task. For instance, for a task to detect association rules, some methods transform symbolic attribute values to binary attributes.

Furthermore, in order to get an insight into the presence of outliers in the data, a range of measurements can be applied based on comparison of the whole data set and the α-quantil trimmed set. If an application has a lot of attributes with possible outliers and if the interesting results are expected in the outlier values, you have to select a method that can handle low support values.

Another measurement belonging to the group of more sophisticated statistical measurements describes the correlation between attributes (for instance, in the case of classification problems, certain properties of discriminant analysis, and its assumptions). The first canonical correlation, for example, describes the degree of correlation between the most significant discriminant function and the class distribution. (A strong correlation exists if the first canonical correlation is close to unity.) If the first discriminant function is the strongest (as uncovered by the eigenvalues), the canonical correlation can nevertheless show that its relation with the classes is only a weak one. In this case it is not likely that a proper prediction can be made with linear discriminating methods.

Another useful measurement is the Wilks Lambda (Wilks Lambda is also known as the U-statistic) value, if the value is near zero, then a good discrimination between the classes can be found. These results along with knowledge about the dimensionality of an alternative data representation that is the minimum needed to solve the current problem can be used for data preprocessing. The number of such dimensions are included, as well as their significance and the general possibilities, in order to distinguish between classes. The number of discrimination functions also shows the complexity of the classification problem.

3.3. Characteristics from Information Theory

In addition to the characteristics of continuous attributes, there is also a need for information on discrete attributes. Information theoretical measurements like information gain (Quinlan,

1986), several entropy measurements (attribute entropy, class entropy, etc.) and measurements of attribute relevance like the Gini-index (Breiman et al., 1984) and g-function (Cooper and Herskovits, 1992) can provide this information.

The class entropy, for example, can be interpreted as the number of binary questions that is needed to distinguish between the classes based on the symbolic attributes. Such measurements describe, for example, the relevance of the symbolic attributes in the domain, so that it could be advisable to select methods like decision-tree learners.

In practice, the experts typically use only a small set of the data characteristic measurements and select an algorithm by using their experience for the identified task. However, in order to offer an automatic decision support for method selection, a sufficient set of data characteristic measurements has to be exploited.

4. Decision Support for Algorithm Selection

There are two main philosophies of method selection:

- approaches aiming at inducing knowledge from experience. Such approaches have the advantage that they will contain more and more specialized knowledge when applied over a longer period of time, and

- automatic assistant systems that use precompiled knowledge for decisionmaking. This kind of approach has the advantage that it is applicable, in principle, to all domains it is selected for, thereby not depending on a recent case base of applications.

In the following, both approaches are briefly discussed.

4.1. The Induction of Knowledge from Experience

In machine-learning applications, a commonly used approach is to let people become familiar with a number of algorithms. Based on insight and probable experience, one can produce results that are convenient. Following this induction of knowledge from experience philosophy several approaches are developed, of which MLC++ (Kohavi et al., 1997) and WEKA (Machine Learning Group, 1998) are ambassadors. Principally, both systems enable the testing of many algorithms on the same data. However, we want to make it very clear that the strong emphasis on accuracy measurements as commonly found should be altered into approaches that consider more dimensions. Method selection, which is based on accuracy only (often based on single runs of algorithms), is not sufficient on its own for performing method selection. Instead, it is necessary to include more properties, as discussed above with respect to model fitness and kind of model.

4.2. Automated Method Selection Assistant Approaches

Approaches with precompiled knowledge for method selection are interesting at the moment, while delivering better possibilities for support of method selection. In this philosophy, two approaches are well known: the Statlog project (Michie et al., 1994) and the Machine Learning Toolbox (Consortium, 1993) project (MLT). A third one, the UGM approach described by Engels et al. (1997), includes task decomposition (top down) and method selection (bottom up from the data; Lindner and Studer, 1999).

MLT aimed at building an automated assistant (cf. CONSULTANT) that supports the decision process. While CONSULTANT suffers from the problem that it is difficult to extend the set of algorithms with new ones due to the way in which its knowledge was compiled, the Statlog approach contains insufficient measurements for distinction between data sets. This makes the generalization of Statlog knowledge to other domains quite arduous.

There is the interesting possibility of performing meta learning. Based on results from Statlog, the topic of meta learning is discussed in Brazdil et al. (1994) and Michie et al. (1994).

However, this approach has several disadvantages:

- Instead of hard boundaries in rules, it would be preferable to have more fuzzy rules, so that decision surfaces are smoother. It is not acceptable in a real-world application to have hard boundaries and exclude a particular algorithm from further consideration on the fact that 35,040 data sets are present instead of a maximum of 35,000.

- In order to add new algorithms to the decision system, they must be tested against a standard set of data sets. How could this be generalized on other data sets?
- How is it warranted that such a standard set of data sets is representative?
- How is applicability defined? In the Statlog approach applicability is related to the best algorithm on the set of standard data sets.

These considerations lead to a focus on case-based approaches since they enable some of the drawbacks mentioned here to be overcome.

4.3. A Case-Based Architecture for Algorithm Selection

Since the process of method selection is difficult to make explicit (as required in approaches that build on precompiled knowledge bases), and since no generally valid knowledge on method selection seems to exist, case-based approaches might form a proper alternative. In cases where (i) domain knowledge is incomplete, (ii) experts cannot really make knowledge explicit, and (iii) there is a possibility of capturing experiences, case-based reasoning (CBR) approaches can be useful (Leake, 1996). CBR approaches can pick those cases, out of a set of previous experiences, that recapture a similar problem to the one at hand.

Case histories require a representation of cases in such a way that all the factors influencing the case (as discussed in Sections 2 and 3) and the task specification (stemming from the analysis of the application restrictions) can be used. Additionally, the parameter configuration of the learning algorithms can be added. The selection of the parameter configuration is a similar problem to the method selection. Changes in the parameters of a certain method could have totally different results. In a case-based approach, a method is also defined by the parameter configuration.

Lindner and Studer (1999) show the practicality of this approach. Today, the case base contains more than sixteen hundred cases as the result of twenty-one different classification algorithms and more than eighty data sets. At the moment, the system is realized for supervised classification tasks that are an important task type in machine learning and KDD applications. The collected data sets are taken from the UCI repository (Merz and Murphy, 1996) and from available real-world applications. To evaluate the recommendation quality, each data set was tested in turn. For the selected data set each associated case is extracted from the case-base. This means that twenty-one cases are removed from the case base (currently, we handle twenty-one algorithms in our case base). For the selected data set the most similar data set is computed by comparing the data characteristics. (Since the UCI repository does not provide application restrictions, the problem description of the cases are reduced to the data characteristics of the data sets.) If the best algorithm of the most similar data set is applicable to the selected data set, this test is counted as a positive recommendation. This means that the recommended algorithm must be an element of the set of applicable algorithms (like the Stalog definition) for the selected data set.

Over all data sets the best algorithm of the most similar data set is applicable in 79 percent. For applications with only numerical or with numerical and symbolic (mixed) attributes, the rate is higher than 85 percent. These are rather good results. It can be seen that the result for data sets with only symbolic attributes is not so good. This is an indicator that the data characteristics for the symbolic attributes are still insufficient and that some additional measurements are needed.

References

Aha, D. 1997. "Special AI review issue on lazy learning." *Artificicial Rev.* **11**: 1–5.

Brazdil, P., J. Gama, and B. Henery. 1994. "Characterizing the applicability of classification algorithms using meta-level learning." In *Proceedings of the European Conference on Machine Learning (ECML 94),* edited by F. Bergadano and L. De Raedt. Lecture Notes in Computer Science, **784**: 83–102. Catania, Italy: Springer-Verlag.

Breiman, L., J. Friedman, R. Olshen, and C. Stone. 1984. *Classification and Regression Trees*, Pacific Grove, CA: Wadsworth and Brooks.

Cooper, G. and E. Herskovits. 1992. "A Bayesian method for the induction of probabilistic networks from data." *Machine Learning* **9**: 309–347.

Engels, R. and C. Theusinger. 1998. "Using a data metric for offering preprocessing advice in data mining applications." In *Proceedings of the Thirteenth Biennial European Conference on Artificial Intelligence (ECAI-98)*, edited by H. Prade, pp. 430–434. Chichester: Wiley and Sons.

Engels, R., G. Lindner, and R. Studer. 1997. "A guided tour through the data mining jungle." In *Proceedings of the Third International Conference on Knowledge Discovery and Data Mining, Newport Beach, CA, August 14–17*, edited by D. Heckerman, H. Mannila, and D. Pregibon. Menlo Park, CA: AAAI Press.

Engels, R., F. Verdenius, and D. Aha. (eds). 1998. *Workshop on the Methodology of Applying Machine Learning (Problem Definition, Task Decomposition and Technique Selection), vol. WS-98-16, July 27, Madison, WI*, Menlo Park, CA: AAAI Press.

Giraud-Carrier, C. and M. Hilario. 1998. "Upgrading learning to the meta-level: model selection and data transformation." Technical Report CSR-98-02. TU Chemnitz: Computer Science.

Hand, D. 1994a. "Deconstructing statistical questions." *J. R. Stat. Soc.*, pp. 317–356.

Hand, D. 1994b. "Statistical strategy: step 1." In *Selecting Models from Data: Artificial Intelligence and Statistics IV*, edited by P. Cheeseman and R. W. Oldford. Lecture Notes in Statistics, **89**: 3–9. Berlin: Springer-Verlag.

Kohavi, R., D. Sommerfield, and J. Dougherty. 1996. 1997. "Data mining using MLC++, a machine learning library in C++." *Int. J. Artificial Intell. Tools* **6(4)**: 537–566 Also available at http://www.sgi.com/Technology/mlc.

Leake, D. B. (ed). 1996. *Case-Based Reasoning: Experiences, Lessons & Future Directions*, Menlo Park, CA: AAAI Press.

Lindner, G. and R. Studer. 1999. "AST: support for algorithm selection with a CBR approach." In *Principles of Data Mining and Knowledge Discovery, Third European Conference (PKDD'99), Prague*, edited by J. Żytkow and J. Rauch, pp. 418–424. Berlin: Springer-Verlag.

Machine Learning Group. 1998. "Waikato environment for knowledge analysis." University of Waikato. Available at http://www.cs.waikato.ac.nz/ml/weka/index.html.

Merz, C. J. and P. M. Murphy. 1996. UCI repository of machine learning databases. Irvine, CA: University of California, Department of Information and Computer Science. http://www.ics.uci.edu/~mlearn/MLRepository.html.

Michie, D., D. Spiegelhalter, and C. Taylor. 1994. *Machine Learning, Neural and Statistical Classification*. Chichester: Ellis Horwood.

MLT Consortium. 1993. "Final public report of the Machine Learning Toolbox project." Technical report, ESPIRIT II Project 2154.

Quinlan, R. 1986. "Induction of decision trees." *Machine Learning* **1(1)**: 81–106.

Schaffer, C. 1994. "A conservation law for generalization performance." In *Machine Learning: Proceedings of the Eleventh International Conference, Rutgers University, New Brunswick, NJ, July 10–13*, edited by W. W. Cohen and H. Hirsh, pp. 259–265. Palo Alto, CA: Morgan Kaufmann.

Wolpert, D. 1994. *The Mathematics of Generalizations*. Addison-Wesley.

18 DOMAIN KNOWLEDGE TO SUPPORT THE DISCOVERY PROCESS

18.1 Taxonomies

Willi Klösgen

ABSTRACT   We classify methods for generating taxonomies and study the role of taxonomies in the knowledge discovery in databases (KDD) process. First, we summarize methods for generating taxonomies for the values in the domain of a single attribute. We classify these methods using several dimensions, such as scale of the attribute, supervised versus unsupervised, dynamic versus static, and top-down versus bottom-up methods. Then we analyze the role of taxonomies in the KDD process by discussing for which tasks they are important, how they are used for discovery, and the advantages of using such taxonomies.

1. Introduction

Taxonomies have been introduced in Chapter 5.7 as a hierarchical system of (disjoint) classes. Each class contains similar items. The items within a class are thus related under special domain aspects, and the set of classes is partially ordered. The structure given by the partial ordering is typically a tree but can also be a directed acyclical graph (DAG). The partial ordering usually captures the generality or inclusion relation between classes. So each node in such a tree or DAG hierarchy represents a class of items. It is possible to attach items at the leaves of the hierarchy, but typically individual items do not belong to a taxonomy. A taxonomy is generated by a classification method that partitions items into classes and classes into superclasses on the next higher hierarchical level.

Thus, in this context, a classification is interpreted as the result of a classification method that generates a hierarchical partition of items into classes. Classification is used in Chapter 16.1 in a different meaning. There, the mutually exclusive classes are already known, and rules or other functions must be learned on training objects that can afterward be applied to classify new objects, that is, the rules assign a new object (dependent on its values) to the known classes. Thus, in Chapter 16.1, classification deals with the generation and application of classification functions.

Whereas Chapter 5.7 generally introduces taxonomies, we discuss taxonomies in this introduction in the special context of data mining, where they are used to build hierarchical classes of attributes, attribute values, or of objects (analysis units stored in the database and exploited by data mining). There is a duality between taxonomies for attribute values and objects. An object taxonomy can be represented in a database by a special attribute, and an attribute value taxonomy (taxonomy on the domain of an attribute) provides an associated object taxonomy.

Large taxonomies are available in many scientific, bibliographic, business, and official statistics domains. For instance, an extensive classification of astronomic terms is provided by NASA, and official internationally agreed classifications of drugs, diseases, and product codes have been arranged. The Medline Information System maintains a taxonomy of eighteen thousand entries in the biomedical area.

Not only are these large taxonomies useful for KDD, but also very small domains of attributes can be arranged in taxonomies. Consider the attribute family status with only four values: unmarried, married, divorced, widowed. A simple taxonomy can, for example, put together the values unmarried, divorced, and widowed in a single group. Another simple taxonomy is shown in Figure 1 for an age attribute.

Various methods are applied to define and generate taxonomies. These range from direct, often task-dependent specification by an analyst, through discussion and coordination processes within a group of experts partially supported by classification techniques, to fully automatic classification or clustering techniques.

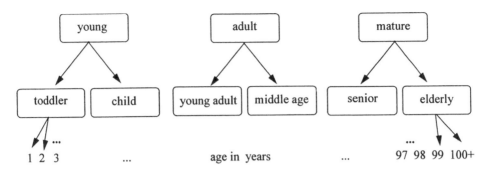

Figure 1 Example of a simple age taxonomy

In the KDD context, two types of items are especially important: objects (the analysis units, e.g., clients or patients) and values of attributes. In the first case, one is interested in clustering methods that generate clusters of objects. Clustering is treated in Chapter 16.5 as a data mining task. In this article, we concentrate on the second case and discuss taxonomies for the values of one attribute with a discrete or continuous-value domain. Such a taxonomy can be exploited in many KDD tasks. On the other hand, a given hierarchical clustering of objects can be represented by an attribute. Then each cluster is a value for this attribute, for example, a label of a cluster is used as the attribute value and this value is associated to each object belonging to the cluster.

Sometimes taxonomies of attributes are also important. In this case, the items are not the values of a single attribute, but the attributes themselves. The attributes captured in a database are then arranged in a taxonomy, for example, by putting together highly correlated attributes in a class. Attributes can be arranged in a set of classes not only by statistical properties (e.g., correlation), but also by domain aspects (e.g., income or education attributes).

A special case of attribute taxonomies relates to a database with (only) binary attributes, for example, a term taxonomy in a text-mining application. Often the binary attributes can be interpreted as values of a more general attribute representing a term category. They are introduced as separate attributes, for example, to handle an attribute with multiple values when objects assume more than one value. Thus, for documents and terms as attributes, usually more than one term of a category is associated to a document.

Taxonomies on the domain of a single attribute often represent monodimensional concepts such as a family status or age taxonomy. But a clustering result derived from many variables can also be included as a new attribute in a data set. Then the taxonomy for this derived attribute captures multidimensional concepts.

Let D be the domain of an attribute A. A may belong to a database schema or be a general attribute defining a set of binary attributes. A taxonomy T consists of a set of subsets of D, which usually form a partition, that is, are mutually disjoint subsets that cover D. A taxonomy is often hierarchically arranged, that is, the subsets are partially ordered by inclusion and, on each hierarchical level, the set of subsets belonging to this level is a partitioning. Besides hierarchies in the form of trees, directed acyclical graphs are also allowed, where a node has several ancestors. This is sometimes useful to represent overlapping or orthogonal hierarchies. The predecessor relation of a taxonomy typically represents an *is-a* relationship. Usually, T will be much smaller than the power set of D. Such a taxonomy can explicitly and statically be given for an attribute, or dynamically and implicitly determined by a special search process that generates and evaluates certain subsets of attribute values during a mining task.

Attributes with taxonomies are usually called structured attributes in machine learning (Michalski, 1983). Basically, two types of taxonomies exist, those that have a strong substantial meaning such as official or agreed classifications of diseases, drugs, countries, and others that are mainly introduced *ad hoc* for grouping purposes, such as income or age classes. But for continuous attributes, domain-related official taxonomies may also exist, for example, income intervals defined in tax legislation. Whereas taxonomies from the first type are fixed, the partial ordering structure of the second taxonomies may be modified within the context of a KDD application.

For continuous attributes, there are usually different ways to group the values into discrete ranges, and unless definitive domain knowledge is available, the optimal organization for a particular KDD task may not be apparent. Often, a particular hierarchy of intervals may be useful for one KDD task but irrelevant to another.

2. Taxonomy Generation

A high-level summary of taxonomy generation methods is presented in this section. Table 1 summarizes the dimensions that are relevant for classifying these methods. A special and very important case of taxonomy generation is presented in much more detail in Chapter 14.4 for the discretization task. Many of the details of discretization methods can be transferred and adapted to the general taxonomy generation task.

The simplest approach for a KDD system to construct taxonomies is to let the user define such a hierarchy. When official taxonomies should be used, they must just be made available or edited. A taxonomy editor allows a comfortable and flexible definition and modification of annotated value subsets that are hierarchically arranged as partitions.

But user-specified *a priori* or predefined taxonomies are static and not adjusted to the knowledge available in the data, that is, to a special analytic question of a data mining task and its data. Sometimes it is useful to provide dynamically constructed taxonomies for a mining task, especially when no official taxonomies exist or are applicable for an attribute. Then it is worthwhile to consider taxonomy construction relating to the question of how appropriate taxonomies, or also, in some cases, not necessarily exhaustive subsets of values, can be found for an attribute A. Dependent on the type of A, diverse methods are used for automatically generating value subsets for A.

Basically, the cases of a nominal, ordinal, or continuous attribute can be distinguished. Sometimes background knowledge on the value domain D can be used for taxonomy construction. An example of background knowledge that can be exploited to construct taxonomies is a nominal attribute representing geographical regions with background information on neighboring regions. An admissible subset of values may then be defined by some conditions on the neighborhood structure of regional value clusters. Such a geographical taxonomy finder is implemented in the Data Surveyor system (Chapter 24.2.2), see (Gebhardt, 1997) for the theoretical foundations of a solution that overcomes the combinatorial explosion and randomness of regional clusters.

Most work in taxonomy construction has been done in the continuous case and the discretization problem (see Chapter 14.4; and, Dougherty et al. (1995) for an overview).

Table 1 Dimensions for Taxonomy Generation

Type of attribute	Nominal	Ordinal	Continuous
Depends on target variables	Yes: supervised	No: unsupervised	
Based on background knowledge	Yes	No	
Depends on subpopulation	Yes: local	No: global	
Integrated into data mining search	Yes: dynamic	No: static	
Taxonomy structure	Nonhierarchical	Tree	Directed acyclical graph (DAG)
Hierarchy generation	Top-down	Bottom-up	

Supervised taxonomy finders are methods that exploit the joint distribution of the taxonomy variable (the variable for which a taxonomy is constructed, e.g., age) with designated target variables for a classification (e.g., incidence of a disease). The found value classes of the taxonomy variable highlight distinct patterns in the behavior of the target variables (age groups with similar disease rates). Supervised discretization methods are mostly applied for the classification problem (Chapter 16.1) and usually deal with a continuous taxonomy variable and a binary target. Then discretizations (discrete intervals) shall be derived for the taxonomy variable that augment the classification accuracy of, for example, a decision tree. But discretization methods for continuous target variables have also been proposed (Subramonian et al., 1997).

Unsupervised methods usually only rely on the univariate distribution of the variable for which a taxonomy shall be derived, for example, for discretization (Chapter 14.4). Quantiles and other simple methods, and also density-based or clustering approaches, which may also exploit all other attributes (not particularly some designated target attributes), are used. Clustering approaches (Chapter 16.5) usually rely on a similarity function measuring the degree of similarity for any two values.

Next, we distinguish global and local methods. Global methods find a taxonomy independent from a special mining task (e.g., classification of a disease) and, for example, a subgroup that has to be expanded in a decision tree by a conjunctive selector. For example, a taxonomy derived for an income attribute in the context of the local subgroup males of the tree (which is constructed for classifying the disease) could be different from a taxonomy in the context of the subgroup females.

Static and global taxonomy generation methods can efficiently be supported by visualization frameworks, in which several generation strategies can be experimented with, and which visually assist analysts in finding an appropriate number and arrangement of hierarchies. An example of such a visual framework is given for attribute discretization by Subramonian et al. (1997).

Top-down methods generate taxonomies by stepwise or recursive specializations of already-found classes on each hierarchical level. For ordinal (and continuous) attributes, a best splitting point into two (or more) intervals is found on each level. However, recursive splitting does not necessarily find the best multi-interval split and some simple splitting heuristics have problems with multimodal or other special dependency forms (e.g., U-form) between target and taxonomy variables. Bottom-up methods generalize the classes already found on a hierarchical level to create the superclasses for the next higher level, for example, by merge techniques.

Sometimes only partial (not exhaustive or covering) taxonomies are needed. These partial taxonomies consist of disjoint classes of similar attribute values that do not cover the whole attribute domain. These partial taxonomies are, for instance, dynamically and locally constructed in rule (Chapter 16.2) or other subgroup mining tasks (Chapter 16.3) when adding further conjuncts to a rule condition or subgroup description.

3. Using Taxonomies for KDD Tasks

Taxonomies are often statically edited or generated when preprocessing the data and then applied in data mining or postprocessing tasks. To avoid some of the problems of static construction, taxonomy generation is sometimes dynamically embedded in a special mining or postprocessing task. Then the coordination between the data mining search and taxomomy generation and time-efficiency of the data mining task must be appropriately solved.

Taxonomies are also important for some preprocessing tasks (see Chapters 13, 14, and 15), especially when applying cross-tabulation, OLAP, or visualization methods. Then a derived discretized variable is sometimes used instead of an original continuous variable. For example, when visualizing relationships in very large databases, scatter diagrams using continuous variables may not be appropriate, because of producing mainly black paper. Then some data reduction achieved with taxonomies may be helpful. Taxonomies provide a high-

Table 2 Advantages of Taxonomies

Data reduction	Very large data sets, categorical analysis methods
Interpretability	Avoid nonsense or odd groupings of attribute(s) (values)
Simplicity	Avoid repetitions, find appropriate hierarchical level
Ordering	General to specific, find deviations and exceptions
Search reduction	Pruning of subnodes
Greediness	Expansion by selectors with higher coverage
Focusing	Support specification of mining task, select aggregation level

level overview of the behavior of target variables by partitioning the taxonomy variable into classes within which the target behavior may be similar.

But taxonomies are predominantly applied in data mining tasks (Chapter 16). In the following, we discuss some advantages of using taxonomies for a data mining search task. These advantages are summarized in Table 2.

Taxonomies are used when a mining method does not allow the exploitation of nominal attributes with many values or continuous attributes. Consider, for example, the task of deriving characteristic rules (Chapter 16.2.2). Then taxonomies are used by generalization operators to include higher-level values of attributes in a generalized relation. As a special case, it may often be advantageous to use intervals for ordinal variables. Taxonomies are especially important for rule generation, subgroup, conceptual clustering, probabilistic network, and some classification methods (e.g., classification trees, rough sets). Attribute-value pairs play a role for all these methods, and instead of using low-level values of the attributes, values on a higher taxonomical level may be advantageous, for example, to identify more significant patterns.

Taxonomies are also helpful to avoid nonsensical or odd models or patterns in data mining. Whenever models or patterns involve sets of values of an attribute (e.g., conceptual clustering, association rules, classification methods, subgroup mining), then faked and noninterpretable sets must not be generated. In order to generate only interpretable models or patterns, not every subset of the domain D of an attribute is usually allowed. A taxonomy for the values of an attribute consisting of a set of subsets of D then holds the allowed subsets. For example, in subgroup mining, taxonomies are important to provide an application relevant and interpretable description language (Chapter 16.3).

When taxonomies are available for attributes, for example, putting similar, highly correlated attributes into a class, nonsense combinations of attributes can be avoided in a similar way. Building regression models based on stepwise forward construction or backward elimination search heuristics can exploit such an attribute taxonomy, for example, by selecting only one representative from a group of highly correlated attributes.

Another advantage of taxonomies is to produce models or patterns that are simpler and present the findings on an appropriate hierarchical level. A finding will thus not be separately presented for all or most items belonging to a taxonomy entry (e.g., individually for the United States, Canada, France, Germany, Great Britain, Italy, and Japan, but taken as a group for the G-7 countries). Thus, repetitions are avoided and appropriate generalizations are produced along the taxonomical structure.

Furthermore, taxonomies can restrict the hypothesis space for a data mining search task. Instead of analyzing all patterns associated with the lower-level values of a taxonomy, it may be sufficient to study only the higher-level patterns. Thus, not only can the search effort be reduced by top-down search strategies, but also nongreedy strategies can be devised. For attributes with many values, elementary selectors built with a single value and added as a further conjunct to a subgroup (or other model or pattern) will often lead to a small resulting subgroup that possibly has too small a statistical significance, so that results can only be found on more general levels. With a taxonomy, implicit internal disjunctions are introduced. Instead of exploring the space of all internal disjunctions (power set of domain) that is often combinatorically prohibitive, a much smaller space is explored.

Finally, taxonomies are also important for the effectiveness of search algorithms: they can avoid algorithms that are too greedy and allow more patient search strategies (see Chapter 11) that can avoid some problems of local optimals in heuristic local search approaches.

Taxonomies are also useful to focus a data mining task. The user can select the level of abstraction for which findings shall be revealed. For example, in association rule applications, nodes in a taxonomical hierarchy may be selected for which association rules shall be found, that is, the analyst only wants association rules that contain children of a specific item in a hierarchical taxonomy. These constraints can be considered in a postprocessing step when filtering all association rules found, but by integrating these constraints into the mining algorithm the execution time of the mining algorithm can be reduced (Srikant et al., 1997). An example of such a taxonomic item constraint is (Jackets and Shoes) or descendants (Clothes) and (not ancestors (Hiking Boots)).

Attributes for which a taxonomy is defined can be used as dependent (target) or independent (exploratory) variables. To deal with structured dependent variables, Kaufman and Michalski (1996) proposed to first focus rules on the top-level nodes. Subsequently, rules are created for descendant nodes in the context of their ancestors. Such a multidimensional search space has also been exploited in Explora (Klösgen, 1996). The same approach can also be applied for the subgroup mining paradigm (Chapter 16.3). First, subgroups for the most general target variables (e.g., all products of a company) are searched, and then exceptions or deviations for more special targets (product groups) are found.

In postprocessing tasks, taxonomies are useful for filtering and generalizing results. Consider association rules as an example. In a brute force search step, many associations are found that are then filtered in a specific application question. When focusing an application question, taxonomies and constraints (Chapter 18.2) are specified.

References

Dougherty, J., R. Kohavi, and M. Sahami. 1995. "Supervised and unsupervised discretization of continuous features." In *Proceedings of the Twelfth International Conference on Machine Learning*, pp. 194–202. San Francisco: Morgan Kaufmann.

Gebhardt, F. 1997. "Finding spatial clusters." In *Proceedings of the First European Symposium on Principles of KDD*, edited by J. Komorowski, and J. Żytkow, pp. 277–287. Berlin: Springer-Verlag.

Kaufman, K., and R. S. Michalski. 1996. "A method for reasoning with structured and continuous attributes in the INLEN-2 multistrategy knowledge discovery system." In *Proceedings of the Second International Conference on Knowledge Discovery and Data Mining*, edited by E. Simoudis, J. Han, and U. Fayyad, pp. 232–237. Menlo Park, CA: AAAI Press.

Klösgen, W. 1996. "Explora: a multipattern and multistrategy discovery assistant." In *Advances in Knowledge Discovery and Data Mining*, edited by U. Fayyad, G. Piatetsky-Shapiro, P. Smyth, and R. Uthurusamy, pp. 249–271. Cambridge, MA: MIT Press.

Michalski, R. S. 1983. "A theory and methodology of inductive learning." In *Machine Learning: An Artificial Intelligence Approach*, edited by R. S. Michalski, J. Carbonell, and T. Mitchell, pp. 83–134. Palo Alto, CA: Tioga Publishing.

Srikant, R., Q. Vu, and R. Agrawal. 1997. "Mining association rules with item constraints." In *Proceedings of the Third International Conference on Knowledge Discovery and Data Mining*, edited by D. Heckerman, H. Mannila, and D. Pregibon, pp. 67–73. Menlo Park, CA: AAAI Press.

Subramonian, R., R. Venkata, and J. Chen. 1997. "A visual interactive framework for attribute discretization." In *Proceedings of the Third International Conference on Knowledge Discovery and Data Mining*, edited by D. Heckerman, H. Mannila, and D. Pregibon, pp. 82–88. Menlo Park, CA: AAAI Press.

18.2 Constraints

Willi Klösgen

ABSTRACT We define constraints as conditions restricting a set of options in order to exclude unreasonable or useless options from being selected by a user or a method. More specifically, we focus on constraints for search tasks performed in the data mining step and describe several types of constraints that restrict large hypotheses spaces. We discuss syntactic constraints, domain, quality, and redundancy constraints, analyzing how they improve search efficiency and contribute to finding interesting results.

1. Introduction

Within a knowledge discovery in databases (KDD) process many tasks are performed, each allowing a set of options. Not all of these options are reasonable or useful within a given context of a special application domain, analytic question, or user preference. Constraints can, very generally, be defined as conditions that restrict an option set. They include expert and domain knowledge that help to automate and focus parts of a discovery process. Constraints can be built into a discovery system, for instance, following an expert system–based approach (Hand, 1992), or be specified by a user. Under this very general view, quite different constraints are relevant for the many diverse KDD tasks. To focus the discussion, in this article we deal with restrictions specified by a user on large hypotheses spaces.

A data mining step is a central step within a KDD process that typically includes a large-scale search task performed within a hypothesis space. Such a search task deals with an analytic question and is specified by a database for which the analytic question has to be answered, a hypothesis language to construct hypotheses of a type that is appropriate for answering the analytic question, (neighbor-) operators defining the topology of the hypothesis space, quality functions to evaluate hypotheses, and a search strategy that is applied to process the hypothesis space. Any instantiation of such a search task typically requires the specification of various options, for example, selecting a subset of the database, setting conditions for hypotheses to be regarded as interesting, or choosing parameters of the search strategy such as the width of a beam search.

This general definition of a data mining search task can be applied to many data mining approaches and covers such hypothesis types as decision trees (Chapter 16.1.3), rules (Chapters 16.1.4 and 16.2), subgroups (Chapter 16.3), equations (Chapter 16.4), clusterings (Chapter 16.5), and probabilistic networks (Chapter 16.6). A formal definition of this view on a data mining task is given by Siebes (1995).

With this focus, we discuss in Section 2 constraints that restrict the hypothesis space of a data mining search task. Restricting the hypothesis space is useful for excluding uninteresting hypotheses and to limit the search effort. To deal with interestingness, constraints refer to the various aspects of interestingness that include statistical significance and several aspects of substantive significance like novelty or usefulness. Specifically, we regard heuristic or exhaustive, general to specific, generate- and test-search approaches (see Chapters 11 and 16.3.1). To achieve search efficiency, pruning conditions are often necessary. These constraints allow the next specialization levels of a general to specific search to be cut off if the condition of a constraint is not satisfied. Thus, for a search node that does not satisfy a pruning constraint, no further generate step producing successors is applied.

According to the components of a search task, constraints can refer to the hypothesis language, the neighborhood operators, the quality function, or the search strategy. The constraints can be applied in a (brute force) search phase, or in a postprocessing refinement phase where large-scale search results are filtered and refined.

Generally, postprocessing constraining is very attractive to save overall exploration time. In a broad and brute force search task, a large number of results are first collected, which are then filtered according to different application views in various postprocessing tasks. This approach is efficient if filtering needs much less computation time than a new search and requires that a broad first search is possible that can be focused afterward by different filtering tasks. Such a broad search is for instance constitutive for association rule approaches.

2. Types of Constraints

Seven dimensions that can be used for classifying constraints are summarized in the rows of Table 1. In this section we describe four types of constraints (first row) that can be used for the three objectives (second row) to restrict the number of hypotheses that are generated and evaluated during search, or presented as results to the user, and to exclude uninteresting results.

2.1. Syntactic Constraints

These constraints limit the construction of hypotheses by fixing some details of the hypothesis language. Thus, they directly influence the size of the hypothesis space of a search task. For subgroup mining patterns (Chapter 5.2), the user typically specifies the maximal number of conjuncts in a subgroup description, whether only positive selectors or also negations of selectors can be included, or if internal disjunctions are allowed in a conjunctive selector. These kinds of constraints can be specified both for the left- and right-hand sides of an association pattern (Chapter 16.2.3). Similar constraints can be given for equation finders, for example, maximal number of terms in an equation, and allowed transformations of variables (Chapter 16.4.2). The details of these constraints depend on the type of hypothesis language. By their syntactic nature, these constraints do not refer directly to an aspect of the application domain. Indirectly, of course, their selection can be influenced by the application area, which, for instance, only considers descriptions with a limited number of conjunctions as potentially interesting because of their being interpretable by the specific users.

Syntactic constraints can often reduce the search space very strongly, which is useful, especially for highly interactive applications. Typically, in the first exploratory analyses, such constraints are specified very restrictively and then relaxed for further refined analyses where the search is focused in subareas identified by the first explorations (compare, e.g., the typical use of the FortyNiner system, Chapter 24.1.4). Often syntactic constraints are pruning constraints, allowing a general to specific search strategy to stop the further specialization. A simple example is the depth of a beam or hill climbing strategy fixing, for example, the maximal number of conjunctions or terms in a hypothesis.

Because these syntactic constraints are domain independent, they can easily be implemented in a data mining system and thus are offered for the specification of a search task in nearly all systems.

Table 1 Dimensions for Classifying Constraints for Hypothesis Spaces

Type	Redundancy:	Syntactic	Domain	Quality
Objective		Restrict search effort	Restrict number of results	Exclude uninteresting results
Pruning potential		Can be directly used for pruning	Needs estimators	No pruning possible
Search component		Hypothesis language or neighborhood operator	Quality evaluation	Search strategy
Interestingness aspect		Statistical significance	Usefulness	Novelty
Generality		Special constraint for single hypothesis type	General constraint for several hypothesis types	

2.2. Domain Constraints

Domain constraints explicitly refer to domain knowledge to restrict the search space or to filter search results. The constraints must be embedded into the representation of a search space and exploited by a general search strategy, and therefore references to domain knowledge must be expressed in a standardized form. Moreover, the type of domain knowledge that can be used for constraints will be different for the various hypotheses types, for example, association rules can refer to domain knowledge other than Bayesian networks.

A common type of domain knowledge for most hypothesis types includes some background knowledge about variables and variable values. Thus, relations defined on the set of variables or their value sets can restrict the variables that are used together in a model (e.g., regression model; see Chapters 16.1.7 and 16.4), or the combinations of variable values that appear together in a subgroup description. Similar variables (e.g., several income variables) are arranged in groups, and to refine a current hypothesis, only the best variable from a group (according to some evaluation measure) not already occurring in the current hypothesis is added. Thus, at most one variable from each group can appear in a model. Similarity of variables is defined from an application or statistical view, for example, by arranging highly correlated variables in a group.

Relations between variable values are primarily used to constrain search spaces in subgroup mining and association rules. Feldman and Hirsh (1997) extend association mining methods by algorithms exploiting these background constraints. Because association rule applications identify very many patterns, some intelligent filtering is needed, either during search or in a postprocessing phase. A template language is defined by Baralis and Psaila (1997) to specify constraints for association rules. Feldman and Hirsh (1997) discuss which special types of unitary or binary domain predicates can significantly reduce the search time for association rules.

Such association rule constraints can, for example, specify that associations between products that appear on the same page in a special advertisement are not interesting, that associations between countries with a common border are uninteresting, or that associations between persons and nations are not interesting when the person possesses the corresponding nationality.

Taxonomies (Chapter 18.1) can also be seen as a special domain constraint type; they constrain the internal disjunctions entering a selector of, for instance, a subgroup description. Consider, for example, a taxonomy on occupations. Then not just any sets of occupations can be used to describe a subgroup of clients, but only disjunctions of occupations that belong to a taxonomical entry in the hierarchy. Srikant et al. (1997) discuss the problem of discovering association rules when constraints are given as Boolean expressions over the presence or absence of the items that can enter an association rule. Items can also be selected from a taxonomy. An example of such a Boolean constraint is ((Jackets and Shoes) or (descendants (Clothes) and not ancestors (Hiking Boots)). They demonstrate that integrating these item constraints into a search can speed up the algorithm by a factor of five to twenty.

Constraints for variables are pruning constraints that very effectively restrict the further expansion of nodes in a search space. Constraints for variable values usually have a lower pruning potential (Feldman and Hirsh, 1997) because they may not be exploited with respect to the general to specific order.

More complex domain constraints have only been exploited in some special mining methods. Specifically for inductive logic programming (ILP) approaches, such constraints are possible because of the very powerful hypothesis language that allows the inclusion of background knowledge. See Chapter 16.2.4 for some specific examples.

2.3. Quality Constraints

A quality constraint typically requires that only hypotheses with a quality greater than a specified threshold are presented as interesting. As discussed below, quality constraints specify conditions on the quality of a single hypothesis, on the context quality of a hypothesis, and also on components of a quality. The quality of a hypothesis usually includes the combined evaluation of several aspects or components of interestingness. Typically, a statistical evaluation of significance (e.g., P-value of a test statistic, or z-score) is an important component of a quality measure, which can be combined with more subjective evaluations of novelty and usefulness aspects, but can also be the only quality aspect considered.

In addition to constraints for the combined quality measure, constraints for the components can also be specified. A statistical significance measure itself typically combines at least two partial aspects, the number of cases that support the hypothesis (e.g., support or size of a subgroup) and the distinctness of the pattern (e.g., deviation size). The support constraint requiring at least a minimal number of cases supporting a hypothesis is, for instance, very effective in restricting the search spaces of subgroup mining; and support and confidence thresholds are used specifically for association rules (Chapters 16.2.3 and 16.3).

The context quality of a hypothesis relates to a search strategy. In a general to specific search, a current node is additionally evaluated in the context of its parent node. Rule finders and subgroup miners provide examples of context quality. The CN2 algorithm (Chapter 16.1.4) requires that a rule is significantly different from its parent rule. A subgroup miner requires that a subgroup behaves in a statistically different way from its parent subgroup (Chapter 16.3.1).

Another context evaluation refers to the mining objective of deriving the best system of hypotheses, for example, a system of rules with the highest classification accuracy to be used for classification (Chapter 16.1.4) or a system of subgroups (Chapter 16.3). Corresponding evaluation constraints can be processed in the search phase or the postprocessing phase. The CWS algorithm (Chapter 16.1.4) integrates a best rule set quality evaluation into the search phase.

These quality constraints primarily address the interestingness evaluation and also contribute to reducing the number of reported hypotheses when data mining methods generate very many results. They can sometimes also be used as pruning constraints that provide very effective conditions for stopping further expansions in a general to specific search. The support constraint is a simple, but effective, pruning example that can be extended to a simple context constraint requiring that the support of a node is in a special range which depends on the parent support (i.e., the subgroup has not nearly the same number of objects as the parent group or is only a very small part of the parent group).

Depending on the search strategy, quality estimates can be exploited. When searching for the best n subgroups, all those subgroups can be pruned for which all successors that fulfill the support constraint cannot have a higher quality than the current nth best subgroup. The optimistic estimate of the highest possible quality of allowed successors depends on the quality function, so that for each function an estimate must be derived. In Klösgen (1996), some general classes of quality functions are analyzed for which an easy calculation of such an estimate is possible. These estimates show a different power, that is, the pruning potential for diverse quality functions is very different. Special estimates have also been derived for some other quality functions, for example, by Smyth and Goodman (1992) for information theoretic measures.

2.4. Redundancy Constraints

The context quality constraint can be seen as a special redundancy constraint that eliminates a hypothesis as redundant with respect to another hypothesis. Meta rules, equivalence classes, and partial orderings are also applied for redundancy elimination. Meta rules or algorithmic approaches determine when a hypothesis is suppressed by another hypothesis. When redundancy elimination is based on equivalence classes or clusterings of hypotheses, one representative from each class or cluster is selected for presentation. In Feldman et al. (1997), several kinds of equivalence classes and partial orderings are defined for associations of subgroups. Redundancy constraints are mainly processed in a search refinement phase. As an example, we discuss several equivalence relations to build equivalence classes of associations for text-mining applications. When equivalence classes of associations are defined, only one representative association from each class is included in the keyword graph presented that visualizes the associations found.

The first equivalence is called cover equivalence. Two associations are cover equivalent if they have the same cover. For example, (Iran, Iraq) ⇒ (Kuwait, U.S.) is equivalent to (Iran, Iraq, Kuwait) ⇒ U.S. because they both have the same cover (Iran, Iraq, Kuwait, U.S.). The association with the highest association or similarity measure is selected as the representative from a cover equivalence class.

Context equivalence is another equivalence relation. Two associations are context equivalent, if, and only if, they are identical up to a different context. That means that the two associations are identical, when from each association those concepts are eliminated that appear on both sides. For example, (Iran, Iraq) ⇒ (Iran, U.S.) is equivalent to (Kuwait, Iraq) ⇒ (Kuwait, U.S.). The first association establishes a connection between Iraq and U.S. in the context of Iran, whereas the second association is related to the context of Kuwait. The context-free associations (or the most general associations with a sufficient quality) are selected as the representatives from this equivalence class (e.g., Iraq ⇒ U.S.).

The next definition relates to a partial ordering of associations. An association A1 is stronger than an association A2, if and only if the cover of A1 is a subset of the cover of A2. As special cases of this ordering, the right- and left-hand sides are treated separately.

Redundancy filters are defined for these equivalences and partial orderings. Selecting the representative of an equivalence class or the strongest associations is applied as a basic redundancy filter. Additional criteria can refine these filters. For example, for the context equivalence, a context-conditioned association is selected in addition to the context-free association, if and only if the association of the context-conditioned association is much higher (e.g., defined by a significance criterion).

References

Baralis, E., and G. Psaila. 1997. "Designing templates for mining association rules." *J. Intell. Inform. Sys.* **9(1)**: 7–32.

Feldman, R., and H. Hirsh. 1997. "Exploiting background information in knowledge discovery from text." *J. Intell. Inform. Sys.* **9(1)**: 83–97.

Feldman, R., W. Klösgen, and A. Zilberstein. 1997. "Visualization techniques to explore data mining results for document collections." In *Proceedings of the Third International Conference on Knowledge Discovery and Data Mining (KDD-97)*, edited by D. Heckerman, H. Mannila, and D. Pregibon, pp. 16–23. Menlo Park, CA: AAAI Press.

Hand, D. 1992. *Artificial Intelligence Frontiers in Statistics*. London: Chapman and Hall.

Klösgen, W. 1996. "Explora: a multipattern and multistrategy discovery assistant." In *Advances in Knowledge Discovery and Data Mining*, edited by U. Fayyad, G. Piatetsky-Shapiro, P. Smyth, and R. Uthurusamy, pp. 249–271. Cambridge, MA: MIT Press.

Siebes, A. 1995. "Data surveying: foundations of an inductive query language." In *Proceedings of the First International Conference on Knowledge Discovery and Data Mining (KDD-'95)*, edited by U. Fayyad, and R. Uthurusamy, pp. 269–274. Menlo Park, CA: AAAI Press.

Smyth, P., and R. Goodman. 1992. "An information theoretic approach to rule induction." *IEEE Trans. Knowledge and Data Engng.* **4**: 301–316.

Srikant, R., Q. Vu, and R. Agrawal. 1997. "Mining association rules with item constraints." In *Proceedings of the Third International Conference on Knowledge Discovery and Data Mining (KDD-'97)*, edited by D. Heckerman, H. Mannila, and D. Pregibon, pp. 67–73. Menlo Park, CA: AAAI Press.

18.3 Previously Discovered Knowledge

Bing Liu and Wynne Hsu

ABSTRACT In this article, we discuss how previously discovered knowledge can be used in future knowledge-discovery processes. This is an important topic as in real-life environments data collected in databases change, and patterns mined in the past may no longer be valid. In such situations, the users always want to know what data and patterns have changed and how they have changed. The ability to mine interesting knowledge and/or changes based on previously discovered knowledge is crucial. This article reviews some main techniques related to this topic.

1. Introduction

The objective of data mining is to find interesting/useful knowledge from databases, not just any regularity or rule. It is well known that a data mining system can discover a huge number of rules, most of which are of no interest to the user (Frawley et al., 1991). In this article we review some techniques that attempt to find interesting rules based on previously discovered knowledge. In particular, we focus on how the current data mining process can make use of previously discovered knowledge to mine those rules that are of interest to the user. This is important because in a dynamic environment, which is the case for almost all businesses, the data collected in databases changes and the patterns mined in the past may no longer be valid. Mining for interesting knowledge based on previously discovered knowledge is crucial. For example, in a supermarket a set of association rules was discovered in the first month. In the second month, based on the newly collected data, a different set of association rules was obtained. Naturally, the supermarket manager would like to know in what way the new set of rules differs from those discovered in the previous month, and/or what the interesting and/or novel rules that denote significant changes are. This knowledge allows him/her to predict changing customer behaviors, detect interesting trends, and perform suitable actions in response to the new situation.

Before reviewing the techniques, let us first discuss what types of information and/or rules are interesting to the user. Past research and applications have shown that those rules and information that are unexpected and/or actionable (Piatetsky-Shapiro and Matheus, 1994; Silberschatz and Tuzhilin, 1995; Liu and Hsu, 1996) are interesting to the user:

- Unexpectedness: rules are interesting if they are new to the user or they contradict previously discovered knowledge.

- Actionability: rules are interesting if the user can do something with them to his/her advantage.

Although both unexpectedness and actionability are important, actionability is perhaps the key concept in most applications because actionable rules allow the user to do their job better by taking some specific action in response to the newly discovered knowledge. However, actionability is an elusive concept because it is not feasible to know the space of all rules and the actions to be attached to them (Silberschatz and Tuzhilin, 1996). Current research has been focused on unexpectedness (Liu and Hsu, 1996; Liu et al., 1997). Actionability is partially handled through unexpectedness because actionable rules are either expected or unexpected (Silberschatz and Tuzhilin, 1996). The techniques reviewed below all attempt to find expected and unexpected rules (with respect to existing knowledge). Expected rules are also called conforming rules as they conform to the existing knowledge. The first technique below is in the context of association rule mining (Agrawal and Srikant, 1994). The other techniques are in the context of classification rule mining (Quinlan, 1992).

2. Using Previously Discovered Rules in Association Rule Mining

Recall that an association rule is of the following form (see Chapter 16.2.3):

$$item_1, ..., item_k \Rightarrow item_{k+1}, ..., item_n[support, confidence],$$

where $item_i$ is a data item. The *support* and *confidence* values must be greater than or equal to the user-specified minimum support (*minsup*) and minimum confidence (*minconf*), respectively. An association rule miner first mines the large item sets, and then produces association rules from the large item sets (see Chapter 16.2.3).

In the association rule-mining context, we can use previously discovered rules in the current mining process to find those conforming (expected) and unexpected rules. The degree of unexpectedness can be expressed in terms of the difference in supports and/or confidences between a new rule and its corresponding old rule in the set of previously discovered rules.

Let E be the set of previously discovered association rules and N be the set of new rules discovered in the current data mining process. If we do not consider the support and confidence information, we have the following situations:

1. Some rules appear in both E and N.

2. Some rules in E do not appear in N.

3. Some rules in N do not appear in E.

In the first case, it is easy to compare the supports and the confidences (or a weighted combination of both) of a rule R in E and the same rule R in N. The differences will tell us how much they deviate from each other. The more they deviate, the more unexpected they are with respect to each other. However, in the second and third cases, we are unable to perform the same comparison because we do not know what the supports and confidences of the missing rules are. For example, in a previous mining session, we discovered the following rule:

milk, cheese $\Rightarrow$ bread [support = 5%, confidence = 70%]

In the new mining process, this rule is not generated (either because its support is too low (<*minsup*) or the confidence is too low (<*minconf*)). As a result, we are unable to compute the differences in supports and confidences. This problem, however, can easily be solved. To obtain the set of (missing) rules M that are in E but not in N in the new mining process, we can consider all the rules in E in the new process (for generating N) as follows:

1. Obtain the item sets L of the rules in E.

2. In the item sets generation phase of the new mining process, record the support information of each item set in L even if it does not meet the minimum support requirement.

3. In the rule generation phase of the new mining process, generate each rule in E even if it does not meet the minimum confidence requirement.

In this way, we can obtain the supports and confidences of all the rules in E that are not in N. We denote the new set of rules, $N'(= N \cup E)$. Likewise, we can do the same for the rules in N but not in E, and obtain E'. Then, N' and E' contain the same rules, but their supports and confidences may be different.

With the availability of all the rules, we can compute the differences in supports and confidences of the new rules and the old rules. Statistical tests (e.g., chi-square test) can also be used to determine whether these differences are significant (Mills, 1955). The rules can then be ranked according to these difference values. Finally, we obtain three types of rules based on the confidence comparison (comparison using support or a weighted combination of support and confidence values can be similarly performed).

1. *Conforming rules* (*expected rules*). Rules that do not change significantly in N' and in E'.

2. *Unexpected positive rules.* Rules whose confidences are larger in N' than in E'.

3. *Unexpected negative rules.* Rules whose confidences are larger in E' than in N'.

The missing rules can also be highlighted to the user.

1. *Totally unexpected rules.* Rules that are in N but not in E.

2. *Totally unexpected missing rules.* Rules that are in E but not in N.

3. Using Previously Discovered Rules to Preprocess the Data

The previous technique only works with discrete (or nominal) attributes. In many real-life databases, especially for classification tasks, continuous attributes are involved. The technique presented below attempts to find interesting rules in such databases by preprocessing the data using previously discovered rules (Liu et al., 1997). It works in the context of classification rule mining.

The essence of this technique is to preprocess the database using previously discovered knowledge and then employ a standard classification system, for example, C4.5 (Quinlan,

1992), to discover interesting rules. The technique does not need any modification to the classification system. Though simple, it is surprisingly effective and flexible. It involves two steps:

1. *Preprocessing the database.* Recall a classification rule is of the following format (see Chapter 16.1.4):

$$P_1, ..., P_i, ..., P_r \Rightarrow C,$$

   where P_i is a test on an attribute and C is a class.

   Let E be the set of previously discovered rules. During the preprocessing step of the new classification rule generation task, we introduce additional classes. A test is carried out on each tuple D_k in the database D. Tuples that are found to be conforming or unexpected with respect to E are assigned the *Conform⟨Oc⟩* or *Unexpected⟨Oc⟩* classes, respectively (i.e., their original classes are replaced). For each tuple, ⟨Oc⟩ is the original class of the tuple (see the example below). The remaining tuples (that are unrelated to E) will retain their original classes. The process uses the following definitions:

   - D_k conforms to a previously discovered rule $E_j \in E$ if D_k satisfies both the conditions and the conclusion of E_j.
   - D_k is unexpected with respect to $E_j \in E$ if D_k satisfies the conditions of E_j but not its conclusion.
   - D_k is unrelated to $E_j \in E$ if D_k does not satisfy the conditions of E_j.
   - D_k conforms to E if $\exists E_j \in E$, D_k conforms to E_j.
   - D_k is unexpected with respect to E if $\forall E_j \in E$, D_k does not conform to E_j, and $\exists E_i \in E$, D_k is unexpected with respect to E_i.
   - D_k is unrelated to E if $\forall E_j \in E$, D_k is unrelated to E_j.

   It must be stressed that these definitions are not unique. See (Liu et al., 1997) for more details.

2. *Running a classification rule-mining system.* After the database has been processed, a classification rule-mining system is used to mine rules in the modified database. This produces conforming and unexpected rules.

Let us see an example. This example uses the credit-screening database created by Chiharu Sano in the University of California–Irvine (UCI) machine-learning repository (Merz and Murphy, 1996). This database has 125 tuples, 10 attributes, and 2 classes *Yes* and *No* representing whether credit has been granted. The rule-mining system used is C4.5 (Quinlan, 1992). Assume we want to study two previously discovered rules:

Previous Rule 1:   *Sex = Female, Age > = 47 ⇒ No*

Previous Rule 2:   *Sex = Female, Bought = Jewel ⇒ No*

There are eleven rules generated using the proposed technique. Below, we only list the conforming and unexpected rules:

Rule 1: *Sex = Female, Age > 52 ⇒ ConformNo*

Rule 2: *Sex = Female, Age > 47, Age <= 52 ⇒ UnexpectedYes*

Rule 3: *Sex = Female, Bought = Jewel, Age <= 52 ⇒ UnexpectedYes*

ConformNo means that this rule conforms to the existing knowledge and its credit-granting class is *No*. *UnexpectedYes* means that the rule is unexpected and its class is *Yes*.

Rule 1 says that only when *Sex = Female* and *Age > 52* will the person not be granted credit. When the age is between 48 (*Age > 47*) and 52 (Rule 2), the person is granted credit, which is unexpected. When *Bought = Jewel*, *Sex = Female*, and *Age* <= 52 (Rule 3), the person is also given credit, which is also unexpected (with regard to the previously discovered Rule 2).

4. Theory Refinement and Finding Unexpected Rules

Theory refinement, which is a branch of machine learning (Mahoney and Mooney, 1994; Towell and Shavlik, 1994; Donoho and Rendell, 1995), can also help to find conforming rules and unexpected rules with respect to the previously discovered knowledge. In theory refinement, the initial knowledge given is an incomplete or incorrect theory of the problem domain. This existing knowledge may be the previously discovered rules or supplied by domain experts. Data examples are used to modify this initial knowledge (or theory) into a more accurate or predictive set of classification rules (Mahoney and Mooney, 1994). In the process, interesting rules may be discovered. There are two main types of theory refinement technique. The first type is based on refinement operators (Ourston and Mooney, 1990), and the second type is based on neural networks (Towell and Shavlik, 1994).

Given a set of existing rules, the first type typically works as follows. A set of refinement operators and a search procedure (e.g., hill-climbing search) are used to modify the existing rules. According to the new data, operators can specialize rules (e.g., add new conditions), generalize rules (e.g., delete some useless conditions), remove old rules, and add new rules. The resulting set of new rules is more accurate (or predictive) with respect to the new data.

Traditional theory refinement systems stop here. However, more can be done to give the user the conforming and unexpected knowledge with respect to the existing rules by comparing the new rules with the existing rules. Those rules that remain unchanged represent conforming rules. Those new rules and modified rules are unexpected with respect to the existing knowledge.

Neural network–based theory refinement typically proceeds as follows:

1. Existing rules are first used to set up the initial network structure. This is done by assigning suitable weights on links and biases of units to reflect the application of these rules.

2. Input units corresponding to attributes of the database that do not appear in any condition of the existing rules are added to the network.

3. Links are added to the network to give existing rules access to items not mentioned in the existing knowledge.

4. After the network is produced, it is refined by using the new data to train the network, for example, using the backpropagation method.

Traditionally, a neural network is seen as a black box. Recent research has shown that symbolic rules can be generated from trained neural networks to explain their behaviors (Setiono and Liu, 1996). These new rules can also be compared with the existing input rules to find conforming and unexpected knowledge for the user.

5. Using Previous Knowledge in the Rule Generation Process

Unlike theory refinement, which modifies existing rules, this technique generates new (classification) rules that are maximally consistent with the existing or previously discovered knowledge (Ortega and Fisher, 1995; Pazzani et al., 1997). That is, it uses the existing rules as references in the new rule generation process.

Given a set of previously discovered rules, the technique works as follows:

1. Assume the existing knowledge is correct. In the rule generation process, the system will try to choose test conditions that are consistent with the existing knowledge. In the event that there are several test conditions that are equally informative or are statistically indistinguishable, the test condition that is both accurate and conforms to existing knowledge will be selected. If a test condition is not consistent with the existing knowledge but appears to be the best according to the normal test selection procedure

(e.g., information gain of the rule generation algorithm in C4.5; Quinlan, 1992), the system will check whether there is a "spurious correlation" in the data. If so, this test condition will not be selected.

2. When the existing knowledge is proved to be incorrect after some statistical testing, the system has to choose test conditions that do not conform to the existing knowledge. In this case, we have found something unexpected because they are against the existing rules.

The resulting set of rules can also be compared with previously discovered rules to obtain conforming and unexpected rules.

One important problem that needs to be noted is that classification rule mining does not find all possible rules that exist in data, but only a subset to form an accurate classifier (Pazzani et al., 1997; Clark and Matwin, 1993). As a result, many unexpected (or novel) rules that exist in the database are left undiscovered. Liu et al. (1998a,b) propose a technique to deal with this problem. It combines methods from both classification and association rule mining to find the complete set of classification rules. It also shows that an accurate classifier can be built by choosing a subset of rules from this complete set.

References

Agrawal, R., and R. Srikant. 1994. "Fast algorithms for mining association rules." In *Proceedings of the Twentieth International Conference on Very Large Databases (VLDB-94)*, pp. 487–499. Santiago, Chile.

Clark, P., and S. Matwin. 1993. "Using qualitative models to guide induction learning." In *Proceedings of International Conference on Machine Learning*, pp. 49–56. San Mateo, CA: Morgan Kaufmann.

Donoho, S. K., and L. A. Rendell. 1995. "Representing and restructuring domain theories: a constructive induction approach." *J. Artificial Intell. Res.* **2**: 411–446.

Evans, R. R., and D. Fisher. 1994. "Overcoming process delays with decision tree induction." *IEEE Expert* **9**: 60–66.

Frawley, W. J., G. Piatetsky-Shapiro, and C. J. Matheus. 1991. "Knowledge discovery in databases: an overview." In *Knowledge Discovery in Databases*, edited by G. Piatetsky-Shapiro, and W. J. Frawley, pp. 1–27. Cambridge, MA: AAAI/MIT Press.

Liu, B., and W. Hsu. 1996. "Post-analysis of learned rules." In *Proceedings of the Thirteenth National Conference on Artificial Intelligence (AAAI-96)*, pp. 828–834. Menlo Park, CA: AAAI Press.

Liu, B., W. Hsu, and S. Chen. 1997. "Discovering conforming and unexpected classification rules." In *IJCAI-97 Workshop on Intelligent Data Analysis in Medicine and Pharmacology (IDAMAP-97)*, pp. 41–48. Nagoya, Japan: IJCAI.

Liu, B., W. Hsu, and Y. M. Ma. 1998a. "Integrating classification and association rule mining." In *Proceedings of the Fourth International Conference on Knowledge Discovery and Data Mining (KDD-98)*, pp. 27–31. Menlo Park, CA: AAAI Press.

Liu, B., W. Hsu, L. F. Mun, and H. Lee. 1998b. "Finding interesting patterns using user expectations." *IEEE Trans. Knowledge and Data Engng* **11(6)**: 817–832.

Mahoney, J. J., and R. J. Mooney. 1994. "Comparing methods for refining certainty-factor rule bases." In *Proceedings of International Conference on Machine Learning (ICML-94)*, pp. 173–180. New York: Kluwer.

Merz, C. J. and P. Murphy. 1996. *UCI repository of machine learning database*. Available at http://www.cs.uci.edu/~mlearn/MLRepository.html.

Mills, F. 1955. *Statistical Methods*. London: Pitman.

Ortega, J., and D. Fisher. 1995. "Flexibly exploiting prior knowledge in empirical learning." In *Proceedings of the Fourteenth International Joint Conference on Artificial Intelligence (IJCAI-95)*, pp. 1041–1047. San Francisco: Morgan Kaufmann.

Ourston, D., and R. Mooney. 1990. "Changing the rules: a comprehensive approach to theory refinement." In *Proceedings of the Eighth National Conference on Artificial Intelligence (AAAI-90)*, pp. 815–820. Menlo Park, CA: AAAI Press.

Pazzani, M., S. Mani, and W. R. Shankle. 1997. "Beyond concise and colorful: learning intelligible rules." In *Proceedings of the Third International Conference on Knowledge Discovery and Data Mining (KDD-97)*, pp. 235–238. Menlo Park, CA: AAAI Press.

Piatetsky-Shapiro, G., and C. J. Matheus. 1994. "The interestingness of deviations." In *Proceedings of the AAAI-94 Workshop on Knowledge Discovery in Databases*, pp. 25–36.

Quinlan, J. R. 1992. *C4.5: Program for Machine Learning*. San Francisco: Morgan Kaufmann.

Setiono, R., and H. Liu. 1996. "Symbolic representation of neural networks." *IEEE Comput.* **29**: 71–77.

Silberschatz, A., and A. Tuzhilin. 1995. "On subjective measures of interestingness in knowledge discovery." In *Proceedings of the First International Conference on Knowledge Discovery and Data Mining (KDD-95)*, pp. 275–281. Menlo Park, CA: AAAI Press.

Silberschatz, A., and A. Tuzhilin. 1996. "What makes patterns interesting in knowledge discovery systems." *IEEE Trans. Knowledge and Data Engng.* **8**: 970–974.

Towell, G., and J. Shavlik. 1994. "Knowledge-based artificial neural network." *Artificial Intell.* **70**: 119–165.

Further Reading

The following papers give a general overview of the existing techniques.

Liu, B., W. Hsu, and S. Chen. 1997. "Discovering conforming and unexpected classification rules." In *IJCAI-97 Workshop on Intelligent Data Analysis in Medicine and Pharmacology* (IDAMAP-97), IJCAI, pp. 41–48. Nagoya, Japan. This paper presents a simple technique that is both effective and flexible. It allows the user to do any *ad hoc* analysis of the new data with regard to the existing rules.

Mahoney, J. J. and R. J. Mooney. 1994. "Comparing methods for refining certainty-factor rule bases." In *Proceedings of International Conference on Machine Learning* (ICML-94), pp. 173–180. New York, NY: Kluwer. This paper gives an overview of two main theory refinement systems and provides a comparison between them.

Pazzani, M., S. Mani, and W. R. Shankle. 1997. "Beyond concise and colorful: learning intelligible rules." In *Proceedings of Third International Conference on Knowledge Discovery and Data Mining* (KDD-97), pp. 235–238. Menlo Park, CA: AAAI Press. This is a recent work on how to use the existing knowledge in classification rules mining to produce better conforming rules. See Ortega and Fisher (1995) for other research on this topic.

Silberschatz, A. and A. Tuzhilin. 1996. "What makes patterns interesting in knowledge discovery systems." *IEEE Trans. Knowledge Data Engng.* **8**: 970–974. This paper studies subjective interestingness measures. It also proposes a number of formal approaches to unexpectedness using belief systems.

18.4 User Preferences

Bing Liu and Wynne Hsu

ABSTRACT The goal of data mining is to discover useful knowledge (or rules) for the user. Past research has produced many efficient techniques for rule discovery from databases. However, these techniques often generate too many rules, which makes it very difficult for the user to analyze them in order to find those truly interesting/useful rules. In this article, we first discuss some issues involved in assisting the user to analyze the discovered rules. We then review a number of existing techniques that employ the user's preferences and knowledge about the domain to identify those potentially interesting/useful rules for the user.

1. Introduction

It is well recognized that a data mining system (DMS) can generate a huge number of rules, and most of them are of no interest to the user (Frawley et al., 1991). Chapter 18.3 discusses how to find interesting rules given previously discovered knowledge (or rules). This article focuses on helping the user find interesting/useful rules based on his or her preferences. The two issues are similar except:

- Previously discovered rules are generated from a DMS, while user preferences have to be acquired from the user, which is a very difficult task.

- Previously discovered rules are precise, but user preferences can be fuzzy and vague.

Discovering interesting rules for the user is not a simple task. A rule can be interesting to one user but not to another. The interestingness of a rule is essentially subjective. To deal with this problem, we need to know what the user's preferences are. This article attempts to answer the following questions:

1. What rules does the user prefer to see, or what rules interest the user?

2. How to obtain the user preferences?

3. How can a DMS find those preferred or interesting rules given the user preferences?

There are many factors that affect the interestingness of a rule. In Silberschatz and Tuzhilin (1995), it is shown that the interestingness of a rule can be measured using two classes of measures: objective measures and subjective measures. Objective measures involve analyzing the rule's structure and the underlying data used in data mining. Such measures include accuracy, significance, support, confidence, and so on (e.g., Quinlan, 1992; Agrawal and Srikant, 1994; Major and Mangano, 1993). These measures will not be discussed in this article as they have been studied in Chapter 16. The focus here is on the subjective aspect of interestingness. Although there are many subjective interestingness measures, such as novelty, relevance, usefulness, and timeliness, the user is essentially interested in two types of rules, unexpected rules and actionable rules (Piatetsky-Shapiro and Matheus, 1994; Silberschatz and Tuzhilin, 1995; Liu and Hsu, 1996).

- Unexpected rules are those that are outside the user's concept space (novel rules) and/or those that contradict the user's existing knowledge.

- Actionable rules are those that allow the user to do something to his or her advantage.

One may say that the user can simply specify the types of rules that he or she wants to see using templates, constraints (see Chapter 18.2), or a data mining query language (Han et al., 1996; Imielinski et al., 1996), and the DMS only generates those matching rules. This, however, is not sufficient for two important reasons (Liu et al., 1998):

1. The user typically does not know what he or she wants to see exactly and completely.

2. Unexpected (or novel) rules are not within the user's concept space and are thus difficult to specify.

We distinguish two types of user preferences: direct preferences and indirect preferences.

1. *Direct user preferences.* The user specifies the class of rules that he or she wants to see.

2. *Indirect user preferences.* The user specifies his or her existing knowledge (or expected rules) about the domain, and the DMS finds those novel (or unexpected) rules.

In this article, we discuss the main issues in using user preferences and review some techniques for finding interesting rules given user preferences.

2. Main Issues in Using User Preferences

2.1. Knowledge Acquisition

The first issue is how to obtain direct user preferences and existing knowledge. This is the same problem as knowledge acquisition in expert systems (Buchanan and Wilkins, 1993; Gonzalez and Dankel, 1993). The user may know a great deal, but it is hard, if not impossible, for him or her to tell what he or she knows completely. To deal with this problem, expert systems research suggests the following:

- Allow interactive and incremental discovery or identification of interesting rules. Through such interactions, the user will be able to provide more preferences and existing knowledge about the domain and to find more interesting rules.

- Actively stimulate the user or suggest what he or she might have forgotten.

2.2. Granularity of Knowledge

User knowledge can be divided into levels according to its granularity (Liu et al., 1997). Some aspects of the knowledge can be quite vague, while other aspects can be quite precise. For example, the user may have the following three levels of knowledge about a domain:

1. *Precise knowledge (PK)*. The user believes that a specific rule should exist in the data. For example, in a loan application domain, the user believes that if one's monthly salary is over $5,000, one will be granted a loan with a probability of 90 percent.

2. *Fuzzy knowledge (FK)*. The user is less sure about the details of the rule. For example, the user may believe that if one's monthly salary is around $5,000 or more, one should be granted a loan. He or she may not be sure that it is exactly $5,000 and is also not sure about the probability.

3. *General impressions (GI)*. The user simply has some vague feelings about the domain. For example, the user may feel that having a higher monthly salary increases one's chance of obtaining a loan but has no idea how much and what probability.

This division of knowledge is important because it determines how a DMS can use the knowledge and also whether it can make use of all possible types of user knowledge to discover interesting rules.

2.3. Knowledge Representation

The next issue is how to represent user preferences and knowledge. It is common to use the same syntax as the discovered rules because when the user is mining a particular type of rules, his or her existing concepts are typically also of the same type.

2.4. Postanalysis versus Incorporating User Preferences in the Mining Algorithm

There is also the issue of which of the following two methods we should adopt:

1. Incorporate the user preferences in the mining algorithm in order to discover only the interesting rules.

   - Advantage: it focuses the search of the mining algorithm on only the interesting rules.

   - Disadvantage: it suffers from the problem of knowledge acquisition. User interaction with the system is difficult because it is not efficient for a mining algorithm to execute whenever the user remembers another piece of preference or knowledge.

2. Postanalyze the discovered rules using user preferences to identify interesting rules.

   - Advantage: the mining algorithm is only run once to discover all the rules. The user then interactively and incrementally analyzes the rules to identify the interesting ones. This also helps to solve the knowledge acquisition problem.

   - Disadvantage: it may generate too many rules initially.

In general, the first approach is ideal if the user is absolutely sure what types of rules are interesting. However, if the user does not have all the specific rules to look for in mind, the second approach will be more appropriate. In many applications, an integrated approach of (1) and (2) is the preferred choice.

Below, we discuss some techniques that employ user preferences to find interesting rules.

3. Template-Based Approach

This is perhaps the most straightforward method for allowing the user to express his or her direct preferences in selecting interesting rules. The user first specifies interesting and uninteresting classes of rules using templates. The system then finds only those matching rules. Klemetinen et al. (1994) proposes such a method for selecting interesting association rules from the set of discovered rules. This is a postprocessing technique. A template describes a set of rules in terms of the items that occurred in the conditional and the consequent parts. Items can be classified into class hierarchies. An example hierarchy is shown below.

$\{grape, apple\} \subset Fruit \subset Fooditem,$

$\{milk,\ cheese\} \subset Dairy\_product \subset Fooditem,$

$\{beef,\ pork\} \subset Meat \subset Fooditem.$

A template is an expression:

$$A_1, ..., A_k \Rightarrow A_{k+1},$$

where each A_i is either an item, a class name, or an expression C+ or C*, where C is a class name. C+ and C* correspond to one or more and zero or more instances of class C, respectively. A rule matches the template if the rule is an instance of the template. For example, the association rule

$$grape,\ milk \Rightarrow pork$$

matches the template

$$Fruit+,\ Dairy\_product* \Rightarrow Meat.$$

Templates can be inclusive or restrictive. Rules that match the inclusive templates are interesting, and rules that match the restrictive templates are not interesting.

This template-based method is simple, but it does not help the user find truly unexpected or novel rules because what the user wants to see is still within his or her existing concept space, and, hence, somewhat anticipated. Other related techniques can be found in (Liu and Hsu, 1998; Srikant et al., 1997; Adomavicius and Tuzhilin, 1997)

4. Belief or Expectation-Based Approaches

In this approach, the user is first asked to state his or her beliefs or expectations about the domain. The system then discovers or identifies those rules that are potentially interesting to the user, that is, conforming (or expected) rules and unexpected rules. This approach also helps to solve the knowledge acquisition problem as follows (Liu et al., 1999):

1. When the unexpected rules identified by the system are not truly unexpected, they serve to remind the user what he or she has forgotten,

2. Like the template-based approach, this approach can be interactive and iterative.

Below we discuss this approach using different granularity of user knowledge.

4.1. Precise Knowledge (PK) Approach

Formal belief systems, such as Bayesian theory and Dempster–Shafer theory, can be used as a general framework to define unexpectedness. For example, in Silberschatz and Tuzhilin (1996), the degree of a belief A is defined as a conditional probability, $P(A|B)$, that A holds, given some previous evidence B. Given a newly discovered pattern p, we can update the degree of belief in A, $P(A|p, B)$, using the Bayes rule. The unexpectedness is defined by how much the degree of belief changed as a result of the new pattern p. Silberschatz and Tuzhilin (1996) surveyed a number of other formal approaches.

The problem with formal approaches is that they all require a large amount of precise knowledge from the user, which is very difficult to obtain in practice. The fuzzy knowledge approach and the general impression approach discussed below aim to relax this requirement.

4.2. Fuzzy Knowledge (FK) Approach

The fuzzy knowledge approach is a postanalysis method (Liu and Hsu, 1996). We discuss the approach in the context of classification rule mining. Extensions to association rule mining are discussed in Liu and Hsu (1998).

Recall that a classification rule is of the following format:

$$P_1, ..., P_i, ..., P_r \Rightarrow C,$$

where P_i is a test on an attribute and C is a class. FK is represented in the same way. An example of FK for a traffic accident domain is

$$P\_Age = OLD,\ Loc = BAD\_VISIBILITY \Rightarrow Class = BAD\_ACCIDENT,$$

where the semantic meanings of *"OLD," "BAD_VISIBILITY,"* and *"BAD_ACCIDENT"* are modeled using fuzzy sets (Zimmermann, 1991).

Some basic definitions for finding interesting rules are given below. Let E be the set of user expectations specified as fuzzy knowledge and N be the set of discovered rules.

1. *Conformity.* $N_i \in N$ and $E_j \in E$ are conforming if both the conditional parts of N_i and E_j and the consequent parts of N_i and E_j are similar.

2. *Unexpectedness.*

   - *Unexpected consequent.* The conditional parts of $N_i \in N$ and $E_j \in E$ are similar, but the consequents of the two patterns are far apart.

   - *Unexpected reason.* The consequents are similar, but the conditional parts of $N_i \in N$ and $E_j \in E$ are far apart.

The computation details for the degrees of conformity and unexpectedness of each $N_i \in N$ with respect to the whole set E can be found in Liu et al. (1999). With these degrees, the rules in N can be ranked in various ways. The top-ranking rules are the most conforming and unexpected rules.

Let us see an example. Suppose we have the following discovered rules from a traffic accident database, and the above example of FK from the user.

Rule 1 : $P\_Age > 50, \quad Loc = straight \Rightarrow Class = slight$

Rule 2 : $P\_Age > 65, \quad Loc = bend, \quad Speed > 50 \Rightarrow Class = killed$

Rule 3 : $P\_Age > 50, \quad Loc = T\text{-}junct \Rightarrow Class = slight$

The ranking according to degrees of conformity is:

Rank 1 Rule 2 : $P\_Age > 65, \quad Loc = bend, \quad Speed > 50 \Rightarrow Class = killed$

Rank 2 Rule 3 : $P\_Age > 50, \quad Loc = T\text{-}junct \Rightarrow Class = slight$

Rank 3 Rule 1 : $P\_Age > 50, \quad Loc = straight \Rightarrow Class = slight$

It shows that discovered Rule 2 conforms to the user's belief that an old person involved in an accident at a bad location will result in a serious injury. In addition, it tells the user that speed also plays a role in serious traffic accidents.

The ranking according to the degree of unexpected consequent is as follows:

Rank 1 Rule 3 : $P\_Age > 50, \quad Loc = T\text{-}junct \Rightarrow Class = slight$

Rank 2 Rule 2 : $P\_Age > 65, \quad Loc = bend, \quad Speed > 50 \Rightarrow Class = killed$

Rank 3 Rule 1 : $P\_Age > 50, \quad Loc = straight \Rightarrow Class = slight$

Rule 3 is against the expected consequent because instead of a serious injury, the old person suffers a slight injury (*T-juncts* are considered to have bad visibility).

4.3. General Impressions (GI) Approach

General impressions attempt to model the vague feelings of a user about a domain (Liu et al., 1997a). Again, we discuss the approach in classification rule mining. Extensions to association rule mining can be found in Liu and Hsu (1998). Let $A = \{a_1, ..., a_s\}$ be the set of attributes in the database D, and $C = \{C_1, ..., C_m\}$ be the set of possible classes in D.

Definition. *A GI is of the following form:*

$$a_1 \ ID_1, ..., a_w ID_w \Rightarrow C_j,$$

where $I = \{a_1, ..., a_w\} \subseteq A, I \neq \varnothing$, *and* $a_p \neq a_q$ *if* $p \neq q$, *and* $ID \in \{<, >, , |, \ [a \ set]\}$. *[A set] represents a subset of values of a discrete (and/or nominal) attribute.*

The meanings of GIs can be illustrated as follows:

- $a < \Rightarrow C_j$. This represents the impression that a smaller value of a will result in a higher likelihood of being in class C_j. It can be used to specify GIs such as "the smaller the period of loan repayment is, the more likely will the loan application be approved."

- $a > \Rightarrow C_j$. This represents the impression that a larger value of a will result in a higher chance of leading to class C_j.

- $a \Rightarrow C_j$. This represents the impression that if the value of a is within some range, then class C_j is likely to be the result. For example, "if one is neither too young nor too old, then the loan application is likely to be approved."

- $a \mid \Rightarrow C_{\text{sub}}$. This represents the impression that some relationships exist between the attribute a and the classes in $C_{\text{sub}}(\subseteq C)$. However, the exact relationships are not known.

- $a[S] \Rightarrow C_j$. This represents the impression that if the value of a is an element in the set S, it is more likely to lead to class C_j.

Some examples of GIs are as follows:

1. *saving* > ⇒ *approved*

2. *jobless* [*no*] ⇒ *approved*

3. *saving* >, *age* ⇒ *approved*

Using GIs to rank the discovered rules according to their conformity and unexpectedness depends on the following assumption: If two or more GIs lead to the same class and they have no common attributes, then their combinations also lead to the same class. Any impression that cannot be composed with a combination of the input GIs are considered unexpected.

The assumption is justified because it conforms to human intuitions (see Liu et al., 1997, for full details). For example, with the above three GIs, it is assumed that

$$saving >, \quad age, jobless[no] \Rightarrow approved$$

also holds. Using the above assumption, we know that the following rule

$$jobless = no, \quad saving > 10 \Rightarrow approved,$$

conforms to the above three GIs as it matches the combined GI formed using (1) and (2) ("*saving*>10" matches "*saving*>" in (1), "*jobless* = *no*" matches "*jobless* [*no*]" in (2)). The following example rule's consequent is unexpected,

$$jobless = no, \quad saving > 10 \Rightarrow not\_approved,$$

because "*saving*>" in (1), "*jobless* [*no*]" in (2) both lead to class *approved*, whereas the rule's class is *not_approved*.

The following rule's conditions are unexpected because we have no GI relating "*age*<" and "*saving*<" to the class *approved*:

$$age < 20, \quad saving < 10 \Rightarrow approved.$$

5. Expert System–Based Approach

Another approach to finding interesting rules is to build an expert system to evaluate the discovered rules. Here, the domain expert's evaluation knowledge is acquired and encoded in an expert system. This approach is taken in the system KEFIR (Piatetsky-Shapiro and Matheus, 1994). KEFIR analyzes health-care information to uncover key findings. Key findings refer to important deviations from the norms for various indicators. The degree of interestingness of a finding is estimated by the amount of benefit that could be realized if an action is taken in response to the finding. The recommended actions for various findings are provided by domain experts. For each action, the expert also estimates the probability of success.

An expert system provides a good application-specific solution. It is suitable for domains that are well understood, and the purpose of data mining is to monitor fixed types of changes in the data. It is not so suitable for general exploratory data analysis.

References

Adomavicius, G., and A. Tuzhilin. 1997. "Discovery of actionable patterns in databases: the action hierarchy approach." In *Proceedings of the Third International Conference on Knowledge Discovery and Data Mining (KDD-97)*, pp. 111–114. Menlo Park, CA: AAAI Press.

Agrawal, R., and R. Srikant. 1994. "Fast algorithms for mining association rules." In *Proceedings of the Twentieth International Conference on Very Large Databases (VLDB-94)*, pp. 487–499. Morgan Kaufmann.

Buchanan, B., and D. Wilkins, eds. 1993. *Readings in Knowledge Acquisition and Learning.* Morgan Kaufmann.

Frawley, W. J., G. Piatetsky-Shapiro, and C. J. Matheus. 1991. "Knowledge discovery in databases: an overview." In *Knowledge Discovery in Databases*, edited by G. Piatetsky-Shapiro and W. J. Frawley, pp. 1–27. Cambridge, MA: AAAI/MIT Press.

Gonzalez, A., and D. Dankel. 1993. *The Engineering of Knowledge-Based Systems: Theory and Practice.* New Jersey: Prentice-Hall.

Han, J., Y. Fu, W. Wang, K. Koperski, and O. Zaiane. 1996. "DMQL: a data mining query language for relational databases." In *Proceedings of the SIGMOD Workshop on Research Issues in Data Mining and Knowledge Discovery*, pp. 27–34.

Imielinski, T., A. Virmani, and A. Abdulghani. 1996. "DataMine: application programming interface and query language for database mining." In *Proceedings of the Second International Conference on Knowledge Discovery and Data Mining (KDD-96)*, pp. 256–260. Menlo Park, CA: AAAI Press.

Klemetinen, M., H. Mannila, P. Ronkainen, H. Toivonen, and A. I. Verkamo. November 1994. "Finding interesting rules from large sets of discovered association rules." In *Proceedings of the First International Conference on Information and Knowledge Management*, pp. 401–408. New York: ACM Press.

Liu, B., and W. Hsu. 1996. "Post-analysis of learned rules." In *Proceedings of the Thirteenth National Conference on Artificial Intelligence (AAAI-96)*, pp. 828–834. Menlo Park, CA: AAAI Press.

Liu, B., W. Hsu, and S. Chen. 1998. "Analyzing the subjective interestingness of association rules." Technical Report. Singapore: School of Computing, National University of Singapore.

Liu, B., W. Hsu, and S. Chen. 1997. "Using general impressions to analyze discovered classification rules." In *Proceedings of the Third International Conference on Knowledge Discovery and Data Mining (KDD-97)*, pp. 31–36. Menlo Park, CA: AAAI Press.

Liu, B., W. Hsu, L. F. Mun, and H. Lee. 1999. "Finding interesting patterns using user expectations." *IEEE Trans. Knowledge and Data Engineering* **11(6)**: pp. 817–832. Los Alamitos: IEEE Computer Society Press.

Major, J. A., and J. J. Mangano. 1993. "Selecting among rules induced from a hurricane database." In *Proceedings of the AAAI-93 Workshop on Knowledge Discovery in Databases*, pp. 28–41. Menlo Park, CA: AAAI Press.

Piatetsky-Shapiro, G., and C. J. Matheus. 1994. "The interestingness of deviations." In *Proceedings of the AAAI-94 Workshop on Knowledge Discovery in Databases*, pp. 25–36. Menlo Park, CA: AAAI Press.

Quinlan, J. R. 1992. *C4.5: Program for Machine Learning.* San Mateo, CA: Morgan Kaufmann.

Silberschatz, A., and A. Tuzhilin. 1995. "On subjective measures of interestingness in knowledge discovery." In *Proceedings of First International Conference on Knowledge Discovery and Data Mining (KDD-95)*, pp. 275–281. Menlo Park, CA: AAAI Press.

Silberschatz, A., and A. Tuzhilin. 1996. "What makes patterns interesting in knowledge discovery systems." *IEEE Trans. Knowledge and Data Engng.* **8**: 970–974.

Srikant, R., Q. Vu, and R. Agrawal. August 1997. "Mining association rules with item constraints." In *Proceedings of the Third International Conference on Knowledge Discovery and Data Mining (KDD-97)*, pp. 67–73. Newport Beach, CA.

Zimmermann, H. J. 1991. *Fuzzy Set Theory and Its Applications.* 2d ed. Boston: Kluwer Academic Publishers.

Further Reading

Klemetinen, M., H. Mannila, P. Ronkainen, H. Toivonen, and A. I. Verkamo. 1994. "Finding interesting rules from large sets of discovered association rules." In *Proceedings of the First International Conference on Information and Knowledge Management*, pp. 401–408. New York: ACM Press. This paper introduces the template-based approach to allow the user to specify the types of rules that he or she wishes to see.

Liu, B., and W. Hsu. 1996. "Post-analysis of learned rules." In *Proceedings of the Thirteenth National Conference on Artificial Intelligence (AAAI-96)*, pp. 828–834. Menlo Park, CA: AAAI Press. This paper introduces how to use fuzzy user knowledge to identify unexpected rules from a set of discovered rules.

Liu, B., W. Hsu and S. Chen. 1997. "Using general impressions to analyze discovered classification rules," *Proceedings of the Third International Conference on Knowledge Discovery and Data Mining (KDD-97)*, pp. 31–36. Menlo Park, CA: AAAI Press. This paper introduces a type of vague user knowledge, called general impressions, and how it can be used to help the user find interesting rules.

Liu, B., and W. Hsu. 1998. "Helping user identifying interesting association rules." Technical Report. Singapore: School of Computing, National University of Singapore. This paper shows how fuzzy knowledge and general impression methods are being used to find interesting rules in the context of association rule mining.

Piatetsky-Shapiro, G., and C. J. Matheus. 1994. "The interestingness of deviations." In *Proceedings of the AAAI-94 Workshop on Knowledge Discovery in Databases*, pp. 25–36. Menlo Park, CA: AAAI Press. This paper presents the expert system–based approach to finding interesting rules, specifically, actionable rules.

Silberschatz, A., and A. Tuzhilin. 1996. "What makes patterns interesting in knowledge discovery systems." *IEEE Trans. Knowledge and Data Engng.* **8**: 970–974. This paper studies the measures of subjective interestingness. It also proposes a number of formal approaches to unexpectedness using belief systems.

19 KNOWLEDGE EVALUATION

19.1 Statistical Evaluations

David D. Jensen

ABSTRACT   This article introduces basic features of error estimators, including bias, variance, and loss functions. It outlines the logic behind classical hypothesis tests and explains the special challenges faced by knowledge discovery algorithms that search large model spaces. It discusses the statistical effects of multiple comparison procedures (MCPs), and several methods to adjust for those effects, including mathematical adjustments, cross-validation, and randomization tests. Finally, it outlines the basic concepts behind overfitting reduction and pruning.

1. Introduction

Many knowledge discovery algorithms estimate error and use those estimates to make important decisions. In particular, many algorithms search a space of alternative models and attempt to select models that best capture useful regularities in the data. Without accurate error estimates, and effective methods to interpret those estimates, algorithms will select suboptimal models and infer the existence of structure in purely random data. Accurate estimates can be obtained, but often only with substantial additional data or computation.

2. Error Estimation

Knowledge discovery algorithms use error estimates to determine the relative utility of alternative models and select among alternative search paths. In addition, human designers evaluate algorithms by estimating the error of models the algorithms produce.

   The error associated with a model m can be estimated by comparing the predictions of m to known values in a data sample S. Many different statistics can be used to estimate the error of a model, including the percentage of misclassified instances, gain or gain ratio, chi-square, and G. Each of these statistics produces a scalar value or score, denoted x. Some statistics take additional inputs (e.g., a loss function or prior knowledge), and some knowledge discovery systems estimate more than one statistic related to error (e.g., precision and recall).

   For example, consider estimating the error of a simple model m_1 on a hypothetical data set S_1 that records diagnostic test results for 73 hospital patients. The aim of m_1 is to predict whether each patient has a given disease. Figure 1 shows the results of applying the model to all patients in S_1. While far from perfect, the model appears to have some predictive ability. The value of the chi-square statistic for this table is 3.946. In the next section, we interpret this score using a statistical hypothesis test.

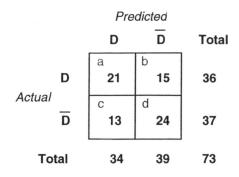

Figure 1 Contingency table

The calculation of many statistics that measure classification error can be explained in terms of a contingency table. For example, using the cell designators in Figure 1 and the additional notation $N = a + b + c + d$, we can calculate statistics such as the percent misclassification $= (b + c)/N$, the false positive rate $= c/(c + d)$, and the positive predictive value $= a/(a + c)$.

The chi-square and G statistics are functions of all cells of a table. For example, chi-square for the table in Figure 1 can be calculated as:

$$\frac{N(ad - bc)^2}{(a + b)(c + d)(a + c)(b + d)}$$

In general, chi-square is the sum, over all cells, of the normalized squared difference between the observed cell count and the expected cell count. Typically, the expected cell count is determined by assuming independence between the row and column variables (e.g., predicted and actual diagnosis).

The score x is an estimate of a population parameter Ψ. Given the population of all possible instances, Ψ could be calculated directly. In practice, however, the values of parameters are estimated based on samples of instances drawn from the population. Samples are used because of logistical limitations (e.g., it may be impractical to survey all possible patients), temporal considerations (data are only available on current patients, but inferences are desired about all current and future patients), or efficiency reasons (the computational complexity of knowledge discovery algorithms almost always depends on the number of instances in a data set and running a particular algorithm on an entire population may be infeasible). Statistics are calculated on these samples and used to estimate population parameters. Many different samples could, in theory, be drawn from the same population, and few samples will produce precisely the same score. Thus, an individual score almost always varies somewhat from the value of the population parameter.

Bias and variance are two criteria often used to describe the quality of the scores produced by an estimator. The bias of an estimator is the difference between the expected value of its scores $E(X)$ and the value of the population parameter Ψ. An estimator is unbiased if $E(X) = \Psi$. While any particular score x produced by an unbiased estimator may be greater or less than Ψ, scores will not vary systematically in either direction. (The fields of statistics and machine learning differ in their definitions of the term bias. Here we use the statistical definition.) Figure 2 shows the distributions of two estimators. One is unbiased and the other has a positive bias. The variance of an estimator is the second moment about the mean of its

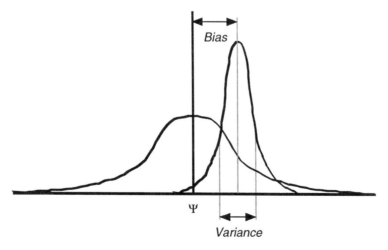

Figure 2 Two estimators of Ψ with different bias and variance

distribution, or $E(X - \mu)^2$, where μ is the mean of X. Variance measures the dispersion of scores around their mean. Given two unbiased estimators, the one with lower variance is preferred. The two estimators in Figure 2 have different variance. The figure shows one situation where a biased estimator might be preferable to an unbiased one because it has lower variance.

A statistic that estimates error can also be described in terms of its loss function. Loss functions describe the consequences or loss associated with a particular estimate. For example, a loss function in a classification task might reflect the costs associated with different types of misclassifications. Many classification tasks are assumed to have zero-one loss. Either a class prediction is correct (a loss of zero) or incorrect (a loss of one). No partially correct classifications are possible and no one misclassification has more serious consequences than another. In contrast, the loss associated with predictions of continuous functions generally varies smoothly between zero and one. Many systems that make predictions of continuous functions use quadratic loss, where the loss is proportional to the squared difference between the predicted and actual values. Despite the widespread use and theoretical tractability of zero-one loss, it is invalid for many tasks (Provost et al., 1998). Different types of misclassification often have different costs, and these costs should affect which models are preferred by knowledge discovery algorithms.

3. Statistical Tests of Hypotheses

An hypothesis test is one common method of interpreting a score. Hypothesis tests are one way of making statistical inferences about the population, based on a score calculated from a sample. Hypothesis tests compare a score to the distribution of scores that would be expected given that a particular null hypothesis is true of the population. The null hypothesis (denoted H_0) makes a quantitative statement about a population parameter (e.g., error on the population) that can be used to derive an expected distribution of scores called a sampling distribution. The null hypothesis and its associated sampling distribution provide a quantitative context for interpreting sample scores.

Once the sampling distribution has been determined, an hypothesis test is performed to determine the probability that a given score, or a more extreme score, would occur given that the null hypothesis (H_0) is true. This probability is referred to as a P-value or merely P. To determine whether to accept or reject the null hypothesis, P is often compared to α, a fixed probability threshold that indicates the maximum acceptable probability of rejecting H_0 when it is true. If $P \leqslant \alpha$, then the null hypothesis is inferred to be false and is rejected. If $P > \alpha$, then the null hypothesis cannot be rejected. Commonly used values of α include 0.05, 0.01, and 0.001. The smallest values of α are used when the loss associated with incorrectly rejecting the null hypothesis is greatest.

The form of the null hypothesis depends on what is being tested. For example, to compare the performance of two models, a possible null hypothesis is that their performance difference in the population is zero. To examine the performance of a single model, a possible null hypothesis is that the model's predictions are independent of the true class labels of instances in the population. Another possible null hypothesis might be that the predictive accuracy of a model on the population does not exceed a given value. In each case there is an alternative hypothesis, H_1, that is paired with the null hypothesis, and it represents the necessary conclusion if the null hypothesis is rejected. For example, if H_0 states that two models have a performance difference of zero, then H_1 would state that the difference is nonzero. If, based on the hypothesis test, H_0 is rejected, then H_1 is accepted.

In nearly all cases, knowledge of the sampling distribution for a statistic is a prerequisite for hypothesis testing. In some cases, the sampling distribution for a statistic has been derived theoretically. For other statistics, sampling distributions must be derived empirically using computationally intensive techniques such as randomization (see Section 6 below).

As an example of an hypothesis test, consider the example of model evaluation discussed in the previous section. As already noted, a chi-square statistic can be calculated from the contingency table in Figure 1, producing a score of 3.946. What does this value imply about the relationship between the model's predictions and the actual disease state in the population

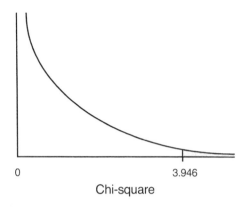

0   3.946

Chi-square

Figure 3 Sampling distribution and sample score

of hospital patients? One reasonable null hypothesis is that the model's predictions and disease state are independent—knowing the prediction of the rule indicates nothing about disease state. Under this null hypothesis, the chi-square statistic has a known sampling distribution parameterized by the number of cells in the table. Comparing the sample score of 3.946 to the sampling distribution of chi-square yields $P = 0.0470$—less than 5 percent of the sampling distribution is greater than or equal to 3.946 (see Figure 3). Given $\alpha = 0.05$, the sample score is judged unlikely to have been drawn from the sampling distribution, and the null hypothesis of independence is rejected. Given $\alpha = 0.01$, the reverse would be concluded, and the null hypothesis would not be rejected.

An alternative approach to the chi-square test is Fisher's exact test (Sachs, 1982). As its name implies, Fisher's exact test produces exact values of P, rather than the approximations provided by comparing the value of statistics to a theoretically derived sampling distribution. Fisher's original formulation applies only to 2 × 2 contingency tables such as the one shown in Figure 1, but generalizations of the test have been formulated for larger tables (Sachs, 1982; Mehta and Patel, 1983). Fisher's exact test can be calculated as the sum of terms of the hypergeometric distribution:

$$\frac{(a + b)!(c + d)!(a + c)!(b + d)!}{n!} \sum_{i} \frac{1}{a_i! b_i! c_i! d_i!},$$

where the summation is over all tables (such as that in Figure 1) that have both identical marginal sums and equal or more extreme cell counts, given the null hypothesis of independence.

Fisher's exact test calculates $P = 0.0618$ for the example above, rather than the value $P = 0.0470$ determined using chi-square. As this example demonstrates, the chi-square test can introduce small but potentially important errors. Fisher's test is particularly useful when cell counts in one or more cells are small (e.g., less than 6), because statistics such as chi-square and G can become inaccurate under such conditions.

When testing an hypothesis, two types of errors are possible. Type I errors are committed by rejecting the null hypothesis when it is true. Type II errors are committed by accepting the null hypothesis when it is false. Hypothesis tests can control the probability of a Type I error, but do not protect against Type II errors. For example, if a very small sample is used to test the null hypothesis of independence between gender and treatment outcome, then we are likely to obtain a very large P-value, and thus be forced to accept the null hypothesis. However, the null hypothesis could still be false, and we would commit a Type II error.

Tests predisposed to Type II errors are said to have low statistical power, such tests will frequently accept the null hypothesis, even when it is false. The probability of a Type II error is denoted by β, where power $= 1 - \beta$. Power depends on several factors, including the size of the effect (in this case, the magnitude of the correlation between predicted and actual diagnosis), the sample size, the inherent variability of scores, and α. Statistical power is ignored in most knowledge discovery algorithms, even in those algorithms that explicitly test statistical significance. However, as knowledge discovery algorithms increase in sophistication, power calculations will become increasingly important. Power calculations can help determine when additional instances should be sampled and, conversely, when the sample is already large enough to identify extremely weak relationships.

Hypothesis tests and power calculations only answer questions about the probabilities of different types of errors. Such tests do not indicate whether a given relationship is important or useful. It is quite possible for a model to represent a relationship that is statistically significant, but practically useless. This is particularly likely with extremely large samples, where statistical power is high and extremely weak relationships can be identified with high statistical confidence. Similarly, it is possible for a relationship to be valid and useful, but not statistically significant. This is particularly likely with extremely small samples, which lack the statistical power to identify all but the strongest relationships. While statistical significance is one of the most basic questions to ask about models and their associated scores, many other possible questions can and should be asked. Among these is whether a relationship is of practical importance within a given domain. For additional discussion about the limitations of significance tests, see Morrison and Henkel (1970) and Glymour et al. (1997).

4. Multiple Comparisons

Search is a hallmark of most knowledge discovery algorithms. (A few knowledge discovery algorithms do not conduct explicit search. For example, neither simple Bayesian classifiers [Domingos and Pazzani, 1997] nor instance-based learning algorithms [Aha et al., 1991] employ explicit search. However, most algorithms explore some sort of space in search of useful models.) For example, algorithms such as A priori (Agrawal et al., 1993) and BRUTE (Segal and Etzioni, 1994) conduct the equivalent of exhaustive search. Greedy algorithms, such as C4.5 (Quinlan, 1993), CN2 (Clark and Niblett, 1989), and FOIL (Quinlan, 1990), search a space of components that can be added to an existing model. Wrapper approaches (e.g., Kohavi and John, 1997) search a space of possible algorithm parameters in order to maximize the performance of induced models.

Each of these search procedures has a similar form:

1. *Generate multiple items.* Generate multiple models $(m_1, m_2, m_3, \ldots m_n)$, components, or algorithm parameters.

2. *Estimate a score for each item.* Estimate a score $x_i = f(m_i, S)$ for each item based on a data sample S (often called a training set).

3. *Select the item with the maximum score.* Select the apparent best item $\text{argmax}(x_1, x_2, x_3, \ldots x_4)$, based on the estimated scores.

We refer to this as a multiple comparison procedure (MCP).

MCPs affect the statistical properties of the score of the selected item. Specifically, the number of items generated in Step 1 of an MCP affects the sampling distribution of the maximum score in Step 3. That is, the extent of the search used to select a given item alters the meaning of the score associated with that item. These effects are covered in greater detail elsewhere (Jensen and Cohen, 2000).

Consider a simple example of an MCP. You are challenged to a game of chance by Sam, a statistically inclined con artist. The game involves simple dice-rolling. You and Sam each bet $10; The person with the higher scoring die receives $20 and the other person receives nothing (ties result in another dice roll). Sam gives you a standard six-sided die and guarantees that it is fair; no score is more likely than any other. You roll the die and obtain a score of four. Sam produces ten dice from his pocket, rolls them, and selects one with the maximum score (a six). He then declares himself the winner, and claims the $20. You assert that Sam's use of ten dice is unfair, but Sam replies that his selected die is just like yours—it is a fair die, and it genuinely obtained a

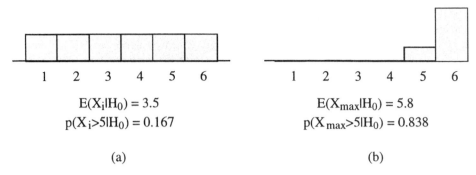

$$E(X_i|H_0) = 3.5$$
$$p(X_i>5|H_0) = 0.167$$

$$E(X_{max}|H_0) = 5.8$$
$$p(X_{max}>5|H_0) = 0.838$$

(a)   (b)

Figure 4 Sampling distributions for one die and ten dice

score of six. Why is selecting the maximum from among ten dice unfair? Why does it differ from rolling only one die?

One way to understand the difference is to examine the sampling distributions of the scores in each case. Figure 4(a) shows the sampling distribution for X_i, the score obtained by rolling a single die where each score in the set {1 2 3 4 5 6} is equally likely. Given this distribution, we can easily calculate the expected value of the die's score, $E(X_i) = 3.5$, and the probability of the score exceeding any particular value, for example, $P(X_i > 5) = 0.167$. Figure 4(b) shows the sampling distribution for X_{max}, the score obtained by selecting the maximum score from among ten dice. The sampling distribution of X_{max} is substantially different from that of X_i. The expected value is much larger, $E(X_{max}) = 5.6$, and the probability of an extreme value is similarly larger, $P(X_{max} > 5) = 0.838$. Comparing scores drawn from the two distributions is unfair, in the sense that values drawn from the distribution of X_{max} will almost always be larger than those drawn from X_i.

Knowledge discovery algorithms produce situations that are directly analogous to this example. Just as Sam started with multiple dice, knowledge discovery algorithms generate multiple models, components, or learning parameters. Just as rolling dice produces a score, knowledge discovery algorithms estimate a score for each model based on a data sample. As noted in Section 2, the scores $x_1, x_2, x_3, \ldots x_n$ are estimates of some population parameter, and thus the probability distribution of each score has nonzero variance. Any two samples, S_1 and S_2, may differ in the degree to which they reflect the population, and thus, $f(m_1, S_1) \neq f(m_1, S_2) \neq \Psi$. Just as Sam selected the die with the maximum score, knowledge discovery algorithms select the item with the maximum score.

If algorithms do not adjust for the effects of multiple comparison procedures (MCPs), they can suffer from various pathologies, including overfitting, oversearching, and feature selection errors. Each of these pathologies results from systematic errors in either the parameter estimates or hypothesis tests. MCPs introduce substantial upward bias into parameter estimates, and they can cause large increases in the probability that a hypothesis test will incorrectly reject the null hypothesis. Sketches of both proofs are given below. Formal proofs can be found elsewhere (Jensen and Cohen, 2000).

As an example of how MCPs affect parameter estimates, consider n models, each with identical performance. That is, $\Psi_1 = \Psi_2 = \Psi_3 = \ldots = \Psi_n$. Suppose that the score X_1 calculated for a single item is an unbiased estimator of Ψ_1. Although x_1 may be larger or smaller than Ψ_1 when calculated on any individual sample, when calculated across all samples, $E(X_1) = \Psi_1$. Now, consider the maximum score $x_{max} = \max(x_1, x_2, x_3, \ldots x_n)$. For any given sample, $x_1 \leqslant x_{max}$. Said differently, the scores $x_2 \ldots x_n$ will never decrease the maximum, and will increase it for some samples. As a result, $E(X_{max}) > E(X_i)$, and thus $E(X_{max})$ is a biased estimator of any Ψ_i.

As an example of how MCPs affect hypothesis tests, consider n classification models, whose predictions are mutually independent, identically distributed, and uncorrelated with the class label. We can determine a threshold x_{crit}, called the critical value, such that $P(x_i > x_{crit} \mid H_0) = \alpha$. If a given score exceeds this critical value, it is deemed statistically significant at the α

level, meaning that there is only a probability of α that x_i will equal or exceed x_{crit} if H_0 is true. However, what is the probability that x_{max} will exceed this critical value if H_0 is true? Assuming score distributions are independently and identically distributed (i.i.d.) and that $P = P(x_i > x_{\text{crit}} \mid H_0)$, then $P(x_{\text{max}} > x_{\text{crit}} \mid H_0) = 1 - (1 - P)^n$. For example, if $P = 0.05$ and $n = 20$, then $P(x_{\text{max}} > x_{\text{crit}} \mid H_0) = 0.64$. Hypothesis tests will be incorrect if they use the sampling distribution appropriate to X_i. Unfortunately, nearly all theoretical sampling distributions are only appropriate for a single score X_i, not the maximum of several scores X_{max}.

The need to adjust for the effects of MCPs is a critical task in knowledge discovery, and it arises in at least two areas. First, empirical evaluations of knowledge discovery algorithms often need to adjust for MCPs. For example, the effects of MCPs underlie the common advice to separate data sets for training and testing when evaluating knowledge discovery algorithms (e.g., Weiss and Kulikowski, 1991). It has also been noted as an important factor in empirical comparisons of multiple algorithms (Feelders and Verkooijen, 1996; Gascuel and Caraux, 1992; Salzberg, 1997). This advice has been standard in the statistical literature on experimental design for decades (Miller, 1981). Second, knowledge discovery algorithms themselves often need to adjust for MCPs, and inadequate adjustments cause a variety of pathological behaviors (Einhorn, 1972; Jensen and Cohen, 2000). Specific pathologies attributable to MCPs include overfitting, oversearching, and feature selection errors.

Overfitting is one of the most commonly identified pathologies of knowledge discovery algorithms. Many algorithms generate models with components that either reduce the model's accuracy on new data, or leave it unchanged (Einhorn, 1972; Dietterich, 1995; Oates and Jensen, 1997, 1998). This behavior, often referred to as overfitting, results from conducting an explicit or implicit hypothesis test with an inappropriate sampling distribution. Algorithms often add components to a model only when the score of those components exceeds some critical value. In many cases, however, algorithms do not adequately adjust this value for the effects of MCPs. Their hypothesis tests use sampling distributions (or critical values) appropriate for X_i, not X_{max}, and thus the tests have extremely inflated probabilities of Type I error. Such errors cause algorithms to infer mistakenly that components will improve model accuracy, and they add those components to the model.

Oversearching is a more recently identified pathology of knowledge discovery algorithms. Several studies (Quinlan and Cameron-Jones, 1995; Murthy and Salzberg, 1995) show that increasing the size of an algorithm's search space can reduce the accuracy of the final model on test data. This contradicts common experience with other AI algorithms, where the quality of the final solution generally increases with the size of the search space. Oversearching occurs because of differing biases in parameter estimates resulting from two MCPs. The maximum scores from two MCPs are compared directly, even though one MCP considers a set of models that is a superset of the other. The maximum score from the larger model space can never be less than the maximum score from the smaller space, although it can be greater. The two maximum scores are not directly comparable because they are drawn from different sampling distributions with different degrees of bias. Algorithms that directly compare these biased scores can construct suboptimal models.

Feature selection errors have been identified most frequently in algorithms for decision tree induction (Quinlan, 1988; Fayyad and Irani, 1992). Most tree induction algorithms apply an MCP to each variable to select a candidate feature to consider using at the root of a new subtree. For example, an MCP might be applied to a discrete variable (eye color) to select which binary feature (e.g., eye color = {blue or green}) provides the greatest increase in classification accuracy if used as the root of a new subtree; here we use the terminology suggested by Kohavi and Provost (1998), where eye color is termed as a variable and eye color = {blue or green} is termed as a feature. An algorithm would generate possible features (e.g., eye color{blue}, eye color = {blue or green}, eye color = {blue or brown}, etc.), score each feature in the context of a current tree, and select the feature with the maximum score. Algorithms then compare the best features from each variable, select the best overall feature, and install that feature at a node in a tree. During classification, instances for which the feature is true are sent down one branch, and instances for which the feature is false are sent down the other. Features drawn from variables with large features sets (e.g., eye color or postal code) are often preferred over features drawn from variables with small sets (e.g., gender), even though the opposite decision would improve performance of the model on test data. As with oversearching, this pathology results from errors in parameter estimates. Algorithms compare the maximum scores from two or more MCPs, where the MCPs consider different numbers of items. Thus, the maximum scores from the MCPs are not directly comparable, because they are biased to differing degrees. The relative ordering of the maximum scores is a poor indicator that the same ordering will hold among the respective population parameter values. As a result, suboptimal features are often selected and added to a model.

The magnitude of the parameter estimation bias introduced by MCPs is determined by several factors other than the number of items compared. First, increasing the sample size of the training set can reduce the variance of the sampling distribution of each score X_i, and this reduces the bias $E(X_{max}) - \Psi$. (The standard deviation of a sampling distribution is called the standard error.) Second, if a small number n_s of population scores is much larger than the other scores, where $n_s \ll n$, then the bias introduced by an MCP will decrease. Finally, if the scores distributions are highly correlated, then bias will also decrease. Additional discussion and proofs for each of these effects are provided elsewhere (Jensen and Cohen, 2000).

5. Mathematical Adjustments

One of the simplest ways to adjust for the effects of an MCP is based on simple probability theory. If each score x_i has some probability P of exceeding a given threshold, then the probability P^* that the maximum of n scores X_{max} will exceed the threshold can be approximated by

$$P^* = nP \tag{1}$$

if P is small. This equation, known as a Bonferroni adjustment, can result in $P^* > 1$ if n or P is large, so the equation is sometimes written

$$P^* = \min(1, nP).$$

A more versatile and precise equation is the Sidak adjustment

$$P^* = 1 - (1 - P)^n. \tag{2}$$

Given equation (1) or (2), a per-comparison threshold can be determined such that $P^* = \alpha$. A variety of related techniques have been developed and are discussed in detail elsewhere (Miller, 1981).

Techniques such as the Bonferroni and Sidak adjustments are efficient and simple to calculate. Despite several assumptions (discussed below), they can be surprisingly accurate, particularly when P is small (Miller, 1981). For these reasons, they have been incorporated into several knowledge discovery algorithms (Kass, 1975, 1980; Gaines, 1989; Jensen and Schmill, 1997; Megiddo and Srikant, 1998).

Unfortunately, Bonferroni and Sidak adjustments make several assumptions that are often violated by knowledge discovery algorithms. First, these adjustments assume that the distributions of individual scores are uncorrelated. This assumption is manifestly false for many situations. For example, multiple models with highly correlated scores are generated by many iterative search algorithms that hill climb in the vicinity of a high-performing model. Second, nonnormal or discrete sampling distributions can lead to substantial errors in adjusted probabilities (Westfall and Young, 1993).

The effects of correlated scores can be demonstrated with a simple experiment. (See Freedman et al., 1986, for a similar experiment.) For each trial, we randomly generate fifty instances with a class variable and twenty predictor variables, each drawn from a uniform distribution of binary values. We introduce varying degrees of correlation among the predictor variables, measured using median pairwise correlation. We search the predictor variables to find the single predictor with the maximum chi-square score, and we accept or reject the hypothesis of independence between the best predictor and the class based on two types of

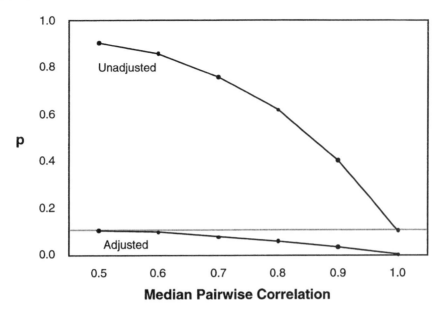

Figure 5 Bounds provided by adjusted probabilities vary with correlation
Previously appeared in D. Jensen and P. Cohen "Multiple Comparisons In Induction
Algorithms," *Machine Learning* **38**: 309–338. Reprinted with permission of Kluwer Publishers

hypothesis tests: an unadjusted chi-square test and an adjusted chi-square test using the Sidak equation. The class and predictors are generated independently, so any rejection of the null hypothesis is a Type I error.

Figure 5 shows the results of this experiment. The x-axis corresponds to the median pairwise correlation among the predictor variables. The results at each level of correlation represent 3,000 trials. The y-axis shows the probability of rejecting the null hypothesis with $\alpha = 0.10$. The correct value is shown by the horizontal dotted line at $P = 0.10$. As would be expected, when predictor variables are independent (pairwise correlation 0.5), the unadjusted test performs quite poorly, rejecting the null hypothesis with a probability of approximately $1 - (1 - 0.10)^{20} = 0.8784$. The adjusted test performs quite well, rejecting the null hypothesis with probability of approximately 0.10. However, as correlation among the predictor variables increases, the probability of rejecting the null hypothesis drops for both tests. When all twenty predictors are perfectly correlated (pairwise correlation $= 1.0$) the adjusted test rejects the null hypothesis with approximately probability $1 - (1 - 0.10)^{1/20} = 0.0053$, and the corresponding probability for the conventional test is 0.10. Perfect correlation among multiple predictor variables is equivalent to testing only a single predictor variable and produces equivalent adjusted and unadjusted P-values. Thus, the adjusted and unadjusted probabilities only bound the correct probability of incorrectly rejecting the null hypothesis, and those bounds become increasingly loose as n increases.

The presence of correlation among scores need not invalidate the use of adjusted probabilities, but it does require substantial modification in how they are used. Many adjustments have been developed for specific correlation structures among the individual scores (see Miller, 1981, for details). In addition, some knowledge discovery techniques (e.g., Kass, 1975, 1980) attempt to adjust n to account for the correlation among individual scores, but these methods are heuristic, at best. A widely applicable and robust theoretical adjustment for MCPs is elusive, and attention has turned to more computationally intensive techiques (Westfall and Young, 1993).

6. Cross-Validation

The simplest method to adjust for the effects of MCPs is to use new data or reserve part of the original data for the sole purpose of adjusting for MCPs. This approach tests the selected item on a data set S' disjoint from the original sample S used to score all items generated by an MCP. Such a disjoint set can be obtained by splitting an original sample into a training set S and a test set S'. However, this approach reduces the size of S, thus increasing the variance of scores and possibly causing the selection of a suboptimal item. Ideally, the size of the S should be maximized.

Cross-validation (Stone, 1974; Weiss and Kulikowski, 1991; Kohavi, 1995) is one way to maximize the size of S while still providing an equivalently sized test set S'. Cross-validation divides the sample S into k disjoint subsets, S_i, where each subset contains approximately $1/k$ of the total instances in S. Then, for $1 \leqslant i \leqslant k$, an algorithm is applied to the sample S with the subset S_i removed $(S - S_i)$. The results of that analysis are then evaluated on the sample S_i, producing k different nearly unbiased scores. The k scores are then combined to produce a single score by some method of aggregation (e.g., averaging).

Cross-validation with k trials is often called k-fold cross-validation. Twofold cross-validation splits the sample evenly, uses each subset alternately for training and testing, and combines the results. Tenfold cross-validation is the most common approach, and it has been shown empirically to be nearly optimal in most cases (Kohavi, 1995). Leave-one-out cross-validation uses $k = N$, so that each subset S_i contains only a single instance. In theory, leave-one-out cross-validation maximizes accuracy by providing the largest training sets. In practice, however, this method can increase both the bias and variance of the resulting estimates.

Several knowledge discovery algorithms use cross-validation to adjust for the effects of MCPs. For example, Breiman et al. (1984) apply tenfold cross-validation within the CART algorithm to determine the value of a pruning parameter they call alpha; this parameter is distinct from the significance level α. Using each subset $S - S_i$, CART constructs a large classification tree. CART prunes that tree by systematically increasing the value of alpha, a parameter that controls the extent of pruning. CART tests each pruned tree on the subset S_i and records the value of alpha corresponding to the tree with maximum accuracy. CART then combines the ten values of alpha to obtain an estimate of its optimal value, and uses that value to prune the tree constructed from the entire set S.

This example illustrates a common approach to using cross-validation in knowledge discovery. Algorithms use cross-validation to estimate the optimal value of some critical parameter—often a parameter that controls the complexity of an induced model. Then that parameter estimate is used to construct a model from the entire data sample S.

Cross-validation is a robust method that can be used to adjust for the effects of MCPs. It makes relatively few assumptions, and it produces nearly unbiased parameter estimates. However, it increases the computational complexity of an algorithm by a factor of nearly k. In addition, cross-validation has significant drawbacks. It can introduce additional variance into parameter estimates (Kohavi, 1995), and, if used incorrectly, it can also introduce significant bias.

Bias can result when cross-validation is used to estimate a population parameter Ψ for the item selected by an MCP, rather than to estimate the optimal value of some critical parameter of an algorithm (as illustrated above). This type of bias can be demonstrated with a simple experiment. For each trial, we randomly generate fifty instances with a class variable and twenty predictor variables, each drawn from a uniform distribution of binary values. To determine whether the best predictor is statistically significant, we use k-fold cross-validation in an attempt to obtain an unbiased estimate of the score associated with the best predictor. In theory, this score can then be compared to a standard sampling distribution appropriate for a single score. The class and predictors are generated independently, so rejection of the null hypothesis is a Type I error.

Figure 6 shows how the probability of incorrectly rejecting the null hypothesis (a Type I error) increases with k, the number of cross-validation folds. As k increases, the sample $S - S_i$ approaches the size of the entire sample S, and an MCP is more likely to select the same predictor as it would if the entire sample S were used. In the extreme case, leave-one-out cross-validation, an MCP applied to each sample $S - S_i$ will select the same predictor nearly every time, approximating the score that would be obtained if cross-validation were never used. Thus, cross-validation with large values of k should not be used to obtain unbiased scores for

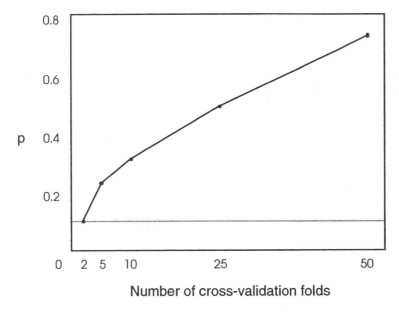

Figure 6 Cross-validation can be biased when used directly to account for MCPs

the items selected by MCPs, but instead should be applied to estimate the optimal value of some critical parameter, as illustrated by CART.

7. Randomization Tests

Randomization tests are a third approach to adjusting for MCPs. Randomization tests, also known as permutation tests, generate an empirical sampling distribution that can be used to test hypotheses about X_{max} (Westfall and Young, 1993; Jensen, 1991, 1992; Edgington, 1995; Noreen, 1989; Cohen, 1995a; Good, 2000). To generate that distribution, randomization tests explicitly generate and test possible samples that could be drawn from the population if the null hypothesis were true. They estimate $P(X_{max} \geq x \mid H_0)$ by estimating the probability density of all samples that would produce a score equal to or greater than x_{max}. Randomization tests are closely related to Fisher's exact test (see Section 3 above).

For example, consider the problem of estimating $P(X_{max} \geq x \mid H_0)$ for the data shown in Table 1, where each x_i corresponds to the classification accuracy of a single-feature rule (e.g., if A3 = T, then Class = +, else Class = −). By applying an MCP, we can determine the rule or rules with maximum classification accuracy x_{max}. We can calculate $P(X_{max} \geq x \mid H_0)$ by applying the same MCP to data samples where the class variable is a permutation of the order of the actual class variable and the predictor variables are identical to the actual data. Under the null hypothesis, each of these data samples S^* is equally likely; thus, the proportion of these randomized samples that result in scores x^*_{max} that equal or exceed x_{max} is equal to $P(X_{max} \geq x \mid H_0)$. For the example data in Table 1, the number of all unique randomized samples is:

$$\binom{6}{3} = \frac{6!}{3!3!} = 20.$$

Each of the class variables for the samples S^* is shown in Table 2.

For most data samples, the number of all unique randomized samples is extremely large. In a data sample in which there are c classes and N_i instances in each class i, the number of unique randomized samples is:

$$\frac{N!}{\prod_i N_i}.$$

Table 1 A Hypothetical Data Sample

Class variable	Predictor variables				
	A1	A2	A3	A4	A5
+	A	X	T	0	F
−	B	Y	T	0	M
+	A	Y	T	1	F
+	B	X	F	1	M
−	B	X	F	0	F
−	A	Y	F	1	M

For example, for a data sample with thirty instances and three uniformly distributed values for the class variable, there are more than 5×10^{12} unique randomized samples.

Fortunately, to estimate $P(X_{max} \geqslant x \mid H_0)$ it is not necessary to consider every possible randomized sample S^*. A randomization test can draw randomly from the space of all samples S^*, and estimate P based on that random sample. Such tests are properly known as approximate randomization tests (Edgington, 1995; Noreen, 1989), but they are far more common than exact randomization tests, and so are commonly known by the abbreviated name. To date, randomization tests have been used only infrequently in knowledge discovery algorithms (Jensen, 1991, 1992; Frank and Witten, 1998; Oates and Jensen, 1998).

Randomization tests produce accurate estimates of sampling distributions in a wide variety of situations. They can be used with nearly any measure of error because they do not require knowledge of the theoretical sampling distribution of a statistic. They avoid making the independence assumption made in the Bonferroni and Sidak adjustments, and they do not assume a specific correlation structure among the scores. Finally, the precision of their estimates of $P(X_{max} \geqslant x \mid H_0)$ can be increased merely by increasing the number of randomization trials.

The drawback of randomization tests is time complexity. Randomization tests typically introduce a constant factor of 100–1,000 into knowledge discovery algorithms. They are also relatively poor at estimating very small P-values, because of the number of randomization trials required. However, most hypothesis tests only require that P-values be less than a relatively large value, typically between 0.10 and 0.01. Determining P to this level of accuracy usually requires no more than 100–1,000 trials.

8. Overfitting Reduction and Pruning

Many knowledge discovery algorithms explicitly correct their tendency toward overfitting by using a two-stage process. First, the algorithm constructs an extremely large model. Second, the algorithm attempts to identify extraneous components in that model and eliminate them. The latter phase is generally called pruning. Algorithms that incorporate pruning include CART (Breiman et al., 1984), C4.5 (Quinlan, 1993), CN2 (Clark and Niblett, 1989), and Ripper (Cohen, 1995b). Pruning can be implemented using any of the previously discussed approaches to adjusting for MCPs, including new data (Quinlan, 1987), mathematical adjustments (Kass, 1975), cross-validation (Breiman et al., 1984), and randomization tests (Oates and Jensen, 1998).

Many algorithms employ pruning because it can increase accuracy. Figure 7 shows the idealized behavior of error as model complexity increases (Breiman et al., 1984; Weiss and Kulikowski, 1991). Initially, error declines sharply as model complexity increases. Error stabilizes as model complexity becomes sufficient for those aspects of the domain that the model can represent. Finally, error increases slightly as extraneous components are added to the model. Curves of roughly this shape have been observed for a variety of knowledge discovery algorithms.

The error curve is distinctly asymmetric with respect to model complexity. Overfitting slightly increases error, but underfitting by the same amount greatly increases error. Thus, if maximizing accuracy is the primary goal, algorithms with high statistical power (but a

Table 2 Randomized Class Variables for Table 1

Actual class variable	Randomized class variables																			
+	+	+	+	+	+	+	+	−	−	−	+	+	+	−	−	−	−	−	−	−
−	+	+	+	+	−	−	−	+	+	+	−	−	−	+	+	+	−	−	−	−
+	+	−	−	−	+	+	+	+	+	+	−	−	−	−	−	−	+	+	+	−
+	−	+	−	−	+	−	−	+	−	−	+	+	−	+	+	−	+	+	−	+
−	−	−	+	−	−	+	−	−	+	−	+	−	+	+	−	+	+	−	+	+
−	−	−	−	+	−	−	+	−	−	+	−	+	+	−	+	+	−	+	+	+

tendency to slightly overfit) are preferable to algorithms that construct models, in which all components have high statistical significance (but may slightly underfit).

In recognition of this asymmetry, some knowledge discovery algorithms incorporate features that encourage slight overfitting. First, some algorithms use the two-phase construction and pruning process rather than attempting to limit the size of the model during the initial construction phase. By intially constructing a model that is likely to have extraneous components, designers hope that their algorithms will identify more useful components than algorithms that risk stopping too early. Second, some algorithms explicitly introduce a tendency toward overfitting into their pruning algorithms. For example, CART (Breiman et al., 1984) explicitly selects the value of a pruning parameter so it is slightly biased in favor of larger classification trees.

Why does overfitting decrease accuracy? Consider the effect of overfitting in the case of classification trees. Given a training sample of fixed size, adding components to a tree reduces the size of the subsample that arrives at a leaf node. Those subsamples are used to estimate parameters of the node (e.g., a class label or a probability distribution over possible class labels). The variance of estimates increases as the size of the subsample decreases. Small subsamples will result in poor estimates and will decrease the accuracy of the model.

However, overfitting does not invariably reduce accuracy. Error curves such as the one in Figure 7 may have a large region over which complexity can vary with little impact on error. This is particularly likely when the training sample is large in relation to the minimum sufficient model size. In these cases, models can contain many extraneous components without affecting accuracy.

Again, consider the case of a classification tree. In cases where error is measured with zero−one loss (e.g., percent correct or chi-square), the leaf parameters are class labels. C4.5 (Quinlan, 1993), for example, estimates a class label based on the majority class of instances at

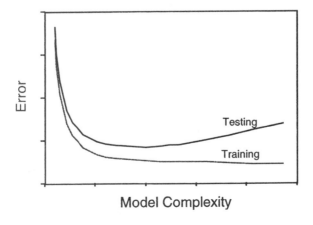

Figure 7 The relationship between model complexity and error.

a leaf. Class labels can be estimated correctly with relatively small samples, and increasing sample size does nothing to improve those estimates, particularly when the correct class represents an overwhelming majority of instances. As a result, moderate amounts of excess structure in the tree have little effect on accuracy. For example, Oates and Jensen (1997, 1998) show that classification trees constructed with C4.5 and pruned with several standard techniques have large amounts of unnecessary structure. In one experiment (Oates and Jensen, 1997) with nineteen data sets, a median value of 32 percent of the nodes in pruned trees was unnecessary, and in a quarter of the data sets, over 50 percent of the nodes were unnecessary, yet eliminating these nodes had little or no impact on accuracy.

In some knowledge discovery tasks, overfitting avoidance can actually impair accuracy. If the training sample contains insufficient data to reach inflection point of an error curve such as the one in Figure 7, then any attempt to limit complexity can increase error. The shape of the error curve depends on the power of induction algorithm, the ability of models to represent knowledge in the domain, and the inherent variability of the data. Thus, overfitting avoidance can be seen as an *a priori* learning bias of a knowledge discovery algorithm (Schaffer, 1993). It does not universally improve accuracy, and its effectiveness depends on how well it corresponds to specific aspects of the domain.

References

Agrawal, R., T. Imielinski, and A. Swami. 1993. "Mining association rules between sets of items in large databases." In *Proceedings of the ACM SIGMOD Conference on Management of Data*, pp. 207–216. New York: Association for Computing Machinery.

Aha, D., D. Kibler, and M. Albert. 1991. "Instance-based learning algorithms." *Machine Learning* 6: 37–66.

Breiman, L., J. Friedman, R. Olshen, and C. Stone. 1984. *Classification and Regression Trees*. Belmont, CA: Wadsworth International.

Clark, P. and T. Niblett. 1989. "The CN2 induction algorithm." *Machine Learning* 3(4): 261–284.

Cohen, P. R. 1995a. *Empirical Methods for Artificial Intelligence*. Cambridge, MA: MIT Press.

Cohen, W. 1995b. "Fast effective rule induction." In *Proceedings of the Twelfth International Conference on Machine Learning*, pp. 115–123. San Francisco, CA: Morgan Kaufmann.

Dietterich, T. 1995. "Overfitting and under-computing in machine learning." *ACM Comput. Surveys* 27: 326–327.

Domingos, P. and M. Pazzani. 1997. "On the optimality of the simple Bayesian classifier under zero–one loss." *Machine Learning* 29: 103–130.

Edgington, E. 1995. *Randomization Tests*. 3rd ed. New York: Marcel Dekker.

Einhorn, H. 1972. "Alchemy in the behavioral sciences." *Public Opinion Q.* 36: 367–378.

Fayyad, U. and K. Irani. 1992. "The attribute selection problem in decision tree generation." In *Proceedings of the Tenth National Conference on Artificial Intelligence (AAAI-92)*, pp. 104–110. Menlo Park, CA: AAAI Press.

Feelders, A. and W. Verkooijen. 1996. "On the statistical comparison of inductive learning methods." In *Learning from Data: Artificial and Intelligence V*, edited by D. Fisher and H.-J. Lenz. New York, NY: Springer-Verlag.

Frank, E. and I. Witten. 1998. "Using a permutation test for attribute selection in decision trees." In *Proceedings of the Fifteenth International Conference on Machine Learning*, pp. 152–160. San Francisco, CA: Morgan Kaufmann.

Freedman, D., W. Navidi, and S. Peters. 1986. "On the impact of variable selection in fitting regression equations." In *On Model Uncertainty and its Statistical Implications*, edited by T. K. Dijkstra, pp. 1–16. Berlin: Springer-Verlag.

Gaines, B. 1989. "An ounce of knowledge is worth a ton of data: quantitative studies of the trade-off between expertise and data based on statistically well-founded empirical induction." In *Proceedings of the Sixth International Workshop on Machine Learning*, pp. 156–159. San Mateo, CA: Morgan Kaufmann.

Gascuel, O. and G. Caraux. 1992. "Statistical significance in inductive learning." In *Proceedings of the Tenth European Conference on Artificial Intelligence*, pp. 435–439. Chichester, England: Wiley.

Good, P. 2000. *Permutation Tests: A Practical Guide to Resampling Methods for Testing Hypotheses*. New York, NY: Springer-Verlag.

Glymour, C., D. Madigan, D. Pregibon, and P. Smyth. 1997. "Statistical themes and lessons for data mining." *J. Data Mining and Knowledge Discovery* 1: 11–28.

Jensen, D. 1991. "Knowledge discovery through induction with randomization testing." In *Proceedings of the 1991 Knowledge Discovery in Databases Workshop*, pp. 148–159. Menlo Park, CA: AAAI Press.

Jensen, D. 1992. "Induction with randomization testing: decision-oriented analysis of large data sets." Ph.D./diss. Saint Louis, MO: Washington University.

Jensen, D. and P. R. Cohen. 2000. "Multiple comparisons in induction algorithms." *Machine Learning* **38(3)**: 309–338.

Jensen, D. and M. Schmill. 1997. "Adjusting for multiple comparisons in decision tree pruning." In *Proceedings of the Third International Conference on Knowledge Discovery and Data Mining*, pp. 195–198. Menlo Park, CA: AAAI Press.

Kass, G. 1980. "An exploratory technique for investigating large quantities of categorical data." *Appl. Stat.* **29**: 119–127.

Kass, G. 1975. "Significance testing in automatic interaction detection (A.I.D.)." *Appl. Stat.* **24**: 178–189.

Kohavi, R. 1995. "A study of cross-validation and bootstrap for accuracy estimation and model selection." In *IJCAI: Proceedings of the Fourteenth International Joint Conference on Artificial Intelligence*, pp. 1137–1143. San Francisco, CA: Morgan Kaufmann.

Kohavi, R. and G. John. 1997. "Wrappers for feature subset selection." *Artificial Intell.* **97**: 273–324.

Kohavi, R. and F. Provost. 1998. "Glossary of terms." *Machine Learning* **30**: 271–274.

Megiddo, N. and R. Srikant. 1998. "Discovering predictive association rules." In *Proceedings of the Fourth International Conference on Knowledge Discovery and Data Mining*. Menlo Park, CA: AAAI Press.

Mehta, C. and N. Patel. 1983. "A network algorithm for performing Fisher's exact test in $r \times c$ contingency tables." *J. Am. Stat. Assoc.* **78**: 427–434.

Miller, R. 1981. *Simultaneous Statistical Inference*. 2nd ed. New York, NY: Springer-Verlag.

Morrison, D. and R. Henkel. (eds). 1970. In *The Significance Test Controversy: A Reader*. Chicago: Aldine.

Murthy, S. and S. Salzberg. 1995. "Lookahead and pathology in decision tree induction." In *IJCAI: Proceedings of the Fourteenth International Joint Conference on Artificial Intelligence*, pp. 1025–1031. San Francisco, CA: Morgan Kaufmann.

Noreen, E. 1989. *Computer-Intensive Methods for Testing Hypotheses: An Introduction*. New York, NY: Wiley.

Oates, T. and D. Jensen. 1997. "The effects of training set size on decision tree complexity." In *Proceedings of the Fourteenth International Conference on Machine Learning*, pp. 254–262. San Francisco, CA: Morgan Kaufmann.

Oates, T. and D. Jensen. 1998. "Large datasets lead to overly complex models: an explanation and a solution." In *Proceedings of the Fourth International Conference on Knowledge Discovery and Data Mining*. Menlo Park, CA: AAAI Press.

Provost, F., T. Fawcett, and R. Kohavi. 1998. "The case against accuracy estimation for comparing induction algorithms." In *Proceedings of the Fifteenth International Conference on Machine Learning*, pp. 445–553. San Francisco, CA: Morgan Kaufmann.

Quinlan, J. R. 1987. "Simplifying decision trees." *Int. J. Man–Machine Studies* **27**: 221–234.

Quinlan, J. R. 1988. "Decision trees and multi-valued attributes." In *Machine Intelligence 11*, edited by J. Hayes, D. Michie, and J. Richards. Oxford: Clarendon Press.

Quinlan, J. R. 1990. "Learning logical definitions from relations." *Machine Learning* **5**: 239–266.

Quinlan, J. R. 1993. *C4.5: Programs for Machine Learning*. San Mateo, CA: Morgan Kaufmann.

Quinlan, J. R. and R. Cameron-Jones. 1995. "Oversearching and layered search in empirical learning." In *IJCAI: Proceedings of the Fourteenth International Joint Conference on Artificial Intelligence*, pp. 1019–1024. San Francisco, CA: Morgan Kaufmann.

Sachs, L. 1982. *Applied Statistics: A Handbook of Techniques*. New York: Springer-Verlag.

Salzberg, S. 1997. "On comparing classifiers: pitfalls to avoid and a recommended approach." *Data Mining and Knowledge Discovery* **1**: 317–328.

Schaffer, C. 1993. "Overfitting avoidance as bias." *Machine Learning* **10**: 153–178.

Segal, R. and O. Etzioni. 1994. "Learning decision lists using homogeneous rules." In *Proceedings of the Twelth National Conference on Artificial Intelligence*. Menlo Park, CA: AAAI Press.

Stone, M. 1974. "Cross-validatory choice and assessment of statistical predictions." *J. R. Stat. Soc. (B)* **36**: 111–147.

Weiss, S. and C. Kulikowski. 1991. *Computer Systems That Learn: Classification and Prediction Methods from Statistics, Neural Nets, Machine Learning, and Expert Systems*. San Mateo, CA: Morgan Kaufmann.

Westfall, P. and S. Young. 1993. *Resampling-based Multiple Testing: Examples and Methods for P-value Adjustment*. New York: Wiley.

19.2 Other Evaluations

19.2.1 Minimum Description Length

Alexander Tuzhilin

ABSTRACT   This article describes the MDL principle that selects the model minimizing the total number of bits needed to encode the model and the data given the model. The article also explores the connection of the MDL principle to the maximum a posteriori (MAP) hypothesis and the Occam's razor principle. Finally, it describes how the MDL principle is applied to the decision tree pruning problem.

1. Introduction

There has been a long-standing discussion in the machine learning community on the applicability of the Occam's razor to KDD problems, Occam's razor states, "choose the simplest explanation that fits the observed data". One of the more recent views on this disscussion is presented in Domingos (1999). The two information-theoretic manifestations of this principle in statistics and data mining are the closely related minimum description length (MDL; Rissanen, 1978) and minimum message length (MML; Wallace and Boulton, 1968) principles. These two principles select a model out of a set of models that minimizes the total number of bits needed to encode the model and the data given the model. They have been applied to several model structures, including classification trees (Mehta et al., 1998; Quinlan and Rivest, 1989; Rastogi and Shim, 1998), finite state automata (Georgeff and Wallace, 1984), clustering (Wallace and Boulton, 1968), DNA string alignment (Allison et al., 1992), and decision graphs (Oliver, 1993). In this article we describe and compare these two principles and present only the most prominent application of the principles to the problem of selecting good decision trees (due to space limitation).

2. The MML Principle

The MML principle can be stated as follows (we follow Oliver and Hand, 1994 in our presentation of MML): Let $D = \{d_1, d_2, ..., d_N\}$ be a set of data points and let $H = \{h_i\}_{i \in I}$ be a set of models (hypotheses) describing data D. Also let C_1 be a coding scheme for hypotheses from H, and C_2 be a coding scheme for data D given hypothesis h from H. Then the minimum message length (MML) principle selects the hypothesis (model) h_0 from H that minimizes the total length of the encoded model and the description of the data given the model, that is,

$$h_0 = \underset{h \in H}{\text{argmin}} \, (L_{C_1}(h) + L_{C_2}(D \mid h)) \tag{1}$$

taken over different possible coding schemes C_1 and C_2.

Example 1.

(Oliver and Hand, 1994). Let $D = \{d_1, d_2, ..., d_N\}$ *be a set of measurements of people's heights that are normally distributed with mean μ and standard deviation σ. Assume that we encode these parameters of our model (μ and σ) using the following encoding scheme C_1. Let the upper and lower bounds on μ be μ_u and μ_l, respectively, and assume that this range is divided into N_μ bins. Similarly, let the upper and lower bounds of σ be σ_u and σ_l, and assume that it is divided into N_σ bins. Using the well-known result from information theory, we can encode μ with $\log_2 N_\mu$ and σ with $\log_2 N_\sigma$ bits.*

Next, given specific parameters of the hypothesis μ and σ, we can code people's heights d_i using the following coding scheme C_2. We first discretize parameters μ, σ, and the height variable as follows. For μ and σ, we determine to which of the N_μ and N_σ bins they belong and then take the midpoints of these bins (μ_d and σ_d). Next, we discretize heights $d_k \in D$ by placing them into K bins $\{(a_i, b_i)\}_{i=1,...,K}$, each bin having width ϵ (i.e., $\mid b_i - a_i \mid = \epsilon$). Then the probability of the *height variable belonging to bin (a_i, b_i) is*

$$P_i = \frac{1}{\sqrt{2\pi}\sigma_d} \int_{a_i}^{b_i} e^{-(x-\mu_d)^2/2\sigma_d^2} \, dx \tag{2}$$

and we assign it to the heights $d_k \in D$ belonging to bin (a_i, b_i), that is, set $\mathrm{Prob}(d_k) = P_i$. Moreover, using the well-known theorem of Shannon, we can encode each height d_k using $-\log_2 \mathrm{Prob}(d_k)$ bits. Therefore, the total length of the encoded set of heights D is equal to $\sum_{k=1}^{N} -\log_2 \mathrm{Prob}(d_k)$.

Finally, the total length of the encoding of the hypothesis (model) h and the data D is

$$L_{C_1}(h) + L_{C_2}(D \mid h) = \log_2 N_\mu + \log_2 N_\sigma + \sum_{k=1}^{N} -\log_2 \mathrm{Prob}(d_k) \tag{3}$$

Then the MML principle selects the discretization scheme for the mean μ and standard deviation σ of the normally distributed height variable (values of $\mu_u, \mu_l, \sigma_u, \sigma_l, N_\mu, N_\sigma$ that determine values μ_d and σ_d) so that the expression (3) is minimal. Note that we kept the discretization parameters of the height variable (including the number and the size of the bins) constant, since it was not included in (3) as a part of the encoding of the model. However, this assumption can be relaxed resulting in a more flexible, but also more complex, encoding and optimization model.

The MML principle has a natural connection to Bayesian theory and the maximum a posteriori hypothesis (MAP), according to which hypothesis h_{MAP} is selected from H that maximizes $P(h|D)$, that is

$$h_{MAP} = \underset{h \in H}{\mathrm{argmax}}\, P(h \mid D). \tag{4}$$

To see the connection, we can rewrite $P(h|D)$ as $P(D \mid h)P(h)/P(D)$, take the logarithm of this expression, and restate (4) as $h_{MAP} = \mathrm{argmin}_{h \in H}(-\log_2 P(D \mid h) - \log_2 P(h))$. Then, according to the well-known theorem of Shannon (Shannon and Weaver, 1949), the optimal encoding of hypotheses from H is $-\log_2 P(h)$ bits and for the data D given h is $-\log_2 P(D \mid h)$ bits. Then

$$h_{MAP} = \underset{h \in H}{\mathrm{argmin}}\, (-\log_2 P(D \mid h) - \log_2 P(h)) = \underset{h \in H}{\mathrm{argmin}}\, (L_{C_2}(D \mid h) + L_{C_1}(h)) = h_0$$

where h_0 is defined in (1). In other words, the MAP hypothesis coincides with the MML hypothesis.

It is important to stress that the MML principle does not state that the shortest encoded hypothesis is the best (in the MAP sense). It says that if we know the prior distributions $P(h)$ and $P(D|h)$ and we select the optimal encoding schemes C_1 and C_2, then the MML principle produces the best (MAP) hypothesis. Unfortunately, we often do not know the distribution $P(h)$ of $h \in H$ and can only guess what the best encoding scheme should be. In this case, the MML principle cannot be grounded in the MAP principle and remains only a heuristic: MML is only as good as the selected encoding scheme.

As stated above, one of the distinguishing features of the MML principle is that it searches for the model with minimal total length over the set of individual models. In the next section, we will describe a closely related MDL principle that searches over the set of model classes.

3. The MDL Principle

As MML, the MDL principle also selects the model that minimizes the code length of the data and the model, as in Equation (1). However, unlike MML, which considers individual models from H, the MDL principle optimizes over classes of models, where a model class defines a set of models with the same parametric form, including the same number of parameters. For example, a class of linear models is defined as $y = a + bx$, where parameters a and b vary over the set of real numbers. A model is a specific instance of the class specified for fixed values of parameters. For example, $y = 2 + 3x$ is a model belonging to the previously specified model class. Of course, individual models in the MML principle can be viewed as special cases of model classes where a class consists of a single model.

In order to describe the MDL principle, we first introduce some notation. Assume that we have a set of model classes $M = \cup_k M_k$, where individual model classes $M_k = \{f(x; \theta)\}$ are specified by the density function f parameterized by $\theta = \{\theta_1, ..., \theta_k\}$, a parameter vector ranging over a subset of the k-dimensional Euclidean space Θ^k. Also let C_1 be a coding scheme for model classes from M, and C_2 be a coding scheme for data D given model class from M. Then, given data $D = (d_1, d_2, ..., d_N)$, the minimum description length (MDL) principle selects the model class M_0 from M that minimizes the total length of the encoded model class and the description of the data given that class, that is

$$M_0 = \underset{M_k \in M}{\operatorname{argmin}}\ (L_{C_1}(M_k) + L_{C_2}(D \mid M_k)) \tag{5}$$

taken over different possible coding schemes C_1 and C_2.

As we can see from (5), the MDL principle (unlike MML) encodes the data for a class of models parameterized by θ, and this makes the problem more challenging. One way to do such an encoding is to use optimal Shannon codes (Shannon and Weaver, 1949) with respect to the marginal distribution of data, that is, define $L_{C_2}(D/M_k)$ as

$$L_{C_2}(D \mid M_k) = -\log \int_{\theta \in \Theta^k} \operatorname{Prob}(D \mid \theta)\operatorname{Prob}(\theta)\ d\theta. \tag{6}$$

In some applications of the MDL principle, it is assumed that the code lengths of the model classes M_k are the same for different values of k. For example, if we assume that there is a finite number of model classes (K) and that they are uniformly distributed, then $L_{C_1}(M_k) = \log K$ for all $k = 1, ..., K$. This means that Equation (5) is reduced to

$$M_0 = \underset{M_k \in M}{\operatorname{argmin}}\ L_{C_2}(D \mid M_k). \tag{7}$$

Also, it is often difficult to compute $L_{C_2}(D \mid M_k)$ in (6), and Rissanen (1999b) proposes to approximate each class M_k (parameterized by θ) by a universal model $f_k(D)$ having a single probability distribution. Such a universal model should imitate any particular model $f(D; \theta)$ in the class M_k across different values of $\theta \in \Theta^k$ (similarly to universal Turing machines).

Moreover, instead of dealing with codes and code lengths, as in (7), Rissanen (1999b) proposes to deal directly with probabilities, that is, select the model class M_k for which $\hat{f}_k(D)$ has the largest probability for data D, since this is equivalent to using optimal codes that minimize the expected code lengths due to the Shannon's result (Shannon and Weaver, 1949). To illustrate these concepts, consider the following example from Rissanen (1999b).

Example 2.

Risannen, 1999b. Let M_k be a parametric class of normal distributions $f(y^n; \mu^n, \tau)$, where τ is a variance and μ^n is a vector of means defined as $\mu^n = \beta X$, where $X = \{x_{it}\}_{i=1,...,k;\ t=1,...,n}$ is a matrix of variables and $\beta = \{\beta_1, ..., \beta_k\}$ is a vector of coefficients. Let $\theta = (\beta, \tau) = (\beta_1, ..., \beta_k, \tau)$ define the set of parameters of the model. Then the MDL principle calls for the selection of the universal model $\hat{f}(y^n; X, k)$ that (1) imitates the class $f(y^n; \theta)$ and (2) selects such k that maximizes probability $\hat{f}(y^n; X, k)$ for the data y^n.

Rissanen (1999b) argues that a good way to define the universal model that approximates $f(D; \theta)$ is through the normalized maximum likelihood (NML) model that is defined as

$$\hat{f}(D) = \frac{f(D; \hat{\theta}(D))}{\int_{\hat{\theta}(y^n) \in \Omega} f(y^n; \hat{\theta}(y^n))\ dy^n}, \tag{8}$$

where $\hat{\theta}(D)$ is the maximum likelihood estimator and Ω is a certain subset of estimates that makes the integral finite. Then the MDL principle calls for the model class M_k, for which the normalized maximum likelihood (NML) model $\hat{f}_k(D)$ defined in (8) assigns the largest probability to data D.

Continuing Example 2, Rissanen shows that $f(y^n; X, k)$ can be expressed as

$$-\log f(y^n; X, k) = \frac{n-k}{2}\log \tau(y^n) + \frac{k}{2}\log(\tau\beta'X'X\beta) + \frac{n-k-1}{2}\log\frac{n}{n-k} - \frac{k+3}{2}\log k + ...,$$

where only the terms that depend on k in a relevant manner are retained. This last formula needs to be minimized over k in order to obtain the first k most important β-coefficients.

4. Comparing MDL and MML Principles

As is shown in the previous two sections, the MDL and MML principles are closely related to each other. Both of them invoke the Occam's razor principle and, as Equations (1) and (5) show, they select a model (or a class of models) that minimizes the total number of bits needed to encode the model and the data given the model.

However, there are also significant differences between the two principles that are highlighted (Baxter and Oliver, 1994; Rissanen, 1999b,c; Wallace and Dowe, 1999a,b). First, the MML principle selects a single model from the set of all possible models. In contrast to this, the MDL principle selects a class of models. As Rissanen (1999a) argues, this provides for a more general approach to the model selection problem than the MML approach. Second, the MDL literature often makes an assumption that the model classes are uniformly distributed (Baxter and Oliver, 1994). This reduces Equation (5) to (7), and only encoding of the data is considered in this case. As a result of this, the MDL encoding of a message is shorter than the MML encoding (Rissanen, 1999a). However, as Wallace and Dowe (1999a, section 6.2; 1999b) show, it is shorter by a rather small margin.

There has been a debate between the founders of the two principles concerning which is better and in what sense (Rissanen, 1999a,c; Wallace and Dowe, 1999a,b). In particular, Rissanen (1999a,c) argues that the MDL principle is more general and has stronger theoretical foundations than MML, is applicable to a broader range of problems, and produces shorter codes than MML. In Wallace and Dowe (1999b), the authors refute the arguments of Rissanen (1999a,c) and reiterate the advantages of the MML principle. Some other points of view on these two principles can be found in Clarke (1999), Dawid (1999), and Shen (1999).

5. Application of MDL to Decision Tree Pruning

The most popular application of the MDL and MML principles, which has received considerable attention in the ML and KDD communities, is the problem of constructing accurate decision trees. The literature describing this application refers to the MDL rather than the MML principle. However, the two principles coincide for this particular application, since the model classes consist of single decision trees in this case. We will follow the established terminology and call it the MDL principle.

Typically, a decision tree is constructed in two phases. However, we will also describe an exception to this two-phase scheme below.) In the first (building) phase, a decision tree is built using standard techniques, such as C4.5 (Quinlan, 1993), CART (Breiman et al., 1984), or SPRINT (Shafer et al., 1996) methods. In the second (pruning) phase, the tree is being pruned using the MDL principle to avoid overfitting (see Chapter 19.1). According to the MDL principle (5), we need to encode the decision tree with schema C_1 and the data for that decision tree with schema C_2.

One way to code decision trees would be through the preorder traversal of its nodes (Quinlan and Rivest, 1989). Internal nodes can be coded with 1 and the code for the attribute and the value of the split corresponding to that node. The leaf nodes can be coded with 0 and the code for the class associated with that leaf. Following the example taken from Quinlan and Rivest (1989), the decision tree from Figure 1 can be coded as follows (Quinlan and Rivest, 1989):

```
1 Outlook 1 Humidity 0 N 0 P 0 P 1 Windy 0 N 0 P
```

In this example, substring 1 Humidity 0 N 0 P corresponds to the left subtree of Figure 1, 0 P to the middle subtree, and 1 Windy 0 N 0 P to the right subtree.

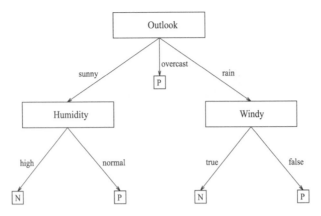

Figure 1 A decision tree

Data for a given decision tree can be encoded recursively as a part of the MDL-based decision tree pruning algorithm presented in Figure 2 (as taken from (Rastogi and Shim, 1998). An important part of this algorithm is the computation of the cost of encoding data $C(S)$ stored at a single leaf node N containing a set S of n records belonging to one of the k classes, each class i ($i = 1, ..., k$) having n_i elements. This cost is derived in Quinlan and Rivest (1989) as

$$C(S) = \log\binom{n+k-1}{k-1} + \log\frac{n!}{n_1! ... n_k!}.$$

According to the algorithm in Figure 2, if node N is a leaf node, then the cost of that node is simply $C(S) + 1$. If node N is an internal node, then we recursively compute the encoding costs of its children (without loss of generality, we assume that there are only two children, N_1 and N_2). Then the total cost of encoding the internal node N is equal to the costs of encoding nodes N_1 and N_2 and the cost of describing the split at node N, $C\_split(N)$, which is equal to the cost of encoding the attribute used in the split and the selected value for that attribute (plus 1 for specifying that this is an internal node). If this total cost is greater than the cost of encoding node N (without children), then we prune children N_1 and N_2 from node N because it is cheaper to keep node N alone than with its children. Otherwise, we keep its children N_1 and N_2.

The cost and the split functions $C(S)$ and $C\_split(N)$ can be computed using different methods. For example, Mehta et al. (1998) use a cost function that is different from the one

```
PROCEDURE computeCost&Prune(Node N)
    IF N is a leaf THEN
        RETURN (C(S)+1)
        /* N1 and N2 are N's children */
    minCost1 := computeCost&Prune(N1);
    minCost2 := computeCost&Prune(N2);
    minCostN := min{C(S)+1, C_split(N)+1+minCost1+minCost2};
    IF minCostN = C(S)+1 THEN
        prune child nodes N1 and N2 from the tree;
    RETURN minCostN
```

Figure 2 Standard pruning algorithm

used in Quinlan and Rivest (1989). However, all these differences fit within the same approach to the MDL pruning that is presented in Figure 2.

The MDL-based pruning algorithm presented in Figure 2 has been tested on several data sets for various cost functions and compared with similar nonMDL-based approaches. In particular, Quinlan and Rivest (1989) compare the decision trees pruned with their version of the MDL algorithm with the pessimistic pruning method described in Quinlan (1987). Quinlan and Rivest (1989) conclude that the accuracy rates of the MDL and pessimistic pruning methods are approximately the same, although the MDL method usually generates shorter decision trees. Similarly, Mehta et al. (1998) compare their version of the MDL algorithm with C4.5 and the pessimistic pruning methods. It reaches similar conclusions by demonstrating that the MDL algorithm generates smaller decision trees, while keeping accuracy rates approximately the same as the other two methods.

One of the problems with the MDL-based methods considered so far is the inefficiency associated with the two-phase approach to decision tree generation. In the first phase, a larger decision tree is built and in the second phase this tree is pruned. As Rastogi and Shim (1998) claim, this pruning can sometimes remove up to 90 percent of the nodes generated in the building phase. To address this problem, they propose an alternative approach in which the building phase is combined with the pruning phase. This method is based on the idea that if during the building phase we know that a certain node is going to be removed in the pruning phase, then there is no need to expand this node in the building phase.

One problem with implementing this idea directly by invoking the pruning algorithm presented in Figure 2 during the building phase is that we do not know the cost of a subtree rooted at a node if that node has not yet been completely expanded. Since this cost can decrease while the tree is expanded in the building phase, we can overprune the tree if we remove the node prematurely.

Rastogi and Shim (1998) present the algorithm PUBLIC that solves this problem by computing a lower bound on the costs of partially built trees. They also show that, using these lower bounds for making pruning decisions, it is impossible to overprune partially built trees. Also, as Rastogi and Shim (1998) demonstrate, the tree will never be underpruned at the time when the building phase is finished because all the pruning costs would be exactly known at that time. As a result, we will produce exactly the same tree at the end as the previous two-phase MDL algorithms would generate. PUBLIC was tested on real-life and synthetic data sets, and it significantly outperforms standard two-phase methods (Rastogi and Shim, 1998).

6. Discussion

MML and MDL are general model selection principles that choose the model(s) that minimize the total number of bits needed to encode the model and the data given the model. These two principles have a nice property of selecting simple models and have strong justifications from the information-theoretic and statistical points of view. In particular, the relationship between these principles and the MAP hypothesis has been described in this article, and the relationship to Kolmogorov complexity is presented in Wallace and Dawe (1999a) and Shen (1999). This combination of simplicity and theoretical justification makes MDL/MML principles attractive model selection methods.

The MML and MDL principles are based on the belief that a model or a model class, which permits the shortest encoding of the data, captures best all the properties in the data we wish to learn (Rissanen, 1989, p. 9). However, the evidence, as presented in this article and elsewhere (Domingos, 1999), does not always support this expectation. For example, the decision trees pruned with the MDL methods described in Mehta et al. (1998), Quinlan and Rivest (1989) and Rastogi and Shim (1998) produce smaller but not significantly more accurate trees in comparison to other popular methods. Moreover, Quinlan and Rivest (1989) report that on some data sets their MDL method overpruned decision trees, resulting in less accurate trees in comparison with the pessimistic pruning method.

The conclusion made by these authors that the MDL method, as applied to decision trees, does not achieve better generalization error rates than alternative approaches is not very surprising because the MDL encoding methods used in these studies do not guarantee the MAP hypothesis. This is the case because we do not know in many applications prior distributions of models (probabilities $P(h)$ for $h \in H$), and we may not be able to select optimal encodings of the models (e.g., of decision trees). In such cases MDL remains just another heuristic trying to reduce generalization error rates.

References

Allison, L., C. S. Wallace, and C. N. Yee. 1992. "Finite-state models in the alignment of macromolecules." *J. Molec. Evol.* **35**: 77–89.

Breiman, L., J. H. Friedman, R. A. Olshen, and C. J. Stone. 1984. *Classification and Regression Trees.* Monterey, CA: Wadsworth Publishers.

Baxter, R. A. and J. J. Oliver. 1994. "MDL and MML: similarities and differences." Technical Report 207. Monash University, Department of Computer Science.

Clarke, B. 1999. "Discussion of the papers by Rissanen, and by Wallace and Dowe." *Comput. J.* **42(4)**.

Dawid, A. P. 1999. "Discussion of the papers by Rissanen and by Wallace and Dowe." *Comput. J.* **42(4)**.

Domingos, P. 1999. "The role of Occam's razor in knowledge discovery." *J. Data Mining and Knowledge Discovery* **3(4)**: 409–425.

Georgeff, M. P. and C. S. Wallace. 1984. "A general criterion for inductive inference." In *Proceedings of the Sixth European Conference on Artificial Intelligence.* North Holland, Amsterdam, pp. 473–482.

Mehta, M., J. Rissanen, and R. Agrawal. August 1995. "MDL-based decision tree pruning." In *Proceedings of the First International Conference on Knowledge Discovery and Data Mining.* Menlo Park, CA: AAAI Press, pp. 216–221.

Oliver, J. and D. Hand. 1994. Introduction to minimum encoding inference. Technical report 205. Monash University.

Oliver, J. J. 1993. "Decision graphs—an extension of decision trees." In *Proceedings of the Fourth International Workshop on Artificial Intelligence and Statistics*, pp. 343–350.

Quinlan, J. R. and R. L. Rivest. 1989. "Inferring decision trees using the minimum description length principle." *Inform. and Comput.* **80**: 227–248.

Quinlan, J. R. 1987. "Simplifying decision trees." *Int. J. Man–Machine Studies* **27**: 221–234.

Quinlan, J. R. 1993. *C4.5: Programs for Machine Learning.* San Mateo, CA: Morgan Kaufmann.

Rissanen, J. 1978. "Modeling by shortest data description." *Automatica* **14**: 465–471.

Rissanen, J. 1989. *Stochastic Complexity in Statistical Inquiry*, Volume 15. Singapore: World Scientific Series in Computer Science.

Rissanen, J. 1999a. "Discussion of paper 'Minimum message length and Kolmogorov complexity' by C. S. Wallace and D. L. Dowe." *Comput. J.* **42(4)**: 327–329.

Rissanen, J. 1999b. "Hypothesis selection and testing by the MDL principle." *Comput. J.* **42(4)**: 260–269.

Rissanen, J. 1999c. "Rejoinder." *Comput. J.* **42(4)**: 343–344.

Rastogi, R. and K. Shim. 1998. "PUBLIC: a decision tree classifier that integrates building and pruning." In *International Conference on Very Large Databases.* San Francisco, CA: Morgan Kaufmann, pp. 404–415.

Shafer, J., R. Agrawal, and M. Mehta. 1996. "SPRINT: a scalable parallel classifier for data mining." In *International Conference on Very Large Databases.* San Francisco, CA: Morgan Kaufmann, pp. 544–555.

Shen, A. 1999. "Discussion on Kolmogorov complexity and statistical analysis." *Comput. J.* **42(4)**: 340–349.

Shannon, C. E. and W. Weaver. 1949. *The Mathematical Theory of Communication.* Urbana, IL: University of Illinois Press.

Wallace, C. S. and D. M. Boulton. 1968. "An information measure for classification." *Comput. J.* **11**: 185–195.

Wallace, C. S. and D. L. Dowe. 1999a. "Minimum message length and Kolmogorov complexity." *Comput. J.* **42(4)**.

Wallace, C. S. and D. L. Dowe. 1999b. "Rejoinder." *Comput. J.* **42(4)**.

19.2.2 Usefulness, Novelty, and Integration of Interestingness Measures

Alexander Tuzhilin

ABSTRACT This article focuses on subjective methods of evaluation of discovered patterns in data that depend not only on the structure of the pattern and the data but also on the user who examines the pattern. The article considers such subjective measures of interestingness as unexpectedness, actionability, template-based measures, including data mining queries, pattern templates, and meta rules, and background knowledge measures. Finally, it describes how these different interestingness measures can be integrated into one common approach.

1. Introduction

The field of knowledge discovery in databases (data mining) has been defined in Fayyad et al. (1996) as the nontrivial process of identifying valid, novel, potentially useful, and ultimately understandable patterns from data. However, most of the work in the knowledge discovery in databases (KDD) field focuses on the validity aspect, and the other two aspects, novelty and usefulness, have been studied to a lesser degree. This is unfortunate because it has been observed both by researchers (Brin et al., 1997; Frawley et al., 1991; Klemettinen et al., 1994; Liu and Hsu, 1996; Silberschatz and Tuzhilin, 1995, 1996) and by practitioners (Stedman, 1997) that many existing tools generate a large number of valid but obvious or irrelevant patterns. Therefore, the problem of evaluation of discovered patterns in terms other than just statistical validity is one of the central problems in data mining.

Chapter 19.1 evaluates discovered patterns in objective terms, that is, in terms of the structure of a pattern and the underlying data used in the discovery process. In contrast, this article focuses on subjective measures of evaluation (Piatetsky-Shapiro and Matheus, 1994; Silberschatz and Tuzhilin, 1995, 1996). These subjective measures depend not only on the structure of a rule and on the data used in the discovery process, but also on the user who examines the pattern and on that user's background knowledge. These subjective measures recognize that a pattern that is of interest to one user may be of no interest to another user who happens to have different background knowledge and/or interests.

In this article, we consider the following subjective measures of interestingness of patterns:

- *Unexpectedness* (Berger and Tuzhilin, 1998; Chakrabarti et al., 1998; Liu and Hsu, 1996; Liu et al., 1997; Padmanabhan and Tuzhilin, 1998, 1999; Silberschatz and Tuzhilin, 1995, 1996; Subramonian, 1998; Suzuki, 1997). Users specify what they know about the application domain, and the system evaluates patterns in terms of how much they contradict this knowledge.

- *Interestingness templates* (Han et al., 1996a,b; Imielinski and Virmani, 1999; Imielinski et al., 1996; Klemettinen et al., 1994; Meo et al., 1998; Shen et al., 1996; Srikant et al., 1997). Users specify in broad terms the classes of patterns in which they are interested, and the KDD system evaluates whether or not the discovered patterns satisfy these criteria.

- *Actionability* (Adomavicius and Tuzhilin, 1997; Matheus et al., 1996; Piatetsky-Shapiro and Matheus, 1994; Silberschatz and Tuzhilin, 1995, 1996). Users specify what is useful, and the KDD system evaluates discovered patterns in terms of how closely they match these criteria.

Before we describe these approaches, we would like to mention that in this section we consider subjective measures in the context of *evaluation* of discovered patterns. If we use the framework for knowledge discovery presented in Silberschatz and Tuzhilin (1995) and shown in Figure 1, then this evaluation process corresponds to part (b) of that figure. According to this, after patterns are discovered by the knowledge discovery system (KDS), they are evaluated by the interestingness filter, and only the most interesting patterns are presented to the user. However, the subjective measures of interestingness could also be incorporated into the discovery engine itself so that the KDS system would only generate patterns interesting according to these measures, as is done in Lee et al. (1998), Padmanabhan and Tuzhilin (1998), and Srikant et al. (1997) and as Figure 1(c) suggests. Although it is an important approach to pattern discovery, it lies outside the scope of this article.

2. Discovery of Unexpected Patterns

As was pointed out in the previous section, subjective measures of interestingness assume some form of background knowledge on the part of the user. The idea of using domain knowledge for

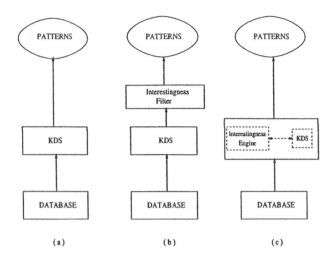

Figure 1 Different approaches to discovering interesting patterns

the purpose of discovering new knowledge is an old one. It can be traced back to early expert systems such as AM (Lenat, 1983) and DENDRAL (Buchanan and Feigenbaum, 1978) that use heuristic search and generate-and-test paradigms for the discovery process. In particular, the AM system discovers new mathematical concepts from the initial set of 115 core set-theoretic concepts by repeatedly applying 1 of the 250 heuristic rules to the set of mathematical concepts already discovered. The newly generated concepts are then tested for their interestingness using such concepts as intuition, aesthetics, utility, richness, and relevance (Lenat, 1983). Similarly, DENDRAL (and subsequently Meta-DENDRAL) helps organic chemists determine the molecular structure of unknown compounds. This is achieved by generating successively larger and larger structures of molecules using a set of heuristic rules and constraints. The initial approaches to discovering new knowledge from existing knowledge using heuristic searches were later extended in the EURISKO system (Lenat and Brown, 1984), in several scientific discovery systems (Shrager and Langley, 1990; Żytkow et al., 1990), and in Lee et al. (1998). In all this work, researchers were interested in discovering a broad range of new knowledge, including unexpected knowledge. However, these approaches only deal with unexpectedness in a limited way and do not directly and formally explain what unexpectedness is and how to discover unexpected patterns in a systematic way. Another stream of work on incorporating domain knowledge into machine-learning methods is described in Michalski and Kaufman (1997), Mitchell (1980), and Pazzani and Kubler (1992). This work deals with inductive learning biases that constrain learning methods to choose one set of rules over others.

The earlier work on using domain knowledge for discovering new knowledge only examined some aspects of unexpectedness and did not focus on this concept *per se.* The first systematic attempt to define unexpectedness of patterns in the data mining community was reported in Silberschatz and Tuzhilin (1995, 1996) where it was defined as follows. First, it was observed in Silberschatz and Tuzhilin (1995, 1996) that, in order to define unexpectedness, one has to introduce prior expectations (or beliefs) and define unexpectedness of a pattern in terms of how it affects these beliefs. In Silberschatz and Tuzhilin (1995, 1996) beliefs are defined as statements in first-order logic and are divided into hard and soft beliefs. A hard belief, such as the belief that a person has a unique Social Security number, is, essentially, an integrity constraint. Any pattern that contradicts one of the hard beliefs is, by definition, unexpected and interesting. A soft belief is defined as a first-order logic expression with the corresponding degree assigned to it. The degree of a belief can be defined using various methods, including the Bayesian (de Finetti, 1970), Dempster–Shafer (Smets, 1988), frequency, and other approaches. This degree changes with additional evidence according to the belief revision strategy specified for that method, and each revision strategy has a corresponding computational procedure that revises the degree. Moreover, different beliefs α_i from the set of beliefs B can be assigned different weights w_i by the user.

If $d(\alpha \mid \xi)$ is the degree of a soft belief α, and ξ is the evidence used in defining this degree, the interestingness of pattern p over a set of beliefs B is defined as

$$I(p, B, \xi) = \sum_{\alpha_i \in B} w_i \mid d(\alpha_i \mid p, \xi) - d(\alpha_i \mid \xi) \mid . \tag{1}$$

This definition measures by how much degrees of beliefs change as a result of a new pattern p. A pattern is expected if it is logically implied from a set of beliefs and is unexpected if its negation is logically implied from the beliefs. It was shown in Silberschatz and Tuzhilin (1996) that, under certain conditions, unexpected patterns are more interesting than expected.

This definition of interestingness is general and, although it is applicable to a broad range of patterns and beliefs, this also makes it difficult to develop efficient algorithms for discovering interesting patterns. In light of this observation, Liu and Hsu (1996) and Padmanabhan and Tuzhilin (1997, 1998) took a logic-based, rather than probabilistic, approach and imposed certain restrictions on the structure of the patterns and beliefs. In particular, Liu and Hsu (1996) define both the set of patterns and of beliefs as rules of the form IF $P_1, P_2, ..., P_n$, THEN C, where expressions P_i are of the form *attr OP value*, where *attr* is the name of an attribute in the data set, *value* is a possible value of that attribute, and OP is one of the relational operators $\{=, \neq, <, >, \leqslant, \geqslant\}$. The consequent C is of the form *Class = value*. The difference between patterns and beliefs in Liu and Hsu (1996) lies in that patterns are defined in precise terms (*attr* in P_is above are fields in the data set), whereas beliefs are expressed using fuzzy logic (*attr* in P_is are fuzzy linguistic variables (Zimmerman, 1991). Moreover, Liu and Hsu (1996) define a distance measure between a belief and a pattern for the purpose of evaluation of patterns discovered with various data mining techniques (e.g., using the C4.5 classifier). According to this measure, similar patterns and beliefs have small distance and different patterns and beliefs have large distance. In particular, they assume that a pattern is similar to a belief if both the conditional and the consequent parts of the belief and the pattern are similar in some fuzzy logic sense.

In many applications it may be difficult for the user to formulate precise beliefs. Instead, the user may have only some vague feelings about the domain. This idea was formalized in Liu et al. (1997) by introducing the concept of general impressions. To illustrate this concept, consider an example of a housing loan domain in which the user may feel that having a high monthly salary increases one's chance of obtaining a loan. These general impressions are less specific than the "reasonably precise knowledge" from Liu and Hsu (1996). Also, Liu et al. (1997) propose a method that discovers patterns that are quite different from the general impressions, and this, by definition, makes them interesting.

As was stated before, the approach presented in Liu and Hsu (1996) and Liu et al. (1997) focuses on discovering patterns that are different from user beliefs or general impressions. Although there is a correlation between concepts of patterns being different from beliefs and unexpected, these two notions are not the same. Therefore, Padmanabhan and Tuzhilin (1997, 1998, 1999) studied the concept of unexpectedness and discovery of unexpected patterns. More specifically, rule $A \rightarrow B$ is defined to be *unexpected* with respect to belief $X \rightarrow Y$ on database D if the following conditions hold:

1. B and Y logically contradict each other ($B \wedge Y \vDash$FALSE);
2. $A \wedge X$ holds on a statistically large subset of tuples in D;[1]
3. the rule $A \wedge X \rightarrow B$ holds on data D.

For example, the rule "people in the month of December shop mostly on weekdays" is unexpected with respect to the belief that "professionals tend to shop on weekends" if the rule "professionals in December tend to shop on weekdays" holds on a statistically large subset of data.

---

[1]"Statistically large" was defined in Padmanabhan and Tuzhilin (1998) as having the support value of a rule greater than a predefined threshold.

This definition captures the meaning of unexpectedness because of the following monotonicity assumption stating that if a belief holds on some data, then it should also hold on all of its statistically large subsets. The definition presented above captures the meaning of unexpectedness because the monotonicity assumption states that the belief must hold on the data defined by expression A, X. Therefore, it is expected that the rule $A \wedge X \rightarrow Y$ holds on the data. However, condition (3) states that rule $A \wedge X \rightarrow B$ holds on the data contrary to this expectation.

In addition, Padmanabhan and Tuzhilin (1998) propose a ZoomUR algorithm that discovers all unexpected association rules in the data for a given set of beliefs. This algorithm was tested on a real-life marketing application in Padmanabhan and Tuzhilin (1999) and generated much fewer rules than the A priori algorithm (Agrawal et al., 1996) did.

In comparison to Padmanabhan and Tuzhilin (1997, 1998, 1999), Suzuki (1997) takes a different approach to unexpectedness that is independent of background knowledge and discovers exceptions, as opposed to more general unexpected rules. In particular, Suzuki (1997) discovered all the association rules $A \rightarrow c$ and their corresponding exceptions $A \wedge B \rightarrow c'$ on the data, where A and B are conjunctions of atoms of the form $Attr = value$, satisfying the following conditions:

1. The confidence and support of the rule $A \rightarrow c$ and of the exception $A \wedge B \rightarrow c'$ are high (above predefined thresholds);[2]

2. The confidence of rule $B \rightarrow c'$ should be smaller than a predefined threshold.

For example, consider the rule stating that if a mushroom has bruises of type f, g_size of type b, and the stalk_shape e, then it is poisonous, that is, bruises $= f$, g_size $= b$, stalk_shape $= e \rightarrow$ class $= p$. Then this rule may have the following exception bruises $= f$, g_size$= b$, stalk_shape$= e$, stalk_root$= ? \rightarrow$ class $= e$ (i.e., if everything else holds but the stalk_root is of type "?", then the mushroom is edible).

This definition captures a meaning of unexpectedness because, given condition (2), one would expect that the confidence of exception $A \wedge B \rightarrow c'$ would also be small. However, according to condition (1), it is unexpectedly high. Suzuki (1997) also presents an algorithm for discovering all pairs of rules and their exceptions and tests it on a data set from the University of California–Irvine Repository.

Yet another approach to unexpectedness was developed by Subramonian (1998), where he introduces a *diff* operator as one of the fundamental data mining operators. The purpose of *diff* is to (1) detect patterns that deviate from the norm, where the norm can be defined in terms of a set of examples or a set of rules, and (2) highlight the differences between two data sets having the same database schema. Subramonian shows how the *diff* operator can be deployed in a variety of settings, including the specification of probabilistic integrity constraints on continuous and discrete attributes, association rules, and clustering.

The approaches described so far deal with the concept of unexpectedness as applicable to patterns that are either explicitly defined as rules or that could be converted to rule representations. The two approaches considered below deal with unexpected patterns defined as temporal sequences, where unexpectedness is defined by some statistical measure based on the underlying data and certain assumptions about the problem (see also Chapter 16.3.1 for related material).

Berger and Tuzhilin (1998) propose an approach to defining and discovering unexpected patterns in temporal sequences expressed as temporal logic formulas. An example of such a pattern is an expression A *Next* (B *Until* C) stating that event A is immediately followed by event B that should occur all the time until event C occurs. Given a sequence and certain assumptions about initial probability distributions for its symbols, one can compute the

---

[2]Suzuki (1997) defines support in nonstandard terms computing only probability $p(A)$ instead of $p(A \wedge c)$. He also computes confidence and support not in terms of the point estimations of these probabilities as is usually done in the association rules literature, but using confidence level measures. See Suzuki (1997) for details.

expected number of occurrences of any temporal logic formula using the methods described in Berger and Tuzhilin (1998). If this expected number of occurrences differs significantly from the actual number of occurrences of the temporal logic formula in the sequence, then such a pattern is unexpected. For example, if it is expected that there should be one hundred occurrences of the pattern *A Next (B Until C)* in a sequence and there are actually only fifteen of these patterns, then the pattern is unexpected. Moreover, Berger and Tuzhilin (1998) show that the problem of discovering unexpected temporal patterns in sequences is NP-complete and proposes an efficient approximate method for discovering most such patterns. This algorithm has been tested on synthetic data, on Web logfile data, and on sequences of operating system calls. The results of these experiments are reported in Berger and Tuzhilin (1998).

The problem of discovering unexpected variations in sequences of item sets changing over time was studied in Chakrabarti et al. (1998). The starting point is a sequence of market baskets, where each market basket consists of an element of the power set $\mathcal{P}(X)$, where X is the set of all items. According to Chakrabarti et al. (1998), an item set is interesting not because it has large support and confidence, as is usually assumed in the association rule literature, but because it is surprising in the following sense. First, the support of an item set is estimated from the marginal supports of the subsets of the item set using Barlett's iterative estimation procedure (Bishop et al., 1975). If this estimated support significantly differs from the actual support of the item set, then such an item set is considered surprising according to Chakrabarti et al. (1998). Moreover, item-set supports are computed in Chakrabarti et al. (1998) using the minimum description length (MDL) principle (Rissanen, 1989; see Chapter 19.2.1). Finally, Chakrabarti et al. (1998) present an algorithm for the discovery of surprising item sets and test it on a real-life market basket data. They compare the performance of their algorithm with the performance of standard statistical methods and demonstrate that their approach was effective in eliminating prevalent and obvious item sets, while extracting item sets with no obvious complementary relationships.

3. Specification of Interestingness Templates

Another way to approach the interestingness problem is to let the users specify in broad terms the types of patterns that are of interest to them. These broad terms can be expressed either by specifying data mining queries that describe the structure of the rules that are of interest to the user (Han et al., 1996a,b; Imielenski and Virmani, 1999; Imielenski et al., 1996; Meo et al., 1998; Shen et al., 1996, Srikant et al., 1997) or by specifying other types of domain knowledge (Clearwater and Provost, 1990; Lee et al., 1998; Liu and Hsu, 1996). Because of the space limitation, we will focus in this section on the specification of interestingness templates expressed with data mining queries.

There are two main approaches proposed in the literature on how to specify data mining queries. They depend on whether underlying rules can explicitly reference various predicates (relational tables) or the rules can reference only attributes (items) from one predicate (table). The first type of data mining queries was described in Han et al. (1996a,b); Kamber et al. (1997), and Shen et al. (1996), and we will call it meta rules (as in Kamber et al., 1997). The second type was described in Klemettinen et al. (1994), Imielenski and Virmani (1999), Imielenski et al. (1996), Meo et al. (1998), and Srikant et al. (1997), and we will call it pattern templates (as in Klemettinen et al., 1994).

3.1. Pattern Templates

In this section we will focus on pattern templates, that is, data mining queries specified over the class of rules referencing only attributes from one table; see Klemettinen et al. (1994), Imielenski and Virmani (1999), Imielenski et al. (1996), Meo et al. (1998), and Srikant et al. (1997).

The first pattern template method was proposed by Klemettinen et al. (1994) for the purpose of identifying and filtering interesting association rules. To define pattern templates, Klemettinen et al. (1994) introduces user-defined taxonomies for individual attributes (items).

For example, the user can impose a taxonomy on the list of courses by grouping them into the classes of basic, undergraduate, and graduate courses. Then a pattern template in Klemettinen et al. (1994) is a rule

$$A_1 \wedge ... \wedge A_k \Rightarrow A_{k+1},$$

where each A_i is either an attribute name, a class name, or an expression $C+$ or $C*$ corresponding, respectively, to one or more and zero or more instances of class C. Such a template defines a class of rules that satisfy the constraints imposed by this template. For example, consider a pattern template

Graduate_Course, Any_Course* $\Rightarrow$ AI_Course

specifying associations between the attribute (item) AI_Course, the class Graduate_Course, and zero or more classes specifying other courses (Any_Course). Then if User_Interfaces is a graduate course and Neural_Networks is a course (as stated before, AI_Course is also a course), then the association rule

User_Interfaces $\wedge$ Neural_Networks $\Rightarrow$ AI_Course

matches the specified pattern template. Moreover, Klemettinen et al. (1994) divide pattern templates into inclusive and restrictive. Then a pattern is interesting if it matches at least one inclusive pattern template and none of the restrictive templates.

Imielinski et al. (1996, 1999) introduced the language M-SQL for the specification of pattern templates. They call these specifications data mining queries—we reserved this term for the overall approach and use the term "pattern templates" instead—and define M-SQL as an extension of SQL that includes a small set of primitive data mining operations. M-SQL queries operate on the underlying database and on a set of previously discovered association rules and return a set of association rules discovered in the data that satisfy the conditions of the user-specified pattern template. For example, the query "Find all rules in Table T involving attributes Disease, Age, and ClaimAmt, which have a confidence of at least 50 percent" can be expressed in M-SQL as (Imielenski et al., 1996)

```
SELECT *
FROM  Mine(T) R
WHERE R.Body < {(Disease = *), (Age = *), (ClaimAmt = *)}
      and {} < R.Body and R.Consequent IN
      {(Disease = *), (Age = *), (ClaimAmt = *)} and R.Confidence > 0.5
```

The Mine operator returns all the association rules that are true in T, and the WHERE-clause imposes conditions on the rules stating that the body of a rule should not be empty and should contain only the attributes Disease, Age, and ClaimAmt. Also, the consequent of the rule must contain one of these attributes, and the confidence should be at least 50 percent. M-SQL queries are evaluated by launching discovery methods described in Imielenski and Virmani (1999) and Imielenski et al. (1996).

In Meo et al. (1998), as in Imielenski et al. (1996), SQL is extended with the MINE RULE operator that integrates with regular SQL statements. MINE RULE operator computes association rules from the table generated as the answer to a regular SQL query (without the MINE RULE add-on). As a part of the MINE RULE operator, the user specifies restrictions on the structure of association rules returned by the operator. These restrictions specify how many items should appear in the body and in the head of a rule, what the minimal level of confidence and support is, and the mining conditions that the discovered association rules must satisfy.

Yet another approach to the specification of pattern templates is presented in Srikant et al. (1997), where item constraints are used for discovering generalized association rules satisfying these constraints (see Chapter 18.2). The generalized association rules assume hierarchies imposed on the items. Then a constraint can be defined as a disjunctive normal form (DNF) statement, where atoms are either items or their negations, or either ancestors or descendants of an item or their negations. Then the discovery problem can be formulated as finding all the association rules satisfying the constraints and having confidence and support above specified threshold levels. Moreover, Srikant et al. (1997) present efficient algorithms for discovering such rules.

3.2. Meta rules

As stated already, meta rules are the data mining queries that can explicitly refer not only to attributes but also to predicates. In general, they have the form

$$P_1 \wedge P_2 \wedge ... \wedge P_n \Rightarrow Q_1 \wedge Q_2 \wedge ... \wedge Q_m, \tag{2}$$

where P_i (for $i = 1, ..., n$) and Q_j (for $j = 1, ..., m$) are either instances of predicates, predicate variables, or expressions of the form *attr θ value*, where *attr* is the name of an attribute, *value* is a value that attribute can take, and θ is one of the relational operators ($=, <, >, \leqslant, \geqslant$). The key feature in definition (2) is the concept of a predicate variable, which is a second-order variable ranging over all the predicates in the database. An example of a meta rule (from Kamber et al., 1997) is

$$P(x, y) \wedge Q(x, w) \Rightarrow buys\ (x, ''Pentium'').$$

This meta rule specifies the class of data mining rules that indicate two factors that simultaneously affect the decision by person x to buy a Pentium PC. In this meta rule, *buys* is an actual predicate (relation) from the database, and P and Q are second-order predicate variables. Then the following rule matches the meta rule specified above

$$owns\ (x, ''laptop'') \wedge income\ (x, ''high'') \Rightarrow buys\ (x, ''Pentium''),$$

where *owns* and *income* are actual predicates (relations) from the database and x is a variable ranging over the domains of predicates *owns, income,* and *buys.*

Different researchers considered different variations of this basic structure of a meta rule. In particular, Fu and Han (1995) adopted it to the case of multilevel, multidimensional association rules. Also Kamber et al. (1997) considered meta rules in the context of a data cube and Han et al. (1996) describes the data mining language DMQL as a part of the DBMiner system (see Chapter 24.1.1).

Shen et al. (1996) take a related but somewhat different approach to the definition of a meta rule. They assume that the body of a rule has the same structure as in (2). However, the head of a rule specifies an action to be applied to the data specified by the body of a rule. They consider four types of actions: computation of the strength of a rule, plotting, classification, and clustering actions. Shen et al. (1996) call their meta rules *meta queries.*

Finally, meta rules were also considered in the context of inductive logic programming (ILP) by Morik et al. (1993), where they are called *rule models.* Rule models in Morik et al. (1993) have the form (2), where $m = 1$ (only one symbol in the head), and Q_1 and P_is are either predicate variables or their negations. Meta rules are used in Morik et al. (1993) as a guiding specification for discovering rules matching them.

4. Discovery of Actionable Patterns

Another important subjective measure of interestingness of discovered patterns is actionability. Intuitively, a pattern is actionable (Adomavicius and Tuzhilin, 1997; Piatetsky-Shapiro and Matheus, 1994; Matheus et al., 1996; Silberschatz and Tuzhilin, 1995, 1996) if we can do something about it, such as act on it to our advantage. In this section we describe two approaches to actionability as presented in Matheus et al. (1996), Piatetsky-Shapiro and Matheus (1994), and Adomavicius and Tuzhilin (1997).

In Piatetsky-Shapiro and Matheus (1994) actionability was studied within the context of the discovery system KEFIR (Matheus et al., 1996) that analyzes health-care insurance claims for uncovering key findings. The key findings in KEFIR are the most important changes from the norms for various indicators assessing different characteristics of provision of health care, such as cost, usage, and quality. The authors in Piatetsky-Shapiro and Matheus (1994) maintain that "a good measure of interestingness of a finding is the estimated benefit that could be realized by taking a specific action in response" (Piatetsky-Shapiro and Matheus, 1994, p. 26). KEFIR classifies all possible findings into a predefined set of types and defines a recommendation, expressed as a production rule, for each type of finding that specifies the actions to be taken in response to the findings. These actions typically indicate how to bring the corresponding indicators back to their norms. For example, a typical recommendation rule can be expressed in KEFIR as (Matheus et al., 1996)

```
IF measure = adm_per_1000 & sector = Premat_Pregn & percnt_chng > 0.10
THEN RECOMMEND ''Initiate an early prenatal care program''
WITH savings_percentage = 0.6
```

Such rules are specified by a domain expert who also assigns a probability of success to the actions in the rule. Once a new finding is discovered by KEFIR, the system determines all the recommendation rules matching this finding and selects the rule with the highest probability of success. It then computes the estimated benefit of taking the action for the selected rule as potential savings realized from the action restoring the deviation back to its norm. This estimated benefit serves as a measure of interestingness in KEFIR. KEFIR provided faster, more accurate, and complete report generation in comparison to the manual process and saved hundreds of thousands of dollars to the organization using it (Matheus et al., 1996). However, the main limitation of the approach taken in KEFIR is that it is very domain specific: it deals only with patterns expressed as deviations, preclassifies all the patterns that can be discovered into a (small) set of classes, and makes several domain-specific assumptions about benefits estimation.

In contrast to this, Adomavicius and Tuzhilin (1997) provide a general definition of actionability and present a generic approach to discovering actionable patterns. This approach is based on the concept of an action hierarchy, which is defined as a tree or a directed acyclic graph of actions with the action/subaction relationship between a parent and a child. For instance, in a supermarket example, the class of product-stocking actions has the class determining what and when to buy as its subactions, which in its own right has the class based on customer demographics as its subactions. For each node of the action tree, a user specifies a set of data mining queries. For example, the user may assign to the node of the action tree hierarchy pertaining to customer demographics the data mining query "find all rules in customer purchase data specifying which product categories the customers with children of various ages are buying" (which can be expressed in the language of Klemettinen et al., 1994, as $ChildrenAge^* \rightarrow Category\,(0.5, 0.01)$). This means that for any rule matching this data mining query, any of the product-stocking actions determining what and when to buy based on customer demographics should take place. More generally, a pattern is actionable in Adomavicius and Tuzhilin (1997) if it can be returned as an answer to one of the data mining queries associated with some action in the action tree hierarchy. Actionable patterns can be discovered by traversing the action tree or its subcomponents and executing selected data mining queries. In addition, Adomavicius and Tuzhilin (1997) present certain optimization techniques based on the data modeling/discovery triggering (DMDT) paradigm described in Tuzhilin and Silberschatz (1996) that make this process more efficient.

5. Integration of Interestingness Measures

So far, individual evaluation criteria have been described in this article for the evaluation of discovered patterns. However, these criteria can be combined and the discovered patterns can be evaluated based on multiple criteria. For example, the user may be interested in statistically strong patterns that are also actionable, or in either actionable or unexpected patterns.

These multiple criteria can be combined together in a pattern discovery algebra. One example of such algebra, called A_{PD}, was described in Tuzhilin (1997). It contains the following three groups of primitive operations:

- *Pattern generation operations.* This class of operations generates new patterns using various data mining algorithms, such as C4.5, CART, A priori, or the algorithms for generating unexpected or actionable patterns.

- *Pattern filtering operations.* This class of operations takes a set of patterns and selects (filters) a subset of this set based on the specified evaluation criteria. One can use any evaluation criteria based on the subjective measures of interestingness described in this section. Alternatively, one can use any of the objective evaluation criteria described in Chapter 19.1. Each type of evaluation criteria corresponds to a specific filtering operator. For example, one can use data mining queries as covered in Section 3 as a filter for selecting interesting patterns. Alternatively, one can use measures introduced in Section 2 for filtering unexpected patterns.

- *Pattern combining operations.* This class of operations takes two sets of patterns and combines them into a new set. There are different methods for combining these two sets. If both sets of rules are unordered, then one can take their union, intersection, or difference. If both sets are ordered, then they can be merged together using different merging schemes. For example, if a pattern is in both lists, then its ranking in the merged list can be based on the average of the rankings in the two lists—details of this method, as well as other ranking methods, are described in Tuzhilin (1997).

The closure of these atomic operations forms the pattern discovery algebra A_{PD}. Each expression from this algebra defines a pattern discovery strategy that allows the users specify discovery strategies with complex criteria of interestingness. For example, the expression

$$Combine\_AVG(F_{ACTION}(C4.5), F_{UNEXP}(CART))$$

first discovers classification rules using C4.5 and CART methods. Then it filters actionable patterns from the set of C4.5 rules, filters unexpected patterns from the set of CART rules, ranks the two sets based respectively on their actionability and unexpectedness measures, and merges the two resulting lists into one list using the averaging criterion.

Pattern discovery strategies, as defined by algebraic expressions from A_{PD}, can be represented using graphical user interfaces similar to the ones developed by Integral Solutions Ltd. for its Clementine product (see Chapter 24.2.1), by IBM for its Intelligent Miner, and by the SAS Institute for its Enterprise Miner (see Chapter 24.2.5; see also Chapter 20.1 for an in-depth discussion of visualization methods of discovered data mining results). An example of

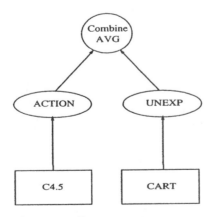

Figure 2 An example of a pattern discovery strategy

a graphical representation of the above A_{PD} expression is presented in Figure 2, where a rectangle defines a pattern generation operation, an oval defines a pattern filtering operation, and a circle defines a pattern combining operation.

As in Clementine and similar systems, pattern discovery strategies can be specified graphically by the user in an *interactive* manner through a trial-and-error process. In particular, the user can build a discovery strategy that is formally expressed in A_{PD}. Moreover, if the user does not like the evaluated strategy, he or she can *backtrack* to some subexpression of that strategy and continue the iterative process from that point until the user builds a satisfactory A_{PD} expression. This process allows the user to explore various evaluation strategies in a flexible manner.

References

Adomavicius, G. and A. Tuzhilin. 1997. "Discovery of actionable patterns in databases: the action hierarchy approach." In *Proceedings of the Third International Conference on Knowledge Discovery and Data Mining*. Menlo Park, CA: AAAI Press, pp. 111–114.

Agrawal, R., H. Mannila, R. Srikant, H. Toivonen, and A. I. Verkamo. 1996. "Fast discovery of association rules." In *Advances in Knowledge Discovery and Data Mining*, chap. 12. Menlo Park, CA: AAAI Press.

Berger, G. and A. Tuzhilin. 1998. "Discovering unexpected patterns in temporal data using temporal logic." In *Temporal Databases: Research and Practice*, edited by O. Etzion, S. Jajodia, and S. Sripada. Berlin, Heidelberg: Springer.

Bishop, Y., S. Fienberg, and P. Holland. 1975. *Discrete Multivariate Analysis: Theory and Practice*. Cambridge, MA: The MIT Press.

Brin, S., R. Motwani, J. D. Ullman, and S. Tsur. 1997. "Dynamic item set counting and implication rules for market basket data." In *Proceedings of ACM SIGMOD Conference*. New York, NY: ACM, pp. 255–264.

Buchanan, B. G. and E. A. Feigenbaum. 1978. "DENDRAL and META-DENDRAL: their applications dimensions." *Artificial Intell.* **11**: 5–24.

Chakrabarti, S., S. Sarawagi, and B. Dom. 1998. "Mining surprising patterns using temporal description length." In *International Conference on Very Large Databases*. San Francisco, CA: Morgan Kaufmann, pp. 606–617.

Clearwater, S. and F. Provost. 1990. "RL4: a tool for knowledge-based induction." In *Proceedings of the Second International IEEE Conference on Tools for Artificial Intelligence*. Washington, DC: IEEE Computer Society Press, pp. 24–30.

Fayyad, U. M., G. Piatetsky-Shapiro, and P. Smyth. 1996. "From data mining to knowledge discovery: an overview." In *Advances in Knowledge Discovery and Data Mining*, chap. 1. Menlo Park, CA: AAAI Press.

de Finetti, B. 1970. *Theory of Probability*. New York, NY: Wiley and Sons.

Frawley, W. J., G. Piatetsky-Shapiro, and C. J. Matheus. 1991. "Knowledge discovery in databases: on overview." In *Knowledge Discovery in Databases*, edited by G. Piatetsky-Shapiro and W. J. Frawley. Menlo Park, CA: AAAI/MIT Press.

Fu, Y. and J. Han. 1995. "Meta-rule guided mining of association rules in relational databases." In *Proceedings of the First International Workshop on Knowledge Discovery with Deductive and Object-Oriented Databases (KDOOD'95)*.

Han, J. et al. 1996a. "DBMiner: A system for mining knowledge in large relational databases." In *Proceedings of the Second International Conference on Knowledge Discovery and Data Mining*. Menlo Park, CA: AAAI Press, pp. 250–255.

Han, J., Y. Fu, W. Wang, K. Koperski, and O. Zaiane. 1996b. "DMQL: a data mining query language for relational databases." In *Proceedings of the SIGMOD Workshop on Research Issues on Data Mining and Knowledge Discovery*. Tech. Report 96-08, CS Department, University of British Columbia.

Imielinski, T. and A. Virmani. 1999. "MSQL: a query language for database mining." *J. Data Mining and Knowledge Discovery* **3(4)**: 373–408.

Imielinski, T., A. Virmani, and A. Abdulghani. 1996. "DataMine: application programming interface and query language for database mining." In *Proceedings of the Second International Conference on Knowledge Discovery and Data Mining*. Menlo Park, CA: AAAI Press, pp. 256–261.

Kamber, M., J. Han, and J. Y. Chiang. 1997. "Metarule-guided mining of multi-dimensional association rules using data cubes." In *Proceedings of the Third International Conference of Knowledge Discovery and Data Mining*. Menlo Park, CA: AAAI Press, pp. 207–210.

Klemettinen, K., H. Mannila, P. Ronkainen, H. Toivonen, and A. I. Verkamo. 1994. "Finding interesting rules from large sets of discovered association rules." In *Proceedings of the Third International Conference on Information and Knowledge Management.* Menlo Park, CA: AAAI Press.

Lee, Y., B. G. Buchanan, and J. M. Aronis. 1998. "Knowledge-based learning in exploratory science: learning rules to predict rodent carcinogenicity." *Machine Learning* **30**: 217–240.

Lenat, D. B. 1983. "AM: discovery in mathematics as heuristic search." In *Knowledge-Based in Artificial Intelligence,* edited by R. Davis and D. Lenat. New York: McGraw-Hill.

Lenat, D. B. and J. S. Brown. 1984. "Why AM and EURISKO appear to work." *Artificial Intell.* **23(3)**: 269–294.

Liu, B. and W. Hsu. 1996. "Post-analysis of learned rules." In *Proceedings of AAAI.* Menlo Park, CA: AAAI Press, pp. 828–834.

Liu, B., W. Hsu, and S. Chen. 1997. "Using generalized impressions to analyze discovered classification rules." In *Proceedings of the Third International Conference on Knowledge Discovery and Data Mining.* Menlo Park, CA: AAAI Press.

Matheus, C. J., G. Piatetsky-Shapiro, and D. McNeill. 1996. "Selecting and reporting what is interesting: the KEFIR application to healthcare data." In *Advances in Knowledge Discovery and Data Mining,* chap. 20. Menlo Park, CA: AAAI Press.

Meo, R., G. Psaila, and S. Ceri. 1998. "An extension to SQL for mining association rules." *J. Data Mining and Knowledge Discovery* **2(2)**: 195–224.

Michalski, R. S. and K. A. Kaufman. 1997. "Data mining and knowledge discovery: a review of issues and a multistrategy approach." Technical report P97-3 Mli 97-2. George Mason University.

Mitchell, T. 1980. "The need for biases in learning generalizations." Technical report CBM-TR-117. Rutgers University.

Morik, K., S. Wrobel, J.-U. Kietz, and W. Emde. 1993. *Knowledge Acquisition and Machine Learning: Theory, Methods and Applications.* New York: Academic Press.

Padmanabhan, B. and A. Tuzhilin. 1997. "Discovering unexpected rules in data mining applications." In *Proceedings of the Workshop on Information Technologies and Systems (WITS).*

Padmanabhan, B. and A. Tuzhilin. 1998. "A belief-driven method for discovering unexpected patterns." In *Proceedings of the Fourth International Conference on Knowledge Discovery and Data Mining.* Menlo Park, CA: AAAI Press, pp. 94–100.

Padmanabhan, B. and A. Tuzhilin. 1999. "Unexpectedness as a measure of interestingness in knowledge discovery." *Decision Support Sys.* **27(3).**

Pazzani, M. and D. Kibler. 1992. "The utility of knowledge in inductive learning." *Machine Learning* **9(1)**: 54–97.

Piatetsky-Shapiro, G. and C. J. Matheus. 1994. "The interestingness of deviations." In *Proceedings of the AAAI-94 Workshop on Knowledge Discovery in Databases,* pp. 25–36.

Rissanen, J. 1989. *Stochastic Complexity in Statistical Inquiry,* vol. 15. Singapore: World Scientific Series in Computer Science.

Shen, W.-M., K.-L. Ong, B. Mitbander, and C. Zaniolo. 1996. "Metaqueries for data mining." In *Advances in Knowledge Discovery and Data Mining,* chap. 15. Menlo Park, CA: AAAI Press.

Shrager, J. and P. Langley. 1990. *Computational Models of Scientific Discovery and Theory Formation.* San Francisco, CA: Morgan Kaufmann.

Silberschatz, A. and A. Tuzhilin. 1996. "What makes patterns interesting in knowledge discovery systems." In *IEEE Transactions on Knowledge and Data Engineering* **8(6)**: 970–974.

Silberschatz, A. and A. Tuzhilin. 1995. "On subjective measures of interestingness in knowledge discovery." In *Proceedings of the First International Conference on Knowledge Discovery and Data Mining.* Menlo Park, CA: AAAI Press.

Smets, P. 1988. "Belief functions." In *Non-standard Logics for Automated Reasoning,* edited by P. Smets, A. Mamdani, D. Dubois, and H. Prade. New York, NY: Academic Press.

Srikant, R., Q. Vu, and R. Agrawal. 1997. "Mining association rules with item constraints." In *Proceedings of the Third International Conference on Knowledge Discovery and Data Mining.* Menlo Park, CA: AAAI Press, pp. 67–73.

Stedman, C. 1997. "Data mining for fool's gold." *Computerworld* **31(48).**

Subramonian, R. 1998. "Defining *diff* as a data mining primitive." In *Proceedings of the Fourth International Conference on Knowledge Discovery and Data Mining.* Menlo Park, CA: AAAI Press, pp. 334–338.

Suzuki, E. 1997. "Autonomous discovery of reliable exception rules." In *Proceedings of the Third International Conference on Knowledge Discovery and Data Mining.* Menlo Park, CA: AAAI Press, pp. 259–262.

Tuzhilin, A. 1997. "A pattern discovery algebra." In *Proceedings of 1997 SIGMOD Workshop on Research Issues on Data Mining and Knowledge Discovery,* pp. 71–76 Tech. Report 97-07, CS Department, University of British Columbia.

Tuzhilin A. and A. Silberschatz. 1996. "A belief-driven discovery framework based on data monitoring and triggering." Technical Report IS-96-26. New York University.

Zimmermann, H. J. 1991. *Fuzzy Set Theory and Its Applications*. Dordrecht, Netherlands: Kluwer Academic Publishers.

Żytkow, J., J. Zhu, and A. Hussam. 1990. "Automated discovery in chemistry laboratory." In *Proceedings of the Eighth National Conference on Artificial Intelligence*. Menlo Park, CA: AAAI Press.

20 PRESENTATION AND VISUALIZATION

20.1 Visualization of Data Mining Results

Willi Klösgen and Stephan R. W. Lauer

ABSTRACT   We discuss some basic principles and examples of efficient visualization techniques for displaying the results of data mining methods. First, the user must immediately be able to capture and compare those properties of the data mining results that indicate why they are significant. Second, the result displays must provide an interaction medium for the user to redirect or refine mining tasks, to filter, focus, or group results, to study sensitivities, to ask for explanations and details, and to link to further (statistical) analyses. After summarizing visualization techniques for some popular data mining methods such as decision trees, association rules, clustering, and Bayesian networks, we outline the architectural principles of an applied interactive graph drawing library and demonstrate its application for the rather different data mining tasks of generalized linear modeling and subgroup mining.

1. Introduction

Knowledge discovery in databases is an iterative and often an exploratory process that can be supported by visualization in various preprocessing, data mining, and postprocessing tasks. Visualization techniques and analytical data mining methods are complementary approaches to help identify patterns and structures. By integrating these approaches, the analytical power of high performance computing can be combined with the human perception system, which is naturally adapted to identify differences and relationships of objects dynamically displayed in different color, shape, size, orientation, and brightness.

Direct data visualization for exploratory analyses is treated in Chapter 15. These data visualization tools are usually applied during preprocessing steps to get familiar with the data and derive a first understanding of the basic distributions of the variables and their relations. In the KDD context, these tools must especially deal with high-dimensional data and also display time and spatially referenced data using animations and (geographical) maps.

An iterative KDD process consisting of various feedback loops of steps that accomplish preprocessing, data mining, and postprocessing tasks can be displayed and manipulated as a graph. This visualization of a KDD process and the operations of the user on a process graph demonstrated in Chapter 24.2.1.

Data mining results can be presented in textual and/or graphical form. Text presentations can be arranged with simple presentation templates or generated by an ensemble of natural language generating methods (Chapter 20.2). In this article, we discuss several approaches that graphically display the results of data mining methods to make them more understandable. Mining algorithms derive results as models or patterns of various types that can be viewed and manipulated by applying interactive visualization tools that are specialized for the model or pattern types. These tools allow the user to interact with data mining results to understand and evaluate the derived models or patterns and to help the user identify potentially interesting results.

Special visualization tools have been developed for some data mining methods, especially for decision trees, association rules, Bayesian networks, and clustering methods. Some of these tools are summarized in Section 2 below. These examples show that an efficient integration of visualization and data mining tools must satisfy the following basic requirements.

At first, a pattern or model must be represented in an appropriate graphical form such that the user can immediately understand and capture the properties that indicate why the pattern or model is interesting. That means that the structure of the pattern or model must be transformed in a graphical structure and the evaluation criteria measuring its interestingness must be represented by graphical characteristics such as location, brightness, color, size, or shape. Effective visualization should reveal interesting properties of patterns or models while avoiding distractions and irrelevancy. With regard to accomplishing this general goal, some basic guidelines for the transformation and selection of graphical items corresponding to a few simple visual principles are discussed in Chapter 15.1. The structure of a pattern or model typically relates to a partially ordered set of components (e.g., a decision tree, generalized linear model, Bayesian network). Focusing or zooming is important, especially when such a structure includes very many components. Three display layers are thus necessary, an overview layer representing the whole structure allowing the user to easily capture the interesting substructures, a zoomed substructure displaying more details for its components, and a component layer representing an individual component (e.g., a node in a graph).

Thus, visualization has to find transparent solutions for the following problems: How can a model or pattern consisting of a set of interdependent components be appropriately displayed? Which interactive operations can be performed on the displayed graph? Which additional displays are important to explain and detail the results and support explorative analyses? The analyst should be able to operate on the results presented to perform comparison, focusing, explanation, browsing, and scheduling operations.

These operations on the displayed graphs allow the user of a mining system to redirect and refine a mining task, to filter or group mining results, to display the sensitivity of the results related to modifications of various parameters (e.g., evaluation criteria), and to browse into the database or link to further statistical analyses. Several graphs can be linked applying the techniques of linked windows of interactive data visualization systems (see Chapter 15). Thus, these graphs provide an interaction medium for the user based on interactive visualization techniques.

A graph as a partially ordered set of nodes is often useful for representing the structure of a model or set of patterns. Thus, a graph representation and manipulation system is important for visualizing data mining results, and graph drawing tools have been used for data mining systems (e.g., Graphviz for MLC++; see 24.1.2). Graph drawing addresses the problem of visualizing structural information by constructing geometric representations of abstract graphs and networks. In Section 3, a Java library of interactive graph drawing tools is summarized which, besides its interactive nature, is distinguished by object-oriented architectural principles including the possibility of three tier implementations (database server, mining server, and client, allowing the interactive presentation and manipulation of results in Internet or Intranet environments). The application of this library is then shown for two rather different data mining tasks: generalized linear modeling (Section 4) and subgroup mining (Section 5).

2. Visualizations in Some Existing Data Mining Systems

Methods to generate decision trees belong to the most popular data mining methods offered in most data mining systems. In this case the structure of the derived model (decision tree) is a simple graph pattern, a partially ordered set of nodes where each node has only one parent node. Because the trees can be rather large, an overview display, as well as focusing and zooming tools must be offered. On a detailed level, an individual node and its statistical characteristics must be presented. A decision tree can be linked to other windows (e.g., a geographical map), where the user can select elements in one window (e.g., nodes of a tree) and the corresponding objects in other windows are highlighted. Examples of visualizing decision trees, including those focusing and linking options, are presented in other chapters of this handbook for the data mining systems Kepler (Chapter 24.2.3), MineSet (Chapter 24.2.4), and Enterprise Miner (Chapter 24.2.5). The possibilities for interactive operations on the displayed trees as indicated in Section 1 above are, however, not yet fully implemented in these systems.

Association rule methods are also offered in most data mining systems, typically presenting the results in textual form. Special association rule visualizers are mostly restricted to simple association rules with only one selector on both the conditional left-hand and conclusive right-hand-side of an association rule. Examples of these visualizations are discussed in the MineSet (Chapter 24.2.4) and Enterprise Miner (Chapter 24.2.5) sections of this handbook. Association rules are also applied in the text mining field. The system Document Explorer offers two visualization types for presenting the associations between keywords (keyword graph) and between keywords belonging to different categories (category map), which are shown in Chapter 24.4.3. The interactive operations offered for implemented association rule visualizers are still limited, compared with the possibilities outlined in Section1.

Clustering methods and Bayesian networks are two areas that have developed special interactive visualizations. Simple visualizations in tree form have already been used for presenting clustering results (dendrograms), and, for instance, for clustering documents with self-organizing map (SOM) algorithms when map-based visualizations show a general view of a document space ordering similar documents near each other (Lagus et al., 1996). The data mining systems MineSet and Enterprise Miner offer cluster visualizers, which display the attribute-by-attribute differences between clusters.

Bayesian networks are directed acyclical graphs and thus visualization is the natural form for result presentation. However, data mining systems that offer Bayesian network methods (e.g., Data Surveyor, Chapter 24.2.2) only include limited interaction possibilities on the derived networks.

Thus, highly interactive visualization as outlined in Section 1 is not yet implemented in most data mining systems and there is still much research and experience needed to determine transparent and operable visualizations for the various special types of data mining patterns and models. On the other hand, efficient explorative analytic work is highly dependent on such tools, thus offering a large potential for the integration of interactive visualization in data mining. In the following sections, we first summarize a basic class-oriented library of graph-based visualization tools that can be easily specialized for quite different data mining methods, as then shown by the examples of generalized models and subgroup mining.

3. Class Library for Interactive Graphs

Basically, the Java class library for displaying and handling interactive graphs consists of three modules.

The first module encapsulates the behavior and the properties of graphs as a mathematical concept. The MathematicalGraph objects implement methods for finding paths, calculating distances, identifying parent nodes, inserting and deleting nodes and edges, etc. In this context, nodes and edges are objects meeting only the most basic requirements for being elements of a mathematical graph: all elements can uniquely be identified, which does not prevent them from having the very same content, and edges have knowledge of two nodes, usually the two nodes connected by that edge. This concept, however, could be extended to other meanings of knowing nodes (for instance, a box grouping together certain nodes has to know which ones are inside and which are outside of the box). Each node or edge is associated to a Payload object, enabling the user to associate each element of the graph separately to virtually unlimited amounts of data, although usually this might be a finite list of real numbers and/or characters. This approach allows users to change the payload without having to tamper with the node and/or edge object itself and thus gives the user a great deal of extensibility. It would even be possible to refer to database entries on other machines via the Internet or to the results of ongoing calculations.

The second module implements the visual aspects of a graph. Nodes have a visual representation on the screen (such as little boxes, circles, icons or complex representations) and so do edges (mostly as lines or arrows connecting two nodes). Furthermore, the VisualGraph classes handle user interactions such as clicking the representations on the screen, moving them with the mouse, interrogating them, zooming in and out, and dragging other objects onto the visual display of the graph.

The third module of the library covers various helper classes to provide the VisualGraph and its elements with the semantics the MathematicalGraph is supposed to have. For instance, if the mathematical graph is meant to represent subgroups of a population, related to each other by the inclusion relation (see Section 5 below), the nodes are meant to represent the subgroups and are associated with a list of additional information such as the size of that group, quality measurements, the definition of that group, et cetera. Now, these properties (size, quality, target value, etc.) must be translated to visual properties, such as size, shape, and color of the visual representation of the node. This is done by a GraphSemanticsTranslator object, which also decides which (and how) information to display if the user issues an interrogation to a specific element of the graph. Other helper objects map the semantics of the mathematical graph to the layout of the visual graph. For instance, if one wishes to display all subgroups with the same number of defining restrictions on the same line (as shown in the example given in Section 5) this piece of extra information, must be handled by a helper class doing the layout of the visual elements.

Therefore, we have a rather abstract mathematical graph, an interactive visual representation of that graph, and helper classes implementing the meaning of the graph by translating abstract properties or mere connotations into visual representations. To use this library, the user only needs to define his own payload objects and a GraphSemanticsTranslator specifying how to translate the contents of the payloads into the appearance of the visual elements of the graph and how to react to user interactions like interrogations. When the user needs very special displays for his nodes and edges, the existing node and edge classes must be extended with special properties (this has been done for the generalized linear model nodes in section 4 below, where we placed a circle representing the parameter value next to the icon of the node). But usually there is no need to interfere with event processing, updating of the display, or the management of the graphs.

4. Interaction Graphs for Generalized Linear Models

Generalized linear models (see McCullagh and Nelder, 1989) state that for a random variable y following a distribution from an exponential family, the expected value of y can be modeled as a nonlinear function of a linear parametric expression, namely that

$$E[y \mid X] = h(\eta),$$

where h is the inverse link-function and η the linear predictor, which expands to

$$\eta = X\beta = \beta_0 + x_1\beta_1 + x_2\beta_2 + ...,$$

where $X = (1, x_1, x_2, ...)$ is a matrix holding the covariables and β is a vector of parameters (β_0, β_1, β_2, ...).

This structure can be represented as a graph; see Figure 1. The nodes are the covariables, each associated with its corresponding parameter, and all connected with the linear predictor η. The linear predictor is connected to the inverse link function h, which in turn leads to the expected value of y.

The variables are displayed as icons representing the type of variable (continuous, binary, discrete but not binary). Parameters are represented by circles adjacent to the variables, with the diameter of the circle giving the numerical parameter value (estimated by a fitting algorithm). The linewidth of the edges connecting elements denotes the amount of influence on the entire model in some measurement such as a P-value or contribution to an F-statistic; the user is able to toggle these definitions interactively, and also for the display of parameters, such as switching to the t-statistic (standardized values) for that parameter.

The user can easily build models by dragging variables (that is, their icons) from a data set window to the graph and connecting the variable to the predictor node or deleting existing variables from the model. The model will be fitted in the background and the results immediately displayed in the graph, giving the user instant feedback on their actions.

Interrogations of elements are context sensitive (a benefit from the object-oriented Java environment), so that various additional information can be retrieved from the graph. Interrogating the parameter circles gives the numerical values behind, and so does interrogation of the edges. Interrogation of the variables displays graphics from an exploratory data analysis tool, such as histograms or barcharts (see Figure 2). In a similar fashion one

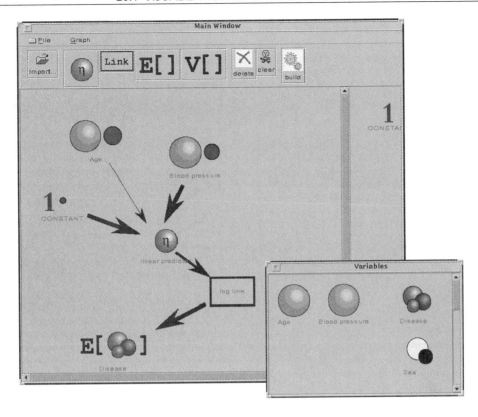

Figure 1 A graph displaying a generalized linear model. Covariables are a constant, age (continuous) and blood pressure (continuous), the variable to be modeled is disease (discrete but not binary). The variable sex (binary) has not yet been added to the model

could interrogate the link function or retrieve model diagnostics plots like residual plots or scatterplots of expected values vs. standard deviations.

In the future, more interactive features will be added. Imagine that possible outliers could be detected from the graphics displaying the variables or the diagnostic plots. Interactively selecting those outliers would exclude them from the model, instantaneously refit the model, and display the results to contrast with the previous model. Another option would

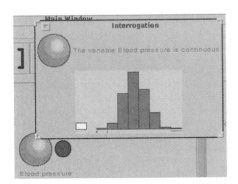
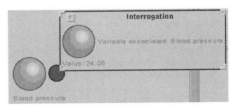

Figure 2 Two examples for interactive interrogations of model elements. Left: interrogations of a variable. Right: interrogation of the associated parameter

condition the model on one or more variables (say, condition on being female) and build the model on this subset of the data set. In an environment like this, modeling would become a genuine exploratory tool to help analyze as yet unknown dependencies in the data.

5. Interaction Graphs for Subgroup Mining

Subgroup mining methods (Chapter 16.3) derive a set of subgroups that have a deviating distribution property from a designated target variable, for example, subgroups with an overproportional share of target objects. Subgroups are partially ordered according to their generality. Thus a graph can be used to represent subgroup results. Since not only partitioning search methods are applied for subgroup patterns, the subgroups can overlap, and since a derived subgroup can thus have several parent nodes, the subgroup graph is typically not a tree. An example of such a subgroup window is presented in Figure 3, displaying a graph representing the results of incrementally and iteratively scheduled subgroup search tasks, for example, subgroups with an overproportional accident rate.

The nodes in this graph represent the subgroups and the edges the specialization relations (e.g., males → single males). A second type of edges is used for the suppression relation when one subgroup is suppressed by other subgroups due to multicollinearities (see Chapter 16.3.1).

A subgroup (node) has a description, a size (number of individuals in the set described by the subgroup), a value for the target variable (e.g., accident share in subgroup), and an absolute quality (significance of deviation related to root node, e.g., total population).

The mapping of interestingness criteria into graphical items has been selected in the following way: the degree of brightness is used to indicate the absolute quality of a subgroup. Thus, in an overview window with many subgroups, the user can easily identify the number and location of highly significant results. The size of a subgroup icon is drawn proportional to the subgroup size.

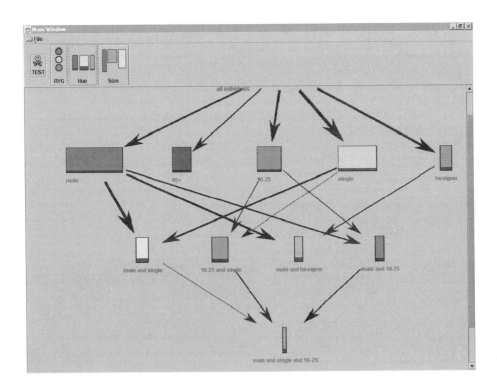

Figure 3 A subgroup window. Subgroups of insured persons with the high accident rate

An edge (e.g., single males as a specialization of the subgroup males) has a relative quality measuring the significance of, for example, the higher accident rate for single males compared to males. The thickness of the edge represents this significance. These edges allow the user to see easily which subgroups are homogeneous (have no deviating specializations), and whether a subgroup is a specialization of all or a few parents or a single parent.

As main interactions on this graph, the user can start further search tasks (which typically extend the graph), manually add and remove nodes, select subgroups, and request special analyses and graphs for the selected subgroups, for example, for multicollinearity analysis, overlapping analysis, and quality analysis (see Chapter 16.3.1). Sensitivity analyses operated on a subgroup graph are typically supported by dividing the domain of a parameter into, say, three intervals and associating a color to each interval by which the subgroups with the parameter in the interval are displayed. By manually modifying the boundaries of the intervals using a slider and parallel updating the subgroup colors, the sensitivity of the subgroups related to the parameter (e.g., a quality parameter) can easily be captured by the user.

In addition, description variables to be used and selected for a subgroup task can be iconized. Both the variables and the subgroup icons can be asked for their properties (e.g., univariate distributions) as shown for the models in Section 4.

As an example for linking the subgroup window with visualization windows of other mining methods, we refer to a spatial clustering mining task (Chapter 16.7). When analyzing the dependency of a target variable both on micro variables (e.g., gender, nationality) and location variables in spatially referenced data (e.g., special properties of regions such as located near a railway line), the subgroup window can be linked to a region window (geographical map, e.g., Descartes system described in Chapter 24.2.3) showing the regional distribution of the target share. In the region window, regions (sets of contiguous districts) with an overproportional target share are identified and shown, either after being selected by the user, or for predefined regional hierarchies, as result of statistical filters, or as results of spatial clustering methods. These regions are special subgroups. Thus, the same analyses for selected regions can be started as for selected subgroups in the subgroup window (e.g., multicollinearity analysis, quality analysis).

Regions can be exported to the subgroup window. There they appear as additional subgroups at a position in the subgroup graph determined by the user (e.g., on the first level or as a specialization of males). In particular, further subgroup searches can then be started from these additional subgroups.

6. Conclusion

Efficient interactive visualization is important for displaying the often voluminous data mining results, to help the user understand these results, and especially to easily capture and compare the evaluation and quality characteristics of the results. Furthermore, the visualizations must stimulate the user to schedule additional analyses. General visualization solutions must be specialized for the various data mining methods. In many existing data mining systems, visualization is included as an add-on based on a rather *ad hoc* design, and interaction on discovery results is only rudimentarily offered. Much research and experience is still needed to develop efficiently integrated visualization and mining approaches. Graph drawing libraries relying on an object-oriented and Internet-based client technology offer useful and powerful general visualization methods that can easily be specialized for the various data mining methods.

References

McCullagh, P. and J. A. Nelder. 1989. *Generalized Linear Models*. London: Chapman and Hall.

Lagus, K., T. Honkela, S. Kaski, and T. Kohonen. 1996. "Self organizing maps of document collections: a new approach to interactive exploration." In *Proceedings of the Second International Conference on Knowledge Discovery and Data Mining*, pp. 238–243. Menlo Park, CA: AAAI Press.

20.2 Natural Language Presentation and Automatic Report Generation

Robert Dale

ABSTRACT This article describes what is involved in the process of natural language generation (NLG), by means of which a textual or spoken presentation can be created from underlying data. We describe the architectural components of an NLG system and the functionality they bring to the overall process, and discuss the applicability of NLG techniques in the context of data mining.

1. Introduction

As an endeavour, data mining is predicated on the observation that our ability to analyze, summarize, and extract knowledge from data has been left behind by our capacity to collect and store that data. Data mining techniques allow us to begin to make sense of that data. An important issue, however, is how we go about expressing the results of a data mining exercise so that they make sense to the user.

In Chapter 20.1, the scope for graphical visualization of data mining results is discussed; in this article, our interest is in what we might think of as the textualization of the results of data mining. We present here the basic ideas that underlie natural language generation, a body of techniques that can be used to express the contents of an underlying information source in linguistic form. The use of such techniques offers possibilities for expressing the results of data mining in a manner that is more directly useful than would be the case if the data were simply presented in their raw form. As we discuss in the conclusion, however, these techniques are likely to be most appropriate for data mining tasks that are regularly repeated on the same type of data.

2. An Overview of Natural Language Generation

2.1. What is Natural Language Generation?

Natural language generation (NLG) is the name we give to a body of research that is concerned with the specification of computational processes that map from some underlying representation of information to a presentation of that information in linguistic form, whether textual or spoken. The underlying representation may be symbolic (for example, it may be the knowledge base of an expert system) or numeric (for example, it might be a database containing time-series data on stock market prices), but it is generally nonlinguistic in nature. NLG systems combine knowledge about language and the domain of their application to produce automatically a wide range of document types, including reports, explanations, and help messages.

As an example, Figure 1 shows a fragment of a database containing stock market price data. The columns here provide values for the date and a number of values relating to stock performance on that day: the highest price reached (in U.S. dollars), the lowest price reached, the closing price, the number of block trades on that day, the change in value of the Dow, and the final value of the Dow. Figure 2 shows a text generated from this data using NLG techniques. (The examples shown here are from an experimental system under development

```
04/01/96     Holiday
04/02/96     103.75  101.5      101.625  41839      -33    5560
04/03/96     103.875 100.875    102.75   46096      +34    5594
04/04/96     103     101.25     101.625  32444      -74    5520
04/05/96     108.875 101.625    107.375  18101      -34    5486
```

Figure 1 Some stock market data for a week in April 1996

Serious Avocado avoided the downwards trend of the Dow Jones average today. There was confined trading by all investors. After shooting to a high of $108.87, its highest price so far for the month of April, Serious Avocado stock eased to finish at an enormous $107.37. The Dow closed after trading at a weak 5486, down 34 points.

Figure 2 An automatically generated stock market report

for the automatic personalized description of share portfolios via the Web or for telephone delivery.)

In recent years, work in natural language generation has taken a particularly practical turn. Wherever large datasets need to be reported on—for example, stock market data, employment statistics, or weather data—NLG offers the possibility of automatic creation of routine texts without costly human authoring. The opportunities here have of course increased vastly with the widespread acceptance of the World Wide Web and the universal access to large datasets this makes possible. NLG applications to date have included, among many others, the composition of weather forecasts (Goldberg et al., 1994); documenting the results of simulations of telephone networking changes (McKeown et al., 1994); helping customer-service representatives write response letters to customers (Coch, 1996); helping technical authors write software manuals (Paris et al., 1995); generating tailored encyclopedia descriptions (Milosavljevic and Dale, 1996); and drafting letters that encourage people to stop smoking (Reiter and Osman, 1997).

2.2. The Architecture of an NLG System

To create a text like that in the example above, a number of subprocesses are implicated. Although alternative architectures exist, it is now commonplace within the natural language generation community to consider the task of NLG to consist of three distinct subprocesses; these are shown diagrammatically in Figure 3.

These stages can be characterized as follows:

1. *Document planning.* This task is concerned with determining the overall content of the text to be generated, and organizing this information into a structure that will lead to a fluent and coherent text. The input, along with the source of information to be reported upon, is some communicative goal: this is something that might be glossed as, for example, "describe the performance of the Serious Avocado stock over the last two weeks," or "compare employment statistics in each of the state capitals." We will refer to the output of this step as a document plan, although one should be wary that this term is used with slightly different connotations by different authors in the field.

2. *Microplanning.* Given a document plan, the process of microplanning involves fleshing this out with more detail. A key activity here is that of working out how best to package the information to be expressed into paragraphs, sentences, and noun phrases within the document as a whole. It is arguably this stage of processing, with its concomitant use of sophisticated linguistic knowledge, that provides the real benefit of using NLG techniques; microplanning permits the generation of texts of higher quality than would be possible simply by using templates and canned text. We will refer to the output of this stage as a text specification.

3. *Surface realization.* Another real benefit of NLG is that it provides scope for a level of abstraction whereby the major reasoning elements of the system can ignore superficial details of the language in which the text is being generated. The surface realization stage is responsible for taking care of the idiosyncracies of grammar and morphology in the target language, so that the earlier stages can focus on higher-level issues in constructing the text; the output is generally referred to as a surface text.

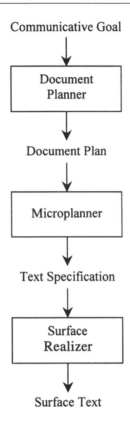

Figure 3 The Architecture of an NLG System

Sections 3, 4, and 5 below elaborate further on what is involved in each of these stages of the NLG process. We will focus here on textual documents, but it should be borne in mind that real documents contain both text and graphics. There is considerable scope, therefore, for integrating the kinds of visualization techniques described in Chapter 20.1 with those described here to produce a comprehensive and multifaceted reporting facility. The integration of text and graphics is currently a topic of considerable interest within the NLG community (see, for example, Wahlster et al., 1993).

3. Document Planning

The document planning task is generally conceived of as encompassing two interrelated subtasks: determining the content of the text to be generated, and working out how that content should be organized so as to produce a coherent text. The determination of content is in essence a task with an expert-systems-like flavor; what is required here is typically very domain-dependent and requires the construction of rules that use knowledge of the application domain to determine what is worth commenting upon. Working out the overall structure of the resulting text is a more linguistically oriented task, although one where the specifics of the domain still have significant impact; for this reason, the kind of knowledge required here has sometimes been referred to as domain communication knowledge (Kittredge et al., 1991).

The information to be conveyed in the text is best thought of as a collection of messages, where each message communicates some piece of information. Content determination then involves constructing the messages to be conveyed. In our simple example above we analyze the input data to identify the following messages as worthy of being conveyed:

- the divergence in direction of the Serious Avocado stock price and the Dow average;
- the profile of trading in the stock;
- how the stock price changed during the day;
- how the highest price reached compared with historical values;
- the price of the stock at the close of trading; and
- the value of the Dow at the close of trading.

Just what messages are to be conveyed will depend on specific properties of the data instances being considered. For example, the fourth message listed above might not be created if the highest price reached by the stock was a value of no great significance; we might think of this as a significant event message. Other messages, such as the price of the stock at the close of trading, are routine messages that are always created. (For a more detailed exposition of this methodology, and the other aspects of NLG described here, see Reiter and Dale, 2000.)

In many contexts, NLG systems are provided with some set of messages, or more generally some collection of information, by some other back-end system. The document planning stage then consists solely of the second subtask identified here, that of organizing this material for presentation. Texts are not just random sequences of sentences: the information to be conveyed generally follows some structure, with that structure often being dictated by the genre of the text type under consideration. Work in the field here generally makes use of one of two distinct approaches. Schema-based approaches (see McKeown, 1985) to determining the overall structure of a plan for a text observe the regularities in structure of texts in the domain of application, and derive a set of grammar rules that dictate both the content and ordering of information to be presented. More sophisticated approaches based on theories of discourse structure, with rhetorical structure theory (RST; see Mann and Thompson, 1988) being the predominant basis, observe that there are underlying generalizations that characterize what it means for a text to be coherent. These theories offer definitions of textuality in terms of the relationships that can hold between parts of a text: one part can elaborate upon another, justify the statements made in another, and so on. Such approaches permit a more principled separation between domain knowledge that relates to information content, and linguistic knowledge about the structure of texts; however, in practice the ideas here are still not sufficiently understood to provide scalable broad-coverage solutions. Hovy (1993) provides an overview of work that has been pursued in this area.

In our example text, a schema-based approach might make use of the observation that, in general, stock market reports first discuss the market overall, then talk about the stock price in more specific terms, then end by commenting on the performance of the Dow overall. A different schema might be invoked if the data warrants it: for example, if the stock price suffers a drop greater than some threshold, this might invoke a schema that presents this significant information first.

An approach based on rhetorical structure theory would carry out more complicated reasoning. Beginning with the core fact to be presented, that of the stock price, the system would then reason as to how this fact might best be elaborated given the available data. This latter approach is generally to be preferred where considerable variations are likely in the texts to be generated, since the overall structure of the texts can be determined dynamically rather than being dictated in advance. It has occasionally been observed that schemas are, in effect, precompiled collections of the kinds of relations used in RST-based approaches.

4. Microplanning

We can think of the process of document planning as being about determining what propositions should be expressed in a text and how those propositions should be organized so as to provide a text where the information flow is coherent. This is, however, no more than a skeletal specification of the text that must eventually be generated. There are a number of respects in which the specification is incomplete:

- There is no *a priori* reason why each message or proposition should be expressed in a single sentence; indeed, doing so generally leads to rather disfluent texts. We have to consider, then, how the material to be conveyed can be packaged into sentence-sized pieces. This is generally referred to as the task of sentence aggregation.

- Strictly speaking, we have not said anything about the words that should be used to express the concepts and relations in the material to be conveyed. In many domains, the mapping from the underlying conceptual elements to the words to be used will be one-to-one and thus a trivial exercise. For example, in our example text, the event of the Dow closing might always be referred to by the verb *closed*. However, in other contexts there will be choices to be made, often for stylistic purposes; and certainly some choice is required if texts are to be generated in multiple target languages from the one underlying source. This step of the process is typically referred to as lexicalization.

- Finally, we have to consider how the entities in the domain will be referred to. In general, the entities in the domain will be represented in the document plan simply by means of symbolic identifiers; for each such identifier we have to determine the properties of the corresponding entity that should be used in referring to it in the text. The goal here is to distinguish the intended referent from all other entities with which it might be confused; at the same time, it is appropriate to use abbreviated forms of reference—and in particular, anaphoric expressions such as *it* and the *stock*—to increase the fluency of the text and to avoid stiltedness. Achieving an appropriate balance between these two constraints is the task of referring expression generation.

We have collected these tasks together here under the component NLG process of microplanning; in some work this is also referred to as sentence planning, although this more specific term ignores the fact that there are also related issues at the level of paragraph structuring. In earlier work on NLG (see in particular Thompson, 1977), there were seen to be two major aspects to generating a text: deciding what to say (often referred to as the strategic component) and deciding how to say it (often referred to as the tactical component). In more recent years there has been widespread awareness that it makes sense to postulate something in the middle; it is this stage of microplanning that provides much of the value of NLG techniques above simpler methods.

The aggregation capabilities required in an NLG system will depend on the granularity of the messages to be conveyed. Consider the third sentence in our example text: "After shooting to a high of $108.87, its highest price so far for the month of April, Serious Avocado stock eased to finish at an enormous $107.37." If one of our predefined message types expresses both the highest value reached and also the closing price, then this sentence represents an aggregation of that message with the more historically oriented message that compares today's high with the month overall. If, on the other hand, we have separate message types for the highest price reached on the day and for the closing price, then this sentence represents an aggregation of three messages, which if realized as separate sentences would result in a less fluent output: "Serious Avocado shot to a high of $108.87. This was its highest price so far for the month of April. The stock eased to finish at an enormous $107.37."

Clearly the types of messages that are constructed from the underlying source have some impact on the possibilities here. When defining a set of message types, it is best to opt for the largest granularity possible without compromising the later opportunities for rearranging information. So, for example, if analysis of a corpus of human-authored texts indicates that stock closing price and the highest price reached are sometimes expressed in quite separate parts of the text, this argues for representing these two pieces of information in separate messages. If, on the other hand, the two pieces of information are generally always mentioned together, then it is safe to combine them in one message. This limits the scope for aggregation but at the same time makes the aggregation process simpler.

Lexicalization and referring expression generation are closely related tasks, since both are concerned with the particular words to be used in the text. The example above demonstrates both processes. For example, the use of the word *enormous* to describe the closing price is a lexicalization decision, based on a mapping from value ranges to words that are considered appropriate expressions of these ranges in the application domain. The example demonstrates several instances of referring expression generation: the stock is introduced using the proper name *Serious Avocado*, then referred to by the pronoun *it* in the second sentence, and finally by a reduced noun phrase *the stock* in the third sentence. Note also that highest price is subsequently referred to by means of the demonstrative *this*. The development of algorithms for referring expression generation is a well-developed area (see, for example, Dale and Reiter, 1996, and Horacek, 1997).

5. Surface Realization

By this stage, we now have a quite detailed specification of how our final text will look. It remains for the third component task in NLG, the surface realization stage, to map this specification into sentences in accordance with the rules of syntax and morphology that apply in the language being generated. The concern here is with ensuring that the sentences generated are grammatical, so that, for example, rules about number agreement between subject and verb are enforced, correct function words are used, and so on. Similarly, the morphological rules of the language are applied at this stage, so that the correct inflections are used on words, and irregular forms of verbs are used appropriately. By isolating this kind of processing inside the surface realizer, we gain the advantage that all of the surface linguistic knowledge is maintained in one place, thus enabling maintainability, and the earlier stages of the NLG process can avoid concern with these fine details, thus supporting modularity.

Surface realization is, then, the most linguistically oriented and least domain-dependent of the three stages in the overall NLG process; accordingly, there are a number of reasonably general purpose reusable surface realizers that have been developed in the research community. It makes sense to consider using these instead of building a surface realizer from scratch, although it should be borne in mind that the use of any such system involves a steep learning curve and may require some commitment to the theoretical underpinnings of the particular approach adopted. The KPML system (Bateman, 1997) provides a surface realizer founded on systemic functional grammar (SFG; see Halliday, 1985); this particular grammatical theory is based on the notion of a speaker's choice among alternatives, and so is well suited to the task of language generation. Elhadad's (1989) FUF/SURGE package is similarly based on SFG, but pragmatically incorporates ideas from other grammatical theories. Both systems have been used extensively in a number of research projects. More recent candidate surface realizers that can be easily obtained are CoGenTex's RealPro (Lavoie and Rambow, 1997), which is based on a grammatical approach called meaning text theory, and Busemann's (1996) TG/2, which in the interests of practical utility combines mechanisms for using canned text, templates, and more linguistically motivated surface realization. In general, earlier approaches here have been driven by linguistic theory, and more recent approaches by pragmatic issues; few current applied NLG systems warrant the full sophistication and broad-coverage offered by linguistically well-motivated models.

6. Conclusions

In this article, we have outlined the kinds of tasks that are addressed in work on natural language generation. These methods provide a way of producing human-readable representations of data that might otherwise be unfathomable. The scope for the application of these techniques in data mining is clear, but so far relatively unexplored.

There are a number of factors to be considered in determining whether NLG techniques can prove useful in the context of a data mining exercise. It must be realized, of course, that there is no magic here, and no free lunch: building a natural language reporting facility is a substantial exercise in its own right, and thus only warranted where the volume of text production required justifies the expenditure of this effort. This is particularly the case for the earlier stages of the NLG process as we have described it here. The need for domain-specific rules for constructing and selecting messages, and for organizing these for coherent presentation, means that the system developer already needs to have a well-developed idea of the kinds of data elements and their configurations that will be reported on. These needs are likely to change frequently in the context of data mining.

At the later stages of processing, where the burden of impact shifts from domain-specific knowledge to linguistic knowledge, there is a considerable increase in reusability of the components used. Even the use of relatively simple surface realization tools such as TG/2 can significantly ease the developer's task of presenting results.

In many data mining contexts, the data mining process itself carries out the task of content selection; provided appropriate abstractions across these results can be carried out ahead of time, this process can then fit comfortably with an NLG component whose task is to organize this information for presentation and realize it as fluent text.

Given the current state of the art, there is a careful balance to be struck. The use of NLG techniques requires some prior assumptions to be made regarding the variations in data that will need to be described and in the presentation that is appropriate for that data; at the same time, if the reporting required is completely regularized, then NLG techniques are overkill, and simple templates are more than adequate. This is particularly the case where the results can be expressed in just one or two sentences. However, as the length of the report output increases, NLG techniques play an increasingly important role in enhancing the quality of the output; married with techniques in document presentation and visualization, NLG provides methods for consistent automated reporting that would otherwise be difficult or economically infeasible.

References

Bateman, J. 1997. "Enabling technology for multilingual natural language generation: the KPML development environment." *Natural Lang. Engng* **3**: 15–55.

Busemann, S. 1996. "Best-first surface realization." In *Proceedings of the Eighth International Workshop on Natural Language Generation*. Sussex: Herstmonoeux, pp. 101–110.

Coch, J. 1996. "Evaluating and comparing three text production techniques." In *Proceedings of the Sixteenth International Conference on Computational Linguistics*. Copenhagen, Denmark: Centre for Sprogteknologi, pp. 249–254.

Dale, R. and E. Reiter. 1996. "The role of the Gricean maxims in the generation of referring expressions." In *Proceedings of the AAAI Spring Symposium on Computational Implicature*. Stanford: American Association for Artificial Intelligence, March 25–27, pp. 16–20.

Elhadad, M. 1989. "FUF: the universal unifier user manual." Technical report. New York: Department of Computer Science, Columbia University.

Goldberg, E., N. Driedger, and R. Kittredge. 1994. "Using natural-language processing to produce weather forecasts." *IEEE Expert* **9(2)**: 45–53.

Halliday, M. A. K. 1985. *An Introduction to Functional Grammar*. London: Edward Arnold.

Horacek, H. July 1997. "Generating referential descriptions in multimodal environments." In *Proceedings of the Workshop on Referring Phenomena in a Multimedia Context and Their Computational Treatment, The 35th Annual Meeting of the Association for Computational Linguistics*: Association for Computational Linguistics, July 11th. Madrid, Spain, pp. 59–66.

Hovy, E. H. 1993. "Automated discourse generation using discourse structure relations." *Artificial Intell.* **63(1–2)**: 341–385.

Kittredge, R., T. Korelsky, and O. Rambow. 1991. "On the need for domain communication language." *Comput. Intell.* **7(4)**: 305–314.

Lavoie, B. and O. Rambow. 1997. "A fast and portable realizer for text generation." In *Proceedings of the Fifth Conference on Applied Natural-Language Processing*. Washington, DC: Association for Computational Linguistics, pp. 73–79.

Mann, W. and S. Thompson. 1988. "Rhetorical structure theory: towards a functional theory of text organisation." *Text* **3**: 243–281.

McKeown, K. 1985. *Text Generation*. Cambridge, UK: Cambridge University Press.

McKeown, K., K. Kukich, and J. Shaw. 1994. "Practical issues in automatic document generation." In *Proceedings of the Fourth Conference on Applied Natural-Language Processing*. Stuttgart: Association for Computational Linguistics, pp. 7–14.

Milosavljevic, M. and R. Dale. 1996. "Strategies for comparison in encyclopedia descriptions." In *Proceedings of the Eighth International Workshop on Natural-Language Generation*. Sussex: Herstmonoeux, pp. 161–170.

Paris, C., K. Vander Linden, M. Fischer, A. Hartley, L. Pemberton, R. Power, and D. Scott. 1995. "A support tool for writing multilingual instructions." In *Proceedings of the Fourteenth International Joint Conference on Artificial Intelligence*, pp. 1398–1404.

Reiter, E. and L. Osman. 1997. "Tailored patient information: some issues and questions." In *Proceedings of the ACL 1997 Workshop on From Research to Commercial Applications: Making NLP Work in Practice*. Madrid: Association for Computational Linguistics, pp. 29–34.

Reiter, E. and R. Dale. 2000. *Building Natural Language Generation Systems*. Cambridge, UK: Cambridge University Press.

Thompson, H. 1977. "Strategy and tactics: a model for language production." In *Papers from the Thirteenth Regional Meeting of the Chicago Linguistics Society*. Chicago, IL: Chicago Linguistics Society. pp. 651–668.

Wahlster, W., E. André, W. Finkler, H.-J. Profitlich, and T. Rist. 1993. "Plan-based integration of natural language and graphics generation." *Artificial Intell.* **63**: 387–427.

21 FROM DISCOVERED KNOWLEDGE TO DECISIONMAKING

Arno Siebes

1. Introduction

Data mining is not so much pursued for its own sake but as a means to an end. That is, the knowledge gained with data mining is only acquired so that it can be applied. This application-driven nature of data-mining is apparent in two stages of the KDD process. First, right at the beginning when a business problem is translated into a data mining solution, and, second, at the very end when the data mining solution is to be translated into a business solution; see Chapter 2 and, for example, `http://www.crisp-dm.org` for the CRISP data mining process.

The problem of translating a data mining solution into a business solution consists of two rather different subproblems. The first, relatively straightforward one is that of exporting a discovered model into some other tool. For example, exporting a client response model into a campaign management tool in a marketing application.

The second subproblem is less easy to pin down, and also much harder. It is a consequence of the fact that data mining is in general secondary analysis. That is, the data has not been collected with this specific analysis task in mind, but for other, perhaps administrative, purposes. Suppose, for example, that we mine a database to determine whom to send a certain mailing to. If the database has been created using a small trial mailing, it is reasonable to assume that if 99 percent of a certain age group responded, a high percentage of that age group will respond in the real mailing. However, if the database used is simply the set of customers with the products they own, such an assumption is far less reasonable.

In this chapter both subproblems will be discussed.

2. Interfacing

Connectivity is an important aspect of any data mining system. On the one hand, it should connect to database management systems (DBMSs) either to import data easily, or, even better, to mine the data in the database directly. On the other hand, it should connect to application tools, such that the mining results can be used by those systems. An example is a campaign management tool as mentioned above.

Clearly, for both types of connectivity, one can write special software to link two software products. However, this is costly and may have to be redone for every new release of one of the two tools. For the database connectivity case, other options are available. There are middleware products in existence that provide a common interface to many different DBMSs and file systems. Moreover, there are standards such as ODBC (Open Database Connectivity); see `http://www.microsoft.com/data/ODBC`.

For connectivity to other applications, life is less simple as such middleware and/or standards to application systems do not exist yet. In fact, to make such solutions possible, the data mining community will have to create standards. For example, a standard way to describe the models and patterns found using data mining.

Such standards are not only of benefit to the connectivity between a mining system and another application, but could also be useful in distributed data mining and makes sharing models in general more easy. In fact, this latter reason is why the uncertainty in the artificial intelligence (AI) community strives toward the creation of a Bayesian network interchange format. Since this appears to be the only such effort toward a model describing language, this chapter will focus on this effort.

Unfortunately, there doesn't seem to be an accepted standard yet. However, the Decision Theory and Adaptive Systems group of Microsoft Research has made two proposals for such a standard. The newer approach uses XML (extensible markup language) and is called XBN; see `http://www.research.microsoft.com/dtas/bnformat`.

The DTD (document type definition) allows for multiple networks to be described in a document. For one such network, the DTD has the following entries:

Static properties. This section describes aspects such as the creator, the version, and the format.

Dynamic properties. This section describes user-defined properties.

Variables. This section describes the nodes (i.e., variables or attributes) in the network. Such a description covers, for example, the name and the type of the variables.

Structure. This section describes the network topology, that is, it lists the arcs in the network. This covers not only the (parent, child) pairs, but also has an extra proviso for variables without parents (the sources in the network).

Distributions. This section gives the conditional probability distributions for the nodes in the network.

Clearly, XML documents as such are not very easily read by humans; however, with general-purpose XML viewers (such as your favorite browser), this is not a problem. The main advantage of a model description language based on XML is that parsing such a description becomes an easily automated task.

3. Using Results Carefully

Data mining always begins with a business problem. That is, a business problem is translated into a data mining problem. For example, the business problem may be that one wants maximal return of investment on a mailing for a given, fixed budget. This may be translated to the data mining problem: find me those customers that are likely to order the item on offer.

After solving the mining question, one has to return to the original business question. That is, one has to make the step from acquired knowledge to decisionmaking. Unfortunately, this is often less easy than assumed. The reason is that in data mining, one often has to use the data that is available, and that is not always the data one would have liked to have.

Take the marketing example introduced above. In the ideal case, one first sends this mailing to a random subset of the population and analyzes the behavior of this subset. Subsequently, one uses the results of this analysis to determine whom to send the mailing to. If all of this has been done carefully, one can predict the return on investment of the final mailing pretty accurately. In fact, that is exactly what a random subset of the population means.

There are many reasons why the ideal case is not often the real case. Sometimes there are not enough resources (time, money, or otherwise) to produce and analyze such a proper random subset of the population. In other cases, it is simply impossible to acquire the required input data. In all such cases, one has to do with the data that is available. For example, rather than the data of a trial mailing, one has to do with the data on what clients have what products already.

3.1. The Ideal Case

Even in the ideal case, that is, the available data matched the analysis requirements, some care has to be taken in applying the results of data mining in practice. An important class of problems is caused by the costs of wrong decisions. In simple cases, such as sending mailings, these costs are limited and well known. In other cases, for example, in a fraud examination, such costs are almost boundless and far harder to predict. What happens, for example, if you accuse one of your largest customers wrongly of fraud?

In those cases where the potential costs and profits can be reasonably estimated beforehand, they should be taken into account even before the actual mining takes place. For many popular mining tasks, such as classification, there are techniques available that use such cost matrices.

The theoretical framework in which this fits is called decision theory; quite often this entails Bayesian decision theory (see, e.g., Robert, 1994). As usual in the Bayesian approach, the statistical analysis yields a probability distribution over all possible models. Combining this with the costs, one can compute the estimated costs of each possible decision and take the one that minimizes these costs, or, phrased more positively, maximizes the profits. More formally, the Bayes optimal prediction for a tuple x is the class that minimizes the conditional risk:

$$R(i \mid x) = \sum_j P(j \mid x)C(i,j)$$

in which $C(i, j)$ are the costs of predicting class i for x, whereas it should have been j and $P(j \mid x)$ is the probability that x belongs to class j.

Even if the costs are hard to estimate, the Bayesian framework in principle tells you what to do, viz., make a probability distribution over the possible costs. Although this makes for an elegant theory, it is not always that applicable in practice. Especially in cases where not too many clients will be singled out, such as for fraud, it makes sense to use common sense. That is, to have a human expert peruse the results and ultimately decide which cases do warrant a follow-up and in what way.

As already said above, if known beforehand, cost matrices should be used as early in the mining as possible. Either by using a tailor-made algorithm that is cost sensitive, or by using a procedure that converts error-based classifiers into cost-sensitive classifiers. One approach in this latter direction is by using stratified sampling. That is, by changing the frequency of classes in the data based on their costs (see Breiman et al., 1984; Kohavi et al., 1998; Stolfo and Chan, 1998).

Another approach is that of meta cost (Domingos, 1999). The basic idea here is that the classified examples in the database are not necessarily labeled with their optimal label. That is, it may be far less risky to assign a class j to a tuple x although the database lists class i for x. For example, because the costs for misclassifying a tuple of class j are far more expensive that misclassifying a tuple of class i. Meta cost relabels the tuples in the database with their optimal class, and then normal classification learning can proceed.

3.2. Reality Strikes

As argued above, quite often one has to cope with the problems of using data that do not really match the analysis requirements. In a sense, this can be seen as falling under the heading of missing (and superfluous) information. It is a severe case, however, in that complete attributes can be missing as well as (very informative) tuples.

A prime example of the latter occurs in credit scoring. If a bank wants to establish a new credit-scoring function, that is, to whom should it give credit, they do not have a credit history on those cases that they refused. In general, however, they do retain the application details of those loans that were refused. Making inferences on the probable behavior of those refused creditors is what they call reject inference and is absolutely crucial in credit scoring.

The general approach toward this problem is, again, to take it into account as much as possible during the mining. There are different ways to attack this problem, most of which rely on model assumptions (see Jacka and Hand, 1998, for a brief overview). To give an example of the work in this area, the work of Feelders (1996) will briefly be discussed here.

This approach is based on mixture distributions. For example, the income density function is expressed in the form:

$$f(\text{income}) = f_1(\text{income}; \ b)\pi_b + f_2(\text{income}; \ g)\pi_g,$$

in which $f_1(\text{income}; b)$ describes the income density for the bad creditors and π_b is the probability that a creditor is bad. Given that some bad creditors and some good creditors have been accepted, parameters can be inferred from the database.

In the general, multivariate case, one has

$$f(x) = \sum_{i=1}^c \pi_i f_i(x; \ \theta_i),$$

and the goal is to estimate the π_i and the θ_i under the assumption on the type of the density functions. In Feelders (1996) it is shown that the EM algorithm will do this for you.

The final, and probably most frequent, case to consider is that you know (and you ought to know) that your data don't really match your requirements and there isn't much you can do about it. In such cases, all you can do is use your common sense and start by distrusting your results.

Consider again the earlier example: you try to find the right groups to send a mailing to based on the products clients actually own. If you proceed by classifying clients into owners and nonowners of, for example, product X, it is possible that you'll find groups, for example, retired lawyers, that have a high percentage of X owners. Does this mean that retired lawyers who do not yet own X have a high probability of reacting to your mailing? Not necessarily.

Perhaps your famous product X is a set of law books. Why would these retired lawyers buy your books? They would probably rather play golf than read about the law. How do you find this out? In this case, looking at your results should help.

How do you find out in general? Well, there are no golden rules that will ensure that you'll never make mistakes. But, you can take precautions that will help you. The first rule is: mistrust your results. If you have used a tree-induction algorithm, you should be aware that these tend to prune off insignificant branches. The problem is that significance is only used in the statistical sense. That is, the (statistically) insignificant bits may have had the information that would tell you why this group scores so high. So, check the insignificant bits. In other words, try to distinguish the owners from the nonowners in this group. Do this by any means and algorithms you have got.

In the same vein, you should be aware that many classification algorithms are highly unstable. That is, if you use a slightly different training set, the resulting tree could look rather different (see, e.g., Breiman, 1996). So, use the algorithm on a slightly different training set: Do the same people still turn up? And if so, for similar reasons, or suddenly completely different reasons? In the same way, it makes sense to use another algorithm: again, Do these people turn up again? And, if so, why?

The second and most important rule is that results only make sense if they make sense to a domain expert. That is, let a domain expert scrutinize the proposed groups. Does it make sense to the expert that you would like to send the mailing to those people or not? If not, don't do it. Whatever promises the statistics of your model make.

In fact, one could phrase all of this differently. If the results of data mining are to be applied, the mining should be done by those that are going to apply the results. The mining system used possibly together with a data mining expert, should ensure that the results are technically all right. The domain expert should do the rest. And this is more than just ensuring that the results are both technically and logically sound. For, the results should also be actionable.

Not too long ago there was an insurance company in the Netherlands that offered discounts to female drivers. This makes perfect sense since women tend to drive safer. However, if such a rule is found, it is not directly applicable. For, not only was such a discount unconstitutional (one is not allowed to discriminate on sex, race, religion...) but also not very smart. On whose name would we insure our family car? Simply leaving out the attributes on which one cannot or should not discriminate is also not very good. For, it is still worthwhile to know that women are safer drivers. There are many ways to get more female applicants. For example, send your advertisements to magazines predominantly read by single females.

4. Conclusion

If you want to apply the results of data mining in practice, you should be constantly aware of the intended application. Do your data fit the business problem? Do your results make sense from a business point of view? Is it wise to use these results? All of this means that the domain expert should be intimately involved in the mining itself. In fact, if the data mining results are to be used in the everyday business context, the domain expert should be the data miner. This doesn't necessarily mean that the domain expert should become a data mining expert. It could also mean that a mining expert sets up the tools in such a way that they are intuitively useful for the domain expert.

References

Breiman, L. 1996. "Bagging predictors." *Machine Learning* **22**: 123–140.

Breiman, L., J. H. Friedman, R. A. Olshen, and C. J. Stone. 1984. *Classification and Regression Trees*. Wadsworth.

Domingos, P. 1999. "Metacost: a general method for making classifiers cost-sensitive." In *Proceedings of the Fifth International Conference on Knowledge Discovery and Data Mining (KDD-99)*.

Feelders, A. 1996. "Learning from biased data using mixture models." In *Proceedings of the Second International Conference on Knowledge Discovery and Data Mining (KDD-96)*. Menlo Park, CA: AAAI Press. pp. 102–107.

Jacka, S. and D. J. Hand. 1998. *Statistics in Finance*. Arnold.

Kohavi, R., F. Provost, and T. Fawcet. 1998. "Analysis and visualization of classifier performance." In *Proceedings of the Fifteenth International Conference on Machine Learning*.

Robert, C. P. 1994. *The Bayesian Choice*. Springer-Verlag.

Stolfo, S. and P. Chan. 1998. "Towards scalabale learning with non-uniform class and cost distributions." In *Proceedings of the Fourth International Conference on Knowledge Discovery and Data Mining (KDD-98)*.

22 LEGAL ASPECTS OF KDD

22.1 Privacy

Jason Catlett

ABSTRACT The concept of privacy encompasses various claims by individuals over whether information about them is communicated to others. Knowledge discovery is extending these claims to whether such information is even created. Privacy statutes can be divided into context-specific laws (more common in the United States), often aimed at specific technologies or industries, and omnibus legislation (more common elsewhere), usually based on the principles of fair information practices. Some of these principles may conflict with goals for data mining projects. Such projects should be guided by a coherent privacy strategy maintained by the organization.

1. What is Privacy?

Privacy is a fundamental human right recognized by the United Nations (1948), but what exactly is it? The most widely accepted definition of privacy is due to Alan F. Westin (1967):

> Privacy ... is the claim of individuals ... to determine for themselves when, how, and to what extent information about them is communicated to others ...

Agre and Rotenberg (1997) discuss the difficulties of a single definition. People have differing and changing judgments of which claims merit support by the law, in ethical codes, and in the court of public opinion.

2. Ethics and Public Relations

Computing professionals are considered by some to have a moral and ethical responsibility to ensure their work does not infringe on others' privacy. The Association for Computing Machinery (1998) imposes several relevant requirements on its members:

> As an ACM member I will ...
>
> (1.2) Avoid harm to others ...
>
> (1.7) Respect the privacy of others ...
>
> (3.5) Articulate and support policies that protect the dignity of users and others affected by a computing system.

Organizations often seem less motivated by any moral imperative than by the possibility of a public relations backlash, legislative response, enforcement action, or fall in stock price (Smith, 1994). Recent history provides several spectacular examples of how public scrutiny of companies' privacy-invasive practices can provoke lawmakers, damage their reputation, lower their market capitalization, reduce goodwill, and place stress on their customer service functions. Examples include the Lotus MarketPlace: Households CD-ROM of addresses in 1990, LEXIS-NEXIS' sale of Social Security Numbers in its P-TRAK system in 1996, a 1998 attempt by American Express and KnowledgeBase Marketing to sell to merchants information about the kind of purchases made by 175 million Americans, the Intel Processor Serial Number, the Microsoft Global User ID, a reporting function in RealPlayer in 1999, and DoubleClick's plan to link name and addresses with cookies in 2000. In all these cases the companies decided to modify or abandon their plans under public pressure.

3. The Law

Privacy law sprawls across constitutional law, tort case law, contracts, and many other areas (Smith, 1993), but the most recent and relevant law is statutory.

Privacy statutes can be divided into two types:

1. omnibus laws based on broad principles that are independent of both the technology being used to collect and manipulate the information and the economic context in which they occur, and

2. context-specific laws that restrict the kind of use, the technology, the market sector, or any other parameter formed by the legislative and lobbying process.

An example is the Video Privacy Protection Act of 1988, passed with alacrity by members of the U.S. Congress who perceived the possible disadvantage in having the titles of the movies they rented being obtained by journalists. The United States has many such context-specific laws (Smith, 1997). They have attempted to cover specific harms arising from new technology, but they quickly fall out of date. The Electronic Communications Privacy Act of 1986 prohibits an ISP from providing information about its customers' communications to governmental organizations, but allows disclosures to nongovernmental ones. Some have elaborate exemptions catering to special interest groups. For example, information about the subject matter of videos rented may be sold to direct marketers. The Telecommunications Act of 1996 includes complex restrictions on uses of data, even making distinctions between different divisions of a single carrier. The task of determining or even simply describing the permitted uses of a given data set can be considerable.

The more general kind of privacy laws are most often based on the notion of fair information practices, formulated by the U.S. Department of Health, Education and Welfare (1973), and subsequently expanded into a set of guidelines issued by the Organization of Economic Cooperation and Development (OECD, 1980).

The foundation of these guidelines are eight principles, such as the requirement that personal data should be kept secure from authorized access. The OECD guidelines were intended for countries drawing up data protection legislation, and many nations have since encoded the principles into law (Banisar and Davies, 1999). U.S. laws have only used this approach for government and the credit industry. Model legislation for Internet businesses that goes some distance along these lines has been proposed by the Federal Trade Commission (1998), but some principles are currently being resisted by commercial interests. Here we will discuss those principles that may impact data mining (Cavoukian, 1998).

3.1. Openness Principle

"There should be a general policy of openness about developments, practices and policies with respect to personal data."

A company using data mining in a jurisdiction where fair information practices are not legally mandated for everyone may believe unilateral openness conflicts with several desiderata: to keep such developments secret from competitors, to retain every possible commercial advantage (especially those enjoyed by competitors), and not to scare away the increasingly suspicious consumer. In 1998 the FTC surveyed Web sites looking for privacy policies disclosing whether personal data is collected, used or sold. They were disappointed with the small fraction they found, especially because they publicized their plans widely beforehand. Many companies' fear of liability was reinforced by the FTC's subsequent action against GeoCities, which claimed that GeoCities misled its customers by not abiding by its posted policies.

The individual participation principle states that the data subject 'should have the right to see data held about him', sometimes called "subject access". The Fair Credit Reporting Act of 1974 gave Americans the right to see their credit reports, exposing widespread inaccuracies in these databases, and creating the opportunity for correction. Knowledge discovery goes beyond previously known facts and may create information about the data subject previously unknown to anyone, including the subject. Under this principle the subject should be able to see the derived information, but what if he disagrees with those inferences?

Many companies seem to regard subject access as an expensive burden, and indeed it is likely be so in a large organization where analyses are performed by many disparate employees or subcontractors without planning for such access. But the risks entailed by disregarding fair information practices are also very substantial.

3.2. Purpose Specification Principle

"The purposes for which personal data are collected should be specified not later than at the time of data collection and the subsequent use limited to the fulfillment of those purposes."

This principle conflicts with a common practice in data mining: to obtain new derived data for different purposes. When customers provide their addresses for the primary purpose of delivery or billing, analyzing them to determine (for example) their propensity to make further purchases is a secondary use, and under the use limitation principle requires the customer's consent. The guidelines do not specify whether this must be explicit affirmative consent (called opt-in by marketers) versus passive failure to opt out in response to some kind of notice. National legislation is usually more precise, though subject to dispute (e.g., *U.S. West v. FCC*, 182 F.3d 1224 [10th Cir 1999]).

The OECD guidelines call for free flow of data between states with adequate data protection laws, and for restrictions on export of data to other jurisdictions. The European Commission (1995) issued a Directive to its states to enact harmonized data protection laws within three years. The lack of comprehensive laws in the United States has raised concerns about a possible transatlantic privacy trade war (Davies, 1998) and motivated the U.S. Department of Commerce to work towards a safe harbor agreement.

The Directive is far more detailed and specific than the OECD guidelines, and places weighty responsibilities on companies (Swire and Litan, 1998). For example, the data subject has the right to obtain "without constraint at reasonable intervals and without excessive delay or expense... communication to him in an intelligible form of the data undergoing processing... [and] knowledge of the logic involved in any automatic processing of data concerning him at least in the case of the automated decisions..."

Scientists undertaking an ambitious data mining project (where making the data intelligible is difficult even for an experienced exploratory data analyst) might be daunted by a legal requirement to not only to present it in a form intelligible to a nontechnical person, but also to communicate the logic of any models constructed from the data. Transparency has always been desired in data mining; if it is required absolutely, projects become more difficult and expensive. Of course the extent to which this must be performed is open to interpretation.

4. Can Knowledge About Groups, Not Individuals, Violate Privacy?

Privacy rights vests in individuals rather than groups; with a few limited exceptions groups have not really attempted to assert privacy claims. Groups sometimes act to protect their constituents' rights, such as remaining anonymous in assembling (U.S. Supreme Court, 1958). Class action suits are common, since the monetary damage to an individual is often small or difficult to quantify, and many privacy suits are based on torts rather than a statute that specifies liquidated damages. U.S. Jewish community leaders have sought reassurances that research data about ethnic groups are not used to those groups' disadvantage (Lehrman, 1997). This followed a discovery concerning a particular breast cancer mutation among Ashkenazi Jews, who have been the voluntary subjects of intense studies of genetic defects in recent years. The dangers arising from pseudoscientific knowledge discovered about groups are superbly recounted by Gould (1981).

Artificial persons such as corporations have no privacy rights in the United States, though many other laws protect copyright, confidential information, and trade secrets (Smith, 1993).

Data about groups can impact privacy if individuals can be identified by fusion or triangulation with other data sources: merely removing obvious identifying data before publishing or redistributing it may be inadequate to protect privacy. Sweeney (1997) gives the example that date of birth alone uniquely identifies 12 per cent of the residents of Cambridge, Massachussets. U.S. Federal agencies such as the Census Bureau have long used statistical disclosure control techniques to reduce risks to anonymity. These include aggressive rounding, suppressing sparsely populated cells and even disturbing the data (U.S. Department of Commerce, 1978). Sweeney has extended this idea to "computational disclosure control."

5. Are Some Kinds of Data More Sensitive Than Others?

Various laws distinguished certain data as especially sensitive, such as religion, sex, health, and individual finances, leading data miners to avoid them, and to use less sensitive variables as a proxy, or to treat them with additional care. Data about ethnicity and neighborhood income are often shunned not because they are secret (on the contrary, they are widely available), but because decisions made using them may be challenged as inequitable and illegal (Hsia, 1978). In the United States the Social Security Number (SSN) is used variously to identify and to authenticate individuals, and is therefore regarded as both sensitive and necessary. Mother's maiden name is another unfortunate choice for authentication because it can be inferred from birth records, which are generally public.

Organizations have often found the SSN convenient as a key in databases, but privacy is better preserved by using an internal identifier instead, and restricting access to SSNs. Taking this a step further, some companies follow a practice of removing all personally identifying information from databases used for online analysis, keeping only one identifier, which can be linked back to the individual through a more restricted procedure. This reduces employee browsing for unauthorized or criminal purposes, a major source of privacy violations. The next step is to irrevocably anonymize or destroy data after a certain period. Some data or inferences may be so potentially damaging to the subject (and in consequent litigation, to the organization) that they should never even be created or stored. Presuming that data will never be disclosed is foolish: clerical errors and other accidents happen, and anything kept anywhere in an organization (even on backup tapes) can be subpoenaed.

Data miners' decisions and behavior on privacy should be governed by their organization's privacy strategy (Clarke, 1997). The policies and procedures that arise from a privacy strategy should include processes for employee education and for modification over time. Standards of behavior are a moving target: technology creates new opportunities, people's expectations change, journalists shift their ideas of what is unusual and newsworthy, and the legislative process reacts to the events of the day. The public's concern about privacy and its demands on businesses have been rising for years and show no sign of receding as technology increases the opportunities for invasions (Hagel and Rayport, 1997). Knowledge discovery in the twenty-first century will surely expand the definition of privacy from an individuals' claim over determining what information about them is communicated to others to include determining what information is created by others.

References

Agre, P. E., and M. Rotenberg 1997. *Technology and Privacy: the New Landscape*. An excellent collection of recent essays. Cambridge, MA: MIT Press.

Association for Computing Machinery. 1998. The Code of Ethics and Professional Conduct. Washington, DC. Available at: http://www.acm.org/constitution/bylaw15.html.

Banisar, D., and S. Davies. 1999. *Privacy and Human Rights 1999: an International Survey of Privacy Laws and Developments*. Washington, DC: Electronic Privacy Information Center.

Cavoukian, A. 1998. *Data Mining: Staking a Claim on Your Privacy*. Toronto: Information and Privacy Commission. Available at: http://www.ipc.on.ca/web_site.eng/MATTERS/SUM_PAP/PAPERS/datamine.htm.

Clarke, R. 1997. *Privacy and Dataveillance, and Organizational Strategy*. Canberra, Australia: Xamax Consultancy Pty Ltd. Available at: http://www.anu.edu.au/people/Roger.Clarke/DV/PStrat.html.

Davies, S. 1998. Europe to US: No Privacy, No Trade. *Wired* 6 May 1998, p. 135. Available at: http://www.wired.com/wired/6.05/europe.html.

European Commission, Directorate General XV. 1995. Directive 95/46/EC of the European Parliament and of the Council of 24 October 1995 on the protection of individuals with regard to the processing of personal data and on the free movement of such data. Available at: http://jilt.law.strath.ac.uk/jilt/dp/material/directiv.htm and http://www2.echo.lu/legal/en/dataprot/directiv/chap2.html.

Gould, S. J. 1981. *The Mismeasure of Man*. New York, NY: W. W. Norton & Co.

Hagel, III, J., and J. F. Rayport. 1997. "The coming battle for customer information." *Harvard Business Review* Jan/Feb 1997: pp. 155–171. Argues that consumers 'are going to take ownership of information about themselves and start demanding value in exchange for it.' Abstract available at http://www.hbsp.harvard.edu/frames/groups/hbr/janfeb97/97104.html.

Hsia, D. C. 1978. "Credit scoring and the Equal Credit Opportunity Act." *Hastings Law J.* **30(2)**. Available at: http://www.uchastings.edu/hlj/abstr302.html.

Lehrman, S. 1997. Jewish leaders seek genetic guidelines (News Article). *Nature*, **389(6649)**, 25 September 1997, p. 322.

OECD (Organization for Economic Co-operation and Development). 1980. *Guidelines on the Protection of Privacy and Transborder Flows of Personal Data*. Paris, France: OECD. Available at: http://www.oecd.org/dsti/sti/it/secur/prod/PRIVEN.HTM.

Smith, R. E. 1993. *The Law of Privacy Explained*. Published by Privacy Journal, P.O. Box 28577, Providence, RI 02908.

Smith, H. J. 1994. *Managing Privacy: Information Technology and Corporate America*. Chapel Hill, NC: University of North Carolina Press.

Smith, R. E. 1997. *Compilation of State and Federal Privacy Laws*. Published by Privacy Journal, P.O. Box 28577, Providence, RI 02908.

Sweeney, L. 1997. "Guaranteeing anonymity when sharing medical data." *Proceedings, Journal of the American Medical Informatics Association*. Washington, DC.: Hanley & Belfus, Inc. Available at: http://medg.lcs.mit.edu/people/sweeney/confidentiality.html.

Swire, P. P., and R. E. Litan. 1998. *None of Your Business: World Data Flows, Electronic Commerce, and the European Privacy Directive*. Washington, DC.: Brookings Institution Press. A comprehensive analysis of the problems transatlantic businesses will encounter complying with EU privacy laws.

United Nations. 1948. *Universal Declaration of Human Rights*. New York: UN. (Article 12 asserts the right to privacy.)

U.S. Department of Commerce, Office of Federal Statistical Policy and Standards. 1978. Report on statistical disclosure and disclosure-avoidance techniques. Available at: http://www.bts.gov/NTL/DOCS/sw2.html. See also other references listed by the American Statistical Association's Committee on Privacy and Confidentiality: http://www.erols.com/dewolf/protect/sdlinfo.htm.

U.S. Department of Health, Education and Welfare. 1973. Secretary's Advisory Committee on Automated Personal Data Systems, Records, Computers, and the Rights of Citizens, Washington, DC. Available at: http://www.epic.org/privacy/consumer/code_fair_info.html.

U.S. Federal Trade Commission. 1998. Prepared Statement on 'Consumer Privacy on the World Wide Web'. U.S. House Of Representatives, July 21, 1998. Washington, DC: FTC. Available at: http://www.ftc.gov/os/1998/9807/privac98.htm.

U.S. Supreme Court. 1958. *NAACP* v. *Alabama*, 357 US 449. Available at: http://www.cortland.edu/www/polsci/naacp.html. In the course of litigation in 1956 by the state of Alabama, the NAACP was found in contempt for refusing to turn over its membership lists. The Supreme Court reversed this, recognizing 'the vital relationship between freedom to associate and privacy in one's associations.'

Westin, A. F. 1967. *Privacy and Freedom*. New York: Athaneumz.

22.2 Contractual Issues

David B. Hamilton

ABSTRACT Contracting for data mining services is an art form. The legal issues permeating the negotiation, drafting, and performance of contracts—on cutting edge issues like noncompetition agreements, privacy issues and Y2K compliance—requires in-depth legal and industry knowledge. This article is but an outline, or even more perfunctory, a checklist, of issues that must be addressed in data mining contracts.

1. Introduction

In such limited space, it is impossible to describe comprehensively the reasons and options for drafting and negotiating data mining contracts. Certainly, the subject can be treated at an overview level as it is here through an outline of what can be or should be included in a contract. The specifics of a good contract, for which vendors and users can pay dearly, cannot be covered by an outline. It is these specifics, however, that may create the success of a company, a project or a product—or equally, their failure. Finally, because data mining is an emerging technology, drafting and negotiating data mining contracts requires not only a thorough knowledge of existing legal precedent but also a certain legal prescience to complete a contract that will survive technological and legislative changes.

It is quite true that, while lawyers have become skilled in addressing cutting edge technological issues, their ability to provide invaluable legal services is constrained by existing legal precedent. Published decisions from state and federal appellate courts that provide guidance on contractual issues simply are not designed to keep pace with emerging technologies. An example for data mining contracts is in the very definition of what is being provided: is the contract a services contract? Or is it a contract for the sale of goods, thereby governed by the UCC (Uniform Commercial Code), a legal structure with its own set of rules, warranties and liabilities? Or further, is what is being delivered a product, thereby subject to product liability laws (like cars, washing machines or tobacco products)? Although this latter concept might be viewed in some legal corners dismissively, many courts borrow from these familiar doctrines as the world of algorithms, UNIX, and source code are foreign concepts to many judges.

By outline then, here are issues that should be addressed in data mining contracts:

2. Pre-contract Issues

    A. RFP (Request for Proposal)

        1. Begins to define buyer's objectives

        2. Define format and deadline of response

        3. Gut check for buyer

        4. Eliminating responses/vendors and narrowing competition

            a. Further competition—is it all time and price?

            b. Buyer's budget—disclosed?

                i. Organizational support? Does it fit business plan?

                ii. Financial commitment

                iii. Realistic schedule

                iv. Devotion of nonmonetary resources

                v. Prepared for overruns, missed deadlines?

        5. Gut check for vendor

            a. Organizational support? Does it fit business plan?

            b. Can vendor meet RFP deadlines?

            c. Obtaining project—for profit? for publicity? as an entree?

            d. Schedule—realistic?

            e. Catastrophe plans—what if half of your employees leave?

            f. Preparation for commitment to customer—how to deal with missed deadlines, cost overruns?

    B. Due Diligence

        1. For buyer

a. References from other buyers

b. Financial stability

c. Personnel evaluation and stability

d. Key man concepts—is vendor too dependent on one or two few individuals

e. Other existing (future) commitments

2. For vendor

a. Payment issues

b. Buyer's reputation/history—is this a new venture or routine contract?

c. When to involve lawyers?

d. When to involve investors/board of directors?

3. Contract Issues

A. Who are the parties?

1. Corporate structure matters—corporation v. partnership v. joint venture v. sole proprietor

2. Adding guarantors—what consequences?

B. Defining scope of work

1. Matching RFP—does it matter?

2. What is being delivered—services, product or both?

3. Defining important terms—for example, software, source code, installation, payment, acceptance, defective work

C. Defining performance issues

1. Schedule

a. Defining what must be delivered—Gantt charts

b. Is there flexibility?

c. Milestone payment issues

d. Status reports

2. Personnel commitments

a. For buyer—avoiding bait-and-switching/personnel changes, vendor commitments

b. for vendor—looking for flexibility to make changes

3. The product

a. Defining alpha/beta/final product

b. Defining releases

c. Continuing support/upgrades/enhancements

d. Fixing bugs

e. Defining functionality—speed, quantity, quality, output, content

4. Installation/implementation

a. Defined

b. Physical plant

c. Buyer's purchasing requirements to complete installation—substitutions and or equal issues

    d. Combining products/software—compatibility

    e. Testing—critical to define standards and specifications

    f. Security and privacy issues

    g. Final acceptance definitions

5. Payment issues

    a. Vendor—typically wants heavy front end, none deferred. How to accommodate but protect?

    b. Buyer—typically, wants to tie payment to milestone achievements. Defining milestones may be compromise

    c. Disbursements—reimbursements for per diems, out of pockets? How defined?

    d. Time and material v. product v. value

6. Legal issues

    a. Product ownership

        i. Licensing—defined broadly or narrowly or exclusive/nonexclusive—many other licensing issues

        ii. Assignability

        iii. Source code escrow

        iv. Preserving competitive advantages—proprietary issues

        v. Nondisclosure—defining confidentiality

        vi. Noncompete

        vii. Duration of agreement

    b. Warranty issues

        i. UCC or not?

        ii. Warranty of performance

        iii. Disclaimers—express and implied

        iv. Warranty of Noninfringement

        ii. Warranty response and other satisfaction of warranty obligations issues

    c. Indemnification/contribution

        i. Defined

        ii. Scope—pay for, actively defend, pay judgment

        iii. For limited actions v. all claims

    d. Insurance

        i. Business interruption insurance

        ii. Property damage

        iii. Bodily harm

        iv. Errors and omissions insurance

    e. Limitation of liability—tension between buyer and vendor—consequential damages, lost profits, and other litigation protection

    f. Exclusive remedies limited to the contract—injunctive relief

    g. Integration clause—the contract supersedes all other agreements

    h. Modification requirements

     i. Governing law—<u>critical</u>!

     j. Venue and jurisdiction—where lawsuits must/may be brought

     k. Changes of financial condition/ownership

     l. Financial reporting requirements

     m. Defining material breach

     n. Assignability

     o. Severability

     p. Access to books and records

     q. Responsibility for taxes, permits, other licenses

     r. Patents, copyrights, trade secrets, royalties

     s. Termination

          i. For cause

          ii. For convenience

          iii. Events of default

          iv. Notice—right to cure

     t. Uniqueness—obligation v. ability to mitigate damages

     u. Liquidated damages for schedule/performance failures

     v. Alternative dispute resolution—choosing prelawsuit mediation v. arbitration and rules of conduct

     w. Events of bankruptcy

9. Cutting edge issues

     a. Use of software/product/services with Internet, Intranet, and World Wide Web

     b. Broadcasting and use of e-mail

     c. Licensing issues

     d. Revenue enhancements—start up companies, sharing in profits, acquiring stock for payment, etc.

     e. Viruses, bombs, and bugs

     f. Millennium compliance

     g. Federal and state law compliance and legislative impact

4. Murphy's Law of Contracts

Even the contract constructed by the most prestigious law firms or lawyers at significant costs are susceptible to interpretations that would seem to turn the contract's intent on its head. For example, in a very recent decision by a federal district court in Maryland on the validity of a geographical restriction in a noncompete agreement, the court determined that, because the former employee's tools of the trade were a computer equipped with a fax modem used to solicit and service customers nationally, the former employee should be prohibited from competing against his former employer regardless of where he lived. This interpretation runs against the mainstream, which normally restricts competition geographically based on a reasonableness test. *Intelus Corp.* v. *Barton*, 1998 U.S. Dist. LEXIS 8239 (D. Md. June 4, 1998). Even so, implicit in the court's decision is the recognition that emerging technologies require rethinking traditional legal concepts.

    In data mining contracts, the industry is under attack from regulators and privacy advocates (see Chapter 22.1 of this handbook). The Telecommunications Act of 1996, still unclear in its application and implementation, at least signals regulators' concerns about the use of customer's basic information (name, long distance usage, etc.) for marketing purposes. Trade magazines and other commercial publications often include articles describing concerns over the intrusion in ordinary lives of repeated credit card opportunities, Internet advertising, eerily customized offers, or even more basic, the impersonal paper results of an HMO computer's reimbursement/payment decision on important medical issues. See, for example, You Are For Sale, *PC World* (September 1998 at 97). All of these events, of course, are driven by data and the ingenious use and processing of data by an entrepreneurial industry (who wouldn't like to invent the Microsoft of the data mining industry?).

That said, the need for greater protection for purchasers and vendors in the data mining community may be the most significant future challenge. The "what if" clause—the clause that determines the operation of the contract in the event of a catastrophic event—has traditionally been defined as a *force majeure* act, that is, an act of God, a strike, a war, and so on. Why not include a regulatory "what if" clause? For example, "in the event that the federal or [any state] [the state Government of Mississippi] [Salt Lake City] shall enact any bill that becomes law that substantially or materially (wiggle words!) affects the subject matter of this contract or by law prohibits the completion of the contract, then the parties shall..." Shall what? How can the parties share the risks and rewards created by the often arbitrary land mine environment found in local, state, and federal government? These issues are not Chicken Little issues; litigation has occurred when events that indeed did happen were dismissed earlier as unlikely by seemingly rational thinking. The need to obtain protection and the ability to do so in a cutting edge industry and on cutting edge issues compels great care in the contracting process.

Finally, to the extent that the parties are not domestic companies or where the subject matter concerns services or products delivered abroad, there are many considerations that must be addressed in a contract. Intellectual property rights under the European Union, by the law of some foreign nations or under International Trade Agreements provide many contractual challenges. International transactions are made easier by some uniform rules; however, the rules are byzantine and require subject matter experts. In the face of an awakening to the power of data mining, expect more guidance and more disputes on these international issues.

The end result is obvious: great care must be used in drafting and negotiating data mining contracts. Cookie-cutter forms or contracts drafted by general practitioners are invitations to trouble, should the contractual and business relationship break down. While the data mining industry comes under attack on regulatory and privacy fronts, at least as to those things over which some measure of control can be exercised, the contract is the blueprint for success or failure.

PART FOUR

DISCOVERY SYSTEMS

23 OVERVIEW OF DISCOVERY SYSTEMS

Willi Klösgen

ABSTRACT This chapter introduces the main dimensions that are important for classifying KDD systems. Criteria for comparing and evaluating systems can be arranged into the categories of input, algorithms, output, user, technology, and support. They are applied when presenting examples of data mining tools belonging to different categories such as those in Chapter 24. We outline the need to be alert for new developments and product updates, since the data mining tools market is rapidly developing and very dynamic. Some pointers to regularly updated product information sources and other reports on data mining tools that can be useful for observing the development of this market are also given.

1. Introduction

The tool and system development dimension of the KDD field is treated in this chapter. Since KDD applications are rapidly increasing and diffusing, the market for advanced KDD tools is dynamic and new systems and versions appear regularly. It is difficult for an interested user to keep track of the state of the art in tool developments. Some sources of information about KDD tools are regularly upgraded, such as the software section of the KDD nuggets (`http://www.kdnuggets.com/software/index.html`). This site arranges descriptions of tools by the main mining tasks, such as Bayesian and dependency networks, classification, clustering, and deviation detection, but also includes preprocessing, visualization, and application categories. Additionally, a download option allows the user to access free or commercial systems for a limited trial use.

Special, and mainly commercial, reports (e.g., Two Crows, Aberdeen Group, Gartner Group) provide an extensive overview and evaluation of KDD tools. Those reports, however, sometimes run the risk of being out of date because of new developments and updates. In contrast, in this chapter we introduce some basic dimensions that are important for comparing, summarizing, and evaluating KDD tools. Then in Chapter 24 a sample of KDD tools is described in more detail. There are also some short case studies, including screen shots of tool applications that illustrate the tasks and methods involved in typical KDD processes. Because of the dynamics of the KDD software market, it is difficult for this sample to be representative or weighted by software quality criteria. The systems have been selected to cover a broad range of the market, including both commercial and academic (free) software, as well as tools specialized for a single mining task and workbenches or suites offering a broad spectrum of mining methods. As an example of another selection, Table 1 lists the systems that have been selected by the Gartner Group and deemed most likely to lead the data mining market in the next five years.

These systems have also been selected to include criteria such as viability of vendors and products, service, support, and consulting. It is expected by Gartner Group that IBM, Oracle, and SAS should have a long-term advantage because of their partnerships, size, and experience.

Table 1 Gartner Group's Magic Quadrant of Data Mining Workbenches

Angoss Knowledge Suite	www.angoss.com
Intelligent Miner	www.software.ibm.com/data/iminer/fordata/
Darwin	www.think.com
Enterprise Miner	Chapter 24.2.5
Mine Set	Chapter 24.2.4
Clementine	Chapter 24.2.1

Table 2 Types of KDD Systems

Tasks supported	Single mining task (e.g., classification), only one method (e.g., classification tree)	Single task, multiple methods (e.g., trees, neural nets, nearest neighbors, rules)	Multiple mining tasks (e.g., classification, clustering)	
Process steps supported	Only data mining	Also pre- and postprocessing		
Domains supported	Generic system	Domain specific (e.g., marketing)		
Tool integration approach	Macro integration (plug-in)	Micro integration		
Architectural layers	Data management	Data aggregation (statist. queries)	Pattern and model evaluation	Search
	Search refinement	User interaction		

2. Dimensions for comparing KDD tools

Different types of KDD systems can be defined according to simple dimensions as summarized in Table 2: systems supporting single versus multiple mining tasks, data mining versus KDD systems, and domain specific versus generic systems.

Examples of single task systems are classification systems (e.g., C4.5), clustering systems (e.g., AutoClass; see Chapter 24.3.1), and data visualization systems (e.g., Netmap). Both of the first two systems offer only one mining method (decision tree or AutoClass) for the classification or clustering task. A typical combination of methods that is offered in some systems for the classification task includes classification trees, rules, neural networks, and nearest neighbors, for example, in the systems Clementine (Chapter 24.2.1), Darwin, and Recon. The next dimension differentiates between data-mining and KDD systems. KDD systems are fully integrated systems (or systems with well-established interfaces to databases, statistical systems, and visualization systems) that support the whole KDD process, that is, preprocessing, data mining, and postprocessing.

Domain-specific systems support a special domain. For example, the systems CoverStory, Spotlight (Anand and Kahn, 1992), and Opportunity Explorer are specialized tools for market research applications.

Besides these simple classification dimensions for KDD tools, other dimensions are important when describing and comparing KDD systems. The data input dimension includes: types of data that can be processed in the system, DBMS interface and integration, and data preprocessing operations. Chapter 4 gives an overview on the types of data that are used in KDD applications. Whether a KDD tool can process only simple rectangular tables—or multi-relational, spatial, text, audio, or multimedia data—can be decisive for a planned application. The DBMS interface and integration is discussed in Section 3. Methods for preprocessing and manipulating data (e.g., importing, defining, selecting, combining, and transforming) are important, because these operations are known to be very time-consuming within a discovery process.

KDD tools can also exploit domain knowledge. Some types of domain or background knowledge that are relevant as input for KDD processes are described in Chapter 18.

The algorithmic dimension of a KDD system includes the methods offered in the system from the vast set of mining (and pre- or postprocessing) methods. Mining methods are described in Part 3. The algorithmic aspect also refers to properties like accuracy, scalability, interpretability, robustness, fastness, and the statistical sophistication of algorithms, including advanced techniques like adaptive sampling, bagging, or boosting.

The next dimension refers to the output, that is, the types of knowledge that are generated by a system. This is a function of the algorithms and methods for mining tasks (classification, clustering, etc.) that are available in a system. An overview of knowledge types is presented in Chapter 5. A further aspect of output is the presentation of the generated knowledge and the role of visualization for data mining results (see Chapter 20). Result reporting, especially Web-based reporting, is an increasingly important feature of a discovery system.

The user dimension includes aspects like the intended user (sophistication required from user, analyst versus domain user), user roles, user advice on reasonable next steps, documentation of steps used in a special KDD process, repeatability and automation (by visual programming, macros, wizards, logs, agendas, experiment managing), intuitive graphical or visual user interface, position of the user in the discovery loop, and degree of system autonomy. These are important for the usability of the system and the degree of automation.

As stressed by the Gartner Group, support and consulting is a practically important dimension for a KDD system. While a large consulting practice is claimed as a benefit by the leading vendors (ranked according to market penetration), some smaller developers (for example, DataSurveyor, Chapter 24.2.2; and Kepler, Chapter 24.2.3) are also providing appropriate service and support. Often the main revenue of these specialized companies is not provided by their software, but by the consultancy fees. Technological dimensions referring to platforms, architectures, integration with other systems and the web are discussed in the next section.

3. Architectural layers of KDD tools

A number of architectural layers can be identified in KDD systems: a basic data management layer is responsible for storing and updating the given data. A data aggregation layer dealing with statistical queries operates on the basic data management layer. This layer can be embedded into the data management layer, for example, by using SQL for data aggregations, or can rely on specialized data access operations. The third layer is the hypotheses evaluation or pattern layer, including statistical problem types and methods for their verification and computation of quality. The pattern layer uses the services of the data aggregation level and is used by the search layer. The search layer includes search strategies and operations for the generation of hypotheses. Finally, a refinement layer operates on the search results, including redundancy elimination methods.

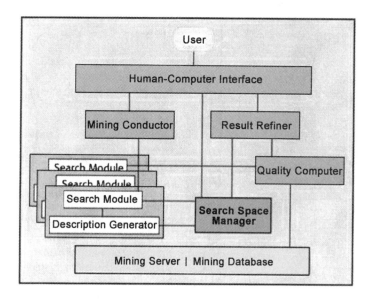

Figure 1 Modular structure of data mining algorithms.

Table 3 Criteria for Data Mining Tools

Input	
Data	Which data types are supported
	Which transformation/preprocessing options
Domain knowledge	Which types of domain knowledge are exploited
Output	
Algorithms	Which mining tasks are supported
	Which methods are available for a task
	Algorithmic properties (accuracy, robustness, scalability, ...)
	Algorithmic sophistication (bagging, boosting, ...)
Presentation	Visualization
	Reporting
User	
	Types and roles of user
	Guidance, documentation of steps, repeatability, automation
	Intuitivity of interface
Technology	
	Platforms
	Programming language
	Integration with other systems (especially database systems)
	Architectural layers and modularity
Support	
	Documentation
	Service and consulting
	Viability of vendor and product

We can distinguish two integration approaches for modular inclusion of mining methods into a system: macro- and microintegration. Macrointegration is based on a frame system that offers general data management, visualization, statistical test functions, and, like the Kepler system (Chapter 24.2.3), is based on a plug-in architecture (Wrobel et al., 1996). This plug-in integration allows a mining algorithm to be included into the system without having to modify the existing implementation of the algorithm. The integration is primarily based on a description of the interface between the system and the algorithm.

Microintegration is a highly modular approach which is realized in, for example, the Data Surveyor system (Chapter 24.2.2). The Data Surveyor architecture (Figure 1) allows a modular and efficient implementation of the search strategies. When including a new algorithm into the system, the modular structure required by the (Data Surveyor) system must be observed and the algorithm usually has to be reimplemented. Data Surveyor is based on an innovative object-oriented representation of a discovery process.

In the core of this architecture there is a search space manager realized in an object oriented database that manages all generated hypotheses. Separate processes operate on this search space manager: a user interface dynamically allows the presentation of the actual state of the search during the search and the search to be redirected. Search modules call a hypothesis or description generator to expand hypotheses by genetic or neighborhood operators and to insert the new hypotheses into the search space manager. A quality module tests the hypotheses and calculates their qualities using an evaluation function. This architecture relies on an object-oriented model for KDD (describing projects, tasks, hypotheses, qualities, etc.) and a procedural mining conductor supporting a general generate-and-test approach that iteratively calls the above processes.

A central architectural topic is the integration of mining algorithms into database management systems. Especially for subgroup mining approaches (Chapter 16.3) requiring many bundles of statistical queries, an SQL-based implementation could be advantageous because of the ease of development, portability, and automatic parallelization possibilities. Within one pass over the database triggered by a SQL statement, all contingency tables can be calculated that are needed for the next level of the search process. Especially for association rules, various architectural alternatives for coupling data mining with relational database systems have been examined (Sarawagi et al., 2000). Constitutive for a tight integration of association rule algorithms is that algorithms like A priori can be expressed in the form of SQL queries. The disadvantage of these SQL-based solutions is their inferior performance compared to implementations using specialized data structures. Contingency tables, for instance, can be very efficiently calculated using bit vector approaches (Klösgen, 1996).

The most basic technological criteria refer to platforms on which the systems are available, which are mainly Unix or NT platforms, but also mainframes (Intelligent Miner from IBM). PC or Unix standalone versions are being replaced more and more by client–server architectures.

Table 3 summarizes the criteria. The descriptions of data mining tools selected in Chapter 24 include these categories.

References

Anand, T. and G. Kahn. 1992. "SPOTLIGHT: a data explanation system." In *Proceedings of the Eighth IEEE Conference on Applied AI*. Washington, DC: IEEE Computer Society, pp. 2–8.

Klösgen, W. 1996. "Explora: a multipattern and multistrategy discovery assistant." In *Advances in Knowledge Discovery and Data Mining*, edited by U. Fayyad, G. Piatetsky-Shapiro, P. Smyth, and R. Uthurusamy, pp. 249–271. Cambridge, MA: MIT Press.

Sarawagi, S., S. Thomas, and R. Agrawal. 2000. "Integrating association rule mining with relational database systems: alternatives and implications." *Data Mining and Knowledge Discovery* 4: 89–125.

Wrobel, S., D. Wettschereck, E. Sommer, and W. Emde. 1996. "Extensibility in data mining systems." In *Proceedings of the Second International Conference on Knowledge Discovery and Data Mining (KDD-96)*, edited by U. Fayyad, E. Simoudis, and J. W. Han. Menlo Park, CA: AAAI Press.

24 CASE STUDIES

24.1 Public Domain, Multiple Mining Tasks Systems

24.1.1 DBMiner

Jiawei Han

ABSTRACT DBMiner is an online analytical mining system, developed for interactive mining of multiple-level knowledge in large relational databases and data warehouses (see Chapters 6.1 and 13). The distinct feature of the system is its tight integration of online analytical processing (OLAP) with a wide spectrum of data mining functions, including characterization, association, classification, prediction, and clustering (see Chapters 16.1, 16.2.2, 16.2.3 and 16.5). The system facilitates query-based, interactive mining of multidimensional databases (see Chapter 6.3) by implementing a set of advanced data mining techniques, including OLAP-based induction, multidimensional statistical analysis, progressive deepening for mining refined knowledge, meta-rule guided mining, and data and knowledge visualization (see Chapter 20). DBMiner integrates smoothly with commercial relational database and data warehouse systems, and provides a user-friendly, interactive data mining environment with high performance. With extensions to the DBMiner system, several specialized data mining system prototypes, including GeoMiner, MultiMediaMiner, and WeblogMiner, have been designed and developed for mining complex types of data with interesting applications.

1. Introduction

DBMiner (http://db.cs.sfu.ca/DBMiner) is a data mining system originating from the Intelligent Database Systems Research Laboratory at the School of Computing Science, Simon Fraser University, Burnaby, British Columbia, Canada V5A 1S6.

With years of research in data-mining and knowledge discovery in databases, Dr. Jiawei Han, his graduate students, and research associates designed and developed the DBMiner system, which integrates online analytical processing (OLAP) with a wide spectrum of data mining functions and performs online analytical mining in relational databases and data warehouses.

The first research paper on data-mining from the research laboratory was published in 1989 (Cai et al., 1991), and the first comprehensive description of the DBMiner system was published in 1996 (Han et al., 1996). A good set of published research papers related to the system can be obtained from the Web at `http://db.cs.sfu.ca`. The system has been demonstrated in major conferences on database systems, artificial intelligence, and data-mining and knowledge discovery. The enterprise version of the system, DBMiner 2.5, has been developed based on a research system prototype and an early version DBMiner 2.5, and was released in 2000 by DBMiner Technology Inc. (`http://www.dbminer.com`).

The major distinct feature of the DBMiner system is its tight integration of online analytical processing (OLAP) with data mining (Han, 1998; Han and Fu, 1996; Han et al., 1998). This integration leads to a promising data mining methodology, called online analytical mining (OLAM), where the system provides a multidimensional view of its data and creates an interactive data mining environment: users can dynamically select data-mining and OLAP functions, perform OLAP operations, such as drilling, dicing/slicing, and pivoting, on data mining results and/or perform mining operations on OLAP results, that is, mining different portions of data at multiple levels of abstraction.

2. Software Architecture

The software architecture of the DBMiner system is shown in Figure 1, which takes data from a relational database and/or a data warehouse, integrates and transforms them into a multidimensional database (portions or all of which could be consolidated into data cube(s)),

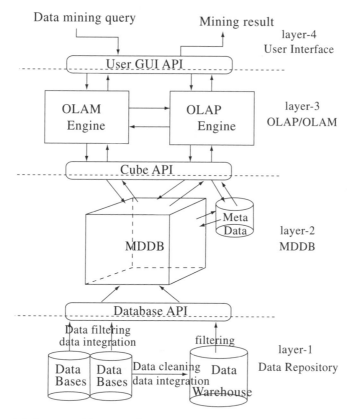

Figure 1 Software architecture of DBMiner: An integrated OLAM and OLAP architecture

and then performs multidimensional online analytical processing and online analytical mining, based on user's data-mining or online analytical processing requests.

The core module of the architecture is an OLAM engine that performs online analytical mining in multidimensional databases in a similar manner to online analytical processing by an OLAP engine. The OLAM engine in the DBMiner system performs multiple data mining tasks, including concept description, association, classification, and sequential-pattern analysis.

More importantly, the system integrates OLAM and OLAP engines, both of which accept users' online queries (or commands) via a User_GUI_API and work on the multidimensional database via an MDDB_API. Notice in the architecture, OLAM and OLAP engines interact each other because the former may take the output of the latter and perform mining on the OLAP results, whereas the latter may take the output of the former and perform OLAP on the mining results. A meta-data directory, which stores (1) database schema, (2) data warehouse schema, and (3) concept hierarchy information (see Chapter 18.1), is used to guide the access of the multidimensional database and the execution of dimension-related OLAP operations, such as drilling and slicing. The multidimensional database can be constructed by accessing database(s), filtering data warehouse(s), and/or integrating multiple such sources, via a Database_API, which is currently supported by MicroJot SQLServer 2000.

3. Input Data and Knowledge

The DBMiner system takes data from a SQLServer database or a SQLServer data cube, which in turn is constructed from single or multiple relational tables, a data warehouse system, and/or other forms of data, such as spreadsheets.

4. Output Knowledge: Manipulation and Visual Presentation

There are many forms of visual presentation of knowledge generated by the DBMiner system, depending on the data mining tasks and user preference: data summarization and characterization generate cross-tabulation tables, generalized rules, bar charts, pie charts, curves, or other forms of graphical outputs using Microsoft Excel 2000. Classification generates visual display of decision trees or decision tables. Association generates association rule tables, association planes, and association rule graphs. Sequential-pattern analysis generates sequential-patterns in both table and rule graph forms.

Moreover, the system provides facilities to view concept hierarchies and data cube contents. Concept hierarchies are presented in a tree form similar to directory/subdirectory structures. Data cube and database contents are presented in a three-dimensional cube form, where the size and color of each cuboid in the three-dimensional cube represent the summarization of corresponding selected measures within a set of three-dimensional intervals.

An important feature of the system is its flexible manipulation, such as performing drilling, dicing, and/or other transformations on the output knowledge. For example, after classification of a combination of dimensions and levels, drilling can be performed on both classified and classifying dimensions to derive a classification tree over the new set of data. Furthermore, one can drill through a node of the decision tree to view the set of detailed data forming the current class.

5. Data Mining Tasks Supported by the System

The DBMiner system supports the following data mining tasks (Han et al., 1997):

- *OLAP analyzer.* This function presents the contents of a data cube at multiple levels of abstraction from different angles by drilling, dicing, slicing, and other OLAP operations. The output can be presented in various visual or graphical forms. Moreover, the OLAP data can be annotated to show the maximal, minimal, and standard deviation values, and other distributions by data dispersion analysis. OLAP operations can be performed on generalized data to drill or dice on the regions of interest for further analysis.

- *Classification.* This function analyzes a set of training data (i.e., a set of objects whose class label is known), constructs a model for each class based on the features in the data, and adjusts the model based on the test data. The model so constructed is presented in the form of decision trees or classification rules, and is used to classify future data and develop a better understanding of data in the database.

- *Association.* This function mines a set of association rules in a multiple dimensional database. The rules so mined can be used for cross-market analysis, correlation analysis, et cetera. A user may specify the rules to be mined in the form of metapatterns (see Chapter 18.4), such as $major(s : student, x) \land P(s, y) \rightarrow grade(s, y, z)$ to confine the search for desired rules. One can also drill along any dimension to mine rules at multiple levels of abstraction.

- *Sequential-pattern analysis.* This function analyzes data in a sequence database to find a set of (sub-) sequences which occur frequently in the database. A user may find that a customer who buys a computer may be likely to buy a CD-ROM and a printer within two months.

6. Support for Task and Method Selection

The DBMiner system supports task and method selection via a Windows-based graphical user interface, where users may choose different mining tasks using a mining wizard or interact with the data mining results for mining at alternative dimensions and levels. Moreover, an SQL-like data mining query language, DMQL, has been designed, and a user-composed mining query is presented in the form of DMQL for examination before submitting for execution.

7. Support of the KDD Process

Since the DBMiner system works with a data warehouse, some essential preprocessing tasks for knowledge discovery, such as data cleaning, data integration, and data consolidation (aggregation grouped by multiple dimensions and levels), are performed, when necessary, by the (supported) underlying data warehouse system. Data selection is performed in the DBMiner system as part of a data mining query.

In DBMiner, most of the postprocessing process on the discovered patterns is integrated with the data mining process, since a data mining query provides not only the selection of task-relevant data and the mining task but also the interestingness measure (see Chapter 19.2), such as mining thresholds, including support, confidence, noise, etc., and desired rule patterns. Such an integration of mining and pattern evaluation not only reduces the search space but also facilitates the focus of the mining process.

8. Main Applications

The DBMiner system can be used as a general purpose, online analytical mining system for both online analytical processing (OLAP) and data mining in relational databases and data warehouses. The system has been used in medium to large relational databases, with excellent results.

Several specialized data mining system prototypes, including GeoMiner, MultiMediaMiner, and WeblogMiner, have been developed by extensions to the DBMiner system. A special purpose data mining system for the banking industry is being developed based on the DBMiner system.

9. Current Status

The DBMiner system has evolved from a research system prototype to an industry product. However, its research innovation and new technology progress is still tightly connected with the university research laboratory.

The minimum hardware requirement for the DBMiner system is a Pentium-500 machine with 64 MB RAM. The system runs on Windows/NT or Windows 2000. The system is directly linked to Microsoft SQLServer 2000, or communicates with various relational database systems, via Microsoft SQLServer 2000.

DBMiner 2.5 can be freely downloaded at `http://db.cs.sfu.ca/DBMiner` or `http://www.dbminer.com` for a 90-day trial use. User licenses for single, group, or educational users can be purchased via `http://www.dbminer.com`.

References

Cai, Y., N. Cercone, and J. Han. 1991. "Attribute-oriented induction in relational databases." In *Knowledge Discovery in Databases*, edited by G. Piatetsky-Shapiro, and W. J. Frawley, pp. 213–228. Menlo Park, CA: AAAI/MIT Press.

Han, J. 1998. "Towards on-line analytical mining in large databases." *ACM SIGMOD Record* **27**: 97–107. New York, NY: ACM Press.

Han, J., and Y. Fu. 1996. "Exploration of the power of attribute-oriented induction in data mining." In *Advances in Knowledge Discovery and Data Mining*, edited by U. M. Fayyad, G. Piatetsky-Shapiro, P. Smyth, and R. Uthurusamy, pp. 399–421. Menlo Park, CA: AAAI Press.

Han, J., Y. Fu, W. Wang, J. Chiang, W. Gong, K. Koperski, D. Li, Y. Lu, A. Rajan, N. Stefanovic, B. Xia, and O. R. Zaïane. August 1996. "DBMiner: a system for mining knowledge in large relational databases." In *Proceedings of the 1996 International Conference on Data Mining and Knowledge Discovery (KDD'96)*, pp. 250–255. Portland, Oregon.

Han, J., J. Chiang, S. Chee, J. Chen, Q. Chen, S. Cheng, W. Gong, M. Kamber, G. Liu, K. Koperski, Y. Lu, N. Stefanovic, L. Winstone, B. Xia, O. R. Zaïane, S. Zhang, and H. Zhu. November 1997. "DBMiner: a system for data mining in relational databases and data warehouses." In *Proceedings of CASCON'97: Meeting of Minds*, pp. 249–260. Toronto.

Han, J., S. Chee, and J. Y. Chiang. June 1998. "Issues for on-line analytical mining of data warehouses." In *Proceedings of the 1998 SIGMOD Workshop on Research Issues on Data Mining and Knowledge Discovery (DMKD'98)*, pp. 2:1–2:5. Seattle.

24.1.2 MLC++

Ronny Kohavi and Daniel A. Sommerfield

ABSTRACT   MLC++, the Machine Learning library in C++, is a set of libraries and utilities that can aid developers in interfacing machine-learning technology, aid users in selecting an appropriate algorithm for a given task, and aid researchers in developing new algorithms, especially hybrid algorithms and multistrategy algorithms.

1. Motivation for MLC++

The ability to test and compare the performance of many algorithms, including hybrid algorithm, and multistrategy algorithms on a given problem motivated the development of MLC++.

It is well known that no one learning algorithm can outperform all others across all domains, a theoretical result called the Conservation Law, or the No Free Lunch Theorem (Mitchell, 1982; Wolpert, 1994; Schaffer, 1994). While the theorem proves that it is impossible for any algorithm to have the highest generalization accuracy over all domains, the theorem assumes that all target concepts are equally likely, an assumption that is rarely true in practice.

In real world domains, not all target concepts are equally likely and some algorithms are clearly better than others. Furthermore, generalization accuracy is not the only way to judge an algorithm; other metrics such as comprehensibility, compactness, speed, and ease of updating are additional factors considered in the selection of an algorithm (Fayyad et al., 1996). These two observations highlight the need to have many algorithms available and to have a strong basis for comparison so that the best algorithms for a given domain may be identified.

While there are many rules of thumb for choosing a learning algorithm, we believe the best method is to try several algorithms, evaluate their results, and use the evaluation as the basis for a decision. MLC++ is ideal for implementing this method.

Although there are many rules of thumb for choosing learning algorithms, we believe the best method is to try several of them and see the results (Kohavi et al., 1997).

MLC++ can serve three types of users:

1. System integrators, developers of tools, and developers of vertical applications can use the libraries to integrate machine-learning technology into products and solutions. MineSet is the best example of this use. MLC++ is integrated into a commercial data-mining product sold by Silicon Graphics (Chapter 24.2.4; Silicon Graphics, 1998; Brunk et al., 1997), which provides access to some of the algorithms in MLC++ through a graphical user interface (GUI). In addition, it provides database access, transformations, and visualizations.

2. Machine-learning researchers developing learning algorithms can use the library itself, modify it, add routines, and build hybrid algorithms.

3. Machine-learning researchers and power users comparing learning algorithms can use the MLC++ utilities to compare performance of different algorithms.

The first two types of users use the library directly. The third type uses a set of MLC++ applications known as the MLC++ Utilities. These command-line driven tools provide easy access to the underlying library functions but require far less programming.

2. Short History of MLC++

The development of MLC++ started at Stanford University in the summer of 1993 and continued there for two years. The original library was public domain. In late 1995 the distribution and support moved to Silicon Graphics (Kohavi and Sommerfield, 1995). Development of MLC++ continues in the analytical data-mining group at Silicon Graphics. The original sources are still available as public domain; the enhanced sources are also available off the Web, although their use is restricted to research use only.

Over fifteen students worked on the project at Stanford, several over multiple quarters. Today, several people at Silicon Graphics work on MLC++ development and maintenance as part of the MineSet product.

The MLC++ mailing list has more than eight hundred subscribers, and over sixteen hundred unique sites have downloaded MLC++ source code.

3. MLC++ Algorithms

While MLC++ is useful for writing new algorithms, most users simply use it to test different learning algorithms. Pressure from reviewers to compare new algorithms with others led us to also interface induction algorithms written by other people. MLC++ provides a uniform interface for these algorithms, termed external inducers.

The following induction algorithms were implemented in MLC++:

A constant predictor based on majority, a decision table (Kohavi and Sommerfield, 1998) ID3 (Chapter 16.1.3; Quinlan, 1986), lazy decision trees (Friedman et al., 1996), nearest-neighbor (Chapter 16.1.6; Dasarathy, 1990), naive-Bayes (Chapter 16.1.5; Domingos and Pazzani, 1997), 1R (Holte, 1993), OODG (Kohavi, 1995b), option decision trees (Kohavi and Kunz, 1997), Perceptron (Chapter 16.1.8; Hertz et al., 1991), and Winnow (Littlestone, 1988).

The following external inducers are interfaced by MLC++:

C4.5 and C4.5 rules (Chapter 16.1.3; Quinlan, 1993), C5.0, CART (Breiman et al., 1984), CN2 (Chapter 16.1.4; Clark and Boswell, 1991), IB (Aha, 1992), neural network: Aspirin/ MIGRAINES (Chapter 16.1.8; Hertz et al., 1991), OC1 (Murthy et al., 1994), PEBLS (Cost and Salzberg, 1993), Ripper (Cohen, 1995), and T2 (Auer et al., 1995).

Because algorithms are encapsulated as C++ objects in MLC++, we were able to build useful wrappers. A wrapper is an algorithm that treats another algorithm as a black box and acts on its output. Once an algorithm is written in MLC++, a wrapper may be applied to it with no extra work.

The most important wrappers in MLC++ are performance estimators, feature selectors, and ensemble creators. Performance estimators apply any of a range of methods, including holdout, cross-validation, bootstrap (Kohavi, 1995a), learning curves, and ROC curves (Provost and Fawcett, 1997) to evaluate the performance of an inducer. Feature selection methods run a search based on performance estimation using the inducer itself to determine which attributes in the database are useful for learning. The wrapper approach to feature selection automatically tailors the feature set to the inducer being run (Kohavi and John, 1997). Ensemble methods create different models and then combine their votes. MLC++ includes bagging, boosting, and several variants (Bauer and Kohavi, 1999; Breiman, 1996; Freund and Schapire, 1996).

In addition to the above, MLC++ supports a discretization wrapper/filter, which pre-discretizes the data, allowing algorithms that do not support continuous features (or those that do not handle them well) to work properly. A parameter optimization wrapper allows tuning the parameters of an algorithm automatically based on a search in the parameter space that optimizes the performance estimate of an inducer using different parameters.

3.1. MLC++ Software Architecture

MLC++ is a class library for development of machine-learning algorithms. Its software architecture is particularly important as it is the foundation of the entire project.

CODING STANDARDS AND SAFETY

MLC++ defines a set of coding standards and conventions. Because MLC++ is a common framework for machine-learning and data-mining research and because research results can easily be ruined by software bugs, the MLC++ coding standards promote safety over efficiency. All major classes in the library contain intensive integrity checks, and MLC++ programs always abort at the first sign of an error. While this method may be inappropriate for real-time systems, it helps guarantee the correctness of the algorithms. MLC++ also incorporates an optional fast mode, which deactivates many of the checks.

PLATFORMS

MLC++ is a cross-platform library. Version 2.01 has been released for SGI IRIX, Windows NT (using the Microsoft Visual C++ compiler), and gnu g++. The g++ version may be used on most UNIX platforms including Solaris and Linux. All compilation is handled by a cross-platform compilation wrapper, which selects the options most appropriate for the target platform. This wrapper script is designed to be extensible so that new platforms may be added with ease.

MCORE

The MLC++ library is built around a set of foundation classes known as MCore. MCore provides common classes such as arrays, hash tables, and link lists, which are used heavily within MLC++. It is a template-based library similar in spirit to the standard template library yet focusing more on code safety.

CENTRAL LEARNING CLASSES

The library contains an extensive set of machine-learning support classes. These classes come in two varieties. The first set forms an application program interface (API) for incorporating algorithms into MLC++. Algorithms writing to this API gain the full benefits of MLC++: for example, an algorithm written as an MLC++ classifier can immediately be run through the cross-validation and feature selection wrappers. The API covers classification, regression, clustering, automatic binning, and search algorithms. Algorithms written outside of the library may be wrapped by external inducers that use the API. Once enclosed in an MLC++ wrapper, the external inducer gains most of the benefits of MLC++. For example, we can use our own bootstrap accuracy estimation to compare results from C5.0 and our internal decision trees. The second set of classes form the building blocks for data-mining and machine-learning algorithms. Code for computing statistics, information-theoretic measures (such as entropy), and basic numerics is included in this set. We also provide a set of data-handling and simple transformation classes. Simple operations such as removing attributes and discretization and all handled within MLC++.

WRAPPERS

The class-based architecture of MLC++ facilitates rapid development of hybrid classification algorithms. Wrapper algorithms are particularly easy to develop in MLC++. MLC++ wrappers use the concept of an inducer, which is a generic model-building class. To build a wrapper, one creates a subclass of inducer that incorporates another inducer class within it. This method allows the wrapper to use any algorithm implemented within the library's API. The library also provides a generic categorizer class that represents a model. Hybrid models may be constructed by embedding categorizer classes within each other. For example, the NBTree model (Kohavi, 1996) embeds a naive Bayes models within a decision tree.

PERSISTENT MODELS

All models (classifiers, regressors, and clustering models) written in MLC++ may be saved to disk in a common persistent format. These models may be read back from disk for deployment or further modification. The MLC++ library provides support tools and APIs for reading and writing these files. New models may be made persistent by following the library guidelines.

Hybrid models are automatically supported by the mechanism once all internal parts are supported. The persistent model files are stored in an extensible ASCII format.

EVALUATION

A main feature of MLC++ is providing an extensible framework for data mining-research. A large portion of this framework is a common set of evaluation classes. These classes support evaluation methods like holdout, cross-validation, bootstrap, and learning curves, and may be applied to any algorithm written as a subclass of the MLC++ inducer. External inducers such as C5.0 may be evaluated with no extra work once they are plugged into MLC++. The evaluation framework is also used as the basis for evaluating nodes in the search space for search algorithms like feature subset search. The framework is designed to be extensible so that new evaluation methods may be added and immediately applied to the full range of algorithms.

TESTING ARCHITECTURE

To guarantee correctness of the code base, MLC++ includes approximately 40,000 lines of automated testing code. Each module in the code is fully tested under a range of conditions. The tests are calibrated so that they produce identical output on different platforms as much as possible. Tests are run in both fast mode (where most integrity checks are disabled for speed) and two different levels of debugging.

UTILITIES

MLC++ contains a set of machine-learning utilities, written using the library. These utilities perform tasks such as induction of models, scoring of records, and evaluation of the model-building process. We also provide utilities for association rule generation, discretization, and clustering. Aside from being useful in themselves, these applications provide good examples on the use of MLC++. The majority of users interested in MLC++ have downloaded the MLC++ utilities, which are available off the Web as a stand alone package for several platforms.

3.2. Integration with MineSet

MLC++ integrates with MineSet (Silicon Graphics, 1998; Brunk et al., 1997) to provide the following features:

DATABASE ACCESS

MLC++ itself can only read data from flat files in the C4.5/UCI format (Blake and Merz, 1998). However, when coupled with MineSet, MLC++ is capable of taking input directly from Oracle, Informix, and Sybase databases.

APPLY MODEL/MODEL DEPLOYMENT

MineSet provides a scoring module using MLC++ to apply classifiers stored in the MLC++ persistent classifier format. Any stored classifier supported by MineSet may be applied using this method. Furthermore, while MLC++ algorithms operate only on data loaded into memory, MineSet provides a model deployment capability that runs directly from disk.

TRANSFORMATIONS

While MLC++ itself provides only limited data transformations, a much more extensive set is available through MineSet. MLC++ itself handles attribute removal (projection), binning, and simple feature construction. MineSet adds aggregation, more binning options, filtering, more advanced feature construction, and an integrated ability to apply saved models to the data. If it is connected to a database, MineSet can also read its data through an SQL query, allowing more complex operations such as joins.

MINING TOOL OPTIONS

MLC++ contains an extensible system for handling the large number of options needed to run a data mining algorithm. Options are passed to MLC++ from MineSet through option files. While the contents of these files are mostly determined by the MineSet user interface, the user may add additional options using a special file called .mineset-classopt. Using this file gives advanced MineSet users access to the full range of MLC++ options, producing greater flexibility in using MineSet.

3.3. MLC++ Visualization

MLC++ interfaces with two visualization packages: MineSet and GraphViz.

MLC++ generates MineSet visualizations for its decision tree, naive Bayes, decision table, clustering, and association rule algorithms. The visualizations are generated in an ASCII format that may be read directly by MineSet. Visualizers may be launched automatically if they are installed on the MLC++ target platform.

MLC++ also generates graph visualizations of all graph-based algorithms using GraphViz (Dot/Dotty) from AT&T (Ellson et al., 1998). These visualizations include decision trees, decision graphs, and visual representations of the search spaces used by the search engine.

ACKNOWLEDGMENT

The MLC++ project could not have started without the support of Nils Nilsson and Yoav Shoham at Stanford University. MLC++ was partly funded by ONR grants N00014-94-1-0448, N00014-95-1-0669, and NSF grant IRI-9116399. After the summer of 1995, Silicon Graphics Inc. provided continued support for MLC++ as part of the MineSet project.

References

Aha, D. W. 1992. "Tolerating noisy, irrelevant and novel attributes in instance-based learning algorithms." *Int. J. Man–Machine Studies* **36(1)**: 267–287.

Auer, P., R. Holte, and W. Maass. 1995. "Theory and applications of agnostic PAC-learning with small decision trees." In *Machine Learning: Proceedings of the Twelfth International Conference*, edited by A. Prieditis, and S. Russell. San Francisco: Morgan Kaufmann.

Bauer, E., and R. Kohavi. 1999. "An empirical comparison of voting classification algorithms: Bagging, boosting, and variants." *Machine Learning* **36**: 105–139.

Breiman, L. 1996. "Bagging predictors." *Machine Learning* **24**: 123–140.

Breiman, L., J. H. Friedman, R. A. Olshen, and C. J. Stone. 1984. *Classification and Regression Trees*. Belmont, CA: Wadsworth International Group.

Brunk, C., J. Kelly, and R. Kohavi. 1997. "MineSet: an integrated system for data mining." In *Proceedings of the Third International Conference on Knowledge Discovery and Data Mining (KDD-97)*, edited by D. Heckerman, H. Mannila, D. Pregibon, and R. Uthurusamy, pp. 135–138. Menlo Park, CA: AAAI Press. Available at http://mineset.sgi.com.

Blake, C. and C. J. Merz. 1998. "UCI repository of machine learning databases." Available at http://www.ics.uci.edu/~mlearn/MLRepository.html.

Clark, P., and R. Boswell. 1991. "Rule induction with CN2: some recent improvements." In *Proceedings of the Fifth European Conference (EWSL-91)*, edited by Y. Kodratoff, pp. 151–163. Heidelberg, Germany: Springer-Verlag. Available at http://www.cs.utexas.edu/users/pclark/papers/newcn.ps.

Cohen, W. W. 1995. "Fast effective rule induction." In *Machine Learning: Proceedings of the Twelfth International Conference*, edited by A. Prieditis, and S. Russell. San Francisco, CA: Morgan Kaufmann.

Cost, S., and S. Salzberg. 1993. "A weighted nearest neighbor algorithm for learning with symbolic features." *Machine Learning* **10(1)**: 57–78.

Dasarathy, B. V. 1990. *Nearest Neighbor (NN) Norms: NN Pattern Classification Techniques*. Los Alamitos, CA: IEEE Computer Society Press.

Domingos, P., and M. Pazzani. 1997. "Beyond independence: conditions for the optimality of the simple Bayesian classifier." *Machine Learning* **29(2/3)**: 103–130.

Ellson, J., E. Gansner, E. Koutsofios, and S. North. 1998. GraphViz. Available at http://www.research.att.com/sw/tools/graphviz.

Fayyad, U. M., G. Piatetsky-Shapiro, and P. Smyth. 1996. "From data mining to knowledge discovery: an overview." In *Advances in Knowledge Discovery and Data Mining*, pp. 1–34. Menlo Park, CA: AAAI Press and the MIT Press.

Freund, Y., and R. E. Schapire. 1996. "Experiments with a new boosting algorithm." In *Machine Learning: Proceedings of the Thirteenth National Conference*, edited by L. Saitta, pp. 148–156. San Francisco, CA: Morgan Kaufmann.

Friedman, J., R. Kohavi, and Y. Yun. 1996. "Lazy decision trees." In *Proceedings of the Thirteenth National Conference on Artificial Intelligence*, pp. 717–724. Menlo Park, CA: AAAI/MIT Press.

Hertz, J., A. Krogh, and R. G. Palmer. 1991. *Introduction to the Theory of Neural Computation*. Boston, MA: Addison-Wesley.

Holte, R. C. 1993. "Very simple classification rules perform well on most commonly used datasets." *Machine Learning* 11: 63–90.

Kohavi, R. 1995a. "A study of cross-validation and bootstrap for accuracy estimation and model selection." In *Proceedings of the Fourteenth International Joint Conference on Artificial Intelligence*, edited by C. S. Mellish, pp. 1137–1143. San Francisco, CA: Morgan Kaufmann. Available at http://robotics.stanford.edu/~ronnyk.

Kohavi, R. 1995b. "Wrappers for performance enhancement and oblivious decision graphs." Ph.D. diss. STAN-CS-TR-95-1560. Stanford University, Computer Science department. Available at http://robotics.Stanford.EDU/~ronnyk/teza.ps.Z.

Kohavi, R. 1996. "Scaling up the accuracy of naive-Bayes classifiers: a decision-tree hybrid." In *Proceedings of the Second International Conference on Knowledge Discovery and Data Mining*. Menlo Park, CA: AAAI Press, pp. 202–207. Available at http://robotics.stanford.edu/~ronnyk.

Kohavi, R., and G. H. John. 1997. "Wrappers for feature subset selection." *Artificial Intelligence* 97(1–2): 273–324. Available at http://robotics.stanford.edu/~ronnyk.

Kohavi, R., and C. Kunz. 1997. "Option decision trees with majority votes." In *Machine Learning: Proceedings of the Fourteenth International Conference*, edited by D. Fisher, pp. 161–169. San Fransisco, CA: Morgan Kaufmann. Available at http://robotics.stanford.edu/users/ronnyk.

Kohavi, R. and D. Sommerfield. 1995. "MLC++ utilities." Available at http://www.sgi.com/tech/mlc.

Kohavi, R., and D. Sommerfield. 1998. "Targeting business users with decision table classifiers." In *Proceedings of the Fourth International Conference on Knowledge Discovery and Data Mining (KDD-98)*, edited by R. Agrawal, P. Stolorz, and G. Piatetsky-Shapiro, pp. 249–253. Menlo Park, CA: AAAI Press.

Kohavi, R., D. Sommerfield, and J. Dougherty. 1997. "Data mining using MLC++: a machine learning library in C++." *Int. J. Artificial Intell. Tools* 6(4): 537–566. Available at http://www.sgi.com/tech/mlc.

Littlestone, N. 1988. "Learning quickly when irrelevant attributes abound: a new linear-threshold algorithm." *Machine Learning* 2: 285–318.

Mitchell, T. 1982. "Generalization as search." *Artificial Intelligence* 18: 203–226. Reprinted in Readings in Artificial Intelligence, Bonnie Webber and Nils Nilsson, eds, San Mateo, CA: Morgan Kaufmann Publishers. pp. 517–542.

Murthy, S. K., S. Kasif, and S. Salzberg. 1994. "A system for the induction of oblique decision trees." *J. Artificial Intell. Res.* 2: 1–33.

Provost, F., and T. Fawcett. 1997. "Analysis and visualization of classifier performance: comparison under imprecise class and cost distributions." In *Proceedings of the Third International Conference on Knowledge Discovery and Data Mining (KDD-97)*, edited by D. Heckerman, H. Mannila, D. Pregibon, and R. Uthurusamy. Menlo Park, CA: AAAI Press.

Quinlan, J. R. 1986. "Induction of decision trees." *Machine Learning* 1: 81–106. Readings in Machine Learning, T. Dietterich and J. Shavlik, eds, San Francisco, CA: Morgan Kaufmann.

Quinlan, J. R. 1993. In *C4.5: Programs for Machine Learning*. San Mateo, CA: Morgan Kaufmann.

Schaffer, C. 1994. "A conservation law for generalization performance." In *Machine Learning: Proceedings of the Eleventh International Conference*, pp. 259–265. San Francisco, CA: Morgan Kaufmann.

Silicon Graphics. 1998. *MineSet User's Guide*. Mountain View, CA: Silicon Graphics. Available at http://mineset.sgi.com.

Wolpert, D. H. 1994. "The relationship between PAC, the statistical physics framework, the Bayesian framework, and the VC framework." In *The Mathematics of Generalization*, edited by D. H. Wolpert. Boston, MA: Addison-Wesley.

24.1.3 ROSETTA Rough Sets

Jan Komorowski, Aleksander Øhrn, and Andrzej Skowron

ABSTRACT   Research in rough sets (Pawlak, 1981, 1982) has resulted in a number of software tools for data mining and knowledge discovery from databases (KDD). Among many of these tools, the ROSETTA system (Øhrn, 1999, Øhrn and Komorowski, 1997; Øhrn et al., 1998) is probably one of the most complete software environments for rough set operations. In ROSETTA, the experimental nature of inducing classifiers from data is explicitly maintained by organizing the workspace in a tree structure that displays how input and output data relate to each other. ROSETTA supports the overall KDD process: from browsing and preprocessing of the data, to reduct computation and rule synthesis, to validation and analysis of the generated rules. Learning may be both supervised (resulting in if-then rules) or unsupervised (resulting in general patterns), and input data may be categorical, numerical, or both. ROSETTA is not tied to any particular application domain, and it has been put to use for a variety of tasks. ROSETTA is a cooperative effort between researchers at NTNU in Norway and Warsaw University in Poland, and is available on the World Wide Web (http://www.idi.ntnu.no/~aleks/rosetta/). The system runs under Windows NT/98/95/2000.

1. Introduction

Rough sets offer an interesting and successful approach to data mining and knowledge discovery. Since the original work of Pawlak (1981, 1982) there has been a systematic growth in theoretical and applied research that relies on this formalism. The theoretical developments have been accompanied by various implementations of rough set tools. There exist today several experimental research systems that support different aspects of developing rough set models. Many prosperous applications using those systems have been reported in the literature.

This article starts with a list of all rough set software systems that are known to us. We then describe the ROSETTA system. It is assumed that the reader is familiar with the basic notions of rough set theory (Pawlak, 1991) and Boolean reasoning (Brown, 1990). A tutorial introduction to rough sets can be found in Chapter 9 of this handbook.

2. Software Systems for Rough Sets

The authors are aware of the following software systems for rough sets. The reader can find more details about these systems in Polkowski and Skowron (1998a,b), or by contacting the respective authors directly.

- Datalogic/R: http://www.reduct.com/.
- Grobian (Roughian): I.Duentsch@ulst.ac.uk, ggediga@luce.psycho.Uni-Osnabrueck.de.
- KDD-R: ziarko@cs.uregina.ca.
- LERS: jerzy@eecs.ukans.edu.
- PRIMEROSE: tsumoto@computer.org.
- ProbRough: zpiasta@sabat.tu.kielce.pl, lenarcik@sabat.tu.kielce.pl.
- ROSETTA: http://www.idi.ntnu.no/~aleks/rosetta/.
- Rough Family: Roman.Slowinski@cs.put.poznan.pl, Jerzy.Stefanowski@cs.put.poznan.pl.
- RSDM: cfbaizan@fi.upm.es, emenasalvas@fi.upm.es.
- RoughFuzzyLab: rswiniar@saturn.sdsu.edu.
- RSL: ftp://ftp.ii.pw.edu.pl/pub/Rough/.
- TAS: zsuraj@univ.rzeszow.pl.
- Trance: wojtek@cs.vu.nl.

3. Background Information

The ROSETTA system (Øhrn, 1999; Øhrn and Komorowski, 1997; Øhrn et al., 1998) has been developed by two groups: the Knowledge Systems Group at NTNU, Norway (Homepage: http://www.idi.ntnu.no/grupper/KS-grp/), and Group of Logic, Warsaw University, Poland (Homepage: http://www.alfa.mimuw.edu.pl/logic/) under the guidance of, respectively, Jan Komorowski and Andrzej Skowron.

In Norway, the main design and programming effort of the graphical user interface (GUI) and kernel architecture has been undertaken by Aleksander Øhrn. Several other people contributed, including (in alphabetical order) Thomas Ågotnes, Merete Hvalshagen, Jørn Nygjerd, Daniel Remmem, Knut Magne Risvik, Ivan Uthus, and Staal Vinterbo.

In Poland, the original work on a library of rough set algorithms, the RSES library, was done (in alphabetical order) by Jan Bazan, Agnieszka Chądzyńska, Adam Cykier, Sinh Hoa Nguyen, Son Hung Nguyen, Piotr Synak, Marcin Szczuka, Dominik Ślęzak, and Jakub Wróblewski.

A public version of ROSETTA is available (see the ROSETTA homepage: http://www.idi.ntnu.no/~aleks/rosetta/), and a reference manual containing a detailed description of the features of the current system can be found at the same location. Readers of the manual should consult Øhrn (1999) and references therein for an overview of the background theory.

ROSETTA runs on 32-bit Windows platforms, both with a GUI and as a command-line utility. It is simple to port ROSETTA to other platforms, albeit not with the GUI. A screenshot of the ROSETTA GUI can be found in Figure 1.

Although the system will run on small configurations, any serious application will benefit from large RAM and fast CPU. Also, since ROSETTA keeps its working data in main memory, machines with low memory may experience degraded performance on very large

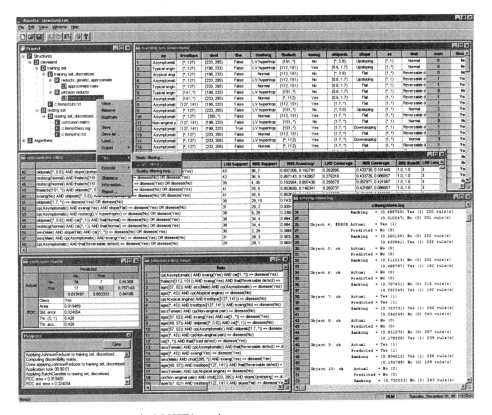

Figure 1 An example ROSETTA workspace.

data sets. For reference, the widest decision tables that we have processed had around 2,500 attributes, and the largest number of objects was about 15,000.

4. Design Issues

The ROSETTA computational kernel is a general C++ class library, and it offers an advantageous code base for researchers to quickly assemble and try out new algorithms and ideas (see the ROSETTA C++ Library home page: http://www.idi.ntnu.no/~aleks/ thesis/source/). Extensibility and flexibility have been chief parameters in its design and construction. By applying suitable object-oriented design patterns, the kernel is maintainable and highly modular, and completely independent of the GUI.

However, a collection of clever algorithms does not in itself make a complete system. In order to comprise a fully usable KDD tool, the algorithms need to be set in an environment such that models can be developed in an interactive manner, data items are organized, and experiments may be conducted in a setting that allows backtracking. These considerations were all made explicit when designing the ROSETTA GUI.

5. Input Data and Background Knowledge

Basic input to ROSETTA are flat data tables describing Pawlak information systems. An information system is a single table, either physically or as a logical view across several underlying tables. Several tables can be present in the system simultaneously. Tabular data may be imported from a wide range of data sources by means of the open database connectivity (ODBC) interface. Possible data sources include spreadsheets, relational database management systems, or plain ASCII files, depending on which ODBC drivers the user has installed on his or her system. Data dictionaries are automatically constructed from the imported data, but hand-crafted dictionaries can also be imported. Dictionaries contain meta data such as attribute names, types, measurement units, coding schemes, et cetera. The user may manually control how raw data is preprocessed, and embed background knowledge in that way. For instance, in a medical setting, known medically relevant cut-off values may be specified during discretization of real-valued attributes.

ROSETTA also has the option of employing user-defined notions of discernibility on a per attribute basis, for example in the reduct computation process. If the domain of an attribute defines a partial order, this knowledge may be input to the system and appropriate discernibility considerations will be made. This feature also enables the user to specify how missing values are to be treated, since missing values may indicate different things from different attributes.

If cost information is available, some of the heuristics for reduct computation can be equipped with a bias for computing inexpensive attribute subsets.

6. System Output

The main output from ROSETTA that may convey discovered knowledge consists of if-then classification rules, or minimal object descriptions, or general patterns, along with several numerical factors associated with these. Such induced rules or patterns may be either as specific as possible, or approximate up to a degree specified by the user. These structures may subsequently be put to use inside the ROSETTA system itself, or exported and applied elsewhere.

Most structures in use by the ROSETTA system such as decision tables, reduct sets, rule sets, indiscernibility graphs, and discernibility functions can be exported to ASCII files. This opens up a link to other systems that support manipulation and visualization of structures in ways not currently supported by ROSETTA. For example, tables can be exported to MATLAB as matrices, and rule sets and tables can be exported to Prolog as sets of clauses and facts. Rule sets can also be exported as C++ source code.

Optional output from computational processes include detailed log files containing information about performance and/or costs. Such files are often directly plottable by external programs.

7. Supported Data Mining Tasks

Data mining is understood as a component of the overall KDD process, and is defined in the rough set framework to be the computation of reducts and their postprocessing, as well as the synthesis of rules (from the reducts) and their postprocessing.

ROSETTA supports computation of both proper and approximate reducts (Bazan, 1998; Pawlak, 1991; Skowron, 1995), and reducts may be relative to an object or relative to a full table. Furthermore, reducts may be relative to a decision attribute or not. Since computing minimal reducts is NP-hard, efficient heuristics are included, such as, for example, genetic algorithms for searching for individual reducts (Wróblewski, 1995, 1998).

As mentioned, the reducts computed by ROSETTA do not necessarily have to be reducts in the strict sense, but can, if specified by the user, be approximations of reducts. Reduct approximations (Bazan, 1998; Skowron, 1995) are generally believed to be more tolerant to noise and other data impurities. Computation of dynamic reducts (Bazan, 1998) is an example of an approximation option that is implemented in ROSETTA.

Postprocessing of reduct and rule sets typically amounts to filtering operations. Such collections of structures may be filtered down to more manageable sizes according to a wide variety of criteria.

8. Support for Task and Method

With respect to supervised learning, ROSETTA can be used to induce classification rules. However, inducing a classifier from raw data is usually composed of several steps that effectively define a pipeline. For instance, discretization may have to be performed before reducts are computed, before rules in turn are generated from the reducts. At each of these steps, choices may have to be made as to which of several candidate algorithms to apply. And different choices at each step define alternative branchings of the induction pipeline. ROSETTA offers a variety of algorithm alternatives at each step, easily selectable through pop-up menus. Furthermore, ROSETTA offers a GUI environment in which the resulting structures in the pipeline branchings can be organized.

9. Support of the KDD Process

KDD is understood to constitute the full process from initial target data selection and preprocessing, to validation and interpretation of the induced models (Fayyad et al., 1996). ROSETTA supports the entire KDD process both in terms of an appropriately designed GUI, and in its offering of relevant algorithms.

The ROSETTA GUI is fully object oriented in the sense that all structural instances are represented as individual icons, each with their own set of operations that can be performed on them. The icons are organized in a project tree where the interrelationship between the icons in the tree immediately reflect how they relate to each other. This aids in data navigation. As a data analysis project is carried out, the tree automatically gets updated and annotated. Annotations help automate the process of generating session logs and project documentation.

Initial browsing and target data selection is done in intuitive, object-oriented grid environments, using data dictionaries to allow communication with the user in terms from the modeling domain. Attributes and objects in a table can be masked out or removed altogether before the table is passed on in the KDD pipeline.

Currently, completion and discretization are the two main preprocessing options offered by ROSETTA. Completion consists of heuristics for eliminating missing values, while discretization consists of converting real-valued attributes into interval attributes. Discretization problems and symbolic value partition problems are of high computational complexity, that is, NP-complete or NP-hard. The Warsaw group has made significant contributions to the development of practical heuristics for these problems (e.g., Nguyen, 1997, 1998; Nguyen and Nguyen, 1998; Nguyen and Skowron, 1995, 1997). Several heuristics for completion and discretization are implemented in ROSETTA.

Support for the data mining component of KDD is described elsewhere in this article. Rules produced by this step may be inspected and interpreted in grid environments using terms from the modeling domain, and may also be applied to new cases in order to assess their predictive capabilities. ROSETTA offers support for cross-validation as well as for simple train-test splits, and allows quantities derived from confusion matrices and ROC curves (Hanley and McNeil, 1982) to be used as performance measures. A handful of statistical tests for hypothesis testing are also implemented.

Although the ROSETTA GUI offers an intuitive environment for interactive model construction, the system also has support for automating the steps in the KDD pipeline. ROSETTA is equipped with a simple scripting language that enables structural objects to flow through a sequence of algorithms. Long KDD pipelines can, thus, be easily assembled and executed without the need for any intervention.

10. Visualization

ROSETTA does not currently offer any means of visualizing data or models graphically. Instead, there is a set of export routines so that the user can do this outside of the system. For example, the indiscernibility relation can be exported to a format recognized by the Graph Viz suite of graph visualization programs (see the Graph Viz home page: `http://www.research.att.com/sw/tools/graphviz`). Such graphs can be used for clustering and unsupervised learning.

11. Main Applications

ROSETTA is a general purpose tool for data mining and KDD within the rough set framework, and is not geared toward any particular application area. Hence, any area in which the fundamental task of constructing a mapping from one domain to another (or forming a minimal description of a domain) comes up, is a potential candidate application area.

Users having downloaded the system report using ROSETTA in fields as diverse as power electronics, analysis of medical data, satellite control, software engineering, finance, public policy generation, medical ethics, history of science, real-time decisionmaking, anthropology, selection of controller gains, environmental modeling, and diagnosis of rotating machinery. For detailed references, see Øhrn (1999).

ACKNOWLEDGMENTS

Numerous people have been involved in the ROSETTA project. We can only express our general thanks to all colleagues, collaborators, reviewers, students, friends, wives, and funding agencies who have contributed to ROSETTA in very many direct and indirect ways.

References

Aamodt, A., and J. Komorowski. eds. 1995. *Proceedings of the Fifth Scandinavian Conference on Artificial Intelligence*. Trondheim, Norway: IOS Press, Frontiers in Artificial Intelligence and Applications, Volume 28.

Bazan, J. G. 1998. "A comparison of dynamic and non-dynamic rough set methods for extracting laws from decision tables." *Rough Sets in Knowledge Discovery 1: Methodology and Applications*, edited by L. Polkowski, and A. Skowron, pp. 321–365. Heidelberg: Physica-Verlag.

Brown, F. M. 1990. *Boolean Reasoning: The Logic of Boolean Equations*. Dordrecht: Kluwer Academic Publishers.

Fayyad, U., G. Piatetsky-Shapiro, and P. Smyth. 1996. "The KDD process for extracting useful knowledge from volumes of data." *Commun. ACM* **39(11)**: 27–34.

Hanley, J. A., and B. J. McNeil. 1982. "The meaning and use of the area under a receiver operating characteristic (ROC) curve." *Radiology* **143**: 29–36.

Komorowski, J., and J. Żytkow, eds. 1997. *Proceedings of the First European Symposium on Principles of Data Mining and Knowledge Discovery (PKDD'97)*. Trondheim, Norway: Springer-Verlag, Lecture Notes in Artificial Intelligence, Volume 1263.

Nguyen, H. S. 1997. "Discretization of real valued attributes—a Boolean reasoning approach." Ph.D. diss. Warsaw University.

Nguyen, H. S. 1998. "From optimal hyperplanes to optimal decision trees." *Fundamenta Inform.* **34**: 145–174.

Nguyen, H. S., and S. H. Nguyen. 1998. "Discretization methods in data mining." In *Rough Sets in Knowledge Discovery 1: Methodology and Applications*, edited by L. Polkowski, and A. Skowron, pp. 451–482. Heidelberg: Physica-Verlag.

Nguyen, S. H., and A. Skowron. 1995. "Quantization of real valued attributes." In *Proceedings of the Second Joint Annual Conference on Information Science*, edited by P. P. Wang, pp. 34–37. Durham: Duke University.

Nguyen, S. H., and A. Skowron. 1997. "Searching for relational patterns in data." In *Proceedings of the First European Symposium on Principles of Data Mining and Knowledge Discovery (PKDD'97)*, edited by J. Komorowski and J. Żytkow, Lecture Notes in Artificial Intelligence **1263**: 265–276. Trondheim, Norway, and Berlin: Springer-Verlag.

Øhrn, A. 1999. "Discernibility and rough sets in medicine: tools and applications." Ph.D. diss. Norwegian University of Science and Technology. Available at: http://www.idi.ntnu.no/~aleks/thesis/.

Øhrn, A., and J. Komorowski. 1997. "ROSETTA: a rough set toolkit for analysis of data." In *Proceedings of the Third Joint Annual Conference on Information Sciences, Durham, NC*, edited by P. P. Wang, pp. 403–407.

Øhrn, A., J. Komorowski, A. Skowron, and P. Synak. 1998. "The design and implementation of a knowledge discovery toolkit based on rough sets: the ROSETTA system." In *Rough Sets in Knowledge Discovery 1: Methodology and Applications*, edited by L. Polkowski, and A. Skowron, pp. 376–399. Heidelberg: Physica-Verlag.

Pawlak, Z. 1981. "Information systems—theoretical foundations." *Inform. Sys.* **6**: 205–218.

Pawlak, Z. 1982. "Rough sets." *Int. J. Comput. Inform. Sci.* **11(5)**: 341–356.

Pawlak, Z. 1991. *Rough Sets: Theoretical Aspects of Reasoning About Data*. Dordrecht: Kluwer Academic Publishers.

Polkowski, L., and A. Skowron, eds. 1998a. *Rough Sets in Knowledge Discovery 1: Methodology and Applications*. Heidelberg: Physica-Verlag.

Polkowski, L., and A. Skowron, eds. 1998b. *Rough Sets in Knowledge Discovery 2: Applications, Case Studies and Software Systems*. Heidelberg: Physica-Verlag.

Skowron, A. 1995. "Synthesis of adaptive decision systems from experimental data." In *Proceedings of the Fifth Scandinavian Conference on Artificial Intelligence*, edited by A. Aamodt and J. Komorowski. Frontiers in Artificial Intelligence and Applications **28**: 220–238. Amsterdam and Trondheim, Norway: IOS Press.

Wang, P. P. 1995. *Proceedings of the Second Joint Annual Conference on Information Sciences*. Wrightsville Beach, NC.

Wang, P. P., eds. 1997. *Proceedings of the Third Joint Annual Conference on Information Sciences*. Durham, NC.

Wróblewski, J. 1995. "Finding minimal reducts using genetic algorithms." In *Proceedings of the Second Joint Annual Conference on Information Science*, edited by P. P. Wang, pp. 186–189. Durham: Duke University.

Wróblewski, J. 1998. "Genetic algorithms in decomposition and classification problems." In *Rough Sets in Knowledge Discovery 2: Applications, Case Studies and Software Systems*, edited by L. Polkowski, and A. Skowron, pp. 472–492. Heidelberg: Physica-Verlag.

24.1.4 49er

Jan M. Żytkow

ABSTRACT 49er is a knowledge discovery system that conducts large-scale searches for regularities in many forms and combines them into multidimensional theories. The system works on data in one relational tables. Regularities are defined as "pattern P holds in range R." 49er starts from two-dimensional contingency tables. Other patterns are recognized as special cases of contingency tables by simple tests. They include functional and multifunctional relations, approximate equivalence, and preference and subset relations. The costly search in a space of equations, for instance, is conducted only when a functionality test shows the presence of an approximate functional relation. When many regularities in one category are detected, an automated method combines them into a concise multidimensional theory, such as a taxonomy, preference graph, or inclusion graph. Taxonomy construction applies when a large number of two-dimensional patterns represent an approximate equivalence relation. 49er combines several searches. Users can selectively turn them off and can set search parameters to direct the exploration and fit computational resources. The system has been applied to many databases in domains such as engineering, science (biology, neurophysiology), medical insurance, education, public opinion questionnaires, juvenile crime, and personnel recruitment and retention.

1. Introduction

49er was developed and improved over a decade (1989–2000) by Jan Żytkow, currently at UNC Charlotte (zytkow@uncc.edu). The main collaborators are John Baker (1989–1990), Mohamed Jafar (1990–1992), Arun Sanjeev (1991–1997, currently at Aurora Biosciences Co. [SanjeevA@aurorabio.com]), and Robert Zembowicz (1990–1995, currently at Vanguard, Charlotte, NC [robert_zembowicz@vanguard.com]). The system was first described by Żytkow and Baker (1991) and in a user manual (Żytkow et al., 1990).

The first version (49er.a) was developed in 1989–1990. It searched through a space of data subsets for significant contingency tables and linear equations (Żytkow and Baker, 1991). The second version (49er.b), developed in 1991–1993 and expanded in 1994–2000, included a search for equations that was triggered by a functionality test, a search for improved discretization of attributes, and generation of multidimensional patterns (Żytkow and Zembowicz, 1993). Gradually, this version was expanded to recognize approximate equivalence and generate taxonomies (1994), to recognize subset relations and construct subset graphs (1995), to discover multifunctional relations (1995), to generate decision trees through correspondence analysis (1997), and to recognize preference relations and construct preference graphs (1999–2000).

2. Input Data and Knowledge

The data model used by 49er is a single relational table of any number of attributes and any number of records. It is up to the user to prepare a view of the data that fits the available main memory. Numerical, ordered, and nominal attributes can be declared and are treated differently. Missing values are allowed for each attribute. Both missing values and all nonmissing values in each record can be used for knowledge discovery, but the user has an option not to use missing values.

49er can seek regularities for all variables or for any subset determined by the user. In many situations the user knows what variables he can control and what other variables he wants to influence by manipulation of the control variables. He may also suspect that other variables influence the control knowledge. 49er allows the user to reflect that knowledge by selection of control (independent) variables, goal (dependent) variables, and variables used to slice data and build conditions that define the range of regularities.

49er is not integrated with a database management system (DBMS), however, Oracle is often used to maintain a multirelational database and to create views for use by 49er. Since data come in many formats, however, reliance on one DBMS is not practical. Often the work required to establish an Oracle database is prohibitive, while it is easy to prepare a data table for the direct use of 49er. During 49er operation, after data are copied to the main memory, relational algebra operations used internally by 49er (select, project, and aggregate) are much more efficient than if they were done externally under the control of DBMS.

3. Output Knowledge

49er works on a single relational table at a time. Let $A_1, A_2, ..., A_M$ be the attributes, $V_1, V_2, ..., V_M$ be the corresponding sets of values for each attribute. The space W of all possible events (situations) is the Cartesian product $W = V_1 \times V_2 \times ... \times V_M$. W includes all possible combinations of attribute values and is very useful for conceptualization of 49er's search and knowledge.

Regularities discovered by 49er can be expressed in the form:

$$\text{PATTERN in RANGE,} \tag{1}$$

where RANGE describes a subset in W (the entire W as a special case), while PATTERN describes a pattern that holds for the records within the RANGE. More specifically, 49er initially tries regularities in the form:

$$\text{REG}(D, I) \text{ in } P_1(S_1) \& ... \& P_k(S_k), \tag{2}$$

where

- $S_1, ..., S_k, D$, I can be any attributes in $\in \{A_1, ..., A_M\}$; but the user can restrict D to a subset of user-defined dependent (goal) attributes; I to a subset of user-defined independent (control) attributes; $S_1, ..., S_k$ to user-defined attributes used to slice data into subsets.

- $P_i(A_i)$ is either $A_i > a_i$, $A_i \leqslant a_i$, or (for nominal attributes) $A_i = a_i$, where a_i is in V_i.

- REG(D, I) is either a function $D = f(I)$ or is a two-dimensional contingency table for all values of I and D, or is a simple summary contingency table for the upper $(A_i > a_i)$ and lower $(A_i \leqslant a_i)$ values of each attribute A_i in $\{D, I\}$. Contingency tables receive regularity status when they show significant dependence between I and D.

Several types of regularities are detected as special cases of contingency tables, for instance, (approximate) equivalence $A_i(x) \equiv A_j(x)$ and (approximate) subset relations $A_i(x) \Rightarrow A_j(x)$. Several theories, represented in graphical form, can summarize large numbers of simple regularities, for instance, taxonomies summarize many equivalence relations, while subset graphs many subset relations (Troxel et al., 1994; Moraczewski et al., 1995; Zembowicz and Żytkow, 1996).

4. Support for Task and Method Selection

With little preparation 49er can mine any single relational table, running a large-scale search and exploring many types of knowledge. This liberates the user from manual exploratory analysis and provides plenty of knowledge that may be further refined under user guidance.

It is difficult to tell *a priori* which forms of knowledge will occur and which will not occur in a given database. 49er's search is open to many possibilities, but at the same time it can be adjusted to fit within the available resources.

In the 49er approach, contingency tables that demonstrate strong and significant relations are the basic form of two-dimensional regularities. Simple tests applied to contingency tables distinguish various special forms of two-dimensional knowledge, leading to automated selection of tasks in two categories. First, different forms of knowledge may require search in different hypotheses spaces, but if data do not fit any hypothesis in a given space, much time could be saved if that space was not searched at all. We solve this problem by testing nonexistence of solutions in particular spaces, such as a space of equations. The search in a particular space is conducted only if the possibility of a solution is not excluded. The second category of tasks becomes active when many regularities of the same type are discovered in a database. 49er uses tests that classify regularities into different types. Then automated methods combine large numbers of regularities in each type into concise, useful forms of taxonomies, inclusion graphs, and other multidimensional theories.

49er seeks regularities that hold in all data, but if no regularity is discovered for attributes A_i and A_j for all data, patterns will be sought for those attributes in many data subsets.

5. Software Architecture

5.1. User Model

Although 49er can run substantial searches autonomously, users play an important role in the data mining loop. It is very useful to run an automatic, exploratory, and shallow search, examine the results, and decide how to set a large-scale search. The user can also select the most interesting regularities and prepare another, more constrained 49er search, in an attempt to refine them (Żytkow and Zembowicz, 1993).

The user may focus the search on specific subsets of control and goal attributes and on specific attributes used for slicing data into subsets.

5.2. System Modularity

Different elements of a regularity in the form (2) are determined (constructed) by separate search components of 49er. All ranges are produced by the slice-data search. It operates depth-first, starting from all data, then using one attribute at a time to slice data until a user-defined depth is reached or until the number of records in a slice becomes insignificantly small. The search is arranged so that each subrange is considered not more than once and a more general range is considered before its subranges. This is important because the search will stop when a regularity is detected, without trying large numbers of possible specializations of that regularity. Although specializations of a regularity R are worth considering because they can strengthen the predictive power of R, this can be done later, when the user decides to use 49er to seek regularity refinement.

For each data subset generated by the slice-data search, the pick-attributes search generates all pairs of attributes, which will subsequently be considered by the find-patterns search. Useful regularities hold between control (independent) variables and goal (dependent) variables: the values of control variables can be changed by user actions, while changes to the goal variables are desirable, but their values can be only controlled indirectly, throughout control variables. If the goal and control attributes are not provided by the user, all attribute pairs are compared in an exhaustive search. Pairs for which a more general regularity has already been detected are excluded in this phase, as described earlier.

Given a range of data and two attributes, the find-patterns search looks for patterns that fit the right-hand side of a regularity (2). The search starts from patterns in the form of contingency tables. If a table that shows significant dependence between D and I is detected, it is further analyzed by several pattern detection tests that seek functional dependence, equivalence, subset relations, and the like.

Contingency tables include many special cases. Relations are special cases, with a count of zero in some cells. The following partial order with contingency tables on the left shows several special cases considered by 49er:

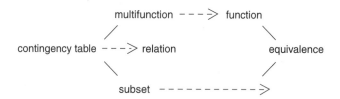

Empirical equations are efficient summaries of data if the data distribution is close to a functional relationship. The search in the space of equations is expensive, so it is better to avoid it altogether on data that are not conducive to functional description. 49er autonomously uses a test that applies to all data sets and is passed only when the data can be approximated by a function (Zembowicz and Żytkow, 1996). Then it looks for equations only on such data, creating a big time saving by skipping many unsuccessful applications of equation finder. 49er uses equation finder (Zembowicz and Żytkow, 1992), a machine discovery system that finds two-dimensional empirical equations from data. Equation finder can detect a broad range of equations useful in different domains. It is applied recursively to find equations for more than two attributes.

Approximate equivalence and subset relations are used to form logic statements, such as $A_i(x) \equiv A_j(x)$ and $A_i(x) \Rightarrow A_j(x)$.

If many such statements are detected, 49er can combine large numbers of those regularities by taxonomy formation modules (Troxel et al., 1994) and subset graph generators (Moraczewski et al., 1995).

5.3. Support for Extendability

49er's modular search and its modular approach to different forms of knowledge make the system easy to expand. If a particular category of patterns that can be recognized in contingency tables is common, then develop criteria that find such tables automatically, and then consider properties of those patterns such as transitivity, to design a specialized theory that combines many tables.

5.4. Performance and Scaling

49er's search is linear in the number of records, quadratic in the number of attributes, and exponential in the number of conditions that describe subranges of data. Since elaborate conditions are not useful or not supported by sufficient data, the search in data subranges is typically shallow and hence feasible.

Search for equations is potentially explosive in terms of candidate equations, so that by default its depth is limited. Depending on the data, up to a few tens of candidate equations are tried. The search is linear in the number of different values of the independent variable that occur in the data, so that it is practically less than linear in the number of records.

49er can search for a long time. Many hours are typical, sometimes it has been used for uninterrupted search several days in a row.

5.5. Platforms

49er can work on any platform that runs Common LISP. For large data sets and large-scale exploration it is important to provide the LISP process with sufficient memory.

5.6. Documentation, Distribution, and Support

Operation of 49er is menu based. Menus provide limited documentation that helps the user understand the meaning of different selections and the data type of user entries. Menus guide the user through preparation of data, allow the key parameters of each search to be set, run 49er, and examine the results.

49er has been distributed individually by zytkow@uncc.edu. Data-mining services and advice are also available.

6. Support of the KDD Process

Menus are designed to guide the user through the knowledge discovery in databases (KDD) process. First they provide help in loading the data and in the entry of background knowledge on the types and roles of different attributes. Menus then provide and explain the options that allow the user to set up search parameters. After the automated search terminates, many menu options guide the examination of the results. Then the same menus can be used to control the repeated process.

Many KDD tasks can be performed within the same framework of discovery. Consider data cleaning and understanding. The user can seek explanation of missing values through contingency tables that show dependencies between missing values of one attribute and values of other attributes. A dependency that holds for missing values may reveal the reasons for which those values are missing.

Wrong values may reveal themselves as exceptions to regularities—patterns. When the same record occurs as an outlier in many contingency tables or other patterns, it is very likely that some of its values are wrong and it is often straightforward to find which value it is.

7. Visualization and Result Presentation

Contingency tables are a useful tool for pattern visualization, engaging the user's pattern recognition mechanisms and allowing the user to decide on the most useful description. In the 49er approach, many relations are initially and uniformly represented as contingency tables, while some are also represented in a concise language of first-order logic. Typically, the logic statements are approximate, so that by comparison of a statement and the corresponding contingency table, the user may decide whether the approximation has been stretched too far.

49er combines many regularities into graphs and tables, subset graphs, and taxonomies (Troxel et al., 1994; Moraczewski et al., 1995), which are useful visualization tools.

8. Main Applications

49er has been applied to many databases in domains such as engineering (Moczulski and Żytkow, 1997), biology (Moraczewski et al., 1995), neurophysiology, medical insurance, education (Sanjeev and Żytkow, 1996), public opinion questionnaires, juvenile crime, and personnel recruitment and retention. In each case, it discovered from hundreds to many thousands of regularities. Especially in scientific and medical domains and in dealing with questionnaires, some of the detected regularities could be combined into taxonomies and subset or preference graphs.

References

Moczulski, W., and J. Żytkow. 1997. "Automated search for knowledge on machinery diagnostics." In *Proceedings of the Sixth Symposium on Intelligent Information Systems*: Polish Academy of Sciences.

Moraczewski, I., R. Zembowicz, and J. M. Żytkow. 1995. "Geobotanical database exploration." In *Working Notes of the AAAI Spring Symposium on Systematic Methods of Scientific Discovery*, pp. 76–80.

Sanjeev, A., and J. M. Żytkow. 1996. "A study of enrollment and retention in a university database." *J. Mid-America Assoc. Educat. Opportunity Prog. Personnel* 8: 24–41.

Troxel, M., K. Swarm, R. Zembowicz, and J. M. Żytkow. 1994. "Concept hierarchies: a restricted form of knowledge derived from regularities." In *Proceedings of Methodologies for Intelligent Systems*, edited by M. Zemankova, and Z. Ras. Germany: Springer-Verlag, pp. 437–447.

Zembowicz, R., and J. Żytkow. 1996. "From contingency tables to various forms of knowledge in databases." In *Advances in Knowledge Discovery and Data Mining*, edited by U. Fayyad, G. Piatetsky-Shapiro, P. Smyth, and R. Uthurusamy, pp. 329–349. Menlo Park, CA: AAAI Press.

Żytkow, J., and J. Baker. 1991. "Interactive mining of regularities in databases." In *Knowledge Discovery in Databases*, edited by G. Piatetsky-Shapiro, and W. Frawley, pp. 31–53. Menlo Park, CA: AAAI Press.

Żytkow, J., and R. Zembowicz. 1993. "Database exploration in search of regularities." *J. Intell. Inform. Sys.* **2**: 39–81.

Żytkow, J., J. Baker, M. Jafar, and T. Tjong. 1990. "Database analyzer; user instruction." Technical Report. Computer Science Department, Wichita State University.

24.2 Commercial Multiple Mining Task Systems

24.2.1 Clementine

Colin Shearer and Peter Caron

ABSTRACT Launched in 1994, SPSS' Clementine was one of the first commercially available tools for data mining. Clementine uses an interface style known as visual programming in which numerous tools used in different stages of the data mining process are represented by icons that are strung together to form visual streams of data mining solutions. Streams can include machine learning and other modeling technologies, data access facilities, record and field manipulation, interactive visualization, conventional analyses, and reporting. The main aim of Clementine was to put data mining in the hands of business users, rather than just technology specialists. This is achieved partly by the easy-to-learn visual programming interface, and also by insulating users from technology details; by default, the modeling algorithms are automatically configured to suit a given data set. Clementine has also proved popular with more sophisticated power analyst users. For them, the visual programming environment provides a highly productive, fluent environment. Compared to a component-based approach, the proportion of the analysts' time needed for noncore tasks such as data manipulation and transformation is reduced, freeing them to concentrate on building models to solve problems. Both types of users value Clementine's openness, which enables integration with existing IT infrastructure, and comprehensive approaches to scalability and deployment of solutions. These approaches take into account all the stages in the data mining process so that, for example, data processing steps are scaled and all steps are exported for deploying solutions to decision makers. Clementine is used by hundreds of organizations worldwide, in sectors including finance, retail, telecommunications, government, and manufacturing. Many applications involve marketing and other aspects of customer relationship management (CRM), but the product has also been used to tackle data mining problems such as product quality analyses, toxicity prediction, and fraud detection.

1. Introduction

Clementine is developed by SPSS Inc., 233 S. Wacker Drive, Chicago, IL 60606, USA (Telephone: (312)-651-3000; Web: www.spss.com).

Development work began in 1992, and the first commercial version of Clementine was shipped in October 1994, with the first implementation of the visual programming environment and a core set of algorithms and functionality. Version 2 added new algorithms, notably Kohonen networks (Kohonen, 1989) for clustering. Version 3 provided ODBC connectivity. Clementine Version 4 added algorithms for association detection and generalized rule induction and a host of other features, and won the Information Age Product of the Year Award in 1997. Version 5, shipped in October 1998, added K-means clustering (MacQueen, 1967) and radial basis function networks and stresses the theme of open data mining. Users could now incorporate their own algorithms and tools, data mining tasks could be automated and embedded in other applications, and interfaces to SPSS and Microsoft Excel were provided. In September 1999, an update to Version 5 added a distributed architecture (Clementine Server) that provided scalable performance across large data sets with a comprehensive approach to scalability that leverages conventional relational databases to speed up all stages in the data mining process. About the same time, a new product, Clementine Solution Publisher, was released. Clementine Solution Publisher drastically cut the time and cost of delivering data mining solutions by exporting the entire process (instead of just models) as C code and embedded SQL.

2. Input

Clementine can access data from any ODBC-compliant data source, retrieving tuples from existing tables and views or using arbitrary SQL queries. Data from extract files in delimiter-based (e.g., CSV) or columnar formats can also be used. There is no concept of migration of data into a Clementine-specific format, although data can be saved in a cache file for faster loading. Multiple data sources can be accessed within a single Clementine visual program. A merge facility joins multiple sources.

3. Output Knowledge

All forms of output—graphs, tables, rule displays, analyses—may be saved as text or bitmapped graphics, or exported as HTML. A project control tool supports collation of output fragments into draft HTML reports. Results data can be written to delimiter-based files or to any ODBC-compliant database.

Visual programs generated by Clementine may be exported as ANSI-standard C code and embedded SQL. This code can be compiled and deployed on other platforms, often for use with other applications. Uses of exported models range from distribution of interactive decision support applications to real-time interception of transactions in mainframe environments to embedded deployment in e-commerce and other Web-based applications.

4. System Architecture

Clementine is controlled through a sophisticated graphical user interface using a metaphor known as visual programming. Pallettes of icons represent tools for accessing data; for manipulating (e.g., pre- or postprocessing) data; for visualizing data; for running machine learning and other modeling algorithms; for reporting on data and results, and for exporting data from the system.

The current set of tools in the core Clementine package (grouped by Clementine palette) comprises:

- Inputting data from ODBC-compliant sources, columnar files, delimiter-structured files, and Clementine's own cache-storage format.

- Selecting, sampling, merging, sorting, and aggregating records; filtering duplicate (or partial duplicate) records; correcting skewed data samples.

- Projecting and renaming fields; entering field information; deriving new fields; recognizing and replacing missing or erroneous values; extracting historical values; mapping set members to flag fields.

- Scatter and line plots; distribution displays; histograms and collections (histograms with numeric overlay); Web (strength of connection) displays, multi- and uni-directional; multiplots, typically used to show multiple values changing over time.

- Tables and cross-tabulations; descriptive statistics; model results analysis; template-based reports; global value calculation; data quality analysis; file and ODBC output.

Modeling algorithms are described below. A further palette, initially empty, holds icons representing generated models.

Users work on a large central workspace, placing icons from the palettes, connecting them to specify data flow and sequencing of operations, and editing their attributes and settings using dialogue boxes associated with each icon.

A rich expression language known as CLEM, comprising about 200 functions and operators, supports selection and derivation operations. CLEM includes standard arithmetic and math functions; string handling; date and time manipulation; and a set of functions which supports time-series or other sequential data by reasoning about values across sequences of records.

Clementine is designed to support a highly interactive style of data mining, maximizing user involvement, which is critical for ensuring the data mining process effectively solves business problems. People, not models, ultimately determine whether results are relevant and actionable. Once users have created visual programs, however, these can be packaged (along with scripts for fine control of execution and process automation) for batch execution outside of the graphical environment.

Clementine Version 5 introduced the ability to add a user's own tools—algorithms, manipulations, visualizations, statistics, etc.—to Clementine's visual programming environment. This makes the system an open platform for data mining, allowing users to benefit from the visual data flow paradigm without restricting them to a fixed set of tools.

5. Search for Knowledge

Clementine's discovery algorithms include:

- Multilayer perceptron (MLP) neural networks trained by backpropagation (Rumelhart and McLelland, 1986).
- Radial basis function networks (Broomhead and Lowe, 1988).
- C5.0 decision tree/rule set induction. (Precursor described by Quinlan, 1993).
- A proprietary ID3 (Quinlan, 1983) derivative, enhanced to estimate numeric values.
- Kohonen self-organizing map (Kohonen, 1989) for clustering.
- K-means clustering (MacQueen, 1967).
- GRI, a proprietary generalized rule induction algorithm. (Precursor described by Mallen and Bramer, 1995).
- The A priori algorithm for association detection (Agrawal et al., 1996).
- Linear regression modeling.

Most of these algorithms have three levels of operation. By default, configuration is automatic, based on Clementine applying rules of thumb to the data. A first level of manual control allows the user to specify high-level strategies, while an expert level gives access to all control parameters.

Clementine's analysis tool provides a range of predefined evaluations of model test results. As well as reporting on the performance of individual models, the tool analyzes the combined performance of models where two or more models that predict the same value have been placed in the same visual program. Combining models—for example, having the outputs of a trained neural network and an induced decision tree work together to support a particular decision—is straightforward, as are other normally complex tasks such as building models whose inputs include the outputs of (possibly many) others.

None of the algorithms in Clementine makes use of explicit background knowledge. Typically, users enter their knowledge by creating new variables that they believe may be relevant, and these variables are available for use by the modeling algorithms. This knowledge entry is often implicit, the user interacting with graphical displays to specify, say, interesting thresholds or groupings which are then automatically translated into variable definitions.

6. User

Clementine is aimed at business-oriented users rather than technologists. The visual programming interface makes the system accessible even to those with limited IT expertise, while the default automatic configuration and management of modeling algorithms insulates such users from technology details (Khabaza and Shearer, 1995).

The system has also proved extremely popular with power users with a much stronger technical background. The main benefit such users experience is a substantial boost in productivity from a fluent environment which integrates a wide range of tools and greatly reduces the need for time-consuming data manipulation and transformation.

7. KDD Process

Clementine's visual programming style can be thought of as visualization of the KDD process. Users draw the process of accessing data, preprocessing it, exploring, modeling from it, evaluating, and applying the results. SPSS was a partner in the consortium that developed and published the industry-standard CRISP-DM data mining process model. Clementine's project tool helps users to organize their work according to the CRISP-DM phases.

8. The Scope of Application Domains

Clementine is a generic data mining tool, not tied to specific sectors or domains. The system has been applied in a wide range of industries, including finance, retail, telecommunications, manufacturing, pharmaceuticals, government, defense, and utilities.

Application-specific stream templates provide a starting point for common applications in particular industries. Templates aimed at telecommunications and e-CRM applications are planned for the next version of Clementine.

9. Visualization and Knowledge Presentation

In addition to a wide range of conventional visualizations (plots, histograms, distribution displays, etc.), Clementine includes a Web tool that produces a graphical display of the strength of relationships in a database. All visualization displays are interactive: users can select interesting regions, outliers, relationships, etc. using the mouse. These can be the basis of selection queries, or they can generate new variables representing, for example, inclusion in a cluster.

Clementine provides textual browsers for models produced by its discovery algorithms (decision trees, rule sets, association rules, etc.). These are interactive: for example, all records corresponding to a specified branch of a decision tree can be fetched.

10. Advantages

Clementine's main strengths are its visual programming interface; the breadth of its support for the data mining process; the ability to combine multiple modeling techniques for a best-fit solution; the export of decision-support models as deployable program code; and its openness in exchanging data and intercalling with other applications and modules.

11. Disadvantages

Most of Clementine's modeling technology is derived from artificial intelligence; traditional statistical techniques are underrepresented. This is addressed, however, by a full link to SPSS, which allows any statistical routines or modeling techniques to be invoked from within Clementine. Closer integration with statistical procedures is planned for the next release of the product.

12. Example of Usage

The following condensed case study illustrates how the Clementine user works through the data mining process to reach a solution. Figure 1 shows the Clementine workbench, with palettes of icons representing tools for use in different stages of the data mining process. Streams are constructed in the large central workspace.

In this application, a bank is modeling sales of a new investment product (in this case, an ISA). The aim is to identify factors associated with purchasing (or not purchasing) this product, and to predict accurately which customers are the best prospects for it. Figure 2 shows initial connection to the data, which is from a test marketing exercise in which the bank attempted to sell the product to a sample of customers; some bought, and many did not. The table shows a simple display of the records. The Web graph uses line thickness to show strength of connection between having a certain number of children and buying an ISA. People with 0 or 1 children appear to be good prospects; people with three children are very unlikely to buy. This is followed by a plot of income versus number of children, with purchase overlayed. This shows a fairly clean relationship: those with more children need to have a higher income to be able to afford this product.

In Figure 3, based on what was discovered by visualization, the user has created a new variable, ScaledIncome, which is the ratio of income to number of children. Moving to the modeling phase, the user defines ISA as the output or target field for models using a type node. Two modeling algorithms—a neural network and C5.0's decision tree induction—are run, producing the gem icons that represent the generated models. Here we can see the C5.0 model being browsed, showing the decision tree.

Figure 4 shows the models being evaluated on unseen test data. The analysis tool provides figures for the individual models and their combined performance. In this case, the best performance is obtained by combining models.

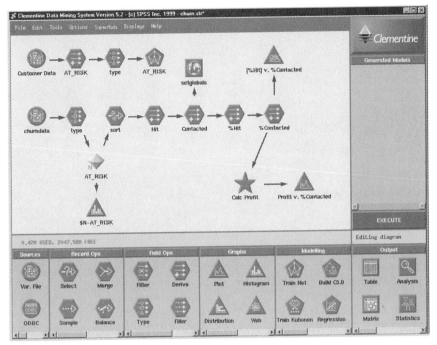

Figure 1 The Clementine Workbench

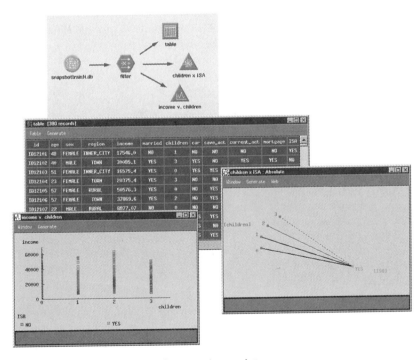

Figure 2 Record display: initial connection to data

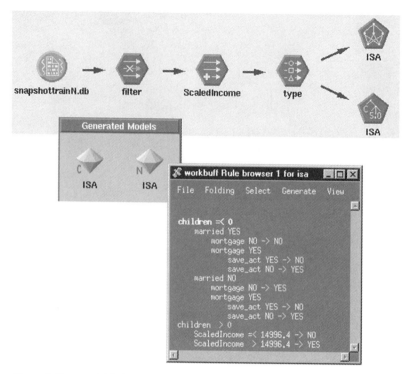

Figure 3 New variable based on visualization discovery

Finally, Figure 5 shows the models being applied to yield business results—in this case, a ranked list of best prospects. Records of customers who have not previously been offered this product are fed through the models. Cases where the models agree are selected, and a score is calculated by combining the models' confidence scores. On a histogram of the score, the user

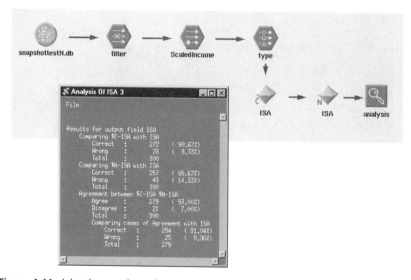

Figure 4 Models when evaluated on unseen test data

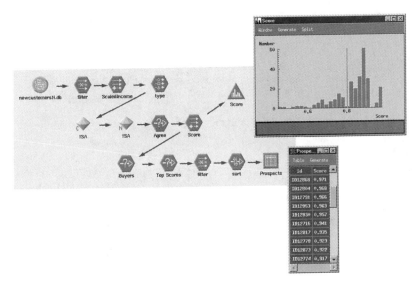

Figure 5 Models when applied to yield business results

places a threshold that generates a selection operation to select the highest-scoring prospects from those cases where the models' combined decision is that they should buy. The selected prospects are ranked by score, and their account numbers and scores displayed; in reality, they would probably be written back to the customer database to form the basis of a marketing campaign.

13. Typical Applications

Across industries, many Clementine applications fall into the category of customer relationship management (CRM). This encompasses customer acquisition (response modeling, profitability prediction, risk scoring), relationship development (cross-selling/up-selling, customer base segmentation and profiling, fraud detection), and retention (churn management).

The system has been used in a wide range of other applications. These include analyzing personnel data; predicting equipment failure to schedule preemptive maintenance; siting retail stores; predicting toxicity of new consumer products, as an alternative to animal testing; cleaning online financial data; predicting electricity demand; giving early warning of possible pollution incidents; and many more (Shearer, 1995).

14. Hardware Implementations

Clementine clients are available on Windows 95, 98, NT, and 2000. Clementine Server is available on Windows NT, 2000, and the most popular Unix platforms: Sun Solaris, HP-UX, and AIX.

15. State of the Art

SPSS is a leader in delivering data analysis capabilities and forging industry standards in data mining and statistics. SPSS runs a wide-ranging program of solo and collaborative research and development, which feeds into the Clementine product line. SPSS is a founding member of the Data Mining Group, which is forging the PMML standard for XML delivery of models.

CRISP-DM (CRoss-Industry Standard Process for Data Mining—Esprit Project 24959) is an initiative to standardize and publish the data mining process model. A core consortium comprising SPSS, Daimler-Benz, NCR, and OHRA has developed and validated the process model, advised and supported by a Special Interest Group of over two hundred data mining vendors, data warehousing suppliers, systems integrators, management consultants, large-scale commercial users, and other interested parties. Clementine includes a process-level CRISP support tool.

MIMIC (Esprit Project 26749) is developing a set of tools and techniques for mining log data representing users' interactions with virtual shopping malls and other e-commerce facilities. The resulting technology, a sequence association algorithm now developed by MINEit Software, is being sold for use with Clementine for finding patterns in Web data and for use in other applications.

ALADIN (Esprit Project 28623) aims to add inductive logic programming to Clementine.

References

Agrawal, R., H. Mannila, R. Srikant, H. Toivonen, and A. I. Verkamo. 1996. "Fast discovery of association rules." In *Advances in Knowledge Discovery and Data Mining*, edited by U. Fayyad, G. Piatetsky-Shapiro, P. Smyth, and R. Uthurusamy: AAAI Press.

Broomhead, D. S., and D. Lowe. 1988. "Multivariable function interpolation and adaptive networks." *Complex Sys.* **2**: 321–355.

Khabaza, T., and C. Shearer. 1995. "Data mining by data owners: presenting advanced technology to non-technologists through the Clementine system." In *Proceedings of Intelligent Data Analysis '95*. Baden-Baden: IIAS Press.

Kohonen, T. 1989. *Self-organisation and Associative Memory*. 3d ed: Springer-Verlag.

MacQueen, J. 1967. "Some methods for classification and analysis of multivariate observations." *Proceedings of the Fifth Berkeley Symposium on Mathematics, Statistics and Probability*, edited by L. M. LeCam, and J. Neyman. Berkeley: University of California Press.

Mallen J. and M. Bramer. 1995. "Cupid—utilising domain knowledge in knowledge discovery." Presented at *Expert Systems XI*, Cambridge.

Quinlan, J. R. 1983. "Learning efficient classification procedures." In *Machine Learning: An Artificial Intelligence Approach*, edited by Michalski, Carbonnel, and Mitchell. Tioga Press.

Quinlan, J. R. 1993. *C4.5: Programs for Machine Learning*: Morgan Kaufmann.

Rumelhart, D. E., and J. L. McClelland. 1986. *Parallel Distributed Processing*: MIT Press.

Shearer, C. 1995. "User-driven data mining applications." Presented at *Unicom Data Mining Seminar*, London.

Further Reading

Clementine User Guide and *Clementine Reference Manual*, SPSS Inc.

24.2.2 Data Surveyor

Arno Siebes

ABSTRACT   Data Surveyor is the collective name of a collection of data mining products. On the one hand, there are the tools that are geared toward the expert data miner, on the other hand there are tools that are for the business end user. The tools for the expert are such that the knowledge discovery in databases (KDD) process is supported as far as possible. The best example of this is the extensive support the user gets in the creation of the mining table. Moreover, the expert tool is set up in such a way as to stimulate interactive data mining. The tools for the end users are built with business applications in mind. That their solution uses data mining is immaterial to the business end user. Using the expert tool, the expert can implement data mining scenarios into the tools of the end user so that the end user will only have to focus on the problems he knows about: the business problems.

1. Introduction

Data Distilleries (DD) started in 1995 as a spinoff company of the CWI, the Dutch national research center in mathematics and computer science. In 1999, DD employed thirty people and was the leading provider of data mining products and consultancy in the Netherlands.

Data Surveyor is the collective name for the data-mining products DD develops and markets. Currently, these products are the Expert Suite and the Customer Care Suite. The mining engine is a complete new implementation based on prototypes developed in the ESPRIT IV project KESO. In addition to DD, developing partners in that project were the data mining groups at CWI, GMD, and the University of Helsinki.

The Expert Suite consists of the Mining Application Server and Expert/Surveyor. The Mining Application Server is the mining engine of the system. That is, it implements the mining algorithms and can be used to store the data on which one wants to mine. The MAS will be described in more detail in Section 2. Expert/Surveyor is the front-end tool for expert users and supports the KDD process interactively and online. Moreover, it allows scenarios to be built for the business user applications of the Customer Care Suite. Expert/Surveyor will be described in Section 3.

The Customer Care Suite, comprising business solutions for end users, consists of several products for application areas. At the moment these are Mailshot/Surveyor, Retention/Surveyor, Xsell/Surveyor, Credit/Surveyor, and Upsell/Surveyor. This suite will be described in Section 4.

This article on Data Surveyor can only give you a snapshot that describes the product suite. However, the main message of this article is the underlying philosophy of the products. This philosophy will remain more or less the same for a long time. For up-to-date information, the reader is referred to the company's Web site: http://www.datadistelleries.com.

2. System Architecture

As explained in the introduction, the Mining Application Server (MAS) is the mining engine of Data Surveyor. One of the main ideas in the architecture of the MAS is that a basic mining algorithm is concerned with just a few components. First, there is a description language in which the models can be expressed. Second, there is a quality function that determines how well a model fits (part of) the database. Finally, there is a search algorithm, which consists of a search strategy (e.g., hill climbing or genetic search) and one or more search operators that generate new models from existing models. An example of the latter is a neighbor operator for the hill-climbing search strategy.

This idea is reflected directly in the architecture of the MAS, which contains a search manager, a description generator, and a quality computer. More complex data mining algorithms consist of a number of such basic algorithms, for example, a tree induction algorithm may employ an algorithm for on-the-fly discretization of continues attributes and another algorithm to prune the resulting tree. The orchestration of these different basic algorithms is done by the mining conductor (see Siebes, 1996, for more details).

An important aspect of this modular approach toward the implementation of mining algorithms is that the different components communicate via a database. That is, all intermediate results as well as their construction history are maintained in a database. In other words, the search space, as far as explored, is maintained in a database. This aspect not only facilitates interactive mining, but also ensures that the user can always return to an arbitrary point in the search and continue in some other direction.

The MAS actually contains more algorithms than the user can employ using the interface. The main reason for this is that it is little work to implement a new algorithm in the MAS, but it requires a lot of work to design and implement a good user interface for that algorithm. The algorithms that the user can employ are for decision rules, decision lists, decision trees, and association rules. Among those that are not yet supported by the interface are Bayesian networks.

In addition to the mining engine, the MAS also supports the storage of the mining table. This capability is based on the main memory database engine Monet (see, e.g., Boncz and Kersten, 1995; Boncz et al., 1996). Monet is based on vertical partitioning, that is, the data is stored columnwise. It has been shown in Holsheimer et al. (1996) and by others that such a storage structure is highly beneficial for data mining. Moreover, Monet has built-in primitives for data-mining, such as the data cube operator and performs multiquery optimization (see Siebes and Kersten, 1997, for the benefits of this). As an aside, note that the search space is also stored in Monet.

One can import data from Oracle databases, file systems, and ODBC-compliant database management systems (DBMSs) in a straightforward way (see the next section). For Oracle 8, a special data cartridge called the Mining Booster has been developed that allows mining on Oracle directly. Basically, the Mining Booster adds that functionality of Monet to Oracle that allows for efficient data mining.

3. KDD Process

Expert/Surveyor is the interface to the MAS that is tailored toward the expert user. This is the interface that supports the KDD process.

Data mining in Expert/Surveyor is organized along projects. One project may have many mining questions, but they all have to use the same mining table. The construction of this table is supported by Expert/Surveyor.

A project is visualized in the interface by a project window. Such a project window consists of different layers. Bottom up, these are the following:

Source back end. In this layer, the user clarifies the types of the data sources that are to be used in the mining. The types supported at the moment are Oracle databases, file systems, and ODBC-compliant DBMSs.

Source data sources. In this layer, the user gives the actual sources to be used. So, if Oracle is used, the correct Oracle databases are selected.

Source data sets. In this layer, the user selects which data sets within the sources are actually used. That is, which tables in the database or which files in the file system are to be used.

Source schema. In this layer, the schema that connects the different source data sets is specified. That is, it gives the logical tables (i.e., the source data sets) and their relationships as customary in many database design formalisms. Note, that as far as these details are known within the sources, this schema is generated automatically. For data sets from different sources, one has to add such links by hand.

While working in this layer, the user can at any time view the properties and the contents of that data set. So, one can see which attributes a table has, the tuples in that table, but also the distribution of the values of an attribute, for example, via histograms.

A very important feature of this layer is that one can add new, derived attributes to existing tables. The expression editor is the tool with which these new attributes can be created.

As a final step in this layer, one has to create a mining table since the algorithms in Data Surveyor currently all expect only one table. To do this, one can create a new table in which all the relevant attributes are copied (note that the implicit joins are computed along the links selected by the user).

Mining questions. In this layer, the user can formulate all of his or her mining questions. This is done by entering the algorithm, the quality, the mining table, and the (optional) selection on that mining table. Note that such a mining question could consist of only one step in a complete algorithm. That is, the user can mine interactively.

Mining answers. By executing mining questions, mining answers are generated. Interactive mining means that one switches back between this layer and the previous one. One determines a question, inspects the results, and then extends the initial question, and so on.

Models. All the intermediate results that are found can be annotated. In fact, all the steps taken so far have plenty of scope for annotation. By annotating steps on the way, the user automatically creates the documentation of his or her mining process.

The results that the user wants to be used can be selected and copied to the model layer. For specific applications, there are layers that allow the user to export these models to that application.

In general, creating the right data set is the most time-consuming step in the whole KDD process. The ease with which the user can go back and forth through the various layers of an Expert/Surveyor as well as the various tools offered in these layers do make this task a lot simpler. It almost forces the user to use the tool in an interactive way.

4. Application Domains

Clearly, Expert/Surveyor can be used for any application for which the algorithms it offers are sufficient. Moreover, if necessary, more algorithms can be implemented rather simply. However, the selection of algorithms is not the only factor that is important for a given application. Just as, or even more, important is the intended user.

Another important set of programs in the Data Surveyor family are those in the Customer Care Suite. Whereas the intended user of the Expert Suite is the experienced data miner, the intended user of the products in the Customer Care Suite is the domain expert. The basic idea behind this is that many mining tasks will be performed often in basically the same settings.

The idea is then that an expert user uses Expert/Surveyor, together with a domain expert, to determine the right settings for a problem at hand. For example, what sources to use, what derived attributes, what the final mining table is, and what the optimal parameters for the algorithms are. If both the expert and the domain expert are satisfied by the results, all settings are frozen into a scenario. This scenario can be loaded into the products in the Customer Care Suite, and a domain expert mines the data via such a product.

The main difference is that for this domain expert this mining will be done automatically. The Customer Care Suite products are in the language of the end user rather than in terms of data mining. With the Mailshot/Surveyor, the marketeer determines which groups to send a mailing to, based on the costs and the expected results. These expected results are based on the models that Mailshot/Surveyor will generate automatically for him based on the implemented scenario.

Other products in this suite are Retention/Surveyor for customer loyalty, Xsell/Surveyor for cross-selling, and Credit/Surveyor for credit scoring and credit control. More products will be added to the suite upon customer demand.

References

Boncz, P. A., and M. L. Kersten. July 1995. "Monet: an impressionist sketch of an advanced database system." In *Proceedings of the Basque International Workshop on Information Technology*. San Sebastian, Spain.

Boncz, P. A., W. Quak, and M. L. Kersten. June 1996. "Monet and its geographical extensions: a novel approach to high-performance GIS processing." In *Proceedings of the EDBT'96*. Avignon, France, pp. 147–166.

Holsheimer, M., M. Kersten, and A. Siebes. 1996. "Data surveyor: searching the nuggets in parallel." In *Advances in Knowledge Discovery and Data Mining*, pp. 447–467. AAAI/MIT Press.

Siebes, A. 1996. "Data mining and the KESO project." In *SOFSEM'96: Theory and practice of Informatics*. Lecture Notes in Computer Science, **1775**: 161–177: Springer-Verlag.

Siebes, A., and A. L. Kersten. 1997. "KESO: minimizing database interaction." In *Proceedings of the KDD-97*, pp. 102–107.

24.2.3 Kepler and Descartes

Stefan Wrobel, Gennady Andrienko, Natalia Andrienko, and Andrea Lüthje

ABSTRACT   Kepler is an extensible data mining platform that supports the entire knowledge discovery process from data access and preparation to analysis and visualization. One of its particular strengths is its open plug-in architecture, which allows third-party developers to easily integrate analysis tools and to import formats or preprocessing operators without the need to re-implement existing software. A large number of popular analysis algorithms can be used as Kepler plug-ins, including such classics as regression, decision trees, association rules, and clustering, as well as instance-based methods, Bayesian approaches, and subgroup discovery. Furthermore, Kepler is able to work with data that is stored in more than one table. Foreign links can be defined and used by several analysis techniques. For most of the tasks mentioned above, both single-relational and multirelational plug-ins are available. Kepler is scriptable, and thus, a good workbench for analysts and developers. Kepler employs a Java client and features a three-tier architecture that links to relational databases. The architecture allows specialized vertical data mining solutions to be constructed in domains such as marketing/finance, electronic commerce, and science/engineering. The analysis of geographically referenced data is now also possible through a link to the Descartes interactive geographical data exploration environment.

1. Introduction

Kepler's plug-in concept was designed by the data mining group of GMD, the German National Research Center for Information Technology, and published at the 1996 KDD conference (Wrobel et al., 1996). Following user requests, the research prototype was reimplemented and extended into a product by GMD and Dialogis.

2. Support of the KDD Process

Kepler supports data import, preprocessing, and actual analysis through an intuitive graphical user interface. With the optional fine tuning of parameters, the system is as suitable for data mining experts as it is for application domain experts.

2.1. Input Data and Knowledge

Data from a variety of ASCII formats as well as SPSS® and dBase® formats can be imported into Kepler. Data can also be imported via JDBC/ODBC from a wide variety of database systems, or natively from an Oracle® database. Naturally, data can also be exported in these formats.

   Kepler is based on the data model of relational databases (RDBMS), and therefore it allows multiple interlinked tables to be analyzed (Wrobel, 1999). Tables can reside in Kepler's internal persistent storage or can be linked to tables from multiple RDBMS servers, allowing manipulation of internal and external data in the same environment. In addition, Kepler allows the definition and utilization of nontabular background knowledge in textual or special purpose formats, as sometimes required by multirelational and other special purpose analysis algorithms.

   At present, in the SPIN! project (see section 3.2), GMD is working on the next generation of data analysis software for spatial and nonspatial data, and the resulting software will ultimately be an integrated successor to Kepler and Descartes. (Please contact GMD for details on availability: GMD AiS, Schloß Birlinghorne, 53754 Sarkt Augustin, Germany, http://ais.gmd.de)

   Kepler's ability to analyze multirelational data is quite unique in the field of data mining tools. Of course, this type of analysis is just an option, and it does not interfere with the analysis of propositionally represented data. Any single relational table can be analyzed with a multitude of analysis methods.

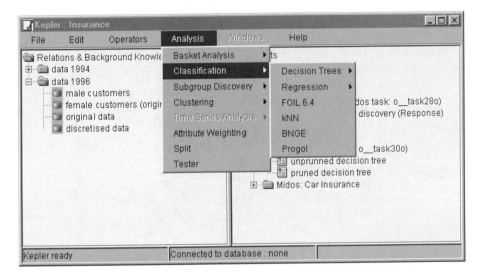

Figure 1 Data mining methods in Kepler.

2.2. *Organization and Output of Knowledge*

The top-level organizational entity in KEPLER is a workspace (see Figure 1). The workspace includes every part of the current application: data in original and transformed versions, background knowledge, and results. Everything in a workspace can be edited and stored in a user-preferred manner in a system of folders so that previous steps can be overviewed easily at any point in time.

Kepler has general task-oriented mechanisms for managing and documenting the results generated by analysis tools, preprocessing operators, and input formats. The kind of output knowledge depends on the plug-ins that are used.

2.3. *Exploration*

Kepler offers a variety of methods for the exploration of data. Overview statistics and graphics help to examine the distribution of attribute values and the overall properties of the data to be analyzed. The special plug-in operator InfoZoom® (Spenke and Beilken, 1999) allows inspection of the characteristics and interactions between attributes in a style similar to the parallel coordinates style through an interactive zoom in and zoom out mechanism.

Geographical data can be explored via interactive cartographic visualization with the Descartes system (see Section 3 below).

2.4. *Preprocessing*

Preprocessing is supported by plug-in operators. A set of standard operators is supplied which includes:

- PowerQuery: point-and-click construction of conjunctive multirelational SQL queries, including data selection, computation of new attributes, replacing specific attribute values, and sampling of large data sets (random or nonrandom).
- aggregation of instances that agree on certain attributes.
- discretization of continuous attributes (Figure 2).
- user-defined transformations in a logical script language.

The user can interactively input preprocessing procedures in Kepler's script language, which is based on standard Prolog, or code them as new plug-in operators. Each preprocessing (and analysis) step is maintained as a task that can be inspected, repeated, and documented.

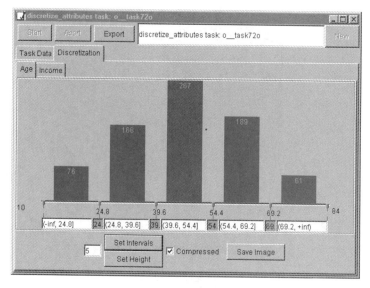

Figure 2 Discretization with Kepler: the graphical presentation can be changed by moving the sliders, editing boundary values or interval sizes

2.5. Data Mining Tasks Supported by the System

All tasks from data access and preparation to analysis and visualization are extensible with plug-ins. Currently, plug-in interfaces (wrappers) are available in Kepler for prediction, classification, clustering, subgroup discovery, and association rule discovery tools. Several tools are included with the system or are available directly from Dialogis; others are third-party tools available from their respective developers.

In order to conduct these tasks, different data mining techniques are required. The algorithms usable in Kepler as plug-ins produce

- regression formulas and trees,
- decision trees,
- classification rules,
- association rules,
- clustering, and
- subgroup descriptions.

Many of these result types are supported by interactive visualizations.

Automated batch preprocessing and analysis are possible through scripting at the task level. Prediction and classification results can be evaluated by testing of the training and/or separate test data, and further evaluation methods can be integrated as plug-ins.

2.6. Support for Task and Method Selection

The Kepler documentation describes standard methods and approaches for using the system and its plug-in algorithms, and it recommends starting points for analysis. Specialized guides are being developed for individual application domains.

2.7. Visualization, Result Presentation, and Export

Results are presented and visualized in a task-oriented fashion, always allowing easy access to the task that created a particular result. Each plug-in can specify how its results are to be visualized. For this purpose, plug-in developers can rely on Kepler's built-in functions for visualizing decision trees, classification rules, association rules, and subgroup discovery results.

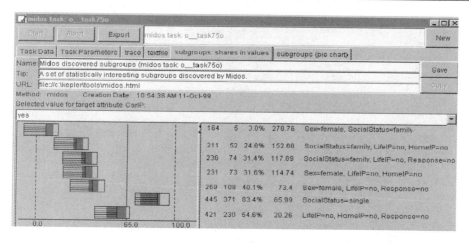

Figure 3 Subgroup discovery with Midos (Wrobel, 1997) discovers interesting deviations in the distribution of a target attribute: subgroups defined by combinations of values of independent attributes are evaluated. The most interesting are selected based on their size and unusualness of their distribution

Figure 3 shows the visualization of a subgroup discovery result, while Figure 4 shows the interactive graphical display produced by Kepler's plug-in wrapper for the popular decision tree software C4.5 (Quinlan, 1993; http://www.cse.unsw.EDU.AU/~quinlan/).

Different views and several display options help the user to explore results, and every result can be exported as an image for further presentation. Results can also be exported as Java applets, allowing for the interactive presentation of the results in the Internet or Intranet without the need for the entire data mining system to be accessible in this manner.

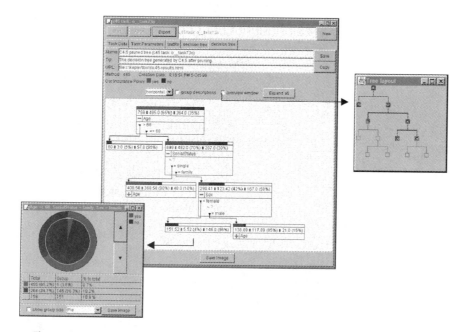

Figure 4 Decision-tree result with tree overview and detailed information for one leaf

3. Geographic Data-Mining with Descartes and Kepler

Geographic information systems (GIS) and knowledge discovery in databases have been developed as two separate technologies until now. Recently, as organizations have accumulated huge databases with a high percentage of geographically referenced data, they have begun to recognize the enormous potential of information hidden in these databases. Applying data mining technologies to geographic information systems is now extremely relevant for most commercial applications. Current results of our integration of the geographic information (analysis) system, Descartes, and the data mining workbench, Kepler, are very promising. The following examples analyze macrodata (small geographical units as analysis objects). The integration is currently extended to geographically referenced microdata (e.g., persons living in districts).

3.1. Descartes: A Tool for Exploratory Visual Analysis of Spatial Data

Descartes (Andrienko and Andrienko, 1999a) provides two unique features:

1. Intelligent mapping support.
2. A wide spectrum of functions for the interactive visual analysis of spatially referenced data.

Descartes automates the generation of maps presenting user-selected data, and it supports various interactive manipulations of map displays that can help to reveal visually important features of the spatial distribution of data. Descartes also supports some data transformations effective for visual analysis, such as dynamic computing of derived variables by means of logical queries and arithmetic operations over existing variables.

Fundamentally speaking, both Kepler and Descartes are designed to serve the same goal: acquiring knowledge from data. Kepler and Descartes are complementary instruments with a high potential for synergy.

3.2. Integrating the Tools: A New Generation of Spatial Data Analysis in the SPIN! Project

To further support the analysis of spatially referenced data, we implemented a link between Kepler and Descartes, thus integrating data mining instruments with interactive cartographic visualization tools (Andrienko and Andrienko, 1999b,c). The present coupling will ultimately lead to a new generation of spatial data analysis and data mining software developed in the ongoing EU-funded SPIN! project at GMD.

The basic idea is that an analyst can view both source data and the results of data mining processes using maps to allow the inspection of spatial information in a natural way. The analyst can detect spatial relationships and patterns much more easily and quickly in this manner.

Conceptually the integrated system combines three kinds of links:

1. *From geography to mathematics.* When visually exploring and manipulating a map, the user may detect some spatial phenomenon. He could then try to find an explanation or justification for this by applying data mining methods.
2. *From mathematics to geography.* Data mining methods produce results that could then be visually presented and analyzed on maps.
3. *Dialogue between mathematics and geography (linked displays).* Graphics representing the results of data mining in the usual (noncartographic) form could be viewed in parallel with maps. Dynamic highlighting would visually connect the corresponding elements in both types of displays.

Some analysis algorithms requires the user to define classes in the data set before the data can be analyzed. The definition of arbitrary classes in some kinds of data can be made easier through the interface to a geographical analysis tool. The Descartes tool, an interactive classification map, allows the user to create arbitrary classes and to include objects in a class by selecting them in the map. By using the map to select the new classes, the user is able to take various kinds of spatial information into account. The relative positions of objects with

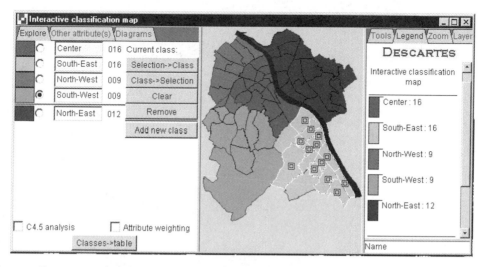

Figure 5 Results of user-generated classification of arbitrary districts in the city of Bonn. The classification was carried out by the Descartes interactive classification map tool, and illustrates one of the benefits of the integration between Kepler and Descartes

respect to other objects of the same kind (north-south, center-periphery, etc.) or spatial relationships with other kinds of geographical objects (closeness to sea, mountains, roads, etc.) are examples of the information gained through this graphical approach.

Figures 5–7 illustrate the integration between Kepler and Descartes. The arbitrary regions (center, north-west, north-east, south-west, and south-east) were classified in the city of Bonn, Germany, using Descartes in order to analyze the demographic data available for these regions with the data mining method C4.5 (Quinlan, 1993). To carry out this analysis, we started C4.5 from Kepler via the built-in plug-in wrapper. The table submitted to Kepler contained various demographic data about the districts of Bonn, such as percentages of different age groups in the population. The classification tree derived from the analysis of these data is displayed in Kepler in an interactive panel shown in Figure 6.

The tree exposes substantial differences among the geographical regions that we specified. For instance, the central part of the city is characterized by a high percentage of young people (18–30 years) and a low percentage of children. In the south eastern part of Bonn, the percentages of children and young people are low, but the percentage of foreigners is high.

The tree displayed in Kepler is dynamically linked with the maps and other displays in Descartes. This means that the user may select a node in the tree and have the geographical objects covered by this node highlighted in all of the displays in Descartes. To illustrate this, we have selected the left node on the bottom of the tree in Figure 6. The districts covered by this node are highlighted in the map shown in Figure 5. The link also works in the opposite direction. That is, when the user selects an object from a map or another display in Descartes, the nodes of the tree covering this object are highlighted.

The rules generated by the C4.5 method as a result of this analysis vividly demonstrate the new insights gained about the demographic data due to the ability to arbitrarily choose new boundaries within the city of Bonn (Figure 7 shows Kepler's graphical display of these rules).

4. Software Architecture

Kepler is meant to be an analyst's workbench for the exploratory and subsequent phases of a data mining project. Specialized vertical solutions can also be constructed based on Kepler modules for nontrained end user deployment. Kepler is an interactive system controlled at

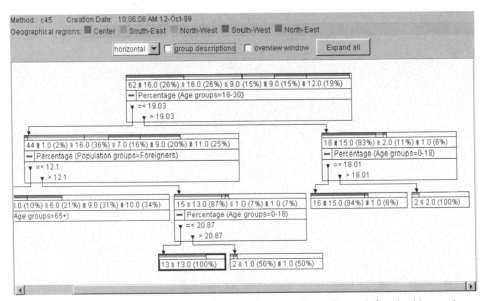

Figure 6 The classification tree generated by C4.5 analysis of user-defined arbitrary classes within Bonn

every step of the data mining process by the user, but it can also employ batch scripts to automate time-consuming tasks.

The three-tier system architecture features a Java front-end client, the Kepler server, and links to RDMBS servers. The system is extensible through its plug-in concept. Plug-in wrappers around existing or new analysis modules allow these modules to be deployed later or to be integrated into other software without the Kepler platform.

| Geographical regions=Center if Percentage (Age groups=0-18)=<18.01,Percentage (Age groups=18-30)>19.03 |
| Center |
| Geographical regions=North-East if Percentage (Population groups=Foreigners)=<9.8,Percentage (Age groups=18-30)=<19.03,Percentage (Age groups=65+)>10.12,Percentage (Age groups=65+)=<18.28 |
| North-East |
| Geographical regions=South-East if Percentage (Population groups=Foreigners)>12.1,Percentage (Age groups=0-18)=<20.87,Percentage (Age groups=18-30)=<19.03 |
| Geographical regions=South-East if Percentage (Population groups=Male)>45.7,Percentage (Population groups=Foreigners)>5.3,Percentage (Age groups=65+)>18.28 |
| South-East |
| Geographical regions=South-West if Percentage (Population groups=Foreigners)=<12.1,Percentage (Age groups=18-30)=<19.03,Percentage (Age groups=60-65)=<5.11 |
| South-West |
| Default rule: Geographical regions =North-West |

Figure 7 Classification rules produced by C4.5 analysis of arbitrarily chosen subgroups in the city of Bonn demographic data

Kepler is best used for medium-sized applications that can be handled directly by the system's internal persistent storage. Large-scale data repositories are best kept on linked-to RDMBS servers. Scalability of analysis methods varied depending on the plug-in algorithm, most of which use memory-resident data. Kepler is currently available on Solaris and Windows NT platforms, and support for HP and AIX is planned.

Descartes has a client–server architecture. The server is implemented in C++, and the client in Java. The system is available for various dialects of UNIX and Windows, as well as Internet application running within any WWW browser. The reader is invited to visit the Web page http://nathan.gmd.de/, which includes additional information and online demonstrators.

5. Main Applications

- Marketing/finance.
- Electronic commerce.
- Engineering/scientific applications.
- Telecommunications.
- Exploratory analysis of georeferenced statistical data.

ACKNOWLEDGMENTS

The authors are grateful for the contributions made to this text by K. Astrahantseff, Dialogis, A. Savinov, GMD, and D. Wettschereck, Dialogis.

Kepler® is a trademarked name of the product available from Dialogis Software and Services GmbH. For reasons of simplicity, we will use its name without trademark references in this article.

DialoGIS® is Descartes' trademarked name as a product available from Dialogis Software and Services GmbH. For reasons of simplicity, we will use its research name in this article.

References

Andrienko, G., and N. Andrienko. 1999a. "Interactive maps for visual data exploration." *Int. J. Geogr. Inform. Sci., IJGIS* **13(4)**: 355–374.

Andrienko, G., and N. Andrienko. 1999b. "Data mining with C4.5 and cartographic visualization." In *User Interfaces to Data Intensive Systems*, edited by N. W. Paton, and T. Griffiths, pp. 162–165. Los Alamitos, CA: IEEE Computer Society.

Andrienko, G., and N. Andrienko. 1999c. "Knowledge-based visualization to support spatial data mining." In *Advances in Intelligent Data Analysis. Third International Symposium, IDA-99, Amsterdam, August 9–11, Proceedings*, edited by D. J. Hand, J. N. Kok, and M. R. Berthold. Lecture Notes in Computer Science, **1642**: 149–160. Berlin: Springer-Verlag.

Quinlan, J. R. 1993. *C4.5 Programs for Machine Learning*. San Mateo, CA: Morgan Kaufmann Publishers.

Spenke, M., and C. Beilken. 1999. *Visual, Interactive Data Mining with InfoZoom®—the Financial Data Set*. In *"Discovery Challenge"*, Third European Conference on Principles and Practice of Knowledge Discovery in Databases, PKDD '99, September 15–18, 1999, Prague. Available at: http://lisp.vse.cz/pkdd99/Challenge/.

Wrobel, S. 1997. "An algorithm for multirelational discovery of subgroups." In *Proceedings of the First European Symposium on Principles of Data Mining and Knowledge Discovery (PKDD-97)*, edited by Jan Komorowski, and Jan Żytkow, pp. 78–87. Berlin: Springer-Verlag.

Wrobel, S. 1999. "Inductive logic programming for knowledge discovery in databases." In *ILP and KDD*, edited by S. Dzeroski, and N. Lavrac. Berlin: Springer-Verlag.

Wrobel, S., D. Wettschereck, E. Sommer, and W. Emde. 1996. "Extensibility in data mining systems." In *Proceedings of the Second International Conference On Knowledge Discovery and Data Mining*, edited by E. Simoudis, and J. Han, pp. 214–219. Menlo Park, CA: AAAI Press.

24.2.4 MineSet

Cliff Brunk and Ronny Kohavi

ABSTRACT MineSet[TM] is a commercial data mining product from Silicon Graphics. It provides an interactive platform for data mining, integrating three powerful technologies: database and file access, analytical data mining engines, and data visualization. MineSet supports the knowledge discovery process from data access and preparation through iterative analysis and visualization to deployment. MineSet uses a client-server architecture for scalability and support of large data. The data access component provides a rich set of transformations that can be used to process stored data into forms appropriate for visualization and analytical mining. MineSet's two- and three-dimensional visualization capabilities allow direct data visualization for exploratory analysis. The analytical mining algorithms create models that can be viewed using visualization tools specialized for the learned models or deployed as part of a larger system. Third party vendors can interface to the MineSet tools for model deployment and for integration with other packages.

1. Introduction

MineSet (Silicon Graphics, 1998; Brunk et al., 1997) is a general purpose data analysis tool that provides database access, analytical data mining, and data visualization in a highly integrated environment that supports the knowledge discovery process (Fayyad et al., 1996). In addition, MineSet is a platform for developing vertical applications that require analytical data mining and visualization. MineSet is an evolving product. The following is a description of the 2.6 release.

   We begin with an overview of the system architecture, and then describe the analytical algorithms, visualization techniques, and support for KDD process management. We conclude with a brief history of the project and commercial uses.

2. Architecture

MineSet employs a three-tiered architecture (Figure 1). The first tier is the client, which includes Tool Manager and the visualization tools. Tool Manager is the graphical user interface through which the user interacts with MineSet. The visualization tools are used to display data and models of data generated by the mining algorithms. After invoking a visual tool with Tool Manager, the user interacts directly with that tool and sends information from it to other tools via Tool Manager. The second tier is the server, which includes Data Mover and the analytical mining engine. Data Mover is the database access and data transformation component of

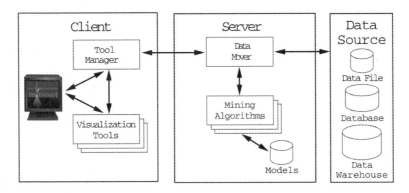

Figure 1 MineSet's three-tiered architecture

MineSet. It extracts data from the source, transforms it, and orchestrates moving it from one MineSet component to another. The mining tools are used to generate models of the transformed data, which can be applied to new data or visualized. The third tier is the data source, which includes the storage subsystem that maintains the user's data. It can be either a file or a commercial database. The tiers are not tied to specific machines: all three can reside on a single hardware platform or three separate platforms. This architecture provides the flexibility needed to scale with the size of the problem. Its allows large mining tasks to be performed on a powerful server machine, while smaller pilot projects can be performed on a desktop machine.

Knowledge discovery is a time consuming and iterative process involving modeling data and then understanding and validating the model. Useful tools facilitate this process by generating models of the data quickly and allowing the user to interact with and understand those models. Because speed is of primary importance, MineSet's analytical mining algorithms operated on data in core memory and key components have been parallelized to further reduce execution time on multiprocessor machines. Although limited to core memory, MineSet supports 64-bit addressing, allowing access to large amounts of memory.

3. Analytical Algorithms

MineSet uses MLC++ (Chapter 24.1.2; Kohavi et al., 1997) as its analytical engine. The naive Bayes (Domingos and Pazzani, 1997), decision tree (Quinlan, 1993), option tree (Kohavi and Kunz, 1997), k-means clustering (Dasarathy, 1990), regression tree (Breiman et al., 1984), decision table (Kohavi and Sommerfield, 1998), association rule generation (Srikand and Agrawal, 1995), and feature selection algorithms (Kohavi and John, 1997) in MLC++ have been made accessible through MineSet's Tool Manager. The emphasis has been on selecting algorithms that generate interpretable models that facilitate data understanding. Algorithms that create black box models, like neural networks, provide little insight into the data and have not yet been included in MineSet.

A plug-in API provides support for algorithms developed outside the MLC++ framework. For instance, Ultimode has released a MineSet add-on plug-in called ACPro for clustering based on AutoClass (Cheeseman et al., 1988). This is extremely important because it is unrealistic to expect a single off-the-shelf tool to provide all the algorithms needed to analyze data in every problem domain. Instead MineSet provides the infrastructure common to the discovery process and allows users to extend the tool as needed by plug-in algorithms specific to their task.

4. Visualization

MineSet provides a rich set of visualization tools that enable users to interactively explore data and quickly discover new patterns, trends, and relationships. These two- and three-dimensional visualization capabilities allow direct data visualization for exploratory analysis, including tools for displaying high-dimensional data taking advantage of geographical and hierarchical information. In addition, the visualization techniques have been specialized for displaying the models generated by the analytical mining algorithms. The algorithms help the user identify potentially interesting models of the data. The visual tools help make these models more understandable and allow the user to interact with the models to gain more insight into the model and the underlying data.

The human perception system can identify anomalies and patterns much faster in a representative landscape than in a spreadsheet. The visual tools utilize three-dimensional landscapes that take advantage of a person's ability to navigate in space, track movement, and compare objects of different sizes, colors, and shapes. In addition to visualization and navigation, the tools contain filtering and search facilities that allow users to quickly reduce the landscape to items of interest.

MineSet includes eight visualization tools. The Statistics Visualizer displays basic statistics in histograms and box plots. The Cluster Visualizer extends the Statistics Visualizer to

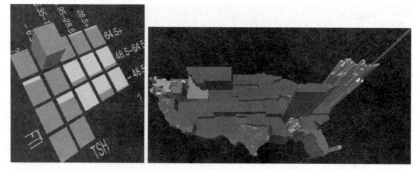

Figure 2 Visualization of a decision table for the hypothyroid database (left). The figure shows the top-level view with two attributes: FTI and TSH. Users can see that several intersections are empty: high TSH values imply unknown FTI (probably not measured) and that most data is in the low range of TSH (below 6.3). High values for FTI (above 64.5) are negative hypothyroid with high probability (dark gray). The interesting intersections are for low FTI and high TSH. MineSet's map visualizer (right) shows refinancing costs, mapped to height, for every U.S. county based on FIPS codes. Deviations from each state's average are colored from blue (zero deviation) to yellow (0.005) to red (0.01)

show the attribute by attribute differences between clusters identified by the clustering algorithms. The Tree Visualizer displays data hierarchically. Users can determine the hierarchy and map attributes to a histogram at each node. The Map Visualizer (Figure 2) displays data with a spatial component. A polygonal map must be provided and two attributes can be mapped to the polygon's height and color. Multiple maps may be linked together to show different attributes for the same spatial geography. The Scatter Visualizer displays scatter plots with up to eight dimensions: three axes, entity color, entity size, entity rotation, and two independent attributes shown through animation. It is also used to visualize the confidence and support of one-to-one association rules. The Splat Visualizer (Becker, 1997; Figure 3) extends the scatter plots when there are more than tens of thousands of records. It blurs the points using Gaussian smoothing. The Decision Table Visualizer (Kohavi and Sommerfield,

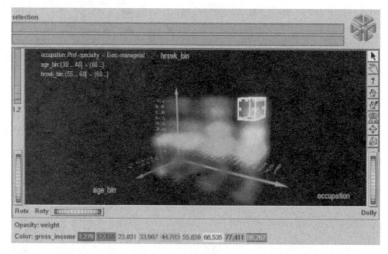

Figure 3 A Splat Visualizer view of census data on adults working in the United States. The plot shows how gross income is affected by age, occupation, and the number of hours worked per week. The density of each splat represents the number of people, and its color represents the average gross income. The selected cube represents people over thirty, who work over fifty-five hours per week in a professional specialty or an executive managerial position

1998; Figure 2), shows the break down of class label according to attribute value. Initially, the two most predictive attributes are shown, but the user can show additionally informative attributes by clicking on the cakes of interest and drilling down. This provides visual OLAP (OnLine Analytical Processing) capability. The Evidence Visualizer (Becker et al., 1997) shows a graphic representation of the naive Bayes model (Chapter 16.1.5) and allows the user to interact with the model by selecting known values, providing what-if analysis.

Additional capabilities shared by most visual tools include mapping attributes to graphical attributes (color, height, shape); manipulating the scene using thumb-wheels and mouse movements for rotation, translation, and zoom; data slicing and animating by manipulating sliders for two additional independent variables as shown on the left; searching and filtering of data; drilling down by pointing to elements in the scene; and sending records associated with selected visual elements to the Tool Manager for further analysis.

As with the analytical algorithms, emphasis has been placed on selecting visualization techniques that are relatively simple to interpret. Techniques that require extensive training to understand like parallel coordinates and grand tours have yet to be included in MineSet.

5. KDD Process Management

MineSet is more than an ensemble of data access, transformation, analytical mining, and visualization techniques connected by a common user interface. In addition to providing a consistent interface to all the tools, MineSet's Tool Manager provides a history mechanism that allows users to review and edit the steps performed in the current analysis, and to change data sources and perform the same analysis on different data sets. Once satisfied with an analysis sequence, it can be stored permanently and applied automatically to future data, or updated to account for changing future conditions.

6. History

MineSet was first released in early 1996 primarily as a visualization product. The importance of connecting to commercial databases was recognized early, with a native connection to Oracle® in MineSet 1.0, followed by connections to Sybase®, Informix®, and to (ASCII) files in MineSet 1.02.

MineSet 1.1 integrated machine learning algorithms from MLC++ (Kohavi et al., 1997), including decision trees, naive Bayes (evidence), column importance, and automatic (entropy-based) discretization. Support for unknown (null values) was added, as well as support for session management (save/restore), a batch mode, integration with the desktop environment (icon launching), and the ability to define new columns with expressions. MineSet 1.2 added Web launching capabilities from machines that have MineSet installed.

MineSet 2.0 added drill-through, the Splat Visualizer, Statistics Visualizer, Record Viewer, binary file format, sampling, option trees, loss matrices, learning curves, probability estimates from classifiers, and backfitting of data.

MineSet 2.5 added boosting of classifiers, parallelization, clustering, regression trees, and decision tables. Support for multibyte characters for internationalization and 64-bit support for large memory models was added in MineSet 2.6. Also added was a Java-based record viewer and a plug-in architecture for adding new data mining tools.

The engineering effort in product development is estimated at over 55 person years, with the engineering team consisting of 18 people.

7. Commercial Uses

MineSet has been used commercially since 1996, but most customers are reluctant to publicize the exact uses as they perceive data mining as a competitive advantage. In the summer of 1998, there were several hundred commercial sites and close to a thousand universities using MineSet. In this section we mention a very restricted set of commercial uses. More information can be found in Adhikari (1998).

Incyte Pharmaceuticals (www.incyte.com) provides genomic technologies to aid in the understanding of the molecular basis of diseases. Incyte created the LifeSeq® 3D software to give scientists powerful visualization tools for sifting through the vast amounts of genomic data in the LifeSeq database (Incyte Pharmaceuticals, 1997, 1998). LifeSeq 3-D is based on MineSet, displaying genomic information as interactive, multidimensional graphics, enabling scientists to navigate large data sets easily and to uncover hidden relationships and important trends in gene expression.

Risk Monitors conducts statistical analyses of loan and mortgage data nationwide, building the models upon which mortgage servicers and banks rely to calculate their underwriting risks. It analyzes 11 million loans nationwide dating back to 1989, and applies up to two hundred variables to them during statistical analyses. Typical analysis was previously done in group, or cohorts. With MineSet, Risk Monitors was able to work with loans at the individual level. More details are available in Goodarzi et al. (1998).

Procter & Gamble Co.'s healthcare division uses MineSet for clinical trials and efficacy tests of over-the-counter drugs. On average, the total cost of bringing a pharmaceutical drug to market is approximately $500 million, making it important to run clinical trials and process the data effectively. Using data mining, scientists try to find an active molecule in a drug, ensuring that it works, testing it for harmful side effects, and eventually testing it on humans. More information can be found in Stevens (1998).

8. Conclusion

MineSet provides a set of scalable analytical mining algorithms for identifying interesting patterns in data. MineSet also provides a rich selection of visualization techniques that help make these patterns understandable. The primary feature that differentiates MineSet from other KDD tools, however, is the integrated environment in which these algorithms and techniques are combined.

References

Adhikari, R. 1998. "Data mining muscle." *Information Week*, pp. 65–67. Available at http://www.informationweek.com/695/95iudat.htm.

Becker, B. 1997. "Volume rendering for relational data." In *Proceedings of Information Visualization*, pp. 87–90. IEEE Computer Society.

Becker, B., R. Kohavi, and D. Sommerfield. 1997. "Visualizing the simple bayesian classifier." In *KDD Workshop on Issues in the Integration of Data Mining and Data Visualization*.

Breiman, L., J. H. Friedman, R. A. Olshen, and C. J. Stone. 1984. *Classification and Regression Trees*. Wadsworth International Group.

Brunk, C., J. Kelly, and R. Kohavi. 1997. "MineSet: an integrated system for data mining." In *Proceedings of the Third International Conference on Knowledge Discovery and Data Mining*, edited by D. Heckerman, H. Mannila, D. Pregibon, and R. Uthurusamy, pp. 135–138. AAAI Press. Available at http://mineset.sgi.com.

Cheeseman et al. 1988. "AutoClass: a Bayesian classification system." In *Proceedings of the Fifth International Conference on Machine Learning*, pp. 54–64. Morgan Kaufmann.

Dasarathy, B. V. 1990. *Nearest Neighbor (NN) Norms: NN Pattern Classification Techniques*. Los Alamitos, CA: IEEE Computer Society Press.

Domingos, P., and M. Pazzani. 1997. "Beyond independence: conditions for the optimality of the simple Bayesian classifier." *Machine Learning* **29(2/3)**: 103–130.

Fayyad, U. M., G. Piatetsky-Shapiro, and P. Smyth. 1996. "The KDD process for extracting useful knowledge from volumes of data." *Commun. ACM* **39(11)**: 27–34.

Goodarzi, A., R. Kohavi, R. Harmon, and A. Senkut. 1998. "Loan prepayment modeling." In *KDD Workshop on Data Mining in Finance*, edited by T. H. Hann and G. Nakhaeizadeh, pp. 62–69.

Incyte Pharmaceuticals. 1997. "Incyte releases LifeTools 3D." Available at http://www.incyte.com/news/1997/PR9712-LT3D.html.

Incyte Pharmaceuticals. 1998. "LifeSeq 3D: Data mining and visualization software." Available at http://www.incyte.com/products/lifeseq/lifeseq3d.html.

Kohavi, R., and G. H. John. 1997. "Wrappers for feature subset selection." *Artificial Intelligence* **97(1–2)**: 273–324. Available at http://robotics.stanford.edu/users/ronnyk.

Kohavi, R., and C. Kunz. 1997. "Option decision trees with majority votes." In *Machine Learning: Proceedings of the Fourteenth International Conference*, edited by D. Fisher, pp. 161–169. Morgan Kaufmann. Available at http://robotics.stanford.edu/users/ronnyk.

Kohavi, R., and D. Sommerfield. 1998. "Targeting business users with decision table classifiers." In *Proceedings of the Fourth International Conference on Knowledge Discovery and Data Mining*, edited by R. Agrawal, P. Stolorz, and G. Piatetsky-Shapiro, pp. 249–253. AAAI Press.

Kohavi, R., D. Sommerfield, and J. Dougherty. 1997. "Data mining using MLC++: a machine learning library in C++." *Int. J. Artificial Intell. Tools* 6(4): 537–566. Available at http://www.sgi.com/Technology/mlc.

Quinlan, J. R. 1993. *C4.5: Programs for Machine Learning*. San Mateo, CA: Morgan Kaufmann.

Silicon Graphics. 1998. *MineSet User's Guide*. Mountain View, CA: Silicon Graphics, Inc. Available at http://mineset.sgi.com.

Srikand, R., and R. Agrawal. 1995. "Mining generalized association rules." In *Proceedings of the Twenty-first International Conference on Very Large Databases*.

Stevens, D. 1998. "Mineset's data visualization enhances clinical studies at Procter & Gamble." *DM Review* 8(7): 135. Available at http://www.dmreview.com/issues/1998/jul/reviews/jul98_135.htm.

24.2.5 Overview of SAS Enterprise Miner

Kelly Sang

ABSTRACT SAS/Enterprise Miner is a comprehensive software product that provides an end-to-end business solution for data mining. It provides a proven data mining methodology SEMMA (Sample, Explore, Modify, Model, Assess), ease-of-use capabilities, as well as a wide breadth of data mining functionality. All of the functionality needed to implement the SEMMA process is accessed through a single graphical user interface (GUI). The SEMMA process is driven by a process flow diagram (PFD), which one can modify and save. However, the GUI is designed in such a way that the business technologist with little statistical expertise can quickly and easily navigate through the SEMMA process, while the quantitative expert can go behind the scenes to fine-tune the analytical process. SAS/Enterprise Miner contains a collection of sophisticated data mining functionalities with a common user-friendly interface that enables the user to create and compare multiple models. Data mining modeling tools include decision trees, linear and logistic regression, neural networks, ensemble models memory based reasoning, two stage models, time series, principal components, as well as clustering and association rule discovery. Data preparation tools include outlier detection, variable transformations, missing data imputation, sampling, and the partitioning of data sets. Advanced visualization tools enable the user to examine large amounts of data in multidimensional histograms quickly and easily, and to compare modeling results graphically.

1. Introduction

Enterprise Miner is developed by SAS Institute Inc., one of the ten largest independent software vendors in the world, whose headquarters are in Cary, North Carolina. Now in existence for over 25 years, SAS Institute provides an integrated suite of information delivery tools that allow companies to transform the wide variety of data within their organization into information that business users need to make decisions. Currently, SAS software and business solutions are being used in more than 30,000 business, government, and university sites in over 120 countries.

Leveraging its experience in statistical analysis and predictive modeling, SAS Institute introduced Enterprise Miner, a comprehensive data mining solution, to the market early in 1998. Enterprise Miner is a client-server application with an easy-to-use graphical user interface (GUI). By October 1998, Enterprise Miner had gone into production on Windows NT and all

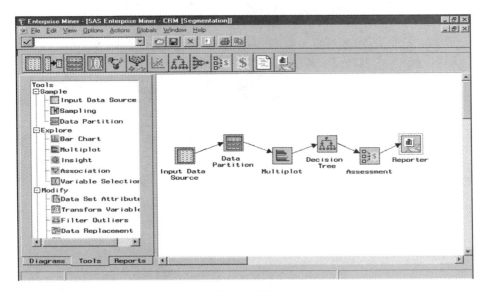

Figure 1 Enterprise Miner's GUI facilitates SEMMA methodology

popular UNIX server platforms, including Sun/Solaris, HP/UX, IBM/AIX, and DIGITAL UNIX.

2. SEMMA Methodology

Regardless of how procedural and analytical in nature, data mining should always start with a clear business objective in mind followed by the identification of related data sources. The data mining process entails steps that are best deployed if a framework for analysis exists.

SAS Institute defines this framework as the SEMMA Methodology. SEMMA stands for Sample, Explore, Modify, Model, and Assess, and it describes a sequence of steps that may be followed during a data mining analysis.

This logical superstructure provides users with a scientific, structured way of conceptualizing, creating, and evaluating data mining projects. The graphical user interface and functionality of Enterprise Miner have been developed to support this methodology. As Figure 1 shows, the tool window on the left consists of all the analysis options organized according to the SEMMA process. Users can choose the tool nodes either from the tools window or by customizing their own tool bar at the top of the window. By dragging and dropping the tool nodes onto the diagram editor, the user can construct a process flow diagram (PFD) of their own data mining project. Although guided by the overall SEMMA process, users are not constrained by the GUI or the SEMMA methodology. The interface is designed with tremendous flexibility to add/drop nodes, change connections, and repeat or omit certain parts of SEMMA to best fit individual data mining needs.

3. Data Access

3.1. Data Access Capabilities in Enterprise Miner

Accessing all relevant data is the starting point for defining any data mining model. Enterprise Miner offers a flexible input data source node that enables the user to specify the data sources to be used in analysis, whether they be SAS data sets or views of any of the over one hundred different data structures SAS software can read, including Oracle, DB2, Sybase, Excel, and others. This functionality is enabled by SAS Institute's Multiple Engine Architecture (MEA) technology, which offers transparent access to a wide variety of data structures, often natively with pass-through SQL for maximum performance. MEA also includes access to data in legacy systems (such as VSAM and ISAM) and supports open standards such as ODBC.

3.2. Input Knowledge

Once the user specifies an input data source, a metasample is automatically generated. Information about the input data, such as variable name, model role, measurement level, data type, and format is recorded. Simple summary statistics are also calculated and displayed for each variable based on the metasample. This sample is also used for several other tasks, such as viewing a variable's distribution in a histogram, determining variable hierarchies in the variable selection node, and as input to the insight node, all serving the purpose of gaining initial knowledge of the input data. Note that this sample is not used in any of the model building.

3.3. Integration with Data Warehouse

Data mining is usually a part of the overall data warehousing initiative in most corporations. Streamlining the process of accessing data from the data warehouse for data mining, sharing the meta data and reducing administrative costs has been a challenge for companies. Enterprise Miner provides a unique solution to meet this challenge by integrating the Institute's award-winning SAS/Warehouse Administrator software. With this integration, a data mining–ready data mart can easily be created using Warehouse Administrator; Enterprise Miner is able to calculate meta-information from the warehouse level.

4. Data Mining Process and Tasks Supported

4.1. Sample

Enterprise Miner allows the user to conduct analysis either on the entire data set or on a representative sample to decrease the model fitting time. The sampling node performs simple random sampling, nth-observation sampling, stratified sampling, first-n sampling, or cluster sampling of the input data set.

In order to ensure that the data mining results generalize well, Enterprise Miner provides the data partition node, which enables the user to partition the input data source or sample into data sets for the following purposes:

Training data—used to fit initial models.

Validation data—used for model assessment and fine tuning.

Testing data—used for a final, unbiased estimate of the generalization error of the model.

Partitioning provides a mutually exclusive data set(s) for cross-validation and model assessment and also helps to speed preliminary model development.

4.2. Exploration and Modification

Data mining is a dynamic, iterative process through which one can gain insights at various stages. One perspective on a problem can lead to another and to the need for further modification and exploration. Enterprise Miner gives users numerous tools and techniques to help them explore and modify their data.

DATA VISUALIZATION TOOLS

Enterprise Miner offers multiple advanced visualization tools, including SAS/Insight, Distribution Explorer, and Multiplot, which enable the user to explore large volumes of data graphically. These tools will be covered in detail in Section 5.

DATA MANIPULATION TOOLS

Many data mining databases have hundreds of potential model inputs (independent variables). The variable selection node can assist the user in reducing the number of inputs by dropping those variables that

- are unrelated to the target,
- have a high percentage of missing values,
- have determinative relationships in hierarchies,
- are class variables that have more than a specified number of values.

The transform variables node helps the user to create new variables that are transformations of existing variables in their data. Transformations are useful when one wants to improve the fit of a model to the data. For example, transformations can be used to stabilize variances, remove nonlinearity, improve additivity, and correct nonnormality in variables. The user can choose from the following types of transformations:

Simple transformations (log, square root, inverse, square, exponential, standardize).

Binning transformations (bucket, quantile, optimal binning for relationship to target).

Best power transformations (maximize normality, maximize correlation with target, equalize spread with target levels).

Users can also create custom transformations and derived variables by defining variables based on their own formulas.

Data sources can contain records that have missing values for one or more variables. Discarding incomplete observations may lead to loss of useful information and biased samples. Enterprise Miner enables the user to replace missing values for interval and class variables with the data replacement node. The node provides the following interval imputation statistics:

- Mean
- Median
- Midrange
- Midminimum spacing
- Tukey's biweight
- Hubers
- Andrew's wave
- Default constant
- Distribution-based
- Tree Imputation
- None

Missing values for class variables can be replaced with the most frequently occurring data value (mode), distribution-based, tree imputation, or default constant. The user can customize the default imputation statistics by specifying his own replacement values for missing and nonmissing data.

The filter outliers node provides the capabilities of automatically eliminating rare values for class variables, extreme values for interval variables based on standard deviation from the mean, extreme percentiles, modal centroid, and median absolute deviations. Filtering extreme values from the training data tends to produce better models because the parameter estimates are more stable.

The data set attributes node enables the user to modify data set attributes, such as data set names, descriptions, and roles.

DESCRIPTIVE ANALYSIS TECHNIQUES

Although predictive modeling is the core of data mining tasks, much of the analysis in the data mining process is descriptive in nature, such as association rule discovery (also known as market basket analysis, affinity analysis) and clustering (also known as unsupervised classification). While the purpose of association rule discovery is to identify items that occur together in a given event or record, the purpose of clustering is often to segment current databases into homogeneous groups in order to develop profiles with each group.

Enterprise Miner provides sophisticated tools for both kinds of the descriptive analysis. The association node performs association rule discovery based on frequency counts of the number of times items occur alone and in combination in the database. Taking the analysis one step further, the association node also facilitates sequence discovery by taking into account the ordering of the relationships (time sequence) among items.

Clustering analysis can be accomplished through both the clustering node and the SOM/Kohonen node in Enterprise Miner. K-means clustering is a computationally efficient method that computes Euclidean distances from one or more quantitative variables and seeds that are automatically generated and updated by the algorithm. While the clustering node can automatically determine the optimal number of clusters, the user has the flexibility to specify the clustering criterion that is used to measure the distance between data observations and seeds as well as the maximum number of clusters allowable by analysis. After clustering is performed, the characteristics of the clusters can be examined graphically using the result browser. Three-dimensional charts and plots are also available to graphically compare the clusters. The SOM/Kohonen node enables the user to create Kohonen networks, self-organizing maps (SOMs), and VQ networks. It provides the analysis results in the form of an interactive map illustrating the characteristics of the clusters. Furthermore, it provides a report indicating the importance of each variable.

4.3. Model

"Predictive modeling (also known as supervised prediction, supervised learning) is the fundamental data mining task" (Potts, 1998). Enterprise Miner supports this task by offering seven major modeling tools: decision trees, linear and logistic regression, neural networks, principal components/dmneural, two-stage model memory based reasoning, and the ensemble model.

The Tree node enables the user to create decision trees that either classify observations based on the values of nominal, ordinal, or binary targets, predict outcomes for interval targets, or predict the appropriate decision when one specifies decision alternatives. It finds multiway splits based on nominal, ordinal, and interval inputs. Users choose the splitting criteria that they would like to use to create the tree. The available options represent a hybrid of the options from CHAID (chi-squared automatic interaction detection), classification and regression trees and C4.5 algorithms. The user can also set the options to approximate traditional CHAID, classification and regression trees or C4.5. The decision tree node supports both automatic and interactive training.

The Regression node enables the user to fit both linear and logistic regression models to a predecessor data set in an Enterprise Miner process flow. Linear regression attempts to predict the value of a continuous target as a linear function of one or more independent inputs. Logistic regression attempts to predict the probability that a binary or ordinal target will acquire the event of interest as a function of one or more independent inputs. The node includes a point-and-click Interaction Builder to assist the user in creating higher-order modeling terms. The Regression node, like the Tree and Neural Network nodes, also provides a directory table facility, called the Model Manager, in which one can store and access models on demand. The node supports forward, backward, and stepwise selection methods.

An artificial neural network is a computer application that attempts to mimic the neurophysiology of the human brain in the sense that the network learns to find patterns in data from a representative data sample. More specifically, it is a class of flexible nonlinear regression models, discriminant models, and data reduction models, which are interconnected in a nonlinear dynamic system. By detecting complex nonlinear relationships in data, neural networks can help people make predictions about real-world problems.

Enterprise Miner supports a sophisticated neural network modeling capability through the Neural Network node. An important feature of the neural network node is its built-in intelligence about neural network architecture. The node surfaces this intelligence to the user by making functions available or unavailable in the GUI according to what is mathematically compatible within a neural network. Unavailable functions are grayed out, which simplifies the building process for the user and ensures that all available functions are compatible with neural network architecture. The user interface is further organized into basic and advanced tabs. The basic tab allows novice users to answer a few simple questions about their data, and the node then sets the parameters of the network accordingly. The advanced tab allows more sophisticated users to adjust manually all of the parameters that control the network.

The following neural network architectures are available in Enterprise Miner:

- Generalized linear model (GLIM)

- Multilayer perceptron (MLP), which is often the best architecture for prediction problems

- Radial basis function (RBF), which is often best for clustering problems

- Equal-width RBF

- Normalized RBF

- Normalized equal-width RBF

The Ensemble node enables the user to combine the results from multiple modeling runs to create a single, integrated model for your data. In particular, it performs:

- Stratified modeling

- Bagging

- Boosting

- Combined modeling

The models generated by the ensemble node are fully integrated with the Model Manager and assessment node and can be compared with other models generated by Enterprise Miner.

The Princomp/Dmneural node enables the user to fit an additive nonlinear model using bucketed principal components as inputs to predict a binary or an interval target variable. For the final model prediction, the tool chooses the activation function from a set of eight functions that yields the smallest SSE or misclassification rate. Training is faster than traditional neural networks, and the problem of collinearity is also avoided since bucketed principal components are used for prediction. The Princomp/Dmneural node also supports "stand alone" principal components analysis, allowing users to pass the scored principal components to the successor nodes, such as the regression node.

The Two Stage Model node computes a two-stage model to predict a class target and an interval target. The interval target variable is usually the value that is associated with a level of the class target variable. For example, the binary variable PURCHASE has two levels: Yes and No, and the interval variable AMOUNT can be the amount of money that a customer spends on the purchase. The node automatically recognizes the class target and the value target, as well as the probability, classification, and prediction variables. A class model and a value model are fitted for the class target and the interval target, respectively, in the first and second stages. By defining a transfer function and using the filter option, users are able to specify how the class prediction for the class target is applied and whether to use all or a subset of the training data in the second stage for interval prediction. The prediction of the interval target is computed from the value model and optionally adjusted by the posterior probabilities of the class target through the bias adjustment option. It also runs a posterior analysis that displays the value prediction for the interval target by the actual value and prediction of the class target. The score code of the Two Stage Model node is a composite of the class and value models. The value model is used to create the assessment plots in the Model Manager and also in the Assessment node.

The Memory Based Reasoning node is an experimental modelling tool that uses a k-nearest neighbor algorithm to categorize or predict observations. Memory-based reasoning is a process that identifies similar cases and applies the information that is obtained from these cases to a new record.

A Time Series node is also available to convert transactional data to time series data, and performs seasonal and trend analysis on an interval target variable. This tool enables users to understand trends and seasonal variation in their customers' buying patterns. For example, the user may have many suppliers and many customers as well as transaction data that is associated with both. The size of each set of transactions may be very large, which makes many traditional data mining tasks difficult. By condensing the information into a time series, users can discover trends and seasonal variations in customer and supplier habits that may not be visible in transactional data.

In addition to the three main predictive modeling tools, Enterprise Miner also provides the User Defined Model node to enable users to incorporate models built outside of Enterprise Miner and compare them to models generated by Enterprise Miner.

4.4. Assess

Assessment statistics are automatically computed when a model is trained in one of the modeling nodes. As the last step of the SEMMA methodology, the assessment node provides a common framework to compare models generated by the modeling nodes. The common criterion for all modeling and predictive tools is a comparison of the expected-to-actual profits obtained from model results. This criterion enables the user to make cross-model comparisons and assessments, independent of all other factors (such as sample size, modeling node, etc.).

Going beyond the SEMMA process, Enterprise Miner also automates the generation of the end result of most data mining problems: score code. Scoring is the process of applying the chosen model to produce predictions for each case in a new data set that may not contain a target. The Score Node of Enterprise Miner enables the user to manage, edit, export, and execute the SAS scoring code that is generated from trained models. The score code is generated automatically and captures any manipulation of records/fields that occur during the data mining process, such as transformation of variables, data replacement, and missing value imputation. A C score node is also available to convert the SAS score code to C functions to enable scoring outside of the SAS system. SAS code that you write in the SAS code node is not supported by the C score node.

4.5. Utilities

In order to make the data mining process even easier to manage, Enterprise Miner provides multiple utility nodes to add extra functionality. The SAS code node gives access to a wide range of packaged multivariate and time-series modeling as well as any other SAS System procedures in the data mining analysis. Thus, it greatly extends the functionality of Enterprise Miner. The data mining database node creates a data mining database (DMDB), which contains a meta data catalog with summary statistics for numeric variables and factor-level information for categorical variables. The DMDB enhances performance by reducing the number of passes that the analytical engine needs to make through the data. If part of the processing needs to be repeated then the group processing node might be useful. It enables the user to define group variables, such as gender, in order to obtain separate analyses for each level of the grouping variable(s). It also enables the user to perform bootstrapping, bagging, and boosting when used in conjunction with the ensemble node. There are two more utility nodes, control point node and subdiagram node, used to simplify the complex process flow diagrams.

5. Visualization and Result Presentation

Data visualization is one of the most unique knowledge discovery techniques, and it has "proven to be reliable, easy to learn, and extremely cost effective" (Westphal and Blaxton, 1998). Enterprise Miner supports a rich set of advanced data visualization techniques for the following three areas in the data mining process:

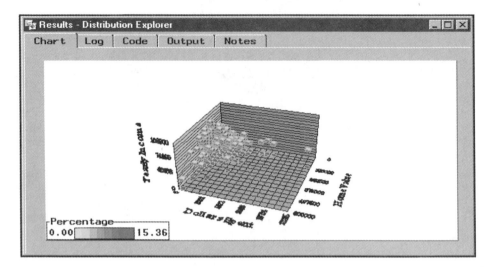

Figure 2 3-D bar chart created in Enterprise Miner

5.1. Visualization of Discovery Results

In the data exploration phase, four visualization tools are available for users to reveal graphically the patterns and trends in the data. The distribution explorer node allows the user to create multidimensional histograms. The user can interact with the graph by rotating a chart and also probing the data from the chart. An example of a three-dimensional bar chart is shown in Figure 2.

The Multiplot node automatically generates distribution plots for each variable as well as plots illustrating the relationship of each variable to the target as shown in Figure 3.

The Insight node is designed for the exploration of the data through graphs and analyses linked across multiple windows. The user can analyze univariate distributions, investigate multivariate distributions, create scatter and box plots, display mosaic charts, examine correlations, and so on. An example is shown in Figure 4.

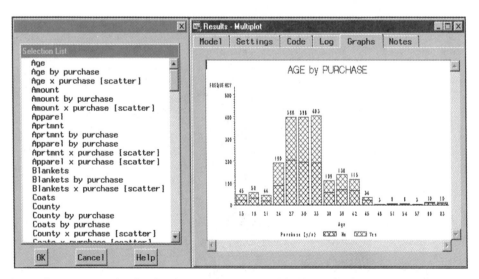

Figure 3 Example of a distribution plot generated by the multiplot node in Enterprise Miner

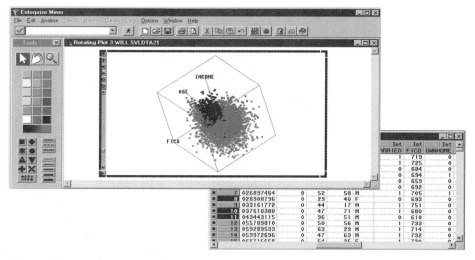

Figure 4 Example of a rotating plot and corresponding data window generated by the insight node in Enterprise Miner

Link analysis is the examination of the linkages between effects in a complex system. Analysts typically employed a variety of techniques including OLAP, associations, sequences, clustering, and most important, graphics to examine the relationships between entities in a complex system. They try to discover patterns of activity that can be used to derive useful conclusions. Some applications include forms of fraud detection, criminal network conspiracies, telephone traffic patterns, Web site structure and usage, database visualization, and social network analysis. The Enterprise Miner Link Analysis node transforms data from differing sources into data model that can be graphed. The data model supports simple statistical measures, presents a simple interactive graph for basic analytical exploration, and generates cluster scores from raw data that can be used for data reduction and segmentation.

More visualization tools are available to display the descriptive analysis and predictive modeling results, such as clustering analysis, association analysis, and decision tree models (see Figures 5–7).

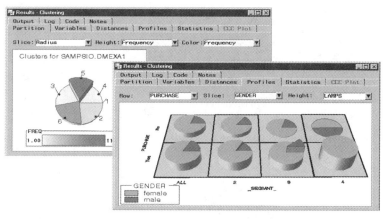

Characteristics of each cluster, the relationship among clusters, and the performance of all the variables in the clusters can all be graphically presented in Enterprise Miner

Figure 5 Graphical presentation of cluster analysis in Enterprise Miner

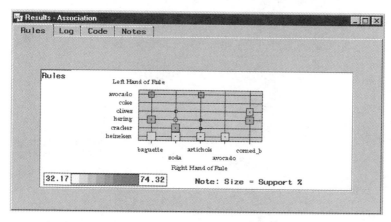

The results of association analysis can be displayed in a plot showing relationships between rules and the associates.

Figure 6 Graphical presentation of association analysis results in Enterprise Miner

Model assessment in Enterprise Miner is also strongly supported by visualization techniques. The assessment results can be presented with a large number of optional charts:

- Lift charts (or gains charts)
- Profit charts
- Return on investment (ROI) charts
- Diagnostic classification charts
- Statistical receiver operating characteristic (ROC) charts
- Business ROC charts
- Threshold-based charts
- Interactive profit/loss assessment charts.

An example of a lift chart presenting the comparison of a neural network model, a regression model, and a decision tree model is shown in Figure 8.

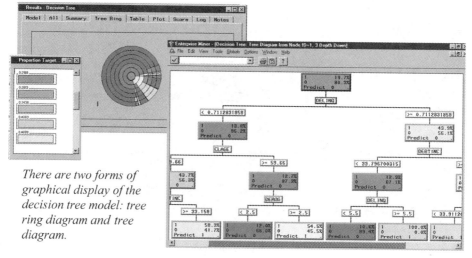

There are two forms of graphical display of the decision tree model: tree ring diagram and tree diagram.

Figure 7 Graphical presentation of decision tree analysis in Enterprise Miner

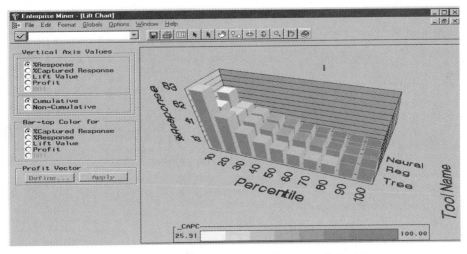

Figure 8 Lift chart showing model assessment results in Enterprise Miner

5.2. Visualization for Management of the Discovery Process

Enterprise Miner is packaged into a central application workspace window, giving users access to all of the product's functionality, and it facilitates the management of the discovery process (Figure 9).

The primary components of the SAS Enterprise Miner Window include the following:

Project navigator. Used to manage projects and diagrams, add tools to the diagram workspace, and view HTML reports that are created by the reporter node.

Diagram workspace. Used for building, editing, and running process flow diagrams (PFDs).

Tools bar. Contains a subset of the Enterprise Miner tools that are commonly used to build PFDs in the diagram workspace. One can add or delete tools from the Tools Bars.

Message and indicator panels. These are positioned across the bottom of the display.

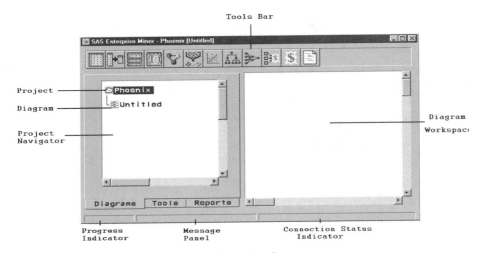

Figure 9 Enterprise Miner integrated user interface

With these easy-to-use tools, users can map out their entire data mining project, launch individual functions, and modify PFDs simply by pointing and clicking.

5.3. Natural Language Presentation and Automatic Report Generation

The rules from the decision tree model are automatically generated in English. For example, a rule may take the form: If *income* > $42 000 and 4 < *order_ freqency* < 7, then *purchase* = yes. Different kinds of analysis reports are available, ranging from summary statistics and modeling statistics to crosstabulations.

Another exciting functionality in Enterprise Miner is the automatic report generator. The Reporter node assembles the details and results from an Enterprise Miner process flow analysis into an HTML report that can be viewed with any Web browser. The node provides a convenient avenue for disseminating the results of a data mining analysis. Each report contains descriptive information about the report, an image of the process flow diagram, and a separate subreport for each node in the flow.

6. Software Architecture (Client-Server Enablement)

Enterprise Miner is a client-server application that runs on windows 95, 98, 2000 and NT client and on windows:2000/NT server as well as popular UNIX server platforms, including HP-UX, Solaris, Digital Unix, and IBM/AIX as well as MUS and INTEL/LINUX. The client-server functionality in Enterprise Miner provides advantages since it allows the user to:

distribute data-intensive processing to the most appropriate machine,

minimize network traffic by processing the data on the source machine,

minimize data redundancy by maintaining one central data source,

distribute server profiles to multiple clients,

regulate access to data sources, and

toggle between remote and local processing.

The software comes with comprehensive online documentation, and it is backed with quality service and support. Resources are dedicated in Technical Support and Profession Services to help customers. Courses on general data mining practices and hands-on software training are available to the public all over the world. In addition, SAS Institute's Quality Partner Program and strategic partnerships with leading consulting organizations are available as supplemental resources to ensure enhanced customer service and support.

7. Conclusion

"No one technique solves all data mining problems" (Berry and Linoff, 1997). With SAS Enterprise Miner, modelers and business analysts are equipped with an integrated software solution that encompasses all steps of the data mining process facilitated through a proven methodology. From data access to every phase of SEMMA, Enterprise Miner enables users to incorporate data mining into their business process and generate actionable results in a reliable and timely fashion.

References

Berry, M., and G. Linoff. 1997. *Data Mining Techniques: for Marketing, Sales, and Customer Support*, edited by R. M. Elliott, pp. 113. New York: Wiley Computer Publishing.

Potts, W. J. E. 1998. *Data Mining Primer: Overview of Applications and Methods*, p. 17. Cary, NC: SAS Institute Inc.

Westphal, C., and T. Blaxton. 1998. *Data Mining Solutions. Methods and Tools for Solving Real-world Problems*, edited by R. M. Elliott, pp. 123. New York: Wiley Computer Publishing.

24.2.6 GainSmarts

Nissan Levin and Jacob Zahavi

ABSTRACT GainSmarts is a data mining system in support of database marketing decisions, encompassing the entire range of the KDD process, including data import, exploratory data analysis, transformation of variables, feature selection, data mining, knowledge evaluation, and model validation (see Chapters 12, 14.2, 16.1.3, 16.1.7, 19, and 34). The data mining engine contains a profiling module to segment an audience employing automatic decision trees, and predictive modeling involving discrete and continuous regression models and AI-based models to predict customers' choice. Numerous statistical tests are used to evaluate knowledge and validate results. GainSmarts' most unique component is feature selection. Governed by a set of rules, the process automatically selects the best predictors explaining customers' choice. GainSmarts also provides for scoring customer lists and using economic criteria to select customers for promotion. Detailed reporting and visualization tools facilitate understanding and interpretation of the model results. GainSmarts is designed for use either as a standalone or an open system. Migration of the system to additional applications is easy. Written primarily in SAS, GainSmarts can run on many SAS-supported platforms. GainSmarts has already been applied to a variety of problems in diverse industries. It is the two-time winner of the Gold Miner award in the KDD-CUP 97 and KDD-CUP 98 competitions, organized by the American Association of Artificial Intelligence.

1. Introduction

GainSmarts, the winner of the 1997 and 1998 KDD-CUP knowledge discovery and data mining tool competitions organized by The American Association of Artificial Intelligence (AAAI), is a state-of-the-art data mining system in support of database marketing decisions. GainSmarts encompasses the entire range of the KDD (knowledge discovery in databases) process, including data import, exploratory data analysis, transformation of variables, feature selection, data mining and analysis, knowledge interpretation, and model validation (see Chapters 14.2 and 19). GainSmarts also allows the user to apply the model results to score customers in the universe, possibly on a different platform, and select customers for promotion based on economic analysis. The types of decisions supported by GainSmarts include, but are not limited to:

- Targeting audiences for cross and up selling
- Improving response through better segmentation
- Incentive management
- Contact strategy
- Churn and attrition management
- Acquisition of new customers

GainSmarts' KDD process, including the modeling engines and pre- and postprocessing, the scoring and selection module, and the documentation, was developed by the authors, Drs. Jacob Zahavi and Nissan Levin; the user interface and the on line help by Urban Science Applications Inc. (USAI). The system is developed in SAS with CPU-intensive routines written in C.

Dr Zahavi is with the Faculty of Management, Tel Aviv University, Tel Aviv 69978, Israel. Dr Levin is a partner in the software company Q-Ware Ltd. in Israel.

USAI is a marketing consulting and software development firm with offices throughout the world, headquartered at 200 Renaissance Center, 19th floor, Detroit, Michigan 48243 (www.urbanscience.com).

The system has been under development since 1993, the user interface and online help since 1996. The beta version was released in April 1997 and the production system in October 1997.

2. Input Data and Knowledge

The input to GainSmarts consists of individual-level data (see Chapter 4). In consumer marketing applications, the input contains data at the customer/prospect level, including:

- Transaction data, such as purchase and promotion history
- Demographic information
- Lifestyle indicators
- Credit and payment history

and any other relevant data. In business-to-business applications, the data set contains data at the individual business level.

Usually individual transactions are aggregated for mining purposes. For example, purchase/promotion history is summarized by categories/time segments/geography/events— as appropriate for the application. Often data for modeling comes from a data warehouse, where data is already summarized (see Chapter 13). Otherwise, one needs to summarize the data in preparation for modeling. Since GainSmarts is written in SAS, users can directly access databases managed by most DBMS (e.g., Oracle, Informix, DB2, SQL Server, or any ODBC-compatible DBMS).

Data is input to GainSmarts via either a flat file or a DBMS table. Using a data dictionary, raw attributes are transformed automatically into statistical predictors to form GainSmarts' knowledge base. If no data dictionary exists, data is input manually via a wizard. Advanced users can add content-specific transformations, such as response rates for past promotions (the ratio of the number of responders to the number of mailings), by directly editing the knowledge base (via the GUI).

3. Output Knowledge

The output knowledge of GainSmarts varies by the type of data mining algorithm. The major outputs are:

Decision trees, created by the profiling module, with nodes (or leaves) representing segments of the population (see Chapter 16.1.3).

Rules expressing segments, made up of the collection of all splitting criteria along the path connecting the segment to the root node (see Chapter 16.1.4).

Functional relations (equations) are the output of regression-based predictive models (see Chapter 16.1.7). These equations express the choice decisions (discrete or continuous) as a function of a set of predictors. Depending upon the model, more than one equation may be created. For example, in multinomial logistic regression, one equation is generated for each choice value.

In neural networks (see Chapter 16.1.8), the functional relation is represented by a weighted directed graph connecting the input to the output nodes via a set of hidden nodes.

Finally, the output knowledge of Bayesian models (see Chapter 16.1.5) consists of logistic-regression-type relations for naive models and neural network type relations for boosted models.

The model results are written out in the form of SAS code, which allows scoring of the appropriate universe on a different platform. The scoring process produces a contact list output containing the resulting decision recommendation for each customer.

4. Data Mining Tasks

GainSmarts supports two types of data mining tasks: classification (see Chapter 16.1) and prediction.

In classification, GainSmarts assigns a record to one of several predefined classes, or segments (e.g., buyers and nonbuyers). GainSmarts uses three tree classifiers to partition an audience into segments (see Chapter 16.1.3):

- STA (standard tree algorithm): a modified version of AID (automatic interaction detection) to allow splitting a node. Also based upon two-way interactions of predictors.

- CHAID (Chi-square AID): expanded to deal with multiple-valued and continuous-choice dependent variables.

- Genetic algorithm (GA): allows node splits based upon several predictors at a time, currently as many as seven predictors.

Starting with the entire population, tree classifiers systematically partition the data into homogenous segments with respect to some criteria (e.g., purchase behavior). The user has the flexibility to chose from two families of criteria to evaluate splits—node-value criteria and partition-value criteria. See Breiman et al. (1984) and Chapters 5.4 and 16.1.3 for more on decision trees.

In prediction, one uses existing values, such as purchase history, to predict future values, such as, for example, the probability of responding to the next offering. GainSmarts offers a variety of models, both statistically based and AI-based, to support the many types of problems encountered in the real world, which include:

- Binary logistic regression (see Chapter 16.1.7) to model yes/no decisions (e.g., buy/no-buy, pay/no-pay, loyal/nonloyal, etc.).

- Multinomial logistic regression to model cases where the customer faces several (up to four) nominal choices (e.g., no-buy, buy a used car, buy a new car).

- Ordinal regression where the choice variable possesses some inherent order (e.g., agree, indifferent, disagree) for up to four ordinal choice values.

- Sequential regression where the decision is taken in sequence (e.g., ask for information, test drive, sale) for up to four sequential choices.

- Linear regression to model continuous choice (e.g., the amount of money spent on purchasing from a catalog).

- Tobit regression to model continuous choice with a censored response.

- Two-stage model for a continuous response involving two models—the first, a logistic regression model applied on all observations; the second, a linear regression model applied only on responders.

- Neural networks for binary choice, involving the back-propagation model and a novel analytical model.

- Bayesian models for binary response, both naive and boosted.

An excellent discussion of the regression models can be found in Long (1997), and of neural networks in Rumelhart and McLelland (1969).

5. Task and Method Selection

Often no single model exists that is perfect for all applications. Thus, one needs to find the most suitable model for the occasion, and for each model calibrate the model parameters; both may require an extensive experimentation process. For example, binary choice prediction problems may be addressed by logistic regression, Bayesian models, neural networks, and even decision trees. Classification can be handled by a variety of decision trees, neural networks, and others. To select the best model, according to some predefined criteria, the user must run GainSmarts successively, each time invoking a different model, and comparing the results. Plans are underway to automate the comparison process. The first step in this direction has already been taken to automate the parameter setting of CHAID to maximize the resulting fit.

6. Support of the KDD Process

The data mining engine is only one component in the KDD process, others being a series of tools to prepare the data for modeling (preprocessing) and knowledge evaluation tools to analyze and interpret the model results (postprocessing). See Fayyad et al. (1996) for a discussion of the KDD process (also see Chapter 18).

GainSmarts offers several preprocessing tools:

- Exploratory data analysis (EDA) to check data integrity. The output consists of a set of frequency tables for all the input attributes that the user can browse for irregularities, outliers, missing values, et cetera. The user can request additional tables, if necessary, such as cross tabs.

- Automatic transformations of attributes to create predictors (explanatory variables) of response based on the data type. For example, continuous attributes (e.g., money spent) are categorized by quartiles or chi-square grouping, or they are expressed by means of a piecewise linear representation. Nominal and character attributes (e.g., marital status) are expressed by means of a set of dummy 0/1 predictors, one for each possible attribute value, which may be further grouped using chi-square analysis.

- Feature aggregation (see Chapter 14.3) of attributes that possess many individual values, such as lifestyle indicators, themes of products bought, state of residence, etc. These attributes are aggregated by similarity measures to render them more prediction power.

- Feature selection (specification) to choose the set of predictors that best explains customers' choice decisions (see Chapter 14.2). Typically this is the most complex component of the model-building process, because the set of potential predictors is often very large. GainSmarts addresses the feature selection issue in two ways:

1. Utilizing decision trees to partition the audience into segments, and using the features affecting the terminal segments as the model's predictors.

2. By means of an expert system that mimics the way an experienced statistician goes about specifying a model. The process consists of eight steps governed by a set of predefined rules, reflecting statistical theory and practice, that determine which predictors to retain or eliminate in each step. The objective is to attain the best fit as defined by the rules (e.g., maximizing the adjusted R-square in linear regression, or the likelihood function in logistic regression).

Knowledge evaluation (see Chapter 19), or postprocessing, is interwoven into the model-building and specification process. Testing of hypotheses is performed throughout to evaluate the statistical significance of predictors; overfitting is controlled by keeping the model parsimonious and by treating the set of predictors corresponding to a given attribute (e.g., a categorical representation of a continuous variable) as a whole unit, either introducing or eliminating the entire set from the model; correlation analysis is used to eliminate redundancy and multicollinearity; statistical measures are used to evaluate interactions; and finally, a validation process involving a holdout sample is conducted to check the stability and accuracy of the modeling results.

7. Visualization and Results Presentation

Model results are presented in tabular and graphical form.

The segmentation (profiling) results are exhibited by means of a tree, with each node representing a segment (terminal or intermediary), with captions that describe the characteristics of the segment (see a section of a tree in Figure 1).

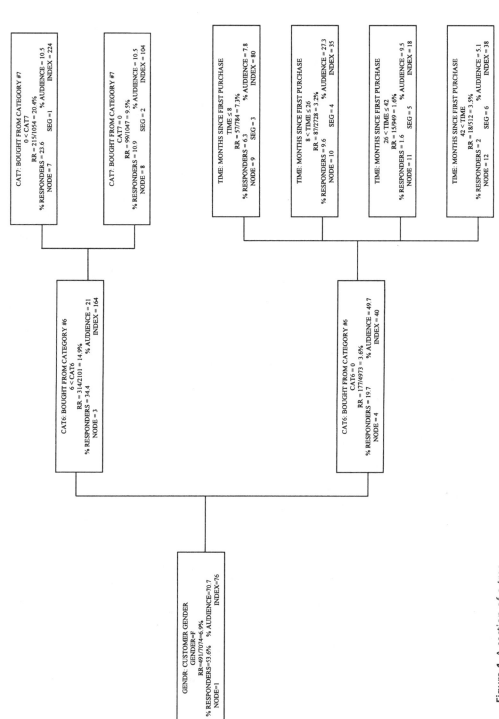

Figure 1 A section of a tree

Table 1 Gains Table

Response prob %	# of prospects	% prospects	# of responses	% response	Actual RR %	Index	Predicted responses	Predicted RR %	Actual profit	Predicted profit
35.90	500	5.0	269	29.60	53.80	5.90	264	52.80	1383	1348
22.20	1000	10.0	403	44.30	40.30	4.40	402	40.18	1821	1814
16.36	1500	15.0	502	55.20	33.47	3.70	496	33.08	2014	1972
12.97	2000	20.0	570	62.70	28.50	3.10	568	28.42	1990	1976
10.40	2500	25.0	621	68.30	24.84	2.70	626	25.04	1847	1882
8.65	3000	30.0	665	73.20	22.17	2.40	673	22.43	1655	1711
7.34	3500	35.0	713	78.40	20.37	2.20	712	20.35	1491	1484
6.30	4000	40.0	758	83.40	18.95	2.10	746	18.65	1306	1222
5.34	4500	45.0	785	86.40	17.44	1.90	775	17.22	995	925
4.59	5000	50.0	797	87.70	15.94	1.80	800	16.00	579	600
4.01	5500	55.0	813	89.40	14.78	1.60	821	14.93	191	247
3.42	6000	60.0	837	92.10	13.95	1.50	839	13.99	-141	-127
2.94	6500	65.0	849	93.40	13.06	1.40	855	13.16	-557	-515
2.47	7000	70.0	866	95.30	12.37	1.40	869	12.41	-938	-917
1.94	7500	75.0	877	96.50	11.69	1.30	880	11.73	-1361	-1340
1.66	8000	80.0	884	97.20	11.05	1.20	889	11.11	-1812	-1777
1.40	8500	85.0	890	97.90	10.47	1.20	896	10.55	-2270	-2228
1.06	9000	90.0	898	98.80	9.98	1.10	902	10.03	-2714	-2686
0.66	9500	95.0	907	99.80	9.55	1.10	907	9.55	-3151	-3151
0.05	10000	100.0	909	100.00	9.09	1.00	909	9.09	-3637	-3637

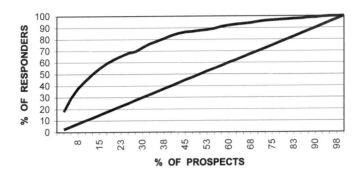

Figure 2 Gains chart

The overall model results are summarized in a gains table (see Table 1) and visualized through a DDE link to Excel, using Excel macros to control the visualization in a flexible manner (see Figures 2–4):

- Gains charts reflecting the lift in response attained at each audience level by the model over a random mailing.
- Bar charts to compare actual versus predicted response.
- Profit charts expressing the net profit (returns from orders minus promotion costs) as a function of the audience mailed.

The user can easily conduct sensitivity analysis to explore how profits are affected by varying the promotion costs and the order value.

Individual attributes may be visualized using SAS GRAPH (e.g., at the audience decile level), to allow the user to discern how important each attribute is in explaining response.

All output results of GainSmarts are held in SAS data sets, which opens up many opportunities for the experienced SAS user to manipulate the output and visualize the results.

8. Software Architecture

In GainSmarts, only the knowledge base is project specific. The KDD process and the reasoning engine are independent of the project domain. Consequently, only the knowledge base needs to be configured when setting up the system for another project. Furthermore, the

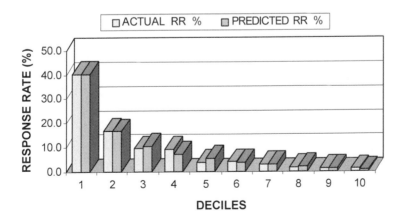

Figure 3 Response rate by deciles

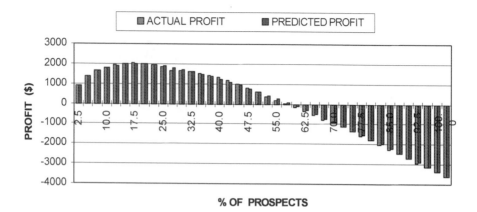

Figure 4 Profit by percentage of prospects

knowledge base may be created automatically using data dictionaries. This allows the end-user to use GainSmarts either as a black box, employing the automatic knowledge base and the default rules and parameters, or as an open box, by editing the knowledge base to add content-dependent predictors, modify parameters, and vary the rules. The user can also invoke selection rules to override model decisions (e.g., contact all females, including those rejected for promotion by the model, or do not contact customers living outside a given radius from a dealers location, etc.).

In terms of programming, GainSmarts is written in a modular form to facilitate adding/modifying models and routines.

Written in SAS, GainSmarts may run on any SAS (version 8.X) supported platform (perhaps with some minor modifications). Currently, versions exist for Windows 95/98/NT, Sun Solaris, compaq True 64 Alpha, HP-UX and IBM AIX.

Context sensitive, online help/documentation is provided in hyperlinked Windows standard help or through HTML browser technology.

Finally, support for GainSmarts is provided by USAI through its network of offices around the world. Support is delivered by telephone, e-mail and, if required by the customer, on-site help and training.

9. Applications

GainSmarts has already been implemented in a variety of applications, including the automotive, financial services, retail catalog, book club, travel, and charitable donation industries. Some selected examples include the following:

- Targeting households for promoting pickup trucks.
- Prospecting new households for home equity loans.
- Targeting audiences for catalog promotions.
- Targeting individuals for credit card promotions.
- Contact strategy for a leading book/music club.
- Forecasting donation amounts in a charitable campaign.

We describe the charitable application in more detail. This study was conducted as part of the KDD-CUP 98 mentioned above, held in conjunction with the 1998 annual KDD conference. The data set for the competition was contributed by PVA (Paralyzed Veterans of America), and consisted of about 200,000 lapsed customers, who participated in a recent mailing campaign, with almost five hundred pieces of data per record. The data set was split into two equal parts, the first, the training set, which also included the value of the dependent variable (the actual amount donated in the campaign), for building the model; the second, which did not include the donation amount, for validating the model. The task was to predict the donation amount for each customer in the validation file. The objective was to maximize the net donation amount by approaching only customers worthy of promotion (net expected donation amount after direct marketing cost > 0).

Fifty-seven research groups participated in the competition, about half from academia and half from industry, but only twenty-one submitted final results. GainSmarts won the Gold Miner award, increasing the net donation amount by more than 40 percent through better targeting of the mailing audience and eliminating unprofitable people from the campaign.

References

Breiman, L., J. Friedman, R. Olshen, and C. Stone. 1984. *Classification and Regression Trees*. Belmont, CA: Wadsworth.

Fayyad, U., G. Piatetsky-Shapiro, and P. Smyth. 1996. "The KDD process for extracting useful information from volumes of data." *Commun. ACM* **39**: 27–34.

Long, S. J. 1997. *Regression Models for Categorical and Limited-dependent Variables*. New York: Sage Publications.

Rumelhart, D. E., and J. L. McLelland. 1986. *Parallel Distributed Processing*, Volume 1. Cambridge, MA: MIT Press.

24.3 Public Domain, Single Mining Tasks Systems

24.3.1. AutoClass (Clustering)

John Stutz

ABSTRACT   AutoClass seeks intrinsic clusters or classes in an instance vector database. It applies a user-specified probabilistic class model and searches for a maximum posterior probability parameterization of a set of such classes. The number of classes is one of these parameters. The resulting clustering is locally optimal with respect to the data and class model. The class model is a product of mutually independent probability distribution or density functions that relate regions of the data space to the individual classes. The fully parameterized classes thus define relative probability of class membership with respect to location in data space. Class membership of instances is then a probability mass distribution over classes. The use of maximum posterior probability parameter estimation, based on minimum information prior parameter probabilities, precludes the overfitting problems that bedevil maximum likelihood methods. The approach is implicitly applicable to any kind of data for which data space clusters can be defined in terms of parameterized probability distributions. In practice, the public domain AutoClass-C is limited to combinations of discrete and number valued data.

1. Introduction

AutoClass began as an experimental proof-of-concept exercise, attempting to demonstrate the utility of combining mixture models with Bayesian maximum posterior probability parameter estimation, for the task of finding intrinsic clusters/classes in scientific data. The initial LISP version was developed in 1986 by Peter Cheeseman and John Stutz. Matthew Self, Jim Kelly, Don Freeman, and Will Taylor all contributed to early versions. These proved the concept, and led, with Robin Hanson's help, to experimental versions for large databases, hierarchical class parameterizations, and parallel implementations. Joe Potts translated the basic LISP version into C. This, with interface work and continued support by Will Taylor, is the public domain version comprising AutoClass-C. AutoClass research has been quiescent since the early 1990s.

In 1998, Ultimode Systems marketed a commercial version combining the basic ideas with improved search techniques and links to graphical interface and visualization facilities.

The initial description of the AutoClass work is in Cheeseman et al. (1987). Though sparser, Cheeseman et al. (1988a,b) is more accessible. Elaborations on the theme are discussed in Hanson et al. (1991) and Stutz and Cheeseman (1996). The currently definitive description is in Cheeseman and Stutz (1996).

2. Input Data and Knowledge

AutoClass-C operates on a single file of independent, fixed attribute data vectors. Appropriate values are integer or real-valued numbers, or discrete symbols taken from a fixed set for each attribute. Missing values are allowed. Binary formatted data is accommodated with restrictions. Neither relational nor set valued data is allowed. There is no integration with database management systems (DBMSs).

Data file formatting is defined in a separate input file that specifies attribute types and auxiliary information. Allowed types are real (integer and floating point), discrete (strings, symbols, or integers), and dummy (anything). Numerical attribute error ranges and optional zero points, and discrete attribute ranges, are also specified here. Data separator and comment characters and missing value symbols may be specified.

Class (cluster) models are specified in terms of a set of supported probability distribution functions. This set varies with different versions and is extendible with some difficulty. AutoClass-C includes an independent multinomial model, an independent Gaussian normal model with missing value option, and a covariant Gaussian normal model. Real-valued attributes specified as scalars with zero points, and modeled as normals, are automatically converted to logarithms, implementing a log-normal model. Attributes may also be ignored. Within the limits of the allowed value type matches and covariant/independent combinations, the user is free to determine how each attribute will be modeled.

Background knowledge must be applied indirectly, in choosing what preprocessing to do, what attributes to model, how to model the chosen attributes, and how to interpret the resulting classes.

3. Output Knowledge (See Chapter 5)

AutoClass generates a maximum posterior probability classification (clustering) of the data, conditioned on the attribute and modeling choices and on the extent of search over the parameter space. Output files describe probability of membership distributions for both the data and classes and the maximum probability parameterizations of the probability distribution functions defining the classes. The latter may be used as input for classification of previously unclustered data or to generate maximum probability decision surfaces in the attribute space. Output files can be formatted either for human readability, or for machine input.

4. Data Mining Tasks Supported by System (See Chapter 16)

AutoClass performs maximum posterior probability intrinsic classification (clustering) of the data and modulates the choice of attributes and of probability distribution functions applied to those attributes. AutoClass provides minimal information priors for the distribution parameters, thus implicitly limiting the maximally probable number of classes. Some preprocessing of data is done automatically, for certain combinations of type and model. In general, both pre- and postprocessing is up to the user.

AutoClass supports a prediction mode where, given a previously determined set of classification parameters, additional data can be classified without further search.

4.1. Support for Task and Method Selection (See Chapter 17)

AutoClass-C supports essentially one task: intrinsic probabilistic clustering.

4.2. Support of KDD Process

AutoClass-C provides no direct support for preprocessing or postprocessing, other than using a log transformation of scalar real-valued attributes.

4.3. Visualization and Result Presentation (See Chapter 20)

There is no support for visualization in AutoClass-C. The LISP versions have an extensive user interface with graphics capabilities for plotting data instances and class parameters. AutoClass-C output files may be optionally formatted for input to user-supplied postprocessing systems.

5. Software Architecture

The user is preeminent when using AutoClass for data mining, and a degree of domain expertise is generally essential for the generation of useful results. The user determines what attributes are used, how they are modeled, what the results mean, and what changes are needed to the data and modeling in order to improve the results in following cycles. Given data and models, AutoClass searches the parameter space, including number of classes, for maximum posterior probability classification parameter sets, reporting a number of the best ones found. In essence, AutoClass searches at the parameter level while the user searches at the model level.

AutoClass was originally written with a fair degree of system modularity, which has since degraded. In particular, the probability distribution functions are implemented as stand-alone modules, each providing common functionality to the input, initialization, search and output modules. The intent was that users should be able to implement distribution functions appropriate to their domain. This has not proved practicable. True to its heritage as a research project, AutoClass supports a number of variations on parameter space search initialization, control and termination methods.

AutoClass run times increase roughly as a product of data volume (instances × attributes modeled), number of classes, and number and duration of searches needed to make a reasonable sampling of the parameter space. The latter can be quite uncertain. The standard search mode is multiple descent EM, with semirandom class reinitializations seeded from the data instances. EM's exponential approach to stationary parameter states forces a cutoff decision, trading search coverage against accuracy of convergence. While defaults are provided, the optimal decision point depends upon the data, models, and available search time.

The C language version runs about 10 times as fast as the corresponding LISP version. Parallel versions of AutoClass have shown a speedup that is approximately linear with the number of processors.

The public domain AutoClass-C is available for UNIX, Windows, and DOS platforms. As the time of writing, complete information on these versions is available from `http://ic-www.arc.nasa.gov/ic/projects/bayes-group/autoclass/`. Limited documentation files are distributed with each system. Since this is no longer an active project, only limited support is available from the authors, though we do make a point of fixing any reported bugs. A thesis class parallel version of AutoClass-C is available from Professor Diane Cook of the University of Texas at Arlington (cook@centauri.uta.edu)—this is neither supported nor maintained and is minimally documented. AutoClass-3, a LISP version with graphics facilities, is available at cost from NASA's Cosmic software distribution agency.

6. Main Applications

AutoClass-C has been copied by many, but with relatively few reports back on applications and results. The first three items describe applications we have done ourselves. These are distinctly biased toward scientific applications such as astronomy, remote sensing, biology, and medicine, largely due to the nature of our employment. They are discussed in some detail in Cheeseman and Stutz (1996), where we emphasize the meta level problems that make or break any data mining project.

An early real-world application was classification of Infra-Red Astronomy Satellite (IRAS) Low Resolution Spectra (LRS). This consisted of 5,425 high-quality point-source spectra, each with 93 infrared fluxes recorded between 8 and 22 micrometers. The results were published as Cheeseman et al. (1989), with an astronomical analysis in Goebel et al. (1989).

A somewhat similar application involved Landsat Thematic Mapper (TM) data. While Landsat TM pixels record energy fluxes in only seven visible and infrared bands, their sheer number is sufficient to swamp any clustering algorithm. AutoClass IV, a LISP variant running on the 32,768 processor Thinking Machines CM-2, was developed to handle 100^20 pixel segments. Results are given in Kanefsky et al. (1994).

Introns are DNA codes that get spliced out when messenger RNA is constructed. Their length varies from about 80 to several thousand bases. The beginning and end of an intron are denoted donor and and acceptor sites. We applied AutoClass to base sequences from these sites, using 40 bases from the intron and 10 from the adjacent sequence, and classifying donor and acceptor sites separately. Each instance thus consists of a string of 50 symbols, drawn from the set of four possibilities (A, G, C, T) in the DNA code.

AutoClass has been used in a number of attempts to duplicate known classifications, such as medical diagnosis. This is not the task for which it was designed, and results have been quite mixed. Success is entirely dependent on presenting AutoClass with a (sub)set of data that yields clusters aligning with the desired classes. When too many attributes fail to inform about the desired classes, the discovered classes are often orthogonal to the desired ones.

Some projects mentioned by AutoClass users:

Compositional groups in geochemical data of archaeological artifacts, using concentrations of 15–20 trace elements.

Centrifugal pump failure modes from the fast Fourier transform of a noise spectrum. Tourism market research questionnaires, with "rate from 1 to 10" data.

Psychosocial data consisting of ratings, scores on personality tests, numbers of symptoms present, etc.

Unsupervised learning problems in natural language processing.

Identifying and isolating reusable components in legacy software systems by using AutoClass to identify "common code" or pieces of code with similar function.

ACKNOWLEDGMENTS

The following have contributed to AutoClass development: Peter Cheeseman, RIACS/NASA, MS 269-2, Ames Research Center, Moffett Field, CA 94035 (cheesem@ptolemy.arc.nasa.gov); John Stutz, NASA, MS 269-2, Ames Research Center, Moffett Field, CA 94035 (stutz@ptolemy.arc.nasa.gov); Robin Hanson, School of Public Health, 140 Warren Hall, UC Berkeley, CA 94720 (http://hanson.berkeley.edu/); Will Taylor, Caelum/NASA, MS 269-2, Ames Research Center, Moffett Field, CA 94035 (taylor@ptolemy.arc.nasa.gov); Matthew Self, Replay Networks Inc., Palo Alto, CA (mself@mself.com); Jim Kelly, Kana Communications, 87 Encina Avenue, Palo Alto, CA 94301 (jkelly@kana.com); Don Freeman; and Joe Potts.

References

Cheeseman, P., J. Kelly, M. Self, and J. Stutz. 1987. "Automatic Bayesian induction of classes." In *Proceedings of the Second Annual Artificial Intelligence Research Forum (Palo Alto, CA)*, edited by P. Friedland, pp. 224–239. Moffett Field, CA: NASA Ames Research Center.

Cheeseman, P., J. Kelly, M. Self, J. Stutz, W. Taylor, and D. Freeman. 1988a. "AutoClass: a Bayesian classification system." In *Proceedings of the Fifth International Conference on Machine Learning (Ann Arbor, MI)*, edited by J. Laird, pp. 54–64. San Mateo, CA: Morgan Kaufmann.

Cheeseman, P., M. Self, J. Kelley, J. Stutz, W. Taylor, and D. Freeman. 1988b. "Bayesian classification." In *The Seventh National Conference on Artificial Intelligence (Saint Paul, MN)*, pp. 607–611. San Mateo, CA: Morgan Kaufmann.

Cheeseman, P., and J. Stutz. 1996. "Bayesian classification (AutoClass): theory and results." In *Advances in Knowledge Discovery and Data Mining*, edited by U. M. Fayyad, G. Piatetsky-Shapiro, P. Smyth, and R. Uthurusamy, pp. 153–180. Menlo Park, CA: AAAI/MIT Press.

Cheeseman, P., J. Stutz, M. Self, W. Taylor, J. Goebel, K. Volk, and H. Walker. 1989. "Automatic classification of spectra from the infrared astronomical satellite (IRAS)." NASA Reference Publication #1217. Springfield, VA: National Technical Information Service.

Goebel, J., K. Volk, H. Walker, F. Gerbault, P. Cheeseman, M. Self, J. Stutz, and W. Taylor. 1989. "A Bayesian classification of the IRAS LRS Atlas." *Astronomy and Astrophysics* **222**: L5–L8.

Hanson, R., J. Stutz, and P. Cheeseman. 1991. "Bayesian classification with correlation and inheritance." In *The Twelfth International Joint Conference on Artificial Intelligence (Sydney, Australia)*, edited by J. Mylopoulos, and R. Reiter, pp. 692–698. San Mateo, CA: Morgan Kaufmann.

Kanefsky, B., J. Stutz, P. Cheeseman, and W. Taylor. 1994. "An improved automatic classification of a Landsat/TM image from Kansas (FIFE)." TR FIA-94-01. Moffett Field, CA: NASA Ames Research Center.

Stutz, J., and P. Cheeseman. 1996. "AutoClass—a Bayesian approach to classification." In *Maximum Entropy and Bayesian Methods*, edited by J. Skilling, and S. Sibisi, pp. 117–126. Dordrecht, Netherlands: Kluwer Academic Publishers.

24.3.2 VisDB

Daniel A. Keim

ABSTRACT The VisDB system is an interactive data visualization and exploration that uses novel pixel-oriented visualization techniques for effective exploration of large multidimensional data sets. Pixel-oriented techniques use each pixel of the display to visualize one data value and therefore allow the visualization of the largest amount of data possible. Using a slider-based direct-manipulation interface, the user may explore the data interactively and discover interesting patterns in the visualizations generated. The system can be used for the discovery of correlations, functional relationships, and clusters. It has proven to be effective even for data sets with small clusters and a high degree of noise. Application areas include stock market analysis, environmental science, computer-aided design, and molecular biology. The pixel-oriented techniques implemented in the VisDB System may be divided into query-independent techniques, which directly visualize the data (or a certain portion of it) and query-dependent techniques, which visualize the relevance of the data with respect to a specific query. Recently, new pixel-oriented techniques have also been developed for geographically related data, such as telecommunication or census data.

1. Introduction

Most of the original VisDB system (Keim and Kriegel, 1994) was developed by Daniel A. Keim and a number of students (especially Thomas Seidl, Juraj Porada, and Mihael Ankerst) in Hans-Peter Kriegel's group at the University of Munich. Currently, the VisDB system and follow-up systems such as the VisualPoints system (Keim and Herrmann, 1998) are being developed at the University of Halle. A brief history of the development of the VisDB system is given below:

1993 First prototype of the VisDB system

1994 C++/Motif-based reimplementation of the VisDB system (Keim and Kriegel, 1994)

1995 Development of the recursive pattern technique (Keim et al., 1995)

1996 Development of the circle segments technique (Keim, 2000)

1998 VisualPoints System (Gridfit Technique) (Keim and Herrmann, 1998)

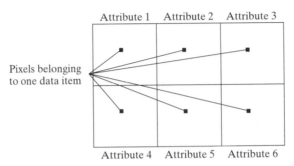

Figure 1 Arrangement of windows for data with six attributes

The VisDB system allows visualization of large amounts of multidimensional data as they occur, for example, in relational tables. The basic idea is to map each data value to a colored pixel and present the data values belonging to one attribute in separate windows (cf. Figure 1). The colors are chosen such that bright colors correspond to small distances and dark colors correspond to large distances (see Keim, 1995a, for details on the color mapping). Since pixel-oriented techniques in general use only one pixel per data value, the techniques allow the user to visualize the largest amount of data that is possible on current displays (up to about 1,000,000 data values). If each data value is represented by one pixel, the main question is how to arrange the pixels on the screen. Pixel-oriented techniques use different arrangements for different purposes. If a user wants to visualize a large data set, the user may use a query-independent visualization technique, which sorts the data according to some attribute(s) and uses a screen-filling pattern to arrange the data values on the display. Query-independent visualization techniques are especially useful for data with a natural ordering according to one attribute (e.g., time series data). However, if there is no natural ordering of the data and the main goal is an interactive exploration of the database, the user will be more interested in feedback to some query. In this case, the user may turn to the query-dependent visualization techniques that visualize the relevance of the data items with respect to a query. Instead of directly mapping the data values to color, query-dependent visualization techniques calculate the distances between data and query values, combine the distances for each data item into an overall distance, and visualize the distances for the attributes and the overall distance, sorted according to the overall distance. The arrangement of the data items centers the most relevant data items in the middle of the window, and less relevant data items are arranged to the outside of the window.

To help understand query-dependent visualization techniques, imagine a simple one-table database containing cars and their properties, such as horsepower of the engine, maximum speed, et cetera In the case of query-dependent techniques, we visualize the database with respect to a user-provided query (e.g., cars with a horsepower of 150 and a maximum speed of 100 mph). In this example, the distances between query values and database entries are the simple numerical differences and the overall distance could be determined as the (weighted) arithmetic mean. The visualization would then show the database ordered according to the overall distance to the query and the colors would represent the single attribute distances to the corresponding query values.

2. Query-independent Visualization Techniques

In dealing with arbitrary multidimensional data without any 2-D or 3-D semantics, one major problem is to find meaningful arrangements of the pixels on the screen. Even if the data has a natural ordering according to one attribute (e.g., time series data), there are many possibilities for arranging the data. One straightforward possibility is to arrange the data items from left to right in a line-by-line fashion. Another possibility is to arrange the data items top-down in a column-by-column fashion. If these arrangements are done pixelwise, in general, the resulting

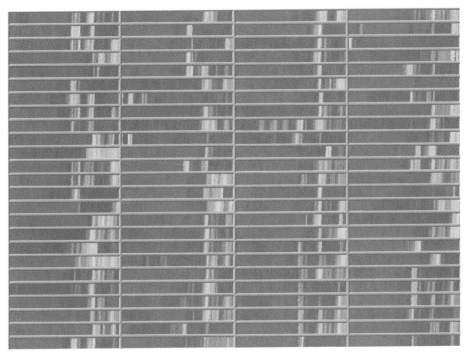

Figure 2 Recursive pattern visualization of one hundred stocks from January 1974 to April 1995 (about 530,000 data values) (cf. Keim et al., 1995)

visualizations do not provide useful results (Keim et al., 1995). Techniques that provide a better proximity of closely related pixels are more useful, such as space-filling curves (e.g., the well-known curves of Peano, 1890, Hilbert, 1891, and Morton, 1966). For data-mining, even more important are techniques that provide nice clustering properties as well as an arrangement that is semantically meaningful. An example of a technique that provides these properties is the recursive pattern technique. The recursive pattern technique is based on a generic recursive scheme, which allows the user to influence the arrangement of data items. The basic arrangement is based on a simple back and forth movement: First, a certain number of elements is arranged from left to right, then below that backwards from right to left, then again forward from left to right, and so on. The same basic arrangement is done recursively where the building elements on recursion level i are the pixel arrays (in the following we call them patterns) resulting from the arrangement on recursion level $(i-1)$. Let w_i be the number of elements arranged in the left-right direction on recursion level i and h_i be the number of rows on recursion level i. On recursion level $i (i \geqslant 1)$, the algorithm draws w_i level $(i-1)$ patterns h_i times alternately to the right and to the left. The pattern on recursion level i consists of $w_i \times h_i$ level $(i-1)$-patterns, and the maximum number of pixels that can be presented on recursion level k is given by $\prod_{i=1}^{k} w_i \times h_i$. An example for a recursive pattern visualization of a database containing the one hundred stocks of the FAZ index (Frankfurt Stock Index) from twenty years of stock price data (altogether 532,900 data values) is presented in Figure 2. The arrangement is rather simple and uses just two recursion levels with the parameter settings $(w_1, h_1) = (1, 22)(w_2, h_2) = (243, 1)$, which means that in each of the one hundred attribute subwindows a column of pixels corresponds to about one month. Using the visualization, it is easy to find stocks with similar stock price developments; for example, the stock price developments of the first, fourth, eighth, tenth, and fifteenth stock in the fourth column (Südzuker Thyseen, Veba, Volkswagen, Bayer, Hypobank) are similar, although the companies are working in completely different areas. Another example is the stock price development of the third- and second-last stock in the third column and the fourth- and fifth-last stock in the fourth column (Binding-Brauerei, Siemens, Lufthansa, Allianz), all four having multiple peaks in 1987, 1990 and 1993. Also interesting is that in more than 50 percent of all price boxes, there is a light green stripe at nearly the same position, especially the bottom boxes in the first and second columns and the top boxes of the third column. This means that those stocks had their peak price around the same time which was in spring 1990. From the visualization, it becomes obvious that many of those stocks did not completely recover from the crash that followed. Further interesting stocks are those that do not follow the overall trend. An example is the eleventh and nineteenth stock in the first column (Daimler-Benz, DYWIDAG), which did not have serious fluctuation over the last few years and continuously remained on the same relatively high price level. Another example is the seventh and tenth stock in the second column (Harpen, MAN ST), which have their peak prices right at the beginning of the considered time interval (about twenty years ago). For details on the recursive pattern technique, the reader is referred to Keim et al. (1995).

Note that for the query-independent techniques, it is not mandatory that the data has some natural ordering. In searching for dependencies among attributes, one might sort the data according to one attribute and use visualization techniques for examining the dependencies of the other attributes. Consider, for example, a large database of personal data. If one wants to find dependencies between the parameter sales (of a person) and other attributes such as salary, age, and travel expenses, one might sort the data according to the sales parameter and visually examine the dependencies of the other attributes.

3. Query-Dependent Visualization Techniques

Query-independent visualization techniques visualize attribute values by directly mapping them to color. The idea of query-dependent visualization techniques is to visualize the data in the context of a specific user query to give the users feedback on their queries and to direct their search. Instead of directly mapping attribute values to colors, the distances of attribute values to the query are mapped to colors. Since the focus of query-dependent techniques is on the relevance of the data items with respect to the query, different arrangements of the pixels are appropriate. Experiments with several arrangements, such as the left-right or top-down arrangements, show that for visualizing the results of a database query it is most natural to present the data items with highest relevance to the query (e.g., data items fulfilling the query) in the center of the display. The first approach described in Keim (1995a) and Keim and Kriegel (1994) arranges the data items with lower relevances in a rectangular spiral shape around the center. The more recent generalized spiral and the circle-segments techniques are generalizations of those techniques.

In the case of the generalized-spiral technique, the original spiral arrangement (Keim and Kriegel, 1994) is extended to a generic snake- or Hilbert-like form, of which the user may choose the height (cf. Figure 3). As in the case of query-independent visualization techniques, a separate visualization for each of the attributes is generated (cf. Figure 1). An additional subwindow shows the overall distances. In all subwindows, the pixels for each data item are placed at the same position as the overall distance for the data item in the overall distance

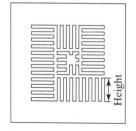

Figure 3 Generalized-spiral technique

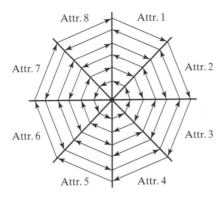

Figure 4 The circle-segments technique for eight-dimensional data

subwindow. By relating corresponding regions in the different windows, the user is able to perceive data characteristics such as multidimensional clusters or correlations. Additionally, the separate subwindows for each of the selection predicates provide important feedback to the user, for example, on the restrictiveness of each of the selection predicates and on single exceptional data items. Note that the original spiral technique is a special case of the generalized-spiral technique with a height of one pixel. The advantage of the generalized-spiral technique is that the degree of clustering is higher. For details on the different variants of the generalized-spiral technique and a first examination of their effectiveness the reader is referred to Keim (1995b).

A second query-dependent technique is the circle-segments technique. The basic idea of the circle-segments visualization technique is to display the distances for the attributes as segments of a circle (cf. Figure 4). If the data consists of k attributes, the circle is partitioned into k segments, each representing the distances for one attribute. Inside the segments, the distance values belonging to one attribute are arranged from the center of the circle to the outside in a back and forth manner orthogonal to the line that halves the segment. An example for a circle-segments visualization of fifty stock price developments from the FAZ index database used in the example above is presented in Figure 5. The main advantage of circle-segments over recursive pattern and other techniques is that the overall representation of the whole data set is more perceivable—including potential dependencies, analogies, and correlations between the dimensions. For details on the circle segments technique, the reader is referred to Ankerst et al. (1996).

4. The VisDB System

Several pixel-oriented visualization techniques, including the techniques described in the previous sections, are implemented as part of the VisDB system (Keim and Kriegel, 1995). In addition to pixel-oriented techniques, the VisDB system also supports the parallel coordinates technique developed by Inselberg and Dimsdale (Inselberg, 1981; Inselberg and Dimsdale, 1990) and the stick figure technique developed by Picket and Grinstein (1988) from the University of Massachusetts, Lowell. The VisDB system is implemented in C++/Motif and runs under X-Windows on HP, Sun, SGI, and Linux machines. The system consists of an interactive interface, which is divided into the visualization portion and the query specification portion for query-dependent techniques (see Figure 6). The query specification portion provides a slider-based direct-interaction interface, which allows an intuitive specification of queries (Keim, 1995a; Keim et al., 1994). Different types of sliders are available for different data types. Other options that support the data exploration process are the ability to focus on certain colors and the ability to retrieve the data values corresponding to a pixel of the display. The current version of the VisDB system is main memory based and allows interactive query-dependent visualizations of databases with less than 100,000 data values; for larger databases,

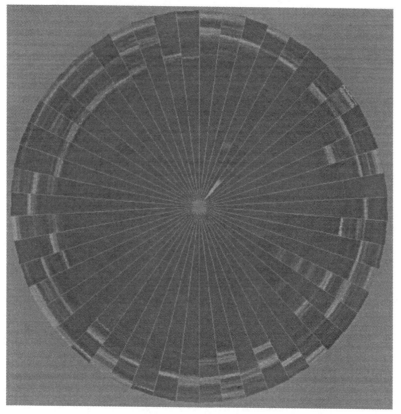

Figure 5 Circle-segments visualization of fifty stocks from January 1974 to April 1995 (about 530,000 data values; cf. Keim, 2000).

the time is still in the range of the few seconds (for 1,000,000 data values, for example, the response time is about twenty seconds).

The VisDB system has been successfully used in several application areas including a financial application where the system has been used to analyze multidimensional time-dependent data, a CAD database project where the system has been used to improve the similarity search, as well as a molecular biology project where the system has been used to find possible docking regions by identifying sets of surface points with distinct characteristics (Keim, 1995a). A preliminary evaluation and comparison of multiple visualization techniques using different data sets and queries is reported in Keim and Kriegel (1996).

5. The VisualPoints System

In a large number of applications, data are referenced by their spatial locations. Visualizing large amounts of spatially referenced data on a limited-size screen display often results in poor visualizations due to the high degree of overplotting of neighboring data points. The VisualPoints system (Keim and Herrmann, 1998) implements a new approach to visualizing large amounts of spatially referenced data. The basic idea is to intelligently use the unoccupied pixels of the display instead of overplotting data points. The VisualPoints system implements three solutions to the problem which are based on:

1. Placing overlapping data points on the nearest unoccupied pixel.
2. Shifting data points along a screen-filling curve (e.g., Hilbert-curve).
3. Hierarchically partitioning and reorganizing the data space.

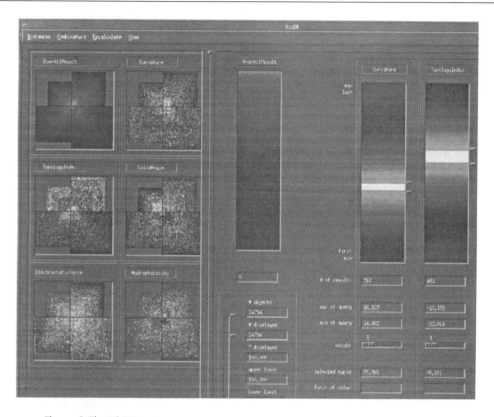

Figure 6 The VisDB system.

Extensive experiments and evaluations of mathematically defined effectiveness criteria show the superior effectiveness and efficiency of the third approach, which is also called the Gridfit-approach (Keim and Herrmann, 1998). Applications of the VisualPoints system include all types of spatial data, such as telecommunications and census data. An application example of lightning strike data in Southern Germany is presented in Figure 7.

Figures 1, 3, 4, 5, 6, and 7 were previously published in Keim "Designing Axel-oriented Visualization Technique. Theory and Application," in *Transactions on Visualization and Computer Graphics*, 2000. Reprinted by permission of IEEE.

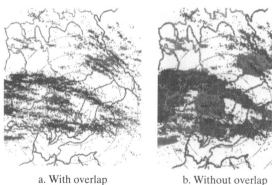

a. With overlap   b. Without overlap

Figure 7 Lightning strike data.

References

Hilbert, D. 1891. "Über stetige Abbildung einer Liner auf ein Flächenstück." *Math. Annalen* **38**: 459–460.

Inselberg, A. 1981. "N-dimensional graphics Part I: lines & hyperplanes."IBM LA Science Center Report # G320-2711.

Inselberg, A., and B. Dimsdale. 1990. "Parallel coordinates: a tool for visualizing multi-dimensional geometry." In *Visualization '90*, pp. 361–370. Los Alamitos, CA: IEEE Press.

Keim, D. A. 1995a. *Visual Support for Query Specification and Data Mining*. Aachen, Germany: Shaker-Publishing Company. Originally released as Ph.D. diss., University of Munich, July 1994.

Keim, D. A. 1995b. "Enhancing the visual clustering of query-dependent database visualization techniques using screen-filing curves." In *Proceedings of the Workshop on Database Issues for Data Visualization*. Lecture Notes in Computer Science, No. 1183, pp. 101–110. Berlin: Springer.

Keim, D. A. 2000. "Designing rival oriented visualization techniques: theory and applications." *Trans Visualization and Computer Graphics* **6**: 59–78.

Keim, D. A., and A. Herrmann. 1998. "The Gridfit Algorithm: an efficient and effective approach to visualizing large amounts of spatial data." In *Visualization '98*. Research Triangle Park, NC, pp. 181–188, 531. New York: ACM Press.

Keim, D. A., and H.-P. Kriegel. 1994. "VisDB database exploration using multidimensional visualization." *Comput. Graphics & Appl.*, pp. 40–49.

Keim, D. A., and H.-P. Kriegel. 1995. "VisDB: a system for visualizing large databases, system demonstration." In *ACM SIGMOD International Conference on Management of Data*, pp. 482. New York, and San Jose, CA: ACM Press.

Keim, D. A., and H.-P. Kriegel. 1996. "Visualization techniques for mining large databases: a comparison." *Trans. Knowledge and Data Engng* **8**: 923–938.

Keim, D. A., H.-P. Kriegel, and M. Ankerst. 1995. "Recursive pattern: a technique for visualizing very large amounts of data." In *Visualization '95*, pp. 279–286. Los Alamitos, CA: IEEE Press.

Keim, D. A., H.-P. Kriegel, and T. Seidl. 1994. "Supporting data mining of large databases by visual feedback queries." In *Proceedings of the International Conference on Data Engineering*, pp. 302–313. Los Alamitos, CA: IEEE Press.

Morton, G. M. 1966. In *A Computer Oriented Geodetic Data Base and a New Technique in File Sequencing*. Ottawa, Canada: IBM Ltd.

Peano, G. 1890. "Sur une courbe qui remplit toute une aire plaine." *Math. Annalen* **36**: 157–160.

Pickett, R. M., and G. G. Grinstein. 1988. "Iconographic displays for visualizing multidimensional data." In *Proceedings of the IEEE Conference on Systems, Man and Cybernetics*, pp. 514–519. Los Alamitos, CA: IEEE Press.

24.4 Commercial Domain, Single Mining Task Systems

24.4.1 TETRAD II

Clark Glymour ·

ABSTRACT The TETRAD programs, now in their third edition, use independence and conditional independence relations found in a data set to suggest a causal Bayes net, or directed graphical model, or collection of such models. Users can specify background knowledge restricting the possible causal explanations and can search with or without the assumption that there are no unmeasured common causes or confounders. Models with discrete variables or linear models can be produced. The program includes a facility for Monte Carlo simulations, and TETRAD III includes a Gibbs sampler for Bayesian estimation of linear models. The programs have been applied to a variety of scientific problems.

The TETRAD II program provides a flexible aid for searching for linear and nonlinear causal models, and for constructing and operating data-based expert systems. The program has multiple modules, some designed for discovering the graphical structure of a Bayes network (or networks) from data and prior knowledge, some designed for estimating the parameters of a Bayes network given the directed graph of the network and a data set, and some designed for simulation studies. The search procedures in the program have been extensively tested in simulation studies and have proved more flexible and more reliable than the search procedures in linear modeling packages such as LISREL and EQS. The program is unique in including search procedures that can be applied when the user does not know whether unmeasured variables confound associations among measured variables or when there are similar uncertainties about sample selection bias. It is also singular in using algorithms for which proofs of asymptotic correctness are available.

The program has been used both for classification and for causal analysis. For example, Spirtes et al. (1993) predicted the outcome of a randomized greenhouse experiment from nonrandomized, observational data; Druzdzel and Glymour (1999) predicted the effect on college dropout rates of policies that altered the mean SAT scores of entering students; Akleman et al. (1999) predicted market prices for corn from exchange rates; DeFazio et al. (1999) identified the composition of rock samples from reflectance spectra; Scheines (1997) found more negative effects of low-level lead exposure on children's verbal IQ scores; and Shipley (2000) has analyzed a variety of biological data using the program and related procedures.

TETRAD II is commercially available as a DOS program, distributed by Lawrence Erlbaum publishers. The algorithms used in TETRAD II are described in Spirtes et al. (1993), and uses of the modules are described and illustrated in an accompanying manual. The program has a very simple interface without graphics and is limited to thirty variables. TETRAD III, an experimental program not commercially available, incorporates improved search procedures, allows an unlimited number of variables, and includes a Gibb's sampling estimator. The TETRAD III program can be accessed through the TETRAD Project Homepage (http://hss.cmu.edu/philosophy/TETRAD/tetrad.html). A Java version, TETRAD IV, can be found at the same site.

The program modules in TETRAD II include the following:

BUILD takes data as input, plus the user's knowledge of the domain, and outputs a description of graphs of causal models that explain patterns in the data, consistent with the prior knowledge specified by the user. BUILD includes features to detect the presence of latent variables in linear systems—unmeasured variables that act upon two or more measured variables—and can make inferences when prior knowledge does not exclude confounding variables. BUILD can be used with raw data assuming the variables are jointly multinormal or jointly multinomial, or with conditional independence results from other procedures. The program conducts a series of conditional independence tests, with significance levels that can be set by the user.

ESTIMATE takes as input discrete, raw data and a graphical Bayes net model with unspecified parameters and provides a maximum likelihood estimate of the model. Run in sequence on discrete data, BUILD and ESTIMATE can produce a Bayes network that can be used as an expert system. To do so, the user must choose a specific network from among the alternatives that BUILD proposes.

UPDATE uses a Bayes network to estimate the probability of any value of any variable of interest given the value of any subset of other variables in the network. With the user's help in model selection, BUILD, ESTIMATE, and UPDATE together form and operate a standard Bayes net expert system based on data and the user's knowledge of the domain.

PURIFY takes as input covariance data for continuous variables and a preliminary clustering of variables; for each cluster, PURIFY outputs a subset of variables for which there is a unidimensional measurement model, or, in other words, within each cluster the program finds a set of measured variables related only by a single unmeasured factor.

MIMBUILD takes as input covariance data, the user's prior knowledge, and measurement models obtained from PURIFY and outputs information about structural relations among the latent factors.

SEARCH performs the same function as the original TETRAD program: from input consisting of covariance data, a linear model, and other prior knowledge, it searches for elaborations of the initial model that offer improved explanations of the data.

STATWRITER takes TETRAD II model formats and writes corresponding input files for several statistical estimation packages, including CALIS, EQS, and LISREL. Using the STATWRITER and BUILD or MIMBUILD, a user can search for linear models with TETRAD and estimate and test models with these packages.

MONTE is a program for generating simulated data from models of continuous or discrete data.

Under specified assumptions about the connection between probability distributions and structure, the outputs of BUILD, PURIFY, and MIMBUILD have been proved correct in the large sample limit.

References

Akleman, D. G., D. A. Bessler, and D. M. Burton. 1999. "Modeling corn exports and exchange rates with directed graphs and statistical loss functions". In *Computation, Causation and Discovery*, edited by C. Glymour, and G. Cooper. Cambridge, MA: MIT/AAAI Press.

DeFazio, J., C. Glymour, J. Ramsey, T. Richardson, T. Roush, and R. Scheines. 1999. "Automated identification of mineral composition from near-infrared reflectance spectra." Technical report. Pittsburgh: Carnegie Mellon University.

Druzdzel, M., and C. Glymour. 1999. "Causal inferences from databases: why universities lose students." In *Computation, Causation and Discovery*, edited by C. Glymour, and G. Cooper. Cambridge, MA: MIT/AAAI Press.

Scheines, R. 1997. "Estimating latent causal influences: TETRAD II model selection and Bayesian parameter estimation." edited by C. Glymour, and G. Cooper, In *Computation, Causation and Discovery*. Cambridge, MA: MIT/AAAI Press.

Shipley, B. 2000. *Cause and Correlation in Biology*. Oxford: Oxford University Press.

Spirtes, P., C. Glymour, and R. Scheines. 1993. *Causation, Prediction and Search*. New York: Springer-Verlag.

24.4.2 Visual Insights

Stephen G. Eick

ABSTRACT Visual Insights is a Lucent Technology New Ventures company focused on building visual applications for understanding customer-related information. Visual Insights software provides both better presentation than existing displays and also interactive analysis and querying capability.

1. Introduction

Visual Insights (http://www.visualinsights.com), a venture of Lucent Technologies, was launched in December 1997 and is positioned as an emerging-growth software company with an outside board and sponsorship in Lucent's New Ventures Group. The company was formed to commercialize Bell Labs research technology in visual data mining. Visual Insights produces a suite of visual data mining products aimed at specific information discovery tasks, based on a common technology.

The motivating idea for visual data mining is to combine the two most powerful information processing machines: the modern computer and the human brain. Using visual attributes such as color, size, shape, layout, and dynamic interaction, it is possible to display usefully large amounts of information. Humans, using pattern recognition skills that have evolved over millions of years, can instantly recognize patterns that would otherwise be buried in masses of details. Human intuition and recognition abilities complement the far more powerful algorithmic capability and processing power of machines. The visual data mining approach is to leverage both by providing macroscopic overviews of relationships and complex interdependencies along with detail-specific, drill-down views showing algorithm results.

The research technology described in Section 2 is a set of interactive views that functions as a dynamic presentation layer for information intensive systems. Visual Insights applications typically involve combining the presentation layer, a data collection system, and domain-specific mining algorithms. Visual Insights' ADVIZOR product set, as of May, 1999, includes three products:

ADVIZOR: a complete visual query and analysis application.

ADVIZOR/Vz: for cost effective deployment of ADVIZOR-based applications and application templates.

ADVIZOR/Developers Edition: for original equipment manufacture (OEMS) and value-added resellers (VARs) to author interactive visual applications.

The aim of Visual Insights technology is to help businesses analyze the ever-increasing amounts of data, find patterns and trends previously unrecognizable, decrease the time between problem identification and solution implementation, and communicate decisions effectively and clearly.

2. Technology Description

Visual Insights technology consists of a rich set of views, each embodying a unique graphical representation or visual metaphor for representing data. Some of the metaphors are conventional, as with the line, pie, and scatterplot view (Figure 1), whereas others are novel, such as, for example, the data constellations view (Figure 2).

The views work together to provide a multiview, visual data analysis environment. Each provides a different perspective, and by combining them into an analysis environment, the total power is significantly more than the sum of the individual contributions. One key idea that makes the environment successful is a very careful choice of interactive operations. Some operations are view-specific, but most, such as selections, automatically propagate among all open views. The core technology is based on a library implementing linked views for interactive statistical graphics (cf. Chapter 15.1). The views implement a number of highly multivariate interaction techniques as discussed in Chapter 15.2 and animation methods as discussed in Chapter 15.4.

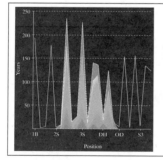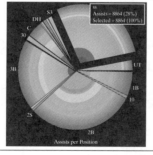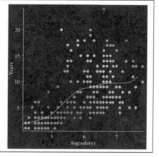

Figure 1 Line chart, pie chart, and scatterplot

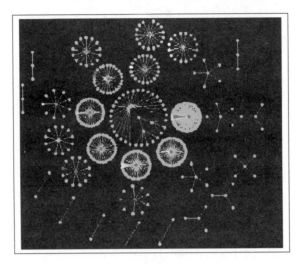

Figure 2 Data constellations graph layout view

There are several special features of the views that make them powerful:

High interactivity. Each view functions both as a display of data and as an input environment accepting user commands. Interactive operations are fast, dynamic, intuitive, and reversible.

View Linking. Interactive operations, such as filtering, selection, highlighting, labeling, and identifying, automatically propagate instantly among all views (Wills, 1999; cf. Chapter 15.1).

Filtering. Mouse-operated filters dynamically reduce the amount of information displayed, thereby eliminating visual clutter that overwhelms static displays.

Colorful. The views use several rich color scales to layer information on top of the display, thereby adding another data dimension.

Scalable. By careful choice of algorithms, the views work with much larger data sets.

Drill down and aggregation. Providing easy mechanisms for users to drill down for details and to aggregate up increases the utility of the views.

2.1. Architectural Vision Drivers

There are eight architectural forces that have influenced view creation and how the software is structured:

1. *Intuitive and easy to use.* The software is designed to make new users productive as quickly as possible while simultaneously providing shortcuts to avoid frustrating experienced users.

2. *Easy to integrate and deploy.* The software must be compatible with existing applications, have clean program APIs, and be easy to install.

3. *Broad problem solving capability.* The views and algorithms must address a wide set of user problems and tasks.

4. *Robust across many different patterns and types of data.* For wide applicability, the views must work across a range of data sets from different problem classes.

5. *High performance delivering fast interactive responses.* A key idea, leveraged in Visual Insights technology, is that users interactively manipulate the views to discover patterns.

This technique, frequently called *parameter focusing*, is similar to focusing the lens on a camera. As users manipulate controls, images suddenly pop into focus revealing patterns. Two things are required for parameter focusing to be effective. The manipulation controls must be easy to use and the client computer must have a powerful graphics card to deliver continuous screen updates.

6. *Broad data access.* It is important to be able to import and process data from all standard sources.

7. *Scalability to work with large data sets.* Many interesting data mining problems involve large data sets.

8. *Ubiquity.* Our aim is to support all standard platforms, in particular, Web-based browser interfaces.

3. Visualization Views

The initial product release of Visual Insights ActiveX Components contains ten production views, with another dozen as research prototypes that may be included in future releases. The views may be divided into four classes: elementary and presentation-oriented (lines, pies), aggregate (bar chart, histogram), drill down for showing details (data sheet, counts), and relationship discovery views (scatterplot, parabox, data constellations, time table).

3.1. Interactive Barchart

The barchart shown in Figure 3, improves on traditional bar charts by including:

Animation, to select and highlight each bar sequentially (cf. Chapter 15.4).

Sorting (Figure 3b), to reorder the bars by name, count, category, selected, or percent selected.

Axis flipping (Figure 3b), to reorient the plot.

Spine plots (Figure 3c), where the bar thickness rather than bar height encodes the statistic.

Integrated color coding, to highlight subcategories within each bar.

3.2. Smoothed Histogram

Figure 4 shows a smoothed frequency distribution. Users manipulate the amount of smoothing by adjusting an interactive slider (not shown), and they can transform the data using either log, linear, or square roots.

3.3. Data Sheet

Data sheet, in Figure 5, is a view for drilling down on individual data items. It shows values using text (Figure 5a), and uses a sequence of progressively smaller fonts to pack more

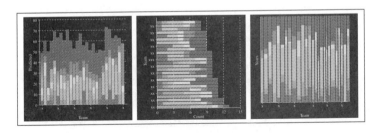

Figure 3 Interactive bar chart. (a) Stacked bar chart, (b) axis flipped and sorted in increasing order, (c) spine plot where bar thickness encodes the statistic rather than the bar height

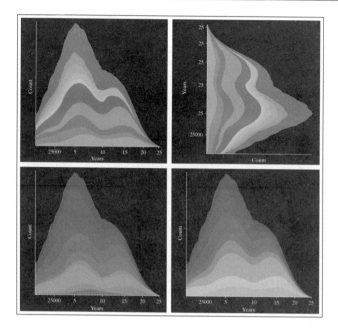

Figure 4 Histogram with different orientations. The densities displayed have been coded using another variable

information onto the display. To the extreme right in Figure 5b, each data entry is represented by a thin single row whose length encodes the value.

3.4. Counts

Counts, in Figure 6, provide statistical summaries of data. The summaries include the mean, mode, minimum, and maximum for each variable in the table.

3.5. Line Chart, Pie Chart, Scatterplot

Figure 1 shows the Visual Insights line chart, pie chart, and scatterplot. These views are conventional, but considerably more powerful due to their interactivity, linking, and scalability.

3.6. Parabox

A Parabox, Figure 7, is a combination of a boxplot and a parallel coordinates plot. It consists of a series of boxplots with parallel coordinates plotted on top. This combination is powerful

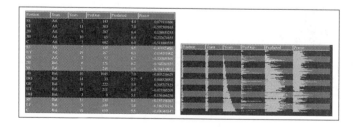

Figure 5 (a) Data sheet showing text and (b) collapsed and sorted

Statistic	log(Salary)	Errors	Position	Team	Years
	Number	Number	String	String	Number
Count	261	261	261	261	261
Selected	261	261	261	261	261
Deleted					
Mean	5.9356	8.6054			7.3678
Mean Sel	5.9356	8.6054			7.3678
Std Dev	0.05495	0.4112			0.2963
Std Sel	0.05495	0.4112			0.2963
Min	4.2000				1
Min Sel	4.2000				1
Max	7.8000	32			24
Max Sel	7.8000	32			24
Sum	1549.2	2246			1923
Sum Sel	1549.2	2246			1923
Unique			23	26	
Uniq Sel			23	26	
Mode			3B	S.E.	
Mode Sel			3B	S.E.	

Figure 6 Count showing a statistical summary of a data table

because boxplots show single variable distributions, and the parallel coordinates show unusual multidimensional observations. The combination shows both.

3.7. Data Constellations

Data constellations show relationships among data items that can be represented as nodes and links on a graph. Associations between items are represented by link thickness, color, and style. Item statistics are encoded in node size, color, and shape.

There are two innovative aspects to data constellations (Wills, 1997). First, they include a suite of scalable graph layout algorithms that exploit hierarchy and sparseness. These layout algorithms produce novel layouts for very large graphs. Second, they implement interactive techniques including panning, zooming, scaling, and filtering that help users navigate and understand the graph.

3.8. Time Table

Time table, in Figure 8, shows discrete time-stamped events that are grouped by a predefined, possibly hierachal, categorical variable. Time table displays events on a X-Y grid with time running along the X-axis and event category along the Y-axis. Each event is represented by a tick mark, with different mark colors and styles corresponding to different types of events. An event spawning a sequence of related events appears in this view as an easily identifiable vertical ladder.

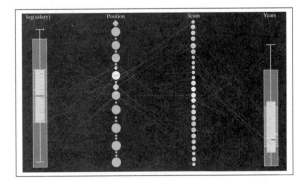

Figure 7 Parabox is a combination of boxplot and a parallel coordinates plot

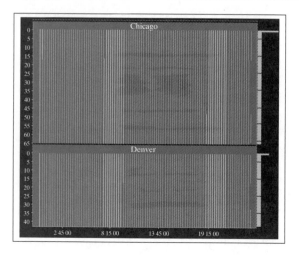

Figure 8 Time table showing time-stamped events

4. Software Architecture

The software is partitioned into three layers. At the lowest level is the Vz C++ class library. Vz is an object-oriented cross-platform C++ library that encapsulates interaction, graphics, and view linking and provides core objects and data structures for visualizations. Vz currently runs under Unix and MS Windows, and it supports OpenGL, X11, and Microsoft graphics APIs. The views are built using Vz primitives.

Above Vz are C++ wrappers that package the views as ActiveX controls. For each view, the wrappers provide dialogue boxes for setting common properties, such as which data table to display, and view-specific properties, such as the smoothing level for the histogram.

The data to be visualized is stored in tables kept in the data pool. When multiple views display data from the same table, they are automatically linked. The data tables are populated using the Structured Data Reader. SDR can access data from flat files, or from relational databases using an ODBC interface.

At the highest level, the Visual Insights platform provides window management, data table population, and scripting. This MS Windows applications is built using the Microsoft Foundation Class. It can host any ActiveX controls including, of course, the Visual Insights views. The platform windows are optimized for hosting the views, and they perform window housekeeping tasks. For screen real estate management, the views automatically resize as the main window resizes and the platform contains a general splitter window for hosting any number of views in an any arbitrary rectangular layout.

As an automation server, the platform is easily integrated with MS Windows applications from different vendors. The integrating program can range from a simple script to a complex front-end written in Visual Basic or C++. The most-used automation method to date is scripting. Scripting languages such as VBscript, Jscript, and Perl are ideal for building platform-based applications. Every platform operation is scriptable and our experience has been that this environment is ideal for rapid prototyping.

5. Supported Knowledge Discovery Tasks

There are several broad classes of knowledge discovery tasks that Visual Insights technology addresses:

Exploratory data analysis through using the aggregate views to provide an overview of a data set, the relationship discovery views to make discoveries, drill downs for confirmation, and the presentation views for communication.

Gestalt involves understanding a data set and complex relationships at different levels of detail. The view set supports fusion by providing macroscopic views showing broad slices of data with microscopic detail-oriented views.

Cleaning is perhaps one the most time consuming tasks with any analysis of real data. Real data sets frequently contain errors, missing values, outliers, and unusual events that bias automatic techniques. It is often a manual task to find the unusual values in a data set and figure out if they are real or spurious. Interactivity in the views makes it easy to spot unusual data items, select them, and check their validity (cf. Chapter 13.1).

6. Brief History

Visual Insights began as a research project in Bell Labs focused on mining corporate databases for business actionable results. The initial research project involved analyzing software source code databases to understand complexity in large software projects. The essential problem is that the complexity in large software projects overwhelms the intellectual capability of any individual or even any team of individuals. The focus of this research was to develop visual tools to enable software engineers to extract information latent in change management databases. This led to a suite of novel views for showing change patterns in text, the integrity constraint structure of relational databases, and the evolution of a large software system (Eick et al., 1992; Baker and Eick, 1995; Ball and Eick, 1996; Antis et al., 1996).

The technology has matured over several years and has been applied to a wide variety of corporate mining problems. Interesting examples include analyzing time-stamped failure events generated by network equipment and captured in log files (Eick and Lucas, 1996) and detecting fraud in streams of international phone calls (Cox et al., 1996).

References

Antis, J. M., S. G. Eick, and J. D. Pyrce. 1996. "Visualizing the structure of relational databases." *IEEE Softw.*, pp. 72–79.

Baker, M. J., and S. G. Eick. 1995. "Space-filling software displays." *J. Visual Lang. Comput.* **6(2)**: 119–133.

Ball, T. A., and S. G. Eick. 1996. "Software visualization in the large." *IEEE Comput.* **29(4)**: 33–43.

Cox, K. C., S. G. Eick, G. J. Wills, and R. J. Brachman. 1997. "Visual data mining: recognizing telephone calling fraud." *J. Data Mining and Knowledge Discovery* **1(2)**: 225–231.

Eick, S. G., and P. J. Lucas. 1996. "Displaying trace files." *Softw. Practice and Experience* **26(4)**: 399–409.

Eick, S. G., J. L. Steffen, and E. E. Sumner, Jr. 1992. "Seesoft™—a tool for visualizing line oriented software statistics." *IEEE Trans. Softw. Engng* **18(11)**: 957–968.

Wills, G. J. 1997. "Nicheworks—interactive visualization of very large graphs." In *Graph Drawing '97 Conference Proceedings*. Lecture Notes in Computer Science, pp. 403–414. Springer-Verlag.

Wills, G. J. 1999. "Natural selection: interactive subset creation." *J. Comput. Graphical Stat.*

24.4.3 Document Explorer

Ronen Feldman

ABSTRACT Document Explorer is a data mining system for document collections. Such a collection represents an application domain, and the primary goal of the system is to derive patterns that provide knowledge about this domain. Additionally, the derived patterns can be used to browse the collection. Document Explorer searches for patterns that capture relations between concepts of the domain. The patterns that have been verified as interesting are structured and presented in a visual user interface allowing the user to operate on the results to refine and redirect mining queries or to access the associated documents. The system offers preprocessing tools to construct or refine a knowledge base of domain concepts and to create an intermediate representation of the document collection that will be used by all subsequent data mining operations. The main pattern types the system can search for are frequent sets, associations (see Chapter 16.2.3 of this handbook), concept distributions, and keyword graphs.

1. Introduction

The information age has made it easy for us to store large amounts of text. The proliferation of documents available on the Web, on corporate intranets, on news wires, and elsewhere is overwhelming. However, while the amount of information available to us is constantly increasing, our ability to absorb and process this information remains constant. Search engines only exacerbate the problem by making more and more documents available in a matter of a few key strokes; so-called push technology makes the problem even worse by constantly reminding us that we are failing to track news, events, and trends everywhere. We experience information overload, and we miss important patterns and relationships even as they unfold before us. As the old adage goes: We can't see the forest for the trees.

Document Explorer offers a new approach to help the user tackle large textual collections. Rather than overwhelm the user with documents, Document Explorer provides the user with knowledge. The system provides the user with a high-level picture of the relevant collection, automatically identifying patterns, correlations, key terms and features, and presenting them to the user in a concise way. Once the user has the larger picture, he or she can then drill down to the relevant documents. With Document Explorer, the user can effectively navigate through large document collections.

Document Explorer is an integrated suite, offering a large variety of tools combined in a single, easy to use platform. The system provides interactive browsers, analysis, and discovery tools, combined with interactive views for viewing and browsing the results, and novel visualization tools (see Chapter 20).

2. Architecture of the Document Explorer System

One of the main drawbacks of the current implementation of text mining systems (e.g., KDT; see Feldman and Dagan, 1995, and Chapter 38 of this handbook) is that they have a fixed set of KDD tools and there is no possibility to generate new tools upon demand. If the user would like to perform a task that is not within the capability of any of the current tools, then this task simply cannot be done within the current systems. In order to overcome this drawback, we have developed a high-level language that will be used to specify the KDD tasks that should be performed. This language, called KDTL (knowledge discovery in texts language), is expressive enough to allow the specification of most KDD operations that might be requested by the user. At the same time, KDTL is simple enough to be used easily. This language is based on a set of primitives that are suitable for the specification of KDD tasks on text collections.

The Document Explorer system contains three main modules. The first module is the backbone of the system and it includes the KDTL query front-end, where the user can enter his queries for patterns; the interpreter, which parses a query, translates it into function, and calls in the lower levels; and the data mining and data management layer. These two layers are responsible for the actual execution of the user's query. The data mining layer contains all the search (see Chapter 11) and pruning strategies that can be applied for mining patterns. The main patterns offered in the system are frequent concept sets (Agrawal et al., 1993; Mannila et al., 1994; associations, Agrawal et al., 1993; and distributions, Feldman and Dagan, 1995).

The embedded search algorithms control the search for specific pattern instances within the target database. This level also includes the refinement methods that filter redundant information and cluster together closely related information. The data management layer is responsible all access to the actual data stored in the target database. This layer encapsulates the target database from the rest of the system.

The second module is the source preprocessing and categorization module. This module includes the set of source converters and the text categorization software. It is responsible for converting the information fetched from each of the available sources into a canonical format and tagging each document with the predefined categories, and for extracting all multiword terms from the documents. In this preprocessing component, the system extracts all the information that will subsequently be used by the data mining methods.

The target database is represented as a compressed data structure, namely a Trie. The fact that we represent the documents as sets of phrases and keywords (concepts) has several implications. We have only binary attributes, and these attributes are sparse (i.e., only a fraction of the attributes appears in any given record, typically around 2–3 percent), and finally the number of records is of medium size (between 20,000 and 500,000 documents). The Trie is an efficient data structure that encapsulates all the information of the document collection. In this Trie, all aggregates existing in the target database are managed in a compressed format. In addition, the Trie provides an efficient approach to incrementally calculate all the aggregates, and to store and access these aggregates. Several forms of Tries can be used that treat the trade-off between space of storing the Trie and time of calculating results derived from the Trie in different ways. For more details on our Trie methods, we refer the reader to Amir et al. (1997).

Besides the target databases, the data mining methods in Document Explorer also exploit a knowledge base on the application domain. The terms of the domain are arranged in a DAG (directed acyclic graph). The terms belong to several hierarchically arranged categories. In the application area of the Reuters newswire collection, used in this paper for application examples, the main categories correspond to countries, economic topics, persons, et cetera. Each category, for example, economic topics, has subcategories (currencies, main economic indicators, etc.). Relations among these categories give further background knowledge. The knowledge base for the Reuters collection includes relations between pairs of countries (e.g., countries with land boundaries), between countries and persons (nationality), countries and commodities (exports), and so on. These relations can be defined by the user or transformed by special utilities from general available sources (such as the CIA World Fact Book, or companies' home pages).

Finally, the third module is the visualization module, which is responsible for providing an attractive set of GUI-based KDD tools (see Section 4) and graph-based visualization techniques that give the user much easier access to the system. Keyword graphs (Feldman and Klösgen, 1997) are a special interactive visualization technique for presenting data mining results. Keyword graphs extend the notion of association rules to relations between keywords and phrases occurring in different documents. A diagram of the Document Explorer system architecture is shown in Figure 1.

We now describe the key components and features of the system.

3. Preprocessing Tools

3.1. Document Annotation

The input for Document Explorer is a collection of textual documents. In the first, preprocessing phase, the documents are analyzed to obtain a set of concepts or terms for each document, characterizing each document in the collection. Document Explorer provides an automatic tool for analyzing and annotating the documents (Currently only English language documents are supported). The documents in the collection are linguistically analyzed, and the significant terms in each document are extracted. Document Explorer provides an interactive tool for viewing the results of the term extraction process, and for manually adding and deleting annotations.

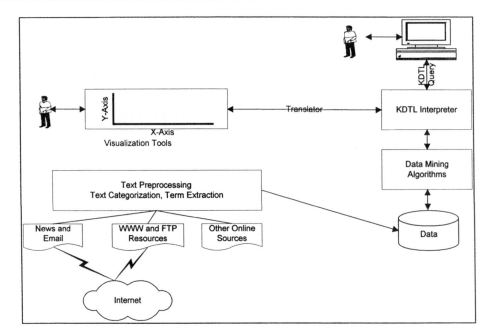

Figure 1 Architecture of the Document Explorer system

3.2. *Term Hierarchy Editor*

In order to make full use of Document Explorer's knowledge discovery tools, it is best if the documents' annotations are grouped into categories of related terms (e.g., country names, machine parts, etc.), and placed in a hierarchical structure. The Term-Hierarchy editor, included in Document Explorer, provides a graphical tool for easy construction and manipulation of such hierarchies. Document Explorer also comes with a predefined term hierarchy for common topics (e.g., company names, people, etc.).

3.3. *The Knowledge Discovery Toolkit*

The heart of Document Explorer is a full suite of knowledge discovery tools, which allow the user to get the large picture emerging from the document collection. In Document Explorer, discovery is an interactive process. The user dynamically both guides and is guided by the discovery process. The interaction between the two is what gives the system much of its power.

Document Explorer provides the user with extensive visualization and browsing tools for viewing the results of the discovery process. The user is provided with dynamic browsers, which allow dynamic drill down and roll up, in order to focus on the relevant results. We note that any part of the discovery process can be applied either to the entire collection or to any subsets of the collection.

Throughout the mining operation, the system maintains the links to the original documents. Thus, at any stage in the discovery process, the user can always access the actual documents that contributed to the discovered pattern.

Document Explorer tools can be grouped into four main categories: browsers, profile analysis, clustering, and pattern discovery tools. In addition, the system provides novel visualization techniques. A brief description of each of the main discovery tools follows. The visualization tools are described in the subsequent section.

3.4. Browsers

Browsers provide the user with the basic means to access and comprehend the data at hand. With Document Explorer, the discovery process already starts at the browsing level.

Document Explorer provides the user with dynamic, content-based facilities. Thus, the browsing is guided by the actual data at hand, not by fixed rigid structures. Document Explorer provides two content-based browsers: Distribution Browser and Interactive Distribution Browser.

DISTRIBUTION BROWSER

The distribution browser presents the user with the frequency of all terms (= concepts) in the collections, grouped by category, and allows the collection to be browsed based on these frequencies. In addition, the Distribution Browser allows the user to specify a base concept and the browser presents the user with the distribution of all other concepts with respect to the base concept. Using this tool, the user can immediately gain information as to what are the most relevant terms related to whatever he or she is interested in. For example, given a collection of news articles, the user may immediately learn that the main business of Philip Morris is tobacco, or that Wang Yeping is strongly affiliated with China (she is the President's wife). Note that this information is obtained before even reading a single document. At any time, the user may drill down and access the actual documents of interest. Thus, Distribution Browser provides a content-based browsing tool, where navigation through the collection is guided by the distribution and relations of concepts within the given collection.

INTERACTIVE DISTRIBUTION BROWSER

The Interactive Distribution Browser provides the user with a flexible interactive browsing facility, allowing him or her to navigate through the data while being guided by the data itself. The Interactive Distribution Browser allows the user to zoom in and out on sets of concepts in the collection, and to obtain online information on the distribution of these concepts within the collection, as well as their relation to other concepts. At any time, the user may drill down and access any document of interest.

3.5. Profile Analysis

Document Explorer provides the user with tools to analyze the profiles of the terms represented in the collection. Thus, the user can gain understanding on the overall nature of a term even before reading any actual document. Document Explorer provides two profile analysis tools: Group Profile Analyzer and Profile Comparison.

GROUP PROFILE ANALYZER

This tool allows the user to specify a group of terms and compute their average profile. The system then presents the user with the overall group profile, and for each individual member, an indication on areas where it is most similar and most different from the group profile. Thus, the user obtains a high-level picture of the overall nature of the group, as well as the special characteristics of the individual members.

PROFILE COMPARISON

The Profile Comparison tool allows the user to specify two terms and to compare their profile. The system presents the user with the key similarities and differences between the two terms. Thus, the user is provided with knowledge on the relationship between the different concepts in the collection.

3.6. Clustering

The clustering tool provides the user with an automatic tool to cluster together related documents (see Chapter 16.5 of this handbook). Each cluster represents a set of documents with common characteristics. The clustering procedure gives the user the intrinsic grouping of the documents within the collection, thus providing him or her with insight into the structure of the collection. Any cluster can be subject to further analysis (including reclustering).

3.7. Pattern Discovery Tools

The Document Explorer system is designed to help the user find the hidden knowledge buried in the large collection. To this end, Document Explorer is equipped with tools that automatically present the user with significant, outstanding patterns discovered within the collection. The Pattern Discovery tools automatically bring to the surface significant information, pointing the user to the possibly most important phenomena. Document Explorer provides three discovery tools: High Correlation Pairs, Association Discovery, and Maximal Sets.

HIGH CORRELATION PAIRS

The High Correlation Pairs tool automatically locates, and presents to the user, pairs of terms that are highly correlated with each other. Thus, the user is automatically presented with the most important relationships within the collection.

ASSOCIATION DISCOVERY

The Association Discovery tool exhibits the ultimate in unaided knowledge discovery. With this tool, the system automatically finds all significant associations between any sets of concepts, based on the entire collection. For example, the system may find that whenever Microsoft and the Justice Department appear in a document, so does Explorer, in most cases. Thus, the system automatically reveals the buried structure of the information at hand. Efficient browsing tools help in finding the relevant associations.

MAXIMAL SETS

The Maximal Sets tool automatically identifies groups of terms, which are highly correlated within themselves, but uncorrelated with other terms. Thus, the tool helps identify pockets of related concepts.

4. Visualization Tools

Document Explorer is equipped with novel visualization tools, which aid the user in gaining a quick understanding of the main features of the collection. The visualization tools provide a graphical representation of the connection between terms (concepts) in the collection. The graphical representations provide the user with a high-level bird's-eye summary of the collection. We describe three of Document Explorer's main visualization tools: keyword graphs, trend graphs, and category connection maps.

4.1. Keyword Graphs

A keyword graph consists of a set of vertices and edges. The vertices of the graph represent terms (concepts). The (weighted) edges represent the affinity between the concepts. Each vertex in the keyword graph represents a single concept, and two concepts are connected by an edge if their similarity, with respect to a predefined similarity function, is larger than a given threshold. A keyword graph is defined with respect to a context, which determines the context in which the similarity of keywords is of interest. Figure 2 shows a keyword graph for the country category in the context of crude oil.

Keyword graphs can either be defined for an entire collection, or for subsets of the collection, and for arbitrarily complex contexts. The system provides the user with an interactive tool for defining and refining the graphs.

4.2. Trend Graphs

Trend graphs provide a graphical representation of the evolution of the collection over time. The user is presented with a dynamic picture, whose changes reflect the changes in the collection. The user can focus on any slice in time, and obtain the state of the information at

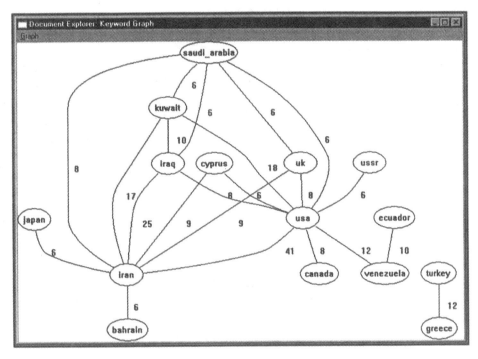

Figure 2 A keyword graph—countries in the context of crude oil

the given time. The user can also define the granularity at which the information is analyzed and presented.

4.3. Category Connection Maps

This visualization tool enables the user to view the connections between a number of different categories, in relation to a given context. Figure 3 presents the connections between the

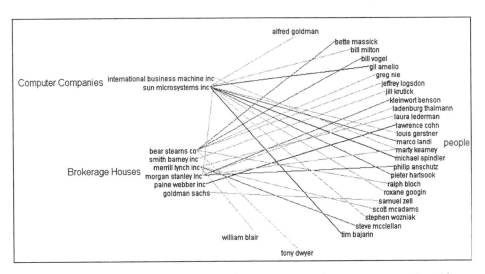

Figure 3 Category map for people, brokerage houses, and computer companies with respect to mergers

categories of people, brokerage houses, and computer companies with respect to the context of mergers.

Any results obtained by Document Explorer can be automatically generated as a report. This includes all figures, tables, and so forth. Reports are generated in MS Word format.

DEVELOPERS

Ronen Feldman, Yonatan Aumann, David Landau, Orly Lipshtat, Amir Zilberstien, and Moshe Fresko.

STATUS

The Document Explorer system has been commercially available from Instinct Software since August 1998. The current implementation for Document Explorer runs under MS Windows NT. The code is written in C++. The design employs a client = server architecture, with the entire engine written in pure C++.

References

Agrawal, A., and R. Srikant. 1994. "Fast algorithms for mining association rules." In *Proceedings of the VLDB Conference*. Santiago de Chile.

Agrawal, A., T. Imielinski, and A. Swami. 1993. "Mining association rules between sets of items in large databases." In *Proceedings of the ACM SIGMOD Conference on Management of Data*, pp. 207–216.

Agrawal, R., H. Mannila, R. Srikant, H. Toivonen, and I. Verkamo. 1995. "Fast discovery of association rules." In *Advances in Knowledge Discovery and Data Mining*, edited by U. Fayyad, G. Piatetsky-Shapiro, P. Smyth, and R. Uthurusamy, pp. 307–328: AAAI Press.

Amir, A., Y. Aumann, R. Feldman, and O. Katz. 1997. "Efficient algorithm for association generation." Technical Report. Department of Computer Science, Bar-Ilan University, Israel

Apte, C., F. Damerau, and S. Weiss. 1994. "Towards language independent automated learning of text categorization models." In *Proceedings of ACM-SIGIR Conference on Information Retrieval*.

Feldman, R., and I. Dagan. August 1995. "KDT—knowledge discovery in texts." In *Proceedings of the First International Conference on Knowledge Discovery (KDD-95)*.

Feldman, R., and H. Hirsh. 1997. "Exploiting background information in knowledge discovery from text." *J. Intell. Inform. Sys.*

Feldman, R. and W. Klösgen. 1997. "Visualization techniques for exploring data mining results in document collections." Technical Report. Department of Computer Science, Bar-Ilan University, Israel.

Feldman, R., I. Dagan, and W. Klösgen. April 1996. "Efficient algorithms for mining and manipulating associations in texts." In *Proceedings of EMCSR96*. Vienna, Austria.

Feldman, R., A. Amir, Y. Aumann, A. Zilberstein, and H. Hirsh. 1997. "Incremental Algorithms for Association Generation." In *Proceedings of the First Pacific Asia Conference on Knowledge Discovery and Data Mining (PAKDD97)*. Singapore.

Iwayama, M., and T. Tokunaga. 1994. "A probabilistic model for text categorization based on a single random variable with multiple values." In *Proceedings of the Fourth Conference on Applied Natural Language Processing*.

Klemettinen, M., H. Mannila, P. Ronkainen, H. Toivonen, and A. Verkamo. 1994. "Finding interesting rules from large sets of discovered association rules." In *Proceedings of the Third International Conference on Information and Knowledge Management*.

Klösgen, W. 1995. "Efficient discovery of interesting statements." *J. Intell. Inform. Sys.* **4(1).**

Klösgen, W. 1996. "Explora: A multipattern and multistrategy discovery assistant." In *Advances in Knowledge Discovery and Data Mining*, edited by U. Fayyad, G. Piatetsky-Shapiro, P. Smyth, and R. Uthurusamy. Cambridge, MA: MIT Press.

Klösgen, W. 1997. "Tasks, methods and applications of knowledge extraction." In *New Technologies and Techniques for Statistics*, edited by Eurostat. Amsterdam, The Netherlands: IOS Press.

Mannila, H., H. Toivonen, and A. Verkamo. 1994. "Efficient algorithms for discovering association rules." In *KDD-94: AAAI Workshop on Knowledge Discovery in Databases*, pp. 181–192.

PART FIVE

INTERDISCIPLINARY LINKS OF KDD

25 STATISTICS

David J. Hand

ABSTRACT Statistics and knowledge discovery in databases (KDD) have intersecting aims—the discovery of structures and patterns in data sets—but they also have differences. KDD, for example, is almost always concerned solely with the analysis of data, while statistics is also concerned with optimal strategies for collecting data. On the other hand, statisticians are rarely concerned with efficient strategies for searching large databases, while this is often an important concern in KDD exercises. The data sets examined by KDD researchers tend to be larger than those examined by statisticians, and this has implications for the nature of the analytic tools. Sometimes analysis can be based on subsamples of the data—and statistical inferential procedures adopted. Often, however, there is no alternative to analyzing the entire data set, and the relevance of inferential procedures is less obvious. Likewise, in the past, statisticians have mainly been concerned with static data sets, while data miners are often concerned with data sets that are constantly evolving. This also has implications for the nature of analysis—a method that may be optimal from a statistical perspective may not be optimal from a KDD perspective. In modern statistics, models play a central role. In KDD, however, algorithms are more often regarded as central. Indeed, in much knowledge discovery work, patterns rather than models are the structure being sought. There is then a very real danger that the detected structures will either be artifacts of data contamination or will be simply due to chance.

1. Introduction

It is probably impossible to produce a definition of statistics with which everyone will agree. The discipline certainly includes condensing and summarizing data so as to encapsulate and present the main features in a simple way, as well as the application of formal probability theory to cope with uncertainty. It also includes theories and strategies for the efficient collection of data, where efficient means that the data are collected in the best (cheapest, smallest, quickest, etc.) way to answer the research questions.

Likewise, as will be evident from entries elsewhere in this handbook, the term knowledge discovery and data mining means different things to different people. It includes extensive searches through large data sets for curious or interesting patterns, as well as more formal model-building exercises. One informal definition (Hand, 1998a) is that data mining (as we shall call it for short) is the process of secondary analysis of large databases aimed at finding unsuspected relationships that are of interest or value to the database owners.

What will be clear, even from these brief descriptions, is that there is considerable overlap between the aims and methods of data mining and the aims and methods of statistics. Both are concerned with analyzing data to find patterns and structures within those data. In what follows, some of the similarities are spelled out. However, there are differences, which will also be examined in detail, so that it is legitimate to regard statistics and data mining as distinct disciplines, albeit with some intersecting aims. Moreover, an appreciation of the similarities and differences between the disciplines can lead to more effective data analysis, since one can then borrow strengths from each side as appropriate. Indeed, one can go further than this: both statistics and data-mining are undergoing rapid development (statistics has been described as being in its most exciting stage ever). This in turn means that theoretical problems are being generated and examined. Insight into these theoretical problems and progress in tackling them can be facilitated by an understanding and awareness of concepts and tools from elsewhere. In particular, insight into issues in data-mining can be obtained from the theory underpinning statistics and vice versa. Examples of such issues are: (i) When is it legitimate to base analyses of very large data sets on only subsets, and how should those subsets be drawn? (ii) How can one best search through an astronomically huge space of possible structures to find ones that fit the data well? and (iii) How can one tell if a structure, discovered after a large search, represents a real feature of the underlying process that led to the data or is just a chance fluctuation?

Although, in this chapter the focus is on the relationship between the knowledge discovery process and statistics, it is perhaps useful to note here that data mining also intersects with other disciplines. In particular, it also overlaps with machine learning, artificial intelligence, pattern recognition, and database technology. Looking at this list, one can see that data-mining is an eclectic discipline. It has taken ideas and tools from a wide variety of areas to apply to the particular kind of problems its practitioners wish to solve.

The sections that follow examine each component of the informal definition of data mining from Hand (1998a), given above. While not everyone may agree with the details of this definition (or may not agree that each specific item is always necessary), it seems likely that there will be agreement about the broad picture it paints.

2. KDD as Process

The informal definition above describes data-mining as a process. One does not simply mine data and have done with it. Rather, it is a continuing activity in which one probes a data set in various ways (as described in Section 5 below), examines the results, and then probes the data again, in a slightly different way, informed by the results from the first step. This is repeated, typically many times. Moreover, since the databases encountered in data mining problems (especially commercial problems) are often dynamic and evolving, such examination can go on indefinitely. Furthermore, this process does not merely involve an interaction between the analyst and the data. It also involves an interaction between the analyst and a domain expert. Having found apparently interesting structures, one describes them to the domain expert who then characterizes them as interesting or (perhaps more frequently) otherwise. But this characterization then serves to guide the direction of future searches. By this means, one slowly learns what is interesting and important in the eyes of the database owners.

The process just outlined also occurs in statistical data analysis. It is notable that this contrasts with the apparent nature of statistical analysis as described in many basic texts. The emphasis there is typically placed on the analysis of single (and small and clean; see Section 4) data sets. A question is given; the data are analyzed; and an answer is found. This is unrealistic. Statistical data analysis, like data-mining more generally, is an iterative and cyclic process. (Having said that, perhaps it is worth remarking that the approach taken in many basic texts is understandable. They have limited space and time in which to communicate the essence of the ideas. It is thus natural to concentrate on the key points, even if it does give a rather misleading impression of the real nature of the exercise.)

3. KDD as Secondary Data Analysis

Data mining is secondary data analysis. That is, it is the analysis of data that have been collected to answer some question, or collected as a side effect of some purpose, other than that the data mining exercise is exploring (e.g., in supermarkets, point of sale data acquisition originally arose as a side effect of the simple need to add up the individual prices of the items being purchased). Once collected and stored, the possibility arises that the data set might well contain other information of value to the database owner, perhaps especially if it is large. To return to the supermarket example, one can explore the purchasing behavior of the customers and also see what items tend to be bought together. Analysis can lead to information on how best to serve the customers, and also information on how best to market goods.

Statistics is also often concerned with secondary data analysis. But it is also often concerned with primary data analysis. That is, a question is posed and data collected (and then analyzed) with the specific aim of answering that question. This means that there are other subdisciplines within statistics that are generally not regarded as within the purview of data-mining. These are concerned with how to collect data so that the most accurate (or perhaps cheapest or quickest or . . .) answer may be found to a question. They include the disciplines of experimental design, survey sample design, and (arguably) questionnaire design.

4. Data for Data-Mining

The data sets examined in data-mining were characterized as large in the opening paragraphs. To a classical statistician trained not too many years ago, a large data set might have involved 1,000 data points. Certainly, 10,000 would have been large, and 100,000 or a million would have been very large. But data-mining often concerns itself with data sets of billions of points (see Hand et al., 1999, for some examples). Such large data sets arise from official sources (e.g., census data), scientific and medical sources (e.g., pharmaceutical data, genetics data, astronomical data), but perhaps especially from commercial sources. This is the economic driving force behind most work in data-mining: the possibility that the large body of data one has on one's customers may contain information that could result in a market edge.

Although statistics is a young discipline, its genesis still predates the computer. This has meant that many of the basic statistical tools were developed for application to small data sets. Of course, things are changing as statistics comes to terms with the opportunities provided by the computer, but such changes take time. There is tremendous inertia incorporated in the standard software that is widely used for statistical analysis, as well as in the very process of disseminating scientific results: the editors of scientific journals prefer to see the established way of summarizing and analyzing data, rather than some radically new approach that most of the readers will not have been taught and will probably not understand.

The sizes of the data sets necessarily mean that there must be a separation between the data and the analyst. One can engage directly with 100 data points, plot them this way and that way, and see exactly which points fail to conform to a proposed model. This is not possible with a billion data points. Hand et al. (1999, Figure 6) illustrate how even so basic a statistical tool as a scatterplot collapses under the weight of numbers. A computer program necessarily lies between the data and the analyst. Of course, this very program is what makes any analysis feasible, but it also risks concealing structures. A program that searches for a good linear regression fit will throw up the best such fit but will not reveal the fact that the data are nonlinearly related.

Perfect data exist only in a perfect world, of course. This is true both for the data that statisticians analyze and also for the data subjected to the KDD process. However, the implications may be more important in a data mining context for two reasons. First, the large sizes of data sets subjected to data mining mean that data contamination can produce effects that would be undetectable and unnoticeable in a statistical context with a small data set (even a small effect is significant if the data set is large enough). Second, data mining is often concerned with seeking small structures, anomalous behavior, or something different from the norm (see Section 5). Data contamination is likely to be a source of precisely such anomalies. A data mining exercise may thus throw up patterns satisfying all the appropriate criteria, but which then turn out to be due to the inadequacies of the data collection process. Indeed, Hand (2000) suggests that most of the unexpected patterns detected through data mining may prove to be due to data contamination of some kind, and not to be of any genuine substantive interest. (Of course, data contamination may be of interest in its own right—or may indeed shed light on relationships.)

Data contamination and corruption can be of two types. Low-level contamination refers to distortion or omission of information describing single records—for example, omission of components of a vector of numbers describing an individual (case, person, etc.). High-level problems refer to records that are missing in their entirety: nonresponse, selection bias, and so on. Recognizing, coping with, and correcting such problems is not straightforward, though statisticians have made some headway (with algorithms like the EM algorithm, or by elaborating the statistical model and including a model for the missing data mechanism). It is a problem that few data miners have yet addressed. The solution of an automatic preprocessing stage to clean the data is not an answer (it would typically have to be automatic because of the large data sets involved) because it is likely to remove the very patterns one might hope to detect in the data mining exercise.

Another difference between most statistical work and much data mining work (though there are exceptions in both directions) is that statisticians are often concerned with static data sets, whereas data miners (perhaps especially in commercial contexts) are often concerned with dynamic data sets. For example, a statistician may analyze the data set arising from a clinical trial under the certain knowledge that no further cases will be added to the set. In contrast, a data miner may be analyzing banking transaction data on a daily basis. Moreover, the decisions may be needed the day after. This has several implications.

It means that the analysis must be fast. There is little point in taking three months to analyze a supermarket's Monday's sales if the information is needed to inform shelf-stocking policy for later that week. This means that scalable algorithms are needed (algorithms that increase in a reasonable way with sample size). It can mean that suboptimal models (in the sense that they are not very realistic) are more useful than a statistician's theoretical ideal. For example, the explicit solution that is possible with a linear regression model may be preferable to the iterative solution that is necessary for a logistic regression model, even when one is trying to predict membership of just one of two classes. It has also meant that data mining has placed more emphasis on sequential or adaptive algorithms than has statistics. Here, data-mining has inherited ideas from machine learning where, as the very name suggests, gradual updating of estimates as more data become available is a key aspect. Section 5 has more to say about algorithms.

Of course, in many cases the entire data set does not need to be analyzed. It is sufficient to analyze a sample; that is, provided a proper sampling frame can be identified and a probability sample drawn. This is an area where statisticians are likely to be able to provide highly effective input. The problems are not all trivial or straightforward, as is illustrated by the example of measuring e-commerce interactions on the World Wide Web. Here, the foundations of what one is seeking to measure are changing even as one samples, and at a pace greater than that ever experienced before.

Sampling is an appropriate strategy (to consider, at least) when one is trying to model fairly gross features of the data. However, if one is seeking anomalies, then sampling is clearly inappropriate. For example, if one was trying to identify stolen credit cards from the transaction patterns, sampling would be pointless. It is a necessary condition of the exercise that one looks at all cases.

Occasionally, of course, one is presented with a sample of data at the start. This is typically the case in statistics, where it is rare to be presented with the entire population. The reverse holds in data-mining. One would normally have available (whether one chose to analyze it or not) all of the transactions on a particular day, records of all a company's employees, or details of all the chemical structures. (And in such circumstances, one has to be careful about what one means by inference.)

Finally, one issue that can arise as a consequence of the large size of the databases examined in data mining exercise is how to search the databases efficiently. This is not a problem with which statisticians generally have to concern themselves.

5. The Search for Relationships

Modern statistics is almost entirely model driven. That is, the statistical and inferential exercise is seen as being one of constructing a summary of the data, either to provide a convenient description of its main points or as a reasonable approximation to the process underlying the data generation (which may then be used for predictive purposes, for example, as in regression and discriminant analysis). There are only few exceptions to this—the Gifi (1990) school of nonlinear multivariate analysis and a sample-based approach to survey work are examples.

In contrast, data mining places great emphasis on algorithms. This is perhaps not so surprising when one recalls the necessity of the place of the computer between the data and the analyst in data-mining, discussed above. Of course, statisticians have also been concerned with developing algorithms, but these are generally seen as serving simply to yield the model. The difference in emphasis can be illustrated by the example of regression analysis. To a statistician, regression analysis involves fitting a model by maximizing the likelihood, where the error distribution is assumed to be normal. A data miner, on the other hand, chooses a score function and develops an algorithm to optimize that function. In the case of regression analysis, this score function will be the sum of squared differences between the predicted and observed values. Of course, these two approaches reduce to the same thing, but they do represent different perspectives. From here, statisticians will go on to develop more elaborate models, with appropriate error distributions being a component of the model, and will then use likelihood (or some variant, extension, or probabilistically-based alternative) to derive parameter estimates. In contrast, data miners may simply take alternative measures of difference between the data and the model—alternative score functions derived perhaps on pragmatic grounds—and optimize these.

Although, in data-mining, the algorithm is often regarded as the primary feature, in place of the model, much data-mining work is concerned with seeking a summary description of data—with building a model. As far as this aspect of data-mining goes, the ultimate objective is the same as that of modern statistics, even if the emphasis on how to get there differs. Having said that, we should note that the types of models sought in data mining exercises are of a particular kind. Broadly speaking, there are two kinds of models (Hand, 1998b): iconic (or mechanistic) and empirical (or operational) models. The former are based on some kind of theory or understanding of the process or phenomenon being studied. This is analogous to a toy airplane as a model of a real one. The latter are simply convenient summaries of the data, which nevertheless include features matching the major aspects of the data and which are useful in practice (e.g., for predictive purposes). Statistics is concerned with models of both kinds, but data mining, in general (there may be the occasional exception) is chiefly concerned with the latter kind: after all, data-mining is a search for the unexpected, not a confirmation of an existing theory.

A wide variety of tools is used in model-building data mining exercises. Some are closely related to corresponding statistical tools, and some are more closely related to machine-learning tools. Examples include regression analysis, classification trees, cluster analysis, conceptual clustering, time-series analysis, Bayesian belief networks, and mixture modeling. There is considerable overlap with the conventional statistical area of exploratory data analysis (Tukey, 1977) although the sizes of the data sets mean that new methods are also required. Data visualization is an important area—the power of the human eye is just as effective when there are many data points as when there are few, though new approaches have to be developed to cope with the large data sets (as with the scatterplot example from Hand et al., 1999, referred to above).

The introductory section noted that data mining was not solely concerned with model building. It was also concerned with seeking small interesting structures, or anomalies, in data sets. This seems to be an activity that has not been pursued by statisticians except in a few special situations. Hand (1998b) calls such work "pattern detection" to distinguish it from model building. Note that it is not the same as pattern recognition, which is an alternative name for supervised classification. Examples of the sorts of pattern sought in data mining are small local concentrations of data points in otherwise sparse areas, small sequences of values that occasionally recur in time series, strikingly high correlations between variables in situations where most correlations are small, or patterns of values that are quite different from most patterns in the data set. This last corresponds to outlier detection in statistics, which is one of the few areas of pattern detection that statisticians seem to have examined.

Statisticians have expended much effort over the years on developing tools for critical assessment of models and model-building procedures. To date, however, the data-mining community has put rather little effort into the assessment of algorithms: the number of papers comparing different methods is small (except in some relatively well-defined areas, such as classification, which have been under investigation by other intellectual communities, including statisticians, for many years). Rather, the tendency is simply to develop yet another algorithm (as a glance at the proceedings of any recent conference on data mining will show). I think this is a sign of the youth of the discipline, and hope that, as it matures, more critical assessment will take place, so that users can make informed choices between different tools. An ideal, of course, would be a sound theoretical base, analogous to the theoretical base underlying the statistical view of model building.

6. Real, Interesting, Valuable?

Section 4 drew attention to the very real danger that many relationships unearthed in the data would turn out to be attributable to data contamination. There is also a danger, perhaps particularly in pattern detection exercises, that many of the (remaining) relationships will be due simply to chance: the intrinsic random variation in the data-generating process simply leading to an apparent coincidence of data points. Given the large number of data points and the large number of pattern shapes typically sought, such coincidences are only to be expected. (Some ten years ago, a woman won the New Jersey lottery twice within four months. The chance of any particular entrant buying winning tickets twice in four months is about 1 in 17 trillion. But we are talking about a large data set here; a great many people buy lottery tickets each month. Taking this into account, we find that the chance that someone, somewhere in the United States, will win twice in four months is about 1 in 30.) Statistical significance tests might be used to try to thin out the candidate patterns, but the large search space means that a very low α level must be used for each test. This means that only patterns corresponding to a very large substantive effect will be identified as possibly interesting—which defeats the aim of the exercise.

The general strategy adopted in the data mining community is to abandon the probabilistic interpretation of the test statistics associated with the patterns. Instead, these are merely regarded as score functions, as noted above, and those with the highest scores are passed over to a domain expert for close examination. Again, the notion of data mining as an interactive process, involving both the data miner and the domain expert, is apparent.

7. Conclusion

Data mining represents the confluence of a wide variety of disciplines concerned with data analysis. It is concerned with seeking structures and relationships within large data sets. It overlaps in many cases with statistics, especially in those areas where a global model is sought. However, there are also important differences. The large data sets mean that there is an emphasis on algorithms rather than on models. Simple suboptimal algorithms may be better than optimal ones. Although model building is an important class of data mining activity, so also is pattern detection: apart from in a few isolated areas, pattern detection has not been the focus of much statistical interest, though it seems likely that statisticians will have much to contribute. In general, the sound principled theoretical base underlying statistics (even if there are differences of opinion about what this base should be—the Bayesian and frequentist schools being just two) is not matched in data mining. This is probably because of its youth— and we might hope to see it change in the future. Once again, statisticians have much to contribute here.

There is one other area of overlap between statistics and data-mining. This is in the software actually used to carry out the analyses. In many cases, data-mining software is simply statistical software repackaged. As time progresses, however, so other data-mining tools are gradually being integrated. Statisticians have a long history of assessing the value of statistical software packages, and this experience will be of value in evaluating data mining packages. Questions to be considered include. Does the package permit the discovery of new information? Is it quicker or easier to find old answers using these new tools? How easy are the new tools to learn and then to use? and How valuable are the discoveries?

Other discussions of the relationship between statistics and data mining are given by Elder and Pregibon (1996), Glymour et al. (1997), and Hand et al. (2001).

References

Elder, J. and D. Pregibon. 1996. *Advances in Knowledge Discovery and Data Mining*, edited by U. Fayyad, G. Piatetsky-Shapiro, P. Smyth, and R. Uthurusamy. Menlo Park, CA: AAAI Press.

Gifi, A. 1990. *Nonlinear Multi-variate Analysis*. Chichester, England: Wiley.

Glymour, C., D. Madigan, D. Pregibon, and P. Smyth. 1997. "Statistical themes and lessons for data mining." *Data Mining and Knowledge Discovery* 1: 11–28.

Hand, D. J. 1998a. "Data mining: statistics and more?" *Am. Stat.* 52: 112–118.

Hand, D. J. 1998b. "Data mining—reaching beyond statistics." *Res. Official Stat.* **2**: 5–17.

Hand, D. J. 2000. "Data mining: new challenges for statisticians." *Social Science Computer Review* **18**: 442–449.

Hand, D. J., G. Blunt, M. G. Kelly, and N. M. Adams. 1999. "Data mining for fun and profit." *Stat. Sci* **15**: 111–131.

Hand, D. J., H. Mannila, and P. Smyth. 2001. *Principles of Data Mining.* Cambridge, Mass.: MIT Press.

Tukey, J. W. 1977. *Exploratory Data Analysis.* Cambridge, Mass: Addison-Wesley.

26 USING RELATIONAL DATABASES IN KDD

Heikki Mannila

1. Introduction

In data mining we repeatedly have to access some subset of the data and compute different statistical quantities from that subset. In this chapter we describe the basic concepts behind relational database management systems, which provide a unified mechanism for fast access to parts of the data, exactly as we wish.

We start with some definitions. In database terminology, a data model is a set of constructs that can be used to describe the structure of data, plus a set of operations for manipulating the data. The relational data model is based on the idea of representing data in tabular form. A table header (schema) consists of the table name and a set of named columns; the column names are also called attributes. The actual table, also called a relation, is a set of rows. Each table entry in the column for attribute A is a value from the domain $Dom(A)$ of A. When the attributes are defined, the domain of each also has to be specified. An attribute can be of any data type: categorical, numerical, etc. The order of the rows and columns in a table is not significant.

As an example, consider a retail outlet with bar-code readers. For each customer transaction, also called a basket, we can collect information about which products the customer bought, and how many of each product. In principle, this data could be represented as a table, where there is an attribute for each product and a row for each transaction. For row t and attribute A, the entry $t(A)$ in the matrix indicates how many A's the customer bought. That is, for each attribute A, the domain $Dom(A)$ is the set of nonnegative integers. See Table 1 for an example table.

As product selection probably changes rapidly, encoding the names of products into attributes is probably not a very good idea. An alternative representation would be to use a table such as that in Table 2, where the product names are represented as entries. This table has three attributes, basket-id, product, and quantity, and the domain of product is the set of all strings, while the domain of quantity is the set of nonnegative numbers. Note that there is no unique way of representing a given set of data as a relational database.

In addition to the data about the transactions, the retailer maintains information about the prices of individual products. This could be represented in a table such as Table 3.

The product data can be too detailed for useful summaries. Therefore, the retailer could use a classification of different products into larger product categories. An example is shown in Table 4.

Table 1 Representing Market Basket Data as a Table with an Attribute for Each Product

			Transactions				
Basket-id	Chips	Mustard	Sausage	Pepsi	Coca-Cola	Miller	Bud
t_1	1	0	0	0	0	1	0
t_2	2	1	3	5	0	1	0
t_3	1	0	1	0	1	0	0
t_4	0	0	2	0	0	6	0
t_5	0	1	1	1	0	0	2
t_6	1	1	1	0	0	1	0
t_7	4	0	2	4	0	1	0
t_8	0	1	1	0	4	0	1
t_9	1	0	0	1	0	0	1
t_{10}	0	1	2	0	4	1	1

Table 2 A More Realistic Representation of Market Basket Data

	Baskets	
Basket-id	Product	Quantity
t_1	Chips	1
t_1	Miller	1
t_2	Chips	2
t_2	Mustard	1
t_2	Sausage	3
t_2	Pepsi	5
t_2	Miller	1
	. . .	

Table 4 describes a hierarchy in saying that Pepsi and Coke are soft drinks, and that soft drinks and beers are drinks.

The schemas of the tables in this example can be described succinctly just by listing the names of the tables and their attributes:

```
baskets(basket-id, product, quantity)
prices(product, price)
product-hierarchy(product, category)
```

Thus, the relational data model is based on the idea of tabular representation. The values in the cells may be arbitrary atomic values such as real numbers, integers, or strings: sets or lists of values are not allowed. This restriction is called the first normal form. That is, if, for example, we want to represent information about people, their ages, and phone numbers, we cannot store multiple phone numbers in one attribute.

The relational model is widely used in data management, and virtually all major database systems are based on it. Some systems provide additional functionality, such as the possibility of using object-oriented data-modeling methods.

Even in relatively small organizations, relational databases can have hundreds of tables and thousands of attributes. Managing the schema of the database can, therefore, be a complicated task.

A relational database typically contains several tables. Sometimes it is claimed that for data analysis purposes, it suffices to combine all the tables into a massive observation matrix, or universal table, and that therefore in data mining, one does not have to care about the fact that the data are in a database. An examination of simple examples shows that this is not feasible, however. Consider the example of products in a supermarket, and see what it would look like in a more realistic setting. Instead of having a table with the attributes product and price, we probably would have a table with at least attributes product, supplier, and price, and an additional table about suppliers, with attributes supplier, address, phone number, etc.

Table 3 Representing Prices of Products

	Prices
Product	Price
Chips	$1.00
Miller	$0.55
Mustard	$1.25
Sausage	$2.00
Pepsi	$0.75
Coke	$0.75
. . .	

Table 4 Representing the Hierarchy of Products as a Table

Product hierarchy	
Product	Category
Pepsi	Soft drink
Coke	Soft drink
Budweiser	Beer
Miller	Beer
Soft drink	Drink
Beer	Drink
. . .	

If we combined all the tables into one table, we would have attributes transaction ID, product, number, supplier address, phone number, product price, etc. in the same table. Furthermore, if each product belongs on the average to K different product groups, inclusion of the information from the product-hierarchy table would increase the size of the representation by a factor of K. For even a moderately sized database, this combining process would lead to a huge table that would be far too large to be stored explicitly.

In pure relational algebra, the selections are based on exact equalities or inequalities. For data mining, we often need concepts of inexact or approximate matching. If a predicate match for approximate matching between attribute values is available, we can (at least in some database systems) use that directly in database operations to select rows that satisfy the approximate matching condition.

2. Index Structures

The goal in data organization is to find ways of quickly locating all the data points that satisfy a given selection condition Q. In data mining, the condition Q can be considered to be the definition of the subgroup of interest. Usually, the selection condition is a conjunction of conditions on individual attributes, such as Product_ID $= 708,014$, Age $\leqslant 40$, and Income $\leqslant 10$. We first consider data structures that are especially applicable to situations where there is only one conjunct.

An index on an attribute A is a data structure that makes it possible to locate points with a given value of A more efficiently than by a sequential scan of the whole data set. Indexes are typically built either by the use of hash functions or by B*-trees. Using such an index, one can locate any record that has a given value for the index attribute A in a few disk accesses. A B*-tree index is also applicable for finding all records that satisfy an inequality constraint such as Age $\leqslant 40$.

Traditional index structures such as hashing and B*-trees provide fast access to rows of tables on the basis of values of a given attribute or collection of attributes. In some applications, however, it is necessary to express selection conditions on the basis of several attributes, and normal index structures do not help. Consider, for example, the case of storing geographic information about cities. Suppose we wish to find all the cities with latitude between 30° N and 40° N, longitude between 60° W and 70° W, and population at least 1,000. Such a query is called a rectangular range query. Suppose the cities table is large, containing millions of city names. How should the query be evaluated? A B*-tree index on the latitude attribute makes it possible to find the cities that satisfy the conditions for that attribute, but for finding the rows that satisfy the conditions on longitude among these, we have to resort to a sequential scan. Similarly, an index on longitude does not help much. What is needed is an index structure that makes it possible to directly use the conditions on both attributes.

Multidimensional indexing refers to techniques for finding rows of tables on the basis of conditions on multiple attributes. One widely used method is the R*-tree. Each node in the tree corresponds to a region in the underlying space, and the node represents the points within that region. For up to about 10 dimensions, the multidimensional index structures speed up searches in large databases. Fast evaluation of range queries in large data sets with hundreds of dimensions is still an open problem.

3. Query Execution and Optimization

A query can be evaluated in various different ways. Consider for example the query

```
Select t.product
from baskets t, baskets u
where t.transaction = u.transaction
  and u.product = ''beer''
```

Here, the notation baskets t, baskets u means that in the query, t and u refer to rows of the basket table; the notation is needed because we want to be able to refer to two rows of the same table. The query finds all the products that have been bought in a transaction that also included beer.

The trivial method for evaluating such a query would be to try all possible pairs of rows from the baskets table, check whether they agree on the basket-id attribute, and test that the second row has beer in the product attribute. This would require n^2 operations on rows, where n is the size of the baskets table.

A more efficient method is to first locate the rows from the baskets table that have beer in the product attribute and sort the basket-ids of those rows into a list L. Then one can sort the baskets table using the basket-id attribute as the sort key and extract the products from the rows whose basket-id appears in the list L. This approach requires $O(n)$ operations for finding the rows with beer, $O(n \log n)$ operations for sorting the rows, and $O(n)$ operations for scanning the sorted list and selecting the correct values, that is, altogether $O(n \log n)$ operations are needed. This is a clear improvement over the $O(n^2)$ operations needed for the naive method.

Query optimization is the task of finding the best possible evaluation method for a given query. Typically, query optimizers translate the SQL query into an expression tree, where the leaves represent tables and the internal nodes operations on the children of the nodes. Next, algebraic equalities between operations can be used to transform the tree into an equivalent form that is faster to evaluate. In the example above, we have used the equation $\sigma_F(r \bowtie s) = \sigma_F(r) \bowtie s$, if F is a selection condition that only concerns the attributes of r. After a suitable expression tree is found, evaluation methods for each of the operations are selected. For example, a join operation can be evaluated in several different ways: by nested loops (as in the trivial method above), by sorting, or by using indexes. The efficiency of each method depends on the sizes of the tables and the distribution of the values in the tables. Therefore, query optimizers keep information about such changing quantities to find a good evaluation method. Theoretically, finding the best evaluation strategy for a given query is an NP-hard problem, so finding the best method is not feasible. However, good query optimizers can be surprisingly effective. One of the authors of this book once spent a couple of days rewriting a complicated SQL query accessing a large database so that the query would be executed as efficiently as possible. The resulting version of the query was about 25 percent *slower* than the straightforward version of the query optimized by using the optimizer of the database management system.

Database management systems strive to provide good performance for a wide variety of queries. While for a single query it can be possible to write a program that computes the result more efficiently than a database management system, the strength of databases is that they provide fast execution for most of the queries. In data mining applications this is useful, as the queries are typically not known in advance.

4. Data Warehousing and Online Analytical Processing (OLAP)

A retail database is a typical example of an operational database: the database is used to conduct the daily operations of the organization, and the operations can rely quite heavily on it. Other examples of operational databases include airline reservation systems, bank account databases, etc. Strategic databases refer to databases that are used in strategic decisionmaking in the organization: the purpose of such databases is to help in decisionmaking.

Typically, an organization has several different operational databases. For example, our retail outlet might have a database about market baskets, a warehouse system, a customer database (or several), a payroll database, a database about suppliers, etc. (A diversified service company might have several customer databases.) Large organizations can have tens or hundreds of operational databases. For decision support purposes, one needs to combine information from various operational databases to find out overall patterns of activity within the company and with its customers. Building decision support applications that directly access the operational databases is quite difficult. The decision support viewpoint is quite closely aligned with the goal of data mining. Indeed, one could say that a major goal of data mining is decision support.

Operational databases, such as our hypothetical retail database, any customer database, or the reservation system of an airline, are most often used to answer well-defined and repetitive queries such as "What is the total price of the products in this basket?" "What is the address of customer NN?" or "What is the balance of account 123456?" Such databases have to support a large number of transactions consisting of simple queries and updates on the contents of the data. This type of database use is called online transaction processing (OLTP).

Decision support tasks require different types of queries: aggregation is far more important. A typical decision support query might be "Find out the sales of all products by region and by month, and the difference compared to last year." The term online analytical processing (OLAP) refers to the use of databases for obtaining summaries of the data, with aggregation as the principal mechanism.

The tables of the database of the retailer had the following form:

```
baskets(basket-id, item, quantity)
products(product, price, supplier)
product-hierarchy(product, category)
basket-stores(basket-id, store, day)
stores(store, sname, city, country)
```

Here we have added the table basket-stores that gives which store and on what date a certain basket was produced. For decision support purposes, a more useful representation of the data might be using the table

```
sales(product, store, date, amount)
```

for representing the amount of a product sold at a given store on a given date. We can add rows to this table by SQL statements:

```
insert into sales(product, store, date, amount)
select item, store, date, sum(quantity)*price
from baskets, basket-stores, prices
where baskets.basket-id = basket-stores.basket-id and item = product
group by item, store, date
```

After this, we can find the total dollar sales of all product categories by countries by giving the following query:

```
select products.product, store.country, sum(amount)
from sales, stores, dates, products
where dates.year ≥ 1997
  and sales.product=products.product
  and sales.store=stores.store
```

```
and sales.date=dates.date
group by products.category, store.country
```

OLTP and OLAP pose different requirements for the database management system. OLTP requires that the data is completely up-to-date and the queries can modify it, several transactions have to be able to execute concurrently without interfering with each other, responses have to be fast, but the queries and updates are relatively simple. In OLAP the queries can be quite complex, but normally only one executes at a given time. OLAP queries do not modify the data, and in finding out facts about last year's sales it is typically not crucial to have today's sale information. The requirements are so different that it makes sense to use different types of storage organizations for handling the two applications.

A data warehouse is a database system used to store information from various operational databases for decision support purposes. A data warehouse for the retailer might include information from the market basket database, the supplier database, customer databases, etc. The data in the payroll database might not be in the data warehouse if it is not considered to be crucial in decision support. A data warehouse is not created just by dumping the data from different databases onto a single disk: several integration tasks have to be performed, such as resolving possible inconsistencies between attribute names and usages, finding out the semantics of attributes and values, etc. Building data warehouses is often an expensive operation, as it requires lots of manual operations and a detailed understanding of the operational databases.

The difference between OLAP and data mining is not clear-cut. One can in fact see a continuum of queries: find out the address of a customer; find out the sales of this product in the last month; sales of all products by region and month; trends in the sales; what products have similar sales patterns; rules that predict the sale of a certain product customer segmentation/clustering. The first query is typically done by using a database system, while the second is a typical OLAP query, and the last two might be called data mining queries. But it is difficult to define exactly where data mining starts and OLAP ends.

5. Data Structures for OLAP

OLAP requires the computation of various aggregates from large base tables. As many aggregates will be needed over and over again, it makes sense to store some of them. The data cube is a clever technique for viewing the results of various aggregations in a tabular way.

In the above example we had a sales table with the schema:

```
sales(product, store, date, amount)
```

A possible row from this table might be:

```
sales(Olvi, store 1, August 25, 17.25)
```

indicating that the sales of Olvi at store number 1 on August 25 were $17.25. Inventing a new value **all** to stand for any product, we might consider rows like

```
sales(all, store 1, August 25, 14214.70)
```

with the intended meaning that the total sales of all products in store 1 on August 25 were $14,214.70.

The data cube for the sales table contains all rows

```
sales(a, b, c, d)
```

where a, b, and c, are either values from the domains of the corresponding attributes or the specific value **all**, and d is the corresponding sum.

6. String Databases

The interest in text databases has increased a lot in recent years. One reason for this is molecular biology: modern biotechnology provides huge amounts of protein and DNA data that is basically in the form of strings. Even more important has been the rise of the Web:

search engines require efficient methods for finding documents that include a given set of terms.

Relational databases are fine for storing data in a tabular form, but they are not well suited for representing and accessing large volumes of text.

Given a large collection of text, a typical query might be "Find all occurrences of the word 'mining' in the text." More generally, the problem is to find occurrences of a pattern P in a text T. The pattern P might be a simple string, a string with wild cards, or even a regular expression. The occurrence of P in T might be defined as an exact match or an approximate match, where errors are allowed.

The occurrences of P in T can obviously be done by sequentially scanning the data T and for each position testing whether P matches or not. Much more efficient solutions exist, however. For example, using the suffix trie data structure we can find the list of all occurrences of pattern p in time that is proportional to the length of p (and not dependent on the size of the text), and outputting the occurrences of p can be done in time $O(|p|+L)$, where L is the number of occurrences of p in the text. The suffix trie can be constructed in linear time in the size of the original text, and it is also fast in practice.

Schematically, a Web search engine might have two data structures: a relational table pages (page-address, page-text) and a suffix trie containing all the text of all the documents loaded into the system. When a user performs a query such as "Find all documents containing the words 'data' and 'mining,' the suffix trie is used to find two lists pages: those containing the word 'data' and those containing 'mining.'" Assuming the lists are sorted, it is straightforward to find the documents containing both words. Note, however, that the number of documents containing both "data" and "mining" is probably much less than the number of documents containing one of the terms.

7. Databases and the Data Mining Process

Databases provide relatively fast access to almost arbitrary subsets of the data. However, when actually running a data mining algorithm, finding patterns, or fitting models, accessing the data only through a database interface can be much slower than loading the data into a flat file and running the algorithm against that.

One of the reasons for this problem is that transfer of data from the data mining program to the database system and vice versa takes considerable time. As an example, consider the case of finding association rules from databases (see Chapter 16.2.3). Recall that the algorithm first asks for the frequency of each individual attribute A, that is, for the number of rows with $A = 1$. This, of course, can be computed easily with an SQL query: select count(*) from R where $A = 1$. However, to compute the frequencies of each attribute requires (if using this simple strategy) the use of p queries, where p is the number of attributes. For databases with a large number of columns, this first stage of the association rule discovery algorithm already becomes time consuming. The next stages of the algorithm require the computation of the frequency of each pair A, B of attributes such that both A and B are individually frequent. Again, the computation of the frequency of the pair is in principle easy using SQL: select count(*) from R where $A = 1$ and $B = 1$. However, for each candidate pair A, B, we would need a separate query.

Thus, one of the efficiency problems in using a relational database system for knowledge discovery in databases (KDD) is that the algorithms cause lots of separate queries. If the separation of the database system and the data mining algorithm is strict, then the database management system will not know that the frequencies of all the attributes will have to be computed, and thus the database system cannot use the optimization provided by computation of the whole set of candidate frequencies in one pass through the data.

A similar situation occurs in the construction of decision trees (see Chapter 5.4). At each node of the tree, we have to select between different ways of partitioning the remaining data set. The evaluation of the quality of each way of partitioning requires (at least when done in the naive way) one pass through the database. If a database system is used to answer the queries, then these passes through the data cannot be combined and much time is lost.

The question of how a database should be integrated into the process is still open. From the architectural point of view, it would be best if all the data were in the database and the data mining algorithms would access it from there. Unfortunately, this induces a considerable decrease in performance.

Does this mean that databases are irrelevant for data mining? Definitely not. Data mining is a complex iterative and interactive process involving several steps. The actual task of finding interesting patterns or fitting models against the data is only a small part of the whole process. Using a database system is essential in controlling the data mining process, and in keeping track of the multiple versions of the data that arise in any real data mining process.

27 ARTIFICIAL INTELLIGENCE

Jan M. Żytkow

ABSTRACT We investigate the bidirectional links between knowledge discovery in databases (KDD) and artificial intelligence (AI). Both are concerned with intelligent agents, search, knowledge representation, knowledge acquisition, and knowledge application, but they differ in many ways. We contrast them first and explain why they differ. Then we outline several ways in which AI can increase its influence on KDD, as well as several areas where KDD can impact AI.

1. Contrasting Artificial Intelligence and KDD

It has been common for the AI community to treat knowledge discovery as a subfield. Discovery and creativity were always considered the particularly advanced form of intelligence. But there is another, practical reason that emerged during the 1990s. Huge amounts of data, supported by a fast-growing infrastructure for storage, retrieval, and computation created a lasting need for intelligent analytical tools, so that KDD became AI's new and major application area.

The KDD community considers AI as one of the foundations. Intelligent agents, search, knowledge representation, and knowledge acquisition are particularly relevant to KDD. Since these are the key areas of AI, both domains are well positioned for long-term interaction. We will now contrast the state of the art in both fields, so that the many ways in which each can influence the other become more apparent.

1.1. Intelligent Agents versus Toolboxes

From its conception in the 1950s, the main goal of AI was the development of intelligent systems, also called intelligent agents. Although the initial goal of making the agents as intelligent as humans is far from realized, several decades of research have led to remarkable results, and the theory of intelligent agents has become one of the key elements of AI (Russell and Norvig, 1995). Agents are distinguished by several components. One is an explicit representation of goals, another is a capability to perceive and assess the external situation, which in search terminology gives knowledge of the current state. Further, agents can plan how to reach the goals from the current state and can act on their plans. The more explicit the representation of each element, the easier it is to maintain and expand an agent.

Intelligent agents increase their appeal in KDD and in the long run may dominate the field. But at present, KDD methods are mostly individual algorithms combined manually by human analysts to fit larger goals. This applies to both research systems and commercial products such as SAS and SPSS/Clementine, which are human-operated toolboxes rather than intelligent agents. Toolbox integration is not trivial. It requires common data structures so that output of one tool can be used as input to another. But missing from toolboxes are (1) mechanisms for autonomous reasoning about goals, (2) control mechanisms that would automatically direct the output of one tool as input to another, and (3) evaluation mechanisms that would, without human help, decide whether a result has been successful, whether alternative results should be sought or a search should be terminated due to lack of success. As the interest in knowledge mining keeps growing, the manual operation of tools becomes a serious limitation, so that the intelligent agents approach will be increasingly practical and attractive.

1.2. Search: Explicit versus Hidden

Search is one of the foundations of AI. AI textbooks describe the theory of search based on simple theoretical principles, supported by clear algorithms that include operators, evaluation, and control strategies. Search algorithms are supported by well-established data structures such as search states and lists of open and closed nodes.

KDD is far from this ideal. An explicit treatment of search is uncommon. While all discovery tools must conduct search, how this is done in concrete cases is rarely clear. Different research groups, especially if their background is not in AI, neglect a clear description of search so that it is difficult to understand what specific contributions they propose and what the competitive advantage of those contributions is.

KDD must work out a clear and standard presentation of search. Without it, hundreds of new methods conceived each year cannot be presented in a succinct way, compared and appreciated. The vast effort contributes far too little to the joint discovery method of KDD. Lack of understanding threatens fragmentation of the domain. For the sake of simple and effective professional communication, KDD should adapt the standard theory of search presented in AI textbooks (Rich and Knight, 1991; Russell and Norvig, 1995). An example of a systematic treatment of search on many learning tasks is Langley's (1996) textbook on machine learning.

1.3. Knowledge Representation

The AI community realized long ago that without unified knowledge representation, it will not create general intelligent agents and will be limited to very selective problem solvers. The challenge resulted in knowledge-based systems that combine knowledge of different kinds and can be used in various applications. The main knowledge representation frameworks include first-order logic, production systems, and frames combined with semantic networks.

KDD has not reached this state. It has a minimal approach to knowledge representation, by adding new forms as new discovery applications emerge. KDD uses many separate mini representations for trees, rules, cluster hierarchies, patterns in time series, and numerous other forms of knowledge. They are combined in different ways with indeterministic, statistical components. None is accepted as a standard. Mechanisms for joint treatment of knowledge in different forms are missing. This case-by-case representation is also detached from the use of knowledge in decision support systems.

Meta knowledge and meta-level reasoning about knowledge is another common subject in AI. For instance, reasoning schemes of epistemic logic (see Chapter 7) are used in many ways. In KDD, reasoning on meta level is limited to narrow tasks, prompted by situations when large numbers of knowledge items of a particular form are generated by a learning or discovery system. For instance, large numbers of classification rules and even larger numbers of association rules (Agrawal et al., 1993) prompted mechanisms that seek minimal rule sets that provide the same coverage as the original, much larger, sets.

Another weakness of KDD in comparison to AI concerns knowledge about structure. Such knowledge is very common and important in AI. It is at the core of many systems, as different as Dendral (Lindsay et al., 1980), R1/XCON (McDermott, 1982), and the block world planners (Rich and Knight, 1991; Russell and Norvig, 1995). With a few exceptions, knowledge about structure is neglected in KDD, even though such knowledge may be inferred from tables that explicitly represent structure and from many multitable databases. Arguably, frequent item sets can be viewed as a special case of simple structures that can be found in transactions. Spatial databases can also lead to knowledge about spatial structures.

1.4. Knowledge Acquisition: Experts versus Data

Throughout the early years of AI it became increasingly clear that domain knowledge can be a very useful part of intelligent systems. For about two decades, domain knowledge was provided by experts. But even though experts possess plenty of domain knowledge, knowledge acquisition proved to be a difficult and long process. Expert systems textbooks covered the process extensively (Jackson, 1990). Standard steps included interviews with experts, prototype building, and confronting experts with the conclusions made by prototypes. Deficiencies of knowledge captured in a prototype stimulate expert thinking and sharpen the knowledge engineering effort in repeated cycles of prototype reconstruction.

While experts can capture trends and contributing factors, they can rarely provide quantitative and probabilistic details of a regularity. Those details make a big difference, however, as the quantitative impact of each factor can determine whether it should be taken into account in a given situation. Here, KDD offers a niche in which knowledge mining can surpass experts. In the fast-changing business world, expert knowledge can and should be augmented by direct data analysis. Expert knowledge can and should be verified against data, too, by drawing empirical conclusions and checking them against data in a process that uses knowledge miners' hypothesis verification mechanisms.

2. The Flow of Ideas from AI to KDD

KDD can draw many lessons from AI. It is worthwhile to follow not only specific solutions, but also the main elements of AI's research paradigm. We will consider the potential of intelligent agents, search, and knowledge representation.

2.1. Intelligent Agents

One worthwhile direction for KDD is organizing discovery systems as intelligent agents. The main advantage is system autonomy that would free human knowledge seekers from many minute problems to which they must currently attend. The current practice in KDD involves frequent human intervention and guidance. But it takes a very skilled person, typically an experienced tool developer, to make meaningful decisions. Sometimes a Ph.D. degree does not prevent pitiful errors. As the applications spread to new databases, we cannot clone tool developers along with tools. It is too costly to place an experienced system developer in a loop where he must attend to minute and numerous details.

In the future, humans who will operate KDD technology will be domain experts and general information technology workers rather than KDD system developers. Their general intelligence may be high and they can understand domain knowledge better than KDD experts, but their experience with data preparation for the sake of various discovery methods and their experience with controlling parameters of those methods will be low. Equally low will be their motivation to learn details of numerous discovery methods.

Agent architectures developed in AI can guide KDD agent construction. One important element is the explicit representation of goals and subgoals. They are often organized in AND–OR trees and implemented as production rules that invoke subgoals and control intergoal transitions. AND-nodes are used for subgoaling, while OR-nodes provide alternative plans that can satisfy the same goal. To be feasible, subgoals must be linked to plans that reach those goals. Because discovery goals require search in different spaces of hypotheses, terms, procedures, and the like, most of the plans are algorithms that arrange for effective search in the corresponding spaces. The lore of AI promotes goals represented declaratively by data structures. An explicit representation of goals and plans facilitates reasoning about them, making it easy to understand the operation of a system and to change the goals.

An intelligent agent-discoverer cannot rely on an *a priori* grand plan if the process must reach knowledge that reflects regularities in the domain represented by data and not merely a particular tool at hand. Such a discovery process, which "allows the data to speak" must be guided by both successful and unsuccessful discovery steps. Here comes situation assessment as the next component of an agent. In KDD, one part of the situation is data that can be partitioned, projected, joined, and aggregated. The other part is the results of the current discovery step. When a regularity has been found in a set of data, several new discovery questions apply: How general is this regularity? Can it be refined by introduction of a new variable? Can it be combined with other known regularities?

When a given step was unsuccessful, an alternative method may be invoked or another hypothesis space may be considered. Ultimately, a particular focus may be abandoned, for instance, a particular combination of variables, and search may shift to other variables.

The distinction between a static network of goals and plans and a dynamic network of the resultant knowledge was introduced in the MYCIN expert system (Shortliffe, 1976) and modified for use in scientific discovery systems such as FAHRENHEIT (Żytkow, 1996). Concrete knowledge is represented in a dynamically changing network that is constructed and maintained according to the steps provided in the static network. As new discoveries are made, the dynamic network grows to include new knowledge. Goals and plans are selected dynamically, at the run time, by analysis of the current state of the knowledge network. After a given task has been completed, the knowledge network is searched for missing elements that suggest new goals.

The concept of intelligent agents can be extended to a network of agents who specialize in different discovery tasks and communicate as they perform their search (Zhong et al., 1997).

But aren't humans going to do better than automated agents? A common argument attributes special insights to humans not available to computer systems. This may be true, but even if deep insights occur to some of us, the repetitive and massive search will wear us out. Even though we may mistrust the judgment of an automated discovery agent, we can use it for clues. After a piece of knowledge has been automatically discovered, there is always room for human-guided verification, and human-guided knowledge refinement.

2.2. Search Is Essential for Discovery

In AI, the vast majority of problems, including discovery problems, cannot be solved by algorithms that directly lead to the goal. Intelligent agents explore possibilities that, from the perspective of eventually accepted solutions, can be called dead ends because they are not included in the solutions. This process is called search. A substantial portion of plans carried out by autonomous intelligent agents are plans that require search.

As we argued, agent-discoverers will be required to conduct many large-scale searches in different hypothesis spaces. Agent autonomy requires that those searches are set up automatically. This can be done when search is programmed in a clear and schematic way so that it is easy to set up and to alter. Here, AI offers serious help. A large part of any AI textbook is devoted to search (Jackson, 1990; Rich and Knight, 1991; Russell and Norvig, 1995). The problem space, also called the search space or state space, is the foundation of the theory of search (Simon, 1979). A search space is defined by a set of states S and a two-argument relation E on S, called a move or a state expansion relation. E contains all direct state-to-state transitions. In practice, the states are not given in advance. Because search spaces are very large, often infinite, states are constructed by search operators from the existing states.

It is imperative that discovery systems are understood in terms of the search spaces they explore. We must clearly see how knowledge is gradually constructed by search. Each operator application is a concrete construction step. It augments the state of knowledge or the proposed model in a specific way, for instance, by adding a new concept, or assembling a new hypothesis (see Chapter 16.4.2). Alternative versions of knowledge are proposed by different instantiation of the same operator.

The search process may be conducted in many ways, that is, by different search controls. It is imperative for KDD that search control is made explicit. Typically, discovery search may start from an empty state. Breadth-first search control tries simpler possibilities before more complex ones. If a simple solution is successful, more complex hypotheses are not tried. Various search control mechanisms differ by the order in which they select states and by the number of states they remember. AI oscillates between exhaustive and selective (heuristic) search. There are reasons for this ambivalence. When resources are available, it is worthwhile to do an exhaustive search, since it often leads to optimal solutions or reveals possibilities that have been overlooked by humans. But exhaustive search is explosive, so search in large spaces must be selective. Hill climbing is a particularly useful selective search. Beam search and genetic algorithms are more complex but also more resilient variations of hill climbing.

Exhaustive search for hidden structure in systems such as GELL-MANN (Fischer and Żytkow, 1991), MECHEM (Valdés-Peréz, 1993), and Dendral (Lindsay et al., 1980) uses nonrepetitive (nonredundant) structure generators, exhaustive in each simplicity class. As an extra benefit, it generates more general hypotheses before their special cases.

A mechanism of search control should evaluate a hypothesis as early as possible. If a partial hypothesis is inconsistent, and a search mechanism accumulates knowledge, there is no sense in further expansion. Because each state can be expanded in many ways, early rejection of a hypothesis H eliminates the search over the entire subtree that could be grown from H.

In the domain of discovery, the goal states are not known in advance. States are constructed in the discovery process and evaluated by various tests, which we can call evaluators. Evaluators must be made very clear in each presentation of a discovery system. They play the opposite role to operators, limiting the search. Boolean tests accept or refute concrete knowledge states. Other tests assign numerical values to states. Goal states are typically required to exceed threshold values of tests such as statistical significance or predictive strength. Without reaching the threshold, even the best goal state in the discovery process is insufficient.

2.3. Knowledge Representation: A Program for KDD

One of the main targets of AI is a uniform and global knowledge representation for use by intelligent agents. Research on such knowledge representations has provided common languages in which knowledge can be organized and shared, and common reasoning mechanisms for the use of knowledge. Without them, AI would be a collection of many tools, each made individually for the treatment of a small class of problems.

In contrast, the focus of different KDD communities is still very narrow, compared to global knowledge representations of AI. The classification rules community, association rules community, decision-trees community, clustering community, Bayesian networks community, and neural networks community each use another representation and each mines for a limited type of knowledge. So the first natural question is how can these forms of knowledge be put together and used jointly, especially when they propose competing results for the same data.

But even more troubling is the following observation: when different tools analyze the same data, each comes up with different results and each is blind to other forms of knowledge. Knowledge, however, should not be a reflection of a tool, but of the regularities in the domain represented by data.

A unified approach to knowledge will open plenty of questions that are customary in logic-driven AI, but still rare in KDD, on completeness of knowledge, consistency, the best form of knowledge to represent a given domain, and the like.

Since many forms of knowledge are still not considered in KDD, one can propose a challenge that applies to each form and even to each piece of knowledge: From what database and by what methods could it be discovered; in what database can it be verified? KDD's perspective on knowledge can be also broadened by another challenge: for each piece of knowledge, consider how it can be applied as background knowledge in support of data mining. Both challenges are very practical when we consider knowledge of an enterprise that possesses substantial databases in support of the enterprise's business process.

One system of knowledge representation is offered by predicate calculus. It is commonly used in different areas of artificial intelligence, and it supports applications by theorem proving. Metaphorically, in this representation each new piece of knowledge is thrown inside a bag. The main strengths are uniform and time-proven mechanisms for knowledge expression and application. Logic representation is very tempting for KDD, as knowledge in the form of rules and equations is already represented in the right form. But as the body of knowledge grows, purposeful access to individual pieces in a bag is difficult. On average, many irrelevant pieces must be considered before the right one will be found. KDD typically uses the bag representation, while successful automated scientific discovery systems use graphs to represent relationships between pieces of knowledge (see Chapter 29). Knowledge graphs are close to another AI knowledge representation using frames and semantic networks. The advantages of frames and semantic networks include fast appropriate access and easy assessment of missing knowledge elements.

Logic representation in KDD takes on new challenges. One of the main advantages of logic representation is deductive inference. In KDD and in ML, however, low thresholds of accuracy for rule acceptance create obstacles for the use of deductive reasoning. For instance, $A \rightarrow B$ and $B \rightarrow C$ may be acceptable, while it may not be the case that $A \rightarrow C$.

Unified knowledge representation is also instrumental in opening up opportunities for knowledge sharing, knowledge accumulation, and synthesizing different pieces of knowledge into new models. At present, KDD revels in first applications of knowledge derived from a new database. But in the long run, incremental growth of knowledge must be more typical than one-time applications. A useful piece of knowledge should be shared and reused in different ways. This requires a systemic approach to knowledge that calls for knowledge accumulation rather than abandoning knowledge after one use.

3. KDD Contributions to AI

The main direct contributions of KDD to AI are (1) the alternative it provides to AI's manual knowledge acquisition and (2) the use of databases as a new extensive knowledge source. But other, less obvious and more hypothetical possibilities are worth mentioning, too, including a new perspective on the debate on the boundaries of artificial intelligence.

3.1. New Source for Knowledge Acquisition

For use in AI's expert systems and knowledge-based systems, typical knowledge sources required an extensive process of knowledge engineering conducted by humans (Jackson, 1990). Automated knowledge acquisition in the fields of automated scientific discovery (ASD) and machine learning (ML) were exceptions, the first specializing in limited scientific domains, while the second in concept learning from examples. KDD can play a similar role, on a scale compatible with the use of databases. It has a long way to go before it becomes an adequate knowledge source to feed AI systems, but it already provides an alternative knowledge source in simple applications and allows AI to draw from vast data resources.

KDD can complement but it may also supersede traditional knowledge acquisition from human experts. First, it can utilize large bodies of data that capture details of the business process. Second, detailed probability distributions and parameter values are best inferred from data. Third, KDD can promptly utilize the most recent data that represent new business trends and behavior patterns, which may not be known to human experts. Even though human experts may be aware of general trends, they may easily overlook new relevant variables and budding exceptions to known regularities.

3.2. Perfecting the Human-Computer Synergy

At the current state of the art, KDD sanctions and even encourages a human in the loop. It is thus well suited to explore human-computer synergy, in contrast with traditional AI, which is focused on artificial agent autonomy. Humans excel in envisioning new tasks, proposing new discovery methods and evaluation criteria, and assembling larger KDD systems from pieces. Within the short history of ML and KDD, researchers have relished in inventing thousands of small methods and in applying them manually in creative combinations that suited a particular data analysis. At the other end of the spectrum, true to the spirit of AI, automated discovery systems were also developed. Sooner or later a new larger paradigm of human-computer interaction will emerge from this vast, varied, and uncontrolled effort.

3.3. Search for Knowledge

While search is one of the main specialties of AI, AI does not specialize in search for knowledge. Here, KDD can be a key contributor. Special challenges concern not only hypotheses generation and evaluation, but also search control specific to the search for knowledge.

Search control should consider, as a standard option, that a particular search for knowledge is unsuccessful, and suspend or abandon the search as appropriate. But the challenge is even bigger: a search may appear successful while it creates poor substitutes or even illusions of knowledge. Many ML and KDD methods always succeed: decision trees are created or sets of classification rules are returned. They may poorly represent knowledge in a given data set, but this can only become clear when the search goes beyond one hypothesis space. As not all data contain knowledge in every form, the search mechanism should ask (1)

Is the best solution in a given space acceptable? and (2) Would knowledge in other forms be more appropriate?

Search for knowledge can be unsuccessful for various reasons. Search spaces are usually very large, often infinite, for instance, the space of equations that can be formed by recursive application of a given set of operations. But a solution may not exist even in an infinite space. For instance, if data are periodic, we can only find local approximations in the space of algebraic equations. KDD systems should be able to recognize that a search in a particular space cannot be successful.

Solutions may exist but be practically unreachable if they are distant from the initial states. In general, there is no cure. But the scope of search can be expanded within given resources of time and memory if repetitive search is reduced. For instance, it is a well-recognized danger in AI that the same state can be constructed many times. Search for knowledge offers a new impediment: different but equivalent or isomorphic pieces of knowledge are plentiful. Ideally, search should generate only one hypothesis in each equivalence class. Testing for equivalence and isomorphism can be prohibitively inefficient, but if equivalent states are permitted, they occur in explosive numbers. This problem occurred in the early discovery systems, Dendral (Lindsay et al., 1980) and BACON1 (Langley et al., 1987). There are many isomorphic descriptions for the same state, and many further descriptions are equivalent based on the domain theory. Ideally, redundant states should not be constructed at all. Dendral and other systems responded with different mechanisms that generate nonredundant descriptions (Lindsay et al., 1980; Żytkow and Fischer, 1996; Valdés-Pérez, 1993). Similar problems must be solved for new forms of knowledge in KDD, contributing to the foundations of AI.

Huge data sets of interest to the KDD search prompted rethinking the requirements for the scaling-up of algorithms, potentially useful to the entire field of AI. Dimensions of complexity in KDD include the numbers of records, attributes, values per attribute, attribute types, and relational tables. They affect search efficiency in different ways. Most algorithms are only linearly affected by the number of records, so they can see all data without much problem. But the requirement that all data must be seen is often not necessary. Sampling can further improve the efficiency of a search, unless it prevents the significance of findings. Combinations of attributes and their values may require a search for frequent item sets to walk through the same data many times. Here, a simple solution uses a fixed minimum support threshold for item sets of interest. This cuts down on search, although it may be impractical to put inexpensive and expensive items, bread and refrigerators, on the same scale of support. Many similar problems of interest to AI are proposed and solved by KDD.

3.4. Consolidation of the Method

At present, KDD permits development of thousands of alternative methods, each applicable to a very limited knowledge-mining task. But as those methods become reasonably successful, the next step must be method consolidation into more general and capable mechanisms. Some commercial systems offer the first steps: output–input integration allows effective manual combinations of methods supported by tools such as SAS and SPSS/Clementine. Research systems such as 49er (Chapter 24.1.4; Zembowicz and Żytkow, 1993), EXPLORA (Klösgen, 1996) and KDW (Piatetsky-Shapiro and Matheus, 1991) exploit large-scale automation. As discovery and creativity are tasks most characteristic to human intelligence, KDD research on large-scale method integration may have a big impact on AI. Artificial agents without discovery capabilities cannot be truly intelligent.

3.5. Limitations of AI and KDD

Are automated discoverers limited in comparison to humans? Can some of these limitations be proved? Critics of discovery systems often challenge research on machine discovery with different tasks, alleging that they are essential to discovery while they cannot be captured by discovery systems. Many such claims were soon refuted by progress in the automation of discovery (Langley et al., 1987). By focusing on small-scale methods, KDD is avoiding this sort of challenge, but consolidation of KDD methods will invite them in the future.

Some arguments have been put in the form of a proof that certain tasks are impossible for computers while they are ostensibly achieved by humans. For instance, Penrose (1989) repeatedly uses the distinction between recursive and nonrecursive problems to argue that computers are limited to the former while humans can also deal with the latter. Consider a search in an infinite space. If a solution exists, it can eventually be found, although perhaps after an impractically long time. But if there is no solution, the search will continue forever. Penrose argues that humans are not so limited. They start asking meta-level questions, and rather than endlessly trying to continue the search at hand, humans can prove that search cannot be conclusive. For a given search problem, this can be done by finding a property that is present in the initial state, is conserved by each move, but is absent in the acceptable solutions. In the cases of search for knowledge, data analysis can suggest such properties: no functional relation holds in a data set, so that search for equations cannot be successful, while another set of data follows a periodic pattern, so that algebraic solutions are not appropriate. A more sophisticated discovery system can mimic the ways human intellect reasons about search. Consider a program that can monitor its own performance. After spending some time on an unsuccessful search in one space, the system can switch to another search or try to demonstrate that no solution exists in a given space.

References

Agrawal, R., T. Imielinski, and A. Swami. 1993. "Mining association rules between sets of items in large databases." In *Proceedings of ACM SIGMOD Conference on Management of Data*, edited by P. Buneman, and S. Jajodia, pp. 207–216. Washington, DC.

Fischer, P., and J. M. Żytkow. 1991. "Constructing models of hidden structure." In *Methodologies for Intelligent Systems*, edited by Z. Ras, and M. Zemankova, pp. 441–449. Berlin: Springer-Verlag.

Jackson, P. 1990. *Introduction to Expert Systems*. Reading, MA: Addison-Wesley.

Klösgen, W. 1996. "Explora: a multipattern and multistrategy discovery assistant." In *Advances in Knowledge Discovery and Data Mining*, edited by U. Fayyad, G. Piatetsky-Shapiro, P. Smyth, and R. Uthurusamy, pp. 249–271. Menlo Park, CA: MIT Press.

Langley, P. 1996. *Elements of Machine Learning*. San Mateo, CA: Morgan Kaufmann.

Langley, P. W., H. A. Simon, G. Bradshaw, and J. M. Żytkow. 1987. *Scientific Discovery: An Account of the Creative Processes*. Boston: MIT Press.

Lindsay, R., B. G. Buchanan, E. A. Feigenbaum, and R. Lederberg. 1980. *Applications of Artificial Intelligence for Organic Chemistry: The Dendral Project*. New York: McGraw-Hill.

McDermott, J. 1982. "R1: a rule-based configurer of computer systems." *Artificial Intell.* 19: 39–88.

Piatetsky-Shapiro, G., and C. J. Matheus. 1991. "Knowledge discovery workbench: an exploratory environment for discovery in business databases." In *Proceedings of Knowledge Discovery in Databases Workshop*, edited by G. Piatetsky-Shapiro, pp. 11–24. Menlo Park, CA: AAAI Press.

Penrose, R. 1989. *The Emperor's New Mind*. New York: Oxford University Press.

Rich, E., and K. Knight. 1991. *Artificial Intelligence*. Boston: McGraw-Hill.

Russell, S., and P. Norvig. 1995. *Artificial Intelligence: A Modern Approach*. Upper Saddle River, NJ: Prentice-Hall.

Simon, H. A. 1979. *Models of Thought*. New Haven, CT: Yale University Press.

Shortliffe, E. H. 1976. *Computer-Based Medical Consultations: MYCIN*. Amsterdam, Netherlands: Elsevier.

Valdés-Pérez, R. E. 1993. "Conjecturing hidden entities via simplicity and conservation laws: machine discovery in chemistry." *Artificial Intell.* 65: 247–280.

Zembowicz, R., and J. M. Żytkow. 1993. "Database exploration in search of regularities." *J. Intell. Inform. Sys.* 2: 39–81.

Zhong, N., C. Liu, Y. Kakemoto, and S. Ohsuga. 1997. "KDD process planning." In *Proceedings of the Third International Conference on Knowledge Discovery and Data Mining (KDD-97)*, pp. 291–294. Menlo Park, CA: AAAI Press.

Żytkow, J. M., and P. Fischer. 1996. "Incremental discovery of hidden structure: application to elementary particles." In *Proceedings of the Fourteenth National Conference on Artificial Intelligence*, pp. 750–756. Menlo Park, CA: AAAI Press.

Żytkow, J. M. 1996. "Automated discovery of empirical laws." *Fundamenta Inform.* 27: 299–318.

28 MACHINE LEARNING

Pedro Domingos

ABSTRACT Machine learning's focus on ill-defined problems and highly flexible methods makes it ideally suited for knowledge discovery in databases (KDD) applications. Among the ideas machine learning contributes to KDD are the importance of empirical validation, the impossibility of learning without *a priori* assumptions, and the utility of limited-search or limited-representation methods. Machine learning provides methods for incorporating knowledge into the learning process, changing and combining representations, combatting the curse of dimensionality, and learning comprehensible models. KDD challenges for machine learning include scaling up its algorithms to large databases, using cost information in learning, automating data preprocessing, and enabling rapid development of applications. KDD opens up new directions for machine-learning research and brings new urgency to others. These directions include interfacing with the human user and the database system, learning from nonattribute-vector data, learning partial models, and learning continuously from an open-ended stream of data.

1. Use of Machine-Learning Methods for KDD

Machine learning is characterized by a focus on complex representations, ill-defined problems, and search-based methods. Representations studied include most of those described in Chapter 5, but particularly decision trees, sets of propositional or first-order rules, sets of instances, clusters, concept hierarchies, and probabilistic networks. Ill-defined problems studied include generalizing from a set of tuples in the absence of a known model structure (Chapter 16.1), clustering (Chapter 16.5), combining logic theories of a domain with learning (de Raedt, 1996), and learning from delayed feedback in very large decision spaces (Sutton and Barto, 1998). Search methods (Chapter 11) used for learning include greedy search, gradient descent, expectation maximization, genetic algorithms, and some forms of look-ahead and pruned breadth-first search. Other types of search frequently found in artificial intelligence, like best-first search and simulated annealing, tend to see less use in machine learning, for reasons discussed below.

The flexibility of most machine-learning methods makes them well suited to applications where little is known *a priori* about the domain, and/or relevant knowledge is hard to elicit. This flexibility also means they are often able to successfully learn from data that was not gathered by a purposely designed experimental procedure, but rather obtained by some process whose end goal was not necessarily knowledge discovery. The flip side of this is that theoretical analysis of machine-learning methods is often difficult, and strong guarantees regarding the correctness of results are consequently seldom available. This is compensated for by the fact that machine learning makes full use of the power of the computer to experimentally validate its methods and results. The same approach would seem to be indispensable in KDD. Standard elements of machine learning's empirical toolbox include the use of holdout sets and cross-validation (Chapter 19.1) to verify generalization, comparison of systems on large collections of benchmark problems (e.g., Blake et al., 1999), lesion studies to elucidate the contribution of specific system components, and experiments with carefully designed synthetic data sets to test specific hypotheses on when and why a given approach will work (Kibler and Langley, 1998).

Difficulties notwithstanding, a significant body of theory has been developed within machine learning (see Kearns and Vazirani, 1994, for an introduction) and has produced highly successful practical algorithms like boosting (Freund and Schapire, 1996), Winnow (Littlestone, 1997), and support vector machines (Scholkopf et al., 1998). Much of this theory is in the form of bounds on the generalization error of a learner, given its empirical error and a measure of the effective size of the hypothesis space it explores (its cardinality, for finite spaces; or its Vapnik–Chervonenkis dimension, for infinite ones Vapnik, 1995). The wealth of theoretical results produced is made possible by not insisting on absolute guarantees (e.g., error will always be less than 5 percent), but instead aiming for probabilistic ones (e.g., error will be less than 5 percent with greater than 99 percent probability).

Machine learning's readiness to perform generalization in the absence of strong guiding assumptions has led it to face squarely the problem of what, and how much, is needed to generalize successfully. The lessons learned form an important part of any KDD practitioner's baggage. One is that generalization is impossible in the absence of assumptions or biases; purely empirical learning is a chimera (Mitchell, 1980; Schaffer, 1994; Wolpert, 1996). Induction can be seen as a knowledge lever, with much higher leverage than deduction, but still of no use without an applied force. The converse lesson is that there is no general-purpose learning method; each method's utility is contingent on the assumptions it makes, and each application requires individual attention. "Universal laws" of discovery like "simple hypotheses are more accurate" (sometimes known as "Occam's razor") should be viewed with suspicion (Schaffer, 1993; Webb, 1996; Domingos, 1998). Having made the notion of bias explicit, machine learning has gone on to study the changes in bias (Gordon and desJardins, 1995) and combinations of different biases (Michalski and Wnek, 1996) that are often required for practical success. Awareness of the importance of knowledge has led to development of methods for explicitly incorporating it into the learning process. This knowledge can appear in the form of a propositional or first-order logic theory (e.g., Pazzani and Kibler, 1992; Saitta et al., 1993; Ourston and Mooney, 1994; Towell and Shavlik, 1994), or in a variety of weaker forms (e.g., Clearwater and Provost, 1990; Donoho and Rendell, 1996; Pazzani et al., 1997).

Machine learning is concerned simultaneously with statistical soundness and computational efficiency. This has led it to explore issues that tend not to arise when either is considered in isolation, but that will often be of concern in KDD applications. One such issue is deciding where a KDD algorithm should fall in the lazy–eager computational spectrum. In the eager extreme, where most traditional modeling approaches fall, all generalization (and therefore most computation) is performed at learning time. In the lazy extreme, exemplified by nearest-neighbor algorithms (Chapter 16.1.3), all generalization and computation occur at performance time. Machine learning has gone between the extremes, identifying the entire lazy–eager spectrum as a useful design dimension, and proceeding to explore it (Aha, 1997). For example, the RISE system autonomously determines the best combination of rules and neighbors to use (Domingos, 1996b).

A central issue that involves both statistical soundness and computational efficiency is the effect of (often massive) search on the significance of the patterns discovered. When thousands or even millions of hypotheses are generated in the course of search, the probability that apparently meaningful discoveries are simply the result of chance cannot be neglected. However, quantifying it is notoriously difficult. Traditional significance testing assumes that a single hypothesis is being tested. Techniques exist for multiple comparison or simultaneous inference problems (Chapter 19.1; Miller, 1981; Klockars and Sax, 1986), but they tend to overpenalize and consequently reject valid patterns. Machine learning provides a number of techniques for assessing hypotheses in a search-conscious fashion, and controlling search to make the best use of computational power without falling into the trap of noise mining (Quinlan and Cameron-Jones, 1995; Freund, 1998; Domingos, 1999a; Jensen and Cohen, 1999). Although this is still very much an open problem, one of the hard-and-fast heuristics to emerge so far has been that apparently impoverished search methods (e.g., greedy search) are often preferable to more powerful ones (e.g., exhaustive search; Quinlan and Cameron-Jones, 1995; Murthy and Salzberg, 1995; Dietterich, 1995). Like all subfields of computer science, machine learning is constrained by finite computational resources, but unlike most others, it is also constrained by another finite resource: the quantity of data available for learning. Either type of resource can be the bottleneck in any given application. If computation is the bottleneck, underfitting can result; if data, overfitting. In KDD projects, where large computational resources and large quantities of data are both frequent, either can be the case.

A generalization of the previous observation is that less can be more. Machine-learning researchers have found that more powerful representations do not necessarily lead to better results (Holte, 1993; Domingos and Pazzani, 1997). Flexibility can have a price in instability.

This trade-off can be captured by the notions of statistical bias and variance, which were first developed for regression, but have been extended to classification (Geman et al., 1992; Kong and Dietterich, 1995; Kohavi and Wolpert, 1996; Friedman, 1997; Domingos, 2000). A related observation is that computational power is often better used to induce multiple models and combine them, instead of searching more for a single best one. This is the approach followed by some of the best-performing learning methods available, including boosting (Freund and Schapire, 1996), bagging (Breiman, 1996a), stacking (Wolpert, 1992), and error-correcting output codes (Kong and Dietterich, 1995).

Another instance of less can be more is the curse of dimensionality (Duda and Hart, 1973). Human intuitions from the three-dimensional world fail in high dimensions. Although we might expect adding attributes to the data to improve learning, given that they provide additional information, after a point the reverse is typically the case. This is because increasing the dimension of the tuple space exponentially increases the quantity of data needed to populate it densely enough for reliable learning. This problem is particularly acute in large KDD applications where the attributes can often number in the hundreds or thousands. Machine learning provides some of the best techniques available for very high-dimensional problems (e.g., decision-tree induction (Chapter 16.1.3) and rule induction (Chapter 16.1.4) and for attribute selection (e.g., Moore and Lee, 1994).

A hallmark of machine learning is the focus on comprehensible results. While comprehensibility is difficult to define precisely and is ultimately subjective, it is essential to the insights that are often the main goal of KDD. Many machine-learning methods produce models that are comprehensible even to someone without mathematical training. For example, they can be sets of "If...Then..." rules, or in graphical form. Besides inducing such models directly, machine learning provides methods for converting less-comprehensible ones into them (e.g., neural networks into decision trees [Craven, 1996]).

2. Research Problems in Machine Learning Relevant to KDD

From the point of view of accurate generalization, machine-learning algorithms are often the most appropriate ones for a great variety of KDD applications. However, the volume of data available in many of these applications far outstrips the capacity of classical machine-learning algorithms. Often, the solution adopted is simply to learn from a small-enough subset of the data, but the selection of this subset is typically done in a very *ad hoc* fashion, often randomly, potentially missing much of the learnable structure. The effort is now under way to enable machine-learning algorithms to learn from several orders of magnitude more data than they were originally designed for.

The most basic requirement for algorithms that mine large databases is that they have linear or only slightly superlinear running time as a function of the database size. Since this is not true for most learning algorithms, it is necessary to adapt them. This can sometimes be done partly in a lossless fashion by optimizing the algorithms without changing their output, but typically requires a lossy approach: developing related algorithms that may not produce exactly the same results but achieve similar levels of performance. Cohen's (1995) RIPPER and Domingos's (1996a) CWS algorithm are examples of this approach for the case of rule induction. Further, when the learning data are too large to fit in main memory, learning algorithms must be able to efficiently retrieve it from disk. This implies making only sequential passes through the data, as opposed to randomly accessing it, and making as few passes as possible. The SLIQ and SPRINT algorithms for decision-tree induction exemplify this approach (Mehta et al., 1996; Shafer et al., 1996), as does the A priori algorithm for finding association rules (Agrawal et al., 1996). The ability to learn efficiently from disk will increasingly be seen as one of the fundamental characteristics of machine-learning algorithms appropriate to KDD. Ideally, algorithms should use only constant RAM and be able to learn from less than one full disk scan, making useful results available at any time after they start running (Smyth and Wolpert, 1997), and taking advantage of additional time to scan further and gracefully improve the output.

For still larger quantities of data, the use of data reduction becomes inevitable. Two classes of approaches can be distinguished here: sampling and summarization. One sampling approach is to divide the examples into multiple subsets, learn on each, and combine the results (Chan and Stolfo, 1995; Breiman, 1996b). Another is to start with a small subset of the examples and iterate, adaptively selecting which new examples to include so as to obtain the maximum possible improvement from each new addition (Catlett, 1991; Musick et al., 1993). Summarization approaches attempt to produce summaries of the data that will fit in main memory, while still containing all or most of the information necessary to learn in an efficiently accessible form. These summaries may be in the form of sufficient statistics (e.g., Moore and Lee, 1997; Graefe et al., 1998) or they may be the result of applying compression techniques to the data (e.g., Davies and Moore, 1999). The sampling and summarization approaches are complementary and can be used together (e.g., Bradley et al. 1998).

For many problems, large quantities of data may be available, but may not be necessary to learn the desired concepts to the required level of accuracy (Oates and Jensen, 1997). For others, even the large quantities available may not be sufficient to capture all the relevant structure. It would thus be useful to have methods, even if heuristic in nature, to estimate early on how much data will be needed. Examples of research in this direction are the fitting of power laws to learning curves (Frey and Fisher, 1999) and statistical tests on the slope of these curves (Provost et al., 1999). A complementary approach is to attempt to estimate the Bayes rate, that is, the error rate at which even an infinite-capacity learner will necessarily asymptote (Dasarathy, 1991; Cortes, 1995; Tumer and Ghosh, 1996), and to stop learning once this level is reached.

The numbers of examples, attributes, and classes presented by KDD applications effectively constitute a previously unexplored region of the machine-learning space. Because of its empirical nature, the validity of much painstakingly assembled machine-learning knowledge in these new circumstances is an open question. Therefore, it is important to determine which elements of this knowledge need to be revised, and how.

Another type of adaptation to machine-learning algorithms needed to make them useful for KDD involves aspects of KDD problems that they currently do not capture well. An example of this is cost information. Most machine-learning algorithms assume that all errors have the same cost, but this is seldom the case in practice. A related problem is that of imbalanced classes: when there is a large majority of one class, it is easy to obtain high accuracy without useful results. Implicitly, misclassifying minority tuples incurs a higher cost, although this may be hard to quantify. Research on adapting machine-learning algorithms for these problems is growing (e.g., Pazzani et al., 1994; Turney, 1995; Provost and Fawcett, 1997; Domingos, 1999b).

More generally, an important research direction involves methods for formulating problems in terms amenable to machine-learning. Integrating, cleaning up, and preprocessing the learning data is the stage of the machine-learning application process that typically consumes the most time because it is the one that requires the most human intervention. Automating this stage would produce an order-of-magnitude speedup in the process, with the corresponding reduction in cost and increase in the number of viable applications.

Although the main focus of machine-learning research has been on classification problems (Chapter 16.1), a significant motivation for this has been the belief that classifiers can be used as building blocks for solutions to many other types of problems. Since many such problems are present in KDD (see Chapter 16), research on the interface between classification and those problems has become particularly relevant.

The perspective of widespread, large-scale application of machine learning creates the need for rapid development and deployment of learning systems. It should be possible for computer scientists with only minor knowledge of machine learning to produce a robust and reliable learning component for whatever system they are building. This requires developing libraries of standard machine-learning components and of ways of putting them together. Despite a number of early developments in this direction (Gilks et al., 1994; Buntine, 1994; Kohavi et al., 1996), for the most part it is still not clear how best to do this. Deciding what representations and techniques to use is still a black art. The designer's personal preferences and a long trial-and-error process are often what determines the outcome. Many imprecise intuitions and rules of thumb exist, but more theoretical and empirical research is needed on what conditions favor what approaches and why, and on systematizing the current jungle of techniques. The results of this research can then be codified in a form that is easily used by nonexperts, or directly incorporated into more self-sufficient learning modules.

3. Impact of KDD on Machine Learning

KDD presents a veritable treasure of new research opportunities for machine learning. In many respects, it allows a renewed focus on problems that were original concerns of the field but that have received decreasing attention over time, arguably in large measure due to the previous limited availability of relevant real-world data sets. Perhaps serendipitously, machine learning's powerful methods often find their most compelling applications in today's large databases, which were not available when the methods were originally developed. KDD also allows machine learning to extend its ideas and motivations in new directions, and to develop productive interfaces with disciplines like databases, statistics, human–computer interfaces, visualization, information retrieval, and high-performance computing.

Applying machine learning to the very large databases found in KDD involves qualitative changes that go beyond simply scaling up the algorithms. For example, the traditional goal of creating a model of everything that is represented in the database must often give way to finding only local patterns or deviations from the norm. Compared to the model-building case, very little theory has been developed so far for this type of problem. Current practical KDD approaches are often more concerned with efficiency than with sound generalization. Since the latter is a central concern of machine learning, analyzing and improving these approaches is potentially fertile ground for new theoretical and methodological developments. Also, if a database is too large to model in its entirety, even through the use of sampling, sufficient statistics, or compression, then a focus of attention mechanism becomes necessary. Many heuristics and sources of information could be brought to bear on the design of such mechanisms. Furthermore, in large databases gathered over a period of time (sometimes many years) and without learning in mind, the usual assumption of i.i.d. (independently and identically distributed) data often does not hold. Thus, an important research direction is taking into account that examples are not independent and that past, present, and future data is not necessarily from the same population.

The majority of work to date in machine learning has focused on learning from examples represented as attribute vectors, where each attribute is a single number or symbol, and a single table contains all the vectors. However, much (or most) of the data in KDD applications is not of this type. For example, relational databases typically contain many different relations/tables, and performing a global join to reduce them to one without losing information is seldom computationally feasible. (Inductive logic programming [de Raedt, 1996] can handle data in multiple relations, but simultaneously focuses on learning concepts that are themselves in first-order form, thus addressing a doubly difficult problem.) The World Wide Web is mostly composed of a combination of text and HTML, plus image and audio files. The data recorded by many sensors and processes, from telescopes and Earth-sensing satellites to medical and business records, have a spatial and temporal structure. In the customer-behavior mining applications that are of central concern to many companies, people can be hierarchically aggregated by occupation and other characteristics, products by category, et cetera. Simply converting data of all these types to attribute vectors before learning, as is common today, risks missing some of the most significant patterns. Although in each case traditional techniques for handling these types of data exist, they are typically quite limited in power compared to the machine-learning algorithms available for the attribute vector case, and there is much scope for extending the ideas and techniques of machine learning in this direction.

A machine-learning system appropriate to future KDD applications should be able to function continuously, learning from an open-ended stream of data and constantly adjusting its behavior, while remaining reliable and requiring a minimum of human supervision. The future is likely to see an increasing number of applications of this type, as opposed to the one-shot, stand-alone applications common today. Early indicators of this trend are e-commerce sites that potentially respond to each new user differently as they learn his or her preferences, and systems for automated trading in the stock market. The trend is also apparent in the increasing preoccupation among corporations to instantly and continuously adapt to changing market conditions, leveraging for this purpose their distributed data-gathering capabilities. While there has been some relevant research in machine learning (Widmer and Kubat, 1998), learners of this type must address several interesting new issues. One is smoothly incorporating new relevant data sources as they come online, coping with changes in them, and decoupling from them if they become unavailable. Another is maintaining a clear distinction between two types of change in the learner's evolving model(s): those that are simply the result of accumulating data and consequently progressing in the learning curve, and those that are the result of changes in the environment being modeled.

In KDD applications, learning is seldom an isolated process. More typically, it must be embedded into a larger system. Addressing the multiple problems this raises will be an opportunity for machine learning to expand its focus and its reach. The need to efficiently integrate learning algorithms with the underlying database system creates a new interface between machine learning and database research: finding query classes that can be executed efficiently while providing information useful for learning, and simultaneously finding learning approaches that use only efficiently executable queries. Some relevant questions are: What types of sampling can be efficiently supported, and how can they be used? What is the best use that can be made of a single sequential scan of the entire database? The outcome of this iterative process may be query types and learning algorithms that are both different from those known today. The interface between machine learning and databases also involves the use for learning purposes of the *meta-data* that is sometimes available in database systems. For example, definitions of fields and constraints between their values may be a valuable source of background knowledge for use in the learning process.

To be used to its full potential, KDD requires a well-integrated data warehouse. Assembling the latter is a complex and time-consuming process, but machine learning can itself be used to partially automate it. For example, one of the main problems is identifying the correspondences between fields in different but related databases (Knoblock and Levy, 1998), or other data sources, like the results of Web searches (Perkowitz and Etzioni, 1995). This problem can be formulated in learning terms: given a target schema $\{X_1, X_2, ..., X_n\}$ and examples of data in this schema, induce general rules as to what constitutes an X_i column. Given a table in a source schema $\{Y_1, Y_2, ..., Y_n\}$, the goal is now to classify each of the Y columns as one of the Xs (or none), with the results for one Y potentially constraining those for the others. Data cleaning is another key aspect of building a data warehouse that offers many research opportunities for machine learning. Very large databases almost invariably contain large quantities of noise and missing fields. More significantly, noise is often of multiple types, and its occurrence varies systematically from one part of the database to another (e.g., because the data comes from multiple sources). Similarly, the causes of missing information can be multiple and can vary systematically within the database. Research enabling machine-learning algorithms to deal with noise and missing data was one of the main drivers of their jump from the laboratory to widespread real-world application. However, example-independent noise and missing data are typically assumed. Modeling systematic sources of error and missing information, and finding ways of minimizing their impact, is the next logical step.

The need to produce learning results that contribute to a larger scientific or business goal leads to the research problem of finding ways to integrate these goals more deeply into the learning process, and of increasing the communication bandwidth between the learning process and its clients beyond simply providing, for example, class predictions for new examples. The importance in KDD of interaction with the human user (expert or not) gives a new urgency to traditional machine-learning concerns like comprehensibility and incorporation of background knowledge. Today's multiple KDD application domains provide a wealth of driving problems and testing grounds for new developments in this direction. Many major application domains (e.g., molecular biology, Earth sensing, finance, marketing, fraud detection) have unique concerns and characteristics, and developing machine-learning algorithms specifically for each of them is likely to occupy an increasing number of researchers.

Most machine-learning research to date has dealt with the well-circumscribed problem of finding a classification model given a single, small, relatively clean data set in *attribute-vector* form, where the attributes have previously been chosen to facilitate learning and the end goal (accurate classification) is simple and well defined. With KDD, machine learning is now breaking out of each one of these constraints. Machine learning's many valuable contributions to KDD are reciprocated by the latter's invigorating effect on it. No doubt this mutually beneficial interaction will continue to develop in the future.

ACKNOWLEDGMENTS
The author is grateful to David Aha, Tom Dietterich, Doug Fisher, Rob Holte, David Jensen, Ryszard Michalski, Foster Provost, Ross Quinlan, and Lorenza Saitta for valuable comments and suggestions regarding this article.

References

Agrawal, R., H. Mannila, R. Srikant, H. Toivonen, and A. I. Verkamo. 1996. "Fast discovery of association rules." In *Advances in Knowledge Discovery and Data Mining*, edited by U. M. Fayyad, G. Piatetsky-Shapiro, P. Smyth, and R. Uthurusamy, pp. 307–328. Menlo Park, CA: AAAI Press.

Aha, D. W. (ed). 1997. "Special issue on lazy learning." Issue 1–5. *Artificial Intelligence Review* 11.

Blake, C., E. Keogh, and C. Merz. J. 1999. *UCI repository of machine learning databases* (Machine-readable data repository). Irvine, CA: Department of Information and Computer Science, University of California at Irvine. Available at http://www.ics.uci.edu/ ~ mlearn/MLRepository.html.

Bradley, P. S., U. Fayyad, and C. Reina. 1998. "Scaling clustering algorithms to large databases." In *Proceedings of the Fourth International Conference on Knowledge Discovery and Data Mining*, pp. 9–15. New York: AAAI Press.

Breiman, L. 1996a. "Bagging predictors." *Machine Learning* **24**: 123–140.

Breiman, L. 1996b. "Pasting bites together for prediction in large data sets and on-line." Technical Report, Berkeley: Statistics Department, University of California at Berkeley.

Buntine, W. 1994. "Operations for learning with graphical models." *J. Artificial Intell. Res.* **2**: 159–225.

Catlett, J. 1991. "Megainduction: machine learning on very large databases." Unpublished Ph.D. diss. Australia: Basser Department of Computer Science, University of Sydney.

Chan, P. K. and S. J. Stolfo. 1995. "Learning arbiter and combiner trees from partitioned data for scaling machine learning." In *Proceedings of the First International Conference on Knowledge Discovery and Data Mining*, pp. 39–44. Montreal: AAAI Press.

Clearwater, S. and F. Provost. 1990. "RL4: a tool for knowledge-based induction." In *Proceedings of the Second IEEE International Conference on Tools for Artificial Intelligence*, pp. 24–30. San Jose, CA: IEEE Computer Society Press.

Cohen, W. W. 1995. "Fast effective rule induction." In *Proceedings of the Twelfth International Conference on Machine Learning*, pp. 115–123. Tahoe City, CA: Morgan Kaufmann.

Cortes, C. 1995. "Prediction of generalization ability in learning machines." Unpublished Ph.D. diss. NY: Department of Computer Science, University of Rochester.

Craven, M. W. 1996. "Extracting comprehensible models from trained neural networks." Unpublished Ph.D. diss. Department of Computer Sciences, University of Wisconsin—Madison.

Dasarathy, B. W. (ed). 1991. *Nearest Neighbor (NN) Norms: NN Pattern Classification Techniques*. Los Alamitos, CA: IEEE Computer Society Press.

Davies, S. and A. Moore. 1999. "Using Bayesian networks for lossless compression in data mining." In *Proceedings of the Fifth International Conference on Knowledge Discovery and Data Mining*. San Diego, CA: ACM Press.

de Raedt, L. (ed). 1996. *Advances in Inductive Logic Programming*. Amsterdam: IOS Press.

Dietterich, T. G. 1995. "Overfitting and undercomputing in machine learning." *Comput. Surveys* **27**: 326–327.

Domingos, P. 1996a. "Linear-time rule induction." In *Proceedings of the Second International Conference on Knowledge Discovery and Data Mining*, pp. 96–101. Portland, OR: AAAI Press.

Domingos, P. 1996b. "Unifying instance-based and rule-based induction." *Machine Learning* **24**: 141–168.

Domingos, P. 1998. "Occam's two razors: the sharp and the blunt." In *Proceedings of the Fourth International Conference on Knowledge Discovery and Data Mining*, pp. 37–43. New York: AAAI Press.

Domingos, P. 1999a. "Process-oriented estimation of generalization error." In *Proceedings of the Sixteenth International Joint Conference on Artificial Intelligence*, pp. 714–719. Stockholm: Morgan Kaufmann.

Domingos, P. 1999b. "MetaCost: a general method for making classifiers cost-sensitive." In *Proceedings of the Fifth International Conference on Knowledge Discovery and Data Mining*, pp. 155–164. San Diego, CA: ACM Press.

Domingos, P. 2000. "A unified bias-variance decomposition for zero-one and squared loss." In *Proceedings of the Seventeenth National Conference on Artificial Intelligence*, pp. 564–569. Austin, TX: AAAI Press.

Domingos, P. and M. Pazzani. 1997. "On the optimality of the simple Bayesian classifier under zero–one loss." *Machine Learning* **29**: 103–130.

Donoho, S. and L. Rendell. 1996. "Constructive induction using fragmentary knowledge." In *Proceedings of the Thirteenth International Conference on Machine Learning*, pp. 113–121. Bari: Morgan Kaufmann.

Duda, R. O. and P. E. Hart. 1973. *Pattern Classification and Scene Analysis*. New York: Wiley.

Freund, Y. 1998. "Self bounding learning algorithms." In *Proceedings of the Eleventh Annual Conference on Computational Learning Theory*, pp. 247–258. Madison, WI: Morgan Kaufmann.

Freund, Y. and R. E. Schapire. 1996. "Experiments with a new boosting algorithm." In *Proceedings of the Thirteenth International Conference on Machine Learning*, pp. 148–156. Bari: Morgan Kaufmann.

Frey, L. J. and D. H. Fisher. 1999. "Modeling decision tree performance with the power law." In *Proceedings of Uncertainty '99: The Seventh International Workshop on Artificial Intelligence and Statistics*, pp. 59–65. Fort Lauderdale, FL: Morgan Kaufmann.

Friedman, J. H. 1997. "On bias, variance, 0/1 – loss, and the curse-of-dimensionality." *Data Mining and Knowledge Discovery* **1**: 55–77.

Geman, S., E. Bienenstock, and R. Doursat. 1992. "Neural networks and the bias/variance dilemma." *Neural Comput.* **4**: 1–58.

Gilks, W. R., A. Thomas, and D. J. Spiegelhalter. 1994. "A language and program for complex Bayesian modelling." *The Statistician* **43**: 169–178.

Gordon, D. F. and M. desJardins. (eds). 1995. "Special issue on evaluation and selection of biases in machine learning." *Machine Learning* **20(1).**

Graefe, G., U. Fayyad, and S. Chaudhuri. 1998. "On the efficient gathering of sufficient statistics for classification from large SQL databases." In *Proceedings of the Fourth International Conference on Knowledge Discovery and Data Mining*, pp. 204–208. New York: AAAI Press.

Holte, R. C. 1993. "Very simple classification rules perform well on most commonly used data sets." *Machine Learning* **11**: 63–91.

Jensen, D. and P. R. Cohen. 2000. "Multiple comparisons in induction algorithms." *Machine Learning* **38**: 309–338.

Kearns, M. J. and U. V. Vazirani. 1994. *An Introduction to Computational Learning Theory*. Cambridge, MA: MIT Press.

Kibler, D. and P. Langley. 1998. "Machine learning as an experimental science." In *Proceedings of the Third European Working Session on Learning*. London: Pitman.

Klockars, A. J. and G. Sax. 1986. *Multiple Comparisons*. Beverly Hills, CA: Sage.

Knoblock, C. and A. Levy. (eds). 1998. *Proceedings of the AAAI-98 Workshop on AI and Information Integration*. Madison, WI: AAAI Press.

Kohavi, R., D. Sommerfield, and J. Dougherty. 1996. "Data mining using MLC++, a machine learning library in C++." *Int. J. Artificial Intell. Tools* **6**: 537–566.

Kohavi, R. and D. H. Wolpert. 1996. "Bias plus variance decomposition for zero-one loss functions." In *Proceedings of the Thirteenth International Conference on Machine Learning*, pp. 275–283. Bari: Morgan Kaufmann.

Kong, E. B. and T. G. Dietterich. 1995. "Error-correcting output coding corrects bias and variance." In *Proceedings of the Twelfth International Conference on Machine Learning*, pp. 313–321. Tahoe City, CA: Morgan Kaufmann.

Littlestone, N. 1997. "Learning quickly when irrelevant attributes abound: a new linear-threshold algorithm." *Machine Learning* **2**: 285–318.

Mehta, M., A. Agrawal, and J. Rissanen. 1996. "SLIQ: a fast scalable classifier for data mining." In *Proceedings of the Fifth International Conference on Extending Database Technology*, pp. 18–32. Avignon, France: Springer.

Michalski, R. S. and J. Wnek. (eds). 1996. *Proceedings of the Third International Workshop on Multistrategy Learning*. Harpers Ferry, VA: AAAI Press.

Miller, R. G. Jr. 1981. *Simultaneous Statistical Inference*. 2d ed. New York: Springer.

Mitchell, T. M. 1980. "The need for biases in learning generalizations." (Technical Report). New Brunswick, NJ: Computer Science Department, Rutgers University.

Moore, A. W. and M. S. Lee. 1994. "Efficient algorithms for minimizing cross validation error." In *Proceedings of the Eleventh International Conference on Machine Learning*, pp. 190–198. New Brunswick, NJ: Morgan Kaufmann.

Moore, A. W. and M. S. Lee. 1997. "Cached sufficient statistics for efficient machine learning with large data sets." *J. Artificial Intell. Res.* **8**: 67–91.

Murthy, S. and S. Salzberg. 1995. "Lookahead and pathology in decision tree induction." In *Proceedings of the Fourteenth International Joint Conference on Artificial Intelligence*, pp. 1025–1031. Montreal: Morgan Kaufmann.

Musick, R., J. Catlett, and S. Russell. 1993. "Decision theoretic subsampling for induction on large databases." In *Proceedings of the Tenth International Conference on Machine Learning*, pp. 212–219. Amherst, MA: Morgan Kaufmann.

Oates, T. and D. Jensen. 1997. "The effects of training set size on decision tree complexity." In *Proceedings of the Fourteenth International Conference on Machine Learning*, pp. 254–262. Madison, WI: Morgan Kaufmann.

Ourston, D. and R. J. Mooney. 1994. "Theory refinement combining analytical and empirical methods." *Artificial Intell.* **66**: 273–309.

Pazzani, M. and D. Kibler. 1992. "The utility of knowledge in inductive learning." *Machine Learning* **9**: 57–94.

Pazzani, M., S. Mani, and W. R. Shankle. 1997. "Beyond concise and colorful: learning intelligible rules." In *Proceedings of the Third International Conference on Knowledge Discovery and Data Mining*, pp. 235–238. Newport Beach, CA: AAAI Press.

Pazzani, M., C. Merz, P. Murphy, K. Ali, T. Hume, and C. Brunk. 1994. "Reducing misclassification costs." In *Proceedings of the Eleventh International Conference on Machine Learning*, pp. 217–225. New Brunswick, NJ: Morgan Kaufmann.

Perkowitz, M. and O. Etzioni. 1995. "Category translation: learning to understand information on the Internet." In *Proceedings of the Fourteenth International Joint Conference on Artificial Intelligence*, pp. 930–936. Montreal: Morgan Kaufmann.

Provost, F. and T. Fawcett. 1997. Analysis and Visualization of Classifier Performance: Comparison under Imprecise Class and Cost Distributions. In *Proceedings of the Third International Conference on Knowledge Discovery and Data Mining*, pp. 43–48. Newport Beach, CA: AAAI Press.

Provost, F., D. Jensen, and T. Oates. 1999. "Efficient progressive sampling." In *Proceedings of the Fifth International Conference on Knowledge Discovery and Data Mining*. San Diego, CA: ACM Press.

Quinlan, J. R. and R. M. Cameron-Jones. 1996. 1995. "Oversearching and layered search in empirical learning." In *Proceedings of the Fourteenth International Joint Conference on Artificial Intelligence*, pp. 1019–1024. Montreal: Morgan Kaufmann.

Saitta, L., M. Botta, and F. Neri. 1993. "Multistrategy learning and theory revision." *Machine Learning* **11**: 153–172.

Schaffer, C. 1993. "Overfitting avoidance as bias." *Machine Learning* **10**: 153–178.

Schaffer, C. 1994. "A conservation law for generalization performance." In *Proceedings of the Eleventh International Conference on Machine Learning*, pp. 259–265. New Brunswick, NJ: Morgan Kaufmann.

Scholkopf, B., C. Burges, and A. Smola. 1998. *Advances in Kernel Methods: Support Vector Machines*. Cambridge, MA: MIT Press.

Shafer, J. C., R. Agrawal, and M. Mehta. 1996. "SPRINT: a scalable parallel classifier for data mining." In *Proceedings of the Twenty-Second International Conference on Very Large Databases*, pp. 544–555. Mumbai, India: Morgan Kaufmann.

Smyth, P. and D. Wolpert. 1997. "Anytime exploratory data analysis for massive data sets." In *Proceedings of the Third International Conference on Knowledge Discovery and Data Mining*, pp. 54–60. Newport Beach, CA: AAAI Press.

Sutton, R. S. and A. Barto. 1998. *Reinforcement Learning: An Introduction*. Cambridge, MA: MIT Press.

Towell, G. G. and J. W. Shavlik. 1994. "Knowledge-based artificial neural networks." *Artificial Intell.* **70**: 119–165.

Tumer, K. and J. Ghosh. 1996. "Classifier combining: analytical results and implications." In *Proceedings of the AAAI-96 Workshop on Integrating Multiple Learned Models for Improving and Scaling Machine Learning Algorithms*, pp. 126–132. Portland, OR: AAAI Press.

Turney, P. 1995. "Cost-sensitive classification: empirical evaluation of a hybrid genetic decision tree algorithm." *J. Artificial Intell. Res.* **2**: 369–409.

Vapnik, V. N. 1995. *The Nature of Statistical Learning Theory*. New York: Springer.

Webb, G. I. 1996. "Further experimental evidence against the utility of Occam's razor." *J. Artificial Intell. Res.* **4**: 397–417.

Widmer, G. and M. Kubat. (eds). 1998. "Special issue on context sensitivity and concept drift." *Machine Learning* **32(2).**

Wolpert, D. 1992. "Stacked generalization." *Neural Networks* **5**: 241–259.

Wolpert, D. 1996. "The lack of *a priori* distinctions between learning algorithms." *Neural Comput.* **8**: 1341–1390.

Further Reading

Aha, D. W. (Ed.) (1997). *Lazy Learning*. Boston: Kluwer. A collection of recent research on lazy learning.

Cohen, P. R. (1995). *Empirical Methods for Artificial Intelligence*. Cambridge, MA: MIT Press. A useful primer on the use of experiments in machine learning and other subfields of AI.

Dasarathy, B. W. (Ed.) (1991). *Nearest Neighbor (NN) Norms: NN Pattern Classification Techniques*. Los Alamitos, CA: IEEE Computer Society Press. One-stop source for the main papers from last three decades of pattern recognition research on learning concepts represented by sets of instances.

Dietterich, T. G. (1997). "Machine learning research: four current directions." *AI Magazine*, **18(4)**, 97–136. An overview of recent developments in some of the main subareas of machine learning, including scaling-up algorithms to large databases. A very useful complement to this article.

Duda, R. O. and P. E. Hart. (1973). *Pattern Classification and Scene Analysis*. New York: Wiley. The classic textbook on statistical pattern recognition.

Jordan, M. I. (Ed.) (1998). *Learning in Graphical Models*. Boston: Kluwer. Tutorials and recent research on learning with probabilistic representations.

Kearns, M. J. and U. V. Vazirani. (1994). *An Introduction to Computational Learning Theory*. Cambridge, MA: MIT Press. An accessible introduction to the theory of machine learning.

Kibler, D. and P. Langley. (1998). "Machine learning as an experimental science." In *Proceedings of the Third European Working Session on Learning*. London: Pitman. Reprinted in J. W. Shavlik and T. G. Dietterich (Eds.) (1990), *Readings in Machine Learning*, San Mateo, CA: Morgan Kaufmann. A very useful introduction to the methodology of machine learning.

Langley, P. (1996). *Elements of Machine Learning*. San Mateo, CA: Morgan Kaufmann. A systematic introductory presentation of the field.

Michalski, R. S., I. Bratko, and M. Kubat. (Eds.) (1998). *Machine Learning and Data Mining: Methods and Applications*. New York: Wiley. Collects a variety of recent research at the interface of machine learning and KDD.

Michalski, R. S., J. G. Carbonell, and T. M. Mitchell. (Eds.) (1983). *Machine Learning: An Artificial Intelligence Approach*, vols. 1–3. Palo Alto, CA: Tioga. A series of books containing much of the early research.

Michalski, R. S. and G. Tecuci. (Eds.) (1994). *Machine Learning: A Multistrategy Approach*. San Mateo, CA: Morgan Kaufmann. Continuation of the previous series, with a focus on combining multiple machine learning biases and using background knowledge.

Michie, D., D. J. Spiegelhalter, and C. C. Taylor. (Eds.) (1994). *Machine Learning, Neural and Statistical Classification*. New York: Ellis Horwood. Describes a large-scale experimental comparison of many algorithms. Also contains introductions to the algorithms and discussion of their strengths and weaknesses. Now out of print, but available online at http://www.amsta.leeds.ac.uk/~charles/statlog/.

Mitchell, T. M. (1997). *Machine Learning*. New York: McGraw-Hill. The standard introductory machine-learning textbook.

Provost, F. and V. Kolluri. (1999). A survey of methods for scaling up inductive algorithms. In *Data Mining and Knowledge Discovery*, 2. An excellent overview of scaling-up research. The place to start if you're looking for a way to scale up your algorithm.

Quinlan, J. R. (1993). *C4.5: Programs for Machine Learning*. San Mateo, CA: Morgan Kaufmann. Describes the most widely used machine learning system.

de Raedt, L. (Ed.) (1996). *Advances in Inductive Logic Programming*. Amsterdam: IOS Press. A collection of articles on learning with examples, background knowledge, and concepts expressed in a subset of first-order logic.

Scholkopf, B., C. Burges, and A. Smola. (1998). *Advances in Kernel Methods: Support Vector Machines*. Cambridge, MA: MIT Press. Expanded papers from a workshop on support vector machines.

Shavlik, J. W. and Dietterich, T. G. (Eds.) (1990). *Readings in Machine Learning*. San Mateo, CA: Morgan Kaufmann. A collection of classic machine-learning papers from the 1980s.

Sutton, R. S. and A. Barto. (1998). *Reinforcement Learning: An Introduction.* Cambridge, MA: MIT Press. Introduction to one of the most active research areas in machine-learning, where the focus is on learning from delayed feedback.

Vapnik, V. N. (1995). *The Nature of Statistical Learning Theory.* New York: Springer. Introduction to the Vapnik–Chervonenkis dimension, the theory of structural risk minimization, and its application to the development of support vector machines.

Weiss, S. M. and C. A. Kulikowski. (1991). *Computer Systems that Learn: Classification and Prediction Methods from Statistics, Neural Nets, Machine Learning, and Expert Systems.* San Mateo, CA: Morgan Kaufmann. An older textbook that also compares machine-learning algorithms with alternative techniques.

The *Machine Learning* journal, published by Kluwer, is the single most important repository of research in the field. Machine-learning articles also appear in the *Artificial Intelligence* journal, in the online *Journal of Artificial Intelligence Research* (http://www.cs.washington.edu/research/jair/home.html), in the *Neural Computation* journal, in the *IEEE Transactions on Pattern Analysis and Machine Intelligence*, and others. The main conference in the field is the *International Conference on Machine Learning*, whose proceedings are published by Morgan Kaufmann. Recent machine-learning research is also reported in the *European Conference on Machine Learning*, the *International Joint Conference on Artificial Intelligence*, the *National Conference on Artificial Intelligence (AAAI)*, the *European Conference on Artificial Intelligence*, the *Annual Conference on Neural Information Processing Systems*, the *International Workshop on Multistrategy Learning*, the *International Workshop on Artificial Intelligence and Statistics*, and others. Research on the theory of machine learning appears in the *International Conference on Computational Learning Theory*, the *European Conference on Computational Learning Theory*, and elsewhere. Useful online machine learning resources include: the UCI repository of machine-learning databases (http://www.ics.uci.edu/~ mlearn/MLRepository.html); the list of home pages of machine-learning researchers maintained by David Aha (http://www.aic.nrl.navy.mil/ ~ aha/people.html); the online bibliographies of several subareas of machine learning maintained by Peter Turney (http://www.iit.nrc.ca/bibliographies/); the *Machine Learning List*, maintained by Michael Pazzani (mailto:ml-request@ics.uci.edu); and the *AI and Statistics List*, maintained by Doug Fisher (mailto:Majordomo@watstat.uwaterloo.ca, with "subscribe ai-stats"). Publicly available machine-learning software includes the MLC^{++} and Weka libraries, found respectively at http://www.sgi.com/Technology/mlc/ and http://www.cs.waikato.ac.nz/ml/weka/.

29 AUTOMATED SCIENTIFIC DISCOVERY

Jan M. Żytkow

ABSTRACT   We investigate the bidirectional links between knowledge discovery in databases (KDD) and automated scientific discovery. Both are concerned with discovery of knowledge, but they differ in many ways. We contrast them and explain why they differ. Then we propose the interchange of ideas and ways of thinking between automated scientific discovery and KDD, so that results in each area can influence the other.

1. Contrasting Automation of Discovery in Science and in Databases

Research on automation of scientific discovery (ASD) has been active since the 1970s. It belongs to the area of artificial intelligence and is motivated by intellectual curiosity about discovery and by the quest for automating intelligence. Discovery, especially scientific discovery, employs the most sophisticated forms of intelligence and is considered the most difficult or even impossible to automate. Research on discovery progressed initially by demonstrating that different isolated steps of scientific discovery can be done by computer systems. When a number of methods that provide such existential proofs became available, the next natural task was integration of many discovery capabilities into one system.

Samples of discovery tasks and results were drawn from sciences, in particular from some of the best-known and most important scientific discoveries of knowledge. Expertise in natural sciences and appreciation for philosophy of science were common and expected among ASD researchers. In the rich history of ASD, many computer systems were developed and applied on discovery tasks in physics, chemistry and biology, economics, technology, medicine, and other domains. Books by Langley et al. (1987), and Shen (1994), and collections edited by Shrager and Langley (1990), Żytkow (1993, 1995), Edwards (1993), Valdés-Pérez (1995), and Simon et al. (1997) are a good starting point in the search for details of discovery tasks, systems, and applications.

Knowledge discovery in databases has been an established research area since 1989. It was motivated by practical interest in mining knowledge from databases, at the time when they became abundant. Databases became not only numerous but also large, beyond the capabilities of traditional methods of analysis. They were not collected for the purpose of knowledge discovery but to support business operations, so that initially it was not even clear whether they would yield interesting and useful knowledge. Today, emboldened by a positive experience, we expect a variety of discoveries to be made by discovery systems in sizable databases. The use of such discoveries, however, is limited to the domain described by data, such as a particular company's catalog sales or enrollment at a particular university.

1.1. Automation of Discovery versus Practical Knowledge Mining

ASD has been occupied with discovery methods that can repeat some of the well-known scientific discoveries. It is clear that it will take long time before a discovery system can make discoveries that are original and significant by scientific standards. In contrast, KDD aims at practical results that can be reached at present. It is satisfied with discoveries of a lesser value because they apply to individual domains, while ASD is concerned with scientific knowledge that applies to an unbound range of situations.

The long-term ambition of ASD is the automation of discovery in a broad sense that matches the activities of human-made science. This includes empirical interaction with the physical world, collection of data, construction of theories from empirical data, and theory revision. Discovery systems have gradually been enriched with new capabilities. This research program was originated with the BACON system. It started from a heuristic equation finder BACON.1, followed by BACON.3, which generates data and applies BACON.1 recursively, then by BACON.4, which converts nominal variables to numerical, and uses both BACON.3 and BACON.1 to generate numerical laws. Finally, BACON.5 augments earlier BACONs with discovery methods that postulate symmetry of the laws and conservation of physical quantities

(Langley et al., 1987; Cheng and Simon, 1992). Similar programs led to the increased discovery capabilities of FAHRENHEIT (Żytkow, 1987; Żytkow and Zhu, 1991, 1994), IDS (Nordhausen and Langley, 1993), BR (Kocabas, 1991), and MECHEM (Valdés-Pérez, 1993, 1994).

But how can we tell whether a particular combination of discovery modules really automated a larger task? The key requirement is autonomous execution of the discovery process. This hands-off approach shaped up the domain of ASD and was used to demonstrate the degree of real automation. It was obvious, both to ASD contributors and critics, that a human operator of a discovery system can make discoveries. Each time a human makes an input, it raises critics' suspicions that a significant know-how is introduced into the process, so the contribution of the machine is disputable.

In contrast, in KDD, user input is sanctioned because the results matter more than automation and more than process understanding.

But practical results were not neglected in ASD. Many systems have been applied in domains of current scientific interest and demonstrated practical results. Meta-DENDRAL was the first system, whose results were published in a domain journal. It created rules for the fragmentation processes of several classes of ketoandrostanes in mass spectrometry (Buchanan et al., 1976). Since then, machine discoverers have scored plenty of small successes. None has been important, measured by its impact on the overall knowledge of humankind, but each would be a legitimate step forward for a scientist. MECHEM found a simple, plausible, seemingly overlooked reaction mechanism for a long-studied chemical reaction in hydrocarbon catalysis (Valdés-Pérez, 1994). It continues producing similar results on other reactions. Applied to experiments in chemistry, FAHRENHEIT discovered empirical equations that are more precise than equations discovered manually by humans working on comparable data (Żytkow et al., 1990). It can be of similar help in other searches for empirical equations.

1.2. Cognitive Reconstruction or Norm

ASD was occupied with scientific episodes of proven significance. Efforts were made to repeat the same results as originally derived by scientists on the same data or even to repeat many episodes in their historical order (Żytkow and Simon, 1986). Such a descriptive approach, also called cognitive simulation, can be evaluated by the accuracy of the method in reproducing historical facts and steps. Reconstruction of the historical details, for instance, the order in which discoveries were made, indicated understanding of the method used by scientists. The accuracy of the method was also confirmed if the same mechanism reconstructed both the successes and failures in reasoning of a particular scientist or a particular school of thinking.

The descriptive approach, which may be viewed as computationally practiced history of science, can be confronted with the normative approach, which is computational methodology of discovery. To evaluate the latter, we confront a method with the goals to determine what progress it provides toward those goals. While ASD uses both approaches, the KDD paradigm is distinctly normative. Methods are evaluated by their efficiency and accuracy of results. Huge numbers of algorithms that result from KDD research provide methods conceived by their authors. The concern for reconstruction of reasoning that underlies spectacular cases of discovery is absent in KDD.

The difference between solutions motivated by both approaches is not that big in ASD, since a method applied by a good scientist will satisfy both the descriptive and the normative criteria.

1.3. Empirical Contents

Scientific knowledge is often used in making verifiable conclusions. When a prediction is falsified, we must revise our knowledge from which that prediction was inferred. Since untestable theories behind many influential ideologies are often presented as knowledge, Popper postulated that falsifiable predictions are a necessary requirement for knowledge. If no falsification is possible, a belief should not be considered knowledge.

KDD is interested in useful predictions, but many KDD methods do not aim at predictive knowledge. Normative concept definitions, data clusters, and many results of similarity-based methods are examples (Żytkow, 1997). In contrast, within the scientific paradigm used by ASD, new concepts are permitted only when used to express empirical knowledge that can explain and predict many new facts (Langley et al., 1987; Shen and Simon, 1993). Discovery of intrinsic concepts and hidden structure is supported by the bootstrap verification criterion (Glymour, 1980) that relies on testability of predictions.

1.4. Objective Knowledge

The frequently declared main goal of KDD is the discovery of patterns in data (Fayyad et al., 1996). In contrast, scientists use data to uncover knowledge about objects in the real world, their properties and behavior. Objective knowledge, that is, knowledge about the domain described by data, is verified by application of domain knowledge to new situations that provide new testable predictions.

While ASD follows science in its drive toward objective knowledge, KDD is often satisfied with patterns in data. Consider the use of cross-validation, which can produce hundreds of alternative decision trees, each similarly accurate. If so many alternatives apply, which among them captures the underlying structure of the domain? Bagging, a popular method in statistically oriented machine learning, which combines many alternatives and uses the majority vote, has similar problems with objectivity.

While ASD distinguishes between objective knowledge and the use of knowledge, KDD often seeks knowledge combined with cost optimization. In the scientific paradigm, both can be developed separately and then put together in different ways depending on concrete tasks. The current KDD lore supports the combination of truth and utility into a single search.

1.5. Forms of Knowledge

A typical ASD task is discovery of scientific laws. Laws of physics and chemistry take on the form of multidimensional equations. Discovery of such equations (Falkenhainer and Michalski, 1986; Wu and Wang, 1989; Moulet, 1992; Schaffer, 1993; Dzeroski and Todoroski, 1993), expanded by simultaneous introduction of intrinsic properties (Langley et al., 1987) that are numerical counterparts of nominal variables and can be used in equations, and augmented by discovery of equation boundaries (FAHRENHEIT: Żytkow and Zhu, 1991), is an important area in ASD. While equations are used in KDD, for instance, as approximate definitions of concepts, they are seldom sought and their criteria of acceptance are much weaker than scientific standards.

Another important focus of ASD, discovery of hidden structure, is also missing in KDD. Provided with facts and theories about macro structures, many ASD systems discover hidden components, their properties, reactions, and the makeup of observable objects (Valdés-Pérez et al., 1993). Some of those systems repeat key discoveries in the history of science, such as discoveries of chemical elements, atoms, genes. Some others respond to recent tasks (Rose, 1989; GELLMANN: Żytkow and Fischer, 1991; MECHEM: Valdés-Pérez, 1994), such as discovery of quarks and other particles and discovery of intermediate steps in chemical reactions. Because of their systematic and exhaustive search, they can notice solutions missed by humans.

In contrast, KDD exploits several forms of knowledge rare in sciences and in ASD, such as association rules, clustering, and decision trees. One form of knowledge that attracted the attention of both KDD and ASD is taxonomies.

1.6. Drive Toward Complete Knowledge

Knowledge should be as complete and adequate as possible. An important component of a machine discoverer is a knowledge representation schema that can handle many pieces of knowledge. One alternative is offered by predicate calculus. It is commonly used in artificial intelligence based on theorem proving. Metaphorically, in this representation each piece of knowledge is a separate statement, thrown inside a big bag of all knowledge pieces. Purposeful access to individual statements in a bag is difficult. Many irrelevant pieces must be considered before the right one is found. This holds for typical results of the KDD search for knowledge in the form of a set of rules. Taxonomies, decision trees, causal graphs, and Bayesian networks are exceptions.

In ASD, many discovery systems use graphs to represent relationships between pieces of knowledge (DIDO: Scott and Markovitch, 1993; IDS: Nordhausen and Langley, 1990, 1993; FAHRENHEIT: Żytkow and Zhu, 1991, 1994). Instead of bags of separate pieces, their knowledge representation resembles jigsaw puzzles, in which every piece of knowledge is supposed to stay in the right place and be connected to other pieces, without holes and overlaps. Not only is access fast, but in addition, holes indicate missing knowledge while overlaps represent redundancies and alternatives that must be resolved by mechanisms of knowledge refinement. Completeness and clarity of knowledge are much easier to verify than in a bag representation. Knowledge graphs can drive further discoveries (DIDO, FAHRENHEIT). It is a good idea to arrange discovery algorithms so that they construct, maintain, and analyze networks of knowledge.

1.7. Data Sources

The large amounts of data available in modern databases created a competitive advantage for discovery systems. The overwhelming amounts of data cannot be examined manually, yet they may conceal plenty of useful knowledge. But how much knowledge can be discovered is not clear. The majority of databases were not created with discovery tasks in mind, and even if they were, the discovery process would create demand for new data about new focus areas. In contrast, a database resembles an archive. In the majority of data mining situations, data are limited to those available in the existing records. We can neither increase their number nor improve their accuracy. We cannot define new observational attributes nor improve the accuracy of the data. Data transformation is possible, but it is limited to pencil-and-paper operations on the existing records, which can neither improve the accuracy nor the reach of data.

The archival mode in which KDD treats data is in sharp contrast with the experimentalist approach of scientists. Experimental scientists actively create new physical situations in order to collect data fitting their research tasks. The emphasis on experimentation is a distinguishing characteristic of science in modern times. Even in domains that do not allow experiments but must rely on observations, we may refocus observations on new areas of interest and we may refine the methods to get better data.

ASD follows natural sciences and uses automated experiment design (Kulkarni and Simon, 1987; Żytkow and Zhu, 1991, 1994; Scott and Markovitch, 1993). This way it can exploit the feedback between theory formation and experimentation strategies. New research problems that are noticed by examination of knowledge graphs lead to new requests for specific experiments.

2. ASD Contributions to KDD

Many results of ASD are worth trying in KDD. Algorithms, knowledge representation schemas, principles that guide system development, discovery tasks, and the ways they are approached are all worth attention. In this section we propose several ways in which KDD can benefit from the experience of ASD.

2.1. A Drive toward Autonomy

The current level of automation in KDD is low. Huge numbers of alternative algorithms perform single tasks, such as decision-tree induction or the search for association rules. But task setup and the use of results to guide the next automated step are done manually.

Automation must increase, however, under the pressure of practical necessities, to improve generation of practical results. In addition, as KDD consolidates and the need for an underlying theory grows stronger, automation will be more popular because autonomy means process understanding at the detailed, algorithmic level, including the representation of knowledge that supports the automation. The ASD program in automation of discovery, over two decades long, can help KDD to move to the next level of knowledge-mining complexity.

An agent becomes more autonomous when it can investigate a broader range of goals. This can be achieved by implementing new components of the discovery process for each new goal. Autonomy can grow much beyond that, however. The components can be integrated so that they feedback to one another in many ways, without human intervention. Integration must be coordinated with knowledge representation mechanisms (IDS, FAHRENHEIT) and must rely on autonomous evaluation of knowledge. As a result, many discovery steps in succession can be performed without external intervention.

Evaluation of knowledge by a discovery system can improve by automation of many steps. A single step rarely creates a sufficient platform for a sound judgment about the results. A combination of steps provides a broader perspective on knowledge and more informed feedback on the reasons for acceptance.

Consider fitting data with empirical equations. Candidate equations can be evaluated by their fit to data, but experience shows that even in a limited search space, several equations of comparable simplicity can often fit the same data with a similar accuracy. Each equation is an equally close approximation to the truth, at least according to the input data. A discoverer may not be able or should not make a choice in this situation. Greater autonomy of a discoverer, however, gives a broader perspective on regularities, improving their evaluation. Further cognitive steps can help to choose among competing regularities. For instance, additional data can be collected in an area in which different equations offer distinguishable predictions. Some equations are more susceptible to generalization; some can be reduced to a known theory while others cannot. Some equations can be transformed to a form that affords a more plausible interpretation (GALILEO: Żytkow, 1990). For each of these reasons, the broader perspective created by further activities of the discoverer can remove ambiguity from that choice.

2.2. Empirical Contents

Scientific knowledge is shaped by the interplay between discoveries of laws and concepts used to express them. New concepts are introduced rarely and cautiously, and they cannot be discovered in isolation from the discovery of knowledge. Many ASD systems implement different versions of such feedback. This mechanism of concept verification is missing in KDD even though it is very important, as it weeds out an unbound variety of concepts that can trash a knowledge system. It is important to be very suspicious and careful about the need for concept learning and clustering. KDD should pay more attention to regularities and less to concepts.

When proclaiming a new piece of knowledge K, it is prudent to ask about the empirical contents of K, which are observational predictions that can be derived from K. Such predictions can be derived from regularities (statements, laws), not from concepts.

2.3. Modeling with Objective Knowledge

In KDD we are happy when we discover regularities in a given database. They lead to predictions about situations very similar to those captured in the existing records. But soon we will be challenged with transfer of knowledge to situations that are more distant. This is typical in science, when knowledge is used to create models of surprisingly new situations. None of the previously known statements that expressed knowledge fit those situations. But when we pay attention to the meaning of each term in a given statement rather than treat it as a black box (a predicting device), we may recombine those terms into a description of a complex empirical situation S. In such a description, objects that constitute S, their properties, and interaction should have their counterparts in different terms that jointly describe S.

A model of a new situation is built from terms and predicates that correspond to objects and interactions occurring in that situation. Statements are built from terms and predicates.

Representing knowledge in a form suitable for modeling and model construction is very difficult to automate. Some discovery systems capture pieces of this process: symmetry heuristics of BACON.5 (Langley et al., 1987) and GALILEO's equation analysis mechanism (Żytkow, 1990).

Unless KDD research recognizes this process, we may be producing huge amounts of knowledge, but each piece will be narrowly applied to a single database.

2.4. Knowledge Graphs

Knowledge graphs have proved very useful in representing knowledge in discovery systems. It is worthwhile considering them in KDD, too. Experience proves that large numbers of knowledge pieces can be discovered in a large database. No user will be happy receiving a bag of loose pieces, however, if the pieces can be arranged into graphs that are far more appealing not only to the customer but also to the knowledge miners. A knowledge graph allows them to understand the impact of many regularities at one time. It also allows the missing pieces of knowledge to be found in order to set new discovery tasks. Our jigsaw puzzle metaphor helps to understand the advantage of graphs: rather than keeping the pieces of a jigsaw loose, we should put them together and present the whole image.

2.5. Data Acquisition

When we sift through megabytes of data, approaching them from different angles, we may have the impression that the data are abundant rather than sparse. However, the situation can be the opposite. We often seek regularities among attributes in small subsets of data. Consider a disease that may depend on age, sex, profession, and habits. If we keep slicing medical data so that we create increasingly uniform data segments about which we try to make justified generalizations, we exponentially reduce the segment of data under consideration. If, in addition, some of the values on which we slice the data are rare, very soon we reach insignificantly small subsets.

Unlike an experimental scientist, a database explorer must be prepared to deal with sparse data of low quality. Not much can be changed since data collection is beyond the control of knowledge miners. But KDD as a domain, knowing the benefits of experimentation and directed observation, may influence data collection.

For the sake of improved knowledge mining, KDD also can and should influence data archiving into a warehouse. It is important to retain in a warehouse those attributes that can be used to express knowledge. This is an important scientific principle, followed by ASD. But what are those attributes and what aggregation should be applied? Before answering those questions, knowledge miners should explore the source database in an open pursuit of knowledge. Such an exploration can indicate which attributes may be worthwhile, as they are critical in expressing large amounts of useful knowledge.

3. KDD Contributions to ASD

We have considered a number of ways in which ASD can be a role model for KDD. But KDD can help ASD in a number of ways, too, so that ASD should pay attention to developments in KDD. Even though their niches are now different, as we argued in the first section, methods of both KDD and ASD apply in a common area formed by scientific and engineering databases, some of them created by simulation. The overlap will slowly grow through demand for high-quality data.

One of the most important factors that will stimulate growth of both domains is the number of KDD researchers trained in knowledge mining who can understand different forms of knowledge, methods of discovery, statistical techniques, and data management.

3.1. Human Involvement

Autonomy is a far-reaching goal of ASD, but the existing systems would not make discoveries without human help. We have argued for the benefits of automation, but we can also see how far we can go if we augment automated tools with human intuitions and choices.

Consider, for instance, the discovery of empirical equations from data. A human operator can limit the space of a search to a well-chosen set of terms and equations. Narrowing down the space allows an automated discoverer to conduct a deeper search, enabling the discovery of complex equations in a limited space. Domain-specific expectations can also guide the search. For instance, human operators may know that empirical analysis of efficiency of computer programs requires functions such as polynomials, logarithms, exponents, and their combinations. When analyzing periodic phenomena, the operator may focus the system on equations built from trigonometric functions.

Breaches of autonomy can be justified by practically useful results. Human intervention becomes essential when a discovery system finds a large number of simple regularities. We are still far from understanding how large amounts of knowledge in a given form can be organized into clear theories, easy to communicate and to apply. So we want the user to examine them because, given an effective visualization, the eyes are able to quickly capture the specificity of regularities. If a particular category of regularities is common, the user can develop criteria that select them automatically, and then combine their large number into a specialized theory.

3.2. Statistical Thinking

The statistical component was typically neglected in ASD. But different combinations of deterministic and statistical knowledge are increasingly useful. Statisticians developed tests that were traditionally calibrated to tens or hundreds of records. But when induction applies to millions of real-world records, and a search covers millions of hypotheses, empirical investigation conducted by KDD faces new challenges, such as the appropriate setup of significance thresholds for massive search. ASD will be wise to adopt those solutions.

Scientific facts are usually highly repeatable, leading to regularities described by deterministic mathematical formulas. We cannot expect the same quality regularities in databases. For this reason, KDD concentrates on search for weaker, statistical regularities. But those weak forms of knowledge can be practically useful and may follow systematic patterns, similar to patterns that are used to express deterministic knowledge. In the long run, it will be possible to define hypothesis spaces that consist of combined deterministic and statistical components and can be automatically searched by ASD algorithms.

3.3. Access to Large Amounts of Data

KDD offers access to very large data sets. ASD mechanisms traditionally used modest amounts of well-prepared data. It is interesting what can be inferred from massive data. It is also challenging to scale up ASD algorithms so that they can handle much larger data sets. Scaling up is interesting but should not become a golden calf. Most scientific results have been reached by analysis of small but well-prepared data sets. A large data set does not have to be analyzed in one session.

Multitable data present other challenges. In what ways can they be joined for the purpose of KDD? What sort of structures can be used to capture knowledge from many tables? For instance, in a medical trauma database, multiple injuries can be recorded for one patient, multiple treatments can be recorded for some injuries, and so forth. Similar problems occur when data are combined from various sources, such as census, federal and local government data, satellite data, and medical records of the population. This is a similar challenge to modeling complex situations, so we can consider it a natural task for ASD.

References

Buchanan, B. G., D. H. Smith, W. C. White, R. J. Gritter, E. A. Feigenbaum, J. Lederberg, and C. Djerassi. 1976. "Automatic rule formation in mass spectrometry by means of the meta-DENDRAL program." *J. Am. Chem. Soc.* **98**: 6168–6178.

Cheng, P. C. and H. A. Simon. 1992. "The right representation for discovery: finding the conservation of momentum." In *Proceedings of the Ninth International Conference on Machine Learning*, edited by Sleeman, D. and P. Edwards, pp. 62–71. San Mateo, CA: Morgan Kaufmann.

Dzeroski, S. and L. Todorovski. 1993. "Discovering dynamics." In *Proceedings of the Tenth International Conference on Machine Learning*, pp. 97–103. San Mateo, CA: Morgan Kaufmann.

Edwards, P. ed. 1993. *Working Notes MLNet Workshop on Machine Discovery*, Blanes, Spain.

Falkenhainer, B. C. and R. S. Michalski. 1986. "Integrating quantitative and qualitative discovery: the ABACUS system." *Machine Learning* **1**: 367–401.

Fayyad, U., G. Piatetsky-Shapiro, and P. Smyth. 1996. "From data mining to knowledge discovery: an overview." In *Advances in Knowledge Discovery and Data Mining*, edited by U. Fayyad, G. Piatetsky-Shapiro, P. Smyth, and R. Uthurusamy. Menlo Park, CA: AAAI Press.

Glymour, C. 1980. *Theory and Evidence*. Princeton, NJ: Princeton University Press.

Kocabas, S. 1991. "Conflict resolution as discovery in particle physics." *Machine Learning* **6**: 277–309.

Kulkarni, D. and H. A. Simon. 1987. "The processes of scientific discovery: the strategy of experimentation." *Cognitive Sci.* **12**: 139–175.

Langley, P., H. A. Simon, G. L. Bradshaw, and J. M. Żytkow. 1987. *Scientific Discovery: Computational Explorations of the Creative Processes*. Cambridge, MA: MIT Press.

Moulet, M. 1992. "A symbolic algorithm for computing coefficients' accuracy in regression." In *Proceedings of the Ninth International Conference on Machine Learning*, edited by D. Sleeman and P. Edwards. San Mateo, CA: Morgan Kaufmann.

Nordhausen, B. and P. Langley. 1990. "An integrated approach to empirical discovery." In *Computational Models of Scientific Discovery and Theory Formation*, edited by J. Shrager and P. Langley, pp. 97–128. San Mateo, CA: Morgan Kaufmann Publishers.

Nordhausen, B. and P. Langley. 1993. "An integrated framework for empirical discovery." *Machine Learning* **12**: 17–47.

Rose, D. 1989. "Using domain knowledge to aid scientific theory revision." In *Proceedings of the Sixth International Workshop on Machine Learning*. San Mateo, CA: Morgan Kaufmann Publishers.

Schaffer, C. 1993. "Bivariate scientific function finding in a sampled real-data testbed." *Machine Learning* **12**: 167–183.

Scott, P. D. and S. Markovitch. 1993. "Experience selection and problem choice in an exploratory learning system." *Machine Learning* **12**: 49–67.

Shen, W. M. 1994. In *Autonomous Learning from the Environment*. New York, NY: W. H. Freeman and Company.

Shen, W. M. and H. A. Simon. 1993. "Fitness requirements for scientific theories containing recursive theoretical terms." *Br. J. Phil. Sci.* **44**: 504–520.

Shrager, J. and P. Langley. (eds). 1990. *Computational Models of Scientific Discovery and Theory Formation*. San Mateo, CA: Morgan Kaufmann.

Simon, H. A., R. E. Valdés-Pérez, and D. H. Sleeman 1997. eds. "Scientific Discovery and Simplicity of Method." In *Artificial Intelligence* **91**: 177–181.

Valdés-Pérez, R. E. 1993. "Conjecturing hidden entities via simplicity and conservation laws: machine discovery in chemistry." *Artificial Intelligence* **65**: 247–280.

Valdés-Pérez, R. E. 1994. "Human/computer interactive elucidation of reaction mechanisms: application to catalyzed hydrogenolysis of ethane." *Catalysis Lett.* **28**: 79–87.

Valdés-Pérez, R. E. ed. 1995. *Working Notes: AAAI Spring Symposium on Systematic Methods of Scientific Discovery*. Menlo Park, CA: AAAI Press.

Valdés-Pérez, R. E., J. M. Żytkow, and H. A. Simon. 1993. "Scientific model-building as search in matrix spaces." In *Proceedings of the Eleventh National Conference on Artificial Intelligence*, pp. 472–478. Menlo Park, CA: AAAI Press.

Wu, Y. and S. Wang. 1989. "Discovering knowledge from observational data." In *Knowledge Discovery in Databases, IJCAI-89 Workshop Proceedings, Detroit, MI*, edited by G. Piatetsky-Shapiro, pp. 369–377. Menlo Park, CA: AAAI Press.

Zembowicz, R. and J. M. Żytkow. 1991. "Automated discovery of empirical equations from data." In *Methodologies for Intelligent Systems*, edited by Z. Ras and M. Zemankova, pp. 429–440. Berlin, Germany: Springer-Verlag.

Żytkow, J. M. 1987. "Combining many searches in the FAHRENHEIT discovery system." In *Proceedings of the Fourth International Workshop on Machine Learning*, pp. 281–287. Los Altos, CA: Morgan Kaufmann Publishers.

Żytkow, J. 1990. "Deriving laws by analysis of processes and equations." In *Computational Models of Scientific Discovery and Theory Formation*, edited by P. Langley and J. Shrager, pp. 129–156. San Mateo, CA: Morgan Kaufmann.

Żytkow, J. M. ed. 1993. Cognitive autonomy in machine discovery, In: *Machine Learning*, **12**: pp. 7–16.

Żytkow, J. M. ed. 1995. Creating a discoverer: an autonomous knowledge seeking agent, In: *Foundations of Science*, **1**: 253–283.

Żytkow, J. M. 1997. "Knowledge = concepts: a harmful equation." In *Proceedings of KDD-97*. Menlo Park, CA: AAAI Press.

Żytkow, J. M. and H. A. Simon 1986. "A theory of historical discovery: the construction of componential models." In *Machine Learning*, **1**: March 1986, pp. 107–137.

Żytkow, J. M., and P. Fischer 1991. Constructing models of hidden structure, in Ras Z. and Zemankova M. eds. *Methodologies for Intelligent Systems*. Berlin: Springer-Verlag. pp. 441–449.

Żytkow, J. M. and J. Zhu. 1991. "Automated empirical discovery in a numerical space." In *The Proceedings of the Third Annual Chinese Machine Learning Workshop, July 15–19, 1991*, pp. 1–11. Harbin Institute of Technology.

Żytkow, J. M. and J. Zhu. 1994. "Experimentation guided by a knowledge graph." In *Learning Action Models*, edited by W. Shen. Menlo Park, CA: AAAI Press.

Żytkow, J. M., J. Zhu, and A. Hussam. 1990. "Automated discovery in a chemistry laboratory." In *Proceedings of the AAAI-90*, pp. 889–894. Menlo Park, CA: AAAI Press.

30 FUZZY AND ROUGH SETS

Witold Pedrycz and Andrzej Skowron

ABSTRACT We discuss various relationships of fuzzy sets and rough sets with knowledge discovery in databases (KDD). We describe the main advances of rough set and fuzzy set methods in solving KDD problems, point out research directions in fuzzy sets and rough sets stimulated by KDD, as well as characterize potential impact of these methodologies on KDD.

1. Introduction

Fuzzy set and rough set constructs as presented in Chapters 9 and 10 are essential for a general conceptual and algorithmic setting in data mining. However, it is apparent that fuzzy sets and rough sets arise as realizations of far more general and fundamental concepts of information granulation and granular computing. We outline relationships between granular computing and KDD. This will help to present the relationships of fuzzy sets and rough sets with KDD. Information granulation (and granular computing afterward) is the process of constructing information granules and their further processing. Information granules are conceptual entities embracing collections of detailed data, for example, numbers into the form of a single entity. The elements are pulled together owing to their functional similarity, similarity (proximity), or some other criterion of likeness (Zadeh, 1979, 1996). Processing of information granules is more general. It does not concentrate on details and captures a way in which information granules are transformed. The concept of granules is appealing. The way in which information technology (IT) is realized at the formal end is not unique: depending on the application, we may use classical set theory (where information granules are modeled as sets), fuzzy set theory (in case of fuzzy sets), or rough set theory (for rough sets). When information granules are expressed as probability density functions, then we exploit the framework of probability theory. We reveal relationships between granular computing and data mining showing that there is an ongoing mutually beneficial interaction and impact between these two. In particular, we show how fuzzy sets and rough sets provide a conceptual and algorithmic environment for data mining. At the same time, we highlight how data mining impacts the research agenda of these two environments.

In general, as illustrated in Figure 1, we may consider a general two-phase scheme of data mining. The first phase is devoted to granulation of information: here, we identify or express the chunks of information that are deemed essential for knowledge representation and data summarization. Afterward, in the second phase we employ one of the formal platforms of granular computing (rough sets, fuzzy sets, rough-fuzzy sets, etc.), with which we develop associations between such granules, carry out classification tasks, communicate results to an end user, etc. It is very likely that an interaction with the user may call for some modifications or further enhancements; these are realized via a feedback link as again indicated in Figure 1.

The above scheme fully complies with one of the key objectives of all data mining activities, that is, user-friendliness manifested in the granular form of discovered patterns. Obviously, various relationships (associations), on data mined and revealed at the level of information granules, are compact and easy to understand by the user. The language of associations is more comprehensive than the language of plain formulas (for instance, regression lines) developed at the level of numerical data. Information granules hide all detailed and inessential relationships as not being pertinent to understanding the essence of the data. The level of specificity can easily be affected by changing the level of granularity, that is, using information granules that are less or more detailed and consisting of the respective number of elements. Both fuzzy sets and rough sets support a construction of information at different levels of granules. They also provide a formal way of quantifying the notion of granularity.

680

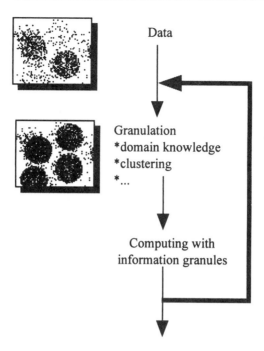

Data

Granulation
*domain knowledge
*clustering
*...

Computing with
information granules

Figure 1 Two-phase model of data mining involving information granulation and granular computing

2. Fuzzy Sets and KDD

Fuzzy sets, as discussed in Chapter 10, are granular constructs that promote representation and processing of concepts with gradual boundaries. Continuity and gradual changes in membership values are essential features of many pursuits of human beings dealing with classification or decisionmaking problems (Pedrycz, 1998c; Zadeh, 1979).

2.1. The Role of Fuzzy Sets in KDD

A number of key pursuits support the use of fuzzy sets as an essential technology of KDD.

In a nutshell, the role of fuzzy sets is to make KDD systems more user friendly and user oriented. This becomes crucial as the relevance of fuzzy set–based architectures depends very much upon an efficient interaction with the user/designer. By their nature, the role of fuzzy sets can substantially enhance the front- and back-end interfaces of KDD systems. In the first case, the user can define a vocabulary of linguistic terms (modeled via fuzzy sets and fuzzy relations) that are exploited afterward as the generic conceptual entities—linguistic landmarks throughout the ensuing algorithms revealing the web of associations in databases. Recall that each fuzzy set or fuzzy relation (in the multidimensional case) are models of information granules in the setting of fuzzy sets. Interestingly, the structure (i.e., granularity), often reflected by size, and distribution of information granules imply the form of associations to be discovered. These information granules help establish relevance and interestingness of the associations. In this way, the user/designer can assume a more proactive role in the data mining activities. The user can query the data mining system through its interface by modifying the size of some information granules. When building a back-end interface, fuzzy sets help interpret the results. Rather than relying on a single number (being the outcome of some data mining activities and describing various notions such as confidence level, correlation coefficients, etc.), fuzzy sets help quantify these in terms of a collection of elements with varying degrees of membership. As a consequence, the results are more descriptive and easy to interpret and visualize. They may also raise awareness as to the quality of data mining by signaling to the user the need for further analysis or advise the user to proceed with more caution with the interpretation of the presented results. These two interfaces realized with the aid of fuzzy sets are in line with the philosophy of visualization for KDD. Fuzzy sets are easy to define to reflect the intuitive meaning of the information granules exploited by the user. The formal apparatus is well established so that these two interfaces can be easily designed and modified.

In some cases, information granules–fuzzy sets need to be constructed from numerical data. Here, fuzzy clustering is an important endeavor leading to the construction of information granules–fuzzy sets or fuzzy relations. Objective function-based clustering algorithms form one of the essential classes of the grouping (Dave and Krishnapuram, 1997; Hoppner et al., 1999; Kaufman and Rousseeuw, 1990). An interesting generalization of the clustering comes in the form of partial supervision (Pedrycz, 1998b) or context-based clustering (Pedrycz, 1996). These scenarios are aimed at capturing hints coming from the user/designer of the data mining system (e.g., directions as to the structure to be looked for). Clustering with partial supervision is positioned in between supervised learning and unsupervised learning algorithms.

The technology of fuzzy sets is useful in the design of rule-based systems. Fuzzy sets help avoid a severe brittleness problem that is inherently associated with any rule-based representation. The rule

if input is A then output is B

fires (becomes activated or relevant) if a given fact X is embraced by A. If A is modeled as a set, then if X is included in A, the output (conclusion) is equal to B. Note, however, that if A may have a variety of interpretations (e.g., A denotes the concept of high temperature, low inflation rate, safe speed, etc, and the rule-based system hinges on set theory), then depending upon the interpretation of A that may be subjective and vary from person to person, the conclusion is either B or not. In this sense, the use of the set-theoretic machinery in this framework associates with the brittleness effect. Fuzzy sets help alleviate this problem: as A is a fuzzy set, any X activates A to a certain degree. This, in turn, implies the activation of B to some degree. The same process of gradual rule firing occurs for all rules in the rule-based system, which, all in all, eliminates the effect of a binary switching between the rules.

Fuzzy sets augment some well-known algorithms of machine learning such as decision trees (Mitchell, 1997). Here, the role of fuzzy sets manifests in several ways:

- Through the formation of the attribute space whose elements are modeled as fuzzy sets or fuzzy relations (Hayashi et al., 1998; Ichihashi et al., 1996; Janikow, 1998, 1999; Umano et al., 1994). Decision trees require attributes with finite values (i.e., they have to be discretized), and this discretization becomes accomplished via fuzzy sets.

- By providing the vehicle for propagating levels for matching the available data with the attributes of the decision tree (Janikow, 1998). As attributes, fuzzy sets can be activated to a certain extent, a number of nodes on the decision trees are involved in the propagation of the activation levels and finally a number of final nodes of the tree. A detailed mechanism for computing how the activation levels are propagated down the tree has been developed based on the techniques of fuzzy sets.

2.2. Influence of KDD on Fuzzy Sets

There is a visible impact of KDD (and its key thrusts) on the research agenda of fuzzy sets. Several clear points to be made deal with the following:

- Complexity analysis and complexity reduction of fuzzy set constructs. Interestingly, fuzzy sets for dealing with gradual membership grades are quite complex and demanding on the processing side. KDD makes this point clear: huge databases require a lot of processing. Processing that is excessively time consuming, no matter how useful and general it could be, may not be acceptable. This situation calls for a thorough review of the basic constructs of fuzzy sets and in-depth analysis of various alternatives (such as different models of fuzzy set operations with an emphasis on those that save on the computational side).

- The same complexity analysis may require some approximation (and simplification) of fuzzy sets, for example, those arising in the form of sets and rough sets.

- Well-advanced, fully developed knowledge representation schemes of KDD as well as efficient KDD schemes can be a starting point for further generalizations pursued in the realm of fuzzy sets.

3. Rough Sets and KDD

In recent years we have witnessed a rapid, worldwide growth in interest in rough set theory and its applications (see, e.g., Lin and Cercone, 1997; Orlowska, 1997; Pawlak, 1991; Pal and Skowron, 1999; Polkowski and Skowron, 1998a; Słowiński, 1992; Tsumoto et al., 1996; and Polkowski et al., 2000). The theory has been followed by the development of software systems that implement rough set methods. Rough sets are applied in domains as diverse as medicine, finance, telecommunication, vibration analysis, conflict resolution, intelligent agents, pattern recognition, control theory, signal analysis, process industry, and marketing.

3.1. The Role of Rough Sets in KDD

A family of approximation spaces defines the search space for data models in the rough set approach. Any approximation space in this family is distinguished by some parameters. Searching strategies for optimal (suboptimal) parameters are basic rough set tools in searching for data models and knowledge. There are two main types of parameters. The first are used to define object sets, called neighborhoods, the second measure the inclusion or closeness of neighborhoods. We are going to describe them informally (a formal definition of parameterized approximation space can be found, e.g., in Pawlak and Skowron, 1999). The basic assumption of the classical rough set approach (Pawlak, 1991), shared with other approaches like machine learning, pattern recognition, and statistics, is that objects are perceived by means of some features (e.g., formulas being the result of measurements of the form *attribute* = *value* called descriptors Pawlak, 1991). Hence, some objects can be indiscernible (indistinguishable) or similar to each other. The sets of indiscernible or similar objects expressible by some formulas are called neighborhoods. In the simplest case, the family of all neighborhoods creates a partition of the universe. In more general cases, it defines a covering. Formulas defining the neighborhoods are basic building blocks from which approximate descriptions of other sets (decision classes or concepts) are induced. Usually, like in machine learning, the specification of concepts is incomplete, for example, given by examples and counterexamples. Having an incomplete specification of concepts, one can only induce an approximate description of concepts by means of formulas defining the neighborhoods. Hence, it follows that it will be useful to have parameterized formulas (e.g., in the simplest case, $a > p$ & $b < q$ are attributes and p, q are parameters) so that by tuning their parameters, one can select formulas relevant for inducing concept approximation. A formula is relevant for concept description if it defines a large neighborhood still included to a sufficient degree in an approximated concept.

In the simplest case, the formulas defining neighborhoods are conjunctions of descriptors. Parameters to be tuned can be of different sorts like the number of conjunction connectives in the formula or the interval boundaries in case of discretization of real-value attributes. In more general cases, these formulas can express the results of measurement or perception of observed objects and represent complex information granules. Among such granules can be decision algorithms labeled by feature value vectors (describing an actual situation in which an algorithm should be performed), clusters of such granules defined by their similarity, or hierarchical structures of such granules (see, e.g., Skowron et al., 1999). These complex granules become more and more important for qualitative reasoning, particularly for spatial reasoning (Roddick and Spiliopoulou, 1999).

3.2. Extraction of Relevant Partitions (Coverings) Defined by Neighborhoods

The process of approximation concept is in rough set framework can be described as searching for partitions (coverings) coarser than defined by actual neighborhoods, relevant to inducing the concept approximations of high quality. There are two main characteristic steps of rough set methods. First is based on computing the appropriate basic constructs of rough sets, that is, reducts, and the second on tuning them, by computing reduct approximations, to receive the best neighborhoods. The reducts are constructed using Boolean reasoning (see Chapter 9) and object discernibility (Skowron and Rauszer, 1992). The quality of concept approximation can be measured using machine-learning techniques but can be also measured by taking into account other measures than those used in KDD, such as covering a sufficiently large part of the concept by a small number of strong patterns.

Searching for concept approximations is related to feature extraction and feature selection, which are well known in pattern recognition or machine learning (see Chapter 9). Moreover, it is also crucial to knowledge discovery (Fayyad et al., 1996), in particular, to scientific discovery (Langley et al., 1997; Shrager and Langley, 1990; Valdés-Pérez, 1999). For example, scientific discovery (Valdés-Pérez, 1999) uses, as a main source of power, relatively general knowledge, including knowledge to search combinatorial spaces. Hence, it is important to discover efficient searching strategies. This includes the processes of inducing the relevant features and functions over which these strategies are constructed as well as the structure of the searching strategy induced from such constructs. The goal of discovery (Langley et al., 1997; Shrager and Langley, 1990) is to find knowledge that is, novel, plausible, and understandable. Certainly, these soft concepts should be induced to a sufficient degree, that is, their approximations should be induced to specify the main constraints in searching for knowledge. In this sense, concept approximation is the basic step not only for machine learning or for pattern extraction, but also for knowledge discovery and scientific discovery. Certainly, in the latter cases, inducing processes of concept approximations is much more complex, and searching for such approximations creates a challenge for researchers.

The process of concept approximation in a rough set framework can be described as searching for partitions (coverings) coarser than defined by actual neighborhoods, relevant to inducing concept approximations of high quality. There are two main characteristic steps of rough set methods. First is based on the computing of appropriate basic constructs of rough sets, that is, reducts, and the second on tuning them, by computing reduct approximations, to receive the best neighborhoods. The reducts are constructed using Boolean reasoning (see Chapter 9).

3.3. Tuning the Inclusion Degree between Sets of Objects

From the point of view of KDD, it is important to consider two relations on formulas, namely, inclusion and closeness. For KDD, instead of classical crisp inclusion or equivalence, it is more appropriate to consider inclusion to a degree and closeness to a degree. Several approaches have been developed based on this idea (see, e.g., Agrawal et al., 1996; Polkowski and Skowron, 1994; Troxel et al., 1994; Zadeh, 1965). A typical example of such inclusion appears in the case of association rules (Agrawal et al., 1996). Another example is related to extracting the default rules from data (for details, see Mollestadt, 1997; Nguyen et al., 1998). Using the rough set approach, different kinds of reduct approximations allow for a degree of impurity in preserving partition, covering, or set inclusion (see, e.g., Skowron and Nguyen, 1999, Chapter 9). Assuming a fixed partition (covering) of objects, the set approximations are induced by tuning of parameters specifying the degree of set inclusion. In this way, data models are extracted from data using the rough set approach.

3.4. Tuning Set Approximations by Tuning Inclusion Degree

The classical rough set approach (Pawlak, 1991) relies on crisp inclusion (see Chapter 9). For applications in KDD, more relaxed approaches have been developed than the classical case discussed. Instead of crisp (exact) inclusion, one can use inclusion in a degree and define the set approximations on this basis (Polkowski and Skowron, 1996; Stepaniuk, 2000; Ziarko, 1993). This helps to solve various KDD tasks like searching for dependencies in a degree instead of exact ones, or for simple, understandable, and interesting approximate concept description instead of complex exact descriptions.

3.5. Quality Measures

Optimization of approximation space parameters is based on searching for relevant degrees of inclusion and relevant partitions (coverings) in the sense that, for example, the concept description based on corresponding approximations performs better while classifying new objects.

Extracting relevant parameters is usually based on optimization of measures of the concept approximation quality on a given set of objects. The quality measure should be chosen in such a way that once the optimal (or suboptimal) description of the concept has been extracted with respect to the chosen quality measure, then the induced description also turns out to be valid for so far unseen objects. Let us note that constructs generated by rough set methods are controlled using statistical testing procedures (see Chapter 9). Examples of typical measures are based on the size of the boundary regions, positive region, entropy of these regions, or on the minimal description length principle (Duentsch and Gediga, 2000; Polkowski and Skowron, 1998b; Skowron and Nguyen, 1999; Rissanen, 1978).

The last principle, often used in machine learning, has been also adopted by the rough set approach. There are some specific steps offered by the rough set approach, which we now briefly discuss. The extraction of shorter descriptions of concepts is realized by searching for the most general neighborhoods still relevant for concept approximation, that is, included to a sufficient degree in approximated concept. In the rough set approach, this process is realized in a special way, namely, by searching for constructs called reducts and their approximations. It can be characterized as extraction of coarser partitions (or coverings) of the object universe still relevant for concept description (for details, see Chapter 9).

It has been shown (Polkowski and Skowron, 1998b; Skowron and Nguyen, 1999) that the process of searching for different kinds of reducts can be realized by Boolean reasoning procedures. Combination of the rough set approach with Boolean reasoning (Brown, 1990) creates a unified methodology for efficiently specifying and extracting different kinds of reducts and their approximations, which are used as basic constructs of concept approximations, and more general knowledge discovery (for more details, see Chapter 9).

Generated knowledge, in particular, data models, are usually suboptimal with respect to the minimal description length principle. This is because of the high computational complexity of problems searching for the optimal models. Moreover, models extracted by using the minimal length principle usually have to be tuned (because of incomplete and/or noisy data) to obtain solutions of satisfactory quality. Typical methods are based on tuning entropy (Duentsch and Gediga, 2000) or on sampling (see, e.g., Bazan, 1998).

Rough sets offer sound and solid theoretical foundations in the process of inducing concept descriptions. The developed methodology based on rough sets and Boolean reasoning provides tools for construction of efficient heuristics for problem solving. At the same time, it allows understanding of the common core and computational complexity of all these problems: the necessity of efficient derivation of short implicants of large Boolean functions (Selman et al., 1997).

3.6. Influence of KDD on Rough Sets

We would like to mention some new research directions in rough sets stimulated by research in KDD.

New approaches have been developed to deal with large databases (Imielinski and Mannila, 1996). For example, one technique is based on the decomposition (into binary trees) of large data tables using so-called templates (see, e.g., Nguyen et al., 1998). Templates are descriptions of regular subdomains of the universe of objects, for example, large groups of bank customers have many common features. They label nonleaf nodes of decomposition binary trees. Any leaf of decomposition trees is labeled by subtables of objects satisfying conditions on the path from the root to that leaf. The data are decomposed until the tables labeling the leaves are of a feasible size with respect to the methods for decision rule generation. Another method for discretization of real-value features of large relational databases (Ganti et al., 1999) is presented in Nguyen (1999). The method is based on some statistical information of discretized data and enables a semioptimal cut (partition) of the discretized range to be found, using only $O(\log n)$ SQL queries, where n is the number of records.

Rough set methods are reported as a useful front end for neural networks (for references, see the papers and bibliography in Pawlak, 1991; Polkowski and Skowron, 1998a; and Szczuka, 2000), in particular, for reducing the number of input variables.

The need to develop data mining methods from data tables with hierarchical attributes and complex values of attributes, for example, representing algorithms or plans, stimulated research on developing rough set methods for solving problems related to such data. One can consider here prediction of biological models changing on the basis of molecular DNA data (Schultze-Kremer, 1999) or prediction of plan changing by an autonomous system (Roddick and Spiliopoulou, 1999).

Several other interesting research projects based on rough sets have recently been reported, such as learning from data of conflict resolutions between different classifiers (Szczuka, 2000) or developing visualization interfaces for rough set methods including, for example, geometry of reducts (Polkowski and Skowron, 1998a). Some other research directions on rough sets are discussed in other sections of this handbook related to rough sets.

We have mentioned above that the goal of knowledge discovery can be identified with searching for strategies constructing complex information granules aimed at representing approximations of soft concepts, such as novel, interesting, plausible, and understandable, in the considered domains. Let us also observe that qualitative process representation, qualitative reasoning, spatial reasoning, perception and measurement instruments, collaboration and communication, and embodied agents are only some of the topics of research directions mentioned in Shrager and Langley (1990) as important for scientific reasoning and discovery. The above-mentioned topics are very much within the scope of computing with words and granular computing (Zadeh, 1996). A rough set extension called "rough mereology" (Polkowski and Skowron, 1994, 1996; 1999) has been proposed as a tool for approximate reasoning to deal with such problems (Polkowski and Skowron, 2000; Skowron et al., 1999). Schemes of reasoning in rough mereology approximating soft patterns seem to be crucial for making progress in knowledge discovery (Polkowski and Skowron, 1998b). In particular, this approach has been used to build a calculus on information granules (Polkowski and Skowron, 1999; Skowron et al., 1999) as a foundation for computing with words (Zadeh, 1996). Among the issues discussed relating to KDD are generalized soft association rules, synthesis of interfaces between sources exchanging concepts and using different languages, problems in spatial reasoning (Roddick and Spiliopoulou, 1999), and data-mining in the Internet. Further interactions of rough mereology and KDD will certainly bring new results for both areas.

4. Hybridization of Fuzzy Sets and Rough Sets

In the previous sections, we have identified the roles played by fuzzy sets and rough sets in KDD. It has become apparent that there is a need for some hybridization to make the processes of information granulation more efficient with regard to the computing requirements posed by real-world data. Furthermore, one may think of building hybrid constructs that capture the essence of fuzzy sets and rough sets (Dubois and Prade, 1990, 1992; Pawlak and Skowron, 1999). Rough-fuzzy hybridization methods provide tools for KDD.

4.1. Fuzzification of Rough Concepts

The classical rough set approach is based on crisp sets. Reducts, the basic constructs of rough sets, define crisp sets used for concept definition. Often, making these sets more soft by their fuzzification helps achieve a higher quality of concept approximations. Examples of such constructs are fuzzy cut and hyperplanes (Nguyen, 1997) or fuzzification of decision rules generated from corresponding reducts.

Let us also mention that set approximations based on a fuzzy indiscernibility relation (e.g., defined by a fuzzy similarity relation [Greco et al., 1998]) have shown to be useful for concept approximation.

Further investigations of techniques transforming rough concepts into fuzzy ones will certainly show further interesting results.

4.2. Approximation of Fuzzy Concepts by Rough Concepts

Rough set methods can be used to define fuzzy concepts approximately. In this case, first one can look for relevant α-cuts of the fuzzy set and next approximate them with respect to known condition features (Yao, 1997). The problem of choosing relevant cuts is analogous to the problem of relevant feature extraction. From a computational complexity point of view, it is a hard problem and can be solved approximately by discovery of learning strategies. The relevant cuts should be well approximated (i.e., new objects with a high chance should be properly classified to sets defined by them) as well as giving a good approximation of the target fuzzy set. This approach can be used for constructive definition of fuzzy membership functions by the rough set approach. Its importance for KDD can be illustrated by data summarization in natural language (i.e., using soft concepts) or flexible query answering (Kacprzyk and Zardrożny, 1999).

4.3. Hybrid Models of Information Granules, Information Granulation, and Granular Data Mining

We have pointed out above how models of information granules and granulation processes enrich the processes and models of data mining. The need for studies of the hybrid models of information granules arises when we are faced with an issue of interoperability between various tasks or subsystems of data mining that could be realized in various frameworks of granular computing. This is a place for hybridization of rough and fuzzy approaches. In particular, rough-fuzzy hybrid systems (see, e.g., Pal and Skowron, 1999) have great potential for further application in KDD to extract approximations of soft patterns in complex environments.

ACKNOWLEDGMENTS
Support from the Natural Sciences and Engineering Research Council of Canada (NSERC) is gratefully acknowledged by W. Pedrycz. A. Skowron was supported by the Wallenberg Foundation, by the ESPRIT-CRIT 2 project 20288, and by the grant 8T11C02519 from the State Committee for Scientific Research (KBN) of the Republic of Poland.

References

Agrawal, R., H. Mannila, R. Srikant, H. Toivonen, and A. Verkano. 1996. "Fast discovery of association rules." In *Advances in Knowledge Discovery and Data Mining*, edited by U. M. Fayyad, G. Piatetsky-Shapiro, P. Smyth, and R. Uthurusamy, pp. 307–328. Menlo Park, CA: AAAI/MIT Press.

Bazan, J. G. 1998. "A comparison of dynamic and non-dynamic rough set methods for extracting laws from decision system." In *Rough Sets in Knowledge Discovery, 1: Methodology and Applications*, edited by L. Polkowski and A. Skowron, pp. 321–365. Heidelberg: Physica-Verlag.

Brown, F. M. 1990. *Boolean Reasoning*. Dordrecht, Netherlands: Kluwer Academic Publishers.

Dave, R. N. and R. Krishnapuram. 1997. "Robust clustering methods: a unified view." *IEEE Trans. Fuzzy Sys.* **5**: 643–662.

Dubois, D. and H. Prade. 1990. "Rough fuzzy sets and fuzzy rough sets." *Int. J. General Sys.* **17**: 191–209.

Dubois, D. and H. Prade. 1992. "Putting fuzzy sets and rough sets together." In *Intelligent Decision Support. Handbook of Applications and Advances of the Rough set Theory*, edited by R. Słowiński, pp. 203–232. Dordrecht: Kluwer Academic Publishers.

Duentsch, I. and G. Gediga. 2000. "Rough set data analysis." In *Encyclopedia of Computer Science and Technology*, vol 43. New York: Marcel Dekker, pp. 281–301.

Fayyad, U. M., G. Piatetsky-Shapiro, P. Smyth, and R. Uthurusamy, eds. 1996. In *Advances in Knowledge Discovery and Data Mining*. Menlo Park, CA: AAAI/MIT Press.

Ganti, V., J. Gehrke, and R. Ramakrishnan. 1999. "Mining very large databases." *Computer*, pp. 38–45.

Greco, S., B. Matarazzo, and R. Słowiński. 1998. "Rough set theory to decision analysis." In *Proceedings of the Third European Workshop on Fuzzy Decision Analysis and Neural Networks for Management, Planning and Optimization, June 16–19,* edited by R. Felix, pp. 1–28. Germany: University of Dortmund.

Hayashi, I., T. Maeda, A. Bastian, and L. C. Jain. 1998. "Generation of fuzzy decision trees by fuzzy ID3 with adjusting mechanism of AND/OR operators." In *Proceedings of the 1988 International Conference on Fuzzy Systems (FUZZ-IEEE 98),* pp. 681–685. NJ: IEEE Press.

Hoppner, F., F. Klawonn, R. Kruse, and T. Runkler. 1999. *Fuzzy Cluster Analysis.* Chichester, UK: J. Wiley.

Ichihashi, H., T. Shirai, K. Nagasaka, and T. Miyoshi. 1996. "Neuro-fuzzy ID3: a method of inducing fuzzy decision trees with linear programming for maximizing entropy and an algebraic method for incremental learning." *Fuzzy Sets and Sys.* **81(1)**: 157–167.

Imielinski, T. and H. Mannila. 1996. "A database perspective on knowledge discovery." *Commun. ACM* **38(11)**: 58–64.

Janikow, C. Z. 1998. "Fuzzy decision trees: issues and methods." *IEEE Trans. Sys., Man Cybernet., Part B* **28(1)**: 1–14.

Kacprzyk, J. and S. Zardrożny. 1999. "Data mining via fuzzy querying over internet." In *Knowledge Management in Fuzzy Databases,* edited by O. Pons, M. Amparo Vila, and J. Kacprzyk, pp. 211–233. Heidelberg: Physica-Verlag.

Kaufman, L. and P. J. Rousseeuw. 1990. *Finding Groups in Data.* New York: J. Wiley.

Komorowski, J., Z. Pawlak, L. Polkowski, and A. Skowron. 1999. "Rough sets: a tutorial." In *Rough Fuzzy Hybridization: A New Trend in Decision-Making,* edited by S. K. Pal and A. Skowron, pp. 3–98. Singapore: Springer-Verlag.

Langley, P., H. A. Simon, G. L. Bradshaw, and J. M. Żytkow. 1987. *Scientific Discovery, Computational Explorations of the Creative Processes.* Cambridge, MA: MIT Press.

Lin, T. Y. and N. Cercone, eds. 1997. *Rough Sets and Data Mining—Analysis of Imperfect Data.* Boston: Kluwer Academic Publishers.

Mitchell, T. 1997. *Machine Learning.* New York: McGraw Hill.

Mollestadt, T. 1997. "A rough set approach to data mining: extracting a logic of default rules from data." Ph.D. diss. Trondheim, Norway: Norwegian University of Science and Technology.

Nguyen, H. S. 1997. "Discretization of real value attributes: Boolean reasoning approach." Ph.D. diss. Warsaw, Poland: Warsaw University.

Nguyen, H. S. 1999. "Efficient SQL-learning method for data mining in large data bases." In *Proceedings of the Sixteenth International Joint Conference on Artificial Intelligence (IJCAI'99),* pp. 806–811. San Francisco: Morgan Kaufmann.

Nguyen, H. S., A. Skowron, and P. Synak. 1998. "Discovery of data patterns with applications to decomposition and classification problems." In *Rough sets in Knowledge Discovery,* edited by L. Polkowski and A. Skowron, vol 1–2, pp 55–97. Heidelberg: Physica-Verlag.

Orłowska, E., ed. 1997. *Incomplete Information: Rough Set Analysis.* Heidelberg: Physica-Verlag.

Pal, S. K. and A. Skowron, eds. 1999. *Rough-Fuzzy Hybridization: A New Trend in Decision Making.* Singapore: Springer-Verlag.

Pawlak, Z. 1991. *Rough Sets—Theoretical Aspects of Reasoning about Data.* Dordrecht, Netherlands: Kluwer Academic Publishers.

Pawlak, Z. and A. Skowron. 1999. "Rough set rudiments." *Bull. Int. Rough Set Soc.* **3(4)**: 181–185.

Pedrycz, W. 1996. "Conditional fuzzy-means." *Pattern Recognition Lett.* **17**: 625–632.

Pedrycz, W. 1998b. "Conditional fuzzy clustering in the design of radial basis function neural networks." *IEEE Trans. Neural Networks* **9(4)**: 601–612.

Pedrycz, W. 1998c. "Fuzzy set technology in knowledge discovery." *Fuzzy Sets Sys.* **3**: 279–290.

Polkowski, L. and A. Skowron. 1994. "Rough mereology." In *Proceedings of the Eighth International Symposium on Methodologies for Intelligent Systems (ISMIS'94), Charlotte, October 1994.* Lecture Notes in Artificial Intelligence, 869, pp. 85–94. Berlin: Springer-Verlag.

Polkowski, L. and A. Skowron. 1996. "Rough mereology: a new paradigm for approximate reasoning." *Int. J. Approx Reasoning* **15(4)**: 333–365.

Polkowski, L. and A. Skowron. 1999. "Towards adaptive calculus of granules." In *Computing with Words in Information/Intelligent Systems,* edited by Zadeh and Kacprzyk, **1–2**: 201–227. Heidelberg: Physica-Verlag.

Polkowski, L. and A. Skowron. (eds). 1998a. In *Rough sets in Knowledge Discovery* Volumes 1–2. Heidelberg: Physica-Verlag.

Polkowski, L. and A. Skowron. 1998b. "Rough mereological foundations for design, analysis, synthesis, and control in distributive systems." *Inform. Sci. Int. J.* **104(1–2)**: 129–156.

Polkowski, L. and A. Skowron. 2000. "Rough mereology in information systems. A case study: Qualitative spatial reasoning." In *Rough Sets: New Developments in Knowledge Discovery in Information Systems,* edited by L. Polkowski, S. Tsumoto, and T. Y. Lin, pp. 89–135. Heidelberg: Physica-Verlag.

Rissanen, J. J. 1978. "Modeling by shortest data description." *Automatica* **14**: 465–471.

Roddick, J. F. and M. Spiliopoulou. 1999. "A bibliography of temporal, spatial, and temporal data mining research." *Newsletter of the Special Interest Group (SIG) on Knowledge Discovery and Data Mining* **1(1)**: 34–48. Available at: http://www.acm.org/sigkdd/explorations/issue1-1.htm.

Schultze-Kremer, S. 1999. "Discovery in human genome project." *Commun. ACM* **42(11)**: 62–64.

Selman, B., H. Kautz, and D. McAllester. 1997. "Ten challenges in propositional reasoning and search." In *Proceedings of the IJCAI'97*. Japan.

Shrager, J. and P. Langley. 1990. "Computational approaches to scientific discovery." In *Computational Models of Scientific Discovery and Theory Formation*, edited by J. Shrager and P. Langley, pp. 1–25. San Mateo, CA: Morgan Kaufmann.

Skowron, A. and H. S. Nguyen. 1999. "Boolean reasoning with some applications in data mining." In *Third European Conference of Principles and Practice of Knowledge Discovery in Databases, September 15–18, 1999, Prague, Czech Republic*. Lecture Notes in Artificial Intelligence 1704, pp. 107–115. Heidelberg: Springer-Verlag.

Skowron, A. and C. Rauszer. 1992. "The discernibility matrices and functions in information systems." In *Intelligent Decision Support. Handbook of Applications and Advances of the Rough Set Theory*, edited by Słowiński, pp. 311–362. Dordrecht: Kluwer Academic Publishers.

Skowron, A., J. Stepaniuk, and S. Tsumoto. 1999. "Information granules for spatial reasoning." *Bull. Int. Rough Set Soc.* **3(4)**: 147–154.

Słowiński, R., ed. 1992. *Intelligent Decision Support. Handbook of Applications and Advances of the Rough Set Theory*. Dordrecht: Kluwer Academic Publishers.

Stepaniuk, J. 2000. "Knowledge discovery by rough set methods." In *Rough Sets: New Developments*, edited by L. Polkowski, S. Tsumoto, and T. Y. Lin. Heidelberg: Physica-Verlag.

Szczuka, M. 2000. "Symbolic and neural network methods for classifiers construction." Ph.D. diss. Warsaw, Poland: Warsaw University.

Troxel, M., K. Swarm, R. Zembowicz, and J. M. Żytkow. 1994. "Concept hierarchies: a restricted form of knowledge derived from regularities." In *Proceedings of the Eighth International Symposium on Methodologies for Intelligent Systems (ISMIS'94), Charlotte, October 1994*. Lecture Notes in Artificial Intelligence, 869, pp. 448–457. Berlin: Springer-Verlag.

Tsumoto, S., S. Kobayashi, T. Yokomori, H. Tanaka, and A. Nakamura. eds. 1996. *The Fourth Internal Workshop on Rough Sets, Fuzzy Sets and Machine Discovery, Proceedings. November 6–8*. Tokyo, Japan: The University of Tokyo.

Umano, M., H. Okamota, I. Hatono, H. Tamura, F. Kawachi, S. Umedzu, and J. Kinoshita. 1994. "Generation of fuzzy decision trees by fuzzy ID3 algorithm and its application to diagnosis by gas in oil." In *Proceedings of the 1994 Japan–USA Symposium on Flexible Automation*, pp. 1445–1448. Japan: Kobe Asian Technology Information Program (ATIP), Albuquerque, New Mexico and Tokyo, Japan.

Valdés-Pérez, R. E. 1999. "Discovery tools for science apps." *Commun. ACM* **42(11)**: 37–41.

Yao, Y. Y. 1997. "Combination of rough and fuzzy sets based on alpha-level sets." In *Rough Sets and Data Mining—Analysis of Imperfect Data*, edited by T. Y. Lin and N. Cercone, pp. 301–321. Boston: Kluwer Academic Publishers.

Zadeh, L. A. 1965. "Fuzzy sets." *Information and Control* **8**: 333–353.

Zadeh, L. A. 1996. "Fuzzy logic = computing with words." *IEEE Trans. Fuzzy Sys.* **4**: 103–111.

Zadeh, L. A. 1979. "Fuzzy sets and information granularity." In *Advances in Fuzzy Set Theory and Applications*, edited by M. M. Gupta, R. K. Ragade, and R. R. Yager, pp. 3–18. Amsterdam: North-Holland.

Ziarko, W. 1993. "Variable precision rough sets model." *J. Comput. Sys. Sci.* **46(1)**: 39–59.

31 NEURAL NETWORKS

Witold Pedrycz

ABSTRACT This chapter elaborates on the connections and interdisciplinary links between knowledge discovery in databases (KDD) and neural networks and neurocomputing, in general. We identify a number of basic categories of synergistic links existing therein. We show that data mining can benefit from the learning abilities of neural networks. Similarly, there are ways in which data mining can augment the research agenda of neurocomputing by drawing attention to the issues of processing large data sets and identifying possible ways of learning enhancement through data granulation. The aspect of increased transparency of neural networks is another essential topic promoted by KDD.

1. Introduction

Neurocomputing (Golden, 1996) is an actively pursued and frequently exploited paradigm of computing. In a nutshell, neural networks are universal approximators of numerical functions. From the user's standpoint, neural networks are black boxes, as the knowledge captured through learning is not provided in an explicit format. The distributed architectures of neural networks and inherently asynchronous processing promote an implicit form of knowledge representation. Neural networks capture experimental data by exploiting an array of architectures and utilizing a panoply of learning algorithms. The objective of neurocomputing is to make sense of data by building nonlinear models. In this sense, the neural model condenses the experimental data into the form of a nonlinear relationship. The agenda of data mining sounds familiar and similar to that delineated for neural networks. The target is different, though: the results of data mining are geared to a user. Neural networks are far less user oriented and less user friendly. In spite of this difference, a synergy of these two technologies seems to be advantageous, desired, and inevitable. Undoubtedly, as neural networks and data mining develop their own suites of algorithms, methodologies, and specific approaches to data processing, in some cases they become highly complementary. This complementarity promotes the synergy.

The objective of this study is to delineate several key interdisciplinary links between neural networks and data mining. We look into the nature of their symbiosis as well as elaborate on possible algorithmic aspects of such synergistic interaction.

First, we briefly review the key features of neural networks concentrating on those that are of particular interest in this synergistic environment of data mining and neurocomputing (Section 2). Various neural architectures allow for different levels of interpretability. We focus on the selected topologies that are characterized by a substantial level of transparency or by intuitively transparent and easily understood learning schemes. Then, in Section 3, we study the role of neural networks whose learning abilities can help develop rules from the data sets. In this way, neural networks serve as a provider of a blueprint of the most essential (and data stable) relationships within data. The reciprocal relationships between neural networks and data mining pursuits are discussed in Section 4. Here, we analyze the impact of the approach of data mining and its underlying methodology as it affects neurocomputing. Interestingly, research in neural networks can be augmented by raising awareness about many essential issues of knowledge representation (e.g., those arising when contrasting rules with associations), transparency of computing models, as well as a need for information processing at a certain granular level being regarded as a vehicle of effective learning.

Figure 1 may serve as a leitmotif of this study and point to the key aspects of such interdisciplinary links. It points out that data mining technology and neural networks augment each other with essential features: neural networks are enriched with a knowledge-based slant specific to data mining, while data mining benefits from the learning abilities of neural networks that help find regularities (patterns) in data being preprocessed in the framework of neurocomputing.

In the remainder of the chapter we use the notion of information granules. While detailed studies of these issues are covered in Chapters 10 and 30 of this handbook, here we

690

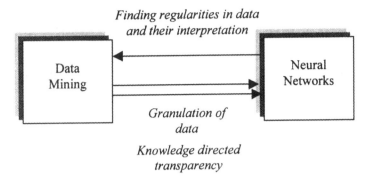

Figure 1 Interdisciplinary links between data mining and neurocomputing leading to their synergy

focus on sets (intervals) and fuzzy sets. At this point, it is worth emphasizing that information granules can be perceived at the intuitive level by considering them as collections of entities (especially numbers) that are combined and discussed together.

2. Neural Networks: Main Features

The list of the outstanding features of neural networks that distinguish them from other architectures and approaches exploited in data mining includes the following (Gallant, 1988; Golden, 1996; Pedrycz and Gomide, 1998):

- Distributed architecture (and the associated distributed character of knowledge representation). Neural networks are composed of simple processing units (artificial neurons).
- Learning abilities (networks can modify their connections to follow experimental data).
- Generalization aspects (neural networks can perform well in instances never seen before).
- Robustness and fault tolerance (neural networks are potentially capable of surviving minor deterioration in their structures due to some loss of connections or a malfunction of some neurons).

In neurocomputing, there are three basic modes of learning: supervised learning (when the networks are given detailed targets they have to adjust to), unsupervised learning (where there are no training guidelines), and reinforcement learning where the supervision signal is temporally or spatially distributed.

In general, relationships between variables can be categorized into two groups: directional and nondirectional. Feedforward neural networks are directional structures. They subscribe to a certain direction between variables meaning that some of them are independent (inputs) and others are dependent (outputs). For instance, the statement "x implies y" states that the values of y depend on x. There are situations where there is no direction indicated (when we do not know what causes what or we want to maintain this level of structural generality for further investigations). With no direction identified, such relationships are associations or relations (in a mathematical sense). When associations are of interest, we concentrate on unsupervised learning such as Hebbian learning, clustering techniques such as Kohonen's self-organizing maps, and the like.

3. From Neural Networks to Data-Mining

In this section, we elaborate on several ways neural networks can impact in data mining activities. In particular, this concerns various aspects of so-called connectionist expert systems (Ciesielski and Palstra, 1966; Gallant, 1988; McSherry, 1997).

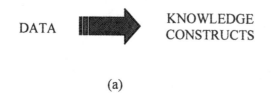

DATA

KNOWLEDGE
CONSTRUCTS

(a)

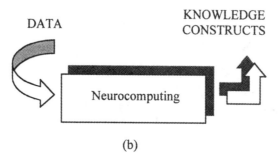

DATA

KNOWLEDGE
CONSTRUCTS

Neurocomputing

(b)

Figure 2 Two fundamental approaches to rule induction: (a) direct one-step approach: data used directly in the formation of knowledge constructs, (b) two-step approach: neural networks serve as a computational "filter," the rules are generated through experimentation with the neural network rather than exploring raw data

3.1. Generation of Rules: From Data to Rules

Neural networks, especially multilayer feedforward architectures, are useful in rule generation from massive numerical data. The paradigm can be schematically portrayed as in Figure 2. Instead of constructing rules directly from data by utilizing data mining techniques such as decision trees, the process consists of two phases. First, a neural network is designed. It captures most of the data, eliminates outliers and noisy patterns, and reveals the main associations in the data set. In the second phase, the network is used to generate the rules. As the neural network adheres to the property of continuity (meaning that if inputs are similar, so are the outputs), generation of the rules can easily be accomplished through the second phase of the entire scheme. Furthermore, in this paradigm, one can be more creative as far as the conditions of the rules are concerned, namely, input is formed (either as a numerical quantity or some information granule) and the response of the network is viewed as the condition part of the rule. Moreover, the construction (revealing) of the rules, as it relies on the network's outcomes rather than on raw data, is more legitimate. In this way, we may hope to derive more stable and meaningful rules in comparison to those obtained when working with raw

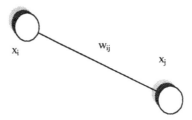

Figure 3 An idea of Hebbian (correlation-like) learning; the strength of the connection between the nodes (concepts defined in the problem) depends on the level of firing (activation) of the nodes

data. The essence of the process is to let the neural network complete all preprocessing and regularization activities and build (implicitly) the relationships within the data.

There are two general approaches to knowledge extraction from neural networks (Andrews et al., 1995; Fu, 1994; McSherry, 1997; Nowlan and Hinton, 1992; Towell and Shavlik, 1993; Wartenberg and Decker, 1996; Yuanhui et al., 1997):

1. *Decompositional.* During this extraction process each component (part) of the network is examined and the knowledge extracted at this level is combined afterward. As we concentrate on the individual components, this is an open-box approach.

2. *Pedagogical (input–output) approach.* This approach concentrates on the derivation of the input–output behavior of the network. In essence, the method falls under the category of the black-box approaches.

3.2. Neural Generation of Associations

Rules are far more general and descriptive than functions, yet they reflect a certain direction assumed in data mining. The notion of input and output variables (attributes or the like) plays a primordial role. There are situations when this direction is not known in advance or we are not interested in any type of directional constraint. In this case, neurocomputing provides us with various models of Hebbian learning. This type of unsupervised learning reveals associations between some entities used to represent the problem. The model can be portrayed as a graph. The nodes of the graph represent variables (attributes) in the data-mining problem. The edges represent links between the variables (see Figure 3).

The strength of the connections is completed in an unsupervised mode: the level of firing of the nodes, x_i and x_j, contributes to the current value of the connection w_{ij}, that is (Golden, 1996),

$$w_{ij}(\text{iter}) = w_{ij}(\text{iter} - 1) + \alpha x_i x_j,$$

where α is a positive learning rate and $w_{ij}(\text{iter} - 1)$ denotes the previous value of the connection.

Such neural models of Hebbian learning constitute an alternative to well-known correlation methods.

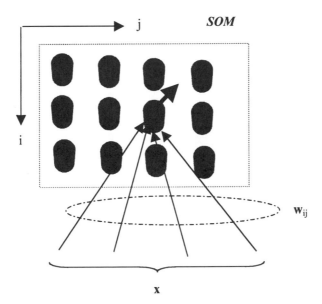

Figure 4 A general architecture of SOM: each neuron is identified through its coordinates (i, j) in the rectangular grid; note the connections bundled together

3.3. *Self-Organizing Maps as a Vehicle for Data Organization*

Self-organizing maps (SOMs) as introduced by Kohonen (see also Golden, 1996) are neural architectures developed through unsupervised learning. The network maps highly dimensional patterns onto a low-dimensional (usually two-dimensional) space in such a way that the topology of the data is preserved. In other words, the similarity between the data is preserved: the patterns that are close in the original space are located close in the map. The patterns that are different are distant in the low-dimensional space.

The network is usually formed as a rectangular grid of linear neurons, see Figure 4, whose connections are updated through competitive learning. Given the input $\mathbf{x}$, the level of activation of each neuron in the grid is determined and a winning node $I^* = (i^*, j^*)$ is found

$$(i^*, j^*) = \arg[\max_{i,j=1,2,...P}(\mathbf{w}_{ij}^T\mathbf{x})],$$

where $\mathbf{w}_{ij}$ denotes a vector of the connections of the node (neuron) at (i, j), $i, j = 1, 2, ..., P$. Afterward, the connections of the winning node and its neighboring neurons are updated in the form

$$\mathbf{w}_{i^*j^*}(\text{new}) = \mathbf{w}_{i^*j^*} + \rho(i,j)[\mathbf{w}_{ij} - \mathbf{x}],$$

where $\rho(i, j)$ is a neighbor function specifying a region in the map over which the connections are updated. This function attains 1.0 for the winning neuron and reduces when moving away from the winner.

The main advantage of the SOM lies in its ability to organize and visualize data so that the user can get a better insight into the structure in the data set and reveal groups therein.

4. From Data Mining Environment to Conceptual and Computational Enhancements of Neurocomputing

The principles of data-mining along with their realizations and algorithmic aspects have an impact on the development of neural networks and result in a shift in the generic learning paradigm. First, we encounter the issue of granulation of data that substantially reduces the learning effort. Note that granulation is used as general term; quite often we refer to

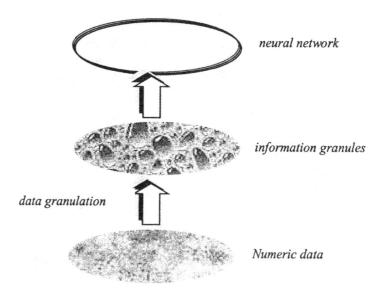

Figure 5 The development process of granular neural networks perceived as a two-phase design; the construction of the network (including its learning) is followed by data granulation sets

discretization, binning, et cetera. In these two cases, the fundamental formalism being used deals with set theory and interval analysis. Second, data mining promotes an important role that is played by knowledge representation mechanisms. Visibly, these have not played a primordial role in neurocomputing so far. It is worth emphasizing that neural networks are apparently committed to numerical computing and processing of numerical data.

Informally speaking, information granules, especially fuzzy sets and rough sets (Bortolan, 1998; Pal and Skowron, 1999; Pawlak, 1982; Pedrycz, 1996; Pedrycz and Gomide, 1998) are viewed as linked collections of objects (data points, in particular) drawn together by the criteria of indistinguishability, similarity, or functionality. Information granules and the ensuing process of information granulation is a vehicle of abstraction leading to the emergence of concepts. One of the possibilities (used commonly in practice) dwells on the use of clustering methods such as fuzzy clustering (Bezdek, 1981). A certain drawback coming with this approach lies in the computational overhead that grows rapidly when faced with huge data sets.

Once the information granules have been formed, they are pivotal components in the design of the neural networks. Figure 5 emphasizes these two design phases. As the number of information granules is substantially lower than the number of original numerical data, this contributes to faster learning and significantly reduces the danger of oversizing the network and/or the memorization effect (poor or total lack of generalization abilities). Information granules can be given in some parametric form such as triangular fuzzy numbers (Pedrycz and Gomide, 1998).

4.1. A Need for Transparency of Knowledge Representation in Neural Networks

Neural networks are ensembles of simple processing units. Their computing capabilities are limited, yet their ensemble gives rise to powerful processing capabilities and exhibits learning abilities. The black-box nature of the network carries a heavy price tag. First, one cannot interpret the network directly (note that what we were doing in Section 3 dealt with the input–output interpretation of the neural networks and it also required two interpretation layers composed of information granules). Second, as the network is not interpretable, one cannot accommodate any prior knowledge that may eventually shorten the process of learning or make it more efficient. To address these shortcomings, one should seek some other functional neurons that are easily interpretable and give rise to at least graylike boxes (as opposed to the black-box nature of the commonly encountered neural networks). There are a number of possibilities. One that is intuitively appealing dwells on the notion of logic-based neurons as studied by Pedrycz (1996, 1998). Let us reiterate the main ideas exploited in this framework. First, one distinguishes between AND and OR neurons. They are logic constructs and generalizations of standard two-valued AND and OR operators encountered in digital systems. The generalization is twofold: these neurons are anchored in the setting of multiple-valued logic as well as equipped with the learning abilities that come with adjustable connections. The neurons use triangular norms (originating from the theory of fuzzy sets). In

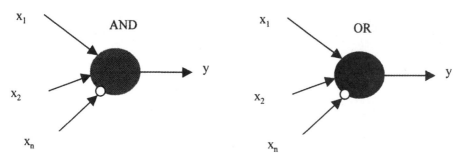

Figure 6 Basic logic (AND and OR) neurons; the complements of the inputs are denoted by small circles

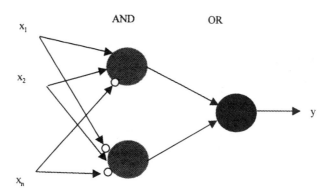

Figure 7 A generic neural architecture leading to logic-based style of approximation

particular, one may resort to the max and min operators regarded as basic logic operators. The diagrams of such neurons are illustrated in Figure 6. Note that the neuron comes with inhibitory inputs whose values are complemented.

The basic architecture of the neuron is that developed in the Shannon theorem. While the theorem applies to two-valued logic, we follow it in this case. The two-valued case is straightforward: any Boolean function is represented as a sum of products (min terms). Here, this translates into AND neurons in the first layer followed by the OR neurons distributed in the second layer (Figure 7). Owing to the logical nature of the neurons, the network can easily be interpreted in the form of if-then statements. It is worth stressing that the approximation carried out by this class of networks is logic driven. More specifically, the network can learn disjunctive normal forms from Boolean data or from continuous data. It is worth stressing that this form of logic-based approximation is more specific than the general form of approximation supported by neural networks. Nevertheless, this narrowed scope of approximation is helpful in interpretation activities.

5. Conclusion

In this study, we have elaborated on essential links between data mining and neurocomputing. In this interaction, an important learning–knowledge representation synergy manifests itself in many possible ways. In general, neurocomputing provides the environment of data mining with another style of constructing relationships existing in data sets. Rather than eliciting rules or associations directly from the data, one constructs a neural network and then uses it to reveal essential relationships. We have discussed the advantages of this approach over direct structure elicitation. In this sense, neural networks can be regarded as a provider of learning tools (both supervised and unsupervised) for data mining. On the other side of the synergistic interaction, data mining raises awareness about the richness of data and knowledge representation schemes and the need for the proper treatment of such structures within neurocomputing. Furthermore, KDD provides an insight into the problems of coping with large data sets that would not be feasible for handling in the standard setting of neural networks.

ACKNOWLEDGMENTS
Support from the Natural Sciences and Engineering Research Council of Canada (NSERC) is gratefully acknowledged.

References

Andrews, R., J. Dieterich, and A. Tickle. 1995. "Survey and critique of techniques for extracting rules from trained artificial neural networks." *Knowledge-Based Sys.* **8**: 373–389.
Bezdek, J. C. 1981. *Pattern Recognition with Fuzzy Objective Function Algorithms*. New York: Plenum Press.

Bortolan, G. 1998. "An architecture of fuzzy neural networks for linguistic processing." *Fuzzy Sets Sys.* **100**: 197–215.

Ciesielski, V. and G. Palstra. 1996. "Using a hybrid neural/expert system for database mining in market survey data." In *Proceeding of the 1996 International Conference on Data Mining and Knowledge Discovery KDD-96*, pp. 38–43. Menlo Park, CA: AAI.

Fu, L. M. 1994. "Rule generation from neural networks." *IEEE Trans. Sys., Man Cybernet.* **24(8)**: 1114–1124.

Gallant, S. 1988. "Connectionist expert systems." *Commun. ACM* **31(2)**: 152–169.

Golden, R. M. 1996. *Mathematical Methods for Neural Network Analysis and Design.* Cambridge, MA: MIT Press.

McSherry, D. August 1997. "A strategy for increasing the efficiency of rule discovery in data mining." In *Advances in Intelligent Data Analysis, Second International Symposium (IDA-97), London, U.K.*, edited by X. Liu, P. Cohen, and M. Berthold, pp. 465–475. Berlin: Springer-Verlag.

Nowlan, S. J. and G. E. Hinton. 1992. "Simplifying neural networks by soft weight-sharing." *Neural Comput.* **4(4)**: 473–493.

Pal, S. K. and A. Skowron, eds. 1999. *Rough Fuzzy Hybridization.* Singapore: Springer-Verlag.

Pawlak, Z. 1982. "Rough sets." *Int. J. Comput. Sci.* **11**: 341–356.

Pedrycz, W. 1996. *Fuzzy Sets Engineering.* Boca Raton, FL: CRC Press.

Pedrycz, W. and F. Gomide. 1998. *An Introduction to Fuzzy Sets: Analysis and Design.* Cambridge, MA: MIT Press.

Towell, C. G. and J. W. Shavlik. 1993. "Extracting refined rules from knowledge-based neural networks." *Machine Learning* **13**: 71–101.

Wartenberg, F. and R. Decker. 1996. "Analysis of sales data: a neural net approach." In *From Data to Knowledge*, edited by W. Gaul and D. Pfeifer, pp. 327–333. Berlin: Springer.

Yuanhui, Z., L. Yuchang, and S. Chunyi. August 1997. "A connectionist approach to extracting knowledge from databases." In *Advances in Intelligent Data Analysis, Second International Symp (IDA-97), London, UK*, edited by X. Liu, P. Cohen, and M. Berthold, pp. 465–475. Berlin: Springer-Verlag.

32 EVOLUTIONARY COMPUTATION

Alex Alves Freitas

ABSTRACT This chapter addresses the integration of knowledge discovery in databases (KDD) and evolutionary algorithms (EAs), particularly genetic algorithms and genetic programming. First, we provide a brief overview of EAs. Then the remaining text is divided into three parts. Section 2 discusses the use of EAs for KDD. The emphasis is on the use of EAs for discovering high-level prediction rules, but we also discuss the use of EAs in attribute selection and in the optimization of parameters for other kinds of KDD algorithms (such as decision trees and nearest neighbor algorithms). Section 3 discusses three research problems in the design of an EA for KDD, namely, how to discover comprehensible rules with genetic programming, how to discover surprising (interesting) rules, and how to scale up EAs with parallel processing. Finally, Section 4 discusses what the added value of KDD is for EAs. This section includes the remark that generalization performance on a separate test set (unseen during training, or EA run) is a basic principle for evaluating the quality of discovered knowledge, and then suggests that this principle should be followed in other EA applications.

1. Introduction

The evolutionary algorithms paradigm consists of stochastic search algorithms that are based on abstractions of the processes of Neo-Darwinian evolution. The basic idea is that each individual of an evolving population encodes a candidate solution (e.g., a prediction rule) to a given problem (e.g., classification). Each individual is evaluated by a fitness function (e.g., the predictive accuracy of the rule). Then these individuals evolve toward better and better individuals via operators based on natural selection, that is, survival and reproduction of the fittest, and genetics, such as crossover and mutation operators (see Goldberg, 1989; Michalewicz, 1996; Koza, 1992, 1994; Koza et al., 1999; Banzhaf et al., 1998).

The crossover operator essentially swaps genetic material between two individuals. Figure 1 illustrates a simple form of crossover between two individuals, each represented as a string with four genes. In the context of KDD, each gene could be, say, an attribute-value condition of a rule (see below). Figure 1(a) shows the individuals before crossover. A crossover point is randomly chosen, represented in the figure by the symbol "|" between the second and third genes. Then the genes to the right of the crossover point are swapped between the two individuals, yielding the new individuals shown in Figure 1(b).

The mutation operator simply changes the value of a gene to a new random value. Both crossover and mutation are stochastic operators, applied with user-defined probabilities. The probability of mutation is usually much lower than that of crossover. However, mutation is still necessary to increase the genetic diversity of individuals in the population. Note that mutation can yield gene values that are not present in the current population, unlike crossover, which only swaps existing gene values between individuals.

An important characteristic of evolutionary algorithms is that they perform a global search. Indeed, evolutionary algorithms work with a population of candidate solutions, rather than working with a single candidate solution at a time. This, together with the fact they use

$$
\begin{array}{cc}
\text{X1 X2} \mid \text{X3 X4} & \text{X1 X2} \mid \text{Y3 Y4} \\
\\
\text{Y1 Y2} \mid \text{Y3 Y4} & \text{Y1 Y2} \mid \text{X3 X4}
\end{array}
$$

(a) Before crossover   (b) After crossover

Figure 1 Simple example of crossover

698

stochastic operators to perform their search, reduces the probability that they will get stuck in local maxima, and increase the probability that they will find the global maximum.

2. Use of Evolutionary Algorithms for KDD

2.1. Evolutionary Algorithms for Rule Discovery

Among the several kinds of evolutionary algorithms described in the literature, genetic algorithms (GA) and genetic programming (GP) have been used the most in rule discovery. These two kinds of algorithms differ mainly with respect to the representation of an individual.

In GA an individual is usually a linear string of rule conditions, where each condition is often an attribute-value pair. The individual can represent a rule, as illustrated in Figure 2(a), or a rule set, as illustrated in Figure 2(b). In both illustrations the individual only encodes the conditions of the antecedent (IF part) of a classification rule, and conditions are implicitly connected by a logical AND. In Figure 2(b) the symbol "||" is used to separate rules within the individual. The predicted class (the THEN part of the rule) can be chosen in a deterministic, sensible way as the majority class among all data instances satisfying the rule antecedent. Supposing that the rules in Figure 1 refer to a credit data set, the system would choose a predicted class such as $credit = good$ for those rules.

The several-rules-per-individual approach has the advantage that the fitness of an individual can be evaluated by considering its rule set as a whole by taking into account rule interactions. However, this approach makes individual encoding more complicated and syntactically longer, which in turn may require more complex genetic operators. Some algorithms following this approach are proposed by De Jong et al. (1993), Janikow (1993), and Pei et al. (1997).

The single-rule-per-individual approach makes individual encoding simpler and syntactically shorter. However, it introduces the problem that the fitness of an individual (a single rule) is not necessarily the best indicator of the quality of the discovered rule set. Some algorithms using one-rule-per-individual encoding are proposed by Greene and Smith (1993), Giordana and Neri (1995), Freitas (1999a), and Noda et al. (1999).

In GP an individual is usually represented by a tree, with rule conditions and/or attribute values in the leaf nodes and functions (e.g., logical, relational or mathematical operators) in the internal nodes. An individual's tree can grow in size and shape in a very dynamic way. Figure 3 illustrates a GP individual representing the rule antecedent: IF $(Employed = "yes")$ AND $((Salary - Mortgage\_debt) > 10,000)$. Assuming, again, a credit application domain, the rule consequent (THEN part) would be a prediction such as '$credit = good$'.

We emphasize that encoding rules into a GP individual is a nontrivial problem, due to the closure property of GP. This property requires that the output of a node can be used as the input to any parent node in the tree. This is a problem in the context of KDD. For instance, the operator $<$ can be used in a parent node if its children contain Age and 18, but not if they contain Sex and $female$.

| Salary = "high" | Age > 18 | ... (other rule conditions) |

(a) GA individual = one rule antecedent

| Employed = "yes" | C/A_balance = "high" | || | Salary = "high" | ||... (other rules) |

(b) GA individual = a set of rule antecedents

Figure 2 Examples of individual encoding in GA for rule discovery

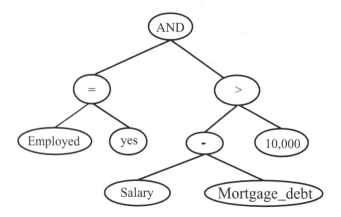

Figure 3 Example of genetic programming individual for rule discovery

Several solutions have been proposed to cope with the requirement of closure in GP. Most of these solutions involve some kind of constrained-syntax GP, often exploiting domain-related semantics (Bhattacharyya et al., 1998; Ngan et al., 1998). A simpler approach is to booleanize all attribute values and use only logical (AND, OR, etc.) functions in the internal nodes (Hu, 1998; Eggermont et al., 1999; Bojarczuk et al., 1999).

THE MOTIVATION FOR USING EVOLUTIONARY ALGORITHMS IN RULE DISCOVERY

One of the major contributions of evolutionary algorithms for rule discovery is that they tend to cope well with attribute interactions, as a consequence of their global search. This is in contrast to the local, greedy search performed by often-used rule induction and decision-tree algorithms.

Most rule induction algorithms generate (prune) a rule by selecting (removing) one-rule-condition-at-a-time. The problem with this approach is illustrated in Figure 4. The figure contains data instances having either positive (+) or negative (−) class, depending on the value of two boolean attributes A_1 and A_2. The goal is to find rule conditions that discriminate between instances with positive and negative classes. The rule condition $A_1 = $ "*false*" (covering instances at the left of the vertical dashed line) is not useful, since it covers as many positive-class examples

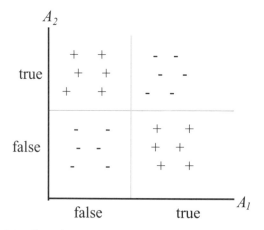

Figure 4 Attribute interaction in classification

as negative-class examples. The same holds for its dual condition $A_1 = $ "*true*." The rule condition $A_2 = $ "*false*" (covering instances below the horizontal broken line), as well as its dual $A_2 = $ "*true*," are not useful either, for the same reason. Hence, an algorithm that selects one rule condition at a time would consider A_1 and A_2 irrelevant attributes and choose another attribute to form a rule condition. However, an algorithm that selects two or more conditions at a time could easily form a rule such as:

IF $(A_1 = $ "*false*") AND $(A_2 = $ "*true*") THEN (*positive – class*).

Evolutionary algorithms usually evaluate a rule as a whole via the fitness function, rather than evaluating the impact of adding/removing one condition to/from a rule. In addition, crossover usually swaps several-rule-conditions-at-a-time between two individuals. Therefore, evolutionary algorithms tend to cope well with attribute interaction.

This is not to say that evolutionary algorithms are inherently superior to rule induction algorithms. No rule discovery algorithm is superior in all cases (Domingos, 1998; Michie et al., 1994).

2.2. Use of Evolutionary Algorithms in Attribute Selection

Evolutionary algorithms have been quite successful in attribute selection (see Chapter 14.2; see also Bala et al., 1995a,b; Vafaie and De Jong, 1993; Guerra-Salcedo and Whitley, 1998, 1999; Martin-Batista and Vila, 1999; Hsu et al., 1999). The reason is that the core problem of attribute selection is to cope with attribute interaction, since the original attributes can be redundant and correlated in a highly nonlinear manner. This seems to be the kind of problem in which the global search performed by evolutionary algorithms tends to present better results than a local search-based approach selecting one attribute at a time.

Most evolutionary attribute selection methods are based on a simple GA, where an individual directly represents a candidate attribute subset. In essence, an individual is a binary string with m genes, where m is the number of attributes. Each gene can take on the value 1 or 0, indicating whether or not the corresponding attribute is selected. For instance, the individual 0 1 1 0 1 0 0 0 represents a candidate solution where the second, third, and fifth attributes are selected.

A more elaborate individual encoding has been proposed by Cherkauer and Shavlik (1996). In their approach, each gene of an individual contains either an attribute name or no attribute, denoted by 0. All the attributes occurring in any of the genes of an individual are the attributes selected by the individual. For instance, the individual 0 0 A_7 A_7 A_2 0 A_7 A_5 0 0 represents a candidate solution where the attributes A_7, A_2, and A_5 are selected. This unconventional individual encoding has some advantages, such as, for example, the fact that occurrences of very relevant attributes may be replicated across the genome.

Regardless of the internal details of individual encoding, the attribute subset selected by an individual is given to a KDD algorithm. The fitness of that individual depends on the result (e.g., predictive accuracy) achieved by that algorithm using only those selected attributes. Hence, the GA acts as a wrapper around the KDD algorithm.

2.3. Optimization of Parameters for Other KDD Algorithms

Genetic algorithms (GA) have also been successfully used as a wrapper to optimize parameters of several other kinds of KDD algorithms. Some examples are as follows.

Kelly and Davis (1991) and Punch et al. (1993) used a GA to optimize the attribute weights of a k-nearest neighbor classifier (see Chapter 16.1.6). Each individual consists of m real-valued weights, where m is the number of attributes. The fitness of an individual is measured by the predictive accuracy of a k-nearest neighbor classifier, by using the attribute weights contained in the individual. Raymer et al. (1996) extended this approach by using a genetic programming system to construct new attributes.

Turney (1995) proposed a hybrid GA/decision tree system (see Chapter 16.1.3) where each individual of the GA consists essentially of attribute costs to be given as input to a cost-sensitive decision tree algorithm. The fitness of an individual is measured by the misclassification cost of the decision tree generated by the cost-sensitive decision-tree algorithm.

Janikow (1995) proposed a GA to optimize the fuzzy sets (see Chapter 10) used to build a decision tree. The decision-tree algorithm is given fuzzy attributes taking on linguistic values such as low, medium, or high, each of which is a fuzzy set with an associated membership function. The GA optimizes the shape of the membership function of each fuzzy set.

3. Research Problems in Evolutionary Algorithms Relevant for KDD

3.1. Discovering Comprehensible Rules with Genetic Programming (GP)

The usually large size and complexity of GP trees makes it difficult to understand them. A partial solution for this problem is to include a penalty term in the fitness function that penalizes complex (syntactically long) rules (Bojarczuk et al., 2000).

More elaborate approaches for improving discovered-rule comprehensibility include the use of hybrid GP/decision trees systems. For instance, Ryan and Rayward-Smith (1998) proposed a hybrid system where a decision-tree algorithm is called not only to generate each individual of the initial population but also to modify individual trees during the GP run. The fitness function favors the discovery of small, accurate trees.

Marmelstein and Lamont (1998) proposed a system to construct a decision tree using GP to implement the decision nodes. Each node of the decision tree evolves a GP to separate the data into two classes. Hence, each GP node in the decision tree is relatively small (due to the divide-and-conquer approach of decision trees) and can be separately analyzed.

3.2. Discovering Surprising Rules

Overall, evolutionary algorithms seem to have a good potential to discover truly surprising rules, due to their ability to cope well with attribute interaction. The rationale for this argument is as follows.

Most users have a reasonably good idea of the relationship between a single predicting attribute and the goal (class) attribute. For instance, in credit datasets the higher the salary of an employee the better his or her credit.

What users do not usually know is the more complex relationship between several-attributes-at-a-time and the goal attribute. For instance, credit quality depends on the interaction between salary, number of dependents, mortgage debt, et cetera.

Recently, there has been a growing interest in rule surprisingness measures in rule induction literature (Liu et al., 1997; Suzuki and Kodratoff, 1998; Padmanabhan and Tuzhilin, 1998; Freitas, 1998a, 1999b). An interesting research direction is to adapt these measures or design new ones to evaluate the rules produced by evolutionary algorithms (Noda et al., 1999).

3.3. Scaling Up Evolutionary Algorithms with Parallel Processing

In the context of mining very large databases, the vast majority of the processing time of an evolutionary algorithm is spent on evaluating an individual's fitness. This processing time can be significantly reduced by using parallel processing techniques (Freitas and Lavington, 1998; Anglano et al., 1997; Neri and Giordana, 1995; Araujo et al., 1999; Flockhart and Radcliffe, 1995; Braud and Vrain, 1999; Freitas, 1998b).

There are two broad ways of parallelizing the computation of the fitness of individuals. The first approach is a kind of inter-individual parallelization, distributing the population individuals across the available processors and computing their fitness in parallel. At a given time different processors compute the fitness of different individuals, but each individual's fitness is computed by a single processor. It is common to replicate all the data being mined in all the processors, so that the fitness of an individual can be computed without accessing data in other processors. However, this strategy reduces scalability for large databases.

The second approach is a kind of intra-individual parallelization, where the fitness of each individual is computed in parallel by all processors. This is a data-parallel approach, where the data being mined is partitioned across the processors. At a given time, each processor is using its local data to compute a partial quality measure for the individual. These partial measures are then combined to compute the individual's fitness. Note that these two parallelization approaches can be combined into a hybrid approach.

4. Added Value of KDD for Evolutionary Algorithms

KDD offers several research opportunities for new methodological developments in evolutionary algorithms. We briefly draw attention here to two possibilities.

First, KDD has an extremely interdisciplinary nature, and it uses many different paradigms of knowledge-discovery algorithms. This motivates the integration of evolutionary algorithms with other knowledge discovery paradigms, as discussed in Section 2.3. There has also been research on the integration between genetic programming and database systems (Martin et al., 1998; Freitas, 1997; Ryu and Eick, 1996).

Second, several KDD tasks involve some kind of prediction, where generalization performance on a separate test set is much more important than the performance on a training set. This is a basic principle for evaluating the quality of a solution in several KDD tasks, and it should be followed in other kinds of problems where evolutionary algorithms are being applied.

Consider, for instance, the problem of simulating the navigation behavior of an ant aiming at collecting all the food lying along an irregular trail. Having implemented a GP system to solve this problem in a particular trail, Koza (1992) states (p. 150): "As we will see this one fitness case is sufficiently representative for this particular problem to allow the ant to learn to navigate this trail and reasonable generalizations of this trail." However, Kuscu (1998) has shown that training the GP on a single trail does not lead to a good performance in other similar trails. Kuscu has also shown that it is possible to achieve a good generalization performance on test trails by using more training trails.

References

Anglano, C., A. Giordana, G. Lo Bello, and L. Saitta. 1997. "A network genetic algorithm for concept learning." In *Proceedings of the Seventh International Conference on Genetic Algorithms (ICGA-97)*, edited by T. Back, pp. 434–441. San Mateo, CA: Morgan Kaufmann.

Araujo, D. L. A., H. S. Lopes, and A. A. Freitas. 1999. "A parallel genetic algorithm for rule discovery in large databases." In *Proceedings of the 1999 IEEE Systems, Man and Cybernetics Conference*. Piscataway, NJ: IEEE.

Bala, J., K. De Jong, J. Huang, H. Vafaie, and H. Wechsler. 1995a. "Using learning to facilitate the evolution of features for recognizing visual concepts." *Evolut. Comput.* **30**: 441–451.

Bala, J., J. Huang, H. Vafaie, K. De Jong, and H. Wechsler. 1995b. "Hybrid learning using genetic algorithms and decision trees for pattern classification." In *Proceedings of the Fourteenth International Joint Conference on Artificial Intelligence (IJCAI-95)*, edited by C. S. Mellish, pp. 719–724. San Mateo, CA: Morgan Kaufmann.

Banzhaf, W., P. Nordin, R. E. Keller, and F. D. Francone. 1998. *Genetic Programming—An Introduction: On the Automatic Evolution of Computer Programs and Its Applications*. San Mateo, CA: Morgan Kaufmann.

Bhattacharyya, S., G. Zumbach, and P. Olivier. 1998. "Representational semantics for genetic programming based learning in high-frequency financial data." In *Genetic Programming 1998: Proceedings of the Third Annual Conference*, edited by J. R. Koza, W. Banzhaf, K. Chellapilla, K. Deb, M. Dorigo, D. B. Fogel, M. H. Garzon, D. E. Goldberg, H. Iba, and R. L. Riolo, pp. 11–16. San Mateo, CA: Morgan Kaufmann.

Bojarczuk, C. C., H. S. Lopes, and A. A. Freitas. 1999. "Discovering comprehensible classification rules using genetic programming: a case study in a medical domain." In *Proceedings of the 1999 Genetic and Evolutionary Computation Conf. (GECCO-99)*. Orlando, FL. July 1999. San Mateo, CA: Morgan Kaufmann.

Bojarczuk, C. C., H. S. Lopes, and A. A. Freitas. 2000. "Genetic programming for knowledge discovery in chest pain diagnosis." *IEEE Engng Med. Biol. Magazine* **19(4)**: 38–44.

Braud, A. and C. Vrain. 1999. "Parallelisation d'Algorithmes Genetiques fondee sur le modele BSP" (in French). *Rapport de Recherche No. 99-06*. France: Universite d'Orleans, LIFO.

Cherkauer, K. J. and J. W. Shavlik. 1996. "Growing simpler decision trees to facilitate knowledge discovery." In *Proceedings of the Second International Conference on Knowledge Discovery and Data*

Mining (KDD-96), edited by E. Simoudis, J. Han, and U. Fayyad, pp. 315–318. Menlo Park, CA: AAAI.

De Jong, K. A., W. M. Spears, and D. F. Gordon. 1993. "Using genetic algorithms for concept learning." *Machine Learning* 13: 161–188.

Domingos, P. 1998. "Occam's two razors: the sharp and the blunt." In *Proceedings of the Fourth International Conference on Knowledge Discovery and Data Mining (KDD-98)*, edited by R. Agrawal, P. Stolorz, and G. Piatetsky-Shapiro, pp. 37–43. Menlo Park, CA: AAAI.

Eggermont, J., A. E. Eiben, and J. I. vanHemert. August 1999. "A comparison of genetic programming variants for data classification." In *Proceedings of the Third International Symposium on Intelligent Data Analysis (IDA-99)*. Berlin: Springer-Verlag.

Flockhart, I. W. and N. J. Radcliffe. 1995. "GA-MINER: parallel data mining with hierarchical genetic algorithms—final report." *EPCC-AIKMS-GA-MINER-Report 1.0*. UK: University of Edinburgh.

Freitas, A. A. 1997. "A genetic programming framework for two data mining tasks: classification and generalized rule induction." In *Genetic Programming 1997: Proceedings of the Second Annual Conference*, edited by J. R. Koza, K. Deb, M. Dorigo, D. B. Fogel, M. Garzon, H. Iba, and R. L. Riolo, pp. 96–101. San Mateo, CA: Morgan Kaufmann.

Freitas, A. A. 1998a. "On objective measures of rule surprisingness." In *Principles of Data Mining and Knowledge Discovery (Proceedings of the Second European Symposium, PKDD-98)*, edited by J. M. Żytkow and M. Quafafou. Lecture Notes in Artificial Intelligence 1510, pp. 1–9. Berlin: Springer-Verlag.

Freitas, A. A. 1998b. "A survey of parallel data mining." In *Proceedings of the Second International Conference on Practical Applications of Knowledge Discovery and Data Mining (PADD-98)*, edited by H. F. Arner and N. Mackin, pp. 287–300. London: The Practical Application Company.

Freitas, A. A. 1999a. "A genetic algorithm for generalized rule induction." In *Advances in Soft Computing— Engineering Design and Manufacturing (Proceedings of the WSC3, Third On-line World Conference, hosted on the Internet, 1998)*, edited by R. Roy, T. Furuhashi, and P. K. Chawdhry, pp. 340–353. Berlin: Springer–Verlag.

Freitas, A. A. 1999b. "On rule interestingness measures." *Knowledge-based Sys. J* **12(5–6)**: 309–315.

Freitas, A. A. and S. H. Lavington. 1998. *Mining Very Large Databases with Parallel Processing*. Boston, MA: Kluwer.

Giordana, A. and F. Neri. 1995. "Search-intensive concept induction." *Evolut. Comput.* **3(4)**: 375–416.

Goldberg, D. E. 1989. *Genetic Algorithms in Search, Optimization and Machine Learning*. Reading, MA: Addison-Wesley.

Greene, D. P. and S. F. Smith. 1993. "Competition-based induction of decision models from examples." *Machine Learning* 13: 229–257.

Guerra-Salcedo, C. and D. Whitley. 1998. "Genetic search for feature subset selection: a comparison between CHC and GENESIS." In *Genetic Programming 1998: Proceedings of the Third Annual Conference*, edited by J. R. Koza, W. Banzhaf, K. Chellapilla, K. Deb, M. Dorigo, D. B. Fogel, M. H. Garzon, D. E. Goldberg, H. Iba, and R. L. Riolo, pp. 504–509. San Mateo, CA: Morgan Kaufmann.

Guerra-Salcedo, C. and D. Whitley. 1999. "Feature selection mechanisms for ensemble creation: a genetic search perspective." In *Proceedings of the AAAI-99 and GECCO-99 Workshop on Data Mining with Evolutionary Algorithms: Research Directions*, edited by A. A. Freitas. Menlo Park, CA: AAAI.

Hsu, W. H., W. M. Pottenger, M. Welge, J. Wu, and T.-H. Yand. 1999. "Genetic algorithms for selection and partitioning of attributes in large-scale data mining problems." In *Proceedings of the AAAI-99 and GECCO-99 Workshop on Data Mining with Evolutionary Algorithms: Research Directions*, edited by Freitas. Menlo Park, CA: AAAI.

Hu, Y.-J. 1998. "A genetic programming approach to constructive induction." *Genetic Programming 1998: Proceedings of the Third Annual Conference*, edited by J. R. Koza, W. Banzhaf, K. Chellapilla, K. Deb, M. Dorigo, D. B. Fogel, M. H. Garzon, D. E. Goldberg, H. Iba, and R. L. Riolo, pp. 146–151. San Mateo, CA: Morgan Kaufmann.

Janikow, C. Z. 1993. "A knowledge-intensive genetic algorithm for supervised learning." *Machine Learning* 13: 189–228.

Janikow, C. Z. 1995. "A genetic algorithm for optimizing fuzzy decision trees." In *Proceedings of the Sixth International Conference on Genetic Algorithms (ICGA-95)*, edited by L. J. Eshelman, pp. 421–428. San Mateo, CA: Morgan Kaufmann.

Kelly, J. D. and L. Davies. 1991. "A hybrid genetic algorithm for classification." In *Proceedings of the Twelfth International Joint Conference on Artificial Intelligence (IJCAI-91)*, pp. 645–650. San Mateo, CA: Morgan Kaufmann.

Koza, J. R. 1992. *Genetic Programming: on the Programming of Computers by Means of Natural Selection*. Cambridge, MA: MIT.

Koza, J. R. 1994. *Genetic Programming II: Automatic Discovery of Reusable Programs.* Cambridge, MA: MIT.

Koza, J. R., F. H. Bennett III, D. Andre, and M. A. Keane. 1999. *Genetic Programming III: Darwinian Invention and Problem Solving.* San Mateo, CA: Morgan Kaufmann.

Kuscu, I. 1998. "Evolving a generalized behaviour: artificial ant problem revisited." In *Proceedings of the Seventh Annual Conference on Evolutionary Programming,* edited by V. W. Porto, N. Saravanan, D. Waagen, and A. E. Eiben. Lecture Notes in Computer Science 1447. Berlin: Springer-Verlag.

Liu, B., W. Hsu, and S. Chen. 1997. "Using general impressions to analyze discovered classification rules." In *Proceedings of the Third International Conference on Knowledge Discovery and Data Mining (KDD-97),* edited by D. Heckerman, H. Mannila, D. Pregibon, and R. Uthurusamy, pp. 31–36. Menlo Park, CA: AAAI.

Marmelstein, R. E. and G. B. Lamont. 1998. "Pattern classification using a hybrid genetic programming—decision tree approach." In *Genetic Programming 1998: Proceedings of the Third Annual Conference,* edited by J. R. Koza, W. Banzhaf, K. Chellapilla, K. Deb, M. Dorigo, D. B. Fogel, M. H. Garzon, D. E. Goldberg, H. Iba, and R. L. Riolo, pp. 223–231. San Mateo, CA: Morgan Kaufmann.

Martin, L., F. Moal, and C. Vrain. 1998. "A relational data mining tool based on genetic programming." In *Principles of Data Mining and Knowledge Discovery: Proceedings of the Second European Symposium (PKDD-98),* edited by J. M. Żytkow and M. Quafafou. Lecture Notes in Artificial Intelligence 1510, pp. 130–138. Berlin: Springer-Verlag.

Martin-Batista, M. J. and M. A. Vila. July 1999. "A survey of genetic feature selection in mining issues." In *Proceedings of the Congress on Evolutionary Computation (CEC-99).* Piscataway, NJ: IEEE.

Michalewicz, Z. 1996. *Genetic Algorithms + Data Structures = Evolution Programs.* 3d ed. Berlin: Springer-Verlag.

Michie, D., D. J. Spiegelhalter, and C. C. Taylor. 1994. *Machine Learning, Neural and Statistical Classification.* New York: Ellis Horwood.

Neri, F. and A. Giordana. 1995. "A parallel genetic algorithm for concept learning." In *Proceedings of the Sixth International Conference on Genetic Algorithms (ICGA-95),* edited by L. E. Eshelman, pp. 436–443. San Mateo, CA: Morgan Kaufmann.

Ngan, P. S., K. S. Leung, M. L. Wong, and J. C. Y. Cheng. 1998. "Using grammar based genetic programming for data mining of medical knowledge." In *Genetic Programming 1998: Proceedings of the Third Annual Conference,* edited by J. R. Koza, W. Banzhaf, K. Chellapilla, K. Deb, M. Dorigo, D. B. Fogel, M. H. Garzon, D. E. Goldberg, H. Iba, and R. L. Riolo, pp. 254–259. San Mateo, CA: Morgan Kaufmann.

Noda, E., A. A. Freitas, and H. S. Lopes. July 1999. "Discovering interesting prediction rules with a genetic algorithm." In *Proceedings of the Congress on Evolutionary Computation (CEC-99).* Piscataway, NJ: IEEE.

Padmanabhan, B. and A. Tuzhilin. 1998. "A belief-driven method for discovering unexpected patterns." In *Proceedings of the Fourth International Conference on Knowledge Discovery and Data Mining (KDD-98),* edited by R. Agrawal, P. Stolorz, and G. Piatetsky-Shapiro, pp. 94–100. Menlo Park, CA: AAAI.

Pei, M., E. D. Goodman, and W. F. Punch. 1997. "Pattern discovery from data using genetic algorithms." In *Proceedings of the First Pacific-Asia Conference on Knowledge Discovery and Data Mining (PAKDD-97).* World Scientific.

Punch, W. F., E. D. Goodman, M. Pei, L. Chia-Sun, P. Hovland, and R. Enbody. 1993. "Further research on feature selection and classification using genetic algorithms." In *Proceedings of the Fifth International Conference on Genetic Algorithms (ICGA-93),* edited by L. E. Eshelman, pp. 557–564. San Mateo, CA: Morgan Kaufmann.

Raymer, M. L., W. F. Punch, E. D. Goodman, and L. A. Kuhn. 1996. "Genetic programming for improved data mining—application to the biochemistry of protein interactions." In *Genetic Programming 1996: Proceedings of the First Annual Conference,* edited by J. R. Koza, D. E. Goldberg, D. B. Fogel, and R. L. Riolo, pp. 375–380. Cambridge, MA: MIT.

Ryan, M. D. and V. J. Rayward-Smith. 1998. "The evolution of decision trees." In *Genetic Programming 1998: Proceedings of the Third Annual Conference,* edited by J. R. Koza, W. Banzhaf, K. Chellapilla, K. Deb, M. Dorigo, D. B. Fogel, M. H. Garzon, D. E. Goldberg, H. Iba, and R. L. Riolo, pp. 350–358. San Mateo, CA: Morgan Kaufmann.

Ryu, T.-W. and C. F. Eick. 1996. "Deriving queries from results using genetic programming." In *Proceedings of the Second International Conference on Knowledge Discovery and Data Mining (KDD-96),* edited by E. Simoudis, J. Han, and U. Fayyad, pp. 303–306. Menlo Park, CA: AAAI.

Suzuki, E. and Y. Kodratoff. 1998. "Discovery of surprising exception rules based on intensity of implication." In *Principles of Data Mining and Knowledge Discovery (Proceedings of the Second European Symposium, PKDD-98),* edited by J. M. Żytkow and M. Quafafou. Lecture Notes in Artificial Intelligence 1510, 10–18. Berlin: Springer-Verlag.

Turney, P. D. 1995. "Cost-sensitive classification: empirical evaluation of a hybrid genetic decision tree induction algorithm." *J. Artificial Intell. Res.* **2**: 369–409.

Vafaie, H. and K. De Jong. 1993. "Robust feature selection algorithms." In *Proceedings of the 1993 IEEE International Conference on Tools with Artificial Intelligence*, pp. 356–363. Piscataway, NJ: IEEE.

Further Reading

Banzhaf, W., P. Nordin, R. E. Keller, and F. D. Francone. 1998. *Genetic Programming—An Introduction: On the Automatic Evolution of Computer Programs and Its Applications.* San Mateo, CA: Morgan Kaufmann. A comprehensible book on genetic programming, discussing both fundamentals and advanced topics in the area.

CEC-99. 1999. *Proceedings of the 1999 Congress on Evolutionary Computation (CEC-99),* Washington, D.C. July 1999. These proceedings include recent research papers presented at a special session on data mining with evolutionary algorithms, chaired by Jan Żytkow.

Dhar, V. and R. Stein. 1997. *Seven Methods for Transforming Corporate Data into Business Intelligence.* Upper Saddle River, NJ: Prentice Hall. A pedagogical book discussing several data mining methods. One of the discussed methods is genetic algorithms.

Freitas, A. A., ed. 1999. *Proceedings of the AAAI-99 and GECCO-99 Workshop on Data Mining with Evolutionary Algorithms: Research Directions,* Orlando, FL. July 1999. Menlo Park, CA: AAAI. A collection of recent research papers on data mining with evolutionary algorithms.

Goldberg, D. E. 1989. *Genetic Algorithms in Search, Optimization and Machine Learning.* Reading, MA: Addison-Wesley. Although some parts of this book are out of date (it was written in 1989), it is a very pedagogical book and it is still highly recommended reading.

Koza, J. R. 1992. *Genetic Programming: On the Programming of Computers by Means of Natural Selection.* Cambridge, MA: MIT Press. The pioneering book on genetic programming, showing how to apply genetic programming to a wide range of problems. Recommended reading, as well as the second and third volumes, mentioned in the reference list—Koza (1994) and Koza et al. (1999).

Koza, J. R., W. Banzhaf, K. Chellapilla, K. Deb, M. Dorigo, D. B Fogel, M. H. Garzon, D. E. Goldberg, H. Iba, and R. L. Riolo, eds. 1998. *Genetic Programming 1998: Proceedings of the Third Annual Conference* San Mateo, CA: Morgan Kaufmann. These proceedings include several research papers on genetic programming for knowledge discovery and data mining.

Michalewicz, Z. 1996. *Genetic Algorithms + Data Structures = Evolution Programs.* 3d ed. Berlin: Springer-Verlag. Good introduction to genetic algorithms in general. It also includes one chapter on genetic algorithms for machine learning and rule discovery.

33 VISUALIZATION

Graham J. Wills

ABSTRACT   This chapter describes visualization methods. It describes their relationship both to scientific visualization and to statistical graphics. The use of visualization for knowledge discovery in databases (KDD) is described with attention to large databases, textual analysis, networks, time-based data, highly multivariate data, and usage by domain experts. Visualization methods are proposed as an aid both in pre- and postmodeling.

1. Use of Visualization Methods for KDD

1.1. Visualization Approaches

The term *visualization methods* refers to a collection of tools and techniques from several disciplines. These methods take a collection of data and produce a visual display that gives insight into the structure of the data. Although the term can be used for static or paper displays, it is generally used to refer to visual displays of data shown on a computer screen. Typically, the user can interact with a visualization, zooming in and out to different parts of the representation, rotating three-dimensional views, indicating parts of the views, displaying detailed information on views and view elements, changing view parameters, and modifying the display.

One branch of visualization methods is derived from statistical graphics and is described in detail in Chapter 15.1. These tools concentrate on showing summary properties of the data and exploring relationships between variables. Exploring census data is one example of the sort of task these techniques are most suitable for. Although most early work in the field concentrated on continuous variables, categorical data is now receiving an increased share of attention. Within this discipline, visualization methods are often termed dynamic graphics, interactive graphics, or a combination of both terms. The former term is often used for views that continuously modify their appearance in a semiautomatic way. Rotating plots, displays of maps that evolve over time, and grand tour plots are examples of these type of views. The second term is used more for views that allow a high degree of interaction with a user. They respond rapidly to a user indicating a feature of interest, requesting details on view elements and marking sets of data as potentially interesting. Scatterplot brushing is an early example of these types of plot, as are many views in DataDesk (Velleman, 1988).

A second branch of visualization methods is motivated by computer scientists searching for ways of investigating large databases and displaying the results of queries. Typically, these methods are highly interactive and focus more on conveying lots of information rather than on exploring relationships. Another goal of these methods is to help the database user formulate a query. Eick et al. (1994) give an example of this kind of visualization. Database queries can be complex, and often the results of a query give either too few results or too many. Visualization techniques can ameliorate this problem by allowing users to display many returned items at once and explore them in order to see how to refine their queries. For these types of problems, the phrases *dynamic queries* or *information visualization* are often used.

Scientific visualization forms a third branch, which is often referred to in its own literature simply as visualization. Here, the task is to analyze a body of data that has some geographic or other spatial location. Classic examples of such problems are displaying results of medical scans and analyzing solutions to fluid flow problems. Usually, there is a large data set to be analyzed, and the primary goal is to present this large data set in a display that uses the physical location as the most important characteristic, with as much additional data as possible superimposed on this basis. There is some overlap between this goal and the production of interactive geographic maps, but the world of geographic information systems (GISs), in which research is being done on interactive mapping (see Muller, 1993 for an overview, and MacEachren, 1992 for an example of related work), does not in practice have much contact with the scientific visualization community, whose focus is more on displaying three-dimensional data than on flat maps. So far, there has only been limited work within the GIS community on interactive visual techniques, of which Dykes (1998) is the best recent example.

A fourth branch concerns itself with visualizations that show the structure of data elements, rather than characteristics of those elements. Graph drawing literature (see Di Battista et al., 1994 for a good introduction) is a branch of visualization with a long history, but techniques such as cognitive maps and meta visualizations—visualizations that show the results of analyses or sequences of data mining algorithms—are attracting recent attention.

1.2. Relationship between KDD and Visualization

Both KDD and visualization have the same goal, namely, to take a body of data and extract information or knowledge from it. Both disciplines use computation to manipulate data and analyze it—discovering patterns, pointing out unusual cases, finding relationships and groups, and giving insight into the real-world processes that gave rise to the data. They face many similar challenges, including the following:

- *Large databases.* The need to adapt and develop methods for larger and larger data sets continues to be a key challenge. Methods that are quadratic or worse in the number of cases become a liability when applied to gigabyte-sized databases. Within visualization, methods that attempt to display cases individually on the screen run into the obvious problem with even moderate-sized data sets; there are too few pixels available on the screen. Both disciplines are seeking new methods that can process large data sets.

- *Highly multivariate data.* Another size issue is that of exploring databases with many variables. Techniques that work well for five variables can fail dramatically when faced with a hundred variables. A problem common to both disciplines is deciding which variables influence each other and which can be regarded as extraneous to an analysis.

- *Heterogeneous data.* Examining a single table of data is a relatively straightforward affair. When we have multiple tables of related data, or when we have data in unusual formats, such as text documents, network connections, or spatially referenced data, then current approaches often prove inadequate.

- *Accessibility for domain experts.* When used in real-world situations, it is vital that any analytic technique be made accessible to people who have little formal training in visualization, data mining, computer science, or statistics, yet who have a great deal of knowledge about the data set being studied. Techniques that domain experts can understand and control are very important.

- *Integration.* As young disciplines, both KDD and visualization started by producing stand-alone tools that experts could use for that purpose only. As these disciplines mature, one challenge is to create tools and methods that can be used with other necessary features in an integrated environment. Database access, Web delivery systems, report generation, systems for combining multiple tools and methods—these are a sample of the challenges facing both disciplines today.

Although similar in goals and challenges, there is clearly a major difference in the approach the two disciplines take. To make a broad generalization, KDD methods attempt to analyze the data as automatically as possible, minimizing human interaction, whereas visualization methods attempt to maximize human interaction so that people's innate analytic ability can be brought to bear on problems. An ideal KDD computer program would, after reading the data, ask a few simple questions of the user and then present the user with a complete answer to their query. An ideal visualization computer program would, after reading the data, present a set of views that the user could interact with and in which they could immediately see valuable information.

The difference is illustrative of how the two disciplines can be used to aid each other. Visualization is a powerful technique for aiding users in understanding the data and suggesting relationships. It is weak at predictive and quantitative tasks. It does not build formal models of the data, but instead suggests models and aids the analyst in deciding what to model. Knowledge discovery techniques tend toward the opposite approach; they are powerful for generating quantitative models and for predictive purposes, but provide little guidance in deciding on the modeling method itself.

The example in Chapter 15.1 illustrated how KDD and visualization methods can be used to complement each other. The analyst had a goal in mind at the start; modeling the dependence of baseball players' salaries on their performances. After building a neural net model, visualization was used to explore the errors in the predictions, and one extremely poor prediction was found to be inexplicable given the available data. This validated the results of the formal analysis and suggested that more data were necessary to explain the wide discrepancy between this one player's predicted and actual salary. The example suggests the following as a basis for interdisciplinary ties between KDD and visualization.

1.3. Visualization as a Pre- and Postmodeling Tool for KDD

With this motivation, we suggest that visualization should be used both before and after building a formal model. In this paradigm, analysts would first look at data using visual tools to explore the data. They can look for data errors and possible data transformations as well as informally checking that domain knowledge about the data is correct; they would be surprised to see salary decreasing as batting prowess increased in a display, for example. Then, analysts would build a qualitative model in which they hypothesize about plausible relationships. This qualitative model would suggest which formal KDD techniques might be most applicable and the analysis would move to the next stage, fitting a formal model.

After a suitable model has been chosen, analysts can use visualization tools to explore the fit of the model. It might be that this examination of the model would reveal deficiencies in the model that require a new model to be built, or it may indicate that certain subsets of the data are unsuitable for this model and should be treated separately. Several iterations between modeling and exploration of the results of the model may be required. At the end of this phase, visual tools can then be used to present the results and to explain what they mean in terms that domain experts can understand. Again, a domain expert might be able to offer suggestions that would improve the model.

This paradigm has a long history in statistical literature. When performing a linear regression analysis, the student is invariably told to look at the data graphically before the analysis to ensure that the model can be applied, and also to examine the results of the analysis afterward in case remedial action is required. Neter et al. (1985) write: "When a regression model...is selected for an application, one can usually not be certain in advance that the model is appropriate for that application.... Hence it is important to examine the aptness of the model for the data before further analysis on that model is undertaken" (p. 109). The rest of their chapter is devoted to describing graphical methods for this task. They suggest drawing a scatterplot of residuals against independent variables to check for a variety of problems with the model. They also suggest that "residuals should be plotted against variables omitted from the model.... The purpose of this additional analysis is to determine whether there are any other key independent variables that could provide important additional descriptive and predictive power to the model" (ibid., p. 120). Unfortunately, while they discuss postanalysis visualization to some length, they underplay preanalysis visualization. Especially for large data sets and computationally intensive algorithms, modeling and then exploring residuals is an expensive technique for uncovering data problems. Even simple visual exploration will highlight common data quality problems by highlighting unusual values, showing rounding or truncation problems, indicating poor choices of coding missing data values and impossible combinations of variables that might cause an otherwise good model to behave badly.

What is true for statistical models holds equally true for data mining models, if not more so, due to the lesser number of diagnostic statistics that are available for the analyst to use. In Sections 2 and 3 below, the interactions between the disciplines are explored with the thought in mind that visualization and modeling of a domain should proceed hand in hand.

2. Research Problems in Visualization Relevant to KDD

2.1. *Visualization of Large Data Sets*

As discussed in Section 1.2, exploring data sets with large numbers of cases or large numbers of variables is an important area of research. One approach that has proved fruitful is to pre-process a large database and create a smaller one (by aggregation) that captures a large proportion of the information inherent in the original. One such method is to discretize numerical variables into a few ranges and create a large multiway table of counts. For example, if we wished to examine a database of everyone in the United States, with information recorded on age (A), sex (S), education (E), and income (I), we could discretize age into decade ranges and income into a few ranges. Sex and education are usually recorded as categorical variables, so we can store this information as a table of $A \times S \times E \times I$. With five recorded levels of education and six income ranges, we would have a table of size $10 \times 2 \times 5 \times 6 = 600$—a small-sized table. Clearly, this approach only works well for few variables, since with even 20 variables taking on 3 values each, we have over 3 billion cells in the table. It is likely that this table will be sparse, and clever allocation methods can be used so that empty cells take up no space, but even so, this method is restricted in the number of variables that can be used.

Mihalisin et al. (1991) has used a modification of this method in which statistical information is stored on predefined response variables for each cell in a multiway table of independent variables. To visualize this table, the user defines a grid, where each grid cell corresponds to a combination of independent variables' values. Figure 1 is an example of such a layout for the sample data discussed above. To construct the grid, assign each independent variable to an axis. When more than one variable maps to an axis, vary one of the variables within each category of the other. In Figure 1, the education level is varied within each sex category. Within this table, cell **X** should produce a representation of the response variable (income) when age is in the third level for females who dropped out of college. Similarly, table cell **Y** should represent males who completed a postdoc who are in the sixth age range. The method of representation within a cell can be varied; a small histogram can be displayed, a color to indicate the average income, or a more specialized representation. If this same display was used to present the results of a decision-tree analysis by choosing a cell representation that shows how the model would classify that cell, we might additionally use the cell to display information on the accuracy and support of the corresponding leaf of the tree. Note that this

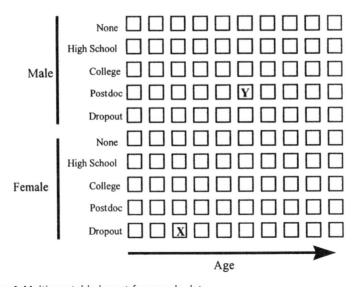

Figure 1 Multiway table layout for sample data

recursive method of defining cell entries to create a grid layout of conditional plot is also used in mosaic plots (Friendly, 1994; Unwin et al., 1996 presents an interactive version) and trellis displays (Becker et al., 1996).

The problem of many variables has been approached using parallel coordinates to display up to a hundred variables simultaneously (Inselberg and Dimsdale, 1990). An example of that method has been introduced briefly in Chapter 15.1. Projection methods where highly multivariate data are projected into two or three dimensions under interactive control have been explored, notably, in Cook et al. (1995). Chapter 15.2 has indicated other approaches to this problem.

Visualization of the results of database queries is another area where the number of variables makes the problem challenging from a research perspective. Shneiderman's dynamic queries (Shneiderman, 1994) give the user intuitive one-dimensional controls to set parameters of a query where each control is linked to the rest so that changing a query on, for example, education, will alter the appearance of the control for age, so that the relationship between these variables can be taken into account when constructing the query.

Techniques for visualization of large data sets are of fundamental importance to KDD. Models built on large data sets are expensive to calculate, so premodeling visualization is vital to ensure that time is not wasted discovering simple data errors. Visualization of the model performance as it iterates to a solution can be useful for a wide variety of algorithms. Again, the goal is to spend compute cycles working on useful models, so understanding how a model is behaving and in what areas it is having trouble allows the analyst to refine techniques more rapidly. In the postmodeling stage, large amounts of input data lead to large amounts of output data, requiring good visual techniques for exploration. Finally, domain experts are not necessarily computer scientists, and visual tools that help domain experts understand large, complex models are valuable.

2.2. Visualization of Textual Data

There are many applications where users want to analyze the relationships between textual documents or within documents. These include applications where users want to search for articles that have a certain set of phrases or are similar to a given document, applications that seek to cluster documents into meaningful groups and applications where insight is sought into the structure of documents. N-gram and similar analysis tools (Suen, 1979; Chapter 16.5) can be used to construct similarities between documents, and Kohonen self-organizing maps have been used to organize documents into "landscapes" that represent the results of document queries (Kohonen, 1995). These landscapes are then typically visualized using a three-dimensional surface rendering that shows the density of documents at each point in the map as a height, with significant peaks being labeled. Such systems are an example of how visualization and data mining techniques complement and enhance each other, with the automatic procedure producing a visual display that can be investigated and explored by a domain expert.

In order to understand structure within text, some systems have been developed for specific areas where the text has certain well-known properties. An example of this is the SeeSoft application (Eick et al., 1992), which represents tens of thousands of lines of source code on one screen, coding it by variables associated with its modification history such as date of change, programmer name, purpose of change, et cetera. The same application has been used to discover relationships between story elements such as key characters in prose. Another challenging growth area in text visualization is the analysis of Web pages, which combine well-defined elements with free-form text and images. Web pages also form a network, which is another active area of visualization research.

2.3. Network Visualization

A large important analysis area consists of graphs with multivariate data on both the nodes and links. Telecommunication networks, computer networks, traffic flows, and migration paths are examples of such information. Although there is a large body of knowledge on displaying small, static networks (Di Battista et al., 1994), relatively little has been done for large, time-evolving networks. Wills (1999) has created a tool for exploring networks with up to a few millions of nodes and links within a linked windows (Chapter 15.1) environment, but this remains a challenging area for both formal modeling and visualization.

For data mining, rule discovery (Chapter 16.2) often leads to large sets of rules. Using a network visualization tool to display these rules as connections between the items they relate allows the analyst to understand the interactions between the rules more easily than a list representation would allow.

Another interesting line of research is in exploring ways of visualizing networks that are produced as part of the modeling process itself. Artificial neural nets are a prime candidate as they are a common tool, yet it is often difficult to form intuition about their internal workings. Modifying existing network visualization tools for this purpose might prove valuable for model building, evaluation, and sensitivity analysis.

2.4. Visualization of Time-Based Data

Time-series data are ubiquitous and important. It is surprising, therefore, that tools for visualizing time series have not progressed further than displaying series as simple traces, with little interactivity or ability to modify representations. Visual detection of autocorrelation within a series, or correlation at some lag between series, can be performed easily by allowing the user to drag one series over another. Human beings have an excellent ability to spot similarities in sections of series this way, and the crude method of printing series onto transparencies and overlaying them on paper versions has been used for many years. It is then surprising that computer techniques for doing this and other similar tasks have yet to become more available.

The analysis of sequences of categorical data is another important area. Visual methods and data mining techniques for exploring sequences can be applied to many problem domains including genetic sequencing (Wu et al., 1993) and visualization of multimedia events (Hibino and Rundensteiner, 1997).

3. Added Value of KDD for Visualization

3.1. Enhancement of Subtle Effects

Within an analysis, some interesting features will be readily apparent in a display. Others are more subtle and might be missed. A common example is a multivariate outlier; a case that does not appear unusual when examined on a variable-by-variable basis, but does look unusual when combinations of variables are taken. A frequent occurrence in census data is the three-year-old with two children. Three-year-old children are not unusual, and people with two children are common, but the combination is indicative of a data error.

By building models that explain the main effects relating variables, KDD algorithms allow more subtle features to stand out clearly. In Chapter 15.1, the neural net drew our attention to a multivariate outlier that had much lower salary than the performance indicated. The rule here is that once the main effects have been noted, a model should be built that accounts for these effects so that the next level of effects can be explored visually.

3.2. Variable Selection and Guided Visualization

With many variables, the user of a visualization system is often overwhelmed. It is hard to decide what to explore and where to start. Ways of helping the user decide which variables to consider initially are needed. One possibility would be to run some naive, fast data mining algorithm for a large number of variables and let the user look at the results to decide which relationships might need exploring in more detail. By looking at the rules in a decision tree, the user would be able to see which variables are most useful for predicting a given categorical variable. This gives an initial starting point from which a visual exploration can be launched. In neural net analyses, this is a common methodology already. The user builds a model using all of the variables and then discards variables until the model deteriorates. A similar process in statistics is termed stepwise regression (Neter et al., 1985, Section 16.4).

A related problem is aiding the user when they have created a view and would like to explore it in more detail. Context-sensitive help such as in DataDesk (Velleman, 1988) is useful, but what is really needed is for some analytic engine to explore possible variations of the plot and point out useful ones to the user. A simple example would be to look at a matrix of scatterplots and suggest which additional variables have strong correlations with the selected ones and so might be added to the display.

3.3. Confirmatory Analysis

One of the strongest and most persistent criticisms of visualization methods is the lack of quantitative results, often phrased along the lines of "I can't make a million-dollar decision based on a pretty picture." Sometimes making decisions based on displays is justified— especially when the display is unambiguous. (For an excellent example, Tufte [1997, p. 45] gives a plot of O-ring damage against temperature that, had it been created, would have shown immediately the danger of the Challenger shuttle launch.) Often that is not the case, and the user is justified in asking whether the pattern he or she sees has any real meaning, or if it is an artifact or product of random effects.

KDD methods can be used to take a qualitative model and give it quantitative meaning. If a series of views indicates a certain model for how the data interact, the user should be able to create such a model and see if there is any justification for it. Sometimes this might involve a fair amount of work if the user wanted to quantify a complex model. But often the questions are more of the order of "I see what appear to be several clusters in this scatterplot. Are they really there?" In such cases, simple algorithms can be run to help determine if that is the case. An ideal system for data mining will allow the user to confirm any visual pattern detected, and to visually explore the results of every model created.

References

Becker, R. A., W. S. Cleveland, and M. J. Shyu. 1996. "The design and control of trellis display." *J. Comput. Stat. Graphics* 5: 123–155.

Cook, D., A. Buja, J. Cabrera, and C. Hurley. 1995. "Grand tour and projection pursuit." *J. Comput. Graphical Stat.* 4: 155–171.

Di Battista, G., P. Eades, R. Tamassia, and I. Tollis. 1994. "Algorithms for drawing graphs: an annotated bibliography." *Comput. Geometry* 4: 235–282.

Dykes, J. A. 1998. "Cartographic visualization: exploratory spatial data analysis with local indicators of spatial association using Tcl/Tk and cdv." *The Statistican* 47: 485–497.

Eick, S., J. Steffen, and E. Sumner. 1992. "Seesoft—a tool for visualizing line oriented software statistics." *IEEE Trans. Softw. Engng.* 18: 957–968.

Eick, S., E. Sumner, and G. Wills. 1994. "Visualizing bibliographic databases." *Database Issues for Data Visualization*, edited by J. P. Lee and G. C. Grinstein, pp. 186–193. New York, NY: Springer-Verlag.

Friendly, M. 1994. "Mosaic displays for n-way contingency tables." *J. Am. Stat. Assoc.* 89: 190–200.

Hibino, S. and E. A. Rundensteiner. 1997. "Interactive visualizations for temporal analysis: application to CSCW multimedia data." *Intelligent Multimedia Information Retrieval*, edited by M. Maybury, pp. 313–335. Boston, MA: MIT Press.

Inselberg, A. and B. Dimsdale. 1990. "Parallel coordinates: a tool for visualizing multidimensional geometry." *Proceedings of the First IEEE Conference on Visualization*, p. 361. Los Alamitos, CA: IEEE Computer Society Press.

Kohonen, T. 1995. *Self-Organizing Maps*. Berlin: Springer.

MacEachren, A. 1992. "Visualizing uncertain information." *Cartographic Perspective* 13: 10–19.

Mihalisin, T., J. Timlim, and J. Schwegler. 1991. "Visualization and analysis of multi-variate data: a technique for all fields." *Proceedings of the 1991 IEEE Visualization Conference*. Los Alamitos, CA: IEEE Computer Society Press, edited by G. M. Nielsen and L. Rosenblum, pp. 171–178.

Muller, J.-C. 1993. "Latest developments in GIS/LIS." *Int. J. Geogr. Inform. Sys.* 7: 293–303.

Neter, J., W. Wasserman, and M. Kutner. 1985. *Applied Linear Statistical Models*. Homewood, IL: Irwin.

Shneiderman, B. 1994. "Dynamic queries for visual information seeking." *IEEE Softw.* 11: 70–77.

Suen, C. Y. 1979. "N-gram statistics for natural language understanding and text processing." *IEEE Trans. Pattern Anal. Machine Intell.* **1**: 164–172.

Tufte, E. 1997. *Visual Explanation*. Cheshire, CO: Graphics Press.

Unwin, A., G. Hawkins, H. Hofmann, and B. Siegel. 1996. "Interactive graphics for data sets with missing values—MANET." *J. Comput. Graphical Stat.* **5**: 113–122.

Velleman, P. F. 1988. *The Datadesk Handbook*. Cornell, NY: Odesta Corporation.

Wills, G. 1999. "Nicheworks—interactive visualization of very large graphs." *J. Comput. Graphical Stat.* **8(2)**: 190–212.

Wu, D., J. Roberge, D. Cork, N. Bao, and T. Grace. 1993. "Computer visualization of long genomic sequences." *IEEE Visualization* **93**: 308–315.

PART SIX

BUSINESS PROBLEMS

34 MARKETING

Lynd D. Bacon

ABSTRACT Data mining applications in marketing should complement marketers' sources of knowledge and provide results that are relevant to the kinds of business problems that marketers want to solve. Marketers have a well-developed knowledge domain that is expressed in the practice of marketing management. They have evolved their own methods for using data that are consonant with important marketing issues. Many of these are not well suited for use on large and complex data sets, so there is great potential for data mining to make useful contributions to the marketing discipline. These consist of providing analyses that are not feasible using traditional methods and of providing direction for traditional, expensive marketing research activities so that the overall research process is more efficient. The important problems for marketers involve maximizing marketing effectiveness. They include increasing sales and profitability, market segmentation, and customer retention management. Marketers will also benefit by having more knowledge extracted from the legacy data sets produced by panel and tracking studies. Data mining procedures can in general be a very useful addition to the set of methods used to manage and analyze marketing information.

1. Introduction

Marketing is a set of social and managerial activities that include the exchange of products of value between individuals and groups. When marketing is accomplished through an organized process called marketing management, it involves planning and executing the conception, pricing, promotion, and distribution of products so that an organization's goals can be met (Bennett, 1995). In most modern corporations and in many other kinds of organizations, marketing management is a formal business function like finance or operations.

The value of data mining activities for marketing management depends on the business value of the results. Marketers, like other managers, are a practical bunch. They are usually not interested in the technology used to produce knowledge *per se*, but in the utility obtained from the knowledge produced (Little, 1979; Little and Cassettari, 1984). They are interested in problems like discovering new marketing opportunities or improving marketing effectiveness. They have their own well-developed vocabulary and knowledge domain, and an existing set of methods and procedures for learning and for making decisions.

Data mining applications in marketing must produce results that address the concerns of marketers and that complement their various ways of obtaining and using information. To do this, data miners need to understand what data marketers use and how they use it. They also need to appreciate the process of marketing, and the business problems that marketers want to solve.

2. Marketing, Information Systems, and Decision Support

The fundamental activities for marketing management are analyzing marketing opportunities, developing strategies, planning marketing programs, and managing the marketing effort (Kotler, 1997). Each of these activities has critical information needs. For example, searching for new opportunities often requires analyzing both internal and external data. These may include data in customer information files, sales transaction data, and data on competitors. As another example, managing a specific marketing program will usually include monitoring program performance by tracking sales or other outcome measures over time, and making comparisons to specific objectives defined in a marketing plan.

As marketing has evolved from just selling to a core set of business activities, marketers have developed a variety of data management, analysis, and reporting procedures to support their decisionmaking. A marketing information system is a technological and organizational solution for gathering and analyzing marketing information (Kotler, 1997). The technical component has been called a marketing decision support system by Little (1979) and others. In its most general form, such a system integrates internal and external data with analysis and reporting methods. The data may include sales transaction data, data from customer surveys, and data obtained from third parties. The creation of many of the first systems was stimulated by the development of technologies that enabled the capture of large amounts of retail transaction data. These technologies included point-of-sale (POS) systems and supermarket scanners, as well as widely available low-cost storage and computing capacity.

The more useful examples of marketing information systems go beyond just reporting on product performance and market conditions. They also provide managers with information about interdependence and possible cause-and-effect relationships, like what factors are contributing to sales in a particular period (McCann and Gallagher, 1990). These relationships are usually described in tables and graphs, and summarized using statistical models or methods from the field of artificial intelligence. The results may be embodied in decision support tools that managers use to do forecasting and scenario analysis. Market information systems have traditionally been designed to deliver model results, rather than to facilitate data exploration and pattern discovery.

Much of the data collected for marketing research—that is, the "planning, collection, and analysis of data relevant to marketing decision making and the communication of the results of this analysis to management" (McDaniel and Gates, 1993, p. G-5)—is not incorporated into a marketing decision support system of the kind described by Little (1979). Many companies do primary field research that produces data on samples of customers or potential customers. These studies have specific objectives and the data that are collected for them are specific to their purpose. They may be conducted to support decisions regarding the design of new products, to estimate demand, to make pricing decisions, to monitor customer satisfaction, to measure attitudes and values, or to test advertising strategies or promotional tactics.

Primary research that directly produces primarily quantitative responses for the purpose of doing statistical analyses is called quantitative research. Examples of quantitative responses include responses on rating scales and reported or observed product purchase frequencies. Common data collection methods for quantitative research include surveys and experiments. Interviews and focus groups are commonly used qualitative research methods. The responses captured in such research are natural language answers to open-ended questions and the content of group discussions. Qualitative efforts are more exploratory than quantitative studies and are usually used to test concepts and to generate ideas. Qualitative research often precedes quantitative studies in an overall process of obtaining specific marketing knowledge. Most primary research studies collect data during only one period of time. Others are designed to estimate changes over time, and data are collected on a periodic basis. These are usually called longitudinal, panel, or tracking studies.

The data for quantitative research are often collected based on sophisticated plans, or sampling designs, that reflect the research objectives and the importance of specific comparisons. A common methodological issue is the extent to which the results of studies can be generalized to markets of interest. The sampling plans for qualitative research usually emphasize heterogeneity at the cost of representativeness.

Marketing researchers store and manipulate primary research data using a variety of technologies. Storage methods range from rectangular ASCII files to data warehouses. Specific research objectives are addressed by using commercially available and proprietary software to do descriptive summaries, perform statistical tests, and to fit and evaluate models. Statistical programs that are used by many marketing researchers include SAS (SAS Institute Inc.) and SPSS (SPSS Inc.)

3. Direct and Database Marketing

The growth of direct marketing (Stone, 1996) has further fueled the use of data by marketers. Direct marketing is an interactive marketing approach using one or more advertising media to affect a measurable response and/or transaction at any location (Stone, 1996). Interactive refers to one-to-one communication between marketer and customer. Since its early days, direct marketing's scope has expanded from considering only how products are distributed, to include enhancing the relationships between an organization and its customers.

Marketers have long recognized the importance of long-term relationships with customers. The pursuit and maintenance of them as a general approach to marketing has been called relationship marketing (McKinna, 1991). Because of the strategic importance of customer relationships, issues like brand loyalty, customer satisfaction, and customer acquisition and retention garner the attention of many marketers. The direct marketing version of a relation-based approach has been called "targeted relationship marketing" (Stone, 1996).

Using a database for contacting customers and executing transactions with them is called "database marketing" (Kotler, 1997; McCorkle, 1997). Database marketers use their data to identify and target customers with offers and to develop customer loyalty. Their databases include information on current customers and on prospective customers, and perhaps on other stakeholders, such as distributors and retailers.

Database marketers often enhance their data with information from organizations that specialize in compiling consumer or business data. Established providers of this kind of information in the United States include companies like R. R. Donnelly, National Demographics & Lifestyles, and R. L. Polk. The added data often include demographic information. It may also include measures of preferred leisure-time activities, or taxonomical indicators for one or more commercially available, proprietary segmentation schemes. Well-known consumer segmentation systems include the VALS lifestyle system from SRI Inc. (Stanford Research Institute), the PRIZM system from Claritas Inc., ACORN from CACI Inc., and CLUSTER PLUS from Donnelly.

A defining characteristic of direct marketing is that marketing efforts, and individual customers' responses to them, can be directly measured. This makes it much easier to evaluate marketing programs' effectiveness and costs than in other areas of marketing. It is also conventional practice for database and direct marketers to do direct evaluations of the performance of the predictive models they develop.

Being able to measure customer responses directly means that customer feedback can be used to revise programs and to continuously craft new offers. This kind of learning process makes it possible to execute custom tactics for each customer, resulting in adaptive one-to-one marketing. The ability to engage in one-to-one marketing is a goal of many marketing organizations, regardless of whether what they do is called direct marketing, or not.

4. Marketing Problems

There are several important problem areas in marketing that data mining can be useful for. These areas are important in the sense that they are at the core of what marketers try to achieve in most settings. They include the following.

4.1. Increasing Sales and Profitability

Most marketing organizations are interested in increasing their products' sales or increasing their market share. (Market share is a measure of how an organization is performing relative to its competitors. Various measures of share are used, the most common being the percentage of total sales in a market that an organization garners.) Ansoff's (1957) classic product/market expansion grid (Table 1) neatly summarizes potential sources of growth in current businesses. Ansoff's product development strategy consists of developing new offers for existing customers. Market development involves finding new markets for existing products.

Table 1 Product/Market Expansion Grid of Business Growth Strategies. Based on Ansoff (1957)

	Current Products	New Products
Current Markets	Market penetration	Product development
New Markets	Market development	Diversification

Penetration consists of increasing the share or sales garnered by existing products in current markets. Diversification is extension into new markets with new products. Data mining methods are most obviously applicable to penetration, followed by product development.

Greater penetration can come about by stimulating current customers to make more purchases, by selling to competitors' customers in the same markets, or by creating new customers. Increased sales can be obtained through cross selling, the activity of selling products to current customers based on other things the customers have bought (Berry and Linoff, 1997; McCorkle, 1997; Stone, 1996). Cross selling programs can be supported by using data mining methods to target customers based on purchase history or other information. Such programs may involve inbound or outbound telemarketing, direct mail (including e-mail), or direct selling.

Under some circumstances it is possible to convert competitors' customers by focusing on the ones that are similar in important respects to existing customers. These potential customers can be targeted based on associations between customers characteristic purchasing, or purchasing-related, behaviors. Doing this requires having data on competitors' customers, of course. Conversion efforts will often be more effective when new strategy or new marketing tactics are used. It is unlikely that customers end up buying products or services from different firms based on chance alone. The reasons that they buy what they do, however, may have to do with differences in their needs and wants, differences in marketing programs that impinge on them, or both. In any case, data mining methods can be used to identify prospective customers so that their responsiveness can be tested, and so that factors affecting their responsiveness can be evaluated.

New customers might be created in a particular market by targeting prospects that are likely to have wants and needs that match the benefits provided by a product. Unlike customers of competing firms, these customers are part of the potential market but are not participating in the market defined in terms of transactions. Therefore, there is likely to be less data available for them, at least at the individual level. As with the case of converting competitors' customers, additional research, new strategy, and new tactics may be required. Data mining can support developing an approach to these new customers, assuming that the available data are adequate.

Growth from product development can be accomplished by exploiting relationships between customer characteristics and the features of substitute and complementary products. (Product substitutes are products that to varying degrees satisfy the same needs or wants of consumers. They compete with each other. Different brands of microcomputers are product substitutes, as are long-distance telephone services. Complements are products that combine to meet needs, and so they have positively correlated demand. Examples are motor oil and oil filters, surgical procedures and suture material.) For example, a pharmaceutical manufacturer might identify and target doctors for a new drug. This targeting might be based on how many prescriptions they write for existing drugs used to treat the same condition that the new drug is for. The new drug is expected to be a substitute for the existing drugs and should therefore compete with them in the market.

As a second example, a new method of administering drugs, like a transdermal patch, might be marketed to patients or physicians as an alternative means of delivering doses of a drug that the manufacturer already produces. The patch and the drug will be product complements. In each example, the opportunity for the new product lies both in use patterns for existing products, and in the expected relationship between the existing products and the new one. The latter depend on the customer needs met by the products. Data mining methods can be used to identify potentially relevant patterns but are not likely to provide much insight into needs-based relationships unless data on customer needs are available. They can also help to reveal customer characteristics or other variables that might moderate the relationship between products used by customers.

Data mining can also be applied to detecting product development opportunities. For example, analysis of purchase co-occurrences can suggest ways of bundling existing products, or their attributes, into new ones. Doing market basket analysis using association rule induction or another kind of algorithm is one way to summarize these co-occurrences. As an example, a provider of financial services might find new product possibilities by searching for particular combinations of services that are purchased across different customer segments. These candidate product bundles can then be researched further to find out whether the segments value the service component differently, a condition that is critical for bundling to work (Nagle and Holden, 1994).

Sales by themselves don't enable firms or other organizations to survive, of course. It is also necessary to have revenues that exceed expenses, or to make a profit, at least in the long run. (Not-for-profit organizations call their profits a budget or operating surplus. It is usually a goal of theirs to avoid continuing operating deficits, just as for-profits strive to be profitable). Assuming prices are constant, total profits can be increased by either selling larger quantities of products, or by making more of a profit on each product sold.

Data mining can be used to help increase profits in several ways. Total profits can be increased if market penetration is increased, assuming of course that profit contributions per sale are positive. Data mining can be used to reduce total expenses through selective targeting of responsive customers. Effective customer targeting reduces overall costs and therefore leads to increased profitability. Data mining methods can be used to detect complex relationships in data sets of satisfaction and loyalty data so as to reveal opportunities to allocate resources more efficiently across product or service attributes. They can also be used to identify unprofitable customers.

4.2. Segmentation

The term *segmentation* has deep meaning in marketing. The concept was first formally introduced to marketing by Wendell Smith (1956), and since then, segmentation has become a core part of marketing strategy and tactics. Segmentation consists of approaching a market that is heterogeneous in terms of customer wants and needs, as a set of smaller, homogeneous markets. The segments are homogeneous in terms of how customers in them respond to particular marketing activities, or on some other basis that is relevant to marketing planning. A particular way of putting customers into segments is called a segmentation scheme, a segmentation solution, or sometimes just a segmentation.

Segmentation is closely related to the activities of segment selection, or targeting, and product positioning (Myers, 1996). Positioning a product means to develop it and its image so that its perceived position among other available products is meaningful, distinct, and competitive. Developing a product positioning usually includes making segments more understandable by profiling them on different variables. This kind of profiling is similar to what data miners call "profiling"; (Edelstein, 1997). Targeting means to focus on a particular segment.

Using a segmentation strategy means that the segments have their own strategies and tactics, and this usually costs more than not segmenting. Whether it is worthwhile to use a segmentation strategy depends on whether the additional revenues obtained outweigh the additional costs (Blattberg and Sen, 1976). The additional revenues, if any, will be obtained from better meeting the wants and needs of customers who differ across the segments. Whether a segmentation strategy will be rewarding financially can be difficult to determine *a priori*.

The data that are used to identify segments measure what marketing researchers call basis variables. Basis variables can be classified as either general or product specific, and either observable or unobservable (Frank et al., 1972; Wedel and Kamakura, 1997). Observable variables include demographic measures, and measures of purchase frequency or product use. Purchase frequency and product use are product specific, whereas measures of customer demographics are general variables. Unobservable variables include values, lifestyle preferences, perceived benefits of products, attitudes toward products, and purchase intentions. The latter three are product specific, while the first two are general. Unobserved variables are variables for which values must be inferred, and generally primary research is required to do this.

Data on observable variables are much more likely to be available for developing segmentation solutions, and for other purposes. Unobservable variables can be important, however, since they may be causally prior to consumers' behaviors, and therefore may contain unique information about future behavior. For example, for planned purchases, intention to purchase in theory should precede the purchase itself. Unobserved variables may also moderate the relationship between past and future behavior. The relationship between purchase history and future purchases may be moderated by beliefs about a brand, for example. The problem with unobserved variables is that they are difficult, and expensive, to measure.

Using different types of variables can provide better support for a broader range of marketing decisions and for strategy (Wind, 1978). Therefore, marketers often consider more than one kind when developing segmentation solutions. It is also not unusual for a firm to develop and use more than one segmentation scheme. There is probably no single best way to segment for all purposes. This is an important notion for data miners and marketing researchers alike.

Methods for forming segments are basically grouping or clustering methods. The methods marketing researchers use can be *a priori* or *post hoc*, and descriptive or predictive (Wedel and Kamakura, 1997). *A priori* methods are procedures where the type and number of segments are determined in advance. An example is grouping customers based on whether they are heavy users of a product or not, using median product purchase or usage rate as a decision criterion. *Post hoc* methods are those in which the results indicate the number and type of segments. The segments formed using either type of *post hoc* method may be mutually exclusive, or overlapping.

The difference between predictive and descriptive procedures is that the former type distinguishes between dependent variables and independent variables. It is the association between these two variable types that is analyzed. Examples of predictive, *post hoc* methods used by marketers are tree-based classifiers, like CHAID (Magidson, 1994) and CART (Breiman et al., 1984), and finite mixture regression models (Wedel and Kamakura, 1997). Hybrid approaches based on hierarchical models estimated using Markov chain Monte Carlo (Allenby and Ginter, 1995) and combinatorial optimization (Desarbo and Grissaffe, 1998) procedures have also been described.

Descriptive *post hoc* procedures for describing segments make no distinction between criterion and predictor variables. These procedures include k-centroid clustering procedures like k-means and k-medians, hierarchical clustering methods, unsupervised neural networks, and finite mixtures models. Descriptive segmentation by clustering is historically the most common application of clustering procedures in marketing research (Arabie and Hubert, 1994).

Predictive *post hoc* methods are becoming increasingly popular in marketing research, as more software becomes available for using them (Wedel and Kamakura, 1997). Many of the predictive and descriptive methods in use today were developed for small data samples, and many are computationally intensive because their algorithms are iterative in nature. They don't scale well for use on large data sets and often can only be applied to samples drawn from large data sets.

There is some consensus in marketing on what makes a segmentation solution a good one (e.g., Frank et al., 1972; Wedel and Kamakura, 1997; Desarbo and Grissaffe, 1998). The important criteria include the following:

1. *Differential responsiveness.* Consumers in different segments should behave differently toward marketing programs directed at them.

2. *Identifiability.* It should be possible to classify customers into distinct segments.

3. *Accessibility.* It should be possible to reach the segments with the tactics designed for them.

4. *Feasibility.* Satisfying the wants and needs of segments should be consistent with the firm's mission and competencies.

5. *Substantiality*. The potential demand in the segments should allow targeting them to be profitable.

6. *Stability*. The segments should be stable enough over time so that strategy and tactics developed for them can be executed.

These criteria are in terms of usefulness for managerial decisionmaking. They also are independent of the technology used to obtain them. Therefore, they provide a useful set of goals for segmentation solutions developed using data mining tools or with other techniques. They are not, however, easy to evaluate, and few studies have attempted to assess segmentation solutions on them (Desarbo and Grissaffe, 1998).

Segmentation in direct and database marketing tends to be more tactical than strategic. A common segmentation objective in database marketing is to identify groups that will be responsive to a particular offer delivered by way of a particular vehicle, such as a direct-mail piece or a telemarketing call. Predictive tree-based classification methods have become particularly popular for this kind of application since they produce a classification in their terminal nodes that is directly related to differences on the response variable of interest.

The evolution of segmentation theory and practice seems to be in the direction of what has been called microsegmentation (Clemons and Weber, 1994; Rangan et al., 1992). Microsegmentation recognizes the special attributes of individual customers and is consistent with the philosophy of one-to-one marketing. Data mining methods combined with techniques from interactive marketing may allow microsegmentation for situations in which segments are both small and transitory, a sort of dynamic microsegmentation (Rigdon and Bacon, 1998).

4.3. Customer Retention, Status, and Loyalty

One of today's generally accepted business truisms is that it is less expensive to keep customers than to get new ones (e.g., Aaker, 1991). One reason is that attracting new customers generally requires greater marketing expenditures than selling to existing customers. Therefore, marketers are interested in understanding factors that are related to retention so that those that are controllable can be managed.

One approach to analyzing customer attrition, or churn, is by using predictive classification techniques. Frequently used methods include tree-based models, limited dependent variables generalized linear models (McCullagh and Nelder, 1989) and generalized additive models (Hastie and Tibsurani, 1992), artificial neural networks, and rule induction procedures. The dependent variable is often a binary indicator of customer status: still a customer, or not. The goal is to model status so that turnover can be anticipated, and so interventions or programmatic changes can be made.

Customer status indicators can be right censored in time. This means that the true values of the indicator are not observed for all customers because data haven't been collected over a long enough period of time. The customers classified as being current may include both customers that will be customers indefinitely and customers who at various times in the future will cease to be customers.

Techniques developed for doing what is called survival analysis (Cox, 1972; Kleinbaum, 1996) provide methods for modeling customer attrition under censoring. Some techniques from survival analysis have been incorporated in tree-based classifiers (Therneau and Atkinson, 1997) and also in tree regression models (Ahn and Loh, 1994; Segal, 1988). A capability to model censored criteria has also been incorporated in neural networks (Ripley, 1996). Some survival analysis methods handle time-varying predictor variables in a direct manner, which make them particularly useful for predicting attrition.

Another customer behavior that can be important to predict is whether their purchasing patterns are changing. In some cases, changes in volume or regularity can be as important to know about as whether a customer is still a customer. For example, credit card issuers are interested in knowing whether valued credit card holders' use of their cards is declining. This knowledge can trigger tactical interventions, like offers of lower rates or of premiums. For pharmaceutical manufacturers, detecting when a doctor's prescription-writing behavior indicates a decline in the use of their products can enable the manufacturer to execute targeted sales tactics (Kallakuran, 1997).

Closely related to customer retention and buying behavior is the concept of customer loyalty. A loyal customer is one who has "a deeply held commitment to rebuy or repatronize a preferred product or service consistently in the future, despite situational influences and marketing efforts having the potential to cause switching behavior" (Oliver, 1997, p. 392). Loyalty to firms and to their brands is considered to be an important component of brand equity (Aaker, 1991; Keller, 1998). Because of the strategic importance of customer loyalty, firms have made substantial investments in measuring and trying to improve customer satisfaction (Oliver, 1997), and also in tracking and improving the relative value that customers perceive they get from products and services (Gale, 1994).

Loyalty is not just historical behavior. And, given the above definition, it is a latent variable—that is, one that cannot be observed directly, but must be inferred—as are concepts like customer satisfaction and customer perceived value. It is important to note that loyalty cannot be adequately measured just using the customer transaction data of a single firm. The reason is that measures of potentially important aspects of customer behavior or its determinants may be unavailable. For example, a customer may decrease her use of a particular credit card because she has acquired a new card from a competing financial services institution, or because she is making fewer purchases in general. On the other hand, her credit card purchases may remain unchanged, while she buys more, or less, with credit cards from competitors. Some of these behaviors are consistent with being a loyal customer, and some aren't. They can't be distinguished based on the card issuer's transaction data alone.

Customer relationship management (CRM) is a general strategy for enhancing marketing performance. It constitutes an integrated approach to customer acquisition, customer value enhancement, and customer retention. The basic goal of CRM is to use the data obtained from all contacts, or touchpoints, between a firm and its customers, along with any available background data on the customers, to maximize the value of exchanges with those customers. CRM programs often require significant investment in data management and data warehousing, and produce large and complex data sets to be analyzed. (By *complex* we mean that there is more than one type of observational unit or entity. The entities may be hierarchically related by way of partial or complete nesting relationships.) CRM provides a natural way to organize data mining efforts supporting marketing (e.g., Berry and Linoff, 2000; Berson et al., 2000) through traditional channels and via e-commerce. CRM is a relatively new activity for organizations, and best practice standards for it have yet to emerge.

Regardless of how data mining efforts for marketing are organized, they are usually focused on customer transaction data of some kind. Using such data to make causal inferences can be problematic because data on variables that may be relevant to your conclusions are not available. As a result you can misjudge relationships between the variables that you do have data on. To statisticians this is known as the omitted variables problem (Bollen, 1989; Judge et al., 1985; Rigdon and Bacon, 1998). The effect of omitting important variables from statistical models include biased estimators and decreased predictive accuracy. When the estimators are used to support managerial decisionmaking, the result can be invalid conclusions, bad decisions, and less than optimal performance by the firm. There is no reason that data mining methods should be immune to this problem. An important problem in making the results of data mining useful for marketing management is making sure that important variables aren't being ignored just because data on them are unavailable.

4.4. Getting Additional Value from Existing Marketing Data, and Other Marketing Problems

The data sets collected for primary research efforts are usually small in terms of the number of observations, or rows, they contain, but they often include a relatively large number of variables. The production schedules that typify primary research projects allow little time to manually search for complex patterns. Automated procedures, such as those sometimes used in data mining, can be useful in this regard.

Some firms collect marketing research data on an ongoing basis over long periods of time. These studies are often called tracking studies, and they are usually designed to monitor product performance or market conditions over time. Such studies sometimes span decades, and large quantities of data are amassed. Common examples include studies of customer satisfaction, studies of product purchasing, and studies of perceptions of competing brands. When research of this kind is conducted by a research organization for the purpose of selling the data to subscribing organizations, it may be referred to as syndicated research or as panel research. The data produced by this kind of ongoing research provide an opportunity to use data mining methods in marketing. The data sets are usually moderate in size and are not usually explored in a comprehensive way.

It should be apparent to the reader by now that data mining as an activity is clearly relevant to several kinds of problems in marketing. It is particularly applicable to direct marketing, to database marketing, and to customer relationship management. Data mining is also relevant to primary research, given the availability of data on variables that should be important given theory and practice. Peacock (1998a) and Berry and Linoff (1997) describe other applications of data mining in marketing.

5. Maximizing the Data Mining Yield

Data miners can improve their success rate in marketing by ensuring that their efforts complement the activities of marketers. Two means for doing this are to work closely with marketers during the course of data mining efforts and to provide complements to other sources of marketing information.

The major benefit of working closely with marketers is that they are the best source of domain knowledge and can provide in-depth understanding of the relevant business problems. Making sure their ideas and feedback are incorporated into the process of data mining and knowledge discovery is a good way to ensure that the outcomes provide good value. A successful data mining application can be thought of as a product design and development effort whose objectives are to satisfy the wants and needs of the customers it is intended for. The customers who are supposed to benefit by it are the place where the effort should start by defining goals and objectives.

Peacock (1998b) has suggested using a multidisciplinary team approach for data mining in marketing research, and that the team leader be a marketing manager. The idea is that a manager is in the best position to define business-relevant goals and objectives, and to understand how to convert results into business answers. The manager should also function as a champion for the effort in its organizational setting. The marketing manager is the marketer for it.

There are a number of ways that the fruits of data mining can complement other means by which marketers obtain information. One obvious way is when data mining is used to identify the need for primary research. For example, an analysis of customer complaints about the handling of product technical support calls may indicate a consistent pattern of higher than average complaint rates during particular time periods and for certain types of calls. Based on the need indicated by this result, primary research would be conducted on customers calling during those periods to find out how they differed from other customers in terms of their characteristics, needs, expectations, and experiences. The results would be used to decide whether service changes need to be made and what kinds of changes seem to be the most useful.

There is great potential benefit in combining data mining methods with the knowledge and techniques of marketing and marketing research. The techniques of data mining enable exploration, identification of interesting relationships, and prediction, and they can be applied to data sets that are very large in terms of either the number of observations, the number of measures on the observations, or both. Some are also relatively automatic in terms of the particular kinds of relationships considered. Marketers are increasingly awash in an embarrassment of data (Rigdon and Bacon, 1998), and many current marketing modeling techniques do not scale well with data-set size or are very labor intensive and time consuming to use. Data mining methods are therefore a welcome and useful addition to the quantitative marketing toolkit.

The critical contributions of marketing theory and practice to any marriage of data mining and marketing are obvious. Theory and practice provide important domain knowledge that should be used for developing problem descriptions and for defining what makes patterns interesting. They should also be brought to bear on decisions about the design and implementation of data warehouses to support data mining activities. For example, an important design criterion may be to be able to span the entire relationship between a firm and any given customer.

Marketing research can contribute in important ways because of its sophistication about sampling issues, statistical estimation, and modeling problems, and issues related to the validity of conclusions about the causes of observed patterns. The data used for data mining are seldom collected using procedures designed to minimize the risk of incorrect conclusions about how markets work. The data are often the result of selection factors that limit the extent to which the obtained results can be generalized. Therefore, some care must be taken in trying to generalize findings. Such limitations are not always so obvious, so attention to their possibility and impact is important.

Edward Tufte (1983) has made some recommendations about designing graphs that generalize to what we consider here, and so they provide us with a final prescription. To borrow from Tufte, successful data mining applications in marketing demonstrate the following characteristics. First, they reflect marketing domain knowledge. Marketing knowledge is integral to their planning and execution. Second, they represent quantitative expertise. They represent the best deployment of methods given the prevailing constraints and data limitations, and the most valid interpretation of findings. Finally, they reflect a sense of the aesthetic and local culture of the management comprising the consumers for the fruits of data mining. Professionals experienced in providing information to management will recognize the need to do it in a way that is consonant with management's beliefs and attitudes. One might think of this part of our prescription as a requirement for good taste.

References

Aaker, D. 1991. *Managing Brand Equity*. New York: Freeman Press.

Ahn, H. and W.-Y. Loh. 1994. "Tree-structured proportional hazards regression modeling." *Biometrics* **50**: 471–485.

Allenby, G. and J. Ginter. 1995. "Using extremes to design products and to segment markets." *J. Marketing Res.* **32**: 392–403.

Ansoff, I. 1957. "Strategies for Diversification." *Havard Business Rev.*, pp. 113–124.

Arabie, P. and L. Hubert. 1994. "Cluster analysis in marketing research." *Advanced Methods for Marketing Research*, edited by R. Bagozzi, pp. 160–189. Malden, MA: Blackwell Publishers.

Bennett, P., ed. 1995. "Dictionary of Marketing Terms." 2d ed. Chicago: American Marketing Association.

Berry, M. and G. Linoff. 1997. *Data Mining Techniques: For Marketing, Sales, and Customer Support*. New York: Wiley.

Berry, M. and G. Linoff. 2000. *Mastering Data Mining: The Art and Science of Customer Relationship Management*. New York: Wiley.

Berson, A., S. Smith, and K. Thearling. 2000. *Building Data Mining Applications for CRM*. New York: McGraw-Hill.

Blattberg, R. and S. Sen. 1976. "Market segments and stochastic brand choice models." *J. Marketing Res.* **13**: 34–45.

Bollen, K. 1989. *Structural Equation Models with Latent Variables*. New York: Wiley.

Breiman, L., J. Friedman, R. Olshen, and C. Stone. 1984. *Classification and Regression Trees*. Belmont, CA: Wadsworth.

Cox, D. 1972. "Regression models and life-tables." *J. R. Stat. Soc., Series B* **34**: 187–202.

Desarbo, W. and D. Grisaffe. 1998. "Combinatorial optimization approaches to constrained market segmentation: an application to industrial market segmentation." *Marketing Lett.* **9(2)**: 115–134.

Edelstein, H. 1997. "Data mining: technology and products." Annual Spring Conference of the Chicago Chapter of the American Statistical Association, Chicago.

Frank, R., W. Massey, and Y. Wind. 1972. *Market Segmentation*. Englewood Cliffs, NJ: Prentice-Hall.

Gale, B. 1994. *Managing Customer Value*. New York: Free Press.

Hastie, T. and R. Tibshirani. 1990. *Generalized Additive Models*. New York: Chapman and Hall.

Judge, G., W. Griffiths, R. Carter Hill, H. Lutkepohl, and T.-C. Lee. 1985. *The Theory and Practice of Econometrics*. New York: Wiley.

Kallukaran, P. 1997. "How does data mining relate to statistics and what can it do for business?" Annual Spring Conference of the Chicago Chapter of the American Statistical Association, Chicago.

Keller, K. 1998. *Strategic Brand Management*. Upper Saddle River, NJ: Prentice-Hall.

Kleinbaum, D. 1996. *Survival Analysis: A Self Learning Text*. New York: Springer-Verlag.

Kotler, P. 1997. *Marketing Management: Analysis, Planning, Implementation, and Control*. Upper Saddle River, NJ: Prentice-Hall.

Little, J. 1979. "Decision support systems for marketing managers." *J. Marketing* **43**: 9–27.

Little, J. and M. Cassettari. 1984. *Decision Support Systems for Marketing Managers*. New York: American Management Association.

Magidson, J. 1994. "The CHAID approach to segmentation modeling: chi-squared automatic interaction detection." *Advanced Methods of Marketing Research*, edited by R. Bagozzi. Malden, MA: Blackwell Publishers.

McCann, J. and J. Gallagher. 1990. *Expert Systems for Scanner Data Environments*. Boston: Kluwer Academic Publishers.

McCorkle, G. 1997. *Direct and Database Marketing*. London: The Institute of Direct Marketing.

McCullagh, P. and J. Nelder. 1989. *Generalized Linear Models*. 2d ed. New York: Chapman and Hall.

McDaniel, C. Jr. and R. Gates. 1993. *Contemporary Marketing Research*. 2d ed. Minneapolis/Saint Paul: West Publishing.

McKinna, R. 1991. *Relationship Marketing*. Reading, MA: Addison-Wesley.

Myers, J. 1996. *Segmentation and Positioning for Strategic Marketing Decisions*. Chicago: American Marketing Association.

Nagle, T. and R. Holden. 1994. *The Strategy and Tactics of Pricing*. Englewood Cliffs, NJ: Prentice-Hall.

Oliver, R. 1997. *Satisfaction: A Behavioral Perspective on the Consumer*. New York: McGraw-Hill.

Peacock, P. 1998a. "Data mining in marketing: Part I." *Marketing Mgmnt*, pp. 9–18.

Peacock, P. 1998b. "Data mining in marketing: Part II." *Marketing Mgmnt*, pp. 15–25.

Rigdon, E. and L. Bacon. 1998. "Data warehousing and data mining: possibilities, pitfalls, and implications for marketing management and research." Atlanta: Department of Marketing, Georgia State University.

Ripley, B. 1996. *Pattern Recognition and Neural Networks*. Cambridge: Cambridge University Press.

Segal, M. 1988. "Regression trees for censored data." *Biometrics* **44**: 35–47.

Smith, W. 1956. "Product differentiation and market segmentation as alternative market strategies." *J. Marketing* **21**: 3–8.

Stone, R. 1996. *Successful Direct Marketing Methods*. 6th ed. Lincolnwood, IL: NTC Business Books.

Therneau, T. and E. Atkinson. 1997. "An introduction to recursive partitioning using the RPART routines," Technical Report. Rochester, MN: Mayo Clinic.

Tufte, E. 1983. *The Visual Display of Quantitative Information*. Chesire, CT: Graphics Press.

Wedel, M. and W. Kamakura. 1997. *Market Segmentation: Conceptual and Methodological Foundations*. Boston: Kluwer Academic Publishers.

Weiss, S. and N. Indurkhya. 1998. *Predictive Data Mining*. San Francisco: Morgan Kaufmann Publishers.

Wind, Y. 1978. "Issues and advances in segmentation research." *J. Marketing Res.* **15**: 317–337.

35 FRAUD DETECTION

Tom E. Fawcett and Foster Provost

ABSTRACT Fraud is the deliberate use of deception to conduct illicit activities. Automatic fraud detection involves scanning large volumes of data to uncover patterns of fradulent usage, and as such it is well suited to data mining techniques. We present three general types of fraud that have been addressed in data mining research, and we summarize the approaches taken. We also discuss general characteristics of fraud detection problems that make them difficult, as well as system integration issues for automatic fraud detection systems.

1. Introduction

Fraud is the deliberate use of deception to conduct illicit activities. Fraud is common wherever money changes hands, as with insurance fraud, credit fraud, wire fraud, and money laundering; or where barriers protect highly desired services, as with telecommunications fraud and computer intrusion. Fraud detection involves monitoring the behavior of customers, users, or accounts in order to detect or avoid undesirable behavior.

Because of the volume of data involved, most fraud problems require automated detection tools. For example, credit card companies process millions of transactions each day, so it is impossible to manually inspect all accounts and transactions for suspicious activity. Companies and government agencies typically build models of normal or suspicious activity, which are then used by computers to ferret out potential cases of fraud. The cases discovered can then be dealt with automatically or referred to a human investigator. Because of the large volume of data, knowledge discovery and data mining methods are natural tools for building models of such activity.

Some fraud is self-revealing, meaning that in time the fraudulent activity necessarily will become apparent. Stolen credit card fraud is self-revealing because the account's true owner will eventually discover and report the fraudulent charges. Another example is a fraudulently acquired loan: eventually the company will realize that the customer has no intention of repaying the debt. On the other hand, money laundering is not self-revealing, and consequently most money laundering goes undetected.

Self-revealing fraud often is characterized by large volumes of labeled historical data (e.g., previously defrauded accounts). Fraud that is not self-revealing typically has few labeled cases from which fraud patterns can be mined. In either situation, data mining tools can be used to help learn patterns of activity. Once such patterns are discovered, manual inspection can often identify illicit activities. Whether or not fraud is self-revealing, normal behavior patterns may be modeled, and the models can be used to indicate suspicious deviations from normal behavior.

2. General Types of Fraud

Before discussing technical issues, we define three classes of fraud. These classes transcend application area and are based on common features of problems that may be superficially different. By highlighting the common structure, it becomes clear that similar data mining methods may apply.

Subscription fraud involves obtaining under false pretenses money or services, often in the form of a customer account. The term *subscription fraud* is commonly used by telecommunications companies, whose customers are service subscribers. The perpetrator never intends to pay the provider, thereby stealing money or services. Subscription fraud is also called application fraud because in many cases the deception involves making false statements when applying for a service. Subscription fraud is ubiquitous in the business world. Common examples are the fraudulent procurement of credit cards, mortgages, and wireless telephone accounts.

Note that subscription fraud is closely related to nonfraudulent account defaulting and may be difficult to distinguish by behavior. To fit a strict definition of *fraud*, there must be deception involved, for example, false statements on an account application. In principle, the issue of intent is also important: If a customer exaggerates annual income on an application, but fully intends to pay, is it fraud? Deducing the truth of statements and inferring intent are fundamentally difficult problems. Therefore, except for purposes of litigation, subscription fraud is often practically inseparable from nonfraudulent risk analysis (see Chapter 36), which estimates a potential customer's likelihood of default.

Superimposition fraud occurs when a perpetrator gains illicit access to an existing legitimate account. The term *superimposition fraud* denotes that fraudulent behavior is superimposed upon (added to) the legitimate behavior, because the legitimate usage often continues concurrently with the fraudulent. Examples of superimposition fraud are the fraudulent use of credit card and calling card numbers, cellular-phone cloning and computer intrusion. Although much less common, there are cases where the fraudulent activity is conducted by the legitimate account holder; for example, the same person may submit both legitimate and fraudulent medical claims.

Collusive agent fraud is the most complex of the three types. It involves several agents acting in concert to take unfair or illegal advantage of a system. Examples are money laundering, wire fraud, securities fraud, and many forms of insurance fraud. Companies often have safeguards in place to detect individual fraudulent transactions, but fraud that spans multiple transactions made among several cooperating agents is much more difficult to catch. Because of its very nature, collusive agent fraud usually involves large payoffs and is rarely self-revealing.

3. Technical Challenges: What Makes Fraud Detection Hard?

One of the foremost difficulties in developing fraud detection systems is defining a suitable performance objective. To be effective, a data mining system must satisfy performance criteria that reflect the true business goals, and these are notoriously difficult to specify. Both the benefit of catching fraud and the cost of issuing a false alarm must be estimated. These are difficult to quantify and may change, for example, with changes in workforce procedures or agreements. The target environment is also dynamic: the amount of fraud may change from month to month unpredictably, which in turn changes the expected cost of a fraud detection strategy. Therefore, it is important to build systems that are robust in dynamic environments.

The need for careful goal definition is magnified by factors such as the tremendously skewed class distributions common in fraud detection domains. The number of fraudulent transactions or accounts is always dwarfed by the number of legitimate ones. For example, even if a credit card company has a severe fraud problem, the incidence of fraud may still be less than 1 percent of all active accounts per day. Unfortunately, most data mining methods are designed to minimize undifferentiated error rate, and this is of limited use in fraud detection. Consider that a system that never issues alarms, in an environment with 1 percent fraud, is correct 99 percent of the time.

Because of the large number of legitimate transactions, fraud detection systems must usually operate with very low false positive rates. The false positive (false alarm) rate is the percentage of legitimate instances that are incorrectly labeled fraudulent by the system. Even a system that has the seemingly quite low daily false positive rate of 1 percent will create 10,000 false alarms per day on a universe of only 1 million customers. Creating useful models with extremely low false positive rates is a significant challenge for existing data mining methods.

Fraud detection is unique among data mining problems because of the existence of intelligent, adaptive adversaries who have a strong interest in defeating the system. As patterns of fraud are discovered and incorporated into a fraud model, they are abandoned by perpetrators who then develop new tactics to avoid detection. Because of this, concept drift is inherent in these domains, and fraud models risk becoming outdated soon after deployment. A challenge is to institute a cyclic process where field data are periodically sampled and mined for new fraud patterns, which are then incorporated back into the deployed system. A related challenge is for fraud detection systems to conceal their strategies in order to prolong their effectiveness.

4. Business and System Integration Issues

The size and sensitivity of fraud detection problems have a significant impact on the data mining methods that can be applied. Fraud detection systems, of which the patterns and models are a small but essential part, typically handle tremendous data feeds and deal with huge databases. For example, systems for detecting cellular-phone fraud usually process millions of calls per day. Timely detection often demands that these systems produce fraud alerts in near real time. Therefore, all operations on a transaction must be done in a fraction of a second, including recording it, accessing relevant account-specific data, processing the transaction and historical data through the fraud model, and issuing an alarm if warranted. Since the account database may contain millions of accounts, each with many historical transactions, a very fast database system and first-rate integration are paramount.

The size of the account database presents a related challenge. Not only must fraud models be computationally efficient, the account-specific models must be very space efficient. For example, storing a neural network or decision tree with each customer record is impractical; it may be possible only to store a few parameters to a general model with each customer. Thus, both time and space constraints argue for very simple fraud detection models.

Another important criterion for fraud models is explainability: the reasons for an alarm must be clear enough to support whatever follow-up actions may be required. Such actions may include a fraud analyst initiating a follow-up investigation, a customer service representative contacting a customer, an account being closed down, or data being provided to a law enforcement agency for criminal prosecution. Each of these requires some degree of explainability from the fraud detection system. If a customer demands to know why an account was shut down, the customer service representative should be able to identify and explain suspicious transactions.

As described above, individual transactions are rarely sufficient to conclude the existence of fraud. Instead, a case is usually built from a transaction history; often a single suspicious transaction triggers the creation of a fraud case, within which other transactions may appear suspicious. Fortunately, fraud is relatively rare, so the processing constraints on fraud cases are not nearly as severe.

5. Data Mining Approaches and Examples

5.1. Subscription Fraud

The task in subscription fraud detection is to determine whether a given account has been applied for fraudulently. As mentioned earlier, detecting subscription fraud is closely related to determining bad credit risks, a task in risk management (see Chapter 36). Customers who default on payments may be indistinguishable from truly fraudulent customers who had no intention of paying.

If this decision is to be made once, at the time of application, the task is to determine whether an account should be granted. If sufficient historical data exist, in the form of fraudulent and nonfraudulent applications, they may be used to train a classifier (see Chapter 16.1). A binary classifier may be used to issue alarms on applications, or a probabilistic classifier may be used to provide a probability or suspicion rank for each application. Applications that are flagged or highly ranked may be referred to customer service personnel for investigation. Alternatively, high-risk applications may be granted with a stipulation, such as a lower credit limit or a mandatory deposit. High-risk applications may also be scheduled for periodic reexamination.

A common problem with subscription fraud is that reliable labeled data may be rare or nonexistent. In this case, clustering (see Chapter 16.5) of account applications may be done. Clustering of applicants is often useful when patterns are unknown because outliers are likely to be suspicious.

Haimowitz and Schwartz (1997) used clustering techniques to detect risky credit applications. Their work addressed a larger problem in risk management (see Chapter 36), that of determining optimal credit-line assignments for new customers. The goal was to determine the best initial credit line to offer applicants, based on the applicant's expected net present value to the company.

Much historical data from existing accounts were available for data mining. Each account was represented using static customer information combined with extensive data about the customer's spending habits, credit usage, and bill payment history. Haimowitz and Schwartz (1997) applied hierarchical clustering (see Chapter 16.5) to a sample of the accounts and determined experimentally the number of customer clusters. These cluster centers were then used as inputs to k-means clustering (see Chapter 16.5) for the remainder of the training set. The resulting five clusters corresponded to different styles of credit usage, for example, "on time with payments, use some credit, profitable" and "high sales, late with payments, pays high delinquency charges, very profitable." One of these clusters corresponded to very delinquent (write-off) customers who were uniformly unprofitable; this cluster is likely to include the high-risk subscription fraud applicants.

Probabilistic rules were then generated that related credit bureau data to the clusters. Seventeen rules were generated in their experiments; each rule, when matched, specified the probability of membership of a new customer in each of the five clusters. For fraud detection, the system need only determine that a customer has been assigned to the subscription fraud cluster with a high enough probability.

Examining account applications is not the only strategy for detecting subscription fraud. Another is to track customer behavior after the account is granted in order to detect suspicious behavior indicative of intent to default. For example, if a cellular-phone customer purchases a low-use plan (appropriate if the phone is to be used only in emergencies) and suddenly starts making hundreds of dollars of cellular calls, the account should be flagged for investigation. Although such checks are used in some fraud detection systems, we are aware of no work in data mining on generating them automatically.

5.2. Superimposition Fraud

In superimposition fraud detection, the task is to scan a stream of transactions associated with an account and determine whether (and when) fraudulent usage has appeared. In some domains, a large-usage increase alone may be enough to indicate fraud, but in most domains the individual transactions must be examined for suspicious behavior.

There are two general strategies for detecting superimposition fraud. One strategy is to learn characteristics of fraudulent behavior and issue alarms when such behavior is seen; the other is to characterize typical behavior of legitimate users and issue alarms when significant deviations are seen. With the latter strategy, user behavior can be modeled individually or each account can be placed into predefined behavior classes (e.g., 9-to-5 business user).

Some fraudulent behavior may be distinguishable at the individual transaction level. For example, perpetrators of credit card fraud often test new cards by using them to purchase small amounts of gasoline at self-service stations. Data mining can be used to identify such patterns by applying a classification learning algorithm (see Chapter 16.1) to a large set of labeled fraudulent and legitimate transactions. This approach will work when fraudulent transactions are prevalent enough in the fraud population and uncommon in the legitimate population. Unfortunately, much fraudulent behavior may be unusual only in the context of a given account; in the universe of legitimate transactions, it may be unremarkable. If this is the case, an account-specific approach must be taken.

Fawcett and Provost (1997) used an account-specific approach to detect cellular-phone (cloning) fraud. In this domain, calling behavior varies considerably between users, so account context must be taken into consideration when issuing alarms. A hybrid approach was used that is sensitive to this context and combines the advantages of modeling fraud and modeling legitimate behavior.

Their system begins by examining the call records of individual accounts that have been defrauded, and generating rules that distinguish fraudulent from legitimate calls. Because these rules are derived from specific accounts, their applicability over the general population of accounts is unknown, so the system applies a covering algorithm that identifies rules common to many accounts. The resulting rules serve as general indicators of fraud.

However, the system does not know the extent to which a given indicator may already apply to the legitimate behavior of any given account. Therefore, the next step is to profile each rule against each account. The system examines a thirty-day sequence of legitimate calls for each account and extracts statistics on how closely each rule matches the normal calling behavior. These statistics are stored with the account, and they collectively represent the account's behavior profile with respect to the fraud indicators.

To detect fraud, the system is applied to one account-day of calls at a time. The system retrieves the profile information previously stored with the account, then applies each rule to the account-day of calls. Each rule contributes a vote on the abnormality of the behavior; when the weighted votes exceed a threshold, an alarm is issued on the account. Experiments showed this system to be superior to several alternative strategies for detecting cloning fraud, including a hand-crafted ensemble strategy combining the best detection methods in existence.

5.3. Collusive Agent Fraud

Collusive agent fraud occurs when several agents collaborate to take unfair or illegal advantage of a system. It is usually the most difficult form of fraud to detect. Such fraud is rarely self-revealing since it is typically perpetrated by otherwise legitimate users who have a strong interest in concealing the fraud, and whose legitimate transactions are far more prevalent.

Unlike other forms of fraud where individual transactions may be labeled as fraudulent, in collusive agent fraud, the fraud case is spread over many transactions and multiple users. Individual actions are not inherently fraudulent; it is only the combination of actions demonstrating intent to take illegal advantage of a system that constitutes fraud. Detection and prosecution usually involves building a case spanning multiple grouped transactions over a long period of time. Classification techniques, which may be effective with other forms of fraud, are less useful here because fraud cannot be described using the attributes of individual transactions. Collusive fraud detection is more similar to plan recognition in artificial intelligence (AI) than to classification.

Because collusive agent fraud involves multiple agents, detecting it usually requires link analysis. Link analysis involves identifying the relationships and transactions between entities in a system. For example, detecting money laundering requires knowing the relationships between businesses, individuals, and financial institutions, and analyzing the money transfers between them. Once links have been established, suspicious associations may be detected either visually or with graph algorithms.

Because of the complexity of collusive agent fraud, systems are usually used as visualization aids (see Chapter 15) for fraud analysts rather than as autonomous fraud detection systems. Dealing with the full complexity of collusive agent fraud in a principled manner is beyond the current state of data mining research and practice. The potential of AI techniques in this area has been evaluated by the Congressional Office of Technology Assessment, whose study is summarized by Jensen (1997).

In spite of the difficulties, some progress has been made on autonomous detection of collusive agent fraud. Goldberg and Senator (1997) describe a system being developed jointly by NASD Regulation and SRA International. The system tracks market transactions and identifies breaks (suspected violations of proper conduct), which are proposed for review by market analysts. The system recognizes specific significant events within the transaction stream and organizes the events into sequences, which match known fraud (break) scenarios. The system currently relies on manually engineered knowledge structures, and the role of data mining is limited. Further work includes using decision-tree discovery (see Chapter 16.1.3) and association rule learning (see Chapter 16.2.3) to uncover indicators of violative behavior in the profiles of firms.

ACKNOWLEDGMENTS

The following sources were useful in preparing this chapter: many discussions with Nicholas Arcuri and others in the Fraud Control Department at Bell Atlantic Mobile; the papers and discussions of the AAAI-97 Workshop on AI Approaches to Fraud Detection and Risk Management; and notes from a tutorial by Steven Donoho and Scott Bennett.

References

Fawcett, T. and F. Provost. 1997. "Adaptive fraud detection." *Data Mining and Knowledge Discovery* **1**(3): 291–316.

Goldberg, H. G. and T. E. Senator. 1997. "Break detection systems." In *AI Approaches to Fraud Detection and Risk Management*, edited by T. Fawcett, I. Haimowitz, F. Provost, and S. Stolfo, pp. 22–28. Menlo Park, CA: AAAI Press.

Haimowitz, I. and H. Schwartz. 1997. "Clustering and prediction for credit line optimization." In *AI Approaches to Fraud Detection and Risk Management*, edited by T. Fawcett, I. Haimowitz, F. Provost, and S. Stolfo, pp. 29–33. Menlo Park, CA: AAAI Press.

Jensen, D. 1997. "Prospective assessment of AI technologies for fraud detection: a case study." In *AI Approaches to Fraud Detection and Risk Management*, edited by T. Fawcett, I. Haimowitz, F. Provost, and S. Stolfo, pp. 34–38. Menlo Park, CA: AAAI Press.

36 RISK ANALYSIS

Ira J. Haimowitz and Tim K. Keyes

ABSTRACT   In this chapter, we discuss both quantitative and qualitative aspects of data mining, as a process for uncovering information related to risk exposure buried in large amounts of data, and its exploitation for enterprise benefit. Section 1 introduces a general foundation for the application of data mining in a risk setting. Section 2 offers some typical business problems data mining can help address. Section 3 suggests potential uses of company internal and external information in the data mining/risk analysis process. Sections 4 and 5 delve into a more technical discussion on data mining methods, tools, and applications. Finally, we focus on the most important and challenging task in data mining—implementation of results—in Section 6.

1. Introduction to Risk Management

Risk is a general term applied to future losses, and *risk management* refers to the general deployment of resources to control exposure (potential loss). Risk management is a growing national need; for example, in 1997 in the United States there was $528 billion in consumer credit card debt and $37 billion in charge-offs (Credit Card Management, 1998). A data miner's duty is to engage in the proactive generation and use of pertinent data to uncover obscured exposures that may result in risk. Example risks are those to net income, stock price, market share, new product introduction, capital, or company prestige.

Future losses that are predictable are not inherently risky. The more relevant issue is whether the future losses are controllable. The uncertainty of losses generates risk, and the inability to characterize this uncertainty makes a business operation (or life, for that matter) unmanageable, or out of control. A proactive data miner will parlay his understanding of risk (the uncertainty of losses) into enterprise advantage through competitive gain or through product, process, or service innovation.

For illustrative purposes, we will include examples from the consumer credit card industry. This is reasonably representative of the world of financial risk, but perhaps not for physical risk (e.g., military, terrorism, medical).

1.1. Anatomy of Risk

There are two dimensions of risk: frequency is the rate at which undesirable events exhibit themselves, while severity is the magnitude of the loss, once exhibited. Using this definition, one can categorize business risks into various tranches (segments) and address them with the appropriate resources (see Figure 1).

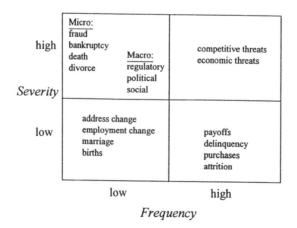

Figure 1 Dimensions of consumer risk

One could argue that data mining activity generally applies to risk problems in the high-frequency and low-severity quadrant. Application to other areas is not unheard of, however (see Chapter 35 on fraud detection). Data mining can help in making more severe risks less frequent, and more frequent risks less severe, as well as lessening risk or severity, by identifying controllable drivers of severity or frequency of risk.

EXAMPLE

A risk manager in the credit card industry is concerned with defaults in monthly customer payments due. An established credit card portfolio experiences a bad rate (percent) on new accounts that follows a normal (2, 0.5) statistical distribution in the first six months. Risk, in this case, manifests itself via the bad rate coming in above or below the mean of 2 percent (or not following a normal distribution). If this expected loss range is maintained in future acquisitions, then the bad rate is a manageable risk (or controllable exposure), an uncertainty that can be prepared for. Data mining could reveal cardholder segments with greater default rates than others, or more uncertainty, and the credit risk manager could use this information to enhance bottom-line growth in risk-based pricing (e.g., percentage rate, credit line, or fees).

2. Business Problems of Data Owners in Risk Management

The stakeholders in a risk management data warehouse (risk analysts, as well as computing specialists) are ultimately concerned with making good decisions based on the assessed risk of their customers. Conclusions derived from the risk data warehouse may ultimately decide important customer management strategies including new customer acquisition, customer life-cycle management, and portfolio review.

Decisions for new customer acquisition govern whether a firm accepts a new applicant for credit and, if so, under what terms. Example decisions are:

- What types of new credit applicants should be granted or denied credit in the future?

- How much of a credit line, interest rate, and repayment terms are granted to individuals?

Customer life-cycle management refers to the ongoing monitoring of, and interaction with, existing customers:

- Whose credit is extended or shortened, and by how much?

- What is the correct allocation of collection activities to delinquent accounts (ignore, contact by mail, telephone, or in person)?

- Which customers are too risky in one product to refrain from offering another product?

To a data miner, these customer decisions are potentially always individualized and dynamic. Rather than setting uniform policies for approval, pricing, and restrictions, these can all be based on an individual's recent historical data, and can be updated.

Finally, there are portfolio review decisions that risk managers make, such as:

- What customer segments should be sold to another firm because they are too risky? At what price?

- Should our firm acquire a set of accounts as possible new customers? At what bid?

- Is there a group of customers sharing some common characteristic making that group risky?

These portfolio review questions can require more domain knowledge and reasoning about aggregates than the customer-based questions. For example, a large group of customers with a collective large outstanding balance may all live in a town dominated by federal military bases. This makes the potential for national defense cuts a very risky event.

Paramount in all decisionmaking about risk must be profitability. Many successful credit-granting firms manage very risky accounts, yet price accordingly, charging high interest rates and demanding short repayment terms. Glasgow (1997) notes that for segments of insurance policyholders, "the risk rating is fair if the premium paid and the investment income earned is sufficient to cover their payout." Later we discuss data mining using expected net present value, which incorporates both risk and profitability.

3. Risk Management Data for the Data Warehouse

Data for risk management can be divided into two types: internal data giving historical performance for a firm's own customers and external data summarizing how customers have purchased products and handled credit for other companies and marketplaces.

3.1. Internal Customer Data

As in other data mining business applications, internal customer data includes both account demographics as well as transaction summaries. Account demographics include basic contact information like name, address, phone, and so on, that are rarely used for modeling, as well as customer attributes like age, gender, occupation, salary level, and original terms (credit line, interest rate) of the customer relationship. Many of these fields originate from the time of customer acquisition and are updated occasionally as needed by customer service organizations. Account demographics may be used as cohorts or segmentation variables in data mining, as well as independent variables.

Transaction summaries in a data warehouse give snapshots of relevant customer credit variables. Examples include periodic purchasing, balance, payments, delinquency status (number of days late) and finance charges. Throughout this paper we will assume a monthly summary, simply because many banks and credit institutions have monthly billing cycles.

Risk data warehouses usually retain twenty-four to thirty-six months of transaction summaries per customer. Internal data are almost always kept on a rolling basis, with each new recent month of customer data taking the place of the oldest month. Also stored are various aggregations like "number of times more than sixty days due" as a measure of delinquency or "number of months since last nonzero balance" as a measure of account dormancy. Thus, hundreds of account variables are potentially available, and the challenge to the data miner is to select customer variables and aggregations that are relevant for predicting future risk as well as nonredundant. Schuermann (1997) notes that in using large data sets for (statistical) modeling in financial risk management, the challenge comes not from the large number of observations, but in limiting the number of independent variables. Elder and Pregibon (1996) note that machine-learning techniques, such as decision trees or CART, can be valuable for determining which variables are most relevant for statistical prediction. Stepwise regression is similarly valuable in selecting variables explaining the most variation in risk—but one whose selections should be reviewed in light of variable interdependencies (i.e., multicollinearity).

One way to reduce the risk analysis data set is to mine a customer aggregation table rather than the raw customer data. Haimowitz et al. (1997) aggregated commercial customer data by location, industry, and financial product line to produce a three-dimensional cube. Each cell of the cube contained risk-related numerical information like total exposure (e.g., credit outstanding). The data mining employed a generalized linear model to search for outlying cube values in a third categorical dimension that were inconsistent with the two-dimensional aggregation. An example outlier might be: high risk in equipment leasing to the construction firms in Chicago, even when Chicago construction is not risky overall, or equipment leasing to construction is not risky nationwide.

3.2. External Third-Party Data for Purchase

Credit bureaus supply information on how consumers, commercial businesses, and governments manage their credit, usually by collecting information from a large set of contributing lending companies. Dun and Bradstreet is the largest American commercial credit bureau; consumer credit bureaus include Equifax, Experian (formerly TRW), and Trans Union. Moody's is a well-known agency that rates municipal and corporate bonds. Credit agencies not only supply delinquency and payment information but also compute credit scores, often the result of a logistic regression model that predicts likelihood of future delinquency conditioned on account characteristics (Lewis, 1992). A credit bureau model may be viewed as an independent variable in another risk model. For data quality, a firm might consider comparing the consistency among multiple credit bureaus for the same sets of customers.

External demographic marketing data, from firms like Equifax, Infobase, Claritas, or Axciom, match each ZIP code or city block to a set of fifty to sixty purchasing or consumer segments. That segment can also be used as an independent variable for risk-related data mining. These can be coarse measures, and data miners should note that the reliability of this data can affect risk decisions and risk uncertainty.

3.3. Contractual Obligations in the Credit Industry

Personal information is quite predictive of credit behavior, and many risk management and data mining operations, with the right to do so, readily take advantage of it. In some countries, federally regulated consumer credit repositories have been established to make personal financial information available to stakeholders with permissible purposes, that is, rights to access. In the United States, the Equal Credit Opportunity Act (ECOA) and the Fair Credit Reporting Act (FCRA) legally restrict the use of personal financial information to those credit and insurance companies to which a consumer has applied or with which the consumer has a current account. In effect, these acts represent legally binding contracts between each credit or insurance grantor in the United States and all consumers. Some examples of where these laws apply:

1. Redlining, or discriminatory use of gender, marital status, and age, is strictly prohibited.

2. Targeted marketing is a data mining activity in which the use of personal financial information is closely monitored. Credit grantors use data mining to discover the relationships between personal financial and demographic characteristics and credit performance (risk) on current or past credit accounts. In a new marketing campaign, for example, the credit grantor in the United States will forward a set of rules (discovered via mining proprietary data) that comprises the relationship (a regression equation, for instance) to a credit bureau or list provider (e.g., ACXIOM/Trans Union), who will apply the scoring rules (Lewis, 1992) to an entire database of potential future customers. The FCRA requires the credit grantor to issue credit to each consumer satisfying the scoring rule for extending credit. The list provider serves the purpose of hiding specific consumer information from the credit grantor looking for acquisitions.

3. Adverse action, or the denial of credit to an applying consumer according to a scoring rule, is regulated in that the consumer has a legal right to know the reasons why credit was denied. This has implications on the types of models that can be used for credit scoring: the credit grantor must deploy models from which he or she can explain why an applicant was denied credit, that is, identify the driving variable(s).

In addition to the well-known legal restrictions such as ECOA and FCRA, there are myriad others imposed in regional jurisdictions: state-by-state insurance laws, bankruptcy laws, and the like. Data miners must be aware of all illegal uses of data available to them for their particular application.

4. Risk Patterns in Data Mining

4.1. Binary Risk Predicates

Most commonly, a firm will define a meaningful binary predicate as the dependent variable in a risk model. An example is: "credit customer will be delinquent for ninety days or more within the next six months." Thus, the predicate includes an account status as well as a future time window. Existing customers in a training data set can be labeled as 1 (risky) or 0 (not risky) based on this predicate for some time frame during their existing account life, and a data miner can predict the likely risk based on data prior to that label. Prediction of a binary outcome variable is conducive to several data mining techniques.

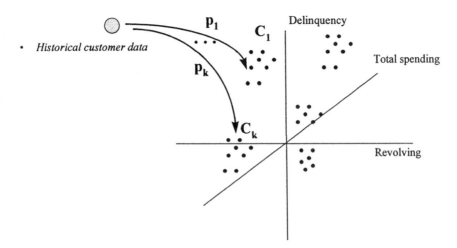

Figure 2 Segmentation of customers for prediction

4.2. Segmenting Customers into Risk-Related Groups

Alternatively, one may cluster a customer data set based on risk-related performance data to find customer groups that are homogenous with respect to risk. Example performance data are aggregations for delinquency, credit revolving, and total spending. Haimowitz and Schwarz (1997) combined risk-related segmentation with likelihood prediction in a credit-line assignment task. Figure 2 from their work illustrates that the prediction was of a probability vector, p_1 to p_k, specifying membership in a variety of customer clusters, some quite risky, others less so.

Cluster membership is a function of time, and therefore one can model the customer life cycle with a state transition diagram. Customers can be modeled by assigning a probability of moving between more and less risky states over time (Figure 3), with probabilities determined as a function of account characteristics. Makuch et al. (1992) used delinquency status as the state and then learned transition probabilities for credit card customers for which certain collection actions were taken, such as do nothing, tape messages, mailings, and so on.

State in period t+1

	current	1-due	2-due	. . .	n-due	chrg-off
current	$P_{0,0}$	$P_{0,1}$	0	. . .	0	0
1-due	$P_{1,0}$	$P_{1,1}$	$P_{1,2}$	. . .	0	0
2-due	$P_{2,0}$	$P_{2,1}$	$P_{2,2}$	. . .	0	0
.	.	.	.	.	.	.
n-due	$P_{n,0}$	$P_{n,1}$	$P_{n,2}$	. . .	$P_{n,n}$	$P_{n,m}$
chrg-off	0	0	0	. . .	0	1

State in period t

Figure 3 Delinquency transition probability matrix

The matrix in Figure 3 illustrates the state-transition model, where 1-due, 2-due, and so on, are the number of months the customer is in arrears. This matrix can also be used to determine roll rates, that is, the rate at which accounts advance in due stage over the course of time.

4.3. Net Present Value Computations and Predictions

The net present value (NPV) of an investment is defined as the net income the investment generates, with future income discounted to the time of the original investment. Net present value is a standard used by corporations in budgeting capital investments (Brealy and Myers, 1991), and is recommended as a good quantitative measure of the success of a targeted marketing campaign (Hughes, 1994). NPV is also a natural measure of the profitability of an individual customer, such as a catalog recipient (Bitran and Mondschein, 1996). Another example is a credit customer making payments over years.

An NPV calculation is dependent on the financial application and includes both expenses and revenue. Expenses include costs of acquiring the account, mailing bills, managing delinquency, and written-off dollars from unpaid balances. Revenue includes payments of bills received and service charges received. The NPV of a customer is essentially future expected revenues minus future expected costs discounted to the time of decisionmaking. Inherent in an NPV calculation is a time frame. Thus, it can be used as a risk predicate; one may wish to predict "likelihood of NPV greater than $10 over the next six months," or isolate a customer segment with the highest possible NPV with little variation. NPV analysis can distinguish customers that are risky (e.g., often delinquent) yet profitable (due to high pricing) from those that are risky with negative NPV that have cost the company money.

5. Aspects of Data-Mining

One goal of data mining, and, indeed, that of all modeling, is prediction. Our efforts to understand historical data are only useful if they improve our analysis and ultimately our capability to predict. Data miners employ a synthesis of analytic approaches, typically relying on one or more of the following:

1. Estimation of the parameters of past performance: means, standard deviations, correlations, associations, and so on, for hypothesis testing

2. Classification, segmentation, or clustering of units (clients, suppliers, regions, etc.) to facilitate the modeling process

3. Construction of a functional relationship, or model, between responses and explanatory variables. Below we briefly list some specific tools data miners use for risk analysis. For a more complete treatment, see, for example, Berry and Linoff (1997).

5.1. Data Mining Techniques

While the strategic goal of data mining is to predict key enterprise phenomenon, the tactical goal is to gather and understand pertinent data, with an aim of discovering relationship patterns that further knowledge, support intelligence, and lead to action (see Figure 4).

1. *Estimation.* Summary statistics (means, medians, modes, standard deviations, correlations), Pareto analysis, nonparametric analysis, and graphical analysis. These tools do not specifically result in the construction of a model relating inputs to outputs, but do, however, contribute to domain knowledge and aid in focusing effort on activities with greater return. Sometimes this activity is called exploratory data analysis.

2. *Clustering/segmentation.* k-means, distance matrices (Euclidean/non-Euclidean), association rules. These approaches result in a logical grouping of observations by similarity in their characteristics, reducing the level of heterogeneity in the data. They are usually performed as a prelude to further modeling.

3. *Classification/discrimination.* CHAID (chi-squared automatic induction), CART (classification and regression trees; Breiman et al., 1993), regression, discriminant

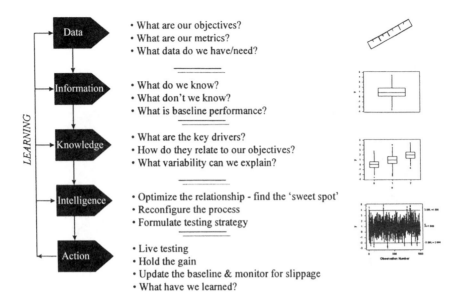

Figure 4 The data mining paradigm

analysis, rule induction. In classification, there are usually a predetermined number of classes to which observations will be assigned, unlike in clustering, where the number of classes or segments is determined empirically, or otherwise allowed to vary. Another contrast is that classification and discrimination approaches are aided by supervision: class assignments are constructed by an associated objective measure, such as the ones described in
Section 4.

4. *Prediction.* Linear/nonlinear regression, CART, MARS (multiple adapted regression splines), artificial neural nets, genetic algorithms, time-series regression (transfer function) models, stochastic models (Markov decision processes), and hybrid models. With these techniques, formal mathematical models are built for the purpose of executing change from a current level of performance to an improved future one, that is, for optimization. Each approach carries its unique baggage of assumptions and shortcomings, and one must remain critical and vigilant when putting them to use (Berry and Linoff, 1997).

5.2. Problems Confronting Data Miners

Below, we categorize the problems data miners in risk management often experience:

1. *Data collection.* Data available for mining are often retrospective (i.e., gathered from historical circumstance) and not the result of carefully planned experimentation and random selection. Factors that drive risk may therefore be buried in the rubble of the actual data elements that describe a confusing amalgam of historical policy changes, economic environments, and system changes. Whenever possible, data mining should begin with defining and measuring the factors that may prove useful in future mining activity, as opposed to being held captive by existing data.

2. *Data hygiene.* Quality of the data to be mined is usually questionable, owing typically to human intervention somewhere along the data entry and maintenance path. There can be missing data or inconsistent entries, and one must assess the potential impact on prediction of data scrubbing methods such as imputation or elimination.

3. *Sampling.* Stratified random sampling may be needed in situations where the data are too voluminous, yet may be troublesome when there may be too few items of interest (e.g.,

defaults, frauds, and so on). One should utilize resampling schemes that can be used to assure consistency of conclusions.

4. *Aging.* Information used in constructing models may become stale by deployment time. Similarly, one faces score drift: by deployment, or over time, a model may no longer predict performance; and one must monitor the model's predictiveness for degradation.

6. Implementation of Data Mining Results

Data mining, to be a key enabler of risk management, must be viewed in the business context. Even after the best of all data and methods has been employed, only half the risk management battle has been won. The data mining team must achieve buy-in from the various corporate stakeholders, including the implementers to make sure the solution is translated correctly, and a good system for monitoring impact and degradation is developed, installed, and used.

6.1. Organizational

Rolling out a risk model for managing customers requires agreement and coordination from several organizations besides the risk management department itself. Sales must agree to risk-based pricing and to segmenting of potential new customers by risk. Marketing must agree to structure and communicate promotions differently to customers having different risk profiles. Information systems must be able to implement the risk-scoring model for new account acquisitions, as well as design new reports related to risk measures. Furthermore, customer service phone and mail representatives may need to change training and customer protocols to ensure consistency of messages to customers given the new risk policy.

6.2. Computational

Project managers must not underestimate the computer and networking challenges to fully implementing a new risk system, and should involve key information systems leaders as soon as possible. New fields and tables may be needed in the customer database to record risk model results for each customer, as well as external credit bureau scores. Scoring algorithms must be reencoded (often in SAS, C, or COBOL on mainframes) for efficient processing on all customers. Implementation within a point-of-sale purchase or credit-line approval system pose further challenges. In this case, a risk score for a new customer must be computed rapidly on demand and a decision communicated by network to the sales or customer service representative.

6.3. Experimental Economic Justification

Like any commercial activity, the economic value proposition of data mining must be quantified to justify its continued existence. While this is admittedly self-serving, it is also representative of good scientific method: the benefit of implicitly quantitative endeavors should be borne out in reality to the maximum possible degree. In the case of models that result from data mining, this justification is tantamount to comparing, in a carefully controlled experiment, a champion strategy (for current process settings) to at least one challenger strategy proposed by the model(s). While this activity is not free, it does have the benefit of measuring process improvement and quantifying the new process baseline if an improvement occurs. Careful experimentation, in this context, means randomly allocating similar observations or homogeneous segments (credit accounts, for example) to the champion strategy and the challenger strategies, with consideration given to the cost of the challenger strategies, and with close monitoring over time. The statistical concepts of experimental design, adaptive control, and control charting can be gainfully employed in this regard (see Lewis, 1992, Section III.4)

ACKNOWLEDGMENTS
Ira Haimowitz conducted his research for this chapter while an employee of the General Electric Company.

References

Berry, M. J. A. and G. Linoff. 1997. *Data Mining Techniques for Marketing, Sales, and Customer Support*. New York: Wiley.

Bitran, G. R. and S. V. Mondschein. 1996. "Mailing decisions in the catalog sales industry." *Mgmnt Sci.* **42(9)**: 1364–1381.

"The boom in bad-debt bonds." *Credit Card Management*. February 1998, pp. 73–76, New York.

Brealy, R. A. and S. C. Myers. 1991. *Principles of Corporate Finance*. 4th ed., New York: McGraw-Hill.

Breiman, L., J. H. Friedman, R. A. Olshen, and C. J. Stone. 1993. *Classification and Regression Trees*. New York: Chapman & Hall.

Elder, J. and D. Pregibon. 1996. "A statistical perspective on knowledge discovery in databases." *Advances in Knowledge Discovery and Data Mining*, edited by U. M. Fayyad, J. Elder, and D. Pregibon. Cambridge, MA: MIT Press.

Glasgow, B. 1977. "Risk and fraud in the insurance industry." *AI Approaches to Fraud Detection and Risk Management*, pp. 20–21. Menlo Park, CA: AAAI Press.

Haimowitz, I. J., O. Ozden Gur-Ali, and H. Schwarz. 1997. "Integrating and mining distributed customer databases." *Proceedings of the Third International Conference on Knowledge Discovery and Data Mining*, pp. 179–182. Menlo Park, CA: AAAI Press.

Haimowitz, I. J. and H. Schwarz. 1997. "Clustering and prediction for credit line management." *AI Approaches to Fraud Detection and Risk Management*, pp. 29–34. Menlo Park, CA: AAAI Press.

Hughes, A. M. 1994. "Lifetime value, the criterion of strategy." *Strategic Database Marketing*. Chap. 3. Toronto: Irwin Professional Publishing.

Lewis, E. M. 1992. *An Introduction to Credit Scoring*. San Rafael, CA: Fair, Isaac and Co.

Makuch, W., J. Dodge, J. Ecker, D. Granfors, and G. Hahn. 1992. "Managing consumer credit delinquency in the US economy: a multi-billion dollar management science application." *Interfaces* **22(1)**: 90–109.

Schuermann, T. 1997. "Risk management in the financial services industry: through a statistical lens." *AI Approaches to Fraud Detection and Risk Management*, pp. 78–82. Menlo Park, CA: AAAI Press.

Further Reading

In addition to those references cited in the text, the following references give further information on this subject.

Bernstein, P. L. 1996. *Against the Gods: The Remarkable Story of Risk*. New York: Wiley.

Nelson, R. W. 1997. *Credit Card Risk Management*, Kalamazoo, MI: Warren Taylor Publishing.

Rosenberg, E. and Gleit, A. 1994. "Quantitative methods in credit management: a survey." *Oper. Res.* **42** (4), 589–613.

37 PRODUCTION CONTROL

Pieter W. Adriaans

ABSTRACT Production control is a rich source of potential data mining applications. Gathering and cleaning the data are relatively easy. Organizations own their own production data so there are almost no legal and privacy issues. Cost justification and return on investment estimates are easy to do because organizations have a long history of setting up administrative procedures to optimize production processes. On the other hand, the penetration of data mining in this segment of industry is small. This is partly caused by the success of traditional operations research techniques that have already removed a lot of the low-hanging fruit. Another explanation is the specialized nature of production processes in various organizations. We distinguish between horizontal and vertical data mining applications. Horizontal applications can be transferred from one production industry to another. In the coming years, we expect the emergence of standard horizontal data mining solutions based on standard ERP platforms. Vertical applications are restricted to one organization or a very small group of companies. There is an abundance of examples of successful applications of vertical data mining. Although these individual applications are too specific to be generalized, one can distinguish classes of application paradigms that can be used across industry to solve similar types of data mining problems.

1. Introduction

Production control is a rich source of potential applications of data mining techniques. On the other hand, there is probably no area where data mining solutions have to compete to this degree with alternative options from traditional decision support approaches. This might explain the relatively slow acceptance of data mining in production control, compared with areas like marketing and fraud detection (see Chapters 34 and 35). In a survey by the Meta group in 1997, 22 percent of data mining users were manufacturing companies. Sales and marketing are driving these investments. In 62 percent of the cases, the investment rationale for data mining in manufacturing was increasing competitiveness. Typical goals associated with production control such as cost reduction seem to play a smaller role. Currently, we see isolated applications of data mining techniques in factories, plants, and warehouses in such diverse areas as planning, visual inspection of the production process (Barani et al., 1997), inventory control (Greuter and Wildöer, 1998), and quality management (Wirth and Reinartz, 1996). The expectation is that in coming years the use of data mining techniques in production control will grow strongly, because there is definitely a class of problems for which data mining seems to be the appropriate approach.

Ever since mass production of goods was introduced into Western society in the late nineteenth century, man has searched for new techniques for the optimization and control of the production process. In 1911, Frederick W. Taylors' *The Principles of Scientific Management* appeared. Taylor's intention was to gain maximum efficiency from workers and machines in the factory by means of so-called time-and-motion studies, which would help to determine the best methods for performing a task in the least amount of time. This illustrates the fact that systematic gathering of data and a scientific approach to production control have been around for a long time. The use of quantitative methods in management has developed into a separate field called operations research (OR), the application of scientific methods to the study of complex systems. Within the context of OR, a number of powerful mathematical techniques for planning scheduling and control exist: linear programming, dynamic programming, game theory, network analysis (PERT-CPM), probability theory, queueing theory, Markovian decision processes, and simulation. There is an established body of knowledge on the application of these techniques in the context of production control. Although data mining techniques could be applied to solve similar problems, OR techniques have a distinct advantage in cases where the problems are mathematically well defined and well within the processing power of current computers: their application is transparent, there is an established methodology, the complexity of the problem is known, and the results are predictable. The big opportunity for data therefore lies in the application of the techniques in areas where traditional OR techniques fail: the analysis of highly complex or nonlinear production systems, the presence of noise in the data, an abundance of parameters, and a lack of systematic knowledge about the domain. Most manufacturing companies have a good overview of the costs involved in the production process so the return on investment is in general relatively easy to calculate.

2. Vertical versus Horizontal Application of Data Mining

In general, the aim of production control is to produce, with the minimum amount of material and effort, an exact number of products of the highest quality at exactly the right time. Yet, in different companies the problems one has to solve are of a very diverse nature. Production processes consist of a variety of different operations. Consider for instance chemical plants, nuclear power plants, wastewater treatment, or car manufacturing. In all those contexts, data mining might be applied to specific phases of the production process. Because of this diversity it is difficult to give a general overview of the techniques used in this field. Therefore, in the analysis of the application of data mining in production control, we distinguish between horizontal and vertical data mining:

Horizontal data mining is applied to general admininstrative processes around production control, for example, data in standardized enterprise resource planning (ERP) systems. Vertical data mining application deals with specific aspects of the production process that exist in a small group of companies. We will apply the distinction in the rest of this article.

2.1. Available Data

The difference between horizontal and vertical data mining also extends to the availability of data. For horizontal applications, data are available whenever a good ERP system is installed. It is clear that organizations with an operational ERP system have a potentially rich source of data to mine.

For vertical applications, the situation is different. In vertical applications of data mining, the data are in general not gathered and stored systematically. It seems that in those contexts data mining often has to be preceded by the creation of an environment to gather the data; for example, sensors, video camera's interfaces to machines, and so on.

2.2. Security

Data mining in production control in most cases is a process that is completely internal. The organization produces and owns the data that is involved in the process. Therefore, legal issues (see Chapter 22) and security problems are relatively easy to deal with. On the other hand, the results of the data mining process are, in general, highly competition sensitive. It is relatively difficult to get information about successful applications of data mining techniques in this context.

2.3. Data Quality

The quality of data varies according to the specific application. In horizontal applications, the quality of the data is mainly dependent on the quality of the administrative processes of the organization. In vertical applications, one finds typical problems of data collection with physical devices, sensors, video cameras, and so on.

3. Application Paradigms

In order to discuss the use of data mining techniques in production control, we will introduce the notion of an application paradigm of a data mining technique. This notion helps us to distinguish the neutral aspect of a learning technique from the different contexts in which the techniques can be used. Induction of decision trees (see Chapter 16.1.3) for instance has been used in:

- *Marketing.* Induction of different profiles of groups of people interested in a certain product based on historic data concerning buying behavior.

- *Aviation.* Learning to fly a plane based on the analysis of sequences of actions of experienced pilots (Sammut et al., 1992).

- *Production control.* Learning combinations of parameters based on a historic analysis of the production process that influences the quality of a product negatively, and thus should be avoided (Chapter 46.5).

In these three examples there is one technique—induction of decision trees—that can be used in various application paradigms: marketing, aviation, and production control. Another example is the different application paradigms that exist for association rules (see Chapter 16.2.3): one could use them to do basket analysis in a marketing context, to do causal modeling of complex production systems, or to find correlations between error conditions in a computer network. The set of application paradigms of neural networks (see Chapter 16.1.8) in production control is almost without limit. These application paradigms form in themselves an important body of knowledge in the practical deployment of data mining in business and industry. They encompass the definition of specific problem types that can be solved with data mining techniques, various ways to gather data, specific discretizations of the search space, and the analysis of specific bias that make the application of data mining feasible. The basic challenge for the data mining community in general, but specifically in production control, is to find the right application paradigms for existing data mining techniques. In the following sections we will outline some of the current paradigms.

4. Horizontal Data-Mining in Production Control

There is a long tradition in standardization of information management in production control. Material requirements planning (MRP) deals with the creation of work and purchase orders based on inventory data, product descriptions, and a master production schedule. Capacity requirements planning (CRP) project the machine loads from the material plan. Manufacturing resource planning (MRP II) is an extension of MRP that plans all resources needed for running a business. A development that will contribute greatly to the success of data mining in industry is the emergence of so-called enterprise resource planning (ERP) systems. ERP updates MRP with a relational database management system (DBMS), a graphical user interface (GUI), and a client/server architecture. Active vendors are SAP and Baan. Their products create an excellent environment for systematic gathering and analysis of production data. Recently, these vendors have started to add rich decision support capabilities to their platforms. An example is the SAP Business Intelligence initiative that, according to the vendor, provides a holistic, closed-loop system that provides the most current, nearly real-time information encompassing operational data, analytical intelligence, and contextual knowledge. Using these tools, decisionmakers can make informed business decisions, drive the decisions to operational systems and monitor the results. Although their application is scarce right now, it will only be a matter of time before standard data mining techniques are integrated in this kind of business intelligence module on top of ERP systems. MRP II modules are: forecasting, customer order entry, production planning, master production scheduling, product structure, bill-of-material processor, inventory control, material requirements planning, capacity planning, shop-floor control, accounting, and financial analysis. In principle, it is conceivable that data mining can be used to optimize all of these activities in some form or another. At this moment, vendors of ERP platforms have not yet added structural facilities for data mining to their products. They rely on the emergence of specialized service providers and tool vendors in this area.

4.1. An Example: Proactive Material Planning

An example of the application of data mining in an ERP context is the optimization of inventory control. Material requirements planning concepts assume a production environment in which the material that is needed is known beforehand. Determining which parts to keep in stock and in what quantity is a complex task. Most stocks are currently managed based on historical consumption, not taking into account planned maintenance activities. Data mining can help in defining material consumption models that can be used to perform proactive stock management. There are a lot of situations where it is difficult to predict material consumptions. Market demands can vary, but also maintenance of production units can cause considerable material consumption. Greuter and Wildöer (1998) describe the application of proactive data mining material planning. We will follow their presentation:

When performing preventive maintenance, the material that is required is dependent on the outcome of the inspections. This uncertainty about part usage makes it impossible to maintain a stock that accurately represents the actual need for parts. An inaccurate prediction of part consumption causes:

- Parts not being available when they are needed for maintenance, leading to:

  - delay during maintenance;
  - higher ordering costs for these parts, because of the high expense of making this part available as soon as possible;
  - higher stock costs, since a minimum safety level is needed to guarantee a reasonable availability for the execution of maintenance.

The costs of low availability and large stock can be very high. Therefore, improving the balance between available and required material will result in significant business benefits. Figure 1 shows how an improved stock content improves availability levels with the same stock costs.

The question as to what availability level is acceptable and which stock costs are acceptable is dependent on the specific business situation. Proactive stock management is only possible if maintenance processes have a repetitive structure and are scheduled a relatively long time before they are executed.

Each material consumption will have its own specific cause. The challenge of proactive planning is to find a way to describe these causes in such a way that they can be compared to the content of scheduled maintenance activities. From that comparison it becomes possible to generate predictions of material consumption for the future.

One way to find these causes is to look for patterns in the historical consumption of each part. For this, information is needed about historical requests for this part, along with information about the circumstances in which the part was needed. By using data mining techniques, prediction models for all parts can be generated. When these prediction models are combined with maintenance planning, they result in a prediction of the consumption of material in the planned period. This prediction can then be used as an input to the material planning process. This process is shown below in Figure 2.

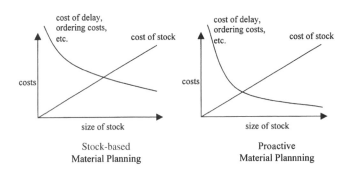

Figure 1 Cost of stock vs. cost delay etc.

The advantages of this new structured process are numerous:

- Clear insight into the causes of material consumption for each part.
- Quantitative information about part consumption in time.
- Possibility to define structured material planning policies.
- Self-optimizing process, increasing the corporate knowledge level.

In maintenance environments we are dealing with a large number of maintenance activities (typically 10,000–500,000 each year) and a large set of possible parts (typically 1,000–25,000 different parts), whereas the actual consumption of parts is relatively low (e.g., 1 consumption in every 25 inspections). By using decision trees, the consumption of parts can be localized to their specific areas, and within these areas chances of occurrence can easily be calculated. For each individual part, a separate decision tree is generated. This means that 1,000–25,000 trees are created in total, which can be done in an automated way using data mining tools. All executed maintenance activities are divided into (1) activities with consumption for the given part and (2) activities without consumption for this part. In practice, ± 99 percent of all activities will have no consumption for a given part. Using these techniques, one can realize better predictions and thus make significant cost reductions.

5. Vertical Application of Data Mining in Production Control: Some Application Paradigms

There is an abundance of isolated vertical applications of data mining in production control. All these applications have their specific data collection, cleaning, and feature selection problems. Different application paradigms have emerged around different learning techniques.

Sometimes different techniques are used to solve similar problems. Barani et al. (1997) describe an automatic knowledge discovery process from a database of images in the context of automatic visual quality inspection of industrial products under informal quality models.

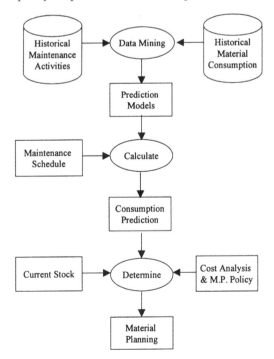

Figure 2 Proactive material planning

One of the key problems in this application is feature selection (see Chapter 16.1.7): What are the right visual primitives? They analyze the appropriateness of different learning methods (FOIL and C4.5). C4.5 (see Chapter 16.1.3) seems to have the best overall perfomance. Lindner and Klose (1997) study trend prognosis of fault rate behavior using linear regression (see Chapter 14.2), C4.5, and neural networks.

Sometimes the same technique is used for completely different purposes. Markov decision processes are used in robot control problems as well as in inventory control. Kimura et al. (1997) have worked on controlling a robot arm using reinforcement learning to learn Markov decision processes. Mahadevan et al. (1997) have studied factory optimization problems, from inventory control to scheduling and reliability as continuous-time Markov decision processes. A key feature of this study is the integration of a reinforcement learning algorithm with discrete-event simulation packages. Others have used decision trees to optimize inventory control (Greuter and Wildöer, 1998).

Another area of interest is applying knowledge-based systems to automate hazard identification methods such as HAZOP (hazard and operability studies), fault-tree analysis, and checklists that have traditionally been carried out manually (Wang and McGreavy, 1997). Data mining in connection with case-based reasoning can be used to analyze large databases with historical data effectively, and to extract knowledge in the form of rules to be used by hazard identification experts.

It is difficult to categorize all these applications under a common denominator. In order to give the reader an impression of the possibilities, we discuss two typical application paradigms briefly.

5.1. The Nondeterministic, Noncausal Black-Box Approach

A big opportunity for data mining lies in domains where both traditional OR and expert system approaches fail. Sometimes one is confronted with complex problems where OR techniques do not work and experts with systematic knowledge are simply not available. The following situation is typical. Suppose one has a unit in a production process that can be in two states, good and bad, that is, it functions properly or not. Causal models of the unit are not available. They may be unknown or the processes in the black box may be too complex to analyze properly. Yet, a machine-learning algorithm may construct a decision model based on historical observation of the behavior of the black box. Interestingly enough, this decision model only helps us to take decisions on the parameter configurations that we have to avoid in order to keep the unit in good health. It does not necessarily lead to a deterministic, or a causal, model of the black box. This means that data mining may teach us to use some device without helping us to understand how it works. This is a fairly normal situation for human beings. We all use our hands and legs without understanding completely how they work, but from the perspective of artificial intelligence (AI) research, this is quite an interesting novelty. So far AI research has focused on understanding systems, that is, human rationality. Data mining and machine learning seem to be focused on what we do, not on what we can explain. This pragmatic pitch partly explains why data mining succeeds in situations where traditional techniques fail.

There are a number of examples of such a black-box approach in industry. Chapter 46.5 have used induction of decision trees to significantly mitigate one kind of process delay, called banding, at a plant of the world's largest printing company. Experts did not possess strong knowledge of banding causes but were able to supply relevant features. Approximately thirty features that might influence this process were selected. Decision trees were created on the basis of historical observations. In a process of interactive induction, combinations of parameter values that needed to be avoided because they apparently caused the banding phenomema were identified. Neither a deterministic nor a causal model needed to be constructed in order to reduce the banding considerably.

Den Heijer and Adriaans (1996) have used genetic algorithms (see Chapter 11) to analyze behavior of pilots in the context of a career and simulator planning application at KLM. In the analysis of planning and scheduling problems, the human planner often has some rules of thumb, but these rules lack structural cohesion. They are insufficient for the construction of an automatic planning system. A critical factor was the prediction of bid behavior of the pilots. The genetic algorithm was able to learn a model that predicted the right behavior in 90 percent of the cases, but it gave no real insight into the factors that determined the behavior of the pilots.

5.2. *Learning Models of Complex Dynamic Systems*

In production control, one is often confronted with the need to construct models of complex dynamic systems. When historical data are available, process plants consist of equipment units linked by pipelines. Inside the equipment, chemical processes (e.g., reactions) and physical processes (e.g., mass and heat transfer) take place. Liquid and vapour fluids are transported between the units via pipelines. The plant is provided with control, instrumentation, and alarm systems. Operability studies require the simulation of disturbance and fault propagation in a process structure. Analyzing these environments with traditional analytical methods is very complicated, if not impossible. One has to solve complex algebraic and differential equations in order to model the highly nonlinear behavior of these plants. Also, the volume of data is a problem. An incident database of a medium-sized company may easily contain 10,000 abnormal occurrence reports. Neural networks in combination with expert systems seem to be a workable solution. Neural networks can learn rules that can be incorporated into the knowledge base of an expert system. Wang and McGreavy (1997) have studied the application of these techniques on heat exchangers. Knobbe et al. (1998, 1999) describe the application of decision trees and association rules to analyze extremely complex information technology (IT) systems.

6. Conclusion

In general, one can say that the applications of data mining in production control are diverse but successful. It is relatively easy to set up a data mining project in production control, especially in organizations with an ERP environment. Data security is not a big problem. Return of investment is relatively easy to calculate. Data availability is sometimes problematic when data collection is done with physical devices. Still, there is an abundance of opportunities. The future will bring considerable growth to this field.

References

Barani, M., R. Cucchiara, P. Mello, and M. Picardi. April 1997. "Data mining for automated visual inspection." In *Proceedings of the PADD97*. London.

"Data Mining Market Trends 1997–1998: A multiclient study." Meta Group, May 23, 1997.

Den Heijer, E. and P. W. Adriaans. 1996. "The application of genetic algorithms in a career planning environment." *Int. J. HCI.*

Greuter, M. M. and R. P. Wildöer. 1998. "Material requirement planning in a maintenance environment through data mining". Internal report. Syllogic.

Kimura, H., K. Myazaki, and S. Kobayashi. 1997. "Reinforcement learning on POMDP's with function approximation." In *Machine Learning, Proceedings of the Fourteenth International Conference (ICML 97)*. Nashville.

Knobbe, A., B. Marseille, O. Moerbeek, and D. van der Wallen. 1998. "Results in data mining for adaptive system management." In *Proceedings of Benelearn '98*.

Knobbe, A., D. van der Wallen, and L. Lewis. 1999. "Experiments with data mining in enterprise management." In *Proceedings of Integrated Management '99*.

Létourneau, S., A. Famili, and S. Matwin. 1997. "Discovering useful knowledge from aircraft operational/maintenance data" In *Proceedings of the Workshop on Machine Learning Application in the Real World: Methodological Aspects and Implications*. Nashville, edited by R. Engels, B. Evans, J. Herrmann, and F. Verdenius.

Lindner, G. and A. Klose. 1997. "ML and statistics for trend prognosis of complaints in the automobile industry" In *Proceedings of the Workshop on Machine Learning Application in the Real World: Methodological Aspects and Implications*. Nashville, edited by R. Engels, B. Evans, J. Herrmann, and F. Verdenius.

Mahadevan, S., N. Marchalleck, T. K. Das, and A. Gosavi. 1997. "Self-improving factory simulation using continuous-time average-reward reinforcement learning." In *Machine Learning, Proceedings of the Fourteenth International Conference (ICML 97)*. Nashville.

Sammut, C., S. Hurst, D. Kedzier, and D. Michie. 1992. "Learning to fly". In *Machine Learning, Proceedings of the Ninth International Workshop (ML92)*, edited by D. Sleeman and P. Edwards. Aberdeen.

Wang, X. Z. and C. McGreavy. April 1997. "Data mining for safety and operability studies in process industries." In *Proceedings of the PADD97*. London.

Wirth, R. and T. Reinartz. 1996. "Detecting early indicator cars in an automitive database: a multi strategy approach." In *Proceedings of the Second International Conference on Knowledge Discovery and Data Mining*. Portland, OR.

38 TEXT MINING

Ronen Feldman

ABSTRACT The information age is characterized by a rapid growth in the amount of information available in electronic media. Traditional data handling methods are not adequate to cope with this flood of information. Knowledge discovery in databases (KDD) is a new paradigm that focuses on automatic or semiautomatic exploration of large amounts of data and on discovery of relevant and interesting patterns within them. While most work on KDD is concerned with structured databases, it is clear that this paradigm is required for handling the huge amount of information that is available only in unstructured textual form. To apply KDD on texts, it is necessary to impose some structure on the data that would be rich enough to allow for interesting KDD operations. On the other hand, we must consider the severe limitations of current text processing technology and define rather simple structures that can be extracted from texts fairly automatically and at a reasonable cost. One of the options is to use a text categorization/term extraction paradigm to annotate text articles with meaningful concepts that are organized in a hierarchical structure. This relatively simple annotation is rich enough to provide the basis for a novel KDD framework, enabling data summarization, exploration of interesting patterns, and trend analysis.

1. Introduction

Most informal definitions (Fayyad et al., 1996) introduce knowledge discovery in databases (KDD) as the extraction of useful information from databases by large-scale search for interesting patterns. The vast majority of existing KDD applications and methods deal with structured databases, for example, client data stored in a relational database (see Chapter 6.1), and thus exploit data organized in records structured by categorical, ordinal, and continuous variables. However, a tremendous amount of information is stored in documents that are virtually unstructured. The availability of document collections and especially of online information is rapidly growing, so that an analysis bottleneck often also arises in this area.

A document collection represents a special application domain and each document is related to a set of the concepts that play a role in this domain. Therefore, one knowledge discovery approach for document collections is targeted at these concepts, that is, seeking patterns that describe (co-occurrence) relations between concepts of the domain. Data mining methods thus extract knowledge about a document domain by searching and structuring interesting concept relations and tracking their changes over time. Additionally, they supply new browsing capabilities using the interdocument information contained in the patterns discovered.

Following this approach, it is obvious that knowledge discovery in the document area is a process (see Chapter 12) that involves preprocessing, data mining, and refinement tasks. Methods of term extraction or text categorization belong to the main preprocessing tasks in this area. Data mining methods, because typically based on large-scale brute force search, produce many patterns. As in KDD for structured databases, one of the main discovery tasks relates to constraining the search by operationalizing interestingness (see Chapter 19.2.2), especially to prevent the user from becoming overwhelmed with too many results.

An additional goal aspires to provide a complemental retrieval approach. Traditionally, retrieval is supported by a query approach selecting all the documents in a collection that include some boolean combinations of keywords. Moreover, clustering approaches are applied in the classical retrieval area that constructs extensional clusters of documents using a distance function for documents. Documents can then be accessed via these query results or clusterings. Data mining approaches provide complemental retrieval possibilities that are given by accessing those documents that support the detected patterns. Thus, the data mining system detects groups of potentially interesting documents that could be browsed. Such a group can be seen as a potentially useful query that the system has identified and that was unknown to the user.

In traditional retrieval it is assumed that the user knows in advance the concepts of documents he could be interested in, or that he selects a constructed cluster of documents (e.g., Salton, 1989; Cutting et al., 1993). Applying KDD tools like Document Explorer (see Chapter 24.4.3) means that the system takes an active role in suggesting concepts of interest to the user, as well as supplying new browsing methods that rely on interdocument information. The discovery framework of Document Explorer may thus be viewed as an intermediate point between user-specified retrieval queries and unsupervised document clustering. The user typically provides some guidance to the system about the type of patterns of interest, but then the system identifies groups of pattern instances applying filtering, ordering, generalization, statistical validation, and clustering techniques.

2. What is Unique About Text Mining?

The most noticeable feature of document collections is the very large number of features that represent each of the documents. Typically, some thousands of keywords or concepts may be relevant for an application domain. The number of attributes in a relational database that are analyzed in a data mining task for structured data is usually much smaller. Additionally, the features are very sparse, that is, only a small percentage of all possible features appears in a single document, so that when a document is represented as a binary vector of features, nearly all values of the vector are zero. Sparseness is also given for the tuple dimension: some features often appear in only a few documents, so that the support of many patterns is quite low.

Features can be arranged in a directed acyclic graph with several hierarchical categories or taxonomies (see Chapter 18.1). These taxonomies are very important, since they allow the user to group the patterns in an adequate hierarchical level. Due to the very large feature set, the overabundance problem of identified patterns is still more relevant for these document applications than for data applications structured the usual way.

Relations between term categories can easily introduce background knowledge. Thus, an additional structure is given for the feature set. They are not just elements in a flat set as in most structured data applications.

These special characteristics of the data mining task for document collections stress the importance of efficient filtering (during and after search) or refinement techniques (see Chapter 19.1), including suppressing, ordering, pruning, generalization, and clustering approaches.

In the subsequent sections we describe the term extraction module of a typical text mining system (such as Document Explorer) (Feldman and Hirsch, 1966; Feldman and Dagan, 1995), and we provide some examples of how the terms extracted from the documents are used for mining the document collection.

3. Alternative Text Representations as a Basis for Text Mining

The simplest form is to represent each document as a vector of words. However, when trying to apply association rule generation (see Chapter 16.2.3) on such representations, we would produce meaningless results. For instance, in Rajman and Besançon (1997), the association generation process detected either compounds, that is, domain-dependent terms such as [wall, street], or [treasury, secretary, james, baker], which are not potentially useful associations, or extracted uninterpretable associations, such as [dollars, shares, exchange, total, commission, stake, securities], which are not easily understandable.

Another paradigm is based on the automatic construction of text classifiers (see Chapter 16.1) based on a set of training articles, typically using statistical methods (for example Lewis, 1992; Iwayama and Tokunaga, 1994). This paradigm can be viewed as an instance of inductive learning (Quinlan, 1993; Kulikowski and Weiss, 1991), which attempts to extrapolate from a collection of labeled examples a classifier capable of accurately assigning labels to future unlabeled examples. Accordingly, there has been some recent work that has applied general inductive learning methods to text categorization (Apte et al., 1994; Lewis and Catlett, 1994;

> Profits at Canada's six big banks topped C$6 billion ($4.4 billion) in 1996, smashing last year's C$5.2 billion ($3.8 billion) record as Canadian Imperial Bank of Commerce and National Bank of Canada wrapped up the earnings season Thursday. The six banks each reported a double-digit jump in net income for a combined profit of C$6.26 billion ($4.6 billion) in fiscal 1996 ended Oct. 31.
> But a third straight year of record profits came amid growing public anger over perceived high service charges and credit card rates, and tight lending policies.
> Bank officials defended the group's performance, saying that millions of Canadians owned bank shares through mutual funds and pension plans.

Figure 1 Example of the output of the term extraction module. Terms chosen to label the document are underlined

Iwayama and Tokunaga, 1994). This paradigm can be viewed as an instance of inductive learning (Quinlan, 1993; and Kulikowski and Weiss, 1991).

Another alternative is to use normalized terms, that is, sequences of one or more lemmatized word forms (or lemmas) associated with their part-of-speech tags. Stock/N market/N or annual/Adj interest/N rate/N are typical examples of such normalized terms.

In the next section, we will describe the term extraction algorithms and the organization of the terms in taxonomies.

4. Term Extraction

Term extraction is used for labeling each document with a set of terms extracted from the document. An example of the output of the term extraction module is given in Figure 1. The excerpt is taken from an article published by Reuters Financial on 12 May 1996. Terms in this excerpt that were identified and designated as interesting by the term extraction module are underlined.

The overall architecture of the term extraction module is illustrated in Figure 2. There are three main stages in this module: linguistic preprocessing, term generation, and term filtering.

The documents are loaded into the system through a special reader. The reader uses a configuration file that informs it of the meaning of the different tags annotating the documents. In such a way, we are able to handle a large variety of formats. The TPL reader packages the information into a SGML file.

The next step is linguistic preprocessing that includes tokenization, part-of-speech tagging, and lemmatzations, (i.e., a linguistically more founded version of stemming; Hull, 1996). The objective of the part-of-speech tagging is to automatically associate morphosyntactic categories such as noun, verb, adjective, et cetera, to the words in the document. In our

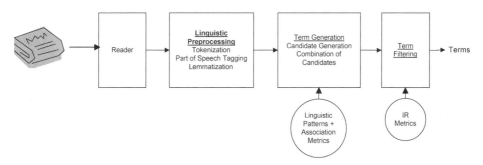

Figure 2 Architecture of the term extraction module

system, we used a rule-based approach (see Chapter 16.1.4) similar to the one presented in Brill (1995), which is known to yield satisfying results (96 percent accuracy), provided that a large lexicon (containing tags and lemmas) and some manually hand-tagged data are available for training.

The term generation and term filtering modules are described in the following subsections.

4.1. Term Generation

In the term generation stage, sequences of tagged lemmas are selected as potential term candidates on the basis of relevant morphosyntactic patterns (such as noun-noun, noun-preposition-noun, adjective-noun, etc.). The candidate combination stage is performed in several passes. In each pass, an association coefficient between each pair of adjacent terms is calculated and a decision is made whether they should be combined. In the case of competing possibilities (such as $(t_1 \ t_2)$ and $(t_2 \ t_3)$ in $(t_1 \ t_2 \ t_3)$), the pair having the better association coefficient is replaced first. The documents are then updated by converting all combined terms into atomic terms by concatenating the terms with an underscore. The whole procedure is then iterated until no new terms are generated.

The nature of the patterns used for candidate generation is an open research question. Daille et al. (1994) and Daille (1996) propose specific operators (such as overcomposition, modification, and coordination) to select longer terms by using combinations of shorter ones. In Dagan and Church (1994), candidate terms are taken to be noun-noun sequences (i.e., noun sequences of length 2 or more). This technique has improved the precision but reduced recall. Justeson and Katz (1995) suggest accepting prepositions as well as adjectives and nouns. This approach generates a much larger number of term candidates, while in Frantzi (1997), only (noun|adjective)-noun sequences are accepted to reduce the amount of bad terms.

In Document Explorer we used two basic patterns: noun-noun and adjective-noun, but we also allowed the insertion of any kind of determiner, preposition, or subordinating conjunction. Therefore, sequences such as "health program for the elderly," "networking software for personal computers," "operating system of a computer," or "King Fahd of Saudi Arabia" are accepted as well.

We have tested four different association coefficients: co-occurrence frequency, ϕ^2, association ratio (Church and Hanks, 1990), and log likelihood (Dunning, 1993; Daille, 1996). The co-occurrence frequency is the simplest association measure that relies on the number of times that the two terms match one of the extraction patterns. ϕ^2 has been used to align words inside aligned sentences (Gale and Church, 1991) and for term extraction (Daille, 1996). The association ratio was used for monolingual word association and is based on the concept of mutual information. Log likelihood is a logarithmic likelihood probability. Our candidate combination phase uses two thresholds. The first is a threshold T_{freq} for the co-occurrence frequency. The second is a threshold T_{metric} for additional filtering on the basis of a complementary association coefficient.

4.2. Term Filtering

The term generation stage produces a set of terms associated with each document without taking into account the relevance of these terms in the framework of the whole document collection. A consequence of this is a substantial overgeneration of terms. Additional filtering is therefore necessary and several approaches can be tested.

The goal of the term filtering stage is to reduce the number of term candidates produced by the term generation stage on the basis of some statistical relevance scoring scheme. After scoring all the terms generated in the term generation stage, we sort them based on their scores and select only the top M terms.

For example, the following are all two-word terms that were identified in the term generation stage but later filtered out in the term filtering stage: *right direction*, *other issue*, *long way*, *question mark*, and *same time*. These terms were determined not to be of interest in the

Table 1 The Scores of the Terms Found by the Term Generation Stage for the Document Shown in Figure 1

Term	Score
Net_income	17.17
Bank	14.88
Earnings	11.41
Canada	10.39
Mutual_fund	8.22
National_bank_of_Canada	7.68
Bank_official	6.56
Pension_plan	6.34
Profit	6.20
Performance	6.09
Anger	5.82
Record_profit	5.63
Canadian_imperial_bank_of_commerce	5.56
Big_bank	5.39
Canadian	5.29
Lending	4.73
Credit_card	4.56
Jump	**4.03**
Season	**3.86**
Group	**3.77**
Policy	**2.84**
Share	**1.50**

context of the whole document collection either because they do not occur frequently enough or because they occur in a constant distribution among the different documents.

We have tested three approaches for scoring terms based on their relevance in the document collection:

1. *Deviation-based approach.* The rationale behind the deviation-based approach is the hypothesis, often used in lexicometry, that terms with a distribution uniform over a collection of documents correspond to terms with little semantic content (i.e., uninteresting words that should be filtered out; Bookstein et al., 1995). We use the standard deviation of the relative frequency of a given term t over all the documents of the collection as the score of t.

2. *Statistical significance approach.* The underlying idea is to test whether the variation of the relative frequency of a given term t in the document collection is statistically significant. This is done using the χ^2 significance test on the relative frequency of a given term t.

3. *Information retrieval approach.* The notion of term relevance with respect to a document collection is a central issue in information retrieval (Salton and Buckley, 1988). We assign each term its score terms–based maximal $tf - idf$ (term frequency − inverse document frequency) score (maximal with respect to all the documents in the collection).

An example of the results of the term filtering stage is given in Table 1. The table shows the scores of the terms found in the excerpt given in Figure 1. Terms appearing in bold were discarded in the filtering stage.

5. Taxonomy Construction

One of the crucial issues in performing text mining at the term level is the need for a term taxonomy. A term taxonomy also enables the production of high-level association rules that are similar to general association rules (Srikant and Agrawal, 1995). These rules capture

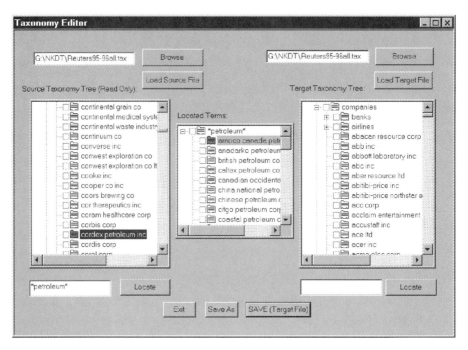

Figure 3 Taxonomy editor.

relationships between groups of terms rather than individual terms. A taxonomy (see Chapter 18.1) is also important in other text mining algorithms such as maximal association rules and frequent maximal sets (Feldman et al., 1997).

A taxonomy also enables the user to specify mining tasks in a concise way. For instance, when trying to generate association rules, rather than looking for all possible rules, the user can specify interest only in the relationships of companies in the context of business alliances. In order to do so, we need two nodes in the term taxonomy marked business alliances and companies. The first node contains all terms related to alliance such as joint venture, strategic alliance, combined initiative, et cetera, while the second node is the parent of all company names in our system (we used a set of rules and knowledge extracted from WWW directories to generate company names).

Building a term taxonomy is a time consuming task. Hence, a typical text mining system must provide a set of tools for semiautomatic construction of such a taxonomy. An example of such a tool is the taxonomy editor shown in Figure 3. This tool enables the user to read a set of terms or an external taxonomy, and use them to update the system's term taxonomy. The user can drag entire subtrees in the taxonomies or specify a set of terms via regular expressions. In Figure 3, we can see the terms found when specifying the pattern "petroleum". The initial set of terms is the set of all terms extracted from the Reuters 52,000 document collection (shown in the left tree), the terms matching the query are shown in the middle tree, and the right tree is the target taxonomy.

The taxonomy editor also includes a semiautomatic tool for taxonomy editing called the taxonomy editor refiner (TER). The TER compares generated frequent sets against the term taxonomy. When most of the terms of a frequent set are determined to be siblings in the taxonomy hierarchy, the tool suggests adding the remaining terms as siblings. For example, if our taxonomy currently contains fifteen companies under tobacco companies and the system generated a frequent set containing many tobacco companies, one of which does not appear in

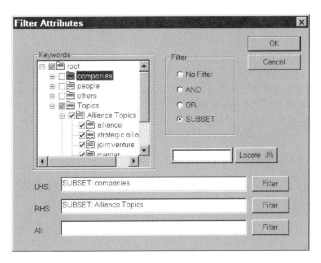

Figure 4 Specifying a filter to display only association rules with companies on the left-hand-side of the rule and alliance topics on the right-hand-side

the taxonomy, the TER will suggest adding this additional company to the taxonomy as a tobacco company. The TER also has a term clustering module that suggests that terms clustered together be placed as siblings in the taxonomy.

6. Mining Association Rules from Document Collections

In the example presented below, the user is interested in business alliances between companies. She therefore specifies a filter (see Chapter 18.4) for the association rules generation algorithm, requesting only association rules with companies on the left-hand side of the rule and business alliance topics on the right-hand side. Figure 4 shows the filter definition window.

Example 1. *Using a collection of financial Reuters articles from 1995–1996, the association generation module generates 12,000 frequent sets that comply with the restriction specified by the filter (with a support threshold of five documents and confidence threshold of 0.1). These frequent sets generated 575 associations. A further analysis removed rules that were subsumed by other rules,*

america online inc, bertelsmann ag $\Rightarrow$ joint venture 13/0.72

apple computer inc, sun microsystems inc $\Rightarrow$ merger talk 22/0.27

apple computer inc, taligent inc $\Rightarrow$ joint venture 6/0.75

sprint corp, tele-communications inc $\Rightarrow$ alliance 8/0.25

burlington northern inc, santa fe pacific corp $\Rightarrow$ merger 9/0.23

lockheed corp, martin marietta corp $\Rightarrow$ merger 14/0.4

chevron corp, mobil corp $\Rightarrow$ joint venture 11/0.26

intuit inc, novell inc $\Rightarrow$ merger 8/0.47

bank of boston corp, corestates financial corp $\Rightarrow$ merger talk 7/0.69

Figure 5 A sample of the association rules found by TextVis that comply with the restrictions specified in the rule filter shown in Figure 4

resulting in a total of 569 rules. A sample of these rules is presented in Figure 5. The numbers presented at the end of each rule are the rule's support and confidence.

The example above illustrates the advantages of performing text mining at the term level. Terms such as *joint venture* would be totally lost if working at the word level. Company names, such as Santa Fe Pacific Corp and Bank of Boston Corp, would also not have been identified. Another important issue is the construction of a useful taxonomy such as the one used in the example above. Such a taxonomy cannot be defined at the word level, as many logical objects and concepts are, in fact, multiword terms.

References

Apté, C., Damerau, F., and S. M. Weiss. 1994. "Automated learning of decision rules for text categorization." *TOIS* **12(3)**: 233–251.

Bookstein, A., S. T. Klein, and T. Raita. 1995. "Clumping properties of content-bearing words." In *Proceedings of SIGIR'95*. Seattle, WA: ACM Press.

Brill, E. 1995. "Transformation-based error-driven learning and natural language processing: a case study in part-of-speech tagging." *Comput. Linguistics* **21(4)**: 543–565.

Church, K. W. and P. Hanks. 1990. "Word association norms, mutual information, and lexicography." *Comput. Linguistics* **16(1)**: 22–29.

Cutting, C., D. Karger, and J. Pedersen. 1993. "Constant interaction-time scatter/gather browsing of very large document collections." In *Proceedings of ACM-SIGIR Conference on Information Retrieval*. Pittsburgh: ACM Press.

Dagan, I. and K. W. Church. 1994. "Termight: identifying and translating technical terminology." In *Proceedings of the European Chapter of the Association for Computational Linguistics* EACL-94: 34–40. Las Cruces, New Mexico: Morgan Kaufmann.

Daille, B. 1996. "Study and implementation of combined techniques for automatic extraction of terminology." In *The Balancing Act: Combining Symbolic and Statistical Approaches to Language*, edited by J. Resnik and P. Klavans, pp. 49–66. Cambridge, MA: MIT Press.

Daille, B., E. Gaussier, and J. M. Lange. 1994. "Towards automatic extraction of monolingual and bilingual terminology." In *Proceedings of the International Conference on Computational Linguistics, COLING'94*, pp. 515–521.

Dunning, T. 1993. "Accurate methods for the statistics of surprise and coincidence." *Comput. Linguistics* **19(1)**: 61–74.

Fayyad, U. M., G. Piatetsky-Shapiro, and P. Smyth. 1996. "From data mining to knowledge discovery: An overview." In *Advances in Knowledge Discovery and Data Mining*. AAAI/MIT Press. pp. 1–34.

Feldman, R. and H. Hirsh. 1996. "Exploiting background information in knowledge discovery from text." *J. Intell. Inform. Sys.* AAAI Press. pp. 343–346.

Feldman, R., Y. Aumann, A. Amir, W. Klösgen, and A. Zilberstein. 1997. "Maximal association rules: a new tool for mining for keyword co-occurrences in document collections." In *Proceedings of the Third International Conference on Knowledge Discovery, KDD-97*. Newport Beach, CA: AAAI Press.

Feldman, R. and I. Dagan. 1995. "KDT—knowledge discovery in texts." In *Proceedings of the First International Conference on Knowledge Discovery, KDD-95*. Montreal, Canada: AAAI Press.

Gale, W. A. and K. W. Church. 1991. "Concordances for parallel texts." In *Proceedings of the Seventh Annual Conference of the UW Centre for the New OED and Text Research, Using Corpora*, pp. 40–62. Berkeley, CA: ACL, University of California.

Hull, D. 1996. "Stemming algorithms—a case study for detailed evaluation." *J. Am. Soc. Inform. Sci.* **47(1)**: 70–84.

Iwayama, M. and T. Tokunaga. 1995. "Cluster-based text categorization: a comparison of category search strategies." *SIGIR*. ACM. pp. 273–280.

Justeson, J. S. and S. M. Katz. 1995. "Technical terminology: some linguistic properties and an algorithm for identification in text." *Natural Language Engng* **1(1)**: 9–27.

Kulikowski, C. A. and S. Weiss. 1991. *Computer Systems that Learn: Classification and Prediction Methods from Statistics, Neural Nets, Machine Learning, and Expert Systems*. Morgan Kaufmann Publishers.

Lewis, D. 1992. "An evaluation of phrasal and clustered representations on a text categorization problem." In *Proceedings of ACM-SIGIR Conference on Information Retrieval*. Copenhagen, Denmark: ACM.

Lewis, D. D. and J. Catlett. 1994. "Heterogenous uncertainty sampling for supervised learning." In *ICML*. Morgan Kaufmann. pp. 148–156.

Quinlan, J. R. and M. Cameron-Jones. 1993. "FOIL: A midterm report." In *ECML*. Springer. pp. 3–20.

Rajman, M. and R. Besançon. October 7–10, 1997. "Text mining: natural language techniques and text mining applications." In *Proceedings of the Seventh IFIP 2.6 Working Conference on Database Semantics (DS-7)*. Leysin, Switzerland: Chapman & Hall.

Salton, G. and C. Buckley. 1988. "Term-weighting approaches in automatic text retrieval." *Inform. Process. and Mgmnt.* **24(5)**: 513–523.

Salton, G. and M. Smith. 1989. "On the application of syntactic methodologies in automatic text analysis." *SIGIR*. ACM. pp. 137–150.

Srikant, R. and R. Agrawal. 1995. "Mining generalized association rules." In *Proceedings of the Twenty-first VLDB Conference*. Montreal, Canada: AAAI Press.

39 MULTIMEDIA APPLICATIONS

Duminda Wijesekera and Daniel Barbará

ABSTRACT As multimedia proliferate throughout the computing domain, ever more documents are being made using semantically rich audiovisual media. Consequently, mining knowledge hidden in multimedia documents is a complex task that involves fusing data from many media and depends upon basic capabilities of identifying basic features in audio and video streams. Existing work in this area mines for cinematic structures, interesting audiovisual sequences and spatiotemporal rules, and medical imaging.

1. Introduction

Efforts in data mining have largely concentrated in developing or perfecting techniques for mining knowledge from conventional data types such as numbers and text. Meanwhile, a rich and vast amount of multimedia data, currently available on the Internet and other sources, remain to be explored. Although we have witnessed the increased importance of multimedia in all areas where computers are used, extracting interesting and semantic knowledge out of data contained in audio, video, and other streams has met with limited success.

Part of the reason for this can be found in the fact that data mining is still in its infancy and researchers are still busy trying to tackle problems that deal with more conventional data types. Additionally, extracting semantic information from audio, image, and video data has proved to be a challenging problem with limited success in only very specific applications. Notice that this problem does not arise in conventional data types. While it may be possible to extract and track faces and gestures from surveillance video, it is still difficult to translate those gestures and facial movements to meaningful information, such as abnormal behavior, emotion. Problems in doing so are twofold: one is that with the current state of the art in image and audio synthesis, it is not easy to identify such semantic information. The second is that higher semantic content may be contained in more than one stream of data and, consequently, needs some mechanisms to fuse their components from streams. However, we believe that although not directly stated as multimedia data mining, there is a considerable body of work that attempts to understand and extract knowledge hidden in multimedia data. The literature on understanding the semantics of video and audio is extensive, and we present only some of them as representatives.

Traditional data mining work attempts to mine for interesting patterns hidden in traditional data types such as texts and numbers. Due to potential application areas, mining for association rules, event patterns, patterns in time-sensitive data, and clustering have been analyzed. Such analyses have been useful in discovering hidden facts such as consumer buying patterns, fault propagation in large telecommunication networks, and exploration patterns on the World Wide Web. In looking for interesting patterns hidden in multimedia data, it is worthwhile to examine some common applications of multimedia and, consequently, attempt to discover interesting patterns hidden in them. Starting with this view, there have been a number of attempts to formulate what constitutes interesting patterns in multimedia data, and try to mine them. One consequence of this point of view has been that multimedia data mining has not totally concentrated on mining for association rules, clustering and interesting event sequences, but on other concepts that will be described shortly.

Multimedia traditionally include video, audio, closed captioning, accompanying text, transparencies, written notes and scripts (such as production notes in cinema and diagnostic notes in medicine), radio, radar, sonar, and other images. Products that use these media include audiovideo recordings of meetings, cinema, medicine, searching through multimedia libraries, usage of electronic maps, monitoring physical security et cetera. In producing multimedia documents, one or more of these media types are used, and producers and consumers depend upon having all of them to convey the intended semantics. Consequently, in extracting interesting knowledge from them, one has to mine data out of a collection of media with varying synchronization granularities. Second, since most lively media capture continuous streams using analog or digital devices, there are bound to be some quantization artifacts, such as encoding and synchronization errors. Conversely, some artifacts such as cinematic scene cuts, pans, and tilts are used as a part of the production and are necessary in conveying the intended semantics. The consequence of this duality is that mining techniques have to be resilient to the former, but sensitive to the latter. In order to get a feeling for data mining issues related to multimedia, we examine some existing applications.

Many people get their daily news from newspapers, radio, and television newscasts. Among them, TV newscasts are gaining worldwide popularity as a major source of news. Consequently, there has been a proliferation of news channels and broadcasts of daily events. Therefore, having an intelligent agent monitor a large number of TV newscasts and present items of interest to an individual result in saving energy and time. There have been attempts to provide such services. In particular, News-on-Demand (Hauptmann et al., 1995) is an application developed within the Informedia (http://www.informedia.cs.cmu.edu/) digital libraries project (described in this chapter) at Carnegie Mellon University to monitor evening news from major American networks and allow users to retrieve stories that are of interest to them. This is a fully automated process requiring no human intervention. The Name-It (Satoh et al., 1999) system developed at the same university is capable of extracting faces and names in newscasts, and associating names with popular faces in contemporary TV newscasts. It does so by using a multimodal video analysis approach, where face sequences are extracted out of the video sequence and names are extracted from textual transcripts of the audio track and video captions. Providing automated extraction and analysis of news in this form can become a very useful application of multimedia data mining.

We continue to produce many multimedia documents in the form of audio and video all the way from small family gatherings and vacations to documents of meeting and professional movies. They are becoming numerous in nature, and without having a summary, it would be like having publications without abstracts. The results would be having too many documents that are difficult to keep track of in a hierarchical fashion. In order to satisfy this need, there has been some work in producing abstracts of videos (Lienhart et al., 1997, 1998; Nam and Tewfik, 1999; Srinivasan et al., 1999). One issue that needs to be addressed in this process is that of intent: that is, an abstract made for documenting purpose has to provide the story, but for an advertisement may create excitement and show some highlights without revealing the end (Lienhart et al., 1997). Usually, abstracts are produced for the former purpose using the original document, and the process first detects cinematic structure such as scenes, and then selects representative video frames for each of them. In unedited home videos there may not be any such structure, and hence another approach must be taken (Lienhart, 1999). Going beyond a traditional linear representation of video abstracts, there have been attempts to show panoramic views of them (Taniguchi et al., 1977; Teodosio and Mills, 1977).

Another application of data mining in multimedia is in cinema (MOCA, the movie content analysis project: http://www.informatik.uni-mannheim.de/informatik/pi4/projects/MoCA/). This application consists of detecting the structure of the movie by detecting cinematic artifacts, categorizing (Fischer et al., 1995), and detecting patterns between meta information such as the director, studio, financial data, and ratings (Wijesekera and Barbara, 2000). One of the major problems encountered in mining for cinema is the difficulty in mining the story (Davenport, 1998; Davenport et al., 1991). Potential future applications in this area are in devising an automated rating system and classifying movies along different dimensions such as adult oriented, violent, soap operas.

An area where multimedia applications have had some degree of success is in medical imaging, where there is a lot of information about tumors and other artifacts relating to demographics, age, gender, and so on, (Khosla et al., 2000). Other studies have shown how to use data mining techniques to connect functional areas of the brain to human activities by using MRI images (Tsuimoto and Morita, 1998).

Naturally, one area where multimedia data mining can be used is in monitoring and maintaining physical security (see http://www.tascvideo.com/). Such applications depend upon having advanced video and audio recognition capabilities that go beyond simple edge detection. Already there are some prototype systems and commercial applications that are emerging in this area (http://www.tascvideo.com/).

The rest of this chapter is organized as follows: Section 2 surveys large projects that have contributed to multimedia data mining. Section 3 describes some techniques that have been used in these projects or have the potential to be used in near future. Section 4 describes basic science used in building these techniques and some tools that have been used. Finally, Section 5 has concluding comments.

2. Survey of Large Projects

This section surveys large projects that have contributed to mining interesting hidden facts from multimedia data. They were designed primarily for many purposes: from video and audio content analysis to indexing multimedia databases, from analyzing cinema and exploring the Internet to providing physical security. This section is not exhaustive, as there have been numerous other large-scale efforts in understanding the semantics captured in multimedia data, both in industry and academia, and the ones presented appear in no particular order in this survey.

2.1. QBIC

Query By Image Content, or QBIC (Ashley et al., 1995; see also http://www.almaden. ibm.com/pub/cs/reports/vision), is an image-querying system that allows a user to retrieve images by color, texture, shape, and layouts. Queries to the system are presented through a graphical user interface. A typical query made to QBIC would be to find images like the one drawn on a drawing tool (shape based) or to find images that are 15 percent red and 15 percent white. The dimension of queries are color, texture, shape, and location of objects within a frame.

The color dimension is further divided into average color, which is based on the Munsell color of an image or an identified object, and histogram color, which is based on a 256- or 64-dimensional color vector histogram. Textual features are based on the coarseness, contrast, and directionality (such as grass is directional, but a smooth surface is not). Location is the two-dimensional Euclidean distance of the centroid of an object with respect to the origin of the frame. Shape matching uses a 20-element shape vector including area, circularity, eccentricity, orientation, and other invariants related to higher-order moments of orientation.

QBIC creates some pertinent information at database population time such as color histograms and texture features automatically. Other features such as object identification are semi-automated and require manual intervention for example to complete flood fill and enhanced snake-based edge detection.

The QBIC search engine matches the features of the presented query in the form of a vector, and matches them with similar vectors of stored objects in the form of an enhanced Euclidean distance function. It is our understanding that this project has been superseded by the CueVideo project at the IBM Almaden Research Center.

2.2. CueVideo

CueVideo (http://www.almaden.ibm.com/cs/cuevideo/cuevideo_papers.html) is an ongoing research project at IBM Laboratories at Almaden, California; Yorktown Heights, New York; and Haifa, addressing challenges that arise in understanding and indexing large multimedia files. It is based on combining video and audio analysis, speech recognition, and artificial intelligence techniques. Currently, it is packaged as a modular system having two basic components: an offline indexing engine that computes indexes that are saved on the CueVideo multimedia server, and a toolkit for browsing (Amir et al., 2000; Srinivasan et al., 1999) media stored on this server.

Intended for the purposes of getting the story contained in movies, the CueVideo browsing interface is divided into four components: storyboard, animation (or motion storyboard), audio event view, and statistics.

The storyboard consists of a sequence of video frames, each representative of the shot containing it. Clicking on a frame results in playing out the audio segment corresponding to the containing shot. In addition, the user can browse and navigate forward and backward in the timeline. Segment detection software used in CueVideo has been enhanced to account for quantization artifacts found in compressed video such as MPEG and JPEG.

Animation or the Motion Storyboard (MSB) in CueVideo is intended to provide a sense of motion and to address the fatigue in viewing too many still frames in the storyboard view. In MSB, a frame representing the animation in a segment is played out with the corresponding audio segment. Experimental results with MPEG-1 encodings show that an MSB of a movie takes about 2 to 3 percent of the original space. This kind of a movie summary has been found to be suitable for news, educational, or commercial use, but not in segments where high motion content plays a key role in conveying the content and associated emotion such as in tennis games, car races, and theater.

The audio events view gives semantics derived from the audio track. Audio analysis algorithms used in CueVideo can classify the audio track into silence, music, and speech. Then, CueVideo lets users decide what constitutes an interesting audio event, with the hope that it can be detected by CueVideo. Under the assumption that this can be done, the audio events view shows audio-based segments with a representative video frame. Published work specifies entire speech segments as interesting audio events, and, consequently, this can be done with fair accuracy. The more challenging part is to extend this to include events such as the user humming, or playing a part of another soundtrack and having the CueVideo system detect the corresponding segments.

The statistics part provides statistics on the automated analysis results such as the number and length of segments, type of cuts used, and the representative frames selected for scenes. They are useful for more technical purposes and also in providing auxiliary contextual information for other views, such as playing the video when a user clicks on the key frame.

One of the most striking features of the CueVideo project is its reliance on user studies to verify the relevance of developed technology. As multimedia is very much dependent on user perception, this will become a significant component in the search for interesting knowledge hidden in multimedia data.

2.3. Informedia Digital Libraries

The Informedia digital library project (`http://www.informedia.cs.cmu.edu/`) at the Carnegie Mellon University was designed to create large digital libraries of video, audio, text, and images. It provides content-based retrieval from a vast collection (about 1 terabyte) of educational material, government documents, and newscasts. Many techniques to understand or recognize knowledge hidden in multimedia documents were developed within this project. They include analyzing video, images, text, and audio.

Informedia can be queried by typing text or speaking. Spoken queries are translated using the SPHINX-II (`http://www.cs.cmu.edu/user/air/SpeechGroup`) speech recognition system developed at Carnegie Mellon.

Informedia has three main components to process texts, images, and audio. As with any extensive database, all relevant components are used first during content creation time to produce relevant meta data and later during the retrieval process.

Textual processing gets their input from ASCII translations of spoken words, closed captioning, or other annotations and production notes. The processing unit segments text in to paragraphs (Hauptmann, 1995). Important sections are identified using keyword prominence of subject-dependent importance. That is done by using traditional information retrieval metrics such as term frequencies and inverse document frequencies (Slaton and McGill, 1983) used to identify critical keywords and their relative importance. Furthermore, structural pronunciation markers such as punctuation marks are used to identify video paragraphs (segments) and their granularity.

Standard image analysis techniques (Zhang et al., 1995) are used to identify scene cuts and calculate primitive image-related statistics, such as color histograms and construction of thumbnails or image icons for segments of video. More sophisticated audio-video-based scene cut detection techniques were also developed (Zhang et al., 1995) during this project. This project also developed some techniques for video skimming and creation of panoramas out of video skims.

The speech analysis software SPHINX-II uses a semicontinuous hidden Markov model (HMM) to model between-word and context-dependent phones (Hauptmann, 1995). The software processes verbal utterances in four steps where they are processed forward and backward, generate a number of hypotheses, and finally select one for possible begin–end pairs for sentences. Breaks in energy levels of audio signals are used to detect transition between speakers or topics. The success rate of speech analysis shows that the best results of 83 to 90 percent of success rates are obtained under laboratory conditions and worst results of about 15 percent are obtained from TV commercials. These experimental results show that obtaining the story from the audio track is highly context dependent and may have a large margin of error. It is also known that speaker-independent speech recognition in general is sensitive to environmental conditions such as microphone placement, and background noise.

This project also prototyped a system, News-on-Demand (Hauptmann et al., 1995), which monitors evening news from major American broadcasters and allow users to retrieve stories of interest without human intervention.

In a follow-up project, Experience-on-Demand (EOD; Wactlar et al., 1999), tools and techniques were developed for users to carry small personal EOD units to record and integrate their experiences in the form spatiotemporal (obtained through global positioning system [GPS]) multimedia streams. These can be used by emergency personnel and crisis managers that are geographically dispersed, yet need some coordination between them.

2.4. The MoCA (Movie Content Analysis) Project

The movie content analysis project MoCA (http://www.informatik.uni-mannheim.de/ informatik/pi4/projects/MoCA/) at the University of Mannheim is an ongoing effort in understanding semantics of multimedia data. The project uses detectable features of video and audio to identify characteristics of relevance in frames (such as brightness and color), sequences of frames (such as motion and cinematic artifacts), and both of them (such as existence of commercials). Some of the technical contributions (see Pfeiffer et al. [1998] for a summary of contributions) of this work are recognizing commercials in TV broadcasts (Kuhmünch and Effelsberg, 2000), recognizing text in video (Lienhart, 1996; Lienhart and Effelsberg, 2000), querying for similar sequences of video (Lienhart et al., 1998, 2000), and abstracting video sequences (Lienhart et al., 1997, 1998a).

Commercial segmentation and recognition in MoCA (Kuhmünch and Effelsberg, 2000) are done in two ways. The first is based on feature statistics such as scene cuts, existence of monochrome frames in between, and shot lengths. The second method is based on using stored information about known commercial spots in telecasts. It uses either video or audio footprints of commercials.

Text appears in video sequences in many forms: in movies they appear in the preamble with names of actors, studio, et cetera, and inside they appear on garments, street signs, billboards, et cetera. This work (Lienhart et al., 1996; Lienhart and Effelsberg, 2000) tries to recognize them by first segmenting them (i.e., extract all pixels that are a part of text) and then recognizing them. Techniques for both parts were developed in MoCA.

Querying similar sequences of video, referred to as VisualGREP (Lienhart et al., 1998, 2000) in MoCA (in comparison with the UNIX grep command), allows users to search for similar video sequences. It is done in two stages. First, the levels of the video hierarchy (i.e., consisting of frames, shots, and scenes) are identified. Second, the user specifies a threshold for most similar and most dissimilar sequences. Then, VisualGREP searches for sequences that are above the similarity measure by using suitable aggregations over frame sequences. Experimental results show that substantial aggregations can be achieved in this process.

In addition, the MoCA group has produced the MoCA Workbench (MoCA-WB; Lienhart et al., 1996) which can be used to experimentally verify new hypothesis about feature extraction from multimedia data. MoCA-WB is based on the Tcl/Tk (Ousterhout, 1994; Welch, 1995) toolkit where, as expected, the underlying functions are written in C/C++. In MoCA-WB, one can define new operators to extract interesting features out of multimedia streams and clearly visualize experimental results.

2.5. VisualSEEk and the Advent Project at Columbia University

This work (http://www.ctr.columbia.edu/VisualSEEK and http://www.ctr. columbia.edu/advent/home-full.html) is an ongoing research effort at Columbia University in mining multimedia knowledge mostly available on the Internet. It uses a sequence of Web agents or spiders to seek new videos and images. Three spiders working together collect videos and images available on the Internet, along with their meta data such as HTML tags, file and directory names, file name extensions, et cetera. The work has been prototyped in the form of an extensive, searchable engine available on the Internet (http:// www.ctr.columbia.edu/VisualSEEK).

Meta data corresponding to image and video files are used to manually identify key terms that characterize contents of corresponding multimedia data. This system contains an extensive taxonomy of subject matter that is used to classify videos or images. Using this taxonomy along with keywords extracted through analyzing meta data and other feature statistics, such as color histograms for images, the system creates indexes and maintains an extensive catalog of multimedia clips.

The system can be searched or browsed in an interactive way to retrieve multimedia clips by both content- and text-based tools. In this process, users can interactively refine their original queries by rejecting some entries in a rank ordered list of items.

2.6. MultiMediaMiner

The MultiMediaMiner (Zaiane et al., 1996, 1998) is a system designed to discover intersecting phenomena in multimedia data. It is built on an enhanced content-based image retrieval system, C-BIRD (Li et al., 1998a,b), and mines for association rules, classifications, and characterizations in videos and images. The MultiMediaMiner consists of four functional modules—image excavator, preprocessor, search kernel and data miner—with a Web-based interface.

The image excavator extracts images and video sequences from multimedia repositories, including the World Wide Web. The image excavator uses image contextual information such as HTML tags and file names to derive keywords. These keywords are cleaned to eliminate common and semanticless words and normalized to build concept hierarchies using hypernamy and hyponamy relationships between words.

The preprocessor extracts features and other meta data from images and stores precomputed data in a database. It also detects scene cuts and, based on them, segments video clips and stores one or more representatives frames of the video sequences or images. The database does not directly store images but information such as feature and layout descriptors in the form of meta data. Stored meta data consist of image URL, file name, video-encoding format, and a list of keywords and a set of descriptive vectors for color and shape parameters. These descriptive vectors are the color histogram of the image quantized to 256 values of RGB (8 for each component of the RGB spectrum), most frequent color (consisting of the five most frequent colors used in the image), and the most frequent orientation, consisting of the five most frequent orientations using edge orientations of $0°$, $45°$, $90°$, and $135°$. Further, these parameters are kept for each 8×8 grid in the image, allowing a drilling-down capability toward image segments.

The search kernel matches queries with images in the database. The querying interface is a Web-like browser.

The mining module has three major functionalities: characterization, classification, and association rule mining. The characterizer discovers features at multiple levels of abstraction such as size, Internet domain, color, et cetera. At any given moment, two of these domains can be visualized using the browser interface. One major problem is having too many dimensions for any data point in the image database. The associator finds sets of association rules of the form $X \rightarrow Y[s\%, c\%]$, with support $s\%$ and confidence $c\%$. A typical association rule is *If image is small and related to sky, then it is dark blue with confidence 55 percent and support 65 percent.* Measures such as "small" are taken from conceptual hierarchies built for the size dimension. The classifier module uses the class labels provided to classify the database, resulting in a characteristic description of each class, and represents them as a decision tree. This last feature can be used for prediction, and this module provides the ability to drill down and roll up the class hierarchy.

The unavailability of large multimedia databases other than the World Wide Web and the dynamic nature of the Web were obstacles encountered in this work. The latter results in constant updates to the database.

Because association of keywords with images is crucial to the MultiMediaMiner, it needs automatic support. In order to provide specialization and generalization capabilities for the rule finder algorithm, it is necessary to have keyword hierarchies. Building natural language concept hierarchies is problematic and time consuming, and, consequently, the authors have decided to build one with Yahoo directories, but due to the too general and inflexible nature of the former, have decided to use WordNet (Beckwith et al., 1990). Nevertheless, since some technical terms do not appear in WordNet, it had to be enhanced to fit the chosen examples, such as the domain of military aircraft sites.

The MultiMediaMiner uses a data cube to store and organize multimedia data in the database with size, width and height of frames, data format, frame sequence duration, last modified date, Internet domain, Internet domain of referring pages with a predefined domain hierarchy, keyword hierarchy, color dimension, edge orientation, popularity of images (counted by the number of other pages referring to it), and the richness of the Web page (measured by the number of Web pages referred in the given Web page) as dimensions. This leads to too many dimensions with some being multivalued. Proliferation of dimensions leads to problems such as including many dimensions in a physical data cube and the consequent memory problems. Consequently, several data cubes had to be created with many overlapping dimensions. This decision brings other issues such as difficulties in discovery of correlations among dimensions in different data cubes, and also in merging rules discovered in dimensions from nonoverlapping data cubes. Due to this reason, the authors are developing new techniques in view of materialization for data cubes.

2.7. Multimedia-Based Monitoring and Physical Security

Concurrently, Loriax and Litton-TASC are developing and in the process of installing an advanced security monitoring system around the U.S. Capitol in order for the Capitol police to monitor, predict, and react to potential security problems (http://www.tascvideo.com/). Stated application domains for similar systems (TASC, 2000) are in supermarket surveillance, transportation, and space-based military systems. In supermarket surveillance, recognizing patterns, such as detecting suspicious repetitive behavior by individuals, which may mean a shoplifter casing an area, and detecting wet spills, results in avoiding costly litigation. In transportation, intelligent video technology can spot erratic traffic patterns, such as cars moving at high speeds, irregular turning, or other atypical traffic behavior. By using intelligence extracted from the video, law enforcement officials could isolate trends and proactively manage problem spots. Highway officials could also monitor critical safety areas like railroad crossings more effectively.

2.8. The CONQUEST System

The CONQUEST (Sheck et al., 1996; Stolorz et al., 1995) system was designed for the analysis of geoscientific data with spatiotemporal properties. Listed publications describe a multidimensional data model consisting of cells to store data values that may span many dimensions, (such as three spatial dimensions and one time dimension to store ocean temperatures) and a distributed parallel query-processing engine that is capable of processing spatiotemporal queries from stored raster data. The data model also extends the standard set-oriented algebraic operation with sequence, grouping, and space conversion operators. This system has been used to predict cyclone formations and blocking event formations—a particular class of persistent atmospheric anomalies in which a westerly jet stream in midaltitude splits into two branches.

The CONQUEST system addresses a lot of issues that arise in extracting knowledge from large image databases. In addition, it distinguishes itself from others by having the capability to address spatiotemporal queries that span large data sets.

3. Basic Technology for Mining Multimedia Data

Projects surveyed in the previous section and others have addressed some basic problems. Most work, reported here or elsewhere, has contributed to solving these problems in some form or other, or used results obtained by others. This section describes them.

3.1. Getting the Story

Because multimedia have been used largely to capture and display ongoing activity, there have been efforts to reverse-engineer existing audiovisual documents in order to unfold the captured story. Many proposals submitted to standardization committees, such as the one developing the MPEG-7, call for incorporating more semantic information. In mining the story out of a multimedia document, there are two issues to be addressed. First, at a more fundamental level, storytelling by itself is quite complex (Davenport, 1996a,b, 1998, 1999), evolving, and depends on many cultural stylistic and other influences. Consequently, gathering and summarizing a story after it has been told involves uncovering these complexities and structures used to present it. Even if mining a story did not encounter the technical problems associated with multimedia, it is not expected to be an easy task. For example, automatically mining and summarizing a written story encounters these problems. Second, when producing stories in the electronic media, cinematography has employed a few techniques, such as scenes and shots. These structural components have been detected with varying degrees of success, as evidenced by a large number of publications (Boreczky and Rowe, 1996; Zabin et al., 1999; see also http://www.almaden.ibm.com/cs/cuevideo/cuevideo_papers.html and http://www.informatik.uni-mannheim.de/informatik/pi4/projects/MoCA/).

In understanding structural components of multimedia documents, two important issues are addressed by many researchers. One is to decrease false positives and increase detection probability of existing structures. The second is to be resilient to digitization artifacts such as quantization and synchronization errors. In doing so, segmentation techniques based on video, audio (Amir et al., 2000; Pfeiffer et al., 1998), or both have been used with a large measure of success. Most of them depend on sudden variations of energy levels or color histograms.

3.2. Abstraction

The issue of abstracting (Lienhart et al., 1997; 1998a; http://www.almaden.ibm.com/cs/cuevideo/cuevideo_papers.html) the story has also been addressed in many research projects that have been surveyed in the previous section. There have been many attempts to find a collection of representative frames for each structural segment of the original document and glue them in an understandable way. A particularly innovative approach that has been developed is to produce panoramas out of multimedia abstracts (Taniguchi et al., 1977; Teodosio and Mills, 1977). Producing video abstracts encounters two difficulties beyond detecting structures. The first is the purpose. As stated earlier in this chapter, an abstract produced for documenting purposes is different from an advertisement for a movie, which is also a kind of abstract produced for a different purpose. The second issue is, even when the structure is detected, choosing the representation or an abstract of that component. Most systems choose the frame in the middle of the scene, or the one approximating the average color or some such index. Some abstracting mechanisms also depend on the audio track. They choose video frames that correspond to interesting and detectable sounds such as crying and laughter.

3.3. Outlier Detection

An interesting consequence of knowing trends is that any deviations from them can be flagged to receive special attention. This is the basic tenet behind multimedia-based monitoring for physical security. Although there are products coming out in the marketplace in the near future, there have been some noteworthy attempts at outlier detection in multimedia.

For example, prototype stereophonic video systems developed at SRI (Small vision system: http://www.ai.sri.com/konolige/svs/), and at the University of British Columbia and Digiclips (Triclops stereovision system: http://www.ptgrey.com) are capable of counting and tracking individual and group movements within enclosed areas. These systems have been used to mine normal walking patterns and paths in sensitive areas such as bank lobbies. Based on such knowledge of normal patterns, it is possible to prealarm some potential abnormal movement patterns.

The work reported in Knorr et al. (1999) describes an interesting application in this area. Their system is capable of identifying unusual paths taken by people traveling in a common area such as a lobby or an atrium. In this experiment, a laboratory is equipped with a three-lensed stereophonic camera to track and record trajectories of people's movement. These cameras are capable of tracking time-stamped two- or three-dimensional coordinates of trajectories traversed by moving people. This information is then used to track their motion using segmented background modeling (Eveland et al., 1998). In this experiment, trajectories of people are parameterized by four quantities: (1) coordinates of start and end points in appropriate dimension; (2) the number of points tracked—effectively giving the length of the trajectory; (3) heading, giving the directional vectors; and (4) velocity. For the start and end points (X, Y), coordinates were taken. For heading (direction) and velocity, the minimum, average, and the maximum were taken. The outlier detection algorithm used in this work was an extension of the work reported in Knorr and Ng (1998) on distance-based outlier detection in large data sets. This algorithm requires a distance function between data points to detect outliers.

3.4. Spatiotemporal Data

Multimedia is said to incorporate more than one medium; and usually involves audio, video, text, still images, et cetera. Concurrently, many multimedia presentations have a temporal dimension—such as a frame rate or a data rate associated with them. Both the multitude of the media and the timing parameters contribute to the richness of multimedia presentation.

Consequently, any data mining knowledge gained in any component medium is relevant, but has not been reviewed under this chapter except to show their relevance. Video and still images are an important component of multimedia, and there is a large amount of images stored from satellite and other images in spatial databases. A separate body of knowledge exists in mining for knowledge in spatial databases, as given in Koperski et al. (1996). The algorithms and techniques developed for spatial data mining such as clustering (Ng and Han, 1994), classification (Koperski et al., 1998b), association rule mining (Koperski and Han, 1995; Koperski et al., 1998a) can be applied for multimedia data mining. But they need to be adapted to multimedia applications in two ways: (1) to include the temporal dimension and (2) to be used in conjunction with other media types.

4. Basic Issues and Tools

Summarized projects and technologies used within them show that multimedia has a lot of richness that can be exploited in discovering hidden knowledge and rules. Harnessing that richness requires us to address some basic issues such as clearly understanding the nature of objects that are of interest.

First, we are mostly interested in higher-order concepts, such as: Do movies have a happy beginning and a sad ending? Characterizing higher-order concepts such as happy and sad are both subjective and difficult from a technical standpoint. Second, in addition to high-order constructs, we encounter multifaceted ones. For example, the sadness may be indicated by a cry in the audio stream and appropriate gestures and facial expressions in the video.

Second, we must have the ability to mine for structure, starting with all the basic objects of interest. Multimedia events, episodes, or scenes are examples of these. In order to do so, a data miner has to resort to a wealth of tools, such as image understanding and recognition, gesture recognition, scene classifiers, speech recognition tools, audio recognizers, and the like. Some of them are given at the end of this section. As object, motion, and speaker recognition becomes more developed, so will knowledge mined out of multimedia streams.

The third is the spatiotemporal nature of multimedia data. Human satisfaction in audio-visual presentations depends upon the quality of individual streams and their synchronization. In addition, size and position of objects appearing in the video streams and their motion also contribute to captured knowledge. As multimedia is delivered and available with a wide variety of qualities, the mining algorithms will have to adapt to them. Notice that this aspect is largely absent in mining knowledge from traditional data types.

4.1. Some Tools for Multimedia Data Mining

Many tools are necessary to mine multimedia data. Some of them are audio recognition and analysis, image analysis and understanding, detecting objects and motion, and detecting and classifying of production artifacts such as scene cuts in movies.

For the audio recognition part, speech recognition software already exists in the marketplace. Tools such as AudioMine (`http://dragonsys.com`) can provide audio-to-text translations. Translations using AudioMine with linguistic structures can be used in mining for interesting audio data or to detect parts of speech through detecting translated text.

For video, there are numerous systems used at an experimental or commercial stage. The work done at the University of Maryland (Haritaoglu et al., 1998) can detect and track people in an outdoor environment on a monocular gray-scale imagery or infrared video camera. W^4 uses a combination of shape analysis and does not depend on color cues. Similarly, Pfinder (Wren et al., 1995) is a real-time system for tracking a person based on a multistatistical model of color and shape to segment a person from a background scene. The Triclops stereovision systems from Point Gray Research (`http://ptgrey.com`) use a stereo camera system consisting of three genlocked cameras to record three-dimensional images in either color or black and white. They come with software that is able to detect and track groups of people in the field of vision. This camera system has already been used in detecting unusual behavior (Knorr and Ng, 1998).

Detection and analysis of scene cuts and other production artifacts such as fade-ins and fade-outs can be used to mine important structural and/or production techniques in motion pictures. While Boreczky and Rowe (1996) provide a pre-1996 survey of available techniques for detecting production artifacts, work done at Cornell University (Zabin et al., 1999) provides some improvements and downloadable code for artifact detection in MPEG or JPEG movies.

5. Conclusion

This chapter is devoted to describing the current status in multimedia data mining. We have described some large projects followed by some techniques that have been useful in multimedia data mining. Mining for multimedia data requires cross-fertilization of ideas and techniques from many areas such as

- Domain-specific knowledge from other disciplines such as cinematography, geography, security, and digital surveillance.

- Techniques from audio and video processing, such as image analysis, image comprehension, object recognition, and key phrase recognition.

- Appropriate adaptations of known algorithms from traditional data mining.

In the previous section, we have attempted to show how some of these techniques can be used to mine for interesting phenomena in multimedia data. What is interesting is to see what is considered interesting in multimedia data mining. Traditional data types, such as numbers and text, have concentrated in mining for association rules and event patterns. Content-based semantic methods in multimedia have concentrated in mining for movie abstracts, stories, and structure. Other areas, such as spatial and geographical data mining, have concentrated on adapting association rules appropriately.

References

Amir, A., D. Ponceleon, B. Blanchard, D. Petkovic, S. Srinivasan, and D. Cohen. January 2000. "Using audio time scale modification for video browsing." In *Hawaii International Conference on System Science* **1**: 33–55. CA: IEEE Computer Society.

Ashley, J., R. Barber, M. Flickner, J. Hafner, and D. Lee. 1995. "Automatic and semi-automatic methods for image annotation and retrieval in qbic." In *Proceedings of the SPIE*. pp. 24–35.

Beckwith R., C. Fellbaum, D. Gross, K. Miller, G. A. Miller, and R. Tengi, eds. 1990. Five papers on WordNet. *J. Lexicography*, **3**(4).

Boreczky, J. S. and Larry A. Rowe. 1996. "A comparison of video shot boundary detection techniques." *J. Electronic Imaging* **3**: 122–128.

Davenport, G. 1996a. "Indexes are 'out', models are 'in'." *IEEE Multimedia* **3**: 10–15.

Davenport, G. 1996b. "Smarter tools for storeytelling: are they just around the corner?" *IEEE Multimedia* **2**: 10–14.

Davenport, G. 1998. "Curious learning, cultural bias and the learning curve." *IEEE Multimedia* **5**: 14–19.

Davenport, G. 1999. "Get a life: thinking outside the box." *IEEE Multimedia* **6**: 5–9.

Davenport, G., T. A. Smith, and N. Pincever. 1991. "Cinematic primitives for multimedia." *IEEE Comput. Graphics Appl* **8**: 17–34.

Eveland, C., K. Konolige, and R. C. Bolles. 1998. "Background modeling for segmentation of video rate stereo sequences." In *Conference on Vision and Pattern Recognition*. CA: JEEE, pp. 266–271.

Fischer, S., R. Lienhart, and W. Effelsberg. 1995. "Automatic recognition of film genres." In *Proceedings of the ACM Multimedia*, pp. 295–304. San Francisco: ACM.

Haritaoglu, I., D. Harwood, and L. S. Davis. 1998. "w^4: who? when? where? what?: a real time system for detecting and tracking people." In *FGR'98*. PA: IEEE. Available at http://umiacs.umd.edu/users/lsd/vsam/Pubs.html.

Hauptmann, A. G. 1995. "Speech recognition in the informedia digital library system: uses and limitations." In *Proceedings of the ICTAI-95, Seventh IEEE International Conference on Tools with AI*. Washington, DC: IEEE.

Hauptmann, A. G., M. J. Witbrock, A. I. Rudnicky, and S. Reed. 1995. "Speech for multimedia information retrieval." In *Proceedings of the User Interface Software Technology*. Washington, DC: IEEE, pp. 15–17.

Khosla, R., I. K. Sethi, and E. Damiani. 2000. *Intelligent Multimedia A Multi-Agent Systems*. Boston: Kluwer Academic Publishers.

Koperski, K. and J. Han. 1995. "Discovery of spatial association rules in geographic information databases." In *Proceedings of the International Symposium of Spatial Databases (SDD'95), Portland, Maine*, pp. 47–66. Berlin: Springer-Verlag.

Koperski, K., J. Han, and J. Adhikary. 1998a. "Mining knowledge in geographical data." Available at http://dt.cs.sfu.ca/publications.

Koperski, K., J. Adikary, and Jaiwei Han. 1996. "Spatial data mining: progress and challenges." In *SIGMOD Workshop on Research Issues on Datamining and Knowledge Discovery (DMKD'96)*, pp. 27–32. Montreal: ACM.

Koperski, K., J. Han, and N. Stefanovic. 1998b. "An efficient two-step method for classification of spatial data." In *Proceedings of the International Symposium Spatial Data Handling (SDH'98)*: Springer-Verlag, pp. 47–66.

Knorr, E. and R. T. Ng. 1998. "Algorithms for mining distance-based outliers in large dataset." In *Proceedings of the Twenty-Fourth VLDB Conference* **24**: 392–403. NY: Morgan Kaufmann.

Knorr, E. M., V. Tucakov, and R. T. Ng. 1999. "Identifying unusual people behavior: a case study of mining outliers in spatio-temporal trajectory databases." *VLBD J*. NY: Morgan Kaufmann. pp. 212–222.

Kuhmünch, C. and W. Effelsberg. 2000. *Handbook of Multimedia*. Boca Raton, FL: CRC Press. pp. 735–743.

Li, Z. N., O. R. Zaiane, and Z. Tauber. 1998. "Illumination invariance and object model in content-based image and video retrieval." *J. Visual Commun. Image Representation* **10**(3): 219–244.

Li, Z. N., O. R. Zaiane, and B. Yan. 1998. "C-BIRD: content-based image retrieval in digital libraries using chromaticity and recognition kernal." In *International Workshop on Storage and Retrieval Issues in Image and Multimedia Databases, in conjunction with the Ninth International Conference on Database and Expert Systems (DEXA'98)*, pp. 361–366. Vienna.

Lienhart, R. November 1996. "Automatic text recognition for video indexing." In *Proceedings of ACM Multimedia 96*, pp. 11–20. NY: ACM Press.

Lienhart, R. 1999. "Abstracting home video automatically." In *Proceeding of ACM Multimedia*, pp. 37–39. NY: ACM.

Lienhart, R. and W. Effelsberg. 2000. "Automatic text segmentation and text recognition for video indexing." *ACM/Springer Multimedia Systems Magazine* 8(1): 69–81.

Lienhart, R., W. Effelsberg, and R. Jain. 2000. "VisualGREP: a systematic method to compare and retrieve video sequences." *Multimedia Tools Appl* 10(1): 47–72, January 1999.

Lienhart, R., W. Effelsberg, and R. Jain. 1998. "Towards a visual grep: a systematic analysis of various methods to compare ideo sequences." In *Storage and Retrieval for Image and Video Databases*, edited by K. Sethi, VI: 271–282. NY: SPIE.

Lienhart, R., S. Pfeiffer, and W. Effelsberg. June 1996. "The MoCA workbench: support for creativity in movie content analysis." In *IEEE Conference on Multimedia Computing and Systems*, pp. 314–321. NY: IEEE Press.

Lienhart, R., S. Pfeiffer, and W. Effelsberg. 1997. "Video abstracting." *Commun. ACM* 40(12): 55–62.

Lienhart, R., S. Pfeiffer, and W. Effelsberg. 1998. *Automatic Trailer Production*. NY: CRC Press.

Nam, J. and A. Tewfik. 1999. "Dynamic video summarization and visualization." In *Proceedings of the ACM Multimedia*, pp. 53–56. NY: ACM Press.

Ng, R. T. and J. Han. 1994. "Efficient and effective clustering methods for spatial data mining." In *Proceedings of the International Conference of Very Large Databases (VLDB'94)*, pp. 144–155. San Francisco: Morgan Kaufmann.

Ousterhout, J. K. 1994. *Tcl and the Tk Toolkit*. Reading, Mass: Addison-Wesley.

Pfeiffer, S., R. Lienhart, G. Kühne, and W. Effelsberg. September 1998. "The MoCA project—movie content analysis research at the University of Mannheim." In *Informatik '98: Informatik zwischen Bild und Sprache, Heidelberg*, edited by J. Dasso and R. Kruse, 28: 329–338. Berlin: Springer-Verlag.

Satoh, S., Y. Nakamura, and T. Kanade. 1999. "Nameit: naming and detecting faces in news media." *IEEE Multimedia* 6: 22–35.

Sheck, E. C., R. Muntz, E. Mesrobian, and K. Ng. 1996. "Scalable exploratory data mining of distributed geoscientific data." In *Proceedings of the Second International Conference of Knowledge Discovery and Data Mining (KDD '96), Portland, Oregon*, pp. 32–37. Menlo Park, CA: AAAI Press.

Slaton, G. and M. J. McGill. 1983. *Introduction to Modern Information Retrieval*. NY: McGraw-Hill.

Srinivasan, S., D. Ponceleon, A. Amir, and D. Petkovic. June 1999. "What is in that video anyway? In search of better browsing." In *Proceedings of the IEEE International Conference on Multimedia Computing and Systems*, 1: 388–392. Italy: IEEE.

Stolorz, P., E. C. Sheck, R. Muntz, E. Mesrobian, and K. Ng. 1995. "Fast spatio-temporal data mining of large geographical datasets." In *Proceedings of the First International Conference of Knowledge Discovery and Data Mining (KDD'95), Montreal, Quebec*, pp. 300–305. Menlo Park, CA: AAAI Press.

Taniguchi, Y., A. Akutsu, and Y. Tonomura. 1977. "Panoramaexcerpts: extracting and packing panoramas for video browsing." In *Proceedings of the ACM Multimedia*, pp. 427–436. NY: ACM Press.

TASC. 2000. "Loronix and litton tasc announces partnership to develop next-generation video surveillance system." TASC News Release, April 13th 2000.

Teodosio, L. A. and M. Mills. 1977. "Panoramic views for navigating real-world scenes." In *Proceedings of the ACM Multimedia*, pp. 325–376. NY: ACM Press.

Tsuimoto, H. and C. Morita. 1998. "The discovery of rules from brain images." *Discovery Sci.*, pp. 198–209.

Wactlar, H. D., M. G. Christel, A. G. Hauptmann, and Y. Gong. 1999. "Informedia experience on demand." Available at: http://www.informedia.cs.cmu.edu/eod.

Welch, B. 1995. *Practical Programming in Tcl and Tk*. NY: Prentice-Hall.

Wijesekera, D. and D. Barbara. 2000. "Mining cinematic knowledge." In *Proceeding of the Workshop in Multimedia Data Mining in KDD*. Boston: ACM.

Wren, C., A. Azarbayejani, A. Darrel, and A. Pentland. October 1995. "Pfinder: real-time tracking of human body." In *Proceedings of the SPIE Conference on Integration Issues in Large Commercial Media Delivery Systems*, pp. 89–98. WA: SPIE.

Zabin, R., J. Miller, and K. Mai. 1999. "A feature-based algorithm for detecting and classifying production effects." *ACM Multimedia Sys.* 7: 119–128.

Zaiane, O. R., J. Han, Z.-N. Li, S. H. Chee, and C. Jeny. 1998. "Multimediaminer: a system prototype for multimedia data mining." In *Proceedings of the ACM-SIGMOD Conference on Management Data (System Demo)* 38: pp. 581–589.

Zaiane, O. R., J. Han, Z.-N. Li, and J. Hou. 1996. "Mining multimedia data." In *Proceedings of the CASCON'96 Meeting of Minds*, pp. 27–32. Toronto: ACM.

Zhang, H., C. Low, and S. Smoliar. 1995. "Video parsing and indexing of compressed data." *Multimedia Tools Appl.* 1: 89–111.

PART SEVEN

INDUSTRY SECTORS

40 BANKING AND FINANCE

Gholamreza Nakhaeizadeh, Elmar Steurer, and Kai Bartlmae

ABSTRACT New technology is dramatically changing the role of business systems and practices in the banking and insurance world. Computers, mass storage, and electronic datacapture are now all commonplace. However, to analyze and transform financial data or customer portfolio information into useable knowledge is difficult and very time consuming. The use of KDD and data mining as an analysis and decision support tool has become widely accepted within financial services. Here we give an overview of techniques applicable, in particular, to the fields of market and credit risk management, trading, portfolio management, customer care, and marketing in financial institutions.

1. Introduction

Global competition, dynamic markets, and rapidly decreasing cycles of technological innovation provide important challenges for the banking and finance industry today. Financial services all over the world use databases to store a large quantity and variety of information. Worldwide just-in-time availability of information allows enterprises to improve their flexibility significantly.

Much research has been conducted on the efficient retrieval of raw data from databases. But for many applications, it is as important to discover new knowledge from the data as it is to retrieve the raw data itself. The use of computing in the form of data mining as an analysis and decision support tool has become widely accepted within the financial service industry. Data mining can contribute to solving business problems in finance by finding patterns, causalities, and correlations in business information and market prices that are not immediately apparent to managers because the volume of data is too large or is generated too quickly to be screened by experts. The methods range from standard quantitative and statistical techniques to the use of neural networks that have proved their worth already in detecting defaults of credit loans or in forecasting currencies, interest rates, or stock market prices and to optimize mailing actions in marketing.

The aim of this chapter is to give an overview of the data mining techniques applicable to banking and finance. In Section 2, we discuss the main business issues in banking and finance that can be addressed by data mining techniques. In section 3, we describe how these topics can be transferred to data mining tasks. In this section we also present some case studies. Section 4 is devoted to special aspects of data mining in finance. A summary of the chapter is given in the last section.

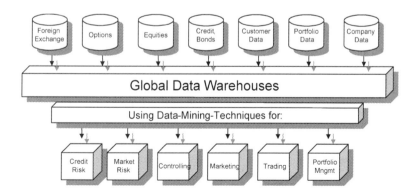

Figure 1 The use of data mining techniques is a global and firmwide challenge for financial businesses. Firmwide data sources can be used through data mining for different business areas

2. Main Business Issues in Banking and Finance

Advanced data mining approaches have become possible since the finance business is able to aggregate all business information on a daily basis within one or more data warehouses. All client and market information is collected and can then be evaluated via data mining techniques for firmwide credit and market risk management, trading, portfolio management, controlling, marketing, and customer care (Figure 1).

Data mining appeals to financial services firms because it allows them to restructure their risks globally and increase their return on capital. The major application fields of data mining techniques in banking and finance are

- Risk management
- Trading
- Portfolio management
- Marketing and customer care

2.1. Risk Management

Managing and measuring risk is at the core of every financial institution. Today's major challenge in the banking and insurance world is therefore the implementation of risk management systems in order to identify, measure, and control business exposure. Here credit and market risk present the central challenge, and one can observe a major change in the area of how to measure and deal with them, based on the advent of advanced database and data mining technology. (Other types of risk are also of importance in banking and finance, i.e., liquidity risk, operational risk, or concentration risk. See Alexander, 1996, for an overview.)

Today, the integrated measurement of different kinds of risk (i.e., market and credit risk) is moving into focus. These all are based on models representing single financial instruments or risk factors, their behavior, and their interaction with the overall market (Figure 2), making this field a highly important topic of research.

FINANCIAL MARKET RISK

For single financial instruments, that is, stock indices, interest rates, or currencies, market risk (the risk of a price change of the instrument) measurement is based on models depending on a set of underlying risk factors, such as interest rates, stock indices, or economic development. One is interested in a functional form between the instrument price or risk and the underlying risk factors as well as in a functional dependency of the risk factor itself. The identification and modeling of these are the primary data mining tasks.

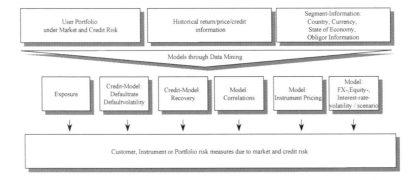

Figure 2 Using data mining techniques for customer, financial instrument, and portfolio risk evaluation. Different sources of information are evaluated with data mining techniques in order to build models which taken together best describe the behavior of a customer, instrument, or portfolio. These include credit behavior, default rate, default volatility, recovery and market information, and they can be aggregated into single risk measures

Today different market risk measurement approaches exist (see Beckers, 1996). All of them rely on models representing single instruments, their behavior, and their interaction with the overall market. Many of these can only be built by mining the proprietary portfolio data, since data is not publicly available and needs consistent supervision.

CREDIT RISK

Credit risk assessment is a key component in the process of commercial lending. Without it the lender would be unable to make an objective judgment of whether to lend to the prospective borrower, or of how much to charge for the loan. Credit risk management entails solving numerous problems which can be classified into two basic groups:

- *Credit scoring/credit rating.* Assignment of a customer or product to a risk level (i.e., credit approval, bond rating).
- *Behavior scoring/credit rating migration analysis.* Valuation of a customer's or product's probability of a change in risk level within a given time frame (i.e., default rate volatility, credit rating migrations).

In commercial lending, risk assessment is usually an attempt to quantify the risk of loss to the lender when making a particular lending decision. Here credit risk can be quantified by the changes of value of a credit product or of a whole credit customer portfolio, which is based on the change in the instrument's rating, the default probability, and the recovery rate of the instrument in case of default. Further diversification effects influence the results on a portfolio level (Wilson, 1997a,b). Thus, a major part of the implementation and care of a credit risk management system will be a typical data mining problem: the modeling of the credit instrument's value through default probabilities, rating migrations, and recovery rates.

Three major approaches exist to model credit risk on the transaction level: accounting analytic approaches (Altman and Bencivenga, 1995), statistical prediction (Altman et al., 1993) and option theoretic approaches (Kealhofer, 1998). Since large amounts of information about clients exist in financial businesses, an adequate way to build such models is to use their own database and data mining techniques, fitting models to the business needs and the business current credit portfolio.

2.2. Portfolio Management

Risk measurement approaches on an aggregated portfolio level quantify the risk of a set of instruments or customers including diversification effects. On the other hand, forecasting

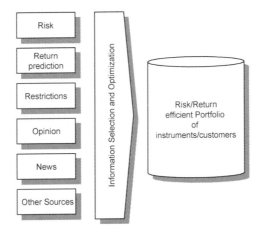

Figure 3 The management of an institutional portfolio is based on all reachable information, that is, risk, expected scenarios, and predicted credit ratings, but also on news and other information sources

models give an indication of the expected return or price of a financial instrument. Both make it possible to manage a firmwide portfolio actively in a risk/return efficient manner. The application of modern risk theory is therefore within portfolio theory (Sharpe et al., 1995), an important part of portfolio management.

With data mining and optimization techniques, investors are able to allocate capital across trading activities to maximize profit or minimize risk. This feature supports the ability to generate trade recommendations and portfolio structuring from user supplied profit and risk requirements (Figure 3).

Using data mining techniques it is possible to provide an extensive scenario analysis capability concerning expected asset prices or returns and the risk involved. With this functionality, what-if simulations of varying market conditions (e.g., interest rate and exchange rate changes) can be run to assess impact on the value and/or risk associated with a portfolio, business unit, counterparty, or trading desk. Various scenario results can be regarded by considering actual market conditions. Profit and loss analyses allow users to access an extensive view of the business' historical profit and loss. Furthermore, the business unit-trader, asset class, region, counterparty, or custom subportfolio can be benchmarked against common international benchmarks.

2.3. Trading

For the last few years a major topic of research has been the building of quantitative trading tools using data mining methods based on past data as input to predict short-term movements of important currencies, interest rates, or equities. The goal of these quantitative techniques is to spot times when markets are cheap or expensive by identifying the factors that are important in determining market returns. The trading system examines the relationship between relevant information and the price of financial assets, and gives buy or sell recommendations when they suspect an under- or overvaluation (Figure 4). Thus, even if some traders find the data mining approach too mechanical or too risky to be used systematically, they may want to use it selectively as a further opinion.

2.4. Marketing and Customer Care

Given the high stakes and intense competition in the finance industry, intelligent business decisions in marketing are more important than ever. Financial institutions are finding it more difficult to locate new, previously unsolicited buyers, and as a result they are implementing aggressive marketing programs to acquire new customers from their competitors. The uncertainties of the buyer make planning of new services and media usage almost impossible.

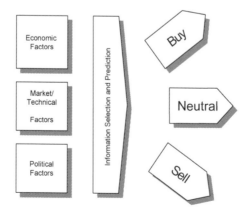

Figure 4 Market participants examine the relationship between relevant information and the price of financial assets, and buy or sell securities when they suspect an under- or overvaluation

The classical solution is to apply subjective human expert knowledge as rules of thumb. Until recently, replacing the human expert by computer technology has been difficult.

An interesting tool available to financial institutions is an analysis of the client's account data. This allows the calculation and analysis of key indicators that help the bank to identify factors that have affected the customer's demand in the past and may well affect the customer's need in the future. Insights gained from the analysis of the account data can provide a basis to optimize mailing actions.

Information about the customer's personnel data can also give indications that affect future demand. In the case of analysis of retail debtors and small corporations, marketing tasks will typically include factors about the customer himself, his credit record, and ratings made by external rating agencies like Moody's or Dun & Bradstreet. Through the advent of electronic commerce, the customer's buying behavior can be evaluated better than ever before and can be used to offer the customer an individualized product.

3. Applicable Data Mining Techniques in Banking and Finance and Some Case Studies

In the last section we described the main business issues in banking and finance and how they can be addressed by data mining techniques. In this section we introduce the data mining techniques that can be used to help decisionmakers with these issues. In the second part of this section we will also introduce some case studies.

3.1. Appropriate Data Mining Techniques in Banking and Finance

Many promising data mining techniques are available and in use for the business issues in finance and banking described above. The theoretical approaches behind such techniques are mainly based on statistics, neural networks, decision trees, rule-generating approaches, association rules, and complex stochastic models. There are many references to these topics in the literature (see Chapter 16 and Mitchie et al., 1994; Mitchell, 1997; Nakhaeizadeh et al., 1998).

In banking and finance, as in the other fields, the main data mining tasks are either one of the tasks we discuss below, or they can be reduced to one of the following:

Segmentation. The data mining task is to find clusters in data (Chapter 16.5). The objects in each cluster should be similar to each other. But each cluster should differ significantly from the other clusters. Often one encounters this data mining task in dealing with credit risk (application and behavior scoring) and, especially, in the case of marketing. Classical statistical approaches (Jobson, 1992), neural nets (Kohonen, 1988), and conceptional clustering methods (Fisher, 1987a,b) can be used to manage these segmentation tasks.

Classification. Using a set of objects belonging to different known classes, the aim is to develop a classifier that can be applied to assign the new object to one of the known classes. Classification finds many applications in risk management, trading, marketing, and customer care, and many data mining techniques to handle these classification tasks (Chapter 16.1). Mitchie et al. (1994) give a comprehensive overview of these techniques.

Applications of such techniques for credit risk can be found in Singleton and Surkan (1995) and Varetto (1998). Methods for balance sheet scoring as for company or country rating are analyzed by Poddig (1995). Furthermore, in the case of behavior scoring or rating migration analysis, the use of classification approaches can help to give better performing and more explainable models (Hosemann and Fritz, 1999). Predictive modeling of customer responses to mailing actions or product offers is another application. It is a common task in the marketing of financial products like credit cards, home loans, or car financing (Furness, 1994a,b).

Forecasting. Perhaps this is the most frequently encountered data mining task concerning the application of data mining techniques in banking and finance. Currency, stock price, and interest rate forecasting are classical examples. In addition to classical statistical approaches like regression modeling (Pindyck and Rubinfeld, 1991), there are many other techniques, such as regression trees (Breiman et al., 1984) and neural networks (Graf and Nakhaeizadeh, 1994), that can be used for forecasting. While the prediction of the mean of an instrument has been broadly investigated by the data mining community, conditional forecasting of volatility has currently moved into focus (Weigend, 1996; Alexander, 1996).

Automated trading of financial instruments and the building of trading systems is a topic that has been covered by the data mining and AI community from early on. The use of forecasting methods like neural networks (Diekmann and Gutjahr, 1998; Green and Pearson, 1994; Rawani et al., 1993), chaos theory (Guillaume et al., 1997), rule systems and fuzzy logic (Tano, 1995), or genetic algorithms (Tayler, 1995) for the generation of trading signals started in the early 1990s and is still a broadly covered topic.

Applications of forecasting methods can be found in portfolio management, which embraces risk measurement, prediction, and optimization: one wants to maximize the risk adjusted return of a portfolio over a given time horizon using all of the introduced techniques. Furthermore, the incorporation of diversification effects and real-world restrictions must be considered. The management of an institutional portfolio is based on all reachable information, that is, risk, expected scenarios, and predicted credit ratings, but also on news and other documents. It can be seen as an optimization step based on risk assessment and market prediction. Efficient and intelligent portfolio management in all areas can therefore be regarded as the strategic goal of all financial institutions (see Hill et al., 1994; Illmanen, 1995; Burgess, 1997).

Dependency analysis. The main goal here is to find dependencies between different financial variables. The typical questions addressed are: What are the main factors having a significant impact on the development of certain stock indices like Dow Jones or DAX? What is the probability that a customer who is interested in financial product X is also interested in product Y? (Webber, 1995). In recent years many complex stochastic models have been developed addressing such issues (Von Hasseln and Nakhaeizadeh, 1997). For association rules see also Chapter 16.2.3 and Agrawal et al. (1993) or for the Bayes network approach, Chapter 16.6 and Pearl (1988).

Deviation Analysis. This data mining task deals with the identification and handling of deviations in the data. These techniques can be used to develop early warning systems in different areas of banking and finance. For example, the identification of the customers whose payments are delayed over a defined interval might be useful in credit risk management. Most of the methods used for deviation analysis are based on statistical approaches (Jobson, 1992).

Deviation analysis can be used further for quality control. This is an important topic of interest in risk management. Generally, one is not only interested in a good predictive model, but also in one that is able to react to changes in the structure of the domain. Difficulties arise when the composition of a portfolio or the economic environment is changing. Monitoring changes is therefore an important area of research connected with deviation analysis (see Diebold et al., 1998, for monitoring changes in market risk management or Lanquillon, 1998, for monitoring the composition of a credit customer portfolio using Sheward control charts).

3.2. Some Case Studies

FORECASTING MARKETS WITH NEURAL NETS AT THE LANDESBANK HESSEN THÜRINGEN
In cooperation with the universities of Karlsruhe and Bremen, the Landesbank Hessen Thüringen have used neural networks for forecasting financial markets since 1995. They use neural networks to predict the short-term movement of financial instruments like the US$/DEM exchange rate, and interest rate-related products like the Bund-Future or T-Bond-Future. The daily recommendations of the networks are used not only as a further opinion but are

executed directly by LHT dealers. Thus far, the bank is successfully dealing with a substantial amount of Futures based only on these systems (see Gutjahr et al., 1997).

CREDIT RISK MANAGEMENT WITH MACHINE LEARNING AT DEBIS FINANCIAL SERVICES
The goal of this project has been the support of complex decisionmaking processes in credit risk management with the use of data mining technology. Together with the Mercedes-Benz Credit Corporation (MBCC) in the United States (an entity of the Debis Financial Services), a system for processing delinquent customers has been established. Customers are classified by the forecasted severity of the delinquency and processed by experts for this class of customers, that is, in uncritical cases by part-time employees or in severe cases by MBCC lawyers. The use of data mining resulted in a reduction in operational costs at the MBCC collections office through matching the customer to the appropriate collector. The classification is being done by a model tree (see Quinlan, 1992), which forecasts the customer's probability of further delinquent payments.

The model trees are fully integrated into MBCC's credit risk process and has been operational since mid-1998 (see Kauderer et al., 1999).

4. Special Aspects of Data Mining in Finance

4.1. Data Protection Aspects

When using data mining techniques in banking and finance, the issue of data protection aspects is an important topic due to the high sensitivity of the data collected. Especially when working with sensitive customer information, special requirements must be fulfilled (Clarke, 1997; see Chapter 22).

When highlighting data protection aspects the case of sensitive customer information is of major concern: if customer information has been collected only for a specific reason, and then if it is going to be used for other purposes, it might be necessary to inform and to receive further consent from the customer in order to process, enhance, or derive further knowledge from this data. Since the task of data mining is to generate new knowledge, solving legal issues is therefore an integral part of the process.

The case of joining different sources of information might be checked by the legal department of the institution conducting business. Difficulties arise when information used and

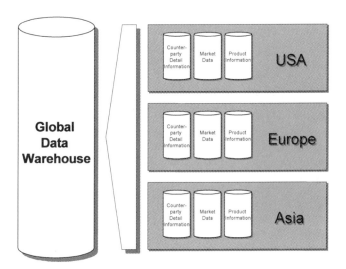

Figure 5 Financial institutions aggregate globally business and market information in an integrated and consistent way from databases worldwide

collected for a specific purpose is subsequntly used for other activities. Here is an example of the use of customer data for marketing activities.

4.2. Data Architecture, Data Availability, Data Consistency, and Global Data Warehouses

Many banking and financial businesses operate worldwide, around-the-clock processing information on millions of financial transactions or customers, reevaluating their portfolio value or scoring their risk. The case of global financial transactions where local systems save similar but not the same information, and the continuously changing customer, portfolio, or financial data make a consistent data source a necessity upon which the data mining process can be based.

An appropriate data architecture using data warehouses can help to base the data mining process on a common ground. Here a data warehouse can be viewed as a data source that repeatedly collects data in an integrated and consistent way from databases worldwide. Since banks and financial institutions must deal with huge amounts of transaction data, one single data warehouse will not be appropriate to handle it all. One will therefore build regional data and information storage segmented by region and collected type of data (customer, market, credit data) that are consistent with each other (Figure 5). Information from different regions must be collected, transformed, and forwarded in a way that data can be aggregated and compared worldwide in order to derive correct knowledge. Furthermore, worldwide time gaps have to be taken into account, since a portfolio value can change dramatically within minutes. These aspects of firmwide data consolidation and consistency are a major problem in business and finance, which will consume large resources during the implementation of a data warehouse and the following mining action. In a last step all the data can be integrated in a global data source or directly used by distributed data mining techniques (see Chapter 13). Since data mining activities can be initiated worldwide, the aspect of 24-hour data availability for each subsystem is of importance. Therefore, global risk management systems operate daily on worldwide data. They collect and aggregate data at a predefined moment and calculate the firmwide portfolio value or risk measures.

5. Summary

In financial institutions considerable developments in information technology and information systems have led to a huge demand for continuous analysis of the resulting data.

Evaluating the customer responses to a new product in the field of marketing, determining the credit-worthiness of individuals or companies in credit risk management, or forecasting markets for daily trading are examples for the application of data mining in this field. Data mining techniques can always be used if one is interested in finding knowledge and structure within the data. So it is quite natural that it is being used by financial institutions, where large amounts of data are common place. But, data mining is a difficult task, a financial business planning to use data mining has to make large efforts, even if the approaches introduced in this chapter seem to be general.

Taken together, the implementation and maintenance of models used in risk management, trading, portfolio management, and marketing offer many opportunities for the use of data mining techniques; hence, it will play a critical key to the success in the finance industry.

References

Agrawal, R., T. Imielinski, and A. Swami. 1993. "Mining association rules between sets of items in large databases." *SIGMOD Record* **22(2)**: 207–216.

Alexander, C. 1996. "Volatility and correlation forecasting." In *The Handbook of Risk Management and Analysis*, edited by C. Alexander, pp. 233–260. Chichester, UK: Wiley.

Altman, E. I. and J. C. Bencivenga. 1995. "A yield premium model for the high yield debt market." *Financial Analysts J.* **51**: 49–56.

Altman, E. I., G. Marco, and V. Varetto. 1993. "Corporate distress diagnosis: comparisons using linear discriminant analysis and neural networks." Working Paper Series. New York University Salomon Center, NY.

Beckers, S. 1996. "A survey of risk measurement theory and practice." In *The Handbook of Risk Management and Analysis*, edited by C. Alexander, pp. 171–192. Chichester, England: Wiley.

Breiman, L., J. H. Friedman, A. Olshen, and C. J. Stone. 1984. *Classification and Decision Trees*. NY: Wadsworth.

Burgess, A. N. 1997. "Modelling asset prices using the portfolio of cointegration models approach." Discussion Paper. London: London Business School, Department of Decision Science.

Clarke, R. 1997. "Customer profiling and privacy implications for the finance industry." Invited Address to AIC Conference on Customer Profiling for Financial Services, 26–27 May, Sydney. Available at http://www.anu.edu.au/people/Roger.Clarke/DV/CustProfFin.html.

Diekmann, A. and S. Gutjahr. 1998. "Prediction of the Euro-Dollar Future using neural networks—a case study for financial time series prediction." In *Intelligent Data Engineering and Learning*, edited by L. Xu, L. W. Chan, I. King, and A. Fu. Singapore: Springer.

Diebold, F. X., T. Gunther, and A. Tay. 1998. "Evaluating density forecasts, with applications to financial risk management." *Int. Econ. Rev.* **39**: 863–883.

Fisher, D. H. 1987a. "Knowledge acquisition via incremental conceptional clustering." *Machine Learning* **2**: 139–172.

Fisher, D. H. 1987b. "Knowledge acquisition via incremental conceptional clustering." Ph.D. diss. Irvine, CA: University of California at Irvine.

Furness, P. 1994a. "New pattern analysis methods for database marketing, Part 1." *The Journal of Database Marketing* **1(3)**: 220–232.

Furness, P. 1994b. "New pattern analysis methods for database marketing, Part 2." *The Journal of Database Marketing* **1(4)**: 297–306.

Graf, J. and G. Nakhaeizadeh. 1994. "Application of learning algorithms to predicting stock prices." In *Logistic and Learning for Quality Software Management and Manufacturing*, edited by V. Plantamura et al., pp. 241–257. New York: Wiley & Sons.

Green, H. and M. Pearson. 1994. "Neural nets for foreign exchange trading." In *Trading on the Edge*. New York: Wiley.

Guillaume, D. M., M. M. Dacorogna, R. D. Davé, U. A. Müller, R. B. Olsen, and O. V. Pictet. 1997. "From the bird's eye to the microscope: a survey of new stylized facts of the intra-daily foreign exchange markets." *Finance and Stochastics* **1**: 95–129.

Gutjahr, S., M. Riedmiller, and J. Klingemann. 1997. "Daily prediction of the foreign exchange rate between the US Dollar and the German Mark using neural networks." In *Proceedings of the 1997 PACES/SPICIS*. Singapore: Springer.

Hill, T., M. Marquez, O'Conner, and W. Remus. 1994. "Artificial neural network models for forecasting and decision making." *Int. J. Forecasting* **10**: 5–15.

Hosemann, D. and S. Fritz. 1999. "Behavior scoring of Deutsche Bank's german corperates." In *Application of Machine Learning and Data Mining in Finance*, edited by G. Nakhaeizadeh and E. Steurer, ECML'98 Workshop Notes, April 1998, Chemnitz.

Illmanen, A. 1995. "Time varying expected returns in international bond markets." *J. Finance* **50(2)**: 481–506.

Jobson, J. D. 1992. *Applied Multivariate Data Analysis. Volume II: Categorical and Multivariate Methods*. University of Chemnitz, Chemnitz, Germany: Springer-Verlag.

Kauderer, H., G. Nakhaeizadeh, F. Artiles, and H. Jeromin. 1999. "Optimization of collection efforts in automobile financing—a KDD supported environment." In *KDD-99, Proceedings of the Fifth ACM SIGKDD International Conference on Knowledge Discovery and Data Mining, San Diego*, edited by S. Chaudhuri and D. Madigan. New York: ACM.

Kealhofer, S. 1998. "Uses and abuses of bond default rates." In *CreditMetric's Monitor First Quarter 1998*, edited by J. P. Morgan, New York.

Kohonen, T. 1988. *Self-organization and Associative Memory*. Berlin: Springer-Verlag.

Lanquillon, C. 1998. "Dynamic aspects in neural classification." In *Application of Machine Learning and Data Mining in Finance*, ECML'98 Workshop Notes April 1998, edited by G. Nakhaeizadeh and E. Steurer. Chemnitz, Germany: University of Chemnitz.

Mitchie, D., D. J. Spiegelhalter, and C. C. Taylor. 1994. *Machine Learning, Neural and Statistical Classification*. New York: Ellis Horwod.

Mitchell, T. 1997. *Machine Learning*. McGraw-Hill.

Nakhaeizadeh, G., Th. Reinartz, and R. Wirth. 1998. "Wissensentdeckung in Datenbanken und Data Mining: Ein Überblick." In *Data Mining. Theoretische Aspekte und Anwendungen*, edited by G. Nakhaeizadeh, pp. 1–33. Heidelberg: Physica Verlag.

Pearl, J. 1988. *Probabilistic Reasoning in Intelligent Systems*. Morgan Kaufmann.

Pindyck, R. S. and D. L. Rubinfeld. 1991. *Econometric Models and Econometric Forecasts*. New York: McGraw-Hill.

Poddig, T. 1995. "Bankruptcy prediction: a comparison with discriminant analysis." In *Neural Networks in the Capital Markets*, edited by A.-P. Refenes, pp. 301–307. Chichester, UK: Wiley.

Quinlan, J. R. 1992. "Learning with continuous classes." In *Proceedings of the Fifth Australian Joint Conference on Artificial Intelligence*, edited by A. Adams and L. Sterling. Singapore: World Scientific.

Rawani, A. M., D. Mohapatra, S. Srinivasan, P. Mohapatra, M. Mehta, and G. Rao 1993. "Forecasting and trading strategy for foreign exchange market." *Inform. Decision Technol.* **19(11)**: 55–62. North-Holland.

Sharpe, W., G. Alexander, and J. Bailey. 1995. *Investments*. Englewood Cliffs, NJ: Prentice-Hall.

Singleton, J. C. and J. Surkan. 1995. "Bond rating with neural networks." In *Neural Networks in the Capital Markets*, edited by A.-P. Refenes, pp. 301–307. Chichester, UK: Wiley.

Tano, S. 1995. "Fuzzy logic for financial trading." In *Intelligent Systems for Finance and Business*, edited by S. Goonatilake and P. Treleaven, pp. 209–224. Chichester, UK: Wiley.

Tayler, P. 1995. "Modeling artificial stock markets using genetic algorithms." In *Intelligent Systems for Finance and Business*, edited by S. Goonatilake and P. Treleaven, pp. 271–288. Chichester, UK: Wiley.

Varetto, F. 1998. "Genetic algorithms applications in the analysis of insolvency risk." *J. Banking and Finance* **22**: 1421–1439.

Von Hasseln, H. and G. Nakhaeizadeh. 1997. "Dependency analysis and learning structures for data mining." In *Proceedings of the Fifth European Congress on Intelligent Techniques and Soft Computing*, edited by H. J. Zimmermann, pp. 1526–1531. Aachen, Germany: Verlag Mainz, Wissenschaftsverlag.

Webber, R. 1995. "Intelligent systems for market segmentation and local market planning." In *Intelligent Systems for Finance and Business*, edited by S. Goonatilake and P. Treleaven, pp. 271–288. Chichester, UK: Wiley.

Weigend, A. S. 1996. "Data mining in finance: report from the Post-NNCM-96 workshop on teaching computer intensive methods for financial modeling and data analysis." In *Decision Technologies for Financial Engineering (Proceedings of the Fourth International Conference on Neural Networks in the Capital Markets, NNCM-96)*, edited by A. S. Weigend, Y. S. Abu-Mostafa, and A.-P. N. Refenes, pp. 399–412. Singapore: World Scientific.

Wilson, T. 1997a. "Portfolio credit risk I." *RISK* **10(9)**: 111–117.

Wilson, T. 1997b. "Portfolio credit risk II." *RISK* **10(10)**: 56–66.

41 TELECOMMUNICATIONS

Leonardo Carbonara

ABSTRACT   As the telecommunications market becomes increasingly competitive, it is essential for operators to target their customers effectively, minimize churn, combat fraud efficiently, and optimize the performance of their networks. KDD technology opens new avenues of opportunity in all of these areas thanks to the wealth of data available for exploration and analysis. In fact, telecommunications companies store vast amounts of data such as customer accounts, call data, equipment records, and fault logs, which represent an invaluable source of information that can be exploited through data mining for a number of purposes. This chapter examines three main application areas of data mining in telecommunications: marketing, fraud detection, and network fault prediction. For each area, the main problems and data mining techniques used are described with the help of examples.

1. Introduction

Telecommunications companies store vast amounts of data such as customer accounts, call data, equipment records, and fault logs. This data represents an invaluable source of information that can be exploited through data mining for a number of purposes. In telecommunications, we find three main areas of application for data mining:

- *Marketing.* As in many other industries, the analysis of transactional data for customer profiling and segmentation can significantly improve the effectiveness of marketing activities.

- *Fraud detection.* Fraud against telecommunications operators is becoming increasingly widespread, taking many different forms, such as cellular cloning, and subscription and Internet fraud. Worldwide, fraud costs the telecommunications industry a reported $12 billion annually.

- *Network fault prediction.* The elements composing a telecommunications network can generate tens of thousands of different types of alarm, each relating to different problems with the network. The complexity of the task makes data mining particularly suitable to analyzing alarm data and improving network performance.

Before we move on to presenting in some detail each of these areas, it is worth spending a few words on the impact of data protection legislation on the use of telecoms data for data mining. As a result of the liberalization of the telecommunications market, in many countries various degrees of regulation are been imposed to ensure fair trading and promote competition. This also affects the way in which customer information can be used and transferred within an organization. These restrictions are often enforced to prevent operators that for historical reasons have a dominant position in the market from using information about customers gained in one part of the business to give another part of the business an unfair advantage over their competitors. Obviously, this also restricts the use of customer information for data mining purposes. In addition, like any other company, telecoms are required to comply with the data protection directives of the markets in which they operate. Interestingly, the new Data Protection Act, recently approved by the European Union, is composed of two directives. The first of these, known as the Framework Directive, lays down the general data protection rules, which apply to everybody. The second Directive is specific to telecommunications and reflects the need felt by the EU to provide additional protection to telecoms customers, especially in relation to privacy issues.

In the following sections each of the application areas listed above is described at length, together with the help of real-world examples.

2. Customer Profiling for Marketing

As a result of deregulation, real competition exists in the telecommunications industry for the first time in a long time. Carriers are offering new services (long distance, cellular, paging, Internet, etc.) through new channels in markets that were previously restricted to them. This section explores various ways in which data can be exploited to help operators face the challenges in the new market.

2.1. Calling Behavior Analysis for Improved Campaign Effectiveness

Direct marketing campaigns can consume large amounts of revenue in the expectation of increasing sales. In order to maximize the revenue generated by a campaign, it is important to identify and target the correct audience for the product or service advertised. Two sources of information are available to the marketers to help the selection of the customers to be targeted by a campaign:

1. Internal data, that is, customer information stored in the company's own databases; and

2. External data, that is, additional information, which can be bought from market research agencies.

As an example, the number of telephone lines owned by a customer would be the sort of information typically stored in a telecom's databases, while the number of children in the customer's family normally would not be found, but could potentially be acquired from an external agency. If, for instance, the aim of a campaign were to sell a second line to residential customers, the combination of these two pieces of information would allow the marketers to target large families with only one line.

As external data can be expensive to acquire and of unproven quality, telecoms are increasingly driven to maximizing the exploitation of their own internal sources of information. This is now being made possible by the convergence of data warehousing and data mining technology.

As explained more extensively in Chapter 34, data mining can be used to analyze the early response to a marketing campaign, and refine the selection criteria for subsequent shots of the campaign. While this kind of analysis is common to many different businesses, telecoms have the advantage of possessing an invaluable source of information in their customers' call records. Call records typically contain the source and destination of the call, its duration, cost, and date and time at which it was made, and provide data miners with a unique opportunity to identify likely campaign responders based on an accurate profile of their calling behavior. Since mining individual call records would be unpractical (consider that, for instance, British Telecom's customers generate more than 120 million calls a day), normally calls are summarized to make them more amenable to analysis. Typical summarizations are at a weekly level, aggregating the calls according to their locality (local, regional, national, and international) and their tariff (daytime, evening, and weekend). This level of detail is generally sufficient to extract from the data meaningful behavioral patterns. Based on the relevance to the specific task at hand, other variables can be created, such as the average duration of calls and the number of distinct international destinations contacted. Moreover, calling data can be coupled with other information (e.g., discount schemes, number of lines, geographical data) to produce an even more detailed picture of a particular segment of customers.

As an example, BT used this methodology to show how the targeting for a marketing campaign for the Friends and Family option could be improved. The data consisted of nearly 2,700,000 calls from over 27,000 telephones in the Oxford area. Fifty-nine different summary variables were created for each of the source telephones. A tree induction algorithm (see Chapter 16.1.3) was used to generate rules that categorized those people who had bought into the Friends and Family discount scheme. The results of this analysis, combined with the visualization of the distribution of Friends and Family customers over the selected area, suggested various ways to improve the marketing campaign. Note that visualization of customer calling behavior was also used by Eick and Fyock (1996) to identify potential customers for advanced services.

2.2. Customer Churn Modelling

Customer churn (or attrition) is the process of customer turnover. In the mobile telecommunications market it is estimated that the cost of churn is between $300 and $400 per new subscriber. Churn is not restricted to the telecommunications market; it occurs wherever increasing competition provides incentives for customers to switch providers. Industries such as credit card issuers, insurance companies, and ISPs (Internet Service Providers) are all subject to increasing levels of churn. In the mobile telecommunication market the churn rate appears to vary around the 30 percent mark.

Modisette (1999) makes a distinction between three different types of churn: unavoidable churn, involuntary churn, and voluntary churn. Unavoidable churn occurs when a customer terminates the contract for reasons beyond the control of the customer or the provider (e.g., customer moving out of the provider's operating area). Involuntary churn is the result of the provider terminating the service for some reason (e.g., failed payments, fraud). Voluntary churn implies service termination on the part of the customer when switching to another operator. Most of the efforts of telecommunications providers are focused on preventing this third type of churn.

In order to combat the high cost of churn, data mining can be employed to understand why customers churn and which customers are most likely to churn in the future. Such information can be utilized by marketing departments to better target recruitment campaigns, and by active monitoring of the customer call base to highlight customers who may, by the signature in their usage pattern, be thinking of migrating to another provider.

Conceptually, churn analysis is no different than any other customer profiling exercise. Classification techniques (see Chapter 16.1) such as decision trees and neural nets can be used to identify customers at risk by comparing churned customers with a sample of "loyal" customers. The so-derived model can then be applied to the rest of the customer base to detect likely defectors.

2.3. Internet Usage Analysis

The provision of services over the Internet is a major strategic opportunity for telecommunications companies. As customers use this infrastructure, large amounts of data about their usage of services and their buying and browsing habits are generated. Customers' navigation patterns through the Internet can be analyzed to answer a number of important questions about the usage of a WWW (World Wide Web) site. Major WWW site owners need to know how people navigate around their site, whether there are places in the site where people have problems finding the information they want, whether people who are interested in certain products or information are interested in others, how effective are the advertisements on their site, and even to which pages this visitor is likely to go next.

When clients visit an Internet site, their access logs record several pieces of information about their usage of the site. First, we have the identification of each visitor making a request to the server. Secondly, the documents requested are also recorded in the form of URLs (Uniform Resource Locators). Other information contained within access logs includes the amount of data sent to the client on each request, the date and time the request was registered, and a status code associated with the status of the request.

Visualization (see Chapter 15) and association rule discovery (see Chapter 16.2.3) allow us to analyze the accumulation of all of these paths. By means of visualization techniques it is possible to discover "heavily trodden paths," which identify regions of the site that are of key interest to its visitors. Association rule discovery, on the other hand, can detect subsets of pages consistently visited by a large number of visitors. If, for instance, in a commercial web site each product is advertised on a different page, this analysis can spot cross-product interests and suggest improvements to the site (easy links between associated products), or promotions based on popular product groupings. Mace (1996) describes in detail a case study of this type of analysis.

3. Fraud Detection

Telecommunications fraud takes many different forms. Among the most important examples are cellular cloning, calling card fraud, and illegal call reselling. It is estimated that the cost of telecommunications fraud to corporations worldwide amounts to $15 billion annually.

What makes fraud detection particularly challenging is the fact that fraud events are relatively rare. For a telecommunications operator, fraudulent customers might amount to just 1 or 2 percent of the entire customer base. This can pose serious limitations to the application of data mining methods, as the performance of some classification techniques tends to deteriorate dramatically when presented with highly skewed data. The pruning mechanisms of efficient decision tree learners, for instance, cannot effectively cope with widely disparate class proportions, in most cases returning a single node tied to the majority class. (Consider, in fact, that, if only 1 percent of the customers were fraudulent, a tree classifying all customers as nonfraudulent would still be correct in 99 percent of the cases.) This problem can be addressed in a number of ways. The performance of decision tree algorithms can be improved by artificially balancing the training data, by attaching a higher misclassification cost to the rare class (Pazzani et al., 1994), or by using boosting (Freund and Schapire, 1996) and bagging (Breiman, 1996) techniques. Alternatively, other classification techniques can be used, which are less sensitive to uneven class distributions in the data. As an example, Ezawa and Norton (1995) describe a system to detect nonpaying AT&T customers, using a Bayesian network (see Chapter 16.1.5).

In this section, two examples of fraud will be discussed: the first example is concerned with cellular cloning, one of the most common types of telecommunications fraud, while the second case, premium rate number fraud, shows how data visualization alone can sometimes be very effective.

3.1. Cellular Cloning Fraud

Fraud control is the number-one problem in the wireless industry today, with cellular fraud in the United States alone costing $1 billion a year. Every cellular phone transmits two unique identification numbers: its Mobile Identification Number (MIN) and its Electronic Serial Number (ESN). These two numbers are broadcast unencrypted and can be received, decoded and stored using special equipment that is relatively inexpensive. Cloning occurs when a customer's MIN and ESN are programmed into a cellular phone not belonging to the customer. To some extent, calling-card fraud is based on the same principle, as it involves the fraudster observing the calling-card account numbers and codes when they are dialed, or recording the dial tones representing the numbers. Standard methods of fraud detection include analyzing call data for overlapping calls (collisions), or calls in temporal proximity that could not have been placed by the same user due to geographical dispersion (velocity checks). Fawcett and Provost (Chapters 35 and 46.3) describe a system that integrates these methods with more sophisticated data mining techniques in order to profile user behavior and detect significant deviations from normal patterns. The data mining stage uses a standard rule learning program (RL) (see Chapter 16.1.4) to derive a general covering set of certainty factor rules that serve to distinguish the fraudulent calls from the legitimate ones. The rules are then used to generate a set of profilers. The profiler constructor has a set of templates which are instantiated by rule conditions. The profiler constructor is given a set of rules and a set of templates, and it generates a profiler for each rule-template pair. Each profiler is trained on typical (nonfraud) account activity, and is then used to describe how far from the typical behavior a current account-day is. In the final stage, the profilers' outputs are used as features to a standard ML program to learn which combinations of profiler outputs indicate fraud with high confidence. The final output is a detector that profiles each user's behavior and produces an alarm if there is sufficient evidence of fraudulent activity.

3.2. Premium Rate Service Fraud

Premium rate services (e.g., chat lines) work as follows: the service users (i.e., the people calling the chat line) pay the operator for the use of the service through their telephone bills.

The operator in turn passes on part of the revenue generated by these calls to the service provider (i.e., the people running the chat line). In a case of fraud against BT, the fraud perpetrators were setting up bogus premium rate services and generating large volumes of calls to these numbers. The bills for these calls were never paid, but BT was required to pay the service providers. When BT began to realize that there was a connection between the Premium Rate services and the unpaid bills, the problem was to identify the various telephone numbers involved in the fraud and understand how they were linked together.

The visualization tool NetMap^{TM} proved particularly successful at providing an intuitive graphical representation of the patterns of calls to be analyzed. The whole study involved some 360,000 telephone calls between about 10,000 telephones (many of which were international destinations). Figure 1 shows one such visualization. Around the circumference of the circle are boxes, or nodes, one for each telephone number. Lines between nodes denote telephone calls, and the thickness of the line is proportional, in this case, to the number of calls between two numbers. The analysis started by identifying a group of suspect London telephone numbers and a set of highly active Premium Rate services. The study then moved on to consider all the other numbers called by the suspect London numbers. This led to the discovery that a small set of mobile numbers were consistently called by the suspects. The emergence of these strong patterns brought the investigators to believe that, while the premium rate numbers were the numbers being exploited in the fraud, the mobile numbers were being used by the organizers of the fraud to coordinate the operations. Further investigation confirmed this hypothesis and led to the identification of the organizers of the fraud. For more details on this work, see Roberts and Totton (1996).

Visualization has also been used successfully by AT&T (Eick and Fyock, 1996) to detect international calling fraud by displaying the calling activity in a way that lets the user see unusual patterns quickly. Activity is visualized in terms of nodes (users and countries) and links between the nodes (calls). Unusual patterns become candidates for further investigation.

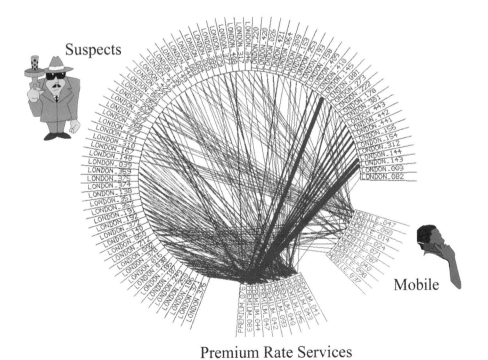

Figure 1 A NetMaP visualization of calling activity

4. Network Fault Prediction

Telecommunications networks consist of many elements. Many of these components generate an alarm when an abnormality occurs in the system. Thousands of these alarms are generated daily. There are tens of thousands of different types of alarms, each relating to different problems with the network. This makes the task of monitoring telecommunications networks extremely difficult and often results in misinterpretation of the alarm data (Jakobson and Weissman, 1993).

A typical example of a problem common to many telecommunications operators is the successful prediction of faults in the access network. Telecommunications networks generally comprise two parts: the main trunk network and the access network. The trunk network is a highly modernized, switched network using mainly optical fiber systems to route traffic between exchanges. This may be managed effectively, with most components being able to flag possible and actual faults using alarms and self-test facilities. The access network provides the connection between the customer's premises and the nearest local exchange, and predominantly comprises twisted copper pairs. As there are no testing components between the network termination in the customer's premises and the telephone exchange, testing must be managed from the exchange, which houses one or more line test systems. Unfortunately, line test data is often of poor quality. Records can be corrupt due to faulty line test equipment, or might have missing values. In addition, the line tests can be wrongly categorized, as faulty lines might never be complained about (if, for instance, the house is empty, or the customer is tolerant of noise), or healthy lines might suddenly have faults that cannot be predicted (e.g., the network might be damaged by road work). Finally, as in the case of fraud (see Chapter 46.3), as actual faults are relatively rare events, it is often difficult to collect a sizeable set of cases to analyze.

Most fault detection problems share some of the above features, making them particularly hard to solve. In the literature, several examples can be found to use neural networks, which generally are less affected by noisy data than symbolic learners, or hybrid systems combining neural and symbolic approaches. Sone (1993) describes a system that employs a distributed neural network architecture to identify faults in switching systems. The system consists of several networks that take into account the switching system architecture. The output of these networks is then interpreted by an expert system that produces the final diagnosis. A similar approach was used by Chattel and Brook (1993) to detect faults in the access network.

Among the purely symbolic systems, we find TASA (Hatonen et al., 1996), which uses a novel framework for locating frequently occurring alarm episodes from the alarm stream and presenting them as rules. Large sets of discovered rules are explored with flexible information retrieval tools supporting interactivity and iteration. In this way, TASA offers pruning, grouping, and ordering tools to refine the results of a basic brute force search for rules. The system has discovered rules that have been integrated into the alarm handling software of the telephone networks. AT&T (Cortes et al., 1995) used classification to predict failures in end-to-end network paths and fiber-optic links, thus guiding maintenance technicians. They have also developed a method for estimating the limiting performance of learning machines imposed by the quality of the data, and applied it to network performance monitoring data. Rough sets theory (see Chapter 16.2.1) has been employed to analyze dependencies amongst alarm data and derive a belief network, which helps engineers filter noncritical alarms and predict faults (Shao, 1996). Finally, Lewis and Sycamore (1993) developed a case-based reasoning approach to fault detection.

Visualization has also proved very effective for displaying and analyzing network traffic data. NYNEX, for instance, uses a visualization tool as a component in its "network exploratorium" (Sevitsky et al., 1996), while Eick and Fyock (1996) describe various visualization techniques used by AT&T.

5. Conclusions

In this chapter some of the main application areas of knowledge discovery techniques in the telecommunications industry have been presented. The variety of data generated and held by telecoms is such that this review did not intend by any means to be exhaustive, but rather it sought to introduce some of the main business problems that can be addressed with the help of KDD. Other applications that were not discussed include credit assessment and tariff allocation, as well as network traffic forecasting and optimization.

Telecoms, while sharing a number of business problems with other industries, such as fraud investigation and customer churn, have a unique source of information in the call records. As it has been shown in this chapter, this data can be exploited in several ways to address a variety of problems. However, the recent legislation on data protection imposes a number of restrictions on their use, aimed at safeguarding customers' privacy.

As the telecommunications market becomes increasingly competitive, it is essential for operators to target their customers effectively, minimize churn, combat fraud efficiently, and optimize the performance of their networks. KDD technology opens new avenues of opportunity in all of these areas thanks to the wealth of data available for exploration and analysis.

References

Breiman, L. 1996. "Bagging predictors." *Machine Learning* **24(2)**: 123–140.

Chattel, A. D. and J. B. Brook. 1993. "A neural network pre-processor for a fault diagnosis expert system." In *Proceedings of the International Workshop on Applications of Neural Networks to Telecommunications*. Hillsdale, NJ: Laurence Erlbaum Associates Inc.

Cortes, C., L. D. Jackel, and W-P. Chiang. 1995. "Limits on learning machine accuracy imposed by data quality." In *Proceedings of the First International Conference on Knowledge Discovery in Databases*, pp. 57–62. AAAI Press.

Eick, S. G. and D. E. Fyock. 1996. "Visualizing corporate data." *AT&T Technol. J.* Jan/Feb 1996.

Freund, Y. 1995. "A decision-theoretic generalisation of on-line learning and an application to boosting." In *Proceedings of the Second European Conference on Computational Learning Theory*. Springer-Verlag.

Hatonen, K., M. Klemettinen, H. Mannila, P. Ronkainen, and H. Toivonen. 1996. "Knowledge discovery from telecommunication network alarm databases." In *Proceedings of the Twelfth International Conference on Data Engineering, New Orleans*, pp. 115–221. IEEE Computer Society Press.

Jakobson, G. and M. D. Weissman. 1993. "Alarm correlation." *IEEE Network* **7(6)**: 52–59.

Lewis, L. and S. Sycamore. 1993. "Learning index rules and adaptation functions for a communications network fault resolution system." In *Proceedings of the International Workshop on Applications of Neural Networks to Telecommunications*. Hillsdale, NJ: Laurence Erlbaum Associates Inc.

Mace, J. 1996. "Mining the net: a case study." In *Proceedings of Data Mining and Data Warehousing '96*. UNICOM Conference, London.

Masand, B. and G. Piatetsky-Shapiro. 1996. "A comparison of approaches for maximizing business payoff of prediction models." In *Proceedings of the Second International Conference on Knowledge Discovery in Databases*. AAAI Press.

Modisette, L. 1999. "Milking wireless churn for profit." *Telecommunications Online*, February 1999.

Pazzani, M., C. Merz, P. Murphy, K. Ali, T. Hume, and C. Brunk. 1994. "Reducing misclassification costs." In *Proceedings of the Eleventh International Conference on Machine Learning*. Springer-Verlag.

Roberts, H. and K. Totton. 1996. "Data mining in BT." In *Proceedings of Data Mining '96, UNICOM Conference*. London.

Shao, J. 1996. "Knowledge discovery in alarm data analysis." In *Proceedings of the Twenty-third Seminar on Theory and Practice of Informatics*, pp. 433–440. Springer-Verlag.

Sevitsky, G., J. Martin, M. Zhou, A. Goodarzi, and H. Rabinowitz. 1996. "The NYNEX network exploratorium visualization tool: visualizing telephone network planning." *Proc. Int. Soc. Optical Engng* **2656**: 170–180.

Sone, T. 1993. "Using distributed neural networks to identify faults in switching systems." In *Proceedings of the International Workshop on Applications of Neural Networks to Telecommunications*. Hillsdale, NJ: Laurence Erlbaum Associates Inc.

42 NEURAL AND ROUGH SET BASED DATA MINING METHODS IN ENGINEERING

Anna L. Buczak and Wojciech Ziarko

ABSTRACT This chapter reviews data mining methods used in engineering. It addresses neural network, neural-fuzzy, neural-genetic, and rough set methods. The peculiarities of engineering data, as well as how these properties influence the data mining process, are described. Multiple real-world engineering applications of data mining are addressed.

1. Data Mining Problems in Engineering

Data mining techniques are derived from many research areas including statistics, neural networks, fuzzy set theory, genetic algorithms, rough sets, and symbolic machine learning. In this chapter we will concentrate on neural network, neural–fuzzy, neural–genetic, and rough set approaches to data mining. We will put special emphasis on application of the methods mentioned in engineering.

Data mining for engineering applications is done mainly for classification and prediction. Not all applications developed in the past are explicitly termed data mining applications (quite a few of them are actually older than the term *data mining*), but in the context of the objectives of the data mining process, they fit the definition well. The goal of classification is to derive a classificatory procedure that would divide observed data patterns into disjoint meaningful categories. Classification in engineering is often done for diagnostics, that is, fault recognition of various machinery parts or full machines. Specific diagnostic applications have been developed for laminar flow table rolls in steel sheet manufacturing mills (Loskiewicz-Buczak and Uhrig, 1992), helicopter gear boxes (Essawy et al., 1997), rolling element bearings (Alguindigue et al., 1993), rotating machinery (see Chapter 46.6), oil lubrication systems (Garga and Hall, 1997), nuclear power plant components (Uhrig, 1992; Uhrig et al., 1995), and so on. Prediction involves building a model that will forecast information about the future, for example, predicting electric load in the next twenty-four-hour time period (Park et al., 1991). Other engineering problems involving prediction are predictive health monitoring for forecasting the remaining useful life of a piece of equipment (Hansen et al., 1996), and city water consumption prediction (An et al., 1997). Prediction is also used in control applications, for estimating the response of a complex system, such as the temperature in an air-conditioned room, to changes in the ambient temperature and heating/cooling rate (Masanori, 1995). Specific examplary applications of prediction in control of nonlinear dynamic systems include noise cancellation (Widrow and Winter, 1988), adaptive echo canceling (Widrow and Winter, 1988), wind energy conversion control (Mayosky and Cancelo, 1998), fuel injection control (Manzie et al., 1998), inverted pendulum control (Mrozek and Plonka, 1998), and cement kiln production control (Mrozek and Plonka, 1998). Other kinds of engineering applications are new material design (Jackson et al., 1996), control algorithm acquisition from process control log data (Mrozek and Plonka, 1998), environmental modeling (An et al., 1997; Grzymala-Busse, 1998), and process optimization based on past process data (Szladow and Ziarko, 1993).

2. Engineering Data Characteristics

When comparing engineering to other applications of broadly understood data mining, one factor becomes apparent: engineering applications most typically use data from sensors (similarly to most medical applications). Business data, on the other hand, are dominated by transactional information such as customer information, employee information collected via questionnaires, cash registers, and so on, usually with a human being the essential part of the information collection process. The difference in the data-gathering methodology leads to differences in data quality (more errors in the business data because of human involvement) and quantity (data files collected from sensors sampled with high frequency are usually huge).

Sensory data are often characterized by high dimensionality of inputs. Sensory data include images from visual or infrared cameras, frequency spectra generated from accelerometers or microphones, and so on. When dealing with those highly dimensional patterns (by patterns we mean representative samples), a common preprocessing technique is to compress the signatures. Signature compression is the process of mapping highly dimensional data into a vector of lower dimensions and is valid if the compressed and original vectors depict the same statistical properties. Signature compression is often used rather than input vector selection because signatures contain generalized information about the whole waveform type. In other words, the general shape of the waveform may be more important for a given problem than the exact amplitude or brightness values. Another approach is feature extraction, common in speech recognition, in which signal processing techniques are used to extract characteristic properties of a waveform.

Certain engineering applications employ sensory readings that are not highly dimensional (e.g., temperature, pressure). In this case, the situation more closely resembles business applications because each input has a well-defined meaning and can be used as a separate attribute. Input compression is not performed in that case, and often methods are devised for input vector selection.

Another peculiarity of engineering applications, especially the ones dealing with diagnosis, is that patterns describing faulty conditions are often very costly to accumulate. In order to obtain a truly valuable pattern, we need to experience the actual failure of a complex machinery or system, and this can be prohibitively costly. It means that not only would the input vector be of very high dimensionality in this case, but also the number of patterns describing faulty conditions would be limited.

3. Modeling Using Neural Network–Based Techniques

Artificial neural networks (ANNs) have been successfully used for system modeling for many years. ANN's robustness to noise and to incomplete patterns makes them a very powerful and flexible tool. From the myriad of different types of neural networks, the ones that are most often used for classification include backpropagation, radial basis function, adaptive resonance theory, and probabilistic neural networks. When performing time-series prediction, recurrent neural networks are employed such as recurrent backpropagation or the Hopfield network. The reader may find a detailed description of all these neural network types in many books (e.g., in Haykin, 1994). When using a neural network for modeling, a proper internal network structure for the problem at hand has to be designed. This includes deciding the number of network layers and number of nodes in each layer.

Modeling and classification results produced by neural network methods are often highly accurate. They have however one inherent problem: lack of explanation why a particular pattern was classified in a given class. Neural networks have often been criticized for being black boxes and, as such, for not providing explanations of their outputs. For example, when dealing with a loan approval, the lack of explanation is not acceptable. If the customer is rejected, it has to be known why (and he or she will probably ask for an explanation). However in many engineering problems, especially those containing highly dimensional inputs, the lack of explanation is quite frequent. It is also widely accepted because many of the highly-dimensional inputs have no obvious meaning to the users. In the case of ANNs, the knowledge is hidden in network weights, and it is difficult to interpret it. The main reason is the nonlinearities (e.g., sigmoidal transfer functions in the backpropagation network) in transfer functions of network neurons. It is very difficult to represent them by if-then rules. Nevertheless, methods exist to extract rules from trained ANNs (see Chapters 16.1.8 and 31). The most widely used method relies on sensitivity analysis of a neural network. Sensitivity analysis helps to understand which parameters are the most important for a specific model. This can be done by holding all inputs but one constant. By varying this input between the minimum and maximum values allowed, and observing the network's response, we can judge its importance on the model. If the output does not vary, it means that the input is not important. Conversely, if the output value varies considerably, the input is considered to be significant. By repeating this process, in a controlled manner, it is possible to rank the inputs with respect to their importance for the model (Bigus, 1996).

Many other powerful methods for extracting rules from trained neural networks have been developed in recent years (Fu, 1994; Kozma and Kasabov, 1998; Lu et al., 1996; Mar Abad Grau and Molinero, 1998). However, very few methods were applied to engineering problems involving real data. Most of the algorithms consist of two steps: network pruning and rule extraction. Network pruning is the process of removing unnecessary connections and nodes from a trained neural network without increasing the approximation error of the network. Unnecessary connections contributing little to the output are those with small weights. What exactly is meant by small weight is usually decided by trial and error. However, some more structured methods also exist (Sietsma and Dow, 1991; Lu et al., 1996). Independent of the network pruning method used, the network after removal of certain connections needs to be retrained. If the accuracy is acceptable, we can remove more connections (if low weights exist in the retrained network). If the accuracy is unacceptable, the pruning process comes to an end. Nodes are removed when both their input and output connections were removed by the pruning process.

A network with a smaller number of connections and nodes left after pruning allows for the extraction of concise and comprehensible rules. Most rule extraction techniques, and also the method developed by Lu et al. (1996) for backpropagation networks, start by applying a clustering algorithm to find clusters of hidden node activation values. Then, discretized activation values of hidden nodes are related to output-level activation values and rules describing network outputs in terms of the discretized hidden unit activation values are generated. Next, input values are related to hidden activation values and a set of rules to describe the hidden units' discretized values in terms of the inputs is generated. The last step consists of merging the two sets of rules to obtain rules relating the inputs and outputs.

4. Engineering Applications of Neural, Neural-Fuzzy, and Neural-Genetic Methods

In order to give the reader a real understanding of how data mining is performed for engineering systems, we will describe a few representative examples in some detail. These examples will be real-world engineering problems and real solutions. The data mining solutions to the problems described in this section will be representative of neural network, neural-fuzzy, and neural-genetic solutions to data mining problems.

4.1. Neural Network Approach to Steel Sheet Manufacturing

The method for machinery diagnostics in a steel sheet manufacturing plant, described in this section, is representative of other neural network–based methods. Machinery diagnostics are often based on vibration monitoring principles that involve collection and analysis of vibration spectra data obtained from vital components of the system. This analysis leads to the identification of component failures and their causes. The system developed in Loskiewicz-Buczak and Uhrig (1992) performs diagnosis of laminar flow table rolls in a steel sheet manufacturing plant. The data set reflects certain faulty operating conditions. The goal of the data mining is to correctly classify the machines into categories associated with different faults. Signals are acquired by accelerometers located at nine locations on each machine. A 150-point spectrum of each sensor output is generated using FFT (fast Fourier transform) techniques. This results in 1,350 input variables. Developing any system with 1,350 inputs is not reasonable since many of those inputs may be unimportant. We cannot use sensitivity analysis of a trained neural network here for the simple reason that a network with 1,350 inputs, 5 outputs (1 for each fault), and any number of nodes in the intermediate layers is very unlikely to converge. Also, as often in engineering applications, we do not have enough patterns to train such a huge neural network. The problem is solved by compressing individual sensor signatures first and then classifying them. Compression from 150 to 50 points is performed by recirculation neural networks (RNNs; Haykin, 1994). The signature compressed by RNNs is the input to a backpropagation neural network (BPN). Each BPN produces a decision as to what degree a given signature belongs to each of the classes. These nine decisions are input to the data fusion center, which is a probabilistic neural network (Haykin, 1994). This network performs Bayesian decision fusion and generates the final classification.

4.2. *Hybrid Neural-Fuzzy–Genetic Approach to Steel Sheet Manufacturing*

The system described in Section 4.1 provided very good classification results for the steel sheet manufacturing problem. However, it did not provide any information on the importance of sensors used for the classification process. In order to not only perform excellent classification but also to infer information as to which sensors are relevant and which are not, a system composed of neural networks, fuzzy logic, and genetic algorithms was developed. The system (Buczak and Uhrig, 1997) is composed of three phases. The first two phases, involving recirculation and backpropagation neural networks, are the same as in Section 4.1. Phase 3, the fusion of decisions from individual classifiers, is performed by a fuzzy fusion module. Unlike most fuzzy logic-based systems that perform reasoning by fuzzy if-then rules, the reasoning is implemented by means of fuzzy aggregation connectives (Zimmermann and Zysno, 1983). These connectives are capable of combining information not only by union and intersection used in traditional set theories but also by compensatory connectives that mimic the human reasoning process better. The particular set of connectives used in this application are generalized mean aggregation connectives (see Figure 1) defined by:

$$g(x_1, x_2, ..., x_n; \ p, w_1, w_2, ..., w_n) = \left(\sum_{i=1}^{n} w_i \ x_i^p \right)^{1/p}. \tag{1}$$

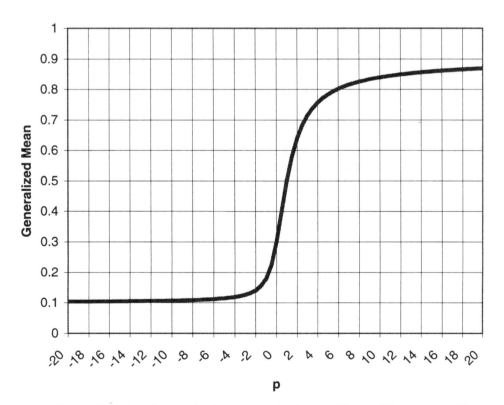

Generalized Mean

Figure 1 Behavior of generalized mean operator for $x_1 = 0.1$, $x_2 = 0.9$, $w_1 = w_2 = 0.5$

The w_i can be thought of as the relative importance factors for the different criteria, where

$$\left(\sum_{i=1}^{n} w_i\right) = 1. \tag{2}$$

The most attractive property of the generalized mean is that by varying the value of p between $-\infty$ and $+\infty$, one can obtain all values between min and max of x_i. Therefore, in the extreme cases, the generalized mean operator can be used as union ($p = -\infty$) or intersection ($p = +\infty$).

In the system described here, the optimal parameters of the aggregation connective are automatically found by a genetic algorithm (GA). The method can be sketched as follows:

1. Code generalized mean parameters (exponent and weights) as bit strings.

2. Generate an initial GA population with different exponents and weights.

3. Perform fusion with the given parameters and calculate the fitness function.

4. Perform genetic algorithm operations to obtain a new population.

5. Repeat Steps 2 and 3 until the stopping criterion is met.

The fitness function describes the classification error of the system. The goal is to have the exponent and weights of generalized mean adjusted by the genetic algorithm in such a fashion that the error for the training patterns is minimized, in the least-squares sense. In the model building process, the system determined the importance of the inputs to be fused (these are the classifications outputted by BPNs) for the diagnosis of laminar flow table rolls. GA converged to a solution in which four out of nine sensor inputs are not necessary for proper classification. The exponent p of generalized mean was found by the genetic algorithm to be 1.397, which means that the system performs a compensative operation in between intersection and union.

4.3. Determining the Importance of Sensor Inputs for a Nuclear Power Plant

When a nuclear power plant is operating normally, the simultaneous readings of hundreds of instruments in a typical control room form a pattern that represents the normal state of the plant (Uhrig, 1992). When some disturbance occurs, the instrument readings undergo a transition to a different pattern, representing a different state of the plant. When the plant is operating at a steady state, the pattern of variables at each sampling instant remains constant or changes slowly. However, when a transient (e.g., loss of coolant in the hot leg of the reactor coolant system or control rod ejection) begins, the sampled values form a different pattern. Each transient is a reason to immediately shut down the nuclear power plant before a serious accident occurs. The goal of the system developed was to identify seven transients and steady-state operations using data from a training simulator at the Tennessee Valley Authority's (TVA's) Watts Bar Nuclear Power Plant. A neural network–based system was developed in Uhrig (1995) for this purpose. The transients present in the data were correctly identified by the system.

From hundreds of plant variables, twenty-two were initially chosen for the study, based on authors' knowledge of plant resources. Genetic algorithms were used to identify the most important of the twenty-two variables associated with each specific transient (Uhrig, 1995). The method consisted of training three-layer backpropagation neural networks for a preset number of training cycles. The networks, depending on different sets of input variables, have different performances (training errors). Network performance and number of input variables can be used in the fitness function whose values are used to guide the selection process in genetic algorithms. The procedure is outlined below:

1. Create an initial population of GA individuals, each of which can be interpreted as a group of selected input variables.

2. Set up and train the population of backpropagation networks with inputs selected by Step 1. The number of hidden nodes and the number output nodes are the same for each network.

3. Use the training error and the number of inputs selected in genetic algorithm fitness function to evaluate the fitness of each network (small number of inputs and small training errors lead to high fitness values).

4. Perform genetic algorithm operations to obtain a new population.

5. Repeat Steps 2 through 4 until a convergence criterion is satisfied.

The method described reduced the number of network inputs from twenty-two to five to nine depending on the particular transient. This input reduction not only allowed the transients to be correctly classified but also gave an important insight into which variables are responsible for each transient. The final system was composed of many simple modular neural networks, each capable of detecting a different transient, using only a few of the most important variables for that transient as inputs. All modular neural networks were integrated to form a diagnostic system capable of monitoring all transients by looking at the outputs of all modular networks.

4.4. Decisionmaking by Pilots

A different type of engineering problem is encountered when the goal is to capture the knowledge of expert personnel. The goal is to understand the decisionmaking process of these highly trained people, derive rules that govern their decision-making, and use it to improve the training of new personnel. Huang and Endsley (1997) study decisionmaking by pilots in complex combat situations, develop a neural network mimicking their decisions, and derive rules from the trained network. Data were collected from a tactical situation display (TSD) in a fighter aircraft cockpit. The TSD was presented to the pilots on a computer screen, and on each trial three to twelve targets were shown for five seconds at which point the targets were blanked from the screen. Experienced aircraft pilots reported the tactical action they would take if the situation displayed occurred.

The TSD is divided into twelve imaginary sectors. For each sector a threat factor can be computed based on the number of targets in that sector and the distance from their own ship. Each threat factor is a continuous-valued input that can be described using a linguistic term such as *High, Medium, Low,* and *None*. With each linguistic term a crisp set can be associated and the input can be coded in a binary representation (e.g., represent High as [0, 0, 1], Medium as [0, 1, 0], etc.). A neural network can be trained with the binary inputs. The method can be sketched in general terms as follows:

1. Classify the continuous-valued inputs into fuzzy sets.

2. Represent the fuzzy sets using a binary scheme.

3. Construct a feedforward neural network with binary inputs identified in Step 2.

4. Train the neural network.

5. Use the large weight approach (Sestito and Dillon, 1993) to identify important inputs.

6. Extract fuzzy rules by using the subset approach (Towell and Shavlik, 1993), i.e., search for subsets of incoming weights that exceed the bias of the neuron.

In the pilot decisionmaking problem, the inputs to the neural network consisted of the threat factors in the sector under consideration, and in two adjacent sectors to the left and two to the right. A simple feedforward network with no hidden layers was trained using a backpropagation learning rule. The output was a binary value (attack/no attack). Since the neural network developed considers only one sector at a time, the results from all the networks had to be combined (fused). The fusion procedure finds the maximum of network outputs for all sectors and declares the sector identified by the maximum as the one to be attacked. In the trained neural network, only three weights had large values. Therefore, only three corresponding inputs were considered important. Next, rule extraction was performed. Only the bias and the weights associated with the three important inputs were considered. The result of the procedure is one rule:

IF (Threat Factor of the sector is High) AND (Threat Factors of the two most adjacent sectors are not High) THEN attack

This fuzzy rule can be used for the purpose of explanation. It can also be used as a decision method instead of the neural network after proper definition of membership functions for the threat factor. These membership functions can be fuzzy, and their construction is independent of the classification method used for converting continuous-valued inputs into binary inputs. In Huang and Endsley (1997), the fuzzy rule gives a better decision accuracy (67.1 percent) than the neural network (61.6 percent). The procedure developed is a general method based on fuzzy logic for extracting rules from feedforward neural networks with continuous inputs and works very well for networks with simple structure.

5. Selected Engineering Applications of the Rough Set Approach

Numerous problems in engineering require constructing models of dependencies existing in natural systems, for instance, in environmental, biological, or chemical systems. These models can be used either for the prediction of future system behavior or to achieve a degree of control over the system. The theory of rough sets seems to fit well into this category of practical problems thanks to the theoretical support it offers to the development of algorithms for constructing empirical models from data. For instance, sample applications were developed in the area of environmental engineering that involved constructing rules for modeling the relation between global temperature and solar energy output, volcanic activity, and so on (An et al., 1997; Grzymala-Busse, 1998). Other applications involved prediction of water-supply consumption based on factors such as day of the week and weather-related factors (An et al., 1997) or capturing structure–activity relationships of chemical compounds.

One important category of knowledge discovery–related engineering applications of rough sets falls in the range of system modeling for the purpose of its control, and acquisition of control algorithms from human operators. In some complex control problems the only way to obtain automated control algorithm is to get the system to learn from the human while observing his actions. Examples of this kind of problem are cement kiln production (Mrozek and Plonka, 1998), balancing an inverted pendulum (Mrozek and Plonka, 1998), and others. It turns out that the methodology of rough sets is particularly well suited to deal with applications of this kind, primarily because of its fundamental objective aimed at acquisition of decision table–based classification models from data. The decision tables produced from data are similar to truth tables known in circuit logic design that have proved their value in countless digital circuits. Similar to truth tables, decision tables are transparent and posses well-defined mathematical properties that can be used for their analysis and simplification. In control applications of rough sets, large amounts of data, typically obtained from sensors, are processed using rough set methodology, which involves data discretization, classification, dependency analysis, and reduction to obtain compact, decision table–based representation of the relationship of interest existing in data. The identified relationships are often nondeterministic, or probabilistic in nature, which means that at best only uncertain decisions or predictions can be made with data-acquired knowledge. This is due to the fact that it is highly unlikely for functional or even partial functional dependencies to exist in this kind of data. The data collections processed in the data mining applications of rough sets are in the range of tens of thousands to several hundred thousand records. The size of the input data is not a real obstacle in the rough sets approach as all records are initially preclassified into a fixed and relatively small number of categories. Because the details of the rough set approach to knowledge discovery have been described elsewhere in this volume, the focus of this section will be the review of some engineering-related applications.

A number of software systems for rough sets-based data analysis were developed and subsequently adapted to different applications (see Polkowski and Skowron, 1998, for a comprehensive list). The engineering applications of rough sets cover a broad spectra of domains. Most of them fall into the following categories: process control and optimization, new material design research, fault diagnosis, engineering design, and environmental engineering. In what follows, due to space limitations, only representative applications are briefly described. More details and more applications' descriptions can be found in Polkowski and Skowron (1998), Slowinski (1992), and Ziarko (1994).

5.1. Control Algorithm Acquisition

Control applications involve using past experience or simulator-generated data reflecting states of a control process to develop a decision table model of a control system. Some exemplary applications of this approach are satellite altitude control (Peters et al., 1998), train control (Khasnabis et al., 1994), balancing inverted pendulum (Mrozek and Plonka, 1998), room temperature control (Masanori, 1995), and cement production control (Mrozek and Plonka, 1998). In the majority of applications the objective is to capture the control knowledge of a human operator controlling a complex device or a process. The data used for that purpose are snapshots of system states taken with a sufficiently high frequency, typically sensor readings of quantities such as spatial coordinates, temperatures, pressures, and so on, and of the information about control actions taken by the operator when operating the system. The control model obtained in this way is subsequently used as a basis of a control algorithm derivation to automatically control the system.

A typical application in this category is the derivation of a cement production control algorithm from data. The quality of the cement produced from slurry in the rotary clinker kiln depends on the interaction of many factors, such as revolution speed and amount of coal being burned. Human operators with significant experience manage to acquire sufficient control skills to produce high-quality clinker. The skills are largely intuitive and not easily convertible into computer control programs. In the industrial application described in Mrozek and Plonka (1998), the control knowledge of the skilled human operator was captured via analysis of the operation log file detailing system states at different times and operator actions taken (setting kiln revolution speed). The unique capabilities of rough set methodology, in particular the ability to measure the degree of dependency between system-state variables and the reduction of redundant variables resulted in choosing this approach to develop an automated control system for cement production. The analysis of the operation log involved rough sets–based detection of dependencies between state variables and the control action variable, identification of redundant state variables, and derivation of an optimized decision table with all redundant variables removed (Table 1). According to standard rough set methodology, in the decision table the detailed values of temperature and of the rate of temperature change have been replaced with qualitative categories corresponding to value ranges (variables TEMP RANGE and TEMP CHANGE). This made it possible to classify all input observations into a relatively small number of classes in terms of the observed combinations of TEMP RANGE and TEMP CHANGE. The rough set theory–based analysis of the relationship between TEMP RANGE, TEMP CHANGE, and REVS (revolution speed in terms of a number of revolutions of the kiln per minute) revealed that the relationship is functional (deterministic) as was summarized in the decision table form. The table was subsequently used for automated control of the cement kiln revolution speed resulting in better quality control than obtained with the help of a human operator (Mrozek and Plonka, 1998).

Table 1 Data-Extracted Cement Kiln Control Table

TEMP RANGE	TEMP CHANGE	REVS
1400–1420	slow-increase	40
1400–1420	fast-increase	20
1400–1420	slow-decrease	40
1420–1440	fast-increase	20
1420–1440	slow-increase	15
1440–1480	fast-increase	0
1440–1480	fast-decrease	20

5.2. Design of New Materials and Other Applications

The key issue in the design of new materials is achieving desirable mechanical, chemical, physical, or biological activity characteristics. In either case, it is necessary to understand the dependencies between chemical or atomic structure of the materials and their target characteristics. Rough sets have been applied to deal with this problem at the stage of building dependency models from experimental material data (Jackson et al., 1996). In the application developed at Wright Laboratory of Wright-Patterson AFB, the objective was to develop a predictive model of energy band gap in the chalcopyrite family of compounds, the primary determinant of electro-optical properties of the materials. These semiconductors are of particular interest because of their role as passive elements in electronic circuits. The rough sets methodology was applied to the chalcopyrite family of crystal structures. The dependency analysis results suggested, the existence of previously unknown correlations between periods of compound elements and band gap energy.

6. Conclusion

Data mining in engineering applications is often geared toward classification of signatures or prediction of future sensor readings. The user is looking for high predictive accuracy of the model rather than for the rules that govern the system. However, as methods for extracting rules from neural networks and neural-fuzzy systems get better, rules extracted will have the same classification/prediction accuracy as the network itself (perhaps even better). At this point, data mining for engineering applications using neural-fuzzy approaches will move toward rule extraction, which is the case in other approaches based on machine-learning algorithms or rough sets. This seems to be the trend for the future for neural-fuzzy approaches.

In rough set–based approaches, the emphasis is shifted toward decision table extraction from data. This is due to the essential advantages of decision tables over rules, as elaborated in detail in Ziarko (1998). Essentially, the empirical decision table is a tabular representation of the relationship existing between some input variables and an output variable, as encoded in the data collection used to derive the table. This aspect of decision tables is similar to neural nets, which also attempt to represent data relationships, but by using complex analytical formulas rather than tables. Using formulas makes it hard to understand and summarize, in human-readable terms, the decisionmaking process. The decision table approach, on the other hand, combines classificatory abilities with transparency of the representation, allowing for easy explanation of factors behind different classificatory decisions.

References

Alguindigue, I. E., A. Loskiewicz-Buczak, and R. E. Uhrig. 1993. "Monitoring and diagnosis of rolling element bearings using artificial neural networks." *IEEE Trans. Industrial Electronics* **40(2)**: 209–217.

An, A., C. Chan, N. Shan, N. Cercone, and W. Ziarko. 1997. "Applying knowledge discovery to predict water-supply consumption." *IEEE Expert* **12(4)**: 72–78.

Bigus, J. 1996. *Data Mining with Neural Networks*. New York: McGraw-Hill.

Buczak, A. L. and R. E. Uhrig. 1997. "Information fusion by fuzzy set operations and genetic algorithms." In *The Industrial Electronics Handbook*, edited by J. D. Irwin, pp. 1325–1337. Boca Raton, FL: CRC Press/IEEE Press.

Essawy, M. A., S. Diwakar, S. Zein-Sabbato, and M. Bodruzzaman. 1997. "Helicopter transmission fault diagnosis using neuro-fuzzy techniques." In *Intelligent Engineering Systems Through Artificial Neural Networks*, edited by C. H. Dagli, M. Akay, O. Ersoy, B. R. Fernandez, and A. Smith, **7**: 661–666. New York: ASME Press.

Fu, L. 1994. "Rule generation from neural networks." *IEEE Trans. Sys. Man, Cybernet.* **24(8)**: 1114–1124.

Garga, A. K. and D. L. Hall. April 1997. "Hybrid reasoning techniques for automated fault classification." In *Proceedings of the Fifty-First Meeting of the Society for Machinery Failure Prevention Technology*. Virginia Beach, VA.

Grzymala-Busse, J. 1998. "Applications of the rule induction system LERS." In *Rough Sets in Knowledge Discovery*, edited by L. Polkowski and A. Skowron, **2**: 366–375: Springer-Verlag.

Jackson, A., S. LeClair, M. Ohmer, W. Ziarko, and Al-Kamhwi. 1996. "Rough Sets Applied to Materials Data." *Acta Metalurgica et Materialia* **44(11)**: 4475–4484.

Hansen, R. J., D. L. Hall, Nickerson, and S. Phoha. 1996. "Integrated predictive diagnostics: an expanded view." In *Proceedings of International Gas Turbine and Aeroengine Congress.*

Haykin, S. 1994. *Neural Networks: A Comprehensive Foundation.* New York: Macmillan.

Huang, S. H. and M. R. Endsley. 1997. "Providing understanding of the behavior of feedforward neural networks." *IEEE Trans. Sys. Man, Cybernet.* **27(3).**

Khasnabis, S., T. Arciszewski, S. Hoda, and W. Ziarko. 1994. "Urban rail corridor control through machine learning: an intelligent vehicle-highway system approach." *Transport. Res. Record* **1453**: 91–97.

Kozma, R. and N. K. Kasabov. May 1998. "Rules of chaotic behavior extracted from a fuzzy-neural network." In *Proceedings of IJCNN'98.* Anchorage, AK.

Loskiewicz-Buczak, A. and R. E. Uhrig. 1992. "Probabilistic neural network for vibration data analysis." In *Intelligent Engineering Systems Through Artificial Neural Networks,* edited by C. H. Dagli, L. I. Burke, and Y. C. Shin. **2**: 713–718. New York: ASME Press.

Lu, H., R. Setiono, and H. Liu. 1996. "Effective data mining using neural networks." *IEEE Trans. Knowledge Data Engng.* **8(6)**: 957–961.

Mar Abad Grau, A., and L. D. H. Molinero. May 1998. "A fast method for rule extraction in neural networks." In *Proceedings of IJCNN'98.* Anchorage, AK.

Masanori, A. 1995. "Design, development and testing of fuzzy logic and rough set controller for HVAC systems." *MSc. Thesis. Faculty of Electronic Systems Engineering,* University of Regina.

Mayosky, M. A. and G. I. E. Cancelo. May 1998. "Adaptive control of wind energy conversion systems using radial basis networks." In *Proceedings of IJCNN'98.* Anchorage, AK.

Manzie, C., M. Palaniswami, and H. Watson. May 1998. "A novel approach to fuel injection control using a radial basis function network." In *Proceedings of IJCNN'98.* Anchorage, AK.

Meidan, A. 1998. "Data mining: issuing predictions and revealing unexpected phenomena." *PCAI,* pp. 24–26.

Mrozek, A. and L. Plonka. 1998. "Rough sets in industrial applications." In *Rough Sets in Knowledge Discovery,* edited by L. Polkowski and A. Skowron, **2**: 214–237. Heidelberg: Springer-Verlag.

Park, D. C., M. A. El-Sharkawi, R. J. Marks, L. E. Atlas, and M. J. Damborg. 1991. "Electrical load forecasting using an artificial neural network." *IEEE Trans. Power Sys.* **6(2).**

Peters, J., K. Ziaei, and S. Ramanna. 1998. "Approximate time rough control: concepts and application to satellite attitude control." In *Rough Sets and Current Trends in Computing,* edited by L. Polkowski and A. Skowron, pp. 491–498. Heidelberg: Springer-Verlag.

Polkowski, L. and A. Skowron, eds. 1998. *Rough Sets and Current Trends in Computing.* Heidelberg: Springer-Verlag.

Sestito, S. and T. Dillon. 1993. "Knowledge acquisition of conjunctive rules using multi-layered neural networks." *Int. J. Intell. Sys.* **8**: 779–805.

Sietsma, J. and R. J. F Dow. 1991. "Creating artificial neural networks that generalize." *Neural Networks* **4**: 67–79.

Slowinski, R., ed. 1992. *Intelligent Decision Support: Handbook of Applications and Advances of the Rough Set Theory,* pp. 77–94. Dordrecht, Heidelberg: Kluwer Academic Publishers.

Szladow, A. and W. Ziarko. 1993. "Adaptive process control using rough sets." In *Proceedings of the International Conference of Instrument Society of America, ISA/93,* pp. 1421–1430. Chicago.

Towell, G. G. and J. W. Shavlik. 1993. "Extracting refined rules from knowledge-based neural networks." *Machine Learning* **13**: 71–101.

Uhrig, R. E. May 1992. "Potential use of neural networks in nuclear power plants." In *Proceedings of Eighth Power Plant Dynamics, Control and Testing Symposium,* pp. 56.01–13. Knoxville: The University of Tennessee.

Uhrig, R. E., A. Loskiewicz-Buczak, and Z. Guo. 1995. "Applications using hybrid neural networks with fuzzy logic and genetic algorithms." In *Hybrid Intelligent Systems,* edited by L. Medsker, pp. 145–172. Norwell, MA: Kluwer Academic Press.

Widrow, B. and R. Winter. 1988. "Neural nets for adaptive filtering and adaptive pattern recognition." *Computer* **21(3)**: 25–39.

Ziarko, W., ed. 1994. *Rough Sets, Fuzzy Sets and Knowledge Discovery.* London: Springer-Verlag.

Ziarko, W. 1998. "Approximation region-based decision tables." In *Proceedings of International Conference on Rough Sets and Current Trends in Computing, Warsaw.* Lecture Notes in AI, 1424, pp. 178–185. Heidelberg: Springer-Verlag.

Zimmermann, H. J., and P. Zysno. 1983. "Decisions and evaluations by hierarchical aggregation of information." *Fuzzy Sets Sys.* **10**: 243–260.

43 MEDICINE

Shusaku Tsumoto

ABSTRACT The development of computer systems has contributed to both medical research and practice and their contribution is now entering into a new phase. Since the early 1980s, there has been a rapid growth in hospital information systems (HISs) leading to a large proportion of laboratory examinations being stored as a huge database. Other types of data, including medical images, will be stored in HISs within the twenty-first century. Thus, it is expected that data mining methods will find interesting patterns from databases of such stored data and will be important for medical research and practice because human beings cannot deal with such a huge amount of data. This chapter provides a practical introduction to knowledge discovery and data mining in medical databases, especially focusing on the following points: (1) the kind of problems medical people want to solve, (2) characteristics of medical data, (3) problems with medical data mining, especially the importance of preprocessing, and (4) an overview of existing research. Discussions show that medical data mining is still in its early days and many problems are still to be solved, even with existing data mining techniques. This suggests that this field should be a hot research topic in medical informatics in the twenty-first century and is awaiting further contributions.

1. Introduction

Medical progress is always supported by data analysis, which not only discovers diseases but also improves the skill of medical experts and establishes the treatment techniques of diseases, although the techniques used are manual or semimanual. One illustrative example is epidemiological research of chronic diseases (Rothman and Greenland, 1998). After statistical approaches had been established, the application of statistics found, from large databases, that hypertension and cholesterol are closely related with cerebral stroke and ischemic heart diseases, which resulted in the development of a large number of chemicals for the control of hypertension. It is already widely accepted that these chemicals contribute to the decrease in the prevalence of cerebral stroke.

It is true that the development of medicine is not supported only by data analysis. Medical practice and research have been changed by the rapid growth of life sciences, including biochemistry and immunology (Levinson and Jawetz, 1996). The mechanism of a disease can be explained as a biochemical process or cell disorder, and the diagnostic accuracy of medical experts is increasing due to the development of laboratory examinations. However, it is also true that data analysis is virtually indispensable when generating a hypothesis. For instance, discovery of HIV infection and Hepatitis type C were inspired by analysis of clinical courses unexpected by experts on immunology and hepatology, respectively (Fauci et al., 1997).

Although life science has rapidly advanced, the mechanisms of many diseases are still unknown, especially neurological diseases, which are very difficult to analyze because their prevalence is very low (Adams and Victor, 1993). Even the mechanism of diseases with high prevalence, such as cancer, are only partially known to medical experts. In this sense, medical research always need a good hypothesis, which is one of the most important motivations for data mining and knowledge discovery for medical people.

Another aspect of interest to medical researchers in data mining is as follows. Since the early 1980s, there has been a rapid growth in hospital information systems, which now store a large proportion of laboratory examinations as databases (Van Bemmel and Musen, 1997). For example, in a university hospital, where more than one thousand patients visit from Monday to Friday, a database system will store more than 1 gigabyte of numerical data from laboratory examinations for each year. Furthermore, storage of medical images and other types of data are discussed as research topics on electronic patient records in medical informatics and all the medical data will be stored in hospital information systems within the twenty-first century.

Thus, it is highly expected that data mining methods will find interesting patterns from databases of such stored data and will be important for medical research and practice because human beings cannot deal with such a huge amount of data.

2. Problems of Data Owners

Data owners (medical researchers or practitioners) would like to extract hypotheses that will lead to good medical research or medical practice. Research and practice do not always overlap, but good medical research will result in medical practice. Medical practice also overlaps with health care, which will have the same social objective. Thus, we will limit our discussions to issues on medical research in this chapter, although much is also applicable to medical practice.

Data owners are interested in the following five problems:

1. Relations between examinations
2. Search for important factors for diagnosis
3. Search for important factors for prognosis
4. Discovery of new diseases
5. Short- and long-term effects of therapeutic procedures

The second to fourth issues are closely related to the first one, so in the subsequent sections, we mainly discuss the first and the fifth issue.

2.1. Relations between Examinations

A final differential diagnosis is often made by the combination of specific examinations, such as medical imaging (CT [computer tomography] or MRI [magnetic resonance image]) and immunological examinations. For example, the introduction of CT has changed the quality of diagnosis of cerebral stroke (Adams and Victor, 1993). Thus, people tend to think that the importance of traditional techniques has slightly decreased in medical practice. However, since highly specific and/or sensitive examinations have several problems with their applications, conventional techniques are still important for medical practice because of the following reasons:

1. *Costs of medical image and immunological tests.* Medical image and laboratory examinations have much higher costs than physical examinations and cannot be applied to each patient so often. Thus, if the specificity and sensitivity of a combination of physical examinations are as good as expensive tests, then the combination will be more applicable and useful.

2. *Estimation of clinical courses and prognosis.* For differential diagnosis of loss of consciousness, medical images, such as CT and MRI, and laboratory examinations, such as concentration of NH_3, are very important. However, in general, they are not so useful for estimation of clinical courses and prognosis. Even now, the combination of physical examinations and medical expertise is useful for detecting the status of each patient with loss of consciousness (Plum, 1992). The construction of a prognostic model is one of the interesting topics in artificial intelligence in medicine (Lucus and Abu-Hanna, 1999), although sufficient models are very difficult to construct.

3. *Discovery of patterns for syndromes.* Although diseases with high prevalence are well examined and their precise classification is established, many diseases with low prevalence are not yet precisely classified and still described as syndromes, which are defined as a set of manifestations for which the pathophysiological processes are unknown (Fauci et al., 1997; Adams and Victor, 1993). Such syndromes may be classified into subclasses of the same etiology: the precise classification of low-prevalence diseases is required for future research, which is a strong motivation for data mining. It is also expected that such classification may lead to discovery of new diseases.

2.2. Short- and Long-Term Effects

For evaluation of treatment, statistical techniques are applied to check whether some chemicals are effective in treating/controlling a disease (Altman, 1991). The time interval for analysis is at most five years, and most of the results are on short-term effects of therapeutic procedures. However, as the treatment of infectious and chronic diseases has become established, most people keep their health until they are seventy to eighty years old in developed countries, which makes us realize the importance of studies on long-term effects. For example, in the case of rheumatic and collagen diseases, oral steroid therapy has become the main therapy to suppress the activities of autoimmune disorders. However, several side effects are observed when it is taken for a long time, and it is a very important research issue to estimate when such side effects will start.

Although these studies on long-term effects are difficult when medical experts maintain the data by themselves, hospital information systems will enable them to store all the data much more easily. Thus, it is expected that data mining techniques greatly contribute to the analysis of data stored for a long period.

3. Available Data

Two types of databases are available in the medical domain. One type is data sets acquired by medical experts that are collected for a special research topic. For example, if a neurologist is interested in meningitis, he may start to collect all the symptoms and laboratory tests with some hypothesis. These data have the following characteristics: (1) the number of records are small; (2) the number of attributes for each record are large, compared with the number of records; and (3) the number of attributes with missing values is very few. These tendencies are general in scientific data, as discussed in Westfall and Young (1993). We refer to this type of database as p-databases (prospective databases). The analysis of those data is called prospective analysis in epidemiology (Kleinbaum and Kupper, 1982; Rothman and Greenland, 1998) because data collection is triggered by the generated hypothesis. Statistical analysis is usually applied to these data sets (Altman, 1991).

The other type is a huge data set retrieved from hospital information systems. These data are automatically stored in a database without any specific research purpose. Usually, these databases only include laboratory tests, although researchers in medical informatics are discussing how to store medical images and physical examinations as electronic patient records (Van Bemmel and Musen, 1997). The standards of data types and their storage will be determined around the year 2000 by ISO/TC215. After establishment of these standards, these different types of data will be stored in HISs, available for data analysis. The data in HIS have the following characteristics: (1) the number of records is huge; (2) there is a large number of attributes for each record (more than several hundred); (3) many missing values will be observed; and (4) many temporal subrecords are stored for each record (patient). We refer to this type of database as r-databases (retrospective databases). The analysis of these data is called retrospective analysis in epidemiology because data will be analyzed after data collection. The data will lose any good features that prospective data hold, and even statistical techniques do not perform well. This type of data is very similar to business databases, where data mining techniques will be useful.

The classification of data is very important for analysis of medical databases. When readers are planning to analyze medical data, they should clarify which type of data they will analyze. In the subsequent sections, each data type will be discussed.

4. Security Problems

With respect to p-databases, medical experts are responsible for their security. Since medical experts are very sensitive to the security of information about their patients, p-databases will not include any personal information except for gender and age.

As for r-databases, security problems are still under discussion. Although almost all the HISs support several security systems, the level of security is variable and dependent on the interest of a system manager. Even researchers in medical informatics feel that the security of HISs is not sufficient. In ISO/TC215, this topic is very important, and standardization of security problems are still being discussed in WG4, the results of which will be available around the year 2000. The discussion focuses on how to make the standards that will be implemented in HISs within several years.

5. Data Mining Problems

Concerning p-databases, data will be prepared with a hypothesis very carefully generated by medical experts. Thus, the quality of data is very high, and any data analysis technique will be applicable and useful. The only problem with p-databases is that the number of measurements is very large, compared with the number of records. Thus, data reduction or rule induction will be useful to detect the important attributes for analysis.

On the other hand, for r-databases there are many difficult issues for data analysis. In the following subsections, three important problems will be discussed.

5.1. Missing Values

There are the following three types of missing values:

1. *Occasional effects.* This type of missing value is very often observed for business databases. Since data collectors may not have clear hypotheses for data collection, several attributes will not be recorded accidentally, irrelevant of whether these attributes are important. Thus, it is difficult for data miners to decide whether such attributes with missing values are important. Data analysis can be applied to such attributes if the importance of these attributes cannot be checked during the preprocessing procedure.

2. *Missing values concerned with medical decisions.* Medical experts usually select physical and laboratory examinations when making a differential diagnosis in order to reach the final diagnosis as quickly as possible. If medical experts decide that some examinations are not useful, they will not select such tests and attributes, and the values of these tests will be stored as blank. In this case, missing values mean that these attributes are not important for a medical decision. Thus, data miners should ask data owners if a database has such attributes.

3. *Progress in laboratory examinations.* Many laboratory tests are developing, which enables us to gain the accuracy of diagnosis and treatment. However, from the viewpoint of data analysis, these tests make data mining more difficult because records taken before the introduction of a test will not include any information about this test. Thus, data miners should check whether a database includes such laboratory examinations.

Data miners should classify attributes with missing values and proceed into preprocessing of data. In the first type, conventional techniques for missing values can be applied (and removal of these attributes should be postponed). In the second type, the context behind the missing values should be extracted and attached to the induced results. Finally, in the third case, data miners should change the strategy. Databases may be split into two subdatabases: one before the introduction of a new examination and the other one after the introduction, and data mining techniques should be applied to each subdatabase.

6. Data Storage

Medical examinations and observations are variable and sometimes difficult to store in a fixed number of attributes. There are the following three types of data storage to be preprocessed:

6.1. List: Multivalued Attributes

Some of the attributes should be represented as a list. For example, traffic accidents may injure several parts of the body. Some patients have damaged only one part of the body, and others suffer from multiple injuries, which makes it difficult to fix the number of attributes. Even if we enumerate all the possibilities of injuries and fix the number of columns corresponding to

Name	Contents
ICD-9,10	International classification of diseases
ICPC	International classification of primary care
DSM	Diagnostic and statistical manual for mental disorders
SNOMED	Systematized nomenclature of human and veterinary medicine
ICD-O	International classification of diseases for oncology
CPT	Current procedural terminology
ICPM	International classification of procedures in medicine
RCC	Read clinical classification
ATC	Anatomic therapeutic chemical code
MeSH	Medical subject headings
DRG	Diagnosis related groups

Table 1 Coding Systems

the worst case, most patients will have only a small number of them. In this case, medical people may input multivalues for each attribute. Concerning this subject, readers may refer to Chapter 4 on types of data.

6.2. Temporal Data

The characteristics of medical temporal databases are: (1) each record is inhomogeneous with respect to time series, including short-term effects and long-term effects; (2) each record has more than one thousand attributes when a patient is followed for more than one year; and (3) when a patient is admitted for a long time, a large amount of data is stored in a very short time period.

Since incorporating temporal aspects into databases is still an ongoing research issue in the database area (Abiteboul et al., 1995), temporal data are stored as a table in hospital information systems. Thus, it is very important for data miners to deal with such irregular temporal data (see Chapter 4).

6.3. Coding Systems

Another difficulty is that medical databases will include specific codes. Medical informatics has a long history for coding systems, which originally comes from statistics of health care. Several important coding systems have been established and widely used in HISs (Table 1; Van Bemmel and Musen, 1997).

One of the major coding systems is ICD (International Classification of Diseases), which represents each disease as a combination of alphabet and numbers. Table 2 shows an example of ICD codes for neurological diseases. It is easy to see that these codes are difficult to interpret and should be preprocessed. For preprocessing, data miners should recognize that most coding systems have their own objectives. While ICD focuses on hierarchical structure of etiology, SNOMED focuses on multiple aspects and has several axes to form a complete hierarchical classification systems (Table 3; College of American Pathologists, 1994). Preprocessing may be dependent on an applied coding system.

Table 2 Examples of ICD-10 Code

Code	Definition
G30	Alzheimer's disease
G30.0	Alzheimer's disease, early onset
G30.1	Alzheimer's disease, late onset
G30.8	Alzheimer's disease, others
G30.9	Alzheimer's disease, unspecified

Table 3 Eleven Axes of SNOMED International

Axes	Definition
T	Topography
M	Morphology
L	Living organisms
C	Chemicals
F	Function
J	Occupation
D	Diagnosis
P	Procedure
A	Physical agents, forces, activities
S	Social context
G	General

Most HIS databases use such coding systems, and raw data retrieved from such systems include such codes, which are difficult to understand. Data miners should check such possibilities: since transformation procedures depend on the coding systems, data miners should always take care of what kind of coding system is used, and they should transform those codes into categorical attributes correctly. Codes are usually used to describe decision attributes and, therefore, data miners should take extreme care.

7. Translate Medical Problems into a Search for Special Forms of Knowledge

Medical experts will view data mining as hypothesis generation, and they need simple hypotheses. For this purpose, simple rule induction, such as association rules, are applicable. However, a large database will generate a huge number of rules, most of which correspond to common sense. It makes data owners disappointed at evaluation of induced results. Thus, a more sophisticated procedure may be required, such as coupling of rule induction with ontological reasoning, and introduction of interestingness or surprisingness. Another important issue is that medical concepts and decisions are hierarchical. Although several researchers focus on this hierarchical nature (Tsumoto, 1998a), generalized techniques have not yet been derived.

8. Data Mining Techniques Used and Results

Medical applications of data-mining are a growing area in medical informatics. However, most of the studies, especially machine-learning applications, fall into the category of induction of predictive classification rules (Cooper et al., 1992; Lavrac et al., 1997; Zupan et al., 1999). Although several interesting results are obtained by such machine-learning applications and rough set approach (Polkowski and Skowron, 1998), they mainly focus on generation of rules with high predictive power, which can be called rules of general information. Unfortunately, those rules, which have general knowledge, often correspond to common sense in domain knowledge. It should be strongly pointed out that interests in data mining and knowledge discovery do not always overlap with such rules of commonsense knowledge, but rather overlap with specific rules, which include new, interesting, and unexpected patterns. In this section, we focus on three methods, the results of which suggest future directions of medical data mining. For other studies, please refer to Cooper et al. (1992), Lavrac et al. (1997) and Zupan et al. (1999).

8.1. Complications of Cardioangiography

Harris (1984) applied exploratory data analysis (Tukey, 1977), statistical methods, and a tree induction method to a database including 995 cases of cardioangiography, which were collected from five army hospitals. This data set is described by fourteen attributes (nine categorical, five continuous), which can be classified as an r-database.

Tree induction is a kind of extension of conventional decision-tree induction (Breiman et al., 1984), called sequential multiple regression analysis, where each node in the tree represents a multiple logistic regression function. In 995 cases, 42 cases include important complications with angiography, and Harris examined important factors for complications. From statistical analysis (t-test and chi-square test) the name of hospital, gender (female), location of inserted catheter, and the period of angiography are significant factors for prediction of the complications. From regression analysis, gender (female), period of angiography, institute, and past history of myocardial infarction are significant factors. Finally, the decision tree selects gender as the first attribute. For both male and female, the second factor is the name of hospital and the location of catheter, respectively.

Harris argues that the most important discovery of this analysis is that the gender is selected as one of the most important factors. From this analysis, he reached one important hypothesis related to gender: one of the main factors may be body size, which is related to the radius of arteries. If the radius of arteries is small, the probability of complications may be high. Since body size is not included in a database, gender is selected as an important factor being associated to body size.

This work suggests several important directions of medical data mining: (1) unexpected attributes will lead to discovery of a new hypothesis; (2) detection of unexpected patterns and their interpretation needs deep background knowledge; and (3) databases collected from different institutes will generate different patterns from each database, and some conflicts will be resolved.

8.2. Analysis of Meningoencephalitis

Tsumoto et al. (1995) and Tsumoto (1999) applied a rule induction method, based on the variable precision rough model (Ziarko, 1993), decision trees (Breiman et al., 1984), and statistical methods, including multivariate analysis (Anderson, 1984; Andersen, 1991), to a database on meningoencephalitis, which was collected by Tsumoto as an r-database. All the induced results were interpreted by the author, a neurologist, and showed that rule induction methods generated rules that are unexpected but interesting to medical experts, whereas decision-tree methods and statistical methods acquired knowledge that matches medical experts' knowledge.

The common data sets collected the data of patients who suffered from meningitis and were admitted to the department of emergency and neurology in several hospitals. These data are collected from past patient records (1979 to 1989) and cases in which the author made a diagnosis (1990 to 1993). The database consists of 121 cases, and all the data are described by 38 attributes, including present and past history, laboratory examinations, final diagnosis, therapy, clinical courses, and final status after the therapy.

The rule induction method based on the variable precision rough set model generated 67 rules for viral meningitis and 95 rules for bacterial meningitis, which included the following rules unexpected by domain experts as shown below. Especially, rules (5) to (7) are new induced results, compared with those discovered by Tsumoto et al. (1995). In this study, grouping of attributes was applied. The attribute risk factor has 12 values, and these attribute value pairs did not contribute to rule generation. Thus, this attribute was transformed into binary attributes. After this transformation, these rules were obtained, which suggests that such transformation is important to induce rules interesting to domain experts.

1. $[WBC < 12000] \wedge [Sex = Female] \wedge [CSF\_CELL < 1000] \rightarrow Viral$

   (Accuracy: 0.97,   Coverage: 0.55)

2. $[Age \geqslant 40] \wedge [WBC \geqslant 8000] \rightarrow Bacterial$ (Accuracy: 0.80,   Coverage: 0.58)

3. $[WBC \geqslant 8000] \wedge [Sex = Male] \rightarrow Bacterial$ (Accuracy: 0.78,   Coverage: 0.58)

4. $[Sex = Male] \wedge [CSF\_CELL \geqslant 1000] \rightarrow Bacterial$ (Accuracy: 0.77,   Coverage: 0.73)

5. $[Risk\_Factor = n] \rightarrow Viral$ (Accuracy: 0.78, Coverage: 0.96)

6. $[Risk\_Factor = n] \wedge [Age < 40] \rightarrow Viral$ (Accuracy: 0.84, Coverage: 0.65)

7. $[Risk\_Factor = n] \wedge [Sex = Female] \rightarrow Viral$ (Accuracy: 0.94, Coverage: 0.60)

These results show that sex, age, and risk factor are very important for diagnosis, which has not been examined fully in the literature (Adams and Victor, 1993). Thus, according to these results, the author reexamined relations among sex, age, risk factor, and diagnosis and discovered the following interesting relations among them:

1. The number of examples satisfying [Sex = Male] is equal to 63, and 16 of 63 cases have a risk factor: 3 cases of DM (diabetes melitus), 3 cases of LC (liver cirrhosis) and 7 cases of sinusitis.

2. The number of examples satisfying [Age $\geqslant$ 40] is equal to 41, and 12 of 41 cases have a risk factor: 4 cases of DM, 2 cases of LC and 4 cases of sinusitis.

These results have not been reported in the literature on neurology. Thus, although these discoveries may not be general knowledge, at least they include knowledge specific to this data set. It can be called discovery of knowledge dependent on the context of data collection. It is notable that these results are also statistically significant by using statistical tests (Tsumoto, 1999). DM and LC are well-known diseases in which the immune function of patients will become very low. Sinusitis has also been pointed out to be a risk factor for bacterial meningitis (Adams and Victor, 1993). It is also notable that males suffer from DM and LC more than females.

In this way, reexamination of databases according to the induced rules revealed several important pieces of knowledge about meningitis. This empirical study also suggests that patterns that are unexpected but interesting to domain experts lead to new discoveries and that interpretation of such patterns needs deep background knowledge.

8.3. Association Rules

Brossette et al. (1998) applied association rule discovery to a database on hospital infection control and public health surveillance, which was essentially a temporal database. They argue that one of the problems with application of association rules (Agrawal et al., 1993) is that high-support and high-confidence rules will be less useful than high-support, low-confidence rules, which may be new, unexpected, and interesting patterns. They, therefore, propose the following process for analyzing surveillance data: (1) for each time-slice or partition of data, discover all high-support association rules; (2) for each rule discovered in the current partition, compare the confidence of the rule from the current partition to the confidences of the rule in previous partitions; (3) if the confidence of the rule has increased significantly from a previous partition, or previous partitions, to the current partition, report this finding as a significant event.

Experimental results were obtained to analyze *Pseudomonas aeruginosa* infection control data collected over one year (1996) at the University of Alabama at Birmingham Hospital. Experiments using one-, three-, and six-month time partitions yielded 34, 57, and 28 statistically significant events, respectively. Although not all of these events are clinically significant, several patterns shows potentially significant shifts in the occurrence of infection or antimicrobial resistant patterns of *P. aeruoginosa*.

Their results are interesting not only in medical context, but also in association rule discovery. The authors reported that for each time partition, more than 2,000, 12,000 and 20,000 rules were obtained. However, from the relations between rules of different partitions, only 34, 57, and 28 events were interesting patterns. This work suggests the following two points: (1) most of the induced results are not unexpected and interesting, and (2) interesting patterns may be obtained by comparison between rules in different settings.

9. Action Taken by Data Owners

Three empirical studies show that medical experts try to interpret unexpected patterns with their domain knowledge, which can be viewed as hypothesis generation. In Harris (1984), gender was an attribute unexpected by experts, which led to a new hypothesis that body size is closely related with complications of angiography. In Tsumoto et al. (1995) and Tsumoto (1999), gender and age are unexpected attributes, which triggered reexamination of data sets and generated a hypothesis that immunological factors are closely related with meningitis.

These actions are summarized into the following three patterns:

1. If induced patterns are completely equivalent to domain knowledge, then the patterns are common sense.

2. If induced patterns partially overlap with domain knowledge, then the patterns may include unexpected or interesting subpatterns.

3. If induced patterns are completely different from domain knowledge, then the patterns may be garbage.

The next step will be validation of a generated hypothesis: a data set will be collected under the hypothesis in a prospective way. After data collection, statistical analysis will be applied to detect the significance of this hypothesis. If the hypothesis is confirmed with statistical significance, these results will be reported.

Another action is to develop a decision support system with generated rules. There are very few studies on this topic: Tsumoto (1998b) reported one preliminary work on the relationship between knowledge discovery and decision support.

10. Future Work

It is notable that data mining tasks achieved in the medical domain are still limited. Most studies, including machine-learning applications, deal with simple tables, which are small pieces of information included in patient data of HISs. In those systems, a large amount of temporal data is left unanalyzed. Even statistical techniques cannot deal with large temporal data, which would be a good opportunity to develop a new method from the data mining side.

Although numerical data are mainly stored in HISs, all other information, such as physical examinations and medical images, will be included as electronic patient records (Van Bemmel and Musen, 1997). Thus, discovery of patterns from those data and images will become an important research area of medical data mining.

Furthermore, the standardization of HISs established by ISO/TC215 will enable us to introduce knowledge discovery in databases from different hospitals as distributed data mining. Medicine has a huge number of data in heterogeneous environments that are waiting for further sophisticated techniques.

In summary, the following future research directions may be important for medical data mining techniques to be widely accepted in medicine:

1. Discovery of relations between rules induced from databases.

2. Coupling of medical knowledge with rules induced from databases.

3. Discovery of temporal diagnostic patterns in hospital information systems.

4. Discovery of short- and long-term effects of therapeutic procedures in hospital information systems.

5. Rule discovery in databases collected from different hospitals.

6. Discovery of new diseases.

Although these tasks are very difficult to achieve, existing techniques are not applicable and new techniques should be introduced.

In the twenty-first century, medical data mining and knowledge discovery will be a hot research topic in medical informatics just after all the techniques for electronic patient records have been established. Problems with medical data mining may inspire the development of general data mining techniques. Then, the growth of data mining techniques will support this hot research topic in medical informatics, which will finally contribute to the development of medical research and practice.

References

Abiteboul, S., R. Hull, and V. Abiteboul. 1995. *Foundations of Databases*. New York: Addison-Wesley.

Adams, R. D. and M. Victor. 1993. *Principles of Neurology*. 5th ed. New York: McGraw-Hill.

Agrawal, R., T. Imielinski, and A. Swami. 1993. "Mining association rules between sets of items in large databases." In *Proceedings of the 1993 International Conference on Management of Data (SIGMOD 93)*, pp. 207–216.

Altman, D. 1991. *Practical Statistics for Medical Research*. London: Chapman and Hall.

Andersen, E. B. 1991. *The Statistical Analysis of Categorical Data*. 2d ed. Berlin: Springer-Verlag.

Anderson, T. W. 1984. *An Introduction to Multivariate Statistical Analysis*. New York: John Wiley & Sons.

Breiman, L., J. Freidman, R. Olshen, and C. Stone. 1984. *Classification and Regression Trees*. Belmont: Wadsworth International Group.

Brossette, S. E., A. P. Spragce, J. M. Hardin, K. B. Wates, W. T. Jones, and S. A. Moser. 1998. "Association rules and data mining in hospital infection control and public health surveillance." *J. Am. Med. Inform. Assoc.* **5**: 375–381.

College of American Pathologists. 1994. *SNOMED*. Chicago: College of American Pathologists.

Cooper, G. F., C. F. Aliferis, J. Aronis, B. G. Buchanan, R. Caruana, M. J. Fine, C. Glymour, G. Gordon, B. H. Hanusa, J. E. Janosky, C. Meek, T. Mitchell, T. Richardson, and P. Spirtes. 1992. "An evaluation of machine-learning methods for predicting pneumonia mortality." *Artificial Intell. Med.* **9**: 107–139.

Fauci, A. S., E. Braunwald, K. J. Isselbacher, and J. B. Martin, eds. 1997. *Harrison's Principles of Internal Medicine*. 14th ed. New York: McGraw-Hill.

Harris, J. M. 1984. "Coronary angiography and its complications—the search for risk factors." *Arch. Internal Med.* **144**: 337–341.

Kleinbaum, D. G. and L. L. Kupper, eds. 1982. *Epidemiologic Research: Principles and Quantitative Methods*. New York: John Wiley & Sons.

Lavrac, N., E. T. Keravnou, and B. Zupan, eds. 1997. *Intelligent Data Analysis in Medicine and Pharmacology*. Dordrecht, Netherlands: Kluwer.

Levinson, W. E. and E. Jawetz. 1996. *Medical Microbiology and Immunology: Examination and Board Review*. 4th ed. New York: Appleton & Lange.

Lucus, P. J. F. and A. Abu-Hanna. eds. 1999. "Special Issue on Prognostic Models in Medicine." *Artificial Intelligence in Medicine* **15(2)**.

Plum, F. 1992. *The Diagnosis of Stupor and Coma*. 3d ed. Philadelphia: F. A. Davis Co.

Polkowski, L. and A. Skowron. 1998. *Rough Sets in Knowledge Discovery*, Vol. 1 and 2. Berlin: Physica-Verlag.

Rothman, K. J. and S. Greenland. 1998. *Modern Epidemiology*. Philadelphia: Lippincott-Raven Publishers.

Tsumoto, S. 1998a. "Extraction of experts' decision rules from clinical databases using rough set model." *J. Intell. Data Anal.* **2(3)**: 215–227.

Tsumoto, S. 1998b. "Automated knowledge acquisition based on rough sets and attribute-oriented generalization." *J. Am. Med. Inform. Assoc.* **5(Supplement)**: 548–552.

Tsumoto, S. 1999. "Knowledge discovery in clinical databases—an experiment with rule induction and statistics." In *Proceedings of the Eleventh International Symposium on Methodologies for Intelligent Systems (ISMIS'99)*, edited by Z. Ras. Berlin: Springer-Verlag.

Tsumoto, S., W. Ziarko, N. Shan, and H. Tanaka. 1995. "Knowledge discovery in clinical databases based on variable precision rough set model." *J. Am. Med. Inform. Assoc.* **2(supplement)**: 270–274.

Tukey, J. 1977. *Exploratory Data Analysis*. New York: Addison Wesley.

Van Bemmel, J. and M. A. Musen. 1997. *Handbook of Medical Informatics*. New York: Springer-Verlag.

Westfall, P. H. and S. Young. 1993. *Resampling-based Multiple Testing: Examples and Methods for p-Value Adjustment*. New York: John Wiley & Sons.

Ziarko, W. 1993. "Variable precision rough set model." *J. Comput. Sys. Sci.* **46**: 39–59.

Zupan, B., N. Lavrac, and E. Keravnou. 1999. "Special Issue on Data Mining Techniques and Applications in Medicine." *Artificial Intell. Med.* **16(1)**.

44 PHARMACOLOGY

Miguel Teodoro and Lydia E. Kavraki

ABSTRACT In the last few decades there have been remarkable advances in the biological and medical fields. Due to this biological revolution, the old trial and error methods routinely used as a tool to discover new drugs are being put aside, as they no longer fulfill the present pharmacological needs. Therefore, new methodologies for drug discovery that make extensive use of data mining are now emerging. Here we describe how data mining can help in the discovery of new drugs, and we give some examples of methods that are currently used, as well as their associated problems. In particular, we will focus on the problem of pharmacophore identification, in which information from diverse sources is integrated to discover the common characteristics that determine the activity of a drug.

1. Data Mining in Pharmacology

Data mining is set to play a critical role for pharmacology as much as it currently does in areas such as marketing, manufacturing, telecommunications, and finance. With the advent of the biotechnology revolution, the pharmaceutical industry has been inundated with a flood of data that cannot be analyzed by traditional methods. This data is stored in a series of annotated databases containing information as diverse as chemical structures of candidate drugs, clinical trial results, three-dimensional structures of proteins and nucleic acids, and chemical structure/ drug activity relationships. More recently, due to advances in DNA sequencing technology, we have entered into a new era in the drug discovery process and the treatment of disease. At the time of this writing, the entire genome of more than thirty organisms has already been sequenced. Among them, the sequencing of the human genome is certainly the most significant achievement. The sequencing efforts are being complemented by the rapidly emerging area of proteomics, which integrates the DNA sequence information with further knowledge of protein structure, function, expression pattern, and post-translational modifications. The management and mining of large genomic and proteomic databases combined with already existing data will prove an exciting challenge for the coming years and will provide an entirely new area for the development of new pharmaceutical drugs and diagnostics.

2. Data Mining for Drug Design

2.1. The Rational Drug Design Cycle

The traditional method of discovering new drugs, used since medicinal drugs were first introduced, is largely a process of trial and error. For a new disease, different compounds would be tested until a cure was found. Rational drug design is a new method of conducting drug discovery based on a detailed knowledge of the molecular mechanisms underlying disease. Molecules called proteins either directly or indirectly mediate all biological processes. These large molecules carry out diverse functions such as catalyzing chemical reactions, transporting oxygen in the blood stream, or acting as molecular switches for the activation of specific genes. A critical feature of proteins is that they are characterized by a specific three-dimensional shape that determines their function. Catalytic proteins also contain a specific region called the active site, which is responsible for binding specific molecular reagents and turning them into final products. With rational drug design, one tries to design a new small molecule that binds to the active site of a specific protein by displaying complementary structural and chemical features. A small molecule that binds strongly to its target protein will disrupt its function and may lead to the desired clinical effect.

The rational drug design cycle is a long and complicated process that integrates data from many different sources as shown in Figure 1. Data mining is performed at various stages of the drug design cycle. During the first stage the goal is to identify a new drug candidate. For this, it is critical to consider other factors besides structural and chemical complementarity between the target protein and the new drug candidate. Information, such as previously

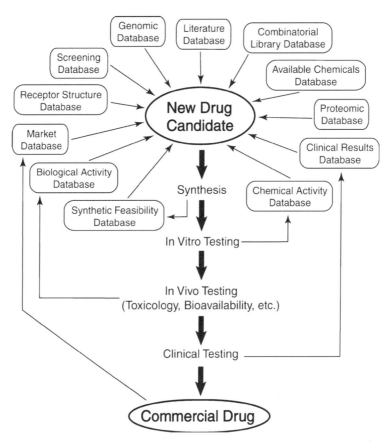

Figure 1 The rational drug design cycle

published work (literature database), preliminary drug screens (screening database), and data from genomics and proteomics databases should be used in order to speed up and cut costs in the development process. Earlier experiments from a synthetic feasibility database can also help in eliminating potential candidates, which although potentially very effective, would not be possible to synthesize in desired quantities at a viable cost. Data mining methods such as clustering of chemical structures and multidimensional regression analysis of clinical trial results can be of invaluable help in analyzing the data stored in diverse databases and in speeding up the identification of new drug candidates. During the second stage of the drug design cycle, the drug candidate must be synthesized and its activity tested *in vitro* and *in vivo*. If the desired effect is verified in these tests, then the drug undergoes a lengthy process of clinical trials whose success determines whether a drug will be commercialized. The information from all tests is again stored and can be mined to identify the causes of failure of a potential drug candidate. These can be exploited to design new leads.

Let us focus our attention on two specific data mining problems encountered in drug design. One problem is docking. Docking consists of identifying compounds that are able to complement the binding site of a known receptor as illustrated in Figure 2(a). The problem is of formidable complexity: drug molecules have internal degrees of freedom (approximately five to thirty) corresponding to torsional rotations around their bonds, and changes in these torsional angles change the shape of the molecule (see Figure 2(b)). Hence, a considered drug candidate can assume widely different shapes when adapting to a protein receptor to reach a minimum energy perfect fit. Information about molecular structure and activity can be used to isolate from chemical databases only those molecules that are likely to result in successful matches or to build a new molecule out of known fragments. In the latter case, the behavior of the new molecule is extrapolated from the properties of the fragments. The docking problem is further complicated by the fact that not only is the drug candidate flexible, but so is the receptor. For a survey on current docking methods, see Finn and Kavraki (1999) and Lengauer and Rarey (1996). Another problem amenable to data mining methods is pharmacophore

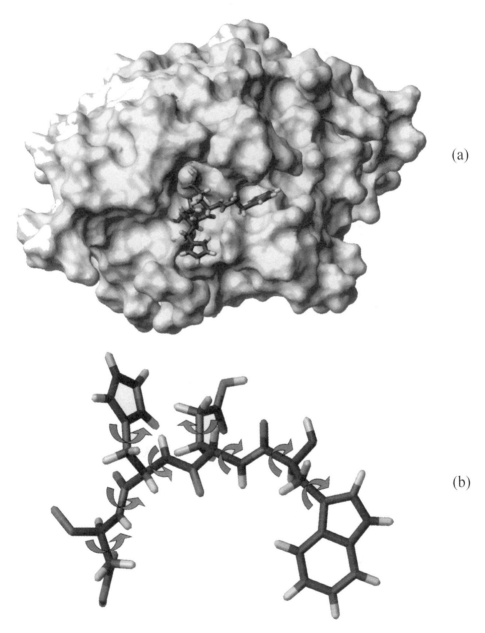

(a)

(b)

Figure 2 (a) A drug molecule docked in a receptor. (b) The drug molecule with some its internal degrees of freedom represented by curved arrows. The drug molecule is capable of changing its overall geometry through torsional rotations of some of its bonds

identification and use. Pharmacophore identification is key to the development of new pharmaceutical drugs when the three-dimensional structure of the receptor's active site is not known (Martin et al., 1993). In this case, it is possible to discover, from preliminary screens, a set of molecules that interact with the given receptor. Pharmacophore identification isolates the molecular components (features) that are responsible for the interaction. These features can later be used to design new drug candidates. Section 3 is devoted to pharmacophore identification.

2.2. Available Resources

Several commercial packages are already available to aid in the data mining process for pharmaceutical drug design. Indicatively, let us mention a few companies. Anvil Informatics (www.anvilinformatics.com) is offering data mining and visualization services to pharmaceutical and biotech companies, Bioreason (www.bioreason.com) is selling automated reasoning systems for drug discovery process, Celera Science (www.celera.com) is working on genomic data and analysis tools, Cellomics (www.cellomics.com) is offering several software solutions for the pharmaceutical industry to facilitate the process of new drug discovery, LION Bioscience (www.lionbioscience.com) markets an IT-platform for drug discovery, MDL Information Systems (www.mdli.com) offers a virtual laboratory for analyzing sequence data using the Bioinformatics Workbench, and Molecular Simulations (www.msi.com), as well as Tripos (www.tripos.com), market software for molecular modeling, simulation, and data mining for computer-assisted drug design.

3. Mining for Pharmacophores

This section defines the pharmacophore identification problem and presents some of the existing methods for its solution. To make the discussion below clear, we first introduce some issues from molecular modeling and some terminology.

3.1. Molecular Modeling

Molecular modeling is a very broad topic and is usually defined as the application of theoretical models to predict or interpret molecular properties. For drug design and pharmacophore determination, there are two critical aspects in this process. The first is energy evaluation. For data mining applications, where a large number of molecules and conformations are probed as possible drug candidates, it is necessary to make energy evaluations as fast as possible while maintaining reasonable accuracy. This precludes the use of highly accurate quantum mechanics methods. Instead, empirical forcefields are used. These represent energy interactions in molecules as a series of experimentally parameterized components such as angle, bond, solvation, and electrostatic energies.

The second critical aspect is the modeling of conformational changes. The conformation of a molecule is the spatial arrangement of the atoms of the molecule. Most molecules are able to change their conformation in order to minimize energetic interactions with the surrounding environment. Most often, the conformation of a molecule stored in a database is different from the conformation that binds to the target protein (active conformation). In order to model conformational changes, kinematic models for molecules have been devised in which the flexibility of the molecule is represented by torsional rotations around some of its bonds as shown in Figure 2(b). These torsional degrees of freedom give an accurate approximation of the flexibility of the molecule, as the other internal degrees of freedom (namely bond angles and lengths) are known to undergo only small changes.

Last but not least, when looking at a molecule, chemists group atoms according to their chemical characteristics and refer to these groups as molecular features. Examples of features include positive and negative charge centers, hydrophobic and hydrophylic parts, hydrogen-bond donors and acceptors, et cetera. By refering to features, it is possible to define a class of molecules with similar characteristics.

3.2. The Problem

The pharmacophore is a three-dimensional arrangement of molecular features that is present in all (or most) of the active conformations of a set of drug molecules that interact with a given receptor. Hence, the pharmacophore can be viewed as a geometric invariant of the active conformations of the considered molecules. A prevailing assumption in rational drug design is that if different ligands exhibit similar activity with a receptor, this activity is due largely to the interaction of the features of the pharmacophore to complementary features of the receptor as illustrated in Figure 3. Thus, if a pharmacophore has been isolated, chemists can use it as a template to search for other molecules that can fit it and exhibit better properties (Glen et al., 1995), or as a scaffold for building new drugs (Finn, 1996).

Both the process of isolating the pharmacophore and the process of finding other molecules that can fit a pharmacophoric pattern are difficult data mining problems. They are also very common tasks in the drug design process. Recent work involves the development of pharmacophores for the benzodiazepine receptor (Filizola et al., 2000), cytochrome P-450 (Ekins et al., 1999), and glutamate receptor (Costantino et al., 1999) ligands.

3.3. Isolating a Pharmacophore

A core data mining problem is to isolate the pharmacophore, given a set of molecules that are known to interact with a receptor. The active conformations of these molecules are not known, but it is assumed that those would be low-energy conformations. Thus far, few solutions to pharmacophore identification have incorporated advanced data mining techniques. Most of the existing solutions start with a collection of distinct low-energy conformations per molecule,

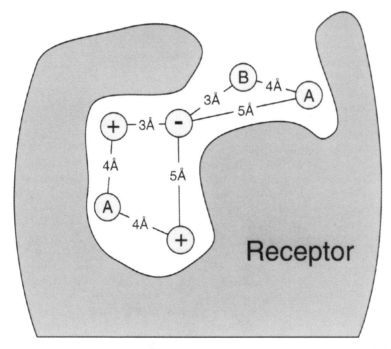

Figure 3 The features of the pharmacophore are primarily responsible for the binding of a molecule to a receptor

obtained by some conformational search procedure (Chen et al., 1999; Finn, 1996). Each conformation is then abstracted to a three-dimensional annotated point set. The points are defined by tracking the molecular features that are considered important for interaction. A search procedure then tries to identify a three-dimensional invariant present in at least one conformation (point set) of the given molecules. The search is often done by pairwise comparisons of conformations. Requiring that the invariant be present in all molecules may unnecessarily exclude solutions, since conformational search methods do not guarantee that all distinct low-energy conformations have been produced. Moreover, the initial set of input molecules may erroneously contain a molecule that does not exhibit the pharmacophore.

Some of the most successful approaches are outlined below. Clearly, pharmacophore identification can be viewed as a problem of determining congruence of point sets. As such, the problem has been studied extensively using graph-theoretic methods (Akutsu, 1994; Akutsu and Halldórsson, 1994; Akutsu et al., 1997; Khanna et al., 1995). Determining the congruence in $\mathscr{R}^3$ is tractable in the absence of complications such as noise (Akutsu, 1994; Akutsu et al., 1997). Undoubtly, invariant identification is more closely related to the problem of identifying the largest common point set (LCP). Unfortunately, the LCP problem turns out to exceedingly difficult; in fact, even for m collections of n points on the real line, the LCP cannot be approximated to within an n^ϵ factor unless $P = NP$, and only weak positive results are known (Akutsu and Halldórsson, 1994; Khanna et al., 1995). Of course, the problem is polynomially solvable when $m = 2$ as shown by Akutsu et al. (1997). However, in the case of pharmacophores, there is noise present in the data and the above methods have limited applicability.

DISCO (Martin et al., 1993) uses clique detection to identify invariants. For each pair of given conformations, the program constructs a graph such that the graph has a clique if and only if the two compared conformations have an invariant in common. The algorithm works well if a small number of initial conformations are available, but there can be a combinatorial explosion in the number of basic operations performed for large data sets (Barnum et al., 1997). Note that subinvariants of all pairwise invariants need to be computed in the end. In an effort to address the combinatorial explosion inherent in methods that reply on pairwise comparisons, some approaches start with small invariants (two to three features) and gradually expand them (Barnum et al., 1997; Drie et al., 1989).

A variety of other methods have been proposed. Optimized geometric hashing techniques from computer vision have been used by Fischer et al. (1992). A genetic algorithm has been described by Jones et al. (1995) in which conformational flexibility is considered during the pharmacophore identification process. The chromosome encodes the torsional angles of the rotatable bonds and the feature mappings. The fitness function is a weighted combination of the feature overlap (the pharmacophore), the common volume occupied by the ligand, and the energy of the ligands to prevent the identification of pharmacophores that use high-energy conformations. The method has been shown to work well in test cases. Distance geometry techniques have been used (Sheridan et al., 1986, 1996), as well as randomized techniques (Finn et al., 1997). Randomization can be introduced both when solving the two-point set matching problem and when considering multiple conformations per molecule. Finn et al. (1997) present two methods for determining congruence. The question of matching with noise is further treated by Indyk et al. (1999), using techniques from combinatorial geometry. The bounds given depend on the diameter of the point set. The problem of matching under noise is a challenging open issue to this date. Methods that utilize some data mining techniques have advocated the use of inductive logic programming (Finn et al., 1998), machine learning (Jain et al., 1994), and recursive partitioning combined with a statistical classification of activities of molecules (Chen et al., 1999).

During pharmacophore identification a major challenge is to be able to work with large heterogeneous chemical data sets. Most existing methods are limited to a small number of low-energy conformations per molecule and to a small total number of molecules. They also presume one binding mode per molecule. Methods that do not have such limitations and can handle a few thousand flexible molecules are now required.

3.4. Finding a Molecule Satisfying a Pharmacophore

Once isolated, the pharmacophore is used as a template to create better drugs. Chemists would search, for example, for molecules that exhibit the pharmacophore but have a different chemical composition. Such molecules could induce an even stronger binding with the considered receptor resulting in a better drug.

It is widely recognized that the problem of matching a single flexible molecule to a pharmacophore is a difficult problem that is currently poorly addressed (Finn, 1996; Willett, 1995). Note that although it is fairly simple to do initial screenings of databases with millions of compounds, it is difficult to narrow down the results at later stages (Willett, 1995). Ligand flexibility can dramatically increase the number of cases that need to be examined before it is decided that a molecule does not match a query. The problem is again clearly amenable to data mining techniques.

Thus far, distance geometry, systematic search, randomized search, and genetic algorithms have been tried but have produced slow algorithms (Blaney et al., 1999; Chang et al., 1989; Clark et al., 1994; Fontain, 1992). The FlexS system (Lemmen et al., 1998) computes a scoring function based on superposition of a known inhibitor, and candidates are ranked and selected on the basis of enrichment factors. One of the most efficient existing techniques for flexible matching is the directed tweak method (Hurst, 1994). The method minimizes a pseudoenergy function, which combines the energy of the molecule and the sum of the squares of the deviations of the distances found in the molecular structure to the distances expressed in the pharmacophore query. Unfortunately the pseudoenergy function contains a large number of local minima, and conformations having high energy are frequently returned (Clark et al., 1994). Work that rigorously treats the kinematics of the molecule while guiding the molecule into low energy conformations was presented by Lavalle et al. (1999). A survey of methods for structural alignment of molecules, some of which could be used for alignment of a molecule to a pharmacophoric pattern, was recently reported by Lemmen and Lengauer (2000). As available data increases, it is a challenge to identify molecules from large heterogeneous data sets that can fit a pharmacophore.

4. Concluding Remarks

Pharmaceutical drug discovery is becoming increasingly dependent on advanced data mining methods in its development cycle. This process requires the analysis of large amounts of complex information stored in diverse databases. Improved methods for data mining, increased computational power and extensive amounts of publicly available biological information are creating a new method of discovery. This new method consists of a data-driven knowledge discovery process that complements the classical scientific method of hypothesis-driven research. The new discovery paradigm will have a large impact on pharmaceutical research not only in the generation of pharmacophores but also in all other stages of the drug design cycle.

ACKNOWLEDGMENTS

Work on this paper by Lydia Kavraki was supported in part by NSF IRI-970228, NSF CISE SA1728-21122N, ATP 003604-0120-1999, and a Sloan Fellowhip. Work on this paper by Miguel Teodoro was supported by the Portuguese Ministry of Science and Technology (PRAXIS XXI BD/13748/97).

References

Akutsu, T. 1994. "On determining the congruence of point sets in higher dimensions." *Lecture Notes Comput. Sci.* **834**: 38–55.

Akutsu, T. and M. Halldórsson. 1994. "On the approximation of largest common subtrees and largest common point sets." *Lecture Notes Comput. Sci.* **834**: 405–413.

Akutsu, T., H. Tamaki, and T. Tokuyama. 1997. "Distribution of distances and triangles in a point set and algorithms for computing the largest common point set." In *Proceedings of the ACM Symposium on Computational Geometry*, pp. 314–322. New York: ACM Press.

Barnum, D., J. Greene, A. Smellie, and P. Sprague. 1996. "Identification of common functional components among molecules." *J. Chem. Inform. Comput. Sci.* **36**: 563–571.

Blaney, J., G. Crippen, A. Dearing and J. Dixon. 1990. "Dgeom: distance geometry." Quantum Chemistry Program Exchange, 590. Department of Chemistry, Indiana University, IN.

Chang, G., W. Guida, and W. Still. 1989. "An internal coordinate Monte-Carlo method for searching conformational space." *J. Am. Chem. Soc.* **111**: 4379–4386.

Chen, X., A. Rusinko, A. Tropsha, and S. Young. 1999. "Automated pharmacophore identification for large chemical data sets." *J. Chem. Inform. Comput. Sci.* **39**: 887–896.

Clark, D., G. Jones, P. Willett, P. Kenny, and R. Glen. 1994. "Pharmacophoric pattern matching in files of three-dimensional chemical structures: comparison of conformational searching algorithms for flexible searching." *J. Chem. Inform. Comput. Sci.* **34**: 197–206.

Costantino, G., A. Macchiarulo, and R. Pellicciari. 1999. "Pharmacophore models of group i and group ii metabotropic glutamate receptor agonists. analysis of conformational, steric, and topological parameters affecting potency and selectivity." *J. Med. Chem.* **15**: 2816–2827.

Drie, J. V., D. Weininger, and Y. Martin. 1989. "Aladdin: an integrated tool for computer-assisted molecular design and pharmacophore recognition, from geometric steric and sub-structure searching of three-dimensional molecular structures." *J. Comput.-Aided Molec. Design* **3**: 225–251.

Ekins, S., G. Bravi, J. H. Wikel, and S. A. Wrighton. 1999. "Three-dimensional-quantitative structure activity relationship analysis of cytochrome p-450 3a4 substrates." *J. Pharmac. Exp. Ther.* **1**: 424–433.

Filizola, M., D. L. Harris, and G. H. Loew. 2000. "Benzodiazepine-induced hyperphagia: development and assessment of a 3d pharmacophore by computational methods." *J. Biomolec. Structure and Dynamics* **17**: 769–778.

Finn, P. W. 1996. "Computer-based screening of compound databases for the identification of novel leads." *Drug Discovery Today* **1**: 363–370.

Finn, P. W. and L. E. Kavraki. 1999. "Computational approaches to drug design." *Algorithmica* **25**: 347–371.

Finn, P. W., L. E. Kavraki, J.-C. Latombe, R. Motwani, C. Shelton, S. Venkatasubramanian, and A. Yao. 1997. "Rapid: randomized pharmacophore identification." In *Proceedings of the International Symposium on Computational Geometry*, pp. 324–333. New York: ACM Press.

Finn, P. W., S. Muggleton, D. Page, and A. Srinivasan. 1998. "Pharmacophore discovery using the inductive local programming progol." *Machine Learning* **32**: 1–33.

Fischer, D., R. Nussinov, and H. Wolfson. 1992. "3-d substructure matching in protein molecules." In *Proceedings of the Third Symposium on Combinatorial Pattern Matching. Lecture Notes in Computer Science, 644*, pp. 136–150. Berlin: Springer-Verlag.

Fontain, E. 1992. "Applications of genetic algorithms in the field of constitutional similarity." *J. Chem. Inform. Comput. Sci.* **32**: 748–752.

Glen, R., G. Martin, A. Hill, R. Hyde, P. Wollard, J. Salmon, J. Buckingham, and A. Robertson. 1995. "Computer-aided design and synthesis of 5-substituted tryptamines and their pharmacology at the 5-HT_{1D} receptor: discovery of compounds with potential anti-migraine properties." *J. Med. Chem.* **38**: 3566–3580.

Hurst, T. 1994. "Flexible 3D searching: the directed tweak method." *J. Chem. Inform. Comput. Sci.* **34**: 190–196.

Indyk, P., R. Motwani, and S. Venkatasubramanian. 1999. "Geometric matching under noise: combinatorial bounds and algorithms." In *Proceedings of the Tenth Annual ACM-SIAM Symposium on Discrete Algorithms*.

Jain, A., T. Dieterich, R. Lathrop, D. Chapman, R. Critchlow, R. Bauer, B. Webster, and T. Laozano-Perez. 1994. "Compass: a shape-based machine learning tool for drug design." *J. Comput.-Aided Molec. Design* **8**: 635–652.

Jones, G., R. C. Glen, and P. Willett. 1995. "A genetic algorithm for flexible molecular overlay and pharmacophore elucidation." *J. Comput.-Aided Molec. Design* **9**: 532–549.

Khanna, S., R. Motwani, and F. F. Yao. 1995. "Approximation algorithms for the largest common set." Technical Report STAN-CS-95-1545. Stanford University.

Lavalle, S., P. Finn, L. Kavraki, and J. Latombe. 1999. "Efficient database screening for rational drug design using pharmacophore-constrained conformational search." In *The Third ACM International Conference on Computational Biology (RECOMB)*, pp. 250–259. New York: ACM Press.

Lemmen, C. and T. Lengauer. 2000. "Computational methods for the structural alignment of molecules." *J. Comput.-Aided Molec. Design* **14**: 215–232.

Lemmen, C., T. Lengauer, and G. Klebe. 1998. "FlexS: a method of fast flexible ligand superposition." *J. Med. Chem.* **41**: 4502–4520.

Lengauer, T. and M. Rarey. 1996. "Computational methods for biomolecular docking." *Curr. Opin. Struct. Biol.* **6**: 402–406.

Martin, Y., M. Bures, E. Danaher, J. DeLazzer, and I. Lico. 1993. "A fast new approach to pharmacophore mapping and its application to dopaminergic and benzodiazepine agonists." *J. Comput.-Aided Molec. Design* **7**: 83–102.

Sheridan, R., M. Miller, D. Underwood, and S. Kearsley. 1996. "Chemical similarity using geometric atom pair descriptors." *J. Chem. Inform. Comput. Sci.* **36**: 128–136.

Sheridan, R., R. Nilakantan, J. Dixon, and R. Venkataraghavan. 1986. "The ensemble approach to distance geometry: application to the nicotine pharmacophore." *J. Med. Chem.* **29**: 899–906.

Willett, P. 1995. "Searching for pharmacophoric patterns in databases of three-dimensional chemical structures." *J. Molec. Recognit.* **8**: 290–303.

45 SCIENCES

45.1 Environmental Sciences

Sašo Džeroski

ABSTRACT Environmental sciences are concerned with the physical, chemical, and biological aspects of the environment. They cover an extremely broad range of topics, such as biodiversity, climate change, forestry, and freshwater ecology, and are relevant to practical issues of environmental management. In this article, we attempt to give an overview of knowledge discovery in databases (KDD) applications in environmental sciences, complemented with a sample of case studies. The latter are described in slightly more detail and used to illustrate KDD-related issues that arise in environmental applications. The application domains addressed range from ecological modeling to remote sensing.

1. Environmental Sciences and Environmental Data

Environmental sciences comprise the scientific disciplines, or parts of them, that consider the physical, chemical, and biological aspects of the environment (Allaby, 1996). A typical representative of environmental sciences is ecology, which studies the relationships among members of living communities and between those communities and their abiotic (nonliving) environment. Environmental sciences are possibly the largest grouping of sciences, drawing heavily on life sciences and earth sciences, both of which are relatively large groupings themselves. Life sciences deal with living (or once-living) organisms and include (among others) agriculture, biology, biophysics, biochemistry, cell biology, genetics, medicine, taxonomy, and zoology. Earth sciences deal with the physical and chemical aspects of the solid Earth, its waters, and the air that envelops it. Included are the geological, hydrological, and atmospheric sciences. The latter are concerned with the structure and dynamics of Earth's atmosphere and include meteorology and climatology.

The field of environmental science is very interdisciplinary. It exists most obviously as a body of knowledge in its own right when a team of specialists assembles to address a particular issue (Allaby, 1996). For instance, a comprehensive study of a particular stretch of a river would involve determining the geological composition of the riverbed, identifying the overlying sediment, measuring the flow of water, determining the chemical and physical properties of the water, as well as sampling and recording the species living in and near the water.

Environmental sciences are highly relevant to environmental engineering, which endeavors to develop processes and infrastructure that preserve the quality of the environment by averting contamination and degradation of air, water, and land resources. They are also relevant to environmental management, which is concerned with directing human activities that affect the environment. Environmental policies and legislation are of crucial importance for environmental management. Here, social sciences enter the picture and topics like environmental impact assessment and environmental economics emerge.

Such a broad, complex, and interdisciplinary field holds much potential for application of KDD methods. As environmental concerns grow and information technology develops, more and more data on many different (physical, chemical, and biological) aspects of the environment are gathered. Environmental monitoring is an important source of such data. Typically, samples of air/soil/water are taken and analyzed for chemical and physical properties, but also for biological properties, for example, the structure of the community of organisms living at the sampled point. Remote sensing is another source of data: meteorological and other satellites continuously provide multispectral images of the Earth that contain information on Earth's atmosphere, geology, and vegetation (among others). Geographical information systems (GISs) are gaining popularity and are a valuable source of environmentally relevant information, such as digital elevation models (DEMs), insolation, and land cover. Other sources include laboratory tests designed to estimate how substances used by humans will affect the environment (and humans themselves): chemicals are (unfortunately not often enough) tested for degradation rates or toxicity.

However, environmental sciences also pose many challenges to existing KDD methods. The data gathered, are of varying quantity and quality. Remote sensing, for example, typically provides large volumes of data. These data, however, can be of varying spatial precision and thus may or may not be of direct use for the problem at hand. Laboratory tests of the toxicity of chemical compounds are typically expensive, and few of the chemicals released in the environment are extensively tested. Analyzing the structure of a community in a biological sample is labor intensive and error prone. Depending on the expertise of the biologist performing the task, the quality of the resulting data may vary significantly.

Given the vast broadness of environmental sciences, any overview of applications of KDD methods in this field is bound to be incomplete. The task is further complicated by the fact that few of the applications are reported in the KDD community. Most are described in publications in one of the many scientific disciplines comprising environmental science, such as soil biology or meteorology. In this article, we attempt to give an overview of KDD applications in environmental sciences, complemented by a sample of case studies in which the author has been involved. The latter are described in slightly more detail and used to illustrate KDD-related issues that arise in environmental applications.

2. Ecological Modeling

Ecological modeling is concerned with the development of models of the relationships among members of living communities and between those communities and their abiotic environment. These models can then be used to better understand the domain at hand or to predict the behavior of the studied communities and thus support decisionmaking for environmental management. Typical modeling topics are population dynamics of several interacting species and habitat suitability for a given species (or higher taxonomic unit).

2.1. Modeling Population Dynamics

Population dynamics studies the behavior of a given community of living organisms (population) over time, usually taking into account abiotic factors and other living communities in the environment. For example, one might study the population of phytoplankton in a given lake (Todorovski et al., 1998) and its relation to water temperature, concentrations of nutrients/pollutants (such as nitrogen and phosphorus) and the biomass of zooplankton (which feeds on phytoplankton). The modeling formalism most often used by ecological experts is the formalism of differential equations, which describe the change of state of a dynamic system over time. A typical approach to modeling population dynamics is as follows: an ecological expert writes down a set of differential equations that capture the most important relationships in the domain. These are often linear differential equations. The coefficients of these equations are then determined (calibrated) using measured data.

Relationships among living communities and their abiotic environment can be highly nonlinear. Population dynamics (and other ecological) models have to reflect this to be realistic. This has caused a surge of interest in the use of techniques such as neural networks for ecological modeling (Lek and Guegan, 1999). Measured data are used to train a neural network that can then be used to predict future behavior of the studied population. In this fashion, population dynamics of algae (Recknagel et al., 1997), aquatic fauna (Schleiter et al., 1999), fish (Brosse et al., 1999), phytoplankton (Scardi and Harding, 1999), and zooplankton (Aoki et al., 1999), among others, have been modeled.

While regression tree induction has also been used to model population dynamics, systems for discovery of differential equations have proved most useful in this respect (Džeroski et al., 1999b), since differential equations are the prevailing formalism used for ecological modeling. Algal growth has been modeled for the Lagoon of Venice (Kompare and Džeroski, 1995; Kompare et al., 1997b) and the Slovenian Lake of Bled (Kompare et al., 1997a), as well as phytoplankton growth for the Danish Lake Glumsoe (Todorovski et al., 1998).

CASE STUDY: MODELING ALGAL GROWTH IN THE LAGOON OF VENICE

The beautiful and shallow Lagoon of Venice is under heavy pollution stress due to agricultural activities (use of fertilizers) on the neighboring mainland. Pollutants are food (nutrients) for algae, which have on occasion grown excessively to the point of suffocating themselves, then decayed and caused unpleasant odors (also noticed by the tourists). Models of algal growth are needed to support environmental management decisions and answer questions such as: Would a reduction in the use of phosphorus-rich fertilizers reduce algal growth?

Kompare and Džeroski (1995) and Kompare et al. (1997b) used regression trees and equation discovery to model the growth of the dominant species of algae (*Ulva rigida*) in the Lagoon of Venice in relation to water temperature, dissolved nitrogen and phosphorus, and dissolved oxygen. The trees give a rough picture of the relative importance of the factors influencing algal growth (cf. Figure 1), revealing that nitrogen is the limiting factor (and thus providing a negative answer to the question in the above paragraph). The equations discovered, on the other hand, give better prediction of the peaks and troughs of algal biomass.

Severe problems of data quality were encountered in this application.

1. Dissolved oxygen, for example, was measured at the water surface at approximately noon (when oxygen is produced by photosynthesis and is plentiful) and does not reveal potential anoxic conditions (which might occur at night)—which it was supposed to reveal.

2. Measurement errors of algal biomass were estimated to be quite large by the domain experts (up to 50 percent relative error).

3. Finally, winds were not taken into account: these might move algae away from the sampling stations and cause huge variations in the observed biomass values.

CASE STUDY: PHYTOPLANKTON GROWTH IN LAKE GLUMSOE

The shallow Lake Glumsoe is situated in a subglacial valley in Denmark. It has received mechanically-biologically treated waste water, as well as nonpoint source pollution due to agricultural activities in the surrounding area. The high concentration of pollutants (food for

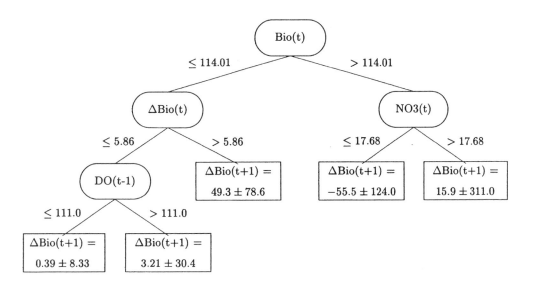

Figure 1 A regression tree for predicting algal growth, that is, change in biomass. Bio(*t*), DO(*t*), and NO$_3$(*t*) stand for the concentrations of biomass, dissolved oxygen, and nitrates at time *t*. Δbio(*t*) stands for Bio(*t*) − Bio(*t* − 1)

phytoplankton) leads to excessive growth of phytoplankton and consequently no submerged vegetation, due to low transparency of the water and oxygen deficit (anoxia) at the bottom of the lake. It was thus important to have a good model of phytoplankton growth to support environmental management decisions.

We used KDD methods for the discovery of differential equations (Džeroski et al., 1999b) to relate phytoplankton (*phyt*) growth to water temperature (*temp*), nutrient concentrations (nitrogen [*nitro*] and phosphorus [*phosp*]) and zooplankton concentration (*zoo*; Todorovski et al., 1998). Some elementary knowledge on population dynamics modeling was taken into account during the discovery process. This domain knowledge tells us that *the Monod term*, which has the form *Nutrient/(Nutrient + constant)*, is a reasonable term to be expected in differential equations describing the growth of an organism that feeds on *Nutrient*. It describes the saturation of the population of organisms with the nutrient.

The model discovered for phytoplankton growth in Lake Glumsoe is shown below:

$$\dot{phyt} = 0.553 \cdot temp \cdot phyt \cdot \frac{phosp}{0.0264 + phosp} - 4.35 \cdot phyt - 8.67 \cdot phyt \cdot zoo$$

Here, $\dot{phyt}$ denotes the rate of change of phytoplankton concentration. The model reveals that phosphorus is the limiting nutrient for phytoplankton growth, as it includes a Monod term with phosphorus as a nutrient. This model made better predictions than a linear model, which has the form

$$\dot{phyt} = -5.41 - 0.0439 \cdot phyt - 13.5 \cdot nitro - 38.2 \cdot zoo + 93.9 \cdot phosp + 3.20 \cdot temp.$$

It was also more understandable to domain experts: the first term describes phytoplankton growth, where temperature and phosphorus are limiting factors. The last two terms describe phytoplankton decay and the feeding of zooplankton on phytoplankton.

The following issues were raised in this application:

1. Data quantity and preprocessing: measurements were only made at fourteen time points during two months (once weekly). Some preprocessing/interpolation was thus necessary to generate enough data for discovering differential equations.

2. Data quality: ecological experts often have poor understanding of modeling concepts, which strongly influences the way data are collected. An electrical engineer with knowledge of control theory would know much better that sampling frequency has to be increased at times when the system under study has faster dynamics (e.g., at peaks of phytoplankton growth).

3. The need for taking into account domain knowledge during the KDD process: this can compensate to a certain extent for poor data quality and quantity (as was the case in this application). This issue is of great importance, yet few KDD methods allow for the provision of domain knowledge by experts.

CASE STUDY: MODELING THE INTERACTIONS OF A RED DEER POPULATION WITH THE NEW GROWTH IN A FOREST

We studied the interactions among a population of red deer and new forest growth in a natural regenerated forest in Slovenia. Ideally, foresters would like to keep the size of the deer population in balance with the rate of regeneration of the forest: if the deer population is large, so are the browsing rates of new forest growth, and regeneration slows down. Understanding the relationship between the two is crucial for managing the balance. Our study has shown that meteorological parameters strongly influence this relationship and have to be taken into account.

A preliminary study using regression trees to model the interactions was performed by Stankovski et al. (1998). Here, we summarize the results of a follow-up study that used a slightly larger data set, cleaner data, and more reliable methods of regression tree induction (Debeljak et al., 1999). The induced models show that the degree of browsing for maple (the preferred browse species of red deer) depends directly on the size of the population. The degree of beech browsing, on the other hand, was most strongly influenced by meteorological parameters, that is, winter monthly quantity of precipitation (snow) and average monthly minimal diurnal air temperature (cf. Figure 2). While beech is not the preferred browse species of red deer, it is consumed yearlong; it is also elastic and snow resistant and thus more exposed to the reach of red deer even in deeper snow.

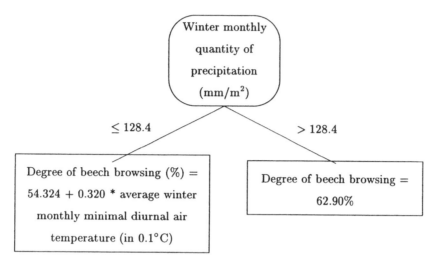

Figure 2 A regression tree for predicting the degree of beech browsing

The following issues were raised by this application:

1. Data quantity: the size of the deer population and browsing rates are only estimated once a year. Even though we were dealing with eighteen years worth of data, these were still only eighteen data points.

2. Data quality: some of the data collected in this domain were unreliable and had to be cleaned/corrected/removed before obtaining reasonable results.

3. Missing information: the outcome of the data analysis process suggested that measuring winter and summer browsing rates separately would greatly improve the models. This information was not measured and could not be reconstructed from the currently measured data, but it should be measured in the future.

2.2. Habitat Suitability Modeling

Habitat suitability modeling is closely related to population dynamics modeling. Typically, the effect of the abiotic characteristics of the habitat on the presence, abundance, or diversity of a given taxonomic group of organisms is studied. For example, one might study the influence of soil characteristics, such as soil temperature, water content, and proportion of mineral soil on the abundance and species richness of *Collembola* (springtails), the most abundant insects in soil (Lek-Ang et al., 1999). The study uses neural networks to build a number of predictive models for collembolan diversity. Another study of habitat suitability modeling by neural networks is given by Ozesmi and Ozesmi (1999).

Several habitat suitability modeling applications of other data mining methods are surveyed by Fielding (1999b). Fielding (1999a) applies a number of methods, including discriminant analysis, logistic regression, neural networks, and genetic algorithms, to predict nesting sites for golden eagles. Bell (1999) uses decision trees to describe the winter habitat of pronghorn antelope. Jeffers (1999) uses a genetic algorithm to discover rules that describe habitat preferences for aquatic species in British rivers.

The author has been involved in a number of habitat suitability studies using rule induction and decision trees. Rule induction was used to relate the presence or absence of a number of species in Slovenian rivers to physical and chemical properties of river water, such as temperature, dissolved oxygen, pollutant concentrations, and chemical oxygen demand (Džeroski and Grbović, 1995). Regression trees were used to study the influence of soil characteristics, such as soil texture, moisture, and acidity on the abundance (total number of individuals) and diversity (number of species) of *Collembola* (Kampichler et al., 2000). We have also used decision trees to model habitat suitability for red deer in Slovenian forests using GIS data, such as elevation, slope, and forest composition (Debeljak et al., 2001). Finally, decision trees that model habitat suitability for brown bears have been induced from GIS data and data on brown bear sightings (Kobler and Adamič, 1999). The model has then been used to identify the most suitable locations for the construction of wildlife bridges/underpasses that would enable the bears to safely cross the highway passing through the bear habitat.

3. Environmental Monitoring and Protection

A typical national environmental protection agency aims to "protect public health and to safeguard and improve the natural environment." It sets and enforces national pollution control standards. To this end, it performs environmental monitoring, that is, "periodic or continuous surveillance or testing to determine the level of compliance with statutory requirements and/or pollutant levels in various media or in humans, plants, and animals" (U.S. EPA Terms, 2000).

Given this context, environmental protection includes, for example, biological and chemical monitoring of river water quality, which further includes regular sampling (fieldwork) and analysis/interpretation (typically, laboratory work) of the samples in terms of, for example, water quality classes. It also includes testing chemical compounds for toxicity and biodegradability. Finally, it includes the study of effects of various pollutants on the health of the population in a given region (environmental epidemiology).

3.1. Environmental Monitoring

Several KDD methods have been used to interpret and classify samples of river water into quality classes. Walley et al. (1992) and Ruck et al. (1993) use Bayesian methods and neural networks respectively, to classify river water quality, and Walley and Džeroski (1996) compare Bayesian classification, neural networks, and regression trees to classify biological samples taken from British rivers. Džeroski and Grbović (1995) apply rule induction to classify biological, as well as chemical, samples taken from Slovenian rivers in terms of water quality classes. Walley et al. (2000) use unsupervised neural networks to diagnose river quality from biological and environmental data.

CASE STUDY: FROM BIOLOGICAL COMMUNITIES TO CHEMICAL PROPERTIES OF RIVER WATER
Physical and chemical properties give a specific picture of river water quality at a particular point in time, while the biota (living organisms) act as continuous monitors and give a more general picture of water quality over a period of time. This has increased the relative importance of biological methods for monitoring water quality. The problem of inferring the chemical properties from the biota is practically relevant, especially in countries where extensive biological monitoring is conducted. Regular monitoring for a very wide range of chemical pollutants would be very expensive, if not impossible. On the other hand, the state of the biota can reflect an increase in pollution and indicate likely causes/sources.

We used data on biological and chemical samples from Slovenian rivers collected through the monitoring program of the Hydrometeorological Institute of Slovenia (Džeroski et al., 2000). Pairs of biological and chemical samples that were taken at the same site at approximately the same time were used: there were 1,061 such pairs, collected over six years. Data on biological samples list all the species/taxa present at the site and their abundances.

Chemical samples contain the measured values of sixteen physical and chemical parameters: biological oxygen demand (BOD), chlorine concentration (Cl), CO_2 concentration, electrical conductivity, chemical oxygen demand COD ($K_2Cr_2O_7$ and $KMnO_4$), concentrations of ammonia (NH_4), NO_2, NO_3, and dissolved oxygen (O_2), alkalinity (pH), PO_4, oxygen saturation, SiO_2, water temperature, and total hardness.

We used regression tree induction to learn predictive models for each of the sixteen parameters separately (Džeroski et al., 2000). The models for the most important indicators of pollution (ammonia, biological oxygen demand, chemical oxygen demand) had the best predictive power. We also used clustering trees (Blockeel et al., 1998) to predict the values for all sixteen parameters at the same time (Blockeel et al., 1999): this actually improved the accuracy as compared to individual predictions for each of the sixteen parameters.

An example clustering tree is shown in Figure 3. In the leftmost leaf (*Chironomus tummi* $\geqslant 3$), highly increased values are predicted for NH_4 (2.3 standard deviations above the average), as well as for BOD, COD ($K_2Cr_2O_7$ and $KMnO_4$), SiO_2, Cl, PO_4, CO_2, and conductivity. On the other hand, highly decreased values are predicted for dissolved oxygen concentration and oxygen saturation (1.66 and 1.77 standard deviations below average). This indicates heavy pollution and is consistent with expert knowledge, as *Chironomus tummi* is an indicator of heavily polluted waters.

The following issues were raised in this application:

1. Varying length data records: biological samples list all the species present. Depending on the site and water quality, the number of taxa present can vary. Methods for handling structural information or careful feature selection are thus needed.

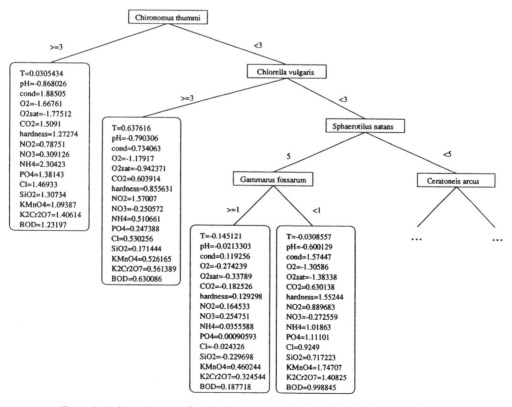

Figure 3 A clustering tree for simultaneous prediction of multiple chemical parameters from biological data

2. Aggregating data: we used detailed data, where organisms were identified to species level, and aggregated data, where species from the same family were grouped together. Domain knowledge on the taxonomy of river water organisms was used.

3. Making multiple predictions: most KDD methods for prediction only deal with one target variable. In many cases, however, it might be beneficial to try to predict several interrelated variables simultaneously.

3.2. Environmental Impact of Chemicals

Large numbers of hazardous organic chemicals are emitted into the environment from anthropogenic and natural sources. Extensive tests on the impact of chemicals are expensive. For example, to test chemicals for carcinogenicity (the capacity to cause cancer), trials are typically performed on rodents (long-term rodent bioassays) that take several years and hundreds of animals. It is thus highly desirable to have reliable models that can be used to both quantitatively and qualitatively describe the fate and behavior of compounds in the environment (Peijnenburg and Damborsky, 1996).

Typically, linear regression would be used to develop a so-called QSAR (quantitative structure–activity relationship) model. A domain expert chooses the features that are relevant to describe the group of compounds studied (which is often very small). As the group of compounds increases and diversifies in terms of chemical structure, this traditional approach becomes less and less appropriate.

A number of KDD methods have been used to derive QSAR models for mutagenicity, carcinogenicity, and biodegradability. Here, methods of inductive logic programming (ILP) are suitable, since they can use structural information and existing domain knowledge. ILP has been used to build a predictive theory for mutagenicity, the capacity to cause genetic change, which is relevant to carcinogenicity (Srinivasan et al., 1996). A set of structurally diverse aromatic and heteroaromatic nitrocompounds (some of which are present in car exhaust gases) were studied, and a new structural alert for high mutagenicity was discovered. ILP was also used to predict the carcinogenicity of a diverse set of chemical compounds (Srinivasan et al., 1997), yielding the most accurate predictor that did not use data from biological tests on rodents in an open competition conducted within the U.S. National Toxicology Program.

ILP has been also used to predict the biodegradability of compounds (Džeroski et al., 1999a; see below). Neural networks have been used to develop QSAR models for predicting biodegradability of organic contaminants in soil systems (Govind et al., 1996). Damborsky et al. (1996) use clustering in combination with linear regression to develop models for the dehalogenation of haloaliphatic compounds. Finally, rule induction was used by Gamberger et al. (1996) to develop biodegradation models for two sets of chemicals.

CASE STUDY: PREDICTING THE BIODEGRADABILITY OF COMPOUNDS

We used a database of 328 structurally diverse and widely used (commercial) chemicals described in a handbook of degradation rates. Complete data on the structure of the chemicals (SMILES notation) were available, as well as data on the overall, biotic, and abiotic degradation rates in four environmental compartments (soil, air, surface water, and ground water). We built models for biotic degradation in surface water, predicting the logarithm of the half-life time of aqueous biodegradation. Half-life times were measured for some compounds and estimated by experts for others: in the latter case, an upper and a lower bound were given, and we took the arithmetic mean of these.

We used several propositional and ILP methods for decision tree, regression tree, and rule induction. In addition to a few global features, such as molecular weight, the main information used for learning was the data on the structure of compounds, that is, the atoms within a molecule and the connections/bonds between them. Domain knowledge about a variety of functional groups and substructures was used. ILP systems use this data directly, while propositional systems use features derived from it, which represent the compounds' structure approximately, but not completely. Several of the derived models perform better than a state-of-the-art biodegradability prediction system based on linear regression.

A relational rule for predicting the biodegradability of a compound is given below:

A compound M degrades fast IF

- M contains an atom A1 and
- atom A1 is a nitrogen atom and
- atom A1 is connected to atom A2 with bond B and
- bond B is an aromatic bond and
- the molecular weight of M is less than 110 units and
- the logP value (hydrophobicity) of M is greater than zero.

Note that this rule is relational, since it makes use of the relations "contains" between a compound and its components (in this case an atom) and "is connected to" between atoms.

Two important issues were raised here:

1. The need to handle structural information, that is, information on the structure of chemicals. The natural representations of chemical structures are not straightforward to squeeze into a fixed-width table.

2. The need for prior/domain knowledge: chunks of knowledge defining functional groups and substructures are essential for good performance.

ILP methods provide facilities for using both types of information directly.

Applications of KDD methods to relate exposure to pollution and human health are also starting to appear. Kontić and Džeroski (1997) study the influence of exposure to polluted air (as a consequence of coal mining) and other environmental/social factors on acute respiratory diseases in children in Slovakia. Rajkumar et al. (2000) use neural networks to assess health risk through inhalation exposure to benzene from vehicular emissions (car exhaust gases).

4. Remote Sensing

Most remote sensing applications of KDD methods fall within the area of earth sciences, such as geosciences, meteorology, and climatology. However, they increasingly often integrate data from other sources, such as geographical information systems, and reach into the realm of environmental management.

An example of a geoscientific data mining application is the detection of earthquakes from satellite images (Stolorz and Dean, 1996). The system Quakefinder automatically detects and measures tectonic activity by comparing satellite images of the same region taken at consecutive points in time. It has been used to automatically map the direction and magnitude of ground displacements along a known seismic fault in southern California and has automatically discovered novel unexplained tectonic activity away from the primary fault studied.

Analysis of atmospheric data is another area where remotely sensed data are used to detect complex spatiotemporal patterns, such as cyclones, hurricanes, and fronts (Stolorz et al., 1995). Data mining methods have been also used in meteorology to address problems such as cloud-type classification (Bankert and Aha, 1995) and intelligent retrieval of archived meteorological data (Jones and Roydhouse, 1995, Mason and Matwin, 1995).

A recent special issue of the *Data Mining and Knowledge Discovery* journal (Brown and Mielke, 2000) is devoted to the analysis of atmospheric data. Satellite radar images have been also used to automatically detect oil spills (Kubat et al., 1998). Air pollution modeling is also an active area of analysis of atmospheric data, where neural networks (Keller et al., 1996) are the most often used among the KDD approaches (Nunnari et al., 1998).

A more traditional remote sensing application of data mining is land cover classification. Given a satellite image of a study area and the land cover for some points in the image as determined by, for example, a ground survey, the task is to learn to predict land cover from the (multi) spectral information in the satellite image. The learned classifier can be then used to determine the land cover of new areas (where ground surveys have not been conducted) by classifying satellite images of the new areas. This has been done at a global scale, where decision trees have been used to predict land cover using data from the Advanced Very-High-Resolution Radiometer (AVHRR; Hansen et al., 2000). The resulting vegetative land cover finds direct use in global biochemical and climate models.

4.1. Case Study: Forest Border Delineation Using Satellite Image and GIS Data

The task addressed here was to identify the forest border and areas of spontaneous afforestation of abandoned farmland in Slovenia with as much accuracy and spatial precision as possible (Kobler et al., 2000). Up-to-date land cover maps are essential for decisionmaking in physical planning and environmental assessment. The starting point was an existing land cover map (CLC or CORINE Land Cover) derived by manual photointerpretation of 1:100,000 scale Landsat TM color prints, where the minimum mapping unit is 20 hectares (ha). The ortorectified, topographically normalized image channels TM2, 3, 4, 5, and 7 of Landsat TM were also used, as well as data from a GIS, including information on the presence/absence of forest at a previous survey, a digital elevation model, insolation, population density, proximity to settlements, and proximity to water.

Clustering or unsupervised classification was first used to group pixels according to their Landsat TM channel values. The clusters were labeled with the predominant CLC label. Decision trees were then learned that reclassify the results of unsupervised classification. Out of 2,558,160 pixels in the study area, a training subset of 127,537 pixels was selected for learning trees. The construction of decision trees proceeded in an interactive fashion, with a domain expert guiding the selection of the variables that appear in the tree. The resulting land cover map has a minimum mapping unit of 0.25 ha (as compared to the original 20 ha). The accuracy and spatial precision of this final map were evaluated on an independent reference sample, obtained by photointerpretation of aerial stereo photographs.

Figure 4 shows a part of the decision tree used to reclassify the land cover obtained from unsupervised learning. If the result of unsupervised learning classifies a pixel as forest, but GIS data indicate that this pixel is actually in a lake, the pixel is reclassified. Depending on the TM5 Landsat TM channel readout, it is classified as either water or marsh.

The final land cover map is slightly more accurate than the original one: 91 percent versus 87 percent at the forest/nonforest level. It has, however, much higher spatial precision: the ratio of the classified to the true border length is 92 percent for the new map, 33 percent for the original one. The new map allows us to assess the rate of spontaneous afforestation: in the study area, about 30 percent of the nonforest has gone to different stages of afforestation in the last twenty years.

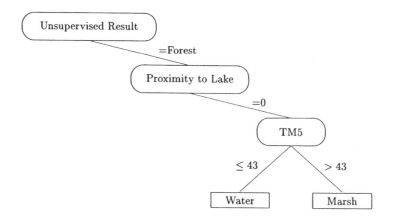

Figure 4 A part of the decision tree used in the first-stage reclassification of land cover

The following issues relevant to KDD have been raised in this application:

1. Handling large amounts of data: even for a small country like Slovenia, the need for spatial precision causes satellite image data sets to be very large.

2. Integrating data from various sources: GIS data give additional quality to satellite images.

3. Integrating multiple KDD methods: more than one data mining method may be needed for a successful application (here, we used clustering and decision-tree induction).

4. Allowing experts to provide domain knowledge by directing the KDD process: in this application it has proved crucial for the domain expert to be able to guide the discovery of patterns (decision trees); however, few KDD tools offer this possibility to their users.

5. Conclusion

In summary, KDD methods have been successfully applied to many problems in environmental science, engineering, and management. Of the case studies presented here, the results of applying KDD methods are most directly relevant to practice in the red deer population modeling case and forest border delineation case. In the latter case, the results (improved forest cover maps) will be of use to decisionmakers in physical planning and environmental assessment.

These applications have raised a number of issues of concern to KDD method developers. These include problems of data quantity (handling large data sets, generalizing from small data sets), data quality (handling missing data, noisy data), and handling nonstandard KDD tasks (where the data do not necessarily reside in a single fixed-width table, e.g., information on chemical structures, images). Especially important is the problem of using existing domain knowledge in the KDD process.

By raising these issues, the applications motivate the further development of KDD methods. An example of KDD method development motivated by environmental applications is the development of a method for detecting changes in images at subpixel level (Stolorz and Dean, 1996). Another example is the development of methods for discovering differential equations that take into account domain knowledge (Džeroski et al., 1999b). To enable comparison of different methods and stimulate further development of KDD methods, some of the data sets from the case studies (e.g., the Lake Glumsoe data set and the biodegradability data set) are available through the author's home page (http://www-ai.ijs.si/SasoDzeroski/).

Given the multitude of existing KDD methods, the issue also arises as to which method to apply to a given problem. This issue is ubiquitous and by no means restricted to the application area of environmental sciences. Unfortunately, this problem is far from solved, even for individual types of data mining tasks (e.g., classification). This is a research topic that has recently attracted many researchers from the areas of machine learning and KDD.

A few rules of thumb may still be stated, however. It is no coincidence, for instance, that decision trees are very often used for handling remote sensing data. Given the efficiency of decision trees and the size of remotely sensed data sets, the two are a likely match. Another example is the use of equation discovery methods in ecological modeling. Given the preference of domain experts for models in the form of differential equations, equation discovery techniques are suitable for use in KDD approaches to ecological modeling

KDD practitioners are faced with many challenges when trying to apply KDD methods in the area of environmental sciences. There is also a pressing need for a more active role to be played by domain experts in providing domain knowledge as input to the KDD process, as well as guiding the search for novel and useful patterns. Given the increasing stress on our environment and the need to preserve it for ourselves and future generations, meeting these challenges is worth the effort.

References

Allaby, M. 1996. *Basics of Environmental Science.* London: Routledge.

Aoki, I., T. Komatsu, and K. Hwang. 1999. "Prediction of response of zooplankton biomass to climatic and oceanic changes." *Ecol. Modelling* 120(2–3): 261–270.

Bankert, R. and D. Aha. 1995. "Automated identification of cloud patterns in satellite imagery." In *Proceedings of the Fourteenth Conference on Weather Analysis and Forecasting.* Dallas, TX: American Meteorological Society.

Bell, J. F. 1999. "Tree based methods." In *Machine Learning Methods for Ecological Applications,* edited by A. H. Fielding, pp. 89–105. Dordrecht, Netherlands: Kluwer Academic Publishers.

Blockeel, H., S. Džeroski, and J. Grbović. 1999. "Simultaneous prediction of multiple chemical parameters of river water quality with TILDE." In *Proceedings of the Third European Conference on Principles of Data Mining and Knowledge Discovery,* pp. 15–18. Berlin: Springer.

Blockeel, H., L. De Raedt, and J. Ramon. 1998. "Top-down induction of clustering trees." In *Proceedings of the Fifteenth International Conference on Machine Learning,* pp. 55–63. San Francisco, CA: Morgan Kaufmann.

Brosse, S., J.-F. Guegan, J.-N. Tourenq, and S. Lek. 1999. "The use of artificial neural networks to assess fish abundance and spatial occupancy in the littoral zone of a mesotrophic lake." *Ecol. Modelling* 120(2–3): 299–311.

Brown, T. J. and P. W. Mielke., guest editors 2000. "Statistical Mining and Data Visualization in Atmospheric Sciences." Special issue of *Data Mining and Knowledge Discovery,* 4(1).

Damborsky, J., K. Manova, and M. Kuty. 1996. "A mechanistic approach to deriving quantitative structure biodegradability relationships. A case study: dehalogenation of haloaliphatic compounds." In *Biodegradability Prediction,* edited by W. Peijnenburg and J. Damborsky, pp. 75–92. Dordrecht, Netherlands: Kluwer Academic Publishers.

Debeljak, M., S. Džeroski, and M. Adamič. 1999. "Interactions among the red deer (*Cervus elaphus,* L.) population, meteorological parameters and new growth of the natural regenerated forest in Snežnik, Slovenia." *Ecol. Modelling* 121(1): 51–61.

Debeljak, M., S. Džeroski, K. Jerina, A. Kobler, and M. Adamič. 2001. "Habitat suitability modelling of red deer (*Cervus elaphus,* L.) in South-Central Slovenia." *Ecol. Modelling* 138(1-3): 321–330.

Džeroski, S. and J. Grbović. 1995. "Knowledge discovery in a water quality database." In *Proceedings of the First International Conference on Knowledge Discovery and Data Mining,* pp. 81–86. Menlo Park, CA: AAAI Press.

Džeroski, S., H. Blockeel, B. Kompare, S. Kramer, B. Pfahringer, and W. Van Laer. 1999a. "Experiments in predicting biodegradability." In *Proceedings of the Ninth International Conference on Inductive Logic Programming,* pp. 80–91. Berlin: Springer.

Džeroski, S., L. Todorovski, I. Bratko, B. Kompare, and V. Križman. 1999b. "Equation discovery with ecological applications." *Machine Learning Methods for Ecological Applications,* edited by A. H. Fielding, pp. 185–207. Dordrecht, Netherlands: Kluwer Academic Publishers.

Džeroski, S., J. Grbović, and D. Demšar. 2000. "Predicting chemical parameters of river water quality from bioindicator data." *Appl. Intell* 13(1): 7–17.

Fielding, A. H. 1999a. "An introduction to machine learning methods." In *Machine Learning Methods for Ecological Applications,* edited by A. H. Fielding, pp. 1–35. Dordrecht, Netherlands: Kluwer Academic Publishers.

Fielding, A. H. (ed). 1999b. *Machine Learning Methods for Ecological Applications.* Dordrecht, Netherlands: Kluwer Academic Publishers.

Gamberger, D., S. Sekusak, Z. Medven, and A. Sabljic. 1996. "Application of artificial intelligence in biodegradation modelling." In *Biodegradability Prediction,* edited by W. Peijnenburg and J. Damborsky, pp. 27–40. Dordrecht, Netherlands: Kluwer Academic Publishers.

Govind, R., L. Lei, and H. Tabak. 1996. "Development of structure–biodegradability relationships (SBRs) for estimating half-lifes of organic contaminants in soil systems." In *Biodegradability Prediction,* edited by W. Peijnenburg and J. Damborsky, pp. 115–138. Dordrecht, Netherlands: Kluwer Academic Publishers.

Hansen, M., R. Defries, J. Townshend, and R. Sohlberg. 2000. "Global land cover classification at 1 km spatial resolution using a classification tree approach." *Int. J. Remote Sensing* 21(6): 1331–1364.

Jeffers, J. N. R. 1999. "Genetic algorithms I." In *Machine Learning Methods for Ecological Applications,* edited by A. H. Fielding, pp. 107–121. Dordrecht, Netherlands: Kluwer Academic Publishers.

Jones, E. and A. Roydhouse. 1995. "Intelligent retrieval of archived meteorological data." *IEEE Intell. Sys.* **10(6)**: 50–57.

Kampichler, C., S. Džeroski, and R. Wieland. 2000. "The application of machine learning techniques to the analysis of soil ecological data bases: relationships between habitat features and *Collembola* community characteristics." *Soil Biol. Biochem.* **32**: 197–209.

Keller, P., S. Hashem, L. Kangas and R. Kouzes, editors. 1996. In *Applications of Neural Networks in Environment, Energy, and Health*. Singapore: World Scientific Publishing.

Kobler, A. and M. Adamič. 1999. "Brown bears in Slovenia: identifying locations for construction of wildlife bridges across highways." In *Proceedings of the Third International Conference on Wildlife Ecology and Transportation*, pp. 29–38. Tallahassee: Florida Department of Transportation.

Kobler, A., M. Hočevar, and S. Džeroski. 2000. "Forest border identification by rule-based classification of Landsat TM and GIS data." *Int. Arch. Photogrammetry and Remote Sensing* **XXXII(6W8/1)**: 93–100.

Kompare, B. and S. Džeroski. 1995. "Getting more out of data: automated modelling of algal growth with machine learning." In *Proceedings of the International Conference on Coastal Ocean Space Utilization*, pp. 209–220. HI: University of Hawaii.

Kompare, B., S. Džeroski, and A. Karalič. 1997a. "Identification of the Lake of Bled ecosystem with the artificial intelligence tools M5 and FORS." In *Proceedings of the Fourth International Conference on Water Pollution*, pp. 789–798. Southampton, UK: Computational Mechanics Publications.

Kompare, B., S. Džeroski, and V. Križman. 1997b. "Modelling the growth of algae in the Lagoon of Venice with the artificial intelligence tool GoldHorn." In *Proceedings of the Fourth International Conference on Water Pollution*, pp. 799–808. Southampton, UK: Computational Mechanics Publications.

Kontić, B. and S. Džeroski. 1997. "Perspective of machine learning in epidemiological studies." In *Proceedings of the International Symposium on Environmental Epidemiology in Central and Eastern Europe*, pp. 27–30. Bratislava, Slovakia: International Institute for Rural and Environmental Health.

Kubat, M., R. Holte, and S. Matwin. 1998. "Machine learning for the detection of oil spills in satellite radar images." *Machine Learning* **30**: 195–215.

Lek, S. and J. F. Guegan, guest editors. 1999. Application of artificial neural networks in ecological modelling. Special issue of *Ecol. Modelling* **120(2–3)**.

Lek-Ang, S., L. Deharveng, and S. Lek. 1999. "Predictive models of collembolan diversity and abundance in a riparian habitat." *Ecol. Modelling* **120(2–3)**: 247–260.

Mason, C. and Matwin, S., guest eds. (1995) Environmental Applications of Artificial Intelligence. Special issue of *IEEE Intell. Sys.* **10(6)**.

Nunnari, G., A. F. M. Nucifora, and C. Randieri. 1998. "The application of neural techniques to the modelling of time-series of atmospheric pollution data." *Ecol. Modelling* **111(2–3)**: 187–205.

Ozesmi, S. L. and U. Ozesmi. 1999. "An artificial neural network approach to spatial habitat modelling with interspecific interaction." *Ecol. Modelling* **116(1)**: 15–31.

Peijnenburg, W. and J. Damborsky, eds. 1996. *Biodegradability Prediction*. Dordrecht, Netherlands: Kluwer Academic Publishers.

Rajkumar, T., H. W. Guesgen, S. Robinson, and G. W. Fisher. 2000. "A new dose model for assessment of health risk due to contaminants in air." *J. Air Waste Mgmnt Assoc.* **50(1)**: 3–20.

Recknagel, F., M. French, P. Harkonen, and K. Yabunaka. 1997. "Artificial neural network approach for modelling and prediction of algal blooms." *Ecol. Modelling* **96(1–3)**: 11–28.

Ruck, B. M., W. J. Walley, and H. A. Hawkes. 1993. "Biological classification of river water quality using neural networks." In *Applications of Artificial Intelligence in Engineering*, edited by G. Rzevski, J. Pastor, and R. A. Adey. *Applications and Techniques* **2**: 361–372. Southampton, UK: Computational Mechanics Publications.

Scardi, M. and L. W. Harding. 1999. "Developing an empirical model of phytoplankton primary production: a neural network case study." *Ecol. Modelling* **120(2–3)**: 213–223.

Schleiter, I. M., D. Borchardt, R. Wagner, T. Dapper, K.-D. Schmidt, H.-H. Schmidt, and H. Werner. 1999. "Modelling water quality, bioindication and population dynamics in lotic ecosystems using neural networks." *Ecol. Modelling* **120(2–3)**: 271–286.

Srinivasan, A., R. D. King, S. H. Muggleton, and M. J. E. Sternberg. 1997. "Carcinogenesis prediction using inductive logic programming." In *Intelligent Data Analysis in Medicine and Pharmacology*, edited by N. Lavrač, E. Keravnou, and B. Zupan, pp. 243–260. Dordrecht, Netherlands: Kluwer Academic Publishers.

Srinivasan, A., S. H. Muggleton, R. D. King, and M. J. E. Sternberg. 1996. "Theories for mutagenicity: a study of first-order and feature based induction." *Artificial Intell.* **85**: 277–299.

Stankovski, V., M. Debeljak, I. Bratko, and M. Adamič. 1998. "Modelling the population dynamics of red deer (*Cervus elaphus* L.) with regard to forest development." *Ecol. Modelling* **108(1–3)**: 145–153.

Stolorz, P. and C. Dean. 1996. "Quakefinder: a scalable data mining system for detecting earthquakes from space." In *Proceedings of the Second International Conference on Knowledge Discovery and Data Mining*, pp. 208–213. Menlo Park, CA: AAAI Press.

Stolorz, P., E. Mesrobian, R. R. Muntz, E. C. Shek, J. R. Santos, J. Yi, K. Ng, S. Y. Chien, H. Nakamura, C. R. Mechoso and J. D. Farrara. 1995. "Fast spatiotemporal data mining of large geophysical data sets." In *Proceedings of the First International Conference on Knowledge Discovery and Data Mining*, pp. 300–305. Menlo Park, CA: AAAI Press.

Todorovski, L., S. Džeroski, and B. Kompare. 1998. "Modelling and prediction of phytoplankton growth with equation discovery." *Ecol. Modelling* **113**: 71–81.

U.S. EPA Terms. 2000. "Terms of the Environment." Document order number EPA175B97001, National Service Center for Environmental Publications. Also available at http://www.epa.gov/OCEPAterms/.

Walley, W. J. and S. Džeroski. 1996. "Biological monitoring: a comparison between Bayesian, neural and machine learning methods of water quality classification." In *Proceedings of the International Symposium on Environmental Software Systems, 1995*, pp. 229–240. London: Chapman and Hall.

Walley, W. J., H. A. Hawkes, and M. Boyd. 1992. "Application of Bayesian inference to river water quality surveillance." In *Applications of Artificial Intelligence in Engineering*, edited by D. E. Grierson, G. Rzevski, and R. A. Adey, pp. 1030–1047. Southampton, UK: Computational Mechanics Publications.

Walley, W. J., R. W. Martin, and M. A. O'Connor. 2000. "Self-organizing maps for the classification and diagnosis of river quality from biological and environmental data." In *Environmental Software Systems: Environmental Information and Decision Support*, edited by R. Denzer, D. A. Swayne, M. Purvis, and G. Schimak, pp. 27–41. Dordrecht, Netherlands: Kluwer.

45.2 Molecular Biology

Aleksandar Milosavljevic

ABSTRACT During the last decade, molecular biology has been transformed by the newly established methods for high-throughput collection of gene-related information such as industrial DNA sequencing, gene amplification by PCR, and microarrays for reading DNA and for measuring gene expression levels. Issues related to the mining of the huge amounts of generated raw data have been addressed by bioinformatics, a new discipline at the interface of molecular biology and computing. This article addresses the following four general areas of computerized knowledge discovery in molecular biology: mining of DNA and protein sequence databases, reconstruction of the molecular past, understanding consequences of genetic variation, and reverse engineering of genetic networks.

1. Introduction

Molecular biology has emerged during the last half century at the interface between biochemistry and genetics. The marriage between the two sciences was made possible by a number of breakthroughs culminating in the discovery by Watson and Crick in 1953 that genes consist of a double helix of DNA. Subsequent discovery of the genetic code (Figure 1) linked genes, the central concept of genetics, to protein enzymes, the central concept of biochemistry. (For a concise historical introduction to molecular biology, see Lander, 1995).

During the last decade, molecular biology has been transformed by the newly established methods for collecting gene-related information such as high-throughput DNA sequencing, gene amplification by PCR, and microarrays for reading DNA and for measuring gene expression levels. The new methods led to the creation of a new discipline called genomics. The availability of genomic methods and information catalyzed a unifying transformation of virtually all life sciences, including evolutionary biology, genetics, epidemiology, medicine, and pharmacology.

An enormous scale-up and industrialization of DNA sequencing was sparked by the Human Genome Project, a government-sponsored program to sequence the complete genome of a human and a number of model organisms (Collins et al., 1998). The project has already provided complete gene catalogues of several organisms, including yeast *S. cerevisiae* and the worm *C. elegans*. Complete DNA sequencing of a bacterium has now become routine. A handful of information factories are expected to produce the complete human genetic blueprint by the year 2003. The industrialization of DNA sequencing is serving as a template for industrialization of other types of data collection experiments.

Data collection throughputs are being dramatically increased by emerging microarray technologies (Debouck and Goodfellow, 1999). Microarrays typically consist of a rectangular array of biological probes. DNA microarrays collect DNA information while gene expression microarrays measure gene activity. Tens of thousands of experiments can now be simultaneously performed on individual biological samples. The increase of density of probes is increasing yearly following a pattern much reminiscent of Moore's law for microprocessors. In contrast to microprocessors, which process information, the microarrays generate information.

The accelerated information collection has produced a glut of raw material for discovery. Integration and analysis of available information are quickly causing a bottleneck. Bioinformatics, a discipline at the interface of biology and computing, has emerged during the last few years in response to this problem.

In the following sections we address a number of selected knowledge discovery topics in molecular biology. The selection is by no means comprehensive. Each section covers a particular situation where an accumulation of genomic information calls for a significant computational component of the discovery process.

2. Mining Databases of DNA and Protein Sequence

From a bird's-eye perspective, biological information may be divided into two general categories: phenome and genome. *Phenome* refers to the totality of information about the outward characteristics of an organism such as anatomy, physiological characteristics, clinical information, and behavior. *Genome* refers to the totality of chromosomal DNA information.

Unlike the phenomic information, which must frequently be accompanied by a precise semantic definition (smoker in one epidemiological study may be defined differently than smoker in another study), a DNA sequence is essentially text in the four-letter alphabet of nucleotides (A, G, C, T). Proteins can be thought of as text in the twenty-letter alphabet of amino acids, a triplet of consecutive nucleotides coding for a single amino acid (Figure 1). Since the triplet code is largely preserved across all living species, meaningful DNA information may be accumulated over time, and may be immediately shared in a meaningful way without semantic definitions.

By applying the computer analogy, we may say that genome corresponds to a genetic computer program, phenome results from the execution of the genetic program, and the environment corresponds to program inputs. *Proteome* (Dove, 1999) is an important subcategory of the phenome that refers to the totality of information about proteins, each protein being encoded by one gene. The term *physiome* has been used to denote the totality of physiological mechanisms.

The availability of the genomic DNA sequence revived the hope of predicting biological phenomena from first principles. A number of projects follow this reductionist vision by focusing on predicting protein-coding regions from genomic DNA sequences and on predicting the three-dimensional structure and function of proteins from the translated amino acid sequence. The reductionist vision has only been partially justified: in addition to physics and chemistry, much of the inference from sequence information involves inference by sequence similarity and reasoning by analogy to known patterns and mechanisms.

(A)

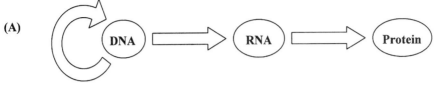

Replication   Transcription   Translation

(B)

		2nd codon position					
		T	C	A	G		3rd
1st	T	TTT F	TCT S	TAT Y	TGT C	T	
		TTC F	TCC S	TAC Y	TGC C	C	
c		TTA L	TCA S	TAA end	TGA end	A	c
o		TTG L	TCG S	TAG end	TGG W	G	o
d	C	CTT L	CCT P	CAT H	CGT R	T	d
o		CTC L	CCC P	CAC H	CGC R	C	o
n		CTA L	CCA P	CAA Q	CGA R	A	n
		CTG L	CCG P	CAG Q	CGG R	G	
p	A	ATT I	ACT T	AAT N	AGT S	T	p
o		ATC I	ACC T	AAC N	AGC S	C	o
s		ATA I	ACA T	AAA K	AGA R	A	s
i		ATG M	ACG T	AAG K	AGG R	G	i
t	G	GTT V	GCT A	GAT D	GGT G	T	t
i		GTC V	GCC A	GAC D	GGC G	C	i
o		GTA V	GCA A	GAA E	GGA G	A	o
n		GTG V	GCG A	GAG E	GGG G	G	n

(C)

DNA sequence: GAG GGG GAC CCC ATT CCC GAG GAG CTT TAT GAG ATG CTG AGT GAC CAC
Translated protein: E   G   D   P   I   P   E   E   L   Y   K   M   L   S   D   H

Figure 1 (A) The flow of biological information. This "central dogma" of molecular biology has been revised only slightly during the last fifty years with the discovery that information may also flow from RNA to DNA through the process called reverse transcription. (B) The genetic code. Each cell in this table contains a triplet codon of DNA nucleotides (A—Adenine, G—Guanine, T—Thymine, C—Cytosine) and the single-letter designation of the amino acid it encodes. Special codons (denoted " end") indicate termination of the translation process. The code for methionine (M) usually also signals initiation of the translation process. Note the redundancy of the code—multiple triplets may code for the same amino acid. (C) Translation of a DNA sequence fragment of the human platelet-derived growth factor protein (PDGF-2).

2.1. Inference by Sequence Similarity

A newly determined DNA sequence fragment is typically compared against a database of known sequences across different organisms. If the DNA sequence is human, the similarity search enables inference by analogy from simpler, well-studied model organisms such as yeast, fruit fly, and mouse. Similarity to a gene of known function is usually interpreted as an indication of possible function of the newly sequenced gene. The hypothesis about function is typically tested experimentally or corroborated based on additional evidence.

    The first major reported discovery that resulted from a sequence similarity search was the discovery that a viral oncogene (viral gene that may cause cancer) functions as a growth factor (Doolittle et al., 1983). This discovery resulted from a comparison of the sequence of the

v-sis oncogene: QGDPIPEELYKMLSGH
sequence similarity: **************** *
growth factor: EGDPIPEELYKMLSDH

Figure 2 Similarity of a short fragment of amino acid sequence of the Simian sarcoma virus onogene v-sis to a fragment of a human growth-factor protein PDGF-2 indicates that cancer-promoting activity of the oncogene can be traced to the stimulation of cell growth (Doolittle, 1983). (The DNA-to-protein sequence translation for PDGF-2 is in Figure 1C.)

oncogene against a database of sequences of genes of known function. The viral oncogene sequence exhibited similarity to a cell growth-factor sequence (Figure 2), indicating that cancer-promoting activity of viral oncogenes can be traced to the stimulation of growth of human cells. The database used in the comparison was compiled by hand by the researchers. The amount of available sequence information has since grown by several orders of magnitude and has enabled numerous discoveries of a similar kind.

Most sensitive algorithms for comparing DNA and protein sequences are based on variations of dynamic programming and suffix tree–like data structures. BLAST (Altschul et al., 1990) and FASTA (Pearson and Lipman, 1988) are the most widely used sequence similarity search algorithms. These heuristic algorithms basically search for local regions of (possibly imperfect) similarity between two sequences. Similarity is measured using variations on the edit distance metric (for an in-depth discussion of mutation models, see Searls and Murphy, 1995). Gusfield (1997) provides a comprehensive survey of sequence analysis algorithms. Waterman (1995) discusses a number of statistics that are helpful in establishing statistical significance of sequence similarity.

Comparison of translated amino acid sequences is often preferred to the comparison of original DNA sequences. The reason for this is the fact that amino acid sequences are more evolutionarily conserved, thus enabling detection of more distant relationships. The key to understanding this phenomenon is the redundancy of the genetic code (Figure 1): not all changes in the DNA sequence cause changes in the amino acid sequence of the translated protein; the silent mutations in DNA that do not change the protein sequence are not likely to cause deleterious effects and thus are more likely to be encountered in living organisms.

2.2. Sequence Patterns

When comparing a new sequence against a database of known sequences, selectivity (low false-positive rate) and sensitivity (low false-negative rate) are the key issues. This is especially true in a situation where a query fragment is compared against a huge database and where even a small false-positive rate may result in a large number of false positives.

A higher level of selectivity and specificity may be achieved by defining sequence patterns and then comparing a newly obtained sequence against a database of patterns. In contrast to sequence-to-sequence comparisons where a heuristic score is assigned to individual edit operations, a sequence-to-pattern comparison is typically based on an explicit probabilistic model and the score is the logarithm of a ratio of likelihoods. The likelihoods correspond to two hypotheses—one is that the sequence contains the pattern, and the other hypothesis is that it does not contain the pattern.

Protein sequence patterns are usually constructed by a semi-interactive analysis of sequence databases. The process typically includes similarity search to find clusters of related sequences and a multiple-sequence alignment step to find corresponding regions and identify conserved patterns (Figure 3). The process may be iteratively repeated until a stable set of patterns is identified. Additional information, such as that about the secondary structure of proteins may also be used to enhance the process (Smith and Smith, 1992).

There are a large number of databases of conserved amino acid sequence patterns. A number of pattern representation languages have been employed. PROSITE (Bairoch, 1992) and BLOCKS (Henikoff and Henikoff, 1996) are widely used databases of regular expression

EVEYI**FKP**S**CV**PLM**R**C**AGCC**
EVEYI**FKP**S**CV**PLM**R**C**AGCC**
STNTF**FKP**P**CV**NVF**R**C**GGCC**
-------------P**SCV**TVQ**R**C**GGCC**
TTNTF**FKP**P**CV**S IY**R**C**GGCC**

Conserved pattern: **FKP   CV   RC   GCC**

Figure 3 Multiple alignment of amino acid sequences (fragments from the growth-factor family) reveals an evolutionarily conserved pattern

patterns describing conserved protein domains. Hidden Markov models (HMMs), which are essentially a probabilistic extension of regular language patterns (Krogh et al., 1994), have recently emerged as a unifying language. Neural net representations (for a sample of pioneering work in this area, see Stormo et al., 1982), as well as hybrid HMM–neural net representations, are also in use (for a recent survey of HMM and neural network representations, see Baldi and Brunak, 1998).

DNA sequence patterns have also been intensively studied. Linguistic frequency analysis (Brendel et al., 1986) and visualization (Levy et al., 1998) of DNA texts revealed words of unusual frequency that convey biologically meaningful information. Most of the interspersed repetitive DNA sequences in the REPBASE database (Jurka, 1998) have been discovered through a semiautomated search for significantly long DNA sequences that occur repeatedly across the human genome.

Some organisms, including humans, contain patterns of local symmetry in their genomic DNA. Most frequent are tandemly repeated short words of different length containing varying levels of mutational noise. A number of methods have been proposed for detecting such patterns (Benson, 1999; Powell et al., 1998; Rivals et al., 1997; Milosavljevic and Jurka, 1993).

Spurious sequence similarity due to the presence of local symmetry may pose a significant problem in a database similarity search. For example, a DNA sequence consisting of twenty consecutive As is at an edit distance 0 to another sequence of twenty consecutive As, yet this apparently high similarity does not indicate evolutionary relationship. This problem has typically been approached by censoring or masking the sequences of high local symmetry (low information content) during database similarity searches. The downside of the censoring approach is that some significant similarities may be missed. To solve this problem, a general measure of similarity that takes into account both internal symmetry (information content) and mutual similarity of compared objects has been proposed (Milosavljevic, 1995).

2.3. Sequence-Related Databases

The main comprehensive publicly accessible DNA sequence databases are GenBank, maintained by the National Center for Biotechnology Information (NCBI) at the National Library of Medicine (NLM), with mirror databases in Europe (European Molecular Biology Laboratory, EMBL, data library) and Japan (DNA DataBase of Japan, DDBJ). A number of companies have also recently developed private databases of DNA sequences. Sequence databases also contain annotation fields indicating sequence features and relevant biological information.

In addition to general sequence databases, there are hundreds of publicly available databases of specialized sequence-related biological information (see the NCBI Web page or the ExPASy server Web page at the Swiss Institute for Bioinformatics for a sampling of links to such databases). Swiss-Prot (Swiss Bioinformatics Institute Protein Database) and the PIR (Protein Information Resource at the National Biomedical Research Foundation) are the most widely used databases of protein sequences.

3. Reconstructing Molecular Past

The theory of evolution owes much to the exhaustive catalogs of biological information and to the hierarchical classification system of Linneaus (Meyr, 1988). The information accumulated by Linneaus and his contemporaries was phenomic; the information accumulated today is mostly genomic DNA sequences and has a similar potential for transforming our view of the history of species.

Zuckerkandl and Pauling (1965) first proposed that the similarity between the amino acid sequences of proteins of different species be used for reconstructing their evolutionary relationships. Most evolutionary reconstructions are now being made based on comparative analyses of macromolecules, both genomic DNA sequences and amino acid sequences. Since evolutionary theories typically cannot be tested in a laboratory, statistics play a major role in validating discovered patterns. A case study analysis of statistical issues involved in sequence-based evolutionary reconstructions may be found in Waterman (1995).

A basic problem in molecular evolution is the reconstruction of phylogenetic (ancestry) trees. A tree may be reconstructed based on homologous (corresponding) sequences of a particular gene across species of interest. Systematic comparison of hundreds of ribosomal genes has led to the discovery of Archaebacteria, the third life kingdom (Woese, 1990). The magnitude of this breakthrough may be best illustrated by the fact that the classification of living organisms in two kingdoms dates back to the Ancient Greek philosophers Aristotle and Theophrastus (Meyr, 1988).

4. Understanding Consequences of Genetic Variation

Predictive genetic patterns may be discovered by correlating information about DNA variation in individual organisms, on one hand, and clinical information, on the other hand. The goal is typically to discover DNA variants that are causative or at least predictive of clinical variables. A study may be hypothesis driven, involving DNA variation in a preselected set of genes, or it may be data driven, involving DNA variation information across a whole genome. The availability of DNA microarrays and similar high-throughput collection devices is expected to enable more data-driven studies.

OMIM (Online Mendelian Inheritance in Man) is a comprehensive online database of current knowledge about human genes and genetic disorders edited by Dr. Victor A. McKusick and colleagues at the Johns Hopkins University and elsewhere and made accessible through the NCBI Web site. The database currently contains over ten thousand entries consisting of textual information, pictures, reference information, and links to MEDLINE articles and sequence information.

4.1. Discovering Disease Genes through Positional Cloning

Positional cloning is based on direct correlation between polymorphic DNA markers evenly spaced throughout a genome, on one hand, and clinical information, on the other hand. The most significant novelty introduced by positional cloning is that a gene may be physically located on a chromosome and isolated (cloned) without any knowledge of the mechanism of action of its protein product. To discover the mechanism of action, the gene may subsequently be sequenced, and the amino acid sequence may be decoded. This is in contrast with the standard biochemical discovery process where protein, the immediate causative agent, is discovered first (Figure 4).

The cystic fibrosis gene was the first major disease gene discovered by positional cloning (Riordan et al., 1989). A number of disease genes have since been identified. However, success has mostly been limited to monogenic diseases, where a mutation in a single gene causes disease. The vast majority of diseases (e.g., psychiatric and cardiovascular) are believed to be multigenic. It is hoped that improved data collection methods will enable the discovery of groups of genes involved in multigenic diseases as well. The discovery process is also being helped by additional information about genes, including the knowledge about related genes in model organisms (Bassett et al., 1995).

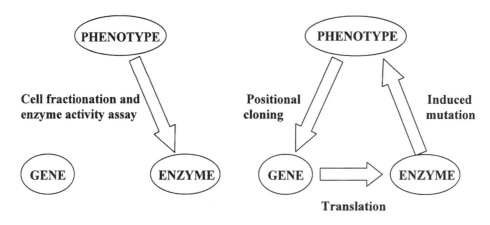

Figure 4 Discovery by positional cloning versus discovery via classical biochemistry. Classical biochemistry discovers the immediate causative agent, the protein enzyme, through a search for a cellular component that exhibits specific enzyme activity. Positional cloning directly reveals the gene; the causal connection may then be proved by artificially introducing mutation in a model organism in order to disrupt enzyme function and induce the disease phenotype

Three types of DNA polymorphisms have been applied in human positional cloning experiments. The first type of polymorphisms that enabled positional cloning were so-called restriction fragment length polymorphisms (RFLPs), first introduced by Botstein et al. (1980). The second generation, mostly used during the last decade, were CA-repeats (individual variations in length of tandem repeats, say, CACA versus CACACACA in a particular position within genomic DNA). The latest generation are the single nucleotide polymorphisms (SNPs), where the difference between two individuals boils down to the difference in a single letter (e.g., A versus G) in a particular position in the DNA text.

Of all types of polymorphisms, SNPs are most frequent—it is expected that every thousand letters there will be a position in the DNA text where there are differences across a significant number of individuals. Given that the size of the human genome is 3×10^9 letters, it is expected that around 3×10^6 SNPs will be discovered. DNA microarray technologies facilitate collection of SNP information in parallel across hundreds of polymorphisms for thousands of individuals per day.

The rapid accumulation of information about the genetic basis of human disease susceptibility raises a number of questions: What is the value of information that somebody will suffer from an incurable disease? Who owns the information? How is the information protected? How should the information be used? How should the information not be used?

To address legitimate concerns regarding the use of DNA information, the U.S. government–sponsored Human Genome Project contains a component that deals exclusively with the ethical, legal, and social implications of the new information and technology (U.S. Department of Energy, Human Genome Project, ELSI Project).

4.2. Genetic Epidemiology

Epidemiology studies the patterns of disease occurrence in human populations and the factors that influence these patterns (Lilienfeld and Stolley, 1994). Modern epidemiology originated with systematic data collection efforts aimed at understanding and controlling spread of disease. Perhaps the most well known study from that early period is John Snow's study that traced the source of the London cholera epidemic to consumption of water from a single London well and led to legislation mandating that all water companies in London filter their water by 1857. It is interesting to note that it was not until 1883 that Robert Koch identified the causative agent, the cholera vibrio (Lilienfeld and Stolley, 1994).

The advent of molecular biology during the past half century has produced numerous molecular markers that are potentially predictive of disease. The term *molecular epidemiology* is used to denote incorporation of molecular, cellular, and other biologic measurements into epidemiologic research (Schulte and Perera, 1993).

The term *genetic epidemiology* is used to denote the study of genetic factors in the origin of disease (for a review of this field, see Khoury et al. [1993].) Variations in genomic DNA are increasingly being recognized as causative agents and confounding factors in disease: for example, a person with a weak copy of a tumor suppressor gene may be more susceptible to colon cancers caused by frequent consumption of grilled meat.

The term *pharmacogenetics* has been used to denote a branch of genetic epidemiology that studies the role of genetic variability in drug response. Consumption of drugs that are harmful or ineffective for patients with particular genetic makeups is a major cause of suffering and economic loss. One well-studied adverse reaction is the sensitivity of some individuals to debrisoquine: certain cytochrome *P450* gene mutations incapacitate the protein enzyme and cause poor drug metabolism, eventually causing poisoning due to the extensive exposure of the organism to the drug (Price Evans, 1993). Another well-known genetically determined adverse reaction is fatal hyperthermia due to administration of succinylcholine during anaesthesia (Price Evans, 1993).

Epidemiological data are typically analyzed using both parametric and nonparametric statistical methods such as contingency tables and logistic regression, and estimation techniques such as maximum likelihood. Selvin (1996) provides an extensive introduction to statistical methods used in epidemiology. A number of statistical packages, such as S-plus and SAS, are widely used for analysis and visualization.

Epidemiological data sets frequently contain private and sensitive information about individuals and their medical histories. Institutions that handle such information usually form so-called internal review boards (IRBs), which ensure that the physical samples and clinical information is handled in an appropriate manner. The use of physical samples, such as blood, is usually governed by consent agreements with the patients. Anonymization of samples is often employed in order to protect privacy.

5. Reverse Engineering of Genetic Networks

While the genomic DNA sequence may be viewed in a computer analogy as the executable program of life, gene expression corresponds to the run-time information on the level of activity of individual genes. While there are in the order of 100,000 genes in the human genome, each of them present in every cell of an organism, only a small fraction of up to a few thousand of them are active in a particular type of cell at any given time. Gene activity is typically measured by the quantity of transcribed messenger RNA (mRNA) or by the amount of translated protein (Figure 1A). Measured quantities of gene expression capture the state of a cell, tissue, organ, or organism.

The floodgates of gene expression information have only been opened during the last few years. The development of discovery methods to deal with the information is now already recognized as a priority.

With the help of expression microarrays, the detailed state of living cells can now be observed as they react to external stimuli or transition from one physiological state to another. For example, changes in mRNA levels of the total set of 6,100 yeast genes have been measured in response to the change in nutrients (Wodicka et al., 1997; DeRisi et al., 1997), in response to temperature change (Lashkari et al., 1997), and during cell division (Chu et al., 1998; DeRisi et al., 1997).

Time profiles of gene expression obtained by microarrays enable the reverse engineering of genetic regulatory networks. Genes have been clustered based on their levels of expression across a number of consecutive timepoints (DeRisi et al., 1997; Chu et al., 1998; Wen et al., 1998), revealing groups of coregulated genes. Two-way clustering of genes and cell states has resulted in the discovery of biologically significant patterns (Alon et al., 1999; Weinstein et al., 1997). Modeling methods developed in the field of digital circuit design have been used to design a model of the well-studied lysis–lysogeny decision circuit of bacteriophage lambda (McAdams and Shapiro, 1995). A relevant case study in this general area may be found in this handbook (Chapter 48.1).

References

Alon, U., N. Barkai, D. A. Notterman, K. Gish, S. Ybarra, D. Mack, and A. J. Levine. 1999. "Broad patterns of gene expression revealed by clustering analysis of tumor and normal colon tissues probed by oligonucleotide arrays." *Proc. Natl. Acad. Sci.* **96**: 6745–6750.

Altschul, S., W. Gish, W. Miller, E. W. Myers, and D. Lipman. 1990. "A basic local alignment search tool." *J. Molec. Biol.* **215**: 403–410.

Bairoch, A. 1992. "PROSITE: a dictionary of sites and patterns in proteins." *Nucleic Acids Res.* **20**: 2013–2018.

Bassett, D. E., M. S. Boguski, F. Spencer, R. Reeves, M. Goebl, and P. Hieter. 1995. "Comparative genomics, genome cross-referencing and XREFdb." *Trends in Genetics* **11**: 372–373.

Benson, G. 1999. "Tandem repeats finder: a program to analyze DNA sequences." *Nucleic Acids Res.* **27**: 573–580.

Botstein, D., R. L. White, M. Skolnick, and R. W. Davis. 1980. "Construction of a genetic linkage map in man using restriction fragment length polymorphisms." *Am. J. Human Genetics* **32**: 314–331.

Brendel, V., J. S. Beckmann, and E. N. Trifonov. 1986. "Linguistics of nucleotide sequences: morphology and comparison of vocabularies." *J. Biomolec. Structure and Dynamics* **4**: 11–21.

Chu, S., J. DeRisi, M. Eisen, J. Mulholland, D. Botstein, P. O. Brown, and I. Herskowitz. 1998. "The transcriptional program of sporulation in budding yeast." *Science* **282**: 699–705.

Collins, F. S., A. Patrinos, E. Jordan, A. Chakravarti, R. Gesteland, and L. Walters. 1998. "New goals for the U.S. Human Genome Project: 1998–2003." *Science* **282**: 682–689.

Debouck, C. and P. N. Goodfellow. 1999. "DNA microarrays in the drug discovery and development." *Nature Genetics* **21(1 Suppl)**: 48–52.

DeRisi, J. L., V. R. Iyer, and P. O. Brown. 1997. "Exploring the metabolic and genetic control of gene expression on a genomic scale." *Science* **278**: 680–686.

Doolittle, R. F., M. Hunkapiller, L. E. Hood, S. Devare, K. Robbins, S. Aaronson, and H. Antoniades. 1983. "Simian sarcoma virus onogene v-sis is derived from the gene (or genes) encoding a platelet-derived growth factor." *Science* **221**: 275–277.

Dove, A. 1999. "Proteomics: translating genomics into products?" *Nature Biotechnol.* **17**: 233–236.

Henikoff, J. G. and S. Henikoff. 1996. "BLOCKS database and its applications." In *Methods in Enzymology,* edited by Doolittle, **266**: 88–105. New York: Academic Press.

Jurka, J. 1998. "Repeats in genomic DNA: mining and meaning." *Curr. Opin. Struct. Biol.* **8**: 333–337.

Khoury, M. J., T. H. Beaty, and B. H. Cohen. 1993. *Fundamentals of Genetic Epidemiology.* Oxford: Oxford University Press.

Krogh, A., M. Brown, I. S. Mian, K. Sjolander, and D. Haussler. 1994. "Hidden Markov models in computational biology: applications to protein modeling." *J. Molec. Biol.* **235**: 1501–1531.

Lander, E. S. 1995. "The secrets of life: a mathematician's introduction to molecular biology." In *Calculating the Secrets of Life,* edited by E. S. Lander and M. S. Waterman. Washington, DC: National Academy Press.

Lashkari, D. A., J. L. DeRisi, J. H. McCusker, A. F. Namath, C. Gentile, S. Y. Hwang, P. O. Brown, and R. W. Davis. 1997. "Yeast microarrays for genome wide parallel genetic and gene expression analysis." *Proc. Natl. Acad. Sci.* **94**: 13057–13062.

Levy, S., L. Compagnoni, E. W. Myers, and G. D. Stormo. 1998. "Xlandscape: the graphical display of word frequencies in sequences." *Bioinformatics* **14**: 74–80.

Lilienfeld, D. E. and P. D. Stolley. 1994. *Foundations of Epidemiology.* Oxford: Oxford University Press.

McAdams, H. and L. Shapiro. 1995. "Circuit simulation of genetic networks." *Science* **269**: 650–656.

Milosavljevic, A. 1995. "Discovering dependencies via algorithmic mutual information: a case study in DNA sequence comparisons." *Machine Learning* **21**: 35–50.

Milosavljevic, A. and J. Jurka. 1993. "Discovering simple DNA sequences by the algorithmic significance method." *Comput. Appl. Biosci.* **9**: 407–411.

Pearson, W. R. and D. J. Lipman. 1988. "Improved tools for biological sequence comparison." *Proc. Natl. Acad. Sci.* **85**: 2444–2448.

Powell, D. R., D. L. Dowe, L. Allison, and T. I. Dix. 1998. "Discovering simple DNA sequences by compression." In *Proceedings of the Pacific Symposium on Biocomputing*. London: World Scientific Publishing Co., pp. 597–608.

Price Evans, D. A. 1993. *Genetic Factors in Drug Therapy*. Cambridge: Cambridge University Press.

Riordan, J. R., J. M. Rommens, B. Kreme, N. Alon, R. Rozmahel, Z. Grzelczak, J. Zielenski, S. Lok, N. Plavsic, J-L. Chou, M. L. Drumm, M. C. Innuzzi, F. S. Collins, and L-C. Tsui. 1989. "Identification of the cystic fibrosis gene: cloning and characterization of complementary DNA." *Science* **245**: 1066–1073.

Rivals, E., O. Delgrange, J. P. Delahaye, M. Dauchet, M. O. Delorme, A. Henaut, and E. Ollivier. 1997. "Detection of significant patterns by compression algorithms: the case of approximate tandem repeats in DNA sequences." *Comput. Appl. Biosci.* **13**: 131–136.

Schulte, P. A. and F. P. Perera. 1993. *Molecular Epidemiology: Principles and Practices*. New York: Academic Press.

Searls, D. B. and K. P. Murphy. 1995. "Automata-theoretic models of mutation and alignment." In *Proceedings of the Third Conference on Intelligent Systems for Molecular Biology*. Menlo Park, CA: AAAI Press.

Selvin, S. 1996. *Statistical Analysis of Epidemiologic Data*. Oxford: Oxford University Press.

Smith, R. F. and T. F. Smith. 1992. "Pattern-induced multi-sequence alignment (PIMA) algorithm employing secondary structure-dependent gap penalties for use in comparative protein modeling." *Protein Engng.* **5**: 35–41.

Stormo, G. D., T. D. Schneider, L. Gold, and A. Ehrenfeucht. 1982. "The use of 'perceptron' algorithm to distinguish translational initiation sites in *E. coli*." *Nucleic Acids Res.* **10**: 2997–3011.

Waterman, M. S. 1995. "Hearing distant echoes: using extremal statistics to probe evolutionary origins." In *Calculating the Secrets of Life*, edited by M. S. Waterman and E. S. Lander. Washington, DC: National Academy Press.

Weinstein, J. N., T. G. Myers, P. M. O'Connor, S. H. Friend, A. J. Fornace Jr. , K. W. Kohn, T. Fojo, S. E. Bates, L. V. Rubinstein, N. L. Anderson, J. K. Buolamwini, W. W. van Osdol, A. P. Monks, D. A. Scudiero, E. A. Sausville, D. W. Zaharevitz, B. Bunow, V. N. Viswanadhan, G. S. Johnson, R. E. Wittes, and K. D. Paull. 1997. "An information-intensive approach to the molecular pharmacology of cancer." *Science* **275**: 343–349.

Wen, X., S. Fuhrman, G. S. Michaels, D. B. Carr, S. Smith, J. L. Barker, and R. Somogyi. 1998. "Large-scale temporal gene expression mapping of central nervous system development." *Proc. Natl. Acad. Sci.* **95**: 334–339.

Wodicka, L., H. Dong, M. Mittmann, M. Ho, and D. J. Lochart. 1997. "Genome-wide expression monitoring in *Saccharomyces cerevisiae*." *Nature Biotechnol.* **15**: 1359–1367.

Woese, C. R., O. Kandler, and M. L. Wheelis. 1990. "Towards a natural system of organisms: proposal for the domains Archaea, Bacteria, and Eucarya." *Proc. Natl. Acad. Sci. (USA)* **87**: 4576–4579.

Zuckerkandl, E. and L. Pauling. 1965. "Molecules as documents of evolutionary history." *J. Theor. Biol.* **8**: 357–366.

Further Reading

Introduction to Molecular Biology

Gonick, L. and M. Wheelis. 1991. *The Cartoon Guide to Genetics*. New York: Harper Perennial. The best one-day introduction to molecular genetics.

Lander, E. S. and M. S. Waterman, eds. 1995. *Calculating the Secrets of Life*. Washington, DC: National Academy Press. A compendium of papers on computational and mathematical problems in molecular biology. Contains a concise introduction to modern molecular biology.

Lodish, H., D. Baltimore, A. Berk, S. L. Zipursky, P. Matsudaira and J. Darnell. 1995. *Molecular Cell Biology*. New York: Scientific American Books. A standard, very readable molecular cell biology textbook.

U.S. Department of Energy, Human Genome Program. 1992. *Primer on Molecular Genetics*. Office of Energy Research, Office of Health and Environmental Research. Washington, DC: U.S. Government Printing Office. This primer provides background information for understanding the relevance of the Human Genome Program.

Watson, J. D., N. H. Hopkins, J. W. Roberts, J. A. Steitz, and A. M. Weiner. 1987. *Molecular Biology of the Gene*. Menlo Park, CA: Benjamin/Cummings. A classic molecular biology text.

Watson, J. D., J. Tooze, and D. T. Kurtz. 1994. *Recombinant DNA: A Short Course*. 2d ed. New York: W. H. Freeman and Co. A concise introduction to basic knowledge and active research methods in molecular biology.

Bioinformatics Journals, Conferences, and Textbooks

Baldi, P. and S. Brunak. 1998. *Bioinformatics: The Machine Learning Approach.* Cambridge, MA: MIT Press. A textbook on bioinformatics with an emphasis on hidden Markov models and neural networks.

Baxevanis, A. D. and B. F. F. Ouellette, eds. 1998. *Bioinformatics: A Practical Guide to the Analysis of Genes and Proteins.* New York: Wiley-Interscience. A practical guide with an emphasis on databases and tools developed at the National Center for Biotechnology Information at the National Institutes of Health. Rich in references and pointers, including a multitude of URLs.

Bioinformatics Journal. Published by Oxford University Press. The flagship journal for bioinformatics.

Cambridge Healthtech Institute (CHI) is a business communication company that organizes industry-oriented conferences on bioinformatics and drug discovery.

Computational Biology Journal. A more theoretically oriented journal.

Conference on Intelligent Systems for Molecular Biology (ISMB). Covers practical and theoretical knowledge discovery problems and systems in molecular biology.

Durbin, R., S. Eddy, A. Krogh and G. Mitchison, 1998. *Biological Sequence Analysis: Probabilistic Models of Proteins and Nucleic Acids.* Cambridge: Cambridge University Press. A tutorial introduction to hidden Markov models, and grammatical and phylogenetic analysis of biological sequences.

Gusfield, D. 1997. *Algorithms on Strings, Trees, and Sequences: Computer Science and Computational Biology.* Cambridge: Cambridge University Press. A thorough reference on the topic of DNA sequence analysis.

IBC-UK Conferences Ltd. is another business communication company that organizes industry-oriented conferences on bioinformatics and drug discovery.

Pacific Symposium on Biocomputing (PSB). Consists of a number of minitracks on the emerging topics in bioinformatics.

Steffen, S.-K. 1995. *Molecular Bioinformatics: Algorithms and Applications.* Berlin: Walter de Gruyter. A sampling of bioinformatics topics, including knowledge representation.

The International Conference on Computational Molecular Biology (RECOMB). A more mathematically oriented conference.

Waterman, M. S. 1995. *Introduction to Computational Biology: Maps, Sequences, and Genomes (Interdisciplinary Statistics).* London: Chapman and Hall. Statistical underpinnings of widely used algorithms in bioinformatics.

Structure of Biological Knowledge

Chaitin, G. 1979. "The maximum entropy formalism," In *Toward a Mathematical Definition of Life*, pp. 477–498. R. D. Levine and M. Tribus, eds. Cambridge, MA: MIT Press. While the chemical and physical laws can in principle be inferred from a relatively small number of well-thought experiments, the quality of biological knowledge critically depends on the size of data sets: the sample size and the number of variables considered may determine whether or not an existing pattern is observed; the amount of available historical information in effect determines the ability to reconstruct evolutionary events. The fact that patterns of life are intrinsically global has in fact been used as a basis for Chaitin's mathematical definition of life. A statistical test for detecting life based on the definition has also been developed (Milosavljevic, 1995).

Meyr, E. 1988. *Toward a New Philosophy of Biology.* Cambridge, MA: Harvard University Press. While chemical and physical knowledge can to a significant degree be expressed mathematically, biological knowledge is less amenable to such representation. Hierarchical classifications, probabilistic inference rules, and conceptual models (formal and pictorial) are more often used. Meyr attempts to address these and related issues from a philosophical perspective.

National Research Council. 1985. *Models for Biomedical Research: A New Perspective.* Washington, DC: National Academy Press. Central to the practice of biomedical research is the concept of a model. According to the report from National Research Council (p. 72), there are two principal types of models, both based on analogy: "The first type seeks similarities between a process or structure within an organism of interest and other organisms, or parts of organisms where analogous processes or structures occur. The second type models processes or structures with conceptual, mathematical, or mechanical analogs. Models are used because they possess simpler or more accessible structure or mechanism in comparison to the object of primary interest, or because certain classes of experiments cannot be carried out in humans."

Ruse, M. and R. M. Burian. eds. 1993. Special Issue on Integration in Biology, *Biology and Philosophy*, **8(3)**. Life sciences are dynamically redefined. Specialization and integration often occur to adjust to emerging experimental methods and knowledge structures. This collection of articles treats the problems of integration of life sciences and biological knowledge from a philosophical perspective.

Schaffner, K. R. 1980. "Theory structure in the biomedical sciences." *J. Med. Phil.* **5(1)**: 57–97. A philosophical perspective on the structure of biological theories, including a number of case studies in molecular biology.

Smith, T. F. and H. J. Morowitz. 1982. "Between history and physics." *J. Molec. Evol.* **18**: 265–282. Biology is a science that has characteristics of both history and physics: on one hand, chemical and physical phenomena form the basis for life processes; on the other hand, the theory of evolution postulates that the living world has emerged through a number of historical frozen accidents such as the emergence of individual species and the emergence of particular anatomies and mechanisms at the molecular, cellular, and organismal levels.

PART EIGHT

KDD IN PRACTICE: CASE STUDIES

46 INDUSTRY

46.1 Database Marketing and Web Mining

Sarabjot S. Anand and Alex G. Büchner

ABSTRACT The four customer-related key disciplines in marketing are attraction, retention, cross-sales, and departure. The same holds for database marketing and its electronic commerce equivalent in Web mining. The case study that is presented tackles the problem of cross-sales in the financial sector in which a particular service had to be cross-sold to the existing customer base. The techniques that were applied are characteristic rule discovery (see Chapter 16.2.2) and deviation detection (see Chapter 16.3.1). We discuss the effect of domain knowledge on the interestingness value of the discovered rules and study techniques for refining the knowledge to increase this interestingness measure. We also investigate the use of externally procured lifestyle and other survey data for data enrichment and discuss its use as additional domain knowledge. The same scenario is then mapped onto its electronic commerce counterpart, where we used log files to discover navigational behavior in order to model potential cross-sales targets.

1. Project Overview

The aim of the project was to identify potential customers for the household insurance product of the client organization from within the organization's current customer base. The project covered all of the typical phases of a data mining undertaking, viz., from data warehousing issues, domain knowledge incorporation, pattern discovery, evaluation, and visualization of the application of results.

The six-month project, with an effort of fifteen person months, involved three different types of expertise. The domain knowledge was provided by a financial marketing adviser from the bank, the data expert was represented by the IT department of the financial institution, and the data mining expertise was provided by the Northern Ireland Knowledge Engineering Laboratory.

Although the data mining process we followed was borrowed from Anand and Büchner (1998), it is very similar to the one described in Part 3 of this handbook. As a result of this, our process has been mapped, where appropriate, onto the one used in this handbook. The following section describes the work undertaken by us within the various stages of the process.

2. KDD Process

2.1. Business Problem

The business problem with which we were confronted was that of cross-selling household insurance to existing customers in a banking database. The problem is depicted in Figure 1. The overall objective was to discover characteristics of current household insurance customers, which could then be used to target all other customer segments, in order to classify them into potential promotion targets and unlikely purchasers (Anand et al., 1997).

2.2. Motivation for a Data Mining Solution

According to Anand et al. (1998), there are four component tasks that can be identified for the cross-sales problem. They are to:

1. Find the sets of customer characteristics that identify, in the customer base, those customers that are most likely to buy a particular product (in this case Household Insurance).

2. Choose the best of these sets of characteristics, in order to identify customers to target in a marketing campaign of some sort (for example, a mail shot).

Bank Customer Base   **Bank Services**

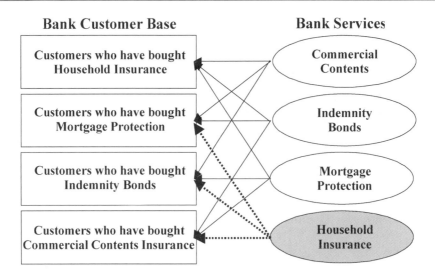

Figure 1 The cross-sales problem

3. Carry out this marketing campaign and analyze the results to see if a high "hit rate" was achieved.

4. Feedback results into the customer database, to carry out refinement of the rules used for targeting customers with the product.

Of these four tasks, tasks (1) and (2) can be identified as data mining tasks, where we were trying to discover the best sets of attributes within the bank's database that identify customers of household insurance. The latter two tasks are of pure marketing nature and will not be discussed further.

The categorization of the first task as having either a classification or characteristic rule discovery goal depends on the data available within their customer database. For a classification goal, the bank must have data on three types of customers, namely those that have household insurance, those that refused to purchase household insurance, and those that did not have household insurance, but did not refuse to purchase it. The first type of customers form the positive examples, the second type of customers form the negative examples, and the third type form the target data set. If, however, the bank only has data on two types of customers, namely those that have household insurance and those who do not, that is, positive examples and a target data set, rather than a classification goal we have a characteristic rules discovery goal (see Chapter 16.2.2). These rules define those characteristics that are prevalent in a particular group of records, which in our case is the group of records that pertain to customers who have household insurance. Given these rules, customers in the target data set with similar characteristics can be targeted with sales campaigns.

The second task is associated with filtering the discovered characteristics using some kind of domain specific mechanism, so as to choose the most relevant characteristics to use for targeting customers. The technique used would clearly depend on the type of goal associated with the first task, which in turn depends on the availability of data. Thus, we postpone further discussion on the second task until Section 2.7.

2.3. The Available Data

With respect to the data held by the bank, two types of the customer data were identified as being relevant to the cross-sales problem. These were the personal information about the customer, for example, demographic information, sex, occupation, and marital status, and transactional information on the different accounts held by the customers. An important aspect of the data was identified at this stage. While data on customers who bought household insurance was available from the bank's databases, no information was available on customers who did not require a household insurance product at all, or who had not taken up the household insurance product with the bank but had household insurance with a competitor organization. This fact confirms that the classification of the first data mining task identified earlier had a characteristic rule discovery goal as opposed to a classification goal.

Three externally available data sets were believed to be relevant to the cross-sales problem, as they provided information about the bank's customers not stored in the bank's database. The Robson's Deprivation Index for Northern Ireland provided information about the level of deprivation of the area in which the customer lived, while the Acorn classification data and lifestyles survey data provided data such as average income, employment rates, and average family size of the area in which the customer lived. Each of these data sets provided information summarized to the enumeration district (artificial geographical boundaries defined by the government based on population density). The bank identifies the geographical location using postal code and not enumeration district.

2.4. Background Knowledge

We formulated various types of domain knowledge in collaboration with the domain expert, all of which were either classified as taxonomies (see Chapter 18.1; in form of concept hierarchies), environment-based constraints (see Chapter 18.2), and user preferences (see Chapter 18.4; represented as syntactic constraints and inter-attribute dependency constraints). At a later stage some of this domain knowledge was refined using previously discovered knowledge (see Chapter 18.3).

2.5. Preprocessing and Data Extraction

In order to create a knowledge discovery view that encompassed relevant customer information, accumulated transactional data, as well as connected external sources, various data preprocessing and extracting steps had to be performed. The preprocessing mainly constituted the removal of outliers, conversion of continuous attributes to discrete attributes, and heterogeneity resolution (achieved through data aggregation and spatial joins) among the three different data sources. Data on 60,000 customers was used in the data mining project, 430 of whom were existing household insurance customers.

2.6. The Discovery Mechanism

An association rule discovery algorithm based on evidence theory, the EAR (evidence-based association rule) algorithm, was used to mine the client's data. The EAR algorithm is a generalization of earlier association algorithms and therefore allows the incorporation of support and uncertainty thresholds and syntactic constraints. In addition to the simple syntactic constraints of the type defined by Agrawal and Srikant (1994), EAR allows the definition, and consequently the incorporation, of inter-attribute dependency constraints. For example, a rule that contains an expression pertaining to the account average balance of a customer is only valid if it also contains an expression regarding the account type as well. In addition to this, the EAR algorithm can discover knowledge from multivalued attributes rather than just binary attributes as in the case of previous algorithms. It allows the incorporation of domain knowledge and can handle missing values in the data. The EAR algorithm requires attributes to be discrete. Therefore, interval bands were provided by the domain expert for continuous variables. Also, domain-specific hierarchies were provided by the domain expert for a number of other attributes.

Through knowledge discovered at various intermediate stages, these taxonomies were refined to achieve more interesting knowledge.

2.7. The Results

In addition to domain knowledge incorporation, the number of rules generated was regulated by setting a threshold on the support of the rule in the data set and by defining an interestingness measure. The interestingness measure used is normally dependent on the problem at hand. In cross-sales, we clearly do not want to base the targeting of a product on customer characteristics that are actually characteristics of the bank's customers in general. Thus, the interestingness measure we used was based on the deviation of the characteristic rules discovered for the customers of the product being targeted from the norm. The norm in our case was defined as the support for these customer characteristics within the complete customer base of the bank, that is, a characteristic rule is interesting if it is a characteristic of the customer of the target product rather than the customer base in general. Thus, we defined the interestingness measure for customer characteristics, c, as:

$$\text{Interest}_c = \frac{S_p - S_o}{\max\{S_o, S_p\}},\tag{1}$$

where, S_p is the support for the characteristics c in the positive example data set and S_o is the support for the characteristics c in the complete customer base. The expression in the denominator is called the normalizing factor, as it normalizes the interestingness measure onto the scale $[-1, 1]$.

Example characteristic rules discovered are shown below:

if Household Insurance = Y

then Occupation = SKILLED

with support = 26.51 percent and interest 0.53

if Household Insurance = Y

then Occupation = SKILLED and Status = Hon-Commits

with support = 21.86 percent and interest 0.68

if Household Insurance = Y

then Occupation = SKILLED and Status = Hon-Commits and Net Credit Turnover > 4000

with support = 12.79 percent and interest 0.74

if Household Insurance = Y

then Occupation = SKILLED and Status = Hon-Commits and Net Credit Turnover > 4000

and Account Type1 = CURRENT

with support = 12.56 percent and interest 0.74

if Household Insurance = Y

then cus_nodeps = 0_Dep and cus_yrnetavgbal = Zero_1500 and CHILDREN = 4

with support = 10.93 percent and interest = −0.77

A positive interest measure suggests that customers with the given consequent are likely to buy household insurance, whereas a negative interest indicates that customers with the given characteristics are less likely to purchase the product.

The effect of the interest value threshold on the number of rules discovered is shown in Table 1. The rules were constrained to a maximum size of seven consequent attributes.

Table 1 Number of Rules Discovered vs. the Interest Measure

Interest Threshold	Number of Rules
0.84	7
0.80	217
0.70	1178
0.50	1739
0.00	3737

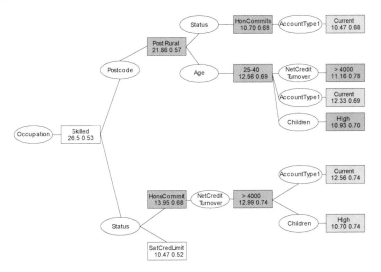

Figure 2 Characteristic rule visualization

Figure 2 presents some of the rules graphically. The oval nodes represent attributes used to specialize the rule specified by the path from the root node to the node preceding the oval node, while the rectangular nodes represent the specialization attribute value. The numbers shown in the rectangular node are the support and interest of the rule. The light gray nodes represent rules that have an interest value less than or equal to another rule of which the present rule is a specialization, while the darker gray nodes represent rules where the specialization attribute has improved the interest value of the rule. Nonshaded nodes represent rules where the specialization has decreased the interest in the rule.

2.8. Applications of the Discovered Knowledge

Before the discovered knowledge was ready for application in the business context of the bank, two knowledge post-processing steps were required. The concept hierarchies were refined to improve the interestingness of the resulting rules, while the attribute relationship rules and constraints were also tuned to improve the quality of the rules discovered. Based on the refined domain knowledge, the same process, as described above, was performed and the results were then used in order to classify the customers into potential promotion targets and unlikely purchasers.

In order to apply the discovered results, we ranked the potential customers according to their associated interest values. From all the rules that applied to the customer, the interest value associated with the customer was that of the rule with the lowest interest measure. The higher the (positive) interest value associated with the customer, the more likely the customer was to buy household insurance.

3. Discovering Internet Marketing Intelligence

From a high-level marketing point of view, the four stages in a marketing life-cycle (attraction, retention, cross-sales, and departure) are identical in traditional retailing and electronic commerce scenarios. However, upon a more detailed examination, there are some subtle differences that require additional efforts in order to apply marketing mechanisms on Internet data (Mulvenna et al., 1998).

The main differences are anchored in the data that is available for knowledge discovery, as well as the type of domain knowledge that can be incorporated. In addition to traditional customer and transaction/purchasing data, we can also collect more sophisticated behavioral data in the form of browsing information, which is stored in Web log files. Additionally, a different type of domain knowledge is available, which represents the topology (structure) of an online trading site. Considering the supplementary elements of electronic commerce business models, we are now in a position to describe briefly a cross-sales scenario based on Web data.

The project has been carried out with one of the largest Irish online book shops, where currently about 2 percent of the overall sales are from Internet users. The objective of the feasibility study was to establish the usability of existing customer, transactional, and browsing data, in order to discover Internet marketing intelligence. The two most interesting types of marketing knowledge were that of attracting new customers and, naturally, that of cross-sales.

The data preparation proved to be the most time-consuming task, since it involved not only the collection of customer information, transactional data, as well as common and cookie log files, but also the organization in a data warehouse in order to build a Web log data cube (Büchner and Mulvenna, 1998). Further activities, which were distinct to traditional retail data, were the performing of reverse DNS lookups on unresolved host names and the handling of relatively large numbers of unknown records, often caused by broken links.

In addition to the traditional cross-sales mechanisms outlined in Sections 1 and 2, a more Internet-specific, and thus less generic, approach was performed for rule discovery. The types of domain knowledge that were considered were the above-mentioned network-like electronic shop topology as well as user-defined hierarchies (for example, generalizations of book topics; [Baumgarten et al., 2000]). The approach we chose was to discover typical sequences that occur before existing customers purchase another product. The unique concept of storing browsing patterns allowed that type of discovery, where navigational behavior can be used as a key factor. In order to discover sequential patterns from Web log files, Agrawal's family of sequential A priori algorithms has been extended, which are also known as A priori All (Agrawal and Srikant, 1995). The main extensions are a more efficient implementation for large amounts of data, as well as support for multiple values in discovered sequences. Both extensions were relevant for the discovery of behavioral navigational patterns for electronic commerce purposes in Internet data, because the amounts of data to be dealt with are usually rather large, and forward and backward browsing on electronic shops as well as double hits have proven important.

The results we found contained a number of sequences pertaining to customers who had bought at least one item in the bookshop within the previous three months and their most typical behavior before they purchased another item. These rules were than mapped onto the most recent log files in order to rank the most likely customers for cross-selling.

The application of the discovered knowledge is similar to traditional retailing, with an essential difference. The targeting can be performed online and for each individual customer, which ideally leads to a one-to-one marketing scenario. For instance, a customer who has all the attributes of a potential cross-selling activity can be shown a specially tailored offer dynamically. Furthermore, the reaction on this offer can be monitored and fed back into the KDD process.

References

Agrawal, R. and R. Srikant. 1994. "Fast algorithms for mining association rules in large databases." In *Proceedings of the Twentieth International Conference on Very Large Databases*, pp. 487–499.

Agrawal, R. and R. Srikant. 1995. "Mining sequential patterns." In *Proceedings of the International Conference on Data Engineering*, pp. 3–14.

Anand, S. S. and A. G. Büchner. 1998. *Decision Support Using Data Mining*. London: Financial Times Pitman Publishers.

Anand, S. S., A. R. Patrick, J. G. Hughes, and D. A. Bell. 1998. "A data mining methodology for cross-sales." *Knowledge-based Sys. J.* **10**: 449–461.

Anand, S. S., J. G. Hughes, D. A. Bell, and A. R. Patrick. 1997. "Tackling the cross-sales problem using data mining." In *Proceedings of the First Pacific-Asia Conference in Knowledge Discovery and Data Mining*, pp. 25–35.

Baumgarten, M., A. G. Büchner, S. S. Anand, M. D. Mulvenna, and J. G. Hughes. 2000. "Navigation pattern discovery from internet data." In *Advances in Web Usage Analysis and User Profiling*, edited by B. Masand and M. Spiliopoulou. Lecturer Notes in Computer Science. Springer-Verlag.

Büchner, A. G. and M. D. Mulvenna. 1998. "Discovering Internet marketing intelligence through online analytical web usage mining." *ACM SIGMOD Record* **27(4).**

Mulvenna, M. D., M. T. Norwood, and A. G. Büchner. 1998. "Data-driven marketing." *Int. J. Electronic Markets* **8(3)**: 32–35.

46.2 The Use of Modern Heuristic Algorithms for Mining Insurance Data

V. J. Rayward-Smith, J. C. W. Debuse and B. de la Iglesia,

ABSTRACT An overview of the use of knowledge discovery in databases (KDD) in the U.K. insurance business is presented. Applications in pricing and marketing are discussed together with the corresponding effectiveness of various data mining algorithms. Rule induction using modern heuristic techniques is seen to be most effective, and a case study in customer profiling is described.

1. Introduction

The U.K. insurance sector has an outstanding range of opportunities for projects involving the extraction of patterns from large databases, a process known as knowledge discovery in databases (Brachman and Anand, 1995; Debuse, 1997; Fayyad et al., 1996; Piatetsky-Shapiro, 1996). Insurance companies within the United Kingdom are allowed to vary the cost of their policies to match the relevant characteristics of their customers; the goal is to charge a given type of customer an amount that covers their probable cost and allows for profit to be made. The types of data that insurance companies are permitted to base the pricing of their policies on include geographical area, gender, car type, social group, and income level. U.K. insurance companies may therefore use the results of KDD projects directly in their pricing process; this can have considerable impact on their competitiveness, since the U.K. insurance market is extremely price sensitive.

The raw material for any KDD project is a large database or set of databases. Successful insurance companies are well provided for in this respect since they maintain enormous databases, containing information across wide areas of their business, and have been doing so for many years. This data can be added to by the purchase of additional databases from external suppliers; such an approach may involve legal issues but can potentially yield significant rewards if the new data proves useful.

An important component of any KDD project is domain knowledge—information regarding the area within which the project is to be carried out. Within insurance companies, a considerable amount of domain expertise is provided by underwriters, actuaries, and statisticians. This domain expertise can prove invaluable in instigating, evaluating, and interpreting KDD projects.

Pricing is obviously a key area for KDD projects within insurance, but marketing is also important. A marketing project may, for example, involve targeting mailshots toward prospective customers who are likely to be interested. The identification of desirable customers, such as those who are likely to be loyal, is another area within which considerable benefit may be gained through KDD. Large savings may also be made through the identification of key characteristics of fraudulent claims; in addition to this, if the company can reduce the number of honest customers that are investigated for fraud, then it will benefit from reduced investigation costs and increased customer satisfaction.

Within many KDD projects in insurance, the desired characteristics of the discovered knowledge are known in advance. For example, if the project involves the identification of key characteristics of fraudulent claims, then the discovered patterns will have to be extremely accurate. If this is not the case, then the company will waste time and money investigating large numbers of genuine claims for fraud and is likely to irritate its customers. In addition to being accurate, the patterns must apply to a reasonable proportion of the fraudulent cases since, otherwise, the benefits realized will be extremely small. A contrasting example is that of mailshot targeting; in this case, the discovered knowledge can be extremely valuable without having to be very accurate. In general, a very small proportion of the customers who are sent mailshots reply; a discovered pattern that identifies a large subset of the customers within which this proportion is doubled is clearly very useful despite having very low accuracy.

The discovered knowledge should also be in a form that can be easily understood, since the management personnel who will decide how and where it is to be used are unlikely to place their trust in something that they cannot understand. In addition, in some instances the company will need to share knowledge with another party. For example, in the case of fraud detection, the company might have to explain to customers why their claims are being investigated, in terms they can understand. These requirements mean that data mining algorithms (which are used to discover patterns) within KDD projects in insurance must usually offer sufficient control to allow users to specify the required characteristics of discovered patterns. These will include accuracy, generality (the proportion of the database to which the pattern applies), and the area of the database to which they apply (such as fraudulent claims).

The discovered knowledge may be in a variety of different forms, such as decision trees (Chapters 5.4 and 16.1.3), rules (Chapters 5.3 and 16.1.4), or neural networks (Chapters 5.9 and 16.1.8). Neural networks (Hertz et al., 1991; Rich and Knight, 1991) represent knowledge in a form that can be difficult and time consuming to comprehend; they are therefore unlikely to be used widely within the field of insurance, since understanding the discovered patterns is often critical. Marketing is a possible exception to this rule. Algorithms such as C5 (Quinlan, 1997) produce trees that represent the discovered knowledge from which rules may be extracted. Trees can be difficult to understand if they are large and complex; in such cases, they suffer similar drawbacks to neural networks. Alternatively, rules may be generated directly, in which case they are not constrained by the structure of the tree; therefore, this approach is often preferred.

Time is an important aspect of KDD projects in insurance. Extracting and making use of knowledge as rapidly as possible maximizes the competitive advantage that the company enjoys. In addition to this, the value of the discovered knowledge may reduce with time as changes occur in the marketplace. As some old patterns become weaker with time, so new patterns are likely to emerge in their place; it is therefore important to regularly rerun KDD projects within the insurance industry using the most recently acquired data.

2. Preprocessing

Within the domain of insurance, a variety of preprocessing operations may prove necessary. The large numbers of records involved mean that size reduction operations can prove useful; the conversion of data from a micro- to a macrolevel is an example of such an operation. Each macro level record represents a set of microlevel records, and may contain a new field that describes the number of microlevel records from which it was formed. For example, if three hundred customers have the same recorded characteristics (i.e., in a motor insurance database they all share the same value for all attributes such as car model, district, age of driver), they can be combined into a single macrolevel record. In that case, the additional field will contain a value of three hundred.

The production of new, high-quality features from the existing set of fields, described as feature construction (FC; Chapters 14.3, Ittner and Schlosser, 1996; Matheus and Rendell, 1989), has considerable potential within insurance. Discovered knowledge may be of significantly higher quality if the new fields produced by feature construction are powerfully predictive. FC may be undertaken by algorithms or, alternatively, can involve domain experts. For example, a domain expert may suggest that, rather than using two fields describing the power and weight of a car, a single field should be used that represents the power-to-weight ratio. The new field is more likely to give an accurate measure of the performance of the car than the two upon which it is based; this may therefore allow patterns of higher quality to be discovered.

Discretization of features (Chapters 14.4, Dougherty et al., 1995) may prove valuable within the insurance sector; this describes the process by which field values are divided into sets of intervals. A common example is customer age for motor insurance policies; this is typically banded into ranges rather than being dealt with in raw form. The process of discretization, if performed correctly, can improve the speed of data mining algorithms by reducing the size of the hypothesis space; the discovered knowledge may also be more simple and accurate. However, it should be noted that low-quality discretization algorithms may result in poor performance from the data mining approaches used.

Visualization may also be a useful preprocessing step within the field of insurance. This approach aims at harnessing the pattern recognition capabilities of the human eye and uses these to extract knowledge. There are numerous ways in which data can be presented graphically; if a suitable approach is chosen, then important patterns may be identified rapidly by eye. These patterns may be used to guide subsequent phases of the KDD process and may also be delivered as part of the discovered knowledge. For example, a simple two-dimensional point graph showing one attribute in each axis and using color to overlay the class attribute may show interesting relationships between the two attributes and the class. From the visualization, it could be inferred that FC should be applied to construct a new attribute as a combination of the two previous attributes. From the same visualization, it may also be possible to spot outliers. Those may need to be removed if they are considered to be the result of some data entry error, or they may form the focus of further mining if they are thought to be interesting exceptional observations.

3. Data Mining: Classification

Classification (Chapters 16.1) is one of the most common data mining tasks within the insurance domain. Classification algorithms build a description of a categorical field or attribute (the class) in terms of other attributes in the database. The high-level goal is to be able to predict the class for a new case.

Decision tree induction is probably the most established and widely used technique for classification. Most commercial data mining packages have a decision tree induction algorithm as part of their data mining tools. The best-known algorithm is C4.5 (Quinlan, 1993) and its successor, C5.

An alternative method for producing a classification is rule induction. Most tree induction algorithms, including C4.5/C5, include functionality to transform the massive set of rules that can be directly deducted from the tree by interpreting each branch as a rule into a smaller and more coherent set (Quinlan, 1987a,b). Rules extracted from trees are far more understandable and have also been shown to give higher accuracy than trees (Perez and Rendell, 1995).

There are many rule induction algorithms available that produce rules outright, without the intermediate stage of building the tree. They mainly follow one of two search strategies. The first, known as separate and conquer, consists of determining the most powerful rule that underlies the data set, separating out those examples that are covered by it, and repeating the procedure on the remaining examples. An example of a system using this approach is CN2 (Clark and Niblett, 1989). The second strategy starts by generating an initial set of rules that covers all the instances in the database (e.g., using decision tree induction). This rule set will normally be very large and contain many rules of low quality. The process continues with a second stage, in which the rule set is optimized (e.g., using pruning techniques [Breslow and Aha, 1996]. This strategy is used, for example, in C5 and in RIPPER [Cohen, 1995]).

Most tree and rule induction algorithms tend to deliver a complete classification of the database, that is, one that covers every record within the training database. But, in a commercial environment such as insurance, the objective of a data mining exercise is not necessarily to provide a comprehensive characterization of a set of classes. This may indeed be detrimental to obtaining interesting and understandable patterns. The objective in many cases is to identify relatively rare, but potentially important, patterns or anomalies relating to some class or classes. This task has been referred to as partial classification (Ali and Srikant, 1997), and the individual rules have been referred to as nuggets (Riddle et al., 1994). In partial classification, the high level goal is not prediction of new cases, it is the description and understanding of the behavior of a particular class. In a motor insurance database, for example, policyholders making claims may be a minority (perhaps only 5 percent of the portfolio), yet those may be the most interesting customers to the company, and the production of high-quality rules that describe those customers could be highly profitable.

The problem of partial classification requires the definition of a measure of interest of a rule. Algorithms for partial classification should seek to maximize that measure. The objective of complete classification algorithms is to produce the highest overall accuracy, and this may not lead to the most interesting individual rules.

There are very few rule induction algorithms constructed specifically for partial classification. Brute force (Riddle et al., 1994) is an example of such an algorithm, but its exhaustive nature makes it computationally expensive for large data sets. We will now examine briefly a powerful rule induction algorithm for extracting high-quality individual classification rules that has been used extensively in an insurance domain (de la Iglesia et al., 1996) and has proved its worth.

The approach of modern heuristic techniques to rule induction is described in more detail in de la Iglesia et al. (1996) and Rayward-Smith et al. (1995). It is based on the use of modern heuristic techniques (Rayward-Smith et al., 1996) such as genetic algorithms (GAs), simulated annealing (SA), and tabu search (TS) to search for high-quality rules underlying the data set. These techniques, inspired by natural processes that perform some form of optimization, have been used extensively to solve optimization problems in a variety of settings. Their versatility is one of their greatest advantages; they work as long as we have a black box that can evaluate proposed solutions. Heuristic techniques do not guarantee finding an optimal solution to a problem, but in practice they have been shown to produce optimal or near-optimal solutions to many real-world problems.

The application of heuristic techniques to the problem of rule induction requires two main aspects to be resolved: how to represent a rule in a form that it can be manipulated by the algorithms (normally as a bit string), and how to measure the quality or interest of a given rule so that the algorithms can distinguish between better and worse rules.

The first aspect is solved by representing a rule as a binary string composed of upper and lower limits (one pair for each of the numerical fields or attributes in the data set) plus sets of individual bits to represent the values that categorical attributes may take. The final part of the string is used to represent the class described by the rule.

The quality or interest of a rule is sometimes known as the fitness (f) of a rule R which is measured in this approach by

$$f(R) = \lambda c - a,$$

where c represents the number of records in the database, D with cardinality d, for which both the antecedent and the consequent of the rule are true, and a represents the number of records for which the antecedent of the rule is true. In other words, a is the number of records for which the rule makes a prediction (correct or incorrect), whereas c is the number of those records for which the prediction is correct.

The fitness function described above supports a partial ordering of rules based on the two most basic properties of a rule: accuracy (sometimes called confidence) and coverage (sometimes called support or generality). The accuracy of an individual rule is defined in this context as

$$\text{Acc}(r) = \frac{c}{a},$$

and its coverage is defined as

$$Cov(r) = \frac{c}{b},$$

where b represents the number of records in the target class.

The fitness function imposes a partial ordering that can be summarized as follows:

- Rules with accuracy above a certain threshold of $\frac{1}{\lambda}$ are preferred to those with accuracy equal to or below the threshold.

- For two rules above the threshold accuracy, if one rule has higher accuracy and coverage than another, then the first rule is preferred.

- For two rules above the threshold accuracy, if they have the same accuracy, then the rule with higher coverage is preferred.

- Similarly, for two rules above the threshold accuracy, if they have the same coverage, the more accurate rule is preferred.

The parameter λ plays a very important part in the fitness measure. It is used to establish the threshold accuracy that will guide the search, so increasing the value of λ decreases the accuracy threshold. At the same time, when rules are not comparable under this partial ordering, the parameter λ can encourage the search toward more accurate or more general rules: increasing the value of λ would increase the reward for generality in the fitness function, and hence encourage the search toward more general rules.

Surprisingly, many of the interest functions used in classification algorithms do not support this partial ordering. For those functions, rules with equal accuracy may have the same interest measure regardless of their coverage. An example of such a function is Laplace accuracy (Clark and Boswell, 1991), used to guide the search in CN2. It seems obvious that if one rule has more coverage than another, with equal accuracy, the former rule should be preferred, as it explains a higher percentage of the database. In an insurance domain, a rule that explains a higher percentage of the database at a given level of accuracy should be translated into increased gains from the exploitation of the knowledge. In conclusion, for partial classification, the selection of an adequate measure of interest is essential for good results.

The fitness of a rule is a very desirable measure of interest as it supports the partial ordering of rules based on accuracy and coverage. It can also be adjusted to include other criteria for rule quality, for example, simplicity. It can also embed feature selection criteria by limiting the number of fields used, or avoiding particular fields. The opportunity to alter the fitness measure, which is the guiding criteria for the search, is a definite strength of this method as the interest of a pattern can be defined in many ways and may encompass many different qualities. The rules produced can also be postprocessed and made simpler, for example, by removing some of the conditions present.

This rule induction method has been used in an insurance environment to produce rules of high quality for a number of data sets. Furthermore, the ability to search for rules with varying levels of accuracy and generality was considered to be a great advantage by the data owners.

4. Case Study in Customer Profiling

The case study that we present here concerns the identification of disloyal customers in an insurance database. Within this example, we define customers that have declined an invitation to renew their policies as *disloyal*. The identification of groups of disloyal customers brings a range of potential benefits. Disloyal customers are likely to be lost to competitors, and it is more expensive for a company to acquire a new customer than to retain an existing one. The knowledge extracted, for example, could suggest that if certain small incentives are offered to potentially disloyal customers, they may be retained by the company.

It is also of interest to identify characteristics of loyal customers, as knowledge in this area can be used by the company to focus its attention on acquiring the type of customers that are likely to be loyal, perhaps by using additional marketing campaigns.

Although the problem requires the modeling of both classes, the emphasis is on creating understandable descriptions of each individual class. The descriptions may not apply to all the members of a class, but may instead apply to a subset of the class. For example, suppose we are able to characterize a group of customers in which 70 percent are classed as disloyal, and which covers 40 percent of the examples of disloyal customers in the database. If offering a small incentive to these customers will result in their retention, the characterization of this group would represent highly desirable knowledge. A complete classification may offer more knowledge in some senses, but overall accuracy of the classification may not be translated into very strong individual descriptions. Also, a complete classification is generally more complex, as it has to cater for every record in the database, and hence the descriptions embedded are more difficult to extract and interpret.

The task to be considered in this case study is therefore that of partial classification. A partial classification may allow us to predict if someone is going to be loyal/disloyal by their characteristics (note, though, that there is no guarantee of a prediction).

The discovered knowledge within this case study is passed on to management. This also imposes some constraints, such as it must be in a form that is easily understood. The customer groups identified within the study must be of reasonable size, since otherwise the benefits that may be gained from them are likely to be negligible. The level of disloyalty/loyalty within the groups must also be sufficiently higher than the overall average to be of use. In other words, patterns must display high coverage and accuracy significantly higher than the percentage of records that belong to the targeted class.

The database that was used for this study contained over 30,000 records. Each record contained a range of customer information, such as claims history and payment method, together with a field describing loyalty. The database was split randomly into a train and test set. The proportion of records used for learning and testing was approximately fifty-fifty.

The study started by the application of algorithms such as C4.5 and CN2 to obtain rules representing a partial classification. The algorithm C4.5 was first used to create a decision tree. The tree created was massive, containing many hundreds of lines, so in its raw format it was too difficult to interpret. This is quite a common problem for tree induction, as for any sizable database the tree generated may contain hundreds or even thousands of lines, and its interpretation as knowledge may require another pattern recognition exercise. Even Quinlan, the creator of C4.5, recognized in Quinlan (1987b) that trees were of limited value if the knowledge embedded in them had to be understood. The tree also showed some signs of overfitting when applied to the test data. The overfitting problem occurs when the tree generated is very accurate at classifying the data used to construct it, but it is less accurate at classifying unseen data. This problem is linked to the problem of tree complexity. A large and complex tree can have a higher error rate than a simple tree because it may have grown to the point that it is actually modeling the noise in the training data, rather than capturing the general characteristics that will be supported by unseen data.

C4.5 and CN2 were used to produce rules for the data set. The rules produced were more suitable for the task in hand, as they represented knowledge in a concise and understandable manner, and they could be assessed individually by their accuracy and coverage. The number of rules generated by both algorithms was manageable, which allowed the examination of each individual rule. However, some of the rules did not display the required coverage and accuracy. Rules of high accuracy covered few records. Furthermore, neither algorithm facilitated the search for rules with varying levels of accuracy and coverage.

The modern heuristic techniques-based approach was particularly well suited to this case study, offering the advantage of being able to control the balance between the accuracy and generality of the discovered rules to suit the aforementioned project requirements. The knowledge is also produced in a form that may be easily understood by management, and the class of interest may be controlled by the user; this allowed groups of either loyal or disloyal customers to be identified. Modern heuristic algorithms were therefore used to extract individual rules of high quality, and the characteristics of those rules were compared to those of the rules found with the previous algorithms.

The rules discovered with the heuristic techniques matched the project requirements very closely. The rules were extremely simple, containing just a few inequalities, and thus could be passed directly to management. The customer groups identified were large, some of them covering over 50 percent of the database; the disloyalty of the groups differed considerably from the average and by over 30 percent in some cases. These rules were of higher quality, when compared using the fitness function, than those obtained with the other algorithms. The company found them more useful because of their wider coverage and high accuracy. For example, a single individual rule containing two conditions highlighted a group of customers in which the percentage of disloyal customers was 41 percent higher than the overall percentage. The rule covered 34 percent of the disloyal customers.

The company found the rules extracted using the modern heuristics the most interesting rules. The knowledge embedded in them was acted upon and was reported to bring considerable commercial advantage to the company. So successful has the approach been that it has now been embedded in a toolkit, Lanner's Datalamp Predictor, which is currently used by a number of U.K. insurance companies.

References

Ali, K., S. Manganaris, and R. Srikant. 1997. "Partial classification using association rules." In *Proceedings of the Third International Conference on Knowledge Discovery and Data Mining*, edited by D. Heckerman, H. Mannila, D. Pregibon, and R. Uthurusamy, pp. 115–118. Menlo Park, CA: AAAI Press.

Brachman, R. J. and T. Anand. 1995. "The process of knowledge discovery in databases: a human-centered approach." In *Advances in Knowledge Discovery and Data Mining*, edited by U. Fayyad, G. Piatetsky-Shapiro, P. Smyth, and R. Uthurusamy. Menlo Park, CA: AAAI Press.

Breslow, A. and D. W. Aha. 1996. "Simplifying decision trees: a survey." *Knowledge Engng. Rev.* **12**: 1–40. Available at www.aic.nrl.navy.mil/papers/1996/AIC-96-014.ps.

Clark, P. C. and R. Boswell. 1991. "Rule induction with CN2: some recent improvements." In *Machine Learning—Proceedings of the Fifth European Conference*, edited by Y. Kodratoff, pp. 151–163. Berlin: Springer-Verlag.

Clark, P. C. and T. N. Niblett. 1989. "The CN2 induction algorithm." *Machine Learning* **3(4)**: 261–283.

Cohen, W. W. 1995. "Fast effective rule induction." In *Proceedings of the Twelfth International Conference on Machine Learning*, edited by A. Prieditis and S. Russell, pp. 115–123. Tahoe City, CA: Morgan Kaufmann Publishers.

Debuse, J. C. W. 1997. "Exploitation of modern heuristic techniques within a commercial data mining environment." Ph.D. diss. University of East Anglia.

Dougherty, J., R. Kohavi, and M. Sahami. 1995. "Supervised and unsupervised discretization of continuous features." In *Proceedings of the Twelfth International Conference on Machine Learning*, edited by A. Prieditis and S. Russell, pp. 194–202. San Francisco, CA: Morgan Kaufmann. Available by anonymous ftp from starry.stanford.edu:pub/ronnyk/disc.ps.

Fayyad, U., G. Piatetsky-Shapiro, and P. Smyth. 1996. "Knowledge discovery and data mining: towards a unifying framework." *Proceedings of the Second International Conference on Knowledge Discovery and Data Mining (KDD-96)*, edited by E. Simoudis, J. W. Han, and U. Fayyad.

Hertz, J. A., R. G. Palmer, and A. S. Krogh. 1991. *Introduction to the Theory of Neural Computation*. Redwood City, CA: Addison-Wesley.

Iglesia, B. de la, J. C. W. Debuse, and V. J. Rayward-Smith. 1996. "Discovering knowledge in commercial databases using modern heuristic techniques." In *Proceedings of the Second International Conference on Knowledge Discovery and Data Mining*, edited by E. Simoudis, J. W. Han, and U. M. Fayyad. Menlo Park, CA: AAAI Press.

Ittner, A. and M. Schlosser. 1996. "Discovery of relevant new features by generating non-linear decision trees." In *Proceedings of the Second International Conference on Knowledge Discovery and Data Mining (KDD-96)*, edited by E. Simoudis, J. W. Han, and U. Fayyad, pp. 108–113.

Matheus, C. J. and L. A. Rendell. 1989. "Constructive induction on decision trees." In *Proceedings of the Eleventh International Joint Conference on Artificial Intelligence*, pp. 645–650. Detroit, NJ: Morgan Kaufmann.

Perez, E. and L. A. Rendell. 1995. "Using multidimensional projection to find relations." In *Proceedings of the Twelfth International Conference on Machine Learning*, edited by A. Prieditis and S. Russell, pp. 447–455. Tahoe City, CA: Morgan Kaufmann Publishers.

Piatetsky-Shapiro, G. 1996. "From data mining to knowledge discovery: the roadmap." In *Proceedings of the Data Mining Conference*, pp. 209–221. Middlesex, England: UNICOM.

Quinlan, J. R. 1987a. "Generating production rules from decision trees." In *Proceedings of the Tenth International Joint Conference on Artificial Intelligence*, pp. 304–307. San Mateo, CA: Morgan Kaufmann Publishers.

Quinlan, J. R. 1987b. "Simplifying decision tress." *Int. J. Man–Machine Studies* **27**: 221–234.

Quinlan, J. R. 1993. *C4.5: Programs for Machine Learning*. San Mateo, CA: Morgan Kaufmann.

Quinlan, J. R. 1997. "Successor to C4.5." In *Knowledge Discovery Nuggets*. http://www.kdnuggets.com/news/97/nog.html.

Rayward-Smith, V. J., J. C. W. Debuse, and B. de la Iglesia. 1995. "Using a genetic algorithm to data mine in the financial services sector." In *Applications and Innovations in Expert Systems III*, edited by A. Macintosh and C. Cooper, pp. 237–252. Cambridge, England: SGES Publications.

Rayward-Smith, V. J., I. H. Osman, C. R. Reeves, and G. D. Smith, eds. 1996. *Modern Heuristic Search Methods*. Chichester, England: John Wiley and Sons.

Rich, E. and K. Knight. 1991. *Artificial Intelligence*. New York: McGraw-Hill.

Riddle, P., R. Segal, and O. Etzioni. 1994. "Representation design and brute-force induction in a Boeing manufacturing domain." *Appl. Artificial Intell.* **8**: 125–147.

46.3 Adaptive Fraud Detection

Tom E. Fawcett

ABSTRACT This article describes the development of a prototype data mining system for detecting cellular phone (cloning) fraud. In cellular cloning fraud, the identity of a legitimate cellular phone is programmed into another; from the second phone, calls can be made illicitly that are charged to the customer's account. The system for detecting such fraud is based on a framework that uses a sequence of data mining techniques. First, a rule learning program discovers general indicators of fraudulent behavior from a large database of defrauded accounts. Next, the indicators are used to create a set of monitors, which profile customer behavior and measure anomalies. Finally, the outputs of the monitors are assigned weights by a linear threshold unit. Experiments with the system indicate that this automatic approach performs better than hand-crafted methods for detecting fraud. Furthermore, the system can be retrained as necessary to accommodate changing conditions of fraud detection environments.

1. Project Overview

Cellular cloning fraud is a classic example of superimposition fraud, as discussed in Chapter 35. In cellular cloning fraud, the identity of a legitimate cellular phone is programmed into another phone. From the second phone, calls can be made illicitly that are charged to the legitimate customer's account. Cellular phone fraud causes inconvenience to customers and expense to cellular service providers.

In 1995, Foster Provost and I began studying the problem of detecting cellular cloning fraud as a domain for data mining. The initial study and subsequent prototype development were done at Bell Atlantic Science and Technology (formerly NYNEX Science and Technology), in cooperation with the Fraud Detection Department of Bell Atlantic Mobile. The project lasted approximately two years.

The project began with a feasibility study that involved familiarizing ourselves with cloning fraud, understanding the detection process, obtaining a sample of billing call data, and undertaking preliminary data analysis. The study also involved implementing an evaluation testbed and experimenting with known techniques for fraud detection.

The initial study was promising, and follow-up work led to the development of a three-step framework for automatically generating fraud detectors from call data. Within the framework, large amounts of cellular call data are analyzed in order to determine general patterns of fraud. Each pattern is then used to generate one or more monitors, which scan customers' accounts for behavior matching the pattern. A monitor measures each customer's typical behavior with respect to its pattern, and when used for new calls reports when behavior has become abnormal. Each monitor's output is provided to a neural network, which weighs the values and issues an alarm when the combined evidence for fraud is strong enough.

Experiments with field data showed that the data mining solution performed better than known strategies for detecting fraud. Furthermore, the system can be retrained as necessary to accommodate changing conditions of fraud detection environments.

2. Motivations for a Data Mining Approach

Data mining was a promising approach to this fraud detection problem for several reasons. First, a large amount of labeled historical data were available. We had reason to believe the data were reasonably clean and reliably labeled. Second, there was a clear and quantifiable business value to solving the problem: the sponsor recognized fraud detection as an important task, and key variables such as the amount of fraudulent call airtime could be measured, at least in principle. Third, because a group of human fraud analysts performed the task already, some acceptable level of performance was known to be possible.

Data mining had several advantages over more traditional systems, such as an expert system. These advantages relate to the dynamic nature of the task, mentioned in Chapter 35. Fraud perpetrators continually modify their tactics in response to new detection techniques or new hardware capabilities. Manual tuning of an expert system is possible, by adding new patterns or adjusting detection parameters, but usually involves trial and error, which may be time consuming. By the time an expert system can be manually tuned, the fraudulent behavior may have changed significantly. In addition, the amount of fraud can change considerably from month to month. Changes in staffing and in fraud levels can affect the costs of dealing with false alarms or with missed fraud. These considerations argue for an adaptive approach, which data mining can provide.

3. Conventional Techniques for Detecting Cloning Fraud

Several techniques are common for detecting cellular cloning fraud. These techniques are evaluated below, along with the detector produced in our data mining project.

One technique involves scanning accounts and checking for call collisions. A collision occurs when two calls overlap in time, which usually indicates that two different users were active simultaneously. Since only a single legitimate customer is licensed to any given phone account, a collision usually indicates cloning fraud.

A velocity check is a similar test between pairs of calls to determine whether a single user could have made both calls while traveling at reasonable speeds (Davis and Goyal, 1993). For example, if a call made in New York is followed by another call made in Boston five minutes later, the system can reasonably infer that two different users must be involved. Collisions and velocity checks are fairly accurate when they occur, but they depend on a moderate level of legitimate activity. Low-usage subscribers (for example, people who only use cellular phones in emergencies) will rarely cause collisions or velocity alarms.

Another method, dialed digit analysis, is a primitive form of data mining in which fraudulent calls are analyzed to build up a database of telephone numbers called during fraudulent episodes. Once this database is created, fraud is detected by scanning accounts and matching the called numbers against this database. An alarm is produced when a sufficient number of hits are found on an account. Various parameters of this method can be adjusted, such as the number of hits needed for an alarm or the amount of time over which the hits must be seen.

4. The KDD Process

4.1. The Data

The data used in the project were records of cellular calls taken from the carrier's billing system. Our data sample consisted of calls placed over four months by users in the New York City area. The sample comprised over 4,000 customer accounts with over two million calls.

In data mining terms, each call constituted an instance vector with a label of fraudulent or legitimate. The billing records contained many attributes from which we chose thirty-one as being potentially informative; for example, the phone number of the caller, the duration of the call, the geographical origin and destination of the call, and any long-distance carrier used. We augmented these attributes with several derived attributes that incorporated knowledge we judged to be potentially useful, such as a categorical TIME-OF-DAY variable representing the time segment of the day in which the call was placed, and a binary TO-PAYPHONE variable that was true if the call was placed to a payphone.

The cellular call data contained errors and noise from various sources. For example, at any point in time the billing records contain some fraud that has not yet been caught and marked. Such fraud would constitute noise in our data. We attempted to minimize this by delaying the data retrieval by two weeks. Some sources of noise were only discovered as a result of data mining. For example, the rule generation process, discussed below, uncovered several unusual attributes (such as CELLSITE = 0) that correlated very strongly with fraud. Investigation and discussion with the data providers revealed that in some cases the billing system would erase or replace certain fields of fraudulent calls after the fraud had been detected. Naturally these values correlated very strongly with fraud, and because they were distracting artifacts they were removed from our data sample.

4.2. Initial Experiments

An important criterion of a data mining solution was that it be fast and impose little storage overhead per account. This ruled out some approaches, such as storing a complete decision tree or neural network with each account.

Because the call data consisted of labeled instances, a straightforward approach would be to treat the problem as a classification task. This would entail applying a standard classification learning algorithm to a large sample of labeled calls, and using the resulting classifier for identifying fraudulent calls. Classification learning has been well explored, so this would be a straightforward application of existing data mining techniques.

Our attempts with such an approach performed poorly. Further analysis of the problem revealed several factors that make simple call classification approaches infeasible. First, context is important: a call that would be unusual for one customer would be typical for another. For example, a call placed from New York is not unusual for a subscriber who lives there, but might be very strange for a Boston subscriber. A data mining approach must discover changes in behavior that are indicative of fraud. Absolute indicators are insufficient when legitimate and fraudulent behavior overlap significantly among individual transactions (calls), as they do in this domain. Second, profiling of individual accounts is important for catching fraud reliably. It is necessary to determine to what extent a given fraud indicator already applies to a customer; otherwise, excessive false alarms may be produced.

We also concluded that call classification could not be done with acceptable accuracy. Our experiments led us to conclude that it is not possible to achieve simultaneously the high degree of accuracy and high level of coverage necessary to classify individual calls effectively. Instead, we chose to aggregate customer behavior into account days. This aggregation smoothes out some of the variation and allows the system to watch for coarser-grained changes that have better predictive power.

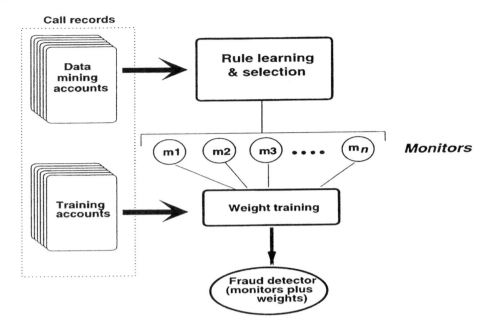

Figure 1 The DC-1 framework. (Reprinted with permission from "Adaptive Fraud Detection" by Tom Fawcett and Foster Provost, *Data Mining and Knowledge Discovery* (code DMKDFD), vol. 1, No. 3, 1997, pp. 291–316, 1997)

4.3. The DC-1 Framework

Results from our initial experiments led us to develop a more complex data mining strategy. The strategy involves finding a small set of general fraud indicators and profiling each account with respect to them. The framework we developed to do this is illustrated in Figure 1. We use the name DC-1 to refer both to this framework and to the system implemented from it. Each of the following sections describes a portion of the framework.

DATA MINING FROM DEFRAUDED ACCOUNTS

DC-1 begins by mining a large corpus of calls of defrauded accounts (denoted data mining accounts in the diagram). The goal is to derive general indicators of cloning activity. The indicators are conjunctive rules discovered by a standard rule discovery (see Chapter 16.1.4) program. DC-1 uses the RL program (Provost and Aronis, 1996) to generate indicators of fraud in the form of classification rules. RL is similar to other Meta-DENDRAL-style rule learners (Buchanan and Mitchell, 1978) and performs a general-to-specific search of the space of conjunctive rules. In DC-1, RL uses a beam search for rules with certainty factors above a user-defined threshold.

In the data mining process the call data are organized by account, with each call record labeled as fraudulent or legitimate. When RL is applied to an account's calls it produces a set of rules that serve to distinguish, within that account, the fraudulent calls from the legitimate calls. These rules may be seen as descriptions of the changes that occurred in transition from legitimate activity to fraudulent activity.

Once all accounts have been processed a rule selection step is performed, the purpose of which is to derive a set of rules that will serve as fraud indicators. Rule selection is necessary because the rule generation step typically generates tens of thousands of rules in total, most of which are specific only to single accounts. The system cannot know *a priori* how general each rule is. Rule selection identifies a small set of general rules that cover the accounts.

For each account, the list of rules generated by that account is sorted by the frequency of occurrence in the entire account set. The highest frequency unchosen rule is selected. An account is skipped if it is already sufficiently covered. The resulting set of rules is used for constructing monitors.

CONSTRUCTING MONITORS

The rule learning step produces a small set of fraud indicators. These rules are common but not universal: for a given account, we do not know to what extent that account's normal behavior already satisfies the rule.

Sensitivity to different users is accomplished by converting the rules into profiling monitors. Each monitor has a profiling step and a use step. Prior to being used on an account to detect cloning fraud, each monitor profiles the account by processing a segment of the account's typical (nonfraud) activity. Statistics from this profiling period are saved with the account. When the monitor is used, it is applied to a single account-day at a time. The monitor references the measures calculated in the profiling step and generates a numeric value describing how far above normal the current account-day is.

In the implementation, monitors describe normal activity by mean ($\bar{X}$) and standard deviation (s). For example, if a rule generated is:

$$(\text{TIME} - \text{OF} - \text{DAY} = \text{EVENING}) \rightarrow \text{FRAUD}$$

The indicator is $(\text{TIME} - \text{OF} - \text{DAY} = \text{EVENING})$, and a monitor using this would calculate the mean and standard deviation of evening calls (both the number and the amount of airtime used) of the account. When scanning the account for fraud, the monitor would calculate the amount of evening usage in an account-day and output the number of standard deviations over the mean profiled usage.

COMBINING EVIDENCE FROM THE MONITORS

The third stage of detector construction assigns weights to the monitors based on their reliability. In this stage, the outputs of the monitors are used as features to a weight training program. Training is done over a set of both defrauded and nondefrauded accounts. Monitors evaluate one entire account-day at a time. The monitors' outputs are presented along with the desired output (the account-day's correct class: fraud or nonfraud). The evidence combination weights the monitor outputs and learns a threshold on the sum.

Our implementation used a linear threshold unit (LTU; Nilsson, 1965) for this evidence combination. An LTU is a one-unit neural network (see Chapter 5.9) with no hidden layer. It is simple and fast, and enables a good first-order judgment of the features' worth.

THE FINAL DETECTOR

The final output of DC-1 is a detector that profiles each user's behavior based on several indicators, and produces an alarm if there is sufficient evidence of fraudulent activity. Figure 2 shows such a detector and how it will be used. Three monitors are shown. The first two are derived from the fraud rule:

$$(\text{FROM\_CITY} = \text{BRONX}) \text{ AND } (\text{TIME\_OF\_DAY} = \text{NIGHT}) \rightarrow \text{FRAUD}$$

The third monitor is derived from the fraud rule:

$$(\text{DAY\_OF\_WEEK} = \text{SUNDAY}) \rightarrow \text{FRAUD}$$

The monitors are given a single day's calls from an account, and each monitor generates a number indicating how unusual that account-day looks. The numeric outputs from the monitors are combined by the LTU. The LTU's output can be thresholded to generate alarms or can be used to produce a sorted list of account-days for investigation by a fraud analyst.

4.4. Evaluating Fraud Detection Performance

Devising a suitable methodology for evaluating fraud detection methods was an ongoing issue in this project. A standard metric in machine learning and data mining is classification accuracy (or equivalently, classification error), which is based on counting correct decisions.

Account-Day

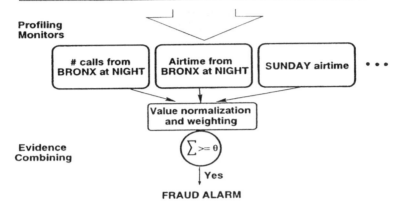

Day	Time	Duration	Origin	Destination
Tue	01:42	10 mins	Bronx, NY	Miami, FL
Tue	10:05	3 mins	Scarsdale, NY	Bayonne, NJ
Tue	11:23	24 sec	Scarsdale, NY	Congers, NY
Tue	14:53	5 mins	Tarrytown, NY	Greenwich, CT
Tue	15:06	5 mins	Manhattan, NY	Westport, CT
Tue	16:28	53 sec	Scarsdale, NY	Congers, NY
Tue	23:40	17 mins	Bronx, NY	Miami, FL

Figure 2 A DC-1 fraud detector processing a single account-day of data. (Reprinted with permission from "Adaptive Fraud Detection" by Tom Fawcett and Foster Provost, *Data Mining and Knowledge Discovery* (code DMKDFD), vol. 1, No. 3, pp. 291–316, 1997.)

Accuracy is insufficient for several reasons related to class skew and error costs (Provost et al., 1998), so a more elaborate evaluation was adopted.

In cellular cloning fraud detection, different types of errors have different costs, and a realistic evaluation should take these costs into account. A false positive error (a false alarm) corresponds to wrongly deciding that a customer has been cloned. Based on the cost of a fraud analyst's time, we estimated the cost of a false positive error to be about $5. A false negative error corresponds to letting an account-day with fraud go undetected. We estimated a false negative to cost $0.40 per minute of fraudulent airtime used on that account day. This figure is based on the proportion of usage in local and nonlocal (roaming) markets, and their corresponding costs.

We also knew that the distribution of fraud and legitimate calls are strongly skewed. (We are unable to discuss the actual amount or proportion of fraud in our data.) In this work we used a stratified sample of 80 percent legitimate and 20 percent fraudulent account days. Stratified sampling was done in both training and testing.

In our experiments we measured both classification accuracy and estimated cost, using standard accuracy equations and the cost assumptions above. In later work we developed an evaluation framework more appropriate for fraud detection and related activity monitoring domains (Fawcett and Provost, 1999).

4.5. Results and Evaluation

The DC-1 system was evaluated on field data along with other fraud detection strategies. In addition, we performed experiments to validate the contributions of individual components in the framework. Details of the experimental designs and their evaluation may be found

Table 1 Accuracies and Costs of Various Detectors

Detector	Accuracy (%)	Cost (US$)
Alarm on All	20	20,000
Alarm on None	80	18,111 ± 961
Collisions + Velocities	82 ± 0.3	17,578 ± 749
High Usage	88 ± 0.7	6,938 ± 470
State of the Art (SOTA)	90 ± 0.4	6,557 ± 541
DC-1 detector	92 ± 0.5	5,403 ± 507
SOTA plus DC-1	92 ± 0.4	5,078 ± 319

elsewhere (Fawcett and Provost, 1997); only the basic performance results will be discussed here.

Table 1 shows some of the accuracy and cost results for the methods we evaluated. All methods were evaluated ten times, with the mean and standard deviation of measurements shown in the table.

Alarm on all and alarm on none represent baseline (knowledge-free) strategies. They correspond to alarming on every account every day, and of never issuing alarms, respectively. Their performance corresponds to the prevalence and costs of the minority and majority classes.

Two strategies for detecting cellular cloning fraud, collisions and velocity checks, were mentioned above. Collisions + velocities is a single detector that performs both tests. DC-1 was used to learn a threshold on the number of collision and velocity alarms necessary to generate a fraud alarm. It was somewhat surprising that these techniques performed poorly in our experiments. Investigation of confusion matrices revealed that the collision and velocity check detectors' errors were due almost entirely to false negatives. When the detectors fired they were accurate, but many fraud days never exhibited a collision or velocity check.

Another fraud detection strategy is simply to check for sudden jumps in usage on an account. We implemented this strategy in the high usage detector. This detector is essentially a monitor that measures undifferentiated usage on an account and alarms when a threshold is exceeded. The threshold was found empirically from training data.

The SOTA (state-of-the-art) detector incorporates a large set of handcrafted methods that were the best individual detectors identified in our initial study. Each method profiles an account in a different way and produces a separate alarm. Weights for combining SOTA's alarms were determined by our weight-tuning algorithm. Details of the SOTA methods are given elsewhere (Fawcett and Provost, 1997).

The DC-1 detector incorporates all the monitors chosen by feature selection. We used the weight learning method described earlier to determine the weights for evidence combining. As the table shows, DC-1 achieved higher accuracy and lower cost than the other fraud detection methods we tested. Finally, SOTA plus DC1 is a hybrid detector incorporating the monitors of both SOTA and DC-1. The resulting detector exhibits no increase in classification accuracy, but does show a slight improvement in fraud detection cost.

5. Conclusions

We have presented a case study on the development of a data mining system for detecting cellular phone cloning fraud. Basic methods in data mining (e.g., rule learning and weight training) could not be used directly to solve this problem, so a more complex system was developed that used basic methods as components. Experiments on field data demonstrated that this method outperforms basic strategies commonly in use for detecting such fraud.

Perhaps the greatest advantage of a data mining solution is the flexibility and adaptability it offers. DC-1 can be retrained at any time as needed to accommodate changing conditions. Such adaptability can save effort in time-consuming manual feature identification and detector tuning. It can save on monetary losses that would occur during the manual identification and tuning process. It can save on less quantifiable damage done due to higher fraud levels, such as perceived network vulnerability. Finally, it can act as a preventative: a service provider that adapts quickly to new patterns of fraud can discourage new fraud from starting.

ACKNOWLEDGMENTS
This work was sponsored by Bell Atlantic. The views and conclusions in this article are those of the author and do not represent official Bell Atlantic policy. We thank Nicholas Arcuri and others in the Fraud Control Department at Bell Atlantic Mobile for many fruitful discussions on cellular fraud and its detection.

References

Buchanan, B. G. and T. M. Mitchell. 1978. "Model-directed learning of production rules." In *Pattern-Directed Inference Systems*, edited by F. Hayes-Roth, pp. 297–312. New York: Academic Press.

Davis, A. and S. Goyal. 1993. "Management of cellular fraud: knowledge-based detection, classification and prevention." In *Thirteenth International Conference on Artificial Intelligence, Expert Systems and Natural Language*. Nanterre, France: EC2, **2**: 155–164.

Fawcett, T. and F. Provost. 1997. "Adaptive fraud detection." *Data Mining and Knowledge Discovery* **1(3)**: 291–316.

Fawcett, T. and F. Provost. 1999. "Activity monitoring: noticing interesting changes in behavior." In *Proceedings on the Fifth ACM SIGKDD International Conference on Knowledge Discovery and Data Mining*, edited by S. Chaudhuri and D. Madigan, pp. 53–62. New York, NY: The Association of Computing Machinery.

Nilsson, N. J. 1965. In *Learning Machines*. New York: McGraw-Hill.

Provost, F. and J. Aronis. 1996. "Scaling up inductive learning with massive parallelism." *Machine Learning* **23**: 33–46.

Provost, F., T. Fawcett, and R. Kohavi. 1998. "The case against accuracy estimation for comparing induction algorithms." In *Proceedings of the Fifteenth International Conference on Machine Learning*, edited by J. Shavlik, pp. 445–453. San Francisco, CA: Morgan Kaufmann Publishers.

46.4 Break Detection Systems

Ted E. Senator and Henry G. Goldberg

ABSTRACT   Break detection systems are a subclass of KDD-based fraud detection applications in which the fraudulent activity is indicated by complex patterns of transactions, typically involving related entities performing multiple activities and playing several distinct roles over a time period, during which they may also be engaged in legitimate activities of the same types with the same or other entities. Break detection systems take as their input a large transaction stream and provide as their output a set of breaks, or leads, which are used to initiate follow-up investigations by trained human analysts. This article discusses two such systems: the FinCEN AI System (FAIS) and the Advanced Detection System (ADS). FAIS was developed for and is used by the U.S. Department of the Treasury's Financial Crimes Enforcement Network (FinCEN). The purpose of FAIS is to detect instances of potential money laundering from the database of reports of large cash transactions. ADS was developed for and is used by the National Association of Securities Dealers (NASD®) Regulation, Inc., the subsidiary of NASD responsible for regulation of the Nasdaq Stock Market. The purpose of ADS is to detect potential instances of violations of the rules of participation in the Nasdaq® and related stock markets subject to NASD Regulation's oversight and jurisdiction.

1. Introduction

This article discusses two similar case study applications of KDD to a subclass of fraud detection problems, which we call break detection systems (BDS). (This term is borrowed from accounting to refer to anomalies, or breaks, in the orderly stream of transactions.) BDS are a subclass of fraud detection applications in which the fraudulent activity is indicated by complex patterns of transactions, typically involving related entities performing multiple activities and playing several distinct roles over a time period, during which they may also be engaged in legitimate activities of the same types with the same or other entities (Goldberg and Senator, 1997). Break detection systems take as their input a large transaction stream and provide as their output a set of breaks, or leads, which are used to initiate follow-up investigations by trained human analysts and typically involve the addition of information from other sources. BDS are appropriately used in complex financial and regulatory environments in which the improper activity of interest is not directly represented in the database. In fact, the key goal of the discovery process is the specification of patterns that define the improper activity. These patterns are then applied to a live transaction stream to detect specific instances of potential improper activity, and the results of this detection are also used to drive additional discovery and pattern refinement.

The two systems discussed in this article are the FinCEN AI System (FAIS) and the Advanced Detection System (ADS). FAIS was developed for and is used by the U.S. Department of the Treasury's Financial Crimes Enforcement Network (further information about FinCEN is available at www.treas.gov/fincen). The purpose of FAIS is to detect instances of potential money laundering from the database of reports of large cash transactions. ADS was developed for and is used by the National Association of Securities Dealers (NASD®) Regulation, Inc., the subsidiary of NASD (Information about the NASD, NASD Regulation, Inc., and the Nasdaq Stock Market, Inc. may be found at www.nasd.com, www.nasdr.com, and www.nasdaq.com) responsible for regulation of the Nasdaq Stock Market. The purpose of ADS is to detect potential instances of violations of the rules of participation in the Nasdaq® and related stock markets subject to NASD Regulation's oversight and jurisdiction. Both systems combine detection and discovery components in an integrated application. The detection components identify specific instances of potential improper activity while the discovery components aid in the identification of patterns or types of improper activities. Detailed descriptions of FAIS and ADS are available in Senator et al. (1995) and Kirkland et al. (1999).

Figure 1 depicts the common architecture of FAIS and ADS, combining specific features from both. In Figure 1, the broad gray arrows represent process flow of data-driven break detection and user-directed special investigations. Ellipses are broad categories of processing, implemented as independent programs, corresponding to steps in the KDD process (labeled in italics), with specifics (labeled in regular fonts) drawn from the two studied systems. The central rectangular box represents the database, with multiple levels of representation as in a blackboard architecture. The hierarchy of representations, created by the data preparation, transformation, detection, analysis and investigation, and data mining steps, and stored in the database, is also shown.

Both systems begin with financial transactions. In FAIS, consolidation and linkage are the fundamental transformation operations that build higher level abstractions of entities and networks. In ADS, data preparation involves computing various aggregates and other summary attributes. ADS also merges multiple temporal data streams to identify episodes of interest. Detection consists of evidence propagation in FAIS and of temporal sequence matching and rule matching in ADS. Data mining techniques are used in both systems in conjunction with the detection engines to identify attributes, patterns, representations, and abstractions suitable for more accurate regular detection. Visualization is used in both systems to depict complex patterns of events and to enable more detailed interactive analyses.

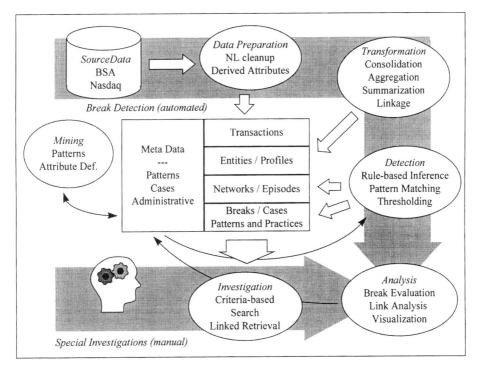

Figure 1 Common architecture of break detection systems

2. The FinCEN AI System: Detecting Potential Money Laundering from Large Cash Transaction Data

2.1. Project Overview

Money laundering is a complex process of placing the profit, usually cash, from illicit activity into the legitimate financial system, with the intent of obscuring the source, ownership, or use of the funds. Money laundering typically involves a multitude of transactions, perhaps by different individuals, into multiple accounts with different owners at different banks or other financial institutions. FAIS links and evaluates cash transaction reports for indications of suspicious activity characteristic of money laundering, with the objective of identifying previously unknown, potential high value leads for follow-up investigation and, if warranted, prosecution.

FAIS operates in two modes: data driven and user directed. The data-driven operation is the regular, scheduled, break detection process of loading, linking, and evaluating new information as it is received. Users regularly review and analyze the end product of the data-driven operation, which is a list of subjects (persons or businesses) sorted by suspiciousness scores. Most of the operational load on the system is the data-driven processing of all transactions. Because data-driven functions operate on all information received by the system, the complexity of the processing is limited by available computing resources. User-directed analysis is *ad hoc*, initiated in response to a specific project or investigation, and based on criteria determined by intelligence leads or investigative priorities. It operates on selected information that is already determined to be of interest, so more complex analyses are possible. After initial subjects and their underlying transactions are identified from either mode, FAIS analysts may iteratively follow a trail of linked subjects, accounts, or transactions using query, evaluation, and visualization tools. The identification of subjects from the transaction information in the database is referred to as consolidation, while the linking together of related subjects, transactions, and accounts into networks of interest is called link analysis. (This use of the term *link analysis* is consistent with law enforcement. Some in the KDD community have (mis)applied the term to graphical causality networks or association rule techniques.) Consolidation is performed as part of data preparation; link analysis is performed by the users. The NetMap (`www.altaanalytics.com`) link analysis tool is used for visualization.

FAIS was developed by a team of about seven FinCEN software engineers with a background in artificial intelligence techniques, supplemented by a group of dedicated experts who were also the primary users. FAIS development began in 1991 and the system was initially deployed in 1993; it has been continually enhanced.

2.2. KDD Process

To combat money laundering, the Bank Secrecy Act (BSA; 12 U.S.C. Sections 1730d, 1829b, 1951–1959, and 31 U.S.C. Sections 5311–5326) requires reporting of cash transactions in excess of $10,000. FAIS receives about 12 million of these transactions per year. About 90 percent are CTRs (Currency Transaction Reports) filed by financial institutions such as banks or credit unions. Casino CTRs and CMIRs (which report transfers of cash across the border) comprise the remainder. The data reported on the forms are subject to errors (e.g., amount of transaction on CMIR reported in foreign instead of U.S. currency), uncertainties (e.g., occupation/business type), and inconsistencies that affect both identification and transaction information, especially in free-text fields.

FAIS initially cleans and restructures the transaction data in a straightforward process of interpretation based on *a priori* knowledge. Since the key entities, subjects (people and organizations), and accounts are sometimes referred to in the transactions ambiguously or with errors, a process of knowledge-based disambiguation, using heuristics such as phonetic name matching and the relative value of various common ID numbers, matches new transactions with prior ones that refer to the same entities. Subject and account records are thus created or updated on a continuing basis. The resulting structures are called clusters and serve to associate sets of transactions referring to each entity. The set of identifiers encountered, as well as frequencies of occurrence, is retained for future matches and serves to summarize the entity. Aggregate attributes (e.g., monthly dollar amounts, maximum transactions, etc.) are computed for the set of transactions. As a practical matter, the disambiguation process is tuned to be very conservative, since it is easier to aggregate further, if needed, than to split clusters that mistakenly combine separate entities.

This process of disambiguation and cluster formation, called consolidation, transforms the database from a purely transactional representation to a form that can support direct link analysis via efficient database operations (Goldberg and Senator, 1995). The linkage of subject and account clusters to the individual transactions, and to each other through these transactions, forms the basis for all further link analysis.

Clusters are evaluated for suspiciousness by an inference network of rules based on domain knowledge of money laundering methods and techniques. This knowledge is based upon law enforcement experience as well as statistical analysis of cash transactions. Knowledge acquisition sessions with investigators originally resulted in rules such as: "Frequent young travelers importing large amounts of cash are likely to be couriers for illicit organizations." Additional rules employing thresholds to detect suspicious amounts of money or numbers of accounts were based on analysis of statistical outliers in the transaction data. A strong motivation for identifying and extracting clusters and networks that accurately represent subject, accounts, and organizations was to provide input for data mining to improve these analyses.

Challenges to data mining include large transaction volume, inability to sample (because sampling interacts with consolidation and link analysis by inhibiting the formation of clusters of interest), and lack of high quality labeled training data. Case-based reasoning techniques and tools were examined during the development process and found to be lacking due to their reliance on a flat feature vector and concerns with scalability. Recognizing money laundering requires detection of specific relationships between entities, as well as recognition of certain signature characteristics of the network as a whole. These are lost when the network is

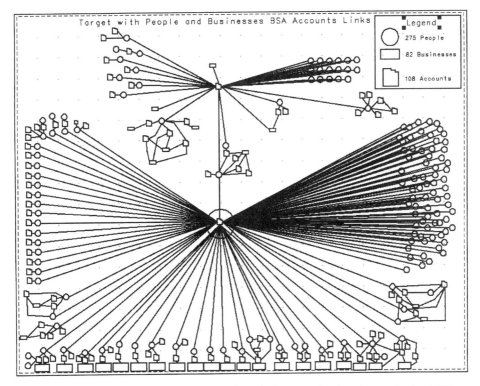

Figure 2 Final presentation of a money laundering organization detected using FAIS

parameterized into a flat feature vector. An example of a detected money laundering network is shown in Figure 2. (Note the critical role of the circled node at the center as a transfer account between two parts of the organization.)

Link analysis plays a critical role in FAIS, in both network acquisition and analysis. The initial consolidation and linkage of transactions forms the basis for rule-based subject evaluation. In addition, detailed analyses by human investigators can greatly enhance the final product. Link analysis enables the analysts to discover relationships, identify key actors and roles in an organization, and understand the structure of the enterprise under investigation. For a more detailed discussion of the role of link analysis in FAIS, see Goldberg and Wong (1998).

In addition to thousands of case reports on individual subjects involved in money laundering—and resultant investigations and prosecutions—FAIS has allowed FinCEN's analysts to identify new methods of money laundering as well as new business and geographic areas for surveillance.

3. The Advanced Detection System: Detecting Potential Regulatory Violations in the Nasdaq Stock Market

3.1. Project Overview

ADS monitors trades and quotations in the Nasdaq® stock market to identify patterns and practices of behavior of potential regulatory interest. (ADS monitors both tiers of the Nasdaq Stock Market, the national market and small cap, as well as the over-the-counter market and the third market). ADS has been in operational use since the summer of 1997 by several groups of analysts. It has grown from supporting one regulatory domain and analyst group to supporting four sharing the same base market data, and it is being extended to several more. It has also grown in data volume from approximately 2 million transactions of all types per day, including approximately 800,000 trades, to the current volume of up to 2.7 million trades per day. Current ADS domains are:

- *Late trade reporting.* Identifies potential trade reporting violations.
- *Market integrity.* Identifies potential instances of coordination between or harassment by market makers.
- *Best execution.* Identifies possible violations of obligation of market makers to provide best price available to a customer given prevailing market conditions.
- *ECN.* Identifies potential misuse of electronic communications networks.

ADS was developed by a team of up to twenty-two NASD employees and contractor personnel from SRA International, Inc. between 1996 and 1998, was placed in production in mid-1997, and is being continually enhanced. (SRA has taken the custom application developed for NASD and converted it into a generic KDD toolkit that meets ADS requirements and can be applied to other application domains. Details of this product are available at www.knowledgediscovery.com/.) ADS makes use of a variety of KDD techniques, including data cleansing, preparation, and transformation, visualization, pattern recognition, data mining, and knowledge management, in support of the activities of regulatory analysis, alert and pattern detection, and knowledge discovery. ADS relies upon two pattern matching techniques for break detection based on rules and temporal sequences of events and includes components for decision tree and association rule methods for data mining. ADS also includes software tools for managing the break workflow, for managing the knowledge discovered by and contained in the system, and for system administration.

ADS is built around a data warehouse containing trades, quotes, orders, associated source and derived attributes, and summary and profile information about issues and firms. Application programs update the warehouse on a daily and weekly basis, and detect breaks using two pattern matches, one of which matches patterns expressed as rules and the other of which matches patterns expressed as time sequences of events. Data mining components include parallel and scaleable decision-tree and association-rule implementations; visualization components include a series of custom-tailored two-dimensional displays, three-dimensional landscapes based on a commercial product, and pseudonatural language and graphical displays of rules discovered by the data mining components. ADS explicitly stores its knowledge as patterns in the database. A complete audit trail of the knowledge—resulting from automated mining, manual crafting, or a combination—that is discovered, validated, and used is maintained as part of ADS.

3.2. KDD Process

ADS' goals were (1) to provide effective, efficient, and comprehensive monitoring of trades and quotations for detection of instances of potential violations of market rules, (2) to support analytical investigations of these instances, (3) to identify patterns and practices of potentially violative behavior, (4) to track the status and disposition of all potential violations, (5) to enable the effective and rapid discovery of unknown behaviors of potential regulatory interest, (6) to support analyses of suspected new behaviors, and (7) to adapt flexibly to new behaviors of interest and to new market structures and rules, for all markets subject to NASD Regulation's jurisdiction. Trade-offs in the KDD process, techniques, and application design for ADS directly support these goals.

Monitoring the daily transaction stream is the primary operational function of ADS. To keep pace with the (ever-increasing) transaction volume, performance is a key consideration in the design of ADS. Only one detection pass over the data stream occurs in regular operations. This necessitates implementation of some computations in the data preparation step, even when greater flexibility might be achieved by leaving the computation to the pattern matching. It has also resulted in the implementation of a replicated database instance, which is used by KDD analysts for discovery of new types of behavior, research into suspected behaviors, and evaluation of new and modified patterns, thus mitigating the effects of KDD analyses on the operational database. A distinct break mart that would replicate the most recent data for detection to improve performance for subsequent investigative analyses is currently under development.

Available data mining tools and techniques have proved limited when applied in ADS due to data volumes and the inability to represent the structure and complexity of the relevant violations. Most violations consist of temporal sequences from multiple data streams (i.e., trades, quotes, insides, and, more recently, orders). Labeled examples of violative activity are rare, making supervised classification techniques ineffective. Sampling of data prior to detection cannot occur because the linkages between transactions are not yet known at this stage in the process. Sampling of individual transactions would result in the reduction of frequency of detected combined regulatory events in inverse proportion to the combined sampling rates. For example, detection of an event consisting of a particular trade followed by a particular quote, with a prior individual sampling rate of 10 percent, would be reduced by a factor of 100. The situation gets worse for more complex events with a greater number of components. We also cannot use sampling because of the regulatory requirement for comprehensive surveillance. Statistical models based on logistic and linear regressions employed in previous systems have been less effective because of highly nonnormal distributions, because of an inability to identify complex structural patterns in the data, and because of the importance of context to distinguish regular market operations from improper behaviors. Decision tree (see Quinlan, 1993) and association rule (see Agrawal et al., 1993) techniques were employed to identify conditions associated with late trade reports early in the project. They yielded far too many rules that were specific to individual firms and were difficult to interpret; however, some rules were generalized manually and others through an automated rule-generalization module, and led to the rule patterns currently in use. Discovery has been primarily accomplished by systematic exploration of the problem space through iterative manual application of the pattern recognition tools under the guidance of domain experts. Background knowledge of the regulatory staff is translated into proposed patterns that correspond to the suspected signatures in the data of scenarios of regulatory interest; these patterns are iteratively evaluated and tuned until they can distinguish potential violations from normal market activity. An unanticipated operational issue has been that discovered knowledge corresponding to previously unknown scenarios may not fit into existing organizational structures, business processes, and investigative protocols, requiring management actions to adapt to the new discoveries. Discovered knowledge is represented and stored explicitly in the database, enabling group access, organizational review, detailed evaluations, and thorough auditing.

Two key components of ADS are rule and sequence pattern matching. A rule pattern identifies an aggregate of violations (e.g., high incidence, on either an absolute or peer-group relative basis, of late trade reports or trades away from the prevailing market price) in a specified time period for a particular firm, and sometimes also in a particular issue. In ADS, the set of rules is applied to the entire market data stream, with variables bound to firm and/or issue. The volume of data matched offers a significant challenge to typical pattern matching algorithms, and special components were designed to use DBMS technology most efficiently to perform the match. The resulting matches are automatically grouped into patterns of similar violations and tested against thresholds for support (rule coverage) and confidence (rule accuracy).

More complex regulatory scenarios in ADS are detected by a specially designed component, which was developed at SRA, drawing upon work in discovery of temporal associations (see Mannila, 1995). Sequences of temporally related data events are described in a sequence description language and are matched by an efficient algorithm that performs a breadth-first search for all matches, either forward or backward in time. (Some sequence patterns cannot be implemented by a one-directional search in time; a bi-directional search capability is being added. These bi-directional patterns would begin with the location of a rare event in the data stream in one temporal direction, either followed or preceded by other events that substantiate the violation.) A major challenge has been to run many patterns against the entire market on an ongoing basis. ADS currently applies about sixty such patterns to cover

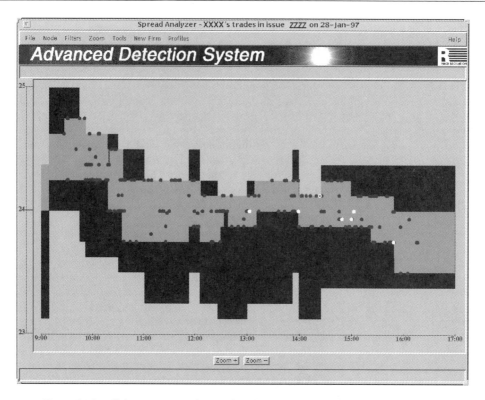

Figure 3 Visualizing quotes, trades, and market insides within ADS

the market in four different regulatory domains. Sequence matching is also an effective way to perform fuzzy temporal joins between, for example, trades and quotes. Example sequences might include large customer trades followed by market movement and preceded by a series of proprietary trades on the same side of the market or drying up of trades to a particular market maker after he ignores common quoting behavior.

Precomputing derived attributes and using the full range of features of the Oracle database engine, such as partitioning and bitmap indexes, is essential to provide the required performance.

Visual discovery techniques are employed extensively in ADS. Several custom displays allow analysts to visualize key market relationships, such as the trading and quotation view of a particular stock from the perspective of an individual market maker during a time period up to a full trading day, or the share flows between all market participants in an individual stock. An example of the most useful and used display, the market spread timeline, is shown in Figure 3. This display depicts all events that contribute to the potential violation in the context of market activity and allows an analyst to evaluate rapidly the validity of the detected instance.

ADS also includes graphical tools for users to introduce new patterns into the break detection and to modify existing patterns. The rule editor/evaluator runs tests immediately on a user specified data set. Thus, a user can take a break from the system, modify the rule constraints, and observe the outcome on the spot.

ADS has resulted in an increase by a factor of three over previous systems in terms of its hit rate of breaks that result in follow-up actions of various types. Knowledge and system maintenance is ongoing as changes occur in the market and as new domains are added. One full-time professional maintains each domain, tuning and developing new patterns corresponding to new scenarios and modifying patterns to take into account changes in data structures and volumes and changes in market behaviors. Knowledge maintenance is enabled by processes and tools. Weekly meetings are held with key users in each domain area to review current breaks and pattern performance. At these meetings, new scenarios are discussed and prototype patterns are evaluated for inclusion in the system. Tuning of operational parameters is done at these reviews. As break quality improves, thresholds can be adjusted to allow more marginal breaks, as well as allowing new patterns to be detected. As a final check on validity, new patterns are introduced into production with Experimental status until they are validated on the operational data stream. Detected breaks must be closed and reasons assigned, both for regulatory accountability and for pattern evaluation and modification. A Knowledge Management Board provides coordination between domains, senior management review of the discovered knowledge, and evaluates and acts on newly discovered knowledge.

The effectiveness of ADS can be measured by the traditional technique of type I and type II errors; however, this method depends highly on the distribution of improper behaviors and does not accurately reflect the regulatory value. We have developed an evaluation metric that counts the number of regulatory operations (ROPS) performed by the system. This method measures the depth and breath of our surveillance coverage. It scales with market activity and with pattern complexity and is independent of the distribution of violations. ADS has grown from about 600 million ROPS in July 1997 to 1.1 billion in July 1998 and almost 3.5 billion in July 1999. We have also tracked the number of potential violations identified by ADS in each domain; the typical experience is an initial increase (as our detection becomes more accurate) followed by a later significant decrease below the initial level (as firms react to regulatory actions).

ADS has resulted in more effective and efficient market surveillance as well as changes in market participant behavior. Analyst staffing has not had to grow as fast as market volumes, due to surveillance efficiency provided by ADS. Investigations resulting from ADS alerts have resulted in specific enforcement actions. (See www.nasdr.com for a list of all NASD Regulation enforcement actions, including those resulting from ADS.) Provision of statistics to firms on both an absolute and peer-group relative basis have resulted in reductions in improper behavior. Even negative results have proven useful in demonstrating the reduction of certain kinds of previously existing or suspected improper behaviors, and the cost of modifying NASD Regulation systems in response to the rapidly changing securities trading industry has been reduced.

4. Common Principles and Techniques

Break detection systems generate leads for further investigation from large volumes of data. This data is almost always received as a series of transactions, with much background information (e.g., lists and characteristics of transactors) not explicitly available. It is assumed that the result of such lead generation is analyzed by a highly-trained investigator; thus break detection systems are not intended for automated investigations or for untrained users. However, automated techniques can be highly effective in supporting these analyses.

Three factors must be present for successful break detection:

1. *Regulatory authority.* What is the legal or regulatory authority that is violated? The clearer the violation of a regulatory rule or policy, the easier it is to define and detect breaks. Where a simple violation can be detected directly in the input data (e.g., late reporting of securities trades), straightforward data mining and pattern recognition techniques are effective. Where more complex and subjective interpretations apply, the system may be able only to detect indicators of potential violations.

2. *Business processes.* How do the users follow up on breaks that are generated? Break detection is often applied in complex, dynamic environments, where lack of labeled data for training or an underlying domain theory impedes knowledge maintenance. Where there is direct feedback of results from breaks and analyses, the knowledge in the system can be rapidly adjusted to track these changes and to improve accuracy. Where the

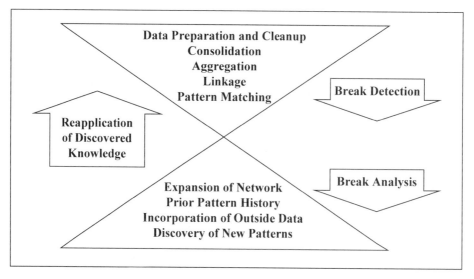

Figure 4 Refinement and expansion of relevant data during break detection and analysis

results of the system pass through many hands and take months or years to ultimately result in regulatory or law enforcement action, alternative metrics must be employed to provide this feedback.

3. *Technical feasibility.* The volume and quality of data, the complexity of patterns that are to be detected or discovered, and the requirements of regulatory coverage and throughput all have a serious impact on performance and ultimately on the feasibility of a break detection system. Techniques must be scaleable to the performance needs of the particular system. However, multistage break detection and analysis can provide a means of reducing the load, as well as provide levels of representation against which data mining can provide useful information.

4.1. A Multistage Process for Detection and Analysis

Break detection is part of a multistage process (see Figure 4) for fraud detection where information in the database is filtered down to a manageable size, using background knowledge. Each stage in the process may be viewed as a transformation to a more efficient representation where the volume of data subject to analysis is reduced.

Once breaks are detected, the resultant leads are investigated by bringing in information from external sources to increase or decrease their suspiciousness. This expansion in the analysis phase is enabled by the same abstractions that support the reduction: consolidation, linkages, pattern detection, and discovery.

Just as data preparation and transformation processes produce a representation in which breaks can be effectively detected, break detection itself produces a representation in which patterns and practices of regulatory or law enforcement interest can be detected. In that representation further analysis can proceed with sufficient speed and effectiveness to allow human involvement.

4.2. Break Evaluation and the Relationship between Break Detection and Discovery

Break detection systems can rank entities of interest with respect to particular time periods (as in FAIS), relying on a score threshold to distinguish breaks from nonbreak entities, or they can generate breaks based on a combined set of conditions (as in ADS). The latter approach is more direct; however, it is less robust, and it makes it harder to ask what-if questions, to combine information about an entity across break types, and to tune the risk-workload trade-off. Since a key trade-off in break detection systems is risk-workload, or false negatives versus false positives, one is tempted to tune detection for high-quality breaks (low false positives; the lift above random choice of subjects for investigation that break detection provides is one measure of the immediate payoff of the system). Provost and Fawcett (1997) introduce a new method of evaluation suitable for BDS.

Another payoff is surveillance coverage. Using break detection, an entire population of transactions can be filtered through the initial phase of regulatory analysis. Moreover, in dynamic and complex domains, break detection may be tuned to allow greater false positives, if doing so also allows detection of previously unrecognized patterns. Detection and discovery may be seen as two sides of the same coin, with detection forming the representation within which discovery can be effective. This is particularly true in situations where violations occur superimposed on normal activity and are not outliers in the statistical sense. Fully automated discovery requires the right abstractions and can only extend what is already known regarding types of violations. This combination of manually designed and tuned break detection patterns and data mining on the results is a way to utilize complex domain knowledge in the discovery process.

ACKNOWLEDGMENTS

The authors would like to thank all of their colleagues at both FinCEN and NASD who contributed to the development of FAIS and ADS. We would especially like to acknowledge the key roles played by James D. Kirkland in developing many of the concepts discussed in this article and of SRA International, Inc. in designing and developing the underlying ADS software. The authors of this paper are employees of the National Association of Securities Dealers (NASD) Regulation, Inc. and were previously employees of the Financial Crimes Enforcement Network of the U.S. Department of the Treasury. The views expressed herein are solely those of the authors and do not represent an official policy statement of NASD Regulation, Inc., the U.S. Treasury Department, or the U.S. Government.

References

Agrawal, R., T. Imielinski, and A. Swami. 1993. "Mining association rules between sets of items in large databases." In *Proceedings of the ACM SIGMOD Conference on Management of Data*, pp. 207–216. New York, NY: ACM Press.

Goldberg, H. G. and T. E. Senator. 1995. "Restructuring databases for knowledge discovery by consolidation and link analysis." In *Proceedings of the First International Conference on Knowledge Discovery and Data Mining (KDD-95)*, pp. 136–141. Menlo Park, CA: AAAI Press.

Goldberg, H. G. and T. E. Senator. 1997. "Break detection systems." In *AI Approaches to Fraud Detection and Risk Management: Collected Papers from the 1997 Workshop* Technical Report WS-97-07. Menlo Park, CA: AAAI Press.

Goldberg, H. G. and R. W. H. Wong. 1998. "Restructuring transactional data for link analysis in the FinCEN AI system." In *Papers from the 1998 Fall Symposium on Artificial Intelligence and Link Analysis October 23–25, Orlando, Florida*, pp. 38–46 Technical Report FS-98-0. Menlo Park, CA: AAAI Press.

Kirkland, J. D., T. E. Senator, J. J. Hayden, T. Dybala, H. G. Goldberg, and P. Shyr 1999. "The NASD Regulation Advanced Detection System (ADS)." *AI Magazine* **20(1)**: 55–67.

Mannila, H., H. Toivonen, and A. Verkamo. 1995. "Discovering frequent episodes in sequences." In *Proceedings of the First International Conference on Knowledge Discovery and Data Mining (KDD-95)*, pp. 210–215. Menlo Park, CA: AAAI Press.

Provost, F. and T. Fawcett. 1997. "Analysis and visualization of classifier performance with nonuniform class and cost distributions." In *AI Approaches to Fraud Detection and Risk Management: Collected Papers from the 1997 Workshop* Technical Report WS-97-07. Menlo Park, CA: AAAI Press.

Quinlan, J. R. 1993. *C4.5 Programs for Machine Learning*. San Mateo, CA: Morgan Kaufman.

Senator, T. E., H. G. Goldberg, J. Wooton, M. A. Cottini, A. F. Umar Khan, C. D. Klinger, W. M. Llamas, M. P. Marrone, and R. W. H. Wong. 1995. "The FinCEN Artificial Intelligence System (FAIS): identifying potential money laundering from reports of large cash transactions." *AI Magazine* **16(4)**: 21–39.

46.5 Using Decision Tree Induction to Minimize Process Delays in the Printing Industry

Robert B. Evans and Douglas Fisher

ABSTRACT Rotogravure printing involves rotating a chrome-plated, engraved copper cylinder in a bath of ink, scraping off the excess ink, and pressing a continuous supply of paper against the engraved cylinder with a rubber roller, thus transferring ink from the engraved image of the cylinder to the paper. The printing process is subject to many types of delays, one of which is cylinder banding. During the course of printing, grooves may become engraved into a cylinder surface. These grooves cause streaks or bands to be printed on the paper, thus ruining the final product. This article describes the application of decision tree induction to identify the conditions under which banding did and did not occur at the Gallatin, Tennessee plant of R. R. Donnelley and Sons. Once found, discovered rules were used to bias printing press parameters toward conditions identified as favorable. This approach has been primarily responsible for reducing bands from 538 in 1989 to 26 in 1998. This article describes the technical and social issues addressed in the banding application.

1. Process Delay Analysis Using Classification

In 1989 only weak human expertise existed regarding cylinder banding. Engineers had good ideas about the attributes relevant to banding, but their knowledge of attribute interactions was not sufficient to reliably predict, and thus guard against, banding incidents. A data mining tool was used to identify conditions under which banding was likely. In our case, each datum was a snapshot of press and environmental conditions that were true when a band occurred or that were true when one was reasonably sure that a band was not imminent. This latter case was not as clearcut as the former. In particular, print orders vary a great deal. Perhaps jobs with small print orders did not experience cylinder bands, but would if the cylinders continued to run. Fortunately, we found that nearly 90 percent of the cylinder bands occurred well before one million copies were printed. To assign a class to a job, we used the following labeling rule. If a cylinder banded at any point, then we took a snapshot of the system and labeled it as Banded. If a print order was greater than one million copies and it ran to completion without a band, a snapshot of the final system was taken and labeled as notBanded. Cylinders that ran to completion in less than one million copies without a band were excluded as indeterminate (see Chapter 14.1).

Approximately thirty attributes described a system snapshot (i.e., tuple). Each attribute represents a characteristic of a particular printing unit (e.g., ink temperature), cylinder (e.g., chrome solution ratio), printing press (e.g., press speed), paper (e.g., paper type), or more general environmental factors (e.g., humidity).

We used top-down induction of decision trees (TDIDT; Quinlan, 1991) to uncover diagnostic rules for cylinder banding (see Chapter 16.1.4). The final product of induction is a decision tree like the one illustrated in Figure 1, which was constructed over a sample of 177 tuples, 98 of which were labeled notBanded and 79 of which were labeled Banded. Experts can use this tree to predict the likelihood of banding on subsequent tuples.

For example, if the chrome solution ratio is high, ink temperature is low, and viscosity of the ink is high, then banding appears unlikely. In conjunction, these three conditions constitute a favorable condition for printing. In contrast, if a cylinder was plated using a chrome solution ratio that is very low, it appears that banding is very likely.

Since many of the measured attributes are continuously valued, our TDIDT variation partitions the numeric attributes so that the resulting finite, discrete values best discriminate the possible outcomes (see Chapter 14.4). The strategy that we developed is a greedy, local (i.e., intervals developed for each decision tree node), n-interval ($2 \leqslant n \leqslant 5$) divisive strategy. For

CHROME SOLUTION RATIO
  = VeryLow (then 0 NotBanded, 9 Banded)
  = Low
    and HUMIDITY
        = Low (then 14 NotBanded, 21 Banded)
        = Neutral (then 7 NotBanded, 4 Banded)
        = High (then 23 NotBanded, 15 Banded)
  = Neutral (then 0 NotBanded, 2 Banded)
  = High
    and INK TEMPERATURE
        = Low
          and VISCOSITY
              = Low (then 6 NotBanded, 5 Banded)
              = Neutral (then 8 NotBanded, 2 Banded)
              = High (then 18 NotBanded, 1 Banded)
        = Neutral (5 NotBanded, 2 Banded)
        = High (17 NotBanded, 18 Banded)

Figure 1 A sample decision tree

purposes of illustration, we have used symbolic labels (e.g., very low, low, neutral, high) in place of discovered ranges in the tree of Figure 1.

2. Interactive Data Mining Using APOS

A TDIDT algorithm called APOS—an acronym for a posterior and a trademark of R. R. Donnelley and Sons—(Evans and Fisher, 1994) was one of three participants in the interactive induction process (Buntine and Sterling, 1990). An analyst, Bob Evans, acted as an interface between TDIDT and an expert on press operations, though Evans, who has more than thirty-five years experience in the printing industry, sometimes played the dual role of analyst and expert.

In our setting, experts did not possess strong knowledge of banding causes, but were able to supply relevant attributes and offer hypotheses about why APOS indicated that certain attribute interactions (i.e., paths in the decision tree) resulted in high incidents of banding or not. The interaction between machine, expert, and analyst is an iterative process where the expert and analyst reflect on machine-induced rules. The expert's background knowledge may expedite induction under sparse data conditions by discounting attributes that would be discounted anyway given more data. This philosophy of using weak knowledge to filter inductive processing also lies behind work by Clark and Matwin (1993). If this strategy is followed naively, however, it may exclude the discovery of novel findings that violate expert expectations.

In general, interactive induction is part of a repertoire of tools for eliciting knowledge from experts, which follows in the tradition of other machine learning approaches to expert system construction (Michalski and Chilausky, 1980; Bareiss et al., 1989). Induction over data enumerates rules that appear consistent with class labelings. The expert can often explain inductively-acquired rules, even if the rules were not known to the expert to begin with. In a system/analyst/expert partnership, the system greatly augments the processing and memory capacity of the expert, promoting an evolving conception of the problem in the expert's mind.

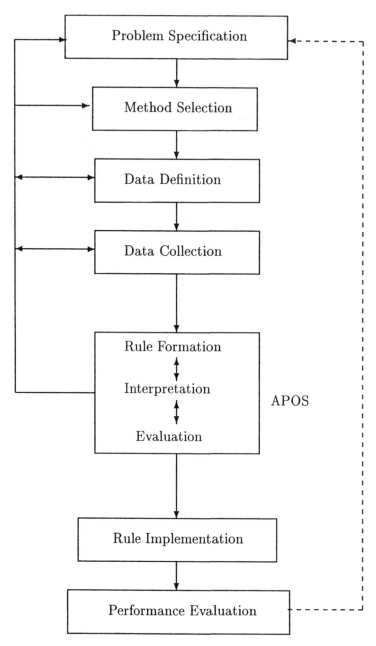

Figure 2 An industrial process improvement model

3. Experiences and Results in Banding Analysis

We have described the methods that we chose to address many of our technological concerns in banding analysis, but our experience also suggests that social and cost issues all play a role in the effective acquisition and implementation of knowledge in an industrial setting. Based on our experience, we posit the general iterative model of Figure 2 as a guide to knowledge acquisition in an industrial setting.

The model suggests that there are many opportunities for feedback and revision of past decisions, but we have distinguished rule implementation and performance evaluation as falling outside the main interactive loop. By this, we stress that analysts and experts must take great care before implementing recommendations that stem from data mining into actual operations.

3.1. Problem Specification

Donnelley management initially had the modest goal of mitigating banding, as opposed to eliminating it completely, though of course the latter would be a desirable outcome. This implied that a deterministic model of banding need not be constructed. Rather, a statistically-reliable model would suffice. An inductive approach was chosen for this reason.

3.2. Method Selection

There are many forms of inductive reasoning. We initially chose decision tree induction because managers and craftsmen were familiar with decision trees. Moreover, the process of attribute selection in decision tree construction was accessible to industry users. In contrast, neural network and statistical models (see Chapters 16.1.8 and 16.1.7 of this handbook; Weiss and Kulikowski, 1991) may be understood by those trained in their proper use, but they may be less accessible to a wider population of professionals.

In addition, an observational study of existing press operations was chosen over controlled, intervention studies (e.g., factorial design), because of weak human expertise concerning banding, and because of the very stringent time constraints on plant operations, which discourages interventions. Had our observational study failed to yield satisfactory results, then controlled experiments may have been appropriate, though the results of the observational study undoubtedly would have informed the design of controlled experiments in any case.

3.3. Data Definition and Engineering

The analyst and experts defined the attributes and class labels, which was not a trivial process. For example, some analysis of initial data produced the class labeling (and data exclusion) rules described earlier. Furthermore, the initial set of attributes was not the final set. Printing engineers initially identified several attributes as relevant only to discard them later based on TDIDT output. For example, the initial set included a subjective attribute called chrome condition with values clear and cloudy. No rules were found using this attribute because the attribute's value could not be reliably determined, and experts eventually dropped the attribute from the data definition.

None the less, in many domains, inductive methods are good at identifying irrelevant attributes, but no inductive method can identify new primitive attributes. Under ideal conditions, it is safer to err by initially generating a liberal superset of the suspected relevant attributes.

3.4. Data Collection

Superficially, data collection may seem trivial, but together with data engineering it constituted the primary bottleneck for interactive induction in our setting. In the banding application, data collection was largely a manual process of completing data collection forms. Unfortunately, craftsmen faced time constraints that did not always allow accurate and complete data collection. The analyst acknowledged these difficulties, and stressed that when faced with conflicts, it is better for data to be incomplete (i.e., some attribute values not recorded) than to record data that was incorrect or even arbitrary.

Data collection may also introduce time conflicts that impact data definition. Although we noted under data definition and engineering that a large set of measurable attributes is desirable under ideal circumstances, measuring too many attributes requires too much time, thus motivating a judicious reduction in the number of attributes being measured. Similarly, we could have also recorded dynamic conditions, such as the change in ink viscosity over time, which may provide useful information. However, such dynamic conditions would have increased the cost of data collection considerably, and they turned out not to be necessary in our application.

Effective induction discriminates conditions that lead to differing outcomes; this requires that data be collected on examples of all the possible outcomes—Banded and notBanded. However, the common wisdom in our setting, and we suspect others, is that examples need only be collected when problems such as banding occur. In part, this tendency undoubtedly stems from the way that the problem is defined—to mitigate or eliminate banding—in which the stress is placed on the undesirable outcome. We revised the problem statement to that of increasing the occurrence of desirable outcomes (i.e., notBanded), which helped motivate craftsmen to collect notBanded data, as well as Banded data.

3.5. Rule Formation, Interpretation, and Evaluation

In an interactive induction setting the tasks of forming, interpreting, and evaluating rules are tightly coupled. Experts compensate for system brittleness in the face of sparse or biased data. In many cases, the expert may reject the system's principle recommendation. For example, in one session APOS recommended that the data be broken up by press (e.g., with identifiers TR802, TR813) since bands seemed to occur more frequently on some presses over others. This line of reasoning may have led to some insights, but the expert preferred an alternative attribute that he felt would produce results more generally applicable to the printing process. Experts also have the option of formalizing their prior biases on attribute informativeness in the form of a heuristics table, which includes entries such as a high value for attribute X is associated with banding. If APOS discovers a rule that seems to contradict a table entry (e.g., high values of attribute X seem associated with no banding), then the user is informed, but this flag does not limit a user's choice of attribute. In general, a user's actions are limited to choosing an attribute for path expansion, or to cease path expansion.

The analyst and the expert must further evaluate the final rule set. The tree of Figure 1 reveals one rule that isolates banding incidents (i.e., chrome solution ratio very low) and one rule strongly suggests no banding (i.e., chrome solution ratio high, ink temperature low, and viscosity high). Other rules (i.e., paths) stemming from the tree are ambiguous as to the outcome. In fact, the large number of ambiguous paths suggests that a system such as Brute (Riddle et al., 1994), which learns decision rules directly, rather than as paths in a decision tree, may be a better basis for interactive induction in a setting like ours. The decision tree learner produced many rules of no interest, because the learner was constrained to forming a tree.

Single applications of decision tree induction uncovered few rules to reliably control cylinder banding. Fortunately, few rules are needed in a setting like ours, since craftsmen can control many attributes, thus effectively biasing the environment in response to even a few discovered rules. In general, our purpose was to discover a modest number of decision tree paths that suggested prescriptions for environmental change, rather than discovering trees that fully described the environment. In practice, several experts applied APOS many times and collected approximately fifteen rules from all of the sessions.

3.6. Rule Implementation

Discovered rules must be implemented. In the case of cylinder banding, press operators should control attributes (e.g., ink temperature) toward values leading to favorable outcomes (i.e., notBanded) and/or away from values leading to undesirable outcomes (i.e., Banded). Induction results in rules of theoretical merit (i.e., following their recommendations will mitigate banding), but experts had to evaluate rules by pragmatic considerations such as cost-effectiveness and social acceptance. Several rules were discarded on pragmatic grounds, reducing the rule set from approximately fifteen to twelve.

For example, some rules suggested that humidifying the plant would mitigate banding, but management discarded this recommendation on an expense basis. In effect, management designated humidity an uncontrollable parameter. Nonetheless, it still may be useful to have such attributes included in rules, because they define differing contexts under which differing actions are in order. In other situations, a rule may indicate an attribute that can be controlled, but to do so would have undesirable side effects. The experts discarded at least one option found to mitigate cylinder banding on the basis of its potential negative impact on print quality along dimensions unrelated to banding.

There are also social issues to be considered. In particular, a table of rules of the form

chrome solution ratio is high, and

ink temperature is low, and

viscosity is high

IMPLIES the cylinder will be notBanded.

present several difficulties. First, individual craftsmen generally control only some of the attributes that participate in a rule. A plater controls the chrome solution, whereas a pressman controls ink temperature and viscosity. Rules that conjoin attributes across several areas of responsibility may, at least in the eyes of craftsmen and managers, make blame assignment difficult and ambiguous. Even within a press team, different team members might be responsible for controlling different parameters. Given the interactions between attributes within and across conjunctive rules, this can make management of press-wide parameters untenable.

For these reasons, an expert and analyst translated the set of conjunctive rules into a list of independent attribute values (or ranges) like those shown in Table 1 using a straightforward process that is not elaborated here. In retrospect, this final choice of representation might motivate a different discovery method than decision tree induction, but a naive approach that discovers simple relationships between single attributes and outcomes directly, would not implicate as many informative attributes as an approach that takes an intermediate step of discovering interacting attributes that collectively inform outcome (e.g., decision tree induction).

The experts posted a complete list of conditions like those shown in Table 1 for the press operators and the plating craftsmen. The printing experts told the craftsmen to stay within the favorable value ranges unless quality considerations dictated otherwise. The experts also explained that, based on the APOS generated trees and the expert's own past experience, operating with two or more attribute values within the unfavorable ranges would greatly increase the risk of banding.

3.7. Performance Evaluation

Table 2 shows the absolute number of bands per year since 1989. The trends are almost identical when the data is expressed in terms of the relative number of bands (per unit work).

The peak during 1994 occurred in September of that year, after contaminated, abrasive ink entered the system in late August. Ink was implicated by rules generated by APOS early in the study. Technicians purged the ink storage facility and cylinder band performance returned to 1993 levels.

Unfortunately, an industrial environment does not facilitate the kind of experimentation that occurs in a laboratory environment. External factors, which may be excluded or at least

Table 1 Recommendations Translated from APOS Rules

Attribute	Favorable	Neutral	Unfavorable
Humidity	High	Medium	Low
Grain screen	Yes	–	No
Anode distance	Wide	Medium	Narrow
Chrome ratio	High	Medium	Low
Ink temperature	Low	Medium	High
Ink viscosity	High	Medium	Low
Blade stroke	Long	Medium	Short
Current density	High	Medium	Low

Table 2 Absolute Number of Bands

1989	1990	1991	1992	1993	1994	1995	1996	1997	1998
538	384	138	66	42	109	21	26	37	26

controlled in a laboratory environment, can impact an industrial operation and preempt precise assignment of cause and effect. One confound in our application was the input of an industrial consultant, who provided some recommendations in 1989. We compared the recommendations of the consultant with those of APOS, and found that APOS produced significantly more rules (12–15) than the consultant (3), which filled important gaps in the consultant's recommendations.

Moreover, APOS also recommended more conservative thresholds on numeric variables in the case where the system and consultant recommendation qualitatively matched. In general, APOS recommendations were specific to the plant from which data was collected, whereas the consultant's recommendations were more general. Finally, one APOS-generated recommendation conflicted with one consultant recommendation. Local engineers performed a deeper analysis and agreed with the APOS rule, though the APOS rule initially seemed counterintuitive.

Our analysis convinces us that APOS-generated rules are primarily responsible for post-1990 improvements: APOS-generated rules subsume, and in one case contradict, those of the consultant, and in any case they are the sole basis for current operations.

Despite our success, rule implementation should proceed cautiously. For example, the experts were very careful to approach a printing crew that seemed most open to input. Even after the experts distributed the APOS recommendations, some time elapsed before all crews were following the recommendations. The continued improvement illustrated by Table 2 is not due to the generation of new rules, but primarily to the craftsmen gradually accepting the recommendations informally distributed in December 1990 and formally distributed in April 1991.

Once recommendations are made and they begin affecting operations, it is very difficult to turn back. If recommendations have a negative effect, then confidence in the knowledge acquisition process will be seriously compromised. In our case, rules were not implemented unless they were justified and explained by plant engineers, but a more cautious strategy might have deferred implementation until these rules were systematically tested on subsequent data. In contrast, if implemented rules have a positive effect, then the sample space is inalterably changed, since management is unlikely to return to the old situation for purposes of hypothesis testing.

4. Concluding Remarks

Though our application did not involve massive data sets (i.e., we worked with about 500 tuples), the interactive data mining approach still significantly extended the processing capabilities of human analysts. Moreover, an interactive data mining approach demands and (management willing) institutionalizes a disciplined approach to problem solving, which includes the systematic collection and analysis of data. Even if a data mining technique were not theoretically required to discover important attribute interactions in the data from a data processing standpoint, it is likely that the long-standing banding problem would not have been mitigated to the extent that it was without the introduction of an induction technique.

We have noted that social factors played a significant role in the success of our project. Along these lines it seemed important that a reward system be in place to promote acceptance of induced rules. At the Donnelley plant this reward system relied on the craftsmen's desire to efficiently produce high-quality products and to receive recognition when they reach remarkable quality or production milestones. In particular, pictures and congratulatory comments were posted on a bulletin board outside the cafeteria about crews who have achieved a year or more of production without any delays due to cylinder bands. Though records are incomplete, it appears that no crew in the plant had ever achieved one year without a cylinder band prior to the application of data mining to the problem. More importantly, the crews regard the accomplishment as noteworthy and the crew members themselves have taken on the role of educating new members on the merits of system-translated recommendations.

References

Bareiss, R. B., B. Porter, and K. Murray. 1989. "Supporting start-to-finish development of knowledge bases." *Machine Learning* **4**: 259–284.

Buntine, W. and D. Sterling. 1990. "Interactive induction." In *Machine Intelligence*, edited by J. E. Hayes-Michie, D. Michie, and E. Tyugu, **12**: 121–138. Oxford, England: Oxford University Press.

Clark, P. and S. Matwin. 1993. "Using qualitative models to guide inductive learning." In *Proceedings of the 1993 International Machine Learning Conference (Amherst, MA)*, edited by P. Utgoff, pp. 49–56. San Francisco, CA: Morgan Kaufmann.

Evans, B. and D. Fisher. 1994. "Overcoming process delays with decision tree induction." *IEEE Expert* **9**: 60–66.

Michalski, R. and C. Chilausky. 1980. "Learning by being told and learning from examples: an experimental comparison of the two methods of knowledge acquisition in the context of developing an expert system for soybean disease diagnosis." *Int. J. Policy Anal. Inform. Sys.* **4**: 125–161.

Quinlan, J. R. 1991. *C4.5: Programs for Machine Learning*. San Francisco, CA: Morgan Kaufmann.

Riddle, P., R. Segal, and O. Etzioni. 1994. "Representation design and brute-force induction in a Boeing manufacturing domain." *Appl. Artificial Intell.* **8**: 125–147.

Weiss, S. and C. Kulikowski. 1991. *Computer Systems That Learn*. San Francisco, CA: Morgan Kaufmann.

46.6 Automated Search for Diagnostic Knowledge on Rotating Machinery

Wojciech Moczulski

ABSTRACT The main task of machinery diagnostics consists of inferring the actual state of a given machine based upon observed symptoms and operating conditions. Diagnostic knowledge is commonly presented in a declarative form. Precise predictions require functional dependencies. Such knowledge can be elicited from data collected during operation of the machine or generated using simulation software, the latter case being discussed in this case study. Several independent attributes representing the operating conditions and technical state of a rotating machine were varied systematically, causing the response—vibrations at several points of the machine. To acquire knowledge from data we used several machine learning techniques and 49er, a system that can discover various forms of knowledge. First we focused the search on detection of groups of attributes that approximate functional relations between control and dependent variables. Then Equation Finder was applied recursively to each group, finding multidimensional equations that capture fine functional relationships. Since diagnostic inference takes place in the direction opposite to causal relationships, the discovered equations had to be inverted, so that the observed vibrations of the machine enabled us to calculate values describing the internal state of the object. The knowledge discovered using this approach was implemented in a diagnostic expert system.

1. Project Overview

The project was concerned with finding knowledge suitable for detection and diagnosis of imbalances of a rotating shaft. Diagnostic knowledge should make inferring the conclusions on

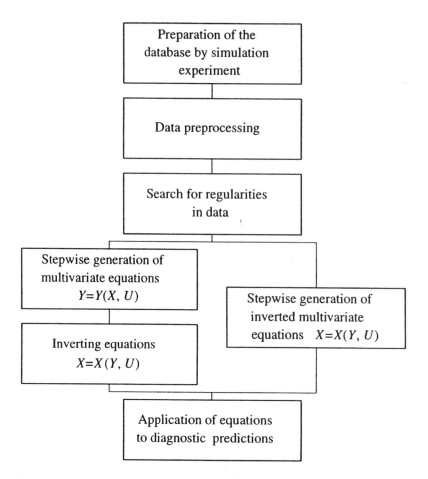

Figure 1 KDD process for discovering diagnostic relationships (in the equations: U—input: operating conditions, X—technical state: imbalance distribution, Y—output: symptoms— parameters of vibrations)

the directly unobservable technical state possible from evidence such as symptoms of the technical state and operating conditions. Specifically, we needed knowledge not only useful in detecting excessive imbalance, but also enabling us to predict the magnitude and location of the imbalance on the shaft. Such knowledge was needed for a computerized monitoring expert system.

This case study is concerned with discovery of diagnostic knowledge from a database of simulation results. Independent variables represented imbalance and operating conditions, while dependent variables represented symptoms of imbalance manifesting themselves in vibrations. Usually such a database would be collected during experiments performed on a real-existing object. However, they are time consuming and often it is quite difficult to observe certain states of the machine, especially if they could cause danger to human operators and/or the environment. Hence, simulation gives a valuable opportunity to collect data as if they were collected in an experiment.

The KDD process (Figure 1) was preceded by preparation of the database and data preprocessing. Then the search was initially focused on regularities found in contingency tables. Guided by such regularities, we extended the search to complex equations that capture functional dependencies between the selected independent and dependent attributes. To enable diagnostic prediction we needed to solve those functional dependencies so that imbalances could be predicted from symptoms. For inversion of equations another method can be used. Independent and dependent variables switch their roles so that functions that predict the technical state can be sought directly (cf., right path in Figure 1). The main advantage of the first path (shown on the left in Figure 1) is that data-imbalance symptoms Y (parameters of vibrations) are collected by systematic variation of input U (operating conditions) and technical state X (imbalance distribution), so that fine equations can be generated recursively. The equation $Y = Y(X, U)$ matches data generated by simulation. The second approach, which was only briefly tested up to now, concerns direct discovery of inverted, that is diagnostic, relationships.

2. KDD Process

2.1. Diagnostic Problem

Our diagnostic task can be categorized as identification of the technical state of a machine based on data collected by observation of this machine. Some observations fall into the category of input, such as raw materials and energy supplies, operating conditions, and values of variables controlling the operation of the machine. Other data describe the internal technical state of the device. Two other categories describe output of the machine: useful products and residual processes that are unwanted but unavoidable results of device operation. Input, operating conditions, and internal state fall into the category of causes, while the useful output and residual processes are considered as the effects, derivable from the input by causal relationships. The measured outputs serve as symptoms of the internal state of the device. A diagnosis starts from symptoms and arrives at conclusions concerning the causes. To make this possible, we need diagnostic relationships which are inverted causal relations.

This case study is focused on a problem of imbalance of a rotating shaft, which is caused by uneven mass distribution with respect to the main central axis of the shaft's inertia. Imbalance is a common problem in rotordynamics that may be caused by phenomena such as cracked parts of the rotor or sediments located on the blades. Not only can identification of imbalance distribution help in detecting the fault, but can also give suggestive evidence on the technical state and enable diagnosticians to detect severe problems early that could result in catastrophic failure in the future.

The most common problems faced by diagnosticians can be reduced to determination of up to two planes with imbalance vectors that are described by location and phase lag (see Figure 2). In such cases we can distinguish four different kinds of shaft imbalance: static, quasi-static, moment, and dynamic.

Imbalance of the rotor causes rotor vibrations. The vibrations propagate to the bearings, their supports and casing of the machine. The greater the imbalance, the more severe the vibrations, manifested in greater dimensions of orbits of motion of the shaft's centerpoint.

We have two tasks: to detect if the imbalance is severe and to diagnose the type of imbalance and estimate the magnitudes of the imbalance vectors and their location along the axis of the shaft as well as the angle between the direction of each imbalance vector and a marker fixed on the shaft. A reliable diagnosis reduces cost of repair, by scheduling the optimal time of the repair and suggesting which part of the machine casing must be disassembled. Maintenance staff may synchronize the repair of the diagnosed machine with other machinery in the plant, thus minimizing the costs of unwanted breaks in the plant's operation. Moreover, costs of both dismounting and spare parts may be reduced.

2.2. Available Data

Diagnostic knowledge may be elicited from both experimental and simulation data. Modern monitoring systems collect plenty of data on machinery operation and malfunctions, but it is difficult to determine the technical state of a machine without a costly disassembling into pieces. It is also difficult to collect data over a broad range of combinations of parameter

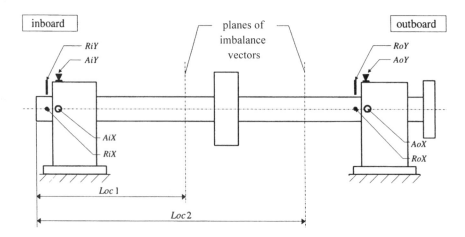

Figure 2 Rotor system considered in the case study. Rotor vibrations are observed in 8 points located in radial planes. In names of quantities prefix *A* denotes absolute vibration and *R*— relative one; *i*—inboard and *o*—outboard bearings, respectively; *X*—horizontal and *Y*— vertical direction of observation.

values. Further, it may be dangerous to humans and to the environment of the machinery to investigate extreme conditions most indicative of catastrophic failures.

For these reasons a database obtained during simulation experiments was generated as an inexpensive alternative to real data. Data were collected systematically over a broad range of values of all independent variables that represent both the state of machinery and its operating conditions.

The dynamic properties of the rotor-bearings-supports system were modeled using a well-established principle of modeling with the application of the finite elements method (Kiciński, 1996).

A strong nonlinear model of kynetostatics of an oil-lubricated journal bearing and linear model of system dynamics were applied to make reliable response calculations. The results of simulation were several parameters of orbits of the shaft centerline, observed in radial planes, perpendicular to the shaft centerline. Kiciński demonstrated that the results are close enough to the observations conducted on the real object.

Raw data collected by simulation describe ellipses of the motion of the shaft's parts, both absolute and relative to stationary parts of the machine's casing. We used data on radial components of vibrations observed as time series in four planes (Figure 2): vibration of the shaft relative to the inboard bearing described by the couple (*RiX*, *RiY*), absolute vibration of the shaft in the inboard bearing (*AiX*, *AiY*), vibration of the shaft relative to the outboard bearing (*RoX*, *RoY*), and absolute vibration of the shaft in the outboard bearing (*AoX*, *AoY*). The location of planes where shaft vibrations were observed corresponded to the location of measuring sensors on the real object. Because a linear model of the system's dynamics was used, the shape of each orbit is elliptic and may be represented by coefficients A, B, C, D of linear combinations of sine and cosine components of the ellipses (Cholewa and Kiciński, 1997):

$$X(t) = A \sin \omega t + B \cos \omega t \tag{1}$$

$$Y(t) = C \sin \omega t + D \cos \omega t, \tag{2}$$

where $X(t)$, $Y(t)$ are two coordinates of an instant position of the shaft center, t is time, and ω is rotation frequency. Thus we obtained $4 \cdot 4 = 16$ parameters (dependent variables) that describe the system's response, that is, absolute and relative vibrations of the shaft. Moreover, we also collected values of independent (control) variables as: rotating speed and imbalance location (independent parameters 7 in total). Our database contains 5,076 records of 23 values each. The number of records corresponds to the plan of the experiment and has been determined arbitrarily.

Although the simulation model was known, for the sake of diagnostic inference we needed an inverted model. Two problems made the inversion difficult or even impractical: equivocal mapping and very time-consuming computations. Obviously, in many real-life problems an adequate model is unknown. Hence, we decided to apply KDD techniques, seeking knowledge that would predict imbalance, given the vibrations, but in addition seeking a method that would work on the future diagnostic problems.

2.3. Background Knowledge

Background knowledge concerns different types of imbalance and how they manifest themselves in relative motion of the shaft against stationary parts of the rotor-bearings-stator system (i.e., vibrations).

Background knowledge was represented by a selected family of relevant attributes and their limiting values, which may either be defined based upon international standards and recommendations (such as VDI 2059 (German Engineers' Association, 1981)), or established individually for the given machine. These limiting values can be applied as cutting points while bining real-valued data.

2.4. Expected Results

Our long-term goal is to elaborate methods that will enable diagnosticians to find knowledge in the form of functional relationships (equations) between observed variables. Equations are the best diagnostic tool, since they lead to precise and unique predictions. In this project we expected to find functional dependencies between symptoms of the technical state and this technical state itself, identified by the imbalance distribution along the shaft. The symptoms were parameters of vibrations observed in several planes perpendicular to the shaft, including the value of the radius of orbits of the relative motion of the shaft against stationary parts and the phase lag of the imbalance vector.

2.5. Data Preprocessing

The simulation data carry complete information on each ellipse. But parameters A, B, C, D cannot be directly measured. Hence, we converted parameters of orbits to new ones that can be measured and directly describe shape and orientation of each ellipse (cf., Figure 3), that is dimensions $D1$, $D2$ of semi-axes of an ellipse, angle TD between its main semi-axis and horizontal (x) axis, and phase TZ of the starting point of the ellipse.

2.6. Data Mining Resources

It only makes sense to search for equations if functional relations are represented in the data. Even if this is the case, the data includes many variables, while only a small subset can be related by an individual equation.

Equations are a rare result of discovery in the databases process, as typical real-world domains are nondeterministic and data sets represent incomplete information about them. Since the search for equations is expensive, it makes sense to seek them only if there is a good chance that they can be discovered. Thus, prior to the search for equations, we estimated whether functional relations were available in the data and what variables were involved in those relations.

Combinatorial complexity of the space of multivariate hypotheses dictates the search strategy of 49er (Żytkow and Zembowicz, 1993). The system initially considers one-dimensional histograms, then two-dimensional contingency tables before trying finer regularities (such as equations) and regularities in more dimensions. Contingency tables are a general tool for expressing statistical knowledge. 49er also uses them to test for approximate functional relations.

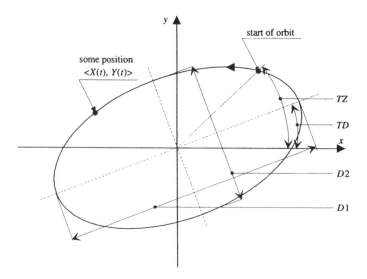

Figure 3 Considered parameters of shaft orbits after data preprocessing

2.7. *Discovery Mechanism*

We had to deal with an object whose properties were described by many attributes and which required an application of multivariate equations. In the following we describe the discovery mechanism applied by Moczulski and Żytkow (1997).

STEPWISE DETECTION OF VARIABLES RELATED BY AN EQUATION

Since the data sets have been generated by systematically varying independent variables, it is possible to use BACON-3 methodology for data collection, followed by stepwise generation of multidimensional equations (Langley et al., 1987). But since data collection is exponential in the number of variables, the approach is impractical unless the right variables are known.

Consider Figure 4. A contingency table that relates an imbalance magnitude to a particular parameter of ellipse measured at one of locations (outboard) is shown in the top row. The relation is nondeterministic, especially when the resolution of the contingency table is low, for instance 5 × 5, as shown in Figure 4. But when the data set is sliced according to the four values of the attribute *Loc*1 available in the data (the middle row in Figure 4), the relation that occurs in each slice is more deterministic. When data are further sliced according to the values of the attribute *RtSp* expressed in RPM (the bottom row in Figure 4), the quality of the functional relation is further improved.

Figure 5 shows a small portion of the search for the best set of variables that improve the contingency tables in the direction of increasingly strong functional relations. The search is guided by the increased values of Cramer's *V* parameter that measures uniqueness of predictions provided by a given table. The value of $V = 0.609$ for all data is improved to $V = 0.740$ and $V = 0.687$ in the slices of data made with the use of different values for *Loc*1. This indicates that *Loc*1 can be used in the search for a multivariate equation.

We used contingency tables to identify functional dependencies. Although we have got high values of Cramer's *V* that suggest very strong functional dependencies, the results obtained were imprecise with respect to diagnostic requirements, where one would like to predict exact distribution of imbalances that could enable the maintenance personnel to reduce the shaft's imbalance to some defined limit. Thus, many approximate dependencies that were found were subsequently further refined by the search for equations.

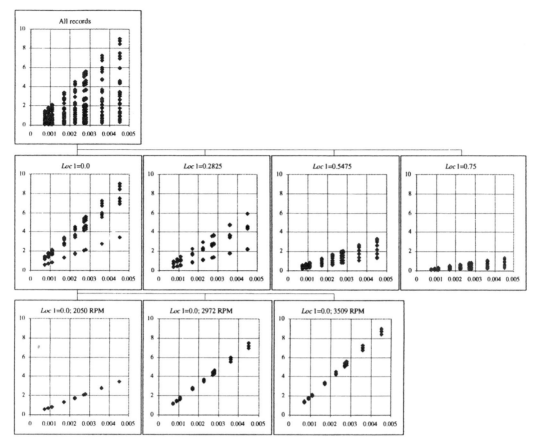

Figure 4 Functional relationship is gradually discovered by slicing the data

STEPWISE GENERATION OF MULTIVARIATE EQUATIONS

Given a set of k attributes that may be related by an equation, $k-1$ independent and one dependent, the search follows the BACON-3 methodology, starting from subsets of data in which all independent variables, except for one variable (X_1), are fixed. If equations of the same form are found in all such data sets, then the next independent variable (X_2) is used to search for equations that link X_2 with parameters in the equations for X_1. Gradually, a multivariate equation can be formed.

It is worth emphasizing that equations were formed by analyses using the original (i.e., continuous) values of attributes. Discretization of data was required only for contingency tables.

INVERTING THE EQUATIONS

The equations are discovered in the form:

$$response = f(operating\_cond, internal\_state) \qquad (3)$$

because data were generated by systematic variation of *operating_cond* and *internal_state*. But to yield concrete diagnoses they must be transformed to the form

$$internal\_state = g(operating\_cond, response). \qquad (4)$$

Equations such as (4) may either be inverted or directly discovered in the final, inverted form.

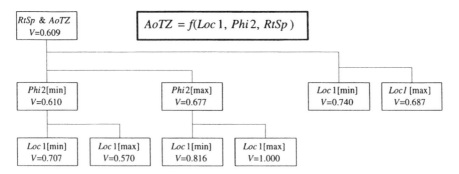

Figure 5 Portion of search for the best set of variables in original data ("causal direction" of equation). Sequences of data slices are shown with values of Cramer's *V*

2.8. Obtained Results

Using the search process described above, equations have been discovered, as for example the following pair:

$$Imbal1 = \frac{AiD1}{-0.862 \cdot RtSp \cdot Loc1 + 830.4 \cdot Loc1 + 0.765 \cdot RtSp - 789} \tag{5}$$

$$Imbal1 = \frac{AoD1}{-2.468 \cdot RtSp \cdot Loc1 + 4007.7 \cdot Loc1 + 2.020 \cdot RtSp - 3217}. \tag{6}$$

We can try to use them to determine two dependent variables: *Imbal*1 and *Loc*1, given the values of *RtSp*, and parameters of the measured ellipses *AiD*1 and *AoD*1. Values of these variables may represent imbalance distribution along the shaft. However, as is clear from Figure 6, both equations lead to ambiguous predictions represented by the area of their overlap in this figure rather that unique predictions, which would be represented by the intersection of both equation diagrams at one point.

Other equations also lead to ambiguous predictions. It is possible, however, that some combinations of variables will lead to new equations that can be solved uniquely. Our search

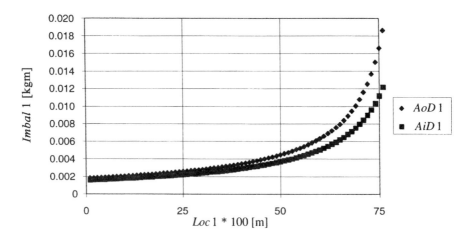

Figure 6 The overlap of diagrams of both equations (5) and (6) represents the diagnosed combination of values of *Loc*1 and *Imbal*1

for such equations has not been successful so far, but plenty of variable combinations have not yet be examined, so the search for diagnostic knowledge in our database will continue.

2.9. *Comparison with Results Obtained by Other Methods*

The database was also used for rule and decision tree learning by induction:

1. Using selective induction with logarithmic and linear transformation of data—we used the AQ15c learning system (Michalski, 1983; Wnek et al., 1995);

2. Using rough classifiers (Pawlak, 1991) with logarithmic transformation of data—we employed the LERS learning system (Chmielewski and Grzymala-Busse, 1992);

3. Using induction of decision trees—we applied the C4.5 induction system (Quinlan, 1986, 1993).

We obtained good accuracy of introductory rule sets (see e.g., Moczulski, 1997, 1998), although the uneven distribution of examples caused some classification problems. However, the most important problem was the impossibility of making quantitative predictions.

Another very promising approach has been proposed by Cholewa and White (1993). They tried to solve a similar task of model inverting, using a neural network approach. The properties of the system were modeled by a direct model represented by a simulation system. Results of the simulation served as training data for a neural network. Although the network was able to classify rough imbalance types, the results did not provide predictions concerning imbalance locations.

A novel attempt (Cholewa and Kiciński, 1997; and recent results of Klimek, 1999) depends on the improvement of local inverse models defined in the neighborhood of a given point in the symptom space. This model makes it possible to achieve quantitative predictions on the imbalance distribution along the shaft. However, inverting each local model requires very extensive computations.

2.10. *Applications of Discovered Knowledge*

Knowledge discovered using the methodology briefly discussed in the case study was applied in an expert system for diagnosing faults on the described object. Discovered knowledge enabled the diagnostician to make accurate predictions and, then, adequate maintenance and repair extent may be estimated without the need to stop and dismount the device.

3. Recapitulation and Conclusions

We deal with a real-life engineering problem. It is important that the discovered knowledge is in good agreement with the common engineering knowledge of domain experts. Therefore, we presented the obtained results to experts, who acknowledged this knowledge base. The experts evaluated results of computations using discovered equations applied to the data with the known vibration characteristics and imbalance distributions. They found good correspondence with the predicted imbalance distribution along the shaft and their qualitative expectations concerning the type of imbalance.

The introductory results obtained are very promising, thus we will continue the research on diagnostic knowledge discovery from databases. In particular we will use real data collected from machinery by diagnostic monitoring systems.

Data preprocessing and data mining are integral parts of the entire KDD process. Thus, problems caused by preprocessing, such as errors in some data values, may be found during data mining, and faulty preprocessing may be identified by contingency tables. Moreover, data mining may advise how to further transform data.

We are going to continue this research taking into consideration the following further issues:

- Comprehensive automation of search for multivariate equations;

- Better measures of accuracy and predictive power of learned knowledge;

- Integration of simulation software, databases, knowledge bases, machine learning and KDD components into a flexible knowledge acquisition system.

ACKNOWLEDGMENTS

The author expresses his gratitude to J. M. Z'ytkow for interesting discussions concerning applications of knowledge discovery methods to acquisition of diagnostic knowledge from databases of examples, and for making accessible the 49er system that was used for all knowledge discovery computations. All signals were generated by P. Maniak and the author, using software kindly made accessible by J. Kiciński, Institute of Fluid Flow Machinery, Polish Academy of Sciences, Gdańsk. This research was partially conducted at Wichita State University, Computer Science Department and was supported by the Polish Scientific Research Committee under grants No. 8 T11F 020 09 and 7 T07B 046 16.

Figures 4, 5, and 6 reprinted with permission from W. Moczulski, J. M. Żytkow, "Automated Search for Knowledge on Machinery Diagnostics", in *Intelligent Information Systems, Proceedings of the Workshop held in Zakopane, Poland, 9–13 June, 1997*, Institute of Computer Science, Polish Academy of Sciences, Warsaw, pp. 194–203.

References

Chmielewski, M. R. and J. W. Grzymala-Busse. 1992. "Global discretization of continuous attributes as preprocessing for inductive learning." TR-92-7. Lawrence, KS: Department of Computer Science, University of Kansas.

Cholewa, W. and J. Kiciński. eds. 1997. In *Machinery Diagnostics. Inverted Diagnostic Models* (in Polish). Gliwice, Poland: Silesian Technical University.

Cholewa, W. and M. F. White. 1993. "Inverse modeling in rotordynamics for identification of imbalance distribution." *Machine Vibration* 2: 157–167.

German Engineers' Association. 1981. *VDI 2059 Part 1: Shaft Vibrations of Turbosets. Principles for Measurement and Evaluation*. Berlin: Beuth Verlag GmbH.

Kiciński, J. 1996. "Nonlinear model of vibration in rotor/bearings system—calculation algorithm." *Machine Dynamics Problems* 15: 45–60.

Klimek, A. 1999. "Methods of improvements of inverse diagnostic models" (in Polish). Ph.D. diss. Gliwice, Poland: Technical University of Silesia, Department of Machine Design Fundamentals.

Langley, P., H. A. Simon, G. L. Bradshaw, and J. M. Żytkow. 1987. In *Scientific Discovery: Computational Explorations of the Creative Processes*. Cambridge, MA: MIT Press.

Michalski, R. S. 1983. "A theory and methodology of inductive learning." *Artificial Intell.* 20: 111–161.

Moczulski W. 1997. "Methods of knowledge acquisition for the needs of machinery diagnostics" (in Polish). Silesian Technical University Science Publication No. 1382, Series: Mechanics No. 130. Gliwice, Poland: Publishing House of Silesian Technical University.

Moczulski, W. 1998. "Methodology of knowledge acquisition for machinery diagnostics." *Comput. Assisted Mechanics Engng. Sci.* 6: 163–175.

Moczulski, W. and J. M. Żytkow. 1997. "Automated search for knowledge on machinery diagnostics." In *Intelligent Information Systems, Proceedings of the Workshop held in Zakopane, Poland, June 9–13, 1997* 194–203. Warsaw: Institute of Computer Science, Polish Academy of Sciences.

Pawlak, Z. 1991. *Rough Sets. Theoretical Aspects of Reasoning About Data*. Dordrecht: Kluwer Academic Publishers.

Quinlan, J. R. 1986. "Induction of decision trees." *Machine Learning* 1: 81–106.

Quinlan, J. R. 1993. *C4.5 Programs for Machine Learning*. San Mateo, CA: Morgan Kaufmann.

Wnek, J., K. Kaufman, E. Bloedorn, and R. S. Michalski. 1995. In *Selective Induction Learning System AQ15c: the Method and User's Guide*. Fairfax, VA: Center for Machine Learning and Inference, George Mason University.

Żytkow, J. M. and R. Zembowicz. 1993. "Database exploration in search of regularities." *J. Intell. Inform. Sys.* 2: 39–81.

Further Reading

Cholewa, W. 2001. "Example-Based Inverse Diagnostic Models". *Bulletin of the Polish Academy of Sciences-Technical Sciences.* 49: 359–377. A novel approach to knowledge discovery in the form of inverted local models of diagnostic relationships and adaptive planning of simulation experiments in technical diagnostics.

46.7 Predicting Telecommunication Equipment Failures from Sequences of Network Alarms

Gary M. Weiss

ABSTRACT The computer and telecommunication industries rely heavily on knowledge-based expert systems to manage the performance of their networks. These expert systems are developed by knowledge engineers, who must first interview domain experts to extract the pertinent knowledge. This knowledge acquisition process is laborious and costly, and typically is better at capturing qualitative knowledge than quantitative knowledge. This is a liability, especially for domains like the telecommunication domain, where enormous amounts of data are readily available for analysis. Data mining holds tremendous promise for the development of expert systems for monitoring network performance since it provides a way of automatically identifying subtle, yet important, patterns in data. This case study describes a project in which a temporal data mining system called Timeweaver is used to identify faulty telecommunication equipment from logs of network alarm messages.

1. Project Overview

Managing the performance of computer and telecommunication networks is an extremely complex task since these networks often contain thousands of components and a problem with one component may quickly propagate through the network. Identifying and isolating faults in these networks is one important aspect of managing network performance. In fact, in order to maintain the availability of these networks, it is critically important to identify a fault before it results in the total failure of a hardware component. To this end, expert systems have been developed to cost-effectively monitor these networks.

One such expert system is AT&T's ANSWER system (Weiss et al., 1998b). ANSWER (automated network surveillance with expert rules) is responsible for monitoring the 4ESS switches that route the majority of the traffic in the AT&T network. When a component within a switch experiences a problem, the switch generates an alarm and forwards it to one of AT&T's two technical control centers. At the technical control center, the alarm is inserted into a relational database and forwarded to ANSWER. ANSWER then analyzes the alarm using rules acquired from domain experts. If ANSWER determines that the alarm requires some action be taken, it forwards an alert describing the problem to a technician for further processing. Because the 4ESS switches in the AT&T network generate in excess of 100,000 alarms per week, it is critical that alarms corresponding to nonrecurring transient problems be filtered so they do not result in an alert. One of the most important functions of ANSWER is to distinguish between recurring and nonrecurring faults.

A key business goal of ANSWER is to minimize the number of service-affecting incidents—such as blocked or lost calls—while keeping development, personnel, and maintenance costs at an acceptable level. Unfortunately, expert systems such as ANSWER require the use of highly trained knowledge engineers to extract knowledge from domain experts and to encode the knowledge in a usable form. This knowledge acquisition process is time-consuming and expensive, and often does not capture important quantitative relationships. For example, a human expert may know that the occurrence of several type-A messages indicates a problem, but may not know specifically how many should be required, or within what time interval, before action is required. Data mining offers an intriguing solution, by making it possible to acquire knowledge directly from the network alarm data. The data mining task in this case study is to identify patterns in network alarm logs that can be used to predict telecommunication equipment failures. These patterns can then be incorporated as rules into the existing ANSWER system.

The data mining team for this project was comprised of a single individual who was familiar with the telecommunication domain through previous involvement with the ANSWER system. The project took approximately two years, of which most of the time was spent developing new data mining software.

2. The KDD Process

The knowledge discovery in databases (KDD) process employed in this case study is very similar to the process described in Chapter 12. The steps in this process, as they relate to our project, are described in this section.

2.1. Understanding the Data Mining Problem

The first step in the process involves gaining an understanding of the application domain and the goals of the KDD task. In this case, such an understanding had been acquired through previous work on the ANSWER expert system. The goal of the project was also influenced by a previous effort that attempted to use data mining techniques to predict catastrophic failures of 4ESS switches (Weiss et al., 1998a). A catastrophic failure is one in which the functioning of the entire 4ESS switch is compromised. The previous effort was seriously hampered by the rarity of catastrophic failures—only fifty such failures had been recorded and were available for study. Because of this experience, and because we wanted our results to be more widely applicable, we focused on the more general goal of predicting individual component failures.

The data mining task, as described in the previous section, is not well defined since neither the term *prediction* nor *pattern* was defined. To be meaningful, a prediction must apply to a specific time period. A prediction of a component failure is said to be correct if, and only if, the prediction occurs more than warning time and less than monitoring time before the actual failure. For example, given a warning time of one minute and a monitoring time of eight hours, a prediction must occur between one minute and eight hours prior to the actual failure for the failure to be considered successfully predicted. The warning time parameter ensures that there is sufficient time to respond to a failure prediction prior to the actual failure, and the monitoring time parameter allows the user to control the specificity of the prediction. A prediction is issued if one of a prespecified set of patterns (i.e., patterns identified by the data mining process) occurs in the stream of alarms coming from the 4ESS switch.

Patterns are described using a pattern language developed for this project. Key features of this language were identified based on knowledge of the telecommunication domain. First, because alarms can be generated as a result of unrelated problems, the pattern language must provide a way of specifying a pattern so that the presence of an alarm does not prevent a pattern from matching. Second, because a fault may manifest itself in slightly different ways at different times—perhaps due to different activity occurring outside the faulty component— there must be a way of specifying a pattern without fixing the order of all alarms within the pattern. Finally, because time is such an important factor, and because the behavior of the system will change in response to a fault, it must be possible to associate a time period with each pattern. Given these three requirements, it should be possible to specify the pattern 3 type-A alarms and 2 type-B alarms occur, in any order, within a five-minute period.

2.2. Selecting a Target Data Set

The target data set was formed by collecting two weeks worth of alarms from the database at one of the two technical control centers. The resulting data set contained 148,886 alarms, where each alarm contained approximately twenty variables. Based on knowledge of the domain and what variables are most important for diagnosis, five variables were selected to describe each alarm. These variables are (1) the time the alarm was generated, (2) a unique identifier for the device associated with the alarm, (3) the type of device, (4) the diagnostic code associated with the alarm, and (5) the severity of the alarm. Thus, an alarm is represented by the tuple <time, device-id, device-type, diag-code, severity>. There are several dozen types of devices in a 4ESS switch, hundreds of diagnostics codes, and three severity levels (warning, minor, and major). Because the 4ESS switch recognizes component failures and automatically generates alarms for such failures, no additional effort was required in order to record these failures in the alarm stream.

2.3. Preprocessing and Transforming the Data

Components can fail for a variety of reasons. Because there is no need to distinguish between different types of failures, the various failure alarms were replaced with a common failure alarm. Also, because routine maintenance testing will cause failed components to generate additional failure alarms, a simple software program was applied to the target data set to prune the redundant failure alarms. The resulting data set yielded 1,045 failure alarms corresponding to 1,045 distinct component failures. The data mining task is then to predict these failure alarms.

2.4. Data Mining

The next major step in the KDD process involves selecting the data mining task and the algorithm to be applied. For this project, the data mining task is clearly a prediction task. Because each alarm record represents an event—an observation that occurs at a specific instant in time—we refer to this as an event prediction task. A temporal data mining algorithm is required because the data set contains events, not examples, and because predicting component failures will require the identification of temporal relationships in the data. Other important considerations in selecting a data mining method include the fact that the component failures are rare and known to be difficult to predict. Given these characteristics, the data mining algorithm may need to find patterns that occur very infrequently in the data and have relatively low predictive accuracy—perhaps well below 50 percent. Most data mining methods are not well suited to problems with these characteristics.

2.5. Interpretation of Results

The data mining algorithm produces a set of patterns for predicting component failures (i.e., each pattern x can be viewed as a rule of the form $x \Rightarrow$ device failure). Recall and precision values are computed for each pattern. For this domain, a pattern's recall is the percentage of the total component failures that it predicts, and its precision is the percentage of times a prediction is correct. Note that if we were to view these patterns/rules as association rules, then recall corresponds to support, and precision corresponds to confidence.

To help select the most appropriate subset of the generated patterns, our data mining software orders the patterns from most to least precise and then uses this ordering to generate a precision/recall curve. This curve is generated by viewing the most precise pattern as a solution, the two most precise patterns as another solution, et cetera, and then plotting the precision and recall for each solution. Such a precision/recall curve is shown in Figure 1. Each point on the curve can then be evaluated given the cost of a component failure that is not predicted (false negative), the cost of incorrectly diagnosing a component as going to fail (false positive), and the value of correctly identifying a failure (true positive). If these values are all known, the optimal point on the curve can be determined. For this domain, as for most domains in the real world, these costs are not precisely known. In this case, these values may be estimated. Alternatively, several of the solutions can be given to a domain expert, who could then choose the most attractive solution based on the precision and recall values.

The KDD process is an iterative process, and it is common to use results as feedback into earlier stages in the KDD process. In this project, the warning and monitoring times are parameters to the data mining software, and preliminary results were used as feedback to modify these parameter values. The values selected for evaluation were partly based on the sensitivity of the results to these parameters. For example, if a small increase in the monitoring time significantly improved our ability to correctly predict a failure, then we explored additional points in this neighborhood. This exploration also provided insight into the nature of the prediction problem. For example, as is shown later, decreasing the warning time enables much better predictions to be made. This indicates that there is information useful for predicting failures that occurs shortly before the actual failure.

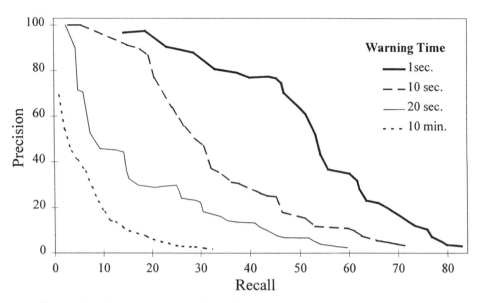

Figure 1 Predictive performance of prediction patterns

2.6. Consolidating Knowledge

The final step involves consolidating the discovered knowledge. This was accomplished by documenting and distributing the key results. More important, these results were then to be incorporated into the ANSWER expert system in the form of rules. Changes were proposed but were not carried out because of a decision, unrelated to this effort, to dramatically change the way the 4ESS switches were monitored.

3. The Data Mining Algorithm

The data mining task requires an algorithm that can identify predictive sequential and temporal patterns in the network alarm data. Because existing methods and software packages were not suitable for performing this task, we developed the Timeweaver data mining software package (TMSP; Weiss, 1999). Timeweaver is a genetic-based data mining system that evolves populations of prediction patterns in order to solve event prediction problems. The decision to utilize a genetic algorithm was based on several factors. One important consideration was that most existing methods are not readily applicable to our data mining task. For example, rule and decision tree learners are not suited to the task because they operate on classified examples, whereas our task involves streams of events. The requirement to find patterns between events caused us to consider methods that could search directly in the space of possible patterns. Given the nature of the data mining task and the requirements on the pattern language, the space of possible patterns is enormous. Given the difficulty of the prediction task and our belief that it is the relationship between alarms that is critical in identifying faults, we felt that a greedy algorithm would not sufficiently explore the search space. For these reasons, a genetic algorithm was chosen—a method that is widely known for its ability to efficiently search through large search spaces.

The first issue in designing a genetic algorithm is how to encode each individual in the population. In this case, each individual represents a pattern. Patterns in Timeweaver are represented as a sequence of pattern events, where each pattern event roughly corresponds to an event in the data set (i.e., an alarm in the context of this project). Patterns also have the following extensions:

- the feature values in each pattern event may take on a wildcard value,

- ordering constraints are specified between successive pattern events in the pattern, and
- a pattern duration is associated with each pattern.

A pattern matches a sequence of events if (1) each pattern event in the pattern matches an event in the sequence, (2) the ordering constraints specified in the pattern are obeyed, and (3) all events involved in the match occur within a time period that does not exceed the pattern duration. For this telecommunication domain, each pattern event is of the form <device-id, device-type, diag-code, severity>. A sample pattern, generated by Timeweaver, is 351:<id20, TMSP,?, Major> * <id20, TMSP, ?, Major> * <id20, TMSP, ?, Minor>. This pattern is matched if, on the same TMSP device, two major alarms occur, followed by a minor alarm, all within 351 seconds. The ? represents a wildcard, indicating that the diagnostic code does not matter, and the * represents the after constraint, which specifies the relative ordering of the events. Note that the presence of other alarms in the alarm stream will not prevent this pattern from matching.

New patterns are generated by combining existing patterns using a crossover operator or by modifying existing patterns via a mutation operator. The patterns selected for combination and mutation are selected proportional to their fitness. The fitness of the prediction pattern is based on both its precision and recall and is computed using the F-measure, defined in Equation (1), where β controls the importance of precision relative to recall.

$$\text{Fitness} = \frac{(\beta^2 + 1) \text{ precision} \cdot \text{recall}}{\beta^2 \text{ precision} + \text{recall}} \tag{1}$$

Any fixed value of β was found to lead to poor performance of the genetic algorithm, so the value of β is continuously varied between 0 and 1. This allows specific patterns, with high precision and low recall, to evolve, as well as general patterns, with high recall but low precision. Over time, patterns evolve that tend to do well with respect to both measures, although some of the general and specific patterns will continue to remain in the population. By employing both precision and recall in the fitness function, the genetic algorithm is able to find patterns that perform well at predicting rare events. Had we only used precision in the fitness function, then the genetic algorithm would have quickly converged to a few extremely specific patterns, and most of the search space would have remained unexplored. The details of the genetic algorithm are described in Weiss (1999). The interested reader may find a general introduction to genetic algorithms in Mitchell (1996) and Goldberg (1989).

4. Results

The target data set was split into disjoint training and test sets by placing all alarms associated with 70 percent of the 4ESS switches into the training set and the remaining alarms into the test set. Timeweaver was applied to the training set, and the mined patterns were then evaluated on the test set. Figure 1 displays the precision/recall curves generated when the monitoring time is held constant at eight hours while the warning time is varied. As expected, the precision of the predictions decreases as the recall of the predictions increases. The figure demonstrates that the performance of the rules is heavily affected by the warning time parameter—the shorter the warning time, the better the predictions. This indicates that the alarms that occur near the actual failure are especially useful in predicting the failure. The mined patterns are not listed since they are only meaningful to a domain expert. However, each curve was formed from approximately thirty patterns, most of which contain three to five pattern events.

5. Alternative Approaches and Related Work

Other approaches to solving the data mining task were considered. Most of these approaches involve reformulating the event prediction problem into a classification problem by transforming the event sequence data into classified examples (Dietterich and Michalski, 1985). These approaches typically involve sliding a window over the data. Events that fall within the window are encoded as a single, fixed-length example. The example is classified based on the proximity of the events in the window to the event to be predicted. A drawback of this approach is that some sequence and temporal information is inevitably lost in the transformation process—and *a priori* we do not know what information is important to preserve. However, one advantage of this approach is that a wealth of existing classification methods can be applied once the transformation has been performed. This approach was evaluated on the telecommunication prediction problem. The network alarm data was transformed into classified examples using a sliding window and the resulting examples were then fed into C4.5 (Quinlan, 1993) and RIPPER (Cohen, 1995); two popular classification systems. The learned rules were not competitive with those generated by Timeweaver (Weiss and Hirsh, 1998), most likely because of the limited amount of sequential and temporal information that was preserved in the transformation process. A similar transformation-based approach, but with a more sophisticated encoding scheme, was employed by Weiss et al. (1998a) to predict catastrophic 4ESS failures and by Sasisekharan et al. (1996) to identify chronic network problems.

A very different data mining approach has also been used to analyze network alarm data. The Telecommunication Network Alarm Sequence Analyzer (TASA) uses specialized data mining algorithms to formulate rules that describe frequently occurring patterns in sequences of network alarms (Hätönen et al., 1996). These rules have been used to filter redundant alarms, locate network problems, and predict network faults. However, the common patterns identified by TASA will not necessarily be useful for prediction. In fact, for our specific data mining task, where the event to be predicted is rare, it is extremely unlikely that common patterns in the alarm data would be helpful in predicting the component failures.

References

Cohen, W. 1993. "Fast effective rule induction." In *Proceedings of the Twelfth International Conference on Machine Learning (Lake Tahoe, Nevada)*, edited by A. Prieditis and S. Russell, pp. 115–123. Menlo Park, CA: AAAI Press.

Dietterich, T. and R. Michalski. 1985. "Discovering patterns in sequences of events." *Artificial Intell.* **25**: 187–232.

Goldberg, D. E. 1989. In *Genetic Algorithms in Search, Optimization, and Machine Learning*. Reading, MA: Addison-Wesley.

Hätönen, K., M. Klemettinen, H. Mannila, P. Ronkainen, and H. Toivonen. 1996. "Knowledge discovery from telecommunication network alarm databases." In *Proceedings of the Twelfth International Conference on Data Engineering (New Orleans, Louisiana)*, pp. 115–122. Los Alamitos, CA: IEEE Computer Society Press.

Mitchell, M. 1996. In *An Introduction to Genetic Algorithms*. Cambridge, MA: MIT Press.

Quinlan, J. R. 1993. In *C4.5: Programs for Machine Learning*. San Mateo, CA: Morgan Kaufmann.

Sasisekharan, R., V. Seshadri, and S. Weiss. 1996. "Data mining and forecasting in large-scale telecommunication networks." *IEEE Expert* **11(1)**: 37–43.

Weiss, G. M. 1999. "Timeweaver: a genetic algorithm for identifying predictive patterns in sequences of events." In *Proceedings of the Genetic and Evolutionary Computation Conference (Orlando, Florida)*, edited by W. Banzhaf, J. Daida, A. Eiben, M. Garzon, V. Honavar, and M. Jakiela, pp. 719–725. San Francisco, CA: Morgan Kaufmann.

Weiss, G. M., J. Eddy, and S. Weiss. 1998. "Intelligent telecommunication technologies." In *Knowledge-based Intelligent Techniques*, edited by L. C. Jain, R. D. Johnson, Y. Takefuji, and L. A. Zadeh, pp. 249–275. Boca Raton, FL: CRC Press.

Weiss, G. M. and H. Hirsh. 1998. "Learning to predict rare events in event sequences." In *Proceedings of the Fourth International Conference on Knowledge Discovery and Data Mining (New York, New York)*, edited by R. Agrawal, P. Stolorz, and G. Piatetsky-Shapiro, pp. 359–363. Menlo Park, CA: AAAI Press.

Weiss, G. M., J. P. Ros, and A. Singhal. 1998. "ANSWER: network monitoring using object-oriented rules." In *Proceedings of the Tenth Conference on Innovative Applications of Artificial Intelligence (Madison, Wisconsin)*, pp. 1087–1093. Menlo Park, CA: AAAI Press.

46.8 Telecommunications Network Diagnosis

Andrea Pohoreckyj Danyluk, Foster Provost and Brian Carr

ABSTRACT The Scrubber 3 system monitors problems in the local loop of the telephone network, making automated decisions on tens of millions of cases a year, many of which lead to automated actions. Scrubber saves Bell Atlantic millions of dollars annually, by reducing the number of inappropriate technician dispatches. Scrubber's core knowledge base, the trouble isolation module (TIM), is a probability estimation tree constructed via several data mining processes. TIM currently is deployed in the Delphi system, which serves knowledge to multiple applications. As compared to previous approaches, TIM is more general, more robust, and easier to update when the network or user requirements change. Under certain circumstances it also provides better classifications. In fact, TIM's knowledge is general enough that it now serves a second deployed application. One of the most interesting aspects of the construction of TIM is that data mining was used not only in the traditional sense, namely, building a model from a warehouse of actual historical cases, but it was also used to produce an understandable model of the knowledge contained in an earlier, successful diagnostic system, which had evolved into opacity over years of operation.

1. Project Overview

This case study describes a data mining application that has resulted in two deployed network diagnosis systems for Bell Atlantic, combining to make tens of millions of classifications annually, many of which result in automated actions.

As is described in detail below, the Scrubber 2 system diagnosed and acted on faults in the local loop of the telephone network. Our job was to build a knowledge base for the diagnostic system's successor, Scrubber 3. The new system is based on a centralized knowledge server, and it covers a network twice as large as the old.

The primary requirement for the system was comprehensibility: the understanding and acceptance by domain experts of how the system makes its decisions. Along with this comprehensibility requirement went a required minimum level of predictive performance, namely, the new system should be at least as good as the prior system. We had additional desiderata, including improving predictive performance and improving extensibility. Finally, we wanted to reduce dependence of the system on weakly supported cost assumptions. The decisions made by the system are based, in part, on the relative costs of the various choices that can be made. These costs are encoded implicitly in Scrubber 2's knowledge base. An additional desideratum for the new system was to build it in such a way that costs could be encoded explicitly. We must stress that these desiderata were seen as far lower priority than the primary requirement.

In fact, to some key players a direct port of the existing system was the optimal solution (to which our additional desiderata were in direct opposition). However, as we describe below, the knowledge inside the existing system was far from comprehensible itself, so a direct port was not a straightforward solution. A large portion of our effort was in modeling the existing system.

The Scrubber 3 team was made up of about two dozen engineers and managers. Individual members of the team were responsible for one or more of the following tasks: (1) development of the Scrubber 3 software; (2) integration of Scrubber 3 with the Delphi system (which, among other tasks, acts as a knowledge server to multiple applications); (3) development of the knowledge base; and (4) evaluation and verification of the encoded knowledge. The team received valuable advice and verification from several local loop diagnosis domain experts.

The Scrubber 2 system to be ported to Scrubber 3 was the most recent of many generations of local loop diagnostic systems, the first of which (MAX) was deployed a decade ago (Rabinowitz et al., 1991). Because the diagnostic knowledge in the system had been

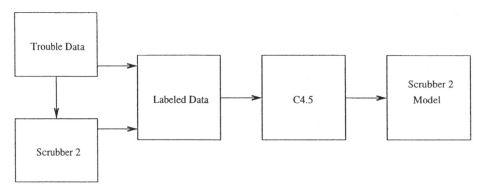

Figure 1 One phase of the KDD process as applied to Scrubber 2

adapted from earlier systems, and because many knowledge engineers had contributed to it over time (as things changed), no single person could claim a complete understanding of the knowledge base. In order to port the system, the knowledge would have to be understood and then re-coded, which was estimated to take at least one person-year. We will concentrate on the data mining applied here—used to build a model of the knowledge base, which had evolved into opacity.

The KDD process applied to this project can be summarized as in Figure 1. What was desired was a model of the classifier as encoded in the Scrubber 2 knowledge base. To build this model, a decision-tree learner (see Chapters 5.4 and 16.1), C4.5 (Quinlan, 1993) was applied to examples of Scrubber 2's diagnostic behavior. (We had performed similar data mining analyses of the MAX system; Danyluk and Provost, 1993; Provost and Danyluk, 1999.) The training set consisted of trouble cases analyzed by Scrubber 2, along with Scrubber 2's diagnoses. The learned classifier not only summarized the knowledge used by Scrubber 2 for diagnosis, but (important for our purposes) it identified the attributes used most heavily by the system for diagnosis.

The model indicated that, of a large set of possible attributes, only a small subset was necessary to model its performance accurately. The ability to focus on this smaller set of attributes opened up the possibility of obtaining significantly more data from a database that contained relevant data in abridged form. These additional data were used to refine the model built by the decision tree inducer, in particular to estimate the probabilities at the leaves of the tree.

2. KDD Process

2.1. Business Problem

Scrubber diagnoses problems in the local loop of the telephone network. The local loop is that part of the network between the customer and the central office. Problems in this part of the telephone network may be due to trouble with customer premise equipment (such as telephones, answering machines, or wiring, for example); trouble with the facilities connecting the customer premise equipment to the cable to the central office; trouble with the cable; or trouble in the central office itself (e.g., in connecting a cable to a switch). Millions of problems (customer-reported problems) are reported each year. Fixing a problem can cost hundreds of dollars.

The first expert system to diagnose problems in the local loop, MAX, was deployed in 1990 (Rabinowitz et al., 1991). MAX (Maintenance Administrator eXpert) performed the task of a maintenance administrator (MA), an employee who studies the relevant data and decides how to resolve the problem. When a customer detects a problem with his line and calls the company to report it, a phone company representative handles the call, recording information reported by the customer. While recording this information, the representative also initiates electrical tests on the line. When MAX was in heavy use, all of this information, along with other information, such as the type of switching equipment to which the customer was connected, was then sent either to a human MA or to MAX for diagnosis. The diagnostic task was to determine roughly where the trouble lay so that the appropriate type of technician could be dispatched. Over the years, the knowledge base of MAX was updated, extended, and migrated to several other systems, including Scrubber and Delphi.

The Scrubber 2 system performed a task at a later point in the diagnostic pipeline. Because action to correct problems is not immediate, many troubles are resolved exogenously. For instance, a customer might have reported a trouble, only to discover that the trouble was that another phone had been left off the hook. If the customer replaces the phone receiver properly, a technician may be dispatched unnecessarily. As another example, heavy rain sometimes causes lines in an old or damaged cable to become wet, resulting in problems that then appear to go away as soon as the weather dries up. Finding and fixing such a problem is very difficult, and a routine dispatch will be fruitless. The job of Scrubber 2 was to survey the lists of troubles waiting to be dispatched, to determine whether the dispatch indeed (still) appeared to be appropriate.

In its first year of operation, the MAX system was estimated to have saved NYNEX approximately six million dollars. Due to the sheer volume of local loop troubles handled at that time, even a single percentage point increase in accuracy was estimated to be worth three million dollars a year in savings to the company. Given the merger of NYNEX and Bell Atlantic, the volume of local loop troubles is now significantly higher.

2.2. Motivation for a Data Mining Solution

The primary goal of the Scrubber 3 team was to create a new Scrubber knowledge base, appropriate for the new applications platform, that performed as well as Scrubber 2. Because of platform incompatibilities, Scrubber 2's code, developed in a no-longer-supported expert system shell, could not simply be transferred to Scrubber 3. Instead, it would have to be re-coded. Unfortunately, as discussed above, Scrubber 2's knowledge base had evolved over a decade, and various knowledge engineers had worked on it during that time, many of whom had moved on and were not available for building Scrubber 3. More important, because of years of continual tweaking and updating, a complete understanding of the resultant knowledge base never truly existed.

In order to port the system, it would first have to be understood and then re-coded, which was estimated to take at least one person-year. An alternative to understanding the Scrubber 2 knowledge might have been re-engineering the knowledge base from scratch. This option was dismissed because (1) time estimates for this task were greater than the one person-year required for the port, and (2) the collective knowledge gained over the years of modifying the local loop knowledge base would have been lost. The evolution of local loop knowledge had produced a system well regarded from several important perspectives (users, experts, analysts, researchers).

Rather than poring over the knowledge base manually, we used data mining techniques to gain an understanding of the classification rules encoded in Scrubber 2. Training and test sets were built from actual cases diagnosed by the system. Labels on individual examples were based on the diagnoses of Scrubber 2. The task was to use a classifier learner (in our case, C4.5) to build a classification model that would model Scrubber 2's performance with high fidelity. Our hope was that the model would give us important insights into the knowledge encoded in Scrubber 2, and would automate to a large degree the construction of the knowledge base for Scrubber 3.

We had evidence that such a model could be built, having used the same modeling process for MAX (Danyluk and Provost, 1993; Provost and Danyluk, 1999). Although MAX was successful and had gained general acceptance, it was also clear that it could be improved. We sought to improve the system in a number of ways, including (1) improving the core knowledge base; and (2) building specialized knowledge for different geographic locations. We constructed a database of problems that had been handled by MAX across the company. For many of these cases we had two sources of labeling: the diagnosis given by MAX and the resolution ultimately reported by the technician who had been dispatched to resolve the trouble. We sought to use the technicians' diagnoses to tune the knowledge already encoded in the system. We applied a number of classifier learning algorithms to our data both to model and to tune MAX. The algorithms included decision tree learners, rule learners, and neural networks. For the problem of modeling MAX, we trained and tested various methods on data labeled with MAX's diagnoses. In all cases we found that we were able to model MAX with a fidelity of at least 0.98 with as few as 10,000 training examples. This led us to believe that we also could model Scrubber with high fidelity, since it was a descendant of MAX, and each operated on a different subset of the same distribution of data.

2.3. The Available Data

The initial data available to us consisted of approximately 26,000 problems that had been handled by Scrubber 2. These data were extracted from Scrubber's log files. Each problem was described by over forty attributes. Of those, approximately half were continuous-valued attributes and half were symbolic-valued. For each problem, we had the diagnosis that had been assigned by Scrubber 2. As a first pass, we framed the learning problem (see Chapter 16.1) as a two-class problem, where the problem should either be dispatched or not. In the former case, the problem is left in the dispatch queue. In the latter case, Scrubber removes the problem from the queue and sends it to a voice-response unit, which calls the customer with an automated message and asks the customer to verify whether the problem indeed is no longer apparent. (A second level of classification is required to choose between different messages.)

No background knowledge was encoded explicitly for use by the classifier learner. However, our own background knowledge, developed over years of working with the MAX system and its derivatives, was used in selecting the appropriate learning program (C4.5, in this case) and the appropriate attributes that were given as input to the learner. Of over forty possible attributes, we selected seventeen.

2.4. Data Mining Resources

Decision tree learning was applied to the data in order to construct a high fidelity model that would also be more understandable than the complex rule base into which the original diagnostic knowledge had evolved. The resultant model needed to be understood by the data miners, domain experts, and in many cases by the system users. The decision tree learner C4.5 was ultimately used to model the behavior of Scrubber 2. While other algorithms were also applied, among them Ripper (Cohen, 1995), we have found over the years that for the local loop diagnosis problem, C4.5 consistently produces classifiers with high predictive accuracy that are also comprehensible by the domain experts. The local loop diagnosis domain is one in which broad general rules can capture approximately half of the diagnoses, but where the other half are covered by many small exception rules, that is, small disjuncts (Danyluk and Provost, 1993). C4.5's greedy algorithm for attribute selection captures this type of domain well. The trees produced, even when large, are considered reasonably comprehensible by the experts, because they understand the general decision tree model and its selection of variables makes sense.

As mentioned above, we had other desiderata for the new knowledge base. For instance, different classification errors have different associated costs. The existing Scrubber 2 model was optimized for a certain set of cost assumptions, but there was continual disagreement as to whether these were best. Furthermore, it became clear that debates over the best set of cost assumptions was misplaced. Costs were different depending on location (compare rural Maine to Brooklyn), and costs change based on changes in problem load and changes in the workforce. Thus, there was a tension between the primary need to build a comprehensible model, and the need for flexibility in the face of the diverse and changing environment. Since we had found decision trees to be highly preferable for explanatory purposes, and very accurate for a fixed set of cost assumptions, our solution was to convert the standard classification trees to probability estimation trees. This conversion is described below.

3. Results

3.1. What Knowledge Has Been Discovered?

As discussed above, data mining techniques were applied to the Scrubber 2 data in order to model the Scrubber 2 knowledge base, which had evolved into opacity. There were two important criteria for the model constructed: readability and consistency with the behavior of Scrubber 2.

Applying C4.5 to the Scrubber 2 data, we were able to produce high-fidelity replicas of Scrubber 2's knowledge base. With a training set of as few as 10,000 examples, C4.5 produced decision trees with fidelity of over 0.99 (accuracy replicating Scrubber 2's diagnoses from its inputs). While the trees produced provided us with a readable model of Scrubber 2's knowledge, we sought to simplify the model where possible in order to gain a better understanding of the system's behavior.

The decision trees produced by C4.5 consistently indicated that a small subset of all the attributes figured prominently in Scrubber 2's diagnoses. Focusing on this subset alone, we used C4.5 to build a new model. While we traded off some fidelity for simplicity of the model produced, the resulting model still fell in a range of acceptable behavior according to guidelines set out at the beginning of the project. These guidelines required not only that overall fidelity of the model be high, but that the number of false positives and false negatives be in appropriate ranges as well.

This model satisfied our criteria for a high-fidelity, yet simple and comprehensible model. This was critical both for our own understanding of Scrubber 2's behavior and for the approval of the managers and domain experts who needed to accept the model for transfer into Scrubber 3. The restriction of the attribute set also had important implications for our construction of the final probability estimation tree.

3.2. Scrubber 3

A base requirement for Scrubber 3 was that it be at least as good as the original system. As discussed above, we had additional desiderata as well, including improving the performance of the system over that of Scrubber 2, and designing it for extensibility. We wanted a comprehensible, locally modifiable, extendable, probabilistic classifier that could accept (naturally) both discrete and continuous attributes. Because of its readability, and because it fit well with the rule-based paradigm used for prior systems, a probabilistic decision tree was the obvious choice.

We modified C4.5 to label examples with class probability estimates (Laplace-corrected class frequencies), rather than with binary decisions. The deployed system reads a probability estimation tree from a file and instantiates it as a lookup table. For a particular problem, it also reads in appropriate decision thresholds, which can be adjusted as needed independently of the learned model.

Even after attribute selection, the resultant tree had over 2,500 leaves, some of which were very small. The problem of small disjuncts has received considerable attention in machine learning literature as one of the fundamental challenges of data mining and of this domain in particular (Holte et al., 1989; Danyluk and Provost, 1993). Small disjuncts cause even more problems in building probabilistic decision trees. For example, consider the case where a leaf comprises five positive examples and one negative. What probability would it be appropriate to assign to that leaf? How confident might we be that that probability was accurate? Notice two things. First, the heuristics used to build decision trees do a great deal of search to find relatively pure leaves (with mostly one class) on the training data. All this search may result in producing example distributions at the leaves that are overly pure, simply as an effect of searching too hard (Chapter 19.1; Jensen and Cohen, 2000). Second, even if the example distributions are more-or-less correct, the corresponding probability estimates may not be precise simply due to the size of the leaves. For simple classification this will not be too much of a problem if the estimate is significantly far from the threshold.

Fortunately, our reduction of the attribute space helped us with both of these problems. We obtained access to a huge database of abridged problem histories, which did not comprise all the attributes, but did comprise the subset used in the final tree. This database had not only the values for these attributes, but also the resolution reported by the technician for the trouble. After cleaning these data (for example, a resolution cannot be considered to be correct if the customer called back shortly thereafter and reported that the trouble in fact had not been resolved), we used them to instantiate the probabilities at the leaves of the tree. The database comprised several million cases; interestingly, the tree still had some small disjuncts.

3.3. Applications of the Discovered Knowledge

Scrubber 3 is currently deployed and is making automated decisions about millions of problems and saving the company over ten million dollars annually.

The probabilistic model was judged to be general enough to apply to a wider variety of local loop diagnosis problems, including front-end diagnosis. Scrubber 3 and the earlier MAX system share the property by which they analyze a problem from data gathered after the customer has finished speaking with a CSR (customer service representative). Often problems cannot be resolved while the customer is on the phone, because electrical tests on the customer's line require that the line not be in use. If the customer calls from a different phone line, however, the possibility arises of gathering relevant data and making an assessment immediately. The Delphi system, introduced above, acts as the knowledge server to Scrubber and also to a system that makes recommendations to assist with the CSR interaction.

We developed a probabilistic model for the front-end closeout problem by training the probabilities of the Scrubber 3 tree with a distribution of troubles appropriate for front-end closeouts. Delphi now also uses the probability estimation tree built for Scrubber 3 to serve knowledge for assisting the CSRs with the front-end task. The ability to use the learned probabilistic model in this way is extremely valuable, because a great deal of knowledge can be gathered by an informed interaction between the CSR and the customer. For example, if the model were to indicate with very high probability that the problem is in the customer's own equipment, the CSR may be able to guide the customer much more aggressively to search for malfunctioning modems or chair legs puncturing extension cords. Precisely quantifying the benefit of such assistance is more difficult than with a fully automated system like Scrubber. However, the incremental development cost was quite small.

References

Cohen, W. W. 1995. "Fast effective rule induction." In *Proceedings of the Twelfth International Conference on Machine Learning (Tahoe City, CA)*, edited by A. Prieditis and S. Russell, pp. 115–123. San Francisco, CA: Morgan Kaufmann.

Danyluk, A. P. and F. J. Provost. 1993. "Small disjuncts in action: learning to diagnose errors in the local loop of the telephone network." In *Proceedings of the Tenth International Conference on Machine Learning (Amherst, MA)*, pp. 81–88. San Mateo, CA: Morgan Kaufmann.

Jensen, D. and P. R. Cohen. 2000. "Multiple comparisons in induction algorithms." *Machine Learning* **38(3)**: 309–338.

Holte, R. C., L. E. Acker, and B. W. Porter. 1989. "Concept learning and the problem of small disjuncts." In *Proceedings of the Eleventh International Joint Conference on Artificial Intelligence (Detroit, MI)*, edited by N. S. Sridharan, pp. 813–818. San Mateo, CA: Morgan Kaufmann.

Provost, F. J. and A. P. Danyluk. 1999. "Problem definition, data cleaning and evaluation: a classifier learning case study." *Informatica* **23**: 123–136.

Quinlan, J. R. 1993. *C4.5: Programs for Machine Learning*. San Mateo, CA: Morgan Kaufmann.

Rabinowitz, H., J. Flamholz, E. Wolin, and J. Euchner. 1991. "NYNEX MAX: a telephone trouble screening expert." In *Innovative Applications of AI 3 (Anaheim, CA)*, pp. 213–230. Menlo Park, CA: AAAI Press.

46.9 Text Mining with Self-Organizing Maps

Dieter Merkl

ABSTRACT Today's information age may be characterized by constant massive production and dissemination of written information. More powerful tools for exploring, searching, and organizing the available mass of information are needed to cope with this situation. This need is our starting point for applying data mining techniques on unstructured information as present in text archives. The users will particularly benefit from cluster techniques that uncover similar documents and bring these similarities to the user's attention. In our approach to text mining we suggest relying on the utilization of self-organizing maps for the analysis of a document archive. The benefit of this approach is the intuitive visualization of document similarities thanks to the spatial ordering of the documents within the self-organizing map. We augment the basic capabilities of the neural network with a data description technique that, based on the features learned by the map, automatically selects the most descriptive features of the input patterns mapped onto a particular unit of the map, thus making the associations between the various clusters within the map explicit. We demonstrate the benefits of this approach by using a real-world document archive comprised of articles from *Time* magazine.

1. Introduction

While there is a vast number of research reports addressing data mining on structured information as it may be found in traditional database systems, data mining on unstructured information, as in text archives, has found much less attention. However, due to the explosion in the amount of information available in textual form, we believe that the utilization of data mining methods on such unstructured information will be crucial in discovering related documents and to assist the user in the exploration of unknown document archives.

An attractive way to assist the user in document archive exploration is based on unsupervised artificial neural networks, especially self-organizing maps, for document space representation. A number of research publications show that this idea has found appreciation in the community (Kohonen, 1998; Lagus et al., 1996; Lin et al., 1991; Merkl, 1995, 1997a,b; 1998; Merkl and Rauber, 1999a; Roussinov and Ramsey, 1998). Self-organizing maps are used to visualize the similarity between documents in terms of distances within the two-dimensional map display. Hence, similar documents may be found in neighboring regions of the map.

Many of the above-mentioned papers focus on the visualization of cluster structure. It still remains a tedious task, however, to interpret the mapping performed by the self-organizing map as such, that is, to analyze which attributes were relevant for a particular mapping or, in other words, to uncover the reason that a particular input pattern is represented by a specific neural processing element. When we look at present applications of the self-organizing map, we usually find it labeled manually in such a way that after inspection of the trained map, a set of keywords is assigned to each unit or cluster to provide the user with some hints on the contents of the map. Apart from the fact that assigning labels manually is highly labor intensive by requiring manual inspection of all data items mapped onto the units, it is difficult, if not impossible, for very high-dimensional data sets as in text mining applications. In order to enable the discovery of associations between documents, we proposed the LabelSOM method (Rauber and Merkl, 1999) to automatically label the units and clusters of a self-organizing map to make the structures learned by the map explicit, that is, to give a justification for a particular mapping.

In this study we provide an overview of our work on text mining based on self-organizing maps. We describe the steps of data preprocessing, clustering results, and the effects of semantic labeling of the neural network.

The material presented in the remainder of this study is organized as follows. In Section 2 we describe the document collection used for the experiments and the necessary steps of data preprocessing. Section 3 provides a description of our approach to text mining. In particular, in

Section 3.1 we give a brief outline of the neural network used for data mining and we provide experimental results from text mining with self-organizing maps and subsequent semantic labeling of the units. A brief review of related work in text mining is contained in Section 4. Finally, we present our conclusions in Section 5.

2. Document Preprocessing for Text Mining

Generally, the task of document classification aims at uncovering the semantic similarities between various documents. First, the documents must be mapped onto some representation language in order to enable further analyses. This process is termed indexing in information retrieval literature. A number of different strategies have been suggested over the years. Still one of the most common representation techniques is single-term full-text indexing, where the text of the documents is accessed and the various words forming the document are extracted. These words may be mapped to their (often just approximate) word stem yielding the so-called terms that are further used to represent the documents. The resulting set of terms is usually cleared from so-called stop-words, that is, words that appear either too often or too rarely within the document collection and thus have only little influence on discriminating between different documents and therefore would only unnecessarily increase the computational load during classification.

In a vector-space model of information retrieval, the documents contained in a collection are represented by means of feature vectors $\mathbf{x}$ of the form $\mathbf{x} = [\xi_1, \xi_2, ..., \xi_n]^T$. In such a representation, the $\xi_i, 1 \leqslant i \leqslant n$, correspond to the index terms extracted from the documents as described above. The specific value of ξ_i corresponds to the importance of index term i in describing the particular document at hand. One might find many strategies to prescribe the importance of an index term for a particular document (Salton and Buckley, 1988). Without loss of generality, we may assume that this importance is represented as a scalar in the range of [0, 1] where zero means that this particular index term is absolutely unimportant to describe the document. Any deviation from zero towards one is proportional to the increased importance of the index term at hand. In such a vector space model, the similarity between two text documents corresponds to the distance between their vector representations (Turtle and Croft, 1992).

In the experiments presented hereafter we use a classic information retrieval test set, namely the *Time* magazine document collection. This collection comprises 420 *Time* magazine articles from the early 1960s. During indexing we omitted terms that appear in less than 10 percent or more than 90 percent of all documents, and we applied some basic stemming rules. Subsequently, the terms are weighted according to a *tf* × *idf* weighting scheme (Salton, 1989), that is, term frequency times inverse document frequency. In particular, we use the weighting function given in Expression (1) below. In this formula, w_{td} is the weight of term t in document d. The higher the weight the more important this term is for describing the contents of the document. tf_{td} refers to the term frequency of term t in document d, df_t is the document frequency of term t, which is the number of documents containing term t, and N is the number of documents in the text archive.

$$w_{td} = tf_{td} \cdot \log \frac{N}{df_t} \tag{1}$$

Such a weighting scheme obviously favors terms that appear frequently within a particular document yet rarely within the whole document collection. The indexing process for the *Time* magazine collection identified 5,923 content terms, that is, the various articles are described by means of a 5,923-dimensional feature space.

3. Uncovering Associations in Text Archives

3.1. Self-Organizing Maps

In our approach to text mining we rely on artificial neural networks, particularly the self-organizing map (Kohonen, 1982, 1995), for uncovering the similarities between documents. The self-organizing map is a general unsupervised tool for the ordering of high-dimensional data in such a way that similar input items are grouped spatially close to one another. The model consists of a number of neural processing elements, or units. These units are arranged according to some topology where the most common choice is marked by a two-dimensional grid. Each of the units i is assigned an n-dimensional weight vector $\mathbf{m}_i$, $\mathbf{m}_i = [\mu_{i_1}, \mu_{i_2}, ..., \mu_{i_n}]^T$, $\mathbf{m}_i \in \mathscr{R}^n$. It is important to note that the weight vectors have the same dimensionality as the input patterns, which are the document representations in our application.

The training process of self-organizing maps may be described in terms of input pattern presentation and weight vector adaptation. Each training iteration t starts with the random selection of one input pattern $\mathbf{x} = [\xi_1, \xi_2, ..., \xi_n]^T$, $\mathbf{x} \in \mathscr{R}^n$. This input pattern is presented to the self-organizing map and each unit determines its activation. Usually, the Euclidean distance between the weight vector and the input pattern is used to calculate a unit's activation. In this particular case, the unit with the lowest activation is referred to as the winner, c. Finally, the weight vector of the winner as well as the weight vectors of selected units in the vicinity of the winner are adapted. This adaptation is implemented as a gradual reduction of the difference between corresponding components of the input pattern and the weight vector, as shown in Expression (2). Note that we make use of a discrete time notation with t denoting the current training iteration.

$$\mathbf{m}_i(t + 1) = \mathbf{m}_i(t) + \alpha(t) \cdot h_{ci}(t) \cdot [\mathbf{x}(t) - \mathbf{m}_i(t)]. \tag{2}$$

Geometrically speaking, the weight vectors of the adapted units are moved slightly toward the input pattern. The amount of weight vector movement is guided by a so-called learning rate, α, decreasing in time. The number of units that are affected by adaptation as well as the strength of adaptation depending on a unit's distance from the winner is determined by a so-called neighborhood function, h_{ci}. This number of units also decreases in time such that toward the end of the training process only the winner is adapted. Typically, the neighborhood function is a unimodal function that is symmetric around the location of the winner and that monotonically decreases with increasing distance from the winner.

The movement of weight vectors has the consequence that the Euclidean distance between input and weight vectors decreases and, thus, the weight vectors become more similar to the input pattern. Hence, the respective unit is more likely to win at future presentations of this input pattern. The consequence of adapting not only the winner alone but also a number of units in the neighborhood of the winner leads to a spatial clustering of similar input patterns in neighboring parts of the self-organizing map. Thus, similarities between input patterns that are present in the n-dimensional input space are mirrored within the two-dimensional output space of the self-organizing map. In other words, the training process of the self-organizing map describes a topology preserving mapping from a high-dimensional input space onto a two-dimensional output space. Such a mapping ensures that patterns that are similar in terms of the input space are represented in geographically close locations of the output space.

It still remains a challenging task, however, to label the map, that is, to determine those features (index terms in our application) of input patterns mapped onto a particular unit that are most characteristic for a specific cluster. In order to improve the document space representation, we provide the user with semantically labeled units of the self-organizing map derived by our LabelSOM method (Merkl and Rauber, 1999b, 2000).

Basically, we are interested in those index terms that best characterize the documents mapped on a particular unit. These terms may then be regarded as a kind of summary of the documents represented by a specific unit. For labeling we analyze the co-occurrence patterns of index terms within the document representations. In particular, we compute the deviation between weight vector components and the respective components of the input vectors. With $\mathscr{D}_i$ denoting the set of documents represented by unit i we may write the deviation δ_{i_k} of a particular vector component k, that is, of an index term, as given in Expression (3). Those index terms that have a deviation below a certain threshold τ_1 are candidates for labeling.

$$\delta_{i_k} = \sum_{x \in \mathscr{D}_i} \sqrt{(\mu_{i_k} - \xi_k)^2}. \tag{3}$$

In an application arena such as text mining, however, we must take care of a second criterion. A keyword-based document representation as used in our work is characterized by the fact that the term-document matrix is populated only very sparsely. Thus, quite a large number of index terms are simply not used to represent a particular document, that is, they have a term weight of zero, and would therefore yield a very small deviation according to Expression (3). A deviation of zero is even possible for index terms that are not used to represent any of the documents mapped onto a particular unit; we should expect that a large number of such index terms will exist. Since we are usually more interested in terms that describe a set of documents rather then in terms that do not, we use only those index terms as labels that have a corresponding weight vector value above a second threshold parameter τ_2. The rationale behind this criterion is that the weight vector entry for a particular index term tends to represent the average of this term's weight in the documents represented by a unit. Hence, high values of weight vector entries correspond roughly to index terms that are important for each of the documents that are mapped onto a particular unit.

3.2. Associations in the Time Magazine Collection

Based on the document description as outlined in Section 2, we trained a 10×15 self-organizing map to represent the contents of the *Time* magazine document collection. The size of the map has been found empirically after a number of training cycles with different network setups. We are currently working toward a novel neural network model that determines the necessary number of units during its unsupervised training process (see Merkl and Rauber, 2000 for preliminary results).

Figure 1 gives a graphical representation of the training result of the self-organizing map. In this figure each unit is marked with the document numbers of those documents the unit has won after training. It is quite obvious that one needs to have profound knowledge of the document archive in order to determine the quality of the training result. This situation would not change dramatically if we used, say, document titles instead of document numbers (see Table 1 for a listing of three document titles).

We believe that it is much easier to uncover the contents of the document archive by looking at the units' descriptions as provided by the LabelSOM technique. The labels for selected units are presented in Figure 2. We cannot show the labels for all units in this work because of space considerations. The complete map, however, is available for interactive exploration at http://www.ifs.tuwien.ac.at/ifs/research/ir.

With such a labeled document space representation, it is obviously much easier to explore the contents on an unknown document collection. For the following discussion, we will use the notation (x/y) to refer to the unit located at row x and column y; starting with $(1/1)$ in the upper left corner. Consider, for example, unit $(4/4)$ labeled with *soviet, moscow, nuclear, khrushchev, negotiation, treaty, berlin, west, russia, agreement, pact, undergo,* and *test*. This unit represents four documents, that is, T062, T380, T392, and T404 (see Figure 1), which are concerned with the negotiations that finally led to the nuclear test ban treaty.

On the right-hand side of the map we find units $(1/8)$ and $(2/8)$ representing four and six documents, respectively. Both units are labeled quite similarly. When we look at the documents, we recognize that unit $(1/8)$ contains documents that discuss a U.S. suggestion to staff NATO ships equipped with Polaris nuclear missiles with multilateral crew members. Unit $(2/8)$ contains documents covering a similar subject matter, namely the British and French efforts in building their own nuclear forces. The United States suggested transferring submarine-based Polaris missiles under European command. The British government accepted this suggestion, which caused continuing disputes with former French president General de Gaulle.

The upper-right unit $(1/10)$ contains eight documents, each of which deals with the problems related to the birth of Malaysia as an independent state. The other countries affected by this issue are clearly visible from the labels and so is the name of Malaysia's prime minister Tunku Abdul Rahman.

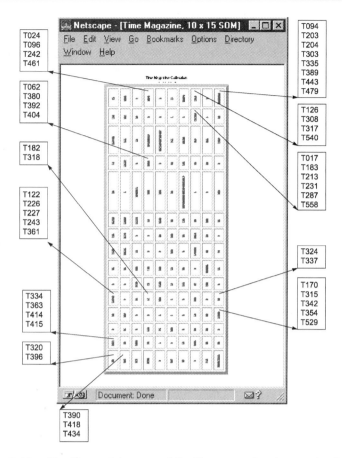

Figure 1 10 × 15 self-organizing map of the *Time* magazine document collection

Turning now to the lower-left part of the map we find three units, that is, (14/1), (15/1), and (15/2), which are again labeled with quite similar terms. The corresponding documents report the religious problems in South Vietnam between Buddhist monks and the Roman Catholic government of Ngo Dinh Diem. The neighboring units to the right, that is, (14/2), (14/3), (14/4), (15/3), (15/4), and (15/5), are all concerned with the Vietnam war.

As a final example, consider units (11/10) and (12/10). From the labels it is obvious that the corresponding documents deal with the British Profumo-Keeler scandal. The script behind this scandal is that British minister of defense John Profumo had an affair with Christine Keeler, who had connections to the Soviet secret service.

4. Related Work

Text mining is a relatively young research area and the number of published reports is quite limited. Among the first, we must mention the work of Feldman and his colleagues (Feldman and Dagan, 1995; Feldman and Hirsh, 1996; Feldman et al., 1997). In their work, text mining relies on heavy document preprocessing where the text is annotated with a set of keywords, organized as a hierarchy in a knowledge base.

In Lent et al. (1997) the authors describe the PatentMiner system, which is based on data mining techniques for sequential patterns. In this system, a phrase is considered as a list of words that occur within a particular part of a document, for example, within one sentence or within one paragraph. The goal now is to identify frequent phrases within the document collection using sequential patterns mining (Agrawal and Srikant, 1995) and to uncover

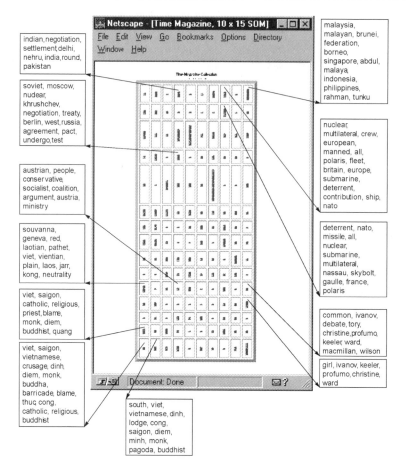

indian, negotiation, settlement, delhi, nehru, india, round, pakistan

soviet, moscow, nuclear, khrushchev, negotiation, treaty, berlin, west, russia, agreement, pact, undergo, test

austrian, people, conservative, socialist, coalition, argument, austria, ministry

souvanna, geneva, red, laotian, pathet, viet, vientian, plain, laos, jarr, kong, neutrality

viet, saigon, catholic, religious, priest, blame, monk, diem, buddhist, quang

viet, saigon, vietnamese, crusage, dinh, diem, monk, buddha, barricade, blame, thug, cong, catholic, religious, buddhist

south, viet, vietnamese, dinh, lodge, cong, saigon, diem, minh, monk, pagoda, buddhist

malaysia, malayan, brunei, federation, borneo, singapore, abdul, malaya, indonesia, philippines, rahman, tunku

nuclear, multilateral, crew, european, manned, all, polaris, fleet, britain, europe, submarine, deterrent, contribution, ship, nato

deterrent, nato, missile, all, nuclear, submarine, multilateral, nassau, skybolt, gaulle, france, polaris

common, ivanov, debate, tory, christine, profumo, keeler, ward, macmillan, wilson

girl, ivanov, keeler, profumo, christine, ward

Figure 2 Labels for a 10 × 15 self-organizing map of the *Time* magazine document collection

phrases that satisfy a specific trend, such as, for example, to be used increasingly often. Quite a similar approach is presented in Ahonen et al. (1997), where the main focus is on discovering phrases and word co-occurrences. Another report on the analysis of word co-occurrences is provided in Swanson and Smalheiser (1997). In this paper the authors demonstrate that from various pieces of evidence extracted from articles in biomedical literature, causes of migraine headaches can be uncovered. The analysis of co-occurrences in a text corpus is also the backbone of the LINDI project (Hearst, 1999).

Most similar to our approach, however, is the work done within the WEBSOM project (Honkela et al., 1997; Kohonen, 1998; Lagus et al., 1996). The main focus of this project is text archive exploration based on self-organizing maps. The major difference with our approach may be found in document preprocessing. The documents are not represented by means of a list of weighted terms extracted from the documents but rather by using the self-organizing map to produce word category maps, that is, maps where similar words are represented by the same unit. The information on the particular words forming a document, however, gets

Table 1 Document Titles of Three Articles

Document No.	Document Title
T317	The allies: Three on a horse
T392	Cold war: The spirit of Moscow
T434	South Viet Nam: Coping with Capricorn

lost. A technique such as LabelSOM as described in this study cannot be applied to text archive description.

5. Conclusions

In this work we have shown how the self-organizing map, which is a neural network model adhering to the unsupervised learning paradigm, may be used for text mining. The essential benefit of self-organizing maps is that similar documents are represented in neighboring regions of the neural network. Hence, the relationship between various documents can easily be seen by visual inspection of the map display. We further presented the LabelSOM method, which provides a straightforward way of assigning labels to the units of a self-organizing map. Attributes, that is, index terms, that are shared by the input patterns mapped onto a particular unit are used to describe that unit. The usage of the LabelSOM method obviously facilitates the interpretation and understanding of the contents of a self-organizing map and the features that it learned, which is hardly possible without the additional information provided by the automatically created labels.

We believe that the utilization of the LabelSOM method largely improves the applicability of the self-organizing map in the field of text mining. The reason is that the various clusters identified by the map not only become intuitively visible as with the enhanced cluster visualization methods developed thus far, but may also be characterized in terms of shared keywords. Hence, the various subject matters of documents contained in an archive are easily accessible to the user. The document archive can now actually be read and understood in the way one would expect from manually indexed document archives.

References

Agrawal, R. and R. Srikant. 1995. "Mining sequential patterns." In *Proceedings of the International Conference on Data Engineering.* Taipei, Taiwan. Los Alamitos, CA: IEEE CS Press. pp. 3–14.

Ahonen, H., O. Heinonen, M. Klemettinen, and A. I. Verkamo. 1997. "Mining the phrasal frontier." In *Proceedings of the European Symposium on Principles of Data Mining and Knowledge Discovery.* Berlin: Springer-Verlag. pp. 343–350.

Feldman, R. and I. Dagan. 1995. "Knowledge discovery in textual databases (KDT)." In *Proceedings of the International Conference on Knowledge Discovery and Data Mining,* Montreal. Menlo Park, CA: AAAI Press. pp. 112–117.

Feldman, R. and H. Hirsh. 1996. "Mining associations in text in the presence of background knowledge." In *Proceedings of the International Conference on Knowledge Discovery and Data Mining,* Portland, OR. Menlo Park, CA: AAAI Press. pp. 112–117.

Feldman, R., W. Klösgen, Y. Ban-Yehuda, G. Kedar, and V. Reznikov. 1997. "Pattern based browsing in document collections." In *Proceedings of the European Symposium on Principles of Data Mining and Knowledge Discovery.* Berlin: Springer-Verlag. pp. 112–122.

Hearst, M. A. 1999. "Untangling text data mining." In *Proceedings of the Annual Meeting of the Association for Computational Linguistics.* College Park, MD. pp. 3–10.

Honkela, T., S. Kaski, K. Lagus, and T. Kohonen. 1997. "WEBSOM—self-organizing maps of document collections." In *Proceedings of the Workshop on Self-Organizing Maps.* Espoo, Finland. pp. 298–303.

Kohonen, T. 1982. "Self-organized formation of topologically correct feature maps." *Biol. Cybernet.* **43**: 59–69.

Kohonen, T. 1995. In *Self-organizing Maps.* Berlin: Springer-Verlag.

Kohonen, T. 1998. "Self-organization of very large document collections: state of the art." In *Proceedings of the International Conference on Artificial Neural Networks,* Skövde, Sweden. Berlin: Springer-Verlag. pp. 65–74.

Lagus, K., T. Honkela, S. Kaski, and T. Kohonen. 1996. "Self-organizing maps of document collections: a new approach to interactive exploration." In *Proceedings of the International Conference on Knowledge Discovery and Data Mining,* Portland, OR. Menlo Park, CA: AAAI Press. pp. 238–243.

Lent, B., R. Agrawal, and R. Srikant. 1997. "Discovering trends in text databases." In *Proceedings of the International Conference on Knowledge Discovery and Data Mining.* Menlo Park, CA: AAAI Press. pp. 227–230.

Lin, X., D. Soergel, and G. Marchionini. 1991. "A self-organizing semantic map for information retrieval." In *Proceedings of the ACM SIGIR International Conference on R&D in Information Retrieval*, Chicago. New York: ACM Press. pp. 262–269.

Merkl, D. 1995. "A connectionist view on document classification." In *Proceedings of the Australasian Database Conference* **17(2)**: 153–161.

Merkl, D. 1997a. "Exploration of document collections with self-organizing maps: a novel approach to similarity representation." In *Proceedings of the European Symposium on Principles of Data Mining and Knowledge Discovery*, Trondheim, Norway. Berlin: Springer-Verlag. pp. 101–111.

Merkl, D. 1997b. "Exploration of text collections with hierarchical feature maps." In *Proceedings of the International ACM SIGIR Conf on R&D in Information Retrieval*, Philadelphia. New York: ACM Press. pp. 186–195.

Merkl, D. 1998. "Text classification with self-organizing maps: some lessons learned." *Neurocomput.* **21(1–3)**: 61–77.

Merkl, D. and A. Rauber. 1999a. "Self-organization of distributed document archives." In *Proceedings of the International Database Engineering and Applications Symposium*, Montreal, Canada. Los Alamitos, CA: IEEE CS Press. pp. 128–136.

Merkl, D. and A. Rauber. 1999b. "Uncovering associations between documents." In *Proceedings of the IJCAI'99 Workshop on Text Mining*. Stockholm. pp. 89–98.

Merkl, D. and A. Rauber. 2000. "Uncovering the hierarchical structure of text archives by using an unsupervised neural network with adaptive architecture." In *Proceedings of the Pacific Asia Conference on Knowledge Discovery and Data Mining*, Kyoto, Japan. Berlin: Springer-Verlag. pp. 384–395.

Rauber, A. and D. Merkl. 1999. "Automatic labeling of self-organizing maps: making a treasure-map reveal its secrets." In *Proceedings of the Pacific Asia Conference on Knowledge Discovery and Data Mining*, Beijing, China. Berlin: Springer-Verlag. pp. 228–237.

Roussinov, D. and M. Ramsey. 1998. "Information forage through adaptive visualization." In *Proceedings of the ACM International Conference on Digital Libraries*, Pittsburgh. New York: ACM Press. pp. 303–304.

Salton, G. 1989. *Automatic Text Processing: The Transformation, Analysis, and Retrieval of Information by Computer*. Reading, MA: Addison-Wesley.

Salton, G. and C. Buckley. 1988. "Term weighting approaches in automatic text retrieval." *Inform. Process. Mgmnt* **24(5)**: 513–523.

Swanson, D. R. and N. R. Smalheiser. 1997. "An interactive system for finding complementary literatures: a stimulus to scientific discovery." *Artificial Intell.* **91**: 183–203.

Turtle, H. R. and W. B. Croft. 1992. "A comparison of text retrieval models." *Comput. J.* **35(3)**: 297–290.

Further Reading

Baeza-Yates, R. and B. Ribeiro-Neto. 1999. *Modern Information Retrieval*. Harlow, UK: Addison-Wesley. This book provides an in-depth coverage of contemporary research issues in information retrieval.

Kohonen, T. 1997. *Self-Organizing Maps*, 2d ed. Berlin: Springer-Verlag. This is by far the most comprehensive review of self-organizing maps and their applications.

Ripley, B. 1996. *Pattern Recognition and Neural Networks*. Cambridge, UK: Cambridge University Press. An excellent introduction to neural networks, which covers a wide spectrum of models and relates them to traditional pattern recognition methods.

Sparck Jones, K. and P. Willett, 1997. *Readings in Information Retrieval*. San Francisco, CA: Morgan Kaufmann. A prime source for classic articles in the area of information retrieval.

46.10 Predicting Daily Stock Indices Movements from Financial News

B. Wüthrich

ABSTRACT   The World Wide Web contains mostly unstructured textual information. Hence, with the growth of the Internet and the World Wide Web, the need for technology to analyze and mine textual information automatically is becoming increasingly important. We developed such a text mining system, which predicts daily closing values of major stock market indices in Asia, Europe, and America from financial news articles retrieved from the Web. Textual statements contain not only the effect (e.g., stocks went down) but also the possible causes of the event (e.g., stocks went down because of panicking investors). Exploiting textual information therefore increases the quality of the input. The forecasts are available daily via www.cs.ust.hk/~beat/Predict at 7:45 a.m. Hong Kong time. A simple trading strategy based on the predictions is presented and to be shown potentially more profitable than the actual index movements.

1. Project Overview

These days an increasing amount of crucial and commercially valuable information is becoming available on the World Wide Web. The *Wall Street Journal* (www.wsj.com) and *Financial Times* (www.ft.com) maintain excellent electronic versions of their daily issues. Reuters (www.investools.com), Dow Jones (www.asianupdate.com), CNN (www.cnnfn.com) and Bloomberg (www.bloomberg.com) provide real-time news and quotations of stocks, bonds, and currencies. All of these electronic information sources contain global and regional political and economic news, citations from influential bankers and politicians, as well as recommendations from financial analysts. This kind of information is primarily responsible for moving bond, stock, and currency markets across Asia/Pacific, Europe, and the Americas.

Numerical data in electronic news feeds contains only information regarding events, for example, "the Dow Jones Industrials fell." Textual statements, on the other hand, contain both events and the main causes of these events, "Dow Jones Industrials fell—because of earnings worries." Exploiting the additional information contained in textual feeds, can dramatically increase the accuracy of financial market predictions versus conventional forecasting techniques as described in Foscolos and Wüthrich (1999).

The data mining tool developed is specifically designed to predict daily movements of major stock market indices such as the Dow Jones Industrial Average (Dow), the Nikkei 225 (Nky), the Financial Times 100 Index (Ftse), the Hang Seng Index (Hsi), and the Singapore Straits Index (Sti). Until now, five researchers and developers have been involved part-time in developing this system over a period of about three years.

Each morning at 6:45 A.M. Hong Kong time, an agent (software application) downloads Web pages from the *Wall Street Journal* and the *Financial Times* containing financial analysis and information on the world's stock, currency, and bond markets. This electronic news is stored in a series of text files (labeled "Today's Web pages" in Figure 1). The latest closing values of each market index are downloaded by an agent (software application) on stock trading days, see Figure 1. These are stored in a numeric data file represented in Figure 1 by "Last day's closing value of the index".

The sample or training data, which is used to develop as set of induction rules for predicting market indices, is stored in a series of text files labeled "Previous Web pages" and numeric data files labeled "Closing values of the index." These files contain data for the last one hundred trading days.

The file labeled "Keyword tuples" in Figure 1 contains over four hundred individual sequences of words, for example, *bond strong, dollar falter, property weak, Dow rebound, technology, rebound, strongly*. These sequences of words (either pairs, triples, or quadruples) have been judged by a domain expert to be influential in moving stock market indices.

2. KDD Process

The data mining system predicts stock market indices in the following manner:

1. The number of occurrences of the key word records in the sample electronic news files on each day is counted. These occurrences are then transformed into a real number between zero and one. This transformed value is the weight assigned to the particular key word tuple.

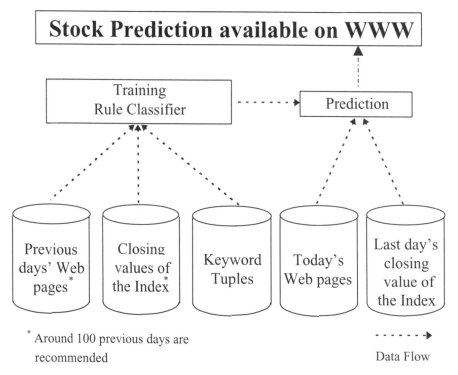

Figure 1 Architecture and main component of the prediction system

2. From the weights and the closing values of the sample data, classification rules (see Figure 1) are generated (see Wüthrich, 1997; and Cho et al., 1999, for the precise algorithm used).

3. The rules produced are applied to the weights derived from today's news. This determines whether a particular index, such as the Dow, will rise (appreciate at least 0.5 percent), move down (decline at least 0.5 percent), or remain steady (change less than 0.5 percent from its previous closing value).

4. From the prediction (Dow rises, falls, or remains steady) and from the latest closing value the forecasted closing value of the index is determined (see Figure 2).

The generated predictions are then moved to the Web page (`www.cs.ust.hk/~beat/ Predict`), where each day at 7:45 A.M. local time in Hong Kong (6:45 P.M. Eastern time) the daily stock market forecast can be followed (see Figure 2).

Following is a detailed description of the individual steps outlined above.

2.1. Keyword Record Counting

The counting of key word tuples or records is case insensitive and stemming algorithms scan the text. Hence, not only exact matches are considered. For example, if a keyword record is stock drop, and a Web page contains a phrase stocks have really dropped, the system still counts this as a match. An example of the result of this counting is shown in Table 1.

2.2. Transformation of Counts into Weights

In a next step, a weight (i.e., a real number between zero and one) for each keyword tuple is computed, as shown in Figure 3.

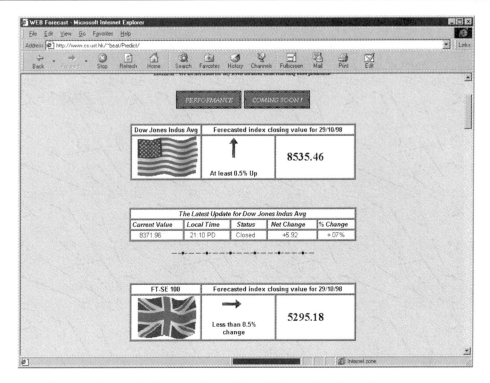

Figure 2 Index predictions provided daily at 7:45 A.M. Hong Kong time

There is a long history in text retrieval literature concentrating on using key word weighting to classify and rank documents. Keen (1991) and Salton and Buckley (1988) provide an overview on term weighting approaches in automatic text retrieval.

There are numerous approaches by which to conduct term weighting. One commonly used approach is to use three components: term frequency, document discrimination, and normalization.

Term frequency (TF) is the number of occurrences of a key word tuple or record appearing in a day's Web page. Key word records that are mentioned frequently are assigned a larger weight. Term frequency factor alone is not a good indicator of the strength or importance of a key word record. This is due to the fact that if a key word record appears on each day's Web pages, then the key word record is not necessarily a characteristic for a particular day. Therefore, category frequency (CF) is introduced. For each possible category: stock index up, down, or steady, the CF of a key word record is the number of training days containing the key word record in that particular category at least once, as shown in Table 2.

For example, the key word record bond lost appeared on twenty-three days when the index went down. Based on the CF, the category discrimination factor (CDF) is computed:

$$CDF_i = \frac{\max(CF_{i,\mathrm{up}}, CF_{i,\mathrm{down}}, CF_{i,\mathrm{steady}})}{t_i},$$

Table 1 Number of Occurrences of Key Word Record at Each Day

	Mar 15	Mar 16	Mar 17
Bond lost	3	1	4
Stock mixed	1	0	8
Interest rate cut	2	4	5

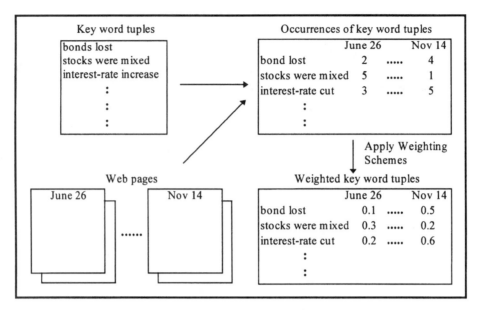

Figure 3 Weights are generated from key word record occurrences

where $CF_{i,c}$ is the category frequency of a key word record i in category c, and t_i is the number of days that the key word record i appears.

The training data set is categorized into the three outcomes (rising index, steady index, and falling index). The CDF takes into account the key word tuples or records that concentrate on a particular category in the sample data and assigns this a higher weight. Table 3 shows such weights. They are calculated by multiplying the term frequency with category discrimination (TF × CDF).

The third weighting term is the normalization factor. For each day the maximum weight of a key word record (day's maximum) is found. Each key word weight is divided by this maximum. This assures that the final weight is a real number between zero and one. While other weighting schemes were tried during the development of this application (see Cho et al., 1999 for more information on different weighting schemes), the method described is simple and provides rather high forecasting accuracy.

Table 2 Category Frequency of Key Word Records with Respect to an Index

Key Word Record	Index up	Index down	Index steady
Bond lost	13	23	18
Stock mixed	2	31	1
Interest rate cut	20	18	9

Table 3 Maximum Values Used to Do Normalization

	Mar 15	Mar 16	Mar 17
Bond lost	1.26	0.42	1.70
Stock mixed	0.86	0.0	6.88
Interest rate cut	0.85	1.70	2.13
Day's maximum	1.26	1.70	6.88

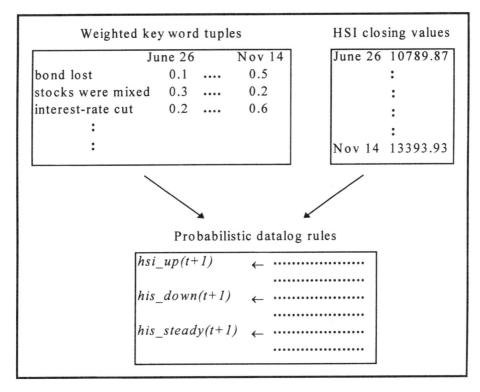

Figure 4 Rules are generated from weighted key words and closing values

2.3. Training the Probabilistic Classifier

Once the key word counts are transformed into weights, three rules sets are generated for each index (see Figure 4). Unlike other rule-based approaches, probabilistic rules are quantitative and can deal with weights (Wüthrich, 1995).

The rule bodies consist of the key word records, and their evaluation yields a probability that specifies the likelihood that the particular index is rising, falling, or remaining steady. The following is the sample rule set generated on 28 October 1998, which calculates the likelihood that the Dow is rising today.

```
DOW_UP (T)←STOCK_ROSE (T−1), NOT INTEREST_WORRY (T−1), NOT BUND_STRONG (T−2),
        NOT INTEREST_HIKE (T−2)
DOW_UP (T)←STERLING_ADD (T−1), BOND_STRONG (T−2)
DOW_UP (T)←YEN_PLUNG (T−1), NOT GOLD_SELL (T−2),
        STOCK_ROSE (T−1)
```

Therefore, the likelihood of the Dow's rising depends, for instance, on the weight computed for the key word *stock rose yesterday* and on the weight of the key word *bond strong two days ago*. Unlike other rule-based approaches, these rules can also deal with weights and are hence more powerful. Suppose the following weights were generated for the last two days, say day 99 and day 100.

```
STOCK_ROSE (100)    : 1.0
INTEREST_WORRY (100) : 0.2
BOND_STRONG (99)     : 0.7
INTEREST_HIKE (99)   : 0.0
```

```
STERLING_ADD (100)      : 0.5
YEN_PLUNG (100)         : 0.6
GOLD_SELL (99)          : 0.1
```

Applying the rules on those weights computes the probability of the index rising. More specifically, the rules compute how likely it is for the index to rise on day 101.

$$\text{DOW\_UP}(101) = 1 * (1 - 0.2) * (1 - 0.7) * (1 - 0) + 0.5 * 0.7 + 0.6 * (1 - 0.1) * 1$$

likelihood that first rule is true, or the second

rule is true, or the third rule is true

-0

since first and second rule are contradictory

$-1 * (1 - 0.2) * (1 - 0.7) * (1 - 0) * 0.6 * (1 - 0.1)$

likelihood that first and third rule are

both true; note stock_rose is taken only once

$-0.5 * 0.7 * 0.6 * (1 - 0.1) * 1$

likelihood that second and third rule true

$+0$

three rule bodies together are contradictory

$=0.811$

2.4. Generating the Forecasts

Once the rules are generated, they are applied to the most recently collected textual news and analysis results. Therefore, the likelihood of the Dow going up on 28 October depends, for instance, on the weight computed for STOCK_ROSE on the 27th and the weight computed for STERLING_ADD on the 26th. From these probabilities, the final decision is taken regarding the likelihood of the Dow rising, falling, or remaining steady. For example, the final decision is that the Dow moves up.

Each of the three rule sets (DOW_UP, DOW_STEADY, DOW_DOWN) yields a probability that specifies how likely the respective event will occur on 29 October. For example, suppose the likelihoods are 0.81, 0.1, and 0.09. For each rule set j a threshold v_j is computed such that if the computed likelihood $f_j(t)$ is above the threshold then it is taken as true; otherwise it is taken as false. The threshold is determined by testing the values $v_j = 0, 0.05, 0.1, 0.15, ...,1$ and selecting the threshold that results in the least error on the sample. Given the three thresholds v_j and the three likelihoods $f_j(t)$, there are three possible cases:

1. Exactly one of three likelihoods is above its threshold, which is $f_j(t) \geqslant v_j$ for one j: class j is the final prediction.

2. None of the three likelihoods is above its threshold, which is $f_j(t) < v_j$ for all j: we compute $d_j(t)$ and select that j to be true, for which the deviation $d_j(t)$ is maximal.

$$d_j(t) = \frac{f_j(t) - v_j}{v_j}$$

3. All likelihoods are above their threshold, which is $f_j(t) \geqslant v_j$ for all j: as before, we select that j with maximal deviation $d_j(t)$.

After the direction of the stock market movement is determined (up, down, or steady), the closing value of the stock index is computed. Suppose the generated rules expect an upward movement for the next day and the Dow closed on the previous day at 8371. The generated rules are now also applied to the training data and the average real percentage change x for those days for which the rules indicate an upward movement is determined. The forecasted closing value for the Dow is therefore $8371 * (1 + x) = 8535$.

Table 4 Performance in the Period 6 December 1997 to 6 March 1998

	Correct	*Slightly wrong*	*Wrong*
Dow Jones Indus.	45.0%	46.7%	8.3%
FT-SE 100	46.7%	36.7%	16.6%
Nikkei 225	41.7%	38.3%	20.0%
Hang Seng	45.0%	26.7%	28.3%
Singapore Straits	40.0%	38.3%	21.7%
Average	43.6%	37.4%	19.0%

3. Out of Sample Testing

The training period or sample is always the most recent 100 trading days. That is, to forecast on the 6 March, the system is first trained on the period 5 December 1997 to 5 March 1998. This ensures that the behavior of the system reflects changes in the financial market environment as the training window slides forward. The performance of the data mining system reported in Table 4 and discussed subsequently is based on the three-month period from 6 December 1997 to 6 March 1998. This provides an out-of-sample period of ninety-nine trading days.

As a measure of accuracy, the percentage of correct predictions is used. For instance, if the system predicts a rise in the index and the index indeed rises, then the observation is correct, otherwise (that is, if the index is steady or falls), the observation is incorrect. This measure of accuracy is shown in the second column of Table 4. The third column in Table 4 indicates how many times the system predicts an index will rise or fall, and it actually remained steady; or, the system predicts the index will remain steady and the index actually rises or falls. The last column indicates the percentage of totally wrong predictions. That is, the system expects the index to rise and it falls, or vice versa.

It is not surprising that the results for the Dow and Ftse are the best, since most of the electronic news feeds concentrate on these mature markets. Singapore, with rather modest results, is the smallest market in terms of capitalization and turnover; hence it was expected to be the least predictable.

The distribution of the actual outcomes and the distribution of the forecast is shown in Table 5.

The latest performance statistics produced by this data mining tool, for ten major stock market indices, are posted on `www.cs.ust.hk/~beat/Predict`. This page is recomputed each day and displays the information discussed in Tables 4 and 5. Additionally this Web page provides:

1. The predicted closing values as compared to the actual outcome (see Figure 5).

2. The actual and forecast direction of the index over the last twenty trading days (see Figure 6).

Table 5 Distribution in the Period 6 December 1997 to 6 March 1998

	Actual outcome			*Distribution of the forecast*		
	Up	*Steady*	*Down*	*Up*	*Steady*	*Down*
Dow	48.3%	26.7%	25.0%	45.0%	33.3%	21.7%
Ftse	35.0%	43.3%	21.7%	51.7%	33.3%	15.0%
Nky	33.3%	41.7%	25.0%	33.3%	30.0%	36.7%
Hsi	35.0%	21.7%	43.3%	26.7%	28.3%	45.0%
Sti	40.0%	20.0%	40.0%	31.7%	26.6%	41.7%
Average	38.3%	30.7%	31.0%	37.7%	30.3%	32.0%

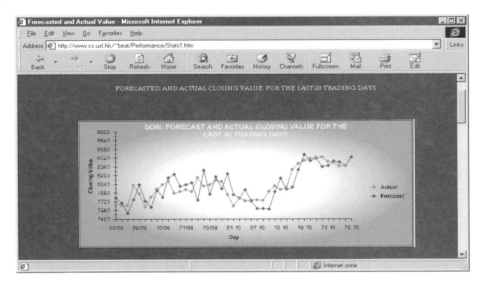

Figure 5 Predicted and actual closing values

3. Conditional probabilities $P(x, y)$, which measure the likelihood of the outcome x (see Figure 7).

4. A Simple Trading Strategy

The accuracy of the data mining system described is sufficient for an investor to construct a simple trading strategy based on purchasing index futures.

The trading strategy exemplified assumes that whenever the market rises it appreciates on average by 0.5 percent, when it is steady there is on average 0 percent change, and when the market falls it slumps on average by 0.5 percent. In other words, the assumption is made that a stop loss is applied at + or −0.5 percent. In reality, markets move on average by much more. Thus, in this regard the trading strategy is conservative with respect to calculated profits.

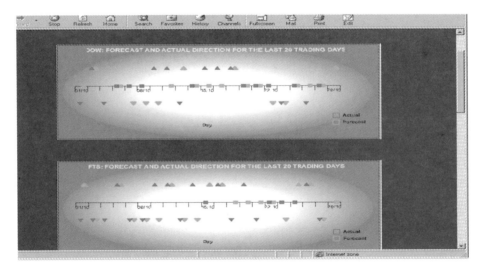

Figure 6 Predicted and actual index directions

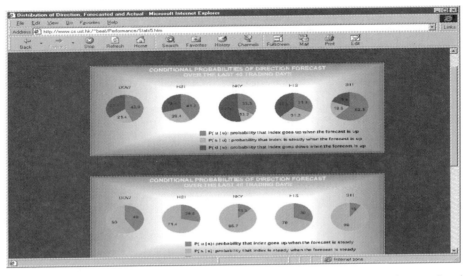

Figure 7 Conditional probabilities, for example, how likely is it to go up when predicted down

This trading strategy assumes that no trading costs are incurred when buying or selling. Trading costs actually depend on the amount traded, the specific futures exchange, and the brokerage. The trading strategy also assumes no slippage, at market open the future is bought or sold at yesterday's closing price. However, as this trading strategy is daily rather than intraday, it is anticipated that slippage would be minimal.

If the data mining tool predicts that the index will rise, the investor goes long on the index future. If the data mining tool predicts the index will fall, the index future is shorted. At market close on each day the strategy requires the investor to close out of all positions.

To understand the potential of the strategy, consider using the strategy to invest in Dow Jones Industrial futures during a ninety-nine-trading-day period from 6 December to 6 March. Referring back to Tables 4 and 5, the future would have been bought on twenty-seven days and short sold on thirteen days. The profit made in the twelve days of buying into the market would be 0.5 percent and profit by short selling the index on six days would have been 0.5 percent. The trading strategy would have been slightly wrong on nineteen of the forty trading days; hence, neither a profit nor loss would have been booked. On the remaining three days a loss of 0.5 percent would have occurred as the data mining tool made incorrect predictions. Assuming an equivalent amount was invested in Dow Jones Industrial futures on each trading day, the profit produced by the strategy over the three month period would be $(12 + 6 - 3) * 0.5$ percent or 7.5 percent, in other words a 30 percent capital appreciation over one

Table 6 Performance of the Index Versus an Active Trading Strategy Based on the System's Forecast, 6 December 1997 to 6 March 1998

	Actual performance		Trading strategy	
	3 months	12 months	3 months	12 months
Dow	5.1%	20.4%	7.5%	30.0%
Ftse	11.4%	45.6%	5.5%	22.0%
Nky	4.3%	17.2%	5.0%	20.0%
His	− 4.6%	−18.4%	3.5%	14.0%
Sti	− 8.8%	−35.2%	4.5%	18.0%
Average	1.5%	5.9%	5.2%	20.8%

year. In the same period, 6 December to 6 March, the Dow itself appreciated by only 5.1 percent. Table 6 provides the full results.

References

Cho, V., B. Wüthrich, and J. Zhang. 1999. "Text processing for classification." *J. Comput. Intell. Finance* **7(2)**: 6–23.

Foscolos, M. and B. Wüthrich. 1999. *A Guide to Data Mining in Investment Management, Quantitative Research Seminar 1999.* Sydney: SBC Warburg Dillon Read Australia Equities Ltd, Warburg Publisher.

Keen, E. M. 1991. "Query term weighting schemes for effective ranked output retrieval." In *Fifteenth International Online Information Meeting*, pp. 135–142.

Salton, G. and M. J. McGill. 1983. *Introduction to Modern Information Retrieval.* New York: McGraw-Hill.

Wüthrich, B. 1995. "Probabilistic knowledge bases." *IEEE Trans. Knowledge Data Engng* **7(5)**: 691–698.

Wüthrich, B. 1997. "Discovering probabilistic decision rules." *Int. J. Intell. Sys. Accounting, Finance Mgmnt* **6**: 269–277.

46.11 Internet Usage Analysis

Gavin Meggs

ABSTRACT An ever-increasing amount of information is being stored in electronic form, both on the Internet and on corporate Intranets. Beyond the effort expended in creating such knowledge bases comes the task of raising users' awareness of the availability of information and encouraging the use of it. Without constant use and feedback, such stores turn from valuable living resources into static outdated libraries. In this case study we show how an understanding of users' interactions with knowledge is used to facilitate and encourage further use of that knowledge. By capturing the significant patterns in user behavior, it is possible to determine which sections of a knowledge base are being used, how they are being used, and by whom. We then consider groupings of like users and develop communities of interest such as active groups of knowledge workers who not only access common areas of knowledge, but also behave in similar ways when doing so. A deeper understanding of how knowledge is used also facilitates the ongoing maintenance and structuring of that knowledge.

1. Project Overview

In this section we present a component view of the project. We focus on the key data mining phase, the phase that takes us from available data to discovered knowledge. A detailed discussion of the more general process of knowledge discovery is given in Part 3 of this handbook, with the detail for this study being given in subsequent sections.

Figure 1 depicts a task-oriented view of the data mining phase.

We begin with the tasks of gathering data to support the analysis. We gather transaction data in the form of access logs that describe the behavior of users with a knowledge store, and background knowledge in the form of hierarchies that describe taxonomies related to the transaction data. Gathered data is supplied to a discovery mechanism where we employ rule discovery methods (see Chapter 16.2). We discover associations between pages; rules derived from these associations; and sequences of pages accessed by users over time. In the final task we determine which users are active in the creation of these patterns, and we cluster (see Chapter 16.5) them together based upon the similarity of their activity. Our output consists of groups of users who share similar behavioral patterns, which we call communities of interest.

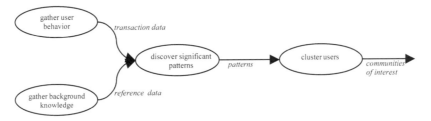

Figure 1 The core data mining phase

2. KDD Process

The need to understand the increasing amount of knowledge available within an organization is a significant one. The pace of change of the relevance of knowledge demands that it be kept up to date; it is a living store of information that must be nurtured if it is not to become outdated. The people in the best position to update knowledge are those who are active in its use, but with such complex relationships within the knowledge and between its users this is not a simple task.

It is not enough to create knowledge bases and inform users of them. We must become involved in the ongoing maintenance of knowledge bases; we must become learners instead of knowers. Herein lies the problem. In order to determine which groups to gather knowledge from, we must first identify those groups. We would prefer this to be an emergent process that requires little or no intervention on the user's part and to identify those users who are active, as opposed to casual users of the knowledge.

We arrive at the need to work away from the behavior of individuals—a community of users of a knowledge base—toward the development of communities of interest, active groups of users who share common interests in a section of a knowledge base. We aim to build these communities from the ground up, using information about individual users' interactions with the knowledge to group them together. By identifying such communities and encouraging interaction within them, we aim to move from disconnected lookups on information to a living relationship between users and knowledge. Subsequently, we will build a deeper understanding of how a knowledge base is used and how it might be maintained.

The analysis of complex relationships within large data volumes is not possible without some form of data mining. The framework provided by data mining process models, such as the CRoss Industry Standard Process model for Data Mining (CRISP-DM) and that provided by Fayyad et al. (1996), assist us in addressing these aspects, from defining the scope of the initial task through the identification of roles supporting the project to the analysis itself and the determination of actions required.

2.1. Available Data

Our source of transactions is the Internet access log, which describes the users' interactions with the knowledge base. These data are comprised of a tuple (IP address, URL, timestamp), where the IP address is statically allocated to a user. The URL is the identifier of a static Web page that has been accessed by a user. Finally, the timestamp identifies when the request for the page was made.

In addition to the transaction data, we exploit background knowledge. Background knowledge is stored in the form of hierarchies and represents taxonomies that are associated with the dimensions of the transaction data. For the first dimension (IP address) we use the structure of the IP address as a four-level hierarchy. By linking the IP address to a user we are able to access a reference indicator for that user. The reference indicator places the user within an organization and is a three-level hierarchy. For the second dimension (URL) we have a hierarchy implicit in the directory structure of the URL. This is an arbitrary level hierarchy. Finally, for the time dimension, we use a single hierarchy (see Figure 2).

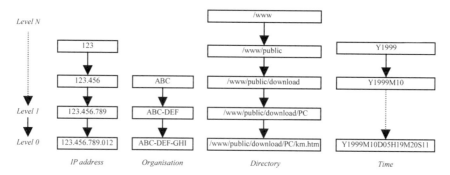

Figure 2 Background knowledge

For the purpose of demonstration, an artificial data set was created with characteristics similar to transactions in the target domain. The data set was comprised of one hundred users. Each user was drawn from one of three user groups (shown as A, B, and C in Figure 3). A total of 65 topics from level 1 of the directory hierarchy were selected and associated with user groups as depicted in Figure 3. User sessions were created by selecting a user at random and then selecting a topic from those associated with the user's group. A URL within the chosen topic was selected at random and assigned to the session. A total of one thousand sessions was created, with the average number of URLs within a session set to five.

From the description of the data set given, we would expect predominant patterns to exist between individual users and topics at level 1 of the directory hierarchy (since the allocation of URLs within a topic is random). Similarities between communities should mirror the distribution of topics in Figure 3.

In addition to the detail of the transaction data and background knowledge, we made use of people who work in the domain. An understanding of the background knowledge at a deeper level than can be captured in the form of the strict hierarchies is crucial. Also, an understanding of how communities of interest are identified, and how they are grown, forms an important part of the analysis process. Such knowledge is used to guide the discovery mechanism toward which sorts of patterns to look for. It also supports recommendations for actions to be taken. For these reasons the developers of the knowledge base and a sample of the user community were involved throughout.

Our aim in using both transaction data and background knowledge to determine patterns was to build an understanding of the level at which patterns became significant. Did users associate with topics in ways that would relate them together or was it organizational groups working with classes of knowledge?

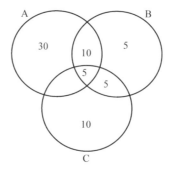

Figure 3 Distribution of topics across user groups

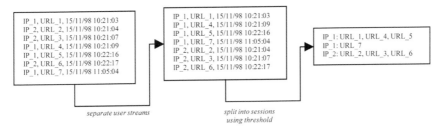

Figure 4 The process of sessionization

The involvement of domain experts would ensure that appropriate action was taken. In this case action would take the form of user groups being put into contact with each other and of links being introduced into the knowledge base between strongly correlated knowledge.

2.2. Pre-Analysis Considerations

The first stage of any analysis of behavior is to build an understanding of what counts as an event. In the analysis of access logs our event is an IP address requesting a page from a server. A behavioral pattern then becomes a chain of events associated with an IP address. Because users may be inactive for periods of time, chains of page accesses for IP addresses are split into sessions using a predefined time threshold (see Figure 4). Sessions form the input to the discovery program.

Background knowledge was either derived from the transaction data (e.g., topics from the directory structure of the URL) or extracted from existing systems (e.g., the organizational hierarchy). For this reason no preprocessing of background knowledge was required; however, background knowledge was inspected to ensure that the lowest levels of the hierarchies could be mapped onto the transactional data.

In some Web systems a user identifier is supplied as part of the URL string and used to link into the user hierarchy; this eventuality was tested, but not included in the final scenario. We also considered mapping users to a geographical hierarchy, but in the target environment many users used laptop machines. They had static IP addresses, but not static office locations.

When deciding which software platform to use for rule discovery, consideration was given to the data mining workbench Clementine (http://www.spss.com/). Clementine supports association rule analysis and also supports the exporting of process streams into executable code that can be used in a stand-alone mode. However, Clementine was not chosen, primarily because it did not allow enough control over the discovery process. First, the tool does not allow access to associations (generated as a necessary precursor to association rules) and does not support the generation of sequences. The requirement to include background knowledge in the analysis could not be supported, despite this knowledge being represented in relational form. Finally, the determination of which users contributed to discovered patterns could only be made through additional processing steps.

These limitations are not just true for Clementine. Other workbenches such as SAS' Enterprise Miner (http://www.sas.com/), Angoss' KnowledgeStudio (http://www.angoss.com/), and K-wiz solutions' k-wiz (http://www.kwiz-solutions.com/) have similar constraints. Supporting, sometimes gracefully, the process view of a data mining study, they fail to address the need to support iterations through the process and the gathering and integration of results for those iterations.

2.3. Performing the Analysis

The task of rule discovery was performed with an in-house consultancy tool that supports the discovery and subsequent analysis of associations, association rules, and sequences. The tool allows access to patterns at the level of associations and supports the incorporation of

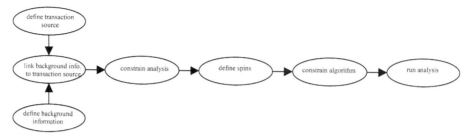

Figure 5 Controlling the analysis

background knowledge into the analysis. By including background knowledge we make it possible to perform the analysis at any level. We also use background knowledge to split data into logical subsets and use the tool to control the analysis across those subsets (see Figure 5).

We begin by specifying a data source for the transaction data. We then define zero or more sources of background knowledge and associate it with transaction data. Our analysis is constrained by specifying which branches of the hierarchies we wish to include in the analysis.

We now have a set of data upon which to perform an analysis, but often we would not want to consider the data set as a whole. For example, we may have many countries involved and perform the analysis for one country at a time, or for different categories of knowledge within the knowledge store. Perhaps most usefully we may build an understanding of how patterns vary over time. To support this we allow the users to specify the level at which they wish to spin for each of the hierarchies used. For example, by spinning on Organization and Month in a data set that contained data for four organizations over the period of a year, we would arrive at forty-eight spins. Each spin would result in a separate run of the pattern discovery algorithm. The results form a rich source of information that is used to analyze patterns within organizations and how their significance varies over time.

Finally, we place constraints upon the algorithm. Do we discover associations, association rules, or sequences? Do we use all of the data or just a sample (perhaps while testing)? What significance must a pattern have before it is reported?

Examples of analyses that could be performed using this approach based on the transaction data and associated background knowledge described are:

- Associations between users and topics in a specified time period.
- Sequences of topics accessed by users in a specific domain (e.g., 146.124.*.*).
- Affinity between topics and how the strengths of those affinities change over time.

For the purpose of the determination of communities of interest, we focused on the patterns of activity between users and topics in the knowledge store.

The final stage of the analysis, the clustering of users contributing to significant patterns, was more straightforward and Clementine was used for this purpose.

3. From Patterns to Action

Three types of patterns were considered. In the first, associations, we search for sets of pages accessed within sessions. The significance of an association is measured in terms of the frequency of its occurrence. The second form of pattern is the association rule. An association rule is developed from an association by considering each of the pages within the set as the consequent of a rule, with the remaining pages forming the antecedents of the rule. We adopt the significance of an association rule as a measure of the likelihood of the consequent occurring given the antecedents, in relation to the likelihood of it occurring in the entire population. For example, if the topic of knowledge discovery features in one in ten sessions, but within the subset of sessions that feature the topic "diapers," it features in one in five sessions, then we say that there was a shift in coverage from 10 percent to 20 percent. This

Table 1 Examples of Patterns Found

		Number of significant patterns		
Organizational level	Directory level	Associations	Association Rules	Sequences
User	URL	50	23	20
User	Topic	72	180	18
Group	URL	84	65	12
Group	Topic	102	68	24

Table 2 Distribution of Pattern Lengths

	Length of pattern				
	2	3	4	5	6
Number of rules	97	61	12	7	3

would be captured as a significance (a shift in coverage) for the rule "diapers -> knowledge discovery" of +10 percent. Finally for sequences we look for temporal chains of topics within a session with the significance of a sequence representing the probability of the user taking the final step in the chain.

In Table 1 we show a summary of significant patterns found for each pattern type when the analysis was run at different levels of the user and directory hierarchy. The threshold for significance in this example was set at a support of 10 percent for associations and a shift in coverage (positive or negative) of 80 percent for both association rules and sequences.

The table shows that the highest number of significant patterns appeared as association rules between users and topics. In the remainder of this paper we focus on these 180 patterns. For simplicity we refer to them as the significant patterns.

The size of a pattern, that is, the number of topics included in a rule, was not constrained. Table 2 shows the distribution of rule lengths for the significant patterns. We see that although the average session length was five, the majority of significant patterns are of length two or three.

3.1. Building Communities

The next stage of the analysis was to extract users involved in the patterns and cluster them. A total of 82 of the original 100 users were involved in the generation of the significant patterns. Their activity was summarized in the form of a matrix relating users to patterns and then normalized. Note that since patterns are made up from observing sessions across users, it is possible for users to feature more than once in any of the patterns. Figure 6 summarizes this process.

The output of this stage of the process is a matrix of similarity between users. The matrix is not simply a comparison of the pages that users access. It is a set of similarities between the behaviors of individuals, patterns that have been deemed to be significant at the global level.

Clustering was performed using the k-means clustering tool within Clementine, with the number of required clusters set to three, our aim being to determine whether clusters of users involved in the significant patterns aligned with the three groups of users defined in the data generation process. Although this is a complex comparison to make, it is intended to give us an insight into the reliability of the approach. Table 3 shows a cross tabulation of cluster membership between derived clusters and the user groups in the source data.

Three distinct clusters have been drawn from the data, but the alignment of those clusters to the organizational groups defined in the data generation process cannot be

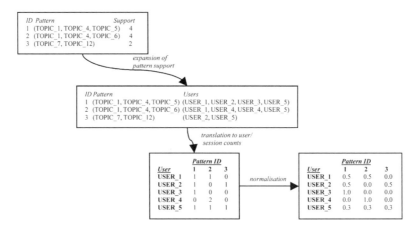

Figure 6 From patterns to user similarities

confirmed. If instead we define three groups that are more closely aligned to the distribution of topics given in Table 3:

CoI-1: users that only access topics accessed by users from organizational group A;

CoI-2: users that access topics accessed by users from organizational group A and organizational group B;

CoI-3: users that access topics only accessed by users from organizational group C;

we arrive at the comparison of clusters and emergent groups shown in Table 4.

Here the alignment of clusters to groups is much closer, as would be expected. The clusters have been formed on patterns of behavior of individuals and not their organizational affiliation.

3.2. Applications of Discovered Knowledge

The focus of this work has been to provide a rich reporting environment where the analyst is able to understand how users interact with knowledge. We have described a study in which we work from a user's interaction with knowledge to better understand how communities of users interact with knowledge. In the process of determining these communities of interest, we

Table 3 Comparison of Derived Clusters and Source Groups

	A	B	C	
Cluster 1	4	7	8	19
Cluster 2	1	4	18	23
Cluster 3	25	5	10	40
	30	16	26	82

Table 4 Comparison of Derived Clusters and Source Groups

	CoI-1	CoI-2	CoI-3	Other	
Cluster 1	1	7	1	10	19
Cluster 2	0	2	16	5	23
Cluster 3	22	5	7	6	40
	23	14	24	21	82

have shown how significant patterns of various types are derived from data at various levels and linked back to users who give rise to those patterns.

There are three primary applications of the knowledge discovered in this process. In the first, we track affinities between topics over time. By building an understanding of how relationships within a knowledge base change, we raise awareness within an organization of the significance of these topics, or perhaps direct attention toward topics that are deemed important, but are receiving little attention. The second major application, and the focus of this paper, is the fostering of communities of interest. By putting active users in touch with each other, awareness across an organization is increased, leading to enhanced connectivity and productivity of individuals. Even conservative estimates of the savings to an organization by reducing the amount of time spent searching for relative knowledge run into millions of dollars. Finally, the maintenance of the knowledge base is made easier as users exploit the value it adds to their work and become more involved in its population.

All three applications lead to the development of the knowledge bases from which we learn.

Relevant Web Sites

CRISP-DM: Cross Industry Standard Process for Data Mining (ESPRIT Project Number 25959), available for download from http://www.crisp-dm.org.

http://www.angoss.com/. Maintained by ANGOSS Software Corporation, Toronto. Company Web site providing links to range of products and services in the fields of data mining and statistics.

http://www.kwiz-solutions.com/. Maintained by K.wiz Solutions Limited, Scotland, UK. Company Web site providing links to a range of products and services in the fields of data mining.

http://www.sas.com/. Maintained by SAS Institute Inc., Cary, NC. Company Web site providing links to a range of products and services in the fields of data mining and statistics.

http://www.spss.com/. Maintained by SPSS Inc., Chicago. Company Web site providing links to a range of products and services in the fields of data mining and statistics.

References

Fayyad, U. M., G. Piatetsky-Shapiro, and P. Smyth. 1996. "Knowledge discovery and data mining: toward a unifying framework." In *Proceedings of the Second International Conference on Knowledge Discovery and Data Mining*, pp. 82–89. Menlo Park, CA: AAAI Press.

47 PUBLIC ADMINISTRATION AND HEALTH CARE

47.1 Data Mining and Hospital Infection Control Surveillance

Stephen E. Brossette and Stephen A. Moser

ABSTRACT The search for signs of emerging infection and antimicrobial resistance is a formidable challenge. To help address this challenge, we developed the data mining surveillance system (DMSS—patent pending), which employs data mining techniques to discover unsuspected, useful patterns in hospital laboratory data. We believe that DMSS will improve infection control surveillance and will have a beneficial impact on both medical and financial outcomes associated with hospital-acquired infections.

1. Project Overview

The project generally follows the knowledge discovery in databases (KDD) model, summarized by the block diagram in Figure 1. Data analysis starts by extracting relevant data from the laboratory database, cleaning it, formatting it, and dividing it into monthly partitions. Data are processed one partition at a time, and discovered patterns are presented to infection control experts after each is completed.

The DMSS project, now five years old, is an ongoing collaborative effort between the departments of Pathology and Computer and Information Sciences at the University of Alabama at Birmingham (UAB). The core development team is composed of four researchers who are members of the UAB Knowledge Discovery Research Group.

2. KDD Process

2.1. The Problem

Each year in the United States, hospital-acquired (nosocomial) infections affect 2 million patients, cost more than $4.5 billion (1992 dollars), and account for half of all major hospital complications (Anonymous, 1992). Additionally, the financial and human cost of drug-resistant infections has reached unprecedented levels (Goldmann et al., 1996). Vancomycin-resistant enterococci, glycopeptide intermediate *Staphylococcus aureus*, extended beta-lactamase producing gram-negative rods, and multidrug-resistant tuberculosis are but a few examples of highly resistant bacteria that now cause significant morbidity and mortality.

2.2. Motivation for Data Mining Solution

Nosocomial infection and bacterial resistance are global problems with local origins. Hospital intensive care units are foci where resistant organisms propagate, only to spread to larger environments as opportunity provides (Jones, 1992; Koontz, 1992; Neu et al., 1992; Shlaes et al., 1997). Early recognition of emerging problems, therefore, requires proactive surveillance at the

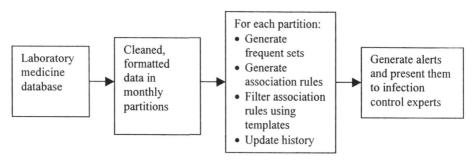

Figure 1 Overview of DMSS

hospital and subhospital levels (Jones, 1992; Koontz, 1992; Neu et al., 1992; Shlaes et al., 1997). Extensive analysis of hospital data, however, requires considerable time and resources, which few hospital epidemiologists have in reserve. Consequently, these data are underutilized.

Traditional hospital infection control surveillance includes the manual review of suspected cases of nosocomial infection and the tabulation of basic summary statistics. Antimicrobial resistance surveillance consists of the daily review of culture results for simple sentinel events and the construction of periodic (i.e., annual or semiannual), hospitalwide antibiogram summaries. Daily review of culture results is unable to detect all but the simplest events while antibiogram summaries are not timely and often mask emerging, complex patterns of resistance (Neu et al., 1992). Consequently, it has been widely recognized that sophisticated, active, and timely intrahospital surveillance is needed (Neu et al., 1992; Shlaes et al., 1997).

2.3. The Available Data

A great deal of hospital data, especially patient care data, are still stored in unstructured paper charts. Traditional hospital infection control surveillance relies heavily on the manual review of these data for the identification of nosocomial infections (Emori et al., 1991). Unfortunately, chart review and the subsequent data analysis are inefficient and often miss patterns of infection and resistance. Additionally, without an efficient way to structure chart information relevant to infection control and a mechanism for getting it into a database in a timely manner, paper charts are useless as a data source for data mining.

Bacterial culture data in the hospital laboratory information system is usually the only available source of timely data related to infection and bacterial resistance. However, not all patients who have bacterial infections are cultured, and databases do not contain other relevant information. Consequently, true rates of infection using traditional denominators cannot be determined using these data.

When properly mined, however, bacterial culture data can be used as an additional source of valuable information that can improve surveillance by suggesting emerging problems not previously suspected. In turn, this can focus the efforts of infection control personnel by guiding investigation, intervention, and follow-up.

In our experiments, bacterial culture data and related patient information are extracted from the UAB clinical laboratory information system. This system collects data from all laboratory tests performed in the healthcare system, which includes a tertiary care academic teaching hospital with an average of 800 beds in service (38,665 admission/year), and a large outpatient clinic with 350,000 visits per year. A subset of data is extracted nightly and compiled into a separate database with approximately 80,000 records per year. After preprocessing, each record ($\approx 60,000$ records/year) describes a single bacterial isolate and contains items for the following attributes: organism name, gram stain/morphology, date collected, nosocomial status, source of isolate (e.g., urine, blood), location of patient in hospital (e.g., Surgical Intensive Care Unit). Each record also contains the set of antimicrobials to which the organism tested resistant or intermediate resistant according to NCCLS criteria (NCCLS, 1999). All attributes are categorical.

2.4. Definitions

Association rules are defined in the traditional way (see Chapter 16.2.3). The support of an item set X is denoted $s(X)$. The incidence proportion, or confidence, of association rule $A \Rightarrow B$ in data partition p_i is the number of times outcome B occurs in group A during time t_i. $s(A)$ is called the precondition support of the rule. A series of incidence proportions for $A \Rightarrow B$ from data partitions $p_1, ..., p_n$ describes the incidence of the outcome B in group A from t_1 through t_n. Therefore, by analyzing the time series of incidence proportions of an association rule $A \Rightarrow B$, it is possible to detect shifts or trends in the incidence of B in A over time.

2.5. The Expected Output

DMSS is expected to produce a set of patterns each month that can be reviewed in no more than one hour by an infection control expert. A pattern consists of an association rule and a sequence of incidence proportions over which a significant change occurs. These patterns are ranked by the domain expert and are used to supplement the traditional surveillance activities of a hospital infection control committee.

2.6. Data Mining Constraints

Time constraints are relatively minor. Monthly, data are extracted from the lab medicine system and preprocessed. The polished data are then processed by DMSS, and the resulting patterns are reviewed by infection control and other experts. Decisions are made regarding the importance of the month's patterns and which actions, if any, are required. All of the above should ideally happen within a week, with the majority of that time taken by pattern interpretation, follow-up investigation, and intervention. Therefore, the time to extract data, format it, run DMSS, and have resulting patterns distributed for review should take no more than two days.

The second constraint is the computational burden of generating small support frequent sets that are necessary to generate association rules with low-incidence proportions. These are necessary to track changes in relatively low-incidence outcomes. The size and complexity of the typical laboratory data sets used allow for the use of traditional frequent set algorithms.

The third constraint is related to pattern evaluation. Patterns generated by DMSS must be manageable in number and useful enough to justify the time required by domain experts to evaluate them. This, of course, is subjective, and is a problem of all descriptive data mining methods. The false-positive rate, that is, the proportion of patterns generated that are uninteresting, must be balanced with the sensitivity of the methodology so that useful patterns are generated and the user is not overwhelmed reviewing inane patterns. DMSS employs rule templates (see Section 4.1) and event capture to address this problem.

2.7. Preprocessing the Data

The data is preprocessed in several ways. First, duplicate records are removed so that the data sets contain no more than one record per patient per organism per month. Second, antimicrobials that an organism is known to be historically resistant to greater than 50 percent of the time are removed since they are of little clinical or therapeutic interest. This significantly reduces the number of frequent antimicrobial items in the data set, thereby reducing the computational burden of generating frequent sets. Finally, all records are split into disjoint monthly partitions.

3. Data Mining Resources

3.1. The Discovery Mechanism

For each frequent set from a data partition, DMSS generates all association rules with a precondition support greater or equal to a preset value, regardless of rule confidence. Each rule in turn is compared to a set of user-defined rule templates that describe flavors of interesting and uninteresting rules. Two types of rule templates are used: include templates and exclude templates (Table 1). An association rule $A \Rightarrow B$ passes a set of rule templates if $A \Rightarrow B$ satisfies

Table 1 Examples of Templates Used to Filter Association Rules

Template Type	Group	Outcome	Explanation
Exclude	(Anything)	(Source)	Exclude rules that contain the source of infection as an outcome.
Include	(Organism OR Location)	(Antibiotic OR Gram/Morph OR Organism)	Include rules whose groups are organism or location specific and whose outcomes are antibiotic, gram/morph, or organism specific.

at least one include template and does not satisfy any exclude template. In DMSS, any number of inclusive and exclusive templates can be specified.

Since rule templates contain domain knowledge, they must be handcrafted by domain experts. In general, an expert usually has an idea of some types of rules that are interesting, or may know of some types that are never interesting. Even if this is not known initially, our experience has indicated that experiments with representative data provide enough insight to facilitate template construction.

3.2. History

Rules that pass the rule templates are stored in the history. For each new rule, the incidence proportion of the current partition and the incidence proportions of several previous partitions are computed and stored. Once a rule is stored in the history, it is updated for each new partition. The history, therefore, contains an up-to-date time series of incidence proportions for every association rule it contains.

3.3. Alerts

High-level patterns, called alerts, are presented to the user. DMSS generates alerts by clustering events.

An event describes a significant change in the series of incidence proportions of an association rule. It is generated by breaking the time series of incidence proportions of an association rule into three contiguous nonoverlapping pieces: the distant past, the not-so-distant past, and the recent past. The not-so-distant past time window w_p and the recent past time window w_c are the only two of interest. If the incidence proportions of the association rule have changed between w_p and w_c, an event is generated. This is done by computing the cumulative incidence proportion of each time window and comparing them by a test of two proportions.

The support of item set X in data partition p is denoted $s(X, p)$. The cumulative incidence proportion of association rule $A \Rightarrow B$ in a time window w is given by

$$\frac{\sum_{p_i \in w} s(A \cup B, p_i)}{\sum_{p_i \in w} s(A, p_i)}.$$

Two cumulative incidence proportions h_1, h_2 are tested under the null hypothesis H_0 : $h_1 = h_2$ by a chi-squared or Fisher exact test of two proportions (Rosner, 1990). If H_0 is rejected, that is, the p-value of the test statistic is less than α, an event is generated.

---

1)   {MICU}$\Rightarrow${A2}
      []Jan: 0/57 | []Feb: 1/60 | []Mar: 2/52 | *Apr: 7/65

2)   {MICU, NP_GNR}$\Rightarrow${A1, A2}
      []Jan: 0/23 | []Feb: 0/20 | []Mar: 2/18 | *Apr: 7/21

3)   {MICU, NP_GNR, nosocomial}$\Rightarrow${A1, A2}
      []Jan: 0/11 | []Feb: 0/10 | []Mar: 1/12 | *Apr: 5/13

4)   {MICU, NP_GNR, nosocomial, *A. baumannii*}$\Rightarrow${A1, A2}
      []Jan: 0/5 | []Feb: 0/5 | []Mar: 1/6 | *Apr: 5/7

5)   {MICU, NP_GNR, nosocomial, *A. baumannii*, sputum}$\Rightarrow${A1, A2,A3}
      []Jan: 0/5 | []Feb: 0/4 | []Mar: 1/4 | *Apr: 5/6

Figure 2 A set of related events. Bracketed partitions (e.g., []Jan) are in w_p. Starred partitions (e.g., *Apr) are in w_c. MICU, medical intensive care unit; NP_GNR, nonpseudomonas Gram-negative rods; An, resistant or intermediate-resistant antibiotic *n*

The choice of α for classifying the result of either statistical test is rather arbitrary, and, indeed, this is a general criticism of significance testing (Rothman and Greenland, 1997). However, since significance testing is used in DMSS for exploratory purposes only, with the value of patterns ultimately depending on user interpretation, the rather arbitrary choice of α is not troublesome so long as the output is manageable and reasonably sensitive. Additionally, no formal claims of statistical inference are presumed.

DMSS uses a subsumption heuristic called event capture to construct event sets. Each event set contains one alert that is presented to the user.

Association rule $A1 \Rightarrow B1$ is called a descendent of association rule $A2 \Rightarrow B2$ if $A2 \subseteq A1$ and $B2 \subseteq B1$. For any two events x and y, x captures y if the association rule of x, $A_x \Rightarrow B_x$, is a descendent of the association rule of y, $A_y \Rightarrow B_y$, the time windows of x and y are equal, and $H_0: h_1 = h_2$, where

$$h_1 = \frac{s(Ay \cup By, w_p) - s(Ax \cup Bx, w_p)}{s(Ay, w_p)},$$

and

$$h_2 = \frac{s(Ay \cup By, w_c) - s(Ax \cup Bx, w_c)}{s(Ay, w_c)},$$

is not rejected at some α by a test of two proportions. Intuitively, event x captures event y if when x is removed from y, y is no longer an event. For example, in Figure 2 the association rule of event 5 is a descendant of the rule of event 2 and their time windows are equal. When event 5 is removed from event 2, the test of two proportions gives $P = 0.32$. If $\alpha = 0.05$, the altered event is not significant, and event 5 captures event 2. By the same process, event 5 also captures events 1, 3, and 4.

An event set x' contains event x, called alert, together with all events that x captures. The algorithm in Figure 3 is used by DMSS to create event sets. Since the alert of an event set contains all pertinent information for the entire set, only alerts are shown to the user as potentially useful patterns; all other events are redundant. This greatly reduces the number of patterns for the user to review.

---

1) A is the set of all events.

2) while $A \neq \varnothing$:

3)   for each $a \in A$:

4)   if (A does not contain a descendant of a)

5)   Create a new event set a'.

6)   Add a to a' as the $alert$.

7)   Remove a from A.

8)   for each $b \in A$:

9)   if (a captures b)

10)   Add b to a'.

11)   Remove b from A.

Figure 3 Algorithm for generating event sets

3.4. Interaction with the Database Owner

The monthly patterns that DMSS generates are reviewed by hospital infection control experts, microbiologists, and members of the pharmacy and therapeutics committee. Currently, the interaction is crude and consists of manual review of printed results. Efforts are under way to construct a collaborative interpretation system which will allow DMSS patterns to be reviewed and ranked asynchronously by experts over a Web-based interface (Wong et al., 1998).

4. Results

4.1. Applications of Discovered Knowledge

The first version of DMSS and initial experiments were described in Brossette et al. (1998). Further development resulted in significant improvements and modifications to the original system described. This system has been applied to both intensive care units (Moser et al., 1999) and hospitalwide data sets. In this article, our studies on hospitalwide data are summarized and selected findings are presented.

In experiments with hospitalwide data, DMSS processed each one-month data partition in less than four minutes. After fifteen partitions, 4,461 rules were stored in the history and 487 alerts had been generated. Association rule templates along with event capture decreased the number of uninteresting alerts presented to the user by about half. Additionally, important previously unrecognized patterns of nosocomial infection and antibiotic resistance were identified. The false-positive rate, while high, did not overwhelm the expert reviewer since on average only forty-one alerts were generated per month, and truly interesting patterns were found in each month's analysis. The retrospective nature of these studies, however, precluded intervention and outcome analysis. Prospective studies that will determine the effect of DMSS on traditional infection control outcomes are under way but are too young to comment on findings.

Representative findings from a recent analysis of hospitalwide UAB data are presented in Table 2. Alerts 2, 3, 4, 6, and 7 are location specific and are not associated with any single microorganism. Alerts 3 and 4 describe changes in the incidence of nosocomial (hospital acquired) gram-negative rod isolates among the isolates in the given locations. Alerts such as these suggest a possible deficiency in infection control practice in these locations and should prompt further investigation by the infection control committee. Alerts 2, 6, and 7 are antimicrobial specific, which suggests possible misuse or overuse of antimicrobial agents with subsequent changes in resistance patterns in the respective locations. Alerts such as these should trigger evaluations of antimicrobial utilization by the Pharmacy & Therapeutics committee. None of these patterns was known before this analysis.

Alerts 1, 5, 8, 9, and 10 are organism specific, and of these, 1, 5, and 10 are location specific. Alert 5 describes a significant increase in the incidence of *S. aureus* from respiratory isolates in the NICU. Alert 9 describes what is likely a clonal outbreak of a multiple-drug-resistant strain of nosocomial *A. baumannii* in location J10W. None of these patterns was known before analysis, but all, if they had been discovered prospectively, deserve thorough investigation and follow-up by the infection control committee.

4.2. Comparisons with Other Methods

Historically, computer-assisted infection control surveillance research has focused on identifying high-risk patients including those on suboptimal antibiotic regimens (Evans et al., 1998, 1986), the use of expert systems to identify possible cases of nosocomial infections (Kahn et al., 1993), and the detection of deviations in the occurrence of predefined events (Sellick, 1993). Until now, this has not included the use of data mining techniques to uncover unknown patterns in hospital data.

DMSS could potentially be used in conjunction with other computer-assisted surveillance systems. For example, an expert system like GermWatcher (Kahn et al., 1993) could be used to preprocess culture data in order to select only those that describe significant infections. DMSS could then be used to analyze and monitor these data only.

Table 2 Selected Alerts from Analysis of Hospitalwide UAB Data

#	Association Rule	May 98	Jun 98	Jul 98	Aug 98	Sep 98	Oct 98	Nov 98	Dec 98	Jan 99	Feb 99	p
1	LocNICU ⇒ Noso, P. aeruginosa	2/30	2/40	4/35	**10/48**							0.019
2	LocR3 ⇒ Noso, Ciprofloxacin		2/21	0/16	1/20	**5/20**						0.049
3	LocW7NE ⇒ NP_GNR, Noso				1/12	0/1	0/8	**10/22**				0.002
4	LocW9NW ⇒ NP_GNR, Noso				0/21	1/26	2/29	6/24				0.011
5	RESP, LocNICU ⇒ Noso, S. aureus					1/17	2/22	2/12	**9/29**			0.016
6	Noso, LocJ3E ⇒ Ticarcillin/Clav						1/6	0/5	0/6	**6/12**		0.021
7	Noso, WAT LocTBIC ⇒ Ticarcillin/Clav						1/9	0/13	0/13	**4/12**		0.024
8	Noso, P. aeruginosa ⇒ Ticarcillin/Clav, Ciprofloxacin, Gentamicin, Imipenem						0/37	0/34	0/40	**3/37**		0.029
9	All Isolates ⇒ LocJ10W, Noso, A. baumannii, Piperacillin, Ticarcillin/Clav, Cotrimazole, Ciprofloxacin, Ceftazidime, Gentamicin, Tobramycin Ceftriaxone						0/617	0/566	0/578	**3/558**		0.028
10	LocHTIC ⇒ Noso, S. aureus							0/22	0/6	0/8	**4/10**	0.003

Bold values, w_c; Normal values, w_p; Noso, nosocomial; Loc, location; NP_GNR, nonpseudomonas gram negative rod; RESP, respiratory source; WAT, wound, abscess, or tissue source.

5. Conclusion

A framework for the application of data mining to hospital infection control and antimicrobial resistance surveillance has been described. Early experimentation with clinical laboratory data has shown that DMSS can find interesting and previously unknown patterns. Ongoing outcomes studies will determine the value of DMSS when used to assist traditional hospital infection control activities.

References

Anonymous. 1992. "Public health focus surveillance: prevention and control of nosocomial infections." *MMWR* **41**: 783–787.

Brossette, S. E., A. P. Sprague, J. M. Hardin, K. B. Waites, W. T. Jones, and S. A. Moser. 1998. "Association rules and data mining in hospital infection control and public health surveillance." *JAMIA* **5**: 373–381.

Emori, T. G., D. H. Culver, T. C. Horan, W. R. Jarvis, J. W. White, D. R. Olson, S. Banerjee, J. R. Edwards, W. J. Martone, and R. P. Gaynes. 1991. "National nosocomial infections surveillance system (NNIS): description of surveillance methods." *Am. J. Infect. Control* **19**: 19–35.

Evans, R. S., R. A. Larsen, J. P. Burke, R. M. Gardner, F. A. Meier, J. A. Jacobson, M. T. Conti, J. T. Jacobson, and R. K. Hulse. 1986. "Computer surveillance of hospital-acquired infections and antibiotic use." *JAMA* **256**: 1007–1011.

Evans, R. S., S. L. Pestotnik, D. C. Classen, T. P. Clemmer, L. K. Weaver, J. F. J. Orme, J. F. Lloyd, and J. P. Burke. 1998. "A computer-assisted management program for antibiotics and other anti-infective agents." *N. Engl. J. Med.* **338**: 232–238.

Goldmann, D. A., R. A. Weinstein, R. P. Wenzel, O. C. Tablan, R. J. Duma, R. P. Gaynes, J. Schlosser, and W. J. Martone. 1996. "Strategies to prevent and control the emergence and spread of antimicrobial-resistant microorganisms in hospitals. A challenge to hospital leadership." *JAMA* **275**: 234–240.

Jones, R. N. 1992. "The current and future impact of antimicrobial resistance among nosocomial bacterial pathogens." *Diagn. Microbiol. Infect. Dis.* **15**: 3–10.

Kahn, M. G., S. A. Steib, V. J. Fraser, and W. C. Dunagan. 1993. "An expert system for culture-based infection control surveillance." In *Proceedings—the Annual Symposium on Computer Applications in Medical Care*, pp. 171–175.

Koontz, F. P. 1992. "A review of traditional resistance surveillance methodologies and infection control." *Diagn. Microbiol. Infect. Dis.* **15**: 43–47.

Moser, S. A., W. T. Jones, and S. E. Brossette. 1999. "Application of data mining to intensive care unit microbiologic data." *Emerging Infect. Dis.* **5**: 454–457.

NCCLS, 1999. *Performance standards for antimicrobial susceptibility testing; Ninth Informational Supplement.* NCCLS document M100-S9. **19**(1). Wayne, Pennsylvania: NCCLS.

Neu, H. C., R. J. Duma, R. N. Jones, McGowan, Jr, J. E., T. F. O'Brien, L. D. Sabath, et al. 1992. "Antibiotic resistance: epidemiology and therapeutics." *Diagn. Microbiol. Infect. Dis.* **2**: 53–60.

Rosner, B. 1990. *Fundamentals of Biostatistics.* 3d ed. Belmont, MA: Duxbury Press.

Rothman, K. J. and S. Greenland. 1997. *Modern Epidemiology.* 2d ed. Philadelphia: Lippincott-Raven.

Sellick, J. A. 1993. "The use of statistical process control charts in hospital epidemiology." *Infect. Control Hosp. Epidemiol.* **14**: 649–656.

Shlaes, D. M., D. N. Gerding, J. F. J. John, W. A. Craig, D. L. Bornstein, R. A. Duncan, et al. 1997. "Society for healthcare epidemiology of American and Infectious Diseases Society of American Joint Committee on the Prevention of Antimicrobial Resistance: guidelines for the prevention of antimicrobial resistance in hospitals." *Clin. Infect. Dis.* **25**: 584–599.

Wong, D., W. T. Jones, S. E. Brossette, J. M. Hardin, and S. A. Moser. 1998. "A strategy for geomedical surveillance using the Hawkeye knowledge discovery system." In *Geomed 97*, edited by L. Gierl, A. D. Cliff, A.-J. Valleron, P. Farrington, and M. Bull, pp. 204–213. Stuttgart: B.G. Teubner.

47.2 Preterm Birth Prediction

Linda K. Goodwin and Jerzy W. Grzymala-Busse

ABSTRACT Accurately predicting which pregnant women are at risk for giving birth prematurely, or preterm, is a difficult problem in health care. Medical science and research have not offered viable solutions for the prematurity problem. The most persistent limitation for preterm birth risk assessment is our continued lack of understanding about the causes of preterm birth. Data mining and knowledge discovery in database tools are being applied with improved outcomes for predicting birth outcomes in pregnant women. In this project, completed in 1992–1993, three large prenatal databases were acquired. Each database was divided into two halves: 50 percent for training data and 50 percent for testing data. Each data set was then analyzed using statistical and machine learning programs. The best predictive accuracy was accomplished using the system LERS (Learning from Examples using Rough Sets). Manual methods of assessing preterm birth have a positive predictive value of 17 to 38 percent. The data mining methods based on LERS reached a positive predictive value of 59 to 92 percent.

1. Project Overview

The development team consisted of a small business owner with expertise in artificial intelligence (AI) and expert systems (Ms. VanDyne), a perinatal nurse expert (Dr. Goodwin), and a computer science professor with expertise in data mining (Dr. Grzymala-Busse). Numerous other experts were consulted throughout the development process. However, the primary work on the project was divided into the following tasks: LERS inductive machine learning (Dr. Grzymala-Busse), statistical and clinical analyses (Dr. Goodwin), and programming the prototype expert system (Ms. VanDyne).

Three large prenatal data sets were used as input data. First, during preprocessing, obvious erroneous records, such as records with a systolic pressure of 14,000 or a maternal weight of less than 10 pounds, were removed. Also, each of the data sets was divided in half, into training data and test data (see Figure 1). Then rules were induced from training data by the system LERS. At the same time, statistical methods were used for the purpose of classification of testing data as well. However, the LERS classification scheme was more successful.

2. The Preterm Birth Problem: Motivation for a Data Mining Solution

Because 8 to 12 percent of all newborns in the United States are delivered prior to 37 weeks' gestation, the problems associated with low birth weight and prematurity continue to plague childbearing families and our nation's health care system. Full-term babies are born between 37 and 42 weeks of gestation. Babies born prior to 37 weeks are considered preterm, or premature, and babies born prior to 32–33 weeks are sometimes considered very preterm.

Preterm babies account for 70 to 80 percent of all neonatal deaths (Wheeler, 1994). Advances in neonatal medicine over the past two decades have produced amazing improvements in the chances of survival of infants born after 20 weeks' gestation, but they frequently suffer from lifelong and debilitating handicaps and their care sometimes exceeds one million dollars in the first year of life (Feldman and Wood, 1997). The 1980s produced numerous preterm risk scoring tools that were based upon clinical experts' experiences and perceptions about the factors associated with premature delivery. But a decade later, it was determined that preterm risk assessment tools had failed (Creasy, 1991; Edenfield et al., 1995; McClean et al., 1993; Shiono and Klebanoff, 1993). Health care providers and consumers agree that preterm birth prevention is preferable to treatment, but physicians and nurses continue to struggle with assessment of preterm birth risk and decisionmaking related to interventions for pregnant women in the clinical setting (Iams et al., 1998; Meis et al., 1998).

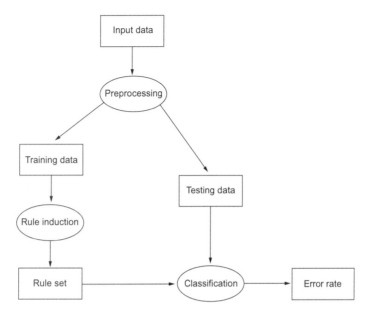

Figure 1 KDD process

3. Input Data

Data mining and KDD methodologies may improve our ability to understand links between massive volumes of patient data and patient outcomes in health care. Issues in mining health care data involve nontrivial obstacles that include data extraction and cleaning, data volume and reduction, repeated measures and temporal data, missing data within a record, and missing variables for all records (Goodwin et al., 1997). A missing variable, for example, frequently includes factors such as occupational work hazards or level of social/psychological support in pregnant women. The literature documents that work-related fatigue and emotional stress may be important considerations for preterm birth risk, but they are rarely contained in prenatal records. Issues related to health care data quality and volume must be solved for data mining methodologies to be seen as valuable for improving patient care.

Historical data sets describing the length of pregnancy, collected by commercial data providers, present each patient as a case (or an example) characterized by a vector of values of many variables. Variables are either independent (attributes) or dependent (decisions). For this application, the decision delivery was a single variable and it had two values (classes or concepts): fullterm and preterm. Frequently, data sets describing pregnant women have conflicting cases (or, briefly, data sets are inconsistent). Examples are conflicting if values for all attributes are pairwise equal but decision values are different. The best tool to deal with inconsistency is rough set theory since it was created especially to handle inconsistencies, and its approach is objective. Thus, the choice of a data mining tool based on rough set theory was natural and the system LERS (Learning from Examples based on Rough Set theory) was selected as a basic KDD tool. The system was developed at the University of Kansas (Grzymala-Busse, 1992).

The majority of patient data is contained in paper records that are all but impossible to analyze. Electronic patient data is proliferating, but prenatal data remains primarily on paper. A wide search for electronic prenatal data yielded three cooperative partners who were willing to share anonymous prenatal data for research purposes. Acquiring the data involved an iterative process with researchers defining data requirements and programmers querying and extracting data for research files. Depending on patient volume and size of the source database, the data

Table 1 Training Data

	Data set 1	Data set 2	Data set 3
Number of cases	1654	1218	6608
Number of unique cases	811	1218	6592
Number of cases in the class fullterm	1482	307	4096
Number of cases in the class preterm	172	911	2512
Number of conflicting cases	179	0	16
Number of attributes	13	73	67
Missing attribute values	No	Yes	Yes

extraction process required anywhere from eight to forty person-hours on the provider's part, and these services were provided without charge to the research project. Subsequent requests for data met with requests for fees by one provider, nonparticipation by a second provider, and continued cooperation with the third provider. A knowledge discovery in database methodology used machine learning programs, inferential statistical analysis, and expert validation techniques to analyze perinatal data sets. The dependent (i.e., decision) variable studied was weeks gestation at delivery, with dichotomous coding of preterm birth (prior to 37 weeks) versus full term birth (37+ weeks). Data verification and cleaning procedures were conducted using both machine learning techniques and multivariate statistical techniques. Frequencies and descriptive statistics were analyzed for each attribute provided for study. Multiple linear regression was used to analyze predictor variables to the birth outcome (decision variable). Finally, expert consultation was used to assist with information-to-knowledge verification procedures in determining the usability of the machine-generated production rules (Woolery et al., 1994; Woolery and Grzymala-Busse, 1994; Grzymala-Busse and Goodwin, 1994, 1996, 1997). In this project three data sets were explored. Tables 1 and 2 present characteristics of these data. In Table 2, unique cases means cases without duplicate records in the data.

4. Background Knowledge: the Preterm Birth Risk Knowledge Domain

Accurate assessment of preterm birth risk enables intervention with appropriate educational programs, bedrest, antibiotic treatment, and early symptom management to prolong gestation and to improve outcomes for infants and their families. The problem of preterm birth risk assessment includes a poorly defined and complex knowledge base. While risk information is increasing at rates that confound traditional techniques of information and patient management, perinatal literature abounds with studies that report contradictory findings. The plethora of information about preterm birth risks remains disorganized, poorly validated through research, and of little guidance to patients and providers of prenatal care.

Emerging consensus suggests that preterm birth risk varies according to different subpopulations (Meis et al., 1998). While African-American women deliver preterm at twice the rate of Caucasian women, most studies conclude that some currently unknown factor associated with black race (and not race itself) increases preterm birth risk (Goldenberg et al., 1996). The

Table 2 Unseen (Testing) Data

	Data set 1	Data set 2	Data set 3
Number of cases	1953	1218	6608
Number of unique cases	1879	1218	6571
Number of cases in the class fullterm	1199	330	4268
Number of cases in the class preterm	394	888	2340
Number of conflicting cases	340	0	32
Number of attributes	13	73	67
Missing attribute values	No	Yes	Yes

specific causative factors for onset of labor remain one of life's great mysteries, whether preterm or full term. Causal categories for preterm birth suggest categories that include sociodemographic (Hickey et al., 1995), infectious (Goldenberg et al., 1998), placenta vasculature (Zygmunt et al., 1997), nutritional status (Hickey et al., 1997), and perhaps stress and psychological factors. Certain medical and obstetrical complications such as bleeding, hypertension, convulsions, and multiple gestation are consistently associated with higher rates of preterm birth. Substance abuse is also associated with higher rates of preterm birth, and this includes a debate about caffeine consumption, cigarette smoking, alcohol, and cocaine. New questions have been raised about the association of fetal gender (James, 1997) and whether seasonal or weather-related variations may be associated with preterm birth risk (Posaci et al., 1995). Lapeer et al. (1995) described the application of neural networks for ranking perinatal variables that influence a baby's birth weight. But their experiment preselected nine variables (mother's height, body mass index, parity, baby's sex, smoking, gravidity, mother's age, social class, and gestational age) and compared neural network outcomes with multivariate linear regression. They concluded that linear regression was faster to accomplish and resulted in only small differences in performance. With an exception where gestational age and birth weight had a 0.5 correlation, other studied correlations between the variables and birth weight ranged from 0.05 to 0.1. Reported statistical significance seems misleading, given the very low correlations, and it would be of doubtful value in making clinical decisions.

5. The Discovery Mechanism

As was explained in the previous section, the LERS system, based on rough set theory, has been selected because some of the input data were inconsistent. LERS checks input data for consistency first. If a class is not involved in conflicts with other classes, rules are induced directly for the class. For a class involved in conflicts, lower and upper approximations are computed. Lower and upper approximations are basic ideas of rough set theory (Pawlak, 1982, 1991).

Let U denote the set of all examples of the input data table and let P denote a nonempty subset of the set A of all attributes. An indiscernibility relation ρ on U is defined for all $x, y \in U$ by $x \, \rho \, y$ if and only if for both x and y the values for all variables from P are identical. Equivalence classes of ρ are called elementary sets of P. An equivalence class of ρ containing x is denoted $[x]_P$. Any finite union of elementary sets of P is called a definable set in P. Let X be a concept. In general, X is not a definable set in P. However, set X may be approximated by two definable sets in P; the first one is called a lower approximation of X in P, denoted by $\underline{P}X$ and is defined as follows.

$$\{x \in U | [x]_P \subseteq X\}$$

The second set is called an upper approximation of X in P, denoted by $\bar{P}X$ and is defined as follows.

$$\{x \in U | [x]_P \cap X \neq \varnothing\}$$

The lower approximation of X in A is the greatest definable set in A, contained in X. The upper approximation of X in A is the least definable set in A containing X.

Rules induced from the lower approximation of the concept certainly describe the concept, so they are called certain. On the other hand, rules induced from the upper approximation of the concept only describe the concept possibly (or plausibly), so they are called possible (Grzymala-Busse, 1988). In this project the algorithm LEM2 (Chan and Grzymala-Busse, 1991) was used to induce rule sets. We cite basic definitions necessary to explain the principles of the LEM2 algorithm.

Let B be a nonempty lower or upper approximation of a concept represented by a decision-value pair (d, w) in A, that is, taking into account all attributes. Set B depends on a set T of attribute–value pairs t if and only if

$$\varnothing \neq [T] = \bigcap_{t \in T} [t] \subseteq B,$$

where $[(a, v)]$ denotes the set of all examples such that for attribute a its values are v. Set T is a minimal complex of B if and only if B depends on T and no proper subset T' of T exists such that B depends on T'. Set T represents a rule. Let $\mathbb{T}$ be a nonempty collection of nonempty sets of attribute-value pairs. Then $\mathbb{T}$ is a local covering of B if and only if the following conditions are satisfied:

1. Each member T of $\mathbb{T}$ is a minimal complex of B,

2. $\bigcup_{T \in \mathbb{T}} [T] = B$, and

3. $\mathbb{T}$ is minimal, that is $\mathbb{T}$ has the smallest possible number of members.

Set $\mathbb{T}$ represents a rule set, a description of the set B. In our experiments, attribute priorities were not used, so the LEM2 algorithm presented does not contain that option. Also, numerical attributes were discretized by experts.

```
Procedure LEM2
(input: a set B,
output: a single local covering T of set B);
begin
  G := B;
  T := ∅;
  while G ≠ ∅
    begin
    T := ∅;
    T(G) := {t | [t] ∩ G ≠ ∅};
    while T = ∅ or [T] ⊈ B
      begin
        select a pair t ∈ T(G) such that |[t] ∩ G| is maximum; if a tie occurs,
          select a pair t ∈ T(G) with the smallest cardinality of [t]; if
          another tie occurs, select first pair;
        T := T ∪ {t};
        G := [t] ∩ G;
        T(G) := {t | [t] ∩ G ≠ ∅};
        T(G) := T(G) − T;
      end while
    for each t in T do
      if [T−{t}] ⊆ B then T := T−{t};
    T := T ∪ {T};
    G := B − ∪   [T];
            T∈T
  end while
  for each T in T do
    if   ∪     [S] = B then T := T−{T};
       S∈T−{T}
```

end procedure.

A classification system uses the rule set, induced from training data, to classify new cases (testing data). The classification system of LERS is a modification of the bucket brigade algorithm (Booker et al., 1990; Holland et al., 1986). The decision to which concept an example belongs is made on the basis of three factors: strength, specificity, and support. They are defined as follows. Strength is the total number of examples correctly classified by the rule during training. Specificity is the total number of attribute-value pairs on the left-hand side of the rule. The matching rules with a larger number of attribute-value pairs are considered more specific. The third factor, support, is defined as the sum of scores of all matching rules from the concept. The concept C, for which the support, that is, the following expression

$$\sum_{\text{matching rules } R \text{ describing } C} \text{Strength}(R) * \text{Specificity}(R)$$

is the largest, is a winner, and the example is classified as being a member of C.

In the new classification system of LERS, if complete matching is impossible, all partially matching rules are identified. These are rules with at least one attribute-value pair matching the corresponding attribute-value pair of an example.

For any partially matching rule R, the additional factor, called Matching factor (R), is computed. Matching factor (R) is the ratio of the number of matched attribute-value pairs of the rule R to the total number of attribute-value pairs of the rule R. In partial matching, the concept C for which the following expression is the largest

$$\sum_{\text{partially matching rules } R \text{ describing } C} \text{Matching\_factor}(R) * \text{Strength}(R) * \text{Specificity}(R)$$

is the winner, and the example is classified as being a member of C.

6. Results

LERS produced 350 rules from Data set 1. There were 170 rules produced from the Data set 2 and 1,133 rules from Data set 3. Data set 3 rules were deemed "not useful" by the experts and were not included in expert system development, because they were primarily based on medical diagnosis and procedure codes. Experts believed it would be more useful to produce a decision support system based on patient biophysical and symptom data. The prototype expert system was built using a Kappa PC expert system shell, and contained 520 rules (350 from Data set 1 and 170 from Data set 2) that were verified by the experts as being accurate (see Table 3). Rules were validated by experts using a manual process of content validity indexing (CVI), where each expert evaluated each rule for accuracy, syntax, and relevance. A rule is considered less specific if the number of attribute-value pairs, or conditions, is small. Results of a study (Grzymala-Busse and Goodwin, 1996) showed that prediction based on less specific rules is not worse than prediction based on more specific rules. Moreover, the shorter, that is, less specific, rules, are computationally more efficient and easier for humans to comprehend and remember. Based on the experts' lack of comfort with simple rules, questions were raised about the predictive power of simple versus complex rules.

A false positive is when the expert system predicted preterm delivery, but the patient delivered full term. The significance of false positives could involve extra (costly) services provided for patients who do not need them. These services would include extra prenatal visits and close monitoring by perinatal providers, although these costs are minimal in comparison to costs generated for a preterm birth. From a patient perspective, false positives have minimal adverse effects on patient outcomes. A false negative is when the expert system predicted full term delivery but the patient delivered preterm. The significance of false negatives is that pregnant women who would benefit from close monitoring and frequent prenatal visits are not likely to receive these services. This lack of needed service could have a negative impact on both patient outcomes and costs, and carries a liability risk for product development. A positive predictive value is defined as the ratio of all true positives to the sum of all true positives and false positives.

Table 3 Results: an Expert System Based on Kappa

	Data set 1	Data set 2	Data set 3
Accuracy	88.83%	59.28%	53.47%
False Positives	3.64%	12.15%	24.91%
False Negatives	7.09%	25.29%	17.40%
Unclassified	0.44%	3.28%	4.22%

Table 4 LERS Positive Predictive Value

	Data set 1	Data set 2	Data set 3
LERS classification scheme	92.5%	75.5%	59.0%

For comparison, the positive predictive value accomplished by the LERS classification scheme, based on specificity, strength, support, and partial matching factor, are cited in Table 4.

7. Comparison with Statistical Analysis

Two programs of machine learning were used as well (ID3 and CONCLUS), but LERS produced the only usable results. The other two programs failed because of hardware and software limitations that were unable to process the volume of data. The accuracy results, presented in Tables 3 and 4, were surprising for several reasons. The majority of the 18,890 subjects in all three databases were Caucasian, married, and well-educated women in their late twenties. From the onset of the research, the sample was not representative of pregnant women perceived to be at risk for preterm birth. Two of the three databases were obtained from home uterine monitoring vendors, and the majority of patients referred to these vendors have already experienced, or are at high risk for preterm labor. The third database was representative of a midwest suburban population, and its primary contribution was that it provided data for both low- and high-risk pregnant women, and also included a more racially diverse population.

Machine learning analysis was conducted simultaneously with statistical analysis with patient records where all variables contained data values. Exploratory factor analysis was conducted using principal components extraction and varimax rotation techniques. Results for Data set 1 used 52 variables and yielded 20 factors that accounted for 61.1 percent of the variance. Data set 2's 77 variables yielded 26 factors that accounted for 68.4 percent of the variance. Continued work with psychometric analyses and conceptual model development of preterm birth risk factors is needed. After exploratory factor analysis was concluded, various regression models were explored. While multicollinearity and redundancy were expected to produce suppression, this phenomenon was not seen in the models analyzed. Multiple regression analysis revealed low to very low correlations between the criterion variable, weeks gestation at delivery, and most of the predictor variables. Data set 3 was not statistically analyzed because a large percentage of the data consisted of ICD9 codes. Data set 1 data produced several statistically significant variables, but clinically these items would be of little use in preventing preterm labor or improving preterm risk assessment. Of 38 items that were analyzed from Data set 2, only last pulse ($r = -0.049$; $P = 0.0528$) and uterine contraction information ($r = 0.165$; $P = 0.0351$) were statistically significant. These two items might prove useful in assessing preterm labor risk and need further study, but low correlations between these two predictors and the criterion variable (weeks gestation at delivery) render these results dubious. Stepwise multiple regression was conducted with Data set 1 data in the spirit of exploration, and results indicated weeks at referral, current use of tocolytic medications, current diagnosis of preterm labor, and premature ruptured membranes were associated with weeks gestation at delivery. These items are expected, and are not helpful in finding predictors that would alert the health care provider before problems began.

The inability to statistically associate known risk factors with preterm birth outcomes, from the data in large perinatal databases, was somewhat surprising. However, these findings can be clarified. First of all, the high volume of dichotomous data yielded numerous variables where the mean was zero, and the variance was at or near zero. Using a preterm/fullterm dichotomous outcome classification, logistic regression analysis may offer solutions to some of the problems encountered, and is currently underway with new data. Also, the inability to predict preterm risk reflected risk factors that were consistent with most preterm risk screening instruments in use at the time of the study (1992–1993). However, review of the literature found that screening indices were not developed with attention to psychometric standards, and they remain invalid and unreliable. Multiple regression statistics did find statistical significance for some of the variables, but the low correlations between the predictor variables and the criterion variable rendered statistical significance meaningless for the purposes of assessment in clinical practice.

8. Conclusions

Data collection for pregnant women who seek prenatal care typically includes thousands of data items. From all this data, the health care provider must combine data elements for decisionmaking related to preterm birth risk, as well as other assessments, decisions, and plans for intervention. The information explosion of the past decade has created a situation where health care providers are unable to assimilate the volumes of information available to make decisions in optimal fashion. In addition to information overload, the perinatal health care provider lacks guidance for preterm birth risk assessment that has been validated as reliable, valid, and generalizable. The literature abounds with prenatal studies and contradictory findings, and it provides little guidance for decisionmaking in perinatal clinical practice. Despite advances in perinatal medicine, the rates of preterm birth have remained at approximately 8 to 12 percent in the United States for the past three decades. It is clear that traditional methods of science have not yielded satisfactory solutions for the problem. KDD results for perinatal data suggest that data mining methodologies may offer improved decision support for identifying women at risk for preterm birth.

ACKNOWLEDGMENTS

Special thanks and acknowledgments to Michele VanDyne (IntelliDyne, Inc.) for her participation in this project and to HealthDyne Perinatal Services, Inc. (Marietta, Georgia), TOKOS Corporation (Santa Ana, California), and Saint Luke's Regional Perinatal Center (Kansas City, Missouri) for providing data.

References

Booker, L. B., D. E. Goldberg, and J. F. Holland. 1990. "Classifier systems and genetic algorithms." In *Machine Learning. Paradigms and Methods*, edited by J. G. Carbonell, pp. 235–282. Cambridge, MA: The MIT Press.

Chan, C. C. and J. W. Grzymala-Busse. 1991. "On the attribute redundancy and the learning programs ID3, PRISM, and LEM2." TR-91-14. Department of Computer Science, University of Kansas, KS.

Creasy, R. 1991. "Preventing preterm birth." *New England J. of Medicine* 325: 727–729.

Edenfield, S. M., S. D. Thomas, W. O. Thompson, and J. J. Marcotte. 1995. "Validity of the Creasy risk appraisal instrument for prediction of preterm labor." *Nursing Res.* 44: 76–81.

Feldman, W. E. and B. Wood. 1997. "The economic impact of high-risk pregnancies." *J. Health Care Finance* 24: 64–71.

Goldenberg, R. L., S. P. Cliver, F. X. Mulvihill, C. A. Hickey, H. J. Hoffman, L. V. Klerman, and M. J. Johnson. 1996. "Medical, psychosocial, and behavioral risk factors do not explain the increased risk for low birth weight among black women." *Am. J. Obstet. Gynecol.* 175: 1317–1324.

Goldenberg, R. L., J. D. Iams, B. M. Mercer, P. J. Meis, A. H. Moawad, R. L. Copper, A. Das, E. Thom, F. Johnson, D. McNellis, M. Miodovnik, D. P. Van, S. N. Caritis, G. R. Thurnau, and S. F. Bottoms. 1998. "The preterm prediction study: the value of new versus standard risk factors in predicting early and all spontaneous preterm births." *Am. J. Public Health* 88: 233–238.

Goodwin, L., J. Prather, K. Schlitz, M. A. Iannacchione, M. Hage, W. E. Hammond, and J. Grzymala-Busse. 1997. "Data mining issues for improved birth outcomes." *Biomed. Sci. Instrumentation* 34: 291–296.

Grzymala-Busse, J. W. 1988. "Knowledge acquisition under uncertainty—a rough set approach." *J. Intell. Robotic Sys.* 1: 3–16.

Grzymala-Busse, J. W. 1992. "LERS—a system for learning from examples based on rough sets." In *Intelligent Decision Support. Handbook of Applications and Advances of the Rough Sets Theory*, edited by R. Slowinski, pp. 3–18. Norwell, MA: Kluwer Academic Publishers.

Grzymala-Busse, J. W. and L. K. Goodwin. 1994. "Improving prediction of preterm birth using a new classification scheme and rule induction." In *Proceedings of the Eighteenth Annual Symposium on Computer Applications in Medical Care (SCAMC), November 5–9*, pp. 730–734. Philadelphia, PA: Hanley & Belfus, Inc.

Grzymala-Busse, J. W. and L. K. Goodwin. 1996. "A comparison of less specific versus more specific rules for preterm birth prediction." In *Proceedings of the First Online Workshop on Soft Computing WSC1 on the Internet*, pp. 129–133. Nagoya, Japan: SOFT.

Grzymala-Busse, J. W. and L. K. Goodwin. 1997. "Predicting preterm birth risk using machine learning from data with missing values." *Bull. Int. Rough Set Soc.* **1**: 17–21.

Hickey, C. A., S. P. Cliver, S. F. McNeal, and R. L. Goldenberg. 1997. "Low pregravid body mass index as a risk factor for preterm birth: variation by ethnic group." *Obstet. Gynecol.* **89**: 206–212.

Hickey, C. A., S. P. Cliver, F. X. Mulvihill, S. F. McNeal, H. J. Hoffman, and R. L. Goldenberg. 1995. "Employment-related stress and preterm delivery: a contextual examination." *Public Health Reports* **110**: 410–418.

Holland, J. H., K. J. Holyoak, and R. E. Nisbett. 1986. *Induction. Processes of Inference, Learning, and Discovery*. Cambridge, MA: The MIT Press.

Iams, J. D., R. L. Goldenberg, B. M. Mercer, A. Moawad, E. Thom, P. J. Meis, D. McNellis, S. N. Caritis, M. Miodovnik, M. K. Menard, G. R. Thurnau, S. E. Bottoms, and J. M. Roberts. 1998. "The preterm prediction study: recurrence risk of spontaneous preterm birth." *Am. J. Obstet. Gynecol.* **178**: 1035–1040.

James, W. H. 1997. "Excess males in preterm birth: interactions with gestational age, race, and multiple birth." *Obstet. Gynecol.* **89**: 156.

Lapeer, R. J., K. J. Dalton, R. W. Prager, J. J. Forsstrom, H. K. Selbmann, and R. Derom. 1995. "Application of neural networks to the ranking of perinatal variables influencing birthweight." *Scand. J. Clin. Laboratory Investigation* **222**: 83–93.

McLean, M., W. A. Walters, and R. Smith. 1993. "Prediction and early diagnosis of preterm labor: a critical review." *Obstet. Gynecol. Survey* **48**: 209–225.

Meis, P. J., R. L. Goldenberg, B. M. Mercer, J. D. Iams, A. H. Moawad, M. Miodovnik, M. K. Menard, S. N. Caritis, G. R. Thurnau, S. F. Bottoms, A. Das, J. M. Roberts, and D. McNellis. 1998. "The preterm prediction study: risk factors for indicated preterm births." *Am. J. Obstet. Gynecol.* **178**: 562–567.

Pawlak, Z. 1982. "Rough sets." *Int. J. Comput. Inform. Sci.* **11**: 341–356.

Pawlak, Z. 1991. "Rough Sets." In *Theoretical Aspects of Reasoning about Data*. Dordrecht, Netherlands: Kluwer Academic Publishers.

Posaci, C., U. Saygili, Y. E. Erata, A. Onvural, D. Issever, and U. Yilmaz. 1995. "Does the incidence of premature labor vary according to the season?" *Rev. Francaise Gynecol. Obstet.* **90**: 481–485.

Shiono, P. H. and M. A. Klebanoff. 1993. "A review of risk scoring for preterm birth." *Clinics in Perinatology* **20**: 107–125.

Wheeler, D. G. 1994. "Preterm birth prevention." *J. Nurse-Midwifery* **39**: 66S–80S.

Woolery, L. K. and J. Grzymala-Busse. 1994. "Machine learning for an expert system to predict preterm birth risk." *J. Am. Med. Inform. Assoc.* **1**: 439–446.

Woolery, L., M. Van Dyne, J. W. Grzymala-Busse, and C. Tsatsoulis. 1994. "Machine learning for development of an expert system to support nurses' assessment of preterm birth risk." In *Nursing Informatics: An International Overview for Nursing in a Technological Era, Proceedings of the Fifth International Conference on Nursing, Use of Computers, and Information Science, San Antonio, TX, June 17–22*, pp. 357–361. Amsterdam, Netherlands: Elsevier.

Zygmunt, M., U. Lang, N. Katz, and W. Kunzel. 1997. "Maternal plasma fibronectin: a predictor of preterm delivery." *Eur. J. Obstet. Gynecol. & Reproductive Biol.* **72**: 121–126.

47.3 Estimating Latent Causal Influences: TETRAD III Variable Selection and Bayesian Parameter Estimation

Richard Scheines

ABSTRACT   The statistical evidence for the detrimental effect of exposure to low levels of lead on the cognitive capacities of children has been debated for several decades. This paper describes how two techniques from artificial intelligence and statistics help make the statistical evidence for the accepted epidemiological conclusion seem decisive. The first is a variable selection routine in TETRAD III for finding causes, and the second a Bayesian estimation of the parameter reflecting the causal influence of actual lead exposure, a latent variable, on the measured IQ score of middle-class suburban children.

1. Introduction

This paper presents an example of causal discovery in which two pieces of artificial intelligence technology proved crucial. The pieces are TETRAD III's Build module, used to identify and discard spurious confounders of the relationship between lead exposure and IQ, and TETRAD III's Gibb's sampler (see: `http://hss.cmu.edu/philosophy/TETRAD/tetrad.html`), used to estimate the influence of lead exposure on IQ within an under-identified model involving the remaining nonspurious confounders.

   In a variety of contexts in KDD, effective variable selection is crucial. For example, identifying a small set of variables that can accurately predict who will be profitable as a credit card customer is a classic KDD problem in the financial realm. Variable selection techniques accompany different models. For example, one can use best subsets, or a forward or backward stepwise procedure with linear or logistic regression. Decision trees all use some variant of a forward stepwise procedure. In each case, the typical desiderata are purely predictive. That is, the goal is to use observations on some variables in order to predict the values of other variables. In contrast, another goal for KDD can be causal discovery. Instead of using a given data set to build a model that will then be used with future data to predict one variable from the observations on the model's inputs, the goal is to use a given data set to build a model that will then be used to predict one variable from interventions that set the values of the model's inputs. Mining a data set might tell us that the amount of stain on a person's teeth is a good predictor of how much tea they will buy, but it does not tell us that a person will buy more tea if we first sell them gum that stains their teeth. In predicting the effects of interventions, causal knowledge is essential, and standard variable selection techniques simply are not designed to identify the causes of a variable. The TETRAD programs (Scheines et al., 1994) implement techniques that are designed to identify the causes and not just the predictors of a variable. In this case study, the difference between standard variable selection in regression and in TETRAD III are made vivid.

   In this paper, the history of lead and IQ research that led to this work is briefly surveyed. Variable selection for prediction vs. variable selection for causal discovery is then discussed, and the difference in this case illustrated. The final sections show how these results allowed a Bayesian estimation of the final causal model, which provides persuasive evidence that exposure to lead does indeed have a deleterious effect on cognition, even at low levels.

2. A Brief History of Lead and IQ Research

By measuring the concentration of lead in a child's baby teeth, Herbert Needleman was the first epidemiologist to reliably measure cumulative lead exposure in children. His work helped convince the United States to eliminate lead from gasoline and most paint (Needleman et al., 1979). Needleman and a few colleagues collected data on over 50 variables on almost 300 New England children. (The data are available in the data sets section of Statlib at Carnegie Mellon University: `www.statlib.cmu.edu`.) The measures included the child's IQ, parental education, parental IQ, SES, teacher evaluations of the child, response time tests, several other possible confounders, and finally a measure of cumulative lead exposure. The goal was causal: to estimate the effect of cumulative lead exposure on the child's IQ.

   Needleman's original statistical analysis, which was basically ANOVA (Needleman et al., 1979) was criticized by the EPA (Grant et al., 1983), which concluded that his data neither supported nor rejected the conclusion that lead was damaging at the doses he recorded in asymptomatic children. Needleman reanalyzed his data with multiple regression. He performed a variable selection search using backwards stepwise eliminative regression, and found five covariates (measured confounders) that he included in a multiple regression to estimate the effect of lead on IQ. He found that even after controlling for the five covariates, the estimated effect of lead on IQ was negative and significant (Needleman et al., 1985).

This helped with the EPA, but it aroused other worries from Steve Klepper, an economist at Carnegie Mellon (see Klepper, 1988; Klepper et al., 1993). Klepper correctly argued that Needleman's statistical model (a linear regression) neglected to account for measurement error in the regressors. That is, Needleman's measured regressors were in fact imperfect proxies for the actual but latent causes of variations in IQ, and in these circumstances a regression analysis gives a biased estimate of the desired causal coefficients and their standard errors.

Unfortunately, an errors-in-all-variables model that explicitly accounts for measurement error is underidentified, and thus cannot be estimated by classical techniques without making additional assumptions. Klepper, however, had worked out an ingenious technique to bound the estimates, provided one could reasonably bound the amount of measurement error contaminating other measured covariates (Klepper, 1988; Klepper et al., 1993). The bounds on the measurement error infecting the measured covariates required to estimate the effect of actual lead exposure in Needleman's model seemed unreasonable, however, and Klepper concluded that the statistical evidence for Needleman's hypothesis was indecisive.

Reanalyzing Needleman's data, TETRAD III was used to check whether backwards stepwise regression had indeed identified the appropriate set of confounders that should be included in the final model. TETRAD III discarded three of the five covariates that stepwise regression had located, and these variables were precisely the ones that required unreasonable measurement error assumptions in Klepper's analysis. With the remaining regressors, an errors-in-all-variables model was specified to parameterize the effect of actual lead exposure on children's IQ. This model is still under-identified, but instead of trying to bound the parameters of interest, a prior distribution was put over the parameters in the model and a Gibbs sampler (Smith and Roberts, 1993; Scheines et al., 1999) was used to do a Bayesian estimation of the resulting model. Under several priors, nearly all the mass in the posterior was over negative values for the effect of actual lead exposure—now a latent variable—on measured IQ.

3. Variable Selection with TETRAD III

In their 1985 article in *Science*, Needleman, Geiger, and Frank gave results for a multivariate linear regression of children's IQ on lead exposure. Having started their analysis with almost forty covariates, they were faced with a variable selection problem to which they applied backwards stepwise regression, arriving at a final regression equation involving lead and five covariates. The covariates were measures of genetic contributions to the child's IQ (proxied by the parent's IQ), the amount of environmental stimulation in the child's early environment (proxied by the mother's education), physical factors that might compromise the child's cognitive endowment (proxied by the number of previous live births and the parents' ages at the birth of the child). The measured variables they used along with the correlations among these variables and the P-value of each correlation are given in Table 1.

The standardized regression solution is as follows, with t-ratios in parentheses. Except for Fab, which is significant at 0.1, all coefficients are significant at 0.05, and $R^2 = 0.271$.

$$\hat{Ciq} = -0.143 \; Lead + 0.219 \; Med + 0.247 \; Piq + 0.237 \; Mab - 0.204 \; Fab - 0.159 \; Nlb \tag{1}$$

$$\quad\quad (2.32) \quad\quad (3.08) \quad\quad (3.87) \quad\quad (1.97) \quad\quad (1.79) \quad\quad (2.30)$$

The intuition behind statistically controlling for covariates in a multivariate regression intended to estimate causal influence is scientifically appealing but can be wrong. It stems from the following plausible story: an association between X and Y might not be due to a direct causal link from X to Y, but rather, at least partly, due to confounders (common causes of X and Y), or intermediate causes; statistically controlling for covariates can remove that part of the association produced by confounders, leaving only the association between X and Y due to an actual causal relationship. In the case of linear regression, β_i (the regression coefficient of the

Table 1 Correlations and P-values (n = 221)

	Lead	Fab	Nlb	Med	Mab	Piq	Ciq
		Correlations					
Lead	1.00						
Fab	−0.08	1.00					
Nlb	0.11	0.39	1.00				
Med	−0.14	0.02	−0.18	1.00			
Mab	−0.15	0.85	0.47	0.003	1.00		
Piq	−0.06	0.17	0.03	0.53	0.16	1.00	
Ciq	−0.23	−0.0003	−0.17	0.41	0.05	0.40	1.00
		P-values					
Fab	0.23						
Nlb	0.10	0.00					
Med	0.04	0.78	0.01				
Mab	0.02	0.00	0.00	0.96			
Piq	0.39	0.01	0.70	0.00	0.02		
Ciq	0.00	0.99	0.01	0.00	0.43	0.00	

Ciq—child's verbal IQ score.
Lead—measured concentration in baby teeth.
Mab—mother's age at birth.
Fab—father's age at birth.
Med—mother's level of education in years.
Nlb—number of live births previous to the sampled child.
Piq—parents' IQ scores.

outcome Y on X_i) is statistically significant just in case the partial correlation of Y and X_i controlling for all of the other regressors is significant.

Measuring whether there is an association between X and Y after controlling for all the other potential confounders is the right test for whether X is a direct predictor of Y, but it is not necessarily the right test for whether X is a direct cause of Y. Clearly Needleman (and Klepper after him) considered the variable selection problem settled by the significance test for coefficients in the multivariate regression, and this seems to be standard operating procedure in the social science and epidemiological community. Unfortunately, the general principle is wrong, and this data set is an exemplar of why.

In the general setting of multivariate regression, linear or otherwise, an outcome Y and a set of regressors X is specified. Assuming that X is prior to Y, in which case Y cannot cause any $X \in X$, we say that X is causally adjacent to Y relative to the set X just in case either X is a direct cause of Y relative to X, or there is a Z not in X such that Z is a common cause of X and Y. TETRAD III requires two assumptions in order to analyze whether any $X_i \in X$ is causally adjacent to Y relative to X from population data: the causal Markov condition and faithfulness. (For discussions of the reliability of regression for determining causal structure, see Spirtes et al., 2000, chapter 8; Scheines, 1993; and Glymour et al., 1994.) The causal Markov condition amounts to assuming that every variable X is independent of all variables that are not its effects, conditional on its immediate causes (Spirtes et al., 1993). The causal Markov condition is necessarily satisfied by structural equation models with independent errors (Kiiveri and Speed, 1982), and it seems to be relatively uncontroversial. Faithfulness amounts to assuming that all independences true in a population determined by a causal structure are due to the absence of causal connection and not due to parameter values that produce independences by perfect cancellation. Although versions of this assumption are used in every science (Spirtes et al., 2000), it is not uncontroversial, and it has been generally challenged by Robins and Wasserman (1996). Allowing these two assumptions, it turns out that X is causally adjacent to Y only if X and Y are dependent conditional on every subset of $X - \{X, Y\}$ (Spirtes et al., 2000). Contrast this criterion with the one used in multivariate regression: X is causally adjacent to Y

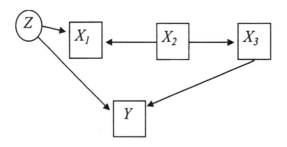

Figure 1 A model that fools regression

only if X and Y are dependent conditional on exactly the set $X - \{X_i, Y\}$. The model in Figure 1, in which $X = \{X_1, X_2, X_3\}$ and Z is unmeasured, makes the flaw in the regression criterion vivid.

This model does not entail that X_2 and Y are independent when we condition on all the other regressors $\{X_1, X_3\}$. It is possible for the model to imply this independence, but only for unfaithful parameterizations. For all faithful parameterizations, a regression of Y on X will produce nonzero coefficients for all three regressors. Although this is not a sampling problem, it is easy to verify that regression will mistakenly conclude that X_2 is causally adjacent to Y on sample data by randomly parameterizing this model, generating a pseudorandom sample, and then running a regression of Y on X_1, X_2, and X_3.

It turns out that the regression criterion is reliable for causal adjacency only when X is known to be prior to Y and the measured variables are known to be confounder complete (in TETRAD III, and many previous publications, we use the terminology of causal sufficiency to mean what is defined here as confounder completeness), that is, all common causes of two variables in $X \cup \{Y\}$ are already in $X \cup \{Y\}$. Assuming confounder completeness in general seems entirely unrealistic, and clearly so for the lead data.

The FCI algorithm executed by the Build module in TETRAD III does not assume confounder completeness, and asymptotically dominates regression as a test for causal adjacency. That is, with correct statistical decisions about independence, the FCI algorithm can detect noncausally adjacent variables that regression cannot, but not vice versa (Spirtes et al., 2000). Run on the correlations in Table 1, TETRAD III indicates that only *Lead*, *Med*, and *Piq* are adjacent to *Ciq*, and that *Mab*, *Fab*, and *Nlb* are not causally adjacent to *Ciq*, contrary to the regression analysis. In Needleman's data, *Mab*, *Fab*, and *Nlb* are more correlated with *Ciq* after conditioning on the other regressors than they are unconditionally. *Mab* and *Fab*, for example, are completely uncorrelated with *Ciq* unconditionally (see Table 1), yet are correlated with *Ciq* conditional upon all the other regressors. Whether *Mab* and *Fab* are measured with error or not, under these assumptions they or the variables they are proxies for cannot be causally adjacent to *Ciq* relative to this set. The regressor *Nlb* is correlated with *Ciq* unconditionally, almost uncorrelated with *Ciq* when conditioned on *Med* ($r_{Nlb,Ciq.Med} = -0.114$, $P = 0.1$), but once again correlated when conditioned on the entire set of regressors.

To finalize the variable selection phase, a regression of *Ciq* was performed on only those regressors found to be causally adjacent to *Ciq*, namely lead, *Med*, and *Piq*.

$$\hat{Ciq} = -0.177\ Lead + 0.251\ Med + 0.253\ Piq \tag{2}$$
$$\phantom{\hat{Ciq} = }(2.89)(3.5)(3.59)$$

The overall R^2 for the regression in equation (2) is 0.243, which is quite close to the R^2 of 0.271 from the full regression on all six variables in equation (1). All coefficients in (2) are significant at 0.01, as expected, and the coefficient on lead is slightly more negative than it was in equation (1).

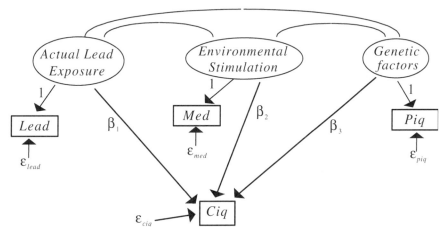

Figure 2 Errors-in-all-variables model for lead's influence in IQ

4. Estimating the Parameters of an Under-identified Model

As Klepper correctly points out, these measured regressor variables are really proxies that almost surely involve substantial measurement error (Klepper, 1988; Klepper et al., 1993). Measured *lead* is really a proxy for actual lead exposure, *Med* is really a proxy for environmental stimulation, and *Piq* is really a proxy for genetic factors related to IQ. Figure 2 shows a full errors-in-all variables specification for the variables included by TETRAD III. The task is now to estimate the coefficient β_1.

Although an errors-in-all-variables linear structural equation model seems a reasonable specification, this model is under-identified in the classical setting. That is, for any implied covariance matrix $\Sigma(\theta)$ that minimizes a discrepancy function of the implied and observed covariances, there are infinite parameterizations θ' such that $\Sigma(\theta) = \Sigma(\theta')$. In this case there are thirteen free parameters in the model but only ten data points in the covariance matrix for *Ciq*, *Lead*, *Med*, and *Piq*; thus the model is under-identified by three degrees of freedom.

Several strategies exist for identifying the model. One is to specify the exact proportion of measurement error for each measured independent variable. Since in this model we have standardized the variables, $\sigma^2(Lead) = 1$. By the model's specification, $\sigma^2(Lead) = \sigma^2(Actual\ Lead) + \sigma^2(\varepsilon_{Lead})$, so the proportion of measured *Lead*'s variance that is due to measurement error is just $\sigma^2(\varepsilon_{Lead})$, which is between 0 and 1. Similarly, this is the case for the other regressors. Using a linear regression to estimate β_1 is equivalent to specifying a measurement error equal to zero for each regressor. We could also simply stipulate that the measurement error for lead is 0.20, or some other number.

Klepper and Leamer (1984) showed that in certain circumstances one can, by imposing bounds on how much measurement error is present, bound the actual coefficients in the under-identified errors-in-variables model. In 1988 and again in 1993 Klepper argued that the upper bounds required by his method to bound the true coefficients in the lead errors-in-variables model (with all five covariates) were unreasonable. For example, one had to bound the measurement error for *Fab* (father's age at birth) at approximately 5 percent, which did not seem justifiable, considering *Fab* is a proxy for physical, emotional, and intellectual factors present in the father that might influence a child's IQ score. Performing Klepper's analysis on the reduced set of regressors identified by TETRAD II, one must be willing to bound the measurement of *Lead*, *Med*, and *Piq* at 0.710, 0.465, and 0.457, respectively, a combination of bounds of which I am reasonably confident. Klepper's technique, however, provides sufficient but not necessary conditions for bounding, and it cannot provide point estimates or standard errors.

Table 2 Multivariate Normal Prior Distribution over the Measurement Error Parameters in the Errors-in-All-Variables Model

Parameter	Mean (μ_0)	Standard Deviation (σ_0)
$\sigma^2(\varepsilon_{Lead})$	0.200	0.10
$\sigma^2(\varepsilon_{Med})$	0.300	0.15
$\sigma^2(\varepsilon_{Piq})$	0.300	0.15

The favored alternative for this study is Bayesian. By putting a prior distribution over the parameters and then computing the posterior, one can compute point estimates; for example, the mean or median in the posterior (θ_{EAP} and θ_{MDAP}), standard deviations around the point estimates [$\sigma(\theta_{EAP})$], percentiles that can be used to compute posterior credibility intervals ($\theta_{0.025}$ and $\theta_{0.975}$), and many other statistics of interest. If the posterior cannot be computed analytically, which is certainly the case for all but the most trivial structural equation models, then one can now compute a sample from the posterior by MCMC simulation methods with TETRAD III (Scheines et al., 1999). (A Gibbs sampler for computing the posterior over the parameters of a structural equation model is now available in TETRAD III: http://hss.cmu.edu/philosophy/TETRAD/tetrad.html.) One can then use the sample from the posterior to estimate the posterior statistics from their sample counterparts, that is $\hat{\theta}_{EAP}$, $\hat{\theta}_{MDAP}$, s($\hat{\theta}_{EAP}$), $\hat{\theta}_{0.025}$, and $\hat{\theta}_{0.975}$. For simplicity, a multivariate normal prior over the t parameters has been used, that is. $p(\theta) \sim N_t(\mu_0, \sigma_0^2)$, and bounds on the parameters enforced; for example, variances are bounded below by 0, by rejecting sampled values outside of the legal parameter bounds. (For details about the Gibbs sampler implementation, see Scheines et al., 1999; and Casella and George, 1992.)

To apply the Bayesian solution to the lead problem, one must put a prior over the parameters. Needleman pioneered a technique of estimating cumulative lead exposure by measuring the accumulated lead in a child's baby teeth. Needleman guesses that between 0 percent and 40 percent of the variance in his measure of dentine lead is from measurement error, with 20 percent a conservative best guess. For the measures of environmental stimulation and genetic factors, he was less confident. We guessed that between 0 percent and 60 percent of the variance in *Med* and *Piq* is from measurement error, with 30 percent as our best guess. Thus the Bayesian analysis was begun by specifying a multivariate normal prior over the model's thirteen parameters. The part of the prior involving measurement error is given in Table 2. The prior is otherwise uninformative.

Using this partially informative prior, 50,000 iterations were produced with the Gibbs sampler in TETRAD III. The sequence converged immediately. Table 3 shows the results of this run, and the histogram in Figure 3 shows the shape of the marginal posterior over β_1, the crucial coefficient representing the influence of actual lead exposure on children's IQ. The results support Needleman's original conclusion, but they require neither unrealistic assumptions about the complete absence of measurement error, nor assumptions about exactly how much measurement error is present, nor assumptions about upper bounds on the measurement error for the remaining regressors.

The Bayesian point estimate of the coefficient reflecting the effect of *Actual Lead* exposure on *Ciq* is negative, and since the central 95 percent region of the posterior lies between −0.420

Table 3 Gibbs Sample Statistics for the Causal Parameters in the Errors-in-All-Variables Model

	$\hat{\theta}_{EAP}$	$\hat{\theta}_{MDAP}$	s($\hat{\theta}_{EAP}$)	$\hat{\theta}_{0.025}$	$\hat{\theta}_{0.975}$
β_1	−0.215	−0.211	0.097	−0.420	−0.038
β_2	0.332	0.307	0.397	−0.358	1.252
β_3	0.321	0.304	0.391	−0.459	1.128

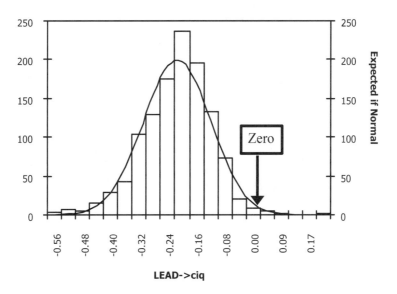

Figure 3 Histogram of relative frequency of β_1 in Gibbs sample

and −0.038, I conclude that exposure to environmental lead is indeed deleterious according to this model and my prior uncertainty over the parameters.

Although my uncertainty about the amount of measurement error associated with *Med* and *Piq*, which are proxies for environmental stimulation and genetic factors respectively, is not sufficient to make β_1 insignificant, it is sufficient to make β_2 and β_3 insignificant. That is, the central 95 percent of the sample from the posterior over both β_2 and β_3 includes 0. Since these coefficients represent the effect of environmental stimulation and genetic factors on a child's cognitive abilities, it seems reasonable to insist that they are at least positive in sign. I thus reran the analysis, but imposed 0 as a lower bound on β_2 and β_3. The posterior distribution over β_1 was slightly less diffuse, and it centered over roughly the same value.

In fact, I sampled from several posteriors corresponding to different priors, and in each case I obtained similar results. Although the size of the Bayesian point estimate for *Actual Lead*'s influence on *Ciq* moved up and down slightly, its sign and significance (the 95 percent central region in the posterior over β_1 was always below zero) were robust.

I also ran the Gibbs sampler on an errors-in-all-variables model that included all six of Needleman's original regressors. In this case the bounds Klepper derived proved important.

Table 4 Informative Part of the Prior in the Errors-in-All-Variables Model Including All Six Original Regressors

Parameter	Mean (μ_0)	Standard Deviation (σ_0)
$\sigma^2(\varepsilon_{Lead})$	0.05	0.05
$\sigma^2(\varepsilon_{Med})$	0.10	0.10
$\sigma^2(\varepsilon_{Piq})$	0.10	0.10
$\sigma^2(\varepsilon_{Fab})$	0.05	0.05
$\sigma^2(\varepsilon_{Mab})$	0.05	0.05
$\sigma^2(\varepsilon_{Nlb})$	0.05	0.05

Distribution of LEAD->ciq

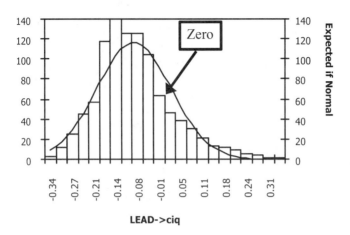

Figure 4 Gibbs sample from model with six regressors.

Recall that the measurement error on *Fab* was required to be below 0.06. Using a prior in which substantial mass violated this bound, the sampler did not converge.

Using a prior that was uninformative except for the parameters shown in Table 4, the histogram of values for β_1 in the Gibbs sample (Figure 4) was substantially different than the one in Figure 3.

A full Bayesian analysis would incorporate uncertainty over these and other model specifications, and in future work I intend to address this problem. Given the two errors-in-all-variables models considered here, however, I am highly inclined to favor the smaller model suggested by TETRAD III's analysis. Given this model, which is perfectly plausible, the data quite clearly support Needleman's original conclusion.

Portions of this article appeared in *Computation, Causation, and Discovery*, edited by C. Glymour and G. Cooper, Cambridge, MA: MIT Press, 1999. Reprinted with permission of MIT Press.

References

Casella, G. and E. I. George. 1992. "Explaining the Gibbs sampler." *The American Statistician* **46**: 167–174.

Grant, L. et al. 1983. "Draft air lead criteria document." Environmental Protection Agency, Washington, D.C., 14 November, Appendix 12-c.

Glymour, C., P. Spirtes, and R. Scheines. 1994. "In place of regression." In *Patrick Suppes: Scientific Philosopher*, edited by Humphreys, Vol. 1. Dordrecht, Netherlands: Kluwer Academic Publishers.

Kiiveri, H. and T. Speed. 1982. "Structural analysis of multivariate data: a review." In *Sociological Methodology*, edited by S. Leinhardt. San Francisco, CA: Jossey-Bass.

Klepper, S. 1988. "Regressor diagnostics for the classical errors-in-variables model." *J. Econometrics* **37**: 225–250.

Klepper, S. and E. Leamer. 1984. "Consistent sets of estimates for regressions with errors in all variables." *Econometrica* **52**: 163–183.

Klepper, S., M. Kamlet, and R. Frank. 1993. "Regressor diagnostics for the errors-in-variables model—an application to the health effects of pollution." *J. Environ. Econ. Mgmnt* **24**: 190–211.

Needleman, H., C. E. Gunnoe, A. Leviton, R. Reed, M. Peresie, C. Maher, and P. Barrett. 1979. "Deficits in psychologic and classroom performance of children with elevated dentine lead levels." *N. Engl. J. Med.* **300**: 689.

Needleman, H., S. Geiger, and R. Frank. 1985. "Lead and IQ scores: a reanalysis." *Science* **227**: 701–704.

Robins J. and L. Wasserman. 1996. "On the impossibility of inferring causation from association without background knowledge." Unpublished manuscript. Pittsburgh, PA: CMU Department of Statistics.

Scheines, R. 1993. "Causation, indistinguishability, and regression." In *Softstat '93: Advances in Statistical Software 4*, pp. 89–99. New York: Gustav Fischer.

Scheines, R., H. Hoijtink, and A. Boomsma. 1999. "Bayesian estimation and testing of structural equation models." *Psychometrika* **64(1)**: 37–52.

Scheines, R., P. Spirtes, G. Glymour, and C. Meek. 1994. *TETRAD II: Tools for Causal Modeling. User's Manual*. Hillsdale, NJ: Erlbaum.

Smith, A. F. M. and G. O. Roberts. 1993. "Bayesian computation via the Gibbs sampler and related Markov chain Monte Carlo methods." *J. R. Stat. Soc., Series B* **55**: 3–23.

Spirtes, P., C. Glymour, and R. Scheines. 2000. *Causation, Prediction, and Search*. 2d ed. Cambridge, MA: MIT Press.

47.4 College Education: Mining University Enrollment Data

Arun P. Sanjeev

ABSTRACT Student information has been collected by universities for several decades. Our research shows that it can be instrumental in providing useful enrollment and retention knowledge. We analyzed university enrollment data, extracted from several databases that contain student records at one university. We started from general goals of understanding enrollment and retention. Then we conducted a broad automated search for regularities that identify the best predictors. Our process of knowledge discovery can be represented as a sequence of queries and quests. Surprising discoveries led to the repeated cycle of asking questions, preparation of relevant data (by queries), defining the search for knowledge (by quests), running the automated search (executing the quests), and interpreting new results. In a number of cases, an important conclusion from large-scale automated search was that no dependencies were found for a particular attribute, while they were expected according to common knowledge. Many discoveries, including negative results, turned out practically useful. Some influenced institutional policies, while others, especially future enrollment predictions help budget officers and university management devise plans and strategies for effective administration.

1. Business Problem

In the educational domain of universities and colleges, the majority of administrative decisions are based on student enrollment. This is because tuition and other revenues are generated by the number of credit hours students enroll in classes. But student enrollment is a complex phenomenon, especially in metropolitan institutions such as Wichita State University (WSU) where the student population is diverse in age, ethnic origin, and socioeconomic status (Sanjeev and Żytkow, 1996). Furthermore, policies in state universities are made to ensure accessibility and equal opportunity. This can make enrollment management more complex. For instance, at WSU, an open admissions policy (admit any high school graduate) prohibits selective admissions.

Understanding the regularities that involve the number of credit hours the students enroll each semester is an open business problem of great importance to the university's well-being. Tuition accountability in universities means retaining extra monies from tuition and fees after the expenses have been met. But an overrun in the predictions will result in serious or even disastrous budget cuts. So, an empirical prediction of the number of students enrolled in a future term and the credit hours students will take can be very useful to the university administrators. It can prepare them for difficult decisions.

Credit hours are taken in the process of gaining academic degrees. Bachelor's degrees are awarded after completing approximately 120 credit hours. Receipt of a degree is a direct measure of student success, so that university administrators desire to increase the percentage of degrees awarded. But nondegree recipients also take credit hours, and it is in the interest of the university that they take more hours and continue to enroll in more terms.

In summary, our first task was understanding enrollment as a part of the university's business process, in terms of process input (characteristics of incoming students), throughput (credit hours taken), duration (number of terms enrolled), and output (degrees received). The next task was selecting the findings that were particularly important and surprising to the administrators. Selected regularities must be explained to the administrators in understandable business terms, or else they will not affect institutional policies.

2. Motivation for a Data Mining Solution

Historical data on students, collected for several decades, exist in large university databases. The databases are used to generate routine reports required by both the university and the state administration. Reports answer specific questions. They are not exploratory, and they do not supply a broader understanding of the university's problems. In contrast, in our approach, knowledge discovery is a broad exploration in search of business process understanding and particularly in search of useful predictive knowledge.

A particularly useful approach to an open and broad exploration is automated search for knowledge. Seeking different kinds of new and useful enrollment and retention, we defined a broad search problem, using all available attributes potentially relevant to new findings, that support, augment, or contradict the expert knowledge of university administrators. New empirical knowledge derived from data can influence changes to established institutional procedures and processes. Especially persuasive are quantitative models that lead to quantitative predictions.

Once discovered, knowledge can be used beyond a specific business goal. A broad and open search is particularly useful, as it leads to a large base of empirical regularities that can be used in many situations and toward many goals.

3. The Available Data

Our student database consists of the following files (tables):

1. Grade tape for each academic term (mainframe, sequential file).
2. Stat tape for each academic term (mainframe, sequential file).
3. Student history file (mainframe, VSAM file).
4. Student transcript file (mainframe, VSAM file).
5. Student financial assistance (mainframe, IMS/DL1 database).

The university collects enrollment data twice every term. It is permanently stored on tapes. The stat tape stores enrollment details by the twentieth day. Both student history and transcript files include all university attendees and contain over six million records. The former provides current demographic and similar data, and the latter contains details of enrollment and grades received by each student. Dollars awarded as aid to students are accounted in the financial aid database.

For our study, we needed data from all sources. First, we selected the attributes that we and several administrators considered related to enrollment and retention analysis. Then, we developed a query that joined different tables and computed new attributes by different aggregates (count, total, etc.) on original attributes.

The first category of attributes used in our study describes students prior to university enrollment. It includes demographics such as age at first term, ethnicity, sex, resident status, home county, et cetera, and high school information like graduation year, grade point average (HSGPA), results on standardized tests (COMPACT), and so on.

The attributes in the second category describe events in the course of study. They include hours of remedial education in the first term (REMHR), cumulative grade point average

(CUMGPA), number of academic terms skipped, number of times changed major, number of times placed on probation, and academic dismissal.

The third category includes the goal attributes. They capture, individually for each student, the global characteristics of the business process: the output, throughput, and duration. We used academic degrees received (DEGREE) as a direct measure of desired output. The total number of credit hours taken by each student (CURRHRS) was used as the most important measure of the process throughput, as it determines the university's budget. Process duration was measured by the number of academic terms enrolled (NTERM) by each student. All these attributes come from the student transcript files.

4. Background Knowledge

Attribute selection was guided by relevance to enrollment and retention. Student selection was another important decision. There are many categories of students. For example, a category called *guests* can include high school students who simultaneously take college classes. To understand the enrollment process, we needed a separate analysis of homogeneous yet large groups. One existing category was particularly useful: the cohort of 1,404 first-time, full-time, freshmen with no previous college experience from the fall 1986 term. This choice allowed sufficient time for the students to receive a baccalaureate degree in spite of skipping several terms (stop-outs). Then, we repeated the same analysis for the identical student subpopulation selected from the fall 1987 to check and verify the stability of the patterns discovered for the fall 1986 cohort.

Later, after we analyzed the initial results, additional attributes were formed with the use of knowledge not available in the data, such as students who need remedial classes. We will later explain both the reasons and the outcome for this attribute.

5. Preprocessing and Data Preparation

Unlike data generated in a scientific laboratory, enrollment data represent students, and as with any personnel data, they are sparse and lead to undeterministic knowledge. To find useful statistical distributions by means of contingency tables, we binned attribute values, to prevent sparse and thus insignificant numbers. We also needed meaningful categories, so that the results could be useful to administrators. For that reason, whenever possible, we used categories that occur in official enrollment reports.

Grade point averages in high school take continuous values. Yet, high school teachers use ranges of average to assign letter grades. For example, averages under 1 are given an F, while A students have at least 3.5. We followed similar guidelines and converted averages into letter grades. Other examples of binned attributes are student age, hours of remedial education (REMHR), and cumulative grade point average in college.

Demographic attributes contain few missing data. But attributes such as ACT test scores contain plenty of missing data. For example, one-third (463 students) of our cohort did not have ACT test scores. Students may not take tests or chose not to report test results. Before missing data are skipped, it is a good idea to consider regularities that treat missing values as one of the values. In the case of ACT test scores we ran the search twice. The first time, we considered only students with valid ACT test scores, and in the second, we included in the search students with missing scores. The results were rewarding. The regularity discovered for students with missing data when compared to the regularity found for only students having ACT test scores was stronger ($V = 0.20$ vs $V = 0.15$) and more significant ($Q = 6 \cdot 10^{-34}$ vs. $Q = 1.91 \cdot 10^{-8}$). The meaning of Cramer's V and significance parameter Q are explained in Chapter 5.1. The results that include missing values are shown in Table 1. A missing value of ACT is a very good predictor of poor performance in college.

One important element of preprocessing is data verification. It should be done whenever possible. Our analysis revealed differences between our enrollment totals and the reports published by our registrar's office. When we considered the entire population of above 15,000 (all) students in fall 1986, our data contained 68 fewer returning students over the course of three terms or one fiscal year. Intrigued, we contacted the manager of our student databases. It turned out that the student databases use Social Security Numbers (SSNs) as record keys. But students, particularly foreign, change their SSN during study. Procedures have been established to address SSN changes. However, updates are made on transactional systems, and tape files remain untouched. They are primarily used for data storage, but not intended for data mining. Fortunately, the differences in student numbers were small, so we decided to ignore them. In our cohort of first-time full-time freshmen, such a discrepancy is at most fourteen students.

6. The Discovery Mechanism

We used the 49er knowledge discovery in databases (KDD) system to search for knowledge. The 49er system (Żytkow and Zembowicz, 1993; 24.1.4 in this handbook) discovers knowledge in the form of statements: Pattern P holds for data in range R. A range of data is the whole data set or a data subset distinguished by conditions imposed on one or more attributes. Examples of patterns include contingency tables (see Chapter 5.1), equations, and logical equivalence.

49er systematically searches for patterns among different combinations of attributes in many data subsets. It uses the statistical test of significance to qualify a hypothesis as a regularity. 49er measures significance by the (low) probability Q (typically of the order of $Q < 10^{-5}$), that a given sample is a statistical fluctuation of random distribution. 49er's measurement of predictive strength of contingency tables is based on Cramer's V coefficient (Chapter 5.1). Both Q and V are derived from χ^2 statistics.

The KDD process can be described by a sequence of queries and quests (Żytkow and Sanjeev, 1998). Queries are used to prepare the data, while quests for specific knowledge (such as knowledge about continuing student enrollment) guide 49er's data mining search.

7. The Results

The initial data table was prepared by Query 1 that (1) selected first-time freshmen enrolled in the fall 1986 from the grade tape; (2) added Category 1 attributes from the student history file; (3) Category 2 attributes computed mainly from attributes in the transcript file; and (4) similarly computed the goal attributes in Category 3. SSNs were used as the key for several join operations.

Since it is a good idea to start the exploration with a broad request for knowledge, the initial discovery tasks that we will call Quest 1 were a broad search request. We requested all regularities between attributes in Category 1 and 2 as independent variables against attributes in Category 3. 49er was supposed to slice data according to the values of attributes in Category 1.

In response to Quest 1, applied to data selected by Query 1, 49er's discovery process resulted in many regularities (Sanjeev and Żytkow, 1996). In this paper we will present a few examples of regularities that led to important applications.

Academic results in high school turned out to be the best predictors of superior performance in college and an excellent indicator of retention (cf. Tables 1–4). Druzdzel and Glymour (1994) reached similar conclusions through application of TETRAD (Spirtes et al., 1993). They used summary data for many universities, in which every university was represented by one record of many attributes averaged over the entire student body. Our study considered records for individual students, so we were able to derive additional conclusions. For instance, seeking regularities in large numbers of data subsets, 49er detected that persistence and superior performance in college differ significantly in age groups and in race groups. Those results, even if they have a high predictive value, were viewed as inconsistent with affirmative action, so that nobody was interested.

Let us consider a few tables that exemplify the most important results. Each table can be viewed as a probability distribution that characterizes the investigated student population. It can be used in many ways (Chapter 5.1). For the sake of university administrators we

Table 1 Observed Absolute Frequency for Fall 1986: COMPACT vs. CURRHRS

120+	40	78	59	108	5
90–119	40	44	24	38	3
60–89	26	32	28	29	0
30–59	57	68	43	36	0
1–29	262	196	65	56	1
0	38	8	4	2	0
COMPACT	missing	<19	$\leqslant 22$	$\leqslant 29$	>29

$\chi^2 = 221$, $Q = 6 \cdot 10^{-34}$, $V = 0.2$

Table 2 Observed Absolute Frequency for Fall 1986: HSGPA vs. CURRHRS

120+	0	11	102	92	73
90–119	0	13	67	26	32
60–89	0	6	54	25	25
30–59	0	34	100	32	22
1–29	4	164	243	60	29
0	0	14	17	5	3
HSGPA	F	D	C	B	A

$\chi^2 = 229$, $Q = 1.7 \cdot 10^{-32}$, $V = 0.19$

Table 3 Observed Absolute Frequency for Fall 1986: DEGREE

Bachelor's	0	15	128	97	91
Associate	0	2	14	8	13
No degree	4	226	443	139	81
HSGPA	F	D	C	B	A

$\chi^2 = 157$, $Q = 1.5 \cdot 10^{-28}$, $V = 0.25$

Table 4 Observed Absolute Frequency for Fall 1986: NTERM

12+	0	10	41	26	8
9–11	0	16	107	70	42
6–8	0	17	98	47	67
3–5	1	42	110	31	31
1–2	3	158	228	69	36
HSGPA	F	D	C	B	A

$\chi^2 = 168$, $Q = 3 \cdot 10^{-23}$, $V = 0.2$

provided several summaries of each probability distribution. For instance, according to Table 2, among the students with a high school grade point average of C/D, the proportion of those who enroll in 30 hours or more to those who enroll in less than 30 credit hours is 47/53. In contrast, as we move to the A/B grade categories, the proportion grows to 77/23. It grows to 83/17 for A students. Table 1 indicates a similar finding for ACT scores. Table 3 indicates that students with an A/B grade (HSGPA) when compared to those with a C/D received bachelor's and associate degrees at a much higher percentage (48.7 percent vs 19.2 percent). Also, the table clearly shows that the higher the HSGPA, the bigger the probability of receiving a degree at WSU: from 0 percent for F students to 56 percent for A students.

Background knowledge of the process of study allowed us to notice several interesting phenomena, which show the complexity of enrollment analysis. Table 4 shows that among the A/B students in high school, 39.1 percent did not stay in college after five terms, which is insufficient to reach a degree. Many may have transferred rather than dropped out, but neither can be verified since universities do not share data. State laws protect privacy by prohibiting data sharing without student consent. Very rarely do students inform administration about their change of the university. At the opposite end of Table 4 we can notice that many students stay in college for an unusually high number of terms. That is characteristic of a metropolitan university where students stop out for one or more semesters, but then continue and eventually reach a degree.

Statistical regularities in the enrollment data are best represented by contingency tables. Although 49er tried other forms of knowledge, such as equations and logic statements, they were very rare in this type of data.

We presented a few examples of the most important regularities found in the data. Now we will focus on the negative results, which are regularities expected by experts but missing in the actual data.

In a series of queries and corresponding quests we generated many attributes that describe financial aid and confronted financial aid attributes with our goal attributes. The results were surprising. No evidence was found to support that awarding financial aid increased college retention and the percentage of degrees awarded. The corresponding tables cannot be produced due to the space limitations. In Table 5 we summarize several negative results. Each number gives the probability Q that a given contingency table could have been generated randomly. None would qualify as a dependency even under the least demanding threshold of 5 percent. High performers are the students with A/B average grade in high school. Many other student subsets were tried, yet there was no evidence to demonstrate the influence of financial aid.

Query 1 used the independent attribute total number of remedial hours taken in the first term (REMHR). An intriguing regularity was returned by Quest 1 (Table 6): Students who took remedial hours in their first term are less likely to receive a degree. The percentage of students receiving a degree decreased from 31 percent for REMHR = 0 to 13 percent for REMHR = 8. This was a disturbing result since the purpose of remedial classes is to prepare students for the regular classes.

Table 5 Financial Aid: Probabilities of Random Fluctuation (Q) for Contingency Tables That Confront an Attribute That Summarizes Financial Aid with the Goal Attributes. Contingency Tables Are Insignificant for All Students and in Different Subsets

STUDENTS	NTERM	CURRHRS	DEGREE
All	0.88	0.24	0.36
Academically Poor	0.11	0.22	0.86
High Performers	0.99	0.99	0.94

Table 6 Observed Actual Values for Fall 1986: DEGREE vs. REMHR

Bachelor's	302	0	27	10	1	7
Associate	32	0	3	3	1	0
No degree	735	2	119	82	10	47
REMHR	0	2	3	5	6	8

$\chi^2 = 31.2$, $Q = 0.0$, $V = 0.106$

After a brief analysis, we realized that Table 6 is misleading. Remedial instruction is intended only for academically underprepared students, while students who do not need remedial instruction are not the right control group to be compared with. So, we identified the criteria that describe students for whom remedial education had been intended and used Query 2 to select those students. In the data table selected by Query 2, those students for whom the remedial education was intended but did not take it played the role of the control group.

A search request (Quest 2) identified REMHR as the control attribute, used all three goal attributes, and allowed data slicing on all attributes in Category 1. 49er's results were again surprising, because no dependencies were detected. For instance, Table 7, which is the counterpart of Table 6, indicates that taking remedial classes does not improve the chances for a student to reach a degree. Consider those students who did not take remedial classes, but needed them according to our criteria. They received bachelor and associate degrees at about the same percentage (10.8 percent vs 9.9 percent) when compared to those who took from three to eight hours of remedial class.

8. Applications of the Discovered Knowledge

On a number of occasions in 1995–1997 the selected results of our enrollment research were presented to senior university administrators including vice presidents and budget officers. We will now outline how our findings have formed the empirical foundation for several strategic decisions made by university administration.

Our research demonstrated that academic results in high school are the best predictor of persistence and superior performance in college. Tables 1–4 show regularities between average grade in high school (HSGPA) and composite ACT as predictors and college performance attributes: cumulative credit hours taken (CURRHRS), total academic terms enrolled (NTERM), and degrees received (DEGREE). Recruitment of one student in the category of A/B is several times more effective than recruitment of a student in categories C/D/E. The limited money that the university can spend on recruitment is most effectively used when it is targeted on the top high school students. At that time the university recruitment effort was not specifically directed, but a new draft of the *Strategic Plan for Wichita State University* includes, as the second of the five goals and objectives: "WSU will recruit and retain high quality students from a

Table 7 Observed Actual Values for Fall 1986: All Students Needing Remedial

Bachelor's	19	4	1	0	4
Associate	2	1	1	0	0
No-degree	174	39	36	4	21
REMHR	0	3	5	6	8

$\chi^2 = 5.06$, $Q = 0.89$, $V = 0.091$

variety of ethnic and socioeconomic backgrounds." This is a big step forward, even if it may not seem like much for those who do not closely follow the politics of state universities.

As a direct result of our research, the eighth-year graduation rate measure has been included as WSU's performance indicator. A strategic planning process called VISION 2020, initiated by the State of Kansas, requires universities to formulate a set of performance indicators (Chambers and Sanjeev, 1997) and report the results. The first of the core indicators concerns undergraduate student retention and graduation rates. The report mandated by the Regents asked for graduation rate measures after four, five, and six years. But students at WSU take often longer than six years to graduate: they tend to stop out for several academic terms during their college careers and enroll in less than fifteen hours in one semester. This phenomenon has been concluded from our studies. It can be partially observed in Table 4. It shows that a considerable percentage of students enroll for over eleven terms. In addition, many students stop out for few semesters. As a result, among the six Regents universities in Kansas, WSU is the only institution in which the graduation rate is also measured at the end of the eighth year.

Our results demonstrated that remedial education is ineffective. Table 7 shows one of many examples of a missing effect. About the same time, in 1996, a review was conducted of the core functionalities of University College, responsible for remedial education, advising students, providing supplemental learning resources such as access to videotapes, and the like. Our results reached the committee and became widely known. A year later, in fall 1997, a cost study was conducted on remedial education programs. Soon an *ad hoc* committee that reviewed academic programs recommended eliminating University College. The move surprised university administrators, and the vice president for academic affairs appointed a new committee. Another year later, in July 1998, that committee recommended that the college be eliminated and replaced by a smaller advising structure designed to enhance retention and student success. Each of these committees was informed in detail about our results. Several committees requested our special presentations. They provided empirical foundation that complemented other arguments. Now, after thirty-seven years of existence, University College no longer exists. The process was long, as policy decisions have many implications and typically require subjective reasons in addition to empirical justification.

Tables 1 and 7 were previously published in A. Sanjeev and J. Żytkow "Modeling the Business Process by Mining Multiple Databases in *Principles of Data Mining and Knowledge Discovery*, edited by J. Żytkow and M. Quafafou, vol. 1510 of the series *Lecture Notes in Computer Science*, pp. 437 and 438. Heidelberg: Springer-Verlag, 1998. Reprinted by permission of Springer-Verlag.

Tables 2, 3, 4, and 6 were previously published in "Discovering Enrollment Knowledge in University Databases" by A. Sanjeev, J. Żytkow, U. M. Fayyad, and R. Uthurusamy. In *Proceedings of the First International Conference on Knowledge Discovery and Data Mining*, pp. 249–250. Menlo Park, CA: AAAI Press, 1995. Reprinted by permission of American Association for Artificial Intelligence.

References

Chambers, S. and A. Sanjeev. 1997. "Reflecting metropolitan-based missions in performance indicator reporting." *Metropolitan Universities* 8(3): 135–152.

Druzdzel, M. and C. Glymour. 1994. "Application of the TETRAD II program to the study of student retention in U.S. Colleges." In *Proceedings of the AAAI-94 KDD Workshop*, pp. 419–430. Menlo Park, CA: AAAI Press.

Sanjeev, A. and J. Żytkow. 1996. "A study of enrollment and retention in a university database." *J. Mid-America Assoc. Educ. Opportunity Program Personnel* VIII: 24–41.

Spirtes, P., C. Glymour, and R. Scheines. 1993. *Causation, Prediction and Search*. New York: Springer-Verlag.

Żytkow, J. and A. Sanjeev. 1998. "Business process understanding: mining many data sets." In *Proceedings of the First International Conference on Rough Sets and Current Trends in Computing (Warsaw, Poland)*, pp. 239–246. Berlin, New York: Springer-Verlag.

Żytkow, J. and R. Zembowicz. 1993. "Database exploration in search of regularities." *J. Intell. Inform. Sys.* 2: 39–81.

48 SCIENCE

48.1 Gene Expression Analysis

Daniel C. Weaver

ABSTRACT Every cell contains all the information necessary to grow, divide, and respond correctly to its environment. The DNA sequence that holds this information is already known for many organisms, and a canonical draft DNA sequence was known for humans by the end of 2000. With this sequence information, biology is poised to enter an era of massively accelerated data collection to elucidate the mechanisms of life and the ailments that result when these mechanisms fail. High-throughput gene expression detection and analysis depends on this genomic information and yields unprecedented amounts of data about the molecular mechanisms that regulate a cell's behavior. Thus, gene expression analysis exemplifies how knowledge discovery techniques are being applied to gene discovery in biology and pharmacological research. This case study will describe what gene expression is, ways in which this data is currently analyzed, and the challenges remaining for effectively deriving biological knowledge from large sets of gene expression data.

1. Problem Definition

A gene is a region of DNA that contains all of the information necessary to produce a molecule (usually a protein) that performs some biological function. The gene is converted from its archival (DNA) form to its functional (protein) form through gene expression, a complex, two-step process by which the DNA coding regions of the gene are transcribed into RNA and subsequently translated into protein. This transfer of coded information from DNA to RNA to protein constitutes the central dogma of molecular biology.

One key to a cell's survival lies in its ability to regulate the rate at which its genes are transcribed and translated. Transcription and translation regulation are complex feedback loops in which some of the cell's gene products control which genes will be expressed in the cell's immediate future. Much of a cell's identity and behavior is determined by the set of expressed genes' products it contains. In other words, a skin cell knows how to be a skin cell because of the genes that it expresses. Furthermore, a skin cell can help to heal a wound by expressing the correct set of genes in response to its proximity to the damaged region. Many diseases act by changing the set of expressed genes in the affected cells. For example, a normal skin cell becomes carcinogenic by inappropriately expressing genes that allow it to divide rapidly and migrate to other tissues. Biologists hope that by studying patterns of gene expression, we will be better able to understand how diseases develop and how they can be prevented and cured.

Recent advances in gene expression detection technologies may help realize this hope by allowing biologists to monitor the expression level of many genes simultaneously. All gene expression detection technologies indirectly count the number of copies or relative number of copies of some or all of the gene products present in the cells of the biological sample of interest. This information can be organized into an experiment-by-gene table such that each row represents one experiment and each column represents one gene (see Table 1). The same gene expression information can also be organized such that each row represents a gene and each column represents an experiment. Both organizations of the data are equally valid and which is used depends on what scientific question the analyst is trying to answer. Gene expression analysis attempts to discover patterns among the expression levels observed for a defined set of genes or experiments. This pattern discovery must take into account the experimental context in which each sample was collected and the known structure and function of the gene, because the goal is to relate a gene's expression pattern and function to the experimental conditions in which its expression changes.

The largest currently published expression study was performed on 6,500 human genes in sixty-two normal and cancerous colon tissue samples, and each gene's expression was measured twenty times in each experiment. The subsequent analysis, therefore, had to find

Table 1 An Example of an Experiment-by-Gene Table

	Experimental variable	Gene 1	Gene 2	Gene 3
Experiment 1	30	1.19	1.32	0.88
Experiment 2	25	1.23	0.77	0.75
Experiment 3	46	1.32	1.33	1.18
Experiment 4	53	1.33	1.18	1.00
Experiment 5	23	0.88	1.00	0.88
Experiment 6	26	1.00	0.92	0.96
Experiment 7	64	1.56	1.19	1.00
Experiment 8	34	1.23	1.15	1.03

relevant gene expression patterns among ~8 million data points (Alon et al., 1999). The human genome has ~35,000 genes in total, so a comparable experiment on the full genome would require >40 million data points. Thus, as more samples are collected on more genes, analysis algorithm efficiency will be one of the primary considerations when evaluating new analytical techniques.

2. KDD Process

2.1. Looking for Diagnostic or Causal Expression Pattern Differences

When a new set of gene expression data is collected, the scientist first asks which genes significantly change their expression levels in response to the tested experimental conditions. This analysis identifies candidate genes that may regulate or execute the cell's response in the experiment. Determining which of the candidate genes actually participate in the cell's activity requires that the biologist perform additional experiments that test this participation directly. In medical research, this analysis identifies genes whose expression significantly increases or decreases during a disease. Some of the identified genes may play a causal role in the disease's establishment or progression and are thus therapeutic targets. Others may be coordinately (but not causally) expressed as the ailment develops and thus are diagnostic for the disease state.

Before knowledge discovery can proceed, the raw expression data must be preprocessed to obtain a normalized final gene expression level. This is usually a two-step process whereby the raw instrument data (frequently image data) is normalized to extract the signal from the background. Then the individual measurements of a gene's expression level are combined into a final single value. Because the background is usually not smooth across the expression detection instrument, one has to measure the local background immediately around each expression measurement. Different gene expression detection instruments have their own background correction considerations, but in general the background is detected by defining the boundaries of the authentic signal (by outlining the corresponding spot in an image or peak on a graph) and calculating the average noise in the immediately adjacent regions (Chen et al., 1997).

After the measurements have been corrected for background, a final expression level must be calculated for each gene. Though multiple gene expression measurements can be taken simultaneously, their results cannot be simply averaged because each measurement could come from a different part of the gene's coding region and some regions will misrepresent the amount of that gene's RNA or protein in the sample. For example, Alon et al. (1999) integrated the twenty measurements collected for each gene by ordering the measurements according to their position in the coding region, throwing out the high and low measurements in a sliding window of five measurements, and calculating the mean of the remaining three measurements. The final gene expression signal was the mean of the intensity values calculated for each window position.

The final expression signals are used to normalize each gene's signal relative to internal or external control measurements or data set(s). These relative expression levels reveal the degree of change that has occurred in each gene's expression levels in the corresponding experimental conditions. Although the specific methods used to process the data differ significantly, the final result is a table like that shown in Table 1. Note that the specific database representation of this information also varies significantly.

Many different but related techniques have been applied to begin identifying candidate genes of interest. Iyer et al. (1999) selected genes that either (1) differed from their control by a factor of 2.20 in at least two of the thirteen data sets collected or (2) whose $\log_2$(relative signal) standard deviation was greater than 0.7. Holstege et al. (1998) also selected genes that differed by greater than a factor of 2 in at least two experiments. DeRisi et al. (1996) used slightly different criteria selecting genes that were greater than 3 standard deviations away from a mean defined by ninety internal control measurements per experiment (which translated into selecting genes whose relative expression was <0.52 or >2.4). From the perspective of data mining, these can be viewed as relatively simple queries to gene-by-experiment tables of properly normalized expression measurements. Once genes of interest are identified by virtue of their expression levels, the next step is to look for gene categorization information that allows the scientist to relate the fact that the gene's expression pattern changes in the experimental conditions to its known or hypothesized biological function.

These techniques have yielded a wealth of knowledge about fundamental biological processes. For example, the study performed by Iyer et al. (1999) repeated a classic experiment in which quiescent cells are induced to resume growth. Though this experiment has been repeated and studied for at least twenty-five years, a single experiment using modern high-throughput gene expression detection and analysis identified many previously unidentified genes that suggest that the cells are not only being induced to resume growth, but also are executing developmental programs to help accelerate wound healing.

2.2. Looking for Co-Regulated Genes and Similar Genetic or Environmental (Pharmacological) Conditions

As more data sets are collected and normalized, the scientist next needs to ask which genes are coordinately expressed and which experimental conditions results in similar patterns of gene expression.

Given a set of genes whose expression levels have been determined across two or more different experimental conditions, the scientist looks for genes that appear to be coordinately expressed. Such coordinate expression frequently occurs when genes are required together to execute biological programs; thus, this type of data mining can identify coherent subsystems of

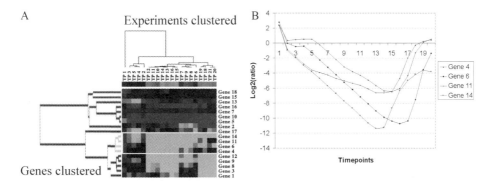

Figure 1 A. Genes and experiments clustered with the software developed by Eisen et al. (1999). A 100-gene network was simulated through twenty timepoints using the linear matrix modeling system developed by Weaver et al. (1999). A subset of genes was used as input to the clustering algorithms, the results of which are shown in A. Each row represents a gene, each column represents a timepoint, and each colored box represents that gene's $\log_2$[Timepoint(n)/Timepoint(0)], where red (dark gray) is positive and green (light gray) is negative. B. The $\log_2$(ratio) of genes 4, 6, 11, and 14 (from the boxed subtree) is plotted to highlight the similarity in their expression patterns

the cell's molecular machinery. Abstractly, this analysis is attempting to find rows in a gene-by-experiment table whose values co-vary. Pragmatically, the analyst clusters the rows (genes) of the table using either hierarchical or nonhierarchical mathematical clustering algorithms.

The data associated with each gene can be viewed as a point in n-dimensional space where the genes' expression has been measured in n experiments. Each row in the gene-by-experiment table defines that gene's position in the n-dimensional space, and cluster analysis attempts to identify sets of points (genes) that are close together according to some mathematical definition of close. Hierarchical clustering methods organize the data into a branching hierarchy of related entities where closely related entities are separated by one or few branch points with short branch lengths. Nonhierarchical clustering algorithms attempt to partition the set of data points into two or more distinct sets of related entities (Mirkin, 1996).

The first algorithm for hierarchical clustering of gene expression data was developed and published by Eisen et al. (1998); this algorithm remains the most commonly used clustering algorithm for gene expression data. After data preprocessing similar to that described in the previous section, their software measures the distance between the input genes' expression patterns by calculating the matrix of correlation coefficient between each pair of genes. Initially all the genes are treated as their own cluster, and the two genes with the highest correlation coefficient are merged. The expression measurements for the merged genes are averaged and a new correlation coefficient matrix is calculated in which the two merged genes are represented by a single row or column with the between-gene distances measured to their averaged values. The algorithm iterates until all the genes are merged into a single cluster. The order in which the genes were merged corresponds to the relatedness of the genes' expression patterns (see Figure 1(A)). To establish the biological significance of the genes whose expression patterns were closely related, the analysts referred to known functional information for each gene. They observed that genes that displayed significant expression pattern similarity were those that are known to participate in common biological programs like nutrient metabolism, DNA replication, and cell division. While this approach works well for a genome like yeast, which contains only $\sim 6{,}000$ genes, it is of order N^4, so it may not scale well to the human genome which is predicted to contain $\sim 35{,}000$ genes. Another hierarchical clustering algorithm that has been applied to gene expression data takes the complementary tactic, iteratively partitioning the genes into two clusters until all the genes have been separated (Alon et al., 1999). While this algorithm is of order $N \log(N)$ (so it will better scale up to large data sets), it is unclear whether this algorithm offers any significant advantages over the average means method described above with respect to the clusters that are identified.

Tavazoie et al. (1999) have recently published a nonhierarchical clustering algorithm of the budding yeast data sets collected by Cho et al. (1998), using the k-means algorithm (Hartigan, 1975). Cho et al. collected gene expression data from fifteen time point samples taken from a population of yeast cells that synchronously progressed through two complete cell division cycles. The analysts took the 3,000 most variable genes across the fifteen timepoints using a metric of variability calculated by a gene's standard deviation divided by its mean. After normalization, the Euclidean distances between all gene pairs were calculated and thirty gene clusters were defined as the starting points for the k-means algorithm to partition the genes based on those distances. The k-means algorithm can partition data into any number of different clusters; that the researchers elected to partition the genes into thirty clusters is arbitrary (but yields good results in this analysis). The first cluster was centered on the centroid of the data set (identified by averaging all the genes) and the remaining clusters were defined by the twenty-nine most distant data points from the centroid. From that starting condition the algorithm iterated until all the genes resided in one of the thirty clusters and cluster membership was stable (i.e., genes had stopped moving from one cluster to another). To substantiate the biological relevance of these clusters, the analysts examined the genes' known functions and showed that genes with known functional similarity tended to co-segregate to the same cluster. Furthermore, the analysts looked for and identified transcription factor binding sites in the regulatory regions of genes that clustered together. Thus, the *k*-means clustering algorithm successfully identified genes that are coordinately expressed and may represent coherent subsystems of the cell.

In addition to clustering genes, scientists use similar techniques to cluster experimental data sets (Alon et al., 1999; Eisen et al., 1998). The complete expression pattern observed for all genes (or some subset thereof) can be viewed as a molecular fingerprint for that experimental, environmental, or disease condition. The expression data is organized into an experiment-by-gene table and the rows (experiments) are clustered to identify similarities between disparate experimental conditions. If successful, such analyses give the biologists a clue about the underlying mechanisms at work in different experimental conditions and could give doctors a means to diagnose disease by virtue of the resulting gene expression patterns.

2.3. Deriving Models of Regulatory Pathways

Scientists are beginning to explore mathematical modeling of gene expression data that may eventually enable discovery of the regulatory feedback that controls each gene's expression. With such a modeling system, the scientist could collect data from diseased tissue and train the model on the disease's gene expression pattern. Theoretically this model would accurately represent the disease's response to various environmental or therapeutic stimuli and could be used to look for therapeutics that reverse the diseased state. Obviously, there are significant technical and theoretical hurdles to overcome, but gene expression monitoring provides some of the required data for this type of modeling. Methods already published model biological regulatory networks with boolean networks (Liang et al., 1998; Wuensche, 1998), differential equations (Chen et al., 1999), and linear matrices (Weaver et al., 1999; Mjolsness et al., 1998).

While there is no space in this paper for a complete treatment of gene expression modeling, consider, for example, the linear matrix models of the gene regulatory network proposed by Weaver et al. (1999). In this approach, the expression state of a gene regulatory network containing n genes is represented by a vector $u(t)$ in n-dimensional space. The regulatory inputs to each gene are modeled with a weight matrix, Z, such that all the inputs for gene i are represented in row z_i. The weights in Z also represent gene i's responsiveness to changes in regulatory input; some genes respond to changing regulation more dramatically than others. Thus, gene i's response to all its regulatory inputs, $s_i(t)$, is calculated by summing across all the genes:

$$\sum_j s_i(t) = z_{i,j} u_j(t). \tag{1}$$

Gene i's resulting expression level, $u_i(t+1)$, is calculated with a dose-response or squashing function that produces a value between complete repression (0) and the gene's maximum observed expression level, m_i.

$$u_i(t+1) = \frac{m_i}{1 + e^{-s_i(t)}}. \tag{2}$$

This mathematical approach lends itself to discovering the regulatory networks because collected data sets can be organized into input-output pairs and these equations can be rearranged to solve for Z. Because these models assume that the regulation of each gene is an independent event, solving for Z only requires calculating one weight matrix row, z_i, at a time.

Thus, to calculate the weight matrix z_i from input and output data set pairs, one must first desquash gene i's expression level $u_i(t+1)$ to obtain s_i, the net regulation and response state of that gene at time t:

$$s_i = -\ln\left(\frac{1}{u_{i(t+1)}} - 1\right). \tag{3}$$

Next, one must calculate the weight matrix row, z_i, that relates the inputs, $u_i(t)$, to the regulation state, $s_i(t)$, which was obtained from desquashing the training outputs. This is a classic linear algebra problem: given a known matrix U (in our case, all the inputs from our training data sets), an unknown vector z_i (the desired weight matrix row), and a known vector

s (gene i's output in each data set), such that $Uz_i = s$, calculate the value of z_i. Rearranging this equation to solve for z_i gives the equation, $z_i = U^{-1}s$, where U^{-1} denotes the inverse matrix of U. Because, in general, fewer data points than genes will be available, the problem is underdetermined and many equally good solutions for z_i are possible, including the correct one. Thus, the problem becomes how to solve for the correct inverse of the input matrix U. The approach to choosing a correct matrix inversion proposed by Weaver et al. (1999) employs the biologically valid assumption that most genes do not regulate most other genes, that is, most of the weights in Z are zero. Therefore, one algorithm for calculating the correct matrix inversion looks at the predicted weights for a row in z_i, identifies the smallest weight absolute value, and sets the corresponding column of the input matrix U to zero (i.e., nullifies that gene's input to calculating the U^{-1}). U^{-1} is recalculated to get a new prediction of z_i, and so forth.

3. Conclusions

Gene expression data is currently used to identify causal or correlated changes in gene expression patterns and to cluster genes that function together in executing biological programs. Causal or correlated expression patterns can be identified through relatively simple statistical tests of the collected data, though more robust analysis algorithms are starting to be used (like principal component analysis). Hierarchical and nonhierarchical cluster algorithms have been published for identifying co-expressed genes, and more algorithms are under development. In both types of analyses, the biological significance of candidate genes or clusters is further substantiated by referencing other known functional information about the identified genes. In the coming years, this field will face additional challenges as it tries to integrate more data, identify more subtle regulatory relationships, and extend the approaches used for gene regulation modeling.

References

Alon, U., N. Barkai, D. A. Notterman, K. Gish, S. Ybarra, D. Mack, and A. J. Levine. 1999. "Broad patterns of gene expression revealed by clustering analysis of tumor and normal colon tissues probed by oligonucleotide arrays." *PNAS* **96**: 6745–6750.

Chen, T., H. L. He, and G. M. Church. 1999. "Modeling gene expression with differential equations." *Proc. Pacific Symp. Biocomput.* **4**: 29–40.

Chen, Y., E. R. Dougherty, and M. L. Bitner. 1997. "Ratio-based decision and the quantitative analysis of cDNA microarray images." *Biomedical Optics* **2**: 364–374.

Cho, R. J., M. J. Campbell, E. A. Winzeler, L. Steinmetz, A. Conway, L. Wodicka, T. G. Wolfsberg, A. E. Gabrielian, D. Landsman, D. J. Lockhart, and R. W. Davis. 1998. "A genome-wide transcriptional analysis of the mitotic cell cycle." *Mol. Cell.* **2**: 65–73.

DeRisi, J., L. Penland, P. O. Brown, M. L. Bittner, P. S. Meltzer, M. Ray, Y. Chen, Y. A. Su, and J. M. Trent. 1996. "Use of a cDNA microarray to analyze gene expression patterns in human cancer." *Nature Gen.* **14**: 457–460.

Eisen, M. B., P. T. Spellman, P. O. Brown, and D. Botstein. 1998. "Cluster analysis and display of genome-wide expression patterns." *PNAS* **95**: 14863–14866.

Hartigan, J. A. 1975. *Clustering Algorithms*. New York: J. Wiley & Sons.

Hilsenbeck, S. G., W. E. Friedrichs, R. Schiff, P. O'Connell, R. K. Hansen, C. K. Osborne, and S. A. W. Fuqua. 1999. "Statistical analysis of array expression data as applied to the problem of tamoxifen resistance." *J. Natl. Cancer Inst.* **91**: 453–459.

Holstege, F. C. P., E. G. Jennings, J. J. Wyrick, T. I. Lee, C. J. Hengartner, M. R. Green, T. R. Golub, E. S. Lander, and R. A. Young. 1998. "Dissecting the regulatory circuitry of a eukaryotic genome." *Cell* **95**: 717–728.

Iyer, V. R., M. B. Eisen, D. T. Ross, G. Schuler, T. Moore, J. C. Lee, J. M. Trent, L. M. Staudt, J. Hudson, Jr., M. S. Boguski, D. Lashkari, D. Shalon, D. Botstein, and P. O. Brown. 1999. "The transcriptional program in the response of human fibroblasts to serum." *Science* **283**: 83–87.

Liang, S., S. Fuhrman, and R. Somogyi. 1998. "REVEAL: a general reverse engineering algorithm for inference of genetic network architectures." *Proc. Pacific Symp. Biocomput.* **3**: 18–29.

Mirkin, B. 1996. *Mathematical Classification and Clustering*. Dordrecht, Netherlands: Kluwer Academic Publishers.

Mjolsness, E., D. H. Sharp, and J. Reinitz. 1998. "A connectionist model of development." *J. Theor. Biol.* **152**: 429–453.

Tavazoie, S., J. D. Hughes, M. J. Campbell, R. J. Cho, and G. M. Church. 1999. "Systemic determination of genetic network architecture." *Nature Gen.* **22**: 281–285.

Weaver, D. C., C. T. Workman, and G. D. Stormo. 1999. "Modeling regulatory networks with weight matrices." *Proc. Pacific Symp. Biocomput.* **4**: 112–123.

Wuensche, A. 1998. "Genomic regulation modeled as a network with basins of attraction." *Proc. Pacific Symp. Biocomput.* **3**: 89–102.

Further Reading

For general background on transcription, translation, and gene expression regulation see the following publications.

Golnick, L. and M. Wheelis. 1991. *The Cartoon Guide to Genetics*. New York: Harper Collins.

Ptashne, M. 1992. *A Genetic Switch: Phage and Higher Organisms*. Palo Alto, CA: Blackwell Scientific Publications.

Tjian, R. 1995. Molecular machines that control genes. *Sci. Am.* **272**: 54–61.

For more on gene expression detection and analysis see the following.

The Chipping Forecast. 1999. *Supplement to Nature Genetics* **21**.

Khan, J., M. L. Bittner, Y. Chen, P. S. Meltzer, and J. M. Trent. 1999. "DNA microarray technology: the anticipated impact on the study of human disease." *Biochim. Biophys. Acta* **1423**: M17–28.

Spellman, P. T., G. Sherlock, M. Q. Zhang, V. R. Iyer, K. Anders, M. B. Eisen, P. O. Brown, D. Botstein, and B. Futcher. 1998. "Comprehensive identification of cell cycle-regulated genes of the yeast *Saccharomyces cerevisiae* by microarray hybridization." *Mol. Biol. Cell.* **9**: 3273–3297.

Somogyi, R. 1999. "Making sense of gene-expression data." *Pharma Informatics: A Trends Guide.* Elsevier Trends Journal, Cambridge, England. 17–24.

Tamayo, P., D. Slonim, J. Mesirov, Q. Zhu, S. Kitareewan, E. Dmitrovsky, E. S. Lander, and T. R. Golub. 1999. "Interpreting patterns of gene expression with self-organizing maps: methods and application to hematopoietic differentiation." *PNAS* **96**: 2907–2912.

Zhang, M. Q. 1999. "Large-scale gene expression data analysis: a new challenge to computational biologists." *Genome Res.* **9**: 681–688.

48.2 Similarities and Differences among Catalysts: Clustering and Profiling Diverse Data on Chemical Reactions

Raúl E. Valdés-Pérez, Andrew V. Zeigarnik, and Jérôme Pesenti

ABSTRACT The science of chemistry has seen less recent use of knowledge discovery techniques than sister sciences like biology, possibly because the comparatively modest size of typical chemical data sets do not obviously call out for data mining. The mistaken impression that small-to-medium sized data sets need at best simple methods is widespread. In this article we apply a combination of classical hierarchical clustering (Hartigan, 1975) and profiling methods (Valdes-Perez et al., 2000) to gain insight into the respective capabilities of different metals to catalyze important reactions in chemistry (see Chapter 16.5.2 in this handbook for further background on clustering methods). As far as we know, this is one of the very few applications of data mining within the broad subfield of chemistry known as catalysis.

1. Project Overview

Any science seeks to understand how the objects or phenomena which it studies are similar and how they are different. Experimental studies of similarities and differences may address either structural or behavioral properties; both types of property need to be studied empirically because there is rarely a theory that reliably predicts one from data on the other. Chemistry is no exception: chemists seek to understand what properties are shared by different metals, as well as how the metals differ from each other. For example, knowledge that the metallic elements nickel and rhodium catalyze similar reactions, but that nickel leads to undesirable poisoning of a catalyst by carbon atoms, is very useful for selecting the right catalysts to carry out some industrial processes.

Chemistry generates its share of theoretical and experimental data, but these data are often not subjected to knowledge discovery techniques, partly because the data sets are not huge, and partly because the objects of study are molecules and reactions that are not representationally simple, and thus the patterns of interest often need to relate diverse representations such as numbers, features, graphs, and other chemistry-specific structures. However, chemistry is not unique in this regard, and there is much unexplored scope for machine discovery. For example, chemical publications often provide lists of steps that are relevant to some class of chemical reactions, together with numbers that represent the rates of these steps, their energetics properties, and so on. One such publication (Hei et al., 1998), with the steps listed therein, is our starting point in this article.

Our team consisted of the three authors, whose training is in computer science (RVP), chemistry (AVZ), and mathematics (JP). RVP and AVZ had collaborated for some time on knowledge-intensive discovery problems in chemistry (the MECHEM system (Zeigarnik et al., 2000b) for elucidating reaction pathways) and were using the mentioned lists of steps and their energetics in the context of pathway elucidation. Separately, RVP and JP were working on new methods for annotating sets of text documents that used clustering as a building block. The juxtaposition of these projects led to the current data mining effort. We have also consulted with the authors of the original chemical publication (Hei et al., 1998) to clarify how some of their calculations were carried out, which affected our use of their results. Also, they kindly made their data available in electronic form upon our request.

2. KDD Process

2.1. Data Source

Our initial data (Hei et al., 1998) consisted of a published list of 168 chemical steps that are thought to be relevant to the conversion of abundant natural gas (methane or CH_4) into more useful gases such as CO and H_2, which themselves are versatile feedstocks that are used to make synthetic fuels. One attempt to carry out this important conversion involves reacting methane with CO_2 at high temperatures; the 168 steps were developed with this reaction in mind.

2.2. Energy Values

The authors of the published data included rough calculations of the difficulty with which each individual step can occur on any of the eight metals studied; the chemical name for the step's difficulty is activation energy; the higher the activation energy (hereafter, just energy), the more unlikely the step is to occur. The metals considered were iron, copper, nickel, and the more expensive metals iridium, palladium, platinum, rhodium, and ruthenium.

It is important to realize that the energy of a step differs from one metal to the next. For example, in our data the step $CH_4 + CO_2 \rightarrow CH_3 + HCOO$ has activation energies ranging from a low of 8.1 kcal/mol on iron to a high of 34.0 on platinum. Thus, the data set consists of a matrix of 168 steps and 8 metals whose $8 \times 168 = 1344$ entries are energies. The energies range from 0 to 86.6 kcal/mol.

In our source list of 168 chemical steps, the bonds between the metal catalyst and C, H, and O atoms are not explicitly accounted for. Since the energy of a step is largely a function of the bonds broken or formed, the discerning reader may wonder why the energies vary over the different metals, since the steps look the same. In fact, the source authors abstracted away the role of the catalyst. The chemist on our team had to re-express all the steps with explicit roles for the catalyst, because we defined step attributes (below) that depend on details of all the bonding changes, including the metal catalyst.

2.3. Clustering

The first question we posed is how the eight metals compare in terms of how easily each of the 168 steps can take place on a metal. Classical hierarchical clustering can answer this question, given the distances between every pair of metals. We used the agglomerative (also known as bottom up) clustering method, which begins by defining each object as a cluster by itself, and then repeatedly merges the two closest clusters to form a new cluster. The result is a hierarchy of clusterings that is a binary tree. The leaves of this tree contain the initial objects, the root contains all objects, and any intermediate node corresponds to the merging of the two nodes below it.

The several variants of hierarchical clustering differ by the measure of distance between two clusters of objects. The three most common measures are the distances between (1) the two farthest members of each cluster (complete-link); (2) the two nearest members of each cluster (single-link); and (3) the mean of the distances between every pair of elements each taken from a different cluster (average-link). Each variant has advantages and disadvantages. Single-link is not sensitive to the order in which objects are presented, but it tends to generate sausage-shaped clusters even if they are not naturally present in the data. On the contrary, average-link and complete-link methods generate more rounded clusters but they are more sensitive to object ordering, and also they are not continuous, that is, a small change to a distance between two objects can drastically change the final tree. In our study, the results of complete-link and average-link clustering turned out the same, and they are similar to single-link: there are two clear clusters (nickel, rhodium, and ruthenium) and (platinum, iridium, and palladium) and two atypical elements copper and iron. This concordance between the several variants, which often happens when single-link gives a balanced tree, gives confidence in the meaningfulness of the result.

We chose the Euclidean distance between two 168-dimensional points as our distance measure between two objects or metals, where each point object is just the energies of the 168 steps. Figure 1 shows the resulting hierarchical clustering. The annotations of the hierarchy are explained in the remainder of this section.

2.4. Other Attributes of Steps

The hierarchical clusters show which metals have similar energies for the various steps relevant to methane conversion, and also reveal which metals are most different. However, no reasons for these differences are apparent; at most one can say that their Euclidean distances in our 168-dimensional space were comparatively large. Hence, we decided to annotate the hierarchy with symbolic expressions of how the metals differ. A different representation of the same data was needed, which we developed by making use of our team's chemical expertise.

Recall that our initial data consisted of a matrix of 8 rows (metals) by 168 columns (chemical steps), whose entries are numeric energies. Thus, a step can be characterized by an energy value that depends on the specific metal. However, a chemical step such as $CH_4 + CO_2 \rightarrow HCOO + CH_3$ can be characterized in other ways that are independent of the metal catalyst. A common characteristic of a step is its transition state, which is a postulated intermediate that the step's reacting molecules (e.g., CH_4 and CO_2) go through during their transition into the step's products (HCOO and CH_3). The transition state can be viewed as a molecule containing all bonds of the reactant molecules and all bonds of the product molecules. If all bonds that are common for both reactant and product molecules are deleted, there remain only those bonds that are changed in an elementary reaction. We label the bonds being broken as $-\times-$ and the bonds being formed as $-$. The resulting subgraph of a transition-state graph describes the structural changes brought about by a chemical transformation; we call this subgraph a core fragment or just core. A core is a graph with vertices labelled by atomic symbols (C, H, O, and metal) and with edges labeled as described above. For example, the core of the reaction in Figure 2 is M$-\times-$O$-$C$-\times-$H$-$M because

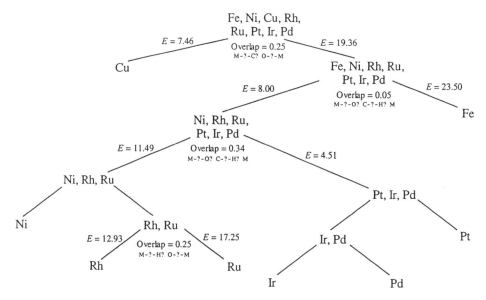

Figure 1 Annotated single-link hierarchical clustering of metals based on the energetics of chemical steps involved in methane conversion (Cu, copper; Fe, iron; Ni, nickel; Rh, rhodium; Ru, ruthenium; Ir, iridium; Pd, palladium; Pt, platinum). Some splits are annotated with the reaction types (cores) whose energetics values diverge the most between the two subclusters created by the split

CH and MO bonds break whereas OC and HM bonds are formed. This core is used in Figure 1 to contrast Fe from six other metals at the second branching.

A key issue is that different steps can have the same core because the same bond types are broken and formed, even though the other, nonreacting atoms are different. Thus, each core can serve as a selector that matches (or mismatches) a number of different chemical steps. However, each step can match only one core selector, since every step can have only one core.

The selectors then become numeric attributes of the form energy of core X, which has the value not applicable for any step that doesn't match the core. Metals will be contrasted among themselves using statements of the form steps that involve such-and-such core fragment occur more readily (face less of an energy barrier) on iridium than on palladium and platinum.

Besides the core of a step, we experimented with other selectors that, for example, indicate whether an oxygen–hydrogen (OH) bond is being broken. Since other bonds besides OH may be broken within a step, such selectors focus on one detail while excluding the larger context. In our case, such selectors did not lead to sharp discriminations between the metal clusters. We also experimented with rather complex selectors that indicated whether a given step was included in a published hypothesis for some important multi-step reactions like water–gas shift, whose net transformation is $CO + H_2O \rightarrow CO_2 + H_2$. However, the best results were obtained with the core selectors which are used in this article.

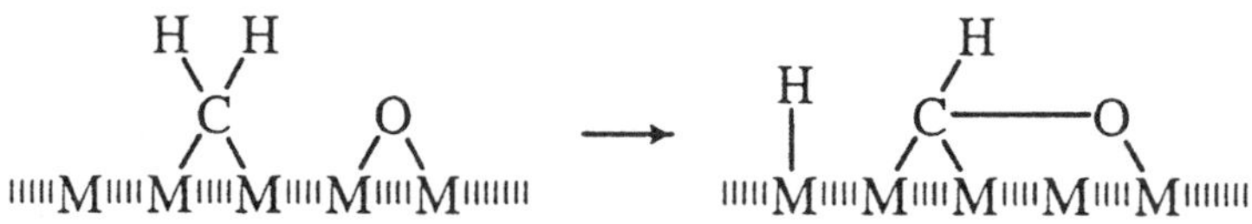

Figure 2 Example of reaction to illustrate the concept of core fragment

2.5. *Annotations*

We tried to annotate each split in the hierarchy with a single attribute that best discriminates the pair of successor metal clusters. For example, the core M– × –C–H– × –M matches seven steps, whose energies on copper are 0, 0, 0, 3.7, 4.8, 24.0, and 30.8 kcal/mol, giving a mean of 9.0 and median of 3.7. Since the first tree split separates copper from the other seven metals, we also collect the 7 metals × 7 steps = 49 energy values from these other metals; their average is 19.4 and median is 16.8. To quantify how separated these two lists of numbers are, we calculate their overlap, that is, how many entries would need to be removed to get all values in one list less than all values in the other list (Valdes-Perez et al., 2000). The overlap measure is normalized to between 0 and 1; its main virtue is that it is nonparametric (doesn't assume anything about the underlying data distributions), is understandable to naive users, and works both on numeric and symbolic attributes, although symbolic attributes are not used here. The best attribute is the one that involves the least overlap between the two clusters of metals.

The final annotated hierarchical clustering appears in Figure 1. For example, the sharpest contrasting attribute at the first branch of the tree is that steps with the core M– × –C–O– × –M occur much more readily on copper (average energy barrier of 7.46 kcal/mol) than on the other metals, whose average energy barrier is 19.36 kcal/mol. The sharpest contrast, at an overlap of only 0.05, was at the next branching between iron and six other metals. Some of the branches are not annotated because we didn't find sharply contrasting attributes that had enough step examples. The annotated tree satisfies our twin goals of expressing concisely how metals are similar and how metals are different, based on how easily the various chemical steps relevant to methane conversion can occur.

As a final experiment, we used the full power of recently developed profiling methods known as CAPP (Valdes-Perez et al., 2000) to generate concise descriptions of the sharpest differentiating characteristics of each metal taken individually. The CAPP method works by comparing all pairs of metals, listing the attributes that can contrast each pair subject to a maximum allowed overlap, and then finding a smallest overall set of attributes that fulfil all the pairwise contrasts. The difference from the previous procedure is that the metals are compared not as clusters but individually, that is, as a flat eight-way classification. All of these results are reported in detail in a companion article written for chemists (Zeigarnik et al., 2000a).

3. Conclusions

Since the early days of chemical catalysis research, chemists have sought data and predictive methods that can guide the design or selection of catalysts (e.g., metals) for specific reactions. For example, the pioneer of catalyst design A. Mittasch carried out in the 1910s about 6,500 tests of around 2,500 different catalysts as part of the development of the Haber–Bosch process for synthesizing ammonia. Essentially the same costly empirical methods are still used by chemists today. The methods of this case study, and of the prior computational work that calculated our initial data, show how a combination of theoretical calculations, clustering, and profiling methods can uncover intelligible patterns that express how catalysts are broadly similar as well as how they are specifically distinct. The obstacle to realizing this goal is still the uneven reliability of theoretical calculations, which give different results when different methods are employed. At the very least, one same method should be used on larger sets of reaction steps.

Our task formulation in this article is an instance of a more general case where one has raw performance data on M benchmark tests (here, reactions) for N designs (metals), and also selectors that state a proposition about the benchmarks and hence serve to match a subset of them, whose performance data will be collected into numeric attributes, just as above. For example, the performance data could be the run times for M benchmark programs (e.g. floating-point routines) on N different computers, a selector is floating-point intensive, and the resulting numeric attribute is run time for a floating-point intensive benchmark. Elsewhere we have applied the same general procedure to benchmarking data in numerical algorithms (Ramakrishnan and Valdes-Perez, 2000).

We close by giving four specific examples of how the discovered knowledge can be used in the chemistry of methane conversion:

1. In complex (multistep) chemical processes, one step is often much slower than others and it, therefore, determines the rate of the overall process. If the core of such a rate-determining step is M– × –O–C– × –H–M, then we conclude that iron is a relatively poor choice of catalyst among the alternatives.

2. If one knows that platinum is a good catalyst for some reaction, it is reasonable to expect that palladium and iridium will also be good.

3. If M– × –C–O– × –M is an important core for some reaction, then copper is likely to be a relatively good catalyst.

4. We confirmed that rhodium and ruthenium behave very similarly, except when the only bond formed is the O–H bond and no other bond is broken between nonmetal atoms (the core M– × –H–O– × –M).

References

Hartigan, J. A. 1975. In *Clustering algorithms*. New York: Wiley.

Hei, M., H. Chen, J. Yi, Y. Lin, Y. Lin, G. Wei, and D. Liao. 1998. "CO_2-reforming of methane on transition metal surfaces." *Surf. Sci.* **417**: 82–96.

Ramakrishnan, N., and R. E. Valdes-Perez. 2000. "A note on generalization in experimental algorithmics." *ACM Trans. Math. Softw* **26(4)**: 568–580.

Valdes-Perez, R. E., V. Pericliev, and F. Pereira. 2000. "Concise, intelligible, and approximate profiling of numerous classes." *Int. J. Human Comput. Studies* **53(3)**: 411–436.

Zeigarnik, A. V., R. E. Valdes-Perez, and J. Pesenti. 2000a. "Comparative properties of transition metal catalysts inferred from activation energies of elementary steps of catalytic reactions." *J. Phys. Chem.* **104(5)**: 997–1008.

Zeigarnik, A. V., R. E. Valdes-Perez, and B. S. White. 2000b. "Proposed methodological improvement in the elucidation of chemical reaction mechanisms based on chemist–computer interaction." *J. Chem. Ed.* **77(2)**: 214.

48.3 Knowledge Discovery in High-Energy Particle and Nuclear Physics

David Zimmerman, Iwona Sakrejda, and Doug Olson

ABSTRACT The fields of high energy and nuclear physics are faced with difficult challenges in terms of both the complexity and volume of data. This article contains a description of some of the tools that have been and will be used in physics data handling. It includes a description of the application of artificial neural network tools to the search for the top quark at the Fermi National Accelerator Laboratory. In addition, this article describes a new data handling framework, which will support deep drill-down data mining in physics analysis.

1. Introduction

High-energy and nuclear physics is concerned with the study of the particles and fields and how they interact to make up our universe. In order to produce these particles for study, physicists perform their experiments at national laboratory facilities that provide large particle accelerators for the production of high-energy particle beams. They build their detectors around interaction regions where the high-energy beams collide. These detectors record information on the types and distributions of particles produced in the collisions.

As experiments have grown in size (in various dimensions) and complexity, physicists have begun to take advantage of knowledge discovery techniques developed in artificial intelligence and computer science research. In particular, neural network analyses have been successfully applied to many standard problems in event classification. Other techniques, such as evolutionary algorithms and Bayesian analysis, have been used in certain cases, but are not yet widely applied or accepted. The forthcoming generation of experiments is using data analysis frameworks that support the process of moving away from the reliance on Fortran and linear cuts event selection and will allow more opportunities to apply data mining techniques in high-energy physics analysis.

1.1. Data Analysis Strategies

Because of the complexity of the phenomena under study in the field of high-energy particle and nuclear physics, the data analysis problem involves significant challenges. Modern detectors are composed of many distinct subsystems. These detector subsystems record information about particle interaction in the detector.

In order to fully analyze and understand a collision detector, physicists create data models. These models maintain relationships not only among the information from each detector that recorded an event, but among larger hierarchies of event information, including calibration data and other meta data that are necessary for a complete event analysis.

In Figure 1 a typical event in the STAR detector (http://www.rhic-bnl-gov/STAR/) is composed of raw electrical signals recorded in the time projection chamber, the electromagnetic calorimeter, the silicon vertex detector, and many other subsystems.

Following the recording of an event, the raw data are processed and stored as tracks that describe the trajectories of particles in the detector. These raw data are immediately transferred to a dedicated computer center where they are stored in a tape archive. After archiving, the raw data, which are composed of electronic signals from the detector, are further processed to create a data summary representation of the events in terms of objects such as tracks and electromagnetic showers.

Each track is described in terms of its kinematic variables, such as its rest mass and momentum. The information hierarchy continues to grow as the data are further analyzed. The goal of the analysis processing stages is to reduce an event to a description that includes only the information relevant to a particular physics interpretation. This leads to a complex event model in which representations of each event are stored in different levels in a hierarchical data store.

ANALYSIS GOALS

In general, most physics analyses aim to produce high precision measurements of relatively rare physical phenomena. An example of such an analysis is the discovery of a new particle, such as the top quark that was discovered by the D0 and CDF experiments at the Fermi

Figure 1 An end-on projection of an event in the STAR detector. A typical central collision at the RHIC accelerator is expected to produce several thousand particles

National Accelerator Laboratory in 1994 (Abe et al., 1994). This discovery involved the recording of data that were taken from many millions of proton-antiproton collisions in the CDF detector. The data from these collisions were analyzed to produce a sample of six events that were candidates as top quarks, against a background of an estimated two events.

A problem of similar difficulty is expected at the STAR experiment at RHIC. This experiment has been designed to search for evidence of the production of a state of matter called The Quark-Gluon Plasma or QGP. The STAR collaboration expects to record data from 10 million collisions per year for approximately ten years of running. The expected volume of data from each year run will be approximately 300 terabytes of event data. Physics analysis groups on STAR will shift through this entire event data set at least once per year in the search for events in which the QGP has formed. The events that are included in this sample will then be further analyzed and compared with simulations in order to define a sample of QGP candidates for detailed study.

DATA VOLUMES

In order to perform high precision measurements, physicists require the analysis of a large number of events. In the present generation of experiments, the typical numbers are tens to thousands of events recorded per year, and data volumes that run from the hundreds to the thousands of petabytes (PB). As the events are processed they take on a hierarchical structure that does not match well to relational database technologies. Most experiments are adopting hybrid data management systems, which include relational databases, object-oriented databases, and home grown storage solutions such as ROOT (http://root.cern.ch) and Java Analysis Studio (http://www-sldnt.slac.stanford.edu/jas/index.htm).

1.2. Other Pattern Recognition Problems in HENP

In addition to the pattern recognition problems associated with the extraction of interesting events from large data samples, there are a number of other problems that arise in high-energy experimental physics.

A typical modern particle physics experiment has hundreds of thousands of channels of electronics that record information about the particle collisions. Since the experiments typically run twenty-four hours a day for periods as long as ten months, physicists have developed extensive monitoring and calibration systems that record meta data to distinct data streams from the data recorded to describe the particle collisions.

The data recorded in the monitoring and calibration streams are used as input to the processing of the physics event data. These data are usually stored in relational databases such as MySQL (http://www.tcx.se/) or Oracle (http://www.oracle.com).

In addition to the fact that calibration and monitoring data are managed in ways that are more amenable to traditional data mining techniques, there is greater need for data mining in the analysis of these data.

Physicists bring a tremendous amount of domain knowledge to bear in their analysis of the collision data. The patterns that arise in calibration and monitoring data often derive from some sort of unexpected behavior such as experimental malfunction.

2. Knowledge Discovery in HENP

A common theme through essentially all of the modern high-energy physics experiments is the need for efficient, automated pattern recognition techniques. Unfortunately, because of the large data volumes and customized data storage solutions, it has proven to be very difficult to utilize conventional off-the-shelf data mining techniques, which are designed for use with smaller numbers of objects and more conventional data management tools, such as relational databases.

In spite of these problems a number of knowledge discovery tools have achieved some level of acceptance in HENP. In particular, neural networks have gained popularity as classification tools. They have been used in analyses of simulation data as part of searches for the Higgs particle (Chiapetta et al., 1994), jet identification (Grahma et al., 1993), and many other classification problems in HENP. Other knowledge discovery tools in use in high-energy and nuclear physics include the training of genetic algorithms for track recognition (Glazov et al., 1993) and entropy-based scaled correlation analysis (Trainor, 1999).

2.1. Artificial Neural Networks

Artificial neural networks (ANN) have become popular tools in HEP analysis. They are well suited to the types of classification problems that arise in HENP analysis. Particle physicists have relied extensively on simulations of their experiments as an important component of traditional analysis techniques (http://www.info.cern.ch/asd/geant/index.html). There are a host of well-accepted simulation tools. Effect simulations of physics processes enable use of simulation data as training samples for neural networks.

In the following section we will present an ANN analysis, which was used to identify a sample of candidate events in which top quarks were produced.

3. Evidence of Top Quark Production in Proton-Antiproton Collisions

The CDF (Abe et al., 1994) collaboration at the Fermilab National Accelerator Laboratory built the CDF detector that detects particles produced in collisions of protons with protons at center-of-mass energies of 800 GigaElectron Volts. The vast majority of the collisions lead to production of standard particles, which form a background against which the production of rare particles such as top quarks must be observed. In spite of the fact that the background processes are typically fairly well understood, they are numerous enough that sophisticated analysis techniques are necessary in order to find a clean sample of events containing particles that are candidates for identification as top quarks. In order to study the analysis efficiency and biases, physicists create simulations that mimic the response of the detector to many different types of events, including both background and signal.

Neural nets are natural tools to be used in event classification because they can be trained on the simulation data. In 1994, CDF published their first evidence for the production of the top quark (Abe et al., 1994). They described an analysis based on linear cuts on a multidimensional parameter space. Their result was a sample of six events with an estimated background contamination of 2.3 ± 0.3 events.

Ametller, Garrido and Talavera performed a neural network analysis (Ametller et al., 1994) in order to explore the potential for improving the selection efficiency for the experiment. In experiments such as CDF that are performing searches for rare events, selection efficiency is very important. In particular, because of the necessity of detector simulations as a basis for determining the selection error, the selection efficiency contributes significantly to the systematic errors associated with background, or misidentification, effects as well as to the statistical significance of this data sample.

Following up on this work they made further studies of the issues that arise in neural networks as classification tools for rare particle searches (Ametller et al., 1996).

3.1. Production of Top Quarks in the CDF Detector

There have been many publications that describe the CDF detector. A good description of the detector and its performance can be found in Abe et al. (1994).

There are two main processes in which top quarks are produced in proton-antiproton collisions. These processes involve the collision of an individual quark from the proton interacting with an individual quark in the antiproton, either directly or through the exchange of a gluon. Symbolically, $q\bar{q} \to t\bar{t}$ and $g\bar{g} \to t\bar{t}$, where q and g signify quark and gluon, respectively, and the t signifies a top quark. The bars above the particle symbols connote the fact that these particles are the antimatter partners, or antiparticle versions.

Each top quark in an event can decay through several possible modes: $t \to qW, W^{\pm} \to l^{\pm}v$, where the top decays to a single lighter quark, and a W particle, which decays to a light charged lepton (e.g., electron or muon) and a neutrino, and $t \to qW, W^{\pm} \to q\bar{q}$, where the top decays to a single lighter quark and a W, and the W decays to two lighter quarks.

Each of the particles that arises from these different event topologies causes a distinct response in the detector. The lighter quarks produced in these decays hadronize and produce a jet of charged particles. The light leptons do not decay in the decay volume, so they are observed directly. The neutrinos do not interact in the detector at all and so yield no signal. The detector response to an event in which a neutrino is created is to observe that there is missing, or undetected, energy and momentum.

These decay modes yield three classes of events in which pairs of top and antitop quarks are produced. Events in which there are six jets (the W particles from each top decay to quarks themselves); events in which there are four jets, one charged lepton, and one neutrino; and events in which there are two jets, two charged leptons, and two neutrinos.

While the events in which the top quark pair leads to six jets in the detector are more numerous than the other two, they are also the most easily mimicked by other particle production processes. The events in which there are two charged leptons are more easily identified, but since they occur in only a few percent of the top events, the yield is too low to make a good estimate of the top quark production rate.

For the purposes of this article, we will follow Ametller et al. (1994) and only discuss the single charged lepton, four jet decay topology.

THE APPLICATION OF NEURAL NETWORK ANALYSIS TO THE TOP SEARCH

Traditional analysis techniques involve performing a series of linear cuts that are chosen to preferentially remove the background versus the signal events from the sample. The determination of the best combination of cuts to use in event selection is a difficult and time-consuming process. Each event corresponds to a particular point in the n-dimensional space described by the n-analysis variables. Since the events themselves couple the information on each access to every other access, a cut on any of the variables changes the event distribution seen on any of the other $n-1$.

In their paper, Ametller, Garrido, and Talavera (1994) describe a neural network analysis of the top quark data from 1994 (Abe et al., 1994). As inputs to their analysis they simulated a set of signal and background events for the four jet type of top events. In studying these events they compared the efficiency (probability of selecting a simulated top candidate event as a top candidate in their selected sample) versus the purity (contamination of their top sample with simulated background events), for the neural network analysis to the linear cutting analysis.

THE NEURAL NETWORK

In order to identify events produced in this channel, a selection criteria is created based on linear cuts against a set of six kinematical variables. They used pT^W, the transverse momentum of the W; E_T, the transverse missing energy in the event; m_W, the invariant mass of the W in the event; S, the sphericity in the event; and A, the acoplanarity in the event. For convenience, each of the variables was normalized to one before being input to the network.

Using the above variables as inputs they created a three-layer feed-forward neural network, which had six input neurons, six hidden neurons, and a single output layer as shown in Figure 2. The neuron response function used was the standard sigmoid function.

The output of the network was 0 for background events and 1 for signal events.

The network was trained on samples of 2,000 simulated top events and 2,000 simulated background events. The learning algorithm used was error back propagation, which is well described in the literature (Webos, 1974).

As a test sample, 570 top simulated events and 2,000 simulated background events were passed through the network.

Figure 3 shows the relationship between the efficiency of the network (which is dependent on the output threshold) versus the purity of the selected sample and the statistical significance of the selected sample. Note the nonlinear coupling between the purity of the selected sample and the efficiency for the selection of candidate events.

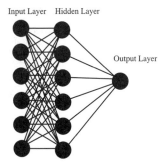

Figure 2 A representation of the topology of the network used in this analysis
This figure previously appeared in LI. Ametller, LI. Garrido, G. Stimpfl-Abele, P. Talavera, and P. Yepes "Discriminating signal from background using neural networks, application to top—quark search at the Fermilab Tevatron." *Phys. Rev.* **D54** (1996), pp. 1233–1236. Reprinted with permission of P. Yepes.

Based on the results obtained from their network, they point out that the neural network has the potential to be an effective cross check on traditional analysis techniques. Artificial neural networks have the potential to automate aspects of the difficult problem of selecting the variables to be used in a linear cutting analysis.

4. Next Generation Knowledge Discovery in HENP

The next generation of experiments in high-energy and nuclear physics will continue to grow both in the volume and complexity of its data. New experiments under construction at the RHIC accelerator at Brookhaven National Laboratory in New York and at the CERN laboratory in Switzerland plan to produce petabytes of data over the course of their data-taking periods, ten years and twenty years, respectively.

Particle physicists continue to develop new tools that will allow more efficient access and analysis of the data coming from the next generation of experiments. These new tools include the widespread adoption of C++ as the development language of choice, dedicated computer centers that include robotic tape archive systems, and multiprocessor analysis farms.

4.1. Grand Challenge Software

The High Energy and Nuclear Physics Data Access Grand Challenge project (`http://www-rnc.lbl.gov/GC`) developed a system designed to optimize deep drill-down mining into high-energy physics data. The size of the data sets is large enough (PB scale) that a tertiary

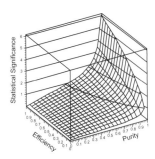

Figure 3 The statistical significance versus the efficiency and purity of the sample as determined by the neural network output

storage level is employed, consisting of a robotically controlled tape archive system (`http://www5.clearlake.ibm.com`). The latencies introduced by this level, as well as the bandwidth limitations (related primarily to cost), lead to a need to provide an optimization strategy that allows a large community of scientists to investigate these data.

The opportunities for optimization are:

- Query estimation—to eliminate unwanted queries.

- Order optimization—to retrieve files from tertiary storage based upon maximizing the amount of sharing between simultaneous queries.

- Look ahead pre-fetch—to analyze queries and retrieve files before they are needed.

- Precise indices—to create indices that permit specification and access to the minimum number of files necessary for a query.

- Clustering—to distribute data in files and on tapes that best matches predicted (clustering) or observed (reclustering) access patterns.

Each of these optimizations has been utilized in the software developed in this project.

The architecture used is that multiple clients connect with the Storage Access Coordination Server (STACS) for submitting queries and retrieving the data (Shoshani et al., 1999). STACS analyzes all active queries and interacts with the tertiary storage system to move files to the file system shared by all clients.

The index is built using application specific attributes for all data objects of interest and includes the identity of the files in which those objects are stored. The model used for this physics data is that it is composed of very many similar objects, called events, and that the components of any particular event may be stored in different files. This permits the optimization of clustering by type. A query specifies which components of the events are desired along with a selection that determines the set of events to be included. The event selection can be specified as a range query on the attribute values in the index or simply be comprised of a list of identifiers for each event in the set.

4.2. Tag Database

The summary information and meta data describing the full data set is kept online in the secondary storage layer (rotating disk) and is called the tag database. The tags are the attribute values associated with each event and they provide the information for the index used by STACS for processing the queries. This tag database can be a VLDB on its own and be several TB in size. A considerable amount of data mining and analysis can be carried out on this database. Mining of the tag database helps ensure that the very expensive queries of the tertiary storage system are well formulated.

4.3. Mining the Physicist's Queries

An additional opportunity that we are looking forward to utilizing is to monitor the access patterns and the queries that scientists submit. Data mining of the queries submitted should provide a very interesting perspective on the practice of scientific research.

The grand challenge software logs queries against the data store. These logs can be stored in a relational database and mined for interesting information. There is great potential for interesting information to be discovered among the patterns that are extracted from the query logs. On a simple level, the queries can yield insight into the physicist's access patterns, which could lead to an altered arrangement of disk resident data in order to improve processing throughput. Potentially of more interest would be to study correlations among the data selected by different analysis teams. Unexpected overlap in the selected samples could be evidence for either unintended biases in the analysis or, possibly, underlying commonality in the physics processes under study.

References

Abe, F. et al. 1994. "CDF Collaboration." *Phys. Rev. D* **50**: 2966.

Ametller, Ll., Ll. Garrido, G. Stimp-Abele, P. Talavera, and P. Yepes. 1996. "Discriminating signal from background using neural networks. Application to top-quark search at the Fermilab Tevatron." *Phys. Rev.* **D54**: 1233–1236.

Ametller, Ll., Ll. Garrido, and P. Talavera. 1994. *Phys. Rev. D* **50**: 5473.

Chiapetta, P., P. Colangelo, P. de Felice, G. Nardulli, and G. Pasquariello. 1994. *Phys. Lett. B* **322**: 219.

Glazov, A., I. Kisel, E. Konotopskaya, and G. Ososkov. 1993. "Filtering tracks in discrete detectors using a cellular automaton." *NIM* **A329**: 262–268.

Grahma, M. A., L. M. Jones, and S. Herbin. 1993. Illinois University Report No. ILL-TH-93-18 (unpublished).

Shoshani, A., L. M. Bernardo, H. Nordberg, D. Rotem, and A. Sim. 1999. "Multidimensional indexing and query coordination for tertiary storage management." *SSDBM*, pp. 214–225.

Trainor, T. A. 1999. *Proceedings of the Fifteenth Winter Workshop on Nuclear Dynamics*. Park City, UT, January 9–16: Plenum Press.

Webos, P. J. 1974. Ph.D. diss. Harvard University.